ELLIOTT AND WOOD'S
CASES AND MATERIALS ON CRIMINAL LAW

D1407445

AUSTRALIA
LBC Information Service
Sydney

CANADA and USA
Carswell
Toronto

NEW ZEALAND
Brooker's
Auckland

SINGAPORE and MALAYSIA
Thomson Information (S.E. Asia)
Singapore

ELLIOTT AND WOOD'S

CASES AND MATERIALS ON CRIMINAL LAW

Eighth Edition

by

MICHAEL J. ALLEN LL.M.

Barrister and Professor of Law, Newcastle Law School

LONDON
SWEET & MAXWELL
2001

D. W. Elliott & J. C. Wood, First Edition 1963
Second Impression 1967
D. W. Elliott & J. C. Wood, Second Edition 1969
Second Impression 1971
D. W. Elliott & J. C. Wood, Third Edition 1974
D. W. Elliott & Celia Wells, Fourth Edition 1982
D. W. Elliott & Michael J. Allen, Fifth Edition 1989
D. W. Elliott & Michael J. Allen, Sixth Edition 1993
Michael J. Allen, Seventh Edition 1997
Second Impression 1988
Third Impression 1999
Michael J. Allen, Eighth Edition 2001
Reprinted 2001, 2002, 2003

Published by
Sweet & Maxwell Limited of
100 Avenue Road, London NW3
http://www.sweetandmaxwell.co.uk
Computerset by Wyvern 21 Limited, Bristol
Printed in Great Britain by MPG Books Ltd

No natural forests were destroyed to make this product; only farmed
timber was used and replanted

A CIP catalogue record for this book
is available from the British Library

ISBN 0 421 71740 8

PREFACE

In the four years since the last edition, there has been considerable judicial activity in many areas of the criminal law. As in the past, however, there has been considerable variability in the quality of the judgments delivered resulting in some areas of uncertainty being resolved but new areas of uncertainty arising. In the House of Lords there has been some clarification of the law on murder and intention in *R. v. Woollin*, strict liability and the presumption of *mens rea* in *B (A Minor) v. D.P.P.*, assault and inflicting grievous bodily harm in *R. v. Burstow; R. v. Ireland*, and murder and joint enterprise in *R. v. Powell and Daniels: R. v. English*. By contrast their Lordships have left the law in a state of confusion by their decisions in *Attorney-General's Reference (No. 3 of 1994)* on transferred malice and murder, *R. v. Smith (Morgan)* on the reasonable man in provocation, and *R. v. Hinks* on the theft of gifts and the meaning of appropriation. In the Court of Appeal there has been considerable activity and overall the quality of judgments at this level is better than in their Lordships House. Decisions worthy of note are those on obtaining services by deception in *Rai*, handling stolen goods in *Forsyth*, joint enterprise and murder in *Uddin*, duress of circumstances in *Abdul-Hussain and Others*, and indecent assault and consent in *Tabassum*. Decisions which leave problems in their wake are to be found in *Martin* on duress, *Marshall* on theft and the meaning of intention permanently to deprive, *Attorney-General's Reference* (No. 2 of 1999) on gross negligence manslaughter and corporate liability, and *Richardson* on assault and consent. A decision which attracted huge media attention and which developed the common law defence of necessity to meet an almost unique problem is that of *Re. A. (Children) (Conjoined Twins: Medical Treatment) (No.1)*. A notable decision by the Divisional Court is that in the case of *D.P.P. v. Armstrong (Andrew)* seeking to resolve the problems created by the Court of Appeal in the cases of *Curr* and *Shaw* relating to the *mens rea* required of a person charged with incitement.

There has been little activity by Parliament touching on the substantive criminal law in the past four years. Some changes have been made to the rules on jurisdiction by the Criminal Justice (Terrorism and Conspiracy) Act 1998 and Part I of the Criminal Justice Act 1993 has finally been brought into force. One piece of legislation whose impact on the substantive criminal law has yet to be fully realised is the Human Rights Act 1998 which came into force in October 2000. Reference is made to decisions of the European Court of Human Rights in several places where it is believed that these will have an impact on our domestic criminal law following the implementation of the 1998 Act.

The subject of law reform is addressed in several chapters with extracts being included from *Violence: Reforming the Offences Against*

v

the Person Act 1861, Home Office, 1998, *Reforming the Law on Involuntary Manslaughter: The Government's Proposals*, Home Office, May 2000, *Setting the Boundaries: Reforming the Law on Sex Offences*, Report of the Sex Offences Review, Home Office, July 2000, and *Legislating the Criminal Code: Fraud and Deception*, (1999) Law Com. C.P. No. 155. Whether any of these will result in legislation in the next four years is open to question.

The law is stated as at January 1, 2001.

Thanks are due to Richard Crouch at Sweet & Maxwell for his editorial support; to the many persons and bodies who kindly allowed us to reproduce copyright material; and to my wife, Nichola, and children Siobhan and Matthew who put up with me hogging the study and computer at home.

Mike Allen
January 2001

CONTENTS

TABLE OF CASES

[Page references in **bold** indicate the page upon which an extract from the report appears.]

TABLE OF STATUTES

REPORTS AND OFFICIAL PROPOSALS

Law Commission Reports

Other Reports

Consultation Papers

Criminal Law Revision Committee Reports

National Penal Codes

ABBREVIATIONS

Blackstone	*Commentaries on the Laws of England*, by Sir William Blackstone (1765) (Chitty's ed., 1826).
Butler Committee	Report of The Committee on Mentally Abnormal Offenders, Cmnd. 6244, 1975.
C.L.J.	*Cambridge Law Journal.*
C.L.R.C.	Criminal Law Revision Committee.
Crim.L.R.	*Columbia Law Review.*
Crim.L.Q.	*Criminal Law Quarterly.*
Crim.L.R.	*Criminal Law Review.*
Fletcher	*Rethinking Criminal Law*, by George P. Fletcher (1978).
Glazebrook	*Reshaping the Criminal Law*, P. Glazebrook (ed.) (1978).
Griew	*The Theft Acts 1968 and 1978*, by Edward Griew (6th ed., 1990).
Hale	*Pleas of the Crown*, by Sir Matthew Hale (1682).
Hall	*General Principles of Criminal Law*, by Jerome Hall (2nd ed., 1960).
Harv.L.R.	*Harvard Law Review.*
Kenny	Kenny's *Outlines of Criminal Law* (19th ed., by J.W.C. Turner, 1966).
L.Q.R.	*Law Quarterly Review.*
M.L.R.	*Modern Law Review.*
Model Penal Code	American Law Institute, *Model Penal Code* (1962).
Russell	*Russell on Crime* (12th ed., by J.W.C. Turner, 1964).
Smith	*The Law of Theft*, by J.C. Smith (7th ed., 1995).
Smith and Hogan	*Criminal Law*, by J.C. Smith and Brian Hogan (8th ed., 1996).
Stephen, H.L.C.	*A History of the Common Law of England*, by Sir James Fitzjames Stephen (1883).
Williams, C.L.G.P.	*Criminal Law, The General Part*, by Glanville Williams (2nd ed., 1961).
Williams, Proof of Guilt	*The Proof of Guilt, A Study of the English Criminal Trial*, by Glanville Williams (3rd ed., 1963).
Williams, T.C.L.	*Textbook of Criminal Law*, by Glanville Williams (2nd ed., 1983).

ACKNOWLEDGMENTS

Grateful acknowledgment is made to the following authors and publishers for permission to quote from their works:

Copyright Permissions

ALDRIDGE, P, "The Coherence of Defences" [1983] Criminal Law Review pp. 665–666

ANDREWS, J, "Robbery" [1966] Criminal Law Review pp. 524–5

ASHWORTH, A, "Belief, Intent and Criminal Liability" in Eekelaar, J and Bell, J (eds) *Oxford Essays in Jurisprudence* (1987) p.1, Clarendon Press, ISBN 0198255071

ASHWORTH, A, *Principles of Criminal Law* (3rd ed., 1999) pp. 24–27, 132, 141–144 OUP, ISBN 0198765576

ASHWORTH, A, "Taking the Consequences" in Shute, S, Gardner, J, and Horder, J (eds), *Action and Value in Criminal Law* (1993) pp.107, 108–110, 113–114, 116–117, 120, 123–124, Clarendon Press, ISBN 0198258062.

BRETT AND WALLER, *Criminal Law Text and Cases* (4th ed., 1978) p.145, Butterworths, Australia.

CROSS, R, "Murder under Duress" (1978) 28 University of Toronto Law Journal, p.377, University of Toronto Press Inc.

DENNIS, I, "The Elements of Attempt" [1980] Criminal Law Review p.768–769

FITZGERALD, PJ, "A Concept of Crime" [1960] Criminal Law Review 257, 259, Sweet & Maxwell, ISSN 0011 135X

FLETCHER, GP, *Rethinking Criminal Law* (1978) pp.362, 368, 396–7, 421, 798–800, 810–812 Boston: Little Brown

GALLIGAN, "The Return of Retribution in Criminal Theory" in *Crime, Proof and Punishment: Essays in Memory of Sir Rupert Cross* (1981) pp.144, 146 *et seq*, Butterworths, ISBN 0406569991

GLAZEBROOK, PR, "Criminal Omissions: The Duty Requirement in Offences Against the Person" (1960) 76 Law Quarterly Review p.387

GOBERT, J, "The Fortuity of Consequence" (1993) 4 Criminal Law Forum p.1, Rutgers University School of Law, ISSN 1046–8374

GRIEW, E, "Consistency, Communication and Codification: Reflections on Two Mens Rea Words" in Glazebrook, P, *Reshaping the Criminal Law* (1978) pp.57–59, Stevens & Sons

GRIEW, E, "States of Mind, Presumptions and Inferences" in Smith, P (ed.) *Criminal Law: Essays in Honour of J.C. Smith* (1987) pp.73–74, Butterworths, ISBN 0406501106

GRIEW, E, *The Theft Acts 1968 and 1978* (7th ed.) Sweet & Maxwell

GROSS, H, *A Theory of Criminal Justice* (1979) pp.13–14, OUP (New York) ISBN 0195023498, 0195023501

HART, HLA, "Act of Will and Responsibility" in *Punishment and Responsibility* (1968) p.90, OUP.

HESTER, S AND EGLIN, P, *A Sociology of Crime* (1992) p.27, Routledge, ISBN 0415073693, 0415073707 (pbk)

HOGAN, B, "Omissions and the Duty Myth" in Smith, P, *Criminal Law: Essays in Honour of J.C Smith* (1986) Butterworths, ISBN 0406501106

HORDER, J, "Pleading Involuntary Lack of Capacity" (1993) 52 Cambridge Law Journal pp.298–302, 313–317

HORDER, J, "Occupying the Moral High Ground? The Law Commission on Duress" [1994] Criminal Law Review pp.334, 339 & 340–342.

HUTCHINSON, AC, "Note on *Sault Ste Marie*" (1979) 17 Osgoode Hall Law Journal p.429

JUSTICE, *Breaking the Rules*, (1980)

KENNY, AJP, *Freewill and Responsibility* (1978) pp.36–38, Routledge.

LACEY, N, "Contingency and Criminalisation" in Loveland, I (ed.) *Frontiers of Criminality* (1995) pp.4 & 14–15, Modern Legal Studies, Sweet & Maxwell, ISBN 0421526300 (pbk.)

LEIGH, K, *Strict and Vicarious Liability* (1982) pp.58–61, Sweet & Maxwell, ISBN 0 421 26770 4

LINDGREN, J, "Unravelling the Paradox of Blackmail" (1984) 84 Columbia Law Review p.670

LLOYD, D, *Introduction to Jurisprudence* (4th ed., 1979) pp.54–59, Sweet & Maxwell

MACKAY, RD AND KEARNS, G, "More Fact(s) about the Insanity Defence" [1999] Criminal Law Review pp.722–723

MACKAY, RD, *Mental Condition Defences in Criminal Law* (1995) pp.155–56, OUP

MACKENNA, B, "Blackmail: a Criticism" [1966] Criminal Law Review p.466

NORRIE, A, "Oblique Intention and Legal Politics" [1989] Criminal Law Review pp.794–796

PACKER, H, *The Limits of the Criminal Sanction* (1969) pp.261 et seq, Stanford University Press

PATIENT, IHE, "Transferred Malice—A Misleading Misnomer" (1990) 54 Journal of Criminal Law 116–124.

PAULUS, I, "Strict Liability: Its Place in Public Welfare Offences" (1978) 2 Criminal Law Quarterly p.445, Canada Law Book Inc.

SAYRE, "Public Welfare Offences" (1933) 33 Columbia Law Review 55

SMITH, ATH, "On Actus Reus and Mens Rea", in Glazebrook, P, *Reshaping the Criminal Law* (1978) pp.95–101, 103–4, Stevens & Sons

SMITH, JC, "Responsibility in Criminal Law" in Bean and Whynes (eds) *Barbara Wootton, Essays in Her Honour* (1986) p.153, Tavistock Publications

SMITH, JC, "Aid, abet, counsel or procure" in Glazebrook, P, *Reshaping the Criminal Law* (1978) pp.122, & 124–125, Stevens & Sons

SMITH, JC, *The Law of Theft* (8th ed., 1997) Butterworths, ISBN 0 406 89545 7, §4–31, 12–02—12–03

SMITH, KJM, "Proximity in Attempt: Lord Lane's Midway Course" [1991] Criminal Law Review p.577

SMITH, KJM, "Duress and Steadfastness: In Pursuit of the Unintelligible" [1999] Criminal Law Review pp.363 & 370

SPENCER, JR, "The Metamorphosis of Section of the Theft Act" [1977] Criminal Law Review p.653

SPENCER, JR, "The Theft Act 1978" [1979] Criminal Law Review p.34

THOMAS, DA, "Form and Function in Criminal Law" in Glazebrook, P, *Reshaping the Criminal Law* (1978) pp.21, 25, 30, Stevens & Sons

TUR, RS, "Subjectivism and Objectivism: Towards Synthesis" in Shute, S, Gardner, J, and Horder, J (eds), *Action and Value in Criminal Law* (1993) pp.219–222, Clarendon Press, ISBN 0198258062

WALKER, N, *Crime and Criminology: A Critical Introduction* (1987), pp.140–141, OUP, ISBN 0192891936, 0192192124 (pbk.)

WALKER, N, "Crime and Punishment in Britain" (1965) p.33, Edinburgh University Press

WASIK, M, "Duress and Criminal Responsibility" [1977] Criminal Law Review 453

WELLS, C, "Whither Insanity?" [1983] Crim. L.R. pp.787–788 & 793–794

WILLIAMS, G, "The Definition of Crime" (1955) Current Legal Problems, pp.107, 116–118, 120–121, 123, 128–129, 130, Stevens & Sons

WILLIAMS, G, *Criminal Law: The General Part* (1961) Stevens & Sons.

WILLIAMS, G, *Finis for Novus Actus"* [1989] Cambridge Law Journal p.391, Cambridge University Press.

WILLIAMS, G, "Oblique Intention" (1987) 46 Cambridge Law Journal pp.417–421, Cambridge University Press.

WILLIAMS, G, *Textbook of Criminal Law* (2nd ed., 1983) Stevens & Sons, pp.75, 138, 148,

WILLIAMS, G, "The theory of excuses" [1982] Criminal Law Review p.739

WILLIAMS, G, "Wrong Turnings in the Law of Attempt" [1991] Criminal Law Review pp. 417 & 419

WILLIAMS, G, "Temporary Appropriation Should be Theft" [1981] Criminal Law Review p.129

WOOTTON, B, *Crime and the Criminal Law* (2nd ed, 1981) pp.46–48, Stevens

Attempt and Impossibility in Relation to Attempt, Conspiracy and Incitement (1980) Law Com. No. 102

A Criminal Code for England and Wales: Commentary on Draft Criminal Code Bill (1989) Law Com No. 177

Legislating the Criminal Code: Offences Against the Person and General Principles, (1993) Law Com. No. 218,

Legislating the Criminal Code: Involuntary Manslaughter, Law Com. No. 237

Offences of Dishonesty: Money Transfers, Law Com. No. 243

Assisting and Encouraging Crime, (1993) Law Com. C.P. No. 131

Legislating the Criminal Code: Fraud and Deception, (1999) Law Com. C.P. No. 155

Criminal Law Revision Committee, 8th Report, *Theft and Related Offences,* Cmnd 2977 (1966)

Criminal Law Revision Committee, 14th Report, *Offences Against the Person,* Cmnd 7844 (1980)

Report of the Advisory Council on the Penal System, "Sentences of Imprisonment" (Home Office) 1978.

Report of the Select Committee of the House of Lords on Murder and Life Imprisonment (H.L. Paper 78–1, Session 1988–89)

Report of the Inter-Departmental Review of the Law on the Use of Lethal Force in Self-Defence or the Prevention of Crime (Home Office) 1996

Violence: Reforming the Offences Against the Person Act 1861, Home Office, 1998

Reforming the Law on Involuntary Manslaughter: The Government's Proposals, Home Office, May 2000

Setting the Boundaries: Reforming the Law on sex offences, Report of the Sex Offences Review, Home Office, July 2000

CHAPTER 1

INTRODUCTORY

The subject matter of this book is the substantive criminal law of England and Wales. In some Commonwealth jurisdictions, *e.g.* Queensland, the criminal law is in the form of a code. In England and Wales, despite an attempt in that direction in the nineteenth century, no general code has reached the statute book. The criminal law is, accordingly, derived from a mixture of common law and statute. Most of the general principles of liability are to be found in the common law and some offences, such as murder, manslaughter and incitement are offences at common law. Parliament has intervened with increasing frequency throughout the past one hundred and fifty years to place more offences and defences on a statutory footing. The various statutes which have been enacted, however, largely represent ad hoc responses to particular problems and do not add up to form a coherent code. The criminal law is replete with inconsistencies and incongruities with the result that discovering what the law is on any point (rather than where it is to be found) can be an immensely difficult task with an uncertain outcome. While this makes the study of criminal law both challenging and interesting, it leaves the practice of law fraught with difficulty and the risk of injustice all the greater as prosecutors, defence advocates, trial judges and juries grapple to discover and apply elusive and even ephemeral principles.

In Law Com. No. 177, *A Criminal Code for England and Wales* (1989) the Law Commission recommended to Parliament a Draft Criminal Code Bill, extracts from which appear throughout this book. This generally was a restatement of the law where the law was clear but where reports of the Law Commission or other public bodies (*e.g.* the Criminal Law Revision Committee) have recommended changes these have been incorporated into the Draft Code. Where the law contained indefensible inconsistency the Draft Code sought to eliminate it. In one case, however, the Law Commission refused to incorporate the effect of House of Lords' decisions with regard to the meaning of "recklessness" (see *R. v. Caldwell, post*, p. 121) preferring their own definition of this term.

Since publication of the Draft Code the Law Commission has come to the view that there is little likelihood of Parliament giving up the time necessary to enact the Code in its entirety. It considers that the best hope for implementation is through a series of Bills each dealing with a discrete area of the criminal law (see Law Com. No. 218, *Legislating the Criminal Code: Offences Against the Person and General Principles* (1993) para. 1.3). As there has been no sign of Parliament

1

enacting the proposed Criminal Law Bill appended to this report, the prospect of a Criminal Code for England and Wales is becoming fainter with the passage of time.

In the remainder of this chapter we will consider some preliminary questions before moving on to look at the substantive criminal law in the chapters which follow. These are: What is a crime? What functions does the criminal law serve? Why is particular conduct classified as criminal?

1. THE CONCEPT OF CRIME

Williams, "The Definition of Crime" (1955) Current Legal Problems 107

Is the effort [to define crime] worth making? The answer is that lawyers must try to clarify the notion of 'crime', because it suffuses a large part of the law. For example: there is generally no time limit for criminal proceedings, whereas civil proceedings are commenced differently, and often in different courts. A criminal prosecutor generally need not be the victim of the wrong, and a private criminal prosecutor is for many purposes not regarded as a party to the proceedings; he is certainly not 'master' of the proceedings in the sense that he can drop them at will; these rules are different in civil cases. The law of procedure may generally be waived in civil but not in criminal cases. There are many differences in the law of evidence, and several in respect of appeal. . . .

. . . The common-sense approach is to consider whether there are any intrinsic differences between the acts constituting crimes and civil wrongs respectively. It is perhaps natural to suppose that since 'a crime' differs from 'a civil wrong', there must be something *in* a crime to make it different from a civil wrong.

As everybody knows, there is one serious hindrance to a solution of this kind. This is the overlap between crime and tort. Since the same act can be both a crime and a tort, as in murder and assault, it is impossible to divide the two branches of the law by reference to the type of act. So also it is impossible to divide them by reference to the physical consequences of the act, for if the act is the same the physical consequences must be the same.

It has occurred to some that there is a possible escape from this difficulty. Although the act, and its consequences, are the same, the act and consequences have a number of different characteristics or aspects; and it may be possible to identify some of these characteristics as criminal and some as civil. Pursuing this line of thought, two separate aspects have been seized upon as identifying crime: the aspect of moral wrong and the aspect of damage to the public. . . .

The proposition that crime is a moral wrong may have this measure of truth: that the average crime is more shocking, and has graver social consequences, than the average tort. Yet crimes of strict responsibility can be committed without moral wrong, while torts and breaches of trust may be, and often are, gross moral wrongs.

Even where a forbidden act is committed intentionally, a court deciding that it is a crime is not committed to the proposition that it is a moral wrong. Thus in holding that a summary proceeding for an offence under the Game Act was criminal in character, Lord Campbell C.J. said: It is our business, not to estimate the degree of moral guilt in the act of the appellant, but to see how such act is treated by the legislature. . . . I cannot be bound by any opinion that I may form of the morality of that act: but I must see what it is that the legislature has chosen to punish: *Cattell v. Ireson* (1858) E.B. & E. at pp. 97–98. There are crimes of great gravity in the legal calendar, such as mercy-killing and eugenic abortion, which are disputably moral wrongs, though they are indisputably crimes. The same is true of numerous summary offences. Lord Atkin put the situation pungently. The criminal quality of an act cannot be discerned by intuition; nor can it be discovered by reference to any standard but one: is the act prohibited with penal consequences? Morality and criminality are far from coextensive; nor is the sphere of criminality necessarily part of a more extensive field covered by morality—unless the moral code necessarily disapproves of all acts prohibited by the state, in which case the argument moves in a circle: *Proprietary Articles Trade Association v. Att.-Gen. for Canada* [1931] A.C. 324 (P.C.). . . .

The second intrinsic difference between crimes and civil wrongs found by some writers is in respect of the damage done. In tort there is almost invariably actual damage to some person, whereas in crime such damage is not essential, the threat being to the community as a whole. . . . Again there are formidable objections. Some torts do not require damage (such as trespass and libel), while many crimes do involve private damage. Some crimes are punished as an affront to the moral feelings of the community although they cause no damage to the community as a whole. This is true of the group of crimes having in differing degrees a religious aspect: blasphemy, attempted suicide, abortion, bigamy. It is also largely true of obscenity and adult homosexuality. Even murder need not cause public damage: for example, when a mother kills her infant child. This creates no general sense of insecurity; the only material loss to society is the loss of the child, and whether that is economically a real loss or a gain depends on whether the country is under- or over-populated at the time. Evidently, the social condemnation of infant-killing rests on non-utilitarian ethics. Some forms of public nuisance, too, are crimes although they positively benefit the community: *Ward* (1836) 4 Ad. & El. 384.

Even where an act injures the community, it need not be exclusively a crime. Thus some crimes, as has already been pointed out, may be made the occasion either of a criminal prosecution or of a civil action (generally a relator action) for an injunction by the Attorney-General; in the latter event the crime is treated not as a crime but as a civil wrong to the public. There are civil public wrongs that are not crimes, for which there is no remedy, but a relator action as where statutory powers are being exceeded. Indeed, an ordinary tort to property may be committed against public property and so become a public wrong. . . .

We have rejected all definitions purporting to distinguish between crimes and other wrongs by reference to the sort of thing that is done or the sort of physical, economic or social consequences that follow from it. Only one possibility now remains. A crime must be defined by reference to the *legal* consequences of the act. We must distinguish, primarily, not between crimes and civil wrongs but between criminal and civil proceedings. A crime then becomes an act that is capable of being followed by criminal proceedings, having one of the types of outcome (punishment, etc.) known to follow these proceedings. . . .

As stated at the outset, there are many differences of procedure between crimes and civil wrongs. Often these differences are of no help in distinguishing between the two, because they are consequential differences—it is only when you know that the act is a crime or a civil wrong respectively that you know which procedure to select. However, some elements in procedure do assist in making the classification. When Parliament passes a statute forbidding certain conduct, it may refer in terms to certain procedural matters—such as trial on indictment, or summary conviction—which indicate that the act is to be a crime. Again, when it is disputed whether a given proceeding, such as a proceeding for a penalty, is criminal or civil, a point can be scored by showing that this proceeding has been held in the past to be governed by some procedural rule which is regarded as indicative of a criminal or civil proceeding, as the case may be. For example, the fact that a precedent decides that a new trial may be granted in a particular proceeding indicates that the proceeding is civil, since new trials are not granted in criminal cases. [But see now Criminal Appeal Act 1968, s.7.] On the other hand a precedent deciding that evidence of character is admissible in a certain proceeding indicates that it is criminal, since evidence of character is not admissible in civil cases, apart from certain quite definite exceptions.

Since the courts thus make use of the whole law of procedure in aid of their task of classification, an attempt to define crime in terms of one item of procedure only is mistaken. This remark applies to the test of crime adopted by Kenny, following Austin and Clark, which links crime with the ability of the Crown to remit the sanction. This test tells you whether an act is a crime only if you already know whether the sanction is remissible by the Crown. Almost always, however, the latter has to be deduced from the former, instead of vice versa. Thus Kenny defines *ignotum per ignotius*. This objection would not be open if Kenny's chosen procedural test were made available *along with all the others*. The procedural test does not give full assistance unless one is allowed to use the whole law of procedure.

. . . In short, a crime is an act capable of being followed by criminal proceedings having a criminal outcome, and a proceeding or its outcome is criminal if it has certain characteristics which mark it as criminal. In a marginal case the court may have to balance one feature, which may suggest that the proceeding is criminal, against another feature, which may suggest the contrary.

P. J. Fitzgerald, "A Concept of Crime" [1960] Crim.L.R. 257, 259

In the question what is a crime there seems to be entangled three different though related questions.

1. The question may be simply the request of the non-lawyer as to how he is to tell whether an act is a crime or not. Here we may give an imperative definition by saying that a crime is a breach of the criminal law. Though dismissed by Glanville Williams as circular, such a definition is useful firstly in emphasising that a crime is not necessarily a moral wrong and vice versa. Secondly, its value is that it directs attention away from abstract speculation on the nature of the act and focuses it on the need to study the provisions of the criminal law itself. . . .

2. The request for a definition of crime may be the request of the non-lawyer to be told what it means for the law to lay down that certain conduct shall be criminal. In other words he may want to know the effect of the law providing that an act is a crime. Here lies the usefulness of the definition proposed by Glanville Williams which distinguishes criminal wrongs from other legal wrongs. . . .

3. The quest for a definition of crime may be a more sophisticated question, of a lawyer reflecting on the criminal law, namely, what have all crimes in common other than the fact that they are breaches of the criminal law? In so far as the motive behind such a question is the desire for a simple test to decide whether conduct is criminal or not without reference to the provisions of the law, Glanville Williams' discussion is helpful

and illuminating in demonstrating that this is a search for the unattainable. But what may lie behind the question 'What is a crime?' may be the idea that Parliament and still more the courts have not created crimes arbitrarily or irrationally. Given that the aim of the criminal law is to announce that certain acts are not to be done, and to bring about that fewer of these acts are done, what is the principle or principles that have led the criminal law to prohibit the acts it has prohibited? . . .

Hester and Eglin, *A Sociology of Crime* (1992) p. 27

Without criminal law there would be no 'crime'. Virtually every form of human action—from taking others' property to taking others' lives—has in some time or place been deemed warranted, if not desirable. For example, until recently, slavery, non-consensual intercourse within marriage, and all forms of execution have been widely practised and have received official approval. This is not to say that people have not objected to these forms of behaviour, but until proscribed by criminal law they cannot be considered 'crimes'. Crime, then, is a relative or legalistic, rather than an absolute, concept. Criminal law is constructed within society. Hence, crime, too, is a social construction.

Question

When Parliament legislates making particular conduct criminal (or abolishing criminal liability for particular conduct) does the nature or morality of that conduct change or is it simply the (potential) consequences of the conduct which change?

2. THE FUNCTION OF THE CRIMINAL LAW

Ashworth, "Belief, Intent, and Criminal Liability" in Eekelaar and Bell (eds.), *Oxford Essays in Jurisprudence* (1987) p. 1.

The fundamental reason for having a system of criminal law is to provide a framework for the state punishment of wrongdoers, and thereby to preserve an acceptable degree of social order. Without criminal laws and their enforcement, each individual's person, property, and family would be substantially less safe from deliberate violation by others. It would hardly be sufficient to declare that individual members of society have certain rights, to physical integrity, security of property, and so on. It is also necessary *inter alia* to take steps to see that rights are not violated, a first step to which is to declare that individuals have duties not to violate the rights of others. Various branches of the civil law require those who negligently breach a duty to pay compensation to those whose rights were thus violated, and other parts of the civil law provide remedies for some deliberate breaches of duty. The specific technique of the criminal law is to provide for the conviction and punishment of those who culpably breach the more serious duties. Typically, the criminal law will declare which forms of conduct and omissions constitute such a serious breach of duty that they call for prosecution, conviction, and sentence under a special 'criminal' procedure and separately from private disputes among citizens. Attached to that declaration will be a system of enforcement and sentencing which operates, by and large, to influence people not to violate these laws. Even those who adopt a retributivist or rights-based approach to criminal liability and punishment surely cannot maintain a general indifference towards the frequency with which these more serious rights and duties are breached. A major part of the reason for having a system of criminal law and punishment is surely to reduce the frequency of those violations.

Note

In the extract which follows Walker, a criminologist, identifies objectives which may be pursued through the use of the criminal law.

Walker, *Crime and Criminology: A Critical Introduction* (1987) pp. 140–141

i. Objectives of the criminal law

Is it possible to discuss the proper content of the criminal law in general terms? If the contents of criminal codes are examined with a sociological eye, no fewer than fourteen different objectives can be discerned:

(*a*) the protection of human persons (and to some extent animals also) against intentional violence, cruelty, or unwelcome sexual approaches;

(*b*) the protection of people against some forms of unintended harm (for example from traffic, poisons, infections, radiation);

(*c*) the protection of easily persuadable classes of people (that is, the young or the weak-minded) against the abuse of their persons or property (for example by sexual intercourse or hire-purchase);

(*d*) the prevention of acts which, even if the participants are adult and willing, are regarded as 'unnatural' (for example incest, . . . bestiality, drug 'trips');

(*e*) the prevention of acts which, though not included under any of the previous headings, are performed so publicly as to shock other people (for example public nakedness, obscene language, or . . . copulation between consenting adults);

(*f*) the discouragement of behaviour which might provoke disorder (such as insulting words at a public meeting);

(*g*) the protection of property against theft, fraud, or damage;

(*h*) the prevention of inconvenience (for example the obstruction of roads by vehicles);

(*i*) the collection of revenue (for example keeping a motor car or television set without a licence);

(*j*) the defence of the State (for example espionage or—in some countries—political criticism);

(*k*) the enforcement of compulsory benevolence (for example the offence of failing to send one's children to school);

(*l*) the protection of social institutions, such as marriage or religious worship (for example by prohibiting bigamy or blasphemy);

(*m*) the prevention of unreasonable discrimination (for example against ethnic groups, religions, the female sex);

(*n*) the enforcement of the processes regarded as essential to these other purposes (for example offences connected with arrest, assisting offenders to escape conviction, and testimony at trials).

Note

Prominent in the objectives outlined above by Walker are those of protection of individuals and the prevention of offending. How these objectives are achieved also depends on the consequences which flow from conviction. Criminalisation cannot be divorced from the purposes which punishment may serve. This, however, is a matter of continuing controversy.

Galligan, "The Return to Retribution in Criminal Theory" in *Crime, Proof and Punishment: Essays in Memory of Sir Rupert Cross* **(1981), pp. 144, 146** *et. seq.*

If one were to attempt to explain the principal functions of that complex amalgam of institutions, persons, rules, and practices which we loosely refer to as the system of criminal justice, then two particular things would seem to call out for special attention. First, criminal justice is concerned centrally with trying, convicting and punishing those who are guilty of breaking the criminal law. Secondly, such systems are concerned to punish those who are convicted with a view to upholding the authority and effectiveness of the criminal law by sanctions that seek to deter, to prevent, to reform, or to incapacitate. These two tasks will often, but not necessarily, be compatible with each other. One view of criminal justice is to emphasise the forward-looking or utilitarian functions while another view sees the backward-looking or retributive aspect as primary. How one perceives the system will largely determine how one explains it and the kind of justifications that one finds acceptable. . . .

Utilitarian accounts usually begin with the assumption that the central purpose of criminal of justice is to reduce crime. This purpose is achieved by taking coercive action against selected individuals, usually those who have broken the law and who can be held personally responsible for so doing. There is an increasing body of offences which do not require responsibility in the usual legal sense, but nevertheless, with respect to the main corpus of criminal laws there is still a meticulous concern to be sure that before a person is punished he is guilty in the sense that he is responsible. But why should this be so? It is an important aspect of forward-looking explanations of criminal justice that the punishment of wrong-doers is not itself part of the general aim or purpose. Rather, confinement of impositions to the guilty law-breaker is a costly constraint on pursuit of the general reductivist aim. One approach faces this problem by suggesting that these constraints are misguided, in that inquiries into matters of personal responsibility are inevitably very crude, and unfairly selective in that there are large areas where action is taken without the requirement of responsibility. According to this view criminal justice should not be thought of as significantly different from other methods of social protection, such as confining dangerous mental defectives. Society has an interest in protecting itself from the person who has or is likely to commit serious crime and may legitimately take whatever preventive action is necessary. Although such an understanding of criminal justice has been anathema to most, a few modifications show it in a much better light. A modified approach might see considerable advantages such as economy, humanitarianism and the reduction of suffering in retaining the basic constraints of the aim of reducing crime, but since these would be conditional they could be departed from if to do so would provide better service to the general aim. It is worth noting that much of the practice of criminal justice is indeed compatible with this position for while coercion is normally based on responsibility, it is also often departed from if we bear in mind the preventive powers of the police and courts, the areas of strict and vicarious liability and the means available for confining mental defectives.

Views of this kind, however, have never dominated explanations of criminal justice. Most forward-looking accounts of criminal justice, no matter how different in other respects, seek to show that while the general purpose of criminal justice is forward looking, the responsibility constraints on that purpose are explicable, justifiable and necessary. Since Bentham's famous but flawed defence of punishing only those responsible for their actions, a range of increasingly subtle and sophisticated explanations have been advanced. There is, for example, the pragmatist argument that as a matter of practicalities it would be virtually impossible to design an efficacious system of criminal justice that did not limit the distribution of sanctions to the responsible offender. Alternatively there is the suggestion that the purpose of criminal justice is not only reduction through-deterrence, but also reduction-through-respect for the law. Unless the administration of criminal justice is in accordance with values esteemed in the community then respect for law is hardly to be earned and naturally most people think that a man should only be punished if he is guilty.

There is much to be said for this view; notice however that it puts forward the responsibility constraint not as an independent value in itself, but of value because it maximises the efficacy of law. . . .

Finally, it is a frequently heard criticism of utilitarian accounts that since the aim is crime control, there are difficulties in finding principles that limit the amount of punishment that may be inflicted on any offender. To the practical reformer this is the central issue, for recent penal history has shown the difficulty of controlling punishment distributed according to forward-looking goals. Retributive accounts, with their emphasis on punishment according to deserts, is naturally an attractive alternative to the unruly policies of rehabilitation and deterrence. . . .

Retributive explanations emphasise the concern of the criminal justice system to punish those who break the law. The core of the idea of retribution is the moral notion that the wrongdoer ought to be punished.

Thus a system that is centrally concerned with punishing offenders is retributive. In explaining the practice of criminal justice in this way, the retributive approach avoids the difficulties in explanation that beset forward-looking accounts. There is no need to distinguish between aim and distribution since the aim provides the criterion of distribution. The person who has not broken the law, or who could not help breaking it, or who can offer some other acceptable excuse is not a wrongdoer and is not liable for punishment. In other words within the context of criminal justice as we know it, punishment means inflicting sanctions on wrongdoers. This does not imply that coercion is never used against people in other ways; all it claims is that the reasons for coercing wrongdoers are different from the reasons that would explain other areas of coercion.

Put in this bald way, retribution includes both a description of criminal justice and a justification. Just as the utilitarian sees criminal justice as primarily concerned with reducing crime, so the retributivist sees the punishment of offenders as the dominant purpose. The logic of punishment consists in singling out an offender, condemning him for his offence and imposing punitive treatment upon him. The retributivist sees these three elements as part of one unified and justifiable social process: the offender has done wrong which, by punishment, is somehow righted. In short, the distinctive feature of retribution as a justifying principle, is that it provides a basis not just for singling out and condemning the offender, but also for inflicting punitive treatment. . . .

3. CLASSIFYING CONDUCT AS CRIMINAL

Note

Decisions whether to criminalise or decriminalise certain behaviour do not occur in a vacuum. The criminal law is not a "given" in any society. Choices are made as to where the boundaries of criminal liability are to be drawn and the drawing of these boundaries can be a highly political process. Quinney, *The Social Reality of Crime* (1970) states:

First, my perspective is based on a special conception of society. Society is characterized by diversity, conflict, coercion and change, rather than by consensus and stability. Second, law is a *result* of the operation of interests, rather than an instrument that functions outside of particular interests. Though law may control interests, it is in the first place created by interests. Third, law incorporates the interests of specific persons and groups; it is seldom the product of the whole society. Law is made by [people], representing special interests, who have the power to translate their interests into public policy.

Lacey, "Contingency and Criminalisation" in Loveland (ed.), *Frontiers of Criminality* (1995) pp. 4 & 14–15

To speak . . . of 'criminalisation' or of the 'frontiers of criminality' appears to presuppose that something or someone is, or has, been 'doing' the criminalising or 'constructing' the frontiers. Here we confront an ambiguity which is central to the idea of 'crime' in contemporary Britain. One culturally endorsed way of looking at crime is as something which is not primarily a legal, but rather a moral, category and hence, on one influential view, as outside the ambit of deliberate legislative change. Hence the role of criminal law is basically to reflect and articulate a pre-existing conception of wrongdoing. Yet from another culturally endorsed point of view, criminal law-making actually creates rather than reproduces categories of 'crime'. The relevance of both perspectives have sometimes been expressed in terms of the ideas of *mala in se* and *mala prohibita*, and reconciled, somewhat uncomfortably, on the basis that they refer to different areas of criminal law. . . .

[It is important to look] beyond the material or instrumental to attend to what are sometimes called the symbolic aspects of criminalisation or decriminalisation policies. Indeed, the recognition of what we might call the 'materiality of discourse' shows that we must be careful not to draw a strong dichotomy between the instrumental and the symbolic. For broader cultural understandings of crime affect particular policies, and are capable of subverting the intended meaning of legal or executive change, or indeed of supplying an astute decision-maker with possibilities of pursuing more than one political end by means of any one reform strategy. For example, observe how government decisions to criminalise or decriminalise by legislation can score political points by exploiting the ambiguity in the notion of crime identified above. On the one hand, government is constructing law and order problems as *political* issues, to which it is responding; formal legislation thus offers government the opportunity to represent itself as instrumentally effective. At the same time, it can draw on a prevailing discourse of crime as in some sense *pre-political*—that is, as wickedness or mere lawlessness or even pathology—as something from which we—that is, any 'good citizen'—would distance him or herself. In this sense, formal criminalisation is exploited as an occasion for the evocation of an underlying, symbolic consensus, appeal to which may be a significant mode of governmental self-legitimation. In such instances, government's legislative shifting of the boundaries of liability itself depends upon and expresses the contingency of crime, yet simultaneously deploys a powerful social discourse which constructs crime as 'given'. The purpose of the legislation is to make criminal that which is not already criminal, yet its rationale is that that behaviour is in another sense already criminal. Conversely, a decision to decriminalise can enjoy a similar dual legitimation; government's liberal credentials are fostered in that it gets credit for actually drawing back the boundaries of 'criminality'; yet its action is justified in part by the implication that the conduct in question was never really criminal in the first place.

It is also important to recognise that deliberate legislative or judicial shifts (perhaps we should say 'attempted shifts') in the frontiers of criminal liability often have symbolic effects which are less obviously envisaged or welcome. For example, the formal criminalisation of a kind of conduct, the practical proscription of which proves for one reason or another to be impossible or very difficult to enforce, may be counterproductive. This counter-productiveness may consist in the proscription's being seen as implicitly legitimating that form of behaviour. Incitement to racial hatred would be a good example here; its virtual non-enforcement is seen by many as implying covert approval of the behaviour formally proscribed. It may also consist in undermining the images of instrumental effectiveness, universality and evenhandedness, which persist even in the face of the general selectiveness and patterning of enforcement practices, and which are central to criminal law's perceived legitimacy (examples here might include those of gaming laws and a variety of offences concerning sexual 'morality').

Note

What conduct should be criminalised? Undoubtedly there will be general agreement on some matters but varying opinions on others. The issue which arises is the extent to which the criminal law should legislate for morality, particularly where views on morality differ and where the conduct involved does not involve harm to others.

Gross, *A Theory of Criminal Justice* (1979) pp. 13–14

It seems obvious that those crimes of violence, theft, and destruction that stand as paradigms of crime and comprise the core of any penal code are also moral wrongs. Everyone has a right to be free of such harm inflicted by others, and when murder, rape, arson, assault, or larceny is committed there is also a moral wrong since a moral duty to refrain from doing harm to others has been breached. The right to be free of such harm does not have its origin in law but in a general consensus on the rights enjoyed by any member of society, or even by any person, no matter how he lives. This consensus is a more fundamental element of society even than the law, and for that reason the violation of such a right is a moral wrong and not simply a legal wrong.

Lloyd, *Introduction to Jurisprudence* (4th ed., 1979) pp. 54–59

A good deal of controversy has arisen in recent years as to whether the fact that conduct is, by common standards, regarded as immoral, in itself justifies making that conduct punishable by law. This controversy was set off by the opinion expressed in the Wolfenden Committee Report on Prostitution and Homosexuality (Cmnd. 247, 1957), which in effect reasserted the answer given by John Stuart Mill, that legal coercion can only be justified for the purpose of preventing harm to others. Accordingly, on this view, there is a moral or ethical limit beyond the appropriate reach of the law. Mill's thesis had been attacked by the great Victorian judge, Stephen, in his *Liberty, Equality and Fraternity*, and the issue was now rekindled by Lord Devlin's critique of *Wolfenden* in a lecture called 'The Enforcement of Morals' delivered in 1959. Lord Devlin has subsequently returned to this theme a number of times [see Devlin, *The Enforcement of Morals*, O.U.P., 1965]. He has argued that there is a public morality which provides the cement of any human society, and that the law, especially the criminal law, must regard it as its primary function to maintain this public morality. Whether in fact in any particular case the law should be brought into play by specific criminal sanctions must depend upon the state of public feeling. Conduct which arouses a widespread feeling of reprobation, a mixture of 'intolerance, indignation and disgust', deserves to be suppressed by legal coercion in the interests of the integrity of society. For this purpose, Lord Devlin has recourse to the common law jury idea, the notion that the 'man in the jury-box' supplies an adequate standard of current morality for the purpose of assessing the limits of legal intervention. The juryman after all does not give a snap judgment; his verdict is the outcome of argument and deliberation after, perhaps, listening to expert evidence and receiving guidance from an experienced judge. And as for reliance upon feeling, this was the ordinary man's best guide where a choice had to be made between a number of reasonable conclusions. He therefore stigmatises as an 'error of jurisprudence' the view in the Wolfenden Report that there is some single principle explaining the division between crime and sin, such as that based upon Mill's notion of what may lead to harmful consequences to third persons.

Devlin concluded that if vice were not suppressed society would crumble: 'The suppression of vice is as much the law's business as the suppression of subversive activities.'

Such a thesis appears to have received some support from the remarkable decision of the House of Lords in the so-called *Ladies' Directory Case* (*Shaw v. D.P.P.* [1962] A.C. 220), but has been strenuously opposed by Professor Hart (H. L. A. Hart, *Law, Liberty and Morality*, O.U.P., 1963). Hart has outlined (35 Univ. of Chicago Law Review, 1, 11–13), in the first place, 'the types of evidence that might conceivably be relevant to the issue'. One could examine 'crude historical evidence', look at disintegrated societies and enquire whether disintegration was preceded by a malignant change in their common morality, considering further any 'causal connection'. Such a survey would have formidable difficulties for, even supposing, which is most unlikely, that moral decadence was responsible for the decline of Rome, would such evidence be persuasive in considering modern technological societies? Hart puts his faith rather in the evidence of social psychology. Depending on one's idealogy, the way of viewing the alternatives to the maintenance of a common morality, this could take one of two forms. One view would be *permissiveness*: one would show how this led to a weakening of individual capacity for self-control and contributed to an increase in violence and dishonesty. But the other side of the coin is *moral pluralism*. Would this lead to antagonism, to a society in the state of nature depicted by Hobbes [see *Leviathan*, Pt. 1, Chap. 13 ('. . . the life of man, solitary, poor, nasty, brutish, and short').] or rather to mutual tolerance, to co-existence of divergent moralities? What evidence there is comes down firmly in favour of co-existence. Having removed the foundations of Devlin's thesis, Hart then sets about to demolish the structure erected upon them. He dismisses as fantastic the notion that all morality forms 'a single seamless web' so that deviation from any one part will almost inevitably produce destruction of the whole. The mere fact that conventional morality may change in a permissive direction does not mean that society is going to be destroyed or subverted. Again, Lord Devlin assumes a degree of moral solidarity in society, which may have existed in mid-Victorian England, but is hardly discernible at the present time. Hart goes on to point out that the real solvent to social morality is not the failure of the law to endorse its restrictions, but rather the operation of free critical discussion, and he goes on to point out the dangers to democracy which might flow from the notion that free discussion should be prohibited on account of its impact on the prevalent social morality. That the moral notions of the majority are matters to which the legislature must pay close account seems beyond question, but what Mill had in mind was that at all costs the idea that the majority had a moral right to dictate how everyone else should live, was something which needed to be resisted. It is essential, therefore, from a libertarian point of view, that public indignation, while given due weight, should be subject to the overriding tests of rational and critical appraisal.

Nevertheless, Hart accepts the need for the law to enforce some morality and the real area of dispute is where the line should be drawn. Mill drew it at harm to others. Hart extends the role of the law by his acceptance of 'paternalism,' in addition to Mill's reliance on harmful consequences to others (*Law, Liberty and Morality*, pp. 30–34). So, where Devlin justified *R. v. Donovan* [1934] 2 K.B. 498, (see, *post*, p. 630) as enforcement of morality, Hart sees the decision as a concession to paternalism. Hart never defines paternalism and Devlin has been critical of its vagueness. 'What, also, I did not foresee was that some of the crew who sail under Mill's flag of liberty would mutiny and run paternalism up the mast.' (*The Enforcement of Morals*, p. 132.) Although Devlin is unable to distinguish paternalism and the enforcement of morals, there is a distinction which centres on the decision-making process of those who are subject to the law. Paternalism thus may intervene to stop self-inflicted harm such as the results of drug-taking or cigarette smoking or of the refusal to use crash helmets or seat belts, not because of a wish to enforce conventional morality, but because of doubts as to the capacity of the 'victim' to make a rational decision, especially where he is mentally disturbed (according to conventional morality) or physically ill.

But Hart goes further than this. He admits, with Devlin, that some shared morality is essential to society, what he calls 'universal values' (*Law, Liberty, and Morality*, p. 71). If *any* society is to survive, if any legal system is to function, then there must be rules prohibiting, for example, murder. But is abortion or euthanasia murder? The standard case remains uncontroversial, the marginal situation is no nearer solution. Hart further argues, in a later formulation (35 Univ. of Chicago Law Review, p. 10), that rules essential for a *particular* society (monogamy might be an example) might be enforced. 'For any society there is to be found . . . a central core of rules or principles which constitutes its pervasive and distinctive style of life.' And he continues: 'it then becomes an open and empirical question whether any particular moral rule is so organically connected with the central core that its preservation is required as a vital bastion'. At this stage a point has been reached where there is not much to choose between the two main contestants.

Question

To what extent does the criminal law, particularly in areas of morality, create criminals? Becker, *Outsiders: Studies in the Sociology of Deviance* (1963) states (at p. 9):

"[T]he central fact about deviance [is that] it is created by society. I do not mean this in the way it is ordinarily understood, in which the causes of deviance are located in the social situation of the deviant or in 'social factors' which prompt his action. I mean, rather, that *social groups create deviance by making rules whose infraction constitutes deviance*, and by applying those rules to particular people and labelling them as outsiders. From this point of view, deviance is *not* a quality of the act the person commits, but rather a consequence of the application by others of rules and sanctions to an 'offender'. The deviant is one to whom that label has successfully been applied; deviant behaviour is behaviour that people so label."

Do you agree in whole or in part with this statement? If the latter, to which offences do you think it more accurately applies?

Packer, *The Limits of the Criminal Sanction* **(1969) pp. 261** *et seq.*

IMMORALITY: A NECESSARY CONDITION

The debate over the relationship between law and morals is perennial. It has rarely taken specific enough account, however, of what kind of law is at issue. The criminal sanction represents a very special kind of law, itself morally hazardous. As we have seen, the rationale of criminal punishment requires that no one should be treated as a criminal unless his conduct can be regarded as culpable. The flouting of this requirement that takes place when offenses are interpreted as being of 'strict liability' contributes to the dilution of the criminal law's moral impact. The ends of the criminal sanction are disserved if the notion becomes widespread that being convicted of a crime is no worse than coming down with a bad cold. The question we now have to face is what role, if any, the moral force of the criminal sanction should have in determining what conduct should be treated as criminal. . . .

Can we then assert that there is any kind of connection between the immorality of a category of conduct and the appropriate use of the criminal sanction? I think we can, but only on a prudential basis. Leaving aside for the moment the question of what we mean by immoral, we may discern an analogy between the requirement of culpability in the individual case and a limiting criterion for the legislative invocation of the criminal sanction: only conduct generally considered 'immoral' should be treated as criminal. Several reasons support this prudential limitation. To begin with, the principles of selection we use in determining what kinds of undesirable conduct to treat as criminal should surely include at least one that is responsive to the basic character of the criminal sanction, *i.e.* its quality of moral condemnation. To put it another way, we should use the strengths of the sanction rather than ignore or undermine them. If the conduct with which the original sanction deals is already regarded as being morally wrong, the processes of the criminal law have, so to speak, a 'leg up' on the job. This is a matter partly of public attitude and partly of the morale maintained by those who operate the criminal processes. The way to keep those processes running at peak efficiency is to ensure that those who operate them are convinced that what they are doing is right. The surest way to persuade them that what they are doing is right is to have them act only against what they think is wrong. If the criminal sanction is widely used to deal with morally neutral behavior, law enforcement officials are likely to be at least subconsciously defensive about their work, and the public will find the criminal law a confusing guide to moral, or even acceptable, behavior.

[Packer dismisses the argument that the criminal sanction can condition people's view of what is moral, and continues]: . . .

The question remains: whose morality are we talking about? It is easy to slide into the assumption that somewhere in society there is an authoritative body of moral sentiment to which the law should look. That assumption becomes particularly dangerous, as we shall see, when it is used to buttress the assertion that the immorality of a given form of conduct is a *sufficient* condition for declaring that conduct to be criminal. But when one is talking about immorality as a *necessary* condition for invocation of the criminal sanction, the inquiry should simply be whether there exists any significant body dissent from the proposition that the conduct in question is immoral. Is there any social group that will be alienated or offended by making (or keeping) the conduct in question criminal? If there is, then prudence dictates caution in employing the criminal sanction.

We can sum up this prudential limitation as follows: the criminal sanction should ordinarily be limited to conduct that is viewed, without significant social dissent, as immoral. The calendar of crimes should not be enlarged beyond that point and, as views about morality shift, should be contracted.

IMMORALITY: AN INSUFFICIENT CONDITION

If the immorality of conduct is a generally necessary condition for invocation of the criminal sanction, is it a generally sufficient one? That is the gist of the "law and morals" debate. Conventional morality, it is asserted, is what holds society together. It must be not only taught but enforced. The enforcement of morals needs no other justification. The usual lines of attack upon this argument are, first, that there is no easy way to determine what should count as immoral and, second, that other considerations (primarily of enforceability) should also be taken into account in determining whether immoral conduct should be made criminal. To these may be added a third: it simply is not true that we use the criminal law to deal with all conduct that we consider immoral; even the most extreme of legal moralists have never pressed for that. Therefore, unless the choice of proscribed conduct is to be purely whimsical, we must take other factors into consideration. . . .

The extent of disagreement about moral judgments is an obvious reason for hesitancy about an automatic enforcement of morals. . . .

In a society that neither has nor wants a unitary set of moral norms, the enforcement of morals carries a heavy cost in repression. We don't begin to agree about the "morality" of smoking, drinking, gambling, fornicating, or drug-taking, for example, quite apart from the gap between what we say and what we do. The more heterogeneous the society, the more repressive the enforcement of morals must be. And the more heterogeneous the society, the more foreign to its ethos that kind of repression is likely to be. . . .

Immorality clearly should not be viewed as a sufficient or even a principal reason for proscribing conduct as criminal. Morals belong to the home, the school, and the church; and we have many homes, many schools, many churches. Our moral universe is polycentric. The state, especially when the most coercive of sanctions is at issue, should not seek to impose a spurious unity upon it. . . .

If a legislator can think of no better reason to proscribe conduct than that he (or his constituency) abhors it, he had better think twice about doing it.

HARM TO OTHERS

[Packer goes on to consider "harm to others" as a limiting principle on the use of the criminal sanction.]

"Harm to others" does not, of course, mean identifiable others. It has become fashionable to talk about "victimless crimes", meaning those in which there is no immediately identifiable victim to lodge a complaint. The absence of an identifiable victim can make enforcement difficult, and can encourage undesirable enforcement practices. But the prospect of these difficulties should not end the inquiry into the wisdom of any given use of the criminal sanction. Many offenses against the administration of government are "victimless crimes" in the sense that there is nobody to complain. Consensual transactions like bribery and espionage are admittedly difficult to detect because of the absence of an identifiable victim; yet they do not necessarily cause so little "harm to others" that we can forget about subjecting them to the criminal sanction.

The "harm to others" formula seems to me to have two uses that justify its inclusion in a list of limiting criteria for invocation of the criminal sanction. First, it is a way to make sure that a given form of conduct is not being subjected to the criminal sanction purely or even primarily because it is thought to be immoral. It forces an inquiry into precisely what bad effects are feared if the conduct in question is not suppressed by the criminal law. Second, it immediately brings into play a host of secular inquiries about the effects of subjecting the conduct in question to the criminal sanction. One cannot meaningfully deal with the question of "harm to others" without weighing benefits against detriments. In that sense, it is a kind of threshold question, important not so much in itself as in focusing attention on further considerations relevant to the ultimate decision. It is for these two instrumental reasons rather than for either its intrinsic rightness or its ease of application that it deserves inclusion.

[Packer summarises as follows the "limiting criteria" he regards as useful for the purpose of establishing a benchmark for the optimal use of the criminal sanction:]

(1) The conduct is prominent in most people's view of socially threatening behavior, and is not condoned by any significant segment of society.
(2) Subjecting it to the criminal sanction is not inconsistent with the goals of punishment.
(3) Suppressing it will not inhibit socially desirable conduct.
(4) It may be dealt with through even-handed and nondiscriminatory enforcement.
(5) Controlling it through the criminal process will not expose that process to severe qualitative or quantitative strains.
(6) There are no reasonable alternatives to the criminal sanction for dealing with it.

Note

Walker in *Crime and Criminology: A Critical Introduction* (1987), pp. 142–150 outlines the following "limiting principles" which if applied would improve the decision-making process on where the boundaries of the criminal law are to be drawn.

Moral limits

(A) Prohibitions should not be included in the criminal law for the sole purpose of ensuring that breaches of them are visited with retributive punishment. (See Beccaria, *Of Crimes and Punishments* (1764).)
(B) The criminal law should not be used to penalise behaviour which does no harm. (See Bentham, *An Introduction to the Principles of Morals and Legislation* (1789).)
(CC) The criminal law should not be used where measures involving less suffering are as effective or almost as effective in reducing the frequency of the conduct in question. (*Cf.* Bentham, *ibid.*)
(DD) The criminal law should not include prohibitions whose by-products are more harmful than the conduct which they are intended to discourage. (*Cf.* Bentham, *ibid.*)
(E) The criminal law should not be used for the purpose of compelling people to act in their own best interests. (Cf. J.S. Mill, *On Liberty* (1859).)

Pragmatic limits

(F) The criminal law should not include prohibitions which do not have strong public support. (*Cf.* James Fitzjames Stephen, *Liberty, Equality, Fraternity* (1873).)
(GG) A prohibition should not be included in the criminal code if only a small percentage of infringements of it could be proved against infringers.

Questions

1. Can you think of conduct which is criminal which does not involve causing harm to non-consenting persons and/or which seeks to compel people to act in their own best interests?
2. What alternative measures are available to reduce the frequency of conduct which currently is criminalised, for example, the taking of proscribed drugs or illicit sexual relationships?
3. Can you identify any by-products of criminalising the above examples of conduct. Do you consider these to be more harmful than the conduct? What criteria would you adopt in making this assessment?
4. Can you identify laws which are virtually unenforceable? Does this undermine respect for the law or do laws, despite their unenforceability, still perform a symbolic function and affirm a common core of morality in society?

Note

Dealing specifically with private consensual sexual behaviour between adults Becker, *op. cit.* p. 304, identified the following reasons why the criminal sanction was an inappropriate response:

(1) Rarity of enforcement creates a problem of arbitrary police and prosecutorial discretion.

(2) The extreme difficulty of detecting such conduct leads to undesirable police practices.

(3) The existence of the proscription tends to create a deviant subculture.

(4) Widespread knowledge that the law is violated with impunity by thousands every day creates disrespect for law generally.

(5) No secular harm can be shown to result from such conduct.

(6) The theoretical availability of criminal sanctions creates a situation in which extortion and, on occasion, police corruption may take place.

(7) There is substantial evidence that the moral sense of the community no longer exerts strong pressure for the use of criminal sanctions.

(8) No utilitarian goal of criminal punishment is substantially advanced by proscribing private adult consensual sexual conduct.

The only countervailing argument is that relaxation of the criminal proscription will be taken to express social approval of the conduct at issue.

Note

The above debate on where the boundaries of the criminal law should be drawn is a continuing one. It features in the speeches of their Lordships in *R. v. Brown*, *post* p. 589 and also featured in debates in Parliament preceding the passage of the Criminal Justice and Public Order Act 1994 which by section 145 reduced the age of consent to homosexual acts to eighteen and which also criminalised trespass in wide-ranging provisions in Part V. It also features in the debate over the decriminalisation of proscribed drugs.

Ashworth, *Principles of Criminal Law*, 3rd ed., pp. 24–27

THE POLITICS OF LAWMAKING

Creating a new criminal offence may often be regarded as an instantly satisfying political response to public worries about a form of conduct that has been given publicity by the newspapers and television. The pressure on politicians to be seen to be doing something may be great, and considered responses such as consultation and commissioning research may invite criticisms of indecision and procrastination. Thus, in many countries, the growth of the criminal law may reflect particular phases in contemporary social history, as written by the mass media and politicians.

We may consider two examples of recent legislative extension of the range of the criminal law: the offences in Part V of the Criminal Justice and Public Order Act 1994 and, first, the offence of causing harassment, alarm or distress in the Public Order Act 1986. In its reform of public order law in the 1980s, the government added to the offences recommended by the Law Commission a further offence, consisting of disorderly behaviour or threatening, abusive or insulting behaviour, likely to cause 'harassment, alarm or distress': Public Order Act 1986, section 5. The reason for adding this offence was to give the police the power to intervene at the early stages of disorder, and also to deal with minor acts of hooliganism. Much could be said about the origins and import of this provision. For present purposes, it is sufficient to note that the new offence is additional to that created by section 4 of the Act, of using threatening, abusive or insulting words or behaviour with intent to cause others to fear violence or with intent to provoke others to use violence. This raises the question whether there was a satisfactory justification for the further police powers and wider offence in section 5: the requirements of section 5 are so modest and broadly-stated that it could be used to cast the net of criminality very wide. Research into the use of section 5 shows just this: although the reliance of the police on section 5 varies considerably from area to area, one feature is that it has been much used to criminalize people who swear at police officers. This demonstrates at once the use by the police of public order offences as 'resources' to use when people show disrespect, and also the way in which criminalization ostensibly aimed at one set of situations (*e.g.* disturbing residents by kicking over dustbins) can then be adapted to deal with situations for which its use was not envisaged (*i.e.* swearing at the police).

The Criminal Justice and Public Order Act 1994 contains various new crimes aimed at penalizing trespassers on land. For many years the general principle has been that trespass to land is not appropriate for criminalization—there are civil remedies, disputes are better decided in the civil courts, and accelerated orders for possession are available to landowners. A few exceptional offences did exist before, but the 1994 Act goes much further by criminalizing aggravated trespass on land with intent to disrupt lawful activities thereon (section 68), by extending the police power to order trespassers off land, with associated offences for non-compliance (section 61), by permitting house owners to take stronger action against squatters (section 72), and by creating a new offence of unauthorized camping (section 77). There may be more political symbolism in these new offences than a real prospect of large-scale police action, but the offences are now on the statute book and several questions arise. Is such conduct so serious that the criminal law ought to be invoked rather than the civil process? Is there not a danger that, as with the Public Order Act 1986, section 5, the wide drafting of these offences will permit their use by the police against other forms of conduct? Aggravated trespass is an offence supposedly aimed at hunt saboteurs, but its wording could encompass many other forms of protest. Unauthorized camping is an offence supposedly aimed at New Age travellers, but its wording is clearly apt to criminalize gypsies for following their long-established way of life. Much will therefore turn on patterns of enforcement. If the experience of the 1986 Act, section 5, is a fair indicator, there will be local variations, with some police forces using the powers fully and others declining to do so, and with much depending on the dynamics of particular situations. Senior police officers have already expressed discomfort about enforcing the new offence of unauthorized camping against gypsies, but perhaps the politicians are content that an offence has been created and thus 'something has been done about it'.

These two examples serve to illustrate the complexity of the issues that arise in the criminalization debate. Even on a theoretical plane, fixing the proper boundaries of the criminal law is likely to involve not sharp distinctions and clearly defined categories, but rather judgments of degree relating to such matters as how proximate the harm should be to justify criminalization, and how relevant the availability of alternative mechanisms for enforcement should be. Although in practice examples of political pressures overcoming principled arguments are abundant, they do not account for all instances of criminalization. In some spheres such as financial regulation there is constant debate about the proper boundaries of criminal and regulatory or civil controls. In others, such as bail offences, law enforcement agents themselves may be the main force behind criminalization. In others it may be a report of the Law Commission or other committee, after due consultation, that results in new criminal law. And in still others, the political argument may be won by a pressure group which has campaigned for expanding the criminal law in areas such as domestic violence, drinking and driving, and so forth. Sheer vote winning, or preserving the position of the powerful over the powerless, accounts for some, but certainly not all, decisions to create new crimes.

Note

While most of the offences considered in the remainder of this book do not fall within the area of morality on which debate as to the location of the boundaries of the criminal law centres, it is, nonetheless, an important debate in which criminal lawyers must engage. This is particularly so in the case of proposals for new criminal offences which may be supported by a section of the populace and where legislation may benefit the popularity of the political party promoting it. It is at such times that the principles suggested by writers such as Packer and Walker must be fed into the debate if all hopes of achieving a rational and principled criminal code are not to be abandoned. At the same time consideration of the European Convention on Human Rights is also pertinent. The Human Rights Act 1998, which came into force on October 2, 2000, gives effect in English law to the rights guaranteed in the Convention. Section 19 of the 1998 Act requires a Minister in charge of a Bill in Parliament to make a statement of compatibility or, if the Bill is not compatible with the Convention, to make a statement to this effect. Consequently lawmakers must now pay particular regard to the Convention to ensure that new laws do not breach the rights guaranteed in the Convention. In addition, the courts in applying all legislation must interpret it, so far as it is possible to do so, in a way which is compatible with the Convention rights (section 3). If a compatible interpretation is not possible the court must apply the existing law to the case before it but the High Court and appellate courts may make a declaration of incompatibility (section 4). Where the common law conflicts with the Convention, courts will likely override the common law because of the obligation on them, as a public authority, not to act in a way which is incompatible with a Convention right (section 6). Accordingly, the Convention will have considerable impact on criminal courts particularly on matters relating to criminal procedure, evidence and sentencing. It will, however, also have relevance in certain areas of the substantive criminal law. In the chapters which follow reference to the European Convention on Human Rights and cases of the European Court of Human Rights will be made where appropriate.

ACTUS REUS

1. ELEMENTS OF CRIME

The terms *actus reus* and *mens rea* when used to describe the elements of a criminal offence are deceptively simple. Not only is there a host of conceptual pitfalls concealed within each, but there is also no agreement amongst lawyers as to the precise divide between them.

A. T. H. Smith, "On Actus Reus and Mens Rea" *in Reshaping the Criminal Law* **(ed. Glazebrook), pp. 95–98**

As the elliptic statements of the basic ingredients of criminal liability that they are frequently taken to be, both expressions [*actus reus* and *mens rea*] are incomplete and misleading. While the term *mens rea* is used in at least three distinct senses, so that failure to distinguish clearly between them leads inevitably to confusion, the terminology of *actus reus* tends to conceal the important principles that are at stake when the courts are deciding what sorts of conduct deserve condemnation as criminal. I do not mean to suggest that the traditional terminology should be abandoned; rather I would argue that a sharper awareness of its limitations might help us to see more clearly what the preconditions to criminal liability really are, and how far they really reflect the principles they are commonly supposed to encapsulate. . . .

This division of crime into its constituent parts is an exercise of analytical convenience: the concepts of *actus reus* and *mens rea* are simply tools, useful in the exposition of the criminal law. Great care should, therefore, be taken to avoid determining questions of policy by reference to definition and terminology. Such observations as that the maxim *actus non facit reum nisi mens sit rea* serves the 'important purpose of stressing two basic requirements of criminal liability', make *actus reus* and *mens rea* seem rather more than analytical tools. They have been converted from the descriptive to the normative: to propositions that criminal liability *should* be based on harmful conduct, and *should* require a mental element. . . .

The raw material of any crime is the particular social mischief that the legislator is seeking to suppress. But for ascertaining the *actus reus* of any given offence, the starting point for the courts is the statute, or, as it may still be, the common law definition. Questions of statutory interpretation must be solved before the exact scope of the proscribed activity can be known. Where the defendant's conduct can fairly be described as coming within the terms of the proscribed activity, an offence has, prima facie, been committed: liability will ensue unless he advances some explanation of his conduct which shows that it was justified, in which case there is no *actus reus*. As one writer puts it, 'the *actus reus* is a defeasible concept'. But some lawyers are content to say that the requirements of *actus reus* are satisfied whenever the terms of the definition are fulfilled. The danger of taking such a very limited view of what is entailed in the *actus reus*, is that it may too readily be concluded that the harm that the law seeks to prevent has occurred. Much depends on the view taken of the role of defences. . . .

Glanville Williams [C.L.G.P., p. 20] inclines to the view that all the elements of a crime are divisible into either *actus reus* or *mens rea* and holds that the *actus reus* includes absence of defence. By implication, therefore, all defences are a denial that the prosecution has proved a requisite part of its case. Although they nowhere clearly articulate the point, Professors Smith and Hogan seem to prefer the view that the constituent ingredients of crime are threefold, and include defences which are themselves composites of physical (or external) and mental elements. This mode of analysis is becoming increasingly widespread amongst academic writers, and has been carried furthest by Professor Lanham [[1976] Crim.L.R. 276]. He says that:

> as a matter of analysis we can think of a crime as being made up of three ingredients, *actus reus*, *mens rea* and (a negative element) absence of a valid defence. Some defences (*e.g.* alibi) negative the *actus reus*. Some defences (*e.g.* I did not mean to do it) negative the *mens rea*. A third group of defences (*e.g.* self-defence) operate without negativing either positive element, in effect as a confession and avoidance. But there is a fourth kind of defence (*sic*) which is perfectly capable of standing as a confession and avoidance but which normally will negative one or other (or both) of the *actus reus* and *mens rea*.

According to this view, then *actus reus* and *mens rea* do not encapsulate all the ingredients of a crime.

Notes

1. The use of Latin terminology is not without its critics; Lord Diplock stated in *Miller* [1983] 2 A.C. 161, 174.

> "My Lords, it would I think be conducive to clarity of analysis of the ingredients of a crime that is created by statute, as are the great majority of offences today, if we were to avoid bad Latin and instead to think and speak . . . about the conduct of the accused and his state of mind at the time of that conduct, instead of speaking of *actus reus* and *mens rea*."

This counsel has been adopted by the Draft Criminal Code Bill (Law Com. No. 177, 1989) which uses the term "act" to describe the external elements of offences in preference to "*actus reus*" in the narrow sense as used by Lanham (*ante*). For "*mens rea*" the phrase "fault element" is used.

2. Most writers seem agreed that the "act" implied in the phrase "*actus reus*" does not stop at bodily movements or overt acts. "Some acts can only be engaged in, some can only be performed, some only are done, and there are even some that can only take place; and this suggests the richness and variety of those bits of the world that we may choose to regard as acts." (Gross, p. 133). Williams takes the view

that "the proposition that an offence requires an act requires to be so qualified by exceptions that its utility comes to seem doubtful. . . . It is therefore less misleading to say that a crime requires some *external state of affairs* that can be categorised as criminal." (T.C.L., p. 31).

(The normal mode of definition of offences is *result-oriented* requiring proof of an act or omission and usually proof that the conduct caused a specified result. This mode of definition is backed up with the law of attempts to cover cases where the intended result does not occur. An alternative mode of definition is that which concentrates on conduct, the *inchoate mode,* making it an offence to do certain acts in order to produce a certain outcome; the offence is committed whether or not the outcome results. An example of a result crime is murder where it must be proved that the deceased died as a result of the accused's conduct. An example of a conduct offence is perjury where the relevant conduct is the making of a statement on oath which the maker does not believe to be true; it is not a requirement of the offence that anyone else should believe the statement. For further discussion of result and conduct crimes see: Smith and Hogan, pp. 31–33; Smith, "The Element of Chance in Criminal Liability" (1971) Crim.L. R. 63; Ashworth, "Defining Criminal Offences Without Harm" in *Criminal Law: Essays in Honour of J. C. Smith* (1987, ed. P. Smith).)

2. VOLUNTARINESS

Criminal liability is founded on the notion of individual autonomy. A person should only be criminally liable where he or she is responsible for his or her conduct. Responsibility presumes that the conduct was voluntarily engaged on by that person. If the conduct is involuntary there should be no criminal liability. This raises the question, however, of what does "voluntary" or "involuntary" mean?

H. L. A. Hart, "Act of Will and Responsibility" in *Punishment and Responsibility* (1968), p. 90

The General Doctrine
   In this lecture I propose to air some doubts which I have long felt about a doctrine, concerning criminal responsibility, which has descended from the philosophy of conduct of the eighteenth century, through Austin, to modern English writers on the criminal law. This is the doctrine that, besides the elements of knowledge of circumstances and foresight of consequences, in terms of which many writers define *mens rea*, there is another 'mental' or at least psychological element which is required for responsibility: the accused's 'conduct' (including his omissions where these are criminally punishable) must, so it is said, be voluntary and not involuntary. This element in responsibility is more fundamental than *mens rea* in the sense of knowledge of circumstances or foresight of consequences; for even where *mens rea* in that sense is not required, and responsibility is 'strict' or 'absolute' . . ., this element, according to some modern writers, is still required. . . .
   In many textbooks there are general assertions that for *all* criminal responsibility conduct must be 'voluntary', 'conduct [must be] the result of the exercise of his will' there must be an 'act with its element of will', 'an act due to the deliberate exercise of the will'. Yet, surely, even if there

is any such general doctrine, these phrases are very dark. What does doctrine mean? What after all is the will? . . .

We know now what the general doctrine means: it defines an act in terms of the simplest thing we can do: this is the minimum feat of contracting our muscles. Conduct is 'voluntary' or 'the expression of an act of will' if the muscular contraction which, on the physical side, is the initiating element in what are loosely thought of as simple actions, is caused by a desire for the same contractions. This is all the mysterious element of the 'will' amounts to: it is this which is the minimum indispensable link between mind and body required for responsibility even where responsibility is strict. . . .

The . . . theory that has got into our law books through Austin is first, nonsensical when applied to omissions, and secondly cannot characterise what is amiss even in involuntary interventions; for the desire to move our muscles, which it says is missing there, is not present in normal voluntary action either.

Consider Hart's alternative definition under which he seeks to classify those acts generally regarded as not voluntary:

". . . We could characterise involuntary movements such as those made in epilepsy, or in a stroke, or mere reflex actions to blows or stings, as movements of the body which occurred although they were not appropriate, *i.e.* required for any action (in the ordinary sense of action) which the agent believed himself to be doing."

Williams, *Textbook of Criminal Law*, p. 148

Lawyers sometimes speak of a voluntary act meaning only that it was willed. Since every act is by definition willed, there is no need to call it voluntary.

The element of volition in an act has greatly exercised the philosophers. I can look at my hand, say to myself 'Hand, move to the left', and then cause it to move to the left. But that is not the way in which I usually live and move. I do not consciously direct orders to my muscles. Two philosophers, Ryle and Melden, have attempted to argue away the notion of will. They build their case upon the difficulty of identifying conscious volitions accompanying bodily movement. Certainly it would be false to assume that every act is the result of deliberation: I may scratch my nose while thinking, without knowing I am doing it or recollecting I have done it. Even when the act is conscious, introspection does not show a conscious exercise of will preceding conduct. When I move my arms, say in writing a letter, I do not consciously decide to move them before moving them. It is true that electrical impulses run from the motor nerve cells in the spinal cord through the nerve fibres to the muscles; and these muscles are under the control of my brain. But the mental functioning that controls movement is not conscious determination, and it takes place at practically the same time as the movement. Will is the mental activity accompanying the type of bodily movement that we call an act. It is, of course, possible to will the absence of an act, as when we sit still.

A bodily movement is said to be willed, generally speaking, when the person in question could have refrained from it if he had so willed, that is, he could have kept still. Movements that are the result of epilepsy, for example, are involuntary or unwilled because the person concerned cannot by any mental effort avoid them. Whatever the difficulties in explaining what we mean by volition, everyone realises the important difference between doing something and having something happen to one; and this distinction is a basic postulate of a moral view of human behaviour.

Note

Voluntariness and consciousness

Where a person performs an act in a state of unconsciousness or impaired consciousness this is referred to as automatism. Automatism may arise from a variety of causes. Where it arises from illness or disease it may amount to insanity. Automatism and insanity are dealt with in Chapter 4. It is not *necessary* for a person to be unconscious before his or her acts are said to be involuntary. A person suffering from St Vitus Dance, or having a muscle spasm, is acting involuntarily under either the Hart "inappropriateness" formula, or the Williams "inability to refrain" test. Nor is unconsciousness in itself *sufficient* to avoid liability. As Lord Denning said in *Bratty v. Att.-Gen. for Northern Ireland* [1963] A.C. 386, 410: "It is not every involuntary act which leads to a complete acquittal." This dictum applies in particular where the defendant is responsible for his or her own incapacity, for example, where he or she is voluntarily intoxicated. In this situation *moral* voluntariness, arising from the prior voluntary act of getting drunk (for which the defendant is responsible), suffices to establish criminal liability for the unconsciously committed subsequent act (see further Chapter 4).

Is voluntariness a purely physical concept or does the law recognise moral involuntariness in the sense that while a person may will an action, other factors may be operating which suggest that the exercise of will in this situation was not free, for example due to a threat emanating from a human agent or to dangers or threats emanating from the situation in which he or she is placed? The law does not recognise moral involuntariness as a denial of the *actus reus* but confines voluntariness to a consideration of the purely physical. Allowances may be made for moral involuntariness through the defences of necessity, duress and duress of circumstances but these are limited by policy considerations which would not be possible if moral involuntariness operated to deny the existence of an *actus reus*, *i.e.* no *actus reus* no crime (see further Chapter 6).

The case which follows has also been criticised for ignoring the requirement of voluntariness.

R. v. Larsonneur
(1933) 97 J.P. 206
Court of Criminal Appeal

The defendant, a French subject, landed in the United Kingdom with a French passport. This was indorsed with conditions prohibiting her employment here. On March 22 these conditions were varied by a condition requiring her to leave the United Kingdom that day. This she did, going to the Irish Free State. The Irish authorities ordered her deportation and she was brought to Holyhead in the custody of the

Irish police and she was there handed over to the English police. She was charged that "she being an alien to whom leave to land in the United Kingdom has been refused, was found in the United Kingdom contrary to Articles 1(3) (*g*) and 18 (1) (*b*) of the Aliens Order, 1920, as amended by S.R. & O. No. 326 of 1923 and 715 of 1931." She was convicted at London Sessions and appealed.

LORD HEWART C.J.: The fact is, as the evidence shows, that the appellant is an alien. She has a French passport, which bears this statement under the date March 14, 1933. "Leave to land granted at Folkestone this day on condition that the holder does not enter any employment, paid or unpaid, whilst in the United Kingdom", but on March 22 that condition was varied and one finds these words: "The condition attached to the grant of leave to land is hereby varied so as to require departure from the United Kingdom not later than March 22, 1933." Then follows the signature of an Under-Secretary of State. In fact, the appellant went to the Irish Free State and afterwards, in circumstances which are perfectly immaterial, so far as this appeal is concerned, came back to England. She was at Holyhead on April 21, 1933, practically a month after the day limited by the condition of her passport. . . .

Appeal dismissed

Notes

Part of the problem with this case is that the prohibition related to a state of affairs rather than a physical act. One way of solving the apparent injustice is by the implication of *mens rea* into the offence: as in *Lim Chin Aik v. R.*, *post*, p. 206. But it may still be possible to reconcile the case with the doctrine of a voluntary act. Lanham defends the decision, though not the reasoning, in "Larsonneur Revisited" [1976] Crim.L.R. 276. He suggests that Miss Larsonneur was herself responsible for her seemingly unfortunate fate, and no more deserved acquittal than a person who becomes an automaton through drink or drugs. It appears from a confession which she made to the police that Miss Larsonneur had gone to Ireland to arrange a marriage between herself and an Englishman, and had been told by the Irish police to leave by April 17: "Miss Larsonneur's story . . . reveals that the defendant brought upon herself the act of compulsion which led to her being charged. . . . No-one could claim that *Larsonneur* stood as a shining example of jurisprudence. But it can hardly be regarded as the last word in judicial depravity. If Miss Larsonneur had been dragged kicking and screaming from France into the United Kingdom by kidnappers and the same judgment had been given by the Court of Criminal Appeal, the defence of unforeseeable compulsion would truly have been excluded and the case would be the worst blot on the pages of the modern criminal law. But she wasn't and it wasn't and it isn't."

See also *Winzar v. Chief Constable of Kent*, *The Times*, March 28, 1983. The appellant had been brought to hospital on a stretcher. He was diagnosed as being drunk and was asked to leave. When he was later found slumped on a seat in the corridor the police were called. They removed him to the highway and then placed him in the police car charging him with being drunk on the highway contrary to section 12 of the Licensing Act 1872. The Queen's Bench Divisional Court upheld his conviction on the basis that as the purpose of the offence was to deal with the nuisance of public drunkenness, it was sufficient to establish guilt to prove that the person was drunk while in a public place; how he came to be there was considered to be irrelevant.

Compare *Kilbride v. Lake* [1962] N.Z.L.R. 590. Kilbride's conviction for failing to display a current warrant of fitness was quashed by the New Zealand Court of Criminal Appeal on the ground that the omission was not within his conduct, knowledge or control, since the warrant was there when he parked his car and inexplicably not there when he returned.

The critics of Larsonneur might be expected to welcome this display of antipodean juristic maturity but an argument is put forward by Budd and Lunch, in "Voluntariness, Causation and Strict Liability" [1978] Crim.L.R. 74 that "it is a form of involuntariness quite unlike those forms usually referred to in the Law. . . . If one believes that strict liability, although entailing the conviction of the morally blameless, is nevertheless beneficial to society, then there is no purpose in excluding from its ambit those who can demonstrate that some unforeseeable intervening event produced the result, or those who can show that they lacked the physical 'opportunity to act otherwise', whether on the extended *Kilbride v. Lake* definition or in the more limited sense of their being in a state of automatism."

It seems that "voluntariness" is a slippery concept which raises, but does not answer, all sorts of questions about responsibility.

For further exploration of the utility of strict liability, see Chapter 3, p. 182.

Questions

1. In both *Larsonneur* and *Winzar* it is possible to identify a prior moral fault on the part of each defendant which preceded the commission of the situational offence. Is it appropriate for a court to delve into history to find such a prior moral fault? If so, how far back should a court be permitted to delve?

2. In *Winzar* could the police officers have been charged with procuring his offence?

3. OMISSIONS

P. R. Glazebrook, "Criminal Omissions: The Duty Requirement in Offences Against the Person" (1960) 76 L.Q.R. 386 at 387

Although a failure to act may have as serious consequences as an act, and although any difference between acts and omissions is often denied, the distinction is deeply embedded in the law. This fact is no less inescapable because there is no precise test for distinguishing an act from an omission. Human conduct may often be described in either positive or negative terms, though usually one way rather than the other will appear more natural. . . . But difficult cases there will be, and their very existence leads to the imposition of liability for omissions. A man is in his spring cart; the reins are not in his hands, but lying on the horse's back. While the horse trots down a hill a young child runs across the road in front of the cart, is knocked down and killed. Had the man held the reins he could

have pulled the horse up. Did he kill the child by driving the cart recklessly, or by recklessly failing to drive the cart?

The facts of the case cited in the last sentence are those of *R. v.
Dalloway* (*post*, p. 47).

One distinction which is important is that between offences whose
essence is an omission and those which, though usually committed by
a positive act, can also be committed by omission. The former are
conduct crimes while the latter are *result* crimes.

Fletcher, *Rethinking Criminal Law* (1978), p. 421

Both 'acts' and 'omissions' can be brought under the general rubric of
'conduct'.... If there is a special problem in punishing omissions, we
can learn what it is only by examining the contexts in which lawyers
conventionally talk about 'omissions' or 'failing to act'. In fact, there is a
radical cleavage between two forms of liability for 'omissions'. According
to one type, the focus of liability is a breach of statutory obligation to act
[appropriate English examples would be failure to display a vehicle tax
disc, failure to report an accident].... We shall call this the field of liability for 'breach of duty to act'. The contrasting field is the imposition of
liability for failing to intervene, when necessary, to prevent the occurrence
of a serious harm such as death or the destruction of property ... we shall
refer to this second type of liability as 'commission by omission'. The
substantive difference [between the two] is that liability for breach of a
statutory duty does not presuppose the occurrence of harm.... In contrast, the death of the victim is essential for committing homicide by
omission.... The gravamen of liability for 'breach of duty' is the breach
itself; for commission by omission, the occurrence of a particular result.

B. Hogan, "Omissions and the Duty Myth" in *Criminal Law: Essays in Honour of J. C. Smith* (1987, ed. P. Smith).

[T]here is no way you can *cause* an event by doing nothing (or is it, more
precisely, by not doing anything?) to prevent it ...

But we immediately encounter the problem of what is meant by doing
nothing, or, rather, not doing anything. The vexing problem of the distinction between act and omission. And 'although any difference between act
and omission is often denied', wrote Mr. Peter Glazebrook, 'the distinction is deeply embedded in the law'. True enough, but my own view is
that the distinction is at best unhelpful and at worst misleading. It is,
however, well entrenched, has found its way into the Draft Criminal Code
Bill and, whatever I say, is likely to stay entrenched for some time yet.
But that does not deter me from putting another view which I believe to
be more logically attractive and even to express more accurately the
common law....

[I]t would be much more conducive to clarity of thought if we spoke
of conduct and causation. If any proposition is self-evident (and, arguably, none is) it is that a person cannot be held to have caused an event
which he did not cause....

This is not to say that I am against liability for omissions.... There are
of course numerous instances where Parliament (and a handful where the
common law) has penalised omissions but what is noteworthy is that the
defendant is penalised for the omission but not visited with liability for
the consequences of that omission. Thus it is an offence under s.6(1) of

the Maritime Conventions Act 1911, punishable with two years' imprisonment on indictment, for the master of a vessel to fail to render assistance
to anyone in danger of being lost at sea. Fair enough, but it is to be noted
that the master is made liable in respect of the omission; he is not, rightly
enough, made liable in respect of any death or injury for any such death
or injury is not of his doing. Exceptionally a statute may punish an omission as severely as the completed offence. A well-known example arises
under the Road Traffic Act 1972, as amended, under which the punishment for a failure to provide a specimen is the same as for driving with
an excessive blood-alcohol concentration. The driver is, however, convicted and punished in respect of the omission; he is not convicted and
punished for the separate offence of driving etc. Since this has not been
proved. In these circumstances it is entirely acceptable to punish the
motorist for his omission as severely as for the driving offence but it
would be wrong to convict him for the driving offence and unnecessarily
to deem him to have driven over the prescribed limit. . . .

[I]n no sense am I against liability for omissions. I would ask only two
conditions of a law punishing omissions. One is that it be clearly articulated and the other is that it seeks to punish the defendant for his dereliction and does not artificially treat him as a cause of the event he has not
brought about by his conduct."

While Hogan's arguments are persuasive they do not yet represent the
law which still speaks in terms of duties. Accordingly, Fletcher's two-fold
classification will be used as a framework for considering the cases in this
area.

i. Breach of Duty to Act

Note

Williams' T.C.L., p. 148 states: "a crime can be committed by omission, but there can be no omission in law in the absence of a duty to
act. The reason is obvious. If there is an act, someone acts; but if there
is an omission, everyone (in a sense) omits. We omit to do everything
in the world that is not done. Only those of us omit in law who are
under a duty to act.

When a statute expressly or impliedly creates an offence of omission,
it points out the person under the duty by the wording of the offence."

The common law rarely imposed liability purely for omissions; an
example was misprison of felony. Occasionally an indictment has been
found to lie at common law for neglect of a duty imposed by common
law or statute; see the following case.

R. v. Dytham
[1979] 3 All E.R. 641
Court of Appeal

The defendant, a police constable, was on duty in uniform near a club
when a man was ejected from the club and kicked to death by a "bouncer". D. took no steps to intervene and drove off. He appealed against
conviction for misconduct whilst acting as an officer of justice.

LORD WIDGERY C.J.: . . . [T]he argument . . . ran deep into constitutional and
jurisprudential history. The effect of it was that not every failure to discharge

a duty which devolved on a person as the holder of a public office gave rise to the common law offence of misconduct in that office. As counsel for the appellant put it, non-feasance was not enough. There must be a malfeasance or at least a misfeasance involving an element of corruption. In support of this contention a number of cases were cited from 18th and 19th century reports. It is the fact that in nearly all of them the misconduct asserted involved some corrupt taint; but this appears to have been an accident of circumstances and not a necessary incident of the offence. Misconduct in a public office is more vividly exhibited where dishonesty is revealed as part of the dereliction of duty. Indeed in some cases the conduct impugned cannot be shown to have been misconduct unless it was done with a corrupt or oblique motive. . . .

[I]n Stephen's Digest of the Criminal Law are to be found these words:

"Every public officer commits a misdemeanour who wilfully neglects to perform any duty which he is bound either by common law or by statute to perform provided that the discharge of such duty is not attended with greater danger than a man of ordinary firmness and activity may be expected to encounter."

In support of this proposition *R. v. Wyat* (1705) 1 Salk. 380 is cited as well as *R. v. Bembridge* (1783) 3 Doug.K.B. 327, a judgment of Lord Mansfield. The neglect must be wilful and not merely inadvertent; and it must be culpable in the sense that it is without reasonable excuse or justification.

In the present case it was not suggested that the appellant could not have summoned or sought assistance to help the victim or to arrest his assailants. The charge as framed left this answer open to him. Not surprisingly he did not seek to avail himself of it, for the facts spoke strongly against any such answer. The allegation made was not of mere non-feasance but of deliberate failure and wilful neglect. This involves an element of culpability which is not restricted to corruption or dishonesty but which must be of such a degree that the misconduct impugned is calculated to injure the public interest so as to call for condemnation and punishment. Whether such a situation is revealed by the evidence is a matter that a jury has to decide.

Appeal dismissed

Question

Did the officer's failure to act cause the death of the victim of the bouncer's assault?

ii. Commission by Omission

Note

An alternative heading would be *"liability for failing to intervene"*. Offences are usually worded in terms requiring active conduct; can liability arise from causing the prohibited result by omitting to act? It is generally recognised that the attitude adopted by the common law is well summarised in the passage below.

Lord Macaulay's Works (ed. Lady Trevelyan), Vol. VII, p. 497

It is, indeed, most highly desirable that men should not merely abstain from doing harm to their neighbours, but should render active services to their neighbours. In general, however, the penal law must content itself with keeping men from doing positive harm, and must leave to public opinion, and to the teachers of morality and religion, the office of furnishing men with motives for doing positive good. It is evident that to attempt to punish men by law for not rendering to others all the service which it is their duty to render to others would be preposterous.

We must grant impunity to the vast majority of those omissions which a benevolent morality would pronounce reprehensible, and must content ourselves with punishing such omissions only when they are distinguished from the rest by some circumstance which marks them out as peculiarly fit objects of penal legislation.

Not all offences are susceptible of commission by omission. Most of the cases concern murder or manslaughter although liability could arise in a similar way for causing grievous bodily harm under section 20 of the Offences Against the Person Act 1861.

Not all omissions give rise to liability; liability depends on there being a duty, recognised by the law, to act or intervene in the circumstances. There are four situations in which such duties have been recognised: duties arising out of contract, duties arising out of relationship, duties arising from care of the helpless and infirm, duty arising from creation of a dangerous situation.

(a) Duty arising out of contract

R. v. Pittwood
(1902) 19 T.L.R. 37
Taunton Assizes

The defendant was a gatekeeper on the Somerset and Dorset Railway. He had to keep the gate shut whenever a train was passing during the period 7 a.m. to 7 p.m. One afternoon the gate was open and a hay cart which was crossing the line was hit by a train. One man was killed and another was seriously injured. Witnesses testified that the road was an accommodation road and not a public road. The accused was charged with manslaughter.

WRIGHT J., without calling upon the prosecution, gave judgment. He said he was clearly of opinion that in this case there was gross and criminal negligence, as the man was paid to keep the gate shut and protect the public. In his opinion there were three grounds on which the verdict could be supported: (1) There might be cases of misfeasance and cases of mere nonfeasance. Here it was quite clear there was evidence of misfeasance as the prisoner directly contributed to the accident. (2) A man might incur criminal liability from a duty arising out of contract. The learned judge quoted in support of this *R. v. Nicholls* (1875) 13 Cox 75; *R. v. Elliott (1889) 16 Cox 710; R. v. Benge* (1865) 4 F. & F. 594; *R. v. Hughes* (1857) Dears. & B. 248. The strongest case of all was, perhaps, *R. v. Instan*, [*post*, p. 31] and that case clearly governed the present charge. (3) With regard to the point that this was only an occupation road, he clearly held that it was not, as the company had assumed the liability of protecting the public whenever they crossed the road. . . .

Verdict: Guilty

(b) Duty arising out of relationship

Note

The existence of close relationships can give rise to a duty to act, such as that owed by parents to their children or spouses to each other. There is little common law authority on the point although it is generally accepted that there is such a duty. In *Gibbins and Proctor* (1918) 13 Cr. App. R. 134 the father of a child and his partner were convicted of murdering the child who had died as a result of their withholding food from it. The father had breached the duty owed by parents to care for their children while Proctor, by taking money to buy food, had assumed a duty towards the child. Statute has largely intervened in the case of parents' duty to their children. For a case on wilful neglect under the Children and Young Persons Act 1933 see *Sheppard, post,* p. 140.

(c) Duty arising from the assumption of care for the helpless and infirm

R. v. Instan
[1893] 1 Q.B. 450
Court for Crown Cases Reserved

The defendant lived with her aunt who was 73 years old. The aunt was healthy until shortly before her death. During the last 12 days of her life she had gangrene in her leg and could not fend for herself, move about nor summon help. Only the defendant knew of this condition. She appeared not to have given her aunt any food nor did she seek medical or nursing aid. She was charged with manslaughter and convicted.

LORD COLERIDGE C.J.: We are all of opinion that this conviction must be affirmed. It would not be correct to say that every moral obligation involves a legal duty; but every legal duty is founded on a moral obligation. A legal common law duty is nothing else than the enforcing by law of that which is a moral obligation without legal enforcement. There can be no question in this case that it was the clear duty of the prisoner to impart to the deceased so much as was necessary to sustain life of the food which she from time to time took in, and which was paid for by the deceased's own money for the purpose of the maintenance of herself and the prisoner; it was only through the instrumentality of the prisoner that the deceased could get the food. There was, therefore, a common law duty imposed upon the prisoner which she did not discharge.

Nor can there be any question that the failure of the prisoner to discharge her legal duty at least accelerated the death of the deceased, if it did not actually cause it. There is no case directly in point; but it would be a slur upon and a discredit to the administration of justice in this country if there were any doubt as to the legal principle, or as to the present case being within it. The prisoner was under a moral obligation to the deceased from which arose a legal duty towards her; that legal duty the prisoner has wilfully and deliberately left unperformed, with the consequence that there has been an acceleration of the death of the deceased owing to the non-performance of

that legal duty. It is unnecessary to say more than that upon the evidence this
conviction was most properly arrived at.

Conviction affirmed

Note

Consider the two following cases in the light of the following extract
from the judgment of Erle C.J., in *R. v. Charlotte Smith* (1865) 10 Cox
82, where a master was charged with the homicide of his servant by,
amongst other things, neglecting to give her sufficient food or whole-
some lodgings. "The law is undisputed that, if a person having the
care or custody of another who is helpless, neglects to supply him
with the necessaries of life and thereby causes or accelerates his death,
it is a criminal offence. But the law is clear, that if a person having the
exercise of free will, chooses to stay in a service where bad food and
lodging is provided, and death is thereby caused, the master is not
criminally liable."

R. v. William Smith
(1826) 2 C. & P. 449; 172 E.R. 203
Gloucester Assizes

The defendants were two brothers and a sister. They had lived with
their mother and with a helpless idiot brother. The mother died and it
was alleged that the idiot brother was neglected and suffered in health.
The defendants were charged with assault and false imprisonment.

BURROUGH J.: I am clearly of opinion that on the facts proved there is no
assault and no imprisonment in the eye of the law, and all the rest of the
charge is nonfeasance. In the case of *Squires* and his wife for starving the
apprentice, the husband was convicted, because it was his duty to maintain
the apprentice, and the wife was acquitted, because there was no such obligation on her. I expected to have found in the will of the father that the defendants were bound, if they took the father's property, to maintain his brother;
but, under the will, they are only bound to pay him £50 a year, and not bound
to maintain him. William Smith appears to have been the owner of the house,
and Thomas and Sarah were mere inmates of it, as their idiot brother might
be; as to these latter, there could clearly be no legal obligation on them: and
how can I tell the jury that either of the defendants had such a care of this
unfortunate man as to make them criminally liable for omitting to attend to
him. There is strong proof that there was some negligence; but my point is,
that omission, without a duty, will not create an indictable offence. There is a
deficiency of proof of the allegation of care, custody and control, which must
be taken to be legal care, custody and control. Whether an indictment might
be so framed, as to suit this case, I do not know; but on this indictment I am
clearly of opinion that the defendants must be acquitted.

Verdict: Not guilty

R. v. Stone and Dobinson
[1977] 1 Q.B. 345
Court of Appeal

S, who was 67, partially deaf, nearly blind and of low intelligence,
cohabited with D, aged 43, who was described as ineffectual and inadequate. Also living with them was S's mentally subnormal son. S's
younger sister, F, came to live there in 1972, suffering from anorexia

nervosa. She stayed in her room most of the time though she was known to creep down and cook herself something to eat when S and D went to the pub.

S and D attempted to find her doctor in spring 1975 though she refused to tell them his name. In July, D and a neighbour washed F who, by this time, was confined to bed and lying amidst her own excrement. The defendants were unable to use the telephone and a neighbour was unsuccessful in getting a local doctor to visit F. No one was informed of F's condition, even though a social worker came to the house from time to time to visit S's son. F died in August. The pathologist's report suggested that she had been in need of urgent medical attention for days, if not weeks. S and D appealed against their convictions for manslaughter.

GEOFFREY LANE L.J.: There is no dispute, broadly speaking, as to the matters on which the jury must be satisfied before they can convict of manslaughter in circumstances such as the present. They are (1) that the defendant undertook the care of a person who by reason of age or infirmity was unable to care for himself; (2) that the defendant was grossly negligent in regard to his duty of care; (3) that by reason of such negligence the person died. . . .

[Counsel for the appellants] submitted that the evidence which the judge had suggested to the jury might support the assumption of a duty by the appellants does not, when examined, succeed in doing so. He suggests that the situation here is unlike any reported case. Fanny came to this house as a lodger. Largely, if not entirely due to her own eccentricity and failure to look after herself or feed herself properly, she became increasingly infirm and immobile and eventually unable to look after herself. Is it to be said, asks Mr. Coles rhetorically, that by the mere fact of becoming infirm and helpless in these circumstances she casts a duty on her brother and the appellant Dobinson. . . .? The suggestion is that, heartless though it may seem, this is one of those situations where the appellants were entitled to do nothing; where no duty was cast upon them to help, any more than it is cast upon a man to rescue a stranger from drowning, however easy such a rescue might be.

. . . Whether Fanny was a lodger or not she was a blood relation of the appellant Stone; she was occupying a room in his house; the appellant Dobinson had undertaken the duty of trying to wash her, of taking such food to her as she required. There was ample evidence that each appellant was aware of the poor condition she was in by mid-July. It was not disputed that no effort was made to summon an ambulance or the social services or the police. . . .

This was not a situation analogous to the drowning stranger. They did make efforts to care. They tried to get a doctor; they tried to discover the previous doctor. The appellant Dobinson helped with the washing and the provision of food. All these matters were put before the jury in terms which we find it impossible to fault. The jury were entitled to find that the duty had been assumed. They were entitled to conclude that once Fanny became helplessly infirm, as she had by July 19, the appellants were, in the circumstances, obliged either to summon help or else to care for Fanny themselves. . . .

Appeal dismissed

Questions

1. Can this case be distinguished from *R. v. William Smith, ante,* p. 32 Does the following statement of principle by Brett J. in *R. v. Nicholls* (1875) 13 Cox 75 help?

"If a grown up person chooses to undertake the charge of a human creature helpless either from infancy, simplicity, lunacy or other infirmity, he is bound to execute that charge without (at all events) *wicked* negligence."

2. Would Stone and Dobinson have been liable if F. was Stone's sister-in-law (*i.e.* his brother's wife)? What was crucial in giving rise to the duty on Stone: the fact that Fanny was his sister; that he allowed her to live in his house; or both?

3. Would they have been liable if they had made no efforts to help at all?

4. Did Stone and Dobinson *cause* F.'s death? Farrier's Note at (1978) 41 M.L.R. 211, n. 6 raises the question whether the restrictive policy adopted in *Blaue, post,* p. 50 should apply where the causal conduct consists of an omission.

Note

The situations in which a duty may arise, however, are not closed: new situations may give rise to the recognition of a duty. In *Khan and Khan* [1998] Crim. L.R. 830 (*cf. Kennedy* [1999] Crim. L.R. 65, pp. 65 and 585 *post*), two drug dealers appealed from convictions of manslaughter arising out of their supply of heroin to the deceased and their failure to summon medical assistance when she went into a coma following her consumption of the drug. In quashing their convictions Swinton Thomas L.J. stated:

To extend the duty to summon medical assistance to a drug dealer who supplies heroin to a person who subsequently dies on the facts of this case would undoubtedly enlarge the class of persons to whom, on previous authority, such a duty may be owed. It may be correct to hold that such a duty does arise . . . . Unfortunately, the question as to the existence or otherwise of [such] a duty . . . was not . . . at any time considered by the Judge, and the jury was given no direction in relation to it.

The Court of Appeal took the view that it was for the judge to rule whether the facts were capable of giving rise to a duty and, if so, for the jury to decide whether there was such a duty. The danger with this approach is that the jury may be unduly influenced by the fact of death and conclude that there must have been a duty to prevent such a death. In a later case, *Singh (Gurphal)* [1999] Crim. L.R. 582 the Court of Appeal affirmed the trial judge's decision that whether a situation gave rise to a duty was a question of law for the judge to determine which, it is submitted, is the better view.

Where a person is under a duty to care for another, whether due to relationship or because the duty is imposed as a result of care rendered to a helpless or infirm person, the question arises whether that person may be released from that duty. See the next case.

Airedale N.H.S. Trust v. Bland
[1993] A.C. 89
House of Lords

Bland had been in a persistent vegetative state for three and a half years being fed artificially and mechanically by a nasogastric tube. The doctors were unanimously of the opinion that there was no hope of recovery or improvement of any kind. The consultant, supported by other distinguished medical experts, was of the opinion that treatment and feeding should cease which would result in death within one to two weeks. The health authority applied for declarations that it and the doctors could lawfully discontinue all life-sustaining treatment (namely artificial feeding and antibiotic drugs) except for such as would be required to enable him to die without pain or distress. The parents and family of Bland supported the application. The judge granted the applications and the Official Solicitor appealed to the Court of Appeal and from its decision to the House of Lords contending that such a withdrawal of life-sustaining treatment would be a breach of the doctor's duty to care for his patient and would constitute a crime.

LORD BROWNE WILKINSON: . . . If I am right so far in my analysis, the critical decision to be made is whether it is in the best interests of Anthony Bland to continue the invasive medical care involved in artificial feeding. That question is not the same as, "Is it in Anthony Bland's best interests that he should die?" The latter question assumes that it is lawful to perpetuate the patient's life; but such perpetuation of life can only be achieved if it is lawful to continue to invade the bodily integrity of the patient by invasive medical care. Unless the doctor has reached the affirmative conclusion that it is in the patient's best interest to continue the invasive care, such care must cease.

LORD MUSTILL: . . .

6. Best Interests: the termination of treatment
After much expression of negative opinions I turn to an argument which in my judgment is logically defensible and consistent with the existing law. In essence it turns the previous argument on its head by directing the inquiry to the interests of the patient, not in the termination of life but in the continuation of his treatment. It runs as follows. (i) The cessation of nourishment and hydration is an omission not an act. (ii) Accordingly, the cessation will not be a criminal act unless the doctors are under a present duty to continue the regime. (iii) At the time when Anthony Bland came into the care of the doctors decisions had to be made about his care which he was unable to make for himself. In accordance with *F v. West Berkshire Health Authority* (*post* p. 315) these decisions were to be made in his best interests. Since the possibility that he might recover still existed his best interests required that he should be supported in the hope that this would happen. These best interests justified the application of the necessary regime without his consent. (iv) All hope of recovery has now been abandoned. Thus, although the termination of his life is not in the best interests of Anthony Bland, his best interests in being kept alive have also disappeared, taking with them the justification for the non-consensual regime and the correlative duty to keep it in being. (v) Since there is no longer a duty to provide nourishment and hydration a failure to do so cannot be a criminal offence.

My Lords, I must recognise at once that this chain of reasoning makes an unpromising start by transferring the morally and intellectually dubious distinction between acts and omissions into a context where the ethical foundations of the law are already open to question. The opportunity for anomaly and excessively fine distinctions, often depending more on the way in which the problem happens to be stated than on any real distinguishing features. ... All this being granted, we are still forced to take the law as we find it and try to make it work. Moreover, although in cases near the borderline the categorisation of conduct will be exceedingly hard, I believe that nearer the periphery there will be many instances which fall quite clearly into one category rather than the other. In my opinion the present is such a case, and in company with Compton J. in *Barber v. Superior Court of Los Angeles County* (1983) 147 Cal App (3d) 1006 at 1017 amongst others I consider that the proposed conduct will fall into the category of omissions.

I therefore consider the argument to be soundly based. Now that the time has come when Anthony Bland has no further interest in being kept alive, the necessity to do so, created by his inability to make a choice, has gone; and the justification for the invasive care and treatment together with the duty to provide it have also gone. Absent a duty, the omission to perform what had previously been a duty will no longer be a breach of the criminal law.

Note

Their Lordships where at pains to distinguish cases such as the present which they categorised as omissions (there being no continuing duty to act due to the futility of the treatment) from those where positive acts are involved, such as the administration of lethal drugs, to bring about a patient's death. They found it difficult to justify the distinction, Lord Browne-Wilkinson confessing:

> Finally, the conclusion I have reached will appear to some to be almost irrational. How can it be lawful to allow a patient to die slowly, though painlessly, over a period of weeks from lack of food but unlawful to produce his immediate death by a lethal injection, thereby saving his family from yet another ordeal to add to the tragedy that has already struck them? I find it difficult to find a moral answer to that question. But it is undoubtedly the law and nothing I have said casts doubt on the proposition that the doing of a positive act with the intention of ending life is and remains murder.

They also sought to explain why the administration of drugs which had a medicinal purpose, such as pain relief, but which inevitably accelerated death, would not give rise to criminal liability on the basis of what was in the patient's best interests. Lord Goff stated:

> It is this principle too which, in my opinion, underlies the established rule that a doctor may, when caring for a patient who is, for example, dying of cancer, lawfully administer painkilling drugs despite the fact that he knows that an incidental effect of that application will be to abbreviate the patient's life. Such a decision may properly be made as part of the care of the living patient, in his best interests; and, on this basis, the treatment will be lawful. Moreover, where the doctor's treatment of his patient is lawful, the patient's death will be regarded in law as exclusively caused by the injury or disease to which his condition is attributable.

The distinctions are fine, even strained, but on such distinctions depend the classification of transactions as lawful or unlawful. Their Lordships could not avoid such distinctions as "active" euthanasia is unlawful and only legislation can change that, Lord Goff stating:

[T]he law draws a crucial distinction between cases in which a doctor decides not to provide, or to continue to provide, for his patient treatment or care which could or might prolong his life and those in which he decides, for example by administering a lethal drug, actively to bring his patient's life to an end. As I have already indicated, the former may be lawful, either because the doctor is giving effect to his patient's wishes by withholding the treatment or care, or even in certain circumstances in which (on principles which I shall describe) the patient is incapacitated from stating whether or not he gives his consent. But it is not lawful for a doctor to administer a drug to his patient to bring about his death, even though that course is prompted by a humanitarian desire to end his suffering, however great that suffering may be: *see R v. Cox* (18 September 1992, unreported) *per* Ognall J. in the Crown Court at Winchester. So to act is to cross the Rubicon which runs between on the one hand the care of the living patient and on the other hand euthanasia—actively causing his death to avoid or to end his suffering. Euthanasia is not lawful at common law. It is of course well known that there are many responsible members of our society who believe that euthanasia should be made lawful; but that result could, I believe, only be achieved by legislation which expresses the democratic will that so fundamental a change should be made in our law, and can, if enacted, ensure that such legalised killing can only be carried out subject to appropriate supervision and control. It is true that the drawing of this distinction may lead to a charge of hypocrisy, because it can be asked why, if the doctor, by discontinuing treatment, is entitled in consequence to let his patient die, it should not be lawful to put him out of his misery straight away, in a more humane manner, by a lethal injection, rather than let him linger on in pain until he dies. But the law does not feel able to authorise euthanasia, even in circumstances such as these, for, once euthanasia is recognised as lawful in these circumstances, it is difficult to see any logical basis for excluding it in others.

Questions

1. Is it simply fortuitous that in this case the transaction could be classified as an omission?
2. Is it possible that death itself may be in a patient's best interests? If so is there a moral difference between the situation where death results from the discontinuance of treatment (an omission) as opposed to the administration of a lethal drug (an act)?

(d) Duty arising from creation of a dangerous situation

R. v. Miller
[1983] 2 A.C. 161
House of Lords

M, a vagrant who lived in an unoccupied house, awoke to find that a cigarette he had been smoking had set fire to the mattress on which he was lying. He did not attempt to extinguish the fire but moved to another room. The house caught fire. M was convicted of arson contrary to section 1 (1) and (3) of the Criminal Damage Act 1971. The Court of Appeal dismissed his appeal against conviction and he appealed to the House of Lords.

LORD DIPLOCK: [T]he Court of Appeal certified that the following question of law of general public importance was involved:

"Whether the actus reus of the offence of arson is present when a defendant accidentally starts a fire and thereafter, intending to destroy or damage property belonging to another or being reckless as to whether any such property would be destroyed or damaged, fails to take any steps to extinguish the fire or prevent damage to such property by that fire?"

The first question to be answered where a completed crime of arson is charged is: "Did a physical act of the accused start the fire which spread and damaged property belonging to another (or did his act cause an existing fire, which he had not started but which would otherwise have burnt itself out harmlessly, to spread and damage property belonging to another)?" I have added the words in brackets for completeness. They do not arise in the instant case; in cases where they do, the accused, for the purposes of the analysis which follows, may be regarded as having started a fresh fire.

The first question is a pure question of causation; it is one of fact to be decided by the jury in a trial upon indictment. It should be answered "No" if, in relation to the fire during the period starting immediately before its ignition and ending with its extinction, the role of the accused was at no time more than that of a passive bystander. In such a case the subsequent questions to which I shall be turning would not arise. . . .

If on the other hand the question, which I now confine to: "Did a physical act of the accused start the fire which spread and damaged property belonging to another?" is answered "Yes", as it was by the jury in the instant case, then for the purpose of the further questions the answers to which are determinative of his guilt of the offence of arson, the conduct of the accused, throughout the period from immediately before the moment of ignition to the completion of the damage to the property by the fire, is relevant; so is his state of mind throughout that period.

Since arson is a result-crime the period may be considerable, and during it the conduct of the accused that is causative of the result may consist not only of his doing physical acts which cause the fire to start or spread but also of his failing to take measures that lie within his power to counteract the danger that he has himself created. And if his conduct, active or passive, varies in the course of the period, so may his state of mind at the time of each piece of conduct. If at the time of any particular piece of conduct by the accused that is causative of the result, the state of mind that actuates his conduct falls within the description of one or other of the states of mind that are made a necessary ingredient of the offence of arson by section 1 (1) of the Criminal Damage Act 1971 (*i.e.* intending to damage property belonging to another or being reckless as to whether such property would be damaged) I know of no principle of English criminal law that would prevent his being guilty of the offence created by that subsection. Likewise I see no rational ground for excluding from conduct capable of giving rise to criminal liability, conduct which consists of failing to take measures that lie within one's power to counteract a danger that one has oneself created, if at the time of such conduct one's state of mind is such as constitutes a necessary ingredient of the offence. I venture to think that the habit of lawyers to talk of "actus reus", suggestive as it is of action rather than inaction, is responsible for any erroneous notion that failure to act cannot give rise to criminal liability in English law.

No one has been bold enough to suggest that if, in the instant case, the accused had been aware at the time that he dropped the cigarette that it would probably set fire to his mattress and yet had taken no steps to extinguish it he would not have been guilty of the offence of arson, since he would have damaged property of another being reckless as to whether any such property would be damaged.

I cannot see any good reason why, so far as liability under criminal law is concerned, it should matter at what point of time before the resultant damage is complete a person becomes aware that he has done a physical act which, whether or not he appreciated that it would at the time when he did it, does in fact create a risk that property of another will be damaged; provided that, at the moment of awareness, it lies within his power to take steps, either himself or by calling for the assistance of the fire brigade if this be necessary, to prevent or minimise the damage to the property at risk.

My Lords, in the instant case the prosecution did not rely upon the state of mind of the accused as being reckless during that part of his conduct that consisted of his lighting and smoking a cigarette while lying on his mattress and falling asleep without extinguishing it. So the jury were not invited to make any finding as to this. What the prosecution did rely upon as being reckless was his state of mind during that part of his conduct after he awoke to find that he had set his mattress on fire and that it was smouldering, but did not then take any steps either to try to extinguish it himself or to send for the fire brigade, but simply went into the other room to resume his slumbers, leaving the fire from the already smouldering mattress to spread and to damage that part of the house in which the mattress was.

The recorder, in his lucid summing up to the jury (they took 22 minutes only to reach their verdict) told them that the accused having by his own act started a fire in the mattress which, when he became aware of its existence, presented an obvious risk of damaging the house, became under a duty to take some action to put it out. The Court of Appeal upheld the conviction, but their ratio decidendi appears to be somewhat different from that of the recorder. As I understand the judgment, in effect it treats the whole course of conduct of the accused, from the moment at which he fell asleep and dropped the cigarette on to the mattress until the time the damage to the house by fire was complete, as a continuous act of the accused, and holds that it is sufficient to constitute the statutory offence of arson if at any stage in that course of conduct the state of mind of the accused, when he fails to try to prevent or minimise the damage which will result from his initial act, although it lies within his power to do so, is that of being reckless as to whether property belonging to another would be damaged.

My Lords, these alternative ways of analysing the legal theory that justifies a decision which has received nothing but commendation for its accord with commonsense and justice, have, since the publication of the judgment of the Court of Appeal in the instant case, provoked academic controversy. Each theory has distinguished support. Professor J. C. Smith espouses the "duty theory"; Professor Glanville Wiliams who, after the decision of the Divisional Court in *Fagan v. Metropolitan Police Commissioner* (*post*, p. 619) appears to have been attracted by the duty theory, now prefers that of the continuous act. When applied to cases where a person has unknowingly done an act which sets in train events that, when he becomes aware of them, present an obvious risk that property belonging to another will be damaged, both theories lead to an identical result; and since what your Lordships are concerned with is to give guidance to trial judges in their task of summing up to juries, I would for this purpose adopt the duty theory as being the easier to explain to a jury; though I would commend the use of the word "responsibility", rather than "duty" which is more appropriate to civil than to criminal law, since it suggests an obligation owed to another person, *i.e.* the person to whom the endangered property belongs, whereas a criminal statue defines combinations of conduct and state of mind which render a person liable to punishment by the state itself.

So, while deprecating the use of the expression "actus reus" in the certified question, I would answer that question "Yes" and would dismiss the appeal.

Appeal dismissed

Questions

1. Was M found guilty because he had fallen asleep while smoking a cigarette or because, when he awoke, he failed to take reasonable steps to put out the fire caused by his lighted cigarette?

2. The facts in the case involved damage to property; would M have been guilty of manslaughter if a fellow squatter sharing the mattress with him had died as a result of asphyxiation?

3. Would M have been liable for arson/manslaughter if the fire had been caused by an electrical fault? Would it make any difference if the fellow squatter was his eight-year-old son?

4. What is the general principle for which *Miller* is authority?

B. Hogan, "Omissions and a Duty Myth" in *Criminal Law: Essays in Honour of J. C. Smith* (1987, ed. P. Smith)

R. v. Miller holds, and with respect rightly, that one who inadvertently (or otherwise faultlessly, presumably) starts a chain of events causing harm may be properly held liable if, having become aware that he was the cause, he fails to take steps reasonably available to him to prevent or minimise the damage that will ensue. . . .

Miller is interesting. One analysis of the case is to say that when the defendant became aware that he had caused (albeit inadvertently) the fire he was under a duty to take steps reasonably available to him to prevent or minimise further harm. Lord Diplock, with whom all their lordships agreed, expressed some support for the duty theory as having the merit of being easier to explain to the jury but then added that he would prefer 'responsibility' instead of duty. He thought that 'duty' was:

> ". . . more appropriate to civil than to criminal law since it suggests an obligation owed to another person, *i.e.* the person to whom the endangered property belongs, whereas a criminal statute defines combinations of conduct and states of mind which render a person liable to punishment by the state itself."

Quite what Lord Diplock is getting at here is not perhaps as clear as crystal, but two things may be said. The first is that he was right to say, if this is what he was saying, that there is no general duty to intervene to prevent or minimise harm to another's property. The second is, in the context of his speech read as a whole, that, having addressed his mind to the question whether it could be said that the defendant caused the fire and inevitably concluding that he did, he sees that it can make no sensible difference that mens rea was formed after the first event in the chain of events leading to the damage. Nor, with respect, can I. The defendant's causal contribution did not end when he inadvertently dropped the lighted cigarette. The fire was causally attributable to him from start to finish; he can hardly be heard sensibly to say that the only damage he caused was the scorch hole in the mattress. When he became aware that steps reasonably available to him would prevent further harm he was still causing the damage. The only difference between the damage caused before and after his awareness was that he was not criminally liable for the damage occurring before his awareness since he lacked mens rea but was liable for the damage he caused after his awareness since he now had mens rea. . . .

So in *R. v. Pittwood* it becomes fruitless to debate whether leaving open the level-crossing gates is to be characterised as omission or commission. The court characterised the conduct as misfeasance and in so doing, though the report is brief, appears to have looked at the totality of the defendant's conduct. And looking at the totality of his conduct it can easily be said that he created a situation of danger which caused harm to the victim.

It is true that in *R. v. Pittwood* the court also said that a duty might arise out of a contract and the cases on 'omissions' are certainly littered with references to 'duty.' In my view these references to duty are unhelpful. The issue in *R. v. Pittwood* was simply whether the defendant had *caused* the deaths of the victims with the relevant mens rea. Most assuredly he had no duty to take employment as a level-crossing keeper but once he did so he must not perform the office (in the same way as one must not drive a car or handle a gun) in such a way as to cause harm to others. No one has a duty to buy a car or a gun, or to obtain employment as a level-crossing keeper, or even to walk down the road to post a letter. But if they choose to do any of these things they must so conduct themselves so as not to cause harm, and if their conduct causes harm with the relevant mens rea they will fall foul of the criminal law. There is no need to complicate such cases by the search for duty.

There is perhaps a stronger case for imputing the duty concept in connection with domestic and similar relationships. So in *R. v. Instan* where the niece failed to summon medical assistance for her aunt who died of gangrene, the court talks of a duty founded in moral obligation. In law, of course, and now as much as then, the niece had no duty whatever to look after her aunt. Had she been paying a casual visit to her aunt, noticed that her aunt would die without prompt medical attention, but had left without taking any measures of assistance then surely the case would have been decided differently. What was determinative in *R. v. Instan* was that the niece had taken it upon herself to look after her aunt. She had no duty to do so, any more than the defendant in *R. v. Pittwood* had any duty to take the job of level-crossing keeper, but having undertaken a certain task (and it is essentially on all fours with driving a car or using a gun or walking down the road to post a letter) it must be performed properly. If it is performed improperly and, with the relevant mens rea, causes harm to another, then criminal liability follows.

I see nothing wrong with the principle in *R. v. Stone* which I take to be that if one chooses to assume the care and control of another then the self-imposed responsibility must be carried out with reasonable care and skill and that liability for manslaughter (or even murder) may be incurred if that responsibility is discharged in a grossly negligent (now reckless)

manner. What is disturbing about *R. v. Stone* is that the evidence hardly
supported the inference that these two elderly incompetents had taken it
upon themselves to discharge the onerous task of looking after the sister.
Did they really *kill* the sister?

I am unhappy about the duty concept in the context of 'omission.' It is
likely to mislead a jury into thinking of duties in other than legal terms;
into a consideration of the immorality of particular conduct; into convicting the defendant merely for his callousness. Better to put the issue as
simply one of causation. For this purpose it is proper to look not merely
at the last link in the causal chain, be it commission or omission, but all
the relevant conduct of the defendant. The questions then become
whether the *conduct* of the defendant caused the actus reus and whether
he did so with mens rea. To introduce an imprecise, ill-defined concept
of 'duty' into the equation only serves to confuse the issue.

Questions

The situations in which the courts have recognised liability for
offences of commission arising from omissions depend on the existence of a duty to act. In the absence of such a duty there can be no
liability. Accordingly, in the absence of a duty arising from relationship, a bystander may watch a child drowning in a puddle and will
not be guilty of any criminal offence. Should there be a specific offence
of failure to render assistance to a person in peril? See further A. Ashworth and E. Steiner, "Criminal omissions and public duties: the
French experience" (1990) 10 *Legal Studies* 153, who discuss, *inter alia*,
article 63(2) of the French Penal Code which provides:

> Any person who voluntarily fails to render assistance to a person in
> peril, which he or she could have given either personally or by calling
> for help, without personal danger or danger to others, is guilty of an
> offence and may be punished by imprisonment from three months to
> five years or by a fine of 360 francs to 20,000 francs or both.

If such a duty were to be imposed in England and Wales should it be
in addition to or in place of the duties which give rise to liability on
the basis of commission by omission?

Contrast the French Penal Code Provision with s. 155 of the Criminal Code, Northern Territory, Australia which carries a maximum
penalty of seven years imprisonment:

> "Any person who, being able to provide rescue, resuscitation, medical
> treatment, first aid or succour of any kind to a person urgently in need
> of it and whose life may be endangered if it is not provided, callously
> fails to do so is guilty of a crime."

See further *Salmon* (1994) 115 FLR, 70 A. Crim. R. 536, (1996) 20 Crim.
L. J. 102.

Draft Criminal Code Bill

Offences of omission and situational offences

16. For the purposes of an offence which consists wholly or in part of
an omission, state of affairs or occurrence, references in this Act to an
"act" shall, where the context permits, be read as including references

to the omission, state of affairs or occurrence by reason of which a person may be guilty of the offence, and references to a person's acting or doing an act shall be construed accordingly.

Causation

17—(1) Subject to subsections (2) and (3), a person causes a result which is an element of an offence when—

(a) he does an act which makes a more than negligible contribution to its occurrence; or
(b) he omits to do an act which might prevent its occurrence and which he is under a duty to do according to the law relating to the offence.

Notes

1. Clause 16 is an interpretation clause which instructs the user of the Code *inter alia* that the requirement of proof of an "act" in Code offences may be satisfied "where the context permits" with proof of an omission. This will be appropriate where there is a recognised duty to act. The Code does not specify when there is such a duty relying on the situations which have already been recognised by the courts. This hardly makes for clarity in the law.

2. Clause 17(1)(b) represents a radical change in the law of causation. It seems that as it is difficult to establish that a consequence has occurred as the result of an omission, the Law Commission is proposing to make it easier to establish causation (or, to be precise, their version of causation) in the case of omissions. Causation will be established where the prosecution prove that the consequence might not have occurred had D acted in performance of his duty to act. By contrast, where an offence of commission is involved, the prosecution must prove that the consequence would not have occurred "but for" D's act. This appears to make criminal liability more stringent in the case of those who omit to act. The Law Commission provides the following illustration of the operation of clause 17(1)(b)—

17(ii) D, E's mistress, lives with E and P. E's child by his wife. While E is away P falls seriously ill. D, wishing P to die, fails to call a doctor. P dies. P's life might have been prolonged by medical attention. If D was under a duty to obtain medical attention for P she is guilty of murder. She has caused P's death intending to cause death."

Questions

1. Is D guilty of murder because of the possibility that medical assistance might have prolonged P's life?

2. If the expert medical evidence was to the effect that swift medical attention might have prolonged P's life for an hour, will D be liable for murder?

3. In the above example if, instead of failing to call a doctor D had done so but the doctor was delayed and P was dead on his arrival, what was the cause of P's death? How does this differ from the situation where D fails to call a doctor? Would D's culpability not be

adequately reflected in a conviction under section 1 of the Children and Young Persons Act 1933 of wilfully neglecting a child in a manner likely to cause injury to his health? (See *Sheppard, post*, p. 143).

4. Is it not the case that the current law imposing liability for omissions in respect of "result crimes" represents a policy decision whereby the existence of a duty combined with a failure to prevent a consequence occurring is treated as equivalent to causing that consequence?

Draft Criminal Law Bill, Law Com. No. 218

Supervening fault

31. Where it is an offence to be at fault in causing a result and a person lacks the fault required when he does an act that may cause, or does cause, the result, he nevertheless commits the offence if—

(a) being aware that he has done the act and that the result may occur or, as the case may be, has occurred and may continue, and
(b) with the fault required,

he fails to take reasonable steps to prevent the result occurring or continuing and it does occur or continue.

Note

This clause restates and generalises the principle applied by the House of Lords in *Miller*. The clause also covers the facts of *Fagan v. Metropolitan Police Commissioner, post*, p. 619.

4. CAUSATION

Brett and Waller, *Criminal Law Text and Cases* (4th ed., 1978), p. 145

Many philosophers have devoted great effort to elucidating the notion of causation. In particular, Hume and Mill have made great contributions in this field of enquiry, and from time to time one finds echoes of or borrowings from their work in judgments and legal writings. It is fair to say, however, that their views (and those of other philosophers also) are concerned with causal statements of general application, such as scientific laws. They are thus of comparatively slight value to lawyers, who are concerned with isolated events in the past which cannot be reproduced in the present or future. . . .

For our purposes it is enough to say that when the law treats a particular act or omission as the cause of an event it makes a choice. It does so for the purpose of attributing the responsibility for that event to a particular person, or of denying that he is responsible for it.

This, however, leaves unanswered the question: how is the choice made? The currently fashionable answer (in many other legal contexts as well as in this) is that the judges resort to considerations of 'policy.' But that tells us very little, and it may indeed be positively misleading. For it conjures up a picture of the judge consciously considering various possible choices and selecting what he thinks to be the 'best' one ('best' here having some rather vague reference to notions of supposed social utility).

And it is reasonably clear that this is not what the judge does, either consciously or (as some would argue) unconsciously.

We think that a more accurate way of answering the question is to say that the judges make use of the common sense notions of the ordinary man (Hart and Honoré, in their *Causation in the Law* (1959), adopt broadly the same view). Nor indeed, is there any good reason why they should not do so. The ordinary common sense notions of causation and responsibility can be shown to have, in most respects, a sound moral basis. . . .

The cases and books make use of a number of phrases in the attempt to clarify these common sense notions. Many of these, however, do little more than state a conclusion which has been reached rather than the reasons for reaching it—as when it is said that the law looks to 'proximate' causes as opposed to 'remote' causes, the notions of proximity and remoteness being taken as self-explanatory, likewise it is sometimes said that the law seeks for the 'primary' cause, or even the 'legal' cause, or that it seeks for the *causa causans* (causing, or operative cause).

Williams (T.C.L., pp. 379–382) elucidates the meaning of some of these phrases:

A convenient English equivalent of the term causation *sine qua non* is but-for causation (properly speaking, but-for . . . not causation). For a factor to be a but-for cause, one must be able to say that *but for* the occurrence of the antecedent factor the event would *not* have happened. . . .

When causation is in issue, the defendant's act (or omission) must be shown to be not only a but-for cause but also an imputable or legal cause of the consequence. Imputable causes are *some* of the but-for causes. In other words, the defendant's act, being a but-for cause, must be sufficiently closely connected with the consequence to involve him in responsibility. The lawyer is interested in the causal parentage of events, not in their causal ancestry. . . .

Several attempts have been made to find a suitable name for this second notion of cause. To call it the "direct" or "proximate" cause (as is often done) is misleading, because several stages may intervene between the so-called direct cause and the effect. D may send poisoned chocolates to V, who lives at the other side of the world; if V eats the chocolates and dies, the law will certainly regard D as responsible for the death, though his act was far removed in space and considerably removed in time from its effect. To call D's act the "effective" cause is unhelpful because every cause must by definition be effective—if an act is not effective to produce a given result, it is not a cause of it. "Substantial" is a less misleading adjective, but it is not illuminating.

Sometimes (looking at the situation backwards instead of forwards) imputable causation is stated in terms of "remoteness of consequence." To say that a particular consequence is "too remote" is only another way of saying that the defendant's act (or omission) is not an imputable cause.
. . . When one has settled the question of but-for causation, the further test to be applied to the but-for cause in order to qualify it for legal recognition is not a test of causation but a moral reaction. The question is whether the result can fairly be said to be imputable to the defendant. If the term "cause" must be used, it can best be distinguished as the "imputable" or "responsible" or "blamable" cause, to indicate the value-judgment involved. The word "imputable" is here chosen as best representing the idea. Whereas the but-for cause can generally be demonstrated scientifically, no experiment can be devised to show that one of a number

of concurring but-for causes is more substantial or important than another, or that one person who is involved in the causal chain is more blameworthy than another.

The remainder of the discussion of causation is divided as follows:

i. *Sine qua non*
ii. Imputability
   (a) Fright and flight
   (b) Weak or intractable victims
   (c) Intervening causes
iii. An alternative approach

i. Sine qua non

R. v. Cato
[1976] 1 W.L.R. 110
Court of Appeal

C and his victim F, were friends. F invited C to have a "fix" of his heroin. Each filled his own syringe and then asked the other to inject it into him. This procedure was repeated several times during one night. F died the next morning. One of the grounds on which C appealed against his conviction for manslaughter concerned causation.

LORD WIDGERY C.J.: . . . It seems to us that the first and most important single factor to which counsel for the appellant directed our attention was concerned with causation, that is to say with the link alleged to exist between the injection of heroin and the death of Farmer. . . .

He pointed out that the medical evidence did not at any point say "This morphine killed Farmer"; the actual link of that kind was not present. The witnesses were hesitant to express such a view and often recoiled from it, saying it was not for them to state the cause of death. It is perfectly true . . . that the expert evidence did not in positive terms provide a link, but it was never intended to. The expert witnesses here spoke to factual situations, and the conclusions and deductions therefrom were for the jury. The first question was: was there sufficient evidence upon which the jury could conclude, as they must have concluded, that adequate causation was present?

When one looks at the evidence it is important to realise that no other cause of Farmer's death was supplied. Dr Robinson thought that there might have been another drug, and she said at one stage it might have been cocaine, but there was never any cocaine found in the body. The only cause of death actually supplied by the evidence was morphine. No natural disease was present and no other drug was identified. Furthermore, the symptoms and the external appearance of the body, and the nature of the final terminal cause, was consistent with poison by the administration of heroin in the way which was described. . . .

Of course behind this whole question of the sufficiency of evidence of causation is the fact that it was not necessary for the prosecution to prove that the heroin was the only cause. As a matter of law, it was sufficient if the prosecution could establish that it was *a* cause, provided it was a cause outside the de minimis range, and effectively bearing upon the acceleration of the moment of the victim's death. When one has that in mind it is, we think, really possible to say that if the jury had been directed to look for heroin as a cause, not de minimis but a cause of substance, and they came back with a verdict of not guilty, the verdict could really be described as a perverse one.

The whole background of the evidence was the other way and there certainly was ample evidence, given a proper direction, upon which a charge of manslaughter could be supported.

But what about the proper direction? [the jury had been asked: "Did [the] injection of heroin by [the appellant] cause, contribute to or accelerate the death of Farmer?"] It will be noted that in none of the versions which I have quoted of the judge's direction on this point, nor in any of those which I have not quoted which appear in the summing up, is there any reference to it being necessary for the cause to be a substantial one. It is said in clear terms . . . that the jury can consider whether the administration of the heroin was a cause or contributed to or accelerated the death, and in precise terms the word "contributed" is not qualified to show that a substantial contribution is required. . . .

Before pursuing that, it is worth reminding oneself that some of the more recent dicta in the textbooks about this point do not support as strongly as was once the case the theory that the contribution must be substantial. In Smith and Hogan, *Criminal Law*, 3rd ed. (1973), p. 217 there is this rather interesting extract:

"It is commonly said by judges and writers that, while the accused's act need not be the sole cause of the death, it must be a substantial one. This appears to mean only that a minute contribution to the cause of death will not entail responsibility. It may therefore be misleading to direct a jury that D is not liable unless his conduct was a 'substantial' cause. Killing is merely an acceleration of death and factors which produce a very trivial acceleration will be ignored."

Whether that be so or not, and we do not propose to give that passage the court's blessing today at all events, if one looks at the circumstances of the present case with any real sense of reality, we think there can be no doubt that when the judge was talking about contribution the jury knew perfectly well that he was talking about something more than the mere de minimis contribution. We have given this point particular care in our consideration of the case because it worried us to some extent originally, but we do feel in the end, having looked at all the circumstances, that there could not have been any question in this case of the jury making the mistake of thinking that the contribution would suffice if it were de minimis. . . .

Appeal dismissed

Model Penal Code

"S.2.03(1) Conduct is the cause of a result when:

(a) it is an antecedent but for which the result in question would not have occurred; and
(b) the relationship between the conduct and result satisfies any additional causal requirements imposed by the Code or by the law defining the offence."

ii. Imputability

The *Model Penal Code* continues:

"S.2.03(2) When purposely or knowingly causing a particular result is an element of an offence, the element is not established if the actual result is not within the purpose or the contemplation of the actor unless: . . .

(b) the actual result involves the same kind of injury or harm as that designed or contemplated and is not too remote or accidental in its occurrence to have a just bearing on the actor's liability or on the gravity of his offence.''

Section 2.03(3) contains a similar provision ''when recklessly or negligently causing a particular result is an element of an offence''.

R. v. Dalloway
(1847) 2 Cox 273
Stafford Assizes

A child ran in front of the defendant's cart and was killed. The reins were not in the defendant's hands but loose on the horse's back.

ERLE J., in summing up to the jury, directed them that a party neglecting an ordinary caution, and, by reason of that neglect, causing the death of another, is guilty of manslaughter; that if the prisoner had reins, and by using the reins could have saved the child, he was guilty of manslaughter; but that if they thought he could not have saved the child by pulling the reins, or otherwise by their assistance, they must acquit him.

Not guilty

Note

This case could also be seen as illustrating the but-for principle. The difficulty here is that the presence of the cart *was* a *sine qua non* of the child's death but D's negligent driving was not.

Problems can also arise where D's act was not the direct cause of death (where, for example, fright exacerbates a medical condition or V dies escaping from D), or where D's act does not cause instantaneous death and a complex chain of causation develops (through, for example, negligent medical care).

(a) Fright and flight

Note

Death may ensue as a result of fright caused by D bringing about a physiological reaction in V, such as a heart attack, or it may occur where V, because he is frightened by D, seeks to flee from him and dies in the process. In *Watson* [1989] 2 All E.R. 865 the Court of Appeal accepted that a jury, properly directed, could have found that the appellants' acts of burgling V's house, wakening and verbally abusing him, V being a frail 87-year-old, caused his death when he died ninety minutes later from a heart attack. See further Busuttil and McCall Smith, ''Fright, Stress and Homicide'' (1990) 54 J. Crim. L. 257.

R. v. Hayward
(1908) 21 Cox 692
Maidstone Assizes

The defendant returned home in a state of violent excitement. He was heard to express the intention of "giving his wife something" when she came in. When she did arrive there were sounds of an altercation and shortly afterwards the woman ran from the house into the road, closely followed by the defendant. She fell into the roadway and the accused kicked her on the left arm. She died and a medical examination showed that the bruise on her arm, caused by the kick, was not the cause of death. The deceased woman was in good health apart from a persistent thyrus gland. Medical evidence was given that a person subject to this condition might die from a combination of fright or strong emotion and physical exertion. The defendant was charged with manslaughter.

RIDLEY J.: . . . directed the jury that if they believed the witnesses there was a sufficient chain of evidence to support a conviction of manslaughter. He pointed out that no proof of actual physical violence was necessary, but that death from fright alone, caused by an illegal act, such as threats of violence, would be sufficient. The abnormal state of the deceased's health did not affect the question whether the prisoner knew or did not know of it if it were proved to the satisfaction of the jury that the death was accelerated by the prisoner's illegal act.

Verdict: Guilty

R. v. Curley
(1909) 2 Cr.App.R. 109
Court of Criminal Appeal

The appellant had been indicted for murder and convicted of manslaughter. He was heard to be quarrelling with the woman with whom he lived. She was heard to cry from her bedroom "Let me out", "murder" and "police". The appellant was heard to go into the room, the window was thrown up. It appeared that the woman jumped from the window.

JELF J.: Appellant told the officer, "I ran at her to hit her. I didn't quite touch her. Out she jumped." On that statement a verdict of murder might well have been returned, but it was mercifully reduced to one of manslaughter. The jumping out of the window was contributed to by the appellant's unlawful act. . . .

Appeal dismissed

R. v. Mackie
(1973) 57 Cr.App.R. 453
Court of Appeal

M was convicted of the manslaughter of a boy aged three whom he was looking after. It was alleged that the boy fell downstairs while running away in fear of being ill-treated.

STEPHENSON L.J. read the judgment of the court:
Where the injuries are not fatal, the attempt to escape must be the natural consequence of the assault charged, not something which could not be expected, but something which any reasonable and responsible man in the

assailant's shoes would have foreseen. Where the injuries are fatal, the attempt must be the natural consequence of an unlawful act and that unlawful act "must be such as all sober and reasonable people would inevitably recognise must subject the other person to, at least, the risk of some harm resulting therefrom, albeit not serious harm": *Church* (*post*, p. 582) . . .

In this case there were two complications: (1) the victim was a child of three and regard must be had to his age in considering whether his reaction was well-founded or well-grounded on an apprehension of immediate violence (in the language of the old cases appropriate to adults) and therefore reasonably to be expected. (2) This defendant was in the position of a parent, which may have entitled him to "assault" the child by smacking or threatening him without breaking the law, and it was not every act which might be expected to cause slight harm to the boy that would be unlawful for a man in his parental position; he might have to do some act in the interests of the boy's own safety, for instance, to keep him away from the upstairs window. The purpose of correcting the child—and perhaps the sole justification for correcting a young child—is to deter; how else can the kind parent of a nervous child save it from danger than by in some degree hurting or frightening it? How far was it reasonable, and therefore lawful, for the appellant to go in punishing this child was one of the questions the jury had to decide. Whether the boy "over-reacted" (as Mr Back put it) in a way which the appellant could not reasonably be expected to have foreseen was another.

. . . At the end of the summing-up the judge came back to these questions in suggesting what the vital points might be: "First, was the boy in fear of Mackie? Secondly, did that cause him to try to escape? Thirdly, if he was in fear, was that fear well-founded? If it was well-founded, was it caused by the unlawful conduct of the accused, that is, by conduct for which there was no lawful excuse even on the part of a man in the position of a father. . . .

We think that the judge directed the jury clearly and correctly as to the law laid down in the cases. . . .

Appeal dismissed

Note

This approach to "manslaughter by 'flight'" was confirmed by the Privy Council in *D.P.P. v. Daley* [1979] 2 W.L.R. 239. Lord Keith of Kinkel summarised it thus:

"[T]he essential ingredients of the prosecution's proof of a charge of manslaughter, laid upon the basis that a person has sustained fatal injuries while trying to escape from assault . . . are: (1) that the victim immediately before he sustained the injuries was in fear of being hurt physically; (2) that this fear was such that it caused him to try to escape; (3) that whilst he was trying to escape, and because he was trying to escape he met his death; (4) that his fear of being hurt there and then was reasonable and was caused by the conduct of the defendant; (5) that the defendant's conduct which caused the fear was unlawful; and (6) that his conduct was such as any sober and reasonable person would recognise as likely to subject the victim to at least the risk of some harm resulting from it, albeit not a serious harm. Their Lordships have to observe that it is unnecessary to prove the defendant's knowledge that his conduct was unlawful."

Daley was further considered in *Williams and Davis* [1992] 1 W.L.R. 380. V was a hitch-hiker who had been picked up by a car driven by W in which D was also a passenger. After about five miles, while the

car was travelling at 30 miles per hour, V jumped from the car and
died from head injuries. It appeared that he had been threatened if
he did not hand over his money. The Court of Appeal quashed W's
convictions for manslaughter and robbery because of misdirections on
evidence, and quashed D's convictions as it regarded a direction based
on *Daley* as insufficient where there was a real issue as to causation.
Stuart-Smith L.J., after referring to the six ingredients in *Daley*, stated:

> "Where the unlawful act was a battery, there was no difficulty with the
> second ingredient. However, where the unlawful act was merely a
> threat unaccompanied and not preceded by actual violence, the position
> might be more difficult. The nature of the threat was important in con-
> sidering both the foreseeability of harm to the victim from the threat
> and the question whether the deceased's conduct was proportionate to
> the threat, that is to say that it was within the ambit of reasonableness
> and not so daft as to make it his own voluntary act which broke the
> chain of causation. The jury should consider two questions: first
> whether it was reasonably foreseeable that some harm, albeit not ser-
> ious harm, was likely to result from the threat itself; and second,
> whether the deceased's reaction in jumping from the moving car was
> within the range of responses which might be expected from a victim
> placed in his situation. The jury should bear in mind any particular
> characteristic of the victim and the fact that in the agony of the moment
> he might act without thought and deliberation."

In *Marjoram* [2000] Crim. L.R. 372, D argued on appeal that for the
purposes of the question whether a reasonable person could have
foreseen the victim's attempt to escape as a possible consequence of
D's assault, the reasonable person should be the same age and sex as
the defendant. In this case D was aged 16. The Court of Appeal ruled
that as the issue concerned the effect of the defendant's conduct on
the victim's mind, the test had to be objective to avoid the absurdity
where there were two defendants of one being held not to have caused
the injury because he had not foreseen the victim's flight, and the
other being held to have caused it because he had foreseen the victim's
flight.

(b) Weak or intractable victims

It is a general rule of criminal liability that defendants take their
victims as they find them. Thus in *R. v. Plummer* (1844) 1 C. & K.
600, where a husband had denied shelter to his wife who died soon
afterwards, Gurney B. said, "It does not appear in evidence what her
disease was, or that she was afflicted with that mortal illness under
which she laboured, or that she was suffering from diarrhoea which
caused her death; but he was, nevertheless, informed that she was
very ill, and had no shelter. If you should be of opinion that her death
was caused or accelerated by his conduct you will say that he is guilty
(of manslaughter)." And in *R. v. Martin* (1832) 5 C. & P. 128 Parke J.
said, "It is said, that the deceased was in a bad state of health; but
that is perfectly immaterial, as, if the prisoner was so unfortunate as
to accelerate her death, he must answer for it." This principle applies
where, for religious or other reasons, the victim refuses medical help.

R. v. Blaue
[1975] 1 W.L.R. 1411
Court of Appeal

The appellant stabbed a woman; the wound penetrated her lung. At the hospital she was told that a blood transfusion and surgery were necessary to save her life. She refused to have a transfusion as it was contrary to her beliefs as a Jehovah's Witness. She died the next day. Medical evidence indicated that she would not have died had she accepted the medical treatment. The appellant was convicted of manslaughter on grounds of diminished responsibility.

LAWTON L.J.: Towards the end of the trial and before the summing up started counsel on both sides made submissions as to how the case should be put to the jury. Counsel then appearing for the defendant invited the judge to direct the jury to acquit the defendant generally on the count of murder. His argument was that her refusal to have a blood transfusion had broken the chain of causation between the stabbing and her death. As an alternative he submitted that the jury should be left to decide whether the chain of causation had been broken. Mr. Herrod submitted that the judge should direct the jury to convict, because no facts were in issue and when the law was applied to the facts there was only one possible verdict, namely, manslaughter by reason of diminished responsibility.

When the judge came to direct the jury on this issue he did so by telling them that they should apply their common sense. He then went on to tell them they would get some help from the cases to which counsel had referred in their speeches. He reminded them of what Lord Parker C.J. had said in *R. v. Smith* [1959] 2 Q.B. 35, 42 and what Maule J. had said 133 years before in *R. v. Holland* (1841) 2 Mood. & R. 351, 352. He placed particular reliance on what Maule J. had said. The jury, he said, might find it "most material and most helpful". He continued:

> "This is one of those relatively rare cases, you may think, with very little option open to you but to reach the conclusion that was reached by your predecessors as members of the jury in *R. v. Holland*, namely, 'yes' to the question of causation that the stab was still, at the time of the girl's death, the operative cause of death—or a substantial cause of death. However, that is a matter for you to determine after you have withdrawn to consider your verdict."

Mr Comyn has criticised that direction on three grounds: first, because *R. v. Holland* should no longer be considered good law; secondly, because *R. v. Smith*, when rightly understood, does envisage the possibility of unreasonable conduct on the part of the victim breaking the chain of causation; and thirdly, because the judge in reality directed the jury to find causation proved although he used words which seemed to leave the issue open for them to decide.

In *R. v. Holland*, 2 Mood. & R. 351, the defendant in the course of a violent assault, had injured one of his victim's fingers. A surgeon had advised amputation because of the danger to life through complications developing. The advice was rejected. A fortnight later the victim died of lockjaw. Maule J. said, at p. 352: "the real question is, whether in the end the wound inflicted by the prisoner was the cause of death". That distinguished judge left the jury to decide that question as did the judge in this case. They had to decide it as juries always do, by pooling their experience of life and using their common sense. They would not have been handicapped by a lack of training in dialectic or moral theology.

Maule J.'s direction to the jury reflected the common law's answer to the problem. He who inflicted an injury which resulted in death could not excuse himself by pleading that his victim could have avoided death by taking greater care of himself: see *Hale's Pleas of the Crown* (1800 ed.), pp. 427–28. The common law in Sir Matthew Hale's time probably was in line with contemporary concepts of ethics. A man who did a wrongful act was deemed *morally* responsible for the natural and probable consequence of that act. Mr Comyn asked us to remember that since Sir Matthew Hale's day the rigour of the law relating to homicide has been eased in favour of the accused. It has been—but this has come about through the development of the concepts of intent, not by reason of a different view of causation. . . .

There have been two cases in recent years which have some bearing upon this topic: *R. v. Jordan* (1956), [*infra*] and *R. v. Smith* [*infra*]. The physical cause of death in this case was the bleeding into the pleural cavity arising from the penetration of the lung. This had not been brought about by any decision made by the deceased but by the stab wound.

Mr Comyn tried to overcome this line of reasoning by submitting that the jury should have been directed that if they thought the deceased's decision not to have a blood transfusion was an unreasonable one, then the chain of causation would have been broken. At once the question arises—reasonable by whose standards? Those of Jehovah's Witnesses? Humanists? Roman Catholics? Protestants of Anglo-Saxon descent? The man on the Clapham omnibus? But he might well be an admirer of Eleazar who suffered death rather than eat the flesh of swine (2 Maccabees, ch. 6, vv. 18–31) or of Sir Thomas More who, unlike nearly all his contemporaries was unwilling to accept Henry VIII as Head of the Church of England. Those brought up in the Hebraic and Christian traditions would probably be reluctant to accept that these martyrs caused their own deaths.

As was pointed out to Mr Comyn in the course of argument, two cases, each raising the same issue of reasonableness because of religious beliefs, could produce different verdicts depending on where the cases were tried. A jury drawn from Preston, sometimes said to be the most Catholic town in England, might have different views about martyrdom to one drawn from the inner suburbs of London. Mr Comyn accepted that this might be so: it was, he said, inherent in trial by jury. It is not inherent in the common law as expounded by Sir Matthew Hale and Maule J. It has long been the policy of the law that those who use violence on other people must take their victims as they find them. This in our judgment means the whole man, not just the physical man. It does not lie in the mouth of the assailant to say that the victim's religious beliefs which inhibited him from accepting certain kinds of treatment were unreasonable. The question for decision is what caused her death. The answer is the stab wound. The fact that the victim refused to stop this end coming about did not break the causal connection between the act and death. . . .

Appeal dismissed

Williams, Note (1976) C.L.J. 15

Although the case follows the precedents, . . . it fails to notice that all of them dated from a time when medical science was in its infancy, and when operations performed without hygiene carried great danger to life. It was therefore open to the court for the benefit of the defendant to consider the question afresh, and there were several reasons for doing so.

It had been held in the law of tort that the test of reasonable foresight applies to facts like those in *Blaue*, but the court refused to bring the criminal law into line. The criminal law should avoid the appearance of harshness, and to make it more stringent than the civil law in the matter of causation is surprising. Lawton L.J., speaking for the court, explained the difference between crime and tort by saying that 'the criminal law is concerned with the maintenance of law and order and the protection of the public generally'. This overlooks that Blaue was in any event punishable severely for wounding with intent. What social purpose is served by giving an attacker *extra* punishment because the person attacked unreasonably refused treatment?

Questions

1. Would the decision in *Blaue* have differed if V had refused treatment because she wanted to die so that Blaue would be charged with murder?

2. Is the decision in *Blaue* inconsistent with the "fright and flight" cases above where an "unreasonable flight" can break the chain of causation.

3. Would Blaue's moral culpability differ any if V had not been a Jehovah's Witness and had accepted a blood transfusion and survived or if V had died before a blood transfusion had been administered? If not is it arguable that the concentration of the criminal law on consequences in determining liability is misplaced given that the consequences of action often depend on chance circumstances which are not within the accused's control? See Gobert below.

J. Gobert, "The Fortuity of Consequence" (1993) 4 Crim. L.F. 1

[T]he moral culpability of Blaue's initial actions is in no way altered by subsequent events, and it is on these actions that his criminal responsibility should be based.

What appears to be happening in cases like *Blaue* is that judges are not prepared to allow a defendant to avoid full liability for morally culpable acts on the basis that the victim was in some way responsible for the ultimate result, whatever logical merit there may be to this argument in pure causation terms. After all, had Blaue's victim bled to death before her plight could be discovered, or had there been no blood of the appropriate type available for a transfusion, there would have been no question regarding his responsibility for the death, for there would have been no intervening cause.

Why should the result be different when there is an intervening cause? The answer to this conundrum is, however, not to say that you must take your victim as you find him but to define crimes so that results are not of criminological significance. Blaue's attack on his victim was intentional, deliberate, and vicious. His criminality should reflect these facts and not the fortuity of whether the victim happened to die. The strained reasoning in *Blaue* resulted from the need to satisfy the legal definition of a crime specified in terms of result and the inevitable corollary of whether the defendant's acts caused that result. Because the court thought that Blaue was morally responsible for his victim's death, it stretched legal principle to find him criminally responsible.

(c) Intervening causes

G. Williams, *"Finis* for *Novus Actus"* [1989] C.L.J. 391

A person is primarily responsible for what he himself does. He is not responsible, not blameworthy, for what other people do. The fact that his own conduct, rightful or wrongful, provided the background for a subsequent voluntary and wrong act by another does not make him responsible for it. What he does may be a but-for cause of the injurious act, but he did not do it. His conduct is not an imputable cause of it. Only the later actor, the doer of the act that intervenes between the first act and the result, the final wielder of human autonomy in the matter, bears responsibility (along with his accomplices) for the result that ensues. . . .

The autonomy doctrine, expressing itself through its corollary the doctrine of *novus actus interveniens*, teaches that the individual's will is the autonomous (self-regulating) prime cause of his behaviour. Although this may sound unbelievably metaphysical, the doctrine is supported because it accords with our ideas of moral responsibility and just punishment, and serves social objectives. The first actor who starts on a dangerous or criminal plan will often be responsible for what happens if no one else intervenes; but a subsequent actor who has reached responsible years, is of sound mind, has full knowledge of what he is doing, and is not acting under intimidation or other pressure or stress resulting from the defendant's conduct, replaces him as the responsible actor. Such an intervening act is thought to break the moral connection that would otherwise have been perceived between the defendant's acts and the forbidden consequence.

Policy arguments in favour of novus actus
(1) The law should not saddle a person with liability for consequences that not only he but also the general public would blame on someone else. The intervention of the responsible actor diverts our retributive wrath from the first actor, who may, in the event, appear to be so much less culpable than the later actor; and this switching of retributive feeling from the first actor to the later actor is expressed in causal language.

(2) Sometimes we may feel that making people responsible for the subsequent behaviour of others, merely because they foresaw or could have foreseen that behaviour, would be too great a restriction upon liberty. . . .

(3) The rule has the beneficial effect of restricting the number of persons made liable for a particular occurrence. Part of the object of the criminal trial is to dramatise society's rejection of the deed, and, generally speaking, this is adequately done by prosecuting the immediate author and his accomplices. No pressing necessity exists to regard more remote authors as responsible for causing the harm . . . though some of them may well be prosecuted for other offences, such as attempt, or in appropriate circumstances as accessories.

Note

A problem which has arisen in several cases is that of medical treatment of wounds inflicted by D on V. If the medical treatment is negligent will this break the chain of causation? Will D only be liable where the original wound is not healed and V dies from it? What happens if the original wound is healed and the medical treatment itself is the immediate cause of death; as D's wounding of V caused him to undergo medical treatment, can it be said that this was still a substantial cause of V's death?

R. v. Jordan
(1956) 40 Cr.App.R. 153
Court of Criminal Appeal

The appellant stabbed the deceased in the abdomen. The deceased was taken promptly to hospital and the wound was stitched. A few days later he died. Jordan was convicted of murder at Leeds Assizes and on appeal sought to adduce further medical evidence. This evidence disclosed that the wound, which had penetrated the intestine in two places, was mainly healed at the time of death. At the hospital terramycin was administered to prevent infection. The deceased was found to be intolerant to this antibiotic. A doctor who was unaware of this ordered its continuance. Two fresh witnesses also testified that abnormal quantities of liquid had been given intravenously. This caused the lungs to become waterlogged and pulmonary oedema was discovered.

HALLETT J.: . . . We are disposed to accept it as the law that death resulting from any normal treatment employed to deal with a felonious injury may be regarded as caused by the felonious injury, but we do not think it necessary to examine the cases in detail or to formulate for the assistance of those who have to deal with such matters in the future the correct test which ought to be laid down with regard to what is necessary to be proved in order to establish causal connection between the death and the felonious injury. Not only one feature, but two separate and independent features, of treatment were, in the opinion of the doctors, palpably wrong and these produced the symptoms discovered at the post-mortem examination which were the direct and immediate cause of death, namely, the pneumonia resulting from the condition of oedema which was found.

Conviction quashed

R. v. Smith
[1959] 2 Q.B. 35
Courts-Martial Appeal Court

The appellant, a soldier, was charged with, and convicted of, the murder of a fellow soldier during the course of a fight between the men of two regiments who shared the same barrack room. The deceased received two bayonet wounds, one in the arm and one in the back which pierced the lung and caused haemorrhage. Another soldier tried to carry the wounded man to the medical reception station. He twice dropped him on the ground. At the station the medical officer and his orderly were extremely busy. There were two other stabbed men to deal with as well as others with minor injuries. The medical staff did not know of the haemorrhage nor was the serious nature of the injury realised. A transfusion of saline solution was tried but failed and when breathing seemed impaired, oxygen and artificial respiration were given. This treatment was "thoroughly bad" and might well have affected his chance of recovery. There was medical evidence at the trial that haemorrhage of this type tends to stop. Had there been a blood transfusion available chances of recovery were assessed as high as 75 per cent. by a medical witness for the defence.

LORD PARKER C.J.: In these circumstances Mr. Bowen urged that not only was a careful summing-up required, but that a correct direction to the court would have been that they must be satisfied that the death of Private Creed was a natural consequence and the sole consequence of the wound sustained by him and flowed directly from it. If there was, says Mr Bowen, any other cause, whether resulting from negligence or not, if, as he contends here, something happened which impeded the chance of the deceased recovering, then the death did not result from the wound. The court is quite unable to accept that contention. It seems to the court that if at the time of death the original wound is still an operating cause and a substantial cause, then the death can properly be said to be the result of the wound, albeit that some other cause of death is also operating. Only if it can be said that the original wounding is merely the setting in which another cause operates can it be said that the death did not result from the wound. Putting it another way, only if the second cause is so overwhelming as to make the original wound merely part of the history can it be said that the death does not flow from the wound. . . .

Mr Bowen placed great reliance on a case decided in the Court of Criminal Appeal, *R. v. Jordan [ante*, p. 56] and in particular on a passage in the headnote which says, ". . . that death resulting from any normal treatment employed to deal with a felonious injury may be regarded as caused by the felonious injury, but that the same principle does not apply where the treatment is abnormal." Reading those words into the present case, Mr Bowen says that the treatment that this unfortunate man received from the moment that he was struck to the time of his death was abnormal. The court is satisfied that *Jordan's* case was a very particular case depending upon its exact facts. It incidentally arose on the grant of an application to call further evidence, and leave having been obtained, two well-known medical experts gave evidence that in their opinion death had not been caused by the stabbing but by the introduction of terramycin after the deceased had shown that he was intolerant to it, and by the intravenous introduction of abnormal quantities of liquid. It also appears that at the time when that was done the stab wound which had penetrated the intestine in two places had mainly healed. In those circumstances the court felt bound to quash the conviction because they could not say that a reasonable jury, properly directed, would not have been able on that to say that there had been a break in the chain of causation; the court could only uphold the conviction in that case if they were satisfied that no reasonable jury could have come to that conclusion.

In the present case it is true that the judge-advocate did not in his summing-up go into the refinements of causation. Indeed, in the opinion of this court he was probably wise to refrain from doing so. He did leave the broad question to the court whether they were satisfied that the wound had caused the death in the sense that the death flowed from the wound, albeit that the treatment he received was in the light of after-knowledge a bad thing. In the opinion of this court that was on the facts of the case a perfectly adequate summing-up on causation; I say "on the facts of the case" because, in the opinion of the court, they can only lead to one conclusion: a man is stabbed in the back, his lung is pierced and haemorrhage results; two hours later he dies of haemorrhage from that wound; in the interval there is no time for a careful examination, and the treatment given turns out in the light of subsequent knowledge to have been inappropriate and, indeed, harmful. In those circumstances no reasonable jury or court could, properly directed, in our view possibly come to any other conclusion than that the death resulted from the original wound. Accordingly the court dismisses this appeal.

Appeal dismissed

R. v. Malcherek
R. v. Steel
[1981] 2 All E.R. 422
Court of Appeal

These two cases raised the same question. M stabbed his wife with a kitchen knife causing a deep abdominal wound. S was accused of attacking a girl causing grave head injuries. Both victims were put on life support machines during normal courses of treatment. In each case the machines were switched off after a number of tests indicated that brain death had occurred. Both M and S were convicted at their trials for murder. The ground of M's appeal and S's application for leave to appeal was that the judge should not have withdrawn the question of causation from the jury. S also sought leave to adduce further medical evidence that the doctors in each case had not complied with all the Medical Royal Colleges' and Faculties of the United Kingdom 1976 suggested criteria for establishing brain death.

LORD LANE C.J.: [After stating the facts] . . . This is not the occasion for any decision as to what constitutes death. . . . There is, it seems, a body of opinion in the medical profession that there is only one true test of death and that is the irreversible death of the brain stem, which controls the basic functions of the body such as breathing. When that occurs it is said the body has died, even though by mechanical means the lungs are being caused to operate and some circulation of blood is taking place. . . .

The question posed for answer to this court is simply whether the judge in each case was right in withdrawing from the jury the question of causation. Was he right to rule that there was no evidence on which the jury could come to the conclusion that the assailant did not cause the death of the victim?

The way in which the submissions are put by counsel for Malcherek on the one hand and by counsel for Steel on the other is as follows: the doctors, by switching off the ventilator and the life support machine, were the cause of death or, to put it more accurately, there was evidence which the jury should have been allowed to consider that the doctors, and not the assailant, in each case may have been the cause of death.

In each case it is clear that the initial assault was the cause of the grave head injuries in the one case and of the massive abdominal haemorrhage in the other. In each case the initial assault was the reason for the medical treatment being necessary. In each case the medical treatment given was normal and conventional. At some stage the doctors must decide if and when treatment has become otiose. This decision was reached, in each of the two cases here, in circumstances which have already been set out in some detail. . . .

There are two comparatively recent cases which are relevant to the consideration of this problem. [His Lordship then considered *R. v. Smith, ante,* p. 55 and *R. v. Jordan, ante,* p. 56].

In the view of this court, if a choice has to be made between the decision in *R. v. Jordan* and that in *R. v. Smith,* which we do not believe it does (*R. v. Jordan* being a very exceptional case), then the decision in *R. v. Smith* is to be preferred.

The only other case to which reference has been made, it having been drawn to our attention by counsel for Steel, is *R. v. Blaue, [ante,* p. 52] . . .

The passage . . . is the last paragraph of the judgment of Lawton L. J. [1975] 1 W.L.R. 1411 at 1416:

"The issue of the cause of death in a trial for either murder or man-slaughter is one of fact for the jury to decide. But if, as in this case, there is no conflict of evidence and all the jury has to do is apply the law to the admitted facts, the judge is entitled to tell the jury what the result of that application will be. In this case the judge would have been entitled to have told the jury that the appellant's stab wound was an operative cause of death. The appeal fails.''

There is no evidence in the present case here that at the time of conventional death, after the life support machinery was disconnected, the original wound or injury was other than a continuing, operating and indeed substantial cause of the death of the victim, although it need hardly be added that it need not be substantial to render the assailant guilty. There may be occasions, although they will be rare, when the original injury has ceased to operate as a cause at all, but in the ordinary case if treatment is given bona fide by competent and careful medical practitioners, then evidence will not be admissible to show that the treatment would not have been administered in the same way by other medical practitioners. In other words, the fact that the victim has died, despite or because of medical treatment for the initial injury given by careful and skilled medical practitioners, will not exonerate the original assailant from responsibility for the death. It follows that so far as the ground of appeal in each of these cases relates to the direction given on causation, that ground fails. . . . Where a medical practitioner adopting methods which are generally accepted comes bona fide and conscientiously to the conclusion that the patient is for practical purposes dead, and that such vital functions as exist (for example, circulation) are being maintained solely by mechanical means, and therefore discontinues treatment, that does not prevent the person who inflicted the initial injury from being responsible for the victim's death. Putting it in another way, the discontinuance of treatment in those circumstances does not break the chain of causation between the initial injury and the death.

Appeal and applications dismissed

Note

In *Jordan* the original wound had healed whereas in *Smith* and *Malcherek* the original wounds were still operating at the time of death. In the case which follows the Court of Appeal had sought to move away from the simplistic analysis of whether or not the original wound had healed at the time of death, as concentration on this may lead to the wrong conclusion. The issue is whether D has caused the death of V not whether the wound D inflicted caused V's death. Even though the actual wound may have healed, D's act may still be an operating and substantial (in the sense of "more than minimal") cause of death.

R. v. Cheshire
[1991] 1 W.L.R. 844
Court of Appeal

In December 1987 D shot V in the leg and the stomach. V underwent surgery and when respiratory complications arose a tracheotomy was performed, the tube remaining in place until early January 1988. In February V developed difficulty in breathing which was diagnosed as being due to anxiety. On February 14, V complained of further problems with breathing. His condition deteriorated and despite attempts at resuscitation V died early on February 15. The cause of death was given

as cardio-respiratory arrest due to a condition produced as a result of
provision of an artificial airway in treatment of gunshot wounds. At
D's trial for murder the defence presented expert medical evidence that
the gunshot wounds no longer threatened V's life and that the cause of
death was the failure to correctly diagnose and treat the cause of V's
breathlessness which was due to a narrowing of V's windpipe near the
site of the tracheotomy scar. The trial judge directed the jury that in
order to find that the chain of causation between the original wounding
and V's death had been broken, they had to be satisfied that the medical
treatment or lack of it was not merely negligent but reckless in the sense
that the doctors had acted or failed to act "careless of the consequences,
careless of the comfort and safety of another person."

BELDAM L.J.: . . . Whilst medical treatment unsuccessfully given to prevent the
death of a victim with the care and skill of a competent medical practitioner
will not amount to an intervening cause, it does not follow that treatment
which falls below that standard of care and skill will amount to such a cause.
As Professors Hart and Honoré comment, treatment which falls short of the
standard expected of the competent medical practitioner is unfortunately only
too frequent in human experience for it to be considered abnormal in the
sense of extraordinary. Acts or omissions of a doctor treating the victim for
injuries he has received at the hands of a defendant may conceivably be so
extraordinary as to be capable of being regarded as acts independent of the
conduct of the defendant but it is most unlikely that they will be.

[His Lordship referred to the cases of *Jordan, Smith* and *Malcherek*.
Referring to the latter case he continued].

[I]t was not suggested that the actions of the doctors in disconnecting
the life support machines were other than competent and careful. The
court did not have to consider the effect of medical treatment which fell
short of the standard of care to be expected of competent medical
practitioners. . . .
[W]hen the victim of a criminal attack is treated for wounds or injuries
by doctors or other medical staff attempting to repair the harm done, it
will only be in the most extraordinary and unusual case that such treatment can be said to be so independent of the acts of the defendant that it
could be regarded in law as the cause of the victim's death to the exclusion of the defendant's acts.
Where the law requires proof of the relationship between an act and
its consequences as an element of responsibility, a simple and sufficient
explanation of the basis of such relationship has proved notoriously elusive.
In a case in which the jury have to consider whether negligence in the
treatment of injuries inflicted by the defendant was the cause of death we
think it is sufficient for the judge to tell the jury that they must be satisfied
that the Crown have proved that the acts of the defendant caused the
death of the deceased adding that the defendant's acts need not be the
sole cause or even the main cause of death it being sufficient that his
acts contributed significantly to that result. Even though negligence in the
treatment of the victim was the immediate cause of his death, the jury
should not regard it as excluding the responsibility of the defendant
unless the negligent treatment was so independent of his acts, and in itself
so potent in causing death, that they regard the contribution made by his
acts as insignificant.

It is not the function of the jury to evaluate competing causes or to choose which is dominant provided they are satisfied that the defendant's acts can fairly be said to have made a significant contribution to the victim's death. We think the word "significant" conveys the necessary substance of a contribution made to the death which is more than negligible.

[His Lordship concluded that although the judge erred when he invited the jury to consider the degree of fault in the medical treatment rather than its consequences, no miscarriage of justice had occurred as he had correctly directed the jury that the prosecution did not have to prove that the bullets were the only cause of death but that they were one operative and substantial cause of death. His Lordship continued:]

Even if more experienced doctors than those who attended the deceased would have recognised the rare complication in time to have prevented the deceased's death, that complication was a direct consequence of the appellant's acts, which remained a significant cause of his death. We cannot conceive that, on the evidence given, any jury would have found otherwise.

Appeal dismissed

Note

The decision in *Cheshire* focuses on the acts of the accused in setting in motion a sequence of events which culminates in the victim's death, *viz.*, had D not injured V, V would not have required medical treatment from which complications might arise which in turn might result in misdiagnosis by the doctor. The Court of Appeal is adamant that only in the most exceptional circumstances will negligent medical treatment relieve the accused of causal responsibility for the victim's death. While *Cheshire* has resolved some of the confusion arising from *Jordan* and *Smith*, the decision itself is not above criticism (see Ashworth below).

A. Ashworth, *Principles of Criminal Law* (3rd ed.) p. 132

No clear reason is offered for discounting the voluntary intervening act of the doctor. If the doctor administers a drug to which the patient is known to be intolerant, or gives some other wrong treatment, should the inappropriateness of the medical treatment affect the casual enquiry? The courts' reluctance to discuss the causal significance of the medical treatment probably stems from a desire to ensure the conviction of a culpable offender, and this suggests a strong attachment to a 'wrongful act' approach to causation, deciding the issue by reference to broader judgments of innocence and culpability. This appears to overlook the fact that D, who inflicted the original wound which gave rise to the need for medical attention, will still be liable for attempted murder or a serious wounding offence even if the medical treatment is held to negative his causal responsibility for the ensuing death. Perhaps, for adherents of the 'wrongful act' approach, this is insufficient: they want to see responsibility for the ultimate result pinned on the defendant. However, a court which declares that it is not the doctor who is on trial but the original wrongdoer is merely offering an unconvincing rationalization of its failure to apply the ordinary causal principle that a voluntary intervening act which accel-

erates death should relieve the original wrongdoer of liability for the
result. If that causal principle is thought unsuitable for medical cases,
should we not be absolutely clear about the reasons, and then look closely
at a doctrine of clinical medical necessity?

Questions

1. If the facts of *Jordan* were to recur how might the question of
causation be decided?
2. What would have happened in *Cheshire* if the doctor, having mis-
diagnosed V's condition, rather than giving no treatment had gone on
to give him drugs which exacerbated his condition?

Note

In *McKechnie* [1992] Crim.L.R. 194, the Court of Appeal upheld D's
conviction of manslaughter on the grounds of provocation, D having
caused serious head injuries to V. V died not from the head injuries
but five weeks later from a burst duodenal ulcer. When V was first
admitted to hospital unconscious from the head injuries, the doctors
decided that they dare not operate on the ulcer. V would not have
died had he had an operation on the ulcer. D's act therefore did not
cause V to undergo medical treatment but rather prevented him
undergoing treatment that would have saved his life. The decision not
to operate was not to be judged on its correctness but its reasonableness. On this basis it could not be considered "extraordinary and
unusual" and was not "so independent of the acts of the accused that
it could be regarded in law as the cause of the victim's death".

R. v. Pagett
(1983) 76 Cr.App.R. 279
Court of Appeal

P, while hiding behind V whom he was holding against her will and
whose body he was using as a shield, fired a shotgun at police officers
who were attempting to arrest him. The officers returned P's fire killing
V. P was charged, *inter alia*, with murder. On the issue of causation the
judge directed the jury that they had to be sure that P had fired first at
the officers and that that act caused the officers to fire back with the
result that V was killed, and that in doing so they had to be satisfied
that the police acted reasonably either by way of self-defence or in the
performance of their duties as police officers. If they were not sure of
those facts then they should acquit P because the chain that linked his
deliberate and unlawful acts to V's death would be broken. The jury
acquitted P of murder and convicted him of manslaughter. P appealed.

ROBERT GOFF L.J.: (for the court) . . . [Two of the] three specific points raised
on behalf of the appellant were as follows (we quote from the grounds of
appeal):
(1) The learned judge erred in law in directing that the jury must as a matter
of law find that the appellant caused the death of the deceased, if they were
satisfied as to the four matters of fact which he set out. The learned judge
ought rather to have left it to the jury to determine as an issue of fact whether

the defendant's act in firing at the police officers was a substantial, or operative, or imputable, cause of the death of the deceased.

(2) In the alternative, if the learned judge was correct in himself determining as a matter of law what facts would amount to causation of the death by the appellant, he ought to have held that the appellant had not in the circumstances of this case caused the death of the deceased. The learned judge, in directing himself upon the law, ought to have held that where the act which immediately resulted in fatal injury was the act of another party, albeit in legitimate self-defence, then the ensuing death was too remote or indirect to be imputed to the original aggressor. . . .

The argument addressed to this Court by Lord Gifford on behalf of the appellant was concentrated primarily on the first and second grounds of appeal, and was as presented concerned with the issue of causation. We find it convenient to deal first with the second ground of appeal. . . .

[I]t was pressed upon us by Lord Gifford [for the appellant] that there either was, or should be, a . . . rule of English law, whereby, as a matter of policy, no man should be convicted of homicide (or, we imagine, any crime of violence to another person) unless he himself, or another person acting in concert with him, fired the shot (or, we imagine, struck the blow) which was the immediate cause of the victim's death (or injury).

No English authority was cited to us in support of any such proposition, and we know of none. So far as we are aware, there is no such rule in English law; and, in the absence of any doctrine of constructive malice, we can see no basis in principle for any such rule in English law. . . .

In our judgment, the question whether an accused person can be held guilty of homicide, either murder or manslaughter, of a victim the immediate cause of whose death is the act of another person must be determined on the ordinary principles of causation, uninhibited by any such rule of policy as that for which Lord Gifford has contended. We therefore reject the second ground of appeal.

We turn to the first ground of appeal, which is that the learned judge erred in directing the jury that it was for him to decide *as a matter of law* whether by his unlawful and deliberate acts the appellant caused or was a cause of Gail Kinchen's death. It is right to observe that this direction of the learned judge followed upon a discussion with counsel, in the absence of the jury. . . .

In cases of homicide, it is rarely necessary to give the jury any direction on causation as such. . . . [H]ow the victim came by his death is usually not in dispute. . . .

Even where it is necessary to direct the jury's minds to the question of causation, it is usually enough to direct them simply that in law the accused's act need not be the sole cause, or even the main cause, of the victim's death, it being enough that his act contributed significantly to that result. . . .

Occasionally, however, a specific issue of causation may arise. One such case is where, although an act of the accused constitutes a *causa sine qua non* of (or necessary condition for) the death of the victim, nevertheless the intervention of a third person may be regarded as the sole cause of the victim's death, thereby relieving the accused of criminal responsibility. Such intervention, if it has such an effect, has often been described by lawyers as a *novus actus interveniens*. . . .

[The phrase is] a term of art which conveys to lawyers the crucial feature that there has not merely been an intervening act of another person, but that that act was so independent of the act of the accused that it should be regarded in law as the cause of the victim's death, to the exclusion of the act of the accused.

. . . Professors Hart and Honoré, *Causation in the Law* . . . consider the circumstances in which the intervention of a third person, not acting in concert with the accused, may have the effect of relieving the accused of criminal responsibility. The criterion which they suggest should be applied in such circumstances is whether the intervention is voluntary, *i.e.* whether it is "free, deliberate and informed". We resist the temptation of expressing the judicial opinion whether we find ourselves in complete agreement with that definition; though we certainly consider it to be broadly correct and supported by authority. Among the examples which the authors give of non-voluntary conduct, which is not effective to relieve the accused of responsibility, are two which are germane to the present case, *viz.*, a reasonable act performed for the purpose of self-preservation, and an act done in performance of a legal duty.

There can, we consider, be no doubt that a reasonable act performed for the purpose of self-preservation, being of course itself an act caused by the accused's own act, does not operate as a *novus actus interveniens*. If authority is needed for this almost self-evident proposition, it is to be found in such cases as *R. v. Pitts* (1842) C. & M. 284, and *R. v. Curley* (1909) 2 Cr.App.R. 96. In both these cases, the act performed for the purpose of self-preservation consisted of an act by the victim in attempting to escape from the violence of the accused, which in fact resulted in the victim's death. In each case it was held as a matter of law that, if the victim acted in a reasonable attempt to escape the violence of the accused, the death of the victim was caused by the act of the accused. Now one form of self-preservation is self-defence; for present purposes, we can see no distinction in principle between an attempt to escape the consequences of the accused's act, and a response which takes the form of self-defence. Furthermore, in our judgment, if a reasonable act of self-defence against the act of the accused causes the death of a third party, we can see no reason in principle why the act of self-defence, being an involuntary act caused by the act of the accused, should relieve the accused from criminal responsibility for the death of the third party. . . .

No English authority was cited to us, nor we think to the learned judge, in support of the proposition that an act done in the execution of a legal duty, again of course being an act itself caused by the act of the accused, does not operate as *novus actus interveniens*. . . . Even so, we agree with the learned judge that the proposition is sound in law, because as a matter of principle such an act cannot be regarded as a voluntary act independent of the wrongful act of the accused. A parallel may be drawn with the so-called "rescue" cases in the law of negligence, where a wrongdoer may be held liable in negligence to a third party who suffers injury in going to the rescue of a person who has been put in danger by the defendant's negligent act. Where, for example, a police officer in the execution of his duty acts to prevent a crime, or to apprehend a person suspected of a crime, the case is surely *a fortiori*. Of course, it is inherent in the requirement that the police officer, or other person, must be acting in the execution of his duty that his act should be reasonable in all the circumstances; see section 3 of the Criminal Law Act 1967. . . .

The principles which we have stated are principles of law . . . It follows that where, in any particular case, there is an issue concerned with what we have for convenience called *novus actus interveniens*, it will be appropriate for the judge to direct the jury in accordance with these principles. It does not however follow that it is accurate to state broadly that causation is a question of law. On the contrary, generally speaking causation is a question of fact for the jury. . . .

But that does not mean that there are no principles of law relating to causation, so that no directions on law are ever to be given to a jury on the question of causation. On the contrary, we have already pointed out one familiar direction which is given on causation, which is that the accused's act need not be the sole, or even the main, cause of the victim's death for his act to be held to have caused the death.

[His Lordship then cited the principle in *R. v. Blaue, ante,* p. 52, as an example of a *statement of legal principle* on causation.]

Likewise, in cases where there is an issue whether the act of the victim or of a third party constituted a *novus actus interveniens*, breaking the causal connection between the act of the accused and the death of the victim, it would be appropriate for the judge to direct the jury, of course in the most simple terms, in accordance with the legal principles which they have to apply. It would then fall to the jury to decide the relevant factual issues which, identified with reference to those legal principles, will lead to the conclusion whether or not the prosecution have established the guilt of the accused of the crime of which he is charged.

In the light of these principles, we do not consider that any legitimate criticism can be made, on behalf of the appellant, of the direction given by the learned judge to the jury on the issue of causation in the present case. . . .

For these reasons, we are unable to accept Lord Gifford's argument based on the first ground of appeal.

Appeal dismissed

Questions

1. Would the outcome have been the same if the victim had been an innocent passer-by?
2. Would P have been guilty of wounding if V had not died?
3. Would P have been guilty if V had escaped from his hold and run in the line of police fire?

Note

In *Pagett*, Robert Goff L.J. spoke of *novus actus interveniens* conveying the idea that there has not merely been an intervening act of another person, but that that act was so independent of the act of the accused that it should be regarded in law as the cause of the relevant consequence to the exclusion of the act of the accused, accepting as broadly correct and supported by authority the Hart and Honoré criterion of whether the intervention is voluntary, *i.e.* "free, deliberate and informed". Consider whether the following cases can be reconciled with this criterion.

1. In *Kennedy* [1999] Crim. L.R. 65, D supplied a syringe filled with heroin to V who paid him and injected it and subsequently died. D was convicted of manslaughter. The Court of Appeal placed considerable emphasis on the fact that D's supply of the syringe amounted to encouragement to V to inject himself. A person who encourages another to commit an offence may be liable as an accessory to that offence because of the encouragement offered, not because the encouragement causes the relevant consequence - it is the principal who

causes it (see chap. 6 *post*). In the instant case, however, V, being the deceased, could not be the principal to manslaughter, only D could be that but V's injection of himself with heroin was the immediate cause of his death (see further *Dalby, post* p. 585).

2. In *Environment Agency v Empress Car Co. (Abertillery)* [1999] 2 A.C. 22, D Co. had on its land a diesel tank which had an outlet pipe connected to it which led to a drum. The outlet pipe was controlled by a tap which was not locked. An unknown person opened the tap resulting in the contents of the tank draining into the drum, overflowing and polluting a river. The appellant was charged with causing polluting matter to enter controlled waters contrary to section 85(1) of the Water Resources Act 1991. D Co. denied causing pollution but was convicted. The House of Lords dismissed D Co's appeal. The leading judgment by Lord Hoffmann drew no distinction between deliberate acts of third parties and interventions of nature stating that:

> "The true common sense distinction is, in my view, between acts and events which, although not necessarily foreseeable in the particular case, are in the generality a normal and familiar fact of life, and acts or events which are abnormal and extraordinary. Of course an act or event which is in general terms a normal fact of life may also have been foreseeable in the circumstances of the particular case, but the latter is not necessary for the purposes of liability. There is nothing extraordinary or abnormal about leaky pipes or lagoons as such: these things happen, even if the particular defendant could not reasonably have foreseen that it would happen to him. There is nothing unusual about people putting unlawful substances into the sewage system and the same, regrettably, is true about ordinary vandalism. So when these things happen, one does not say: that was an extraordinary coincidence, which negatived the causal connection between the original act of accumulating the polluting substance and its escape. In the context of section 85(1), the defendant's accumulation has still caused the pollution. On the other hand, the example I gave of the terrorist attack would be something so unusual that one would not regard the defendant's conduct as having caused the escape at all."

It appears that in cases involving pollution, at least, the free, deliberate, informed and malicious act of a third party will not constitute a *novus actus* as it is not extraordinary.

iii. An Alternative Approach

Fletcher, *Rethinking Criminal Law*, pp. 362, 368

It would be plausible to define a law protecting life in terms that made the occurrence of death irrelevant. The critical issue would be an act endangering life. An attempt to kill, particularly if manifested unequivocally in the actor's behaviour, would be treated the same as an actual killing. Conduct highly dangerous to human life would be treated as equivalent to reckless homicide. The rationale for eliminating the issues of causation and death would be that the purpose of the law should be to punish and to deter blameworthy assaults on the interest in life. The actual occurrence of death and its causal attribution are irrelevant to the sets of acts that should be deterred, and it is also irrelevant to the criteria rendering the accused blameworthy for his conduct. The man who shoots at an apparently alive but dead patient, is arguably no less blameworthy than the assassin who has the bad luck to shoot and kill a living patient. . . .

There is no easy solution to the problem of causation. The metaphysics of proximate cause, degrees of contribution and intervening causes will continue to affect even the most rational penal system. The reasons are several. First, the inquiry into causation is categorical. A death is attributable to someone or it is not. There is no room for a compromise verdict as there is in the assessment of culpability for criminal homicide. Secondly, the issue of causation, along with the elements of acting and the occurrence of death, goes to the foundation of liability. . . .

The third significant factor is that the courts are bound to render these appellate decisions in an all-or-nothing fashion without having a general theory to guide their assessment whether in close cases they should find for the defendant or the prosecution. . . .

Rooted in the practice of tainting, the causal inquiry bears neither on the definition of conduct that should be deterred nor on the criteria for justly blaming someone who endangers human life.

Question

Consider whether any of the above cases would have been decided differently had the question not been one of causation but of an act endangering life, as suggested by Fletcher.

Draft Criminal Code Bill

Causation

17.—(1) (See *ante*, p. 42).

(2) A person does not cause a result where, after he does such an act or makes such an omission, an act or event occurs—

(a) which is the immediate and sufficient cause of the result;
(b) which he did not foresee, and
(c) which could not in the circumstances reasonably have been foreseen.

(3) A person who procures, assists or encourages another to cause a result that is an element of an offence does not himself cause that result so as to be guilty of the offence as a principal except when—

(a) section 26(1)(c) applies; or
(b) the offence itself consists in the procuring, assisting or encouraging another to cause the result.

5. COINCIDENCE OF ACTUS REUS AND MENS REA

Note

Where an offence requires *mens rea* the prosecution must prove that D had *mens rea* at the time he did the act which caused the *actus reus*.

R. v. Jakeman
(1982) 76 Cr.App.R. 223
Court of Appeal

J booked two cases containing cannabis on a flight from Accra to Rome and from there to London. The flight was diverted from Rome to Paris. J did not claim her cases in Paris but flew on to Rome and then to London. Officials in Paris sent the cases to London where they were not collected. The cannabis was discovered and J was charged with being knowingly concerned in the fraudulent evasion of the restriction on the importation of cannabis contrary to section 170(2) of the Customs and Excise Act 1979. J's defence was that on boarding the aircraft she repented of her original intention and tore up the baggage tags. The judge ruled that this provided no defence. J appealed.

WOOD J.: Mr Mansfield . . . submits that for the offence under section 170(2) of the 1979 Act, the participation of the applicant and her *mens rea* must continue throughout the offence—in this case at least until the wheels of the aircraft touched down at Heathrow Airport. . . .

The following propositions are supported by decisions of this court. First, that the importation takes place when the aircraft bringing the goods lands at an airport in this country, see *R. v. Smith (Donald)*; [1973] Q.B. 924, 935G. Secondly, acts done abroad in order to further the fraudulent evasion of a restriction on importation into this country are punishable under this section, see *R. v. Wall (Geoffrey)* [1974] 1 W.L.R. 930, 934C.

For guilt to be established the importation must, of course, result as a consequence, if only in part, of the activity of the accused. If, for example, in the present case the applicant had taken her two suitcases off the carousel at Charles de Gaulle airport in Paris, removed all the luggage tags, placed the suitcases in a left luggage compartment and thrown the key of that compartment into the Seine, and then subsequently, in a general emergency, all left luggage compartments had been opened, a well-known English travel label had been found on her suitcase and those suitcases had been sent to the Travel Agents' agency, care of Customs and Excise at Heathrow, then that undoubted importation would not be the relevant one for the purposes of a charge against the applicant. . . .

Although the importation takes place at one precise moment—when the aircraft lands—a person who is concerned in the importation may play his part before or after that moment. Commonly, the person responsible for despatching the prohibited drugs to England acts fraudulently and so does the person who removes them from the airport at which they have arrived. Each is guilty. . . .

There is no doubt, that . . . the applicant had a guilty mind when at Accra she booked her luggage to London. By that act, she brought about the importation through the instrumentation of innocent agents. In this way, she caused the airline to label it to London, and the labels were responsible for the authorities in Paris sending it on to London.

What is suggested is that she should not be convicted unless her guilty state of mind subsisted at the time of importation. We see no reason to construe the Act in this way. If a guilty mind at the time of importation is an essential, the man recruited to collect the package which has already arrived and which he knows contains prohibited drugs commits no offence. What matters is the state of mind at the time the relevant acts are done, *i.e.* at the time the defendant is concerned in bringing about the importation. This accords with the general principles of common law. To stab a victim in a rage with the necessary intent for murder or manslaughter leads to criminal responsibility for the resulting death regardless of any repentance between the act of stabbing and the time of death, which may be hours or days later. This is so even if, within seconds of the stabbing, the criminal comes to his senses and does everything possible to assist his victim. Only the victim's survival will save him from conviction for murder or manslaughter.

The applicant alleged that she repented as soon as she boarded the aircraft; that she deliberately failed to claim her luggage in Paris, that she tore up the baggage tags attached to her ticket and so on, but none of this could have saved her from being held criminally responsible for the importation which she had brought about by deliberate actions committed with guilty intent. Thus, the learned judge was right in the ruling he made.

Appeal dismissed

Questions

1. If checking in the cases at Accra amounted to an "act which is more than merely preparatory to the commission of the offence" (section 1(1) Criminal Attempts Act 1981), would removal of the luggage in Paris, in the manner suggested by the judge, have provided an answer to a charge of attempted fraudulent evasion of importation restrictions?

2. If checking in the cases at Accra did not amount to "an act which is more than merely preparatory to the commission of the offence," should such an intention be sufficient for conviction of the completed offence which unexpectedly occurs at a time when *mens rea* no longer exists?

Note

Where an *actus reus* may be brought about by a continuing act, it is sufficient that the accused had *mens rea* during its continuance even though he did not have *mens rea* at its inception (see *Fagan v. Metropolitan Police Commissioner*, *post*, p. 619; see also *Kaitamaki* [1985] A.C. 147 *post*, p. 676). A problem which has arisen in relation to homicide, is that of death resulting from a series of acts performed by the accused only some of which were performed with *mens rea*.

Thabo Meli v. The Queen
[1954] 1 W.L.R. 228
Privy Council

The deceased was taken to a hut by the appellants where he was struck over the head with intent to kill him. His unconscious body was then rolled over a small cliff to make the death appear to be an accident. Medical evidence indicated that the appellants had not succeeded in killing the deceased in the hut but that he had died from exposure.

LORD REID: The point of law which was raised in this case can be simply stated. It is said that two acts were necessary and were separable: first, the attack in the hut; and, secondly, the placing of the body outside afterwards. It is said that, while the first act was accompanied by *mens rea*, it was not the cause of death; but that the second act, while it was the cause of death, was not accompanied by *mens rea*; and on that ground it is said that the accused are not guilty of any crime, except perhaps culpable homicide.

It appears to their Lordships impossible to divide up what was really one transaction in this way. There is no doubt that the accused set out to do all these acts in order to achieve their plan and as parts of their plan; and it is too refined a ground of judgment to say that, because they were under a misapprehension at one stage and thought that their guilty purpose had been achieved before in fact it was achieved, therefore they are to escape the penalties of the law. . . .

Note

1. In the next chapter the issue of mistake will be considered. In *Thabo Meli* the appellants made a mistake; they thought they were disposing of a corpse when they threw the victim over the cliff. An intention to destroy or dispose of a corpse is not sufficient *mens rea* for murder; what is required is an intention to kill or to cause grievous bodily harm. Thus, in strict legal principle, the appellants' mistake meant that they did not have the *mens rea* of murder at the time they caused death. If they were to be convicted of murder, the court would have to extend the law on policy grounds to cover this situation where there was no contiguity between the *actus reus* and *mens rea*. As Williams states (C.L.P.G. pp. 174–175):

"In [this case of *Thabo Meli*] the accused intends to kill and does kill; his only mistake is as to the precise moment of death and as to the precise act that effects death. Ordinary ideas of justice and common sense require that such a case shall be treated as murder. If so it is necessary to make an exception to the general principle [that mistake as to an element of the *actus reus* negatives *mens rea*], and to hold that although the accused thinks that he is dealing with a corpse, still his act is murder if his mistaken belief that it is a corpse is the result of what he has done in pursuance of his murderous intent. If a killing by the first act would have been manslaughter, a later destruction of the supposed corpse should also be manslaughter."

2. In the case of *Church* [1966] 1 Q.B. 59 *post*, p. 582, the problem of the supposed corpse arose in relation to a conviction of manslaughter. The appellant struck and attempted to strangle a woman. She fell unconscious and the appellant, believing her dead following his extremely cursory examination of her, threw her into a river where she drowned. He was convicted of manslaughter and on appeal that conviction was upheld. The Court of Criminal Appeal appears to have upheld the conviction on the basis of gross negligence manslaughter although it also made comments on the "series of acts" doctrine in *Thabo Meli*. It adopted "as sound" Williams's view as expressed in the final sentence of the passage above. The court was of opinion that the judge should have directed the jury that—

". . . they were entitled (if they thought fit) to regard the conduct of the appellant in relation to Mrs Nott [the deceased] as constituting throughout a series of acts which *culminated in her death*, and that, if that was how they regarded the accused's behaviour, it mattered not whether he believed her to be alive or dead when he threw her in the river." (emphasis added) (at p. 71).

The problem with this approach is that it begs a question; was it such a series of acts that would have led to conviction under the *Thabo Meli* approach? In *Thabo Meli* the acts of attack and disposal were part of a concerted plan to kill the accused and then dispose of the corpse. There was no such plan in *Church* (nor could there be in a case of manslaughter unless it arose as a result of a plea of diminished responsibility), so were the acts of original attack and the act of disposal part of a series? In *Thabo Meli* the acts formed a series, not because the act of disposal followed sequentially on the attack, but because they were concerted acts in pursuance of a plan. In speaking of *Thabo Meli* the Court of Criminal Appeal stated that, with regard to the charge of murder against *Church* (of which he was acquitted),

"... the jury should have been told that it was still open to them to convict of murder, notwithstanding that the appellant may have thought his blows and attempt at strangulation had actually produced death when he threw the body into the river, if they regarded the appellant's behaviour from the moment he first struck her to the moment when he threw her into the river as a series of acts designed to cause death or grievous bodily harm." (at p. 67)

This statement talks of a "series of acts designed to cause death" whereas, in respect of manslaughter, the court talked of a "series of acts which culminated in . . . death". It is difficult to follow the court's reasoning when it talks of a series of acts designed to cause death as the act of disposal is for the purpose of disposing of a *body*, it being the actor's belief that death had occurred already. Such a direction would be inherently illogical.

In *S. v. Masilela* 1968 (2) S.A. 558 the Supreme Court of South Africa (Appellate Division) held that a conviction of murder could be returned where death resulted from the act of disposal by the assailant even though there was no preconceived plan. In the case which follows there was neither a preconceived plan nor did the accused believe he was dealing with a corpse.

R. v. Le Brun
[1991] 3 W.L.R. 653
Court of Appeal

D and W (his wife) argued in the street, W refusing to go home. D struck W rendering her unconscious. He dragged her from the street either to get her into the house where she did not want to go or to conceal his previous assault and in so doing W's head struck the pavement, fracturing her skull and death resulted. D was convicted of manslaughter and appealed.

LORD LANE C.J.: . . . The question can be perhaps framed in this way. There was here an initial unlawful blow to the chin delivered by the appellant. That, again on what must have been the jury's finding, was not delivered with the intention of doing really serious harm to the wife. The guilty intent accompanying that blow was sufficient to have rendered the appellant guilty of manslaughter, but not murder, had it caused death. But it did not cause death. What caused death was the later impact when the wife's head hit the pavement. At the moment of impact the appellant's intention was to remove her, probably unconscious, body to avoid detection. To that extent the impact may have been accidental. May the earlier guilty intent be joined with the later non-guilty blow which caused death to produce in the conglomerate a proper verdict of manslaughter?

It has usually been in the previous decisions in the context of murder that the problem has arisen. We have had our attention directed to a Privy Council case, *Meli v. The Queen* [1954] 1 W.L.R. 228. . . . That decision of course is not binding upon us. It is of very persuasive authority and it was adopted by another division of this court in 1975 in *R. v. Moore* [1975] Crim.L.R. 229.

However, it will be observed that the present case is different from the facts of those two cases in that death here was not the result of a preconceived plan which went wrong, as was the case in those two decisions which we have cited. Here the death, again assuming the jury's finding to be such as it must have been, was the result of an initial unlawful blow, not intended to cause serious harm, in its turn causing the appellant to take steps possibly to evade the consequences of his unlawful act. During the taking of those steps he commits the actus reus but without the mens rea necessary for murder or manslaughter. Therefore the mens rea is contained in the initial unlawful assault, but the actus reus is the eventual dropping of the head on to the ground.

Normally the actus reus and mens rea coincide in point of time. What is the situation when they do not? Is it permissible, as the prosecution contend here, to combine them to produce a conviction for manslaughter?

The answer is perhaps to be found in the next case to which we were referred, and that was *R. v. Church* [1966] 1 Q.B. 59.

[His Lordship quoted Edmund Davies J.'s judgment where he stated that a manslaughter verdict would have been returned on the basis of a "series of acts which culminated in death", and continued.]

It seems to us that where the unlawful application of force and the eventual act causing death are parts of the same sequence of events, the same transaction, the fact that there is an appreciable interval of time between the two does not serve to exonerate the defendant from liability. That is certainly so where the appellant's subsequent actions which caused death, after the initial unlawful blow, are designed to conceal his commission of the original unlawful assault. . . .

In short, in circumstances such as the present, which is the only concern of this court, the act which causes death, and the necessary mental state to constitute manslaughter, need not coincide in point of time. . . .

[His Lordship concluded that the judge's direction to the jury was satisfactory in so far as it related to manslaughter.]

Appeal dismissed

Questions

1. In all the earlier cases D killed in the course of covering up the homicide he mistakenly believed he had already committed. Is the true principle the following: that D is liable for homicide (murder or manslaughter depending on his *mens rea*) where he performs a series of acts which culminate in death, *mens rea* existing either (a) at the time of the initial act, or (b) at some stage during the transaction? (see *Att.-Gen.'s Reference (No. 4 of 1980), infra*).

2. Lord Lane C.J. also sought to support the conviction of manslaughter in *Le Brun* on the basis of causation. He stated:

"It would be possible to express the problem as one of causation. The original unlawful blow to the chin was a cause sine qua non of the later actus reus. It was the opening event in a series which was to culminate in death: the first link in the chain of causation, to use another metaphor. It cannot be said that the actions of the appellant in dragging the victim away with the intention of evading liability broke the chain which linked the initial blow with the death."

Was the initial assault a substantial cause of death? Could the conviction be supported solely on this causation basis without the "series of acts" doctrine being applied? If it can be supported solely on causation what was the *mens rea* at the time of "the later *actus reus*"?

Note

A problem which the Court of Appeal did not address in *Le Brun* is that which arose in the following case where it was impossible to tell which act caused death.

Attorney-General's Reference (No. 4 of 1980)
[1981] 2 All E.R. 617
Court of Appeal

D and V were arguing. D slapped V causing her to fall backwards down a flight of stairs head first onto the floor where she lay motionless. D tied a rope around her neck and dragged her upstairs, placed her in the bath, cut her throat to let out her blood, and then cut her up and disposed of the pieces. The body was never found so the cause of death could not be determined. V died either from the fall, from being strangled by the rope or from having her throat cut. The defence submitted that there was no case to go to the jury and the judge withdrew the case directing an acquittal on the basis that the Crown had failed to prove the cause of death. The Attorney-General sought the court's opinion on the following point of law: whether a person who has committed a series of acts against another culminating in the death of that person, each act in the series being either unlawful and dangerous or an act of gross criminal negligence, is entitled to be acquitted of manslaughter on the ground that it cannot be shown which of such acts caused the death of the deceased.

ACKNER L.J.: On the above facts this reference raises a single and simple question, *viz.*, if an accused kills another by one or other of two or more different acts each of which, if it caused the death, is a sufficient act to establish manslaughter, is it necessary in order to found a conviction to prove which act caused the death? The answer to the question is No, it is not necessary to found a conviction to prove which act caused the death. No authority is required to justify this answer, which is clear beyond argument, as was indeed immediately conceded by counsel on behalf of the accused.

What went wrong in this case was that counsel made jury points to the judge and not submissions of law. He was in effect contending that the jury should not convict of manslaughter if the death had resulted from the "fall", because the push which had projected the deceased over the handrail was a reflex and not a voluntary action, as a result of her digging her nails into him.

If, however, the deceased was still alive when he cut her throat, since he then genuinely believed her to be dead, having discovered neither pulse nor sign of breath, but frothy blood coming from her mouth, he could not be guilty of manslaughter because he had not behaved with gross criminal negligence. What counsel and the judge unfortunately overlooked was that there was material available to the jury which would have entitled them to have convicted the accused of manslaughter, whichever of the two sets of acts caused her death. It being common ground that the deceased was killed by an act done to her by the accused and it being conceded that the jury could not be satisfied which was the act which caused the death, they should have been directed in due course in the summing up, to ask themselves the following questions: (i) "Are we satisfied beyond reaonable doubt that the deceased's 'fall' downstairs was the result of an intentional act by the accused which was unlawful and dangerous?" If the answer was No, then they would acquit. If the answer was Yes, then they would need to ask themselves a second question, namely: (ii) "Are we satisfied beyond reasonable doubt that the act of cutting the girl's throat was an act of gross criminal negligence?" If the answer to that question was No, then they would acquit, but if the answer was Yes, then the verdict would be guilty of manslaughter. The jury would thus have been satisfied that, whichever act had killed the deceased, each was a sufficient act to establish the offence of manslaughter.

The facts of this case did not call for "a series of acts direction" following the principle in *Thabo Meli v. R.* [*supra*]. We have accordingly been deprived of the stimulating questions whether the decision in *R. v. Church* [*post*, p. 542] correctly extended that principle to manslaughter, in particular to "constructive manslaughter" and if so whether that view was part of the ratio decidendi.

Determination accordingly

Questions

1. If the jury are satisfied that D, with *mens rea*, committed an unlawful and dangerous act in hitting V, could they, applying *Le Brun* (which approved the direction on manslaughter in *Church* based on a series of acts culminating in death), convict of manslaughter even though the cause of death is not determined? Has *Le Brun* rendered nugatory the decision in *Att.-Gen.'s Reference*?

2. Should the dual test articulated by Ackner L.J. be applied if the charge is one of murder or should the "series of acts" doctrine in *Le Brun* be extended to cover murder?

MENS REA

Criminal liability is generally not based solely on the commission of acts and their attendant consequences or the commission of acts in particular circumstances. Generally (but see Strict Liability) liability only arises where an autonomous rational individual performs the act which causes the consequence, or performs the act in the particular prohibited circumstances, with the requisite *mens rea* (*i.e.* fault requirement) for the offence. *Mens rea* builds on ideas of individual autonomy in that an individual should only be liable to the extent that s/he chose to act as s/he did (i) either intending the consequence to occur or being aware of the risk of the consequence occurring, or (ii) knowing or believing the relevant circumstance(s) to exist. *Mens rea* is a means by which responsible actors are identified for the purpose of attributing blame and imposing punishment. But there are a number of problems which arise in analysing *mens rea*. Firstly, is blame or culpability dependent only on the state of mind of the accused when the relevant act was performed or does the incidence of harm resulting from the accused's act raise the degree to which s/he is culpable, that is, is blame a product of state of mind or of the harm caused plus the state of mind? Secondly, where *mens rea* indicators of blame are absent may blame arise from other factors such as intoxication for which the accused is responsible (see chapter 4)? Thirdly, what is the effect on *mens rea* of exculpatory factors such as impaired capacity (e.g due to insanity, see chapter 4), impaired freedom of choice (e.g. due to duress or necessity, see chapter 5), or justifications such as self-defence (see chapter 5)? Finally what do the various terms which import *mens rea* into offences actually mean?

1. THE REQUIREMENT OF MENS REA

Williams, *Criminal Law: The General Part*, p. 30

Nature of the requirement of mens rea

There is no need to go into the remote history of *mens rea*; suffice it to say that the requirement of a guilty state of mind (at least for the most serious crimes) had been developed by the time of Coke, which is as far back as the modern lawyer needs to go. 'If one shoot at any wild fowl upon a tree, and the arrow killeth any reasonable creature afar off, without any evil intent in him, this is *per infortunium.*'

It may be said that any theory of criminal punishment leads to a requirement of some kind of *mens rea*. The deterrent theory is workable only if the culprit has knowledge of the legal sanction; and if a man does not foresee the consequence of his act he cannot appreciate that punishment lies in store for him if he does it. The retributive theory presupposes moral guilt; incapacitation supposes social danger; and the reformative aim is out of place if the offender's sense of values is not warped.

However, the requirement as we have it in the law does not harmonise perfectly with any of these theories. It does not fit the deterrent theory, because a man may have *mens rea* although he is ignorant of the law. On the deterrent theory, ignorance of the law should be a defence; yet it is not. Again, the requirement does not quite conform to the retributive theory, because the *mens rea* of English law does not necessarily connote an intention to engage in moral wrongdoing. A crime may be committed from the best of motives and yet remain a crime. (In this respect the phrase *mens rea* is somewhat misleading). There are similar difficulties with incapacitation and reform.

What, then, does legal *mens rea* mean? It refers to the mental element necessary for the particular crime, and this mental element may be either *intention* to do the immediate act or bring about the consequence or (in some crimes) *recklessness* as to such act or consequence. In different and more precise language, *mens rea* means intention or recklessness as to the elements constituting the *actus reus*. These two concepts, intention and recklessness, hold the key to the understanding of a large part of criminal law. Some crimes require intention and nothing else will do, but most can be committed either intentionally or recklessly. Some crimes require particular kinds of intention or knowledge.

Outside the class of crimes requiring *mens rea* there are some that do not require any particular state of mind but do require negligence. Negligence in law is not necessarily a state of mind; and thus these crimes are best regarded as not requiring *mens rea*. However, negligence is a kind of legal fault, and in that respect they are akin to crimes requiring *mens rea*.

Yet other crimes do not even require negligence. They are crimes of strict or vicarious responsibility, and, like crimes of negligence, they constitute exceptions to the adage *Actus non facit reum nisi mens sit rea*.

Note

Williams regards intention and recklessness as basic *mens rea* in that a defendant's culpability should be dependent on his awareness of the relevant circumstances surrounding, and consequences of, his conduct. The Law Commission in their Draft Criminal Code Bill recognise recklessness as the "presumed minimum requirement for criminal liability" and by clause 20(1) create a presumption for Code offences and offences created subsequent to the Code's enactment:

"Every offence requires a fault element of recklessness with respect to each of its elements other than fault elements, unless otherwise provided."

Is *mens rea* a merely descriptive term or does it serve other purposes? The extracts which follow address this problem.

A. T. H. Smith, "On Actus Reus and Mens Rea" in *Reshaping the Criminal Law* (ed. Glazebrook), p. 103

The idea that *mens rea* is in some sense a basic or indispensable ingredient of criminal liability is deeply rooted. For example, Stroud stated that:

> the guilt of an act charged against a prisoner must always depend upon two conditions . . . [which] . . . may be called the condition of illegality (*actus reus*) and the condition of culpable intentionality (*mens rea*). (*Mens Rea* (London, 1914), p. 7.)

Kenny's view was that:

> no external conduct, however serious or even fatal its consequences may have been, is ever punished unless it is produced by some form of *mens rea*. (*Outlines of Criminal Law* (2nd ed.) (Cambridge, 1904), p. 39).

These writers explicitly discount the phenomenon of strict liability, and they should not be taken to task for failing to elucidate matters with which they were not concerned. Nevertheless, by insisting that *mens rea* is a necessary constituent of crime, they distort the function that that concept really performs. A fully descriptive account of criminal responsibility would be forced to acknowledge that there are many instances where liability is imposed without proof of *mens rea* as to at least some elements in the *actus reus*.

It may be helpful to identify three of the purposes for which the expression *mens rea* is used. It is, first, an expositional tool, when used in sentences such as 'the *mens rea* of X offence is Y', where Y might be (depending on the offence in question) intention, recklessness, malice, dishonesty, an intent to defraud or deceive. We could substitute the expression 'mental element' without any change of meaning. This is the use to which Stephen referred when he said that

> the maxim about '*mens rea*' means no more than that the definition of all or nearly all crime contains not only an outward and visible element, but a mental element, varying according to the different nature of different crimes. (*A History of The Criminal Law of England* (London, 1883), vol. ii, p. 95).

In addition the term is used, as has already been seen, to denote traditional *mens rea*, a catalogue of more or less blameworthy mental states of intention, recklessness and negligence from which the legislator, in defining crime, is free to pick and choose to suit his requirements.

The expression *mens rea* performs, however, another function by acting as an ideal towards which the legal system should evolve. A balance of modern opinion favours imposing liability on the basis of fault, subjectively assessed, and a considerable body of literature criticises such strict liability and constructive liability for deviating from this ideal. Such criticisms are premised on a view of criminal responsibility which has fault as its basis. But when traditional *mens rea* is referred to as the 'fault' element, this fault principle and a purely technical usage are conflated. The two by no means necessarily coincide, since traditional *mens rea* refers only to awareness of circumstances and to the contemplation of particular results. It does not follow that, because a person foresees or intends he is necessarily at fault: the intention may have been formed in a variety of exculpating circumstances such as under provocation, duress or necessity. As the expression of a fault principle, then, traditional *mens rea* is no more than a rule of thumb. Even as a description of the present law, it is necessary to look for a more embracing fault principle within which the

existing excuses can be subsumed. This more fundamental principle has
been formulated by Professor Hart in these terms:

> unless a man has the capacity and a fair opportunity or chance to adjust
> his behaviour to the law its penalties ought not to be applied to him.
> (*Punishment and Responsibility* (Oxford, 1968), p. 181).

This, he argues, is not only a rationale for most of the excuses which the
law already admits; it might also act as a critical principle to ask of the
law more than it already concedes.

An account of criminal liability that treats traditional *mens rea* as a
necessary fault requirement is thus deficient in two respects. It overlooks
the phenomenon of strict liability, and it takes no account of a number of
efficacious excuses which do not negative the element of awareness or
cognition.

Fletcher, *Rethinking Criminal Law*, pp. 396–397

Descriptive and Normative Uses of the Same Terms

One of the persistent tensions in legal terminology runs between the
descriptive and normative uses of the same terms. Witness the struggle
over the concept of malice. The term has a high moral content, and when
it came into the law as the benchmark of murder, it was presumably used
normatively and judgmentally. Yet Fitzjames Stephen and succeeding
generations of English jurists have sought to reduce the concepts of malice
to the specific mental states of intending and knowing. California judges,
in contrast, have stressed the normative content of malice in a highly
judgmental definition, employing terms like 'base, anti-social purpose'
and 'wanton disregard for human life'. For the English, malice is a question of fact: did the actor have a particular state of consciousness
(intention or knowledge)? In California, malice is a value judgment about
the actor's motives, attitudes and personal capacity.

If the English have tried to reduce the normative concept of malice to
a state of fact, other commentators and courts seek to invest nominally
descriptive terms with moral force. Though the terms 'intent', 'state of
mind,' and 'mental state' appear to be descriptive, legislators and courts
use these terms to refer to issues that require normative judgment. . . .

The confusion between normative and descriptive language is so pervasive in Anglo-American criminal law that it affects the entire language
of discourse. There appear to be very few terms that are exempt from
the ambiguity. The term 'intent' may refer either to a state of intending
(regardless of blame) or it may refer to an intent to act under circumstances (such as failing to inquire about the age of a sexual partner) that
render an act properly subject to blame. The term 'criminal intent' does
not resolve the ambiguity, for a criminal intent may simply be the intent
to do the act, which, according to the statutory definition, renders the act
'criminal', *i.e.* punishable under the law. There may be nothing morally
blameworthy in keeping a pair of brass knuckles as a conversation piece,
yet that intent renders the act punishable and, in this sense, is a criminal
intent.

It is obvious that the very word 'criminal' is affected by the same tension between descriptive and normative illocutionary force. When used
normatively, 'criminal' refers to the type of person who by virtue of his
deeds deserves to be branded and punished as a criminal. When used
descriptively, as in the phrase 'criminal act' it may refer simply to any act
that the legislature has declared to be 'criminal'. Thus the term 'criminal
intent' may mean the intent to act under circumstances that make it just

to treat the actor as a criminal in the pejorative sense. . . . But it is equally plausible to use the term 'criminal intent' to refer to the intent or knowledge sufficient to commit a crime as defined by the legislature. The adjective 'criminal' in this context simply means that the intent is sufficient to render the act punishable under the statute. . . .

There is no term fraught with greater ambiguity than that venerable Latin phrase that haunts Anglo-American criminal law: *mens rea*. Glanville Williams defines *mens rea* to mean 'the mental element necessary for the particular crime'. Of course, the term 'mental element' may be employed either descriptively or normatively, yet in this context it seems clear that Williams means to refer to a factual state of affairs. Intent, used descriptively, is an example of a required 'mental element'. In another passage, Williams argues that the issue of duress should not be seen as negating either intention or *mens rea*. Thus he would conclude, . . . that someone who was acquitted on grounds of duress nonetheless acted with *mens rea*. However prestigious this line of analysis might be, the courts fortunately remain unimpressed. Engaged as they are in the processes of judgment and condemnation, the courts repeatedly stress the normative content of *mens rea*,. . . .

This tension between descriptive and normative usage carries significance for the structuring of issues in the criminal law. Descriptive theorists, like Stephen, Turner, Williams and others in the English tradition, are apt to see problems of insanity, duress and mistake as extrinsic to the analysis of *mens rea* and criminal intent. Normative theorists, in contrast, are able to integrate these 'defensive' issues into their formulation of the minimum conditions for liability. If *mens rea* raises a normative issue of just and appropriate blame, then there is no *mens rea* or 'criminal intent' when the intentional commission of the offence is excused by reason of duress, insanity, or reasonable mistake about an attendant circumstance (*e.g.* the age of the girl in statutory rape).

A. Ashworth, "Taking the Consequences" in *Action and Value in Criminal Law* (eds. Shute, Gardner and Horder) p. 107

The consequences of one's acts do not always turn out in the way anticipated. What might be described as the expected result of one's conduct . . . may be overtaken by unexpected contingencies . . . and might therefore be followed by quite unusual consequences. . . . Would it be right if one were blamed for these consequences? . . .

We will focus here on outcome-luck, and begin by enquiring whether there is a plausible distinction between act and result which might be useful in this sphere. In an earlier essay I argued that the only element of an action which lies within the agent's control is the trying, the doing of all the acts which the agent reasonably believes necessary to achieve the desired end. Thus, if A and B each shoot at their victims from a distance of ten yards and A hits but B misses, the argument would be that intrinsically their actions are the same. Each of them tried to kill, and it is that trying alone which is sufficiently within their control, whereas what happens in the physical world thereafter may be affected by other forces and circumstances. . . . It therefore seems possible, for some types of case at least, to identify intrinsic elements of an action which are independent of outcome-luck.

Separating the act of trying from the consequences is purely an analytical device. It is a prelude to, but does not establish, the proposition that it is wrong to blame people for unintended (or at least, unforeseeable) consequences. . . . On this question of moral assessment two opposing

positions have been urged, and they have been termed the subjectivist
and the objectivist. Let us return to the example of A and B who each
shoot at an intended victim, and suppose that A narrowly misses because
the intended victim moves suddenly, but that B succeeds in killing his or
her intended victim. On the subjectivist view, A and B are equally culpable, and the difference between them in terms of outcomes is purely a
matter of chance. Their moral guilt ought to depend on the choices they
make (which are sufficiently within their control), not on chance outcomes
(which are not). As Duff himself has expressed it [*Intention, Agency and
Criminal Liability*, p. 113]:

> It is through the intentions with which I act that I engage in the world
> as an agent, and relate myself most closely to the actual and potential
> effects of my actions; and the central or fundamental kind of wrongdo-
> ing is to direct my actions towards evil—to intend and to try to do what
> is evil.

On this view, the consequences are not significant for moral blame. By
way of contrast, the objectivist view treats the consequences flowing from
conduct as part of the act itself, and regards any separation between act
and consequences as unconvincing. For the objectivist, the consequences
must be taken into account when assessing moral responsibility.

How can the conflict between subjectivist and objectivist views be
resolved?

[I]n terms of moral theory there may be distinct questions of at least
three kinds—causal responsibility, responsibility to compensate, and
moral blame—and that the arguments for one may not conclude the case
for the others.

[Duff argues that a] leading function of the criminal law and punishment is the communicative or censuring function, and a law which drew
no distinction between completed and merely attempted offences would
imply that the actual causing of harm is unimportant. Since this is morally
the wrong message to convey, the presence or absence of harmful consequences should be marked. This argument crosses the boundary from
moral theory to legal theory, and raises questions about the differences
(if any) between moral and legal responsibility. It is to these that we must
now turn. . . .

Without attempting a general survey of the differences between
responsibility in a moral sense and responsibility under the law, a few
relevant distinctions can be identified. One is that, even though it may
not be entirely true that legal responsibility is concerned only with the
more serious wrongs, it is certainly the case that legal responsibility can
give rise to the application of the coercive powers of the State. Moral
sanctions may take the form of verbal criticism, or social ostracism, or
even expulsion from a family home or a club, whereas legal sanctions
may impose compulsory payments, exclusion from premises or from
occupying a certain position, compulsory supervision, and even incar-
ceration. A second distinction is that legal responsibility is declared by a
court in public, as a result of the machinations of a formal system. This
lends an authoritative and, where the proceedings are criminal, an official
censuring element to the judgment which is unlikely to form part of most
moral judgments. Largely because of the declaratory or stigmatizing effect
of legal processes and the powerful impact of legal sanctions, fairness is
generally thought to require that there be reasonably precise rules which
are announced in advance: these are elements of the concept of the 'rule
of law'. . . .

It is not merely that citizens should be able to discover in advance whether their conduct amounts to an offence. It is also that the degree of censure should be proportioned to the degree of wrongdoing, because that both respects the offender as a choosing individual and serves to structure the official response of the courts rather than leaving it as a matter of discretion. It would be manifestly inadequate for a legal system to have a single offence stating that anyone who behaves in a way that is contrary to the good of society may be liable to conviction and punishment of up to life imprisonment. Its communicative function would be intolerably vestigial, its censuring function would be hopelessly vague, and the discretion left at the sentencing stage would confer enormous power on the courts on what would then be the key issue. This suggests that a principle of fair labelling should form part of a system of criminal law, so as to ensure that each offence is defined and labelled in a way which conveys the relative seriousness of the offence, and which confines the court's sentencing powers appropriately. Of course this principle does not dictate particular formulae, and there is room for argument whether a system of criminal law which has a single, compendious offence of damage to property might also have a single, compendious offence of harm to individuals, or ought fairly to distinguish between minor assaults and serious woundings, for example. But this may illustrate a further difference between moral and criminal responsibility: in criminal law the behaviour has to be fitted into a pre-existing category which will specify certain elements and not others, whereas in moral discourse the blame may be expressed in a narrative and more individuated form.

[Ashworth goes on to examine the differences between civil and criminal liability.]

Just as criminal conviction may be followed by punishment, so civil liability may be followed by an award of compensation. Now the very idea of compensation is to provide the person who suffers loss, harm, or damage with 'a full and perfect equivalent', something which 'makes good' the harm. . . .

The criminal law and punishment are differently directed. They are much more concerned with culpability, since their function is to censure, and that should be restricted to those who deserve it, to the extent that they deserve it. Most of the serious offences require proof of intention or recklessness, whereas the normal minimum for compensation through civil law is proof of negligence. More especially, the criminal law would regard attempted murder as a very serious crime, even though the conduct might not have given rise to any claim for compensation at all. . . .

The reason why attempted murder is treated as a serious offence is that the attempter *tried* to commit murder, which is the highest crime—and, in many cases, the failure arose from factors not intended by the attempter (*e.g.* someone else intervened, the aim was slightly inaccurate, the victim moved). The problem of attempts is hardly peripheral to criminal liability: it is crucial to an understanding of the difference between that and civil liability. It demonstrates the central significance of culpability in the criminal law, where the purpose is to censure and the punishment may restrict or deprive of liberty. It also indicates a difference between the concepts of harm used in criminal law and in the civil law: whereas there is no civil liability unless there is proof of harm, the criminal law is composed only partly of 'result-crimes', and many other crimes impose liability on the basis of conduct which is preliminary to the infliction of harm, merely because of the intention with which the person acted.

The preoccupation with the mental or fault element in serious criminal offences has other manifestations. The culpable causing of a death will give rise, let us assume, to a right to compensation in the civil courts. The amount of compensation is unlikely to differ according to the degree of the harm-doer's culpability. But in the criminal courts the dispute will be over the classification of the conduct as murder, manslaughter, or some other grade of homicide. Murder will have the most stringent fault element and the highest sentence, whilst the other grade(s) of homicide will have lower fault elements and lower sentences. The criminal law is chiefly concerned with desert, that is, with whether or not the person deserves to be labelled as a criminal and, if so, what level of offence is fairly applicable. Once again, culpability is a crucial issue.

[Ashworth goes on to examine liability for manslaughter which may arise where the accused commits a battery which harbours the risk of harm but death occurs due to an unforeseen and unlucky turn of events. He continues that the accused does not deserve to be convicted of manslaughter which bears a heavily condemnatory label when his culpability is minor.]

The fault and the result are simply too far apart for a manslaughter label to communicate anything other than the misfortune which befell both the victim and [the accused]. The criminal law is a censuring institution. It should censure people for wrongs, not misfortunes, and should censure them fairly and proportionately. . . .

CONCLUSIONS

The attraction of the subjectivist or the objectivist approach to outcome-luck rests largely on intuitions about fairness. But there are supporting arguments that can be tested, and much of this essay has been devoted to an examination of the arguments invoked by objectivists in favour of the view that wrongdoers should 'take the consequences'—or not—of their conduct. Some objectivists place considerable emphasis on the concordance of their approach with popular sentiments and public opinion. If intuitions lie at the foundation of both the rival approaches, this will be a significant consideration. But it cannot be conclusive unless it is also claimed that moral and legal responsibility should follow popular sentiments even when they can be shown to harbour elements of irrationality.

Three related difficulties with objectivism have been identified here. First, in some versions it fails to distinguish adequately between issues of causation, of liability to compensate, and of moral blame and criminal liability. Indeed, some expressions of popular sentiment perpetrate a gross confusion between punishment and compensation. If it can be shown that the intuitions, or at least what is inferred from feelings of unfairness, are tainted with confusion, their strength as guides to ethical principle is much diminished. Second, objectivists seem to underestimate the censuring function of the criminal law, and to neglect the pivotal importance of culpability in both liability and sentencing. Third, whilst their insistence on the communicative function of the criminal law is right, it does not follow that the criminal law should always communicate what people wish to hear, as it were. The communicative function might be regarded as educative, where it is clear that popular sentiments are tainted by confusion. Political paternalism of this kind is open to abuse, of course. . . .

The legal implications of favouring subjectivism in matters of outcome-luck have been tested here in relation to three types of case: attempts and completed crimes; death resulting from a minor assault and battery; and dangerous driving. If a subjectivist were drafting a new criminal code, all these cases would be made to depend on the defendant's culpability rather than the outcome in the particular case. The effect of this on the form of the criminal law would be quite radical, since many offences are currently defined by reference to the result. . . .

2. THE MEANING OF MENS REA

Note

While there may be differences in theoretical approach, a more pressing problem for any student of criminal law is the bewildering array of words and phrases with which the mental element in offences may be indicated. Lord Simon of Glaisdale in *D.P.P. for Northern Ireland v. Lynch* [1975] A.C. 653, 688, speaking in a wider context than the issue of duress, with which the case was primarily concerned, said:

"A principal difficulty in this branch of the law is the chaotic terminology, whether in judgments, academic writings or statutes. Will, volition, motive, purpose, object, view, intention, intent, specific intent or intention, wish, desire; necessity, coercion, compulsion, duress—such terms which do indeed overlap in certain contexts, seem frequently to be used interchangeably, without definition, and regardless that in some cases the legal usage is a term of art differing from the popular usage. As if this were not enough, Latin expressions which are themselves ambiguous, and often overlap more than one of the English terms, have been freely used—especially animus and (most question-begging of all) mens rea."

For this obfuscation of the law the judges must carry a large share of the blame.

E. Griew, "Consistency, Communication and Codification: Reflections on Two Mens Rea Words" in *Reshaping the Criminal Law* (ed. Glazebrook), pp. 57–59.

A striking feature of English criminal law has been the casual, erratic quality of the use of key terms in its technical language. This has been most marked in the case of important words that Parliament or the judges have used to express aspects of the mental element of crimes: words like 'malice' and 'maliciously' (examples of ancient casualness), 'wilfully' (a once-popular statutory adverb that has left a legacy of confusion), 'intention' and 'recklessness' (the most discussed of the criminal 'states of mind'). Judges in particular, but Parliament as well, have on the whole seemed to care little about achieving consensus or consistency in this department of the legal vocabulary. This indifference in the matter of language has been part of a larger indifference to criminal law analysis as a whole. . . .

There has recently arisen a judicial practice of disposing of problems in the criminal law—some would say, of escaping from them—by explicit reliance on the linguistic competence of the common man. To the extent that consensus about the meaning of a word in a particular context is in the nature of language possible, it can arise in two broad ways. One of these occurs when, as it might be put, 'everyone knows what the word means'. If, however, there is no such spontaneous consensus, or if a special use is to be made of the word, the required consensus must be imposed by authority. The authority stipulates a meaning. Legal authority in this connecction is legislature or court. In relation both to general concepts in the criminal law and to words in particular contexts, the courts have tended to make a virtue of refraining from 'stipulative definition'— from imposing consensus by saying what words are to be understood to mean. This tendency has been reinforced by the proposition, which has recently enjoyed a powerful vogue in appellate criminal courts, that the meaning of an ordinary word of the English language is not a question of law. Those courts have been very ready—though not consistently so—to find that statutory words whose application is in question before them are 'ordinary words', and have 'approved of trial judges' restraint in the explication of the words for their juries' assistance. . . . The result is that even though there is in fact no spontaneous consensus about the meaning of a word, the courts proceed on the fiction that 'everyone knows what it means'. Parliament too has so far been silent in this field. In short, authority has not yet asserted itself in the stipulation of criminal law definitions. . . .

Concern for language, whether as an aspect of the criminal law as a whole or in the expression of particular rules, is a concern for principle and for substance. If lawyers are not involved in understanding and expounding the theory of the criminal law, their operations will tend towards mere ritual. Theory depends upon the development and accurate deployment of a self-consistent language, through the medium of which legal statements may tellingly respond to discriminations of policy and to the relationships between relevant concepts. The theory and its servant language are not matters for the legislator alone. Lawyers and judges are vital participants in the business of communication by which legislative intention is translated into acts of adjudication. Where legislation is wanting, or where it lacks 'definition', the task of making or clarifying the law is with the courts. That task has, by its nature, to be performed as occasion arises and only to the extent demanded by the occasion. When occasion does not arise, the court's contribution ought to be made with two considerations (among others) in mind. One is the larger picture—the total body of criminal law theory into which the court's decision and the language that embodies it must fit; indifference to theory and principle involves the danger of particularistic decision and in the long run of incoherence. The second consideration is that criminal law rules are of general application. To deny explanation of them as required, on the ground that it is not the court's job to explain 'ordinary words', is to risk all upon the assumption that the word, being ordinary, is within the lexical equipment of the adult population at large and understood (if not used) by everyone in the same sense. This is in fact a set of uniformly unsafe assumptions about people's linguistic competence, about the sociology of language, and about the composition of tribunals of fact. The assumptions upon which, for safety, we should proceed, are: that very low levels of linguistic competence are quite general in the adult population; that even 'ordinary' words (and especially abstract words) are variously understood—everyone may 'know what they mean' but, without knowing it, use them with different meanings; and that the decisions of two benches or juries could depend upon quite different collective senses of how the law is using the same undefined abstract word.

i. Intention

"Intention" is the *mens rea* term which conveys the highest level of culpability of an offender. If a person intends to cause a result he is more culpable than a person who acts recklessly, that is, who acts recognising that the result might occur. It is important to define the boundary between intention and recklessness not only to determine the degree of culpability of the offender for sentencing purposes, but also to determine in many cases whether the offender is liable to conviction where the offence charged is one which requires intention to be proved. The *Concise Oxford Dictionary* defines "intend" as "have as one's purpose" and "intention" as "intending, one's purpose ... object ... ultimate aim". The law, however, does not always attribute to words their dictionary meaning. "Intention" is such a word.

G. Williams, "Oblique Intention" (1987) 46 C.L.J. 417

Why is it that intention, or intent, one of the basic concepts of the criminal law, remains so unclear? Judges decline to define it, and they appear to adjust it from one case to another.

Part of the trouble is the disagreement on the subject of intention among jurists generally. The philosophers who have lately arrived on the scene, hoping to help the lawyers to solve their legal problems, in fact give only limited assistance. Their philosophical interest stems from the fact that intention is an important ethical concept, but they do not relate their discussions to any particular ethical theory, and they do not sufficiently consider the specific requirements of the criminal law. Indeed, they mix up the ordinary meaning of the word 'intention' with its desirable legal meaning. To be sure, the meaning of intention as a technical term of the law ought to be close to the literary and popular one, but there are sound reasons for saying that the two should not always be identical.

Added to the confusion of counsel is the fact that judges sometimes wrap up excuses into the meaning of intention, though rationally excuses should have nothing to do with the matter.

Judges reject the proposition that the legal concept of intention in relation to the consequences of action necessarily involves desire of the consequence. This is quite right, and a useful beginning; but the recent pronouncements of the lords get no further. They do not acknowledge the truth that intention generally does involve desire, and they do not say when it does not.

Note

What, then, is the possible meaning of "intention" in the criminal law? Does "doing an act with foresight of its consequences" amount to the same as "doing an act intending to bring about that consequence"? To answer this question it is necessary to examine the various states of mind that might constitute intention. The states of mind competing to be included within the compass of the term *intention* may be illustrated as follows—

Scenario

D has insured V's life. He decides to kill V in order to obtain the insurance moneys. D's *desire* is to kill V and his *motive* is to obtain the insurance moneys. What is his *intention*?

Case (a) D intends a consequence if it is his *aim* or *objective*. If D shoots at V in order to kill him, the consequence, V's death, is both desired and *intended* by D.

Case (b) D intends a consequence if he foresees it as certain to result from his conduct.

So D wishing to kill V shoots at V who is standing behind a window.

In this case D knows that in order to kill V the bullet must pass through the window. With regard to the window, D intends to break it although he does not desire to do so for its own sake; breaking the window is a necessary precondition to shooting V, that is, it is a means to that end. As Lord Hailsham said in *Hyam* [1975] A.C. 55, 74, "intention [includes] the means as well as the end and the inseparable consequences of the end as well as the means". In the circumstances as they exist, it is not possible for D to kill V without breaking the window. Thus it can be said that D has a *direct* intention regarding V and an *oblique* intention regarding the window; breaking the window is his subsidiary or secondary aim which must be achieved if he is to achieve his ultimate or primary aim.

Does D *desire* to break the window? This depends on the width of the definition of desire. Duff, "The Obscure Intentions of the House of Lords" [1986] Crim.L.R. 773, argues that a person may intend to do various unpleasant things without desiring them. For example, a person with tootache visits the dentist; he does not like visiting dentists and thus does not want or desire to go but he does go intentionally. Williams questions this conclusion.

G. Williams, "Oblique Intention" (1987) 46 C.L.J. 417–421

What the courts ought to hold appears to me to be clear. (1) Except in one type of case, intention as to a consequence of what is done requires desire of the consequence. Of course, intention, for the lawyer, is not a bare wish; it is a combination of wish and act (or other external element). With one exception, an act is intentional as to a consequence if it is done with (motivated by) the wish, desire, purpose or aim (all synonyms in this context) of producing the result in question. (2) The one type of case in which it is reasonable to say that an undesired consequence can be intended in law is in respect of known certainties. A person can be held (but will not always be held) to intend an undesired event that he knows for sure he is bringing about.

(1) The first proposition is disputed by some writers, particularly the two philosophers, [Alan White and R. A. Duff], who have taken an interest in the English criminal law. Their principal argument is that one can intend to do various unpleasant things, *e.g.* visiting the dentist; therefore intention need not involve desire. I would have thought that the error in this is too obvious to need stating. The premise is true, but the conclusion does not follow. Obviously, people go to the dentist in order to get certain benefits (relief from pain or the preservation of the teeth). To get these

benefits, the possibility of pain or discomfort is accepted. It is accepted not as an end in itself but as part of the package, and the package as a whole is desired—otherwise one would not go to the dentist. The pain taken by itself is not desired, but the proposition was not that the patient intends the pain but that he intends to visit (intentionally visits) the dentist.

The writers who deny the relevance of desire replace it with the word 'purpose'. But does not purpose imply desire? One can have an undeclared purpose, but not a undesired purpose. 'Undesired purpose' is a contradiction in terms.

(2) The second proposition seemed to be on its way to legal acceptance until recent pronouncements of the lords. Perhaps the lords intended to negative it. Or perhaps they did not. More of this later.

In one application, at least, the second proposition is accepted as almost universally true. Where the defendant desires result x, and anyone can see, by merely considering x, that another result, y (forbidden by law), will also be involved, as the direct consequence of x and almost as part and parcel of it, then the defendant will be taken to intend both x and y.

Three men accidentally killed a girl in horseplay. Being frightened, they hid the body under a pile of stones. It was held that they were guilty of conspiracy to prevent the burial of a corpse [*Hunter* [1974] Q.B. 95]. The Court of Appeal upheld a direction that 'if the defendants agreed to conceal the body and the concealment in fact prevented burial, then the offence was made out, although prevention of burial was not the object of the agreement.'

A result that is either witnessed or foreseen as certain is almost always regarded as sharing the intentional nature of an act where it is either the contemporaneous (concurrent) result or the immediate consequence of the act. A person will normally be taken to intend something that he is consciously doing, or that follows under his nose from what he is then doing. . . .

Using the word 'intention' in this way admittedly involves an extension beyond its normal meaning in the language. The normal meaning connotes desire. [White] writes: 'What I do knowing I am doing it need not be done intentionally, as when I know that I am hurting your feelings but not doing so intentionally.' The remark is true for ordinary speech, and true in law for offences involving the 'hurting of feelings'; but the law is much more concerned with hurting bodies than with hurting feelings. If I drive over you because I am in a hurry and you will not get out of the way, I drive over you intentionally, and it would be no use my saying that my sole intention was to make progress. For legal purposes the meaning of intention has to be widened to this extent.

Similarly, a surgeon intentionally wounds his patient when he inserts the scalpel. He does not, of course, commit a crime of intention, but that is because he has the justification of consent. Lord Hailsham on one occasion denied this, and put the surgeon's defence on lack of intent; this is an example of the judicial tendency already mentioned, to bring in defences under the heading of lack of intention. In the unlikely case of a surgeon kidnapping his recalcitrant patient and making various incisions in him, entirely for the patient's benefit, the surgeon would be guilty of the offence of wounding with intent; yet his intention to make the incisions would be the same as in an ordinary medical operation.

The law should generally be the same where the defendant is aware that a consequence in the future is the certain (though undesired) result of what he does. He is liable for a crime of intention if the foreseen though undesired consequence is inseparably bound up with the desired consequence. This opinion has been supported by some writers, though not all. More importantly, it has been accepted by several of the major reform bodies of the common-law world. If such a variety of intention is accepted we need a name for it, the best being Bentham's coinage of 'oblique intention'. Direct intention is where the consequence is what you are aiming at. Oblique intention is something you see clearly, but out of the corner of your eye. The consequence is (figuratively speaking) not in the straight line of your purpose, but a side-effect that you accept as an inevitable or 'certain' accompaniment of your direct intent (desire-intent). There are twin consequences of the act, x and y; the doer wants x, and is prepared to accept its unwanted twin y. Oblique intent is, in other words, a kind of knowledge or realisation.

When one speaks of the unwanted consequence as being 'certain', one does not, of course, mean certain. 'Nothing is certain save death and taxes.' For example, a person who would otherwise have been the victim of the criminal's act may be warned in time, or providentially happen to change his plans, and so escape what would otherwise have been his fate. Certainty in human affairs means certainty as a matter of common sense—certainty apart from unforeseen events or remote possibilities. Realisation of practical certainty is something higher in the scale than appreciation of high probability.

Case (c) D intends a consequence if it is a virtual, practical or moral certainty that it will result from his actions—in other words, he intends a result where he acts being aware that the result will occur in the ordinary course of events if he succeeds in achieving his purpose.

So D places a bomb under V's seat timed to kill him in mid-flight as he pilots a plane.

In this case D does not desire to kill the crew or passengers but if he realises that their deaths are a *virtual*, *practical* or *moral certainty*, that is, that they will die in the ordinary course of events, he obliquely intends their deaths. The deaths of the crew or passengers are not a pre-condition to killing V but, in the ordinary course of events, they are the inevitable *by-product* of D's killing V; they are an inseparable consequence of that end. If, miraculously, the crew and passengers survive, D will not have failed in achieving his purpose, that is, killing V. This does not necessarily mean that D did not desire their deaths, if desire is given a wider meaning. Norrie is a supporter of the view that an act is intended where it is seen by the actor as having some "desirable characteristic". While agreeing that "intention" should include oblique intention he disagrees that obliquely intended consequences are undesired; this conclusion involves attributing a wider meaning to "desire".

A. Norrie, "Oblique Intention and Legal Politics" [1989] Crim.L.R. 793,
794–796

2. Defining oblique intention

I agree with Williams that intention ought to be defined to include desire but, so long as it is so defined, disagree with his claim that the concept of oblique intention 'involves an extension beyond its normal meaning in the language'. That is not to say that the legal usage of oblique intention corresponds wholly with the ordinary usage.

Intention and desire

Duff argued, I believe correctly, in an earlier paper that the idea of an intended act includes the notion of a desire to bring the act about, using the term 'desire' (or 'want')

'as the most general term of volition, covering attitudes normally contrasted with "wanting", like seeing an action as a duty, as the lesser of two evils, or as an unpleasant but necessary means to a desired end. To intend an action is to see it as having some "desirable characteristic" . . .'

But he later rejected this view:

'It is unnecessary, since it adds nothing to an analysis which talks only of the agent believing that her action might bring X about, and acting because of that belief. Indeed we may ascribe a desire for X to the agent only *because* we realise she intends to bring X about, rather than taking her to intend it because we realise that she desires it. It may be misleading, since it may lead us to treat desire as an independent ingredient or criterion of intention. We may then forget to distinguish the philosophers' use of "desire" (according to which it is an empty truism that all intended results are desired) from its ordinary use (according to which intention need not involve desire).'

The 'philosophers' use', however, is not an empty truism. Desire is analytically distinct from the narrow view of intention proposed by Duff. We may understand that the agent intended to bring X about either by deduction from the patterns of her action *or* by reference to her expressed wishes prior to the action or her *post facto* explanation of why she did it. Desire need not simply be tacked onto an already pre-established deduction of intention. Secondly, it is a moot point whether what Duff regards as ordinary use is not rather narrowly conceived. Take the standard illustration of the person with toothache who, in Duff's view, intends but does not want to go to the dentist. As Williams points out, there is no logical barrier to saying in a real (not technical) sense that the person *does* more broadly want to go to the dentist—as a means to an end, as part of a 'package' which has the ultimate end of removal of the pain at its heart. There seems no objection to saying both 'I didn't want to go to the dentist, but . . .' and 'I wanted to go to the dentist (but only) in order to . . .' Duff's original conception of a 'desirability characteristic' is valuable, and while the recognition of narrow and broader definitions of desire may entail complexity, it does not thereby entail confusion.

Intention, desire and oblique intention

The relevance of this philosophical discussion becomes apparent when we consider the rationale for a doctrine of oblique intent. Oblique intention only becomes a problem for ordinary usage if one separates intention from desire, for one then loses the possibility of seeing what was intended as being that which possesses a 'desirability characteristic', as being part of a 'package' of desires. Williams is wrong to say that oblique intention involves a departure from the ordinary usage of 'intention', for oblique intention can quite naturally be seen as a species of intention once one realises that what is intended is that which is desired in the broad 'package' sense of the term. Williams writes: 'If I drive over you because I am in a hurry and you will not get out of the way, I drive over you intentionally, and it would be no use my saying that my sole intention was to make progress.' Indeed not, but Williams gives the example to illustrate a situation where desire does not go with intent, whereas given his espousal of the 'package' view of desire, it does. I want to drive over you as part of a package which includes my making progress. Your injury is not my direct desire, but it has a 'desirability characteristic' in the broader context. Oblique intention, which includes the intention of means necessary to ends and of necessary side consequences to ends, connotes desire in the broad sense outlined above.

Two further points may be made. First, to identify oblique intention with desire in this way makes good sense for it does away with the need for alternative artificial strategies to cover what normal usage requires. Duff suggests that obliquely intended actions may be intentional but not intended. He writes that 'if I know that my action will cause death, I surely cause that death intentionally, even if I do not act with the intention of causing it: for I voluntarily make myself its agent'. This circuitry could have been avoided had he followed the logic of the broad 'philosophers' sense of desire outlined earlier in the same article, for his definition of 'intentional' action corresponds to the 'philosophers' usage, rendering this distinction unnecessary.

Secondly, the so-called 'test of failure' is only relevant to the narrow sense of intention outlined above and has the effect of artificially constricting commonsensical usage. Where I intend to bring X about and am sure that Y is a necessary corollary, but it turns out that X happens without Y, I have failed to produce the necessary corollary but not failed in my intention. Therefore Y was not part of my intention. But Y *was* part of my intention in that I was prepared to accept its necessity as a means to my end or as a side-consequence of it. I may not directly have wanted Y to happen, but I wanted X sufficiently to will the existence of Y too. I may be quite happy that X occurs without Y, but that does not mean to say the bringing about of Y was not part of my initial intention. . . .

The 'test of failure' is too constricting because it only tests direct intention, and not surrounding circumstances, means to ends, and necessary side-consequences. . . . [It] is only relevant if one has already defined intention in the narrow direct sense, and constrains commonsensical usage.

Case (d) D intends a consequence if he foresees it as a probable or likely consequence of his actions.

So D shoots at V, while he is driving a bus, in order to kill him. D foresees that it is probable that the passengers on the bus or other road users will also be killed.

In this case D does not desire the deaths of the passengers or other road users and will have been successful in his objective if only X dies. Does his foresight of their probable deaths amount to *intention* or does it only constitute *recklessness*?

If there are different states of mind which may be classed as *intention* or *intentional* (as the examples above illustrate), how have the courts dealt with this definitional problem.

Their approach has been far from consistent.

R. v. Steane
[1945] K.B. 997
Court of Criminal Appeal

The appellant, a British film actor, was employed in Germany when war broke out. He was arrested and entered the service of the German broadcasting system reading news bulletins and helping to produce films. He gave evidence that this was done under the pressure of beatings and of threats and with a view to saving his wife and children from a concentration camp. After the war he was convicted of doing acts likely to assist the enemy, with intent to assist the enemy, contrary to Regulation 2A of the Defence (General) Regulations 1939. On appeal it was argued by the Crown that the saving of his wife and children from a concentration camp might have been the motive for his act, but that this was irrelevant on the issue whether he acted with the intent alleged.

LORD GODDARD C.J.: The difficult question that arises, however, is in connexion with the direction to the jury with regard to whether these acts were done with the intention of assisting the enemy. The case as opened, and indeed, as put by the learned judge appears to this court to be this: A man is taken to intend the natural consequences of his acts; if, therefore, he does an act which is likely to assist the enemy, it must be assumed that he did it with the intention of assisting the enemy. . . .

While no doubt the motive of a man's act and his intention in doing the act are, in law, different things, it is, none the less, true that in many offences a specific intention is a necessary ingredient and the jury have to be satisfied that a particular act was done with that specific intent, although the natural consequences of the act might, if nothing else were proved, be said to show the intent for which it was done. . . . The important thing to notice in this respect is that where an intent is charged in the indictment, the burden of proving that intent remains throughout on the prosecution. No doubt, if the prosecution prove an act the natural consequence of which would be a certain result and no evidence or explanation is given, then a jury may, on a proper direction, find that the prisoner is guilty of doing the act with the intent alleged, but if on the totality of the evidence there is room for more than one view as to the intent of the prisoner, the jury should be directed that it is for the prosecution to prove the intent to the jury's satisfaction, and if, on a review of the whole evidence, they either think that the intent did not exist or they are left in doubt as to the intent, the prisoner is entitled to be acquitted. . . .

In this case the court cannot but feel that some confusion arose with regard to the question of intent by so much being said in the case with regard to the subject of duress. Duress is a matter of defence where a prisoner is forced by fear of violence or imprisonment to do an act which in itself is criminal. If the act is a criminal act, the prisoner may be able to show that he was forced into doing it by violence, actual or threatened, and to save himself from the consequences of that violence. There is very little learning to be found in any of the books or cases on the subject of duress and it is by no means certain how far the doctrine extends, though we have the authority both of Hale and of Fitzjames Stephen, that while it does not apply to treason, murder and some other felonies, it does apply to misdemeanors; and offences against these regulations are misdemeanors. But here again, before any question of duress arises, a jury must be satisfied that the prisoner had the intention which is laid in the indictment. Duress is a matter of defence and the onus of proving it is on the accused. As we have already said, where an intent is charged on the indictment, it is for the prosecution to prove it, so the onus is the other way.

Now, another matter which is of considerable importance in this case, but does not seem to have been brought directly to the attention of the jury, is that very different considerations may apply where the accused at the time he did the acts is in subjection to an enemy power and where he is not. British soldiers who were set to work on the Burma road or, if invasion had unhappily taken place, British subjects who might have been set to work by the enemy digging trenches would undoubtedly be doing acts likely to assist the enemy. It would be unnecessary surely in their cases to consider any of the niceties of the law relating to duress, because no jury would find that merely by doing this work they were intending to assist the enemy. In our opinion it is impossible to say that where an act was done by a person in subjection to the power of others, especially if that other be a brutal enemy, an inference that he intended the natural consequences of his act must be drawn merely from the fact that he did it. The guilty intent cannot be presumed and must be proved. The proper direction to the jury in this case would have been that it was for the prosecution to prove the criminal intent, and that while the jury would be entitled to presume that intent if they thought that the act was done as the result of the free uncontrolled action of the accused, they would not be entitled to presume it, if the circumstances showed that the act was done in subjection to the power of the enemy, or was as consistent with an innocent intent as with a criminal intent, for example, the innocent intent of a desire to save his wife and children from a concentration camp. They should only convict if satisfied by the evidence that the act complained of was in fact done to assist the enemy, and if there was doubt about the matter, the prisoner was entitled to be acquitted.

Appeal allowed
Conviction quashed

Questions

1. Is it true to say that Steane had no intention to assist the enemy, or is it not the case that he intended to assist the enemy in order to save his family from the concentration camp? (see A. K. W. Halpin, "Intended Consequences and Unintended Fallacies" (1987) 7 O.J.L.S. 104, 110–111).

2. Is Glanville Williams correct when he states that "a more satisfactory way of deciding the case would have been to say that the accused did in law intend to assist the enemy but that duress was a defence?" (See Williams, C.L.G.P. section 18.)

Note

Following confusion created by *D.P.P. v. Smith* [1961] A.C. 290, the first point raised in *Steane* as to how intention might be proved has been clarified by Parliament by section 8 of the Criminal Justice Act 1967 which provides:

A court or jury, in determining whether a person has committed an offence,—
(a) shall not be bound in law to infer that he intended or foresaw a result of his actions by reason only of its being a natural and probable consequence of those actions; but
(b) shall decide whether he did intend or foresee that result by reference to all the evidence, drawing such inferences from the evidence as appear proper in the circumstances.

As to the meaning of "intention" *Steane* is the leading authority against the view that intention includes foresight of certainty. There are authorities, however, that suggest the opposite. In *R. v. Lemon* [1979] A.C. 617, 638 Lord Diplock, although dissenting on the question whether blasphemous libel required a mental element beyond the intention to publish, stated:

"The fear that, by retaining as a necessary element of the mens rea of the offence the intention of the publisher to shock and arouse resentment among believing Christians, those who are morally blameworthy will be unjustly acquitted appears to me to manifest a judicial distrust of the jury's capability of appreciating the meaning which in English criminal law is ascribed to the expression 'intention' of the accused. When Stephen was writing in 1883, he did not then regard it as settled law that, where intention to produce a particular result was a necessary element of an offence, no distinction is to be drawn in law between the state of mind of one who does an act because he desires it to produce that particular result and the state of mind of one who, when he does the act, is aware that it is likely to produce that result but is prepared to take the risk that it may do so, in order to achieve some other purpose which provided his motive for doing what he did. It is by now well-settled law that both states of mind constitute 'intention' in the sense in which that expression is used in the definition of a crime whether at common law or in a statute. Any doubts on this matter were finally laid to rest by the decision of this House in *R. v. Hyam* [1975] A.C. 55."

But did *Hyam* settle the meaning of intention? See *infra*.

Hyam v. D.P.P.
[1975] A.C. 55
House of Lords

Mrs Hyam's lover became engaged to be married to Mrs Booth. Being jealous of this and wishing to frighten Mrs Booth from the neighbourhood, Mrs Hyam went to her house in the early hours of the morning, poured petrol through the letterbox, stuffed newspaper through it and lit it. Mrs Booth escaped but her two daughters were suffocated by the fumes from the fire. Mrs Hyam was charged with their murder. The question before the House of Lords was whether the mens rea required for murder was established where the accused knew that it was highly probable that her act would result in death or serious bodily harm. The question was not whether foreseeing a consequence as highly probable was the same as intending that consequence, but in the course of their judgments, their Lordships did deliver some dicta on intention.

LORD HAILSHAM OF ST. MARYLEBONE: My Lords, in my view the one point in this case is the intention which it is necessary to impute to an accused person in order to find him guilty of the crime of murder. Is it simply the intention to kill or cause grievous bodily harm (in the sense of really serious injury) as is commonly assumed, or is it enough that he intends wilfully to expose another to the risk of death or grievous bodily harm in the sense of really serious injury? I do not believe that knowledge or any degree of foresight is enough. Knowledge or foresight is at the best material which entitles or compels a jury to draw the necessary inference as to intention. But what is that intention? It is acknowledged that intention to achieve the result of death or grievous bodily harm in the sense of really serious injury is enough to convict. But may the intention wilfully to expose a victim to the serious risk of death or really serious injury also be enough? It is upon the answer to this question that, in my view, depends the outcome of the present appeal. . . .

I know of no better judicial interpretation of "intention" or "intent" than that given in a civil case by Asquith L.J. (*Cunliffe v. Goodman* [1950] 2 K.B. 237) when he said, at p. 253:

> "An 'intention' to my mind connotes a state of affairs which the party intending . . . does more than merely contemplate: it connotes a state of affairs which on the contrary, he decides, so far as in him lies, to bring about, and which, in point of possibility, he has a reasonable prospect of being able to bring about, by his own act of volition."

If this be a good definition of "intention" for the purposes of the criminal law of murder, and so long as it is held to include the means as well as the end and the inseparable consequences of the end as well as the means, I think it is clear that "intention" is clearly to be distinguished alike from "desire" and from foresight of the probable consequences. As the Law Commission pointed out in their disquisition on *Smith* [1961] A.C. 290 [Law Commission Report No. 10], a man may desire to blow up an aircraft in flight in order to obtain insurance moneys. But if any passengers are killed he is guilty of murder, as their death will be a moral certainty if he carries out his intention. There is no difference between blowing up the aircraft and intending the death of some or all of the passengers. . . .

No doubt foresight and the degree of likelihood with which the consequences are foreseen are essential factors which should be placed before a jury in directing them as to whether the consequences are intended.

I do not, therefore, consider . . . that the fact that a state of affairs is correctly foreseen as a highly probable consequence of what is done is the same thing as the fact that the state of affairs is intended. . . .

I do not think that foresight as such of a high degree of probability is at all the same thing as intention, and, in my view, it is not foresight but intention which constitutes the mental element in murder. It is the absence of intention to kill or cause grievous bodily harm which absolves the heart surgeon in the case of the transplant, notwithstanding that he foresees as a matter of high probability that his action will probably actually kill the patient. It is the presence of an actual intention to kill or cause grievous bodily harm which convicts the murderer who takes a very long shot at his victim and kills him notwithstanding that he thinks correctly as he takes his aim that the odds are very much against his hitting him at all.

VISCOUNT DILHORNE: . . . A man may do an act with a number of intentions. If he does it deliberately and intentionally, knowing when he does it that it is highly probable that grievous bodily harm will result, I think most people would say and be justified in saying that whatever other intentions he may have had as well, he at least intended grievous bodily harm. . . .

LORD DIPLOCK: . . . This appeal raises two separate questions. The first is common to all crimes of this class. It is: what is the attitude of mind of the accused towards the particular evil consequence of his physical act that must be proved in order to constitute the offence? . . .

Upon the first question I do not desire to say more than that I agree with those of your Lordships who take the uncomplicated view that in crimes of this class no distinction is to be drawn in English law between the state of mind of one who does an act because he desires it to produce a particular evil consequence, and the state of mind of one who does the act knowing full well that it is likely to produce that consequence although it may not be the object he was seeking to achieve by doing the act. What is common to both these states of mind is willingness to produce the particular evil consequence: and this, in my view, is the mens rea needed to satisfy a requirement, whether imposed by statute or existing at common law, that in order to constitute the offence with which the accused is charged he must have acted with "intent" to produce a particular evil consequence. . . .

Note

The judgments in *Hyam* do not appear to have been as certain and emphatic regarding intention as Lord Diplock suggested in *Lemon*. This, doubtless, was due to the fact that their Lordships were directly concerned with the mens rea for murder rather than a definition of intention. Several cases have suggested a narrower meaning of *intention* somewhere between that adopted in *Steane* and that declared by Lord Diplock in *Lemon*.

In *Mohan* (*post*, p. 447), a case on attempt, the Court of Appeal rejected the argument that in *Hyam* the House of Lords had given intention a meaning which was to be generally applicable in the criminal law. In *Belfon* [1976] 1 W.L.R. 741, a case of wounding with intent where the trial judge had directed the jury that foresight of grievous bodily harm was enough to convict the accused, the Court of Appeal quashed the conviction, Wien J. stating:

". . . we do not find . . . in any of the speeches of their Lordships in *Hyam's* case anything which obliges us to hold that the 'intent' in wounding with intent is proved by foresight that serious injury is likely to result from a deliberate act. There is certainly no authority that recklessness can constitute an intent to do grievous bodily harm. Adding the concept of recklessness to foresight not only does not assist but will inevitably confuse a jury. Foresight and recklessness are evidence from which intent may be inferred but they cannot be equated either separately or in conjunction with intent to do grievous bodily harm."

Both *Mohan* and *Belfon* sought to distinguish intent from evidence from which intent may be inferred. Thus evidence of foresight of likely consequences is not intent but is evidence pointing towards the existence of intent. This point is reiterated in *Moloney* (*infra*), a murder case, where the House of Lords repudiated the definition of intention derived from *Hyam*.

R. v. Moloney
[1985] 1 A.C. 905
House of Lords

The appellant, a soldier, and his step-father had been drinking heavily. His step-father challenged him to a competition to see who could load, draw and fire a shotgun in the shortest time. The outcome was that the appellant shot his stepfather and was charged with murder. The appellant testified that he had no intention to kill and had not aimed his gun at his stepfather. In summing-up the judge gave the following direction on intent: "When the law requires that something must be proved to have been done with a particular intent it means this: a man intends the consequences of his voluntary act (a) when he desires it to happen, whether or not he foresees that it will probably happen; and (b) when he foresees that it will probably happen, whether he desires it or not." He appealed against conviction of murder.

LORD BRIDGE OF HARWICH delivered the following opinion with which the remainder of their Lordships agreed: . . . The fact that, when the appellant fired the gun, the gun was pointing directly at his stepfather's head at a range of about six feet was not, and could not be, disputed. The sole issue was whether, when he pressed the trigger, this fact and its inevitable consequence were present to the appellant's mind. If they were, the inference was inescapable, using words in their ordinary, everyday meaning, that he intended to kill his stepfather. The undisputed facts that the appellant loved his stepfather and that there was no premeditation or rational motivation, could not, as any reasonable juror would understand, rebut this inference. . . .

The definition of intent on which Stephen Brown J. based his initial direction to the jury in this case and which first appeared in the 40th edition but now appears virtually unchanged in the 41st edition of *Archbold Criminal Pleading Evidence & Practice* published in 1982, is, as previously stated, clothed with the spurious authority of quotation marks. I will repeat it here for clarity (para. 17–13, p. 995):

> "In law a man intends the consequence of his voluntary act, (a) when he desires it to happen, whether or not he foresees that it probably will happen, or (b) when he foresees that it will probably happen, whether he desires it or not."

Although in its terms applicable to any offence of specific intent, this so-called definition must be primarily derived from *R. v. Hyam* [1975] A.C. 55. The text embodies a reference to Viscount Dilhorne's opinion, implicit in the passage cited above from p. 82 of the report, that in *R. v. Hyam* itself, as in the vast majority of cases, an explanation of intent was unnecessary and notes the endorsement of this view to which I have already referred in *R. v. Beer*, 63 Cr.App.R. 222. Apart from copious references to *R. v. Hyam*, the ensuing citation in support of the claim that the definition "is in accordance with the great preponderance of authority", refers to many decided cases in which there are to be found obiter dicta on the subject. But looking on their facts at the decided cases where a crime of specific intent was under consideration, including *R. v. Hyam* itself, they suggest to me that the probability of the consequence taken to have been foreseen must be little short of overwhelming before it will suffice to establish the necessary intent. Thus, I regard the *Archbold* definition of intent as unsatisfactory and potentially misleading and one which should no longer be used in directing juries.

The golden rule should be that, when directing a jury on the mental element necessary in a crime of specific intent, the judge should avoid any elaboration or paraphrase of what is meant by intent, and leave it to the jury's good sense to decide whether the accused acted with the necessary intent, unless the judge is convinced that, on the facts and having regard to the way the case has been presented to the jury in evidence and argument, some further explanation or elaboration is strictly necessary to avoid misunderstanding. In trials for murder or wounding with intent, I find it very difficult to visualise a case where any such explanation or elaboration could be required, if the offence consisted of a direct attack on the victim with a weapon, except possibly the case where the accused shot at A and killed B, which any first year law student could explain to a jury in the simplest of terms. Even where the death results indirectly from the act of the accused, I believe the cases that will call for a direction by reference to foresight of consequences will be of extremely rare occurrence. I am in full agreement with the view expressed by Viscount Dilhorne that, in *R. v. Hyam* [1975] A.C. 55, 82 itself, if the issue of intent had been left without elaboration, no reasonable jury could have failed to convict. I find it difficult to understand why the prosecution did not seek to support the conviction, as an alternative to their main submission, on the ground that there had been no actual miscarriage of justice.

I do not, of course, by what I have said in the foregoing paragraph, mean to question the necessity, which frequently arises, to explain to a jury that intention is something quite distinct from motive or desire. But this can normally be quite simply explained by reference to the case before the court or, if necessary, by some homely example. A man who, at London Airport, boards a plane which he knows to be bound for Manchester, clearly intends to travel to Manchester, even though Manchester is the last place he wants to be and his motive for boarding the plane is simply to escape pursuit. The possibility that the plane may have engine trouble and be diverted to Luton does not affect the matter. By boarding the Manchester plane, the man conclusively demonstrates his intention to go there, because it is a moral certainty that that is where he will arrive.

I return to the two uncertainties by the Criminal Law Revision Committee in the Report referred to above as arising from *R. v. Hyam*, which still remain unresolved. I should preface these observations by expressing my view that the differences of opinion to be found in the five speeches in *R. v. Hyam* have, as I believe, caused some confusion in the law in an area where, as I have already indicated, clarity and simplicity are, in my view, of paramount importance. I believe it also follows that it is within the judicial function of your Lordships' House to lay down new guidelines which will achieve those desiderata, if we can reach broad agreement as to what they should be. . . .

Starting from the proposition established by *R. v. Vickers* [1957] 2 Q.B. 664, as modified by *D.P.P. v. Smith* that the mental element in murder requires proof of an intention to kill or cause really serious injury, the first fundamental question to be answered is whether there is any rule of substantive law that foresight by the accused of one of those eventualities as a probable consequence of his voluntary act, where the probability can be defined as exceeding a certain degree, is equivalent or alternative to the necessary intention. I would answer this question in the negative. Here I derive powerful support from the speech of my noble and learned friend. Lord Hailsham of St Marylebone L.C., in *R. v. Hyam* [1975] A.C. 55. He said, at p. 75:

"I do not, therefore, consider, as was suggested in argument, that the fact that a state of affairs is correctly foreseen as a highly probable consequence of what is done is the same thing as the fact that the state of affairs is intended."

And again, at p. 77:

"I do not think that foresight as such of a high degree of probability is at all the same thing as intention, and, in my view, it is not foresight but intention which constitutes the mental element in murder." . . .

I am firmly of opinion that foresight of consequences, as an element bearing on the issue of intention in murder, or indeed any other crime of specific intent, belongs, not to the substantive law, but to the law of evidence. Here again I am happy to find myself aligned with my noble and learned friend, Lord Hailsham of St. Marylebone L.C., in *R. v. Hyam*, where he said, at p. 65: "Knowledge or foresight is at the best material which entitles or compels a jury to draw the necessary inference as to intention." A rule of evidence which judges for more than a century found of the utmost utility in directing juries was expressed in the maxim: "A man is presumed to intend the natural and probable consequences of his acts." In *D.P.P. v. Smith* your Lordships' House, by treating this rule of evidence as creating an irrebuttable presumption and thus elevating it, in effect, to the status of a rule of substantive law, predictably provoked the intervention of Parliament by section 8 of the Criminal Justice Act 1967 to put the issue of intention back where it belonged, viz., in the hands of the jury, "drawing such inferences from the evidence as appear proper in the circumstances". I do not by any means take the conjunction of the verbs "intended or foresaw" and "intend or foresee" in that section as an indication that Parliament treated them as synonymous; on the contrary, two verbs were needed to connote two different states of mind.

I think we should now no longer speak of presumptions in this context but rather of inferences. In the old presumption that a man intends the natural and probable consequences of his acts the important word is "natural". This word conveys the idea that in the ordinary course of events a certain act will lead to a certain consequence unless something unexpected supervenes to prevent it. One might almost say that, if a consequence is natural, it is really otiose to speak of it as also being probable.

Section 8 of the Criminal Justice Act 1967 leaves us at liberty to go back to the decisions before that of this House in *D.P.P. v. Smith* and it is here, I believe, that we can find a sure, clear, intelligible and simple guide to the kind of direction that should be given to a jury in the exceptional case where it is necessary to give guidance as to how, on the evidence, they should approach the issue of intent.

I know of no clearer exposition of the law than that in the judgment of the Court of Criminal Appeal (Lord Goddard C.J., Atkinson and Cassels JJ.) delivered by Lord Goddard C.J. in *R. v. Steane* [1947] K.B. 997 (*ante*, p. 90) where he said, at p. 1004:

> "No doubt, if the prosecution prove an act the natural consequence of which would be a certain result and no evidence or explanation is given, then a jury may, on a proper direction, find that the prisoner is guilty of doing the act with the intent alleged, but if on the totality of the evidence there is room for more than one view as to the intent of the prisoner, the jury should be directed that it is for the prosection to prove the intent to the jury's satisfaction, and if, on a review of the whole evidence, they either think that the intent did not exist or they are left in doubt as to the intent, the prisoner is entitled to be acquitted."

In the rare cases in which it is necessary to direct a jury by reference to foresight of consequences, I do not believe it is necessary for the judge to do more than invite the jury to consider two questions. First, was death or really serious injury in a murder case (or whatever relevant consequence must be proved to have been intended in any other case) a natural consequence of the defendant's voluntary act? Secondly, did the defendant foresee that consequence as being a natural consequence of his act? The jury should then be told that if they answer yes to both questions it is a proper inference for them to draw that he intended that consequence. . . .

Appeal allowed

Questions

1. Lord Bridge spoke of a result being a "natural consequence". Does this mean that a consequence must be substantially more likely than one which is described as being probable if the inference of intention is to be drawn; or does this phrase create an ambiguity in that a

consequence may be considered a *natural consequence* by the fact that it causally follows on directly from the original act?

2. Lord Bridge stated with regard to the term "natural consequences" that "the probability of the consequence taken to have been foreseen must be little short of overwhelming before it will suffice to establish the necessary intent". Was Lord Bridge really speaking of "oblique" intention in the sense in which Glanville Williams uses this term? (see *ante*, p. 85).

3. Lord Bridge sought to distinguish *intention* from *foresight of consequences*; the latter is relevant only as *evidence* of intention. Lord Bridge also sought to distinguish *intention* from *motive* or *desire*. J. Stannard in "Mens Rea in the Melting Pot" [1986] 37 N.I.L.Q. 61, accordingly concludes that *intention* must be equivalent to *purpose*. He states that the "failure test" distinguishes intended consequences from those that are merely foreseen. In the Manchester plane example, if the plane had been diverted from Manchester to Leeds, would the escapee have failed in his purpose?

4. Lord Bridge declared that he knew no clearer exposition of the law than that in *Steane*. Given his Manchester plane example and the expressed outcome, should Lord Bridge not regard Steane's intention as having been to assist the enemy?

Note

Lord Bridge's judgment in *Moloney*, far from clarifying the law, created its own problems which quickly surfaced in *R. v. Hancock and Shankland* [1986] 1 A.C. 455. The appellants, who were striking miners, were charged with the murder of a taxi-driver who was killed taking a miner to work. The appellants pushed a concrete post and concrete block from a bridge over a three-lane highway on to the taxi travelling below. They claimed that they had intended only to block the road and frighten the miner as they believed the block was positioned over the middle lane and the taxi was in the nearside lane. The judge gave a direction to the jury based on Lord Bridge's speech in *Moloney* and the jury convicted. The Court of Appeal quashed the murder convictions substituting convictions for manslaughter holding that the *Moloney* guidelines were misleading. The Crown appealed but the House of Lords dismissed the appeal affirming the decision below that the phrase "natural consequence" used by Lord Bridge required amplification if it was not to mislead. Lord Scarman stated (at p. 473):

[Lord Bridge] omitted any reference in his guidelines to probability. He did so because he included probability in the meaning which he attributed to "natural." My Lords, I very much doubt whether a jury without further explanation would think that "probable" added nothing to "natural." I agree with the Court of Appeal that the probability of a consequence is a factor of sufficient importance to be drawn specifically to the attention of the jury and to be explained. In a murder case where it is necessary to direct a jury on the issue of intent by reference to foresight of consequences the probability of death or serious injury resulting from the act done may be critically important. Its importance will depend on the degree of probability: if the likelihood that death or serious injury will result is high, the probability of that result may ... be seen as overwhelming evidence of the existence of the intent to kill or injure. ... In my judgment, therefore, the *Moloney* guidelines as they stand are unsafe and misleading. They require a reference to probability. They also require an explanation that the greater the probability of a consequence the more likely it is that the consequence was foreseen and that if that consequence was foreseen the greater the probability is that that consequence was also intended. But juries also require to be reminded that the decision is theirs to be reached upon a consideration of all the evidence.

Lord Scarman's focus appears to be on the means by which intention (in its direct sense) may be proved rather than on clarifying any broader conception of intention to incorporate oblique intent. It is arguable that Lord Bridge's ill-framed direction was concerned with the latter. It fell to the Court of Appeal to seek to make sense of the contradictory pronouncements of their Lordships in the case of *Nedrick* below.

Questions

1. In *Moloney* Lord Bridge, while declining to define what *intention* means, did provide guidelines for the jury on how to discover it. Lord Scarman deprecated the use of such guidelines because of the danger that they would be followed slavishly. He opined that the jury should "exercise practical common sense" and base their decision upon a consideration of all the evidence, stating that whereas the law is for the judge to define, the facts are for the jury to decide. But what is the law in relation to intention? Is *intention* an ordinary word with an ordinary meaning known to all? If, rather, it is a word with a technical meaning, what is that technical meaning?

2. If foresight of the probability of a consequence is simply evidence from which intention may be inferred, what is the further mental element the jury must find before they can conclude that the accused intended that consequence? (see R. A. Duff, "The Obscure Intentions of the House of Lords" [1986] Crim.L.R. 771, 772).

Note

In *Nedrick* (below) the Court of Appeal sought to draw together various threads contained in the speeches in *Moloney* and *Hancock and Shankland* to provide some guidance for trial judges.

R. v. Nedrick
[1986] 1 W.L.R. 1025
Court of Appeal

The appellant had a grudge against a woman. He poured paraffin through the letter box and on to the front door of her house and ignited it without giving any warning. A child died in the ensuing fire. The appellant admitted starting the fire but claimed he only wished to frighten the woman and did not want anyone to die. He was convicted of murder following a direction to the jury which equated foresight with intention.

LORD LANE C.J. read the following judgment of the court: . . . That direction was given before the publication of the speeches in the House of Lords in *R. v. Moloney* and *R. v. Hancock*. In the light of those speeches it was plainly wrong. The direction was based on a passage in *Archbold Criminal Pleading Evidence & Practice*, 41st ed. (1982), p. 994, paragraph 17–13, which has been repeated in the 42nd ed. (1985), p. 1162, paragraph 17–13. That passage was expressly disapproved in *R. v. Moloney*, in that it equates foresight with intention, whereas "foresight of consequences, as an element bearing on the issue of intention in murder . . . belongs, not to the substantive law, but to the law of evidence", *per* Lord Bridge of Harwich, at [1985] A.C. 928. The judge was in no way to blame of course for having directed the jury in this way.

What then does a jury have to decide so far as the mental element in murder is concerned? It simply has to decide whether the defendant intended to kill or do serious bodily harm. In order to reach that decision the jury must pay regard to all the relevant circumstances, including what the defendant himself said and did.

In the great majority of cases a direction to that effect will be enough, particularly where the defendant's actions amounted to a direct attack upon his victim, because in such cases the evidence relating to the defendant's desire or motive will be clear and his intent will have been the same as his desire or motive. But in some cases, of which this is one, the defendant does an act which is manifestly dangerous and as a result someone dies. The primary desire or motive of the defendant may not have been to harm that person, or indeed anyone. In that situation what further directions should a jury be given as to the mental state which they must find to exist in the defendant if murder is to be proved? . . .

It may be advisable first of all to explain to the jury that a man may intend to achieve a certain result whilst at the same time not desiring it to come about. In *R. v. Moloney* Lord Bridge gave an illustration of the distinction [the example of the man boarding a plane bound for Manchester to escape pursuit.] . . .

In *R. v. Hancock* the House decided that the *R. v. Moloney* guidelines require a reference to probability. Lord Scarman said, at p. 473:

"They also require an explanation that the greater the probability of a consequence the more likely it is that the consequence was foreseen and that if that consequence was foreseen the greater the probability is that that consequence was also intended."

When determining whether the defendant had the necessary intent, it may therefore be helpful for a jury to ask themselves two questions. (1) How probable was the consequence which resulted from the defendant's voluntary act? (2) Did he foresee that consequence?

If he did not appreciate that death or serious harm was likely to result from his act, he cannot have intended to bring it about. If he did, but thought that the risk to which he was exposing the person killed was only slight, then it may be easy for the jury to conclude that he did not intend to bring about that result. On the other hand, if the jury are satisfied that at the material time the defendant recognised that death or serious harm would be virtually certain (barring some unforeseen intervention) to result from his voluntary act, then that is a fact from which they may find it easy to infer that he intended to kill or do serious bodily harm, even though he may not have had any desire to achieve that result.

As Lord Bridge of Harwich said in *R. v. Moloney*: "the probability of the consequence taken to have been foreseen must be little short of overwhelming before it will suffice to establish the necessary intent". At p. 926 he uses the expression "moral certainty"; he said, at p. 929 "will lead to a certain consequence unless something unexpected supervenes to prevent it".

Where the charge is murder and in the rare cases where the simple direction is not enough, the jury should be directed that they are not entitled to infer the necessary intention, unless they feel sure that death or serious bodily harm was a virtual certainty (barring some unforeseen intervention) as a result of the defendant's actions and that the defendant appreciated that such was the case.

Where a man realises that it is for all practical purposes inevitable that his actions will result in death or serious harm, the inference may be irresistible that he intended that result, however little he may have desired or wished it to happen. The decision is one for the jury to be reached upon a consideration of all the evidence.

> *Appeal allowed.*
> *Conviction quashed.*
> *Conviction of manslaughter substituted.*

Note

Lord Lane C.J. appeared to confine the situations in which a jury could infer intention to those where the consequence (in a murder case death or serious bodily harm) was foreseen as virtually certain. He did not, however, equate such foresight with intention making it clear that whether or not such an inference was to be drawn was a matter for the jury. Speaking extra-judicially, however, in the House of Lords' debate on the *Report of the Select Committee of the House of Lords on Murder and Life Imprisonment* (H.L. Deb., Vol. 512, col. 480) he stated:

> "It is right to say that the decision in *Nedrick* . . . endeavoured to provide a satisfactory definition of the word 'intention'. . . . It is equally true to say . . . that in *Nedrick* the court was obliged to phrase matters as it did because of earlier decisions in your Lordships' House by which it was bound. We had to tread gingerly indeed in order not to tread upon your Lordships' toes. As a result *Nedrick* was not as clear as it should have been. However, I agree respectfully with the conclusions of the committee that 'intention' should be defined in the terms set out in paragraph 195 of the report on page 50. [The Committee adopted clause 18(b) of the Law Commission draft Criminal Code which states that 'a person acts intentionally with respect to . . . a result when he acts either in order to bring it about or being aware that it will occur in the ordinary course of events.'] That seems to express clearly what in *Nedrick* we failed properly to explain."

This seems to go much further than the Court of Appeal sought to go in *Nedrick* as it defines "intention" rather than providing a test from which a jury may *infer* intention. In the case which follows the House of Lords revisited this problem.

R. v. Woollin
[1999] A.C. 82
House of Lords

The appellant was charged with the murder of his three month old son having lost his temper and thrown him on to a hard surface fracturing his skull from which injury he died. The trial judge initially had directed the jury that they could infer that the accused intended to kill (or cause serious bodily harm) if they were satisfied that he appreciated that death or serious bodily harm was virtually certain to result from his actions. Later in his summing up the judge said that if they were satisfied he appreciated that there was a substantial risk of causing serious injury to his son they could find from this that he intended to do so. The jury convicted and the Court of Appeal dismissed his appeal against conviction.

LORD STEYN: . . . The Court of Appeal certified the following questions as of general importance:

"1. In murder, where there is no direct evidence that the purpose of a defendant was to kill or to inflict serious injury on the victim, is it necessary to direct the jury that they may only infer an intent to do serious injury if they are satisfied (a) that serious bodily harm was a virtually certain consequence of the defendant's voluntary act and (b) that the defendant appreciated that fact? 2. If the answer to question 1 is 'Yes,' is such a direction necessary in all cases or is it only necessary in cases where the sole evidence of the defendant's intention is to be found in his actions and their consequence to the victim?"

On appeal to your Lordships' House the terrain of the debate covered the correctness in law of the direction recommended by Lord Lane C.J. in *Nedrick* and, if that direction is sound, whether it should be used only in the limited category of cases envisaged by the Court of Appeal. And counsel for the appellant renewed his submission that by directing the jury in terms of **substantial risk** the judge illegitimately widened the mental element of murder.

The directions of the judge on the mental element
His Lordship outlined the trial judge's initial direction to the jury which followed the *Nedrick* recommended direction. After an overnight adjournment the judge continued his summing up but did not use the *Nedrick* direction, instead referring to appreciation of a substantial risk of serious injury.

It is plain, and the Crown accepts, that a direction posing an issue as to appreciation of a "substantial risk" of causing serious injury is wider than a direction framed in terms of appreciation of a "virtual certainty (barring some unforeseen intervention)." If Lord Lane C.J. correctly stated the law in *Nedrick*, the judge's direction in terms of substantial risk was wrong. But the Crown argued, as I have indicated, that *Nedrick* was wrongly decided or, alternatively, that the principle as enunciated by Lord Lane does not apply to the present case.

The problem facing the Court of Appeal in Nedrick
. . . [His Lordship quoted extensively from *Nedrick* but highlighted the following passage as the critical part of Lord Lane CJ's direction:]

". . . Where the charge is murder and in the rare cases where the simple direc-
tion is not enough, the jury should be directed that they are not entitled to
infer the necessary intention, unless they feel sure that death or serious bodily
harm was a virtual certainty (barring some unforeseen intervention) as a result
of the defendant's actions and that the defendant appreciated that such was the
case . . . ."

The effect of the critical direction is that a result foreseen as virtually
certain is an intended result.

The direct attack on Nedrick

It is now possible to consider the Crown's direct challenge to the correctness of *Nedrick*. First, the Crown argued that *Nedrick* prevents the jury
from considering all the evidence in the case relevant to intention. The
argument is that this is contrary to the provisions of section 8 of the Act
of 1967. This provision reads:

"A court or jury, in determining whether a person has committed an
offence—(a) shall not be bound in law to infer that he intended or foresaw a result of his actions by reasons only of its being a natural and
probable consequence of those actions; but (b) shall decide whether he
did intend or foresee that result by reference to all the evidence, drawing such inferences from the evidence as appear proper in the circumstances."

Paragraph (a) is an instruction to the judge and is not relevant to the
issues on this appeal. The Crown's argument relied on paragraph (b)
which is concerned with the function of the jury. It is no more than a
legislative instruction that in considering their findings on intention or
foresight the jury must take into account all relevant evidence: see Professor Edward Griew, "States of Mind, Presumptions and Inferences," in
Criminal Law: Essays in Honour of J. C. Smith (1987), pp. 68, 76–77. *Nedrick*
is undoubtedly concerned with the mental element which is sufficient for
murder. So, for that matter, in their different ways were *Smith, Hyam,*
Moloney and *Hancock*. But, as Lord Lane C.J. emphasised in the last sentence of *Nedrick*, at p. 1028: "The decision is one for the jury to be reached
upon a consideration of all the evidence." *Nedrick* does not prevent a jury
from considering all the evidence: it merely stated what state of mind (in
the absence of a purpose to kill or to cause serious harm) is sufficient for
murder. I would therefore reject the Crown's first argument.

In the second place the Crown submitted that *Nedrick* is in conflict with
the decision of the House in *Hancock*. Counsel argued that in order to
bring some coherence to the process of determining intention Lord Lane
C.J. specified a minimum level of foresight, namely virtual certainty. But
that is not in conflict with the decision in *Hancock* which, apart from disapproving Lord Bridge's "natural consequence" model direction, approved
Moloney [1985] A.C. 905 in all other respects. And in *Moloney* Lord Bridge
said, at p. 925, that if a person foresees the probability of a consequence
as little short of overwhelming, this "will suffice to *establish* the necessary
intent." Nor did the House in *Hancock* rule out the framing of model
directions by the Court of Appeal for the assistance of trial judges. I
would therefore reject the argument that the guidance given in *Nedrick*
was in conflict with the decision of the House in *Hancock*.

The Crown did not argue that as a matter of policy foresight of a virtual
certainty is too narrow a test in murder. Subject to minor qualifications,
the decision in *Nedrick* was widely welcomed by distinguished academic
writers: see Professor J. C. Smith Q.C.'s commentary on *Nedrick* [1986]

Crim.L.R. 742, 743-744; Glanville Williams, "The Mens Rea for Murder: Leave it Alone" (1989) 105 L.Q.R. 387; J. R. Spencer, "Murder in the Dark: A Glimmer of Light?" [1986] C.L.J. 366-367; *Ashworth, Principles of Criminal Law*, 2nd ed. (1995), p. 172. It is also of interest that it is very similar to the threshold of being aware "that it *will* occur in the ordinary course of events" in the Law Commission's draft Criminal Code (see Criminal Law: Legislating the Criminal Code: Offences against the Person and General Principles, Law Com. No. 218 (1993) (Cm. 2370), Appendix A (Draft Criminal Law Bill with Explanatory Notes), pp. 90-91): compare also Professor J. C. Smith Q.C., "A Note on 'Intention'" [1990] Crim.L.R. 85, 86. Moreover, over a period of 12 years since *Nedrick* the test of foresight of virtual certainty has apparently caused no practical difficulties. It is simple and clear. It is true that it may exclude a conviction of murder in the often cited terrorist example where a member of the bomb disposal team is killed. In such a case it may realistically be said that the terrorist did not foresee the killing of a member of the bomb disposal team as a virtual certainty. That may be a consequence of not framing the principle in terms of risk-taking. Such cases ought to cause no substantial difficulty since immediately below murder there is available a verdict of manslaughter which may attract in the discretion of the court a life sentence. In any event, as Lord Lane C.J. eloquently argued in a debate in the House of Lords, to frame a principle for particular difficulties regarding terrorism "would produce corresponding injustices which would be very hard to eradicate:" Hansard (H.L. Debates), November 6, 1989, col. 480. I am satisfied that the *Nedrick* test, which was squarely based on the decision of the House in *Moloney*, is pitched at the right level of foresight.

The argument that Nedrick has limited application

The Court of Appeal [1997] 1 Cr.App.R. 97, 107 held that the phrase a "virtual certainty" should be confined to cases where the evidence of intent is limited to admitted actions of the accused and the consequences of those actions. It is not obligatory where there is other evidence to consider. The Crown's alternative submission on the appeal was to the same effect. This distinction would introduce yet another complication into a branch of the criminal law where simplicity is of supreme importance. The distinction is dependent on the vagaries of the evidence in particular cases. Moreover, a jury may reject the other evidence to which the Court of Appeal refers. And in preparing his summing up a judge could not ignore this possibility. If the Court of Appeal's view is right, it might compel a judge to pose different tests depending on what evidence the jury accepts. For my part, and with the greatest respect, I have to say that this distinction would be likely to produce great practical difficulties. But, most importantly, the distinction is not based on any principled view regarding the mental element in murder. Contrary to the view of the Court of Appeal, I would also hold that section 8(*b*) of the Act of 1967 does not compel such a result.

In my view the ruling of the Court of Appeal was wrong. It may be appropriate to give a direction in accordance with *Nedrick* in any case in which the defendant may not have desired the result of his act. But I accept the trial judge is best placed to decide what direction is required by the circumstances of the case.

The disposal of the present appeal

It follows that the judge should not have departed from the *Nedrick* direction. By using the phrase "substantial *risk*" the judge blurred the line between intention and recklessness, and hence between murder and manslaughter. The misdirection enlarged the scope of the mental element required for murder. It was a material misdirection. At one stage it was argued that the earlier correct direction "cured" the subsequent incorrect direction. A misdirection cannot by any means always be cured by the fact that the judge at an earlier or later stage gave a correct direction. After all, how is a jury to choose between a correct and an incorrect direction on a point of law? If a misdirection is to be corrected, it must be done in the plainest terms: *Archbold, Criminal Pleading, Evidence & Practice*, 1998 ed., p. 411, para. 4-374.

That is, however, not the end of the matter. For my part, I have given anxious consideration to the observation of the Court of Appeal that, if the judge had used the phrase "a virtual certainty," the verdict would have been the same. In this case there was no suggestion of any other ill treatment of the child. It would also be putting matters too high to say that on the evidence before the jury it was an open-and-shut case of murder rather than manslaughter. In my view the conviction of murder is unsafe. The conviction of murder must be quashed.

The status of Nedrick
In my view Lord Lane C.J.'s judgment in *Nedrick* provided valuable assistance to trial judges. The model direction is by now a tried-and-tested formula. Trial judges ought to continue to use it. On matters of detail I have three observations, which can best be understood if I set out again the relevant part of Lord Lane's judgment. It was:

"(A) When determining whether the defendant had the necessary intent, it may therefore be helpful for a jury to ask themselves two questions. (1) How probable was the consequence which resulted from the defendant's voluntary act? (2) Did he foresee that consequence? If he did not appreciate that death or serious harm was likely to result from his act, he cannot have intended to bring it about. If he did, but thought that the risk to which he was exposing the person killed was only slight, then it may be easy for the jury to conclude that he did not intend to bring about that result. On the other hand, if the jury are satisfied that at the material time the defendant recognised that death or serious harm would be virtually certain (barring some unforeseen intervention) to result from his voluntary act, then that is a fact from which they may find it easy to infer that he intended to kill or do serious bodily harm, even though he may not have had any desire to achieve that result . . . (B) Where the charge is murder and in the rare cases where the simple direction is not enough, the jury should be directed that they are not entitled to infer the necessary intention, unless they feel sure that death or serious bodily harm was a virtual certainty (barring some unforeseen intervention) as a result of the defendant's actions and that the defendant appreciated that such was the case. (C) Where a man realises that it is for all practical purposes inevitable that his actions will result in death or serious harm, the inference may be irresistible that he intended that result, however little he may have desired or wished it to happen. The decision is one for the jury to be reached upon a consideration of all the evidence." (Lettering added.)

First, I am persuaded by the speech of my noble and learned friend, Lord Hope of Craighead, that it is unlikely, if ever, to be helpful to direct the jury in terms of the two questions set out in (A). I agree that these questions may detract from the clarity of the critical direction in (B). Secondly, in their writings previously cited Glanville Williams, Professor Smith and Andrew Ashworth observed that the use of the words "to infer" in (B) may detract from the clarity of the model direction. I agree. I would sub-stitute the words "to find." Thirdly, the first sentence of (C) does not form part of the model direction. But it would always be right for the judge to say, as Lord Lane C.J. put it, that the decision is for the jury upon a consideration of all the evidence in the case.

The certified questions
Given my conclusions the certified questions fall away.

Appeal allowed.
Conviction of murder quashed.
Conviction of manslaughter substituted.
Cause remitted to Court of Appeal (Criminal Division) for sentencing.

Questions

1. If on a trial for murder the evidence indicates that the accused may not have intended the result of death in the sense of that being his aim or purpose, is the trial judge obliged to give the revised *Nedrick* direction?
2. If a jury consider that the accused did foresee the result of death as virtually certain, are they bound to find that he intended that result?
3. If D in **Case (d)** (p. 90, *ante*) believed that death of the bus passen-gers was virtually certain to result from his actions of shooting the driver (even though in reality it was only a probability), and one of the passengers does die, could a jury convict D of murder if they strictly followed the revised *Nedrick*, direction?
4. If D has a good motive for acting, even though death is virtually certain to ensue if he achieves his primary purpose, is the judge in the trial of D for murder obliged to give the revised *Nedrick* direction and, if so, is the jury, if it concludes that D foresaw death as virtually cer-tain, obliged to convict? (See the cases in the next section).

ii. Motive and Intention

Note

In seeking to discover the meaning of "intention" a useful starting place is to distinguish it from a concept with which it is often con-fused, namely *motive*.

Williams, *T.C.L.*, p. 75

In ordinary speech, 'intention' and 'motive' are often convertible terms. For the lawyer, the word 'motive' generally refers to some further intent which forms no part of the legal rule.

If we say that a man shot and killed his aunt with the motive of benefit-ing under her will, the immediate intent, which makes the act murder, is the intention or desire to kill, while the further intent or motive, which forms no part of the definition of the crime of murder, is the intention or desire to benefit under the will. Other motives are the desire to obtain the satisfaction of revenge, or to get rid of a rival, or to promote a political object. (Such motives may also be expressed in abstract terms: 'he killed her from a motive of greed/revenge/jealousy.' Motive in this sense is irrelevant to responsibility (guilt or innocence), though it may be relevant to proof, or to the quantum of punishment. The prosecution may prove a motive for the crime if it helps them to establish their case, as a matter of circumstantial evidence; but they are not legally bound to prove motive, because a 'motiveless' crime is still a crime. Conversely, the defendant may adduce evidence of his good motive in order to reduce his punishment, perhaps to vanishing-point.

Exceptionally, the term 'motive' is used in a sense relevant to responsibility in the crime of libel. Also, crimes of ulterior intent require two intents, one lying behind the other, and the second may be called motive. The crime of burglary is committed where a person enters a building or part of a building by way of trespass with intent to commit one of certain crimes therein. There is an intentional entry, with the ulterior intent of committing a crime in the house; this ulterior intent is the motive of the entry, and is sometimes referred to as such, yet here it forms part of the legal definition.

Note

Exceptionally, a motive may be made an element of an offence. For example, the Crime and Disorder Act 1998 provides for an enhanced penalty where certain offences are racially aggravated, such as assaults, criminal damage or public order offences. An offence is racially aggravated where it "is motivated (wholly or partly) by hostility towards members of a racial group, based on their membership of that group" (see s.28(1)(b)). But generally motive is irrelevant to liability, even where that motive may be good (see, for example, *Smith* [1960] 2 Q.B. 423; *Chandler v. D.P.P.* [1964] A.C.763).

The position that a good motive does not absolve a person from criminal liability has been affirmed recently by both the Privy Council and the House of Lords in two cases involving claims of entrapment. In the first, *Yip Chiu-Cheung v. R.* [1994] 3 W.L.R. 514 (*post*, p. 477), the appellant had been convicted in Hong Kong of conspiracy to traffic in heroin contrary to common law and the Dangerous Drugs Ordinance. The other party to the conspiracy was an American undercover drug enforcement agent who (with the agreement of the Hong Kong authorities) was to meet the appellant and take delivery of the heroin which he was then to take to Australia. The appellant argued that the agent could not be a co-conspirator as he lacked the necessary *mens rea* for conspiracy. Lord Griffiths stated (at p. 518):

> "The crime of conspiracy requires an agreement between two or more persons to commit an unlawful act with the intention of carrying it out. It is the intention to carry out the crime that constitutes the necessary *mens rea* for the offence."

On this basis his Lordship concluded that even though the agent was "acting courageously and with the best of motives", he intended to commit the offence of drug trafficking regardless of whether he would be prosecuted.

On similar facts the House of Lords in *R v. Latif* [1996] 1 All E.R. 353 expressed the view that a customs officer, who brought heroin to England as part of an operation designed to catch a major trafficker, had the necessary intention to evade the prohibition on the importation of heroin and would have been guilty of an offence contrary to s. 50(3) of the Customs and Excise Management Act 1979.

In both *Yip Chiu-Cheung* and *Latif* the statements concerning motive and intention came in the context of appeals by what might be regarded as appellants for whom there would be little moral sympathy. The problem, however, which remains is those actors for whom there would be considerable moral sympathy but whose conduct may appear to fall within the strict letter of the law on intention if it is rigidly applied. There are two antagonistic tensions at play: first, the logic of the *Nedrick/ Woollin* test for oblique intention if applied without moderation could catch those whose motive for pursuing their primary purpose is morally inconsistent with the *mens rea* for the offence, the *actus reus* of which was the side-effect of achieving their primary purpose (cf *Steane, ante* p. 90, *Moor, post*, p. 110, and *Gillick* v *West Norfolk and Wisbech A.H.A., post* p. 327); and secondly, the reluctance of judges to frame a defence (whether based in justification or excuse) to cover those who act from a good motive. This problem is set in even starker contrast when the virtually certain side effect of D achieving his morally commendable primary purpose is death and thus, *prima facie*, could amount to murder, whereas the accepted *mens rea* for murder does not cover, for example, the terrorist bomber who displays "wicked recklessness" towards the bomb disposal team but does not foresee death as a virtual certainty.

Question

P is terminally ill and suffering extreme pain. D, a doctor, prescribes a course of pain relieving treatment involving the administration of diamorphine. The pain relieving treatment involves gradually increasing the amount of diamorphine administered. D knows that diamorphine in large doses eventually kills. After several days of diamorphine treatment P dies. Assuming D is prosecuted for murder should the trial judge give the jury the revised *Nedrick* direction? If so would D's motive provide the jury with a reason for not finding intention should they be satisfied that D foresaw death as being virtually certain to ensue from the administration of diamorphine? Reconsider your answer after reading the following extracts from jury directions in two trials for attempted murder and murder respectively of two doctors. Consider also whether the effect of the two directions is to create a special defence for doctors to protect them from a rigid application of the *Nedrick* test.

R. v. Cox
Winchester Crown Court
September 18, 1992
12 Butterworths Medico-Legal Reports

Dr Cox, a consultant rheumatologist, was charged with the attempted murder of his patient, Mrs Lilian Boyes, who was suffering from rheumatoid arthritis and other conditions. She was dying and suffering extreme pain and pleading for help to die. A short time before her death Dr Cox administered to her an injection of potassium chloride in a quantity which could have no therapeutic purpose. Dr Cox admitted the injection and its quantity. The only issue of contention was his intent in giving it. The prosecution alleged that in administering it Dr Cox's intention was to end her life. The defence argued that his primary purpose was to relieve pain and that there was no intent to kill. Dr Cox was charged with attempted murder as Mrs Boyes' body had been cremated and thus the actual cause of death could not be established - that is whether she died from the effects of the potassium chloride injection or whether she died of natural causes before it took effect.

OGNALL J. directed the jury: . . . We all appreciate that some medical treatment, whether of a positive, therapeutic character or solely of an analgesic kind—by which I mean designed solely to alleviate pain and suffering—some treatment carries with it a serious risk to the health or even the life of the patient. Doctors are frequently confronted with, no doubt, distressing dilemmas. They have to make up their minds as to whether the risk, even to the life of their patient, attendant upon their contemplated form of treatment, is such that the risk is, or is not, medically justified. If a doctor genuinely believes that a certain course is beneficial to his patient, either therapeutically or analgesically, then even though he recognises that that course carries with it a risk to life, he is fully entitled, nonetheless, to pursue it. If in those circumstances the patient dies, nobody could possibly suggest that in that situation the doctor was guilty of murder or attempted murder.

The problem is obviously particularly acute in the case of those who are terminally ill and in considerable pain, if not agony. Such was the case of Lillian Boyes. It was plainly Dr Cox's duty to do all that was medically possible to alleviate her pain and suffering, even if the course adopted carried with it an obvious risk that, as a side effect of that treatment, her death would be rendered likely or even certain.

There can be no doubt that the use of drugs to reduce pain and suffering will often be fully justified notwithstanding that it will, in fact, hasten the moment of death. What can never be lawful is the use of drugs with the primary purpose of hastening the moment of death.

And so, in deciding Dr Cox's intention, the distinction the law requires you to draw is this. Is it proved that in giving that injection, in that form and in those amounts, Dr Cox's primary purpose was to bring the life of Lillian Boyes to an end?

If it was, then he is guilty. If, on the other hand, it was, or may have been, his primary purpose in acting as he did to alleviate her pain and suffering, then he is not guilty. That is so even though he recognised that, in fulfilling that primary purpose, he might or even would hasten the moment of her death. . . .

Disposition: Guilty

R. v. Moor
Newcastle Crown Court,
May 11, 1999

Dr Moor, a General Practitioner, was charged with murdering a patient by administering a large dose of diapmorphine to him. The patient, George Liddell was 85 and suffering from bowel cancer which, according to the hospital, had been operated on successfully. However, Mr Liddell, on leaving hospital and going to live with his daughter, became depressed, immobile and appeared to be in severe pain. He went into decline and Dr Moor, who had been prescribing diamorphine (5mgms later increased to 10mgms) for him for some days gave him a much increased dose (30mgms)—all were administered by a syringe driver (this releases the diamorphine into the patient's bloodstream gradually over a 24 hour period). The following day Dr Moor administered a larger dose (at least 60mgms) by injection when he attended Mr Liddell who was in a coma and breathing in the manner of a person close to death. He claimed his purpose in doing so was to make sure that the patient suffered no break through pain. Within twenty minutes Mr Liddell died.

The case became the subject of an investigation because Dr Moor stated in an article in a Sunday newspaper that he had helped patients to die with large doses of diamorphine. A post-mortem was carried out on Mr Liddell revealing abnormally large levels of diamorphine. This also revealed that he was not terminally ill from cancer, as Dr Moor had thought on the basis of his acute pain. Defence experts, however, gave evidence that he had a serious heart condition which had been missed by the hospital and this was almost certainly responsible for his very sick, terminal, appearance. They also expressed the view that the cancer which remained after the operation could have caused acute pain.

HOOPER J. directed the jury as follows on the question of murder:
"Question 1 Has the prosecution satisfied you so that you are sure that the . . . injection given by Dr Moor to George Liddell contained significantly more than 60 mgms (2 ampoules of 30mg). If the answer to question 1 is 'No', your verdict must be 'not guilty'. If the answer to question 1 is 'Yes', go on to question 2.
Question 2 Has the prosecution satisfied you so that you are sure that the defendant caused the death of George Liddell. If the answer to question 2 is 'No', your verdict must be 'not guilty'. If the answer to question 2 is 'Yes', go to question 3.

A person causes the death of another if his act, in this case the intramuscular injection containing morphine, contributed significantly to the death. It does not have to be the sole or principal cause of death.
Question 3 Has the prosecution satisfied you so that you are sure that Dr Moor's purpose in giving the intramuscular injection was not to give treatment which he believed in the circumstances (as he understood them) to be proper treatment to relieve George Liddell's pain and suffering? If the answer to question 3 is 'No', your verdict must be 'not guilty'. If the answer to question 3 is 'Yes', go to question 4.

Bear in mind that there is no dispute that Dr Moor believed that George Liddell would die shortly of natural causes. In other words of another judge [Devlin J, *R. v. Adams*, Central Criminal Court, April 9, 1957]:

"A doctor aiding the sick or dying does not have to calculate in minutes or hours or weeks the effect on a patient's life of the medicines which he administers. If the first purpose of medicine, the restoration of health, can no longer be achieved there is still much for the doctor to do and he is entitled to do all that is proper and necessary to relieve the pain and suffering even if measures he takes may incidentally shorten life.'

Question 4 Has the prosecution satisfied you so that you are sure that the defendant when he gave the intramuscular injection intended to kill George Liddell. If the answer to question 4 is 'No', your verdict must be

'not guilty'. If the answer to question 4 is 'Yes', then your verdict must
be one of 'guilty' ''.

A person intends to kill another person if he does an act, in this case
giving the injection, for the purpose of killing that person. If Dr Moor
thought or may have thought that it was only highly probable that death
would follow the injection, then the prosecution would not have proved
that he intended to kill and he would be not guilty.''

Disposition: Not Guilty

Note

Hooper J. effectively adopted the special defence approach used in
Cox—if D's purpose is proper medical treatment (pain relief would be
such) his purpose is not to kill and he should be acquitted (even
though he may realise that death is virtually certain). If, however, his
purpose is not proper medical treatment, the question for the jury is
whether his intention was to kill. Hooper J. framed the questions in
the most generous way possible for Dr Moor. The jury acquitted. We
do not know how far they proceeded in their deliberations on the
questions (cf *Gillick v West Norfolk A.H.A.* [1986] A.C. 112, *post* p. 327).

Questions

1. In what way might the direction to the jury and the outcome of
the case have differed if Dr Cox had administered a large dose of
diamorphine to Mrs Boyes and she had died as a result?

2. Consider how a judge might direct the jury in the following circumstances:

D is a retired General Practitioner. P, her husband, is terminally ill
from cancer and in excruciating pain. He begs to be allowed to die.
P's G.P. has prescribed diamorphine which is being administered
by a syringe driver at a rate which will not prove fatal and which
also is not controlling the pain. D alters the setting of the syringe
driver to increase the rate at which the diamorphine is administered
with the result that P dies. D admits that she knew from her experience that this would be the inevitable outcome but also claims that
her purpose was to relieve P's suffering.

3. Should the way in which a judge directs a jury on intention be
dependent upon the professional capacity in which an accused acts?

4. Is the criminal law creeping closer towards the recognition of a
general justificatory defence based on good motive? (See further *Re A
(Children) (Conjoined Twins: Medical Treatment) (No.1)* [2000] 4 All E.R.
961, *post* p. 336.)

iii. Knowledge

Law Com. No. 177

''8.10 'Knowingly': knowledge and 'wilful blindness'. . . .
[T]he state of mind which is to be assimilated to 'actual knowledge' for
the purposes of criminal liability is that of so-called 'wilful blindness'.

English criminal law has commonly treated a person as knowing something if, being pretty sure that it is so, he deliberately avoids making an examination or asking questions that might confirm the fact—he avoids taking advantage of an available means of 'actual knowledge'. It is this state of mind which, we believe, has to be captured by a short form of words. Clause 18(a) therefore treats a person as acting 'knowingly' with respect to a circumstance 'not only when he is aware that it exists or will exist, but also when he avoids taking steps that might confirm his belief that it exists or will exist.'"

Note

Statute may require knowledge expressly by use of that word or one of its variants. But even where an express requirement of knowledge is not included in the statute, the courts have frequently implied such a requirement: see, *e.g. Sweet v. Parsley* (*post*, p. 186). In *Roper v. Taylor's Central Garages* [1951] 2 T.L.R. 284, Devlin J. stated that "knowingly" only says expressly what is normally implied. He went on to explain that there are different degrees of knowledge:

"There are, I think, three degrees of knowledge which it may be relevant to consider in cases of this kind. The first is actual knowledge, which the justices may find because they infer it from the nature of the act done, for no man can prove the state of another man's mind; and they may find it even if the defendant gives evidence to the contrary. They may say, 'We do not believe him; we think that this was his state of mind.' They may feel that the evidence falls short of that, if they do they have then to consider what might be described as knowledge of the second degree; whether the defendant was, as it has been called, shutting his eyes to an obvious means of knowledge. Various expressions have been used to describe that state of mind. I do not think it necessary to look further, certainly not in cases of this type, than the phrase which Lord Hewart C.J. used in a case under this section, *Evans v. Dell* (1937) 53 T.L.R. 310, where he said (at p. 313): '. . . the respondent deliberately refrained from making inquiries, the results of which he might not care to have.'
The third kind of knowledge is what is generally known in law as constructive knowledge: it is what is encompassed by the words 'ought to have known' in the phrase 'knew or ought to have known.' It does not mean actual knowledge at all; it means that the defendant had in effect the means of knowledge. When, therefore, the case of the prosecution is that the defendant failed to make what they think were reasonable inquiries it is, I think, incumbent on them to make it plain which of the two things they are saying. There is a vast distinction between a state of mind which consists of deliberately refraining from making inquiries the result of which the person does not care to have, and a state of mind which is merely neglecting to make such inquiries as a reasonable and prudent person would make. If that distinction is kept well in mind I think that justices will have less difficulty than this case appears to show they have had in determining what is the true position. The case of shutting the eyes is actual knowledge in the eyes of the law: the case of merely neglecting to make inquiries is not knowledge at all—it comes within the legal conception of constructive knowledge, a conception which, generally speaking, has no place in the criminal law."

Where knowledge is required a court may be satisfied that wilful blindness suffices. In *Westminster City Council v. Croyalgrange Ltd* [1986] 2 All E.R. 353, 359, Lord Bridge stated:

"it is always open to the tribunal of fact, when knowledge on the part of a defendant is required to be proved, to base a finding of knowledge on evidence that the defendant had deliberately shut his eyes to the obvious or refrained from inquiry because he suspected the truth but did not want to have his suspicion confirmed."

How precise must a person's knowledge be if he is to be liable for knowingly committing a specified offence? See the case which follows.

R. v. Taaffe
[1984] A.C. 539
House of Lords

On his arraignment on a charge of having been knowingly concerned in the fraudulent evasion of the prohibition on the importation of cannabis resin, contrary to section 170(2) of the Customs and Excise Management Act 1979 and the Misuse of Drugs Act 1971, T pleaded not guilty. No evidence having been called, the recorder was asked to rule on the question whether T's version of events, if accepted by the jury, would entitle him to be acquitted. T's version was: (i) that he had been enlisted by a third party in Holland to import a substance from that country into England in fraudulent evasion of the prohibition on its importation and had so imported it; (ii) the substance had in fact been cannabis, importation of which was prohibited by the 1971 Act; (iii) T had mistakenly believed the substance to be currency; (iv) currency was not subject to any such prohibition; (v) T believed that it was. The recorder ruled that, even on T's version of events, he would be obliged to direct the jury to convict. Thereupon T pleaded guilty and was sentenced. T appealed and the Court of Appeal quashed his conviction. The Crown appealed.

LORD SCARMAN delivered the following opinion with which the remainder of their Lordships agreed: My Lords, the certified question in this appeal by the Crown from the decision of the Court of Appeal quashing the respondent's conviction in the Crown Court at Gravesend, neatly summarises the assumed facts upon which the learned recorder ruled that, even if they were proved to the satisfaction of a jury, the respondent would not be entitled to be acquitted. The question is in these terms:

"When a defendant is charged with an offence, contrary to section 170(2) of the Customs and Excise Management Act 1979, of being knowingly concerned in the fraudulent evasion of the prohibition on the importation of a controlled drug—Does the defendant commit the offence where he: (a) imports prohibited drugs into the United Kingdom; (b) intends fraudulently to evade a prohibition on importation; but (c) mistakenly believes the goods to be money and not drugs; and (d) mistakenly believes that money is the subject of a prohibition against importation?"

In effect, the learned recorder answered the question in the affirmative and the Court of Appeal in the negative. . . .

Lord Lane C.J. [in the Court of Appeal] construed the section under which the respondent was charged as creating not an offence of absolute liability but an offence of which an essential ingredient is a guilty mind. To be "knowingly concerned" meant, in his judgment, knowledge not only of the existence of a smuggling operation but also that the substance being smuggled into the country was one the importation of which was prohibited by statute. The respondent thought he was concerned in a smuggling operation but believed that the substance was currency. The importation of currency is not subject to any prohibition. Lord Lane C.J. concluded, at p. 631:

"[The respondent] is to be judged against the facts that he believed them to be. Had this indeed been currency and not cannabis, no offence would have been committed."

Lord Lane C.J. went on to ask this question:

"Does it make any difference that the [respondent] thought wrongly that by clandestinely importing currency he was committing an offence?"

The Crown submitted that it does. The court rejected the submission: the respondent's mistake of law could not convert the importation of currency into a criminal offence: and importing currency is what it had to be assumed that the respondent believed he was doing.

My Lords, I find the reasoning of the Lord Chief Justice compelling. I agree with his construction of section 170(2) of the Act of 1979: and the principle that a man must be judged upon the facts as he believes them to be is an accepted principle of the criminal law when the state of a man's mind and his knowledge are ingredients of the offence with which he is charged.

Appeal dismissed

Question

Could T have been convicted of attempt to evade the prohibition on importation contrary to section 170(2) of the 1979 Act? (See Chapter 7, *infra.*)

Note

Statute prohibits the importation of many different substances and the penalties available vary depending upon the substance illegally imported. This raises the question whether D believing he is importing prohibited goods the penalty for which is light, may be convicted of, and sentenced for, importing a prohibited substance the penalty for which is heavy? In *Ellis, Street and Smith* (1986) 84 Cr.App.R. 235, the appellants were convicted of being knowingly concerned in the fraudulent evasion of the prohibition on importation of a controlled drug, namely cannabis, contrary to section 170(2) of the Customs and Excise Management Act 1979. Cannabis is a Class B drug and the maximum penalty for its importation is fourteen years imprisonment. The appellants actually believed that they were importing pornographic materials which carries a maximum penalty of two years. The Court of Appeal upheld their convictions following the decision in *Hennessy* (1979) 68 Cr.App.R. 419 (approved in *Shivpuri* [1987] A.C. 1, H.L.) that all that the accused had to know was that he was importing prohibited goods; he need not know their nature. Thus if D believes he is importing prohibited pornography or prohibited birds eggs in a sealed container when, in fact, it contains heroin, he will be guilty of the offence of importing a Class A drug which carries a maximum sentence of life imprisonment even though, had he known the true facts, he would never have considered doing so.

Questions

1. Is D truly knowingly concerned in the fraudulent evasion of the prohibition on the importation of a controlled drug where he knows he is engaging in a smuggling operation but is mistaken as to the substance being smuggled? Why should he not be judged according to the facts as he believed them to be and be convicted of attempting to commit the offence he believed he was committing?

2. Is knowledge previously acquired but subsequently forgotten sufficient to support a conviction? See the case which follows.

R. v. Russell
(1984) 81 Cr.App.R. 315
Court of Appeal

Police officers stopped D's car and found a cosh under the driver's seat. D was convicted of possessing an offensive weapon in a public place. His defence had been that he had forgotten that he had put the cosh there. D appealed arguing that the trial judge had failed to direct the jury that it was for the prosecution to prove that D had the cosh with him "knowingly."

JUPP J.: We were referred to the case of *Cugullere* (1961) 45 Cr.App.R. 108; [1961] 1 W.L.R. 858, brought under the same section of the Prevention of Crime Act 1953, in which the Court of Criminal Appeal said, at the bottom of p. 110 and p. 860 respectively: "This court is clearly of the opinion that the words 'has with him in any public place' must mean 'knowingly has with him in any public place'. If some innocent person has a cosh slipped into his pocket by an escaping rogue, he would not be guilty of having it with him within the meaning of the section, because he would be quite innocent of any knowledge that it had been put into his pocket. In the judgment of this court, the section cannot apply in circumstances such as those. It is, therefore, extremely important in any case under this section for the judge to give a careful direction to the jury on the issue of possession. The first thing the jury have to be satisfied about, and it is always a question for the jury, is whether the accused person knowingly had with him the alleged offensive weapon." . . .

The appellant's defence in the present case is not that, having had a cosh slipped under his driving seat by some third party, he was innocent of any knowledge that it had been put there. It is that he himself put the cosh under the driving seat, but until the police found and showed it him, he had forgotten all about it. Whether or not the jury would have accepted it, this defence should have been properly left to the jury, but it was not.

It was submitted on behalf of the Crown in this Court that there is a distinction between "not knowing" and "having forgotten". The appellant, it is said, always knew how he came to put the cosh under the driving seat, although he only recalled it when the police confronted him with the cosh, and asked him to explain it.

In our judgment, the Court in *Cugullere*, in saying that the words of the statute must be construed as "knowingly had with him", were not merely dealing with the situation where a defendant has an offensive weapon put within his reach by a stranger without his knowing it. They were applying the general principle of criminal responsibility which makes it incumbent on the prosecution to prove full *mens rea*. The well-known observations of Lord Reid in *Sweet v. Parsley* (1969) 53 Cr.App.R. 221, 225, [1970] A.C. 132, are relevant here: "It is firmly established by a host of authorities that *mens rea* is an essential ingredient of every offence unless some reason can be found for holding that that is not necessary. It is also firmly established that the fact that other sections of the Act expressly require *mens rea*, for example because they contain the word 'knowingly', is not in itself sufficient to justify a decision that a section which is silent as to *mens rea* creates an absolute offence. In the absence of a clear indication in the Act that an offence is intended to be an absolute offence, it is necessary to go outside the Act and examine all relevant circumstances in order to establish that this must have been the intention of Parliament. I say 'must have been', because it is a universal principle that if a penal provision is reasonably capable of two interpretations, that interpretation which is most favourable to the accused must be adopted".

It would in our judgment be wrong to hold that a man knowingly has a weapon with him if his forgetfulness of its existence or presence in his car is so complete as to amount to ignorance that it is there at all. This is not a defence which juries would in the ordinary way be very likely to accept, but if it is raised it should be left to them for their decision.

Appeal allowed.
Conviction quashed.

iv. Recklessness

Note

Most crimes may be committed *intentionally* or *recklessly*. As recklessness provides the baseline for liability in most offences it is important that the term be clearly defined. However, as with *intention, recklessness* has thrown up definitional problems in the last fifteen years or so. The word currently is used in two senses when once it appeared to have a single meaning in the context of the criminal law. The word *reckless* (and its variants) has only been used in statutes in recent years, *e.g.* the Criminal Damage Act 1971. Formerly the word *maliciously* was used. This was defined as meaning *intention* or *recklessness*.

In C.L.G.P. Glanville Williams defined recklessness to mean *advertent negligence* as opposed to *inadvertent negligence*.

Williams, *C.L.G.P.* section 24

Negligence is of two kinds, being either advertent negligence (commonly called recklessness) or inadvertent negligence. Both advertent and inadvertent negligence may be found either as to surrounding circumstances, or as to consequences. Here, we are concerned with advertent negligence (recklessness) in relation to consequences. . . .

Recklessness as to consequence occurs when the actor does not desire the consequence, but foresees the possibility and consciously takes the risk. In inadvertent negligence, on the other hand, there is no such foresight. . . .

Convenience requires a narrow use of the term 'negligence' to signify inadvertent negligence unless the context concludes this meaning. Recklessness can thus be contrasted with negligence, though in a more general sense both are species of the same genus.

If the actor foresaw the probability of the consequence he is regarded as reckless, even though he fervently desired and hoped for the exact opposite of the consequence, and even though he did his best (short of abandoning his main project) to avoid it. Judges in speaking of recklessness frequently insert words to the effect that the defendant 'did not care whether he caused damage or not', but the better view is that this is irrelevant. Recklessness is any determination to pursue conduct with knowledge of the risks involved though without a desire that they should eventuate. . . .

Although this meaning of recklessness is now generally accepted, three factors imperil its stability. The first results from the etymology of the word in the English language. A man who is reckless is literally a man who does not reck, that is to say one who does not care; on this line of reasoning, reckless and careless become synonyms. This would matter little if 'careless' kept its primary meaning of one who does not care, but in fact 'careless' has come to be applied to persons who may care very much about the harmful result of their acts but are constitutionally incapable of preventing those results. It is only too easy for this widened meaning of 'careless' to infect the word 'reckless'.

The etymological similarity of 'reckless' and 'careless' is the more unfortunate because of a second factor, the constant pressure to extend the reach of the criminal law on account of the supposed policy of the individual case. Judges sometimes wish to punish a particular defendant who is thought to have been guilty of improper conduct, without remembering an even more imperative requirement of public policy: that the technical terms of the law should retain unequivocal meanings. To allow 'reckless' and 'careless' to become interchangeable would leave us without adequate means to differentiate two concepts.

The third inflationary factor results from another linguistic association, namely in the formulas commonly used to instruct juries. The need for a formula arises from the difficulty of proving recklessness. If the issue is whether the defendant was reckless as to a given consequence, the question is whether he foresaw the possibility of that consequence; but he will probably deny that he foresaw it, and it is impossible to look directly into his mind to know whether he is speaking the truth. Usually the question will have to be solved by examining the defendant's conduct and his opportunities of knowledge. Yet conduct is by no means so certain a guide to the issue of recklessness as it is to that of intention. When a man bends himself to secure a result, he will often leave evidence of telltale pieces of behaviour which are inexplicable except on the assumption that he intended the result. But recklessness may be a mere passing realisation, instantly dismissed, which leaves no mark upon conduct. Also, a man is capable of self-deception: he may decide that an unpleasant result is not likely because he does not want it to be likely.

On the issue of recklessness, these considerations may be put before the jury. There is no objection to instructing the jury to consider whether the defendant *must* have foreseen the consequence, but it is fatally easy to confuse this with the question whether the defendant *ought* as a reasonable man to have foreseen it. The latter question presupposes an objective test of the reasonable man, and the accused person's actual foresight is immaterial. The former question is directed exclusively to the accused's actual foresight, and the test of what a reasonable man would have foreseen is merely a step in reasoning. For example, it may be shown that the accused is mentally subnormal, or that on the occasion in question he was drunk, or suffering from some fear, anger, or other excitement which deprived him of the ability to look circumspectly to the probable outcome of his conduct. These facts would not, according to the usual view, be relevant to an issue of inadvertent negligence, if that were before the court; but they are very relevant to the issue of recklessness. They may lead the tribunal to decide that the accused did not foresee the consequence, even though a person somewhat differently situated would have foreseen it. In short, a judgment of inadvertent negligence rests merely on a comparison between the conduct of the accused and that of a reasonable man, while a judgment of recklessness uses the concept of the reasonable man only as a guide to what went on in the accused's mind, and only so long as it can plausibly be assumed that the accused's mind accorded with the normal at the time of his act.

It must be confessed that, defined in this way, recklessness is not a concept that is likely to secure many convictions, if the law is properly administered. Recklessness as a form of *mens rea* is some enlargement upon the requirement of intention, but not a considerable one. This, at least, is true for recklessness as to the consequence of conduct. There is, however, another application of the concept of recklessness, namely as to the existence of present facts, *i.e.* the circumstances surrounding conduct. A person is said to be reckless as to a surrounding circumstance if he is aware of the possibility that such a circumstance exists and does an act regardless of it.

Question

Williams spoke of three factors which could imperil the stability of the meaning of recklessness; to what extent do the cases which follow establish the prophetic quality of Williams' comments?

Note

The courts originally gave recklessness a *subjective* meaning.

R. v. Cunningham
[1957] 2 Q.B. 396
Court of Criminal Appeal

C stole a gas meter from the cellar of a house and in doing so fractured a gas pipe. Gas escaped, percolated through the cellar wall to the adjoining house, and entered a bedroom with the result that W, when she was asleep, inhaled a considerable quantity of the gas. C was convicted of unlawfully and maliciously causing W to take a noxious thing, so as thereby to endanger her life contrary to section 23 of the Offences Against the Person Act 1861. The judge directed the jury that "maliciously" meant "wickedly"—doing "something which he has no business to do and perfectly well knows it".

BYRNE J. read the judgment of the court: The act of the appellant was clearly unlawful and therefore the real question for the jury was whether it was also malicious within the meaning of section 23 of the Offences Against the Person Act 1861.

Before this court Mr Brodie has taken three points, all dependent upon the construction of that section. Section 23 provides: "Whosoever shall unlawfully and maliciously administer to or cause to be administered to or taken by any other person any poison or other destructive or noxious thing, so as thereby to endanger the life of such person, or so as thereby to inflict upon such person any grievous bodily harm, shall be guilty of felony. . . ."

Mr Brodie argued, first, that mens rea of some kind is necessary. Secondly that the nature of the mens rea required is that the appellant must intend to do the particular kind of harm that was done, or, alternatively, that he must foresee that that harm may occur yet nevertheless continue recklessly to do the act. Thirdly, that the judge misdirected the jury as to the meaning of the word "maliciously". He cited the following cases: *R. v. Pembliton* [*post*, p. 176], *R. v. Latimer* [*post*, p. 177] and *R. v. Faulkner* (1877) 13 Cox C.C. 550. In reply, Mr Snowden, on behalf of the Crown, cited *R. v. Martin* (1881) 8 Q.B.D. 54.

We have considered those cases, and we have also considered, in the light of those cases, the following principle which was propounded by the late Professor C. S. Kenny in the first edition of his *Outlines of Criminal Law* published in 1902 and repeated in 1952: "In any statutory definition of crime, malice must be taken not in the old vague sense of wickedness in general but as requiring either (1) An actual intention to do the particular kind of harm that in fact was done; or (2) recklessness as to whether such harm should occur or not (*i.e.* the accused has foreseen that the particular kind of harm might be done and yet has gone on to take the risk of it). It is neither limited to nor does it indeed require any ill will towards the person injured." The same principle is repeated by Mr Turner in his 10th edition of *Russell on Crime* at p. 1592.

We think that this is an accurate statement of the law. It derives some support from the judgments of Lord Coleridge C.J. and Blackburn J. in *Pembliton's* case (1874) L.R. 2 C.C.R. 119. In our opinion the word "maliciously" in a statutory crime postulates foresight of consequence. . . .

With the utmost respect to the learned judge, we think it is incorrect to say that the word "malicious" in a statutory offence merely means wicked. We think the judge was, in effect, telling the jury that if they were satisfied that the appellant had acted wickedly—and he had clearly acted wickedly in stealing the gas meter and its contents—they ought to find that he had acted maliciously in causing the gas to be taken by Mrs Wade so as thereby to endanger her life.

In our view it should have been left to the jury to decide whether, even if the appellant did not intend the injury to Mrs Wade, he foresaw that the removal of the gas meter might cause injury to someone but nevertheless removed it. We are unable to say that a reasonable jury, properly directed as to the meaning of the word "maliciously" in the context of section 23, would without doubt have convicted.

In these circumstances this court has no alternative but to allow the appeal and quash the conviction.

Appeal allowed

Notes

1. For further consideration of 'maliciously' see Chapter 9 on Non-Fatal Offences Against the Person.

2. The Law Commission, in Working Paper No. 31, *Codification of the Criminal Law, General Principles: The Mental Element in Crime* (1970)

and in its Report, *The Mental Element in Crime* (Law Com. No. 89), attributed a subjective meaning to *recklessness*. The Criminal Damage Act 1971 resulted from the work of the Law Commission (Law Com. No. 29, *Criminal Law Report on Offences of Damage to Property*). The Act sought to revise and simplify the law in relation to offences of damage to property. The term *reckless* as used in section 1 of the Act was construed by the Court of Appeal to mean *subjective recklessness*; the clearest statement of principle was given by Geoffrey Lane L.J. in *R. v. Stephenson* [1979] Q.B. 695. D, who suffered from schizophrenia, crept into a hollow in a large haystack and lit a fire to keep warm. The stack caught fire resulting in £3,500 of damage. Medical evidence was given that D might not have had the same ability to foresee or appreciate risks as the mentally normal person. The trial judge directed the jury that they could find D guilty if satisfied that he had closed his mind to the obvious fact of risk from his act and that schizophrenia might be a reason which made a person close his mind to the obvious fact of risk. In effect he was directing the jury to convict if the risk of damage would have been obvious to a reasonable person. The Court of Appeal quashed the conviction, Geoffrey Lane L.J. stating:

"A man is reckless when he carries out the deliberate act appreciating that there is a risk that damage to property may result from his act. It is however not the taking of every risk which could properly be classed as reckless. The risk must be one which it is in all the circumstances unreasonable for him to take.

Proof of the requisite knowledge in the mind of the defendant will in most cases present little difficulty. The fact that the risk of some damage would have been obvious to anyone in his right mind in the position of the defendant is not conclusive proof of the defendant's knowledge, but it may well be and in many cases doubtless will be a matter which will drive the jury to the conclusion that the defendant himself must have appreciated the risk. The fact that he may have been in a temper at the time would not normally deprive him of knowledge or foresight of the risk. If he had the necessary knowledge or foresight and his bad temper merely caused him to disregard it or put it to the back of his mind not caring whether the risk materialised, or if it merely deprived him of the self-control necessary to prevent him from taking the risk of which he was aware, then his bad temper will not avail him. . . . We wish to make it clear that the test remains subjective, that the knowledge or appreciation or risk of some damage must have entered the defendant's mind even though he may have suppressed it or driven it out."

Note

In 1981 the House of Lords had cause to consider the definition of *recklessness* as used in the Criminal Damage Act 1971. A reversal of the position enunciated in *Stephenson* was the outcome.

R. v. Caldwell
[1982] A.C. 341
House of Lords

In pursuit of a grievance which he thought he had against the proprietor of a hotel, the respondent set fire to the hotel. There were 10 guests living there at the time. The fire was discovered before any serious damage occurred. The appeal was mainly concerned with his defence of intoxication, as to which see *post*, p. 251 but the House took the opportunity to consider the meaning of recklessness in the Criminal Damage Act 1971.

LORD DIPLOCK: ... [The respondent] was indicted at the Central Criminal Court on two counts of arson under section 1(1) and (2) respectively, of the Criminal Damage Act 1971. That section reads as follows:

"1.—(1) A person who without lawful excuse destroys or damages any property belonging to another intending to destroy or damage any such property or being reckless as to whether any such property would be destroyed or damaged shall be guilty of an offence.

(2) A person who without lawful excuse destroys or damages any property, whether belonging to himself or another. . . .

(*a*) intending to destroy or damage any property or being reckless as to whether any property would be destroyed or damaged; and

(*b*) intending by the destruction or damage to endanger the life of another or being reckless as to whether the life of another would be thereby endangered;

shall be guilty of an offence.

(3) An offence committed under this section by destroying or damaging property by fire shall be charged as arson."

Count 1 contained the charge of the more serious offence under section 1(2) which requires intent to endanger the life of another or recklessness as to whether the life of another would be endangered. To this count the respondent pleaded not guilty. . . .

Count 2 contained the lesser offence under section 1(1) to which the respondent pleaded guilty.

The recorder directed the jury that self-induced drunkenness was not a defence to count 1, and the jury convicted him on this count. . . . [u]nder section 1(2)(*b*) there are two alternative states of mind as respects endangering the life of another. . . . One is intention that a particular thing should happen in consequence of the *actus reus*, *viz.*, that the life of another person (should be endangered, (this was not relied on by the Crown in the instant case). The other is recklessness as to whether that particular thing should happen or not. The same dichotomy of *mentes reae*, intention and recklessness, is to be found throughout the section; in subsection (1) and paragraph (*a*) of subsection (2) as well as in paragraph (*b*); and "reckless" as descriptive of a state of mind must be given the same meaning in each of them.

My Lords, the Criminal Damage Act 1971 replaced almost in their entirety the many and detailed provisions of the Malicious Damage Act 1861. Its purpose, as stated in its long title was to *revise* the law of England and Wales as to offences of damage to property. As the brevity of the Act suggests, it must have been hoped that it would also simplify the law.

In the Act of 1861, the word consistently used to describe the *mens rea* that was a necessary element in the multifarious offences that the Act created was "maliciously"—a technical expression, not readily intelligible to juries, which became the subject of considerable judicial exegesis. This culminated in a judgment of the Court of Criminal Appeal in *R. v. Cunningham*, (*ante*, p. 119) which approved, as an accurate statement of the law, what had been said by Professor Kenny in his *Outlines of Criminal Law* (1st Edn., 1902):

"In any statutory definition of a crime, 'malice' must be taken . . . as requiring either (1) an actual intention to do the particular *kind* of harm that in fact was done; or (2) recklessness as to whether such harm should occur or not (*i.e.* the accused has foreseen that the particular kind of harm might be done and yet has gone on to take the risk of it)."

My Lords, in this passage Professor Kenny was engaged in defining for the benefit of students the meaning of "malice" as a term of art in criminal law. To do so he used ordinary English words in their popular meaning. Among the words he used was "recklessness", the noun derived from the adjective "reckless", of which the popular or dictionary meaning is: careless, regardless, or heedless, of the possible harmful consequences of one's acts. It presupposes that if thought were given to the matter by the doer before the act was done, it would have been apparent to him that there was a real risk of its having the relevant harmful consequences; but, granted this, recklessness covers a whole range of states of mind from failing to give any thought at all to whether or not there is any risk of those harmful consequences, to recognising the existence of the risk and nevertheless deciding to ignore it. Conscious of this imprecision in the popular meaning of recklessness as descriptive of a state of mind, Professor Kenny, in the passage quoted, was, as it seems to me, at pains to indicate by the words in brackets the particular species within the genus reckless states of mind, that constituted "malice" in criminal law. This parenthetical restriction on the natural meaning of recklessness was necessary to an explanation of the meaning of the adverb "maliciously" when used as a term of art in the description of an offence under the Malicious Damage Act 1861 (which was the matter in point in *R. v. Cunningham*); but it was not directed to and consequently has no bearing on the meaning of the adjective "reckless" in section 1 of the Criminal Damage Act 1971. To use it for that purpose can, in my view, only be misleading.

My Lords, the restricted meaning that the Court of Appeal in *R. v. Cunningham* had placed on the adverb "maliciously" in the Malicious Damage Act 1861 in cases where the prosecution did not rely upon an actual intention of the accused to cause the damage that was in fact done called for a meticulous analysis by the jury of the thoughts that passed through the mind of the accused at or before the time he did the act that caused the damage, in order to see on which side of a narrow dividing line they fell. If it had crossed his mind that there was a risk that someone's property might be damaged but, because his mind was affected by rage or excitement or confused by drink, he did not appreciate the seriousness of the risk or trusted that good luck would prevent its happening, this state of mind would amount to malice in the restricted meaning placed upon that term by the Court of Appeal; whereas if, for any of these reasons, he did not even trouble to give his mind to the question whether there was any risk of damaging the property, this state of mind would not suffice to make him guilty of an offence under the Malicious Damage Act 1861.

Neither state of mind seems to me to be less blameworthy than the other; but if the difference between the two constituted the distinction between what does and what does not in legal theory amount to a guilty state of mind for the purposes of a statutory offence of damage to property, it would not be a practicable distinction for use in a trial by jury. The only person who knows what the accused's mental processes were is the accused himself—and probably not even he can recall them accurately when the rage or excitement under which he acted had passed, or he has sobered up if he were under the influence of drink at the relevant time. If the accused gives evidence that because of his rage, excitement or drunkenness the risk of particular harmful consequences of his acts simply did not occur to him, a jury would find it hard to be satisfied beyond reasonable doubt that his true mental process was not that, but was the slightly different mental process required if one applies the restricted meaning of "being reckless as to whether" something would happen, adopted by the Court of Appeal in *R. v. Cunningham*.

My Lords, I can see no reason why Parliament when it decided to revise the law as to offences of damage to property should go out of its way to perpetuate fine and impracticable distinctions such as these, between one mental state and another. One would think that the sooner they were got rid of, the better.

When cases under section 1(1) of the new Act, in which the prosecution's case was based upon the accused having been "reckless as to whether . . . property would be destroyed or damaged", first came before the Court of Appeal, the question as to the meaning of the expression "reckless" in the context of that subsection appears to have been treated as soluble simply by posing and answering what had by then, unfortunately, become an obsessive question among English lawyers. Is the test of recklessness "subjective" or "objective"? The first two reported cases, in both of which judgments were given off the cuff, are first *R. v. Briggs* [1977] 1 W.L.R. 605, *R. v. Parker (Daryl)* [1977] 1 W.L.R. 600. Both classified the test of recklessness as "subjective." This led the court in *Briggs* to say: "A man is reckless in the sense required when he carries out a deliberate act knowing that there is some risk of damage resulting from that act but nevertheless continues in the performance of that act." This leaves over the question whether the risk of damage may not be so slight that even the most prudent of men would feel justified in taking it, but it excludes that kind of recklessness that consists of acting without giving any thought at all to whether or not there is any risk of harmful consequences of one's act; even though the risk is great and would be obvious if any thought were given to the matter by the doer of the act. *Parker*, however, opened the door a chink by adding as an alternative to the actual knowledge of the accused that there is some risk of damage resulting from his act and his going on to take it, a mental state described as "closing his mind to the obvious fact" that there is such a risk.

R. v. Stephenson (*ante*, p. 121), the first case in which there was full argument, though only on one side, and a reserved judgment, slammed the door again upon any less restricted interpretation of "reckless" as to whether particular consequences will occur than that originally approved in *Briggs*. . . . The court . . . made the assumption that although Parliament in replacing the Act of 1861 by the Act of 1971 had discarded the word "maliciously" as descriptive of the *mens rea* of the offences of which the *actus reus* is damaging property, in favour of the more explicit phrase "intending to destroy or damage any such property or being reckless as to whether any such property would be destroyed," it nevertheless intended the words to be interpreted in precisely the same sense as that in which the single adverb "maliciously" had been construed by Professor Kenny in the passage that received the subsequent approval of the Court of Appeal in *R. v. Cunningham*.

My Lords, I see no warrant for making any such assumption in an Act whose declared purpose is to revise the then existing law as to offences of damage to property, not to perpetuate it. "Reckless" as used in the new statutory definition of the *mens rea* of these offences is an ordinary English word. It had not by 1971 become a term of legal art with some more limited esoteric meaning than that which it bore in ordinary speech—a meaning which surely includes not only deciding to ignore a risk of harmful consequences resulting from one's acts that one has recognised as existing, but also failing to give any thought to whether or not there is any such risk in circumstances where, if any thought were given to the matter, it would be obvious that there was.

If one is attaching labels, the latter state of mind is neither more nor less "subjective" than the first. But the label solves nothing. It is a statement of the obvious; *mens rea* is, by definition, a state of mind of the accused himself at the time he did the physical act that constitutes the *actus reus* of the offence; it cannot be the mental state of some non-existent, hypothetical person.

Nevertheless, to decide whether someone has been "reckless" whether harmful consequences of a particular kind will result from his act, as distinguished from his actually intending such harmful consequences to follow, does call for some consideration of how the mind of the ordinary prudent individual would have reacted to a similar situation. If there were nothing in the circumstances that ought to have drawn the attention of an ordinary prudent individual to the possibility of that kind of harmful consequence, the accused would not be described as "reckless" in the natural meaning of that word for failing to address his mind to the possibility; nor, if the risk of the harmful consequences was so slight that the ordinary prudent individual upon due consideration of the risk would not be deterred from treating it as negligible, could the accused be described as "reckless" in its ordinary sense if, having considered the risk, he decided to ignore it. (In this connection the gravity of the possible harmful consequences would be an important factor. To endanger life must be one of the most grave). So to this extent, even if one ascribes to "reckless" only the restricted meaning, adopted by the Court of Appeal in *Stephenson* and *Briggs*, of foreseeing that a particular kind of harm might happen and yet going on to take the risk of it, it involves a test that would be described in part as "objective" in current legal jargon. Questions of criminal liability are seldom solved by simply asking whether the test is subjective or objective.

In my opinion, a person charged with an offence under section 1(1) of the Criminal Damage Act 1971 is "reckless as to whether or not any property would be destroyed or damaged" if (1) he does an act which in fact creates an obvious risk that property will be destroyed or damaged and (2) when he does the act he either has not given any thought to the possibility of there being any such risk or has recognised that there was some risk involved and has nonetheless gone on to do it. That would be a proper direction to the jury; cases in the Court of Appeal which held otherwise should be regarded as overruled.

Where the charge is under section 1(2) the question of the state of mind of the accused must be approached in stages, corresponding to paragraphs (*a*) and (*b*). The jury must be satisfied that what the accused did amounted to an offence under section 1(1), either because he actually intended to destroy or damage the property or because he was reckless (in the sense that I have described) as to whether it might be destroyed or damaged. Only if they are so satisfied must the jury go on to consider whether the accused also either actually intended that the destruction or damage of the property should endanger someone's life or was reckless (in a similar sense) as to whether a human life might be endangered. . . .

LORDS KEITH OF KINKEL and ROSKILL agreed with LORD DIPLOCK].

LORD EDMUND-DAVIES, (with whom LORD WILBERFORCE agreed): . . . The words "intention" and "recklessness" have increasingly displaced in statutory crimes the word "maliciously" which has frequently given rise to difficulty in interpretation. [His Lordship then cited the passage from *Cunningham*, quoted by Lord Diplock, *supra*].

My Lords, my noble and learned friend, Lord Diplock, somewhat dismissively describes Professor Kenny as having been "engaged in defining for the benefit of students the meaning of 'malice' as a term of art in criminal law" . . . I have to say that I am in respectful, but profound, disagreement. The law in action compiles its own dictionary. In time, what was originally the common coinage of speech acquires a different value in the pocket of the lawyer than when in the layman's purse. Professor Kenny used lawyers' words in lawyers' sense to express his distillation of an important part of the established law relating to *mens rea*, and he did so in a manner accurate not only in respect of the law as it stood in 1902 but also as it has been applied in countless cases ever since, both in the United Kingdom and in other countries where the common law prevails; see, for example in Western Australia, *Lederer v. Hutchins* [1961] W.A.R. 99, and, in the United States of America, Jethro Brown's "General Principles of Criminal Law", 2nd Edition, 1960, 115. And it is well known that the Criminal Damage Act 1971 was in the main the work of the Law Commission, who, in their Working Paper No. 31 (1970) defined recklessness by saying:

"A person is reckless if, (a) by knowing that there is a risk that an event may result from his conduct or that a circumstance may exist, he takes that risk, and (b) it is unreasonable for him to take it, having regard to the degree and nature of the risk which he knows to be present."

It was surely with this contemporaneous definition and the much respected decision of *Cunningham* in mind that the draftsman proceeded to his task of drafting the Criminal Damage Act 1971.

It has therefore to be said that, unlike negligence, which has to be judged objectively, recklessness involves foresight of consequences, combined with an objective judgment of the reasonableness of the risk taken. And recklessness *in vacuo* is an incomprehensible notion. It *must* relate to foresight of risk of the particular kind relevant to the charge preferred, which, for the purpose of section 1(2), is the risk of endangering life and nothing other than that.

So if a defendant says of a particular risk, "It never crossed my mind", a jury could not on those words alone properly convict him of recklessness simply because they considered that the risk *ought* to have crossed his mind, though his words might well lead to a finding of negligence. But a defendant's admission that he "closed his mind" to a particular risk could prove fatal, for "A person cannot, in any intelligible meaning of the words, 'close his mind to a risk' unless he first realises that there is a risk; and if he realises that there is a risk, that is the end of the matter." (Glanville Williams, *Textbook of Criminal Law*, p. 79).

In the absence of exculpatory factors, the defendant's state of mind is therefore all-important where recklessness is an element in the offence charged, and section 8 of the Criminal Justice Act 1967 has laid down that:

"A court or jury, in determining whether a person has committed an offence,—

(*a*) shall not be bound in law to infer that he intended *or foresaw* a result of his actions by reason only of its being a natural and probable consequence of those actions; but

(*b*) shall decide whether he did intend *or foresee* that result by reference to all the evidence, drawing such inferences from the evidence as appear proper in the circumstances."

My Lords, it is unnecessary to examine at length the proposition that ascertainment of the state of mind known as "recklessness" is a *subjective* exercise, for the task was expansively performed by Geoffrey Lane L.J. (as he then was) in *Stephenson* (*ante*, p. 121).

[The House dismissed the appeal on the grounds that self-induced intoxication was not a defence to section 1(2) where the charge was based on recklessness, see *post*, p. 251].

Appeal dismissed

Questions

1. Do you agree with Lord Diplock that to ask a jury to distinguish between a defendant who foresaw a risk and one who ought to have foreseen a risk calls for 'meticulous analysis'? Is this analysis any more meticulous than that required of a jury in any other case where it is required to decide on the defendant's state of mind?

2. Are the distinctions between *subjective* and *objective* recklessness as 'fine and impracticable' as Lord Diplock suggests?

3. Do you agree with Lord Diplock that the term *reckleness* had not by 1971 become a legal term of art or was Lord Edmund-Davies correct when he stated that the law acquires its own dictionary?

4. If "reckless" is an "ordinary English word" (Lord Diplock) is it not strange that the majority in *Caldwell* "prevails not only over the weighty dissent of Lords Wilberforce and Edmund-Davies but also over the substantial body of judicial opinion in the cases of *Briggs*, *Stephenson* and other cases in the Court of Appeal and Divisional Court". (Smith [1981] Crim.L.R. 393)? One possible answer to this question would be that "even 'ordinary' words (and especially abstract words) are variously understood—everyone may 'know what they mean' but, without knowing it, use them with different meanings." (Griew, "Consistency, Communication and Codification: Reflections on Two Mens Rea Words" in Glazebrook, pp. 57, 58.)

5. Lord Diplock framed his "objective" test of recklessness to catch individuals who might plead that because of rage, excitement or drunkenness they did not appreciate the risk of damaging property; if the accused pleads that he did not appreciate the risk for some other reason, does this mean that he must be found not guilty? (see *Elliot v. C., infra*) *For example*, D. is a 14-year-old girl baby-sitting for neighbours. Feeling cold she decides to light the coal fire. The coal is damp and will not light. She finds paraffin in the garden shed and pours this over the coal. She ignites this thereby causing a conflagration which causes considerable damage to the house. D. has never before lit a coal fire being used to central heating. If the risk of damage was *obvious*, would D. be guilty of arson? If the fire put at risk the children sleeping upstairs, would D. be guilty of recklessly damaging property being reckless whether life was endangered?

Note

In *R. v. Lawrence* [1982] A.C. 510, decided at the same time as *Caldwell*, the House of Lords considered the meaning of "recklessly" in the context of causing death by reckless driving. (The offences of reckless driving and causing death by reckless driving have since been replaced by section 1 of the Road Traffic Act 1991 with the offences of dangerous driving and causing death by dangerous driving.) Their Lordships decided that the *Caldwell* test of recklessness should be applied to reckless driving. Lord Diplock stated:

"Recklessness on the part of the doer of an act does presuppose that there is something in the circumstances that would have drawn the attention of an ordinary prudent individual to the possibility that his act was capable of causing the kind of serious harmful consequences that the section which creates the offence was intended to prevent, and that the risk of those harmful consequences occurring was not so slight that an ordinary prudent individual would feel justified in treating them as negligible. It is only when this is so that the doer of the act is acting 'recklessly' if before doing the act, he either fails to give any thought to the possibility of there being any such risk or, having recognised that there was such risk, he nevertheless goes on to do it."

In *Reid* [1992] 3 All E.R. 673, the House of Lords was again considering a case of causing death by reckless driving. In the course of his speech Lord Goff of Chieveley suggested a slight revision to Lord Diplock's two-part test in *Caldwell*:

". . . Lord Diplock's requirement that the risk must be obvious must logically relate only to his first category of recklessness; it cannot be relevant where the defendant is in fact aware that there is some risk of the relevant kind. I suspect that Lord Diplock's application of this requirement to both categories was due to a desire for brevity. The point is not important; but in the interests of clarity it is, I believe, desirable to put this right when directing juries."

Question

In *Reid* [1992] 1 All E.R. 673, Lord Keith of Kinkel stated (at p. 674):

"Absence of something from a person's mind is as much part of his state of mind as its presence. Inadvertence to risk is no less a subjective state of mind than is disregard of a recognised risk. If there is nothing to go upon apart from what actually happened, the natural inference is that the [accused's] state of mind was one or other of those described by Lord Diplock. It would, however, be quite impossible for any juryman to say which it was, and in particular for him to be satisfied beyond reasonable doubt that it was the first state of mind rather than the second. So logically, if only the first state of mind constituted the relevant mens rea, it would be impossible ever to get a conviction."

Lord Keith was dealing with reckless driving and the "first" state of mind he referred to was advertence to a risk while the "second" was inadvertence. If Lord Keith is correct, is he suggesting that all convictions in cases where only the "*Cunningham*" test for recklessness suffices are unsafe or unsatisfactory?

Notes

1. There is a lacuna in the *Caldwell/Lawrence* recklessness test, namely the situation where, although it is proved there was an obvious risk, the defendant gave thought to the matter and wrongly concluded that there was no risk or that the risk was negligible in the sense that it was one which a reasonable and prudent person might take.

In *Chief Constable of Avon and Somerset Constabulary v. Shimmen* (1986) 84 Cr.App.R. 7, D sought to rely on this lacuna in his defence to a charge of criminal damage. D was a self-defence aficionado who sought to demonstrate his skill to his friends by kicking at and narrowly missing a shop window. In fact D broke the window. D stated in his defence that he believed "he had eliminated as much risk as possible by missing by two inches instead of two millimetres." His submission essentially was that he recognised the risk but thought he had minimized it so that no damage would result. The Divisional Court concluded that D was reckless as he recognised the risk and did not take adequate precautions to eliminate it.

It is arguable that a person cannot be considered reckless where he believes he has taken adequate precautions to eliminate a risk as his state of mind then is one of believing that, because of his precautions, there is no risk; the Divisional Court did not deal specifically with this issue. However, if a person believes he has minimized the risk rather than eliminated it (which would appear to have been Shimmen's belief) and there is no social utility in the act to be performed (as was the case here) then there is no justification for running such a risk, *i.e.* the reasonable and prudent person would not take such a risk. J. C. Smith states in his *Commentary* to the above case [1986] Crim.L.R. 802:

"Taking even the slightest risk with the property of another can be justified only if there is some acceptable reason for taking the risk. This is, of course, an objective question to be answered by the judge and jury or magistrates. It may fairly be assumed that no one would regard as reasonable the taking of any risk of destruction of a valuable shop window in order to demonstrate to a few friends the actor's skill in self-defence."

In *Merrick* [1996] 1 Cr. App. R. 130 D was convicted of damaging property being reckless as to whether life was endangered contrary to s. 1(2) of the Criminal Damage Act 1971. D had, with the householder's consent, removed a repeater box from the ground outside the house and to which television cabling was attached. In the process of carrying out this work a live electrical cable was exposed for approximately six minutes before D took steps to make it safe by sealing it with plastic and burying it in rubble and cementing over it. D. accepted that he had created a risk by exposing the cable but claimed he had taken reasonable precautions to eliminate the dangers by using the materials he had brought to the site for that purpose. The trial judge ruled that any precautions designed to eliminate the risk of endangering life must, to provide a defence, be taken before the damage was caused. D's actions were taken after the danger was caused to remedy the situation. D changed his plea to guilty and appealed. The Court of Appeal upheld the trial judge's ruling Hidden J. stating at p. 137:

"There is clear distinction to be drawn between the avoiding of a risk and the taking of steps to remedy a risk which has already been created. If an accused person is successfully to contend that the taking of certain steps has prevented him from falling within the definition [of reck-lessness] then those steps must be ones directed towards preventing the risk at all, rather than remedying it once it has arisen."

The Court of Appeal did not address two important issues: (1) whether the risk taken by D was a justified one in which case the taking of that risk may have been reasonable in the circumstances where the cable was under D's supervision and action to render it safe was taken immediately; and (2) the question of lawful excuse. Regarding (1) there must be operations which give rise to a risk to life which risk cannot be prevented in advance but only eliminated after it has arisen. Working with electrical cables would seem to fall into such a category. Must all such work now cease if risks cannot be pre-vented in advance? In his original commentary on *Shimmen* Professor Smith states at p. 802 that "It should make no difference whether the defendant's considered conclusion that there is no risk arises from his initial contemplation of the circumstances or from steps taken by him to change those circumstances." With regard to (2) see p. 906, *post*.

2. Another question left undecided by *Caldwell* and *Lawrence* was whether a defendant would be found guilty where the risk was not obvious to him (by reason of age, lack of experience, or lack of understanding) even though such a risk would have been obvious to the reasonably prudent individual. The answer came in the following case.

Elliot v. C. (a minor)
[1983] 1 W.L.R. 939
Queen's Bench Division

C, a 14-year-old schoolgirl, in a remedial class at school, who had been out all night without sleep, entered a garden shed. She found white spirit which she poured on the carpet in the shed and ignited it. The shed was destroyed by the fire. The justices found C not guilty of des-troying the shed and contents contrary to section 1(1) of the Criminal Damage Act 1971. The justices concluded that because of her age, lim-ited understanding, lack of experience of white spirit and exhaustion, the risk of destroying the shed would not have been obvious to her or been appreciated by her if she had given thought to the matter. The prosecution appealed.

GLIDEWELL J.: . . . [T]he magistrates accepted that they were bound to follow the "model direction" of Lord Diplock which I have read. It was, however, argued before them, and again before us by counsel for the respondent . . . that when, in the first part of his test, Lord Diplock referred to "an act which in fact creates an obvious risk that property will be destroyed or damaged", he meant a risk which was obvious to the particular defendant. This argument was accepted by the magistrates. . . .

Before us, counsel for the appellant has argued forcefully that the magistrates were wrong to adopt that interpretation of the decision in *Caldwell*. He submits that the phrase "creates an obvious risk" means that the risk is one which must have been obvious to a reasonably prudent man, not necessarily to the particular defendant if he or she had given thought to it. It follows, says counsel, that if the risk is one which would have been obvious to a reasonably prudent person, once it has also been proved that the particular defendant gave no thought to the possibility of there being such a risk, it is not a defence that because of limited intelligence or exhaustion she would not have appreciated the risk even if she had thought about it.

It is right to say, as counsel for the appellant pointed out to us, that there are passages in the speech of Lord Diplock in *Caldwell* which suggest that his Lordship was indeed using the phrase "creates an obvious risk" as meaning, "creates a risk which was obvious to the particular defendant". Thus, his Lordship said ([1981] 1 All E.R. 961 at 964, [1982] A.C. 341 at 351):

"Among the words [Professor Kenny] used was 'recklessness', the noun derived from the adjective 'reckless', of which the popular or dictionary meaning is 'careless, regardless, or heedless of the possible harmful consequences of one's acts.' It presupposes that, if thought were given to the matter by the doer before the act was done, it would have been apparent to him that there was a real risk of its having the relevant harmful consequences. . . ."

Speaking of another earlier decision of the Court of Appeal, in *R. v. Briggs* [1977] 1 All E.R. 475, [1977] 1 W.L.R. 605, he said ([1981] 1 All E.R 961 at 965, [1982] A.C. 341 at 353): ". . . even though the risk is great and would be obvious if any thought were given to the matter by the doer of the act."

He said ([1981] 1 All E.R. 961 at 967, [1982] A.C. 341 at 355):

"So, in the instant case, the fact that the respondent was unaware of the risk of endangering the lives of residents in the hotel owing to his self-induced intoxication would be no defence if that risk would have been obvious to him had he been sober."

The last passage was based on the earlier decision of the House of Lords in *R. v. Majewski* (*post*, p. 252), a decision relating to the effect of self-induced intoxication on intent. But, quite apart from the *Majewski* test, the decision of the majority in *Caldwell* that intoxication, even if it resulted in the defendant not thinking at all whether there was a risk that property or life would be endangered, nevertheless did not take him out of the state of mind properly described as "reckless" is only consistent in my view with their Lordships meaning by the phrase "creates an obvious risk" creates a risk obvious to the reasonably prudent person.

That the submission of counsel for the appellant is correct is to my mind, however, put beyond a peradventure by two later decisions of the House of Lords.

[His Lordship cited the discussion of "reckless" by Lord Diplock in *Lawrence* (*supra*, p. 127) and *Miller* (*supra*, p. 37).]

In the light of these last two authorities, we are in my judgment bound to hold that the word reckless in section 1 of the Criminal Damage Act 1971 has the meaning ascribed to it by counsel for the appellant. It is only fair to the magistrates in the present case to say that it seems that they were not referred to the decision in *R. v. Lawrence*, and *R. v. Miller* had not, when they reached their decision, been heard by the House of Lords. . . .

ROBERT GOFF L.J.: I agree with the conclusion reached by Glidewell J. but I do so simply because I believe myself constrained to do so by authority. I feel moreover that I would be lacking in candour if I were to conceal my unhappiness about the conclusion which I feel compelled to reach. . . .

[His Lordship quoted Lord Diplock's model direction in *Caldwell* and continued.] Now, if that test is applied literally in the present case, the conclusion appears inevitable that, on the facts found by the magistrates, the respondent was reckless whether the shed and contents would be destroyed; because first she did an act which created an obvious risk that the property would be destroyed, and second she had not given any thought to the possibility of there being any such risk.

Yet, if I next pause . . . and ask myself the question: would I, having regard only to the ordinary meaning of the word, consider this girl to have been, on the facts found, *reckless* whether the shed and contents would be destroyed, my answer would, I confess, be in the negative. This is not a case where there was a deliberate disregard of a known risk of damage or injury of a certain type or degree; nor is it a case where there was mindless indifference to a risk of such damage or injury, as is expressed in common speech in the context of motoring offences (though not, I think, of arson) as "blazing on regardless"; nor is it even a case where failure to give thought to the possibility of the risk was due to some blameworthy cause, such as intoxication. This is a case where it appears that the only basis on which the accused might be held to have been reckless would be if the appropriate test to be applied was purely objective: a test which might in some circumstances be thought justifiable in relation to certain conduct (*e.g.* reckless driving), particularly where the word "reckless" is used simply to characterise the relevant conduct. But such a test does not appear at first sight to be appropriate to a crime such as that under consideration in the present case, especially as recklessness in that crime has to be related to a particular consequence. I therefore next ask myself the question whether I can, consistently with the doctrine of precedent, sensibly interpreted, legitimately construe or qualify the principle stated by Lord Diplock in *Caldwell* so as to accommodate what I conceive to be the appropriate result on the facts of the present case, bearing in mind that those facts are very different from the facts under consideration by the House of Lords in *Caldwell*, where the defendant had set fire to a hotel when in a state of intoxication. . . .

I find it striking that the justices, in reaching their conclusion in the present case, have done so (no doubt in response to an argument advanced on the respondent's behalf) by imposing on Lord Diplock's statement of principle a qualification similar to one considered by Professor Glanville Williams in his article "Recklessness Redefined" (1981) 40 C.L.J. 252 at 270–271. This is that a defendant should only be regarded as having acted recklessly by virtue of his failure to give any thought to an obvious risk that property would be destroyed or damaged, where such risk would have been obvious *to him* if he had given any thought to the matter. However, having studied Lord Diplock's speech, I do not think it would be consistent with his reasoning to impose any such qualification. I say that not only because this qualification does not appear in terms in his conclusion which I have already quoted, but also because, when considering earlier in his speech Professor Kenny's definition of recklessness (which he rejected as being too narrow), Lord Diplock expressly adverted to the fact that that definition presupposed that "if thought were given to the matter by the doer before the act was done, it would have been apparent *to him* that there was a real risk of its having the relevant harmful consequences . . ." (see [1981] 1 All E.R. 961 at 964. [1982] A.C. 341 at 351; my emphasis). It seems to me that, having expressly considered that element in Professor Kenny's test, and having (as I think) plainly decided to omit it from his own formulation of the concept of recklessness, it would not now be legitimate for an inferior court, in a case under this particular subsection, to impose a qualification which had so been rejected by Lord Diplock himself. It follows that for that reason alone I do not feel able to uphold the reasoning of the magistrates in the present case. But I wish to add that, for my part, I doubt whether this qualification can be justified in any event. Where there is no thought of the consequences, any further inquiry necessary for the purposes of establishing guilt should prima facie be directed to the question why such thought was not given, rather than to the purely hypothetical question of what the particular person would have appreciated had he directed his mind to the matter.

Appeal allowed

Questions

1. In *Caldwell* Lord Diplock was concerned to define recklessness in such a way as to ensure that a defendant could not secure an acquittal by pleading that because of his intoxication he failed to recognise an obvious risk. Is it conceivable that C, in the above case, falls within the same category of blameworthiness as the intoxicated Caldwell?

2. Will C's conviction serve as a deterrent to other mentally retarded people? In favour of the judgment in *Caldwell* it can, at least, be argued that Caldwell could choose whether or not to get himself drunk; do people such as C have any choice with regard to their mental deficiencies?

3. If no sympathy was to be shown to the accused who was incapable of foreseeing risks obvious to the ordinary prudent man, would it be possible to improve the accused's chances of acquittal by at least accrediting to the ordinary prudent man the age and such of the accused's characteristics as would affect his appreciation of the risk? The answer was provided in the following case.

R. v. Stephen Malcolm R.
(1984) 79 Cr.App.R. 334
Court of Appeal

The appellant, when aged 15, committed a series of burglaries. He and his accomplices, believing that a woman and her daughter had informed on them to the police, threw three petrol bombs at the woman's house near the daughter's bedroom, causing loud bangs and sheets of flame. The appellant claimed that he intended only to frighten and that he did not realise that if a petrol bomb had gone through the daughter's window it might have killed her. He was convicted of arson contrary to section 1(2)(*b*) of the Criminal Damage Act 1971.

ACKNER L.J.: . . . The point of law which is raised before us is the point which [counsel for the appellant] took before Judge Abdela. It is said that the learned judge erred in law in deciding that the test of recklessness as to whether life was endangered was as follows: A person is guilty of the offence if (i) he does an act which in fact creates a risk to the ordinary prudent man, *i.e.* one of mature years and understanding, that life will be endangered; (ii) he did the act not having given thought to the possibility of such a risk; or (iii) recognising that there was some risk, he nonetheless continued the act.

The learned judge, it is urged, was wrong in law because he failed to apply the law in relation to what constitutes the "ordinary prudent man" and failed adequately to consider *D.P.P. v. Camplin (post*, p. 536). He should have found that the ordinary prudent man is synonymous with the reasonable man and therefore the jury should have had regard to the particular situation of the appellant, namely his age, and any other characteristics which would affect his appreciation of the risk.

This arson, it is accepted by [counsel for the appellant] was serious. For the ordinary prudent adult there was plainly an obvious risk of endangering the life of another. Thus the sole question which this appeal raises is whether the learned judge was wrong in the ruling which he gave. . . . [Counsel for the appellant] submits that the same approach as in *D.P.P. v. Camplin* (*supra*) applies where recklessness is the issue before the jury.

[His Lordship discussed *Camplin*; considered *Caldwell Lawrence* and *Miller* before dealing at length with *Elliot v. C.* (*ante*, p. 130).]

In the face of [these authorities, counsel for the appellant] sought to induce us to adopt a *via media*. He said he accepted it would be wrong to ask the question whether the defendant himself was aware of the risk, but it would be right to inquire whether a person of the age of the defendant and with his characteristics which might be relevant to his ability to foresee the risk, would have appreciated it. He drew our attention in particular to the submission made by the prosecution before the justices in *Elliott's* case "that in relation to the defendant aged 14 years, the proper approach was whether such risk would have been obvious to a normal 14 year old child." Therefore he said he was not seeking to relate the test to the particular defendant, but merely, so to speak, to a class of which he is a member. This, he says, provides him with the same logical basis of approach to the reasonable man or the reasonably prudent person as *D.P.P. v. Camplin* (*supra*) had suggested. We do not think that that *via media* was for one moment in the mind of Lord Diplock. The opportunity so to ingraft this important modification on the principle which he had enunciated had arisen in the subsequent cases and would have been just the sort of point (if it was a valid one) which we would have expected the House of Lords to have desired to have dealt with, thus clearing up the position, when they had the opportunity to do so when considering whether or not to give leave in *Elliott's* case (*supra*). If they had desired to say, for instance, that the age the defendant was a factor to which particular regard must be had in applying the test, then *Elliott* was just the sort of case to do that, excising, if appropriate, any reference to any other ephemeral characteristics such as exhaustion from which the girl was said to be suffering. But they did not take that opportunity. We do not think that we should seek by this subtlety to avoid applying principles which we also have difficulty in accepting. We respectfully share the regrets voiced by Robert Goff L.J. that in essence "recklessness" has now been construed synonymously with "carelessness".

We therefore dismiss the appeal against conviction. Although we would have preferred that the judge should have at least been entitled in law to have left to the jury the question, would a boy of the defendant's age have appreciated that to have thrown petrol bombs very close to the windows of this dwelling house was a danger to the life of the occupants of that house, we have little doubt that on the facts of this case the answer would have been clearly in the affirmative. . . .

Appeal dismissed

Note

Elliot v. C., Stephen (Malcom R.), Bell [1984] 3 All E.R. 842 (where D.'s inability to foresee risks due to schizophrenia was held to be irrelevant) and *Coles* [1995] 1 Cr.App.R. 157 (where the Court of Appeal upheld the decision of the trial judge to refuse to admit evidence from a psychologist to the effect that D., a fifteen-year-old, was of below average intelligence) establish that an accused is to be judged against the standard of the ordinary reasonable person even though this is a standard which he may be constitutionally incapable of attaining. If the reasonable prudent person is not invested with any of the accused's characteristics for the purposes of deciding on recklessness, might s/he nevertheless have the benefit of hindsight or expert knowledge? This question arose in the following case.

R. v. Sangha
[1988] 2 All E.R. 385
Court of Appeal

D set fire to furniture in a flat. There was no risk of the lives of the occupants being endangered as they were not present. Unknown to D there was also no danger to occupants of adjacent flats because of the special construction of the building. D was charged with the offence of damaging property being reckless whether the life of another would be thereby endangered, contrary to section 1(2)(b) of the Criminal Damage Act 1971. It was argued that D could not have been reckless whether life was endangered if there was, in fact, no risk to life. D was convicted and appealed.

TUCKER J.: It is clear that in the present case the relevant time is the time when the two armchairs were set alight. That is the point at which the ordinary prudent man would recognise that some risk of danger to life would be created.

There may of course be cases of arson where the lives not only of the occupants would be endangered, but also of those who might come to their rescue, or of firemen who might have to put out the blaze. But in the present case counsel for the Crown did not stress that aspect.

In our judgment, when consideration is given whether an act of setting fire to something creates an obvious and serious risk of damaging property and thereby endangering the life of another, the test to be applied is this: is it proved that an ordinary prudent bystander would have perceived an obvious risk that property would be damaged and that life would thereby be endangered? The ordinary prudent bystander is not deemed to be invested with expert knowledge relating to the construction of the property, nor to have the benefit of hindsight. The time at which his perception is material is the time when the fire is started.

Section 1(2) of the 1971 Act uses the word "would" in the context of recklessness whether property would be destroyed or damaged, and whether the life of another would be thereby endangered. We interpret this word "would" as going to the expectations of the normal prudent bystander.

Applying this test to the facts of the case before us, it is clear that in setting fire to these armchairs as the jury found the appellant did, he created a risk which was obvious and serious that property would be damaged and that the life of another would thereby be engandered. The fact that there were special features here which prevented the risk from materialising is irrelevant.

Appeal dismissed

Note

The test of recklessness established by *Caldwell* and *Lawrence* is therefore quite clearly objective (although Lord Diplock may have disliked the use of such a label). But to which offences does the objective test of recklessness apply?

Rape

After its decision in *Pigg* [1982] 1 W.L.R. 762, in which the Court of Appeal held, *obiter*, that the *Caldwell* and *Lawrence* test of recklessness applied with regard to the issue of consent, the Court subsequently changed its stance in *R. v. Satnam S. and Kewel S.* (1984) 78 Cr.App.R. 149 (see *post*, p. 684) where Bristow J. held that Lord Diplock's test of recklessness did not apply to section 1(1) of the Sexual Offences (Amendment) Act 1976 stating—

"*Caldwell* [and] *Lawrence* . . . were concerned with recklessness in a different context and under a different statute.

The word 'reckless' in relation to rape involves a different concept to its use in relation to malicious damage or, indeed, in relation to offences against the person. In the latter cases the foreseeability, or possible foreseeability, is as to the consequences of the criminal act. In the case of rape the foreseeability is as to the state of mind of the victim."

Question

Is the distinction drawn between recklessness as to consequences and recklessness as to circumstances a valid one?

Statutory Offences which may be committed recklessly

In *Seymour* [1983] 2 A.C. 493, H.L., (*post*, p. 592) a case of "motor manslaughter", Lord Roskill stated:

"[I]t would be quite wrong to give the adjective 'reckless' or the adverb 'recklessly' a different meaning according to whether the statutory or the common law offence [causing death by reckless driving or reckless manslaughter, respectively] were charged. 'Reckless' should today be given the same meaning in relation to all offences which involve 'recklessness' as one of the elements unless Parliament has otherwise ordained."

This dictum was *obiter* going much further than was required for decision of the case before the House, although the case did conclude that the *Caldwell* test applies to the common law offence of reckless manslaughter.

The offences of common assault, assault occasioning actual bodily harm and indecent assault are statutory offences (see the Criminal Justice Act 1988, s.39 and *D.P.P. v. Taylor and Little* [1992] 1 All E.R. 299, the Offences Against the Person Act 1861, s.47, and the Sexual Offences Act 1956, ss.14 and 15, respectively) but assault is defined at common law. Assault may be committed recklessly (see *Venna* [1976]

Q.B. 421, *post*, p. 623). In *Kimber* [1983] 1 W.L.R. 1118, a case involving indecent assault, the Court of Appeal adopted a subjective test of reck-lessness without making any reference to *Caldwell*. The dictum of Lord Roskill in *Seymour*, however, gave rise to a short period of confusion in relation to other offences involving assault. In *D.P.P. v. K. (A Minor)* [1990] 1 W.L.R. 1067, the Divisional Court held that the *Caldwell* test applied on a charge of assault occasioning actual bodily harm. In *R. v. Spratt* [1990] 1 W.L.R. 1073, the Court of Appeal declared that *D.P.P. v. K.* was wrongly decided, McCowan L.J. going on to state:

"The words 'unless Parliament has otherwise ordained' may well have been intended to refer not only to modern Acts of Parliament which use the word 'recklessly' but also to the 1861 Act, where the word 'mali-ciously' is used. However, the history of the interpretation of the 1861 Act shows that, whether or not the word 'maliciously' appears in the section in question, the courts have consistently held that the mens rea of every type of offence against the person covers both actual intent and reck-lessness, in the sense of taking the risk of harm ensuing with foresight that it might happen. (See *R. v. Ward* (1872) L.R. 1 C.C.R. 356, *R. v. Brad-shaw* (1878) 14 Cox C.C. 83, *R. v. Cunningham* [1957] 2 All E.R. 412, [1957] 2 Q.B. 396 and *R. v. Venna* [1975] 3 All E.R. 788, [1976] Q.B. 421.) Hence, according to judicial interpretation of the 1861 Act, these are all instances where Parliament 'has otherwise ordained'.

The sentence 'Reckless' should today be given the same meaning in relation to all offences which involve 'recklessness' as one of the elements 'unless Parliament has otherwise ordained' seems to us to be obiter. In any event we cannot believe that by the use of those words their Lord-ships intended to cast any doubt either on the decision in *R. v. Cun-ningham* or, more importantly for present purposes, on the decision in *R. v. Venna*, which was approved by the House of Lords in both *D.P.P. v. Majewski* and *R. v. Caldwell*.

Finally, counsel for the Crown argues that while *R. v. Venna* says that *Cunningham* recklessness will amount to guilt under s.47, it does not say that nothing else will do. In other words, it is now possible to add on failure to give thought to the possibility of risk as also qualifying for guilt. We do not accept that interpretation of the decision in *R. v. Venna*. Moreover, we are not attracted by what would be the consequence of accepting the argument of counsel for the Crown, namely that responsibil-ity for the offence of assault occasioning actual bodily harm (in respect of which Parliament used neither the word 'maliciously' nor 'recklessly') would be wider than for the offence of unlawful wounding (in respect of which Parliament used the word 'maliciously').

Accordingly, we consider ourselves bound by *R. v. Venna*."

Statutory Offences which may be Committed "Maliciously"

In *Cunningham* (*ante*, p. 119) *maliciously* was construed to mean *intentionally* or *recklessly*, using the latter term in its subjective sense. Did *Caldwell* effect any change in this area? In *W. (A Minor) v. Dolbey* [1983] Crim.L.R. 681, the Divisional Court held that *Caldwell* did not apply to offences where the *mens rea* was expressed by the term "mali-ciously" and that the definition of this term in *Cunningham* still stood. The House of Lords considered this issue in two appeals which were

heard together, *R. v. Savage, R. v. Parmenter* [1991] 4 All E.R. 698. Lord
Ackner stated:

"III *In order to establish an offence under s.20 of the 1861 Act, must the prosecution prove that the defendant actually foresaw that his act would cause harm, or
is it sufficient to prove that he ought so to have foreseen?*

Although your Lordships' attention has been invited to a plethora of
decided cases, the issue is a narrow one. Is the decision of the Court of
Criminal Appeal in *R. v. Cunningham* [1957] 2 All E.R. 412, [1957] 2 Q.B.
396 still good law, subject only to a gloss placed upon it by the Court of
Appeal, Criminal Division in *R. v. Mowatt* [1967] 3 All E.R. 47, [1968] 1
Q.B. 421, or does the later decision of your Lordships' House in *R. v.
Caldwell* [1981] 1 All E.R. 961, [1982] A.C. 341 provide the answer to this
question? . . .

R. v. Caldwell
Mr Sedley Q.C. [counsel for the respondent Parmenter] has not invited
your Lordships to reconsider the majority decision of your Lordships'
House. He chose a much less ambitious task. He submits that *R. v. Cunningham* cannot be bad law, since it is inconceivable that your Lordships'
House, in its majority judgment, would have steered such a careful path
around it. Your Lordships, having power to overrule it, would, so he
submits, have felt obliged to do so in order to avoid creating a false
double standard of "recklessness". He further submits that it is significant
that Lord Diplock, whose speech represented the views of the majority of
your Lordships, nowhere suggests that his own judgment in *R. v. Mowatt*
[1967] 3 All E.R. 47, [1968] 1 Q.B. 421, which clarified or modified *R. v.
Cunningham*, was of doubtful validity. . . ."

[His Lordship examined the decisions in *Caldwell, Lawrence* and *Seymour* and continued.]

"Before returning to the submission made by Mr. Sedley, to which I
have referred above, I think it is now convenient to go back in time to the
decisions of the Court of Appeal in *R. v. Mowatt* [1967] 3 All E.R. 47, [1968]
1 Q.B. 421, to which reference has already been made. The facts of that
case were simple. On 30 September 1966 in the early hours of the morning
the defendant and a companion stopped a third man in the street and
asked him whether there was a pub anywhere nearby. The defendant's
companion then snatched a £5 note from the third man's breast-pocket
and ran off. The third man chased him without success and returned to
the defendant, grasping him by the lapels and demanding to know where
his companion had gone. The defendant then struck the third man,
knocking him down. Two police officers saw the defendant sit astride the
third man and strike him repeated blows in the face, pull him to his
feet and strike him again, knocking him down and rendering him almost
unconscious. The defendant admitted inflicting the first blow but claimed
it was self-defence. He was tried on an indictment which included a count
for wounding with intent to do grievous bodily harm contrary to s.18 of
the Offences Against the Person Act 1861. In summing up on this count
the trial judge told the jury they were entitled to return a verdict of unlawful wounding under s.20 of the Act. However in his summing up, while
explaining the meaning of the word 'unlawfully' so far as it was relevant
to the defence of self-defence, he gave no direction as to the meaning of
'maliciously'.

The importance of this case is that the Court of Appeal considered *R. v. Cunningham* and, although modifying or explaining an important feature of that decision, in no way queried its validity. The judgment of the Court of Appeal, to which I have already made references, was, as previously stated, given by Diplock L.J., as he then was. It is of course one of Mr Sedley's points that, although *R. v. Mowatt* was not referred to in *R. v. Caldwell*, it was most unlikely that its existence was overlooked, particularly by Lord Diplock. Diplock L.J. observed that 'unlawfully and maliciously' was a fashionable phrase of parliamentary draftsmen in 1861 (see [1967] 3 All E.R. 47 at 49, [1968] 1 Q.B. 421 at 425). It ran as a theme, with minor variations, through the Malicious Damage Act 1861, and the Offences Against the Person Act 1861. He then referred to the 'very special' facts in *R. v. Cunningham* and observed:

'No doubt on these facts the jury should have been instructed that they must be satisfied before convicting the accused *that he was aware* that physical harm to some human being was a possible consequence of his unlawful act in wrenching off the gas meter. In the words of the court '"maliciously" in a statutory crime postulates foresight of consequence" (see [1957] 2 All E.R. 412 at 414, [1957] 2 Q.B. 396 at 399), and on this proposition we do not wish to cast any doubt.' (My emphasis.)

Subsequently, he added ([1967] 3 All E.R. 47 at 50, [1968] 1 Q.B. 421 at 426):

'In the offence under s.20 and in the alternative verdict which may be given on a charge under s.18—for neither of which is any specific intent required—the word "maliciously" does import on the part of the person who unlawfully inflicts the wound or other grievous bodily harm an *awareness* that his act may have the consequence of causing some physical harm to some other person. That is what is meant by "the particular kind of harm" in the citation from *Professor Kenny's Outlines of Criminal Law* (18th edn, 1962, para. 158a, p. 202). It is quite unnecessary that the *accused* should have foreseen that his unlawful act might cause physical harm of the gravity described in the section, i.e., a wound or serious physical injury. It is enough that *he* should have foreseen that some physical harm to some person, albeit of a minor character, might result.' (My emphasis.)

Mr. Sedley submitted that in *R. v. Caldwell* your Lordships' House could have followed either of two possible paths to its conclusion as to the meaning of 'recklessly' in the 1971 Act. These were: (a) to hold that *R. v. Cunningham* (and *R. v. Mowatt*) were wrongly decided and to introduce a single test, wherever recklessness was an issue; or (b) to accept that *R. v. Cunningham* (subject to the *R. v. Mowatt* 'gloss' to which no reference was made) correctly states the law in relation to the Offences Against the Person Act 1861, because the word 'maliciously' in that statute was a term of legal art which imported into the concept of recklessness a special restricted meaning, thus distinguishing it from 'reckless' or 'recklessly' in modern 'revising' statutes then before the House, where those words bore their then popular or dictionary meaning.

I agree with Mr Sedley that manifestly it was the latter course which the House followed. Therefore in order to establish an offence under s.20 the prosecution must prove either that the defendant intended or that he actually foresaw that his act would cause harm."

v. Wilfulness

Arrowsmith v. Jenkins
[1963] 2 Q.B. 561
Divisional Court

The defendant addressed a public meeting on the highway and was convicted on an information alleging wilful obstruction of the highway, by standing on it and causing others to congregate.

LORD PARKER C.J.: The sole question here is whether the defendant has contravened section 121(1) of the Highways Act 1959. That section provides: "If a person, without lawful authority or excuse, in any way wilfully obstructs the free passage along a highway he shall be guilty of an offence and shall be liable in respect thereof to a fine not exceeding forty shillings."

I am quite satisfied that section 121(1) of the Act of 1959, on its true construction, is providing that if a person, without lawful authority or excuse, intentionally as opposed to accidentally, that is, by an exercise of his or her free will, does something or omits to do something which will cause an obstruction or the continuance of an obstruction, he or she is guilty of an offence. Mr Wigoder, for the defendant, has sought to argue that if a person— and I think that this is how he puts it—acts in the genuine belief that he or she has lawful authority to do what he or she is doing then, if an obstruction results, he or she cannot be said to have wilfully obstructed the free passage along a highway.

Quite frankly, I do not fully understand that submission. It is difficult, certainly, to apply in the present case. I imagine that it can be put in this way: that there must be some *mens rea* in the sense that a person will only be guilty if he knowingly does a wrongful act. I am quite satisfied that that consideration cannot possibly be imported into the words "wilfully obstructs" in section 121(1) of the Act of 1959. If anybody, by an exercise of free will, does something which causes an obstruction, then an offence is committed. There is no doubt that the defendant did that in the present case.

Appeal dismissed

Cf. *Eaton v. Cobb* [1950] 1 All E.R. 1016.

Lewis v. Cox
[1985] Q.B. 509
Queen's Bench Division

The defendant's friend was arrested for being drunk and disorderly and placed in the back of a police vehicle. The defendant opened the rear door of the vehicle to ask his friend where he was being taken but a police constable closed the door warning him that he would be arrested for obstruction if he opened it again. When the constable returned to the driver's seat of the vehicle the defendant opened the door once more, whereupon the constable arrested him for obstructing him. The defendant was charged with wilfully obstructing a police constable in the execution of his duty, contrary to section 51(3) of the Police Act 1964. The justices acquitted the defendant and the prosecution appealed.

WEBSTER J.: . . . The justices found as a fact that the opening of the rear door of the van by the defendant was not aimed at the police, and that he did not intend to obstruct the police.

It was accepted by counsel on behalf of the defendant that the arrest of Marsh was lawful, and that the defendant's conduct in opening the door on the second occasion in fact obstructed the police because it prevented the prosecutor from driving the police vehicle away, which he would have done had the defendant not opened the door. The contention before the justices, which was substantially the same as the contention made on his behalf before this court, was that the defendant did not wilfully obstruct the police because his actions were not aimed at the police. The expression "aimed at the police" is an expression taken from the judgment of Griffiths L.J. in *Hills v. Ellis* [1983] Q.B. 680, 685, to which I will refer more fully later in this judgment.

The justices considered that the principle laid down by the decision in that case was that a person is guilty of wilful obstruction of a police constable in the execution of his duty if he deliberately does some act which is aimed at the police and if that act, viewed objectively, obstructs the police. They concluded that on the evidence before them the defendant had done no deliberate aggressive act which was aimed at the police, but that his sole aim was to ask Marsh where he was to be taken and that, as the actions of the defendant were not aimed at the police, the justices were of the opinion that they could not convict him of the offence, and they accordingly dismissed the charge against him.

The question which they ask for the opinion of this court is whether the principles applied by them were those laid down in *Hills v. Ellis*; they also ask whether, given the evidence in the case, the decision to dismiss the charge was perverse and unreasonable. For the moment I will consider only the first of those two questions.

For my part, I approach this question, in the first place, by disregarding any decision as to the meaning of the words "wilful" or "wilfully" in any context other than that of the section in question. This is because whereas, for instance, this court has held in *Arrowsmith v. Jenkins* (*ante*, p. 000) that the wilful obstruction of a highway, contrary to section 121 of the Highways Act 1959, does not import *mens rea* in the sense that a person will only be guilty of that offence if he knowingly did a wrongful act, there is a line of authority, to which I will turn, that the word "wilfully" in the context of section 51(3) of the Police Act 1964 connotes an element of *mens rea*. I find it necessary to consider this line of authority, although not every case in it, in some detail because it cannot, in my view, confidently be asserted that the test, whether the actions of the defendant are "aimed at the police," is the definitive and authoritative test.

It can, however, in my view be confidently stated, as I have already mentioned, that the word "wilfully" imports an element of *mens rea*. In *Betts v. Stevens* [1910] 1 K.B. 1 . . . Darling J., dealing with the question of intention, said, at p. 8: "The gist of the offence to my mind lies in the intention with which the thing is done."

In *Willmott v. Atack* [1977] Q.B. 498 . . . Croom-Johnson J., who gave the first judgment, said, at pp. 504–505.

"When one looks at the whole context of section 51, dealing as it does with assaults upon constables in subsection (1) and concluding in subsection (3) with resistance and wilful obstruction in the execution of the duty, I am of the view that the interpretation of this subsection for which the defendant contends is the right one. It fits the words 'wilfully obstructs' in the context of the subsection, and in my view there must be something in the nature of a criminal intent of the kind which means that it is done with the idea of some form of hostility to the police with the intention of seeing that what is done is to obstruct, and that it is not enough merely to show that he intended to do what he did and that it did in fact have the result of the police being obstructed."

May J. agreed . . .

Lord Widgery C.J. . . . [also] agreed. . . .
   In *Moore v. Green* [1983] 1 All E.R. 663, . . . McCullough J. said at p. 665:

"I do not understand the reference to 'hostility' to indicate a separate
element of the offence. I understand the word to bear the same meaning
as the phrase which Croom-Johnson J. used immediately afterwards,
namely 'the intention of seeing that what is done is to obstruct' . . ."

Griffiths L.J. agreed with the judgment of McCullough J.
   Finally, on this aspect of the matter, I return to *Hills v. Ellis.* . . .
   Griffiths L.J. cited the same passage from the judgment of Croom-
Johnson J. in *Willmott v. Atack* and continued, at p. 685:

"The defendant's counsel argues from that passage that as the motive here
was merely to correct an officer's error, it cannot be said that he, the defendant, was acting with any hostility towards the police. But in my view, the
phrase 'hostility to the police' in that passage means no more than that the
actions of the defendant are aimed at the police. There can be no doubt here
that his action in grabbing the officer's arm was aimed at that officer. It was
an attempt to get that officer to desist from the arrest that he was making.
In my view, this is as clear a case as we can have of obstructing a police
officer in the course of his duty, and the justices came to the right decision."

McCullough J. agreed with the judgment of Griffiths L.J., and added, at
p. 686:

"I am uncertain what Croom-Johnson J. had in mind when he used the
word 'hostility' . . . Hostility suggests emotion and motive, but motive and
emotion are alike irrelevant in criminal law. What matters is intention, that
is, what state of affairs the defendant intended to bring about. What motive
he had while so intending is irrelevant. What is meant by 'an intention to
obstruct?' I would construe 'wilfully obstructs' as doing deliberate actions
with the intention of bringing about a state of affairs which, objectively
regarded, amount to an obstruction as that phrase was explained by Lord
Parker C.J. in *Rice v. Connolly* [1966] 2 Q.B. 414, 419B, that is, making it more
difficult for the police to carry out their duty. The fact that the defendant
might not himself have called that state of affairs an obstruction is, to my
mind, immaterial. That is not to say that it is enough to do deliberate actions
which, in fact, obstruct; there must be an intention that those actions should
result in the further state of affairs to which I have been referring."

Lord Parker C.J. on the same page of his judgment in *Rice v. Connolly* said
that "wilful" in the context of this section "not only in my judgment means
'intentional' but something which is done without lawful excuse;" and his
explanation of "wilfully obstructs" as being something which makes it more
difficult for the police to carry out their duties was taken by him from the
judgment of Lord Goddard C.J. in *Hinchliffe v. Sheldon* [1955] 1 W.L.R. 1207,
where Lord Goddard C.J. said, at p. 1210; "Obstructing, for the present purpose, means making it more difficult for the police to carry out their duties."
   For my part I conclude that, although it may not be unhelpful in certain
cases to consider whether the actions of a defendant were aimed at the
police, the simple facts which the court has to find are whether the defendant's conduct in fact prevented the police from carrying out their duty, or
made it more difficult for them to do so, and whether the defendant intended that conduct to prevent the police from carrying out their duty or to
make it more difficult to do so.
   In the present case the test which the justices applied was whether the
defendant had deliberately done some act which was aimed at the police,
they found that his actions were not aimed at the police and they accordingly

dismissed the charge. In my view, for the reasons which I have given, the justices did not ask themselves the right question for the purposes of the present case, or the whole of the right question.

I turn, therefore, to the second question which they ask, which is whether, given the evidence in the case, the decision to dismiss the charge was perverse and unreasonable. . . .

For my part I conclude . . . that if the justices had directed themselves properly in the way in which I have set out they must, on the evidence, have decided that the defendant, when he opened the door on the second occasion, intended to make it more difficult for the police to carry out their duties, even though that was not his predominate intention, and they ought, therefore, to have convicted him of the charge against him.

My answer to the second part of the question, therefore, is that given the evidence in the case, the justices' decision to dismiss the charge was perverse and unreasonable, and I would accordingly allow this appeal and remit the case to the justices with a direction to them to convict.

KERR L.J.: I agree with Webster J.'s analysis of the authorities. The *actus reus* is the doing of an act which has the effect of making it impossible or more difficult for the police to carry out their duty. The word "wilfully" clearly imports an additional requirement of *mens rea*. The act must not only have been done deliberately, but with the knowledge and intention that it will have this obstructive effect. But in the absence of a lawful excuse, the defendant's purpose or reason for doing the act is irrelevant, whether this be directly hostile to, or "aimed at", the police, or whether he has some other purpose or reason.

Appeal allowed
Case remitted with direction to convict

Questions

1. Is the word "wilfully" in section 121(1) of the Highways Act 1959 (now s. 137(1) of the Highways Act 1980) redundant? *cf. Lewis v. Dickinson* [1976] Crim.L.R. 442.

2. How does the interpretation of "wilfully" in *Arrowsmith v. Jenkins* differ from that in *Lewis v. Cox*?

Note

The courts have also struggled in their search for an appropriate interpretation of "wilful" in the context of "wilful neglect" under the Children and Young Persons Act 1933.

R. v. Sheppard
[1980] 3 All E.R. 899
House of Lords

The youngest child of Mr and Mrs S. died at the age of 16 months from malnutrition and hypothermia. Three appointments to see a paediatrician had been made by the Health Visitor but the appellants had failed to attend. They were convicted of causing cruelty by wilful neglect under section 1 of the Children and Young Persons Act 1933. The Court of Appeal felt bound by authority to uphold the direction of the trial judge that no element of foresight of harm was necessary for the offence, but granted leave to appeal to the House of Lords.

LORD DIPLOCK: . . . In the light of the trial judge's instructions given to the jury as to the law applicable to the offence charged, it can safely be inferred from the verdicts of guilty that the jury found (1) that injury to Martin's health had in fact been caused by the failure of each of the parents to have him examined by a doctor in the period prior to his death and (2) that any reasonable parents, *i.e.* parents endowed with ordinary intelligence and not indifferent to the welfare of their child, would have recognised from the manifest symptoms of serious illness in Martin during that period that a failure to have him examined by a doctor might well result in unnecessary suffering or injury to his health . . .

Their real defence, if it were capable of amounting to a defence in law was that they did not realise that the child was ill enough to need a doctor; they had observed his loss of appetite and failure to keep down his food, but had genuinely thought that this was due to some passing minor upset to which babies are prone, from which they recover naturally without medical aid and which medical treatment can do nothing to alleviate or to hasten recovery.

We do not know whether the jury would have thought that this explanation of the parents' failure to have Martin examined by a doctor might be true. In his instructions the judge had told the jury that to constitute the statutory offence with which the parents were charged it was unnecessary for the Crown to prove that at the time when it was alleged the parents should have had the child seen by a doctor either they in fact knew that their failure to do so involved a risk of causing him unnecessary suffering or injury to health or they did not care whether this was so or not. . . .

The Court of Appeal, regarding themselves as bound by the same line of authority, felt compelled to dismiss the parents' appeal . . . but certified as the point of law of general public importance involved in their decision to dismiss the appeal:

"What is the proper direction to be given to a jury on a charge of wilful neglect of a child under s.1 of the Children and Young Persons Act 1933 as to what constitutes the necessary mens rea of the offence?"

The relevant provisions of section 1 are in the following terms:

"(1) If any person who has attained the age of sixteen years and has the custody, charge, or care of any child or young person under that age, wilfully assaults, ill-treats, neglects, abandons, or exposes him, or causes or procures him to be assaulted, ill-treated, neglected, abandoned, or exposed, in a manner likely to cause him unnecessary suffering or injury to health (including injury to or loss of sight, or hearing, or limb, or organ of the body, and any mental derangement), that person shall be guilty of a misdemeanour, and shall be liable—(a) on conviction on indictment, to a fine, or alternatively, or in addition thereto, to imprisonment for any term not exceeding two years. . . .

(2) For the purposes of this section—(a) a parent or other person legally liable to maintain a child or young person shall be deemed to have neglected him in a manner likely to cause injury to his health if he has failed to provide adequate food, clothing, medical aid or lodging for him, or if, having been unable otherwise to provide such food, clothing, medical aid or lodging, he has failed to take steps to procure it to be provided under enactments applicable in that behalf. . . ."

. . . My Lords, the language in which the relevant provisions of the 1933 Act are drafted consists of ordinary words in common use in the English language. If I were to approach the question of their construction untrammelled (as the House is) by authority I should have little hesitation in saying that where the charge is one of wilfully neglecting to provide a child with adequate medical aid, which in appropriate cases will include precautionary medical examination, the prosecution must prove (1) that the child did in fact need medical aid at the time at which the parent is charged with having failed to provide it and (2) either that the parent was aware at that time that the child's health might be at risk if it were not provided with medical aid or that the parent's unawareness of this fact was due to his not caring whether the child's health were at risk or not.

In view of the previous authorities, however, which reach a different conclusion, it becomes necessary to analyse more closely the wording and structure of sections 1(1) and (2)(*a*). . . .

The presence of the adverb "wilfully" qualifying all five verbs, "assaults, ill-treats, neglects, abandons, or exposes", makes it clear that any offence under section 1 requires *mens rea*, a state of mind on the part of the offender directed to the particular act or failure to act that constitutes the *actus reus* and warrants the description "wilful". The other four adverbs refer to positive acts, "neglect" refers to failure to act, and the judicial explanation of the state of mind denoted by the statutory expression "wilfully" in relation to the doing of a positive act is not necessarily wholly apt in relation to a failure to act at all. The instant case is in the latter category, so I will confine myself to considering what is meant by wilfully neglecting a child in a manner likely to cause him unnecessary suffering or injury to health. . . .

The *actus reus* of the offence with which the accused were charged in the instant case does not involve construing the verb "neglect" for the offence fell within the deeming provision; and the only question as respects the *actus reus* was: did the parents fail to provide for Martin in the period before his death medical aid that was in fact adequate in view of his actual state of health at the relevant time? This, as it seems to me, is a pure question of objective fact to be determined in the light of what has become known *by the date of the trial* to have been the child's actual state of health at the relevant time. It does not depend on whether a reasonably careful parent, with knowledge of those facts only which such a parent might reasonably be expected to observe for himself, would have thought it prudent to have recourse to medical aid. . . . If failure to use the hypothetical powers of observation, ratiocination and foresight of consequences [of the reasonable man] is to constitute an ingredient of a criminal offence it must surely form part not of the *actus reus* but of the *mens rea*.

It does not, however, seem to me that the concept of the reasonable parent . . . has any part to play in the *mens rea* of an offence in which the description of the *mens rea* is contained in the single adverb "wilfully". In the context of doing a child a positive act (assault, ill-treat, abandon or expose) that is likely to have specified consequences (to cause him unnecessary suffering or injury to health), "wilfully", which must describe the state of mind of the actual doer of the act, may be capable of bearing the narrow meaning that the wilfulness required extends only to the doing of the physical act itself which in fact results in the consequences described, even though the doer thought that it would not and would not have acted as he did had he foreseen a risk that those consequences might follow. Although this is a possible meaning of "wilfully", it is not the natural meaning even in relation to positive acts defined by reference to the consequences to which they are likely to give rise; and, in the context of the section, if this is all the adverb "wilfully" meant it would be otiose. Section 1(1) would have the same effect if it were omitted; for even in absolute offences (unless vicarious liability is involved) the physical act relied on as constituting the offence must be wilful in the limited sense, for which the synonym in the field of criminal liability that has now become the common term of legal art is "voluntary."

So much for "wilfully" in the context of a positive act. To "neglect" a child is to omit to act, to fail to provide adequately for . . . its physical needs. . . . For reasons already given the use of the verb "neglect" cannot, in my view, of itself import into the criminal law the civil law concept of negligence. The *actus reus* in a case of wilful neglect is simply a failure, for whatever reason, to provide the child whenever it in fact needs medical aid with the medical aid it needs. Such a failure as it seems to me could not be properly described as "wilful" unless the parent *either* (1) had directed his mind to the question whether there was some risk (though it might fall far short of a probability) that the child's health might suffer unless he were examined by a doctor and provided with such curative treatment as the examination might reveal as necessary, and had made a conscious decision, for whatever reason, to refrain from arranging for such medical examination, *or* (2) had so refrained because he did not care whether the child might be in need of medical treatment or not.

As regards the second state of mind, this imports the concept of recklessness which is a common concept in *mens rea* in criminal law. It is not to be confused with negligence in the civil law of tort (see *Andrews v. Director of Public Prosecutions* [1937] A.C. 576 at 582–583). In speaking of the first state of mind I have referred to the parent's knowledge of the existence of some risk of injury to health rather than of probability. The section speaks of an act or omission that is "likely" to cause unnecessary suffering or injury to health. The word is imprecise. It is capable of covering a whole range of possibilities from "it's on the cards" to "it's more probable than not"; but, having regard to the parent's lack of skill in diagnosis and to the very serious consequences which may result from failure to provide a child with timely medical attention, it should in my view be understood as excluding only what would fail to be described as highly unlikely. . . .

To give to section 1(1) of the 1933 Act the meaning which I suggest it bears would not encourage parents to neglect their children nor would it reduce the deterrent to child neglect provided by the section. It would afford no defence to parents who do not bother to observe their children's health or, having done so, do not care whether their children are receiving the medical examination and treatment that they need or not; it would involve the acquittal of those parents only who through ignorance or lack of intelligence are genuinely unaware that their child's health may be at risk if it is not examined by a doctor to see if it needs medical treatment. And, in view of the abhorrence which magistrates and juries feel for cruelty to helpless children, I have every confidence that they would not readily be hoodwinked by false claims by parents that it did not occur to them that an evidently sick child might need medical care.

In the instant case it seems likely that on the evidence the jury, if given the direction which I have suggested as correct, would have convicted one or both of the accused; but I do not think it possible to say with certainty that they would. It follows that in my opinion these appeals must be allowed and that the certified question should be answered: "The proper direction to be given to a jury on a charge of wilful neglect of a child under s.1 of the Children and Young Persons Act 1933 by failing to provide adequate medical aid is that the jury must be satisfied (1) that the child did in fact need medical aid at the time at which the parent is charged with failing to provide it (the *actus reus*) and (2) either that the parent was aware at that time that the child's health might be at risk if it was not provided with medical aid or that the parent's unawareness of this fact was due to his not caring whether his child's health was at risk or not (the *mens rea*).

[LORD KEITH and LORD EDMUND-DAVIES delivered opinions in which they agreed with LORD DIPLOCK; LORD SCARMAN and LORD FRASER delivered dissenting opinions].

Questions

1. Do you agree with Lord Diplock that, if the word "wilfully" were given a narrow meaning extending only to the doing of the positive act, and not its consequences, it would be otiose in section 1(1)? Is a parent who admonishes a child with a slap committing a voluntary act? Is it therefore a "wilful" assault? Or is it not an assault at all because it is "lawful"?

2. If the parent in question 1 is not committing an assault because parents are allowed to use reasonable disciplinary measures, is Lord Diplock right to assert it is only in the *"mens rea"* of an offence that the reasonable man concept will be found?

3. Both Lord Fraser and Lord Scarman believed that the deterrent effect of the offence would be reduced if the prosecution had to prove foresight of the consequences of neglect. Can this hypothesis be tested?

vi. Proposals for Reform

In the Draft Criminal Code Bill (Law Com. No. 177) the Law Commission used the term *fault element* in preference to the common law phrase *mens rea*. In clause 18 it defined the *fault terms* "knowingly", and "intentionally" and "recklessly". Clause 18 provided that "a person acts—

"(a) 'knowingly' with respect to a circumstance not only when he is aware that it exists or will exist, but also when he avoids taking steps that might confirm his belief that it exists or will exist;"

Since drawing up the Draft Code the Law Commission has taken the pragmatic decision that the best chance of implementing it is through "a series of Bills, each of which will be complete in itself and will contain proposals for the immediate reform and rationalisation of a major, discrete area of the criminal law (*Legislating the Criminal Code: Offences Against the Person and General Principles*, Law Com. No. 218, 1993, para. 1.3). Following some criticisms of its definition of intention in the Draft Criminal Code Bill the Law Commission has revised the definition of intention in the Bill appended to Law Com. No. 218. It has also included some minor revisions of the definition of "recklessly".

Draft Criminal Law Bill

Definition of fault terms

1.—For the purposes of this Part a person acts—

(a) "intentionally" with respect to a result when—
  (i) it is his purpose to cause it, or
  (ii) although it is not his purpose to cause it, he knows that it would occur in the ordinary course of events if he were to succeed in his purpose of causing some other result; and
(b) "recklessly" with respect to—
  (i) a circumstance, when he is aware of a risk that it exists or will exist, and

(ii) a result, when he is aware of a risk that it will occur,
and it is unreasonable, having regard to the circumstances known to
him, to take that risk;

and related expressions shall be construed accordingly.

**Legislating the Criminal Code: Offences Against the Person and General
Principles,
Law Com. No. 218**

"Intention"

7.2 To define "intention" by statute involves a different policy from that
adopted, in the context of the law of homicide, by the House of Lords. However, in that context the absence of definition, whether by statute or in the
practice of the courts, has been productive of serious difficulty, in particular
in relation to a result of conduct that, although not desired by the actor, is
known by him to be the certain, or overwhelmingly likely, outcome of his
actions. As the authorities stand the jury, in a case where it appears that the
defendant did not desire the relevant result of his actions, are only told that
they may nevertheless *infer* his intention to cause that result if he recognised
that result to be a "virtually certain" consequence of his actions. This form
of direction falls short of asserting that such recognition of virtual certainty
is in law a case of intention; and thus does not clarify the nature of the state
of mind that the jury may "infer".

7.3 In LCCP 122 we drew attention to the criticism of that position that
had been made not only in the Code Report but also by the Nathan Committee (*Report of the House of Lords Select Committee on Murder and Life Imprisonment* (H.L. Paper 78–1, 1989) para. 69). We therefore proposed that for the
purposes of the Criminal Law Bill there should be a statutory definition of
intention, and suggested a formula in terms almost identical to those set out
above. . . .

The basic definition: intention as "purpose"
7.4 In all but the most unusual case, courts and juries will only be concerned with the basic rule in clause 1(a)(i) of the Criminal Law Bill: that a
person acts intentionally with respect to a result when it is his purpose to
cause that result.

7.5 The concept of purpose is ideally suited to express the idea of intention
in the criminal law, because that law is concerned with results that the
defendant causes by his own actions. Those results are intentional, or intentionally caused, on his part when he has sought to bring them about, by
making it the purpose of his acts that they should occur. It is for that reason
that distinguished judges have naturally spoken of the concept of intention
in the criminal law in terms of "purpose". We are confident that courts and
juries will find the statutory confirmation of this central nature of intention,
when that word is used in the definition of offences, both easy and helpful
to use.

A special and limited case
7.6 Therefore, in almost all cases when they are dealing with a case of
intention, courts will not need to look further than paragraph (i) of clause
1(a). Paragraph (ii) is however aimed at one particular type of case that, it is
generally agreed, needs to be treated as a case of "intention" in law, but
which is not covered by paragraph (i) because the actor does not act in order
to cause, or with the purpose of causing, the result in question. . . .

7.7 The point was formulated by Lord Hailsham of St Marylebone in *Hyam*. A person must be treated as intending "the means as well as the end and the inseparable consequences of the end as well as the means." If he acts in order to achieve a particular purpose, knowing that that cannot be done without causing another result, he must be held to intend to cause that other result. The other result may be a *pre-condition*: as where D, in order to injure P, throws a brick through a window behind which he knows P to be standing; or it may be a *necessary* concomitant of the first result: as where (to use a much-quoted example) D blows up an aeroplane in flight in order to recover on the insurance covering the cargo, knowing that the crew will inevitably be killed. D intends to break the window and he intends the crew to be killed.

7.8 There is, of course, no absolute certainty in human affairs. D's purpose *might* be achieved without causing the further result; P *might* fling up the window while the brick is in flight; the crew *might* make a miraculous escape by parachute. These, however, are only remote possibilities, as D (if he contemplates them at all) must know. The further result will occur, and D knows that it will occur, "in the ordinary course of events". This expression was used in clause 18 of the Draft Code to express the near-inevitability, as appreciated by the actor, of the further result.

7.9 It is desirable to stress, because the point has been misunderstood in some quarters, that this way of defining "intention" does not have the effect of treating some cases of recklessness as cases of intention by extending liability for an offence requiring intention to every case where the actor foresees the further result as highly likely to occur. On the contrary, the definition extends the meaning of "intention" only very slightly beyond the primary meaning adopted in clause 1(a)(i) of "purpose". The point of the phrase "in the ordinary course of events" is to ensure that "intention" covers the case of a person who knows that the achievement of his purpose will *necessarily* cause the further result in question in the absence of some wholly improbable supervening event. The phrase had earlier been used by the CLRC [Fourteenth Report] in explaining their use of the word "intention" in the context of offences against the person. The Nathan Committee recommended adoption of the Draft Code definition for the purpose of the law of murder. The Lord Chief Justice expressed approval of it in the House of Lords debate on that committee's report.

7.10 Reference to "the ordinary course of events" can, therefore, now be made with some confidence in this part of the definition of "intention". That is the approach of clause 1(a)(ii) of the Criminal Law Bill. However, the Bill's definition, while being fundamentally that of the Draft Code, seeks to improve on and tighten the Draft Code in three respects.

7.11 First, in order to re-emphasise that this part of the definition is not dealing with a case of recklessness, it specifically requires the actor to *know*, and not merely to be aware (of a risk), that the further result would occur in the ordinary course of events if he succeeded in his purpose of causing the result at which he was actually aiming.

7.12 Second, the formulation has to cater for the case in which the actor is not sure that his main purpose will be achieved—he cannot be *sure*, for example, that the bomb that he places on the plane will, as he intends, go off in flight. In such a case he does not know that the secondary result (the death of the crew) will occur. Yet he ought to be guilty of murder if the crew do die because he knows that they *will* die *if* the bomb goes off as he intends. So the definition of "intention" should treat a person as intending a result that he knows to be, in the ordinary course of events, a necessary concomitant of achieving his main purpose *if* that purpose is achieved.

7.13 Third, it is prudent to provide specifically that a result that it is the actor's purpose to *avoid* cannot be intended. . . .

7.14 The extended definition of "intention" employed in clause 1(a)(ii) of the Criminal Law Bill thus takes account of the above three points. It makes plain that the definition is not confined to cases where the actor is certain that he will succeed in his principal objective. However, it treats as intended any result that the actor recognises at the time that he acts as inevitable if his purpose is to be achieved; and he is treated thereafter as having intended that result whether or not the purpose at which he aimed is in fact achieved.

3. MISTAKE

Notes

An area of the law that has been in an unsatisfactory state for some time is that of mistake. What effect does a mistake have on the liability of a defendant where his mistake relates to an element of the *actus reus* of the offence with which he is charged?

There are many mistakes which a defendant may make, some of which may be relevant to his ultimate liability. A mistake may be such as to negate the *mens rea* of the defendant in respect of a circumstance of the offence (*i.e.* an *actus reus* element). However, if *mens rea* is not required in respect of a particular circumstance, a mistake thereto may be of no relevance. A mistake may also be made with regard to circumstances which justify or excuse the commission of an offence such as pleas of self-defence or duress.

A question which has taxed judicial minds over the last century is whether a mistake must be a reasonable one before it serves to relieve a defendant of liability. Unfortunately the judicial answers to this question have differed, lacking consistency and coherent exposition of principle.

There are two basic categories into which mistakes may be grouped: *relevant* mistakes and *irrelevant* mistakes. Most uncertainty and inconsistency has arisen in respect of the first category.

i. Relevant Mistakes

A mistake is *relevant* where it relates to either a definitional element of the offence (*i.e.* an *actus reus* element) or a possible justificatory or excusatory claim (more generally referred to as defences). At one time, if a mistake was to operate to negate liability, it had to be a reasonable one. The House of Lords in *D.P.P. v. Morgan* (*infra*) opened the way for mistakes which were simply honest, although unreasonable, to operate to negate liability in certain circumstances. The effect of this decision, and the offspring it has generated, is that the category of relevant mistakes must now be divided into two sub-categories: mistakes which relate to definitional matters and those which relate to non-definitional matters.

(1) *Mistake as to a definitional element of the offence*

(a) Mistake negating *mens rea*

Where an offence requires intention or recklessness on the part of the defendant, may he be convicted if he makes a mistake as to one of the required circumstances of the offence, *i.e.* the definitional facts? In other words, does the *mens rea* requirement apply only to the doing of the act or does it also apply to the surrounding circumstances? Several cases established that where the word "wilfully" was used to define the *mens rea* requirement, a mistake as to the surrounding circumstances would act to negate the defendant's *mens rea* (see *Eaton v. Cobb* [1950] 1 All E.R. 1016; *Wilson v. Inyang* [1951] 2 K.B. 799; *Bullock v. Turnbull* [1952] 2 Lloyd's Rep. 303; *Willmott v. Atack* [1977] Q.B. 498; *Ostler v. Elliott* [1980] Crim.L.R. 584; but *cf. Cotterill v. Penn* [1936] 1 K.B. 53).

Would the same result ensue where a statute required intention or recklessness?

James L.J., giving judgment in *R. v. Smith (David)* [1974] Q.B. 354, said of section 1(1) of the Criminal Damage Act 1971:

"Construing the language of [the] section we have no doubt that the *actus reus* is 'destroying or damaging any property belonging to another.' It is not possible to exclude the words 'belonging to another' which describe the 'property.' Applying the ordinary principles of *mens rea*, the intention and recklessness and the absence of lawful excuse required to constitute the offence have reference to property belonging to another. It follows that, in our judgment, no offence is committed under this section if a person destroys or causes damage to property belonging to another if he does so in the honest though mistaken belief that the property is his own, and provided that the belief is honestly held it is irrelevant to consider whether or not it is a justifiable belief."

Shortly after the decision in *Smith* the House of Lords was faced with the issue of which parts of the definition of an offence (all or some) are qualified by the requirement of a mental element, and whether a mistake as to such part must be *reasonable* if it is to affect the defendant's liability.

D.P.P. v. Morgan
[1976] A.C. 182
House of Lords

The appellant invited three friends to have intercourse with his wife telling them that her signs of resistance were not to be interpreted as lack of consent: she enjoyed it better that way. In fact she was not consenting and offered considerable resistance to her assailants who in turn used a considerable degree of force to overcome her resistance. The friends were charged with rape, the appellant with aiding and abetting. They appealed against the direction of the trial judge that their belief in her consent must be reasonable. The court of Appeal dismissed their appeals but gave leave to appeal to the House of Lords certifying the following question: "Whether in rape a defendant can properly be convicted notwithstanding that he in fact believed the woman consented, if such belief was not based on reasonable grounds."

LORD HAILSHAM OF ST MARYLEBONE: . . . If it be true, as the learned judge says [in his summing up to the jury] "in the first place," that the prosecution have to prove that

> "each defendant intended to have sexual intercourse without her consent, not merely that he intended to have intercourse with her but that he intended to have intercourse without her consent",

the defendant must be entitled to an acquittal if the prosecution fail to prove just that. The necessary mental ingredient will be lacking and the only possible verdict is "not guilty". If, on the other hand, as is asserted in the passage beginning "secondly", it is necessary for any belief in the woman's consent to be "a reasonable belief" before the defendant is entitled to an acquittal, it must either be because the mental ingredient in rape is not "to have intercourse and to have it without her consent" but simply "to have intercourse" subject to a special defence of "honest and reasonable belief", or alternatively to have intercourse without a reasonable belief in her consent. Counsel for the Crown argued for each of these alternatives, but in my view each is open to insuperable objections of principle. No doubt it would be possible, by statute, to devise a law by which intercourse, voluntarily entered into, was an absolute offence, subject to a "defence" or belief whether honest or honest and reasonable, of which the "evidential" burden is primarily on the defence and the "probative" burden on the prosecution. But in my opinion such is not the crime of rape as it has hitherto been understood. The prohibited act in rape is to have intercourse without the victim's consent. The minimum *mens rea* or guilty mind in most common law offences, including rape, is the intention to do the prohibited act, and that is correctly stated in the proposition stated "in the first place" of the judge's direction. . . .

The only qualification I would make to the direction of the learned judge's "in the first place" is the refinement for which . . . there is both Australian and English authority, that if the intention of the accused is to have intercourse *nolens volens*, that is recklessly and not caring whether the victim be a consenting party or not, that is equivalent on ordinary principles to an intent to do the prohibited act without the consent of the victim.

The alternative version of the learned judge's direction would read that the accused must do the prohibited act with the intention of doing it without an honest and reasonable belief in the victim's consent. This in effect is the version which took up most of the time in argument, and although I find the Court of Appeal's judgment difficult to understand, I think it the version which ultimately commended itself to that court. At all events I think it the more plausible way in which to state the learned judge's "secondly". In principle, however, I find it unacceptable. I believe that *"mens rea"* means "guilty or criminal mind", and if it be the case, as seems to be accepted here, that mental element in rape is not knowledge but intent, to insist that a belief must be reasonable to excuse is to insist that either the accused is to be found guilty of intending to do that which in truth he did not intend to do, or that his state of mind, though innocent of evil intent, can convict him if it be honest but not rational. . . .

I believe the law on this point to have been correctly stated by Lord Goddard C.J. in *R. v. Steane* [1947] K.B. 997, 1004, (*ante*, p. 90) when he said:

> ". . . if on the totality of the evidence there is room for more than one view as to the intent of the prisoner, the jury should be directed that it is for the prosecution to prove the intent to the jury's satisfaction, and

if, on a review of the whole evidence, they either think that the intent did not exist or they are left in doubt as to the intent, the prisoner is entitled to be acquitted."

That was indeed, a case which involved a count where a specific, or, as Professor Smith has called it, an ulterior, intent was, and was required to be, charged in the indictment. But, once it be accepted that an intent of whatever description is an ingredient essential to the guilt of the accused I cannot myself see that any other direction can be logically acceptable. Otherwise a jury would in effect be told to find an intent where none existed or where none was proved to have existed. I cannot myself reconcile it with my conscience to sanction as part of the English law what I regard as logical impossibility, and, if there were any authority which, if accepted would compel me to do so, I would feel constrained to declare that it was not to be followed. However for reasons which I will give, I do not see any need in the instant case for such desperate remedies.

The beginning of wisdom in all the *"mens rea"* cases to which our attention was called is, as pointed out by Stephen J. in *R. v. Tolson* (1889) 23 Q.B.D. 168, that *"mens rea"* means a number of quite different things in relation to different crimes. . . . It follows from this, surely, that it is logically impermissible, as the Crown sought to do in this case, to draw a necessary inference from decisions in relation to offences where *mens rea* means one thing, and cases where it means another, and in particular from decisions on the construction of statutes, whether these be related to bigamy, abduction or the possession of drugs, and decisions in relation to common law offences. It is equally impermissible to draw direct or necessary inferences from decisions where the *mens rea* is, or includes, a state of opinion, and cases where it is limited to intention (a distinction I referred to in *R. v. Hyam* (*ante*, p. 93) or between cases where there is a special "defence," like self-defence or provocation and cases where the issue relates to the primary intention which the prosecution has to prove.

Once one has accepted, what seems to be abundantly clear, that the prohibited act in rape is non-consensual sexual intercourse, and that the guilty state of mind is an intention to commit it, it seems to me to follow as a matter of inexorable logic that there is no room either for a "defence" of honest belief or mistake, or of a defence of honest and reasonable belief or mistake. Either the prosecution proves that the accused had the requisite intent, or it does not. In the former case it succeeds, and in the latter it fails. Since honest belief clearly negatives intent, the reasonableness or otherwise of that belief can only be evidence for or against the view that the belief and therefore the intent was actually held, and it matters not whether, to quote Bridge J. in the passage cited above, "the definition of a crime includes no specific element beyond the prohibited act". If the mental element be primarily an intention and not a state of belief it comes within his second proposition and not his third. Any other view, as for insertion of the word "reasonable" can only have the effect of saying that a man intends something which he does not.

By contrast, the appellants invited us to overrule the bigamy cases from *R. v. Tolson* onwards and perhaps also *R. v. Prince*, L.R. 2 C.C.R. 154 (the abduction case) as wrongly decided at least in so far as they purport to insist that a mistaken belief must be reasonable. . . .

Although it is undoubtedly open to this House to reconsider *R. v. Tolson* and the bigamy cases, and perhaps *R. v. Prince* which may stand or fall with them, I must respectfully decline to do so in the present case. Nor is it necessary that I should. I am not prepared to assume that the statutory offences of bigamy or abduction are necessarily on all fours with rape, and before I was prepared to undermine a whole line of cases which have been accepted as law for so long, I would need argument in the context of a case expressly relating to the relevant offences. I am content to rest my view of the instant case on the crime of rape by saying that it is my opinion that the prohibited act is and always has been intercourse without consent of the victim and the mental element is and always has been the intention to commit that act, or the equivalent intention of having intercourse willy-nilly not caring whether the victim consents or no. A failure to prove this involves an acquittal because the intent, an essential ingredient, is lacking. It matters not why it is lacking if only it is not there, and in particular it matters not that the intention is lacking only because of a belief not based on reasonable grounds. I should add that I myself am inclined to view *R. v. Tolson* as a narrow decision based on the construction of a statute, which prima facie seemed to make an absolute statutory offence, with a proviso, related to the seven-year period of absence, which created a statutory defence. The judges in *R. v. Tolson* decided that this was not reasonable, and, on general jurisprudential principles, imported into the statutory offence words which created a special "defence" of honest and reasonable belief of which the "evidential" but not the probative burden lay on the defence. I do not think it is necessary to decide this conclusively in the present case. But if this is the true view there is a complete distinction between *Tolson* and the other cases based in statute and the present.

I may also add that I am not impressed with the analogy based on the decision in *Wilson v. Inyang* [1951] 2 K.B. 799, 803 which has attracted the attention of some academic authors. That clearly depends on the construction of the words "wilfully and falsely" where they are used in the relevant statute. Also, though I get some support from what I have been saying from the reasoning of the decision in *R. v. Smith (David)* (*post*, p. 911), I nevertheless regard that case as a decision on the Criminal Damage Act 1971, rather than a decision covering the whole law of criminal liability.

For the above reasons I would answer the question certified in the negative, but would apply the proviso to the Criminal Appeal Act on the ground that no miscarriage of justice has or conceivably could have occurred.

Appeal dismissed

Note

The decision in *Morgan* promoted the subjectivist view of criminal liability as opposed to the objectivist approach. The extract below presents a critique of *Morgan* in the context of an article which seeks to identify a more helpful middle ground between the extremes of objectivism and subjectivism.

Richard H.S. Tur, "Subjectivism and Objectivism: Towards Synthesis" in Shute *et al*, *Action and Value in Criminal Law* (1993) 213.

The starting-point in the moral assessment of any offence must be with the definition of that offence. Prior to the decision in *Morgan*, the definition of rape in English criminal law was distinctly minimalist. As Humphreys J put it in *R v. Turner* [[1944] KB 463, 469]: "on a charge of rape the Crown has to prove two things: intercourse and the non-consent of the woman." On this definition, the intercourse had to be intentional, which of its very nature it is most likely to be, but the defendant's perception of the victim's state of mind was relevant, if at all, only at the defence stage of proceedings. On that basis, any mistake about the woman's consent would be a mistake as to a circumstance not qualified by *mens rea*—i.e. Tolson-mistake—and therefore the mistake would have to be reasonable. The question to ask of this model of rape—minimalist definition plus external defence—is whether it produces ethically acceptable outcomes and, if so, what, if anything, is unsatisfactory about it?

Consider a hypothetical character, Adonis. He strongly believes that he is irresistible to women. Thus, believing that no woman could say "No" to him, Adonis has sexual intercourse with a non-consenting woman, but such is the strength of his belief that he misinterprets her resistance and does not register her protests. Adonis honestly believes that the woman consented. Given the definition in *R v. Turner*, together with the *Tolson* requirement that mistake be reasonable, Adonis would be guilty of rape.

Morgan changed all that: "it is no longer disputed that, in England, perception of the woman's consent is an aspect of the mental element in crimes of rape." [*Pappajohn v. R* (1980) 111 DLR (3d) 1, *per* Dickson J. at 11.] The effect of this definitional revision is that Adonis must now be acquitted on a charge of rape because, as a matter of "inexorable logic", an actual belief in consent is incompatible with the existence in the mind of the accused of the (newly) required mental element and the prosecution must fail because it cannot (now) prove all the definitional elements of the offence. Although an acquittal is logically inescapable given the widened definition, there was no a priori necessity to adopt that definition.

The question to ask of the extended *Morgan* definition is in what ways, if any, it is preferable to the *Turner* definition (plus *Tolson* defence). On moral grounds alone it is difficult to see the *Morgan* redefinition as other than a retrograde step: "it can be argued with force that it is only fair to the woman and not in the least unfair to the man that he should be under a duty to take reasonable care to ascertain that she is consenting to the intercourse and be at the risk of a prosecution if he fails to take care." [*per* Lord Cross, at 203B.] Powerful reasons might properly be expected from those who would depart from this moral principle.

The judgments in support of this departure are, however, very disappointing. There is little serious consideration of the social and moral merits of the alternative definitions of rape. Lord Cross founded his decision upon the alleged meaning of rape "according to the ordinary use of the English language"; Lord Fraser relied on an unargued assertion about "forms of immoral conduct . . . not intended to be struck at by the law against rape"; and Lord Hailsham proceeded on the basis of "what seems . . . abundantly clear, that the prohibited act in rape is non-consensual intercourse, and that the guilty state of mind is an intention to commit it". [*per* Lord Cross, at 203B.]

If it is allowed that the mental element in rape includes a perception of the woman's consent, then an honest belief in consent, no matter how unreasonable, necessitates acquittal because it entails the absence of the requisite mental element. The legal argument from that point on is impeccable, but the legal argument for that point is weak and unpersuasive. The House of Lords had a free and unconstrained choice between the two definitions and its adoption of the maximalist approach was not required by logic nor by legal precedent, and is difficult to justify on moral grounds. Ordinarily, on reaching such a conclusion, a commentator on the common law might advocate overruling the unsatisfactory precedent, but that option is foreclosed in England by section 1 of the Sexual Offences (Amendment) Act 1976 which puts the *Morgan* redefinition on a statutory footing.

In view of the reservations that can legitimately be expressed about its *ratio*, it is not surprising that *Morgan has not been very popular and that various attempts have been made to circumvent it. The Morgan* principle actually availed the accused nothing in that the House of Lords applied the proviso, taking the view that the alleged belief was so unreasonable as to be incredible. That move is not available to secure a conviction of Adonis, however, because *ex hypothesi* he does believe that the woman is consenting. . . .

The Canadian Supreme Court qualified the *Morgan* principle in *Pappajohn v. R,* holding that there was no room nor need for the *Morgan* direction unless there was extrinsic evidence supportive of the defendant's claim honestly to have believed that the woman was consenting. In *R v. Taylor,* [(1984) 80 Cr.App.Rep. 327] the English Court of Criminal Appeal adopted substantially the same reasoning and conclusion, though the Canadian case was not mentioned. The general issue was whether the *Morgan* direction on honest belief must always be put to the jury and, if not, when it may be dispensed with.

The court held that in cases of conflicting testimony, where the jury finds that there is evidence of non-consent, and there is no extrinsic evidence supportive of the defendant's claim, there is no room for any so-called defence of honest belief and no need to put the *Morgan* direction to the jury. Just as honest belief is inconsistent with the *mens rea* of the offence, as defined in *Morgan,* so that *mens rea* is inconsistent with honest belief. "Inexorable logic" runs both ways. If, therefore, the jury concludes on all the evidence that any ordinary person in the position of the accused must have realized that the woman was not consenting; that the accused, as an ordinary person, must have so realized and therefore did; then there is no room in the accused's mind for the logically incompatible belief in consent. The doctrinal question is whether *Taylor* qualifies *Morgan* or contradicts it. That is a matter for the House of Lords in the fullness of time. The effect of current English criminal law up to the Court of Appeal would be to convict Adonis so long as his belief in the woman's consent rested merely on his own wishful thinking and mere *ipse dixit.*

If, on moral grounds, one believes that Adonis should be convicted, one is committed to conviction in the absence of *Morgan mens rea.* English criminal law already adopts that position in the case of intoxicated mistake as is illustrated in *R v. Fotheringham* [1988] Crim. LR 846]. If that is morally acceptable then so, too, is conviction of the sober man who makes an unreasonable mistake. That moral commitment calls for restoration of the *Turner* definition and the *Tolson* defence, and this discussion of rape illustrates that definition and redefinition of offences is not merely a matter of dry legal technique for committees of lawyers to determine, but one of pressing moral (and public) concern. With respect, moral commitments should determine legal definitions and not vice versa.

Note

Whilst *Morgan* dealt with the issue of mistakes in relation to the offence of rape, the question which remained to be answered was whether the principle enunciated therein also applied to honest but unreasonable mistakes in respect of definitional elements in other offences. At first, in *Phekoo* [1981] 1 W.L.R. 1117, the Court of Appeal held that *Morgan* was confined to the offence of rape and mistakes as to definitional elements in other offences had to be based on reasonable grounds if they were to operate to negate liability.

In the case below the Court of Appeal considered whether the *Morgan* principles applied where the appellant was charged with indecent assault.

R. v. Kimber
[1983] 1 W.L.R. 1118
Court of Appeal

LAWTON L.J. read the following judgment of the court: The appeal raises these points. First, can a defendant charged with an indecent assault on a woman raise the defence that he believed she had consented to what he did? The trial judge, Mr Recorder Smyth Q.C. ruled that he could not. Secondly, if he could, did the jury have to consider merely whether his belief was honestly held or, if it was, did they have to go on to consider whether it was based on reasonable grounds? Another way of putting these points is to ask whether the principles upon which the House of Lords decided *R. v. Morgan* [1976] A.C. 182 should be applied to a charge of indecent assault on a woman....

The burden of proving lack of consent rests upon the prosecution.... The consequence is that the prosecution has to prove that the defendant intended to lay hands on his victim without her consent. If he did not intend to do this, he is entitled to be found not guilty; and if he did not so intend because he believed she was consenting, the prosecution will have failed to prove the charge. It is the defendant's belief, not the grounds on which it was based, which goes to negative the intent.

In analysing the issue in this way we have followed what was said by the majority in *R. v. Morgan* [1976] A.C. 182: see Lord Hailsham of St Marylebone at p. 214F–H and Lord Fraser of Tullybelton at p. 237E–G. If, as we adjudge, the prohibited act in indecent assault is the use of personal violence to a woman without her consent, then the guilty state of mind is the intent to do it without her consent. Then, as in rape at common law, the inexorable logic, to which Lord Hailsham referred in *R. v. Morgan*, takes over and there is no room either for a "defence" of honest belief or mistake, or of a "defence" of honest and reasonable belief or mistake: [1976] A.C. 182, 214F–H.

The decision in *R. v. Morgan*, probably because of its sordid facts and the improbability of the defence raised, caused unease amongst lawyers and some members of the public. Parliament reacted by passing the Sexual Offences (Amendment) Act 1976. The courts from time to time have shown a propensity to distinguish other offences from the common law concept of rape so as to avoid having to follow the reasoning in *R. v. Morgan*. This has been described by one academic writer as "The Retreat from *Morgan*" (see Cowley [1982] Crim.LR., 198). Since each case must be decided after careful analysis as to what constituted a prohibited act and what is the nature of the *mens rea*, if any, which has to be proved, a detailed consideration of these cases would be *obiter* for the purposes of this judgment. In these circumstances we do not intend to adjudge whether these cases were correctly decided or to attempt to distinguish them from this case. The application of the *Morgan* principle to offences other than indecent assault on a woman will have to be considered when such offences come before the courts. We do, however, think it necessary to consider two of them because of what was said in the judgments. The first is a decision of the Divisional Court in *Albert v. Lavin* [1982] A.C. 546. The offence charged was assaulting a police officer in the execution of his duty, contrary to section 51 of the Police Act 1964. The defendant in his defence contended, *inter alia*, that he had not believed the police officer to be such and in consequence had resisted arrest. His counsel analysed the offence in the same way as we have done and referred to the reasoning in *Morgan*. Hodgson J., delivering the leading judgment, rejected this argument and in doing so said, at pp. 561–562:

> "But in my judgment Mr Walker's ingenious argument fails at an earlier stage. It does not seem to me that the element of unlawfulness can

properly be regarded as part of the definitional elements of the offence. In defining a criminal offence the word 'unlawful' is surely tautologous and can add nothing to its essential ingredients . . . And no matter how strange it may seem that a defendant charged with assault can escape conviction if he shows that he mistakenly but unreasonably thought his victim was consenting but not if he was in the same state of mind as to whether his victim had a right to detain him, that in my judgment is the law."

We have found difficulty in agreeing with this reasoning, even though the judge seems to be accepting that belief in consent does entitle a defendant to an acquittal on a charge of assault. We cannot accept that the word "unlawful" when used in a definition of an offence is to be regarded as "tautologous". In our judgment the word "unlawful" does import an essential element into the offence. If it were not there social life would be unbearable, because every touching would amount to a battery unless there was an evidential basis for a defence. This case was considered by the House of Lords. The appeal was dismissed, but their Lordships declined to deal with the issue of belief.

In *R. v. Phekoo* [1981] 1 W.L.R. 1117 . . . [Hollings J., refering to *Morgan* stated] "It seems to us clear that this decision was confined and intended to be confined to the offence of rape." We do not accept that this was the intention of their Lordships in *Morgan's* case. Lord Hailsham of St Marylebone started his speech by saying that the issue as to belief was a question of great academic importance in the theory of English criminal law.

In our judgment the recorder should have directed the jury that the prosecution had to make them sure that the appellant never had believed that [the woman] was consenting. As he did not do so, the jury never considered an important aspect of his defence.

[Lawton J., however, concluded that no reasonable jury, properly directed, would have accepted the appellant's account and that he was, at least, reckless as to whether the woman was consenting. Accordingly, there had been no miscarriage of justice.]

Appeal dismissed

(b) Mistake as to a justificatory claim

Where a defendant has, *prima facie*, committed the offence charged, having brought about the *actus reus* with the requisite *mens rea*, will a claim of justification serve to negate his liability where it is based upon a mistaken belief. For example, if D intentionally wounds X in the mistaken belief that X is about to attack him, will his plea of self-defence succeed to negate his liability where it is an honestly held belief or must the belief also be a reasonable one?

In *Albert v. Lavin* [1982] A.C. 546, the Divisional Court held that a mistaken belief on the part of the defendant that his act was justified on the basis of self-defence, had to be based on reasonable grounds. Is a claim of justification something separate from the definitional elements of an offence? If so there might be some reason in principle for requiring such mistakes to be reasonable. Alternatively, is the absence of a justificatory claim part of the definitional elements of the offence? If so, does *Morgan* apply or is it to be confined to rape and kindred offences. Glanville Williams has been a strong proponent of the second view.

Williams, T.C.L. p. 138

No other rule of the substantive criminal law distinguishes between the definitional and defence elements of a crime, and it is a distinction that it is impossible to draw satisfactorily. A rule creating a *defence* merely supplies additional details of the scope of the *offence*. To regard the offence as subsisting independently of its limitations and qualifications is unrealistic. The defence is a negative condition of the offence, and is therefore an integral part of it. What we regard as part of the offence and what as part of a defence depends only on traditional habits of thought or accidents of legal drafting; it should have no bearing on the important question of criminal liability. For example, it is purely a matter of convenient drafting whether a statute says, on the one hand, that damaging the property of another without his consent is a crime, or, on the other hand, that damaging the property of another is a crime but that his consent is a defence. In fact we regard the non-consent of the owner as a definitional element, but there is no particular reason why this should be so, and the question of guilt or innocence should not depend on it (see 2 Leg.Stud. 233).

This view was echoed in the Court of Appeal in the following case.

R. v. Williams (Gladstone)
(1984) 78 Cr.App.R. 276
Court of Appeal

Mason saw a youth rob a woman. He chased and caught him but the youth broke free. The appellant then witnessed Mason catch the youth again and knock him to the ground. Mason told the appellant that he was a police officer (which was untrue) and that he was arresting the youth for mugging a woman. The appellant asked to see his warrant card. When Mason failed to produce one, a struggle ensued, during which the appellant punched Mason in the face. He was charged with assault occasioning actual bodily harm. He claimed that he honestly believed that the youth was being unlawfully assaulted by Mason and that he was trying to rescue him. As Mason was acting lawfully, the appellant had made a mistake. The jury were directed that his mistake would be relevant if it was honest and based on reasonable grounds. He was convicted and appealed on the ground that the judge had misdirected the jury.

LORD LANE C.J. gave the judgment of the court: "Assault" . . . is an act by which the defendant, intentionally or recklessly, applies unlawful force to the complainant. There are circumstances in which force may be applied to another lawfully. Taking a few examples: first, where the victim consents, as in lawful sports, the application of force to another will, generally speaking, not be unlawful. Secondly, where the defendant is acting in self-defence: the exercise of any necessary and reasonable force to protect himself from unlawful violence is not unlawful. Thirdly, by virtue of section 3 of the Criminal Law Act 1967, a person may use such force as is reasonable in the circumstances in the prevention of crime or in effecting or assisting in the lawful arrest of an offender or suspected offender or persons unlawfully at large. In each of those cases the defendant will be guilty if the jury are sure that first of all he applied force to the person of another, and secondly that he had the necessary mental element to constitute guilt.

The mental element necessary to constitute guilt is the intent to apply unlawful force to the victim. We do not believe that the mental element can be substantiated by simply showing an intent to apply force and no more.

What then is the situation if the defendant is labouring under a mistake of fact as to the circumstances? What if he believes, but believes mistakenly, that the victim is consenting, or that it is necessary to defend himself, or that a crime is being committed which he intends to prevent? He must then be judged against the mistaken facts as he believes them to be. If judged against those facts or circumstances the prosecution fail to establish his guilt, then he is entitled to be acquitted.

The next question is, does it make any difference if the mistake of the defendant was one which, viewed objectively by a reasonable onlooker, was an unreasonable mistake? . . .

It is upon this point that the large volume of historical precedent . . . is concerned. But in our judgment the answer is provided by the judgment of this Court in *Kimber* (*ante*, p. 157) by which . . . we are bound . . .

We respectfully agree with what Lawton L.J. said [in *Kimber*] with regard both to the way in which the defence should have been put and also with regard to his remarks as to the nature of the defence. The reasonableness or unreasonableness of the defendant's belief is material to the question of whether the belief was held by the defendant at all. If the belief was in fact held, its unreasonableness, so far as guilt or innocence is concerned, is neither here nor there. It is irrelevant. Were it otherwise, the defendant would be convicted because he was negligent in failing to recognise that the victim was not consenting or that a crime was not being committed and so on. In other words the jury should be directed first of all that the prosecution have the burden or duty of proving the unlawfulness of the defendant's actions; secondly, if the defendant may have been labouring under a mistake as to the facts, he must be judged according to his mistaken view of the facts; thirdly, that is so whether the mistake was, on an objective view, a reasonable mistake or not.

In a case of self-defence, where self-defence or the prevention of crime is concerned, if the jury came to the conclusion that the defendant believed, or may have believed, that he was being attacked or that a crime was being committed, and that force was necessary to protect himself or to prevent the crime, then the prosecution have not proved their case. If however the defendant's alleged belief was mistaken and if the mistake was an unreasonable one, that may be a powerful reason for coming to the conclusion that the belief was not honestly held and should be rejected.

Even if the jury come to the conclusion that the mistake was an unreasonable one, if the defendant may genuinely have been labouring under it, he is entitled to rely upon it.

We have read the recommendations of the Criminal Law Revision Committee, Part IX, paragraph 72(a), in which the following passage appears: "The common law defence of self-defence should be replaced by a statutory defence providing that a person may use such force as is reasonable in the circumstances as he believes them to be in the defence of himself or any other person." In the view of this Court that represents the law as expressed in *D.P.P. v. Morgan* and in *Kimber* and we do not think that the decision of the Divisional Court in *Albert v. Lavin* from which we have cited can be supported.

Appeal allowed
Conviction quashed

Williams was considered in *R. v. O'Grady* [1987] 3 W.L.R. 321, C.A. (*post*, p. 273). The Judicial Committee of the Privy Council reviewed the whole area in the following case.

Beckford v. R.
[1988] A.C. 130
Privy Council

At the appellant's trial for murder the judge directed the jury that if the appellant had a *reasonable* belief that his life was in danger or that he was in danger of serious bodily injury he was entitled to be acquitted on the grounds of self-defence.

LORD GRIFFITHS: . . . It is accepted by the prosecution that there is no difference on the law of self-defence between the law of Jamaica and the English common law and it therefore falls to be decided whether it was correctly decided by the Court of Appeal in *R. v. Williams* (*ante*, p. 159) that the defence of self-defence depends upon what the accused "honestly" believed the circumstances to be and not upon the reasonableness of that belief—what the Court of Appeal in Jamaica referred to as the "honest belief" and "reasonable belief" schools of thought.

There can be no doubt that prior to the decision of the House of Lords in *R. v. Morgan* (*ante*, p. 151) the whole weight of authority supported the view that it was an essential element of self-defence not only that the accused believed that he was being attacked or in imminent danger of being attacked but also that such belief was based on reasonable grounds.

The question then is whether the present Lord Chief Justice, Lord Lane, in *R. v. Williams*, was right to depart from the law as declared by his predecessors in the light of the decision of the House of Lords in *R. v. Morgan*. . . .

The common law recognises that there are many circumstances in which one person may inflict violence upon another without committing a crime, as for instance, in sporting contests, surgical operations or in the most extreme example judicial execution. The common law has always recognised as one of these circumstances the right of a person to protect himself from attack and to act in the defence of others and if necessary to inflict violence on another in so doing. If no more force is used than is reasonable to repel the attack such force is not unlawful and no crime is committed. Furthermore a man about to be attacked does not have to wait for his assailant to strike the first blow or fire the first shot; circumstances may justify a pre-emptive strike.

It is because it is an essential element of all crimes of violence that the violence or the threat of violence should be unlawful that self-defence, if raised as an issue in a criminal trial, must be disproved by the prosecution. If the prosecution fail to do so the accused is entitled to be acquitted because the prosecution will have failed to prove an essential element of the crime namely that the violence used by the accused was unlawful.

If then a genuine belief, albeit without reasonable grounds, is a defence to rape because it negatives the necessary intention, so also must a genuine belief in facts which if true would justify self-defence be a defence to a crime of personal violence because the belief negates the intent to act unlawfully. Their Lordships therefore approve . . . *R. v. Williams*, as correctly stating the law of self defence. . . .

Looking back, *R. v. Morgan* can now be seen as a landmark decision in the development of the common law returning the law to the path upon which it might have developed but for the inability of an accused to give evidence on his own behalf. . . .

There may be a fear that the abandonment of the objective standard demanded by the existence of reasonable grounds for belief will result in the success of too many spurious claims of self-defence. The English experience has not shown this to be the case. The Judicial Studies Board with the approval of the Lord Chief Justice has produced a model direction on self-defence which is now widely used by judges when summing up to juries. The direction contains the following guidance:

"Whether the plea is self-defence or defence of another, if the defendant may have been labouring under a mistake as to the facts, he must be judged according to his mistaken belief of the facts: that is so whether the mistake was, on an objective view, a reasonable mistake or not."

Their Lordships have heard no suggestion that this form of summing up has resulted in a disquieting number of acquittals. This is hardly surprising for no jury is going to accept a man's assertion that he believed that he was about to be attacked without testing it against all the surrounding circumstances. In assisting the jury to determine whether or not the accused had a genuine belief the judge will of course direct their attention to those features of the evidence that make such a belief more or less probable. Where there are no reasonable grounds to hold a belief it will surely only be in exceptional circumstances that a jury will conclude that such a belief was or might have been held.

Their Lordships therefore conclude that the summing up in this case contained a material misdirection and . . . the test to be applied for self-defence is that a person may use such force as is reasonable in the circumstances as he honestly believes them to be in the defence of himself or another.

Appeal allowed

Note

See further the discussion of *Scarlett* [1994] 3 All E.R. 629, *post*, p. 364 and *Owino* [1995] Crim. L.R. 743, *post*, p. 366.

(c) The Problem of *Tolson*

The offence of bigamy under section 57 of the Offences Against the Person Act 1861 is committed where a person "being married, shall marry any other person during the life of the former husband or wife". A proviso to the section provides that it shall not extend to a person marrying a second time where their "husband or wife shall have been continually absent from such person for the space of seven years then last past, and shall not have been known by such person to be living within that time" or where the first marriage has been annulled or dissolved. In *Tolson* (1889) 23 Q.B.D. 168, a wife remarried five years after last seeing her husband whom she believed to have been lost at sea. She was charged with bigamy when it was discovered that he was still alive. She was convicted as she did not come within the proviso although the jury found that she believed on reasonable grounds and in good faith that he was dead. The Court for Crown Cases Reserved by a majority quashed her conviction importing into the statute a defence based on honest and reasonable belief. Cave J. stated (at p. 181):

"At common law an honest and reasonable belief in the existence of circumstances, which, if true, would make the act for which a prisoner is indicted an innocent act has always been held to be a good defence."

The defence would apply to statutory offences unless excluded expressly or by necessary implication. In *Gould* [1968] 2 Q.B. 65, it was held that a reasonable belief that the first marriage had been dissolved was also a defence. The effect is to make bigamy an offence of strict liability in respect of the element of "being married" to which a defence of "no negligence" may be raised.

When a statute creates an offence it does not recapitulate all the defences traditionally allowed by the criminal law; yet it must have been the intention of Parliament that these defences should apply. Similarly, since the requirement of *mens rea* is a traditional principle of law, for serious crimes, it is reasonable to suppose that Parliament meant it to govern the statute.

Stephen J. stated this argument in a much-quoted passage. It is too long to reproduce, but may be summarised. The judge begins by saying that 'the full definition of every crime contains a proposition as to a state of mind'. Then he spells this out again by saying that if the mental element is absent there is no crime; and he clearly means this proposition to apply to crimes created by statute as well as at common law, so that all alike require a mental element. There follows a series of instances showing that where a person does not know a fact required for the crime he lacks the mental element and so cannot be guilty. Finally, however, the judge confines his proposition to cases where the defendant's belief that the facts were innocent was not merely in good faith but was based on reasonable grounds. This implies that if the defendant genuinely but unreasonably believed in the existence of justifying facts he has no defence, even though in that case he lacked the mental element that is supposed to be required. The reference to reasonable grounds departs from the purely subjective element that the judge has hitherto been propounding, and introduces an objective test. There is, therefore, a basic contradiction in the judgment. . . .

Stephen J. is assuming that the mental element required for a crime is knowledge of a particular fact, which we may call A (*e.g.* 'I am still married'). The defendant's defence is that he believed that the fact present was not-A ('I am not now married'). A defence of belief in not-A is of course the same thing as denying knowledge of A. But Stephen J. says that belief in not-A is no defence unless it is reasonable. If it is unreasonable, the defendant is convicted although he believed not-A, *i.e.* although he did not know A. Yet the judge says that the defendant must know A. So he contradicts himself: QED. His judgment would make a person guilty of bigamy although the only mental element was that of intending to enter into a valid marriage—a state of mind that almost all of us possess at some time in our lives.

Although the question of reasonable belief was not before the court in *Tolson*, and although Stephen J. and some other members of the court were clearly guilty of self-contradiction, the idea started in

Tolson was perpetuated in later bigamy cases. Time and again the judges have said that a mistake of fact, to be a defence to a charge of bigamy, must be reasonable.

Questions

1. In *Morgan* Lord Fraser said "bigamy does not involve any intention except the intention to go through a marriage ceremony"; if this is correct, wherein lies the guilty state of mind in bigamy which distinguishes a bigamist from every other person who marries?
2. Is there any justification in convicting a person of bigamy who mistakenly believes he or she is free to marry?

Note

In *Sweet v. Parsley* [1970] A.C. 132 (*post* p. 186), Lord Diplock referred to a general principle of construction of statutory offences in terms similar to those used in *Tolson* stating (at p.163):

"a general principle of construction of any enactment, which creates a criminal offence, [is] that, even where the words used to describe the prohibited conduct would not in any other context connote the necessity for any particular mental element, they are nevertheless to be read as subject to the implication that a necessary element in the offence is the absence of a belief, held honestly and upon reasonable grounds, in the existence of facts which, if true, would make the act innocent."

In *B. (A Minor) v D.P.P.* [2000] 2 W.L.R. 452 (*post* p. 193), the House of Lords had to answer the following questions certified by the Divisional Court as points of law of general public importance:

"1. Is a defendant entitled to be acquitted of the offence of inciting a child aged under 14 to commit an act of gross indecency, contrary to section 1(1) of the Indecency with Children Act 1960, if he may hold an honest belief that the child in question was aged 14 years or over? 2. If yes, (a) must the belief be held on reasonable grounds? (b) On whom does the burden of proof lie?"

Their Lordships answered question 1. in the affirmative, question 2.(a) in the negative and question 2.(b) the prosecution. Lord Nicholls of Birkenhead referred to *Tolson* but did not overrule it. Both Lord Nicholls and Lord Steyn referred to Lord Diplock's dictum in *Sweet v. Parsley* which they considered in light of the later decisions in *Morgan*, *Kimber*, *Williams (Gladstone)* and *Beckford* and concluded that his formulation of the common law presumption was out of step with these cases in so far as it required that a mistaken belief had to be based on reasonable grounds. Lord Nicholls stated (at pp.457-8):

"This seems to be a relic from the days before a defendant in a criminal case could give evidence in his own defence. It is not surprising that in those times juries judged a defendant's state of mind by the conduct to be expected of a reasonable person.

[T]he traditional formulation of the common law presumption must now be modified appropriately. Otherwise the formulation would not be an accurate reflection of the current state of the criminal law regarding mistakes of fact. Lord Diplock's dictum . . . must in future be read as though the reference to reasonable grounds were omitted."

Lord Steyn stated (at p.471):

"There has been a general shift from objectivism to subjectivism in this branch of the law. It is now settled as a matter of general principle that mistake, whether reasonable or not, is a defence where it prevents the defendant from having the mens rea which the law requires for the crime with which he is charged. It would be in disharmony with this development now to rule that in respect of a defence under section 1(1) of the Act of 1960 the belief must be based on reasonable grounds. Moreover, if such a special solution were to be adopted, it would almost certainly create uncertainty in other parts of the criminal law. It would be difficult to confine it on a principled basis to section1(1)."

Tolson appears to be an aberrant decision, limited to bigamy, and awaiting the right circumstances to arise for it to be overruled.

(2) *Mistake as to a non-definitional element*, i.e. *as to an excusatory claim*

Peter Alldridge, "The Coherence of Defences" [1983] Crim.L.R. 665–666

The basis of a claim of justification is that it speaks to the act, a claim of excuse to whether the actor is properly regarded as responsible for it. A claim of justification involves saying, 'I am responsible for what was done, but I am not an appropriate object for punishment because what was done, although an invasion of an interest of another which is generally protected by the criminal law, was done in circumstances which gave me a legal right to do it.' The reason for there being such a legal right is that the behaviour was such as should be encouraged (carrying out the order of the court, arresting offenders, preventing crime, some instances of necessity, consent), or at the very least legally tolerated (self-defence, other cases of consent). The claim of excuse is a different sort of claim altogether. Here D admits, 'There was an unjustified invasion of a legally protected interest.' But s/he says, 'the normal inference from the fact that my action caused the invasion to the conclusion that I am responsible for it ought not to be drawn: some factor operates which makes that normal inference unwarranted.'

[A]n exculpatory defence must be an excuse or justification but cannot be both. The point of the claim of justification is that D was a responsible actor. Knowledge of sufficient circumstances to make the invasion of P's interest tolerable, and thus establish the right to invade it, is itself a prerequisite of that right. The point of a claim of excuse is that D was not a responsible actor. A coherent defence cannot contain elements the rationale of which is that D was a responsible actor, together with elements whose rationale is that D was not.

Fletcher, *Rethinking Criminal Law*, pp. 798–800, 810–812

THE THEORY OF EXCUSES

Interposing a claim of excuse concedes that there is a wrong to be excused. The claim challenges the attribution of the wrongdoing to the actor. If the excuse is valid, then, as a matter of definition, the actor is not accountable or culpable for the wrongful act. The focus of the excuse is not on the act in the abstract, but on the circumstances of the act and the actor's personal capacity to avoid either an intentional wrong or the taking of an excessive risk. Insanity and involuntary intoxication are paradigmatic excuses. Duress and necessity are regarded as excuses in some legal systems, but not in others. . . .

In a case of justified conduct, the act typically reflects well on the actor's courage or devotion to the public interest. If he disables an aggressor in order to save the life of another, his conduct speaks well for his courage; if as a police officer he disables a felon seeking to escape, his conduct testifies at least to his devotion to duty. Justifications require good reasons for violating the prohibitory norm; someone who chooses to act on these reasons is likely to deserve respect and praise rather than blame.

The distinguishing feature of excusing conditions is that they preclude an inference from the act to the actor's character. Typically, if a bank teller opens a safe and turns money over to a stranger, we can infer that he is dishonest. But if he does all this at gunpoint, we cannot infer anything one way or the other about his honesty. Typically, if a driver knowingly runs over someone lying in the roadway, we might infer something about the driver's indifference to human life. But we cannot make that inference if the choice open to the driver was going over a cliff or continuing down the incline and running over someone lying in the roadway. Similarly, if someone violates a legal prohibition under an unavoidable mistake about the legality of his conduct, we cannot infer anything about his respect for law and the rights of others. The same breakdown in the reasoning from conduct to character occurs in cases of insanity, for it is implicit in the medical conception of insanity that the actor's true character is distorted by his mental illness. . . .

The single most difficult point in the theory of excuses is the relationship between excuses and the norms that govern our conduct. The nature of a justification is that the claim is grounded in an implicit exception to the prohibitory norm. The 'right' of self-defence carves out a set of cases in which violation of the norm is permissible. When the principles of justification are rendered concrete in particular cases, the result is a precedent that other people may properly rely upon in similar cases. If a court recognises a privilege, based on necessity, to shoot a rabies-stricken dog in order to protect children in the neighbourhood, the result modifies the norm against the destruction of property. If deadly force is adjudged permissible against a threatened rape, the norm against homicide is *pro tanto* contracted. In similar cases arising in the future, similarly situated actors may rely on these recognised privileges in planning their conduct. The only requirement for claiming the precedent is the general legal rule that the new case may not be significantly different in its relevant facts.

Excuses bear a totally different relationship to prohibitory norms. They do not constitute exceptions or modifications of the norm, but rather a judgment in the particular case that an individual cannot be fairly held accountable for violating the norm. This fundamental difference means that cases acknowledging that conduct in a particular situation is excused do not generate precedents that other people may rely on in the future.

This is obvious in cases of mistake of law, for the judgment of the court serves to advise the public of the rule in question, and therefore in the future there is even less excuse for ignorance of the particular law. . . .

Excuses have this peculiar quality, for they occupy a hiatus between two concepts of law. Law in the narrow sense consists solely of the norms prohibiting conduct and laying down the criteria of justification. Law in the broad sense encompasses the total set of criteria that affects the outcomes of particular case. In the ring between these two circles of law, one finds the criteria of excuses as well as other conditions—such as criteria of immunity and the statute of limitations—that affect the outcome of particular cases.

(See further, Glanville Williams, "The Theory of Excuses" [1982] Crim. L.R. 732.)

R. v. Graham
(1981) 74 Cr.App.R. 235
Court of Appeal

LORD LANE C.J.: [I]n general, if a mistake is to excuse what would otherwise be criminal, the mistake must be a reasonable one. . . .

The correct approach [is] (1) Was the defendant, or may he have been, impelled to act as he did because, as a result of what he reasonably believed [X] had said or done, he had good cause to fear that if he did not so act [X] would kill him or (if this is to be added) cause him serious physical injury? (2) If so, have the prosecution made the jury sure that a sober person of reasonable firmness, sharing the characteristics of the defendant, would not have responded to whatever he reasonably believed [X] said or did by taking part in the killing?

Note

Lord Lane C.J.'s dicta were approved by the House of Lords in *R. v. Howe and Bannister* [1987] 2 W.L.R. 568. In neither case was mistake an issue, so what was said was strictly *obiter*. Subsequent cases have accepted that in duress or duress of circumstances the issue is one of reasonable belief (see, for example, *Abdul-Hussain, et al.* [1999] Crim. L.R. 570; *Cairns* [1999] 2 Cr.App.R. 137). It should be noted, however, that the latter case was misconstrued in *Martin* [2000] 2 Cr.App.R.42 as having held that the test in duress was subjective thereby creating further uncertainty.

Questions

1. Is there any basis in principle why a mistake in respect of an excusatory claim must be based on reasonable grounds when a mistake in respect of a justificatory claim need not be?

2. Is it possible to reconcile Lord Lane's statement in *Williams*, that a defendant must be judged on the basis of the facts as he believed them to be, with his pronouncement in *Graham*?

Proposals for Reform

Draft Criminal Code Bill

Proof or disproof of states of mind

14. A court or jury, in determining whether a person had, or may have had, a particular state of mind, shall have regard to all the evidence including, where appropriate, the presence or absence of reasonable grounds for having that state of mind.

Ignorance or mistake of law

21. Ignorance or mistake as to a matter of law does not affect liability to conviction of an offence except—

(a) where so provided; or
(b) where it negatives a fault element of the offence."

In para. 8.32 of the *Commentary on Draft Criminal Code Bill* (Law Com. No. 177) the Law Commission state—
"8.32 *Ignorance or mistake negativing a fault element.* 'Ignorance of the law is no defence' is a popular aphorism with a good deal of power to mislead. It therefore seems worthwhile to state, in paragraph (b), the truth that a mistake as to the law, equally with one as to fact, can be the reason why a person is not at fault in the way prescribed for an offence."
Appendix B of the Code Report provides the following illustrations—

21(i) D, removing property from a flat at the end of his tenancy, intentionally damages a fixture. It is a landlord's fixture but D thinks that it belongs to himself. He is not guilty of intentionally damaging property belonging to the landlord.
21(ii) It is an offence for a person to act as auditor of a company at a time when he knows that he is disqualified from appointment to that office. D, a director of X Ltd., does not know that a director of a company is disqualified from appointment as its auditor. He acts as auditor of X Ltd. He is not guilty of the offence."

Defences

Draft Criminal Code Bill

Belief in circumstance affording a defence

41.—(1) Unless otherwise provided, a person who acts in the belief that a circumstance exists has any defence that he would have if the circumstance existed.
(2) Subsection (1) does not apply in respect of a defence specially provided for a pre-Code offence as defined in section 6 (to which section 2(3) applies).
(3) Any requirement as to proof or disproof of a defence applies to proof or disproof of a belief mentioned in subsection (1).

In paras. 12.6–12.8 of the *Commentary on Draft Criminal Code Bill* (Law Com. No. 177) the Law Commission state—

"12.6 *A statutory presumption*. If knowledge of a particular circumstance is an element of an offence, a belief that that circumstance does not exist means that the offence is not committed. Subsection (1) provides a presumption in favour of a corresponding rule for defences, namely, that a person who acts in the belief that a circumstance exists has any defence that he would have if it existed. The Code thus gives general effect to the *prima facie* principles that a person is to be judged, for purposes of criminal liability, on the facts as he believed them to be. This is the tendency, though not the universal effect, of recent judicial developments in the field of defences. It is desirable that the Code should provide consistently for offences and defences, leaving it to Parliament in particular contexts, if it thinks fit, to exclude the application of this subsection or to limit a defence of belief in the existence of an 'exempting circumstance' to a case of a belief based on reasonable grounds. Where a defendant relies on this subsection, the absence of reasonable grounds for the belief he claims to have held is, of course, relevant in determining whether he did hold it.

12.7 *Mistake as to one element of a defence*. A defence may have two or more elements, each of which is, in the language of the Code, an 'exempting circumstance', and a person's mistaken belief may be as to the existence of one such circumstance. Subsection (1) places him in the position that he would be in if his belief were true. For example, a person may be guilty of manslaughter rather than murder if he kills under provocation—that is, if something done or said causes him to lose his self-control (clauses 55(a) and 58). If he mistakenly believes that just such a thing has been done or said, the supposed provocation is treated as actual provocation, and other elements of this special defence to murder (the alleged loss of self-control and the question whether the provocation was sufficient ground for the loss of self-control) are then considered on that basis.

12.8 *Voluntary intoxication*. Subsection (1) has to be read subject to clause 22 (1)(b) and (3). A person who was voluntarily intoxicated is credited, in the case of an offence requiring a fault element of recklessness, with the understanding of the relevant matter that he would have had if he had been sober. Similarly, in the case of an offence requiring a fault element of failure to comply with a standard of care, or requiring no fault, a person who was voluntarily intoxicated is treated as not having believed that an exempting circumstance existed if a reasonable sober person would not have done so."

Note

If the Draft Criminal Code Bill was to be enacted the fine distinctions between definitional elements and excusatory claims (outlined *supra*) would no longer exist; a defendant would be judged on the facts as he believed them to be whether or not there were reasonable grounds for that belief.

ii. Irrelevant Mistakes

    (1) Mistake and Strict Liability
    (2) Ignorance of the Law
    (3) Transferred Malice
Mistakes can only be relevant in crimes which require proof of some

mental element. As the preceding sections indicate, the courts, in allocating mistake to one category or another, are making decisions as to what that mental element is and to what parts of the *actus reus* it is to apply. The rules deduced from the cases can be stated without reference to mistake as such. Thus of bigamy it can be said that proof of intention is necessary for the act of getting married while as to the circumstances of being married only negligence is needed. Where an offence is interpreted as not even requiring negligence as to an element of the *actus reus* it is said to be an offence of strict liability. *Prince*, below, illustrates how the creation of such an offence renders the mistake of no legal consequence.

The converse of the opening statement of the above paragraph is not true: mistakes are sometimes irrelevant in *mens rea* crimes. Ignorance of the law is often no defence. In these cases, as in *Prince*, the mistake is *rendered* irrelevant by the law even though, had things been as the defendant supposed, there would have been no offence. However, in cases of transferred malice, the mistake is legally irrelevant because it is immaterial to D.'s culpability whether the victim is the intended one or someone else.

(1) *Mistake and strict liability*

R. v. Prince (1875) L.R. 2 C.C.R. 154: Section 55 of the Offences Against the Person Act 1861 provided that it is an offence "unlawfully [to] take . . . any unmarried girl, being under the age of 16 years, out of the possession and against the will of her father. . . ." [see now Sexual Offences Act 1956, s. 20] Prince was convicted under this section despite having reasonable grounds to believe the girl concerned was over 16. The following passage is from the judgment of Blackburn J. in which nine other judges concurred (at L.R. 2 C.C.R. 154, 170): "The question . . . is reduced to this, whether the words in s.55 are to be read as if they were 'being under the age of sixteen, and he knowing she was under that age.' No such words are contained in the statute, nor is there the word 'maliciously,' 'knowingly,' or any other word used that can be said to involve a similar meaning." See also *R. v. McPherson* [1980] Crim.L.R. 654.

Serious doubt has been cast on the continuing authority of *Prince* by the House of Lords' decision in B. *(A Minor. v D.P.P.* [2000] 2 W.L.R. 452 *(ante* p. 164; *post* p. 193). Lord Nicholls of Birkenhead stated (at p. 460) that "some of the reasoning in *Prince's* case is at variance with the common law presumption regarding *mens rea* [and] . . . must be regarded as unsound". Lord Steyn (at p. 469) rejected "the contention that there is a special rule of construction in respect of age-based sexual offences which is untouched by the presumption . . . . Moreover *Prince's* case is out of line with the modern trend in criminal law which is that a defendant should be judged on the facts as he believes them to be . . . it is a relic from an age dead and gone.' Lord Hutton stated (at p. 474) that 'to the extent that *Prince's* case can be viewed as establishing a general rule that mistake as to age does not afford a defence in age-based sexual offences, that rule cannot prevail over the presumption [of *mens rea*] stated by this House in *Sweet v. Parsley*."

R. v. Miller [1975] 1 W.L.R. 1222: The offence of driving a motor vehicle on a road while disqualified under section 99(6) of the Road Traffic Act 1972 (now s.103 of the Road Traffic Act 1988) was held to have been committed despite the defendant's belief that he was driving on a private road. James L.J., p. 1226: "[W]e have reached the clear conclusion that section 99 . . . provides an offence which is proved once the prosecution establish the facts which were not disputed in the present case, namely, that there was driving by a person who was at that time disqualified . . . and that it is not relevant for a defendant to raise the question of his state of mind in order to show . . . a mistaken belief as to the nature of the place where the driving was taking place."

R. v. Howells [1977] 2 W.L.R. 716: It is an offence under section 1 of the Firearms Act 1968 to possess a revolver without a firearm certificate. Under section 58(2) this does not apply to antique firearms, "purchased . . . or possessed as a curiosity or ornament." D thought he possessed an antique; in fact it was a modern reproduction. His appeal against conviction was dismissed by the Court of Appeal, Brown L.J., p. 725: "This court has reached the decision that s.1 should be construed strictly . . . to allow a defence of honest and reasonable belief that the firearm was an antique and therefore excluded would be likely to defeat the clear intention of the Act."

L. H. Leigh, *Strict and Vicarious Liability* (1982), pp. 58–61

. . . Lord Diplock in *Sweet v. Parsley* suggested that a general due diligence defence might be possible at common law. [S]uch a defence [exists] in Australia and Canada. It is appropriate at this juncture to examine its antecedents and extent, before considering the question upon what basis it might be introduced into English law.

The Australian formulation derives from *Proudman v. Dayman* (1943) 67 C.L.R. 536). The charge was that the accused permitted a person, not being the holder of a licence for the time being in force, to drive a motor vehicle on a public road. The question arose whether the accused could raise a defence of honest and reasonable mistake to the charge. Although on the facts there was no basis for such a defence, Dixon J. held that reasonable mistake might be raised as a defence to a charge of a strict liability offence. The reasoning adopted by His Honour was that a holding that the prosecution need not prove intention or recklessness to procure a conviction does not imply that fault has no part in the case. His Honour thus states:

'It is one thing to deny that a necessary ingredient of the offence is positive knowledge of the fact that the driver holds no subsisting licence. It is another to say that an honest belief founded on reasonable grounds that he is licensed cannot exculpate a person who permits him to drive. As a general rule an honest and reasonable belief in a state of facts which, if they existed, would make the defendant's act innocent affords an excuse for doing what would otherwise be an offence.' (at 540)

From this it followed that, save in an exceptional case where liability is truly intended to be absolute, the accused might defend himself by showing that he exercised due diligence to comply with the law. The affinity of this thought to those English cases which insisted that an absence of *mens rea* words simply shifted the burden of proof is plain.

The result of this approach is to create three categories of statutory offences: those in which the prosecution must prove full *mens rea*: those in which it need not prove *mens rea* but the accused may raise as a defence to a charge that he or she exercised all due diligence: and those in which liability is absolute. In this latter case, the legislature must make it clear that absolute liability is intended.

It is impossible to indicate what view English courts will ultimately take of the place of fault as a common law principle. In *Sweet v. Parsley* Lords Reid, Pearce and Diplock intimated that the question of due diligence defences may not be entirely foreclosed by authority. In *R. v. Warner*, Lord Guest had thought that the half-way house represented by the Australian cases was blocked by the decision in *Woolmington v. D.P.P.* that the Crown must prove, beyond a reasonable doubt, all the elements of the case. In *Sweet v. Parsley*, Lord Diplock intimates that this point may need to be reconsidered: *Woolmington*, his Lordship states, is no bar to the use of honest and reasonable mistake as a solvent of strict liability cases since it only decides that where there is evidence of a defence, a jury must consider it and acquit the accused unless they are sure that the accused did not hold a particular belief, or there are no reasonable grounds for it.

Dicta in *Morgan* also suggest that a common law no fault defence is possible, but they are very confused. The *ratio* of the case is that in rape, an honest mistake as to the existence of the elements of the offence is a defence. The House of Lords was, however, obliged to explain away a series of cases on bigamy which held that a mistake had both to be honest and reasonable to afford a defence. Lord Cross drew a distinction between offences which require *mens rea* and those which do not. Some *mens rea* offences specify the mental element required for the offence: in respect of them, mistake need only be honest. Other *mens rea* offences do not specify any mental element: in their case, mistake must be both honest and reasonable. Where no *mens rea* is required at all, mistake will not excuse the defendant. On this view, a mistake defence would only be available where a court was prepared to construe an offence which is silent as to the mental element, as involving *mens rea*. Why there should be a difference between two classes of *mens rea* offences is obscure. Lord Hailsham took a different view of the bigamy cases. He treated the leading case, *Tolson*, as a narrow decision based on the construction of a statute which *prima facie* appeared to create an absolute offence subject to a statutory defence related to a seven year period of absence. His Lordship suggests this explanation:

> 'The judges . . . decided that this was not reasonable, and, on general jurisprudential principles, imported into the statutory offence words which created a special "defence" of honest and reasonable belief of which the "evidential", but not the probative burden lay on the defence.'

If Lord Hailsham's suggestion were adopted, there would be no reason why honest and reasonable mistake, or a showing by the accused that he used due diligence to comply with the law, should not afford a defence to crimes of strict liability generally, subject always to the power of Parliament to legislate so as to exclude it. If the general jurisprudential principle referred to (whatever it may be) can be invoked to prevent injustice in one case, there seems no reason why it could not be invoked in another. No doubt a tendency to do so would be most marked where a penalty of imprisonment was available and sometimes imposed for the offence, or where the stigma attaching to conviction for that offence was very considerable. Where the usual penalty was a fine, an inference that no such defence was intended might well be drawn, as it might where an adequate statutory scheme of defences was already provided. But all these are possibilities latent in *dicta* in leading cases; no court has sought to build upon them. It cannot be said with certainty therefore, whether the courts will continue to recognise defences based upon particular statutory words, or whether they will take the further step of creating a general due diligence defence which would be displaced only where a particular scheme made it clear that no such defence was intended.

Question

Would the defence of honest and reasonable belief stated by Dixon J. in *Proudman v. Dayman* have availed the defendants in *Prince, Miller* and *Howells, supra,* if it had existed in English common law?

(2) *Ignorance of the law*

R. v. Smith, post, p. 911 and *R. v. Gould* [1968] 1 All E.R. 849 indicate that mistake of civil law can preclude a person from having the requisite mental element for a particular offence.

Secretary of State for Trade and Industry v. Hart
[1982] 1 All E.R. 817
Queen's Bench Division

Hart acted as the auditor of two companies although as a director of each company he was disqualified from so doing by virtue of section 161(2) of the Companies Act 1948. He was charged with acting as an auditor of a company knowing that he was disqualified for appointment as auditor, contrary to section 161(2) of the 1948 Act and section 13(5) and (6) of the Companies Act 1976. Hart submitted that as he did not know of the statutory provisions disqualifying him, he could not be guilty. The magistrate dismissed the case because of Hart's ignorance of the law and the Secretary of State appealed.

WOOLF J.: . . . The fact that Mr Hart, during the relevant period, had acted as auditor of those companies, at a time when he was disqualified as alleged in the information, was not in dispute before the stipendiary magistrate. The only matter that was in issue was whether or not Mr Hart had the necessary *mens rea* to constitute the offences which were alleged. . . .
In subs. (2) [of section 161] it is stated:

"None of the following persons shall be qualified for appointment as auditor of a company—(*a*) an officer or servant of the company; (*b*) a person who is a partner of or in the employment of an officer or servant of the company; (*c*) a body corporate."

The term "officer" is defined in s.455 of that Act as including a director, manager or secretary. So clearly, because of the provisions of subs. (2), although Mr Hart had been authorised to act as an auditor, he was not qualified to hold the appointment in a company in respect of which he was a director or secretary. . . .
Subsection (5) [of section 13 of the 1976 Act] provides:

"No person shall act as auditor of a company at a time when he knows that he is disqualified for appointment to that office; and if an auditor of a company to his knowledge becomes so disqualified during his term of office he shall thereupon vacate his office and give notice in writing to the company that he has vacated it by reason of such disqualification."

Subsection (5) therefore creates the disqualification which arises as a result of persons holding particular offices. . . .

Subsection (6) of s.13 of the 1976 Act widens the categories of persons who could be guilty of a criminal offence in relation to this matter. It provides:

"Any person who acts as auditor in contravention of subsection (5) above or fails without reasonable excuse to give notice of vacating his office as required by that subsection shall be guilty of an offence and liable on conviction on indictment to a fine and on summary conviction to a fine not exceeding £40 for every day during which the contravention continues."

It is subss. (5) and (6) of s.13 of the 1976 Act that this court is primarily concerned with in answering the question posed by this appeal. Counsel on behalf of the Secretary of State argues that when subss. (5) and (6) are read together the position is one where a person is guilty of an offence under those provisions if he knows the facts or circumstances which cause him to be disqualified but nonetheless acts as an auditor. He contends that it is not necessary for a person charged with an offence under those subsections also to know as a matter of law he is disqualified. He submits that it is sufficient if he knows the facts and circumstances, because like anyone else a person acting as an auditor should be aware of the provisions of the law which deal with the disqualification for an appointment to the office of auditor.

This is, however, as I have already pointed out, a criminal offence which is created by s.13(5) and (6). In my view it is at least equally consistent with the ordinary meaning of the words which are used in those subsections, that their effect is that a person is not guilty of an offence and is not disqualified from acting as an auditor unless he in fact knows not only the relevant facts but also that in consequence of the facts he is disqualified by the law for appointment to the office. The words in their ordinary interpretation are wholly consistent with a view of the subsections which means that a person in the position of Mr Hart must be aware of the statutory restrictions which exist against his holding the appointment. . . .

[T]he wording we have to consider, introduced by s.13 of the Companies Act 1976, clearly requires some form of *mens rea*, and clearly requires it expressly. . . . Counsel for the Secretary of State concedes that the offence here created is not an absolute offence. . . . However, he wishes to introduce a limited form of knowledge as being necessary. In my view it would be wrong to introduce such a limitation, bearing in mind the express words here are open to the interpretation which I have indicated. Because it is wrong, and would be an undesirable limitation on the normal principles of statutory construction in relation to a criminal offence, to qualify what is required as *mens rea*, it is my view that the stipendiary magistrate in this case came to the right decision.

ORMROD L.J.: [After referring to subsections (5) and (6) of section 13 of the 1976 Act] (T)he offence, as was correctly set out in the information, is that Mr Hart acted as an auditor of a company at a time when he knew that he was disqualified for that appointment. And interpreting the language quite simply, it seems to me to indicate that Mr Hart is not guilty of a criminal offence unless he knew that he was disqualified.

If that means that he is entitled to rely on ignorance of the law as a defence, in contrast to the usual practice and the usual rule, the answer is that the section gives him that right. . . .

Appeal dismissed

Question

Would the result have been different if Mr Hart's submission had been that while he knew he was disqualified under the Companies Acts from acting as an auditor, he did not know that this constituted a criminal offence?

Note

Compare the outcome in *Hart* with *Grant v. Borg* [1982] 1 W.L.R. 638, where the accused (a non-patrial with limited leave to remain in the United Kingdom) was charged with knowingly remaining beyond the time limited by the leave, contrary to section 24(1)(*b*)(i) of the Immigration Act 1971. On the issue whether a mistake, as to whether "leave to remain" had expired, was relevant, Lord Bridge stated:

"The principle that ignorance of the law is no defence in crime is so fundamental that to construe the word 'knowingly' in a criminal statute as requiring not merely knowledge of the facts material to the offender's guilt, but also knowledge of the relevant law, would be revolutionary and, to my mind, wholly unacceptable."

Ignorance of the law in the sense of not realising that a particular act is prohibited is rarely a defence. People are presumed to know the law. Two justifications have been advanced for this constructive knowledge:

Oliver Wendell Holmes, *The Common Law* (1881), p. 48:
"[T]o admit the excuse at all would be to encourage ignorance ... and justice to the individual is rightly outweighed by the larger interests on the other side of the scales."

Hall, p. 382:
"If that plea [mistake of law] were valid, the consequence would be: wherever a defendant in a criminal case thought the law was thus and so, he is to be treated as though the law were thus and so, i.e. *the law actually is thus and so*. But such a doctrine would contradict the essential requisites of a legal system. . . ." (italics in original).

Hall's view seems logically attractive but does any defence of mistake, whether of fact or law, alter either factual reality or the law itself? In any case, this view fails to recognise that ignorance of the law does sometimes affect culpability. When an offence is confined to a particular class of prohibited persons and the means of discovering who is in that class are obscure, ignorance may be excused: Lord Evershed in *Lim Chin Aik v. The Queen, post*, p. 206, [1963] A.C. 160, 171: "[T]he maxim [ignorance of the law is no excuse] cannot apply to such a case as the present where it appears that there is ... no provision ... for the publication in any form of an order of the kind made in the present case or any other provision designed to enable a man by appropriate inquiry to find out what 'the law' is." The United States' Supreme Court has allowed a defence of ignorance to an offence of "failing to register as a convicted person": *Lambert v. California* 355 U.S. 225 (1957). The court drew a distinction between crimes of commission, where ignorance could never be a defence, and crimes of omission, where it may be, unless the failure to act is under circumstances which should alert the doer to the consequences of such failure. Mr Justice Douglas said, at p. 232: "Were it otherwise, the evil would be as great as it is when the law is written in print too fine to read, or in language foreign to the community." Can this be reconciled with Holmes's statement above? See, generally, A. J. Ashworth, "Excusable Mistake of Law" [1974] Crim.L.R. 652.

(3) Transferred malice

Note

Where D makes a mistake as to the identity of his victim, for example he thinks that B is A and he shoots him intending to kill him, his mistake is irrelevant as he intended to kill a person and he did kill a person.

Where some chance factor alters the result from that which D intended, his liability will depend on whether the result amounts to the same offence which D had intended. This is illustrated by the two cases which follow.

R. v. Pembliton
(1874) L.R. 2 C.C.R. 119
Court for Crown Cases Reserved

The defendant was a member of a group who were fighting outside the public-house called The Grand Turk. He picked up a large stone and threw it at those with whom he had been fighting. The stone passed over their heads and broke a window of the public-house. The defendant was indicted for "unlawfully and maliciously" committing damage under the Malicious Damage Act 1861, s.51. The jury found that he had intended to strike the persons at whom he aimed the stone and that he did not intend to break the window.

LORD COLERIDGE C.J.: I am of the opinion that the evidence does not support the conviction. The indictment is under [section 51, Malicious Damage Act 1861] which deals with malicious injuries to property, and the section expressly says that the act is to be unlawful and malicious. There is also the fifty-eighth section, which makes it immaterial whether the offence has been committed from malice against the owner of the property or otherwise, that is, from malice against someone not the owner of the property. In both these sections it seems to me that what is intended by the statute is a wilful doing of an intentional act. Without saying that if the case had been left to them in a different way the conviction could not have been supported, if, on these facts, the jury had come to the conclusion that the prisoner was reckless of the consequence of his act, and might reasonably have expected that it would result in breaking the window, it is sufficient to say that the jury have expressly found the contrary. . . .

BLACKBURN J.: We have not now to consider what would be malice aforethought to bring a given case within the common law definition of murder; here the statute says that the act must be unlawful and malicious, and malice may be defined to be "where any person wilfully does an act injurious to another without lawful excuse". Can this man be considered, on the case submitted to us, as having wilfully broken a pane of glass? The jury might perhaps have found on this evidence that the act was malicious, because they might have found that the prisoner knew that the natural consequence of his act would be to break the glass, and although that was not his wish, yet that he was reckless whether he did it or not; but the jury have not so found, and I think it is impossible to say in this case that the prisoner has maliciously done an act which he did not intend to do.

Conviction quashed

R. v. Latimer
(1886) 17 Q.B.D. 359
Court for Crown Cases Reserved

L, who was quarrelling with C in a public-house aimed a blow at C with his belt. The belt glanced off C and severely injured R. In answer to questions by the recorder the jury found that the striking of R was purely accidental and not such a consequence of the blow as the prisoner ought to have expected to follow. They also found that the blow was unlawful and malicious. L was found guilty of unlawful and malicious wounding.

LORD COLERIDGE C.J.: We are of opinion that this conviction must be sustained. It is common knowledge that a man who has an unlawful and malicious intent against another, and, in attempting to carry it out, injures a third person, is guilty of what the law deems malice against the person injured, because the offender is doing an unlawful act, and has that which the judges call general malice, and that is enough. . . . So, but for *R. v. Pembliton (supra)*, there would not have been the slightest difficulty. Does that case make any difference? I think not, and, on consideration, that it was quite rightly decided. But it is clearly distinguishable, because the indictment in *R. v. Pembliton* was on the Act making unlawful and malicious injury to property a statutory offence punishable in a certain way, and the jury expressly negatived, the facts expressly negatived, any intention to do injury to property, and the court held that under the Act making it an offence to injure any property there must be an intent to injure property. *R. v. Pembliton*, therefore, does not govern the present case, and on no other ground is there anything to be said for the prisoner.

Conviction affirmed

(See also *R. v. Mitchell* [1983] 2 W.L.R. 938.)

Question

If the facts of *Pembliton* recurred today with what offence(s) could he be charged?

Note

The Law Commission in *Legislating the Criminal Code: Offences Against the Person and General Principles* (Law Com. No. 218) favours the retention of transferred fault. Clause 32 of the Draft Criminal Law Bill largely replicates clause 24 of the Draft Criminal Code Bill (Law Com. No. 177).

Draft Criminal Law Bill

Transferred fault and defences.

32.—(1) In determining whether a person is guilty of an offence, his intention to cause, or his awareness of a risk that he will cause, a result in relation to a person or thing capable of being the victim or subject-matter of the offence shall be treated as an intention to cause or, as the case may be, an awareness of a risk that he will cause, that result in relation to any other person or thing affected by his conduct.

(2) Any defence on which a person might have relied on a charge of an offence in relation to a person or thing within his contemplation is open to him on a charge of the same offence in relation to a person or thing not within his contemplation

Law Com No. 218

Transferred fault . . .

42.2 . . . Where a person intends to affect one person or thing (X) and actually affects another (Y), he may be charged with an attempt in relation to X; or it may be possible to satisfy a court or jury that he was reckless with respect to Y. But an attempt charge may be impossible (where it is not known until trial that the defendant claims to have had X and not Y in contemplation); or inappropriate (as not adequately describing the harm done for labelling or sentencing purposes). Moreover, recklessness with respect to Y may be insufficient to establish the offence or incapable of being proved. The rule stated by the subsection overcomes these difficulties.

Transfer of fault required for "the offence"
42.3 The clause assumes that the specified result, such as serious injury, or damage to property belonging to another, is an element of a specific offence. If the actor does not cause such a result, the external elements of the offence with which he is charged are not made out. Accordingly, no question of criminal liability arises. It is only when the external elements of the offence charged have been caused by the defendant that the second question arises, of whether he acted with the fault required for that offence. This clause provides that if he acted with that fault, it can be transferred. What is required is a concurrence of fault in relation to *the result specified for the offence* and the occurrence of such a result, although not in relation to the same person or thing.

Note

In the article which follows the author argues that the doctrine of "transferred fault" is misconceived providing a solution to a perceived problem which does not truly arise if the principles of *actus reus* and *mens rea* are understood and applied.

I. H. E. Patient, "Transferred Malice—A Misleading Misnomer" (1990) 54 J.C.L. 116–124

Assume that X aims a shot at A, intending to kill A. The shot misses the intended victim, but hits and kills B instead. There are two ways of looking at this situation.

The first approach is based on the notion that one must distinguish between a 'killing of victim A' and a 'killing of victim B'. As to A, the intended killing did not succeed. Hence, there might be a charge of attempted murder. As to B, there was no intention to kill 'B', hence no murder of B. However, a lesser form of homicide, namely manslaughter, might be given, either in the form of constructive manslaughter (the unlawful act need not be directed against the eventual victim) or in the form of reckless killing (if B stood close to A there would be at least an obvious risk that B might be hit).

Alternatively, one might ignore the particular identity of the victim. The *actus reus* of homicide is not the 'killing of A' or the 'killing of B', but in more general terms the 'killing of a human being'. Accordingly, the required intention is that of 'killing a human being'. On that basis, X, in our example, has committed a murder of B, for he killed a human being (namely B) and he did so with the required intention of killing a human being (namely A). This second, more streamlined, solution is capable of avoiding certain practical difficulties, especially of proof, and moreover represents, it is submitted, the more correct approach in principle, provided it is clearly seen as resting on the application of the general principles of *actus reus* and *mens rea*. Unfortunately, it is often rationalised in a different manner, namely as an instance of so called 'transferred malice'. In other words, the case is seen as one where the intention to kill victim A is 'transferred' to victim B. Such a view must be based on the assumption that the *mens rea* for murder is the killing (or causing of grievous bodily harm) to a particular victim, namely, in our case, an 'intention to kill A' as opposed to an 'intention to kill B', so that the required intention can then be 'transferred' from one victim to the other. This kind of thinking seems to be, consciously or otherwise, influenced by a preoccupation with the form of the indictment, where, of course, the particular victim is referred to. Now that the principles of *actus reus* and *mens rea* have become more clearly established, not least as the direct and indirect result of increasing codification, such a misleading way of thinking must be challenged, in order to curb the creation of avoidable difficulties. Significantly, one of the early leading cases, *R. v. Latimer* [*ante*, p. 177], which is often relied upon as an authority for the notion of transferred malice, in fact rejects that concept and adopts the approach described above of simply applying the principles of *actus reus* and *mens rea*. The facts of the case were these: the prisoner, X, aimed a blow at A with his belt. The belt bounded off and struck B, who stood close by, and caused wounds to her (B's) face. X was convicted under section 20 of the Offences Against the Person Act 1861. An appeal was taken on the ground that X could not be guilty of injuring B, as he did not intend to injure her.

This argument could only be conceived on the implied assumption that the offence in question was the wounding of a particular victim, namely B, as opposed to the wounding of another victim, A. The court made short shrift of this idea. The *actus reus* of the offence in section 20 is the inflicting of grievous bodily harm upon *any other person* and the prisoner had the necessary *general malice*. It was, therefore, not a question of establishing an intention to injure a particular victim, which would then be 'transferred' to another victim. Rather, the accused had the necessary 'general' *mens rea* of intending to inflict grievous bodily harm upon any (other) person. Whether that person was A or B, was irrelevant. . . .

To summarise the argument so far: In the cases under discussion, the original plan misfires in that a target, other than that envisaged, is affected. . . . Whether there is liability concerning the substituted target, turns solely on whether the necessary *mens rea* relating to the *actus reus* in question, is given. There is no transfer of any kind involved. If the *actus reus* is described as the 'wounding of any other person' (s. 20 Offences Against the Person Act 1861), then an intention to wound another person constitutes the required *mens rea*, irrespective of whether the intention relates to a person called 'A' or 'B'. To use the terminology of the new Draft Criminal Code Bill, A, as much as B, is 'capable of being the victim of the offence', since he is capable of coming under the description 'any other person'. Hence, if X, intending to wound A, wounds B by mistake, X can be guilty of wounding B. He wounds another person and he intends to do so. Both *actus reus* and *mens rea* of the relevant offence are given. Anyone who sees this as involving a transfer, can do so only on the basis of a distorted, artificially narrowed view of *mens rea*. He must assume that section 20 requires an 'intention to wound B' as opposed to an 'intention to wound A', so that, B having actually been injured in place of A, the intention relating to A can be 'transferred' to B. That, as has been explained above, is *not* the approach in the relevant cases. By way of contrast, let it be assumed that B, the substitute-victim in our example, is a police constable and that X is charged with assaulting a constable in the execution of his duty under section 51(1) of the Police Act 1964. X's intention to assault a non-policeman, A, cannot—it is submitted—constitute the necessary *mens rea* for the charge. For the *actus reus* in section 51 requires not 'any person', but 'a constable' and A, not being a constable, is in the words of clause 24 of the Draft Code, not capable of being the victim of the offence in section 51. Thus, it is entirely a matter of testing the *mens rea* against the wording of the relevant *actus reus*. To see this as a situation where a 'transfer from one victim to another is impossible' would be inappropriate and distorting. The victim of the offence in section 51 cannot be A in the first place.

Note

In the case which follows the doctrine of transferred malice arose for consideration in a novel way.

Attorney-General's Reference (No. 3 of 1994)
[1998] A.C. 245
House of Lords

B stabbed his pregnant girlfriend in the abdomen. No injury to the foetus was detected. Subsequently the child was born prematurely and it was discovered that she had received a wound while in the womb. The child died subsequently not from the knife wound but due to complications arising from her premature birth. B was charged with murder. The trial judge directed an acquittal on the ground that no conviction for either murder or manslaughter was possible in law. The Attorney-General referred the matter to the Court of Appeal which, applying the doctrine of transferred malice, arrived at a contrary conclusion to that of the trial judge holding that murder or manslaughter could be committed where unlawful injury is deliberately inflicted either to a child in utero or to a mother carrying a child in utero where the child was subsequently born alive, existed independently of the mother and then died, the injuries in utero either having caused or made a substantial contribution to the death. The requisite intent which had to be proved in the case of murder is an intention to kill or to cause really serious bodily injury to the mother, the foetus before birth being viewed as an integral part of the mother. The case, at B's request, was referred to the House of Lords.

LORD MUSTILL: [His Lordship stated five rules which, regardless of their justice or logic, are undeniable features of the criminal law.]

1. *It is sufficient to raise a prima facie case of murder (subject to entire or partial excuses such as self-defence or provocation) for it to be proved that the defendant did the act which caused the death intending to kill the victim or to cause him at least grievous bodily harm . . . .*
2. *If the defendant does an act with the intention of causing a particular kind of harm to X, and unintentionally does that kind of harm to Y, then the intent to harm X may be added to the harm actually done to Y in deciding whether the defendant has committed a crime towards Y. . . .*
3. *Except under statute an embryo or foetus in utero cannot be the victim of a crime of violence. In particular, violence to the foetus which causes its death in utero is not a murder. . . .*
4. *The existence of an interval of time between the doing of an act by the defendant with the necessary wrongful intent and its impact on the victim in a manner which leads to death does not in itself prevent the intent, the act and the death from together amounting to murder, so long as there is an unbroken causal connection between the act and the death. . . .*
5. *Violence towards a foetus which results in harm suffered after the baby has been born alive can give rise to criminal responsibility even if the harm would not have been criminal (apart from statute) if it had been suffered in utero. . . .*

[His Lordship went on to reject the proposition accepted by the Court of Appeal that a foetus is part of the mother concluding that a foetus is a separate organism to which existing principles could not necessarily be applied. His Lordship also expressed his dislike of the rule that an intent to cause grievous bodily harm is sufficient *mens rea* for murder albeit that the rule was too long established for the House of Lords to abolish it.]

I turn to the second rule, of "transferred malice." For present purposes this is more important and more difficult. Again, one must look at its origins to see whether they provide a theme which can be applied today. Three of them are familiar. [The first] explanation of [the rule is] founded on the notion of risk. The person who committed a crime took the chance that the outcome would be worse than he expected. . . .

Secondly, there is the reversed burden of proof whereby the causing of death is prima facie murder, unless it falls within one of the extenuating categories recognised by the institutional writers. Again, this concept is long out of date. Nobody could seriously think of using it to make new law.

Thirdly, there was the idea of "general malice," of an evil disposition existing in the general and manifesting itself in the particular, uniting the aim of the offender and the result which his deeds actually produced. According to this theory, there was no need to "transfer" the wrongful intent from the intended to the actual victim; for since the offender was . . . "an enemy to all mankind in general," the actual victim was the direct object of the offender's enmity. Plainly, this will no longer do, for the last vestiges of the idea disappeared with the abolition of the murder/felony doctrine.

What explanation is left: for explanation there must be, since the "transferred malice" concept is agreed on both sides to be sound law today?

[His Lordship discussed the cases of *Pembliton, ante* p. 176, and *Latimer, ante* p. 177]

My Lords, I find it hard to base a modern law of murder on these two cases. The court in *Reg. v. Latimer* was, I believe, entirely justified in finding a distinction between their statutory backgrounds and one can well accept that the answers given, one for acquittal, the other for conviction, would be the same today. But the harking back to a concept of general malice, which amounts to no more than this, that a wrongful act displays a malevolence which can be attached to any adverse consequence, has long been out of date. And to speak of a particular malice which is "transferred" simply disguises the problem by idiomatic language. The defendant's malice is directed at one objective, and when after the event the court treats it as directed at another object it is not recognising a "transfer" but creating a new malice which never existed before. As Dr. Glanville Williams pointed out (*Criminal Law: The General Part*, 2nd ed. (1961), p. 184) the doctrine is "rather an arbitrary exception to general principles." Like many of its kind this is useful enough to yield rough justice, in particular cases, and it can sensibly be retained notwithstanding its lack of any sound intellectual basis. But it is another matter to build a new rule upon it. . . .

I turn to deal more briefly with the remaining rules. The third rule, it will be recalled, is that a foetus cannot be the victim of murder. I see no profit in an attempt to treat the medieval origins of this rule. It is sufficient to say that is established beyond doubt for the criminal law, as for the civil law (*Burton v. Islington Health Authority* [1993] Q.B. 204) that the child en ventre sa mère does not have a distinct human personality, whose extinguishment gives rise to any penalties or liabilities at common law.

The fourth rule is an exception to the generally accepted principle that actus reus and mens rea must coincide. A continuous act or continuous chain of causes leading to death is treated by the law as if it happened when first initiated. The development of this into the fifth rule, which links an act and intent before birth with a death happening after a live delivery, causes a little more strain, given the incapacity of the foetus to be the object of homicide. If, however, it is possible to interpret the situation as one where the mental element is directed, not to the foetus but to the human being when and if it comes into existence, no fiction is required.

My Lords, the purpose of this inquiry has been to see whether the existing rules are based on principles sound enough to justify their extension to a case where the defendant acts without an intent to injure either the foetus or the child which it will become. In my opinion they are not. To give an affirmative answer requires a double "transfer" of intent: first from the mother to the foetus and then from the foetus to the child as yet unborn. Then one would have to deploy the fiction (or at least the doctrine) which converts an intention to commit serious harm into the mens rea of murder. For me, this is too much. If one could find any logic in the rules I would follow it from one fiction to another, but whatever grounds there may once have been have long since disappeared. I am willing to follow old laws until they are overturned, but not to make a new law on a basis for which there is no principle.

Moreover, even on a narrower approach the argument breaks down. The effect of transferred malice, as I understand it, is that the intended victim and the actual victim are treated as if they were one, so that what was intended to happen to the first person (but did not happen) is added to what actually did happen to the second person (but was not intended to happen), with the result that what was intended and what happened are married to make a notionally intended and actually consummated crime. The cases are treated as if the actual victim had been the intended victim from the start. To make any sense of this process there must, as it seems to me, be some compatibility between the original intention and the actual occurrence, and this is, indeed, what one finds in the cases. There is no such compatibility here. The defendant intended to commit and did commit an immediate crime of violence to the mother. He committed no relevant violence to the foetus, which was not a person, either at the time or in the future, and intended no harm to the foetus or to the human person which it would become. If fictions are useful, as they can be, they are only damaged by straining them beyond their limits. I would not overstrain the idea of transferred malice by trying to make it fit the present case.

Accordingly, . . . on the presumed facts the judge was right to direct an acquittal on the count of murder.

[His Lordship, adopting the reasoning of Lord Hope of Craighead, went on to conclude that had the trial judge directed the jury on the question of manslaughter, B could have been convicted without the need to resort to the doctrine of transferred malice.]

LORD HOPE OF CRAIGHEAD: . . . It was submitted that, since the foetus was not at the time of the unlawful act a living person, the offence of manslaughter could not be committed; and that, in any event, what constitutes a "dangerous act" for the purposes of the law of manslaughter has always been defined by reference to what all sober and reasonable people would recognise was dangerous towards persons who were alive when the danger manifests itself. . . . For the foetus, life lies in the future, not the past. It is not sensible to say that it cannot ever be harmed, or that nothing can be done to it which can ever be dangerous. Once it is born it is exposed, like all other living persons, to the risk of injury. It may also carry with it the effects of things done to it before birth which, after birth, may prove to be harmful. It would seem not to be unreasonable therefore, on public policy grounds, to regard the child in this case, when she became a living person, as within the scope of the mens rea which B. had when he stabbed her mother before she was born. . . .

I think, then, that the position can be summarised in this way. The intention which must be discovered is an intention to do an act which is unlawful and dangerous. In this case the act which had to be shown to be an unlawful and dangerous act was the stabbing of the child's mother. There can be no doubt that all sober and reasonable people would regard that act, within the appropriate meaning of this term, as dangerous. It is plain that it was unlawful as it was done with the intention of causing her injury. As B. intended to commit that act, all the ingredients necessary for mens rea in regard to the crime of manslaughter were established, irrespective of who was the ultimate victim of it. The fact that the child whom the mother was carrying at the time was born alive and then died as a result of the stabbing is all that was needed for the offence of manslaughter when actus reus for that crime was completed by the child's death. The question, once all the other elements are satisfied, is simply one of causation. The defendant must accept all the consequences of his act, so long as the jury are satisfied that he did what he did intentionally, that what he did was unlawful and that, applying the correct test, it was also dangerous. The death of the child was unintentional, but the nature and quality of the act which caused it was such that it was criminal and therefore punishable. In my opinion that is sufficient for the offence of manslaughter. There is no need to look to the doctrine of transferred malice for a solution to the problem raised by this case so far as manslaughter is concerned.

Questions

1. Is the doctrine of transferred malice based on the fact that the difference between the way in which the *actus reus* occurred and the way D intended it to occur is immaterial, or is it, as Lord Mustill believes, based on a fiction?
2. Lord Mustill stated with regard to *Pembliton* and *Latimer* that he found it "hard to base a modern law of murder on these two cases". Is the law of murder based on them?
3. Lord Mustill expressed dislike for both the doctrine of transferred malice and the rule that intent to cause grievous bodily harm is sufficient *mens rea* for murder if the victim dies. Had B intended to kill his pregnant girlfriend and the baby had been born alive but died subsequently due to injuries she had sustained in the stabbing of her mother, would Lord Mustill have countenanced a conviction of B for murder of the baby?
4. Is the outcome that B could be convicted of manslaughter but not murder not incongruous where B had the *mens rea* for murder, a human being was killed as a result of his acts, and the killing was accepted by their Lordships as being an unlawful homicide?

4. STRICT LIABILITY

If *mens rea* or negligence need not be proved in respect of one or more elements of the *actus reus* of an offence, that offence is one of strict liability. JUSTICE, the British Section of the International Commission of Jurists, estimated that of the 7,200 separate offences listed in *Stone's Justices' Manual* for 1975, over half did not require proof of a mental element. (JUSTICE, *Breaking the Rules* (1980)).

i. The evolution of strict liability

Sayre, "Public Welfare Offences" (1933) 33 Col.L.R. 55

The growth of a distinct group of offences punishable without regard to any mental element dates from about the middle of the nineteenth century. Before this, convictions for crime without proof of a *mens rea* are to be found only occasionally, chiefly among the nuisance cases. In the early days newspaper proprietors might also be punished . . . for libel without proof of *mens rea*, for in libel prosecutions actual criminal knowledge on the part of the owners or publishers of newspapers would often be a matter so difficult to ascertain as to make proof well-nigh impossible. Yet to treat as criminal newspaper owners who were altogether innocent of any criminal intent seemed so harsh and unjust a doctrine and so out of accord with established legal principles that in 1836 an act of Parliament was passed to make this no longer possible [Lord Campbell's Act: s.7 allowed a newspaper proprietor to escape liability by proving that the publication was made 'without his authority, consent or knowledge.'] But apart from exceptional isolated cases criminal liability depended upon proof of a criminal intent. . . .

The decisions permitting convictions of light police offences without proof of a guilty mind came just at the time when the demands of an increasingly complex social order required additional regulation of an administrative character unrelated to questions of personal guilt; the movement also synchronised with the trend of the day away from nineteenth century individualism toward a new sense of the importance of collective interests. The result was almost inevitable. The doctrine first evolved in the adulterated food and liquor cases came to be recognised as a special class of offence for which no *mens rea* was required. . . . The interesting fact that the same development took place in both England and the United States at about the same time strongly indicates that the movement has been not merely an historical accident but the result of the changing social conditions and beliefs of the day. . . .

The problem is how to draw the line between those offences which do and those which do not require *mens rea*. Clearly, it will not depend on whether the crime happens to be a common law or statutory offence. . . . Some courts have suggested that the line depends upon the distinction between *mala in se* and *mala prohibita*; and this seems to depend essentially upon whether or not the offence is inherently immoral. But this also is . . . unsound. . . . Many offences which are held not to require proof of *mens rea* are highly immoral; and many requiring it are not inherently immoral at all. . . .

Neither can the dividing line be drawn according to the gravity or the lightness of the offence. Petty larceny is a much lighter and less dangerous offence than selling narcotics or poisoned food, yet the former requires *mens rea* and the latter not. . . .

How then can one determine practically which offences do and which do not require *mens rea*, when the statute creating the offence is . . . silent? . . . [T]wo cardinal principles stand out upon which the determination must turn.

The first relates to the character of the offence. All criminal enactments in a sense serve the double purpose of singling out wrongdoers for the purpose of punishment or correction and of regulating the social order. But often the importance of the one far outweighs the other. . . .

The second criterion depends upon the possible penalty. If this be serious . . . the individual interest of the defendant weighs too heavily to allow conviction without proof of a guilty mind. . . . Crimes punishable with prison sentences, therefore, ordinarily require proof of a guilty intent.''

ii. Identifying offences of strict liability

If Parliament did its job properly there should never be any room for doubt whether or not an offence is one of strict liability. However, many offences are created without there being a clear indication whether liability is to be strict or whether the absence of words which impose a requirement of proving *mens rea* is simply the result of oversight. Sometimes Parliament makes its intention clear as in the provision which follows.

Contempt of Court Act 1981

Strict liability

1. In this Act "the strict liability rule" means the rule of law whereby conduct may be treated as a contempt of court as tending to interfere with the course of justice in particular legal proceedings regardless of intent to do so.

2. (1) The strict liability rule applies only in relation to publications, and for this purpose "publication" includes any speech, writing, broadcast or other communication in whatever form, which is addressed to the public at large or any section of the public.

(2) The strict liability rule applies only to a publication which creates a substantial risk that the course of justice in the proceedings in question will be seriously impeded or prejudiced.

(3) The strict liability rule applies to a publication only if the proceedings in question are active within the meaning of this section at the time of the publication.

(4) Schedule 1 applies for determining the times at which proceedings are to be treated as active within the meaning of this section.

Defence of innocent publication or distribution

3.—(1) A person is not guilty of contempt of court under the strict liability rule as the publisher of any matter to which that rule applies if at the time of publication (having taken all reasonable care) he does not know and has no reason to suspect that relevant proceedings are active.

(2) A person is not guilty of contempt of court under the strict liability rule as the distributor of a publication containing any such matter if at the time of distribution (having taken all reasonable care) he does not know that it contains such matter and has no reason to suspect that it is likely to do so.

(3) The burden of proof of any fact tending to establish a defence afforded by this section to any person lies upon that person.

In the absence of such express language courts when interpreting penal provisions have to discover the intention of Parliament. Certain factors or considerations may assist the courts in this exercise. However, the weight to be attributed to any factor is more difficult to assess with the result that it is very difficult to predict how a court will construe a particular provision.

(1) The presumption of mens rea

Sweet v. Parsley
[1970] A.C. 132
House of Lords

Miss Sweet, a teacher, let rooms in a farmhouse to students. She did not reside in the farmhouse but retained one room for her own use for occasional overnight stays when she visited to collect the rent and check the property. After the police had searched the premises, finding evidence that cannabis had been smoked there, Miss Sweet was convicted by magistrates of being concerned in the management of premises which were used for the purpose of smoking cannabis, contrary to section 5(*b*) of the Dangerous Drugs Act 1965. The magistrates found that Miss Sweet did not exercise any control over her tenants and that she had no knowledge that the house was being used for the purpose of smoking cannabis. Her appeal to the Divisional Court was dismissed and she appealed to the House of Lords.

LORD REID: A Divisional Court dismissed her appeal, holding that she had been concerned in the management of those premises. The reasons given for holding that she was managing the property were that she was in a position to choose her tenants: that she could put them under as long or as short a tenancy as she desired and that she could make it a term of any letting that smoking of cannabis was not to take place. All these reasons would apply to every occupier who lets out parts of his house or takes in lodgers or paying guests. But this was held to be an absolute offence following the earlier decision in *Yeandel v. Fisher* [1966] 1 Q.B. 440.

How has it come about that the Divisional Court has felt bound to reach such an obviously unjust result? It has in effect held that it was carrying out the will of Parliament because Parliament has chosen to make this an absolute offence. And, of course, if Parliament has so chosen the courts must carry out its will, and they cannot be blamed for any unjust consequences. But has Parliament so chosen?

I dealt with this matter at some length in *Warner v. Metropolitan Police Commissioner* [1969] 2 A.C. 256. On reconsideration I see no reason to alter anything which I there said. But I think that some amplification is necessary. Our first duty is to consider the words of the Act: if they show a clear intention to create an absolute offence that is an end of the matter. But such cases are very rare. Sometimes the words of the section which creates a particular offence make it clear that *mens rea* is required in one form or another. Such cases are quite frequent. But in a very large number of cases there is no clear indication either way. In such cases there has for centuries been a presumption that Parliament did not intend to make criminals of persons who were in no way blameworthy in what they did. That means that whenever a section is silent as to *mens rea* there is a presumption that, in order to give effect to the will of Parliament, we must read in words appropriate to require *mens rea*. . . . [I]t is firmly established by a host of authorities that *mens rea* is an essential ingredient of every offence unless some reason can be found for holding that that is not necessary.

It is also firmly established that the fact that other sections of the Act expressly require *mens rea*, for example because they contain the word "knowingly" is not in itself sufficient to justify a decision that a section which is silent as to *mens rea* creates an absolute offence. In the absence of a clear indication in the Act that an offence is intended to be an absolute offence, it is necessary to go outside the Act and examine all relevant circumstances in order to establish that this must have been the intention of Parliament. I say "must have been" because it is a universal principle that if a penal provision is reasonably capable of two interpretations, that interpretation which is most favourable to the accused must be adopted.

What, then, are the circumstances which it is proper to take into account? In the well-known case of *Sherras v. De Rutzen* (*post*, p. 191), Wright J. only mentioned the subject-matter with which the Act deals. But he was there dealing with something which was one of a class of acts which "are not criminal in any real sense, but are acts which in the public interest are prohibited under a penalty." It does not in the least follow that when one is dealing with a truly criminal act it is sufficient merely to have regard to the subject-matter of the enactment. One must put oneself in the position of a legislator. It has long been the practice to recognise absolute offences in this class of quasi-criminal acts, and one can safely assume that, when Parliament is passing new legislation dealing with this class of offences, its silence as to *mens rea* means that the old practice is to apply. But when one comes to acts of a truly criminal character, it appears to me that there are at least two other factors which any reasonable legislator would have in mind. In the first place a stigma still attaches to any person convicted of a truly criminal offence, and the more serious or more disgraceful the offence the greater the stigma. So he would have to consider whether, in a case of this gravity, the public interest really requires that an innocent person should be prevented from proving his innocence in order that fewer guilty men may escape. And equally important is the fact that fortunately the Press in this country are vigilant to expose injustice and every mani-festly unjust conviction made known to the public tends to injure the body politic by undermining public confidence in the justice of the law and of its administration. But I regret to observe that, in some recent cases where serious offences have been held to be absolute offences, the court has taken into account no more than the wording of the Act and the character and seriousness of the mischief which constitutes the offence.

The choice would be much more difficult if there were no other way open than either *mens rea* in the full sense or an absolute offence; for there are many kinds of case where putting on the prosecutor the full burden of proving *mens rea* creates great difficulties and may lead to many unjust acquittals. But there are at least two other possibilities. Parliament has not infrequently transferred the onus as regards *mens rea* to the accused so that, once the necessary facts are proved, he must convince the jury that on balance of probabilities he is innocent of any criminal intention. I find it a little surprising that more use has not been made of this method: but one of the bad effects of the decision of this House in *Woolmington v. D.P.P* [1935] A.C. 462 may have been to discourage its use. The other method would be in effect to substitute in appropriate classes of cases gross negli-gence for *mens rea* in the full sense as the mental element necessary to constitute the crime. It would often be much easier to infer that Parliament must have meant that gross negligence should be the necessary mental element than to infer that Parliament intended to create an absolute offence. A variant of this would be to accept the view of Cave J. in *R. v. Tolson* (*ante*, p. 162). This appears to have been done in Australia where authority appears to support what Dixon J. said in *Proudman v. Dayman* (1941) 67 C.L.R. 536, 540: "As a general rule an honest and reasonable belief in a state of facts which, if they existed, would make the defendant's act inno-cent affords an excuse for doing what would otherwise be an offence." It may be that none of these methods is wholly satisfactory but at least the public scandal of convicting on a serious charge persons who are in no way blameworthy would be avoided.

If this section means what the Divisional Court have held that it means, then hundreds of thousands of people who sublet part of the premises or take in lodgers or are concerned in the management of residential premises or institutions are daily incurring a risk of being convicted of a serious offence in circumstances where they are in no way to blame. For the greatest vigilance cannot prevent tenants, lodgers or inmates or guests whom they bring in from smoking cannabis cigarettes in their own rooms. It was suggested in argument that this appellant brought this conviction on herself because it is found as a fact that when the police searched the premises there were people there of the "beatnik fraternity". But surely it would be going a very long way to say that persons managing premises of any kind ought to safeguard themselves by refusing accommodation to all who are of slovenly or exotic appearance, or who bring in guests of that kind. And unfortunately drug taking is by no means confined to those of unusual appearance.

Speaking from a rather long experience of membership of both Houses, I assert with confidence that no Parliament within my recollection would have agreed to make an offence of this kind an absolute offence if the matter had been fully explained to it. So, if the court ought only to hold an offence to be an absolute offence where it appears that that must have been the intention of Parliament, offences of this kind are very far removed from those which it is proper to hold to be absolute offences.

I must now turn to the question what is the true meaning of section 5 of the 1965 Act . . . is the "purpose" the purpose of the smoker or the purpose of the management? . . . It is clear that the purpose is the purpose of the management . . . So if the purpose is the purpose of the management, the question whether the offence . . . is absolute can hardly arise.

I would allow the appeal and quash the appellant's conviction.

LORD PEARCE. My Lords, the prosecution contend that any person who is concerned in the management of premises where cannabis is in fact smoked even once, is liable, though he had no knowledge and no guilty mind. This is, they argue, a practical act intended to prevent a practical evil. Only by convicting some innocents along with the guilty can sufficient pressure be put upon those who make their living by being concerned in the management of premises. Only thus can they be made alert to prevent cannabis being smoked there. And if the prosecution have to prove knowledge or mens rea, many prosecutions will fail and many of the guilty will escape. I find that argument wholly unacceptable.

The notion that some guilty mind is a constituent part of crime and punishment goes back far beyond our common law. And at common law mens rea is a necessary element in a crime. Since the Industrial Revolution the increasing complexity of life called into being new duties and crimes which took no account of intent. Those who undertake various industrial and other activities, especially where these affect the life and health of the citizen, may find themselves liable to statutory punishment regardless of knowledge or intent, both in respect of their own acts or neglect and those of their servants. But one must remember that normally mens rea is still an ingredient of any offence. Before the court will dispense with the necessity for mens rea it has to be satisfied that Parliament so intended. The mere absence of the word "knowingly" is not enough. But the nature of the crime, the punishment, the absence of social obloquy, the particular mischief and the field of activity in which it occurs, and the wording of the particular section and its context, may show that Parliament intended that the act should be prevented by punishment regardless of intent or knowledge.

Viewing the matter on these principles, it is not possible to accept the prosecution's contention. Even granted that this were in the public health class of case, such as, for instance, are offences created to ensure that food shall be clean, it would be quite unreasonable. It is one thing to make a man absolutely responsible for all his own acts and even vicariously liable for his servants if he engages in a certain type of activity. But it is quite another matter to make him liable for persons over whom he has no control. . . .

[His Lordship concluded that the "purpose" which had to be proved was that of the person concerned in the management of the premises. Since the appellant had no knowledge of the use being made of the premises, he concluded the appeal had to be allowed.]

Appeal allowed

[The Misuse of Drugs Act 1971 incorporated "knowingly" in this offence.]

Questions and Note

1. How is a court to distinguish between a "truly criminal" offence to which stigma attaches and "quasi-criminal" acts which are prohibited in the public interest? Would no stigma attach to a farmer whose leaking slurry tank pollutes a nearby river killing hundreds of salmon or to a butcher who sells meat unfit for human consumption if in each case the parties had acted with due vigilance?

2. Would a better solution to the position of stark choice between *mens rea* and strict liability be the middle ground of providing a "due diligence" defence for the accused to prove as in *Proudman v. Dayman* (1941) 67 CLR 536 and *R. v. City of Sault Ste Marie* (1978) 85 D.L.R. (3d) 161. See also Misuse of Drugs Act 1971, ss.8&28.

3. Unlike the High Court of Australia in *Proudman v. Dayman* and the Supreme Court of Canada in *R v. City of Sault Ste Marie*, English courts have not developed a general due diligence (or "no negligence") defence to offences of strict liability, although Lord Diplock did suggest in *Sweet v. Parsley* that it might be possible at common law. However, Parliament often does provide for a due diligence defence: see *e.g.* Offices, Shops and Railway Premises Act 1963, section 67; Trade Descriptions Act 1968, ssection 24(3); Weights and Measures Act 1985, ssection 34. A refinement of the due diligence defence in many statutes is the imposition of the requirement that the accused not only prove due diligence but that he also prove that the contravention was due to the act or default of a third party: see *e.g.* Food Safety Act 1990, section 21(2); Medicines Act 1968, section 121. Some statutes merely require disclosure of the identity of the third party alleged to have been responsible for the contravention: see *e.g.* Consumer Safety Act 1978, section 2(6).

Note

The presumption of *mens rea* is merely the starting point in the courts' analysis of statutory provisions. In determining whether the presumption is to be upheld or rebutted in a particular instance the courts will look at other relevant factors.

(2) The statutory context

In construing a particular section of an Act courts may obtain assistance by considering the presence or absence of *mens rea* words in other sections of the Act and by determining the purpose of the provision in question.

Cundy v. Le Cocq
(1884) 13 Q.B.D. 207
Queen's Bench Division

C, a licensed victualler, sold liquor to a person who was drunk. C. was unaware of the drunkenness, but he was nevertheless convicted of unlawfully selling liquor to a drunken person, contrary to section 13 of the Licensing Act 1872. C appealed to the Divisional Court.

STEPHEN J.: I am of opinion that this conviction should be affirmed. Our answer to the question put to us turns upon this, whether the words of the section under which this conviction took place, taken in connection with the general scheme of the Act, should be read as constituting an offence only where the licensed person knows or has means of knowing that the person served with intoxicating liquor is drunk, or whether the offence is complete where no such knowledge is shown. I am of opinion that the words of the section amount to an absolute prohibition of the sale of liquor to a drunken person, and that the existence of a bona fide mistake as to the condition of the person served is not an answer to the charge, but is a matter only for mitigation of the penalties that may be imposed. I am led to that conclusion both by the general scope of the Act, which is for the repression of drunkenness, and from a comparison of the various sections under the head "offences against public order". Some of these contain the word "knowingly", as for instance section 14, which deals with keeping a disorderly house, and section 16, which deals with the penalty for harbouring a constable. Knowledge in these and other cases is an element in the offence; but the clause we are considering says nothing about the knowledge of the state of the person served. I believe the reason for making this prohibition absolute was that there must be a great temptation to a publican to sell liquor without regard to the sobriety of the customer, and it was thought right to put upon the publican the responsibility of determining whether his customer is sober. Against this view we have had quoted the maxim that in every criminal offence there must be a guilty mind; but I do not think that maxim has so wide an application as it is sometimes considered to have. In old time and as applicable to the common law or to earlier statutes, the maxim may have been of general application; but a difference has arisen owing to the greater precision of modern statutes. It is impossible now, as illustrated by the cases of *R. v. Prince* (*ante*, p. 168), and *R. v. Bishop* (1880) 5 Q.B.D. 259, to apply the maxim generally to all statutes, and the substance of all the reported cases is that it is necessary to look at the object of each Act that is under consideration to see whether and how far knowledge is of the essence of the offence created. Here, as I have already pointed out, the object of this part of the Act is to prevent the sale of intoxicating liquor to drunken persons, and it is perfectly natural to carry that out by throwing on the publican the responsibility of determining whether the person supplied comes within that category.

I think, therefore, the conviction was right and must be affirmed.

Conviction affirmed

Sherras v. De Rutzen
[1895] 1 Q.B. 918
Queen's Bench Division

S, a licensed victualler, was convicted under section 16(2) of the Licensing Act 1872, for having unlawfully supplied liquor to a police constable on duty without having the authority of a superior officer of such constable for so doing. S reasonably believed that the constable was off

duty. He appealed to quarter sessions and thence to the Divisional
Court.

DAY J.: I am clearly of opinion that this conviction ought to be quashed. This
police constable comes into the appellant's house without his armlet, and with
every appearance of being off duty. The house was in the immediate neighbourhood of the police-station, and the appellant believed, and he had very
natural grounds for believing, that the constable was off duty. In that belief
he accordingly served him with liquor. As a matter of fact, the constable was
on duty—but does that fact make the innocent act of the appellant an offence?
I do not think it does. He had no intention to do a wrongful act; he acted in
the bona fide belief that the constable was off duty. It seems to me that the
contention that he committed an offence is utterly erroneous. An argument
has been based on the appearance of the word "knowingly" in subsection (1)
of section 16, and its omission in subsection (2). In my opinion the only effect
of this is to shift the burden of proof. In cases under subsection (1) it is for
the prosecution to prove the knowledge, while in cases under subsection (2)
the defendant has to prove that he did not know. That is the only inference I
draw from the insertion of the word "knowingly" in the one subsection and
its omission in the other.

It appears to me that it would be straining the law to say that this publican,
acting as he did in the bona fide belief that the constable was off duty, and
having reasonable grounds for that belief, was nevertheless guilty of an
offence against the section for which he was liable both to a penalty and to
have his licence indorsed.

WRIGHT J.: I am of the same opinion. There are many cases on the subject, and
it is not very easy to reconcile them. There is a presumption that *mens rea*, an
evil intention, or a knowledge of the wrongfulness of the act, is an essential
ingredient in every offence; but that presumption is liable to be displaced
either by the words of the statute creating the offence or by the subject-matter
with which it deals, and both must be considered: *Nichols v. Hall* (1873) L.R.
8 C.P. 322. One of the most remarkable exceptions was in the case of bigamy.
It was held by all the judges, on the statute 1 Jac. 1, c. 11, that a man was
rightly convicted of bigamy who had married after an invalid Scotch divorce,
which had been obtained in good faith, and the validity of which he had no
reason to doubt: *Lolly's Case* (1812) R. & R. 237. Another exception, apparently
grounded on the language of a statute, is *Prince's Case* (1875) L.R. 2 C.C.R.
154, where it was held by 15 judges against one that a man was guilty of
abduction of a girl under 16, although he believed, in good faith and on reasonable grounds, that she was over that age. Apart from isolated and extreme
cases of this kind, the principal classes of exceptions may perhaps be reduced
to three. One is a class of acts which, in the language of Lush J. in *Davies v.
Harvey* (1874) L.R. 9 Q.B. 433, are not criminal in any real sense, but are acts
which in the public interest are prohibited under a penalty.... Another class
comprehends some, and perhaps all, public nuisances.... Lastly, there are
many cases in which, although the proceeding is criminal in form, it is really
only a summary mode of enforcing a civil right.... But, except in such cases
as these, there must in general be guilty knowledge on the part of the defendant, or of someone whom he has put in his place to act for him, generally, or
in the particular matter, in order to constitute an offence. It is plain that if
guilty knowledge is not necessary, no care on the part of the publican could
save him from a conviction under section 16, subsection (2), since it would be
as easy for the constable to deny that he was on duty when asked, or to
produce a forged permission from his superior officer, as to remove his armlet

before entering the public-house. I am, therefore, of opinion that this conviction ought to be quashed.

Conviction quashed

Question

Do the two cases above represent a conflict of authority, as Glanville Williams suggests (C.L.G.P., p. 223)? Or can a rationale be found in the distinction between the risk of serving a drunk, and that of serving a constable on duty?

B. (A Minor) v. Director of Public Prosecutions
[2000] 2 W.L.R. 452
House of Lords

B, aged 15, sat next to a girl aged 13 on a bus and asked her several times to perform oral sex with him which she refused to do. He was charged with inciting a girl under the age of 14 to commit an act of gross indecency with him, contrary to section 1(1) of the Indecency with Children Act 1960. B honestly believed the girl was over 14 but when the justices ruled that this was no defence to the charge he changed his plea to guilty. On a case stated by the justices, the Divisional Court of the Queen's Bench Division dismissed B's appeal. The Divisional Court certified, *inter alia*, that the following point of law of general public importance was involved in its decision, namely, "Is a defendant entitled to be acquitted of the offence of inciting a child aged under 14 to commit an act of gross indecency . . . if he may hold an honest belief that the child in question was aged 14 years or over?"

LORD NICHOLLS OF BIRKENHEAD: [His Lordship referred to the common law presumption that *mens rea* is an essential ingredient of an offence unless Parliament has indicated the contrary intention either expressly or by necessary implication.]

The construction of section 1 of the Indecency with Children Act 1960

In section 1(1) of the Indecency with Children Act 1960 Parliament has not expressly negatived the need for a mental element in respect of the age element of the offence. The question, therefore, is whether, although not expressly negatived, the need for a mental element is negatived by necessary implication. "Necessary implication" connotes an implication which is compellingly clear. Such an implication may be found in the language used, the nature of the offence, the mischief sought to be prevented and any other circumstances which may assist in determining what intention is properly to be attributed to Parliament when creating the offence.

I venture to think that, leaving aside the statutory context of section 1, there is no great difficulty in this case. The section created an entirely new criminal offence, in simple unadorned language. The offence so created is a serious offence. The more serious the offence, the greater is the weight to be attached to the presumption, because the more severe is the punishment and the graver the stigma which accompany a conviction. Under section 1 conviction originally attracted a punishment of up to two years' imprisonment. This has since been increased to a maximum of ten years' imprisonment. The notification requirements under Part I of the Sex Offenders Act 1997 now apply, no matter what the age of the offender: see Schedule 1, paragraph 1(1)(b). Further, in addition to being a serious offence, the offence is drawn broadly ("an act of gross indecency"). It can embrace conduct ranging from predatory approaches by a much older paedophile to consensual sexual experimentation between precocious teenagers of whom the offender may be the younger of the two. The conduct may be depraved by any acceptable standard, or it may be relatively innocuous behaviour in private between two young people. These factors reinforce, rather than negative, the application of the presumption in this case.

The purpose of the section is, of course, to protect children. An age ingredient was therefore an essential ingredient of the offence. This factor in itself does not assist greatly. Without more, this does not lead to the conclusion that liability was intended to be strict so far as the age element is concerned, so that the offence is committed irrespective of the alleged offender's belief about the age of the "victim" and irrespective of how the offender came to hold this belief.

Nor can I attach much weight to a fear that it may be difficult sometimes for the prosecution to prove that the defendant knew the child was under fourteen or was recklessly indifferent about the child's age. . . .

Similarly, it is far from clear that strict liability regarding the age ingredient of the offence would further the purpose of section 1 more effectively than would be the case if a mental element were read into this ingredient. There is no general agreement that strict liability is necessary to the enforcement of the law protecting children in sexual matters. For instance, the draft criminal code bill prepared by the Law Commission in 1989 proposed a compromise solution. Clauses 114 and 115 of the bill provided for committing or inciting acts of gross indecency with children aged under thirteen or under sixteen. Belief that the child is over sixteen would be a defence in each case: see the Law Commission, Criminal Law, A Criminal Code for England and Wales, vol 1, Report and draft Criminal Code Bill, p. 81 (Law Com. No. 177).

Is there here a compellingly clear implication that Parliament should be taken to have intended that the ordinary common law requirement of a mental element should be excluded in respect of the age ingredient of this new offence? Thus far, having regard especially to the breadth of the offence and the gravity of the stigma and penal consequences which a conviction brings, I see no sufficient ground for so concluding.

Indeed, the Crown's argument before your Lordships did not place much reliance on any of the matters just mentioned. The thrust of the Crown's argument lay in a different direction: the statutory context. This is understandable, because the statutory background is undoubtedly the Crown's strongest point. The Crown submitted that the law in this field has been regarded as settled for well over one hundred years, ever since the decision in *Reg v. Prince* (1875) L.R. 2 C.C.R. 154. That well known case concerned the unlawful abduction of a girl under the age of sixteen. The defendant honestly believed she was over sixteen, and he had reasonable grounds for believing this. No fewer than fifteen judges held that this provided no defence. Subsequently, *in R. v. Maughan* (1934) 24 Cr.App.R. 130 the Court of Criminal Appeal (Lord Hewart C.J., Avory and Roche JJ.) held that a reasonable and honest belief that a girl was over sixteen could never be a defence to a charge of indecent assault. The court held that this point had been decided in *Rex v. Forde* (1923) 17 Cr.App.R. 99. The court also observed that in any event the answer was to be found in *Prince's* case. Building on this foundation Mr. Scrivener Q.C. submitted

that the Sexual Offences Act 1956 was not intended to change this established law, and that section 1 of the Indecency with Children Act 1960
was to be read with the 1956 Act. The preamble to the 1960 Act stated
that its purpose was to make "further" provision for the punishment of
indecent conduct towards young people. In this field, where Parliament
intended belief as to age to be a defence, this was stated expressly: see,
for instance, the "young man's defence" in section 6(3) of the 1956 Act.

This is a formidable argument, but I cannot accept it. . . . Where the
Crown's argument breaks down is that the motley collection of offences,
of diverse origins, gathered into the Sexual Offences Act 1956 displays no
satisfactorily clear or coherent pattern. If the interpretation of section 1 of
the Act of 1960 is to be gleaned from the contents of another statute, that
other statute must give compelling guidance. The Act of 1956 as a whole
falls short of this standard. So do the two sections, sections 14 and 15,
which were the genesis of section 1 of the Act of 1960.

Accordingly, I cannot find, either in the statutory context or otherwise,
any indication of sufficient cogency to displace the application of the
common law presumption. In my view the necessary mental element
regarding the age ingredient in section 1 of the Act of 1960 is the absence
of a genuine belief by the accused that the victim was fourteen years of
age or above. The burden of proof of this rests upon the prosecution in the
usual way. If Parliament considers that the position should be otherwise
regarding this serious social problem, Parliament must itself confront the
difficulties and express its will in clear terms. I would allow this appeal.

LORD STEYN: . . . [His Lordship examined the history of section 1(1) offence
and the relationship of the Act of 1960 to the Sexual Offences Act 1956.]

The correct approach

My Lords, it will be convenient to turn to the approach to be adopted to
the construction of section 1(1) of the Act of 1960. While broader considerations will ultimately have to be taken into account, the essential point
of departure must be the words of section 1(1). The language is general
and nothing on the face of section 1(1) indicates one way or the other
whether section 1(1) creates an offence of strict liability. In enacting such
a provision Parliament does not write on a blank sheet. The sovereignty of
Parliament is the paramount principle of our constitution. But Parliament
legislates against the background of the principle of legality. In *Reg. v.
Secretary of State for the Home Department, Ex parte Pierson* [1998] A.C. 539
many illustrations of the application of the principle were given in the
speech of Lord Browne-Wilkinson and in my speech: 573G-575D, 587C-
590A. Recently, in *Reg. v. Secretary of State for the Home Department, Ex parte
Simms* [1999] 3 W.L.R. 328 the House applied the principle to subordinate
legislation: see in particular the speeches of Lord Hoffmann at p. 341F-G,
myself, at p. 340G-H, and Lord Browne-Wilkinson, at p. 330E. In *Ex parte
Simms* Lord Hoffmann explained the principle as follows, at p. 341:

"But the principle of legality means that Parliament must squarely confront what it is doing and accept the political cost. Fundamental rights
cannot be overridden by general or ambiguous words. This is because
there is too great a risk that the full implications of their unqualified
meaning may have passed unnoticed in the democratic process. In the
absence of express language or necessary implication to the contrary,
the courts therefore presume that even the most general words were
intended to be subject to the basic rights of the individual."

This passage admirably captures, if I may so, the rationale of the principle of legality. In successive editions of his classic work Professor Sir Rupert Cross cited as the paradigm of the principle the " 'presumption' that mens rea is required in the case of statutory crimes": *Statutory Interpretation* 3 ed. (1995), p. 166. Sir Rupert explained that such presumptions are of general application and are not dependent on finding an ambiguity in the text. He said they

"not only supplement the text, they also operate at a higher level as expressions of fundamental principles governing both civil liberties and the relations between Parliament, the executive and the courts. They operate as constitutional principles which are not easily displaced by a statutory text."

In other words, in the absence of express words or a truly necessary implication, Parliament must be presumed to legislate on the assumption that the principle of legality will supplement the text. This is the theoretical framework against which section 1(1) must be interpreted.

[His Lordship examined *Sweet v. Parsley* placing emphasis on the speech of Lord Reid.]

Concentrating still on the wording of section 1(1) of the Act of 1960, I now address directly the question whether the presumption is prima facie applicable. Two distinctive features of section 1(1) must be taken in to account. First, the actus reus is widely defined. Unlike the position under sections 14 and 15 of the Act of 1956, an assault is not an ingredient of the offence under section 1(1). Any act of gross indecency with or towards a child under the age of 14, or incitement to such an act, whether committed in public or private, is within its scope. The subsection is apt to cover acts of paedophilia and all responsible citizens will welcome effective legislation in respect of such a great social evil. But it also covers any heterosexual or homosexual contact between teenagers if one of them is under 14. And the actus reus extends to incitement of a child under 14: words are enough. The subsection therefore extends to any verbal sexual overtures between teenagers if one of them is under 14: see the telling examples given by Brooke L.J. in the instant case [1999] 3 W.L.R. 116, 128H-129C. For the law to criminalise such conduct of teenagers *by offences of strict liability* would be far reaching and controversial. The second factor is that section 1(1) creates an offence of a truly criminal character. It was initially punishable on indictment by a custodial term of up to two years and by subsequent amendment the maximum term has been increased to ten years' imprisonment. Moreover, as Lord Reid observed in *Sweet v. Parsley* (at 146H) "a stigma still attaches to any person convicted of a truly criminal offence, and the more serious or more disgraceful the offence the greater the stigma." Taking into account the cumulative effect of these two factors, I am persuaded that, if one concentrates on the language of section 1(1), the presumption is *prima facie* applicable.

[His Lordship examined the arguments of the Crown which sought to rebut the presumption but found no merit in them. He answered the certified question in the affirmative.]

Appeal allowed

Note

A number of sexual offences are age-related. Whether an age-related offence is one of strict liability will have to be determined on a case by case basis. For example, section 6 of the Sexual Offences Act 1956 makes it an offence, punishable with up to two years imprisonment, for a man to have intercourse with a girl under 16. Section 5 makes it an offence, punishable with up to life imprisonment, for a man to have intercourse with a girl under 13. Section 6 is clearly an offence of strict liability as it provides a defence in sub-section 3 where the accused is under twenty-four years of age, has not previously been charged with a like offence, and he believes the girl to be 16 or over and has reasonable cause for that belief. Section 5 is silent on the question of mens rea. Lord Steyn considered that section 5 "plainly creates an offence of strict liability". This view is highly questionable. The reasoning which led to a conclusion that section 1(1) of the Indecency with Children Act 1960 did not create an offence of strict liability would seem to apply with equal or greater force to this offence particularly in light of the extremely severe penalty which may be imposed. This argument is given added force by the fact that where a person over the age of eighteen is convicted of a "serious offence" (as defined in section 109(5) of the Powers of Criminal Courts (Sentencing) Act 2000) and has previously been convicted of a serious offence, a life sentence is mandatory "unless the court is of the opinion that there are exceptional circumstances relating to either of the offences or to the offender which justify its not doing so". The list of serious offences includes the section 5 offence. (See further Professor J.C. Smith's commentary to *B (A Minor) v. DPP* [2000] Crim L.R. 403 for a discussion of the uncertainties relating to indecent assaults of consenting children under the age of sixteen.)

(3) The social context

Courts have sought to distinguish between offences which involve moral obloquy or stigma and those which do not. If an offence is of a regulatory nature it is more likely to fall into this latter category. In determining whether the presumption of *mens rea* has been rebutted two factors are of particular relevance, namely (1) whether the offence is of general application to all members of the public or confined to a specific class of persons engaged in a particular activity, trade or profession and (2) the nature of the social danger which the offence is aimed at preventing. If the offence applies only to a particular class of persons the courts will more readily hold the presumption has been rebutted (see Lord Diplock's speech in *Sweet v. Parsley, ante,* p. 184).

Pharmaceutical Society of Great Britain v. Storkwain Ltd
[1986] 2 All E.R. 635
House of Lords

The respondents brought informations against the appellants alleging they were guilty of offences under section 58(2)(*a*) and section 67(2) of the Medicines Act 1968, having sold on prescription medicines to customers who had presented prescriptions which proved to be forgeries. The appellants believed in good faith and on reasonable grounds that the prescriptions were valid. The magistrates dismissed the informations. The Divisional Court allowed the appeal of the respondents. The appellants appealed to the House of Lords.

LORD GOFF OF CHIEVELEY: My Lords, this appeal is concerned with a question of construction of section 58 of the Medicines Act 1968. . . . The Divisional Court certified the following point of law as being of general public importance:

> "Whether the prosecution have to prove mens rea where an information is laid under Section 58(2)(*a*) of the Medicines Act 1968 where the allegation is that the supply of 'prescription only' drugs was made by the [defendant] in accordance with a forged prescription and without fault on [his] part."

. . . For the appellants, counsel submitted [*inter alia*] that there must, in accordance with the well-recognised presumption, be read into section 58(2)(*a*) words appropriate to require *mens rea* in accordance with *R. v. Tolson* (*ante*, p. 162); in other words, to adopt the language of Lord Diplock in *Sweet v. Parsley* [1970] A.C. 132 at 163, the subsection must be read subject to the implication that a necessary element in the prohibition (and hence in the offence created by the subsection together with section 67(2) of the 1968 Act) is the absence of belief, held honestly and on reasonable grounds, in the existence of facts which, if true, would make the act innocent. . . .

I am unable to accept counsel's submission, for the simple reason that it is, in my opinion, clear from the 1968 Act that Parliament must have intended that the presumption of *mens rea* should be inapplicable to section 58(2)(*a*). First of all, it appears from the 1968 Act that, where Parliament wished to recognise that *mens rea* should be an ingredient of an offence created by the Act, it has expressly so provided. Thus, taking first of all offences created under provisions of Pt. II of the 1968 Act, express requirements of *mens rea* are to be found both in section 45(2) and section 46(1), (2) and (3) of the Act. More particularly, in relation to offences created by Pt. III and Pts. V and VI of the 1968 Act, section 121 makes detailed provision for a requirement of *mens rea* in respect of certain specified sections of the act, including sections 63 to 65 (which are contained in Pt. III), but significantly not section 58, nor indeed sections 52 and 53. . . . It is very difficult to avoid the conclusion that, by omitting section 58 from those sections to which section 121 is expressly made applicable, Parliament intended that there should be no implication of a requirement of *mens rea* in section 58(2)(*a*). This view is fortified by subss. (4) and (5) of section 58 itself. Subsection (4)(*a*) provides that any order made by the appropriate ministers for the purposes of section 58 may provide that section 58(2)(*a*) or (*b*), or both, shall have effect subject to such exemptions as may be specified in the order. From this subsection alone it follows that the ministers, if they think it right, can provide for exemption where there is no *mens rea* on the part of the accused. Subsection (5) provides that any exemption conferred by an order in accordance with subsection (4)(*a*) may be conferred subject to such conditions or limitations as may be specified in the order. From this it follows that, if the ministers, acting under subs. (4), were to confer an exemption relating to sales where the vendor lacked the requisite *mens rea*, they may nevertheless circumscribe their exemption with conditions and limitations which render the exemption far narrower than the implication for which counsel for the appellants contends should be read into the statute itself. I find this to be very difficult to reconcile with the proposed implication.

It comes as no surprise to me, therefore, to discover that the relevant order in force at that time, the Medicines (Prescriptions Only) Order 1980, is drawn entirely in conformity with the construction of the statute which I favour. . . .

For these reasons, which are substantially the same as those which are set out in the judgments of Farquharson and Tudor Price JJ. in the Divisional Court, I am unable to accept the submissions advanced on behalf of the appellants. I gratefully adopt as my own the following passage from the judgment of Farquharson J. ([1985] 3 All E.R. 4 at 10):

"... it is perfectly obvious that pharmacists are in a position to put illicit drugs and perhaps other medicines on the market. Happily this rarely happens but it does from time to time. It can therefore be readily understood that Parliament would find it necessary to impose a heavier liability on those who are in such a position, and make them more strictly accountable for any breaches of the Act."

I would therefore answer the certified question in the negative, and dismiss the appeal with costs.

Certified question answered in negative. Appeal dismissed

Questions

1. What measures would it be necessary for pharmacists to adopt to ensure that drugs were not dispensed on a forged prescription and would any such measures be practicable?
2. If the purpose of the legislation was to encourage pharmacists to take care when dispensing drugs, could this purpose have been achieved in any other way without imposing strict liability?

Note

Courts are vigilant to protect public safety. Where this consideration is weighty the courts may find that the presumption of *mens rea* has been rebutted. This is more likely to be the result where the court considers that the imposition of strict liability will encourage greater vigilance on the part of those regulated by the statute.

Alphacell Ltd v. Woodward
[1972] A.C. 824
House of Lords

In the course of their business the appellants produced large quantities of polluted effluent which they pumped into a settling tank near a river bank. Pumps were installed in the tank to pump out excess water to prevent the tank from overflowing. The pumps were shielded by filters to prevent solid matter from blocking them. They were also regularly inspected. Despite these precautions the pumps became blocked by brambles, leaves and other vegetable matter causing the tank to overflow and polluted effluent to enter the river. The appellants were convicted under s.2(1) of the Rivers (Prevention of Pollution) Act 1951 which made it an offence if a person "causes or knowingly permits to enter a stream any poisonous, noxious or polluting matter". The question certified for the House of Lords was:

"Whether the offence of causing polluting matter to enter a stream contrary to section 2 of the Rivers (Prevention of Pollution) Act 1951 can be committed by a person who has no knowledge of the fact that polluting matter is entering the stream and has not been negligent in any relevant respect."

LORD SALMON. My Lords, I agree that this appeal should be dismissed and I wish to add only a few brief observations of my own. It is undisputed that the river on the banks of which stands the appellants' Mount Sion Works was polluted by contaminated effluent which flowed from those works into the river. The vital question is whether the appellants caused that pollution within the meaning of section 2 (1) of the Rivers (Prevention of Pollution) Act 1951. The nature of causation has been discussed by many eminent philosophers and also by a number of learned judges in the past. I consider, however, that what or who has caused a certain event to occur is essentially a practical question of fact which can best be answered by ordinary common sense rather than by abstract metaphysical theory.

It seems to me that, giving the word "cause" its ordinary and natural meaning, anyone may cause something to happen intentionally or negligently or inadvertently without negligence and without intention. . . .

The appellants clearly did not cause the pollution intentionally and we must assume that they did not do so negligently. Nevertheless, the facts so fully and clearly stated by my noble and learned friend Viscount Dilhorne to my mind make it obvious that the appellants in fact caused the pollution. If they did not cause it, what did? There was no intervening act of a third party nor was there any act of God to which it could be attributed. The appellants had been responsible for the design of the plant; everything within their works was under their control; they had chosen all the equipment. The process which they operated required contaminated effluent being pumped round their works until it came to rest in an open tank which they sited on the river bank. If the pumps which they had installed in this tank failed to operate efficiently the effluent would necessarily overflow into the river. And that is what occurred. It seems plain to me that the appellants caused the pollution by the active operation of their plant. They certainly did not intend to cause pollution but they intended to do the acts which caused it.

The appellants contend that, even if they caused the pollution, still they should succeed since they did not cause it intentionally or knowingly or negligently. Section 2 (1) (*a*) of the Rivers (Prevention of Pollution) Act 1951 is undoubtedly a penal section. It follows that if it is capable of two or more meanings then the meaning most favourable to the subject should be adopted. Accordingly, so the argument runs, the words "intentionally" or "knowingly" or "negligently" should be read into the section immediately before the word "causes." I do not agree. It is of the utmost public importance that our rivers should not be polluted. The risk of pollution, particularly from the vast and increasing number of riparian industries, is very great. The offences created by the Act of 1951 seem to me to be prototypes of offences which "are not criminal in any real sense, but are acts which in the public interest are prohibited under a penalty": *Sherras v. De Rutzen* [1895] 1 Q.B. 918, *per* Wright J. at p. 922, referred to with approval by my noble and learned friends Lord Reid and Lord Diplock, in *Sweet v. Parsley* [1970] A.C. 132, 149, 162. I can see no valid reason for reading the word "intentionally", "knowingly" or "negligently" into section 2 (1) (*a*) and a number of cogent reasons for not doing so. In the case of a minor pollution such as the present, when the justices find that there is no wrongful intention or negligence on the part of the defendant, a comparatively nominal fine will no doubt be imposed. This may be regarded as a not unfair hazard of carrying on a business which may cause pollution on the banks of a river. The present appellants were fined £20 and ordered to pay, in all, £24 costs. I should be surprised if the costs of pursuing this appeal to this House were incurred for the purpose of saving these appellants £44.

If this appeal succeeded and it were held to be the law that no conviction could be obtained under the Act of 1951 unless the prosecution could discharge the often impossible onus of proving that the pollution was caused intentionally or negligently, a great deal of pollution would go unpunished and undeterred to the relief of many riparian factory owners. As a result, many rivers which are now filthy would become filthier still and many rivers which are now clean would lose their cleanliness. The legislature no doubt recognised that as a matter of public policy this would be most unfortunate. Hence section 2 (1) (*a*) which encourages riparian factory owners not only to take reasonable steps to prevent pollution but to do everything possible to ensure that they do not cause it.

I do not consider that the appellants can derive any comfort (as they seek to do) from the inclusion in section 2 (1) (*a*) of the words "knowingly permits" nor from the deeming provision against local authorities in relation to sewage escaping into a river from sewers or sewage disposal units [section 2 (1)]. The creation of an offence in relation to permitting pollution was probably included in the section so as to deal with the type of case in which a man knows that contaminated effluent is escaping over his land into a river and does nothing at all to prevent it. The inclusion of the word "knowingly" before "permits" is probably otiose and, if anything, is against the appellants, since it contrasts with the omission of the word "knowingly" before the word "causes". The deeming provision was probably included to meet what local authorities might otherwise have argued was a special case and cannot, in my opinion, affect the plain and unambiguous general meaning of the word "causes".

For these reasons I would dismiss the appeal with costs.

[Lords Wilberforce, Pearson, Cross of Chelsea and Viscount Dilhorne made speeches dismissing the appeal.]

Appeal dismissed with costs.

Gammon (Hong Kong) Ltd and Others v. Attorney General of Hong Kong
[1954] 2 All E.R. 503
Privy Council

The appellants were respectively the registered contractor, the project manager and the site agent for building works on a site in Hong Kong. Part of a temporary lateral support system collapsed. The company was charged with a material deviation from an approved plan in contravention of subsection (2A)(*b*) of section 40 of the Hong Kong Building Ordinance (revised edn. 1981), and with carrying out works in a manner likely to cause risk of injury or damage in contravention of sub-section (2B)(*b*). The project manager and the site engineer were charged under sub-section (2B)(*b*), respectively, with carrying out works, and permitting them to be carried on in a manner likely to cause risk of injury or damage.

LORD SCARMAN: delivered the judgment of the Board: . . .

i. The general law

. . . The question in the appeal is whether the ordinance, correctly interpreted, provides a sound reason for holding that the offences created by subss. (2A)(*b*) and (2B)(*b*) of section 40 of the ordinance are offences of strict liability. . . .

In their Lordships' opinion, the law relevant to this appeal may be stated in the following propositions: (1) there is a presumption of law that *mens rea* is required before a person can be held guilty of a criminal offence; (2) the presumption is particularly strong where the offence is "truly criminal" in character; (3) the presumption applies to statutory offences, and can be displaced only if this is clearly or by necessary implication the effect of the statute; (4) the only situation in which the presumption can be displaced is where the statute is concerned with an issue of social concern; public safety is such an issue; (5) even where a statute is concerned with such an issue, the presumption of *mens rea* stands unless it can also be shown that the creation of strict liability will be effective to promote the objects of the statute by encouraging greater vigilance to prevent the commission of the prohibited act.

ii. The ordinance

Their Lordships turn to consider the purpose and subject matter of the ordinance. Its overall purpose is clearly to regulate the planning, design and construction of the building works to which it relates in the interests of safety. It covers a field of activity where there is, especially in Hong Kong, a potential danger to public safety. And the activity which the ordinance is intended to regulate is one in which citizens have a choice whether they participate or not. Part IV (section 40) of the ordinance makes it very clear that the legislature intended that criminal sanctions for contraventions of the ordinance should be a feature of its enforcement. But it is not to be supposed that the legislature intended that any of the offences created by the ordinance should be offences of strict liability unless it is plain, from a consideration of the subject-matter of the ordinance and of the wording of the particular provision creating the offence, that an object of the ordinance, *e.g.* the promotion of greater vigilance by those having responsibility under the ordinance, would be served by the imposition of strict liability.

The appellants submit that there is no necessity for strict liability in respect of any of the offences charged. Their first submission is that strict liability would not promote greater vigilance. If the persons charged had no knowledge of an essential fact, what could they have done to avoid its occurrence? Their second submission is more comprehensive. They submit that strict liability in respect of any offence created by the ordinance would run counter to the structure and character of the ordinance. The ordinance, it is submitted, relies not on criminal liability but on the elaborate and stringent provisions for the registration of persons qualified to ensure that its requirements are met.

So far as the first submission is concerned, their Lordships are satisfied that strict liability would help to promote greater vigilance in the matters covered by the two offenders with which this appeal is concerned (the material deviation under subs. (2A)(*b*) and the risk of injury or damage under subs. (2B)(*b*). The second submission is more formidable. Their Lordships, however, reject it also. Their Lordships agree with the view expressed by the Court of Appeal as to the purpose and subject-matter of the ordinance. The Court of Appeal saw no injustice in the imposition of heavy penalties for offences under the ordinance "whether resulting from intentional infringement of the law, negligence or incompetence." They made this powerful comment:

"Any large scale building operation will almost inevitably produce circumstances in which a departure from the generally accepted standards (whether of work or materials) will be likely to cause danger. Indeed, the extent of the danger and of the damage which may be done will frequently be enormous. It therefore behoves the incompetent to stay away and the competent to conduct themselves with proper care. A building contractor who delegates his legal responsibilities to an agent can fairly be held liable if he appoints an agent who is incompetent or careless: he should regulate his business in such a way as to avoid, on the one hand, the appointment of incompetent agents and, on the other, the consequences of any carelessness by a competent agent. Only if he is made responsible for seeing that the statutory standards are maintained can the purpose of the legislature be attained and in such a case as this the presumption of strict liability displaces the ordinary presumption of mens rea: see *Lim Chin Aik v. R. (post,* p. 206)."

Important as are the provisions of the ordinance for the registration, disqualification and discipline of persons qualified, authorised and registered to perform the duties and obligations required by the ordinance, the legislature by enacting Pt. IV (section 40) of the ordinance clearly took the view that criminal liability and punishment were needed as a deterrent against slipshod or incompetent supervision, control or execution of building works. The imposition of strict liability for some offences clearly would emphasise to those concerned the need for high standards of care in the supervision and execution of work. The view that their Lordships have reached, after the thorough review of the ordinance and history . . . is that, where the ordinance provides for an offence in terms which are silent or ambiguous as to the need for full *mens rea* covering all its essential ingredients, the wording of the particular provision must be carefully examined against the background and in the context of the ordinance to determine whether it is necessary to interpret the silence or resolve the ambiguity in favour of *mens rea* or of strict liability.

Put in positive terms, the conclusion of the Board is that it is consistent with the purpose of the ordinance in its regulation of the works to which it applies that at least some of the criminal offences which it creates should be of strict liability. It is a statute the subject matter of which may properly be described as—

"the regulation of a particular activity involving potential danger to public health [and] safety . . . in which citizens have a choice whether they participate or not . . ."

(See [1970] A.C. 132 at 163 *per* Lord Diplock.)

Whether, therefore, a particular provision of the statute creates an offence of full *mens rea* or of strict liability must depend on the true meaning of the words of the particular provision construed with reference to its subject-matter and to the question whether strict liability in respect of all or any of the essential ingredients of the offence would promote the object of the provision. . . .

iii. Subsections (2A) and (2B)

Their Lordships now turn to consider the two subsections in detail and separately; for it does not follow that, if one subsection should create an offence of strict liability, the other must also do so. But first a few observations on certain features common to both.

The first common feature is that both subsections have a characteristic of which Lord Reid spoke in *Sweet v. Parsley* [1970] A.C. 132 at 149. The specific provisions subsections (2A)(*b*) and (2B)() belong to that:

"multitude of criminal enactments where the words of the Act simply make it an offence to do certain things but where everyone agrees that there cannot be a conviction without proof of mens rea in some form."

Each provision clearly requires a degree of *mens rea*, but each is silent whether it is required in respect of all the facts which together constitute the offence created. The issue here is, therefore, a narrow one. Does subs. (2A)(*b*) require knowledge of the materiality of the deviation? Does subs. (2B)(*b*) require knowledge of the likelihood of risk of injury or damage?

The second common feature is that each provision appears in a section which creates many other offences, the wording of some, though not all, of which clearly requires full *mens rea*.

A third common feature is that the maximum penalties for the offences which they create are heavy: a fine of $250,000 and imprisonment for three years. There is no doubt that the penalty indicates the seriousness with which the legislature viewed the offences.

The first of these features raises the determinative question in the appeal. Their Lordships will, therefore, consider it later in respect of each subsection.

The second feature, in their Lordships' opinion, proves nothing. One would expect a wide range of very different offences in a statute which establishes a comprehensive system of supervision and control over a great range of complicated works in diverse circumstances. And it can be said with equal force that a feature of section 40 is that in many cases where *mens rea* is required it expressly says so, and that, where a defence of reasonable excuse or lack of knowledge is to be available, it makes express provision to that end; examples may be seen in subss. (1B), (10), (2A)(*c*), (2C), (6), (7) and (7A).

The severity of the maximum penalties is a more formidable point. But it has to be considered in the light of the ordinance read as a whole. For reasons which their Lordships have already developed, there is nothing inconsistent with the purpose of the ordinance in imposing severe penalties for offences of strict liability. The legislature could reasonably have intended severity to be a significant deterrent, bearing in mind the risks to public safety arising from some contraventions of the ordinance. Their Lordships agree with the view on this point of the Court of Appeal. It must be crucially important that those who participate in or bear responsibility for the carrying out of works in a manner which complies with the requirements of the ordinance should know that severe penalties await them in the event of any contravention or non-compliance with the ordinance by themselves or by anyone over whom they are required to exercise supervision or control.

Subsection (2A)

... The wording of paragraph (*b*) clearly requires knowledge of the approved plan and of the fact of deviation. But in their Lordships' view it would be of little use in promoting public safety if it also required proof of knowledge of the materiality of the deviation. As it was put on behalf of the Attorney-General, if the offence requires knowledge of the materiality of the deviation to be proved, the defendant is virtually judge in his own cause. The object of the provision is to assist in preventing material deviations from occurring. If a building owner, an authorised person or a registered person is unaware of the materiality of the deviation which he authorises (and knowledge of the deviation is necessary), he plainly ought to be. He is made liable to criminal penalties because of the threat to public safety arising from material deviations from plans occurring within the sphere of his responsibility. The effectiveness of the ordinance would be seriously weakened if it were open to such a person to plead ignorance of what was material. In the words already quoted of the Court of Appeal, ". . . it behoves the incompetent to stay away and the competent to conduct themselves with proper care."

Subsection (2B)

The construction of subsection (2B)(*b*) is more difficult, but their Lordships are satisfied that it imposes strict liability for substantially the same reasons as those which have led them to this conclusion in respect of subsection (2A)(*b*). The offence created clearly requires a degree of *mens rea*. A person cannot carry out works or authorise or permit them to be carried out in a certain manner unless he knows the manner which he is employing, authorising or permitting. . . .

Their Lordships find some support for their view that subsection (2B)(*b*) is an offence of strict liability in the wording of the offence created by subsection (2B)(*a*). The wording of paragraph (*a*) points to strict liability, once injury or damage has in fact been caused. Anyone who has carried out, authorised or permitted work to be carried out in a manner which has in fact caused injury or damage is caught.

Conclusion

For these reasons their Lordships conclude that to the extent indicated the offences charged against the appellants are of strict liability.

Appeal dismissed: case remitted to magistrate

Question

In *Alphacell* and *Gammon* the defendants were companies engaging in commercial activities in spheres which involved risk to public safety. With the exception of road traffic offences where the danger to the public is grave, and a few other activities such as possessing firearms (see *R. v. Howells* [1972] 2 W.L.R. 716, *ante*, p. 171) individuals rarely engage in activities which involve serious risks to public safety. Corporate entities do not suffer the stigma which individuals may suffer when convicted of a criminal offence. Professor Andrew Ashworth in *Principles of Criminal Law* (3rd ed) p. 169 states that "the conflict between social welfare and fairness to defendants should be resolved differently according to whether the defendant is a private individual or a large corporation". Do you agree?

(4) *Promoting the enforcement of the law*

Reynolds v. G. H. Austin & Sons Ltd
[1951] 2 K.B. 135
King's Bench Division

A women's guild organised an outing and arranged with a company, who carried on the business of operating motor-coaches, to convey in a motor-coach a party at a fixed price per person. The organiser of the outing caused to be exhibited in a shop an advertisement giving particulars of the trip which stated "Few tickets left. Apply within." The company had no knowledge and no reasonable means of discovering that any such advertisement had been made. The outing took place and the company, who held no road service licence covering the journey in question, were charged with having used the motor-coach in contravention of section 72 of the Act of 1930 on the ground that by the condition of section 25, subsection (1)(*b*), of the Act of 1934, such journey "must be made without previous advertisement to the public of the arrangements therefor." The information was dismissed and the prosecutor appealed.

EVLIN J.: . . . The main weight of the case for the prosecutor rests on the contention that this statute belongs to a class in which *mens rea* should be dispensed with. There is no doubt that some of the provisions of the Road Traffic Acts do fall within that class: see, for example, *Griffiths v. Studebakers Ltd* [1924] 1 K.B. 102. It may seem, on the face of it, hard that a man should be fined, and, indeed, made subject to imprisonment, for an offence which he did not know that he was committing. But there is no doubt that the legislature has for certain purposes found that hard measure to be necessary in the public interest. . . . Thus a man may be made responsible for the acts of his servants, or even for defects in his business arrangements, because it can be fairly said that by such sanctions citizens are induced to keep themselves and their organisations up to the mark. Although, in one sense, the citizen is being punished for the sins of others, it can be said that, if he had been more alert to see that the law was observed, the sin might not have been committed. But if a man is punished because of an act done by another, whom he cannot reasonably be expected to influence or control, the law is engaged, not in punishing thoughtlessness or inefficiency, and thereby promoting the welfare of the community, but in pouncing on the most convenient victim. Without the authority of express words, I am not willing to conclude that Parliament can intend what would seem to the ordinary man (as plainly it seemed to the justices in this case) to be the useless and unjust infliction of a penalty. . . .

I think it a safe general principle to follow (I state it negatively, since that is sufficient for the purposes of this case), that where the punishment of an individual will not promote the observance of the law either by that individual or by others whose conduct he may reasonably be expected to influence then, in the absence of clear and express words, such punishment is not intended.

Appeal dismissed

Lim Chin Aik v. The Queen
[1963] A.C. 160
Privy Council

The appellant was charged with and convicted of contravening section 6(2) of the Immigration Ordinance 1952 of the State of Singapore by remaining in Singapore (after having entered) when he had been prohibited from entering by an order made by the Minister under section 9. At the trial there was no evidence from which it could properly be inferred that the order had in fact come to the notice or attention of the appellant. He appealed, ultimately to the Privy Council.

LORD EVERSHED: That proof of the existence of a guilty intent is an essential ingredient of a crime at common law is not at all in doubt. The problem is of the extent to which the same rule is applicable in the case of offences created and defined by statute or statutory instrument. . . .

Mr Gratiaen founded his argument upon the formulation of the problem contained in the judgment of Wright J. in *Sherras's* case (*ante*, p. 191). The language of that learned and experienced judge was as follows: "There is a presumption that *mens rea*, or evil intention or knowledge of the wrongfulness of the act, is an essential ingredient in every offence, but that presumption is liable to be displaced either by the words of the statute creating the offence or by the subject-matter with which it deals, and both must be considered." . . .

Their Lordships accept as correct the formulation cited from the judgment of Wright J. . . . What should be the proper inferences to be drawn from the language of the statute or statutory instrument under review—in this case of sections 6 and 9 of the Immigration Ordinance? More difficult, perhaps, still what are the inferences to be drawn in a given case from the "subject-matter with which [the statute or statutory instrument] deals"?

Where the subject-matter of the statute is the regulation for the public welfare of a particular activity—statutes regulating the sale of food and drink are to be found among the earliest examples—it can be and frequently has been inferred that the legislature intended that such activities should be carried out under conditions of strict liability. The presumption is that the statute or statutory instrument can be effectively enforced only if those in charge of the relevant activities are made responsible for seeing that they are complied with. When such a presumption is to be inferred, it displaces the ordinary presumptions of *mens rea*. . . .

But it is not enough in their Lordships' opinion merely to label the statute as one dealing with a grave social evil and from that to infer that strict liability was intended. It is pertinent also to inquire whether putting the defendant under strict liability will assist in the enforcement of the regulations. That means that there must be something he can do, directly or indirectly, by supervision or inspection, by improvement of his business methods or by exhorting those whom he may be expected to influence or control, which will promote the observance of the regulations. Unless this is so, there is no reason in penalising him, and it cannot be inferred that the legislature imposed strict liability merely in order to find a luckless victim. This principle has been expressed and applied in *Reynolds v. G. H. Austin & Sons Ltd* (*ante*, p. 205) and *James & Son Ltd v. Smee* [1955] 1 Q.B. 78. Their Lordships prefer it to the alternative view that strict liability follows simply from the nature of the subject-matter and that persons whose conduct is beyond any sort of criticism can be dealt with by the imposition of a nominal penalty. . . . But though a nominal penalty may be appropriate in an individual case where exceptional lenience is called for, their Lordships cannot, with respect, suppose that it is envisaged by the legislature as a way of dealing with offenders generally. Where it can be shown that the imposition of strict liability would result in the prosecution and conviction of a class of persons whose conduct could not in any way affect the observance of the law, their Lordships consider that, even where the statute is dealing with a grave social evil, strict liability is not likely to be intended.

Their Lordships apply these general observations to the Ordinance in the present case. The subject-matter, the control of immigration, is not one in which the presumption of strict liability has generally been made. Nevertheless, if the courts of Singapore were of the view that unrestricted immigration is a social evil which it is the object of the Ordinance to control most rigorously, their Lordships would hesitate to disagree. That is a matter peculiarly within the cognisance of the local courts. But Mr Le Quesne was unable to point to anything that the appellant could possibly have done so as to ensure that he complied with the regulations. It was not, for example, suggested that it would be practicable for him to make continuous inquiry to see whether an order had been made against him. Clearly one of the objects of the Ordinance is the expulsion of prohibited persons from Singapore, but there is nothing that a man can do about it if, before the commission of the offence, there is no practical or sensible way in which he can ascertain whether he is a prohibited person or not. . . . It seems to their Lordships that, where a man is said to have contravened an order or an order of prohibition, the common sense of the language presumes that he was aware of the order before he can be said to have contravened it. Their Lordships realise that this statement is something of an over-simplification when applied to the present case; for the "contravention" alleged is of the unlawful act, prescribed by subsection (2) of the section, of remaining in Singapore after the date of the order of prohibition. Nonetheless it is their Lordships' view that, applying the test of ordinary sense to the language used, the notion of contravention here alleged is more consistent with the assumption that the person charged had knowledge of the order than the converse. But such a conclusion is in their Lordships' view much reinforced by the use of the word "remains" in its context. It is to be observed that if the respondent is right a man could lawfully enter Singapore and could thereafter lawfully remain in Singapore until the moment when an order of prohibition against his entering was made; that then, instanter, his purely passive conduct in remaining—that is, the mere continuance, quite unchanged, of his previous behaviour, hitherto perfectly lawful—would become criminal. These considerations bring their Lordships clearly to the conclusion that the sense of the language here in question requires for the commission of a crime thereunder *mens rea* as a constituent of such crime; or at least there is nothing in the language used which suffices to exclude the ordinary presumption. Their Lordships do not forget . . . the fact that the word "knowingly" or the phrases "without reasonable cause" or "without reasonable excuse" are found in various sections of the Ordinance (as amended) but find no place in the section now under consideration. . . . In their Lordships' view the absence of such a word or phrase in the relevant section is not sufficient in the present case to prevail against the conclusion which the language as a whole suggests. In the first place, it is to be noted that to have inserted such words as "knowingly" or "without lawful excuse" in the relevant part of section 6(3) of the Act would in any case not have been sensible. Further, in all the various instances where the word or phrase is used in the other sections of the Ordinance before-mentioned the use is with reference to the doing of some specific act or the failure to do some specific act as distinct from the mere passive continuance of behaviour theretofore perfectly lawful. Finally, their Lordships are mindful that in the *Sherras* case itself the fact that the word "knowingly" was not found in the subsection under consideration by the court but was found in another subsection of the same section was not there regarded as sufficient to displace the ordinary rule.

Appeal allowed

iii. Critique

It is evident from the cases in the preceding section that a number of justifications are advanced for the imposition of strict liability, such as improved standards of prevention (*i.e.* the public will be better protected from the inherent risks in certain activities), and greater administrative efficiency (*i.e.* that efficacious enforcement is only possible where there is no burden on the prosecution to prove a mental element). On their own both these arguments could be used to favour the abolition of *mens rea* in all crimes. (See Wootton, *infra*).

Two further glosses are thus added. On the one hand it is suggested that strict liability does not eliminate fault as a basis of liability but that the fault element is determined at an earlier stage of the criminal process. Such an argument can lead to different conclusions. (See Paulus, Thomas and Smith, below.) On the other hand, it is said that, since these offences are not "true" crimes, the concept of *mens rea* is not required to prevent the injustice of punishing the "morally" innocent. This approach leads to difficulties in deciding whether it is the nature of the prohibited activity or the fact that no mental element is required which renders these "quasi'" crimes. A vicious circle may arise in which strict liability is imposed to protect the public from the risks inherent in certain activities, while that protection is undermined by sentencing lightly defendants who, by virtue of the use of discretionary enforcement policies, have at the very least been negligent. (See Walker, *infra*). At a different level of analysis, it can be questioned whether either strict liability or negligence acts as an incentive to greater safety precautions (Hutchinson, *infra*).

Ingeborg Paulus, "Strict Liability: Its Place in Public Welfare Offences" (1978) 20 Crim.L.Q.445:

Theoretical legal reasoning repeatedly stresses that strict liability ... is unjust and holds persons liable for offences for which they are morally blameless. Yet empirical researchers assessing the law in action are not alarmed about strict liability offences and their enforcement. ... [W]henever studies have been made investigating the workings of strict liability, the persons involved in the administration of public welfare offences, especially those concerning food and drug laws, have stressed that strict liability generally does not penalise offenders who are not also clearly guilty. ... [T]he personnel in charge of enforcement rarely prosecute unless they find an element of fault or *mens rea* present in the offence. But the *availability* of strict liability prosecutions greatly facilitates their work.

[The studies referred to are: Smith and Pearson, "The Value of Strict Liability" [1969] Crim.L.R. 5; W. G. Carson, "Some Sociological Aspects of Strict Liability and the Enforcement of Factory Legislation" (1970) 33 M.L.R. 396; F. J. Remington, *et al.*, "Liability Without Fault Criminal Statutes" [1965] Wis.L.R. 625. To these can be added: Law Commission, Pub. Working Paper No. 30, Strict Liability and the Enforcement of the Factories Act 1961 (1970) and Law Reform Commission of Canada, "Studies in Strict Liability" (Ottowa, 1974).]

D. A. Thomas, "Form and Function in Criminal Law" in Glazebrook, p. 30:

The effect of imposing strict liability is not necessarily to eliminate fault as a requirement of liability, but to delegate to the enforcer both the responsibility of deciding what kind of fault will in general justify a prosecution (with the certainty of conviction) and the right to determine whether in the circumstances of the particular case that degree of fault is present. The main objections to the concept of strict liability are thus procedural rather than substantive, and the questions to be addressed to the proponent of a statute creating an offence of strict liability are: 'Why is it not possible to incorporate into the definition of the offence the nature of the fault which is likely in practice to be required as a condition precedent to prosecution, and why is it not possible for the existence of this fault to be determined in accordance with the normal processes of the law?' At

the very least, there can be no justification for enacting an offence of strict
liability which is not balanced by a provision allowing the question
whether fault existed or not to be raised in the trial as an affirmative
defence, and any offence of strict liability where the gravity of the offence
would be enhanced by the offender's knowledge of the relevant circumstances should be the lowest step in a hierarchy of offences including
similar offences requiring proof of knowledge or intent.

J. C. Smith [1966] Crim.L.R. 505, commenting on *Lockyer v. Gibb*
[1967] 2 Q.B. 243, a case on possession of drugs where the defendant
did not know that what she possessed *was* a drug:

The interpretation of statutes so as to create offences of strict liability
in fact creates difficulties of sentencing which have not been faced up to
by the courts. Take a case in which the accused is tried on indictment.
The judge tells the jury to convict if they are satisfied that (i) D knew he
was in possession of the thing, and (ii) the thing is a dangerous drug.
They convict. If these are the only facts proved against D it would be
quite scandalous to do other than give him an absolute discharge. If D
ought to have known the thing was a drug, then he is in some degree
blameworthy; if he in fact knew it was a drug, he is more blameworthy.
But the jury need not consider these questions. How does the judge know
on what basis he should sentence? He is discouraged from asking the jury
the question at all. The judge presumably makes up his own mind. His
view of the facts may differ completely from that of the jury—if they have
a view. Thus what is really the fundamental issue of fact in the case is
withdrawn from the jury and decided by the judge alone. The position in
the case of a magistrates' court is a little easier because the magistrates at
least know on what facts the conviction is based; but it is unsatisfactory
that they may come to the sentencing stage without having considered
whether the accused bears any moral responsibility whatever for the
'offence' which has been committed. This question must be considered
before a sentence can be imposed. Presumably it is dealt with in the
informal way in which other findings of fact relating only to sentence
are handled. But this is hardly satisfactory, when it is really the most
fundamental issue of fact in the case which is being considered. On what
basis was the fine of £10 in the present case imposed? The magistrate
must have thought that the defendant was in some degree blameworthy
or he would presumably have granted an absolute discharge. Yet he was
evidently not satisfied beyond reasonable doubt that the defendant knew
that the substance was a dangerous drug. Did he then fine her because
she ought to have known? Or was he satisfied with a lower degree of
proof (she probably knew)?

Nigel Walker, *Crime and Punishment in Britain* (1965), p. 33:

The number of people killed or injured in road accidents each year is
more than ten times the numbers involved in all the forms of assault
recorded in the Criminal Statistics. Many of these casualties were due to
the victim's own negligence or disobedience of rules; but even if we allow
for this by halving the figures, it is clear that anti-social use of vehicles is
a much more important source of death, bereavement, physical suffering
and disablement than any intentional forms of violence. Yet the penal
system treats motoring offences far less seriously than crimes of violence
or even of dishonesty. Inadvertence is the excuse offered by most people

accused of illegal parking, speeding or disobeying traffic signals, and that partly because this defence is so hard to disprove, partly in the hope of making the negligent driver less negligent, the law has been drafted so that even negligent transgressions are offences. This encourages the impression that *most* such transgressions are merely negligent, although it is very doubtful whether this is so.

Allan C. Hutchinson, Note on Sault Ste Marie (1979), 17 Osgoode Hall Law Journal 415, 429 (fn. 78):

An application of the presently favoured 'economic perspective,' as represented by Richard A. Posner and other members of the so-called Chicago School, to the problem offers some interesting insights into the relative efficiency of strict liability and negligence as methods of combating the type of harm and safeguarding the interests that public welfare offences are intended to protect. According to such an analysis, where the primary object of an offence is accident prevention, as is the case with public welfare offences, there is little to choose between strict liability and negligence. Whichever basis of liability is employed, the standard of care taken by the potential injurer is likely to be influenced almost exclusively by the result of balancing the cost of precautions against the predicted cost of the penalty. If the preventive costs are lower, then precautions will be taken whether the offence is one of negligence or strict liability. But if the penalty is lower, then neither negligence nor strict liability is likely to encourage the taking of precautions. Therefore, the choice of liability standards has no effect on the level of safety achieved. Moreover, it is possible, yet surprising to many, that, if either basis of liability is to bring about some long term effect, the imposition of strict liability is more likely than negligence to result in an improvement in accident prevention. As regards negligence, liability is usually determined on the existing state of sophistication of the technology of accident prevention and, as such, presents little or no incentive to advance such knowledge by investing in its research and development. On the other hand, strict liability may engender greater safety, as there is more of an incentive to encourage and engage in the research into and the development of precautionary measures:

> 'If [for example, a railroad company] were liable for all accidents . . ., it would compare the liability that it could not avoid by means of existing safety precautions without the feasibility of developing new precautions that would reduce that liability. If safety research and development seemed likely to reduce accident costs by more than the cost of research and development, the [company] would undertake it. . . . (Posner, *The Economic Analysis of Law* (2nd ed., Boston: Little, Brown, 1977) at 138).'

Such an approach is overly simplistic. The validity of the argument is contingent on two dubious assumptions: that penalties will remain minimal and unrealistic, and that the intangible costs (*i.e.* loss of reputation in the community, political embarrassment, unsettling of shareholders) will be negligible. Moreover, it fails to take into account the possible and positive gains that are available if the polluter shows himself to be a morally and socially responsible member of the community. There is much more to law and life than the cold and relentless logic of economic reasoning.

iv. Proposals for Reform

In contrast to the general trend one commentator has ardently advocated the increase in crimes of strict liability:

Baroness Wootton, *Crime and The Criminal Law* (2nd ed., 1981), pp. 46–48

If, however, the primary function of the courts is conceived as the prevention of forbidden acts, there is little cause to be disturbed by the multiplication of offences of strict liability. If the law says that certain things are not to be done, it is illogical to confine this prohibition to occasions on which they are done from malice aforethought: for at least the material consequences of an action, and the reasons for prohibiting it, are the same whether it is the result of sinister malicious plotting, of negligence or of sheer accident. A man is equally dead and his relatives equally bereaved whether he was stabbed or run over by a drunken motorist or by an incompetent one; and the inconvenience caused by the loss of your bicycle is unaffected by the question whether or not the youth who removed it had the intention of putting it back, if in fact he had not done so at the time of his arrest. It is true, of course, as Professor Hart has argued, that the material consequences of an action by no means exhaust its effects. 'If one person hits another, the person struck does not think of the other as *just* a cause of pain to him. . . . If the blow was light but deliberate, it has a significance for the person struck quite different from an accidental much heavier blow.' To ignore this difference, he argues, is to outrage 'distinctions which not only underlie morality, but pervade the whole of our social life'. That these distinctions are widely appreciated and keenly felt no one would deny. Often perhaps they derive their force from a purely punitive or retributive attitude; but alternatively they may be held to be relevant to an assessment of the social damage that results from a criminal act. Just as a heavy blow does more damage that a light one, so also perhaps does a blow which involves psychological injury do more damage than one in which the hurt is purely physical.

The conclusion to which this argument leads is, I think, not that the presence or absence of the guilty mind is unimportant, but that *mens rea* has, so to speak—and this is the crux of the matter—*got into the wrong place*. Traditionally, the requirement of the guilty mind is written into the actual definition of a crime. No guilty intention, no crime, is the rule. Obviously this makes sense if the law's concern is with wickedness: where there is no guilty intention, there can be no wickedness. But it is equally obvious, on the other hand, that an action does not become innocuous merely because whoever performed it meant no harm. If the object of the criminal law is to prevent the occurrence of socially damaging actions, it would be absurd to turn a blind eye to those which were due to carelessness, negligence or even accident. The question of motivation is *in the first instance* irrelevant.

But only in the first instance. At a later stage, that is to say, after what is now known as conviction, the presence or absence of guilty intention is all-important for its effect on the appropriate measures to be taken to prevent a recurrence of the forbidden act. The prevention of accidental deaths presents different problems from those involved in the prevention of wilful murders. The results of the actions of the careless, the mistaken, the wicked and the merely unfortunate may be indistinguishable from one another, but each case calls for a different treatment. Tradition, however, is very strong, and the notion that these differences are relevant only after the fact has been established that the accused committed the forbidden act seems still to be deeply abhorrent to the legal mind. Thus Lord Devlin, discussing the possibility that judges might have taken the line that all 'unintentional' criminals might be dealt with simply by the imposition of a nominal penalty, regards this as the 'negation of law'. 'It would,' [Devlin, Lord, *Samples of Law Making* (OUP, 1962) p. 73] he says, 'confuse the function of mercy which the judge is dispensing when imposing the penalty with the function of justice. It would have been to deny to the citizen due process of law because it would have been to say to him, in effect: "Although we cannot think that Parliament intended you to be punished in this case because you have really done nothing wrong, come to us, ask for mercy, and we shall grant mercy".... In all criminal matters the citizen is entitled to the protection of the law ... and the mitigation of penalty should not be adopted as the prime method of dealing with accidental offenders.'

Within its own implied terms of reference the logic is unexceptionable. If the purpose of the law is to dispense punishment tempered with mercy, then to use mercy as a consolation for unjust punishment is certainly to give a stone for bread. But these are not the implied terms of reference of strict liability. In the case of offences of strict liability the presumption is not that those who have committed forbidden actions must be punished, but that appropriate steps must be taken to prevent the occurrence of such actions.

J. C. Smith, "Responsibility in Criminal Law" in *Barbara Wootton, Essays in Her Honour* (1986) eds., Bean and Whynes, 141 at 153

This brings me to what I regard as the major difficulty in Lady Wootton's theory. It is essentially a practical one. The only question for the court of trial is to be 'Did he do it?' Whether he did it intentionally, recklessly, negligently, or by sheer accident is irrelevant. In any event the person who did it is to be passed on to the 'sentencer' who will consider what should be done to ensure that he does not do it again. Now if the court of trial has to disregard the question of fault, so too surely do the police and the prosecuting authority (or whatever takes its place). If we allow the police or prosecutor to decide to proceed or not on the basis of whether or not the defendant was at fault, we do indirectly what we will not permit to be done directly. We allow the crucial decision which is now made formally and openly on proper evidence in court to be made informally, privately, and on whatever evidence the prosecutor, in his wisdom, or lack of it, considers relevant. The logic of the system requires the prosecution of *all* cases because even if the forbidden result has resulted from 'sheer accident,' the sentencer is under a duty to consider whether there is anything to be done to ensure that the 'offender' does not have such accidents again. Everyone who causes injury to another person, everyone who damages another's property, could, and should, be brought to court. Every buyer or seller of goods who makes an innocent misrepresentation, every bona-fide purchaser of goods in fact stolen, the surgeon whose patient dies on the operating table, the Good Samaritan who innocently gives help to a person escaping after committing an arrestable offence—all these have brought about the harm which it is the object of the law to prevent; so they should be subject to process of law so as to ensure that they do not cause the harm again. The business of the courts would be enormously multiplied. And to what purpose? What is to be done with all those who (like Ball and Mrs Tolson) have behaved reasonably and have had the misfortune to cause the forbidden result by sheer accident—except to tell them to continue to behave reasonably?

It is reasonably safe to assume that what would in fact happen is that, however illogically, the fault test would be applied at the police or prosecution stage. This would be prompted, not only by the natural sense of justice of those operating the system, but also by their realization of the futility of invoking legal process against one who has behaved entirely reasonably.

A further practical difficulty is that the system would put enormous discretion into the hands of the sentencer. He would apparently have the same power in law over one who caused death accidentally as over a murderer. It is difficult to believe that such a large discretion would be tolerable. It would dilute, if not destroy, the criminal law as a moral force and that at a time when the decline of religious belief has, as Lady Wootton herself says, created a dangerous vacuum. The shift from punishment to prevention may be intended to remove the moral basis of the law; but if, as some believe, one of the major reasons why people do not commit crimes is the sense of guilt which attaches to them, should not the aim be to enhance the sense of guilt rather than otherwise? To remove the element of fault is to empty the law of moral content. If murder were, in law, no different from accidental death, should we be so inhibited from committing murder as most of us are?

The Model Penal Code

S.1.04(1) An offence defined by this Code or by any other statute of this State, for which a sentence of [death or of] imprisonment is authorised, constitutes a crime. Crimes are classified as felonies, misdemeanours or petty misdemeanours.

(5) An offence defined by this Code or by any other statute of this State constitutes a violation if it is so designated in this Code or in the law defining the offence or if no other sentence than a fine, or fine and forfeiture or other civil penalty is authorised upon conviction or if it is defined by a statute other than this Code which now provides that the offense shall not constitute a crime. A violation does not constitute a crime and conviction of a violation shall not give rise to any disability or legal disadvantage based on conviction of a criminal offence.

S.2.05(1) The requirements of culpability prescribed by Sections 2.01 and 2.02 [of which the minimum is negligence] do not apply to:

(a) offences which constitute violations, unless the requirement involved is included in the definition of the offence or the Court determines that its application is consistent with effective enforcement of the law defining the offence; or

(b) offences defined by statutes other than the Code, insofar as a legislative purpose to impose absolute liability for such offences or with respect to any material element thereof plainly appears.

Justice, *Breaking the Rules*, 1980

[In recommending a similar division between "crimes" and "contraventions" in this country, *Justice* envisages the following:]

Section 4.12 In practice, the sort of procedure we have in mind would work something like this:—

(a) whenever the public authority charged with responsibility for the relevant sector of public conduct obtained evidence amounting to a *prima facie* case of a contravention, it would notify the alleged contravenor by letter and invite his explanation;

(b) failing a satisfactory explanation within a fixed time, the authority would impose a prescribed penalty, and notify the contravenor what his options are;

(c) those options would be either to comply with the penalty imposed (*e.g.* to pay a fine) or, if he challenged the imposition of the penalty, to give notice of his objection (on a form supplied to him) to his local Magistrates' Court;

(d) if such a notice is given, the burden would be on the authority to satisfy the Magistrates' Court, by sworn evidence and beyond reasonable doubt, that the alleged contravenor had committed the contravention complained of.

Question

The Law Commission proposal in clause 20(1) of the Draft Criminal Code Bill would create a presumption in favour of *mens rea* which Parliament could rebut. The M.P.C. and "Justice" propose that "offences" of strict liability should be separately classified. Would either of these proposals tend to increase the incidence of strict liability? Is either approach preferable?

CHAPTER 4

MENTAL INCAPACITY

Notes

1. In this chapter defences which relate to the defendant's mental capacity will be considered. Duress, necessity and self-defence are dealt with in Chapter 5. Provocation and diminished responsibility, because they are only available in murder, are dealt with in Chapter 8.

2. In a criminal trial the defendant's mental state at three separate points in time may be relevant:

(i) the time when the *actus reus* was committed;
(ii) the time when the defendant is called to plead to the charge against him;
(iii) the time when the court comes to consider the appropriate sentence where the defendant has been convicted.

In this book (i) will be considered. On (ii) see J. Sprack, *Emmins* on *Criminal Procedure* (2000), pp. 244–245; on (iii) see M. Wasik, *Emmins on Sentencing* (1998).

3. With regard to (i) there are three ways in which the issue of the defendant's mental state may be raised;

(a) on a plea of insanity;
(b) a plea that the *actus reus* was committed while the defendant was in a state of automatism; and
(c) on a plea of diminished responsibility where the charge is murder (see Chap. 8).

4. The section which follows is concerned with the law's treatment of insanity which provides a complete defence to a charge where the defendant was insane at the time the *actus reus* of the offence was committed. Previously the defence carried with it the consequence that the defendant would be ordered by the court to be admitted to a mental hospital under section 37 of the Mental Health Act 1983 subject to restriction without limit of time under section 41. The defendant would be detained until the Home Secretary or a Mental Health Tribunal ordered his release on being satisfied that detention was no longer necessary for the protection of the public. This automatic committal

to a mental hospital for an indeterminate period was one of the deterrents against pleading insanity as a defence. Some defendants preferred to plead guilty and cast themselves upon the mercy of the judge sentencing them rather than rely on a defence which was technically available to them. Between 1975 and 1989 there was a total of 52 verdicts of "not guilty by reason of insanity", with the number in any single year ranging from one to six (see R. D. Mackay, *Mental Condition Defences in the Criminal Law* (1995) p. 102). The Criminal Procedure (Insanity and Unfitness to Plead) Act 1991 has changed this. Section 3 substitutes a new section 5 of the Criminal Procedure (Insanity) Act 1964 providing the judge with discretion in the disposal he chooses. The substituted section 5 provides—

"5.—(1) This section applies where—

(a) a special verdict is returned that the accused is not guilty by reason of insanity; or
(b) findings are recorded that the accused is under a disability and that he did the act or made the omission charged against him.

(2) Subject to subsection (3) below, the court shall either—

(a) make an order that the accused be admitted, in accordance with the provisions of Schedule 1 to the Criminal Procedure (Insanity and Unfitness to Plead) Act 1991, to such hospital as may be specified by the Secretary of State; or
(b) where they have the power to do so by virtue of section 5 of that Act, make in respect of the accused such one of the following orders as they think most suitable in all the circumstances of the case, namely—

(i) a guardianship order within the meaning of the Mental Health Act 1983;
(ii) a supervision and treatment order within the meaning of Schedule 2 to the said Act of 1991; and
(iii) an order for his absolute discharge.

(3) Paragraph (b) of subsection (2) above shall not apply where the offence to which the special verdict or findings relate is an offence the sentence for which is fixed by law."

In the five years immediately following the coming into force of the Criminal Procedure (Insanity) Act 1991 there were 44 findings of "not guilty by reason of insanity" (see Mackay and Kearns, "More Fact(s) about the Insanity Defence" [1999] Crim. L.R. 714, 716). The authors speculate that the reason for this increase is that "the new legislation has started to become more widely known by lawyers and psychiatrists as it has permeated the body of medico-legal knowledge. This in turn may have led to an appreciation that the 1991 Act has removed the more glaring disincentives inherent within the 1964 Act of running a defence of [not guilty by reason of insanity]". The vast majority of offences in respect of which the special verdict was returned were offences of violence. In 17 cases the disposal was as it would have been prior to the passage of the 1991 Act, a restriction order without limit of time. However in 23 cases a community-based disposal was utilised. The authors speculate that this fact will, itself, stimulate greater use of the insanity defence. The fact remains, however, that the 1991 Act has not removed the stigmatising label of "insane" which may still deter some defendants from raising the insanity defence. In addition, the Act did not address the problem of the legal definition of insanity which remains grossly outdated and fails to recognise developments in medical knowledge.

1. INSANITY

Trial of Lunatics Act 1883

2. (1) Where in any indictment or information any act or omission is charged against any person as an offence, and it is given in evidence on the trial of such person for that offence that he was insane, so as not to be responsible, according to law, for his actions at the time when the act was done or omission made, then, if it appears to the jury before whom such person is tried that he did the act or made the omission charged, but was insane as aforesaid at the time when he did or made the same, the jury shall return a special verdict that the accused is not guilty by reason of insanity.

Note

This provision states the consequence of a finding of insanity which is the return of the special verdict. The test for insanity was laid down in the following case.

M'Naghten's Case
(1843) 10 Cl. & F. 200; 8 E.R. 718

M'Naghten was indicted for murder and acquitted on the ground of insanity. In consequence debates took place in the House of Lords, and it was decided to take the opinion of the judges as to the nature and extent of the unsoundness of mind which would excuse the commission of a felony of this sort. Five questions were put to the judges in the terms set out in the following extract from their opinions.

TINDAL C.J.: (Delivering the opinion of all the judges except Maule J.): The first question proposed by your Lordships is this: "What is the law respecting alleged crimes committed by persons afflicted with insane delusion in respect of one or more particular subjects or persons: as, for instance, where at the time of the commission of the alleged crime the accused knew he was acting contrary to law, but did the act complained of with a view, under the influence of insane delusion, of redressing or revenging some supposed grievance or injury, or of producing some supposed public benefit?"

In answer to which question, assuming that your Lordships' inquiries are confined to those persons who labour under such partial delusions only, and are not in other respects insane, we are of opinion that, notwithstanding the party accused did the act complained of with a view, under the influence of insane delusion, of redressing or revenging some supposed grievance or injury, or of producing some public benefit, he is nevertheless punishable according to the nature of the crime committed, if he knew at the time of committing such crime that he was acting contrary to law; by which expression we understand your Lordships to mean the law of the land.

Your Lordships are pleased to inquire of us, secondly, "What are the proper questions to be submitted to the jury, where a person alleged to be afflicted with insane delusion respecting one or more particular subjects or persons, is charged with the commission of a crime (murder, for example), and insanity is set up as a defence?" And, thirdly, "In what terms ought the question to be left to the jury as to the prisoner's state of mind at the time when the act was committed?" And as these two questions appear to us to be more conveniently answered together, we have to submit our opinion to be, that the jurors ought to be told in all cases that every man is to be presumed to be sane, and to possess a sufficient degree of reason to be responsible for his crimes, until the contrary be proved to their satisfaction; and that to establish a defence on the ground of insanity, it must be clearly proved that, at the time of the committing of the act, the party accused was labouring under such a defect of reason, from disease of the mind, as not to know the nature and quality of the act he was doing; or, if he did know it, that he did not know he was doing what was wrong. The mode of putting the latter part of the question to the jury on these occasions has generally been, whether the accused at the time of doing the act knew the difference between right and wrong: which mode, though rarely, if ever, leading to any mistake with the jury, is not, as we conceive, so accurate when put generally and in the abstract, as when put with reference to the party's knowledge of right and wrong in respect of the very act with which he is charged. If the question were to be put as to the knowledge of the accused solely and exclusively with reference to the law of the land, it might tend to confound the jury, by inducing them to believe that an actual knowledge of the law of the land was essential in order to lead to a conviction: whereas the law is administered upon the principle that everyone must be taken conclusively to know it, without proof that he does know it. If the accused was conscious that the act was one which he ought not to do, and if that act was at the same time contrary to the law of the land, he is punishable: and the usual course therefore has been to leave the question to the jury, whether the party accused had a sufficient degree of reason to know that he was doing an act that was wrong: and this course we think is correct, accompanied with such observations and explanations as the circumstances of each particular case may require.

The fourth question which your Lordships have proposed to us is this: "If a person under an insane delusion as to existing facts, commits an offence in consequence thereof, is he thereby excused?" To which question the answer must, of course, depend on the nature of the delusion: but, making the same assumption as we did before, namely, that he labours under such partial delusion only, and is not in other respects insane, we think he must be considered in the same situation as to responsibility as if the facts with respect to which the delusion exists were real. For example, if under the influence of his delusion he supposes another man to be in the act of attempting to take away his life, and he kills that man, as he supposes, in self-defence, he would be exempt from punishment. If this delusion was that the deceased had inflicted a serious injury to his character and fortune, and he killed him in revenge for such supposed injury, he would be liable to punishment.

Question

Do you agree with Glanville Williams that "the three questions a jury must consider under the M'Naghten Rules are principally concerned with *mens rea*" (T.C.L., p. 644)?

C. Wells "Whither Insanity?" [1983] Crim.L.R. 787–788 & 793–794

Insanity, along with the related defences of automatism and intoxication, raises very clearly the social protection role of the criminal law. The recent cases of *Bailey* [*infra*. p. 242] and *Sullivan* [*infra*. p. 224] illustrate this point. At one level they merely confirm the status quo—epilepsy is a 'disease of the mind', diabetes is not. At another, they give an insight into the difficulty of pursuing the dual models of individual responsibility and social protection. In neither case is there any attempt to locate the argument within a theoretical context. And yet unless there is more clarity as to whether insanity is treated as a condition, like infancy, barring the jurisdiction of the court, or as an excuse for the particular act, the operation of the defence and its effect on other defences such as automatism and intoxication will continue to confound . . .

Very few defendants choose to avail themselves of the insanity defence. Although nominally an acquittal, the special verdict of 'not guilty by reason of insanity' is little less than 'a direction to punish but not to punish criminally.' . . . The choice therefore for mentally disordered defendants is that between conviction (and the possibility at least of a determinate sentence) and a rather double-edged acquittal. Some defendants may be able to argue that they were in a state of automatism and thus add the possibility of a full acquittal. Because this represents a more attractive choice it is not surprising that it is in this sort of case that the courts have most often been asked to draw a line between the sane and the insane. But not infrequently the decision can also become entwined with the intoxication defence. The possibility of conceptual confusion on a large scale is thus opened—from insanity as a precluding or excusing condition through automatism on the basis of the 'no act' plea to the qualification of that plea by the doctrine of self-induced automatism. The issue then becomes one of whether to apply the rationale of the intoxication defence to the automaton whose condition is self-induced other than through drink or drugs. This may seem a long way from insanity. The paradigm mad person and the paradigm drunk may have little in common but appeal cases rarely deal with the unitary paradigm. *Bailey* (the case of the diabetic) is no exception. Considered with *Sullivan* (the epilepsy case), it confronts the problematic issue of when automatism should be treated as insanity. *Bailey* also raises the important, related, question of the limitations on automatism as a defence when it is self induced. . . .

> 'It has for centuries been recognised that if a person was, at the time of his unlawful act, mentally so disordered that it would be unreasonable to impute guilt to him, he ought not to be held liable for conviction and punishment.'

This type of 'reason is since reason long has been' argument was employed also by the Butler Committee and is of course a somewhat inadequate starting point for an inquiry into insanity, particularly in view of changing ideas about criminal responsibility. And, as with much discussion in this area, it skates over the dual effect of the insanity verdict, concentrating only on the absolvent quality and ignoring its concomitant of indefinite detention.

One view prevalent in the English literature is that insanity excuses because it negatives the mental element in crime. There are two problems with this. Unless *mens rea* is here being given the wider normative meaning of 'the state of mind stigmatised as wrongful by the criminal law', it is not easy to see that insanity does necessarily negative *mens rea*. It only does so if *mens rea* consists of a subjective mental element. Where it is an objective form of recklessness or negligence, or where there is a crime of strict liability, then the argument that insanity excuses because it precludes *mens rea* breaks down. And if one took the wider normative view of *mens rea*, then the argument would be somewhat tautologous; it would amount to saying that an insane person is not responsible because the stigmatised wrongful state of mind includes only the sane.

The other problem with the *mens rea* view of insanity is that it is an implicit acknowledgement that the insanity defence is about disposal rather than responsibility. A sane person who lacks *mens rea* is normally acquitted. If insanity is a 'defence' because it amounts to lack of *mens rea*, then it is otiose.

Thus an exploration of insanity and responsibility has either to go beyond *mens rea*, or, if a normative view is taken, it has to justify the exclusion of the insane.

Notes

1. *M'Naghten* places the burden of proof on the defendant. It was held in *R. v. Sodeman* [1936] 2 All E.R. 1138 that this requires proof on a balance of probability. Both the Criminal Law Revision Committee (11th Report, Cmnd. 4991 (1972), section 1.40) and the Butler Committee on Mentally Abnormal Offenders (Cmnd. 6244 (1975), section 18.39) recommended that this burden should be on the prosecution. In the Draft Criminal Code, Clause 35, either the defence or prosecution may prove mental disorder on a balance of probabilities.

2. Where the issue of insanity is raised during a trial, the prosecution are relieved of the duty of proving mens rea as the 1883 Act only requires it to be proved that the accused "did the act or made the omission charged" (see *Attorney-General's Reference (No. 3 of 1998)* [1999] 3 W.L.R. 1994).

3. There is a problem with placing a burden of proof on the accused in cases where the effect of the defect of reason is that he did not know the nature and quality of the act he was doing. In such a case he is being asked to prove on a balance of probabilities something the contrary of which the prosecution have not proved. If the prosecution prove beyond reasonable doubt that he knew what he was doing, and thus had *mens rea* that would be an end of the matter. But if they fail to prove this it seems superfluous, and indeed illogical, to require the accused to prove the contrary on a balance of probabilities. The opportunity to confront this problem arose in the context of the next case but was ignored by the Court of Appeal which focused its attention on whether a trial judge may raise the issue of insanity and leave it to the jury.

R. v. Thomas (Sharon)
27 October 1994, Lexis Transcript
Court of Appeal

D was charged with burglary and robbery. At the time of the alleged offences she was drunk. Medical evidence was called on her behalf at the trial to the effect that she had a mental condition, hypomania, which was aggravated by drink, and which, if aggravated, would render her so confused that she would be unable to form the specific intent required for the offences. The trial judge intervened and put questions to D's doctor which elicited answers to the effect that hypomania was a disease of the mind and D would not have been aware of the nature and quality of her acts. The judge raised the question of leaving the defence of insanity to the jury but counsel for D submitted that it should not be so left. The judge directed the jury on insanity. D was convicted of burglary and appealed arguing, *inter alia*, that (1) where medical evidence was called to the effect that D could not have formed the specific intent for the offence, the judge erred in leaving to the jury, against the wishes of D's counsel, the defence of insanity and in ruling he was obliged to do so; (2) to leave such a defence over complicated the case: it failed to differentiate between the ability to form a specific intent and the ability to appreciate the nature and quality of her acts.

ROCH L.J.: . . . The judge's decision to raise the issue of insanity and his direction to the jury on the matter were, in the judgment of this Court, material irregularities for several reasons. First, insanity was not a defence raised by the appellant or her counsel. Her defence was simply that by reason of her hypomania, and the drink that she had taken, the jury could not be sure that she had been capable of forming, and had formed, the specific intents required by Counts 1 and 2 in the indictment. She was entitled, on the evidence . . . to raise that issue. That issue being raised by the defence, it was for the Crown to satisfy the jury that the appellant had had the ability to form, and had formed, one or other of the two specific intents required.

The judge clearly thought that he had a duty to raise the issue of insanity, and that it provided an additional defence for the appellant in this case. In our judgment, it did not, as a practical matter, raise an additional defence for this appellant.

It may well be that a judge has a duty in an appropriate case to raise defences open to a defendant where the burden of disproving that defence rests on the prosecution. However, in our judgment, the situation is not the same where the defence places a burden of proof upon a defendant. In those cases, in our view, the principle is correctly stated in *Archbold*, current edition, Volume 2 at para. 17–111 in these terms:

"In certain exceptional circumstances, a judge can of his own volition raise an issue of insanity and leave the issue to the jury providing there is evidence embracing all the relevant considerations in the M'Naghten Rules."

The editors of *Archbold* then go on to set out what a judge must do if he is minded to take such a course. That statement is consistent with the views expressed by this Court in the case of *R v Dickie* (1984) 79 Cr App Rep 213, in the judgment given by Watkins LJ where, at page 218, the court said:

"We have come to the conclusion that we are unable to say there are no circumstances in which a judge may of his own volition raise an issue of insanity and leave it to a jury, provided that if he chooses to do so there is relevant evidence which goes to all the factors involved in the M'Naghten test. We envisage, however, that circumstances in which a judge will do that will be exceptional and very rare."

Then his Lordship went on to consider the procedural steps that a judge would have to take if a judge decided that he had before him an exceptional and very rare case in which he should take that initiative.

There may be cases, for example, cases of homicide, where an accused has raised a defence of, say, diminished responsibility where a judge would be entitled, of his own volition to raise the issue of insanity with the jury. However, it would have to be a rare and exceptional case. This was not such a case in our judgment.

The evidence of possible insanity arose in answer to questions put by the judge after the cross-examination of Dr O'Riordan had been completed. It is to be regretted, in our view, that the judge chose to ask those questions. A serious consequence of those questions was that the jury may well have supposed that the appellant would only have been incapable of forming the necessary specific intentions if she had been legally insane.

In the . . . summing-up, the judge had correctly indicated that the jury could not find the appellant to have been legally insane unless it was shown to be more probable than not that she had been unaware of the nature and quality of her acts, and that that had been caused by a disease of the mind. This may well have misled the jury as to the burden of proof on the second issue left to them, namely, had the appellant had the necessary intent to support a charge of robbery or, alternatively, a charge of burglary.

These unsatisfactory features were added to by the judge's references on more than one occasion to the uncomfortable consequences of this line of defence. The issue of insanity was, in our view, a complication which the judge should have avoided and from which the jury should have been spared. Leaving the issues raised on behalf of the appellant, and only those issues to the jury, was not simplistic. It was, in the circumstances of this case, the correct thing for the judge to have done.

In our judgment, that first matter was a material irregularity which justifies the quashing of the appellant's conviction.

Appeal allowed and conviction quashed

Note

In the above case D was not pleading automatism or insanity but raising the possibility that due to her intoxication she did not have the requisite intention for the offence. Had she pleaded automatism the judge would have been free to determine as a question of law whether the alleged cause of that condition was a disease of the mind in which case the plea would have been one of insane automatism (see *Sullivan, post,* p. 224).

i. Disease of the Mind

R. v. Kemp
[1957] 1 Q.B. 399
Bristol Assizes

The defendant was charged with causing grievous bodily harm to his wife. He suffered from arteriosclerosis which had not given rise to general mental trouble but caused temporary loss of consciousness during which state the attack was made. He did not plead insanity.

DEVLIN J.: . . . In this case it is conceded that everything [in the third and fourth answers in *M'Naghten's Case*] applies here, except for "disease of the mind. . . ." The law is not concerned with the brain but with the mind, in the sense that "mind" is ordinarily used, the mental faculties of reason, memory and understanding. If one read for "disease of the mind" "disease of the brain", it would follow that in many cases pleas of insanity would not be established because it could not be proved that the brain had been affected in any way, either by degeneration of the cells or in any other way. In my judgment the condition of the brain is irrelevant and so is the question of whether the condition of the mind is curable or incurable, transitory or permanent. There is no warranty for introducing those considerations into the definition in the M'Naghten Rules. Temporary insanity is sufficient to satisfy them. It does not matter whether it is incurable and permanent or not.

I think that the approach of Mr Lee (for the Crown) to the definition in the Rules is the right one. He points out the order of the words "a defect of reason, from disease of the mind". The primary thing that has to be looked for is the defect of reason. "Disease of the mind" is there for some purpose, obviously, but the prime thing is to determine what is admitted here, namely, whether or not there is a defect of reason. In my judgment, the words "from disease of the mind" are not to be construed as if they were put in for the purpose of distinguishing between diseases which have a mental origin and diseases which have a physical origin, a distinction which in 1843 was probably little considered. They were put in for the purpose of limiting the effect of the words "defect of reason". A defect of reason is by itself enough to make the act irrational and therefore normally to exclude responsibility in law. But the Rule was not intended to apply to defects of reason caused simply by brutish stupidity without rational power. It was not intended that the defence should plead "although with a healthy mind he nevertheless had been brought up in such a way that he had never learned to exercise his reason, and therefore he is suffering from a defect of reason". The words ensure that unless the defect is due to a diseased mind and not simply to an untrained one there is insanity within the meaning of the Rule.

Hardening of the arteries is a disease which is shown on the evidence to be capable of affecting the mind in such a way as to cause a defect, temporarily or permanently, of its reasoning, understanding and so on, and so as is my judgment a disease of the mind which comes within the meaning of the Rules.

Verdict: Guilty but insane

R. v. Sullivan
[1984] A.C. 156
House of Lords

The appellant was charged with inflicting grievous bodily harm on P. At his trial he admitted the act but asserted by way of defence that he had done so while in an epileptic seizure. The trial judge ruled that this amounted to a defence of insanity rather than a defence of automatism. The appellant then changed his plea to guilty of assault occasioning actual bodily harm and was convicted of that offence. He appealed against the conviction but the Court of Appeal upheld the judge's ruling and dismissed the appeal. He appealed to the House of Lords.

LORD DIPLOCK: The evidence as to the pathology of a seizure due to psychomotor epilepsy can be sufficiently stated for the purposes of this appeal by saying that after the first stage, the prodram, which precedes the fit itself, there is a second stage, the ictus, lasting a few seconds, during which there are electrical discharges into the temporal lobes of the brain of the sufferer. The effect of these discharges is to cause him in the post-ictal stage to make movements which he is not conscious that he is making, including, and this was a characteristic of previous seizures which Mr Sullivan had suffered, automatic movements of resistance to anyone trying to come to his aid. These movements of resistance might, though in practice they very rarely would, involve violence. . . .

[His lordship reviewed the M'Naghten rules and *Bratty*, p. 235 *infra* and continued.] In the instant case, as in *Bratty*, the only evidential foundation that was laid for any finding by the jury that Mr. Sullivan was acting unconsciously and involuntarily when he was kicking Mr Payne, was that when he did so he was in the post-ictal stage of a seizure of psychomotor epilepsy. The evidential foundation in the case of Bratty, that he was suffering from psychomotor epilepsy at the time he did the act with which he was charged, was very weak and was rejected by the jury; the evidence in Mr Sullivan's case, that he was so suffering when he was kicking Mr Payne, was very strong and would almost inevitably be accepted by a properly directed jury. It would be the duty of the judge to direct the jury that if they did accept that evidence the law required them to bring in a special verdict and none other. The governing statutory provision is to be found in section 2 of the Trial of Lunatics Act 1883. This says "the jury *shall* return a special verdict. . . ."

My Lords, I can deal briefly with the various grounds on which it has been submitted that the instant case can be distinguished from what constituted the ratio decidendi in *Bratty v. Attorney-General for Northern Ireland* [1963] A.C. 386, and that it falls outside the ambit of the M'Naghten Rules.

First, it is submitted the medical evidence in the instant case shows that psychomotor epilepsy is not a disease of the mind, whereas in *Bratty* it was accepted by all the doctors that it was. The only evidential basis for this submission is that Dr Fenwick said that in medical terms to constitute a "disease of the mind" or "mental illness", which he appeared to regard as interchangeable descriptions, a disorder of brain functions (which undoubtedly occurs during a seizure in psychomotor epilepsy) must be prolonged for a period of time usually more than a day; while Dr Taylor would have it that the disorder must continue for a minimum of a month to qualify for the description "a disease of the mind".

The nomenclature adopted by the medical profession may change from time to time; Bratty was tried in 1961. But the meaning of the expression "disease of the mind" as the cause of "a defect of reason" remains unchanged for the purposes of the application of the M'Naghten Rules. I agree with what was said by Devlin J. in *R. v. Kemp* (*ante*, p. 223), that "mind" in the M'Naghten Rules is used in the ordinary sense of the mental faculties of reason, memory and understanding. If the effect of a disease is to impair these faculties so severely as to have either of the consequences referred to in the latter part of the rules, it matters not whether the aetiology of the impairment is organic, as in epilepsy, or functional, or whether the impairment itself is permanent or is transient and intermittent, provided that it subsisted at the time of commission of the act. The purpose of the legislation relating to the defence of insanity, ever since its origin in 1800, has been to protect society against recurrence of the dangerous conduct. The duration of a temporary suspension of the mental faculties of reason, memory and understanding, particularly if, as in Mr Sullivan's case, it is recurrent, cannot on any rational ground be relevant to the application by the courts of the M'Naghten Rules, though it may be relevant to the course adopted by the Secretary of State, to whom the responsibility for how the defendant is to be dealt with passes after the return of the special verdict of "not guilty by reason of insanity".

To avoid misunderstanding I ought perhaps to add that in expressing my agreement with what was said by Devlin J. in *Kemp*, where the disease that caused the temporary and intermittent impairment of the mental faculties was arteriosclerosis, I do not regard that learned judge as excluding the possibility of non-insane automatism (for which the proper verdict would be a verdict of "not guilty") in cases where temporary impairment (not being self-induced by consuming drink or drugs) results from some external physical factor such as a blow on the head causing concussion or the administration of an anaesthetic for therapeutic purposes. I mention this because in *R. v. Quick* [1973] Q.B. 910, Lawton L.J. appears to have regarded the ruling in *Kemp* as going as far as this. If it had done, it would have been inconsistent with the speeches in this House in *Bratty*, (*post*, p. 235) where *Kemp* was alluded to without disapproval by Viscount Kilmuir L.C. at p. 403, and received the express approval of Lord Denning, at p. 411. The instant case, however, does not in my view afford an appropriate occasion for exploring possible causes of non-insane automatism.

The only other submission in support of Mr Sullivan's appeal which I think is necessary to mention is that, because the expert evidence was to the effect that Mr Sullivan's acts in kicking Mr Payne were unconscious and thus "involuntary" in the legal sense of that term, his state of mind was not one dealt with by the M'Naghten Rules at all, since it was not covered by the phrase "as not to know the nature and quality of the act he was doing." Quite apart from being contrary to all three speeches in this House in *Bratty v. A.-G. for Northern Ireland* this submission appears to me, with all respect to counsel, to be quite unarguable. Dr Fenwick himself accepted it as an accurate description of Mr Sullivan's mental state in the post-ictal stage of a seizure. The audience to whom the phrase in the M'Naghten Rules was addressed consisted of peers of the realm in the 1840's when certain orotundity of diction had not yet fallen out of fashion. Addressed to an audience of jurors in the 1980's it might more aptly be expressed as "He did not know what he was doing."

My Lords, it is natural to feel reluctant to attach the label of insanity to a sufferer from psychomotor epilepsy of the kind to which Mr Sullivan was subject, even though the expression in the context of a special verdict of "not guilty by reason of insanity" is a technical one which includes a purely temporary and intermittent suspension of the mental faculties of reason, memory and understanding resulting from the occurrence of an epileptic fit. But the label is contained in the current statute, it has appeared in this statute's predecessors ever since 1800. It does not lie within the power of the courts to alter it. Only Parliament can do that. It has done so twice; it could do so once again.

Sympathise though I do with Mr Sullivan, I see no other course open to your Lordships than to dismiss this appeal.

[The other Law Lords agreed with Lord Diplock's speech.]

Appeal dismissed

Questions

1. If, as Lord Diplock stated, the purpose of the M'Naghten Rules is "to protect society against the recurrence of the dangerous conduct," was this purpose furthered by the procedure followed in *Sullivan* when the guilty plea was accepted? Was it furthered by the outcome in *R. v. Thomas* (*ante*, p. 221) (see E. Lederman "Non-Insane and Insane Automatism: Reducing the Significance of a Problematic Distinction" (1985) 34 I.C.L.Q. 819)

2. Did Sullivan's conviction serve any other purpose such as deterring other epileptics from injuring others while in an epileptic seizure?

3. Does the distinction between external physical factors and internal organic or functional factors provide a sound basis for identifying those who are dangerous and from whom society needs to be protected? (See further *Parks*, *post*, p. 228.)

4. Do, and if so should, the M'Naghten Rules apply to defendants who suffer from retarded development, *i.e.* is mental deficiency a disease of the mind?

5. If the facts of *Sullivan* were to recur with the difference that the victim dies and on a trial for murder the judge refuses to accept a plea

of guilty to manslaughter, and the jury return a verdict of not guilty by reason of insanity resulting in the accused's compulsory indefinite detention in a secure mental hospital, could the accused appeal against this outcome on the grounds that section 5 of the Criminal Procedure (Insanity) Act 1964 is incompatible with his rights under Article 5 of the European Convention of Human Rights? (see Note 1 below)

Note

Article 5 of the European Convention of Human Rights states:

1. Everyone has the right to liberty and security of person.
No one shall be deprived of his liberty save in the following cases and in accordance with a procedure prescribed by law; . . .
(e) the lawful detention . . . of persons of unsound mind . . .

In the leading case before the European Court of Human Rights, *Winterwerp v. Netherlands* (1979) 2 E.H.R.R. 387, the Court stated at para. 39:

"In the Court's opinion, except in emergency cases, the individual concerned should not be deprived of his liberty unless he has been reliably shown to be of 'unsound mind'. The very nature of what has to be established before the competent national authority—that is, a true mental disorder—calls for objective medical expertise. Further, the mental disorder must be of a kind or degree warranting compulsory confinement. What is more, the validity of the continued confinement depends upon the persistence of such a disorder."

It is doubtful whether conditions such as diabetes, epilepsy, or somnambulism would be classified by objective medical experts as mental disorders. Certainly they would not fall within the definition of "mental disorder" in section 1 of the Mental Health Act 1983 which governs the conditions for civil commitment to a mental hospital and covers "mental illness, arrested or incomplete development of mind, psychopathic disorder and any other disorder or disability of mind". Detention of such a person who is not of "unsound mind" would be a breach of Article 5. This form of challenge to the law of insanity, however, will be of limited utility as it will be an option only where a special verdict results in detention and the condition from which the accused suffers is not a mental disorder. If any other disposal under section 5 of the 1964 Act is used, it will not breach Article 5 however much one might consider that, for example, a diabetic should not be labelled as being insane.

2. In *Bratty v. Attorney-General for Northern Ireland* [1963] A.C. 386 (*post*, p. 235) Lord Denning stated, at p. 412:

"It seems to me that any mental disorder which has manifested itself in violence and is prone to recur is a disease of the mind. At any rate it is the sort of disease for which a person should be detained in hospital rather than be given an unqualified acquittal."

This dictum was not approved in *Sullivan* which focused on the cause of the defect of reason rather than the consequences flowing from it. In *Burgess* [1991] 2 W.L.R. 1206, the accused sought to plead automatism due to sleep walking on a charge of wounding with intent to do grievous bodily harm contrary to section 18 of the Offences Against the Person Act 1861. The trial judge ruled that this was a plea of insanity. The appellant appealed against the finding of the jury that he was not guilty by reason of insanity. The Court of Appeal expressed its approval of Lord Denning's "definition" of "disease of the mind". Lord Lane C.J. adding this qualification (at p. 1212):

> "It seems to us that if there is a danger of recurrence that may be an added reason for categorising the condition as a disease of the mind. On the other hand, the absence of the danger of recurrence is not a reason for saying that it cannot be a disease of the mind."

This revival of Lord Denning's dictum is hardly helpful (nor was it necessary for deciding the appeal). Firstly, mental disorders may manifest themselves in other ways which do not involve violence, for example, pyromania or kleptomania; if these conditions are due to an internal cause they will be labelled diseases of the mind. In *Hennessy* [1989] 1 W.L.R. 287, D, whilst in a hyperglycaemic episode due to failure to take insulin which he claimed was due to stress, anxiety and depression, took a motor vehicle without authority and drove whilst disqualified. The offences were not violent but the Court of Appeal held that D's plea was one of insanity as diabetes being an internal factor amounted to a disease of the mind. Stress, anxiety and depression, while they may be caused by external factors, were not themselves external factors. Secondly, there are conditions which manifest themselves in violence which do not fall within the definition of disease of the mind approved in *Sullivan* as the case of *Quick* (*post*, p. 236) discloses.

The Supreme Court of Canada has taken a rather more pragmatic and explicitly policy oriented approach to the "disease of the mind" test.

R. v. Parks
(1992) 95 D.L.R. (4th) 27
Supreme Court of Canada

D was charged with murder and raised the defence of automatism based on somnambulism. Medical evidence indicated that D had been under stress, had been getting very little sleep and that there was a family history of sleep disorders. The medical witnesses also testified that somnambulism is not a disease of the mind in the sense of being a neurological, psychiatric of other illness but rather a disorder of sleep. They testified that a sleep-walker's ability to control voluntarily even complex behaviour is severely limited or not available and that aggression while sleep-walking is quite rare and repetition of violence is unheard of. The trial judge directed the jury that if D was in a state of somnambulism at the time of the killing he was entitled to be acquitted on the basis of non-insane automatism. The jury acquitted and the prosecution appealed.

LAMER C.J.C.: ... For a defence of insanity to have been put to the jury, together with or instead of a defence of automatism, as the case may be, there would have had to have been in the record evidence tending to show that sleep-walking was the cause of the respondent's state of mind ... [T]hat is not the case here. This is not to say that sleep-walking could never be a disease of the mind, in another case on different evidence.

LA FOREST J.: ... In part because of the imprecision of medical science in this area the legal community reserves for itself the final determination of what constitutes a "disease of the mind". This is accomplished by adding the "legal or policy component" to the inquiry.

A review of the cases on automatism reveals two distinct approaches to the policy component of the "disease of the mind" inquiry. These may be labelled the "continuing danger" and "internal cause" theories ... At first glance these approaches may appear to be divergent, but in fact they stem from a common concern for public safety. ...

The "continuing danger" theory holds that any condition likely to present a recurring danger to the public should be treated as insanity. The "internal cause" theory suggests that a condition stemming from the psychological or emotional make-up of the accused, rather than some external factor should lead to a finding of insanity. The two theories share a common concern for recurrence, the latter holding that an internal weakness is more likely to lead to recurrent violence than automatism brought on by some intervening external cause.

The "internal cause" approach has been criticized as an unfounded development of the law. ... These criticisms have particular validity if the "internal cause" theory is held out as the definitive answer to the disease of the mind inquiry. However, it is apparent from the cases that the theory is really meant to be used only as an analytical tool, and not as an all-encompassing methodology. ... [S]omnambulism is an example of a condition that is not well suited to analysis under the "internal cause" theory. The poor fit arises because certain factors can legitimately be characterized as either internal or external sources of automatistic behaviour. For example, the Crown in this case argues that the causes of the respondent's violent sleepwalking were entirely internal, a combination of genetic susceptibility and the ordinary stresses of everyday life (lack of sleep, excessive afternoon exercise, and a high stress level due to personal problems). These "ordinary stresses" were ruled out as external factors by this court in *Rabey* (1980) 54 C.C.C. (2d) 1 (although by a narrow majority). However, the factors that for a waking individual are mere ordinary stresses can be differently characterized for a person who is asleep, unable to counter with his conscious mind the onslaught of the admittedly ordinary strains of life. One could argue that the particular amalgam of stress, excessive exercise, sleep deprivation and sudden noises in the night that causes an incident of somnambulism is, for the sleeping person, analogous to the effect of concussion upon a waking person, which is generally accepted as an external cause of non-insane automatism; see Williams, *Textbook of Criminal Law*, 2nd ed. (1983) at p.666. In the end the dichotomy between internal and external causes becomes blurred in this context, and is not helpful in resolving the inquiry. ...

In this case, then, neither of the two leading policy approaches determines an obvious result. It is clear from the evidence that there is almost no likelihood of recurrent violent somnambulism. A finding of insanity is therefore less likely, but the absence of a continuing danger does not mean that the respondent must be granted an absolute acquittal. At the same time, the "internal cause" theory is not readily applicable in this case. It is therefore necessary to look further afield.

... [citing additional policy considerations in *Rabey*]

It seems unlikely that the recognition of somnambulism as non-insane automatism will open the floodgates to a cascade of sleep-walking defence claims.... Moreover, it is very difficult to feign sleep-walking—precise symptoms and medical histories beyond the control of the accused must be presented to the trier of fact, and as in this case, the accused will be subjected to a battery of medical tests....

As I noted at the outset, it is apparent that the medical evidence in this case is not only significant in its own right, but also has an impact at several stages of the policy inquiry. As such, I agree with the Chief Justice that in another case with different evidence sleep-walking might be found to be a disease of the mind....

Appeal dismissed

Note

While Parks may be celebrating his good fortune to have been tried in Canada one puzzle for other Canadians will be to work out which cases of somnabulism might fall within insane rather than non-insane automatism!

(ii) Defect of Reason

Note

The basis of the M'Naghten Rules is "defect of reason" (not emotion or will) and the result of the defect of reason must be that the accused either did not know what he was doing or did not know that what he was doing was wrong.

R. v. Codere
(1916) 12 Cr.App.R. 21
Court of Criminal Appeal

The appellant had been convicted of murder. Insanity was the only defence raised at the trial. Under section 5(4) of the Criminal Appeal Act 1907, the Court of Criminal Appeal have power to quash the sentence and order the appellant to be detained as insane.

LORD READING C.J.: ... Mr Foote (on behalf of Codere) has addressed an argument to us based on *M'Naghten's Case*, which is the classic authority on the subject, which in substance resolved itself into this, that we must assume that when the law says that the question is whether the accused was labouring under such a defect of reason, from disease of the mind, as not to know the nature and quality of the act he was doing, we must read "nature" to have reference to the physical act, and "quality" to refer to the morality of the act, and that therefore the jury should be asked if he knew he was doing wrong. The argument advanced is that the judge ought to tell the jury that "quality" means, "Did the accused person know that the act was immoral?" and when one stops and asks the meaning of "immoral" we get to the first of the difficulties which faced Mr Foote.

It is said that "quality" is to be regarded as characterising the moral, as contrasted with the physical, aspect of the deed. The court cannot agree with that view of the meaning of the words "nature and quality." The court is of opinion that in using the language "nature and quality" the judges were only dealing with the physical character of the act, and were not intending to distinguish between the physical and moral aspects of the act. That is the law as it has been laid down by judges in many directions to juries, and as the court understands it to be at the present time.

We then come to the second branch of the test, namely, if he knew the physical nature of the act did he know that he was doing wrong? Mr Foote has argued that it is not enough that he knew the act was contrary to law and punishable by law, and that, even if he did know that ... yet the jury ought to have been told that they must find a special verdict (of guilty but insane) ... unless they came to the conclusion that he knew that the act was morally wrong. The question of the distinction between morally and legally wrong opens wide doors. In a case of this kind, namely, killing, it does not seem debatable that the appellant could have thought that the act was not morally wrong, judged by the ordinary standards, when the act is punishable by law, and is known by him to be punishable by law. It was suggested at one time in the course of argument that the question should be judged by the standard of the accused, but it is obvious that this proposition is wholly untenable, and would tend to excuse crimes without number, and to weaken the law to an alarming degree. It is conceded now that the standard to be applied is whether according to the ordinary standard adopted by reasonable men the act was right or wrong. ... Once it is clear that the appellant knew that the act was wrong in law, then he was doing an act which he was conscious he ought not to do, and as it was against the law, it was punishable by law; assuming, therefore, that he knew the nature and quality of the act, he was guilty of murder, and was properly convicted.

The difficulty no doubt arises over the words "conscious that the act was one which he ought not to do", but, looking at all the answers in *M'Naghten's Case*, it seems that if it is punishable by law it is an act which he ought not to do, and that is the meaning in which the phrase is used in that case. There may be minor cases before a court of summary jurisdiction where that view may be open to doubt, but in cases such as these the true view is what we have just said.

Application dismissed

Question

Under an insane delusion that his wife is possessed by evil, D. decides to kill her and does so. Does his delusion relate to the nature and quality of his act entitling him to plead insanity?

R. v. Windle
[1952] 2 Q.B. 826
Court of Criminal Appeal

The appellant gave his wife a fatal dose of aspirin. He admitted that he had done so, and said he supposed he would hang for it. The appellant's only defence was that of insanity. At the trial, Devlin J. ruled that there was no evidence to go to the jury on the defence of insanity.

LORD GODDARD C.J.: The point we have to decide in this case can be put into a very small compass. We are asked to review what are generally known as the M'Naghten Rules, and possibly to make new law. ... The argument before us has really been on what is the meaning of the word "wrong". ... Mr Shawcross (for Windle) ... suggested that the word "wrong" as it was used in the M'Naghten Rules, did not mean contrary to law but has some kind of qualified meaning, such as morally wrong, and that if a person was in such a state of mind through a defect of reason that, although he knew that what he was doing was wrong in law, he thought that it was beneficial or kind or praiseworthy, that would excuse him.

Courts of law can only distinguish between that which is in accordance with law and that which is contrary to law. There are many acts which, to use an expression which is to be found in some of the old cases, are contrary to the law of God and man. For instance, in the Decalogue will be found the laws "Thou shalt not kill" and "Thou shalt not steal". Those acts are contrary to the law of man and also to the law of God. If the seventh commandment is taken, "Thou shalt not commit adultery," although that is contrary to the law of God, so far as the criminal law is concerned it is not contrary to the law of man. That does not mean that the law encourages adultery; I only say that it is not a criminal offence. The law cannot embark on the question, and it would be an unfortunate thing if it were left to juries to consider whether some particular act was morally right or wrong. The test must be whether it is contrary to law. . . .

In the opinion of the court there is no doubt that in the M'Naghten Rules "wrong" means contrary to law and not "wrong" according to the opinion of one man or of a number of people on the question of whether a particular act might or might not be justified. In the present case, it could not be challenged that the appellant knew that what he was doing was contrary to law, and that he realised what punishment the law provided for murder.

Appeal dismissed

Questions

1. Consider the questions raised by these last two cases. Is what is legally wrong always morally wrong? In *Codere* the judge was prepared to conceive of a negative answer only in minor crimes dealt with by courts of summary jurisdiction.

2. Would D be entitled to rely on the insanity defence if he believed his act was morally wrong although because of a disease of the mind he failed to appreciate that it was contrary to law? (Compare the approach of the High Court of Australia in *Stapleton v. R.* (1952) 86 C.L.R. 358 with *Windle.*)

3. *Codere* approves the test "the ordinary standard adopted by reasonable men", *Windle* indicates that the test is "whether it is contrary to law". Does this alter the law? Was the creation of a new test essential for the decision in *Windle*?

4. If the test is one of insanity is an objective test of any sort appropriate? Consider the passage in *Codere* which indicates that a subjective standard would "weaken the law to an alarming degree".

Note

In practice it appears that psychiatrists pay little heed to the arcane distinctions drawn in *Windle* and *Codere* as the following extracts discloses.

R. D. Mackay and G. Kearns, "More Fact(s) about the Insanity Defence" [1999] Crim. L.R. 714, 722–723

Perhaps the most interesting finding is in the way that the "wrongness" limb of M'Naghten continues to be interpreted by psychiatrists. In previous research it was remarked that "the general impression gained from reading the documentation in these cases was that the wrongness issue was being treated in a liberal fashion by all concerned, rather than in the strict manner regularly depicted by legal commentators". [See Mackay, R. D., "Fact and Fiction about the Insanity Defence" [1990] Crim.L.R. 247 at 251. The strict manner referred to is that the defendant did not know that his action was legally wrong. [see *Windle.*] Within the current research sample it was found that in 25 reports (18 cases) the psychiatrists specifically used the term that the defendant did not know that his act was "wrong". However, it is safe to say the vast majority of these reports made no reference to knowledge of legal wrongness. Rather in most of the case reports the "wrongness" limb was interpreted widely to cover whether the defendant thought his/her actions were morally justified, and/or whether the actions were in perceived self-defence of themselves or others, in the sense of protecting their physical or spiritual well-being. [The factual scenarios in many of these cases involved religious delusions relating to the victim being possessed by the devil or concerning the need to save the world. . . .] Indeed, when we include the reports which supported these arguments (but where the phrase contained in the M'Naghten rules "did not know that it was wrong" was not actually referred to) then we find that 35 reports (25 cases) utilised the "wrongness" limb in agreeing that the defendant was NGRI. In short, the overwhelming impression is that the question the majority of psychiatrists are addressing is: if the delusion that the defendant was experiencing at the time of the offence was in fact reality, then would the defendant's actions be morally justified?—rather than the narrow cognitive test of legal wrongness required by the M'Naghten rules. . . .

It seems clear, therefore, that the "wrongness" limb continues to be preferred in psychiatric reports as indicated in the earlier research. In so doing, it may be argued that psychiatrists in many respects are adopting a common sense or folk psychology approach and that the courts by accepting this interpretation are, in reality, expanding the scope of the M'Naghten Rules.

iii. Uncontrollable Impulse

Notes

1. Will an individual be able to rely on the insanity defence where he appreciates the nature and quality of his conduct and knows that it is contrary to the law but, because of a defect of reason due to a disease of the mind, is unable to prevent himself from acting as he did? When the defence of uncontrollable impulse was raised in *Sodeman v. R.* [1936] 2 All E.R. 1138, the Privy Council (at. p. 1140), rejected the proposition "that the rules in *M'Naghten's* Case are no longer to be treated as an exhaustive statement of the law with regard to insanity, and that there is to be engrafted upon those rules another rule that where a man knows that he is doing what is wrong, nonetheless

he may be held to be insane if he is caused to do the act by an irresistible impulse produced by disease."

This was further explained in *Attorney-General for South Australia v.
Brown* [1960] A.C. 432 where, in an appeal to the Privy Council, Lord
Tucker said (at p. 449) "At various times in the past attempts have
been made to temper the supposed harshness or unscientific nature
of the M'Naghten Rules. These attempts were supported by the high
authority of Sir James Fitz-James Stephen, but in the end the Rules
remain in full force and their harshness has in this country been to
some extent alleviated by the recent legislative enactment affording
the defence of diminished responsibility. . . .

"Their Lordships must not, of course, be understood to suggest that
in a case where evidence has been given (and it is difficult to imagine
a case where such evidence would be other than medical evidence)
that irresistible impulse is a symptom of the particular disease of the
mind from which a prisoner is said to be suffering and as to its effect
on his ability to know the nature and quality of his act or that his act
is wrong it would not be the duty of the judge to deal with the matter
in the same way as any other relevent evidence given at the trial."

For the way in which "irresistible impulse" has been treated in the
defence of diminished responsibility, see *R. v. Byrne, post,* p. 565.

2. The "defect of reason" must arise "from a disease of the mind".
The question may arise whether a person's state of automatism (where
clearly reason is not only defective but completely absent) arises from
a disease of the mind. These cases are dealt with in the next section.
A similar problem can be seen in the section on intoxication, *post,*
p. 244.

2. AUTOMATISM

Note

The defence of automatism arises initially as one form of denial that
the prosecution has proved that the *actus reus* was voluntary (see *ante,*
p. 22). But acquittal will not necessarily follow. If the origin of the
automatic state is a disease of the mind, a finding of insanity will
result. *Kemp, Bratty, Quick* and *Bailey, infra* illustrate the problems
facing the courts in this borderland between the two defences. Where
the origin is self-induced intoxication, the defendant is subject to the
limitations of that defence: see *Majewski, post,* p. 252. Even where the
defendant's state is attributable to neither of those factors a person
who is at fault in losing the capacity for voluntary control of his or
her actions cannot rely on this defence: *Quick* and *Bailey, infra.* This
imports a similar notion to that which qualifies intoxication as a denial
of *mens rea*: self-induced incapacity may be culpable.

Thus it is only in extremely confined circumstances that the defence
can be successfully raised. See Williams, T.C.L., 662–666 for a description of the common causes of automatism.

Bratty v. A.-G. for Northern Ireland
[1963] A.C 386
House of Lords

The appellant strangled a girl. He said in a statement to the police that when he was with her he had "a terrible feeling" and "a sort of black-ness" came over him. At the trial there was medical evidence that he might have been suffering from psychomotor epilepsy. To a charge of murder he raised three defences: automatism, lack of intent for murder, and insanity. The judge refused to leave the first two to the jury, and they rejected the plea of insanity. This was affirmed by the Court of Criminal Appeal in Northern Ireland. He appealed to the House of Lords.

VISCOUNT KILMUIR AND LORD MORRIS OF BORTH-Y-GEST delivered speeches dismissing the appeal with which LORDS TUCKER and HODSON agreed.

LORD DENNING: My Lords, in the case of *Woolmington v. D.P.P.* A.C. 462, 482, Viscount Sankey L.C. said that "when dealing with a murder case the Crown must prove (a) death 'as a result of a voluntary act of the accused', and (b) malice of 'the accused' ". The requirement that it should be a voluntary act is essential, not only in a murder case, but also in every criminal case. No act is punishable if it is done involuntarily: and an involuntary act in this context— some people nowadays prefer to speak of it as "automatism"—means an act which is done by the muscles without any control by the mind, such as a spasm, a reflex action or a convulsion; or an act done by a person who is not conscious of what he is doing, such as an act done whilst suffering from concussion or whilst sleep-walking. . . .

The term "involuntary act" is, however, capable of wider connotations: and to prevent confusion it is to be observed that in the criminal law an act is not to be regarded as an involuntary act simply because the doer does not remember it. When a man is charged with dangerous driving, it is no defence to him to say "I don't know what happened. I cannot remember a 'thing' ", see *Hill v. Baxter* [1958] 1 Q.B. 277. Loss of memory afterwards is never a defence in itself, so long as he was conscious at the time . . . see *Russell v. H.M. Advocate* 1946 S.C.(J.) 37; *R. v. Podola* [1960] 1 Q.B. 325. Nor is an act to be regarded as an involuntary act simply because the doer could not control his impulse to do it. When a man is charged with murder, and it appears that he knew what he was doing, but he could not resist it, then his assertion "I couldn't help myself" is no defence in itself, see *A.-G. for South Australia v. Brown* (1960) A.C. 432: though it may go towards a defence of diminished responsibility, in places where that defence is available, see *R. v. Byrne*, [*post*, p. 565]: but it does not render his act involuntary so as to entitle him to an unqualified acquittal. Nor is an act to be regarded as an involuntary act simply because it is unintentional or its consequences are unforeseen. When a man is charged with dangerous driving, it is no defence for him to say, however truly, "I did not mean to drive dangerously. . . ." But even though it is absolutely prohibited, nevertheless he has a defence if he can show that it was an involuntary act in the sense that he was unconscious at the time and did not know what he was doing. . . .

Another thing to be observed is that it is not every involuntary act which leads to a complete acquittal. Take first an involuntary act which proceeds from a state of drunkenness. If the drunken man is so drunk that he does not know what he is doing, he has a defence to any charge, such as murder or wounding with intent, in which a specific intent is essential, but he is still liable to be convicted of manslaughter or unlawful wounding for which no specific intent is necessary, see *Beard* [1920] A.C 479.

Again, if the involuntary act proceeds from a disease of the mind, it gives rise to a defence of insanity, but not to a defence of automatism. Suppose a crime is committed by a man in a state of automatism or clouded consciousness due to a recurrent disease of the mind. Such an act is no doubt involuntary, but it does not give rise to an unqualified acquittal, for that would mean that he would be let at large to do it again. The only proper verdict is one which ensures that the person who suffers from the disease is kept secure in a hospital so as not to be a danger to himself or others. That is a verdict of guilty but insane.

Once you exclude all the cases I have mentioned, it is apparent that the category of involuntary acts is very limited. . . .

My Lords, I think that Devlin J. was quite right in *Kemp's* case in putting the question of insanity to the jury, even though it had not been raised by the defence. When it is asserted that the accused did an involuntary act in a state of automatism, the defence necessarily puts in issue the state of mind of the accused man: and thereupon it is open to the prosecution to show what his true state of mind was. The old notion that only the defence can raise a defence of insanity is now gone. The prosecution are entitled to raise it and it is their duty to do so rather than allow a dangerous person to be at large. . . .

Upon the other point discussed by Devlin J., namely, what is a "disease of the mind" within the M'Naghten Rules, I would agree with him that this is a question for the judge. The major mental diseases, which the doctors call psychoses, such as schizophrenia, are clearly diseases of the mind. But in *Charlson* [1955] 1 W.L.R. 317, . . ., Barry J. seems to have assumed that other diseases such as epilepsy or cerebral tumour are not diseases of the mind, even when they are such as to manifest themselves in violence. I do not agree with this. It seems to me that any mental disorder which has manifested itself in violence and is prone to recur is a disease of the mind. At any rate it is the sort of disease for which a person should be detained in hospital rather than be given an unqualified acquittal. . . .

I am clearly of opinion that, if the act of George Bratty was an involuntary act, as the defence suggested, the evidence attributed it solely to a disease of the mind and the only defence open was the defence of insanity. There was no evidence of automatism apart from insanity. There was, therefore, no need for the judge to put it to the jury. And when the jury rejected the defence of insanity, they rejected the only defence disclosed by the evidence. . . .

I would, therefore, dismiss the appeal.

Appeal dismissed

R. v. Quick and Paddison
[1973] Q.B. 910
Court of Appeal

The appellant, who was a diabetic, was a psychiatric nurse. He was charged with assaulting a patient at the hospital where he worked. He said he could not remember the incident but that on the day it occurred he had taken his prescribed insulin, a small breakfast, some whisky, a quarter of a bottle of rum, and had no lunch. Medical evidence showed he was suffering at the time from hypoglycaemia, a deficiency of blood sugar after an injection of insulin. The appellant changed his plea to guilty after the judge rejected his defence of automatism on the grounds that the only defence open to him was insanity.

LAWTON L.J., for the court: In its broadest aspects these appeals raise the question what is meant by the phrase "a defect of reason from disease of the mind" within the meaning of the M'Naghten Rules. More particularly the question is whether a person who commits a criminal act whilst under the effects of hypoglycaemia can raise a defence of automatism, as the appellants submitted was possible, or whether such a person must rely on a defence of insanity if he wishes to relieve himself of responsibility for his acts, as Bridge J. ruled. . . .

Our examination of such authorities as there are must start with *Bratty* v. *A.-G. for Northern Ireland, supra*, because the judge ruled as he did in reliance on that case. The House of Lords . . . accepted that automatism as distinct from insanity could be a defence if there was a proper foundation in the evidence for it. In this case, if Quick's alleged condition could have been caused by hypoglycaemia Bridge J.'s ruling was right. The question remains, however, whether a mental condition arising from hypoglycaemia does amount to a disease of the mind. All their Lordships based their speeches on the basis that such medical evidence as there was pointed to Bratty suffering from a "defect of reason from disease of the mind" and nothing else. Lord Denning discussed in general terms what constitutes a disease of the mind [His Lordship then quoted the passage on "disease of the mind", *supra*].

If this opinion is right and there are no restricting qualifications which ought to be applied to it, Quick was setting up a defence of insanity. He may have been at the material time in a condition of mental disorder manifesting itself in violence. Such manifestations had occurred before and might recur. The difficulty arises as soon as the question is asked whether he should be detained in a mental hospital? No mental hospital would admit a diabetic merely because he had a low blood sugar reaction; and common sense is affronted by the prospect of a diabetic being sent to such a hospital when in most cases the disordered mental condition can be rectified quickly by pushing a lump of sugar or a teaspoonful of glucose into the patient's mouth.

The "affront to common sense" argument, however, has its own inherent weakness, as counsel for the Crown pointed out. If an accused is shown to have done a criminal act whilst suffering from a "defect of reason from disease of the mind", it matters not "whether the disease is curable or incurable . . . temporary or permanent" (see *R. v. Kemp* [*ante* p. 223], *per* Devlin J.). If the condition is temporary, the Secretary of State may have a difficult problem of disposal; but what happens to those found not guilty by reason of insanity is not a matter for the courts.

In *R. v. Kemp*, where the violent act was alleged to have been done during a period of unconsciousness arising from arteriosclerosis, counsel for the accused submitted that his client had done what he had during a period of mental confusion arising from a physical, not a mental disease. Devlin J. rejected this argument saying:

"It does not matter, for the purposes of the law, whether the defect of reasoning is due to a degeneration of the brain or to some other form of mental derangement. That may be a matter of importance medically, but it is of no importance to the law, which merely has to consider the state of mind in which the accused is, not how he got there."

Applied without qualification of any kind, Devlin J.'s statement of the law would have some surprising consequences. Take the not uncommon case of the rugby player who gets a kick on the head early in the game and plays on to the end in a state of automatism. If, whilst he was in that state, he assaulted the referee it is difficult to envisage any court adjudging that he was not guilty by reason of insanity. Another type of case which could occur is that of the dental patient who kicks out whilst

coming round from an anaesthetic. The law would be in a defective state
if a patient accused of assaulting a dental nurse by kicking her whilst
regaining consciousness could only excuse himself by raising the defence
of insanity. . . . [His Lordship referred to *Hill v. Baxter* [1958] 1 Q.B. 277,
D.C., and *Watmore v. Jenkins* [1962] 2 Q.B. 572.]

In this case, had the jury been left to decide whether the appellant
Quick at the material time was insane, or in a state of automatism or just
drunk, they probably would not have any difficulty in making up their
minds.

[His Lordship then referred to some Commonwealth cases].
. . .

In this quagmire of law seldom entered nowadays save by those in
desperate need of some kind of defence, *Bratty v. A.-G. for Northern Ireland,
supra,* provides the only firm ground. Is there any discernible path? We
think there is—judges should follow in a common sense way their sense
of fairness. This seems to have been the approach of the New Zealand
Court of Appeal in *R. v. Cottle* [1958] N.Z.L.R. 999, and of Sholl J. in *R. v.
Carter* [1959] V.R. 105. In our judgment no help can be obtained by specu-
lating (because that is what we would have to do) as to what the judges
who answered the House of Lords' questions in 1843 meant by disease of
the mind, still less what Sir Matthew Hale meant in the second half of the
17th century [(1682) Vol. J, Ch. IV.] A quick backward look at the state of
medicine in 1843 will suffice to show how unreal it would be to apply the
concepts of that age to the present time. . . . Our task has been to decide
what the law means now by the words "disease of the mind." In our
judgment the fundamental concept is of a malfunctioning of the mind
caused by disease. A malfunctioning of the mind of transitory effect
caused by the application to the body of some external factor such as
violence, drugs including anaesthetics, alcohol and hypnotic influences
cannot fairly be said to be due to disease. Such malfunctioning, unlike
that caused by a defect of reason from disease of the mind, will not always
relieve an accused from criminal responsibility. A self-induced incapacity
will not excuse—see *R. v. Lipman* [1970] 1 Q.B. 152, nor will one which
could have been reasonably foreseen as a result of either doing, or omitting to do something, as, for example, taking alcohol against medical
advice after using certain prescribed drugs, or failing to have regular
meals whilst taking insulin. From time to time difficult borderline cases
are likely to arise. When they do, the test suggested by the New Zealand
Court of Appeal in *R. v. Cottle* is likely to give the correct result, *viz.* can
this mental condition be fairly regarded as amounting to or producing a
defect of reason from disease of the mind?

In this case Quick's alleged mental condition, if it ever existed, was not
caused by his diabetes but by his use of insulin prescribed by his doctor.
Such malfunctioning of the mind as there was, was caused by an external
factor and not by a bodily disorder in the nature of a disease which disturbed the working of his mind. It follows in our judgment that Quick
was entitled to have his defence of automatism left to the jury and that
Bridge J.'s ruling as to the effect of the medical evidence called by him
was wrong. Had the defence of automatism been left to the jury, a number
of questions of fact would have to be answered. If he was in a confused
mental condition, was it due to a hypoglycaemic episode or to too much
alcohol? If the former, to what extent had he brought about his condition
by not following his doctor's instructions about taking regular meals? Did
he know that he was getting into a hypoglycaemic episode? If Yes, why
did he not use the antidote of eating a lump of sugar as he had been
advised to do? On the evidence which was before the jury Quick might

have had difficulty in answering these questions in a manner which would have relieved him of responsibility for his acts. We cannot say, however, with the requisite degree of confidence, that the jury would have convicted him. It follows that this conviction must be quashed on the ground that the verdict was unsatisfactory.

Appeal allowed

Questions

1. Lawton L.J. stated that the law should not give the words "defect of reason from disease of the mind" a meaning which would be regarded with incredulity outside the court. Is it arguable that the distinction between automatism arising from intrinsic causes and that arising from extrinsic causes, itself affronts common sense in that, implicit in the distinction is the conclusion that diabetes is a disease of the mind?

2. Quick's hypoglycaemic condition arose from taking insulin, drinking alcohol and not eating sufficient food. The opposite condition, hyperglycaemia (excess blood-sugar) arises where insulin is missing from the blood; this condition can have similar effects to hypoglycaemia. If Quick had committed the assault in a hyperglycaemic episode, what would have been the result under the principles expounded by the Court of Appeal? (See *Hennessy, ante*, p. 228 and *Bingham* [1991] Crim. L.R. 433.)

3. What would be the position of D, an epileptic, who fails to take drugs which completely suppress epileptic seizures, and who, in the course of a seizure, thrashes violently injuring V? Would it make any difference if D knew that such failure could lead to seizures and violence on his part? (See *Bailey, post*, p. 242.)

4. If the criterion for sane automatism is that it is due to an extrinsic cause, how would the courts react to an automatic act due to the effects of a disease caused by a bacterial or viral infection? For example, D suffering from bacterial meningitis and in a convulsive fit, hits V. On a charge of causing grievous bodily harm D pleads automatism; would he succeed? E, who is suffering from arteriosclerosis, falls into an autonomic state and hits X. On a charge of causing grievous bodily harm E pleads automatism; would he succeed? If the outcome in each case differs, can this be justified on any logical and substantive basis?

Note

Stress, anxiety or depression which lead to impaired consciousness are not themselves external physical factors (see *Hennessy, ante*, p. 228), but where they are due to an external physical factor and they lead to impaired consciousness, automatism may be pleaded successfully (see *R. v. T.* [1990] Crim. L. R. where the issue of automatism was left to the jury on the basis of medical evidence that D was acting in a dissociative state when she committed a robbery and caused actual bodily harm due to post traumatic stress disorder as a result of being raped three days previously. *Cf. Rabey* (1977) 37 C.C.C. (2d) 461.) See further

Horder, "Pleading Involuntary Lack of Capacity", *infra*, who engages in a critique of the non-insane automatism plea, particularly as used in cases such as *T*.

J. Horder, "Pleading Involuntary Lack of Capacity" (1993) 52 Camb.L.J. 298

Defendants may plead involuntary lack of capacity on a number of grounds that raise different theoretical problems. They may claim that the harm complained of was done by them when they were sleepwalking or under hypnosis. Alternatively they may claim that the causing of the harm was linked to an abnormal state of mind induced in them by, for example, Post Traumatic Stress Disorder (PTSD), pre-menstrual tension (PMT), or an unexpectedly violent allergic reaction to food or alcohol of a certain kind. There is, however, a fundamental difference between these two groups of cases. In the sleepwalking and hypnosis cases, the defendants' pleas amount to a claim that they were not truly acting at all. . . . In the latter group of cases, the defendant's pleas amount to a claim that they were not (or not fully) in control of what were admittedly their actions. . . .

We may engage with the world through causing things to happen, through voluntary conduct, or through evaluated conduct. A system of criminal law based solely on causation could not give rise to any difficulties concerning a plea of lack of capacity, for such a plea could gain no purchase. . . . Our system of criminal law is not based . . . on principles of brute deterrence, and presupposes that to become criminals people must be responsible for harm, and not just cause it.

This brings us to the second means by which we may engage with the world, namely through conduct. . . . Under the voluntary conduct model of criminal responsibility, it becomes possible to distinguish between accidents which are attributable to me and those which are not, and (a related point) to plead lack of capacity as a complete denial of responsibility. . . . If . . . voluntary conduct is one of the benchmarks of responsibility (putting aside questions about blame) it becomes possible to distinguish between cases on the grounds of lack of capacity; it becomes possible to distinguish between mere causers of harm, like sleepwalkers, and unwitting agents of harm, like those who leap . . . without looking. The former will lack capacity, whereas the latter will not. . . .

[I]t is the voluntary conduct model of engagement with the world that the criminal law claims to adopt in analysing responsibility, as opposed to blame. Lord Denning's classic definition of non-insane automatism in *Bratty* (*ante*, p. 235) reveals this:

> "Automatism—means an act which is done by the muscles without any control by the mind such as a spasm, a reflex action or a convulsion; or an act done by a person who is not conscious of what he is doing such as an act done whilst suffering from concussion or whilst sleepwalking."

In other words, it is only where defendants are agents and not mere causers of harm that they are to be regarded as responsible for causing that harm, a finding of responsibility being an essential precondition (absent questions of voluntary intoxication) for investigation into *mens rea* or blame. . . . This is as clear an endorsement of the voluntary conduct model of responsibility . . . as one could wish to find.

Despite the fact that, in theory at least, the voluntary conduct model is the model of engagement with the world which underpins the criminal law's conception of responsibility, there are troublesome cases. The law regards young children as beyond (or beneath) criminal responsibility even when they do harm intentionally, and mitigates the offence of intentional killers suffering from diminished responsibility, even though they may unquestionably be voluntary agents rather than mere causers of harm. . . .

Under the evaluated conduct model of engagement with the world, what counts as significant engagement by me is conduct which was or could have been influenced by critical evaluation before I embarked or decided to go ahead. . . . [I]f we return to our troublesome examples, it is the fact that the influence of critical evaluation on an agent's conduct is (virtually) impossible that qualifies the agent's capacities for engagement with the world and enables them to deny (full) responsibility.

In the case of very young children, their exemption from criminal liability might be justified on a number of grounds, such as the wish to avoid undue harshness in the application of criminal process and sanctions. Nonetheless, what gives grounds such as this their force is that, whilst even very young children are quite capable of engaging in intentionally harmful conduct, they do not have developed moral characters as to which such conduct can be related. It is the possession of such a character that makes possible the formation of and action upon an intelligent conception of the good (in) life, and hence makes it possible to subject one's (potential) conduct to critical moral evaluation, and shape it in the light of that evaluation.

By way of contrast, engagement in nothing more than voluntary and intentional conduct does not presuppose the possession of a moral character. . . .

[Analysing the case of *R. v. T.* Horder goes on to state:]

The defendant's condition points clearly in the direction of acquittal or substantial mitigation of the offence on the grounds of non-insane automatism, but non-insane automatism is a plea shaped by the voluntary conduct model of responsibility, which seeks to do no more than distinguish agents from mere causers of harm; and like the victim of post hypnotic suggestion, T seems most plausibly to have been an agent, albeit a morally unwitting agent, and not a mere causer of harm.

There are other agents who may lack capacity under the evaluated conduct model of responsibility but who, in virtue of being voluntary agents, may have difficulty pleading non-insane automatism. Examples are provided by those whose moods are radically affected by PMT or by the violently allergic reaction, even to small quantities of alcohol, known as Pathological Alcoholic Intoxication. The law is forced into an inconsistent attitude to such defendants when they do harm as a result of their violent mood changes. Since they engage in voluntary conduct, the general applicability of the law's voluntary conduct model of responsibility dictates that the presumption of rational capacity has not been displaced, and they must rely on a lack of *mens rea* (that is unless, of course, they are as fortunate as T in persuading the judge that they might have been in a state akin to sleepwalking and thus were indeed not engaged in voluntary conduct). Yet if it should happen that such defendants kill intentionally, and they plead diminished responsibility, the grounding of this plea . . . in the evaluated conduct model of responsibility means that their plea of partial lack of capacity stands a good chance of success, despite the admittedly voluntary character of their conduct. . . .

[W]here defendants may have intentionally done harm through some voluntary conduct of theirs [such as cases concerning PTSD, PMT, Pathological Alcoholic Intoxication and hypoglycaemia], . . . their inability to evaluate conduct ought to excuse them. . . . These are cases best dealt with

through the broadening out of diminished responsibility into a general
defence. [This would require the creation of] an intermediate "diminished
responsibility" verdict . . . distinct from finding the defendant guilty or
not guilty. The verdict would indicate nothing more or less than that
defendants had voluntarily caused harm whilst unable to evaluate their
conduct or control it through moral evaluation. Such a finding would
have the effect of giving the trial judge the power to make an order in lieu
of punishment or outright acquittal, an order which might conceivably be
one ranging from absolute or conditional discharge, through supervision
and treatment, to an order for detention in a secure institution for exceptional cases where the defendant's condition makes them, albeit temporarily, a vivid and violent danger. . . .

It is important to recognise, though that allowing people to plead lack
of moral capacity as an excuse, when they are suffering from the kinds of
(temporary) disorders discussed above, need not give rise to the possibility of unjust leniency for the person who claims "I could not help it; it's
just the way I am." Consider someone whose violent nature is attributable
to the violent abuse they themselves witnessed, or suffered, in their form-
ative childhood years. Such a person is tragically unlucky but nonetheless
fully responsible for their conduct. There are many things for which we
must take responsibility even though we did not deliberately or even
carelessly bring them about, and our moral character is one of these. The
victim of abuse who turns abuser *exhibits* their moral character in the
abuse they inflict, and they must take responsibility for this just because
the moral character exhibited is *theirs*. Those who are violent or dangerous
due to PMT, PTSD, Pathological Alcoholic Intoxication or hypoglycaemia,
however, are not morally responsible for their actions precisely because
they are estranged from their moral characters when they act.

Self-induced automatism

Note

If non-insane automatism leads to a complete acquittal based on the
doctrine of voluntariness, will this principle lead to the same outcome
where it can be shown that the autonomic state was self-induced?

In *Quick* Lawton L.J. stated:

> "A self-induced incapacity will not excuse . . . nor will one which could
> have been reasonably foreseen as a result of either doing, or omitting
> to do something, as, for example, taking alcohol against medical advice
> after using certain prescribed drugs, or failing to have regular meals
> while taking insulin."

On the basis of this dictum Quick's autonomic state appears to have
been self-induced by not eating or taking a lump of sugar when the
first signs of hypoglycaemia manifested themselves. However, his
conviction was quashed as his defence of automatism had not been
left to the jury. The effect of *Quick*, however, appeared categorically
to rule out the defence of automatism where it was self-induced.

R. v. Bailey
[1983] 1 W.L.R. 760
Court of Appeal

The appellant was charged with wounding with intent and with an
alternative count of unlawful wounding contrary to sections 18 and 20

respectively of the Offences Against the Person Act 1861. His defence was automatism caused by hypoglycaemia which was due to his failure to take sufficient food after taking insulin, although he had taken some sugar and water. He claimed, accordingly, that he lacked the specific intent required for the purpose of s.18 and the basic intent required for the purpose of s.20. The judge directed the jury that as the appellant's incapacity was self-induced he could not plead automatism. The appellant was convicted of causing grievous bodily harm with intent, contrary to s.18. He appealed.

GRIFFITHS L.J.: . . . But in [*Quick*] [t]he Court of Appeal held that [the ruling upon which the present trial judge had based his direction] was wrong and that the malfunctioning caused by the hypoglycaemia was not a disease of the mind and that the appellant was entitled to have his defence considered by the jury. . . .

But in that case, the offence, assault occasioning actual bodily harm, was an offence of basic intent. No specific intent was required. It is now quite clear that even if the incapacity of mind is self-induced by the voluntary taking of drugs or alcohol, the specific intent to kill or cause grievous bodily harm may be negatived: see *R. v. Majewski* [1977] A.C. 443 (*post*, p. 252). This being so, as it is conceded on behalf of the Crown, the direction to which we have referred cannot be correct so far as the offence under section 18 is concerned.

But it is also submitted that the direction is wrong or at least in too broad and general terms, so far as the section 20 offence is concerned. If . . . *Quick* correctly represents the law, then the direction given by the recorder was correct so far as the second count was concerned even though the appellant may have had no appreciation of the consequences of his failure to take food and even though such failure may not have been due to deliberate abstention but because of his generally distressed condition. In our judgment the passage from Lawton L.J.'s judgment was obiter and we are free to re-examine it.

Automatism resulting from intoxication as a result of a voluntary ingestion of alcohol or dangerous drugs does not negative the mens rea necessary for crimes of basic intent, because the conduct of the accused is reckless and recklessness is enough to constitute the necessary mens rea in assault cases where no specific intent forms part of the charge: see *R. v. Majewski* (*post*, p. 252). . . .

The same considerations apply where the state of automatism is induced by the voluntary taking of dangerous drugs: see *R. v. Lipman* [1970] Q.B. 152 where a conviction for manslaughter was upheld, the appellant having taken L.S.D. and killed his mistress in the course of an hallucinatory trip. It was submitted on behalf of the Crown that a similar rule should be applied as a matter of public policy to all cases of self-induced automatism. But it seems to us that there may be material distinctions between a man who consumes alcohol or takes dangerous drugs and one who fails to take sufficient food after insulin to avert hypoglycaemia.

It is common knowledge that those who take alcohol to excess or certain sorts of drugs may become aggressive or do dangerous or unpredictable things, they may be able to foresee the risks of causing harm to others but nevertheless persist in their conduct. But the same cannot be said without more of a man who fails to take food after an insulin injection. If he does appreciate the risk that such a failure may lead to aggressive, unpredictable and uncontrollable conduct and he nevertheless deliberately runs the risk or otherwise disregards it, this will amount to recklessness. But we certainly do not think that it is common knowledge, even among diabetics, that such is a consequence of a failure to take food and there is no evidence that it was known to this appellant. Doubtless he knew that if he failed to take his insulin or proper food after it, he might lose consciousness, but as such he would only be a danger to himself unless he put himself in charge of some machine such as a motor car, which required his continued conscious control.

In our judgment, self-induced automatism, other than that due to intoxication from alcohol or drugs, may provide a defence to crimes of basic intent. The question in each case will be whether the prosecution have proved the necessary element of recklessness. In cases of assault, if the accused knows that his actions or inaction are likely to make him aggressive, unpredictable or uncontrolled with the result that he may cause some injury to others and he persists in the action or takes no remedial action when he knows it is required, it will be open to the jury to find that he was reckless.

Turning again to *R. v. Quick* and the passage we have quoted, we think that notwithstanding the unqualified terms in which the proposition is stated, it is possible that the court may not have intended to lay down such an absolute rule. In the following paragraph Lawton L.J. considers a number of questions, which are not necessarily exhaustive, which the jury might have wanted to consider if the issue had been left to them. One such question was whether the accused knew that he was getting into a hypoglycaemic episode and if so why he did not use the antidote of taking sugar which he had been advised to do. These questions suggest that even if the hypoglycaemia was induced by some action or inaction by the accused his defence will not necessarily fail.

In the present case the recorder never invited the jury to consider what the appellant's knowledge or appreciation was of what would happen if he failed to take food after his insulin or whether he realised that he might become aggressive. Nor were they asked to consider why the appellant had omitted to take food in time. They were given no direction on the elements of recklessness. Accordingly, in our judgment there was also a misdirection in relation to the second count in the indictment of unlawful wounding.

But we have to consider whether, notwithstanding these misdirections, there has been any miscarriage of justice and whether the jury properly directed could have failed to come to the same conclusion. As Lawton L.J. said in *Quick's* case at p. 922, referring to the defence of automatism, it is a "quagmire of law seldom entered nowadays save by those in desperate need of some kind of a defence. . . ." This case is no exception. We think it very doubtful whether the appellant laid a sufficient basis for the defence to be considered by the jury at all. But even if he did we are in no doubt that the jury properly directed must have rejected it. Although an episode of sudden transient loss of consciousness or awareness was theoretically possible it was quite inconsistent with the graphic description that the appellant gave to the police both orally and in his written statement. There was abundant evidence that he had armed himself with the iron bar and gone to Mr Harrison's house for the purpose of attacking him because he wanted to teach him a lesson and because he was in the way.

Moreover the doctor's evidence to which we have referred showed it was extremely unlikely that such an episode could follow some five minutes after taking sugar and water. For these reasons we are satisfied that no miscarriage of justice occurred and the appeal will be dismissed.

Appeal dismissed

Questions

1. A drunkard has no defence to a crime of basic intent (see pp. 252–261 *infra*). As a result of *Bailey* an automaton who has brought about his own state of automatism may have a defence. Is this difference one which can be justified on grounds of policy or principle?

2. The court in *Bailey* did not presume recklessness because of the absence of common knowledge amongst diabetics that failure to take food after insulin might result in aggressive behaviour. How might a court come to such a conclusion? What would happen if directions on prescriptions of insulin were to include such a warning?

3. Bailey was charged with an offence for which the test for recklessness was the *Cunningham* one. What ought the result to have been if his offence had been one to which the *Caldwell* recklessness test applied? See *Hardie, post*, p. 266.

4. Schiffer, in *Mental Disorder and the Criminal Trial Process* (1978), gives examples of statistical studies which show that "(1) violent behaviour of any sort is unusual in epileptic automatisms; (2) the vast majority of epileptics have never experienced fugue state automatism; and (3) amongst those who do . . . it is a relatively rare occurrence" (p. 93). In light of the fact that a person in hypoglycaemic coma though unconscious may still perform normal functions, as if a robot, is it tenable to conclude (as a reading of *Bailey* and *Sullivan* would seem to dictate) that epileptics represent a greater danger to the public than diabetics? If not, is the distinction between external and internal organic causes, a fatuous one? (cf. *Parks, ante*, p. 228.)

5. Schiffer (at p. 100) states that hypoglycaemic coma may be caused by overproduction of insulin by the pancreas. How would the courts have treated Bailey if his automatism had resulted from this cause?

3. PROPOSALS FOR REFORM

Draft Criminal Code Bill, Clause 33

"Automatism and physical incapacity
33.—(1) A person is not guilty of an offence if—

(a) he acts in a state of automatism, that is, his act—
   (i) is a reflex, spasm or convulsion; or
   (ii) occurs while he is in a condition (whether of sleep, unconsciousness, impaired consciousness or otherwise) depriving him of effective control of the act; and
(b) the act or condition is the result neither of anything done or omitted with the fault required for the offence nor of voluntary intoxication.

(2) A person is not guilty of an offence by virtue of an omission to act if—

(a) he is physically incapable of acting in the way required; and
(b) his being so incapable is the result neither of anything done or omitted with the fault required for the offence nor of voluntary intoxication."

In paras. 11.2–11.3 of the *Commentary on Draft Criminal Bill* (Law Com. No. 177) the Law Commission state—

"11.2 *Limited function of subsection (1)*. The main function of clause 3(1) is to protect a person who acts in a state of automatism from conviction of an offence of strict liability. It is conceded that he does 'the act' specified for the offence; but the clause declares him not guilty. One charged with an offence requiring fault in the form of failure to comply with a standard of conduct may also have to rely on the clause. On the other hand, a state of automatism will negative a fault requirement of intention or know-ledge or (normally) recklessness; so a person charged with an offence of violence against another, or of criminal damage, committed when he was in a condition of impaired consciousness, does not rely on this clause for his acquittal but on the absence of the fault element of the offence.

11.3 *Conditions within the subsection*. Subsection (1)(a) refers to acts of two kinds:

(i) an act over which the person concerned, although conscious, has no control: the 'reflex, spasm or convulsion'. Such an act would rarely, if ever, be the subject of a prosecution.
(ii) an act over which the person concerned does not have effective control because of a 'condition' of "sleep, unconsciousness, impaired consciousness or otherwise". We believe that the references to 'impaired consciousness' and to deprivation of 'effective' control are justified both on principle and by some of the leading cases. The gov-erning principle should be that a person is not guilty of an offence if, without relevant fault on his part, he cannot choose to act otherwise than as he does. The acts of the defendants in several cases have been treated as automatous although it is far from clear, and even unlikely, that they were entirely unconscious when they did the acts and although it cannot confidently be said that they exercised no control, in any sense of that phrase, over their relevant movements. . . .

Draft Criminal Code Bill, Clauses 34–40

34. In this Act—

'mental disorder' means—

(a) severe mental illness; or
(b) a state of arrested or incomplete development of mind; or
(c) a state of automatism (not resulting only from intoxication) which is a feature of a disorder, whether organic or functional and whether continuing or recurring, that may cause a similar state on another occa-sion;

'return a mental disorder verdict' means—

(a) in relation to trial on indictment, return a verdict that the defendant is not guilty on evidence of mental disorder; and
(b) in relation to summary trial, dismiss the information on evidence of mental disorder;

'severe mental illness' means a mental illness which has one or more of the following characteristics—

(a) lasting impairment of intellectual functions shown by failure of memory, orientation, comprehension and learning capacity;

(b) lasting alteration of mood of such degree as to give rise to delusional appraisal of the defendant's situation, his past or his future, or that of others, or lack of any appraisal;
(c) delusional beliefs, persecutory, jealous or grandiose;
(d) abnormal perceptions associated with delusional misinterpretation of events;
(e) thinking so disordered as to prevent reasonable appraisal of the defendant's situation or reasonable communication with others;

'severe mental handicap' means a state of arrested or incomplete development of mind which includes severe impairment of intelligence and social functioning.

35.—(1) A mental disorder verdict shall be returned if the defendant is proved to have committed an offence but it is proved on the balance of probabilities (whether by the prosecution or by the defendant) that he was at the time suffering from severe mental illness or severe mental handicap.

(2) Subsection (1) does not apply if the court or jury is satisfied beyond reasonable doubt that the offence was not attributable to the severe mental illness or severe mental handicap.

(3) A court or jury shall not, for the purposes of a verdict under subsection (1), find that the defendant was suffering from severe mental illness or severe mental handicap unless two medical practitioners approved for the purposes of section 12 of the Mental Health Act 1983 as having special experience in the diagnosis or treatment of mental disorder have given evidence that he was so suffering.

(4) Subsection (1), so far as it relates to severe mental handicap, does not apply to an offence under section 106(1), 107 or 108 (sexual relations with the mentally handicapped).

36. A mental disorder verdict shall be returned if—

(a) the defendant is acquitted of an offence only because, by reason of evidence of mental disorder or a combination of mental disorder and intoxication, it is found that he acted or may have acted in a state of automatism, or without the fault required for the offence, or believing that an exempting circumstance existed; and
(b) it is proved on the balance of probabilities (whether by the prosecution or by the defendant) that he was suffering from mental disorder at the time of the act.

37. A defendant may plead 'not guilty by reason of mental disorder'; and

(a) if the court directs that the plea be entered the direction shall have the same effect as a mental disorder verdict; and
(b) if the court does not so direct the defendant shall be treated as having pleaded not guilty.

38.—(1) Whether evidence is evidence of mental disorder or automatism is a question of law.

(2) The prosecution shall not adduce evidence of mental disorder, or contend that a mental disorder verdict should be returned, unless the defendant has given or adduced evidence that he acted without the fault required for the offence, or believing that an exempting circumstance existed, or in a state of automatism, or (on a charge of murder) when suffering from mental abnormality as defined in section 57(2).

(3) The court may give directions as to the stage of the proceedings at which the prosecution may adduce evidence of mental disorder.

39. Schedule 2 has effect with respect to the orders that may be made upon the return of a mental disorder verdict, to the conditions governing the making of those orders, to the effects of those orders and to related matters.

40. A defendant shall not, when a mental disorder verdict is returned in respect of an offence and while that verdict subsists, be found guilty of any other offence of which, but for this section, he might on the same occasion be found guilty—

(a) on the indictment, count or information to which the verdict relates; or
(b) on any other indictment, count or information founded on the same facts."

In the *Commentary on Draft Criminal Bill* (Law Com. No. 177) the Law Commission state—

Code provisions on mental disorder

11.9 *Butler Committee.* The Butler Committee [in *Report of the Committee on Mentally Abnormal Offenders* (1975) Cmnd. 6244] proposed substantial reform of the law and procedure relating to the effect of mental disorder on criminal liability and the disposal of persons acquitted because of mental disorder. The necessity of incorporating in the projected Criminal Code an appropriate provision to replace the outdated "insanity" defence was one justification given by the Committee for its review of the subject. We ourselves are persuaded that implementation of the Committee's proposals would greatly improve this area of the law. We have, however, found it necessary to suggest some important modifications of those proposals. Clauses 34 to 40 therefore aim to give effect to the policy of the Butler Committee as modified by us in ways that will be explained in the following paragraphs.

11.10 *The present "insanity defence".* Before considering the structure of the proposed law, it will be convenient to refer to that of the present law. The *M'Naghten Rules,* together with statutory provisions, produce a "special verdict" ("not guilty by reason of insanity") . . . in two kinds of case.

(i) The first case is that where it is proved (rebutting the so-called "presumption of sanity") that, because of "a defect of reason, from disease of the mind", the defendant did not "know the nature and quality of the act he was doing". If the defendant "did not know what he was doing", he must have lacked any fault required for the offence charged; so, in modern terms at least, this first element in the *M'Naghten Rules* has the appearance of a rule, not about guilt, but about burden of proof and disposal. The defendant should in any case be acquitted, but he must prove that he should be; and his acquittal is to be treated as the occasion for his detention as a matter of social defence.
(ii) The second case is that where, because of "a defect of reason, from disease of the mind", the defendant "did not know he was doing what was wrong." This is a case, then, in which the Rules afford a defence properly so called: a person who would otherwise be guilty is not guilty "by reason of insanity". But, once again, social defence requires his detention in hospital.

11.11 *Structure of the proposed provisions*. Clauses 35 and 36, following the structure proposed by the Butler Committee, are similarly concerned with two kinds of case, in each of which there is to be a verdict of acquittal in special form ("not guilty on evidence of mental disorder"). On the return of a mental disorder verdict the court would have flexible disposal powers. . . .

(a) *Clause 35(1)*. In one case all the elements of the offence are proved but severe mental disorder operates as a true defence. This is equivalent to case (ii) above.

(b) *Clause 36*. In the other case an acquittal is inevitable because the prosecution has failed to prove that the defendant acted with the required fault (or to disprove his defence of automatism or mistake); but the reason for that failure is evidence of mental disorder, and it is proved that the defendant was indeed suffering from mental disorder at the time of the act. This differs from case (i) above in casting no burden on the defendant of proving his innocence. . . ."

Clause 35: Case of mental disorder verdict: defence of severe disorder

11.15 Subsection (1) provides that even though he has done the act specified for the offence with the fault required, a defendant is entitled to an acquittal, in the form of a mental disorder verdict, if he was suffering from severe mental illness or severe mental handicap at the time. This implements the Butler Committee's conception with some modifications.

11.16 *Attributability of offence to disorder: a rebuttable presumption*. One aspect of the Committee's recommendation has proved controversial. The Committee acknowledged that—

"it is theoretically possible for a person to be suffering from a severe mental disorder which has in a causal sense nothing to do with the act or omission for which he is being tried";

but they found it "very difficult to imagine a case in which one could be sure of the absence of any such connection". They therefore proposed, in effect, an irrebuttable presumption that there was a sufficient connection between the severe disorder and the offence. This proposal is understandable in view of the limitation of the defence to a narrow range of very serious disorders; and its adoption would certainly simplify the tasks of psychiatric witnesses and the court. Some people, however, take the view that it would be wrong in principle that a person should escape conviction if, although severely mentally ill, he has committed a rational crime which was uninfluenced by his illness and for which he ought to be liable to be punished. They believe that the prosecution should be allowed to persuade the jury (if it can) that the offence was not attributable to the disorder. We agree. Subsection (2) provides accordingly. We believe that it must improve the acceptability of the Butler Committee's generally admirable scheme as the basis of legislation.

11.17 *"Severe mental illness"* is defined in clause 34 in the terms proposed by the Butler Committee. Severe mental illness, for the purpose of this exemption from criminal liability, ought in the Committee's view, to be closely defined and restricted to serious cases of psychosis (as that term is currently understood). The Committee recommended, as the preferable mode of definition, the identification of "the abnormal mental phenomena which occur in the various mental illnesses and which when present would be regarded by common consent as being evidence of severity".

We believe that this symptomatic mode of definition has much to commend it. The psychiatric expert will give evidence in terms of strict "factual tests", rather than of abstractions (such as "disease of the mind" or "severe mental illness" itself) or diagnostic labels. The method allocates appropriate functions to the law itself (in laying down the test of criminal responsibility), to the expert (in advising whether the test is satisfied) and to the tribunal of fact (in judging, by reference to the whole of the case, whether that advice is soundly given). . . .

11.19 *"Severe mental handicap"* is defined in clause 34. The expression used by the Butler Committee was "severe subnormality", which was defined in the Mental Health Act 1959, section 4, in terms apt for the Committee's purpose. But the expression "severe mental impairment" has since replaced "severe subnormality" in mental health legislation (the latter term having fallen out of favour). "Severe mental impairment" has the following meaning:

"a state of arrested or incomplete development of mind which includes severe impairment of intelligence and social functioning and is associated with abnormally aggressive or seriously irresponsible conduct on the part of the person concerned".

This definition is not a happy one for present purposes; exemption from criminal liability on the ground of severe mental handicap ought not to be limited to a case where the handicap is associated with aggressive or irresponsible conduct. We therefore propose that the expression "severe mental handicap" be used, with the same definition as "severe mental impairment" down to the word "functioning". This will give effect to the Butler Committee's intentions and has the approval of our Royal College advisers.

11.20 *Burden of proof.* Subsection (1) permits proof of severe disorder by either prosecution or defendant. Normally it will be for the defendant to prove it, as his defence to the charge. This is as proposed by the Butler Committee. But there may be a case in which the defendant adduces evidence of mental disorder on an issue of fault or automatism and the prosecution responds with evidence of severe disorder and in such a case it may be the prosecution evidence (or a combination of prosecution and defence evidence) which results in a mental disorder verdict under clause 35(1). . . .

Clause 36: Case for mental disorder verdict: evidence of disorder

11.23 *Broad effect of the clause.* Evidence of mental disorder may be the reason why the court or jury is at least doubtful whether the defendant acted with the fault required for the offence. The Butler Committee recommended that, although in such a case there must be an acquittal, this acquittal should be in the qualified form "not guilty on evidence of mental disorder" where it is proved that the defendant was in fact suffering from mental disorder at the time of his act. Clause 36 gives effect to this recommendation, significantly modified by the adoption of a narrower meaning of "mental disorder" than that proposed by the Committee.

11.24 *Cases covered by the clause.* The clause adapts the Committee's proposal to the conceptual structure of the Code. First, it provides that the mental disorder verdict is not to be returned unless evidence of mental disorder is the only reason for an acquittal. The provision must not affect a case in which the defendant is entitled to an acquittal on some additional ground having nothing to do with mental disorder. Secondly, it refers not only to absence of fault but also (a) to automatism and (b) to a belief in a circumstance of defence. (a) Automatism is mentioned because the acquittal of one who acted in a state of automatism is not grounded only in absence of "fault" (see clause 33). (b) A person may commit an act of violence because of a deluded belief that he is under attack and must defend himself. Within the scheme of the Code—which draws a distinction between elements of offences (including fault elements) and defences—such a person would not, when relying on his delusion, be denying "the fault for the offence". His mentally disordered belief must therefore be separately mentioned in the paragraph. . . .

11.28 *"Mental disorder": the proposed definition.* We define "mental disorder" in clause 34 to include (only):

(a) "severe mental illness" (as defined in the same section): the defendant who lacked fault, or believed in the existence of an exempting circumstance, because of a psychotic distortion of perception or understanding, will receive a mental disorder verdict and be amenable to the court's powers of restraint.

(b) "arrested or incomplete development of mind": this category from the Mental Health Act definition of "mental disorder" survives our amendment of the Butler Committee's proposal. We must, however, express a doubt as to whether it should do so. Some persons against whom fault cannot be proved might receive mental disorder verdicts, and become subject to the protective powers of the criminal courts, although under the present law they would receive unqualified acquittals. It may be thought more appropriate to leave any acquitted persons within this category who represent a danger to themselves or others to be dealt with under Part II of the Mental Health Act 1983.

(c) (in effect) pathological automatism that is liable to recur: it would not, we think, be acceptable to propose that the courts should lose all control over a person acquitted because of what is now termed "insane automatism". Paragraph (c) of our definition requires the "state of automatism" (see clause 33(1)) to be "a feature of a disorder . . . that may cause a similar state on another occasion". This qualification confines the mental disorder verdict to those possibly warranting some form of control that the court can impose. It may nevertheless be felt by some that the paragraph includes too much. The Butler Committee wished, in particular, to protect from a mental disorder verdict a diabetic who causes a harm in a state of confusion after failing to take his insulin. We do not think, however, that there is a satisfactory way of distinguishing between the different conditions that may cause repeated episodes of disorder; nor do we think it necessary to do so. There is not, so far as we can see, a satisfactory basis for distinguishing between (say) a brain tumour or cerebral arteriosclerosis on the one hand and diabetes or epilepsy on the other. If any of these conditions causes a state of automatism in which the sufferer commits what would otherwise be an offence of violence, his acquittal should be "on evidence of mental disorder". Whether a diabetic so affected has failed to seek treatment, or forgotten to take his insulin, or decided not to do so, may affect the court's decision whether to order his discharge or to take some other course. What is objectionable in the present law is the offensive label of "insanity" and the fact that the court is obliged to order the hospitalisation of the acquitted person, in effect as a restricted patient. With the elimination of these features under the Butler Committee's scheme, the verdict should not seem preposterous in the way that its present counterpart does.

4. INTOXICATION

Note

A person may become intoxicated through the consumption of drink or drugs. Whatever the cause of the intoxication, the law treats the intoxicated offender the same. Intoxication is not *per se* a defence; rather, a defendant who relies on intoxication is saying that because of his intoxication he did not have the necessary *mens rea* for the offence. Thus, if D, although intoxicated (whether voluntarily or involuntarily) has formed the necessary intent for the crime he will be guilty. See *Kingston, post,* p. 262. If D's intoxication leaves him incapable of forming the *mens rea* for the offence with which he is charged, or if he claims that he did not form the *mens rea* for the offence because he was intoxicated, he will not necessarily be acquitted; the outcome will hinge on whether the offence is one of specific or basic intent.

i. Specific and Basic Intent

D.P.P. v. Majewski
[1976] 2 W.L.R. 623
House of Lords

M appealed against convictions of assault occasioning actual bodily harm and assault of a police constable in the execution of his duty on the ground that he was too intoxicated, through a combination of drugs and alcohol, to form the appropriate *mens rea*. M was a drug addict who, over the previous two days, had consumed a large quantity of amphetamines and barbiturates before spending an evening drinking at the pub where the offences were committed. M admitted that he had sometimes "gone paranoid" but this was the first time he had "completely blacked out". Medical evidence was given that such a state of "pathological intoxication" was uncommon and that automatism due to the ingestion of alcohol together with either amphetamines or barbiturates was unlikely; it was more likely for a person intoxicated in this way to know what he was doing at the time but to suffer an "amnesic patch" later.

LORD ELWYN-JONES L.C.: . . .
The Court of Appeal dismissed the appeal against conviction but granted leave to appeal to your Lordships' House certifying that the following point of law of general public importance was involved:

"Whether a defendant may properly be convicted of assault notwithstanding that, by reason of his self-induced intoxication, he did not intend to do the act alleged to constitute the assault. . . ."

If a man consciously and deliberately takes alcohol and drugs not on medical prescription, but in order to escape from reality, to go "on a trip", to become hallucinated, whatever the description may be, and thereby disables himself from taking the care he might otherwise take and as a result by his subsequent actions causes injury to another—does our criminal law enable him to say that because he did not know what he was doing he lacked both intention and recklessness and accordingly is entitled to an acquittal?

Originally the common law would not and did not recognise self-induced intoxication as an excuse. Lawton L.J. spoke of the "merciful relaxation" to that rule which was introduced by the judges during the 19th century, and he added:

"Although there was much reforming zeal and activity in the 19th century Parliament never once considered whether self-induced intoxication should be a defence generally to a criminal charge. It would have been a strange result if the merciful relaxation of a strict rule of law had ended, without any Parliamentary intervention, by whittling it away to such an extent that the more drunk a man became, provided he stopped short of making himself insane, the better chance he had of acquittal. . . . The common law rule still applied but there were exceptions to it which Lord Birkenhead L.C., *D.P.P. v. Beard* [1920] A.C. 479, tried to define by reference to specific intent."

There are, however, decisions of eminent judges in a number of Commonwealth cases in Australia and New Zealand (but generally not in Canada nor in the United States), as well as impressive academic comment in this country, to which we have been referred supporting the view that it is illogical and inconsistent with legal principle to treat a person who of his own choice and volition has taken drugs and drink, even though he thereby creates a state in which he is not conscious of what he is doing, any differently from a person suffering from the various medical conditions like epilepsy or diabetic coma and who is regarded by the law as free from fault. However, our courts have for a very long time regarded in quite another light the state of self-induced intoxication. The authority which for the last half century has been relied on in this context has been the speech of Lord Birkenhead L.C. in *D.P.P. v. Beard*, at 494:

"Under the law of England as it prevailed until early in the nineteenth century voluntary drunkenness was never an excuse for criminal misconduct; and indeed the classic authorities broadly assert that voluntary drunkenness must be considered rather an aggravation than a defence. This view was in terms based upon the principle that a man who by his own voluntary act debauches and destroys his will power, shall be no better situated in regard to criminal acts than a sober man."

Lord Birkenhead L.C. made an historical survey of the way the common law from the 16th century on dealt with the effect of self-induced intoxication on criminal responsibility. This indicates how, from 1819 on, the judges began to mitigate the severity of the attitude of the common law in such cases as murder and serious violent crime when the penalties of death or transportation applied or where there was likely to be sympathy for the accused, as in attempted suicide. Lord Birkenhead L.C., at 499, concluded that (except in cases where insanity was pleaded) the decisions he cited—

"establish that where a specific intent is an essential element in the offence, evidence of a state of drunkenness rendering the accused incapable of forming such an intent should be taken into consideration in order to determine whether he had in fact formed the intent necessary to constitute the particular crime. If he was so drunk that he was incapable of forming the intent required he could not be convicted of a crime which was committed only if the intent was proved. . . . In a charge of murder based upon intention to kill or to do grievous bodily harm, if the jury are satisfied that the accused was, by reason of his drunken condition, incapable of forming the intent to kill or to do grievous bodily harm ... he cannot be convicted of murder. But nevertheless unlawful homicide has been committed by the accused, and consequently he is guilty of unlawful homicide without malice aforethought, and that is manslaughter: *per* Stephen J. in *Doherty's Case* (1887) 16 Cox C.C. 306, 307. [He concluded the passage:] the law is plain beyond all question that in cases falling short of insanity a condition of drunkenness at the time of committing an offence causing death can only, when it is available at all, have the effect of reducing the crime from murder to manslaughter."

From this it seemed clear—and this is the interpretation which the judges have placed on the decision during the ensuing half-century—that it is only in the limited class of cases requiring proof of specific intent that drunkenness can exculpate. Otherwise in no case can it exempt completely from criminal liability. . . .

[His Lordship quoted Lord Denning in *Gallagher, post,* p. 269, and in *Bratty, ante,* p. 235].

In no case has the general principle of English law as described by Lord Denning in *Gallagher's* case and exposed again in *Bratty's* case been overruled in this House and the question now to be determined is whether it should be.

I do not for my part regard that general principle as either unethical or contrary to the principles of natural justice. If a man of his own volition takes a substance which causes him to cast off the restraints of reason and conscience, no wrong is done to him by holding him answerable criminally for any injury he may do while in that condition. His course of conduct in reducing himself by drugs and drink to that condition in my view supplies the evidence of mens rea, of guilty mind certainly sufficient for crimes of basic intent. It is a reckless course of conduct and recklessness is enough to constitute the necessary mens rea in assault cases: see *R. v. Venna* [*post,* p. 623], *per* James L.J. The drunkenness is itself an intrinsic, an integral part of the crime, the other part being the evidence of the unlawful use of force against the victim. Together they add up to criminal recklessness. On this I adopt the conclusion of Stroud that:

"It would be contrary to all principle and authority to suppose that drunkenness [and what is true of drunkenness is equally true of intoxication by drugs] can be a defence for crime in general on the ground that 'a person cannot be convicted of a crime unless the *mens* was *rea*.' By allowing himself to get drunk and thereby putting himself in such a condition as to be no longer amenable to the law's commands, a man shows such regardlessness as amounts to *mens rea* for the purpose of all ordinary crimes."

This approach is in line with the American Model Code, s.2.08(2),

"When recklessness establishes an element of the offence, if the actor, due to self-induced intoxication, is unaware of a risk of which he would have been aware had be been sober, such unawareness is immaterial."

. . . The final question that arises is whether s.8 of the Criminal Justice Act 1967 has had the result of abrogating or qualifying the common law rule. That section emanated from the consideration the Law Commission gave to the decision of the House in *D.P.P. v. Smith* [1961] A.C. 290. Its purpose and effect was to alter the law of evidence about the presumption of intention to produce the reasonable and probable consequences of one's acts. It was not intended to change the common law rule. In referring to "all the evidence" it meant all the *relevant* evidence. But if there is a substantive rule of law that in crimes of basic intent, the factor of intoxication is irrelevant (and such I hold to be the substantive law), evidence with regard to it is quite irrelevant. Section 8 does not abrogate the substantive rule and it cannot properly be said that the continued application of that rule contravenes the section. For these reasons, my conclusion is that the certified question should be answered Yes, that there was no misdirection in this case and that the appeal should be dismissed.

My noble and learned friends and I think it may be helpful if we give the following indication of the general lines on which in our view the jury should be directed as to the effect on the criminal responsibility of the accused of drink or drugs or both, whenever death or physical injury to another person results from something done by the accused for which there is no legal justification and the offence with which the accused is charged is manslaughter or assault at common law or the statutory offence of unlawful wounding under s.20, or of assault occasioning actual bodily harm under s.47 of the Offences Against the Person Act 1861.

In the case of these offences it is no excuse in law that, because of drink or drugs which the accused himself had taken knowingly and willingly, he had deprived himself of the ability to exercise self-control, to realise the possible consequences of what he was doing or even to be conscious that he was doing it. As in the instant case, the jury may be properly instructed that they "can ignore the subject of drink or drugs as being in any way a defence to" charges of this character.

[LORD DIPLOCK agreed with the speech of Lord Elwyn-Jones and with Lord Russell's explanation of *Beard*.]

LORD SIMON also agreed but added "by way of marginal comment": . . . a considerable difficulty in this branch of the law arises from the terminology which has been used . . . [I]t is desirable that the terms used should be defined, unambiguous and used consistently. . . .

But, in order to understand this branch of the law in general and *D.P.P. v. Beard* in particular, it is desirable to have further tools of analysis. A term that appears frequently in discussion of this aspect of the law and crucially in *Beard* is "specific intent." . . .

I would not wish it to be thought that I consider "ulterior intent" as I defined it in *Morgan* [*ante*, p. 151] as interchangeable with "specific intent" as that term was used by Stephen, for example, in his Digest, by Lord Birkenhead L.C. in *Beard* or by Lord Denning and others in commenting on *Beard*. "Ulterior intent", which I can here summarily describe as a state of mind contemplating consequences beyond those defined in the actus reus, is merely one type of "specific intent" as that term was used by Lord Birkenhead L.C., etc. "Ulterior intent" does not accurately describe the state of mind in the crime of doing an act likely to assist the enemy (*R. v. Steane* [1947] K.B. 997, *ante*, p. 88) or causing grievous bodily harm with intent to do some grievous bodily harm (Offences Against the Person Act 1861, s.18, as amended by the Criminal Law Act 1967) or even murder. None of these requires by its definition contemplation of consequences extending beyond the actus reus.

I still have the temerity to think that the concept of "crime of basic intent" is a useful tool of analysis; and I explained what I meant by it in the passage in *Morgan* generously cited by my noble and learned friend, Lord Elwyn-Jones L.C. It stands significantly in contrast with "crime of specific intent" as that term was used by Stephen's Digest and by Lord Birkenhead L.C. in *Beard*. The best description of "specific intent" in this sense that I know is contained in the judgement of Fauteux J. in *R. v. George* (1960) 128 Can. Crim. Cas. 289, 301:

> "In considering the question of *mens rea*, a distinction is to be made between (i) intention as applied to acts considered in relation to their purposes and (ii) intention as applied to acts apart from their purposes. A general intent attending the commission of an act is, in some cases, the only intent required to constitute the crime while, in others, there must be, in addition to that general intent, a specific intent attending the purpose for the commission of the act."

In short, where the crime is one of "specific intent" the prosecution must in general prove that the purpose for the commission of the act extends to the intent expressed or implied in the definition of the crime . . .

As I have ventured to suggest, there is nothing unreasonable or illogical in the law holding that a mind rendered self-inducedly insensible (short of *M'Naghten* insanity), through drink or drugs, to the nature of a prohibited act or to its probable consequences is as wrongful a mind as one which consciously contemplates the prohibited act and foresees its probable consequences (or is reckless whether they ensue). The latter is all that is required by way of mens rea in a crime of basic intent. But a crime of specific intent requires something more than contemplation of the prohibited act and foresight of its probable consequences. The mens rea in a crime of specific intent requires proof of a purposive element. This purposive element either exists or not; it cannot be supplied by saying that the impairment of mental powers by self-induced intoxication is its equivalent, for it is not. So that the 19th century development of the law as to the effect of self-induced intoxication on criminal responsibility is juristically entirely acceptable; and it need be a matter of no surprise that Stephen stated it without demur or question.

LORD SALMON: . . . [A]n assault committed accidentally is not a criminal offence. . . . A man who by voluntarily taking drink and drugs gets himself into an aggressive state in which he does not know what he is doing and then makes a vicious assault can hardly say with any plausibility that what he did was a pure accident which should render him immune from any criminal liability. Yet this in effect is precisely what counsel for the appellant contends that the learned judge should have told the jury.

A number of distinguished academic writers support this contention on the ground of logic. As I understand it, the argument runs like this. Intention, whether special or basic (or whatever fancy name you choose to give it), is still intention. If voluntary intoxication by drink or drugs can, as it admittedly can, negative the special or specific intention necessary for the commission of crimes such as murder and theft, how can you justify in strict logic the view that it cannot negative a basic intention, *e.g.* the intention to commit offences such as assault and unlawful wounding? The answer is that in strict logic this view cannot be justified. But this is the view that has been adopted by the common law of England, which is founded on common sense and experience rather than strict logic. There is no case in the 19th century when the courts were relaxing the harshness of the law in relation to the effect of drunkenness on criminal liability in which the courts ever went so far as to suggest that drunkenness, short of drunkenness producing insanity, could ever exculpate a man from any offence other than one which required some special or specific intent to be proved.

[His Lordship then discussed *Beard*.]

As I have already indicated, I accept that there is a degree of illogicality in the rule that intoxication may excuse or expunge one type of intention and not another. This illogicality is, however, acceptable to me because the bene-volent part of the rule removes undue harshness without imperilling safety and the stricter part of the rule works without imperilling justice. It would be just as ridiculous to remove the benevolent part of the rule (which no one suggests) as it would be to adopt the alternative of removing the stricter part of the rule for the sake of preserving absolute logic. Absolute logic in human affairs is an uncertain guide and a very dangerous master. The law is primar-ily concerned with human affairs. I believe that the main object of our legal system is to preserve individual liberty. One important aspect of individual liberty is protection against physical violence. . .

My Lords, for these reasons, I would dismiss the appeal.

[LORD EDMUND-DAVIES and LORD RUSSELL OF KILLOWEN delivered speeches in favour of dismissing the appeal].

Appeal dismissed

Questions

1. Lord Elwyn-Jones states that self-induced intoxication is "a reck-less course of conduct" and that "recklessness is enough to constitute the necessary *mens rea* in assault cases." In what sense(s) is the word "reckless" being used in these two statements? (See further Ashworth, *Principles of Criminal Law*, 3rd ed, pp. 220–221.)

2. Although Lord Simon agreed with Lord Elwyn-Jones he also said "Mens rea is . . . the state of mind stigmatised as wrongful by the crim-inal law. . . . There is no juristic reason why mental incapacity . . . brought about by self-induced intoxication, to realise what one is doing . . . should not be such a state of mind stigmatised as wrongful." Is this compatible with describing such intoxication as "reckless?"

3. Lord Salmon and Lord Edmund-Davies admitted that the decision was illogical. Do you agree? See Dashwood: "Logic and the Lords in Majewski" [1977] Crim.L.R. 532 and 591, and Sellers: "Mens Rea and the Judicial Approach to Bad Excuses" (1978) 41 M.L.R. 245.

4. Barlow in "Drug Intoxication and the Principle of *Capacitas Rationalis*" (1984) 100 L.Q.R. 639, at 646 states:

"Given that self induced intoxication creates a risk that harmful conduct of some diverse kind may result, it would almost always be forensically impossible to demonstrate that a specific risk was known and ignored, at the point before the drug was used. Can it really be said that the accused in *D.P.P. v. Majewski* soberly foresaw on Sunday morning before he began intoxicating himself with amphetamines, barbiturates and alcohol that he might consequently commit an assault on Monday evening? The most he could have foreseen at that point was that intox-ication might create a wide range of risks to other people or their prop-erty. That he might become irrational and might be reduced to a socially dangerous entity. That is not the essence of criminal recklessness."

Do you agree?

Notes

1. It is clear from *Garlick* [1981] Crim.L.R. 178 that when intoxication is raised as a defence to a crime of specific intent the question in issue

is not whether the defendant was incapable of forming the intent but whether, even if still capable, he or she did form that intent.

2. The onus of proof remains on the prosecution to prove beyond reasonable doubt that regardless of the alleged intoxication, D had the requisite intent (see *Sheehan and Moore* (1974) 60 Cr.App.R. 308; *Pordage* [1975] Crim.L.R. 575).

3. Where on a charge of an offence of specific intent evidence of intoxication emerges during the trial which might lead a reasonable jury to conclude that there is a reasonable possibility that D did not form the intent, whether or not D expressly raises it, the judge is under an obligation to direct the jury on this matter as intent is an essential element of the offence which the Crown has to prove (see *Bennett* [1995] Crim.L.R. 877; *Brown and Stratton* [1998] Crim.L.R. 485).

4. Unfortunately a line of cases has developed which is undermining the clarity of the above position largely due to two mistakes which are becoming prevalent in judicial reasoning. The first is the assertion (with *Beard* [1920] A.C. 479 being cited as the authority) that evidence of intoxication must be to the effect that it rendered D incapable of forming the requisite intent. This ignores *Garlick, Sheehan and Moore* and *Pordage*. Secondly, there is a tendency to regard intoxication as a defence requiring proof by the accused (again due to reliance on dicta in *Beard* which were made before the leading case on the burden of proof, *Woolmington* [1935] A.C. 462, was decided) when, in fact, it is simply a denial that the Crown has discharged its burden of proving beyond reasonable doubt that D had the requisite intent. Both these mistakes were made by the Court of Appeal in *McKnight, The Times,* May 5, 2000 where Henry LJ placed considerable reliance on the Privy Council case of *Sooklal v. The State of Trinidad and Tobago* [1999] 1 W.L.R. 2011, where both mistakes were also made. *In McKnight,* a murder case, the Court of Appeal held that the trial judge is obliged to direct the jury to consider the question of the accused's claim that he was intoxicated and did not form the necessary intent only where there is a sufficient factual basis established in the evidence for the claim that D was so drunk as to be incapable of forming the intent or was so drunk as not to know what she was doing. Henry L.J. cited with approval the speech of Lord Hope of Craighead in *Sooklal* where he stated (at p.2017):

> Whenever reduction of a charge of murder on the ground of self-induced intoxication is in issue, the ultimate question is whether the defendant formed the mens rea for the crime charged . . . . What is required is specific evidence that the defendant was so intoxicated that he lacked the specific intent which is essential for murder: that is the intent to kill or to inflict grievous bodily harm upon the victim. . . .
>
> This test is not satisfied by evidence that the defendant had consumed so much alcohol that he was intoxicated. Nor is it satisfied by evidence that he could not remember what he was doing because he was drunk. The essence of the defence is that the defendant did not have the guilty intent because his mind was so affected by drink that he did not know what he was doing at the time when he did

the act with which he was charged. The intoxication must have been of such a degree that it prevented him from foreseeing or knowing what he would have foreseen or known had he been sober. . . .

There is little excuse for senior judges making such basic errors which have the unfortunate effect of leaving the law in a state of uncertainty.

Note

Section 1(2) of the Criminal Damage Act 1971 provides:

"A person who without lawful excuse destroys or damages any property, whether belonging to himself or another. . . .
(*a*) intending to destroy or damage any property or being reckless as to whether any property should be destroyed or damaged; and
(*b*) intending by the destruction or damage to endanger the life of another or being reckless as to whether the life of another would be thereby endangered;
shall be guilty of an offence."

In *R. v. Caldwell* (*infra*), the House of Lords held that whether this is a crime of specific or basic intent depends on the basis of the charge.

R. v. Caldwell
[1981] 2 All E.R. 961
House of Lords

The facts appear, *ante*, p. 121.

The certified question was as follows: "Whether evidence of self-induced intoxication can be relevant to the following questions—(a) Whether the defendant intended to endanger the life of another; and (b) Whether the defendant was reckless as to whether the life of another would be endangered, within the meaning of section 1(2)(b) of the Criminal Damage Act 1971."

LORD DIPLOCK: As respects the charge under section 1(2) the prosecution did not rely upon an actual intent of the respondent to endanger the lives of the residents but relied upon his having been reckless whether the lives of any of them would be endangered. His act of setting fire to it was one which the jury were entitled to think created an obvious risk that the lives of the residents would be endangered; and the only defence with which your Lordships are concerned is that the respondent had made himself so drunk as to render him oblivious of that risk.

If the only mental state capable of constituting the necessary *mens rea* for an offence under section 1(2) were that expressed in the words "intending by the destruction or damage to endanger the life of another", it would have been necessary to consider whether the offence was to be classified as one of "specific" intent for the purposes of the rule of law which this House affirmed and applied in R. v. *Majewski*, and this it plainly is. But this is not, in my view, a relevant inquiry where "being reckless as to whether the life of another would be thereby endangered" is an alternative mental state that is capable of constituting the necessary *mens rea* of the offence with which he is charged.

The speech of the Lord Chancellor in *Majewski* with which Lord Simon of Glaisdale, Lord Kilbrandon and I agreed, is authority that self-induced intoxication is no defence to a crime in which recklessness is enough to constitute the necessary *mens rea*. . . .

Reducing oneself by drink or drugs to a condition in which the restraints of reason and conscience are cast off was held to be a reckless course of conduct and an integral part of the crime. The Lord Chancellor accepted as correctly stating English law the provision in section 208 of the American Model Penal Code:

> "When recklessness establishes an element of the offence, if the actor, due to self-induced intoxication, is unaware of a risk of which he would have been aware had he been sober, such unawareness is immaterial."

So, in the instant case, the fact that the respondent was unaware of the risk of endangering the lives of residents in the hotel owing to his self-induced intoxication, would be no defence if that risk would have been obvious to him had he been sober.

. . . [T]he Court of Appeal in the instant case regarded the case as turning upon whether the offence under section 1(2) was one of "specific" intent or "basic" intent. Following a recent decision of the Court of Appeal by which they were bound, R. v. *Orpin* (1980) 70 Cr.App.R. 306, they held that the offence under section 1(2) was one of "specific" intent in contrast to the offence under section 1(1) which was of basic intent. This would be right if the only *mens rea* capable of constituting the offence were an actual intention to endanger the life of another. For the reasons I have given, however, classification into offences of "specific" and "basic" intent is irrelevant where being reckless as to whether a particular harmful consequence will result from one's act is a sufficient alternative *mens rea*. I would give the following answers to the certified questions:

(a) If the charge of an offence under section 1(2) of the Criminal Damage Act 1971 is framed so as to charge the defendant only with "*intending* by the destruction or damage" [of the property] "to endanger the life of another," evidence of self-induced intoxication can be relevant to his defence.

(b) If the charge is, or includes, a reference to his "being reckless as to whether the life of another would thereby be endangered," evidence of self-induced intoxication is not relevant.

Lords Keith of Kinkel and Roskill agreed with this statement of the law. Lord Wilberforce agreed with Lord Edmund-Davies.

Lord Edmund-Davies: [T]he view expressed by my noble and learned friend Lord Diplock "that the speech of the Lord Chancellor in *Majewski* is authority that self-induced intoxication is no defence to a crime in which recklessness is enough to constitute the necessary *mens rea*" . . . is a view which, with respect, I do not share. In common with all noble and learned Lords hearing that appeal, Lord Elwyn-Jones L.C. adopted the well-established (though not universally favoured) distinction between basic and specific intents. *Majewski* related solely to charges of assault, undoubtedly an offence of basic intent, and the Lord Chancellor made it clear that his observations were confined to offences of that nature. . . . My respectful view is that *Majewski* accordingly supplies no support for the proposition that, in relation to crimes of specific intent (such as section 1(2)(*b*) of the 1971 Act) incapacity to appreciate the degree and nature of the risk created by his action which is attributable to the defendant's self-intoxication is an irrelevance. The Lord Chancellor was dealing simply with crimes of basic intent, and in my judgment it was strictly within that framework that he adopted the view expressed in the American Penal Code [s.2.08] and recklessness as an element in crimes of specific intent was, I am convinced, never within his contemplation.

For the foregoing reasons, the Court of Appeal were in my judgment right in quashing the conviction under section 1(2)(*b*) and substituting a finding of guilty of arson contrary to section 1(1) and (3) of the 1971 Act. . . . Having revealed in *Majewski* (pp. 495B–497C) my personal conviction that, on grounds of public policy, a plea of drunkenness cannot exculpate crimes of basic intent and so exercise unlimited sway in the criminal law, I am nevertheless unable to concur that your Lordships' decision should now become the law of the land. For, as Eveleigh L.J. said in *Orpin* (*supra*, at p. 312):

" . . . there is nothing inconsistent in treating intoxication as irrelevant when considering the liability of a person who has willed himself to do that which the law forbids (for example, to do something which wounds another), and yet to make it relevant when a further mental state is postulated as an aggravating circumstance making the offence even more serious."

Appeal dismissed

Law Com. No. 229, Intoxication and Criminal Liability

How the Majewski principle applies to Caldwell recklessness

3.37 *Majewski* is irrelevant in the primary situation governed by *Caldwell* recklessness—namely, that in which there is an obvious risk, to which the defendant gives no thought. In this type of case the *reason* why the defendant does not advert to the risk (whether it be, as in *Caldwell* itself, voluntary intoxication or, say, mental handicap) is immaterial. The test is whether the risk would have been obvious to a reasonable, prudent *and sober* person.

3.38. In a case which would otherwise fall within the "lacuna", however (that is, where the defendant *does* consider whether there is a risk but decides that there is not), the fact that the defendant is intoxicated may be relevant to his liability: it would seem in principle that the *Majewski* rule should apply. It would follow that if, but for his intoxication, the defendant would have been aware of the risk, he is regarded as having been reckless.

Note

Mitchell, "The Intoxicated Offender—Refuting the Legal and Medical Myths" (1988) Int. J. Law & Psych. 77, argues that scientific evidence supports a simple subjective test for the effect of intoxication on *mens rea* in all cases, making the following points:

1. Modern day judicial assumptions about the effects of drugs and alcohol stem from Victorian medical opinion.
2. There is a lack of consensus among scientists as to a link between aggression and psychoactive drugs (including alcohol).
3. Research and scientific literature indicate that intoxicated people almost always know what they are doing and do exactly what they intend; the assumption by the courts that intoxication both causes aggression and negatives intent is anomalous–aggression is necessarily directed and targeted.
4. His research had uncovered no genuine case where intoxication caused an automatic or involuntary act.
5. Medical testimony about intoxication is "biased, inaccurate, harmful and unnecessary" (p. 100).

Mitchell's views would tend to suggest that the *Majewski* rule is unnecessary and that the only question for a jury in any case should be "did D, whatever his state of intoxication, perform a voluntary act and do so with the *mens rea* for the crime with which he is charged?" The need to distinguish between offences of basic and specific intent disappears. This is the position adopted in the non-Code Australian States (see *O'Connor* (1981) 146 C.L.R. 64) and in New Zealand (see *Kamipeli* [1975 2 N.Z.L.R. 610). In "Surviving without Majewski—A View from Down Under" [1993] Crim.L.R. 427, 429, Orchard states:

"In these jurisdictions complete acquittal as a result of intoxication raising doubt as to a required state of mind is not unknown, but it is very unusual. This may in part be due to juries and judges being unwilling to give effect to what they regard as an unmeritorious principle, but it also reflects the reality that while intoxication may often contribute to and explain intentional offending it will seldom result in the absence of the modest mental requirements of intention, awareness and foresight that generally suffice for *mens rea*. Advocacy and expert speculation might obscure this, but it can be appropriately brought home to the jury. In *Kamipeli* it was recognised that it is proper, and often it will be necessary, for the jury to be warned that absence of intent because of intoxication "is a conclusion not to be lightly reached", and the issue may be removed from the jury's consideration if there is no evidence which could reasonably support such a conclusion."

ii. Involuntary Intoxication

R. v. Kingston
[1994] 3 WLR 519
House of Lords

D, who had paedophiliac tendencies, was convicted of indecent assault on a 15 year old boy. The defence was that he had been drugged by his co-defendant who had intended to blackmail him and that he would not otherwise have committed the offence. He appealed against the trial judge's ruling that involuntary intoxication could only serve as a defence if, as a result, the defendant had not formed the necessary mens rea for the offence. The Court of Appeal allowed his appeal against conviction, holding that if a surreptitiously administered intoxicant causes a person to lose his self-control and so form an intent he would not otherwise have formed, the law should exculpate him as the operative fault is not his. The following point of law was certified as being of general public importance: "Whether if it is proved that the necessary intent was present when the necessary act was done by him, a defendant has open to him a defence of involuntary intoxication?" On appeal by the Crown:

LORD MUSTILL: . . . [T]he general nature of the case is clear enough. In ordinary circumstances the respondent's paedophiliac tendencies would have been kept under control, even in the presence of the sleeping or unconscious boy on the bed. The ingestion of the drug (whatever it was) brought about a temporary change in the mentality or personality of the respondent which lowered his ability to resist temptation so far that his desires overrode his ability to control them. Thus we are concerned here with a case of disinhibition. The drug is not alleged to have created the desire to which the respondent gave way, but rather to have enabled it to be released. . . .

On these facts there are three grounds on which the respondent might be held free from criminal responsibility. First, that his immunity flows from general principles of the criminal law. Secondly, that this immunity is already established by a solid line of authority. Finally, that the court should, when faced with a new problem acknowledge the justice of the case and boldly create a new common law defence.

It is clear from the passage already quoted that the Court of Appeal adopted the first approach. The decision was explicitly founded on general principle. There can be no doubt what principle the court relied upon, for at the outset the court [1994] Q.B. 81, 87, recorded the submission of counsel for the respondent:

"the law recognises that, exceptionally, an accused person may be entitled to be acquitted if there is a possibility that although his act was intentional, the intent itself arose out of circumstances for which he bears no blame."

The same proposition is implicit in the assumption by the court that if blame is absent the necessary mens rea must also be absent.

My Lords, with every respect I must suggest that no such principle exists or, until the present case, had ever in modern times been thought to exist. Each offence consists of a prohibited act or omission coupled with whatever state of mind is called for by the statute or rule of the common law which creates the offence. In those offences which are not absolute the state of mind which the prosecution must prove to have underlain the act or omission—the "mental element"—will in the majority of cases be such as to attract disapproval. The mental element will then be the mark of what may properly be called a "guilty mind." The professional burglar is guilty in a moral as well as a legal sense; he intends to break into the house to steal, and most would confidently assert that this is wrong. But this will not always be so. In respect of some offences the mind of the defendant, and still less his moral judgment, may not be engaged at all. In others, although a mental activity must be the motive power for the prohibited act or omission the activity may be of such a kind or degree that society at large would not criticise the defendant's conduct severely or even criticise it at all. Such cases are not uncommon. Yet to assume that contemporary moral judgments affect the criminality of the act, as distinct from the punishment appropriate to the crime once proved, is to be misled by the expression "mens rea," the ambiguity of which has been the subject of complaint for more than a century. Certainly, the "mens" of the defendant must usually be involved in the offence; but the epithet "rea" refers to the criminality of the act in which the mind is engaged, not to its moral character. . . .

[His Lordship referred to *Yip Chiu-Cheung v. R., post*, p. 477.]

I would therefore reject that part of the respondent's argument which treats the absence of moral fault on the part of the appellant as sufficient in itself to negative the necessary mental element of the offence. . . .

[I]t is impossible to consider the exceptional case of involuntary intoxication without placing it in the context of intoxication as a whole. . . .

As I understand the position it is still the law that in the exceptional case where intoxication causes insanity the M'Naghten Rules (*M'Naghten's Case* (1843) 10 Cl. & F. 200) apply: see *Director of Public Prosecutions v. Beard* [1920] A.C. 479, 501 and *Attorney-General for Northern Ireland v. Gallagher* (*post*, p. 269). Short of this, it is no answer for the defendant to say that he would not have done what he did had he been sober, provided always that whatever element of intent is required by the offence is proved to have been present. As was said in *Reg. v. Sheehan* [1975] 1 W.L.R. 739, 744C, "a drunken intent is nevertheless an intent." As to proof of intent, it appears that at least in some instances self-induced intoxication can be taken into account as part of the evidence from which the jury draws its conclusions; but that in others it cannot. I express the matter in this guarded way because it has not yet been decisively established whether for this purpose there is a line to be drawn between offences of "specific" and of "basic" intent. That in at least some cases a defendant cannot say that he was so drunk that he could not form the required intent is however clear enough. Why is this so? The answer must I believe be the same as that given in other common law jurisdictions: namely that such evidence is excluded as a matter of policy. As Mason J. put the matter in *Reg. v. O'Connor* (1980) 146 C.L.R. 64, 110:

"the view is taken that the act charged is voluntary notwithstanding that it might not be ordinarily considered so by reason of the condition of the perpetrator, because his condition proceeds from a voluntary choice made by him. These cases therefore constitute an exception to the general rule of criminal responsibility."

There remains the question by what reasoning the House put this policy into effect. As I understand it two different rationalisations were adopted. First that the absence of the necessary [intent] is cured by treating the intentional drunkenness (or more accurately, since it is only in the minority of cases that the drinker sets out to make himself drunk, the intentional taking of drink without regard to its possible effects) as a substitute for the mental element ordinarily required by the offence. The intent is transferred from the taking of drink to the commission of the prohibited act. The second rationalisation is that the defendant cannot be heard to rely on the absence of the mental element when it is absent because of his own voluntary acts. Borrowing an expression from a far distant field it may be said that the defendant is estopped from relying on his self-induced incapacity.

Your Lordships are not required to decide how these two explanations stand up to attack, for they are not attacked here. The task is only to place them in the context of an intoxication which is not voluntary. Taking first the concept of transferred intent, if the intoxication was not the result of an act done with an informed will there is no intent which can be transferred to the prohibited act, so as to fill the gap in the offence. As regards the "estoppel" there is no reason why the law should preclude the defendant from relying on a mental condition which he had not deliberately brought about. Thus, once the involuntary nature of the intoxication is added the two theories of *Majewski* fall away, and the position reverts to what it would have been if *Majewski* had not been decided, namely that the offence is not made out if the defendant was so intoxicated that he could not form an intent. Thus, where the intoxication is involuntary *Majewski* does not *subtract* the defence of absence of intent; but there is nothing in *Majewski* to suggest that where intent is proved involuntary intoxication *adds* a further defence.

[His Lordship referred to some Scottish cases and continued.]

My Lords, making due allowance for the differences between the laws of the two jurisdictions these cases are clear authority against the proposition that mere disinhibition is sufficient to found a defence.

[His Lordship referred to the American Law Institute's Model Penal Code and continued.]

My Lords, I cannot find in this material any sufficient grounds for holding that the defence relied upon is already established by the common law, any more than it can be derived from general principles. Accordingly I agree with the analysis of Professor Griew, *Archbold News*, 28 May 1993, pp. 4–5:

"What has happened is that the Court of Appeal has recognised a new *defence* to criminal charges in the nature of an exculpatory excuse. It is precisely because the defendant acted in the prohibited way with the intent (the mens rea) required by the definition of the offence that he needs this defence."

To recognise a new defence of this type would be a bold step. The common law defences of duress and necessity (if it exists) and the limited common law defence of provocation are all very old. Since counsel for the appellant was not disposed to emphasise this aspect of the appeal the subject was not explored in argument, but I suspect that the recognition of a new general defence at common law has not happened in modern times. Nevertheless, the criminal law must not stand still, and if it is both practical and just to take this step, and if judicial decision rather than legislation is the proper medium, then the courts should not be deterred simply by the novelty of it. So one must turn to consider just what defence is now to be created. The judgment under appeal implies five characteristics.

1. The defence applies to all offences, except perhaps to absolute offences. It therefore differs from other defences such as provocation and diminished responsibility.

2. The defence is a complete answer to a criminal charge. If not rebutted it leads to an outright acquittal, and unlike provocation and diminished responsibility leaves no room for conviction and punishment for a lesser offence. The underlying assumption must be that the defendant is entirely free from culpability.

3. It may be that the defence applies only where the intoxication is due to the wrongful act of another and therefore affords no excuse when, in circumstances of no greater culpability, the defendant has intoxicated himself by mistake (such as by shortsightedly taking the wrong drug). I say that this may be so, because it is not clear whether, since the doctrine was founded in part on the dictum of Park J. in *Pearson's Case*, 2 Lew. 144, the "fraud or stratagem of another" is an essential element, or whether this was taken as an example of a wider principle.

4. The burden of disproving the defence is on the prosecution.

5. The defence is subjective in nature. Whereas provocation and self-defence are judged by the reactions of the reasonable person in the situation of the defendant, here the only question is whether this particular defendant's inhibitions were overcome by the effect of the drug. The more susceptible the defendant to the kind of temptation presented, the easier the defence is to establish. . . .

[T]he defence appears to run into difficulties at every turn. In point of theory, it would be necessary to reconcile a defence of irresistible impulse derived from a combination of innate drives and external disinhibition with the rule that irresistible impulse of a solely internal origin (not necessarily any more the fault of the offender) does not in itself excuse although it may be a symptom of a disease of the mind: *Attorney-General for South Australia v. Brown* [1960] A.C. 432. Equally, the state of mind which founds the defence superficially resembles a state of diminished responsibility, whereas the effect in law is quite different. It may well be that the resemblance is misleading, but these and similar problems must be solved before the bounds of a new defence can be set.

On the practical side there are serious problems. Before the jury could form an opinion on whether the drug might have turned the scale witnesses would have to give a picture of the defendant's personality and susceptibilities, for without it the crucial effect of the drug could not be assessed; pharmacologists would be required to describe the potentially disinhibiting effect of a range of drugs whose identity would, if the present case is anything to go by, be unknown; psychologists and psychiatrists would express opinions, not on the matters of psychopathology familiar to those working within the framework of the Mental Health Acts but on altogether more elusive concepts. No doubt as time passed those concerned could work out techniques to deal with these questions. Much more significant would be the opportunities for a spurious defence. Even in the field of road traffic the "spiked" drink as a special reason for not disqualifying from driving is a regular feature. Transferring this to the entire range of criminal offences is a disturbing prospect. The defendant would only have to assert, and support by the evidence of well-wishers, that he was not the sort of person to have done this kind of thing, and to suggest an occasion when by some means a drug might have been administered to him for the jury to be sent straight to the question of a possible disinhibition. The judge would direct the jurors that if they felt any legitimate doubt on the matter—and by its nature the defence would be one which the prosecution would often have no means to rebut—they must acquit outright, all questions of intent, mental capacity and the like being at this stage irrelevant. . . .

For these reasons I consider that both the ruling and the direction of the learned judge were correct. Accordingly I would answer the first certified question in the negative and would allow the appeal.

[Lords Keith of Kinkel, Goff of Chieveley, Browne-Wilkinson and Slynn of Hadley agreed with the speech of Lord Mustill.]

Appeal allowed

R. v. Hardie
[1985] 1 W.L.R. 64
Court of Appeal

When the relationship with the woman with whom he had been living broke down, the appellant became upset and took several Valium tablets belonging to the woman. He was unaware of the effect the tablets might have. Several hours later he started a fire in the bedroom of the flat while the woman and her daughter were in the sitting room. He was charged with damaging property with intent to endanger life or being reckless whether life would be endangered contrary to s. 1 (2) of the Criminal Damage Act 1971. He argued in his defence that the effect of the Valium had been to prevent him having *mens rea*. The judge directed the jury that this could not provide a defence as he had voluntarily self-administered the drug. He appealed on grounds of misdirection.

PARKER L.J.: . . . It is clear from *R. v. Caldwell* [1982] A.C. 341 that self-induced intoxication can be a defence where the charge is only one of specific intention. It is equally clear that it cannot be a defence where, as here, the charge included recklessness. Hence, if there was self-intoxication in this case the judge's direction was correct. The problem is whether, assuming that the effect of the Valium was to deprive the appellant of any appreciation of what he was doing it should properly be regarded as self-induced intoxication and thus no answer. . . .

R. v. Majewski was a case of drunkenness resulting from alcoholic consumption by the accused whilst under the influence of non-medically prescribed drugs. *R. v. Caldwell* was a case of plain drunkenness. There can be no doubt that the same rule applies both to self-intoxication by alcohol and intoxication by hallucinatory drugs, but this is because the effects of both are well-known and there is therefore an element of recklessness in the self-administration of the drug. *R. v. Lipman* [1970] 1 Q.B. 152 is an example of such a case.

"Intoxication" or similar symptoms may, however, arise in other circumstances. In *R. v. Bailey* (*ante*, p. 242) this court had to consider a case where a diabetic had failed to take sufficient food after taking a normal dose of insulin and struck the victim over the head with an iron bar. The judge directed the jury that the defence of automatism, *i.e.* that the mind did not go with the act, was not available because the incapacity was self-induced. It was held that this was wrong on two grounds (a) because on the basis of *R. v. Majewski* it was clearly available to the offence embodying specific intent and (b) because although self-induced by the omission to take food it was also available to negative the other offence which was of basic intent only.

[Having referred to the judgment of Griffiths L.J., *ante*, p. 242, his Lordship continued]

In the present instance the defence was that the Valium was taken for the purpose of calming the nerves only, that it was old stock and that the appellant was told it would do him no harm. There was no evidence that it was known to the appellant or even generally known that the taking of Valium in the quantity taken would be liable to render a person aggressive or incapable of appreciating risks to others or have other side effects such that its self-administration would itself have an element of recklessness. It is true that Valium is a drug and it is true that it was taken deliberately and not taken on medical prescription, but the drug is, in our view, wholly different in kind from drugs which are liable to cause unpredictability or aggressiveness. It may well be that the taking of a sedative or soporific drug will, in certain circumstances, be no answer, for example in a case of reckless driving, but if the effect of a drug is merely soporific or sedative the taking of it, even in some excessive quantity, cannot in the ordinary way raise a *conclusive* presumption against the admission of proof of intoxication for the purpose of disproving mens rea in ordinary crimes, such as would be the case with alcoholic intoxication or incapacity or automatism resulting from the self-administration of dangerous drugs.

In the present case the jury should not, in our judgment, have been directed to disregard any incapacity which resulted or might have resulted from the taking of Valium. They should have been directed that if they came to the conclusion that, as a result of the Valium, the appellant was, at the time, unable to appreciate the risks to property and persons from his actions they should then consider whether the taking of the Valium was itself reckless. We are unable to say what would have been the appropriate direction with regard to the elements of recklessness in this case for we have not seen all the relevant evidence, nor are we able to suggest a model direction, for circumstances will vary infinitely and model directions can sometimes lead to more rather than less confusion. It is sufficient to say that the direction that the effects of Valium were necessarily irrelevant was wrong.

Appeal allowed

Questions

1. Is it possible to reconcile *Hardie* with *Caldwell* and *Elliott v. C.* [1983] 1 W.L.R. 939 (*ante*, p. 130)? For example, D is mentally retarded.

He finds some Valium tablets in the medicine cabinet and consumes them rendering himself intoxicated. In this state he sets fire to property. He is charged with criminal damage and in his defence it is argued that D did not realise that Valium could render him intoxicated and incapable of appreciating risks. The prosecution argue that as D is generally incapable of appreciating risks, *Elliott v. C.* should be followed rather than *Hardie*. How might this issue be decided.

2. In determining whether the self-administration of a drug such as Valium "would itself have an element of recklessness," is it the *Cunningham* or *Caldwell* test of recklessness which is applicable? (*Cf. Bailey, ante,* p. 242.)

3. To which drugs does the *Majewski* rule apply and which fall under the *Hardie* exception?

4. If, instead of taking the drug himself, Hardie's drink had been drugged with a proscribed drug leading to the same outcome, what would have been the judge's instruction to the jury?

R.D. Mackay, *Mental Condition Defences in the Criminal Law* (1995) pp. 155–156

The distinction between *Majewski* recklessness and *Bailey* recklessness involves the assumption that, while the antisocial effects of excess alcohol and 'certain sorts of drugs' are well known, the same is not true of drugs such as insulin taken for medicinal purposes nor of drugs taken for soporific or sedative purposes. In the latter types of case, therefore, an added burden is placed on the prosecution to prove a generalised form of 'recklessness' relating to knowledge not only of the incapacity but also how the accused might react during this time. An important point here is that the cases of *Bailey* and *Hardie* involve a number of significant distinctions. In the first place, *Bailey* was a case of automatism while *Hardie* deals with the negation of *mens rea*. Secondly, while Bailey was concerned with an offence of 'subjective' recklessness (see *Cunningham*), *Hardie* faced a charge which clearly consisted of 'objective' recklessness (see *Caldwell*). These points seem to have been ignored by the court in *Hardie* and yet they could have an important bearing on the development of the law within this area, as there is clear authority for the proposition that once the accused's incapacity reaches the stage of automatism, then *Caldwell* recklessness is irrelevant. This was made clear in *R. v. Bell* [1984] 3 All E.R. 842, a decision reached shortly before *Hardie*. Accordingly, it seems clear that, even if *Bailey* had been charged with criminal damage he would still have been acquitted, provided the prosecution was unable to prove 'recklessness' in the sense of an awareness of the risk of becoming unpredictable etc. By way of contrast, however, the defence of *Hardie* was that he lacked *mens rea*, and yet the court applied *Bailey*. This has led the Law Commission to conclude that the principle developed in the latter case 'applies, it would seem, even to offences to which *Caldwell* recklessness applies' while at the same time pointing out that this view seems inconsistent with the reasoning in *Elliot* v. *C:* [as] it is difficult to discern, for the purpose of explaining why the defendant did not give thought to an obvious and serious risk, a principled distinction between reliance upon an innate incapacity and reliance on incapacity caused by taking (even a non-dangerous) drug'. There is much force in this type of criticism which makes it all the more regrettable that the court in *Hardie* did not explore the precise nature of the recklessness required. In this context, however, it can be pointed out that the court does refer at one stage to the fact that, if the jury considered that the effect of the Valium had resulted in a lack of *mens rea*, 'they should then consider whether the taking of the Valium was itself reckless'. This strongly suggests that the fault element is similar to that in *Majewski*, in the sense that, if it is not commonly known that the taking of a non-dangerous drug would lead to incapacity, then the further question the jury must decide is simply '*Majewski* recklessness [in the sense of] *Caldwell* recklessness as to becoming intoxicated.' The rationale behind this is that 'it is recklessness as to becoming intoxicated and not recklessness as to the actus reus occurring; the fault element lying in D allowing himself to become dangerous or destructive'. Whether this is the correct interpretation of the rule in *Majewski* must be open to question. However, there is no doubt that as the law stands at present it is difficult to fully reconcile *Hardie* and *Bailey*. Despite this difficulty it is equally clear that these cases demonstrate a reluctance on the part of the courts to extend the strictures of *Majewski* beyond alcohol and dangerous drugs.

iii. Becoming Intoxicated "With Intent"—the "Dutch Courage" Problem

If D drinks to give himself "Dutch courage" to commit an offence, may he rely on his intoxication in defence to support a plea that when he committed the offence he was so drunk that he either did not form or was incapable of forming the necessary intent? See next case.

Attorney-General for Northern Ireland v. Gallagher
[1963] A.C. 349
House of Lords

The respondent was convicted of the murder of his wife. The defence was that of insanity under the M'Naghten Rules or, in the alternative, that at the time of the commission of the crime the respondent was by reason of drink incapable of forming the intent required in murder and was therefore guilty only of manslaughter. The respondent had indicated an intention to kill his wife before taking the alcohol. The Court of Criminal Appeal in Northern Ireland allowed an appeal on the ground that the judge in his summing-up directed the jury to apply the tests laid down in the M'Naghten Rules to the time when alcohol was taken and not to the time when the actual murder was committed.

LORD DENNING: My Lords, this case differs from all others in the books in that the accused man, whilst sane and sober, before he took to the drink, had already made up his mind to kill his wife. This seems to me to be far worse—and far more deserving of condemnation—than the case of a man who, before getting drunk has no intention to kill, but afterwards in his cups, whilst drunk, kills another by an act which he would not dream of doing when sober. Yet by the law of England in this latter case his drunkenness is no defence even though it has distorted his reason and his will-power. So why should it be a defence in the present case? And is it made any better by saying that the man is a psychopath?

The answer to the question is, I think, that the case falls to be decided by the general principle of English law that, subject to very limited exceptions, drunkenness is no defence to a criminal charge, nor is a defect of reason produced by drunkenness. This principle was stated by Sir Matthew Hale in his *Pleas of the Crown*, I, p. 32, in words which I would repeat here. "This vice" (drunkenness) "doth deprive men of the use of reason, and puts many men into a perfect, but temporary, phrenzy.... By the laws of England such a person shall have no privilege by this voluntary contracted madness, but shall have the same judgment as if he were in his right senses." ...

The general principle which I have enunciated is subject to two exceptions:

1. If a man is charged with an offence in which a specific intention is essential (as in murder, though not in manslaughter), then evidence of drunkenness, which renders him incapable of forming that intention, is an answer: see *Beard's* case. This degree of drunkenness is reached when the man is rendered so stupid by drink that he does not know what he is doing (see *R. v. Moore* (1852) 3 C. & K. 153), as where, at a christening, a drunken nurse put the baby behind a large fire, taking it for a log of wood (*Gentleman's Magazine*, 1748, p. 570); and where a drunken man thought his friend (lying in his bed) was a theatrical dummy placed there and stabbed him to death (*The Times*, January 13, 1951). In each of those cases it would not be murder. But it would be manslaughter.

2. If a man by drinking brings on a distinct disease of the mind such as delirium tremens, so that he is temporarily insane within the M'Naghten Rules, that is to say, he does not at the time know what he is doing or that it is wrong, then he has a defence on the ground of insanity: see *R. v. Davis* (1881) 14 Cox 563 and *Beard's* case.

Does the present case come within the general principle or the exceptions to it? It certainly does not come within the first exception. This man was not incapable of forming an intent to kill. Quite the contrary. He knew full well what he was doing. He formed an intent to kill, he carried out his intention and he remembered afterwards what he had done. And the jury, properly directed on the point, have found as much, for they found him guilty of murder. Then does the case come within the second exception? It does not, to my mind, for the simple reason that he was not suffering from a disease of the mind brought on by drink. He was suffering from a different disease altogether. As the Lord Chief Justice observed in his summing-up: "If this man was suffering from a disease of the mind, it wasn't of a kind that is produced by drink." ...

My Lords, I think the law on this point should take a clear stand. If a man, whilst sane and sober, forms an intention to kill and makes preparation for it, knowing it is a wrong thing to do, and then gets himself drunk so as to give himself Dutch courage to do the killing, and whilst drunk carries out his intention, he cannot rely on this self-induced drunkenness as a defence to a charge of murder, nor even as reducing it to manslaughter. He cannot say that he got himself into such a stupid state that he was incapable of an intent to kill. So also when he is a psychopath, he cannot by drinking rely on his self-induced defect of reason as a defence of insanity. The wickedness of his mind before he got drunk is enough to condemn him, coupled with the act which he intended to do and did do. A psychopath who goes out intending to kill knowing it is wrong, and does kill, cannot escape the consequences by making himself drunk before doing it. That is, I believe, the direction which the Lord Chief Justice gave to the jury and which the Court of Criminal Appeal found to be wrong. I think it was right and for this reason I would allow the appeal.

I would agree, of course, that if before the killing he had discarded his intention to kill or reversed it—and then got drunk—it would be a different matter. But when he forms the intention to kill and without interruption proceeds to get drunk and carry out his intention, then his drunkenness is no defence and nonetheless so because it is dressed up as a defence of insanity. There was no evidence in this case of any interruption and there was no need for the Lord Chief Justice to mention it to the jury.

I need hardly say, of course, that I have here only considered the law of Northern Ireland. In England a psychopath such as this man might now be in a position to raise a defence of diminished responsibility under section 2 of the Homicide Act 1957. . . .

Appeal allowed

iv. Intoxication and Defences

Jaggard v. Dickinson
[1980] 3 All E.R. 716
Queen's Bench Division

The appellant went to a house late one night. She was drunk. She thought it was a house belonging to a friend. She believed, correctly, that her friend would not object to her breaking in. It was the wrong house. She appealed against a conviction under section 1(1) of the Criminal Damage Act 1971, on the ground that, despite her intoxication, she was entitled to rely on the defence of lawful excuse under s.5(2) and (3) of the Act (*post.* p. 848).

MUSTILL J.: . . . It is convenient to refer to the exculpatory provisions of s.5(2) as if they created a defence while recognising that the burden of disproving the facts referred to by the subsection remains on the prosecution. The magistrates held that the appellant was not entitled to rely on s.5(2) since the belief relied on was brought about by a state of self-induced intoxication.

In support of the conviction counsel for the respondent advanced an argument which may be summarised as follows (i) Where an offence is one of "basic intent", in contrast to one of "specific intent", the fact that the accused was in a state of self-induced intoxication at the time when he did the acts constituting the actus reus does not prevent him from possessing the mens rea necessary to constitute the offence: see *D.P.P. v. Morgan* [*ante*, p. 151], *D.P.P. v. Majewski* [*ante*, p. 245]. (ii) Section 1(1) of the 1971 Act creates an offence of basic intent: see *R. v. Stephenson* [1979] Q.B. 695. (iii) Section 5(3) has no bearing on the present issue. It does not create a separate defence, but is no more than a partial definition of the expression "without lawful excuse" in s.1(1). The absence of lawful excuse forms an element in the mens rea: see *R. v. Smith* [*post*, p. 911]. Accordingly, since drunkenness does not negative mens rea in crimes of basic intent, it cannot be relied on as part of a defence based on s.5(2).

Whilst this is an attractive submission, we consider it to be unsound, for the following reasons. In the first place, the argument transfers the distinction between offences of specific and of basic intent to a context in which it has no place. The distinction is material where the defendant relies on his own drunkenness as a ground for denying that he had the degree of intention or recklessness required in order to constitute the offence. Here, by contrast, the appellant does not rely on her drunkenness to displace an inference of intent or recklessness; indeed she does not rely on it at all. Her defence is founded on the state of belief called for by s.5(2). True, the fact of the appellant's intoxication was relevant to the defence under s.5(2) for it helped to explain what would otherwise have been inexplicable, and hence lent colour to her evidence about the state of her belief. This is not the same as using drunkenness to rebut an inference of intention or recklessness. Belief, like intention or recklessness, is a state of mind; but they are not the same states of mind.

. . . Parliament has specifically required the court to consider the defendant's actual state of belief, not the state of belief which ought to have existed. This seems to us to show that the court is required by s.5(3) to focus on the existence of the belief, not its intellectual soundness; and a belief can be just as much honestly held if it is induced by intoxication as if it stems from stupidity, forgetfulness or inattention.

It was, however, urged that we could not properly read s.5(2) in isolation from s.1(1), which forms the context of the words "without lawful excuse" partially defined by s.5(2). Once the words are put in context, so it is maintained, it can be seen that the law must treat drunkenness in the same way in relation to lawful excuse (and hence belief) as it does to intention and recklessness, for they are all part of the mens rea of the offence. To fragment the mens rea, so as to treat one part of it as affected by drunkenness in one way and the remainder as affected in a different way, would make the law impossibly complicated to enforce.

If it had been necessary to decide whether, for all purposes, the mens rea of an offence under s.1(1) extends as far as an intent (or recklessness) as to the existence of a lawful excuse, I should have wished to consider the observations of James L.J., delivering the judgment of the Court of Appeal in *R. v. Smith* [*post*, p. 911]. I do not however find it necessary to reach a conclusion on this matter and will only say that I am not at present convinced that, when these observations are read in the context of the judgment as a whole, they have the meaning which the respondent has sought to put on them. In my view, however, the answer to the argument lies in the fact that any distinctions which have to be drawn as to the relevance of drunkenness to the two subsections arises from the scheme of the 1971 Act itself. No doubt the mens rea is in general indivisible, with no distinction being possible as regards the effect of drunkenness. But Parliament has specifically isolated one subjective element, in the shape of honest belief, and has given it separate treatment and its own special gloss in s.5(3). This being so, there is nothing objectionable in giving it special treatment as regards drunkenness, in accordance with the natural meaning of its words.

In these circumstances, I would hold that the magistrates were in error when they decided that the defence furnished to the appellant by s.5(2) was lost because she was drunk at the time. I would therefore allow the appeal.

Appeal allowed
Conviction quashed

Question

1. Is there any reason in principle or policy why a drunken defendant who believes that property belonging to P is his own and damages it, should be convicted whereas a drunken D who destroys P's property believing it belongs to Q and that Q would consent, will be acquitted because his drunken belief is covered by s.5(2)?

Note

In *Young* [1984] 1 W.L.R. 654, the appellant was charged with possessing a controlled drug with intent to supply. His defence, based on s.28(3) of the Misuse of Drugs Act 1971, was that because of intoxication he "neither believed nor suspected nor had reason to suspect that the substance . . . in question was a controlled drug." The Courts-Martial Appeal Court accepted that where there is an exculpatory statutory defence of honest belief, self-induced intoxication is a factor which must be considered in the context of a subjective consideration of the individual state of mind. However, with regard to the phrase *"nor had reason to suspect"* in s.28(3) the court held that this was not a matter which was entirely personal and individual calling for subjective consideration; rather it involved the concept of objective rationality to which self-induced intoxication is irrelevant.

R. v. O'Grady
(1987) Q.B. 995
Court of Appeal

A was convicted of manslaughter having been charged with murder. A and V, a friend, had been drinking heavily and spent the night at A's flat. During the night they fought. A claimed that he had been attacked by V while asleep and that he had fought to subdue him, stating to the police, "If I had not hit him I would be dead myself." The judge directed the jury that if, due to his intoxication, A mistakenly thought he was under attack, he would be entitled to defend himself but he was not entitled to go beyond what was reasonable because of his mind being affected by drink. A appealed on the grounds that (1) the judge was wrong to limit the reference to mistake as to the existence of an attack; he should have included the possibility of mistake as to the severity of an attack, and (2) the judge in effect divorced the reasonableness of A's reaction from his state of mind at the time.

LORD LANE C.J.: . . . As to the first two grounds, these require an examination of the law as to intoxication in relation to mistake. . . .

As McCullough J., when granting leave, pointed out helpfully in his observations for the benefit of the court:

"Given that a man who *mistakenly* believes he is under attack is entitled to use reasonable force to defend himself, it would seem to follow that, if he *is* under attack and mistakenly believes the attack to be more serious than it is, he is entitled to use reasonable force to defend himself against an attack of the severity he believed it to have. If one allows a mistaken belief induced by drink to bring this principle into operation, an act of gross negligence (viewed objectively) may become lawful even though it results in the death of the innocent victim. The drunken man would be guilty of neither murder nor manslaughter."

How should the jury be invited to approach the problem? One starts with the decision of this court in *R. v. Williams (Gladstone)* (1983) 78 Cr.App.R. 276 [*ante*, p. 159], namely, that where the defendant might have been labouring under a mistake as to the facts he must be judged according to that mistaken view, whether the mistake was reasonable or not. It is then for the jury to decide whether the defendant's reaction to the threat, real or imaginary, was a reasonable one. The court was not in that case considering what the situation might be where the mistake was due to voluntary intoxication by alcohol or some other drug.

We have come to the conclusion that where the jury are satisfied that the defendant was mistaken in his belief that any force or the force which he in fact used was necessary to defend himself and are further satisfied that the mistake was caused by voluntarily induced intoxication, the defence must fail. We do not consider that any distinction should be drawn on this aspect of the matter between offences involving what is called specific intent, such as murder, and offences of so called basic intent, such as manslaughter. Quite apart from the problem of directing a jury in a case such as the present where manslaughter is an alternative verdict to murder, the question of mistake can and ought to be considered separately from the question of intent. A sober man who mistakenly believes he is in danger of immediate death at the hands of an attacker is entitled to be acquitted of both murder and manslaughter if his reaction in killing his supposed assailant was a reasonable one. What his intent may have been seems to us to be irrelevant to the problem of self-defence or no. Secondly, we respectfully adopt the reasoning of McCullough J. already set out.

This brings us to the question of public order. There are two competing interests. On the one hand the interest of the defendant who has only acted according to what he believed to be necessary to protect himself, and on the other hand that of the public in general and the victim in particular who, probably through no fault of his own, has been injured or perhaps killed because of the defendant's drunken mistake. Reason recoils from the conclusion that in such circumstances a defendant is entitled to leave the Court without a stain on his character. . . .

Finally we draw attention to the decision of this court in *R.* v. *Lipman* [1970] 1 Q.B. 152 itself. The defence in that case was put on the grounds that the defendant, because of the hallucinatory drug which he had taken, had not formed the necessary intent to found a conviction for murder, thus resulting in his conviction for manslaughter. If the appellant's contentions here are correct, Lipman could successfully have escaped conviction altogether by raising the issue that he believed he was defending himself legitimately from an attack by serpents. It is significant that no one seems to have considered that possibility. . . .

We have therefore come to the conclusion that a defendant is not entitled to rely, so far as self-defence is concerned, upon a mistake of fact which has been induced by voluntary intoxication. . . .

Appeal dismissed

Questions

1. Under the rule in *Majewski*, D can only use evidence of voluntary intoxication to establish lack of *mens rea* if the offence is one of "specific intent", but D may be convicted of an offence of basic intent. This promotes the policy of protecting the public from those who, by becoming intoxicated, render themselves a danger to society. As *O'Grady* had been convicted of the basic intent offence of manslaughter, was there any need for the court to abandon the *Majewski* rule in relation to a defence of self-defence? Would the court have promoted the policy of protecting the public against the intoxicated offender by applying the *Majewski* rule and upholding *O'Grady's* conviction?

2. In *Gladstone Williams* (*ante*, p. 159), in respect of assault, Lord Lane C.J. stated that "the mental element necessary to constitute guilt is the intent to apply unlawful force to the victim. We do not believe that the mental element can be substantiated by simply showing an intent to apply force and no more." In *Beckford v. R.* [1987] 3 W.L.R. 611 Lord Griffiths stated that "it is an essential element of all crimes of violence that the violence or threat of violence should be unlawful". If this reasoning is followed, is it not the case that a drunken defendant who pleads self-defence is saying that, by reason of his mistake, he did not intend to use unlawful violence but rather he believed he was justified in using force in self-defence? If so, should not *Majewski* be applied thereby providing for acquittal where the offence is one of specific

intent but, if it is one of basic intent, recklessness in becoming intoxicated might be substituted for recklessness in respect of using unlawful violence?

3. In *Gladstone Williams* the Court of Appeal, under Lord Lane C.J., adopted the recommendations of the Criminal Law Revision Committee on self-defence in its 14th Report, declaring that they represented the existing law. Is it not surprising that in the present case, where the law was unclear, the Court of Appeal, again under Lord Lane C.J., ignored the C.L.R.C.'s further recommendations (14th Report, Cmnd. 7844, para. 277) which stated that the defence of self-defence should be available for offences of specific intent where the mistake was wholly or partly induced by drink or drugs, but not for offences of basic intent?

4. If the situation in *O'Grady* arises now will the defendant be convicted of murder or manslaughter?

Note

In *O'Connor* [1991] Crim. L.R. 135, the Court of Appeal treated the *obiter* decision in *O'Grady* as binding on them. D, who was drunk, was arguing with V in a public house. In the course of the argument D head-butted V about three times as a result of which V died. D was convicted of murder having argued in his defence that he believed he was acting in self-defence. The Court of Appeal held that the trial judge was correct to conclude that intoxication was irrelevant on the question whether D believed he was acting in self-defence. The conviction for murder was quashed, however, as the trial judge had not directed the jury to take account of D's intoxication when considering whether he had formed the specific intent to cause grievous bodily harm. The decision in *O'Connor* highlights the illogicality of the decision in *O'Grady*; the jury must ignore D's intoxication when considering whether he believed he was acting in self-defence but they must take it into account in deciding whether he intended to kill or cause grievous bodily harm. It will be surprising if juries are not left confused by such a direction.

Question

D and E are drunk and as a prank they seize V, their friend, and hold him over a balcony believing that he is consenting to their dangerous horseplay. V falls and sustains several broken bones. D and E are charged with unlawfully and maliciously inflicting GBH contrary to section 20 of the Offences Against the Person Act 1861. Will D and E be able to rely in their defence on their drunken belief that V consented to their prank?

Note

You may be surprised to learn that in *Richardson and Irwin* [1999] 1 Cr.App.R. 392, the Court of Appeal held on the facts in the question above that D's and E 's convictions should be quashed as the trial judge should have directed the jury that when considering the question of consent they should have taken account of evidence that the defendants' minds were affected by alcohol. Section 20 is an offence of basic intent and one would have expected the Court to rule that intoxication is irrelevant on such a charge. This decision, however, gives rise to the strange anomaly that D's intoxication relieves the prosecution of the need to prove foresight of some harm but does not relieve them of the need to prove absence of a belief in consent. This decision is consistent with the questionable authority of *Aitken* (1992) 95 Cr.App.R.304 but the Court of Appeal did not consider the cases of *O'Grady* (1987) Q.B. 995 (*ante*, p. 273) or *O'Connor* [1991] Crim LR 135 (*ante*, p. 275) nor did it refer to the cases on rape where the Court of Appeal had disallowed reliance on intoxicated beliefs in consent (see *Woods* (1982) 74 Cr.App.R. 312, *Fotheringham* (1988) 88 Cr.App.R. 206).The authority of *Richardson and Irwin*, accordingly must be open to doubt. It is certainly difficult to find any policy reason to support the decision particularly when one considers that had D and E not been drunk they would not have made the mistake regarding V's consent and most probably would not have engaged in such potentially dangerous horseplay.

v. Proposals for Reform

Law Com. No. 229, Legislating the Criminal Code: Intoxication and Criminal Liability (1995)

The options canvassed in LCCP 127

5.2 In LCCP 127 we put forward the following policy options for consideration:

Options which would retain the Majewski principle
  1. Do nothing.
  2. Codify the *Majewski* approach, in one of three different ways:

(i) codify the present law without amendment;
(ii) adopt the proposals of the CLRC and the rule in the American Model Penal Code, so as to apply *Majewski* only to allegations of recklessness; or
(iii) adopt a simplified version of (ii), under which a state of voluntary intoxication would itself constitute recklessness in law.

Options which would entail disregarding the effect of voluntary intoxication
  3. Disregard the effect of voluntary intoxication in *any* offence, with the effect that the defendant could in no case rely on voluntary intoxication to negative mens rea.
  4. Disregard the effect of voluntary intoxication in *any* offence (as in option 3), but subject to a statutory defence whereby it would be open to the defendant to prove, on the balance of probabilities, that he lacked the mens rea of the offence.

Options which would entail abandoning the Majewski principle
  5. Abolish the *Majewski* approach without replacement, so that the defendant's intoxication would be taken into account with all the other

relevant evidence in determining whether he had the prescribed mental element of the offence.

6. Combine the abolition of the *Majewski* approach with the introduction of a new offence of "criminal intoxication", which would be committed by a person who, when deliberately intoxicated to a substantial extent, caused the harm proscribed by one of a number of offences in a fixed list. We provisionally proposed that the maximum sentence for the new offence should be significantly lower than that for the underlying listed offence.

5.7 As a result, although we had *formulated* six possible options for reform, we provisionally favoured only options 5 and 6, both of which involved the total abandonment of the *Majewski* principle. As with all our law reform work, when we published the consultation paper we looked forward with keen interest to receiving and considering the responses to our provisional views.

Summary of our main recommendations

1.34 Our main recommendations can be summarised as follows:

- The present law of intoxication should be codified, with a few significant amendments.
- Where the prosecution alleges any intention, purpose, knowledge, belief, fraud or dishonesty, evidence of intoxication should be taken into account in determining whether that allegation has been proved.
- For the purpose of any allegation of any other mental element of an offence (in particular, allegations of recklessness or awareness of risk), a voluntarily intoxicated defendant should be treated as having been aware of anything of which he would have been aware but for his intoxication.
- A person should not escape liability on the ground of automatism alone if his automatism is wholly or partly caused by voluntary intoxication.
- Where a voluntarily intoxicated person holds a belief which, had he not been intoxicated, would have negatived his liability for an offence, the belief should not have that effect if he would not have held it but for his intoxication *and* the offence does not require proof of intention, purpose, knowledge, belief, fraud or dishonesty.
- A person should be regarded as "intoxicated" if his awareness, understanding or control is impaired by an intoxicant; and an "intoxicant" should be defined as meaning alcohol, a drug or any other substance (of whatever nature) which, once taken into the body, has the capacity to impair awareness, understanding or control.
- A person's intoxication should be regarded as involuntary if

 (a) when he took the intoxicant he was not aware that it was or might be an intoxicant; or
 (b) he took it solely for a medicinal purpose, and *either*
   (i) was not aware that it would or might give rise to aggressive or uncontrollable behaviour on his part *or*
   (ii) took it on, and in accordance with, medical advice; or
 (c) it was administered to him without his consent; or
 (d) he took it under duress, or otherwise in such circumstances as would afford a defence to a criminal charge.

The extent to which our recommendations would change the law

1.36 First, our recommendations would dispense with the need to classify the offence charged as one of "specific" or "basic" intent in order to determine which régime applies to it. In place of this distinction we propose a set of rules which, instead of applying to some *offences* but not to others, are so formulated as to be capable of applying in relation only to certain kinds of *mental element*.

1.37 Secondly, it seems (though the position is not entirely clear) that the present law treats a mistaken belief brought about by the defendant's voluntary intoxication in different ways according to whether it is categorised as negativing an element of the offence or as forming part of a defence. . . . This rule is inconsistent with the law on mistakes which negative an element of an offence, and with the way in which the law treats defences created by statute. Our proposal will apply the same rules in all of these cases, and will make the law consistent and much simpler to apply.

1.38 Finally, we believe that the present law operates in an inconsistent manner in drawing a distinction between "dangerous" and "non-dangerous" drugs. If the court decides that the drug taken by the defendant is "non-dangerous", a much less strict version of the *Majewski* approach is applied to him. The courts themselves have to decide, without the benefit of medical advice, which drugs are "non-dangerous" for this purpose. Valium, for example, has been held to be "non-dangerous", although medical evidence shows that it can increase aggression. Our proposals would remove this distinction, and instead require the courts to look at the defendant's *purpose* in taking the drug, how drastic he expected its effect on him to be, and whether he obtained—and followed—medical advice.

Draft Criminal Law (Intoxication) Bill

EFFECT OF INTOXICATION ON CRIMINAL LIABILITY

1.—(1) This section applies where it is alleged that any mental element of an offence was present at any material time in the case of a person who was then intoxicated.

(2) If the person's intoxication was voluntary and the allegation is in substance an allegation that at the material time he—

(a) acted intentionally with respect to a particular result,
(b) had a particular purpose in acting in a particular way,
(c) had any particular knowledge or belief, or
(d) acted fraudulently or dishonestly,

evidence of his intoxication may be taken into account in determining whether the allegation has been proved.

(3) If the person's intoxication was voluntary and the allegation is not one to which subsection (2) applies, then, in determining whether the allegation has been proved, he shall be treated as having been aware at the material time of anything of which he would then have been aware but for his intoxication.

(4) If the person's intoxication was involuntary, then (whether the allegation is or is not one to which subsection (2) applies) evidence of his intoxication may be taken into account in determining whether the allegation has been proved.

(5) For the purposes of this section a person acts "intentionally" with respect to a result when—

(a) it is his purpose to cause it, or
(b) although it is not his purpose to cause it, he knows that it would occur in the ordinary course of events if he were to succeed in his purpose of causing some other result;

and this section applies in relation to omissions as it applies in relation to acts.

2.—(1) This section applies with respect to the liability for an offence of a person who was at any material time in a state of automatism wholly or partly caused by intoxication.

(2) If the person's intoxication was voluntary, then (subject to subsection (4))—

(a) the fact that he was at the material time in a state of automatism shall operate to rebut any relevant allegation to which section 1(2) applies; but
(b) that fact shall otherwise be disregarded and, in the case of any other relevant allegation, section 1(3) shall accordingly apply in relation to him as a person who was at that time in a state of voluntary intoxication;

and for this purpose "relevant allegation" means an allegation falling within section 1(1) and relating to that time.

(3) If the person's intoxication was involuntary, the fact that he was at the material time in a state of automatism shall (subject to subsection (4)) operate to negative liability for the offence.

(4) If any such state of automatism was caused partly by such disease of the mind as would, if it had been wholly so caused, require a verdict of not guilty by reason of insanity, then—

(a) it shall be treated as if it had been wholly so caused; and
(b) subsection (2) or, as the case may be, subsection (3) above shall not apply.

3.—(1) Where at any material time a person—

(a) was intoxicated, but
(b) held a particular belief which, had he not been intoxicated, would have operated to negative liability for an offence,

then, unless subsection (2) applies, that belief shall so operate whether the intoxication was voluntary or involuntary.

(2) That belief shall not so operate if—

(a) the person's intoxication was voluntary; and
(b) but for his intoxication he would not have held that belief; and
(c) liability for the offence can be established without proof of any allegation to which section 1(2) applies.

(3) Where at any material time a person charged with murder—

(a) was intoxicated, but
(b) held a particular belief which, had he not been intoxicated, would have operated to reduce the homicide to manslaughter,

that belief shall so operate whether the intoxication was voluntary or involuntary.

(4) Any enactment which (in whatever terms) provides for a person holding a particular belief to have a defence to a criminal charge shall have effect subject to the provisions of this section.

INTOXICATION

4.—(1) For the purposes of this Act—

(a) "intoxicant" means alcohol, a drug or any other substance (of whatever nature) which, once taken into the body, has the capacity to impair awareness, understanding or control; and
(b) a person is "intoxicated" if his awareness, understanding or control is impaired by an intoxicant;

and "intoxication" shall be construed accordingly.

(2) For the purposes of subsection (1)(a) it is immaterial that a particular substance has the capacity to impair awareness, understanding or control only if taken by a person with an increased or abnormal susceptibility thereto attributable to—

(a) his physical or mental condition at the time when it is taken into his body, or
(b) anything done or omitted to be done by him at any time thereafter;

and for the purposes of subsection (1)(b) it is immaterial that a person's awareness, understanding or control is impaired by a particular substance by reason only of any such increased or abnormal susceptibility thereto.

(3) For the purposes of this Act—

(a) references to a person being "involuntarily intoxicated" shall be construed in accordance with sections 5 and 6(3) and (5); and
(b) references to a person's intoxication being "involuntary" shall be construed accordingly;

and a person's intoxication if not involuntary is "voluntary" for the purposes of this Act.

(4) In this Act references to a person "taking" an intoxicant or other substance include references to its being administered to him with his consent.

5.—(1) Subject to subsection (2), an intoxicated person is involuntarily intoxicated if—

(a) at the time when he took the intoxicant he was not aware that it was or might be an intoxicant; or
(b) he took the intoxicant solely for medicinal purposes; or
(c) the intoxicant was administered to him without his consent; or
(d) he took the intoxicant in such circumstances as would, in relation to a criminal charge, afford the defence of duress by threats or any other defence recognised by law.

(2) A person is not involuntarily intoxicated by virtue of subsection (1)(b) if—

(a) he took the intoxicant being aware that, as taken by him, it would or might give rise to aggressive or uncontrollable behaviour on his part, or
(b) having taken the intoxicant, he failed to take reasonable precautions to counteract its effect on him being aware that his failure to do so would or might give rise to any such behaviour,

and (in either case) the intoxicant was taken by him—

(i) otherwise than on medical advice, or
(ii) (if taken on medical advice) otherwise than in accordance with any directions given to him by the person providing the advice.

(3) Where an intoxicated person—

(a) was aware at the time when he took the intoxicant that it was or might be an intoxicant having the capacity to impair awareness, understanding or control only if taken as mentioned in section 4(2), and
(b) is intoxicated by reason only of any such increased or abnormal susceptibility to the intoxicant as is mentioned in that provision,

he is nevertheless involuntarily intoxicated if—

(i) (where the susceptibility was attributable to his physical or mental condition at the time when he took the intoxicant) he was not then aware that he had or might have any such susceptibility, or
(ii) (where the susceptibility was attributable to anything done or omitted to be done by him at any time thereafter) he was not then aware that any such act or omission would or might result in any such susceptibility.

(4) In this section—

"the intoxicant", in relation to an intoxicated person, means the intoxicant by virtue of which he is intoxicated; and
"medicinal purposes" includes sedative and soporific purposes.

(5) A person's intoxication shall for the purposes of this Act be presumed not to have been involuntary unless there is adduced such evidence as might lead the court or jury to conclude that there is a reasonable possibility that it was involuntary.

6.—(1) This section applies where at any material time referred to in sections 1 to 3—

(a) a person was intoxicated following the taking of a combination of two or more intoxicating substances, and
(b) at the time of taking them he—
(i) was aware that any one or more of them was or were, or might be, an intoxicating substance or intoxicating substances, but
(ii) was not so aware in the case of the other or others.

(2) In this section—

"intoxicating substance" means any substance which is or contains an intoxicant;
"known substance" means any substance falling within subsection (1)(b)(i); and
"undetected substance" means any substance falling within subsection (1)(b)(ii).

(3) The intoxicated person shall be treated as involuntarily intoxicated at the material time if he would not have been intoxicated but for having taken the undetected substance or substances.

(4) If subsection (3) does not apply to the intoxicated person in relation to the material time referred to in section 1, he shall not, by virtue of section 1(3), be treated as having then been aware of something if he was unaware of it by reason only of his having taken the undetected substance or substances.

(5) If subsection (3) does not apply to the intoxicated person in relation to the material time referred to in section 2, his intoxication shall nevertheless be treated for the purposes of that section as having then been involuntary if—

(a) he would not then have been in a state of automatism, or
(b) his state of automatism would not have been wholly or partly caused by intoxication,

had he taken only the known substance or substances.

(6) If subsection (3) does not apply to the intoxicated person in relation to the material time referred to in section 3, section 3(2) shall not apply in relation to him if he held the belief in question by reason only of his having taken the undetected substance or substances.

Questions

1. Horder, "Sobering Up? The Law Commission on Criminal Intoxication" (1995) 58 M.L.R. 534, states:

"The main bulk of the provisions are designed to fend off public criticism rather than to provide a principled basis on which the law can operate. If this is true (as it seems to be), then to allow evidence of voluntary intoxication to negative *mens rea* in *any* crime, particularly a serious crime of violence, looks perverse. Yet the policy-driven Commission proposals contain a large set of circumstances in which evidence of voluntary intoxication can be so used. Voluntary intoxication may, for example, negative *mens rea* on a murder charge, but not on a charge of criminal damage. But it can hardly be claimed authoritatively that public outrage would be more provoked by an acquittal-based on evidence of voluntary intoxication—in the latter case than in the former. So why draw the distinction if defensive policy considerations are what are to shape reform?"

Do you agree with Horder's analysis?

2. Clause 2 deals with intoxication and automatism. If enacted what would be the outcome for D in the following cases and is there any moral distinction to be drawn between these cases on the basis of D's actions and his responsibility for them:

a. D takes a drug which causes him to become unconscious. He collapses at the top of a flight of stairs crashing into V who falls down the stairs sustaining serious head injuries from which he dies. D is charged with manslaughter.
b. D takes a drug which causes him to hallucinate. He sees what he thinks to be a monster coming up the stairs and hurls it back down. In fact the "monster" was V who dies as a result of the injuries received. D is charged with manslaughter. (cf. *Lipman, ante*, p. 265).
c. D takes a drug which exacerbates a psychiatric condition from which he suffers. He begins to hallucinate seeing demons everywhere. He hurls one such demon down the stairs. The "demon" was V who dies as a result of the injuries received. D is charged with manslaughter.
d. D's beer is "spiked" with a dangerous drug as a result of which he begins to hallucinate. He hears voices which tell him that V is a paedophiliac killer and that he should kill him to rid the world of his wickedness. D hurls V down the stairs intending to kill him and V dies as a result. D is charged with murder (see also clause 6).

CHAPTER 5

DEFENCES

1. DEFENCES IN GENERAL

A. T. H. Smith, "On Actus Reus and Mens Rea" *in Reshaping the Criminal Law* **(ed. Glazebrook), p. 97–101**

When speaking colloquially lawyers are inclined to call any reason advanced by a defendant in support of an acquittal a 'defence'. These include such explanations as alibi, infancy, mistake, accident, and insanity. When they use the term more precisely, they point out that automatism—for example—is not really a defence at all, but a denial that the prosecution has proved part of its case: the prosecution has failed to show that the defendant acted with *mens rea*. It has now been accepted by no less a body than the House of Lords that, where the definition of any particular crime includes intention or recklessness, any mistake that has the effect of preventing the formation of these states of mind must exculpate, whether it be a reasonable mistake or not. This is so because mistake prevents the formation of the particular *mens rea* which must be established as part of the prosecution case. Duress, necessity, self-defence, and infancy, on the other hand, are said to be properly described as 'defences', because they do not negative either traditional *mens rea* or *actus reus*, but operate in some way independently. . . .

It is possible to make a distinction between defences which are justificatory in character, and those which are excuses. It has not found much favour in Anglo-American jurisprudence, partly no doubt because of Stephen's emphatic assertion that it 'involves no legal consequences,' a reproach guaranteed to deprive it of any significance it might otherwise have enjoyed. Briefly stated, the distinction is that we excuse the actor because he is not sufficiently culpable or at fault, whereas we justify an act because we regard it as the most appropriate course of action in the circumstances, even though it may result in harm that would, in the

283

absence of the justification, amount to a crime. It does not follow that, because the distinction between the two is not formally taken in our law that it is altogether without significance, particularly where the law is in a state of flux. The reasons why, and the circumstances in which, we are prepared to excuse may be altogether different from the corresponding reasons for justification. We admit excuses as 'an expression of compassion for one of our kind caught in a maelstrom of circumstances'. A plea of justification, by contrast, is founded upon the law's preference, in social and policy terms, for one course of action rather than another.

Where a defendant successfully pleads a defence such as prevention of crime or self-defence, he argues that what he did was not unlawful, and he is able to point to a specific rule—in the one case of statutory origin, and in the other, in common law—to substantiate his plea. It may be, however, that a plea of justification has not crystallised into one of these specific defences, but is of a more nebulous sort.

For example, although it appears that there is no general defence of necessity in that there is no rule to which a defendant can appeal to justify his having chosen to bring about a proscribed harm, there is nevertheless a principle infiltrating the legal system, given efficacy through a variety of legal inlets, that where a person is placed by force of circumstance in the position of having to choose between two evils, his act is justified if he chooses the lesser one. In that somewhat fitful sense, necessity operates as a 'defence'. Some would say that a person who commits a prima facie unlawful act as a result of necessity is not blameworthy or at fault and hence lacks *mens rea*. But it does not necessarily follow that we exculpate him for that reason. An alternative explanation is that where the act done is the lesser of two evils, it is justified or lawful—that there was no *actus reus* notwithstanding that the conduct falls literally within the terms of the definition of the offence.

Analysis of crime in terms of *actus reus* and *mens rea*, and the mechanical application of statutes, tend to obscure the principles of harm and illegality on which criminal liability is based. Unless these principles find expression either in the definition of the crime itself (*e.g.* by the inclusion of 'unlawfully') or in some express exculpatory rule, it seems that our legal system is incapable of giving effect to them. Whereas the judges are adept at interpreting legislation in such a way as to introduce traditional *mens rea*, if necessary by reading words into the statutes, they will only infrequently allow considerations of principle to override the plain words of a statute. Only by providing in a code for a defence of necessity, therefore, is it possible to ensure that this principle is preserved in a form in which it will invariably prevail.

See also G. Williams, "The Theory of Excuses" [1982] Crim.L.R. 732.

2. DURESS

Wasik, "Duress and Criminal Responsibility" [1977] Crim.L.R. 453

There seems to be general agreement among lawyers that criminal responsibility should follow when an individual chooses to perform an act proscribed by the criminal law, when he has both the capacity and a fair opportunity or chance to adjust his behaviour to conform with the law. It follows that no individual should be held responsible if he had no opportunity to choose an alternative to breaking the law. As the philosophers put it: there should be no ascription of responsibility to the accused unless 'he could have acted otherwise'. Much attention has been paid to this requirement by philosophers but lawyers, by contrast, have not shown a great deal of interest. Perhaps the main reason for this is the practical rarity of such problems. It is much more common for an accused to plead mistake or lack of intention as an excuse than to plead that he had no choice but to act as he did. Cases in which the defence of duress is raised are probably the most frequent of this small group. . . .

A comparison has sometimes been made between the defence of duress and that of automatism. The suggestion is that in duress, the accused claims that there was no act by *him*; in automatism the accused claims that there was no *act* by him. Both defences are then seen as containing what may in loose terminology be called 'an involuntary act' on the part of the accused. But this is misleading, as the element of voluntariness is quite different in the two excuses. Where the defence of automatism succeeds, the accused has had no opportunity at all to exercise choice with regard to the performing of the act, and thus he cannot be held responsible for it. . . . By contrast, in duress, there is an issue of choice. If a man is threatened with physical injury unless he assists in a criminal enterprise, he has the choice (albeit a difficult one) of assisting in the crime or facing the consequences. The question here is whether the accused had a fair opportunity to make the choice.

i. An imminent threat of death or serious injury

R. v. Hudson and Taylor
[1971] 2 Q.B. 202
Court of Appeal

H and T who were aged 17 and 19 respectively, were charged with perjury in a case in which they were witnesses to an unlawful wounding incident. They admitted that they had given false evidence but raised the defence of duress. This took the form of threats before the trial that unless they did so they would be "cut up". The recorder directed the jury that the defence was not available since the threat was not immediate. On appeal the Crown contended that the plea should have failed on the additional ground that they should have sought police protection before the trial.

LORD WIDGERY C.J.: . . . it is clearly established that duress provides a defence in all offences including perjury (except possibly treason or murder as a principal) if the will of the accused has been overborne by threats of death or serious personal injury so that the commission of the alleged offence was no longer the voluntary act of the accused. This appeal raises two main questions: first, as to the nature of the necessary threat and, in particular, whether it must be "present and immediate"; secondly, as to the extent to which a right to plead duress may be lost if the accused has failed to take steps to remove the threat as, for example, by seeking police protection.

It is essential to the defence of duress that the threat shall be effective at the moment when the crime is committed. The threat must be a "present" threat in the sense that it is effective to neutralise the will of the accused at that time. Hence an accused who joins a rebellion under the compulsion of threats cannot plead duress if he remains with the rebels after the threats have lost their effect and his own will has had a chance to re-assert itself (*McCrowther's Case* (1746) Fost. 13; and *A.-G. v. Whelan* [1934] I.R. 518). Similarly a threat of future violence may be so remote as to be insufficient to overpower the will at the moment when the offence was committed, or the accused may have elected to commit the offence in order to rid himself of a threat hanging over him and not because he was driven to act by immediate and unavoidable pressure. In none of these cases is the defence of duress available because a person cannot justify the commission of a crime merely to secure his own peace of mind.

When, however, there is no opportunity for delaying tactics, and the person threatened must make up his mind whether he is to commit the criminal act or not, the existence at that moment of threats sufficient to destroy his will ought to provide him with a defence even though the threatened injury may not follow instantly, but after an interval. This principle is illustrated by *Subramaniam v. Public Prosecutor* [1956] 1 W.L.R. 965, when the appellant was charged in Malaya with unlawful possession of ammunition and was held by the Privy Council to have a defence of duress, fit to go to the jury, on his plea that he had been compelled by terrorists to accept the ammunition and feared for his safety if the terrorists returned.

In the present case the threats of Farrell were likely to be no less compelling, because their execution could not be effected in the court room, if they could be carried out in the streets of Salford the same night. Insofar, therefore, as the recorder ruled as a matter of law that the threats were not sufficiently present and immediate to support the defence of duress we think that he was in error. He should have left the jury to decide whether the threats had overborne the will of the appellants at the time when they gave the false evidence.

Counsel for the Crown, however, contends that the recorder's ruling can be supported on another ground, namely, that the appellants should have taken steps to neutralise the threats by seeking police protection either when they came to court to give evidence, or beforehand. He submits on grounds of public policy that the accused should not be able to plead duress if he had the opportunity to ask for protection from the police before committing the offence and failed to do so. The argument does not distinguish cases in which the police would be able to provide effective protection, from those when they would not, and it would, in effect, restrict the defence of duress to cases where the person threatened had been kept in custody by the maker of the threats, or where the time interval between the making of the threats and the commission of the offence had made recourse to the police impossible. We recognise the need to keep the defence of duress within reasonable bounds but cannot accept so severe a restriction on it. The duty, of the person threatened, to take steps to remove the threat does not seem to have arisen in an English case but in full review of the defence of duress in the Supreme Court of Victoria (*R. v. Hurley, R. v. Murray* [1967] V.R. 526), a condition of raising the defence was said to be that the accused "had no means, with safety to himself, of preventing the execution of the threat."

In the opinion of this court it is always open to the Crown to prove that the accused failed to avail himself of some opportunity which was reasonably open to him to render the threat ineffective, and that on this being established the threat in question can no longer be relied on by the defence. In deciding whether such an opportunity was reasonably open to the accused the jury should have regard to his age and circumstances, and to any risks to him which may be involved in the course of action relied on.

In our judgment the defence of duress should have been left to the jury in the present case, as should any issue raised by the Crown and arising out of the appellants' failure to seek police protection. The appeals will, therefore, be allowed and the convictions quashed.

Appeals allowed

Notes

1. In *Abdul-Hussain and Others, The Times*, January 26, 1999, the Court of Appeal followed the approach adopted in *Hudson and Taylor*.

The appellants were Shiite Muslims from Iraq who had fled to Sudan. They were over-stayers in Sudan and feared being arrested and returned to Iraq where they expected they would be tortured and executed. They hi-jacked an aeroplane at Khartoum Airport and forced the pilot to fly to London where they sought political asylum. They pleaded duress of circumstances (see *post*, p. 330) to charges of hi-jacking an aeroplane. The trial judge ruled that this defence would not be left to the jury as death or injury would not have immediately followed had they not hi-jacked the aeroplane. The Court of Appeal quashed their convictions holding that the defence should have been left to the jury as the issue for them to consider was whether the threat of imminent death or injury was operating on the mind of the accused so as to overbear his will when he committed the crime and not whether the execution of the threat was immediately in prospect. Rose L.J. stated:

> "[I]f Anne Frank had stolen a car to escape from Amsterdam and been charged with theft, the tenets of English law would not ... have denied her a defence of duress of circumstances, on the ground that she should have waited the Gestapo's knock on the door."

2. In *R. v. Valderrama-Vega* [1985] Crim.L.R. 220 C.A., the appellant was charged with the importation of prohibited drugs from Colombia. He pleaded duress on the basis that a Mafia-type organisation had threatened injury or death to himself and his family. In addition he said that he needed money as he was under severe financial pressure and he had also been threatened with disclosure of his homosexuality. The Court of Appeal held that it was wrong to direct the jury that duress was a defence only where the defendant acted "*solely* as the result of threats of death or serious injury to himself or his family". Rather these threats must be a *sine qua non* of the defendant's decision to commit the offence although he may have had other motives.

3. Most of the cases have involved threats to kill or injure the accused. Will threats to kill or injure others be sufficient to found the defence of duress? In *R. v Ortiz* (1986) 83 Cr.App.R. 173, the Court of Appeal assumed that a threat to injure the accused's wife or family could do so. This is confirmed by *Martin* [1989] 1 All E.R. 652 (*post*, p. 331). In *R. v Hurley* [1967] V.R. 526, the Supreme Court of Victoria held that threats to kill or seriously injure the accused's common law wife could amount to duress. In *Conway* [1989] Q.B. 290 (*post*, p. 330) a threat to the passenger in the accused's car was sufficient. It has still to be determined whether a threat to a complete stranger would suffice to found the defence although this seems to be implicit in the decision in *Pommell*, *post*, p. 330 where the argument focused on other issues.

ii. The test for duress

R. v. Graham
[1982] 1 W.L.R. 294
Court of Appeal

G, a practising homosexual, lived with his wife (W) and K, another homosexual. G took Valium for an anxiety state and this made him

susceptible to bullying. K was a violent man. One night K attacked W
with a knife but G intervened. Next day W left home; K and G remained
drinking heavily and G took more Valium than was prescribed. K suggested killing W and at K's suggestion G telephoned her luring her
back to the flat. When she arrived K put a flex round her neck and told
G to take hold of the other end of the flex and pull on it. He did so, he
claimed, only because he was afraid of K. He was convicted of murder,
the Crown having conceded that duress could be raised as a defence.
G appealed on the ground that the judge had misdirected the jury.

LORD LANE C.J.: The prosecution at the trial conceded that, on those facts, it
was open to the defence to raise the issue of duress. In other words, they were
not prepared to take the point that the defence of duress is not available to a
principal in the first degree to murder. Consequently, the interesting question
raised by the decisions in *D.P.P. for Northern Ireland* v. *Lynch* [1975] A.C. 653
(*post*, p. 299) and *Abbott* v. *The Queen* [1977] A.C. 755 (*post*, p. 302) was not
argued before us. We do not have to decide it. We pause only to observe that
the jury would no doubt have been puzzled to learn that whether the appellant was to be convicted of murder or acquitted altogether might depend on
whether the plug came off the end of the percolator flex when he began to
pull it. . . .

The direction which the judge gave to the jury required them to ask themselves two questions. First, a subjective question which the judge formulated:

"Was this man at the time of the killing taking part . . . because he
feared for his own life (or) personal safety as a result of the words or
the conduct . . . on the part of King, either personally experienced by
him, or genuinely believed in by him . . ."

Neither side in the present appeal has taken issue with the judge on this
question. We feel, however, that, for purposes of completeness, we should
say that the direction appropriate in this particular case should have been
in these words: "Was this man at the time of the killing taking part
because he held a well-grounded fear of death (or serious physical injury)
as a result of the words or conduct on the part of King?" The bracketed
words may be too favourable to the defendant. The point was not argued
before us.

The judge then went on to direct the jury that if the answer to that first
question was "yes", or "he may have been", the jury should then go on
to consider a second question importing an objective test of reasonableness. This is the issue which arises in this appeal. Mr. Kennedy for
the appellant contends that no second question arises at all; the test is
purely subjective. He argues that if the appellant's will was in fact overborne by threats of the requisite cogency, he is entitled to be acquitted
and no question arises as to whether a reasonable man, with or without
his characteristics, would have acted similarly.

Mr Sherrard, for the Crown, on the other hand, submits that such dicta
as can be found on the point are in favour of a second test; this time an
objective test. He argues that public policy requires this and draws an
analogy with provocation.
[Having considered dicta in *Lynch*, *post*, p. 299, *Archbold Criminal
Pleading & Practice* (40th ed, 1979), Smith & Hogan, *Criminal Law* (4th
ed., 1978) and the Law Commission *Report on Defences of General
Application* (1977) (Law Com. No. 83), para. 2.28, his Lordship continued.]

As a matter of public policy, it seems to us essential to limit the defence of duress by means of an objective criterion formulated in terms of reasonableness. Consistency of approach in defences to criminal liability is obviously desirable. Provocation and duress are analogous. In provocation the words or actions of one person break the self-control of another. In duress the words or actions of one person break the will of another. The law requires a defendant to have the self-control reasonably to be expected of the ordinary citizen in his situation. It should likewise require him to have the steadfastness reasonably to be expected of the ordinary citizen in his situation. So too with self-defence, in which the law permits the use of no more force than is reasonable in the circumstances. And, in general, if a mistake is to excuse what would otherwise be criminal, the mistake must be a reasonable one.

It follows that we accept Mr Sherrard's submission that the direction in this case was too favourable to the appellant. The Crown having conceded that the issue of duress was open to the appellant and was raised on the evidence, the correct approach on the facts of this case would have been as follows. (1) Was the defendant, or may he have been, impelled to act as he did because, as a result of what he reasonably believed King had said or done, he had good cause to fear that if he did not so act King would kill him or (if this is to be added) cause him serious physical injury? (2) If so, have the prosecution made the jury sure that a sober person of reasonable firmness, sharing the characteristics of the defendant, would not have responded to whatever he reasonably believed King said or did by taking part in the killing? The fact that a defendant's will to resist has been eroded by the voluntary consumption of drink or drugs or both is not relevant to this test.

We doubt whether the Crown were right to concede that the question of duress ever arose on the facts of this case. The words and deeds of King relied on by the defence were far short of those needed to raise a threat of the requisite gravity. However, the Crown having made the concession, the judge was right to pose the second objective question to the jury. His only error lay in putting it too favourably to the appellant.

The appeal is dismissed.

Appeal dismissed

Question

Lord Lane stated that "[c]onsistency of approach in defences to criminal liability is obviously desirable". Has Lord Lane been consistent in his approach with regard to the issue of mistake in respect of the facts upon which a defence is based? (See R. v. *Gladstone Williams, post*, p. 159).

Notes

1. Lord Lane's formulation of the test for duress was approved by the House of Lords in R. v. *Howe, ante*, p. 303.
2. For duress to be raised as a defence there must be a nexus between the threats made and the offence committed by the accused as a result of the threats. In *Cole* [1994] Crim. L.R. 582, the accused appealed against his conviction for robbery committed as a result of threats of violence made by moneylenders if he did not repay the money he had borrowed. The Court of Appeal upheld the conviction,

holding that the defence of duress by threats can only apply where the offence charged is the very offence nominated by the person making the threats. In this case, the moneylenders had not stipulated that the accused commit robbery to meet their demands and the defence was therefore not available to him. In *Ali* [1995] Crim L.R. 303 the Court of Appeal assumed that a threat "to get the money from a bank or building society" . . . or else, without specifying a particular place, was sufficient to found a defence of duress by threats to a charge of robbery.

iii. Characteristics attributable to the person of reasonable firmness

There is some uncertainty as to which of the accused's characteristics may be relevant to the objective test. In *Graham, ante,* p. 287, Lord Lane C.J. stated that the law requires a defendant "to have the steadfastness reasonably to be expected of the ordinary citizen in his situation". He drew an analogy with provocation (see p. 531 *post*) where the understanding at the time was that an objective standard of self-control was required but characteristics which were relevant to the gravity of the provocation to the defendant could be attributed to the reasonable person (For the current position see *post*, pp. 535ff.) This would suggest that for duress, perhaps with the exception of age and sex in so far as they may be relevant to steadfastness, it is only those characteristics which render the threat more grave to the defendant than the ordinary citizen which should be taken into account. For example, a threat to break D's arm would be more grave to D than the ordinary citizen if D only has one arm. In the case which follows the Court of Appeal attempts to state the relevant principles having examined the earlier cases of *Emery* (1993) 14 Cr.App.R. (S) 394, *Hegarty* [1994] Crim. L.R. 353, *Horne* [1994] Crim.L.R. 584 and *Hurst* [1995] 1 Cr.App. R. 82.

R. v. Bowen
[1996] 2 Cr. App. R. 157
Court of Appeal

D was convicted of obtaining services by deception, having obtained numerous goods on credit over a six month period and then failed to make payments. He claimed he was acting under duress having been threatened by two men that if he did not obtain the goods for them he and his family would be petrol-bombed. He was told that if he went to the police his family would be attacked. The judge excluded from the jury's consideration evidence that D was abnormally suggestible and vulnerable. On appeal the question of D's low I.Q. was also raised.

STUART-SMITH L.J. read the judgement of the Court: . . .
But the question remains, what are the relevant characteristics of the accused to which the jury should have regard in considering the second objective test? This question had given rise to considerable difficulty in recent cases. It seems clear that age and sex are, and physical health or disability may be, relevant characteristics. But beyond that it is not altogether easy to determine from the authorities what others may be relevant. . . .

[His Lordship referred to *Emery, Hegarty, Horne, Hurst, Graham, Camplin, post*, p. 536, and *Morhall, post*, p. 540.]

Questions of duress and provocation are similar, in that the two-fold test applies in each case. . . . In the case of duress, the question is: would an ordinary person sharing the characteristics of the defendant be able to resist the threats made to him?

What principles are to be derived from these authorities? We think they are as follows:

(1) The mere fact that the accused is more pliable, vulnerable; timid or susceptible to threats than a normal person are not characteristics with which it is legitimate to invest the reasonable/ordinary person for the purpose of considering the objective test.

(2) The defendant may be in a category of persons who the jury may think less able to resist pressure than people not within that category. Obvious examples are age, where a young person may well not be so robust as a mature one; possibly sex, though many women would doubtless consider they had as much moral courage to resist pressure as men; pregnancy, where there is added fear for the unborn child; serious physical disability, which may inhibit self protection; recognised mental illness or psychiatric condition, such as post traumatic stress disorder leading to learned helplessness.

(3) Characteristics which may be relevant in considering provocation, because they relate to the nature of the provocation, itself will not necessarily be relevant in cases of duress. Thus homosexuality may be relevant to provocation if the provocative words or conduct are related to this characteristic; it cannot be relevant in duress, since there is no reason to think that homosexuals are less robust in resisting threats of the kind that are relevant in duress cases.

(4) Characteristics due to self-induced abuse, such as alcohol, drugs or glue-sniffing, cannot be relevant.

(5) Psychiatric evidence may be admissible to show that the accused is suffering from some mental illness, mental impairment or recognised psychiatric condition provided persons generally suffering from such condition may be more susceptible to pressure and threats and thus to assist the jury in deciding whether a reasonable person suffering from such a condition might have been impelled to act as the defendant did. It is not admissible simply to show that in the doctor's opinion an accused, who is not suffering from such illness or condition, is especially timid, suggestible or vulnerable to pressure and threats. Nor is medical opinion admissible to bolster or support the credibility of the accused.

(6) Where counsel wishes to submit that the accused has some characteristic which falls within (2) above, this must be made plain to the judge. The question may arise in relation to the admissibility of medical evidence of the nature set out in (5). If so, the judge will have to rule at that stage. There may, however, be no medical evidence, or, as in this case, medical evidence may have been introduced for some other purpose, *e.g.* to challenge the admissibility or weight of a confession. In such a case counsel must raise the question before speeches in the absence of the jury, so that the judge can rule whether the alleged characteristic is capable of being relevant. If he rules that it is, then he must leave it to the jury.

(7) In the absence of some direction from the judge as to what characteristics are capable of being regarded as relevant, we think that the direction approved in *Graham* without more will not be as helpful as it might be, since the jury may be tempted, especially if there is evidence, as there was in this case, relating to suggestibility and vulnerability, to think that these are relevant. In most cases it is probably only the age and sex of the accused that is

capable of being relevant. If so, the judge should, as he did in this case, confine the characteristics in question to these.

How are these principles to be applied in this case? Miss Levitt accepts, rightly in our opinion, that the evidence that the appellant was abnormally suggestible and a vulnerable individual is irrelevant. But she submits that the fact that he had, or may have had, a low I.Q. of 68 is relevant since it might inhibit his ability to seek the protection of the police. We do not agree. We do not see how low I.Q., short of mental impairment or mental defectiveness, can be said to be a characteristic that makes those who have it less courageous and less able to withstand threats and pressure.

Appeal dismissed

Questions

1. In *Hudson and Taylor, ante*, p. 285, the Court of Appeal stated that the defence of duress would be denied a defendant if he "failed to avail himself of some opportunity which was reasonably open *to him* to render the threat ineffective" (emphasis added). If because of his low I.Q. D is not capable of recognising such an opportunity, is it not the case that evidence of his I.Q. is relevant to the subjective question rather than the objective question?

2. As questions whether something constitutes a "mental illness, mental impairment or recognised psychiatric condition" are both matters of degree and opinion on which psychiatrists may differ, would it not be better either (a) to abandon the objective question (see Professor Smith's Commentary below), or (b) to abandon attempts to identify relevant and non-relevant characteristics when considering liability and leave these matters to the judge to taken into account when sentencing?

Professor Sir John Smith, *R. v. Bowen*, Commentary, [1996] Crim. L.R. 577, 579

Clearly a characteristic which has no bearing on ability to resist threats of the kind which have been made in the particular case is irrelevant. If a person of low I.Q. is as well able to resist the threats as a person of high I.Q., the fact that the defendant has a low I.Q. is irrelevant for this purpose. It appears that this is a question for the judge. The court seems to have ruled it out as a matter of law in the present case. Similarly in *Flatt*, [1996] Crim. L.R. 576, with reference to drug addiction. If, however, the defendant is in a 'category of persons who the jury may think less able to resist pressure than people not within that category', then the defendant's membership of that category is relevant; *but* the merely pliable, vulnerable and timid are not a category for this purpose. Those suffering from 'recognised mental illness or psychiatric condition, such as post traumatic stress disorder leading to learned helplessness' apparently are. A jury may have some difficulty with the question: 'Would a woman, displaying the firmness reasonably to be expected of a woman suffering from learned helplessness, have yielded to the threat?' Effectively, this seems to eliminate the objective test for this category of persons. The elimination of the objective test might in principle be a good thing but, if so, it should be done generally and not for limited categories.

The opinion of the court on this last point seems to be based on its interpretation of *Emery*. It is submitted that it is not the correct interpretation. . . . In *Emery* Lord Taylor C.J. said '. . . the question for the doctors was whether a woman of reasonable firmness with the character-istics of Miss Emery, if abused in the manner which she said, would have had her will crushed so that she could not have protected the child.' Lord Taylor cannot have envisaged anything so absurd as 'a woman of reason-able firmness suffering from a condition of dependent helplessness', and that is not what he says. The jury were to consider whether a woman of reasonable firmness *would have been reduced to* a condition of dependent helplessness. If so, the will of the reasonably firm woman would obvi-ously have been overborne. The point surely is that the history of violence which was alleged in that case to have produced the condition of depend-ent helplessness was part of the duress. The jury have to envisage an ordinary woman of reasonable firmness before the history of the violence begins and consider whether, by the time of the final threat, her will would be so overborne that she would fail to resist it.

Note

In the extract below Professor K. J. M. Smith argues that the require-ment of reasonable steadfastness is superfluous as the defence already has a "non-variable threshold" by requiring a threat of death or ser-ious harm.

K. J. M. Smith, "Duress and Steadfastness: In Pursuit of the Unintelligible" [1999] Crim.L.R. 363, 370

It is within these initial objective boundaries that the current law's addi-tional, separate requirement of reasonable steadfastness has to be consid-ered. Just what is its function alongside a fixed minimum level of threat?

Judicial comments suggest it to be a particular manifestation of the ever-present concern over eroding the universal expectation, reinforced by the threat of sanctions, that the law is to be observed. Only exception-ally will the law compromise this expectation. In Lord Lane's frequently quoted words: it was a "matter of public policy . . . to limit the defence . . . by means of an objective criterion formulated in terms of reasonableness". [*Graham*, [1982] 1 All E.R. 801 at 806] But does not the fixed qualifying standard of the threat of serious harm or death perform this role? It is being maintained that, when faced with a belief in the threat of death or serious harm, the question is, *should* that defendant have capitulated bear-ing in mind their personal characteristics? In other words, does the reas-onable steadfastness test envisage some defendants of strong emotional or physical disposition who will be denied a defence of duress and who must not choose self-preservation? Unless some curious, morally unsus-tainable variability exists in the standard of self-sacrifice or self-preservation expected of a defendant *in extremis*, no coherent function can be assigned to the steadfastness requirement.

In suggesting this, a fundamental and vital distinction must be drawn between the emotional impact of a threat of at least serious harm on the defendant (how personally disturbing or intimidating it was), and what the defendant might have done in the circumstances to avoid or neutralise the threat, or how much credibility the threat should have been given. It is with respect to these two latter factors, where reasonableness of response is demanded by the law, that the defendant's personal character-istics could plausibly be drawn into the wider question of whether the defendant has behaved reasonably. However, undoubtedly, this was not

Lord Lane's intended role for "steadfastness". Moreover, most subsequent judicial wrangles over just what personal characteristics may
legitimately be admitted in determining "reasonable steadfastness" were
clearly concerned with the issue of the emotional impact on the defendant's ability to resist threats as distinct from the reasonableness of a belief
in the threat's existence or ways of avoiding it. Thus, these cases would
seem to accept that even where the threat of serious harm is credible and
where there is no reasonable prospect of escape open to the defendants,
the jury must still consider, in effect, whether the defendant's choice of
self-preservation was morally acceptable bearing in mind his personal
characteristics; in other words, in the jury's view did the defendant
deserve to be excused? . . .

Arguably, steadfastness is a superfluous objective test, pointlessly
adding to the complexity of the defence. Steadfastness is superfluous
when set alongside duress's fixed minimum standard of the threat of at
least serious harm. Subject to other distinct requirements, this threat condition marks the threshold of qualifying coercion, submission to which is
deemed to be the fitting basis for excusing a defendant because it constitutes acceptable "human frailty" or self-preference. Moreover, it can
hardly be accidental that the Model Penal Code's duress provisions,
whilst incorporating a "reasonable firmness" condition, do not specify a
fixed universal minimum level of threat. To this extent, the Model Penal
Code formulation of duress implicitly requires juries to balance the level
of threat against the offence committed—a proportionality requirement.
Secondly, the presence of a steadfastness test deflects attention away from
legitimate defence conditions relating to the neutralization or avoidance
of threats. Contrary to an implicit view persisting in an extensive body of
case law from *Graham* onwards (and explicit Law Commission opinion),
the steadfastness requirement cannot coherently relate to anything other
than the distinct conditions that defendants take all reasonable opportunities to escape from or neutralise an aggressor's threat. This is true both
for duress *per minas* and duress of circumstances. It is in satisfying these
objective conditions of the reasonableness of the defendant's capitulation
to threats that reference may plausibly be made to the defendant's characteristics and capacities.

Just what characteristics *ought* to be admissable remains problematic,
even when steadfastness is employed in this defensible fashion. As pointed out, the question is very much akin to that arising in self-defence (and
prevention of crime) and as yet lacks authoritative resolution. For both
defences the question is what characteristics, beyond those of physical
attributes, ought to be regarded as relevant to the defendant's ability to
make a reasonable effort to avoid or neutralise a threat of harm. In both
duress and self-defence the outstanding question may be reduced to
whether, besides physical limitations, evidence of anything less than medically recognised mental impairment affecting the defendant's competence to cope with a threat should [be] admissible in determining whether
the defendant acted reasonably. . . . [T]he inherent difficulty entailed in
a jury weighing up a defendant's moral resilience alone argues against
admitting such evidence. But beyond such practical problems, deeper
conceptual objections exist. Allowing evidence of character to influence
the ascription of criminal responsibility would be a unique departure
from orthodox principles of liability. Drawing into the calculation of reasonableness the defendant's character traits would be to reduce the issue
to something approaching whether the defendant could have acted otherwise . . .

Jettisoning the steadfastness standard, except in relation to matters of escape from or avoidance of a threat, would be a worthwhile simplification.

Note

In determining the first question in duress (whether the accused, because of what he reasonably believed the duressor had said or done, had good cause to fear death or GBH) it was believed that any condition from which D suffered which may have affected his perception should not be taken into account in determining the reasonableness of his belief. In *Martin* [2000] 2 Cr.App.R. 42, D suffered from schizoid-affective disorder which meant that he was more likely than others to regard things said to him as threatening and to believe that such threats would be carried out. The trial judge ruled that evidence of this condition was irrelevant in relation to the first question. The Court of Appeal held that duress and self-defence being analogous (relying on Lord Lane's dictum to this effect in *Graham*), the same subjective approach should be taken in respect of the accused's belief. In other words, D's psychiatric conditions may provide the explanation for his mistaken belief and thus were relevant to the jury's consideration of the first question. While this may be seen by some as a welcome development, the reasoning of the Court of Appeal is difficult to support. Lord Lane's dictum in *Graham* pre-dated his decision in *Williams (Gladstone)* (1984) 78 Cr.App.R. 276, (*ante*, p. 159) which established the subjective approach for self-defence. Secondly, the Court of Appeal placed reliance on the duress of circumstances case of *Cairns* [1999] 2 Cr.App.R. 137 reading this as having established a subjective test for duress of circumstances. However, that case did not establish such a test; the case concerned a direction by the trial judge that the defence could only be availed of where the perceived threat was "an actual or real threat". The Court of Appeal held this to be a misdirection, the issue being whether the accused reasonably perceived a threat of serious injury or death. Consequently it is unclear whether *Martin* has amended the first question to dispense with the requirement that D's belief be a reasonable one or whether the test remains as it was but D's mental condition is to be treated as relevant to the question, that is, whether his belief was reasonable or not was to be judged against the reasonable man having that particular condition.

iv. Voluntary association with criminal organisation

R. v. Sharp
[1987] 1 Q.B. 833
Court of Appeal

A was convicted of manslaughter and pleaded guilty to robbery and attempted robbery. He had joined a gang of robbers which carried out a series of armed robberies of sub-post offices. This series culminated in the offence which resulted in the death of the sub-postmaster who was shot by H. A was tried on a count charging murder and submitted that he had acted under duress as he had only taken part in the last robbery because a gun had been pointed at his head by H who threatened to blow it off if he did not participate. The trial judge rejected this submission and A appealed.

Lord Lane C.J.: . . .

No one could question that if a person can avoid the effects of duress by escaping from the threats, without damage to himself, he must do so. In other words if there is a moment at which he is able to escape, so to speak, from the gun being held at his head by Hussey, or the equivalent of Hussey, he must do so. It seems to us to be part of the same argument, or at least to be so close to the same argument as to be practically indistinguishable from it, to say that a man must not voluntarily put himself in a position where he is likely to be subjected to such compulsion.

. . . But we are fortified in the view . . . that this is part of the common law and always has been, by certain matters which appear in the speeches of their Lordships in *D.P.P. for Northern Ireland v. Lynch* [1975] A.C. 653 (*post*, p. 299). Although *Lynch's* case has been the subject of certain adverse comment since the date of those speeches, nevertheless the passages to which we wish to refer have not, as far as we know, been the subject of criticism.

First of all in the speech of Lord Morris of Borth-y-Gest appears this passage, at p. 668:

"Where duress is in issue many questions may arise such as whether threats are serious and compelling or whether (as on the facts of the present case may specially call for consideration) a person the subject of duress could reasonably have extricated himself or could have sought protection or had what has been called a 'safe avenue of escape'. Other questions may arise such as whether a person is only under duress as a result of being in voluntary association with those whom he knew would require some course of action. In the present case, as duress was not left to the jury, we naturally do not know what they thought of it at all."

A little later Lord Morris of Borth-y-Gest again said, at p. 670:

"In posing the case where someone is 'really' threatened I use the word 'really' in order to emphasise that duress must never be allowed to be the easy answer of those who can devise no other explanation of their conduct nor of those who readily could have avoided the dominance of threats nor of those who allow themselves to be at the disposal and under the sway of some gangster-tyrant. Where duress becomes an issue courts and juries will surely consider the facts with care and discernment."

Here, of course, I interpolate, Hussey was the archetypal gangster-tyrant.

I turn from Lord Morris of Borth-y-Gest to the speech of Lord Wilberforce, at p. 679:

"It is clear that a possible case of duress, on the facts, could have been made. I say 'a possible case' because there were a number of matters which the jury would have had to consider if this defence had been left to them. Among these would have been whether Meehan, though uttering no express threats of death or serious injury, impliedly did so in such a way as to put the appellant in fear of death or serious injury; whether, if so, the threats continued to operate throughout the enterprise; whether the appellant had voluntarily exposed himself to a situation in which threats might be used against him if he did not participate in a criminal enterprise (the appellant denied that he had done so); whether the appellant had taken every opportunity open to him to escape from the situation of duress. In order to test the validity of the judge's decision to exclude this defence, we must assume on this appeal that these matters would have been decided in favour of the appellant."

Finally, so far as the passages in favour of the contention which we are supporting are concerned, in the speech of Lord Simon of Glaisdale appears this passage, at p. 687:

"I spoke of the social evils which might be attendant on the recognition of a general defence of duress. Would it not enable a gang leader of notorious violence to confer on his organisation by terrorism immunity from the criminal law? Every member of his gang might well be able to say with truth, 'It was as much as my life was worth to disobey.' Was this not in essence the plea of the appellant? We do not, in general, allow a superior officer to confer such immunity on his subordinates by any defence of obedience to orders: why should we allow it to terrorists? Nor would it seem to be sufficient to stipulate that no one can plead duress as a defence who had put himself into a position in which duress could be exercised on himself."

We draw assistance from the fact that common law jurisdictions as well as Commonwealth jurisdictions throughout the world have adopted this rule almost unanimously (although the wording in their various statutes differs the one from the other), which is an indication to us that this may well have been, and indeed was, throughout a principle of the common law.

His Lordship referred to *R. v. Hurley and Murray* [1967] V.R. 526.

We are therefore, in the light of that persuasive authority and the indications in their Lordships' speeches in *D.P.P. for Northern Ireland v. Lynch* [1975] A.C. 653 of the opinion that the judge, Kenneth Jones J., was correct in the decision which he reached.

We are further fortified in that view by the judgment of Lord Lowry C.J. of Northern Ireland, in *R. v. Fitzpatrick* [1977] N.I. 20. Let me read the brief headnote once again in order to indicate the nature of the decision. It runs as follows:

"If a person by joining an illegal organisation or a similar group of men with criminal objectives and coercive methods, voluntarily exposes and submits himself to illegal compulsion, he cannot rely on the duress to which he has voluntarily exposed himself as an excuse either in respect of the crimes he commits against his will or in respect of his continued but unwilling association with those capable of exercising upon him the duress which he calls in aid."

... In other words, in our judgment, where a person has voluntarily, and with knowledge of its nature, joined a criminal organisation or gang which he knew might bring pressure on him to commit an offence and was an active member when he was put under such pressure, he cannot avail himself of the defence of duress. Mr Mylne concedes that such a ruling is the end of his appeal. The appeal is therefore dismissed.

Appeal dismissed.

Question

Would the joining of a criminal organisation or gang automatically disentitle a defendant from raising duress as a defence or must the organisation or gang be one which he knew used violence to enforce its discipline? See next case.

R. v. Shepherd
(1988) 86 Cr.App.R. 47
Court of Appeal

A was a member of a gang of shoplifters. At his trial on a charge of burglary, he raised the defence of duress claiming he had played a willing part in a previous offence but, when he expressed a desire to give up, had been threatened by P with violence to himself and his family. (While awaiting trial A had been assaulted by P, for which offence P had been given a prison sentence.) The trial judge withdrew the defence of duress from the jury because of A's original voluntary participation in the criminal organisation. A appealed.

MUSTILL L.J.: At the conclusion of the argument we had arrived at the following opinion:

(1) Although it is not easy to rationalise the existence of duress as a defence rather than a ground of mitigation, it must in some way be founded on a concession to human frailty in cases where the defendant has been faced with a choice between two evils.

(2) The exception which exists where the defendant has voluntarily allied himself with the person who exercises the duress must be founded on the assumption that, just as he cannot complain if he had the opportunity to escape the duress and failed to take it, equally no concession to frailty is required if the risk of duress is freely undertaken.

(3) Thus, in some instances it will follow inevitably that the defendant has no excuse: for example, if he has joined a group of people dedicated to violence as a political end, or one which is overtly ready to use violence for other criminal ends. Members of so called paramilitary illegal groups, or gangs of armed robbers, must be taken to anticipate what may happen to them if their nerve fails, and cannot be heard to complain if violence is indeed threatened.

(4) Other cases will be difficult. There is no need for recourse to extravagant examples. Common sense must recognise that there are certain kinds of criminal enterprises the joining of which, in the absence of any knowledge of propensity to violence on the part of one member, would not lead another to suspect that a decision to think better of the whole affair might lead him into serious trouble. The logic which appears to underlie the law of duress would suggest that if trouble did unexpectedly materialise, and if it put the defendant into a dilemma in which a reasonable man might have chosen to act as he did, the concession to human frailty should not be denied to him.

Having arrived at these conclusions on the argument addressed to us, it appeared to us plain there had been a question which should properly have been put to the jury and that the appeal must accordingly be allowed. We intimated that this would be so, whilst taking the opportunity to put our reasons in writing.

Naturally a proper scepticism would have been in order when the defence came to be examined at the trial, for there were many aspects on which the appellant could have been pressed. In particular, his prior knowledge of P would require investigation. At the same time the trial would not have been a foregone conclusion, since the concerted shoplifting enterprise did not involve violence to the victim either in anticipation or in the way it was actually put into effect. The members of the jury have had to ask themselves whether the appellant could be said to have taken the risk of P's violence simply by joining a shoplifting gang of which he was a member. Of course even if they were prepared to give the appellant the benefit of the doubt in this respect, an acquittal would be far from inevitable. The jury would have then to consider the nature and timing of the threats, and the nature and persistence of the offences, in order to decide whether the defendant was entitled to be exonerated. It may well be that, in the light of the evidence as it emerged, convictions would have followed. But the question was never put to the test. The issues were never investigated. The jury were left with no choice but to convict.

In these circumstances we saw no alternative but to hold that the convictions could not stand.

Appeal allowed
Conviction quashed

Notes

1. In *Lewis* (1993) 96 Cr.App.R. 412 the Court of Appeal held that for a defendant to be precluded from relying on duress, there must be a close connection between the coercion and the offence of violence in which he has joined. D, while serving a prison sentence for armed robbery, was attacked by his former accomplice, C. Following his refusal to give evidence against C, D was convicted of contempt of court. The Court of Appeal allowing his appeal held that although the violence and fear of reprisal arose out of D's participation in the robbery, it was not so closely or immediately connected that it could be said he voluntarily exposed himself to the risk of the subsequent violence by agreeing to take part.

2. The crucial issue in each case will be whether D was aware of the risk of compulsion by threats of death or GBH at the time he voluntarily associated with those who ultimately issued those threats against him. His association with them need not necessarily involve "joining" their gang or organisation. In *Baker and Ward* [1999] 2 Cr.App.R. 335, 346 the Court of Appeal held that voluntary association would cover the situation where:

> "the accused, although not joining a gang or organisation, may have involved himself in criminal activities which bring him into contact with other criminals in circumstances where the accused knew or was aware that if he defaulted in fulfilling his role or in discharging his obligations he assumed in relation to the other criminals he would be subjected to such compulsion. Drug dealing on a scale which is significant could be such a case."

See also *Heath* [2000] Crim. L.R. 109.

v. Duress and murder

The question whether duress is available as a defence to a charge of murder has come before the House of Lords or Privy Council on three occasions. The case which follows was the first occasion.

D.P.P. v. Lynch
[1975] A.C. 653
House of Lords

The appellant was the driver of a car which contained members of the IRA in Northern Ireland on an expedition in which they shot and killed a police officer. He said that he was not a member of the IRA and was convinced that he would be shot if he did not obey the leader of the group. The trial judge held that the defence of duress was not available to an aider and abettor of murder. The Court of Criminal Appeal in Northern Ireland dismissed his appeal.

LORD MORRIS OF BORTH-Y-GEST: . . . The issue in the present case is therefore whether there is any reason why the defence of duress, which in respect of a variety of offences has been recognised as a possible defence, may not also be a possible defence on a charge of being a principal in the second degree to murder. I would confine my decision to that issue. It may be that the law must deny such a defence to an actual killer, and that the law will not be irrational if it does so.

Though it is not possible for the law always to be worked out on coldly logical lines there may be manifest factual differences and contrasts between the situation of aider and abettor to a killing and that of the actual killer. Let two situations be supposed. In each let it be supposed that there is a real and effective threat of death. In one a person is required under such duress to drive a car to a place or to carry a gun to a place with knowledge that at such place it is planned that X is to be killed by those who are imposing their will. In the other situation let it be supposed that a person under such duress is told that he himself must there and then kill X. In either situation there is a terrible agonising choice of evils. In the former to save his life the person drives the car or carries the gun. He may cling to the hope that perhaps X will not be found at the place or that there will be a change of intention before the purpose is carried out or that in some unforeseen way the dire event of a killing will be averted. The final and fatal moment of decision has not arrived. He saves his own life at a time when the loss of another life is not a certainty. In the second (if indeed it is a situation likely to arise) the person is told that to save his life he himself must personally there and then take an innocent life. It is for him to pull the trigger or otherwise personally to do the act of killing. There, I think, before allowing duress as a defence it may be that the law will have to call a halt. May there still be force in what long ago was said by Hale?

"Again, if a man be desperately assaulted, and in peril of death, and cannot otherwise escape, unless to satisfy his assailant's fury he will kill an innocent person then present, the fear and actual force will not acquit him of the crime and punishment of murder, if he commit the fact; for he ought rather to die himself, than kill an innocent."

(see *Hale's Pleas of the Crown*, vol. 1, p. 51). Those words have over long periods of time influenced both thought and writing but I think that their application may have been unduly extended when it is assumed that they were intended to cover all cases of accessories and aiders and abettors. . . .

It is most undesirable that, in the administration of our criminal law, cases should arise in which, if there is a prosecution leading to a conviction, a just conclusion will only be attained by an exercise thereafter of the prerogative of granting a pardon. I would regret it, therefore, if upon an application of legal principles such cases could arise. Such principles and such approach as will prevent them from arising would seem to me to be more soundly based. . . .

LORD WILBERFORCE: What reason then can there be for excepting murder? One may say—as some authorities do (*cf. A.-G. v. Whelan* [1934] I.R. 518, 526 *per* Murnaghan J., *R. v. Hurley and Murray* [1967] V.R. 526, 543 *per* Smith J.) that murder is the most heinous of crimes: so it may be, and in some circumstances, a defence of duress in relation to it should be correspondingly hard to establish. Indeed, to justify the deliberate killing by one's own hand of another human being may be something that no pressure or threat even to one's own life which can be imagined can justify—no such case ever seems to have reached the courts. But if one accepts the test of heinousness, this does not, in my opinion, involve that all cases of what is murder in law must be treated in the same way. Heinousness is a word of degree, and that there are lesser degrees of heinousness, even of involvement in homicide, seems beyond doubt. An accessory before the fact, or an aider or abettor, may (not necessarily must) bear a less degree of guilt than the actual killer: and even if the rule of exclusion is absolute, or nearly so in relation to the latter, it need not be so in lesser cases. Nobody would dispute that the greater the degree of heinousness of the crime, the greater and less resistible must be the degree of pressure, if pressure is to excuse. Questions of this kind where it is necessary to weigh the pressures acting upon a man against the gravity of the act he commits are common enough in the criminal law, for example with regard to provocation and self-defence: their difficulty is not a reason for a total rejection of the defence. To say that the defence may be admitted in relation to some degrees of murder, but that its admission in cases of direct killing by a first degree principal is likely to be attended by such great difficulty as almost to justify a ruling that the defence is not available, is not illogical. It simply involves the recognition that by sufficiently adding to the degrees, one may approach an absolute position.

So I find no convincing reason, on principle, why, if a defence of duress in the criminal law exists at all, it should be absolutely excluded in murder charges whatever the nature of the charge; hard to establish, yes, in case of direct killing so hard that perhaps it will never be proved: but in other cases to be judged, strictly indeed, on the totality of facts. Exclusion, if not arbitrary, must be based either on authority or policy. I shall deal with each. . . .

The broad question remains how this House, clearly not bound by any precedent, should now state the law with regard to this defence in relation to the facts of the present case. I have no doubt that it is open to us, on normal judicial principles, to hold the defence admissible. We are here in the domain of the common law: our task is to fit what we can see as principle and authority to the facts before us, and it is no obstacle that these facts are new. The judges have always assumed responsibility for deciding questions of principle relating to criminal liability and guilt, and particularly for setting the standards by which the law expects normal men to act. In all such matters as capacity, sanity, drunkenness, coercion, necessity, provocation, self-defence, the common law, through the judges, accepts and sets the standards of right-thinking men of normal firmness and humanity at a level which people can accept and respect. The House is not inventing a new defence: on the contrary, it would not discharge its judicial duty if it failed to define the law's attitude to this particular defence in particular circumstances. I would decide that the defence is in law admissible in a case of aiding and abetting murder, and so in the present case. I would leave cases of direct killing by a principal in the first degree to be dealt with as they arise.

It is said that such persons as the appellant can always be safeguarded by action of the executive which can order an imprisoned person to be released. I firmly reject any such argument. A law, which requires innocent victims of terrorist threats to be tried for murder and convicted as murderers, is an unjust law even if the executive, resisting political pressures, may decide, after all, and within the permissible limits of the prerogative to release them. Moreover, if the defence is excluded in law, much of the evidence which would prove the duress would be inadmissible at the trial, not brought out in court, and not tested by cross-examination. The validity of the defence is far better judged by a jury, after proper direction and a fair trial, than by executive

officials; and if it is said that to allow the defence will be to encourage ficti-
tious claims of pressure I have enough confidence in our legal system to
believe that the process of law is a better safeguard against this than inquiry
by a government department.

Lord Edmund-Davies agreed that duress was a defence to a principal in the
second degree to murder and also indicated that he might accept the defence
as being available for the principal offender. Lord Simon and Lord Kilbrandon dissented.

Appeal allowed
Retrial Ordered

Abbott v. The Queen
[1977] A.C. 755
Privy Council

The appellant claimed the defence of duress on a charge of murder as
a principal in the first degree. By a majority of three to two the Privy
Council held that the defence was not available to a principal.

Lord Salmon delivered the majority judgment of their Lordships:
Whilst their Lordships feel bound to accept the decision of the House of
Lords in *Lynch's* case they find themselves constrained to say that had they
considered (which they do not) that that decision is an authority which
requires the extension of the doctrine to cover cases like the present they
would not have accepted it. . . .
Counsel for the appellant has argued that the law now presupposes a
degree of heroism of which the ordinary man is incapable and which therefore
should not be expected of him and that modern conditions and concepts of
humanity have rendered obsolete the rule that the actual killer cannot rely on
duress as a defence. Their Lordships do not agree. In the trials of those
responsible for wartime atrocities such as mass killings of men, women or
children, inhuman experiments on human beings, often resulting in death,
and like crimes, it was invariably argued for the defence that these atrocities
should be excused on the ground that they resulted from superior orders and
duress: if the accused had refused to do these dreadful things, they would
have been shot and therefore they should be acquitted and allowed to go free.
This argument has always been universally rejected. Their Lordships would
be sorry indeed to see it accepted by the common law of England.

Lord Wilberforce and Lord Edmund-Davies: dissenting:
The starting point in this appeal must be the decision of the House of Lords
in *D.P.P. for Northern Ireland v. Lynch* [*supra*] which decision was not available
to the trial judge in this case or to the Court of Appeal. This established that
on a murder charge the defence of duress is open to a person accused as a
principal in the second degree. Not only has the actual decision in *Lynch* to
be respected but also its implications, for it was based upon a consideration
in some depth of topics scarcely adverted to by their Lordships in the present
appeal. The question that immediately arises is whether any acceptable distinction can invariably be drawn between a principal in the first degree to
murder and one in the second degree, with the result that the latter may in
certain circumstances be absolved by his plea of duress, while the former may
never even advance such a plea.
The simple fact is that *no* acceptable basis of distinction has even now been
advanced. In *Lynch* Lord Simon of Glaisdale and Lord Kilbrandon who dis-

sented, adverted to the absence of any valid distinction as a ground for holding that duress should be available to *neither....*

Lynch having been decided as it was, the most striking feature of the present appeal is the lack of any indication, in the judgment of the majority *why* a flat declaration that in no circumstances whatsoever may the actual killer be absolved by a plea of duress makes for sounder law and better ethics. In truth, the contrary is the case. For example D attempts to kill P but, though injuring him, fails. When charged with attempted murder he may plead duress (*R. v. Fagan* (unreported), September 20, 1974, and several times referred to in *Lynch*). Later P dies and D is charged with his murder; if the majority of their Lordships are right, he now has no such plea available. Again, no one can doubt that our law would today allow duress to be pleaded in answer to a charge, under section 18 of the Offences Against the Person Act 1861, of wounding with intent. Yet, here again, should the victim die after the conclusion of the first trial, the accused when faced with a murder charge would be bereft of any such defence. It is not the mere lack of logic that troubles one. It is when one stops to consider why duress is *ever* permitted as a defence even to charges of great gravity that the lack of any moral reason justifying its *automatic* exclusion in such cases as the present becomes so baffling and so important.

The majority have deemed it right to resurrect in the present appeal objections to the admissibility of a plea of duress which, if accepted, would leave *Lynch* with only vestigial authority, even though the decisions resulted from their demolition. One example of this is the alleged ease with which bogus pleas of duress can be advanced, and the so-called "charter for terrorists, gang leaders and kidnappers" originally raised by Lord Simon of Glaisdale in *D.P.P. for Northern Ireland v. Lynch* just as though the pleas of duress had merely to be raised for an acquittal automatically to follow. But the realistic view is that, the more dreadful the circumstances of the killing, the heavier the evidential burden of an accused advancing such a plea, and the stronger and more irresistible the duress needed before it could be regarded as affording any defence....

Appeal dismissed

The issue was finally settled in the following case:

R. v. Howe and Others
[1987] 1 A.C. 417
House of Lords

H and B, with C and M, participated in the assault and then killing of two victims. On the first occasion H and B were principals in the second degree. On the second occasion they jointly strangled the victim. On a third occasion the intended victim escaped. At their trial on two counts of murder and one of conspiracy to murder they pleaded duress claiming that they had feared for their own lives if they had not done as M directed. The judge left the defence of duress to the jury in respect of the first murder and the conspiracy charge but not in respect of the second murder. The appellants were convicted on all three counts.

LORD HAILSHAM OF MARYLEBONE L.C.: [The first of the three questions certified by the Court of Appeal is as follows:] "(1) Is duress available as a defence to a person charged with murder as a principal in the first degree (the actual killer)?" ... In my opinion, this must be decided on principle and authority, and the answer must in the end demand a reconsideration of the two authorities of *D.P.P. for Northern Ireland v. Lynch* and *Abbott v. The Queen.* ...

I therefore consider the matter first from the point of view of authority. On this I can only say that at the time when *Lynch* was decided on the balance of weight in an unbroken tradition of authority dating back to Hale and Blackstone seems to have been accepted to have been that duress was not available to a defendant accused of murder. I quote only from Hale and Blackstone. Thus *Hale's Pleas of the Crown* (1736), vol. 1, p. 51:

> "if a man be desperately assaulted, and in peril of death, and cannot otherwise escape, unless to satisfy his assailant's fury he will kill an innocent person then present, the fear and actual force will not acquit him of the crime and punishment of murder, if he commit the fact; for he ought rather to die himself, than kill an innocent: . . ."

Blackstone, Commentaries on the Laws of England (1857 ed.), vol. 4, p. 28 was to the same effect. He wrote that a man under duress: "ought rather to die himself than escape by the murder of an innocent." . . .

Before I leave the question of reported authority I must refer to . . . *R. v. Dudley and Stephens* (*post*, p. 333). That is generally and, in my view correctly, regarded as an authority on the availability of the supposed defence of necessity rather than duress. But I must say frankly that, if we were to allow this appeal, we should, I think, also have to say that *Dudley and Stephens* was bad law. There is, of course, an obvious distinction between duress and necessity as potential defences; duress arises from the wrongful threats of violence of another human being and necessity arises from any other objective dangers threatening the accused. This, however, is, in my view a distinction without a relevant difference, since on this view duress is only that species of the genus of necessity which is caused by wrongful threats. I cannot see that there is any way in which a person of ordinary fortitude can be excused from the one type of pressure on his will rather than the other. . . .

I do not think that the decision in *Lynch* can be justified on authority and that, exercising to the extent necessary, the freedom given to us by the *Practice Statement (Judicial Precedent)* [1966] 1 W.L.R. 1234 which counsel for the respondent urged us to apply, I consider that the right course in the instant appeal is to restore the law to the condition in which it was almost universally thought to be prior to *Lynch*. . . .

This brings me back to the question of principle. I begin by affirming that, while there can never be a direct correspondence between law and morality, an attempt to divorce the two entirely is and has always proved to be, doomed to failure, and, in the present case, the overriding objects of the criminal law must be to protect innocent lives and to set a standard of conduct which ordinary men and women are expected to observe if they are to avoid criminal responsibility. . . .

In general, I must say that I do not at all accept in relation to the defence of murder it is either good morals, good policy or good law to suggest, as did the majority in *Lynch* and the minority in *Abbott* that the ordinary man of reasonable fortitude is not to be supposed to be capable of heroism if he is asked to take an innocent life rather than sacrifice his own. Doubtless in actual practice many will succumb to temptation, as they did in *Dudley and Stephens*. But many will not, and I do not believe that as a "concession to human frailty" the former should be exempt from liability to criminal sanctions if they do. I have known in my own lifetime of too many acts of heroism by ordinary human beings of no more than ordinary fortitude to regard a law as either "just or humane" which withdraws the protection of the criminal law from the innocent victim and casts the cloak of its protection upon the coward and the poltroon in the name of a "concession to human frailty."

I must not, however, underestimate the force of the arguments on the other side, advanced as they have been with such force and such persuasiveness by some of the most eminent legal minds, judicial and academic, in the country.

First, amongst these is, perhaps, the argument from logic and consistency. A long line of cases, it is said, carefully researched and closely analysed, established duress as an available defence in a wide range of crimes, some at least, like wounding with intent to commit grievous bodily harm, carrying the heaviest penalties commensurate with their gravity. To cap this, it is pointed out that at least in theory, a defendant accused of this crime under section 18 of the Offences Against the Person Act 1861, but acquitted on the grounds of duress, will still be liable to a charge of murder if the victim dies within the traditional period of one year and a day. I am not, perhaps, persuaded of this last point as much as I should. It is not simply an anomaly based on the defence of duress. It is a product of the peculiar *mens rea* allowed on a charge of murder which is not confined to an intent to kill. More persuasive, perhaps, is the point based on the availability of the defence of duress on a charge of attempted murder, where the actual intent to kill is an essential prerequisite. It may be that we must meet this casus omissus in your Lordships' House when we come to it. It may require reconsideration of the availability of the defence in that case too.

I would, however, prefer to meet the case of alleged inconsistency head on. Consistency and logic, though inherently desirable, are not always prime characteristics of a penal code based like the common law on custom and precedent. Law so based is not an exact science. All the same, I feel I am required to give some answer to the question posed. If duress is available as a defence to some crimes of the most grave why, it may legitimately be asked, stop at murder, whether as accessory or principal and whether in the second or the first degree? But surely I am entitled to believe that some degree of proportionality between the threat and the offence must, at least to some extent, be a prerequisite of the defence under existing law. Few would resist threats to the life of a loved one if the alternative were driving across the red lights or in excess of 70 m.p.h. on the motorway. But . . . it would take rather more than the threat of a slap on the wrist or even moderate pain or injury to discharge the evidential burden even in the case of a fairly serious assault. In such a case the "concession to human frailty" is no more than to say that in such circumstances a reasonable man of average courage is entitled to embrace as a matter of choice the alternative which a reasonable man would regard as the lesser of two evils. Other considerations necessarily arise where the choice is between the threat of death or *a fortiori* of serious injury and deliberately taking an innocent life. In such a case a reasonable man might reflect that one innocent human life is at least as valuable as his own or that of his loved one. In such a case a man cannot claim that he is choosing the lesser of two evils. Instead he is embracing the cognate but morally disreputable principle that the end justifies the means.

I am not so shocked as some of the judicial opinions have been at the need, if this be the conclusion, to invoke the availability of administrative as distinct from purely judicial remedies for the hardships which might otherwise occur in the most agonising cases. Even in *Dudley and Stephens* in 1884 when the death penalty was mandatory and frequently inflicted, the prerogative was used to reduce a sentence of death by hanging to one of six months in prison. In murder cases the available mechanisms are today both more flexible and more sophisticated. The trial judge may make no minimum recommendation. He will always report to the Home Secretary, as he did in the present case of Clarkson and Burke. The Parole

Board will always consider a case of this kind with a High Court judge brought into consultation. In the background is always the prerogative and, it may not unreasonably be suggested, that is exactly what the prerogative is for. If the law seems to bear harshly in its operation in the case of a mandatory sentence on any particular offender there has never been a period of time when there were more effective means of mitigating its effect than at the present day. . . .

During the course of argument it was suggested that there was available to the House some sort of half way house between allowing these appeals and dismissing them. The argument ran that we might treat duress in murder as analogous to provocation, or perhaps diminished responsibility, and say that, in indictments for murder, duress might reduce the crime to one of manslaughter. I find myself quite unable to accept this. The cases show that duress, if available and made out, entitles the accused to a clean acquittal, without, it has been said, the "stigma" of a conviction. Whatever other merits it may have, at least the suggestion makes nonsense of any pretence of logic or consistency in the criminal law. It is also contrary to principle. Unlike the doctrine of provocation, which is based on emotional loss of control, the defence of duress, as I have already shown, is put forward as a "concession to human frailty" whereby a conscious decision, it may be coolly undertaken, to sacrifice an innocent human life is made as an evil lesser than a wrong which might otherwise be suffered by the accused or his loved ones at the hands of a wrong doer. The defence of diminished responsibility (which might well, had it then been available to *Dudley and Stephens*, have prevailed there) is statutory in England though customary in Scotland, the law of its origin. But in England at least it has a conceptual basis defined in the Homicide Act 1957 which is totally distinct from that of duress if duress be properly analysed and understood. Provocation (unique to murder and not extending even to "section 18" offences) is a concession to human frailty due to the extent that even a reasonable man may, under sufficient provocation temporarily lose his self control towards the person who has provoked him enough. Duress, as I have already pointed out, is a concession to human frailty in that it allows a reasonable man to make a conscious choice between the reality of the immediate threat and what he may reasonably regard as the lesser of two evils. Diminished responsibility as defined in the Homicide Act 1957 depends on abnormality of mind impairing mental responsibility. It may overlap duress or even necessity. But it is not what we are discussing in the instant appeal.

LORD GRIFFITHS: . . .

There are surprisingly few reported decisions on duress but it cannot be gainsaid that the defence has been extended, particularly since the second war, to a number of crimes. I think myself it would have been better had this development not taken place and that duress had been regarded as a factor to be taken into account in mitigation as Stephen suggested in his *History of the Criminal Law of England* (1883) vol. 2, p. 108. However, as Lord Morris of Borth-y-Gest said in *D.P.P. for Northern Ireland v. Lynch* [1975] A.C. 653, 670, it is too late to adopt that view. And the question now is whether that development should be carried a step further and applied to a murderer who is the actual killer, and if the answer to this question is no, whether there is any basis upon which it can be right to draw a distinction between a murderer who did the actual killing and a murderer who played a different part in the design to bring about the death of the victim. . . .

[A]re there any present circumstances that should impel your Lordships to alter the law that has stood for so long and to extend the defence of duress to the actual killer? My Lords, I can think of none. It appears to me that all present indications point in the opposite direction. We face a rising tide of violence and terrorism against which the law must stand firm recognising that its highest duty is to protect the freedom and lives of those that live under it. The sanctity of human life lies at the root of this ideal and I would do nothing to undermine it, be it ever so slight.

On this question your Lordships should, I believe, accord great weight to the opinion of the Lord Chief Justice [Lord Lane in *Graham, ante,* p. 287] ... and the judges who sat with him, and decline to extend the defence to the actual killer. If the defence is not available to the killer what justification can there be for extending it to others who have played their part in the murder. I can, of course, see that as a matter of commonsense one participant in a murder may be considered less morally at fault than another. The youth who hero-worships the gang leader and acts as lookout man whilst the gang enter a jeweller's shop and kill the owner in order to steal is an obvious example. In the eyes of the law they are all guilty of murder, but justice will be served by requiring those who did the killing to serve a longer period in prison before being released on licence than the youth who acted as lookout. However, it is not difficult to give examples where moral fault may be thought to attach to a participant in murder who was not the actual killer; I have already mentioned the example of a contract killing, when the murder would never have taken place if a contract had not been placed to take the life of the victim. Another example would be an intelligent man goading a weakminded individual into a killing he would not otherwise commit.

It is therefore neither rational nor fair to make the defence dependent upon whether the accused is the actual killer or took some other part in the murder. I have toyed with the idea that it might be possible to leave it to the discretion of the trial judge to decide whether the defence should be available to one who was not the killer, but I have rejected this as introducing too great a degree of uncertainty into the availability of the defence. I am not troubled by some of the extreme examples cited in favour of allowing the defence to those who are not the killer such as a woman motorist being highjacked and forced to act as getaway driver, or a pedestrian being forced to give misleading information to the police to protect robbery and murder in a shop. The short, practical answer is that it is inconceivable that such persons would be prosecuted; they would be called as the principal witnesses for the prosecution.

As I can find no fair and certain basis upon which to differentiate between participants to a murder and as I am firmly convinced that the law should not be extended to the killer, I would depart from the decision of this House in *D.P.P. for Northern Ireland v. Lynch* and declare the law to be that duress is not available as a defence to a charge of murder, or to attempted murder. I add attempted murder because it is to be remembered that the prosecution have to prove an even more evil intent to convict of attempted murder than in actual murder. Attempted murder requires proof of an intent to kill, whereas in murder it is sufficient to prove an intent to cause really serious injury.

It cannot be right to allow the defence to one who may be more intent upon taking a life than the murderer. This leaves, of course, the anomaly that duress is available for the offence of wounding with intent but not to murder if the victim dies subsequently. But this flows from the special regard that the law has for human life, it may not be logical but it is real and has to be accepted.

I do not think that your Lordships should adopt the compromise solution of declaring that duress reduces murder to manslaughter. Where the defence of duress is available it is a complete excuse. This solution would put the law back to lines upon which Stephen suggested it should develop by regarding duress as a form of mitigation. English law has rejected this solution and it would be yet another anomaly to introduce it for the crime of murder alone. I would have been more tempted to go down this road if the death penalty had remained for murder. But the sentence for murder although mandatory and expressed as imprisonment for life, is in fact an indefinite sentence, which is kept constantly under review by the parole board and the Home Secretary with the assistance of the Lord Chief Justice and the trial judge. I have confidence that through this machinery the respective culpability of those involved in a murder case can be fairly weighed and reflected in the time they are required to serve in custody.

LORD MACKAY OF CLASHFERN: . . . The first question . . . that arises in this appeal is whether any distinction can be made between this case and the *Lynch* case. . . . While . . . *Lynch* was decided by reasoning which does not extend to the present case, the question remains whether there is a potential distinction between this case and that of *Lynch* by which to determine whether or not the defence of duress should be available. . . .

I have not found any satisfactory formulation of a distinction which would be sufficiently precise to be given practical effect in law and at the same time differentiate between levels of culpability so as to produce a satisfactory demarcation between those accused of murder, who should be entitled to resort to the defence of duress and those who were not.

The House is therefore, in my opinion, faced with the unenviable decision of either departing altogether from the doctrine that duress is not available in murder or of departing from the decision of this House in *Lynch*. While a variety of minor attacks on the reasoning of the majority were mounted by counsel for the Crown in the present case, I do not find any of these sufficiently important to merit departing from *Lynch* on these grounds. I do, however, consider that having regard to the balance of authority on the question of duress as a defence to murder prior to *Lynch*, for this House now to allow the defence of duress generally in response to a charge of murder would be to effect an important and substantial change in the law. In my opinion too, it would involve a departure from the decision in the famous case of *R. v. Dudley and Stephens*. The justification for allowing a defence of duress to a charge of murder is that a defendant should be excused who killed as the only way of avoiding death himself or preventing the death of some close relation such as his own well-loved child. This essentially was the dilemma which Dudley and Stephens faced and in denying their defence the court refused to allow this consideration to be used in a defence to murder. If that refusal was right in the case of Dudley and Stephens it cannot be wrong in the present appeals. Although the result of recognising the defence advanced in that case would be that no crime was committed and in the case with which we are concerned that a murder was committed and a particular individual was not guilty of it (subject to the consideration of the second certified question) that does not distinguish the two cases from the point of view now being considered.

To change the law in the manner suggested by counsel for the appellants in the present case would, in my opinion, introduce uncertainty over a field of considerable importance. . . .

[His Lordship referred to uncertainties in the defence of duress such as, whether a threat of loss of liberty suffices or whether the threatened harm must be to D or extends to his family, which would require further definition, or to any person.]

To say that a defence in respect of which so many questions remain unsettled should be introduced in respect of the whole field of murder is not to promote certainty in the law. . . .

In my opinion, we would not be justified in the present state of the law in introducing for the first time into our law the concept of duress acting to reduce the charge to one of manslaughter even if there were grounds on which it might be right to do so. On that aspect of the matter the Law Commission took the view that where the defence of duress had been made out it would be unjust to stigmatise the person accused with a conviction and there is clearly much force in that view. . . . It seems to me plain that the reason that it was for so long stated by writers of authority that the defence of duress was not available in a charge of murder was because of the supreme importance that the law afforded to the protection of human life and that it seemed repugnant that the law should recognise in any individual in any circumstances, however extreme, the right to choose that one innocent person should be killed rather than another. In my opinion, that is the question which we still must face. Is it right that the law should confer this right in any circumstances, however extreme? While I recognise fully the force of the reasoning which persuaded the majority of this House in *Lynch* to reach the decision to which they came in relation to a person not the actual killer, it does not address directly this question in relation to the actual killer. I am not persuaded that there is good reason to alter the answer which Hale gave to this question. No development of the law or progress in legal thinking which have taken place since his day have, to my mind, demonstrated a reason to change this fundamental answer. In the circumstances which I have narrated of a report to Parliament from the Law Commission concerned *inter alia* with this very question it would seem particularly inappropriate to make such a change now. For these reasons, in my opinion, the first certified question should be answered in the negative.

It follows that, in my opinion, the House should decline to follow the decision in *Lynch*. . . . Up to the present time, the courts have been declining to allow an actual killer to plead the defence of duress while allowing it to a person charged with murder who was not the actual killer as is illustrated in the circumstances of these appeals. Lord Lane C.J. in *R. v. Graham*, illustrated how technical and puzzling in practice the distinction could be. In my opinion, it would not be right to allow this state of affairs to continue. I recognise that this decision leaves certain apparent anomalies in the law but I regard these as consequences of the fact that murder is a result related to crime with a mandatory penalty. Consequently no distinction is made in penalty between the various levels of culpability. Differentiation in treatment once sentence has been pronounced depends upon action by the Crown advised by the executive government although that may be affected by a recommendation which the court is empowered to make. Where a person has taken a minor part in a wounding with intent and is dealt with on that basis he may receive a very short sentence. If sufficiently soon after that conviction the victim dies, on the same facts with the addition of the victim's death caused by the wounding he may be sentenced to life imprisonment. This is simply one illustration of the fact that very different results may follow from a set of facts together with the death of a victim from what would follow the same facts if the victim lived.

[Lord Bridge of Harwich and Lord Brandon of Oakbrook made speeches dismissing the appeal.]

Appeals dismissed

Questions

1. Lord Hailsham, knowing of many acts of heroism by ordinary people, concluded that a law which protected the "coward and the poltroon" could not be regarded as either "just or humane". Is there a general duty in the criminal law to be a hero? Against what standard is a defendant usually judged? (See self-defence, *post*, p. 343, provocation, *post*, p. 531, and *Miller, ante*, p. 37) Does Lord Hailsham provide any clear refutation of the statement by Wechsler and Michael in "A rationale of the law of homicide" (1937) 37 Col.L.R. 738, that "when a third person's life is also at stake even the path of heroism is obscure"?

2. Lord Griffiths stated "I would do nothing to undermine [the sanctity of human life], be it ever so slight." Does the criminal law unequivocally protect this ideal? (See self-defence, mistake and provocation.)

3. Lord Griffiths supported the view of Lord Lane C.J. in the Court of Appeal that the defence should not be afforded to a murderer as the "defence of duress is so easy to raise and may be so difficult for the prosecution to disprove." If this is the case, does not the same criticism apply to all defences? Is Lord Griffiths' view reconcilable with Lord Hailsham's view that "juries have been commendably robust" in rejecting the defence where appropriate (which they did in the case before their Lordships)? Bearing in mind their Lordships' approval of Lord Lane's statement of the test for duress in *Graham*, whereby the defendant will be judged against the standard of the "sober person of reasonable firmness sharing the defendant's characteristics," is it any more likely that the unmeritorious defendant would succeed on a defence of duress where the charge is one of murder as opposed to theft or wounding or any other offence?

4. Lords Hailsham and MacKay placed considerable emphasis on the precedent of *Dudley and Stephens, post*, p. 333, in dictating the result of the instant appeals. Is it true, as Lord Hailsham asserted, that that case has met with "very wide acceptance"? Is the defence of necessity wholly analogous to duress? Is necessity based on excuse or justification? Is it available for all offences (except murder)?

5. Lords Hailsham, Griffiths and MacKay placed considerable emphasis on the writers of the past (all of whom could be traced back to Hale) who stated that duress was not available as a defence to a charge of murder. Was this approach to be commended in light of the counsel of Lords Wilberforce and Edmund-Davies in *Abbott* at 771, where they stated:

> "Great stress has been laid by the majority of their Lordships upon the apparent unanimity with which great writers of the past have rejected duress as a defence, but, on any view, they have to be read with circumspection in these days, for the criminal courts have long accepted duress as an available defence to a large number of crimes from which those same writers withheld it."?

6. Lord Bridge stated that it is "by legislation alone ... that the scope of the defence of duress can be defined with the degree of precision which, if it is to be available in murder at all, must surely be of

critical importance". Lord MacKay also believed the defence was too uncertain for it to be extended to cover an actual killer. As duress is a common law defence (like self-defence and provocation) how did it develop in the first place? If duress is uncertain, is it not also uncertain in relation to other offences? What role do their Lordships envisage for judges if it is not to develop and clarify the common law? Is it arguable, as Milgate states in "Duress and the criminal law: another about turn by the House of Lords" (1988) 47 C.L.J. 61, that *Howe* is "a major piece of judicial legislation, based on an apparently cursory examination of principle and policy"?

7. Lord MacKay, having rejected the idea that, in relation to a murder charge, duress should operate like the defence of provocation and reduce the charge to one of manslaughter, sought to support his view by quoting from Law Com. No. 83 that "where the defence of duress had been made out it would be unjust to stigmatise the person accused with a conviction". Is Lord MacKay's reasoning convincing in light of the decision in *Howe* and the proposals of the Law Commission (see *post*, p. 317)?

8. Lords Hailsham and Griffiths expressed the view that the issue of duress in murder would best be dealt with by the Executive through the agency of the Parole Board or Royal Pardon. Do you agree in light of Lord Wilberforce's judgment in *Lynch*, *ante*, p. 299?

9. Lord Griffiths was of the opinion that duress should not be available on a charge of attempted murder. Would duress also need to be removed as a potential defence to charges under section 18 of the Offences Against the Person Act 1861? What would happen if, after an acquittal following a defence of duress on a charge under section 18, the victim died from the injuries inflicted by D?

Note

The decision in *Howe* left unresolved the question whether duress was a defence to attempted murder. This question arose for decision in the following case.

R. v. Gotts
[1992] 2 W.L.R. 284
House of Lords

A, aged sixteen, was threatened with death by his father unless he killed his mother who had fled the matrimonial home. A followed his mother and stabbed her in the street but was restrained by bystanders so that, although she sustained serious injuries, she did not die. A pleaded duress on a charge of attempted murder. The trial judge ruled that duress was not available on a charge of attempted murder whereupon A pleaded guilty and an order of three years probation was made against him. The Court of Appeal dismissed A's appeal against his conviction.

LORD JAUNCEY OF TULLICHETTLE (with whom Lords Templeman and Browne-Wilkinson agreed):
[His Lordship, having referred to *Hale's Pleas of the Crown* (1736),

Blackstone, *Commentaries on the Laws of England* (1776), Stephen, *History of the Criminal Law of England* (1883) and Kenny, *Outlines of Criminal Law* (13th ed., 1929) concluded:]

My Lords, there is nothing in the writings to which I have referred which leads me to conclude that at common law duress is or is not a defence to attempted murder. In arriving at this conclusion or lack of it I am fortified by the fact that Lord Lane C.J. [1991] 1 Q.B. 660, 667 came to a similar view where he said:

> "In these circumstances we are not constrained by a common law rule or by authority from considering whether the defence of duress does or does not extend to the offence of attempted murder." . . .

[His Lordship referred to *Lynch*, *Abbott* and *Howe* and concluded that these cases did not decide the question whether duress is available on a charge of attempted murder.]

As the question is still open for decision by your Lordships it becomes a matter of policy how it should be answered. It is interesting to note that there is no uniformity of practice in other common law countries. The industry of Mr Miskin who appeared with Mr Farrer disclosed that in Queensland, Tasmania, Western Australia, New Zealand and Canada duress is not available as a defence to attempted murder but that it is available in almost all of the states of the United States of America. The reason why duress has for so long been stated not to be available as a defence to a murder charge is that the law regards the sanctity of human life and the protection thereof as of paramount importance. Does that reason apply to attempted murder as well as to murder? As Lord Griffiths pointed out in [*Howe*, at p. 303] an attempt to kill must be proved in the case of attempted murder but not necessarily in the case of murder. Is there logic in affording the defence to one who intends to kill but fails and denying it to one who mistakenly kills intending only to injure? If I may give two examples:

(1a) A stabs B in the chest intending to kill him and leaves him for dead. By good luck B is found whilst still alive and rushed to hospital where surgical skill saves his life.

(1b) C stabs D intending only to injure him and inflicts a near identical wound. Unfortunately D is not found until it is too late to save his life.

I see no justification or logic or morality for affording a defence of duress to A who intended to kill when it is denied to C who did not so intend.

(2a) E plants in a passenger aircraft a bomb timed to go off in midflight. Owing to bungling it explodes while the aircraft is still on the ground with the result that some 200 passengers suffer physical and mental injuries of which many are permanently disabling, but no one is killed.

(2b) F plants a bomb in a light aircraft intending to injure the pilot before it takes off but in fact it goes off in mid-air killing the pilot who is the sole occupant of the airplane.

It would in my view be both offensive to common sense and decency that E if he established duress should be acquitted and walk free without a stain on his character notwithstanding the appalling results which he has achieved, whereas F who never intended to kill should, if convicted in the absence of the defence, be sentenced to life imprisonment as a murderer.

It is of course true that withholding the defence in any circumstances will create some anomalies but I would agree with Lord Griffiths (*Reg. v. Howe* [1987] A.C. 417, 444A) that nothing should be done to undermine in any way the highest duty of the law to protect the freedom and lives of those that live under it. I can therefore see no justification in logic, morality or law in affording to an attempted murderer the defence which is withheld from a murderer. The intent required of an attempted murderer is more evil than that required of a murderer and the line which divides the two offences is seldom, if ever, of the deliberate making of the criminal. A man shooting to kill but missing a vital organ by a hair's breadth can justify his action no more than can the man who hits that organ. It is pure chance that the attempted murderer is not a murderer and I entirely agree with what Lord Lane C.J. [1991] 1 Q.B. 660, 667 said: that the fact that the attempt failed to kill should not make any difference.

For the foregoing reasons I have no doubt that the Court of Appeal reached the correct conclusion and that the appeal should be dismissed.

LORD LOWRY: (with whom Lord Keith of Kinkel agreed): . . . The basic proposition for the appellant is that at common law duress has always been a defence for those charged with every crime except murder, most forms of treason and possibly (for a short time) robbery and that to add attempted murder to the exceptions would not be justified. The trial judge, whose words I have cited earlier, may seem to have adopted the first part of this proposition but not the second. The answer by the Crown I suggest, has to be that attempted murder *is* at common law an exception to the general rule and was an exception at the time when the appellant tried to kill his mother. . . .

The foundation of the Crown's argument is that, accepting the sanctity of human life as the basis for denying the defence of duress in murder, both logic and morality demand that that defence must be withheld from one who tried (albeit unsuccessfully), and therefore *intended*, to kill, when one considers that in murder the defence is withheld not only from the deliberate killer but also from the killer who intended only to inflict very serious injury and from all principals in the second degree, whatever their mens rea. . . .

I sympathise with the proposition that attempted murder should be recognised as an exempted crime. But from the point of view of deterrence this idea holds no special attraction. If one makes the somewhat artificial assumption (without which the principle of deterrence has no meaning) that a potential offender will know when the defence of duress is not available, one then has to realise that, whatever the law may be about *attempted* murder, one who sets out to kill under threat will be guilty of murder if he succeeds. Therefore the deterrent is in theory operative already. The moral position, too, is clouded, because *Director of Public Prosecutions for Northern Ireland v. Lynch* [1975] A.C. 653, in this respect alone affirming the majority opinion of the Court of Criminal Appeal in Northern Ireland, affirmed that the offender, even when acting under duress, intends to commit the crime (of murder, not attempted murder). But his guilty intent is of a special kind: "coactus voluit," as the Latin phrase has it. Thus the denial of the duress defence, based on moral principles, is not straightforward. It may not be just a case of the law saying: "Although you did not succeed, you intended to kill. Therefore you cannot rely on duress." The law might equally well say: "As with other offenders who allege duress, your guilty intent was caused by threats. Therefore, since the intended victim did not die, you, like other offenders, can rely on those threats as a defence. If the victim had died in circumstances amounting to murder or if treason had been the crime, it would of course have been different." This emphasises the point that murder is a result-related crime.

The choice is between the two views propounded by Lord Lane C.J. [1991] 1 Q.B. 660, 664F-G and 667B: (1) *if* the common law recognised that murder and treason were the only excepted crimes, then we are bound to accept that as the law, whether it seems a desirable conclusion or not; the fact that there is no binding decision on the point does not weaken a rule of the common law which has stood the test of time; or (2) we are not constrained by a common law rule or by authority from considering whether the defence of duress does or does not extend to the offence of attempted murder.

I consider that the view to be preferred is that which is contained in the first of these propositions and that to adopt the second would result in an unjustified judicial change in the law. It is only with diffidence that I would express an opinion on the criminal law which conflicts with that of such highly respected authorities as the present Lord Chief Justice and my noble and learned friend, Lord Griffiths, but on this occasion I feel obliged to do so. I proceed to give my reasons for this conclusion.

Both judges and textwriters have pointed out that the law on the subject is vague and uncertain. . . . But, in my opinion, this vagueness ought not to encourage innovation which makes a departure from the received wisdom even if that wisdom is imperfect. This is particularly true if the innovation is retrospective in effect, to the prejudice of an accused person. . . .

To withhold in respect of *every* crime the defence of duress, leaving it to the court (or, in relation to fixed penalty crimes, the executive) to take mitigating circumstances into account, seems logical. But to withhold that defence only from a selected list of serious crimes (some of which incur variable penalties) is questionable from a sentencing point of view, as indeed the sentence in the present case shows. The defence is withheld on the ground that the crime is so odious that it must not be palliated; and yet, if circumstances are allowed to mitigate the punishment, the principle on which the defence of duress is withheld has been defeated.

The fact that the sentence for attempted murder is at large is, with respect to those who think otherwise, no justification for withholding the defence of duress. Quite the reverse, because it is the theoretical inexcusability of murder and treason which causes those crimes (the fixed penalty for which can be mitigated only by the executive) to be deprived of the duress defence. . . .

Having referred in the Court of Appeal's judgment [1991] 1 Q.B. 660 to the wise observations of Lord Griffiths in *R. v. Howe* [1987] A.C. 417 on the undesirability of making available the defence of duress to any person who has deliberately killed, Lord Lane C.J. said [1991] 1 Q.B. 660, 667: "It seems to us that if those considerations are well founded, the fact that the attempt failed to kill *should* not make any difference." (Emphasis supplied.) But in my submission everything except the turpitude of attempted murder points away from saying that that offence is already at common law outside the ambit of the duress defence. And I further suggest that actual wickedness is not shown to be a dominant factor in the calculation compared with the result.

As I have said, your Lordships are concerned to say what the law is and not what it ought to be. So far from clearing the way for judges to declare that attempted murder is an excepted crime, the uncertainty and vagueness surrounding duress ought to induce caution before deciding to reject the received wisdom on the subject. What we can be clear about is that the common law regards duress as *generally available* but not available in cases of murder and treason, and the statutory codes treat duress as generally available except as expressly mentioned. . . .

If the common law has had a policy towards duress heretofore, it seems to have been to go by the result and not primarily by the intent and, if a change of policy is needed with regard to criminal liability, it must be made prospectively by Parliament and not retrospectively by a court.

I am not influenced in favour of the appellant by the supposed illogicality of distinguishing between attempted murder on the one hand and conspiracy and incitement to murder on the other and I agree on this point with the view of Lord Lane C.J.: short of murder itself, attempted murder is a special crime. But I am not swayed in favour of the Crown by the various examples of the anomalies which are said to result from holding that the duress defence applies to attempted murder. As Lord Lane C.J. said, at p. 668B, it would be possible to suggest anomalies wherever the line is drawn. The real logic would be to grant or withhold the duress defence universally.

Attempted murder, however heinous we consider it, was a misdemeanour. Until 1861 someone who shot and missed could suffer no more than two years' imprisonment and I submit that, when attempted murder became a felony, that crime, like many other serious felonies, continued to have available the defence of duress.

My Lords, having considered all the arguments on either side, I am of the opinion that your Lordships *are* constrained by a common law rule (though not by judicial authority) from holding that the defence of duress does not apply to attempted murder. Accordingly, I would allow the appeal, quash the conviction and set aside the probation order but, in the special circumstances of this case, I would not propose that a new trial be ordered.

Appeal dismissed

Questions

1. Was the decision of the majority one of principle or policy?
2. J. Raz in "The rule of law and its virtue'" (1977) 93 *L.Q.R.* 195, 198–199 states:

"*All laws should be prospective, open and clear.* One cannot be guided by a retroactive law. It does not exist at the time of action. . . . The law must be open and adequately publicised. If it is to guide people they must be able to find out what it is. For the same reason its meaning must be clear. An ambiguous, vague, obscure or imprecise law is likely to mislead or confuse at least some of those who desire to be guided by it."

Were these principles observed by the majority in *Gotts*? If someone seeking to know the law in advance of action inquired whether duress is a defence to the offences of wounding with intent contrary to section 18 of the Offences Against the Person Act 1861, or incitement to kill or conspiracy to murder, would it be possible to provide a clear answer?
3. Lord Keith of Kinkel stated at pp. 285–286:

"The principal argument against allowing the defence of duress to a charge of attempted murder appears to be what is said to be the illogicality of denying the defence to one who has killed while intending only to wound with intent to inflict grievous bodily harm, while admitting it in the case of one who has intended to kill but chanced to fail to do so. Considering that the intent is more evil in the latter case than in the former, so it is claimed, the person who has intended to kill but failed should not be treated more leniently. But I find it difficult to accept that a person acting under duress had a truly evil intent. He does not actually desire the death of the victim. In the case of a man who is compelled by threats against his wife and children to drive a vehicle loaded with explosives into a checkpoint, the object being to kill those manning it, but that object having fortunately failed, the driver is likely to be as relieved at the outcome as anyone else. It would be hard to condemn him as having had an evil intent. The logical solution may be to withhold the defence in the case of all crimes, leaving the circumstances of the duress to be taken into account in mitigation. But that solution is not open to the court in the present state of the law. It could only be brought about by Parliament.''

Is it likely that the argument in future may move to the meaning of intent with an accused charged with attempted murder who seeks to plead duress relying on authorities such as *Steane* [1947] K.B. 997 (*ante*, p. 90) and *Gillick v. West Norfolk and Wisbech Area Health Authority* [1986] A.C. 112 (*post* p. 000)? See the extract from his commentary on *Howe* by J.C. Smith which follows.

J.C. Smith, Commentary [1987] Crim.L.R. 483–484

. . . *Duress and intent* Lord Hailsham agreed with the opinions of Lords Kilbrandon and Edmund-Davies in *Lynch* that duress does not negative intention. Where the defence of duress is allowed, this is notwithstanding the fact that the defendant intended to commit the crime. It is submitted that this is right—but it is surely inconsistent with *Steane* [1947] K.B. 997, recently accepted as rightly decided by the House in *Moloney* [1985] A.C. 905. Steane, of course, knew that he was doing an act of assistance to the enemy war effort but was held not to intend to assist the enemy because his purpose was to avert the threat of the concentration camp to himself and his family. If that negatived intention, so surely does a purpose of saving one's own life. The present case suggests that *Steane* would have been more properly acquitted on the ground that he acted with intent to assist the enemy under duress. Unfortunately, however, it is likely to continue to bedevil discussion of the meaning of intention.

There is a similar problem with *Gillick's* case [1986] A.C. 112 and the matter of the *mens rea* of an aider and abettor of crime. The reason why a doctor who gives contraceptive advice to a girl under the age of 16 is not guilty of aiding and abetting the commission of an offence under section 6 of the Sexual Offences Act 1956 is nowhere clearly spelt out in the speeches of the majority, but one view for which there is considerable support is that he lacks the necessary intent. But if it is said that the hypothetical doctor, doing an act which he knows will promote, encourage or facilitate the commission of an offence, is not guilty because his real intention is to protect the girl, how can it be said that a person intends to aid and abet murder when his real object is to save himself or others from death? If that object does not negative intention to aid and abet, surely, *a fortiori*, the object of protecting the girl cannot do so.

vi. Proposals for Reform

Draft Criminal Law Bill (Law Com. No. 218)

DURESS

25.—(1) No act of a person constitutes an offence if the act is done under duress by threats.

(2) A person does an act under duress by threats if he does it because he knows or believes—

(a) that a threat has been made to cause death or serious injury to himself or another if the act is not done, and
(b) that the threat will be carried out immediately if he does not do the act or, if not immediately, before he or that other can obtain effective official protection, and
(c) that there is no other way of preventing the threat being carried out,

and the threat is one which in all the circumstances (including any of his personal characteristics that affect its gravity) he cannot reasonably be expected to resist.
It is for the defendant to show that the reason for his act was such knowledge or belief as is mentioned in paragraphs (a) to (c).

(3) This section applies in relation to omissions as it applies in relation to acts.

(4) This section does not apply to a person who knowingly and without reasonable excuse exposed himself to the risk of the threat made or believed to have been made.
If the question arises whether a person knowingly and without reasonable excuse exposed himself to such a risk, it is for him to show that he did not.

Legislating the Criminal Code: Offences Against The Person And General Principles, Law Com. No. 218

The proposed defence

The threat
29.1 As we said at paragraph 18.5 of LCCP 122, the overwhelming tendency of the authorities as of modern codes, is to limit the defence to cases where death or serious injury is threatened. . . . Consultation strongly supported that limitation on the defence of duress, which is imposed by clause 25(2)(a) of the Criminal Law Bill.

The person threatened
29.2 There was very limited support for any formal limitation of the defence to cases in which the threat is to a limited class of person, such as the defendant's close relatives. We adhere to the view that the relevance of the closeness or otherwise of the relationship between the defendant and the person threatened is more appropriately catered for within the general test imposed by clause 25(2) of the Criminal Law Bill of whether "the threat is one which in all the circumstances (including any of his personal characteristics that affect its gravity) he cannot reasonably be expected to resist".

The possibility of official protection
29.3 The threat must be, or the defendant must believe that it is, one that will be carried out immediately, or before he (or the person under threat) can obtain official protection: Criminal Law Bill, clause 25(2)(b). This provision, by allowing the defence if the defendant believes that official protection will be ineffective, differs from previous treatments of the point.

29.4 Clause 26(3) of the Bill accompanying LCCP 122 provided that it would be immaterial that, in fact or as the actor believed, any available official protection would, or might be, ineffective. As we explained at paragraph 18.7 of LCCP 122, this gave effect to the policy of the Commission's 1977 report, in which the Commission said:

" . . . [T]o leave to the jury the question of whether the defendant believed that the protection would be effective, which in itself would involve some consideration of whether the protection would be effective, would be unsatisfactory, both because of the width of the questions and because of the scope for misuse of the defence . . ."

29.5 This approach was supported by the South-Eastern Circuit (Southwark) Scrutiny Group in its comments on the first Draft Code Bill. But we noted that it had been seriously questioned on the ground of inconsistency with the rationale of the defence . . .

Similarly, the Code team had represented to us that a person's belief that he cannot be protected "is surely relevant to the effect of the threat on his freedom of action [and cannot] properly be ignored as one of the circumstances in the light of which the question whether he could reasonably be expected to resist the threat is to be answered".

29.6 The substantial balance of opinion on consultation agreed with the doubts to which we have just referred. On careful re-examination, we are quite persuaded that no such provision as clause 26(3) should be retained. We would regard it as wholly unsatisfactory if a defendant who in every other respect qualified for the defence were to have it withheld because *ineffective* official protection was available, or because he or she had acted on the basis of an honest belief that such protection would be ineffective. The case of a wife committing perjury because subjected to duress by her husband, cited by one respondent in the context of *Hudson* [*ante*, p. 276], is an obvious example of a case in which theoretical but not actual official protection might be available.

29.7 We have therefore removed clause 26(3) as inconsistent with the general approach of the rest of the defence, which has as its guiding principle the reasonable reaction of the defendant in the circumstances as he or she believed them to be. Clause 25(2)(b) of the Criminal Law Bill puts the matter beyond doubt by its reference to "effective" official protection.

The actor's view of the facts

29.8 The emphasis in clause 26(2)(a) of the Bill accompanying LCCP 122 on the actor's *knowledge or belief* that a threat has been made reflected this latter aspect of the defence of duress. The actor is excused because he acted under the pressure of a threat. It is plainly not enough that a threat has been made, for example, to kill his child: he must know that it has been made. But the defence ought therefore equally to be available if the actor mistakenly believes the facts to be such that, were his belief correct, he would have the defence. That aspect of the defence has, however, been a matter of some controversy.

29.9 In *Graham* Lord Lane CJ, on behalf of the Court of Appeal, required a mistaken belief that a person was being threatened to be "reasonable", so that the defendant had "good cause" to fear the supposedly threatened harm. The view to the contrary, which informed the Draft Code and the Bill accompanying LCCP 122, is that the reasonableness or otherwise of a person's asserted belief belongs to the domain of evidence. . . .

29.10 On consultation, there was almost no support for the view that the defendant's belief must be reasonable, and many respondents thought that, in accordance with other areas of the modern law, reasonableness should be a matter of evidence only. We therefore adhere to the view expressed in LCCP 122, as set out in paragraph 29.8 above, and clause 25(2)(a) of the Criminal Law Bill reflects that view.

Is the threat one which the actor should resist?

29.11 Under present law, a threat of death or serious injury excuses the actor whose resistance it overcomes only if the threat might have overcome the resistance of "a sober person of reasonable firmness, sharing the characteristics of the [actor]". The actor is required to have "the steadfastness reasonably to be expected of the ordinary citizen in his situation".... In LCCP 122 we continued to think, however, that the test should simply be whether in all the circumstances the person in question could reasonably be expected to have resisted the threat. We assumed that a person could not under this test rely upon his insobriety as a relevant circumstance; but at the same time, we were not convinced that a person's "characteristics" can be distinguished in the way that the *Graham* test appears to contemplate. Relative timidity, for example, may be an inseparable aspect of a total personality that is in turn part cause and part product of its possessor's life situation; and thus may itself be one of the "circumstances" in the light of which the pressure represented by the duress is to be assessed.

29.14 On consultation, there was strong support for our view that the defence should apply where *the particular defendant in question* could not reasonably have been expected to resist the threat. We do not accept the contrary view, for which there was very little support, that the defence should be withheld from the "objectively weak". First, such an approach would be ineffectual as a means of law enforcement. If a person is in a condition that makes it unreasonable to expect him to resist, then he will not resist, and the fact that a different person in those circumstances might have resisted will not affect the matter. Second, the purpose of the defence is not to enforce unrealistically high standards of behaviour. Rather, the defence acknowledges that where the defendant could not reasonably have been expected to act otherwise he should not be convicted of a crime. Our view on this question therefore remains unchanged, as does the formulation now to be found in the closing words of clause 25(2) of the Criminal Law Bill.

Application of the defence to murder

The consultation

30.8 Of those commentators who addressed the issue, the majority were in favour of the extension of the defence to murder, but there were a significant number who in doing so expressed some reservation....

The arguments of principle and the practical considerations

30.10 The moral argument against extending duress to murder remains that it cannot be right for the State to excuse deliberate killing even where the will of the defendant is overborne by the threat of death or serious injury to himself or another.... Rather than allow duress (or necessity) to excuse the taking of life, the law should "set a standard of conduct which ordinary men and women are expected to observe": a standard, if necessary, of heroism and self-sacrifice, of which ordinary people are capable. . . .

30.11 Powerful though that argument may appear to be, and deeply felt as it clearly is by a minority of those who responded to our consultation, we cannot adopt it. In our view, it is not only futile, but also wrong, for the *criminal* law to demand heroic behaviour. The attainment of a heroic standard of behaviour will always count for great merit; but failure to achieve that standard should not be met with punishment by the State. . . .

30.13 [W]e also respectfully agree with Lord Lowry's observation in *Gotts* that, since the defence of duress could arise in a case where the defendant was seeking to avoid the implementation of threats to third parties, the simple moral equation assumed by treating a defendant as one who kills to save his own life does not necessarily apply.

30.14 To the other arguments of principle for extending the defence of duress to murder, we would certainly add our rejection of the view that the absence of that defence can be sufficiently mitigated by exercise of executive discretion. We remain of the view that reliance on executive discretion is not adequate in principle or in practice. Even if the prosecutor knows of a plea of duress, he may not be able, or think it proper, to judge its merits; and, apart from any other considerations, those responsible for considering a prisoner's release would have to judge his claim to have been coerced without the benefit of a proper trial of the issue.

30.15 The essence of the practical concern felt by those who oppose extension of the defence to murder was expressed by Lord Lane CJ in *Howe* and was strongly influential in the House of Lords in that case: duress is a defence most likely to arise in terrorist, gang or other organised crime offences and, particularly in such circumstances, "the defence of duress is so easy to raise and may be so difficult for the prosecution to disprove beyond reasonable doubt, the facts of necessity being as a rule known only to the defendant himself".

30.16 We feel the force of that concern, and did not lightly adopt the reply to it in LCCP 122 that the defence is not available to a member of a criminal or terrorist group; that the innocent tools of terrorists, on the other hand, should be excused if they could not have been expected to act otherwise; that such defendants should not be denied the right to raise a true defence because others may claim it falsely; and that the question whether the defendant was a terrorist or an innocent tool is a proper question for the jury and for the application of the normal burden of proof. On careful reconsideration, however, we think it important to separate within this reply the principle that the innocent should not be denied a true defence because others may abuse it from the view that the defendant should not bear the burden of proof. To the former principle we adhere. As to the latter question, we have already indicated our recognition that it is in the context of the extension of the defence to murder that the issue of burden of proof is most pressing. . . .

The burden of proving duress

33.1 We have explained above our view that the concerns about the operation of the defence of duress expressed by Lord Lane CJ in the Court of Appeal in *Howe*, and repeated by the House of Lords in that case and in *Gotts*, cannot justly or effectively be met by withholding duress as a defence to murder, or by reducing it, either in relation to that offence or more widely, to a mere ground for mitigation of sentence. In this section we explain why we now believe that those considerations would be met most appropriately and directly by placing on the defendant the persuasive burden of proving the defence.

33.2 Although we provisionally adopted the contrary view in LCCP 122, we noted the response to that paper from some members of the judiciary that the burden of proof ought to be reversed, or that, if the burden were reversed, they might find it easier to support the extension of the defence to murder. . . .

33.3 Once we had reached the provisional view that the burden of proof should be reversed, we decided to conduct a further special consultation on that issue. In response there was strong support for that provisional conclusion, especially among the judiciary and practitioners. . . .

33.5 It is no light matter to propose that the defendant bear the persuasive burden of proof, and that, moreover, not only in the case of murder, but in relation to all other offences, to which duress is already a complete defence, with the burden now resting on the prosecution to disprove it beyond reasonable doubt. Certainly we would not be recommending the change if we thought it might appear to undermine the important general rule that the prosecution must prove its case. On the contrary, we see the arguments for the change in the case of duress as wholly exceptional, depending on factors unique to that defence which distinguish it from all others.

33.6 In our view, duress is a defence like no other in that, at the lowest, it is much more likely than any other defence to depend on assertions which are peculiarly difficult for the prosecution to investigate or subsequently to disprove. By contrast, for example, self-defence, and all the cases included in the wider defence contemplated by clause 27 of the Criminal Law Bill, depend on the immediate circumstances in which the defendant commits (what would otherwise be) the offence. In self-defence, he acts to protect himself from unlawful force; in other applications of the clause 27 defence, he acts to terminate the commission of crime, or interference with property. In all those cases, the evidence of circumstances founding the defence is part and parcel of the incident during which the offence is committed; and it is therefore reasonable to expect the prosecution, who have to prove the offence, also to disprove the existence of circumstances on which the defence might be founded.

33.7 By contrast, in the case of duress by threats the circumstances on which the defence is founded will characteristically have occurred well before, and quite separately from, the actual commission of the offence that the prosecution will know about and must prove. Thus, the threats from A, his cell-mate, that cause B to give perjured evidence; or the coercion exercised on the defendant to make him join the bank robbery; take place far away from the actual commission of the crime, and may well involve no one who is involved in the commission of that crime. That is quite different from a case of self-defence, where the person on whose conduct the alleged defence is founded will (unless of course he is dead) almost certainly already be a leading witness for the prosecution.

The practical effect of reversing the burden
33.10 First, the effect of altering the burden of proof would be to enable the court to concentrate more directly on the plausibility of the defendant's story. To place the burden, on the balance of probabilities, on the

defendant would not mean that a claim by him or her of having been threatened would simply be rejected if there were no separate supporting evidence: that is important because the defendant might find it just as difficult as the prosecution to bring into court the person responsible for the threat as a witness to the truth. Rather, the court would have to decide on all the evidence whether it was more likely than not that what the defendant claimed had in fact occurred. That seems a much more reasonable exercise than to provide that in such a case the prosecution must *dis*prove the unilateral claims of the defendant. . . .

33.11 Second, a shifting of the burden will be of particular importance in giving real effect to clause 25(4) of the Criminal Law Bill, which withholds the defence from one (conspicuously, a member of a criminal gang) who has without reasonable excuse exposed himself to the risk of duress. . . .

Mere denial by a defendant of having voluntarily joined the gang, or mere assertion of coercion to join, perhaps many years ago, are conspicuously difficult to disprove, especially where the criminal standard of proof has to be applied; whereas, if the burden were on the accused, it would simply be a question of whether his explanation was more likely than not.

33.12 We have considered in this connection the suggestion in response to LCCP 122 that the members of a criminal gang might well be capable, not only individually, but in collusion, of concocting a false defence of duress. In such a case, if the burden of proof rested on the defence, proper account could be taken of the fact that others who could have supported the defendant's allegations had not done so. By this we do not mean that a defence case will necessarily, or usually, fail if it is not supported, but only that lack of evidence from other gang members can be given due weight; whereas, if the burden of disproof of the defence is on the prosecution, failure to adduce evidence in support of the defendant's case, even from his co-accused, may not be given proper significance.

J. Horder, "Occupying the Moral High Ground? The Law Commission on Duress" [1994] Crim.L.R. 334, 340–342

One frequent objection to the common law's objectivism in the shaping of defences like duress is that if one requires beliefs to have reasonable grounds, one risks convicting defendants of serious crimes purely because they have been negligent. There is far less in this objection than meets the eye. Defendants who fail in a plea of duress are convicted because they have unlawfully and (*ex hypothesi*) deliberately harmed others or committed some other crime. The question of the circumstances, if any, in which they should be granted an excuse for their unlawful conduct is a collateral but separate issue, in which a consideration of negligence may properly play a role even if the crime for which the defendant falls to be convicted is one of specific intent. In spite of this, the Commission's reforms are a sell-out to subjectivism (see esp. para. 29).

The rot sets in with the Commission's understanding of the excusatory basis of duress. This is said to be that the 'duressee', 'has been in effect compelled to act as he does by the pressure of a . . . threat to which he himself is subject' (para. 35.4). The phrase 'in effect' indicates that the compulsion spoken of here is compulsion in a special sense, not clearly explained but obviously psychological in nature: a compulsion where 'the will of the defendant is overborne by the threat' (para. 30.10). Once one accepts that subjective psychological intimidation is what really matters in duress cases, it is then but a short step to argue that the only test for whether the defence is made out should be almost entirely subjective: whether 'in all the circumstances ... *the particular defendant in question* could not reasonably have been expected to resist the threat' (para. 29.13/ 14; emphasis in the original).

Yet in its explanation for the excusatory basis of duress, the Commission falls prey to a species of crude behaviorism, and hence misrepresents the real explanation. If it were true that defendants in duress cases were 'in effect compelled' to act as they do by the pressure of a threat, there would be no theoretical difference between someone who assisted a terrorist because they had been threatened with death, and someone who assisted a terrorist because they had been wired to receive a very painful electric shock at the first sign of dissent. Both would have to be regarded as 'in effect compelled' to act as they do, even though in fact only the person wired to receive a shock is 'in effect [psychologically] compelled' to comply. By way of contrast, in most excusing duress cases coercion puts D into a genuine dilemma: D is coerced into choosing between two morally unacceptable courses of action (if D had truly been compelled, as in the electric shock case, there would have been no genuine dilemma to face). What makes the dilemma *genuine* is that D has no known or realistic means of escaping the dilemma, *e.g.* by seeking official protection—and would not act for a reason extrinsic to the dilemma (such as: 'I always disliked V anyway, so ...'). Once one sees that the excusatory basis of duress is not compulsion but a coerced choice from morally unacceptable options, one begins to appreciate that moral scrutiny of D's choice itself is just as central to evaluating D's claim to excuse as analysis of the coercion that gave rise to the choice. There must be coercion before there can be excuse through duress, but that is a necessary rather than a sufficient condition. There is no sufficient condition for excuse without an evaluation of D's actual choice: D's choice of course of conduct must be morally understandable, even if (given the authenticity of the dilemma) there is no morally correct course of action available. ...

Most regrettably, however, the Commission proposes (para. 29.8–29.10) to sweep away almost every legal requirement of moral scrutiny of D's choice, a scrutiny that is (along with coercion) at the heart of duress as an excuse. I refer, of course, to the requirements set down in *Graham* that defendants must (a) *reasonably* believe as a result of what the threatener has said or done that they have *good cause* to fear that the threat will be carried out immediately if they do not comply, and (b) have acted in the face of the threat as might a person of reasonable firmness, who shared such of their characteristics as affected the gravity of the threat. (A) was rejected as part and parcel of the Commission's slavish devotion to subjectivism. Under the Commission's redrafted clause (25(2), above), it will cease to matter why D believed she had been threatened in the relevant way, or why she believed the threat would be carried out if she did not do as requested. It is enough that D actually believed these things, however grossly unreasonable the beliefs. This over-hasty abolition of the common law's objectivism (i) overlooks the extent to which requirements of reasonableness can be sensitive to the fact that people may make mistakes under the pressure of circumstances, and (ii) permits defendants to indulge prejudice and act without proper regard for the interests of victims who are then harmed or killed by them. Consider (ii). Suppose D, a racist who considers all Afro-Caribbean people to be by nature violent, had only one ground for believing that the threatener—X, say—would carry out the threat, namely that X was Afro-Caribbean. Under the Commission's proposals, a jury must be told to take this belief at face value, without regard to its unreasonableness. D is to be excused in just the same way as a 'duressee' who has been prepared, in the interests of those believed to be at risk if the (perceived) threat is complied with, to try to check that there is a real threat and that the threatener means business. No one should contemplate this with equanimity. The common law's requirement in (a) above should be left intact.

Turning to (b) above, in order to bring cowards within the scope of the defence the Commission's test requires the jury to ask a subjective question of moral biography: could '*the particular defendant in question*' reasonably have been expected to resist the threat (para. 29.14)? The rationale for this change is the commendable desire 'not to enforce unrealistically high standards of behaviour' (*ibid*). Unfortunately, the test goes much further than this, permitting far too little moral scrutiny of D's decision to comply with the threatener's demand. Suppose D is a practising paedophile who has been threatened with serious injury unless he has intercourse with a child. He thus has intercourse with a child. The fact that D is inured to intercourse with children might well be something that made it less reasonable to expect *him* to resist the threat (even if one assumes that his paedophilia as such did not actually motivate him to comply); but should this really influence a jury in his favour? Moreover, the new test bizarrely requires the jury to consider whether D could reasonably be expected to have resisted the threat in '*all* the circumstances' (clause 25(2); my emphasis). Suppose D kills rather than suffer grave harm himself, and then claims that he could not reasonably have been expected to resist the threat, given that his attitudes to killing had been coarsened (albeit only temporarily) by watching violent videos the night before. Is this one of the circumstances the jury is to consider? No law that requires an affirmative answer to either of these two questions should be passed. If the common law's objectivist requirements in (b) must be altered to remove references to the person of reasonable firmness (and I am far from convinced that this is necessary), the jury should be instructed to consider 'whether the defendant should have resisted the threat, taking into account all the morally relevant circumstances.' Guidance (perhaps updated by Practice Directions) should then be given separately to judges on how to instruct a jury to apply this test, *e.g.* ignoring drunkenness and a temporary or innate indifference to violence, but bearing physical weakness (and, if we must, timidity) in mind.

3. NECESSITY

i. A defence of necessity?

Note

Criminal lawyers have for a considerable time debated the question whether a general defence of necessity exists in English law. Duress by threats relates to the situation where a person commits an offence to avoid a greater evil of death or serious injury to himself or another threatened by a third party. The defence operates to excuse him from criminal liability. Necessity relates to the situation where a person commits an offence to avoid a greater evil to himself or another which would ensue from the circumstances in which he or that other are placed. It was thought that if the defence of necessity existed it operated as a justification rendering the accused's conduct lawful. The dicta in the cases both as to the existence of the defence and its operation as either an excuse or justification are scant and contradictory.

Early writers on English law such as Bracton, Coke and Hale all quoted maxims which conceded that necessity might justify conduct which would otherwise be unlawful. In *Moore v. Hussey* (1609) Hob 96, Hobart J. stated "All laws admit certain cases of just excuse, when they are offended in the letter, and where the offender is under necessity, either of compulsion or inconvenience." The examples of necessity these writers supplied were pulling down a house to prevent a fire spreading, a prisoner escaping from a burning jail although statute made prison-breach a felony, jettisoning cargo to save a vessel in a storm (see *Mouse's Cases*) (1620) 12 Co. Rep. 63). *Obiter dicta* in twentieth century cases have been inconclusive. In *Buckoke v. G.L.C.* [1971] Ch. 655, 668 Lord Denning stated:

"During the argument I raised the question: Might not the driver of a fire engine be able to raise the defence of necessity? I put this illustration: A driver of a fire engine with ladders approaches the traffic lights. He sees 200 yards down the road a blazing house with a man at an upstairs window in extreme peril. The road is clear in all directions. At that moment the lights turn red. Is the driver to wait for 60 seconds, or more, for the lights to turn green? If the driver waits for that time, the man's life will be lost. I suggested to both counsel that the driver might be excused in crossing the lights to save the man. He might have the defence of necessity. Both counsel denied it. They would not allow him any defence in law. The circumstances went to mitigation, they said, and did not take away his guilt. If counsel are correct—and I accept that they are— nevertheless such a man should not be prosecuted. He should be congratulated."

[The particular question in this case is of academic interest only since drivers of fire engines, police cars and ambulances are now allowed in emergencies to regard red traffic lights as warnings to give way (Traffic Signs Regulations and General Directions, S.I. 1975 No. 1536 reg. 34(1)(b)). They are also permitted to exceed speed limits (Road Traffic Regulation Act 1967, s.79).]

Similarly in *London Borough of Southwark v. Williams* [1971] 2 All E.R. 175, 179 Lord Denning stated:

"[I]f hunger were once allowed to be an excuse for stealing, it would open a way through which all kinds of disorder and lawlessness would pass. So here. If homelessness were once admitted as a defence to trespass, no one's house could be safe. Necessity would open a door which no man could shut. It would not only be those in extreme need who would enter. There would be others who would imagine that they were in need, or would invent a need, so as to gain entry. Each man would say his need was greater than the next man's. The plea would be an excuse for all sorts of wrongdoing. So the courts must, for the sake of law and order, take a firm stand. They must refuse to admit the pleas of necessity to the hungry and the homeless; and trust that their distress will be relieved by the charitable and the good."

Edmund Davies L.J. considered that there was a defence of necessity but it would not avail the squatters in the instant case as the defence was dependent on there being "an urgent situation of imminent peril".

In several traffic cases there are *obiter dicta* to the effect that there is a defence of necessity. In *Johnson v. Phillips* [1976] 1 W.L.R. 65, a motorist was instructed by a police officer to reverse the wrong way down a narrow one-way street in order to allow ambulances access to injured persons further up the street. On his refusal he was charged with wilful obstruction of a constable in the execution of his duty. Wien J., p. 69:

"The precise question that has to be answered in the instant case may be put thus: has a constable in purported exercise of his power to control traffic on a public road the right under common law to disobey a traffic regulation such as going the wrong way along a one-way street? If he himself has that right then it follows that he can oblige others to comply with his instructions to disobey such a regulation. If, for example, a bomb had been planted in The Windsor public house and the exit from Cannon Street had in some way been blocked, could he lawfully reverse a police vehicle and oblige any other motorist then present in the road to reverse his own vehicle? The answer is yes, provided that in the execution of his duty he was acting to protect life or property: see *Hoffman v. Thomas* [1974] 1 W.L.R. 374, 379.... In the judgment of this court a constable would be entitled, and indeed under a duty, to give such instruction if it were reasonably necessary for the protection of life or property.'

In *Woods v. Richards* [1977] R.T.R. 201, Eveleigh J. stated—

"In so far as the defence of necessity is relied on ... [t]here is no evidence at all in this case of the nature of the emergency to which the defendant [a police officer] was being summoned. As the defence of necessity to the extent that it exists must depend on the degree of emergency or the alternative danger to be averted, it is quite impossible in the present case to express the view that the defence was open to the defendant."

This view suggests that had there been evidence of the nature of the emergency the defence could have been considered by weighing that emergency against the manner in which the defendant drove his car which had given rise to the charge of careless driving. See also *R. v. O'Toole* (1971) Cr.App.R. 206.

More recently cases involving driving offences have given rise to the recognition of the defence of duress of circumstances (see *post*, pp. 317–319.

In *D.P.P. v. Harris* [1995] 1 Cr.App.R. 170 the Divisional Court spoke in terms of the common law defence of necessity being available to a charge of reckless driving, but held that it was not available on a charge of careless driving in the instant case, being excluded by the terms of regulation 34 of the Traffic Signs Regulations (S.I. 1981 No. 859) which relates to the circumstances in which a police vehicle may ignore a traffic light showing red. In another Divisional Court case, *Cichon v. D.P.P.* [1994] Crim. L.R. 918, the court held that a defence of necessity was not available on a charge of allowing a pit bull terrier to be in a public place without being muzzled, contrary to s.1(2)(d) of the Dangerous Dogs Act 1991, as the offence was an absolute one and Parliament could not have intended that it should apply.

In several other cases the decisions appear to have been based on necessity although that term was not used. In *R. v. Bourne, post*, p. 607 a surgeon in a London hospital performed an abortion on a 14-year-old rape victim. He was charged with *unlawfully* using an instrument with intent to procure a miscarriage, contrary to section 58 of the Offences Against the Person Act 1861, Macnaghten J., in directing the jury, defined the word "unlawfully" to mean an act "not done in good faith for the purpose only of preserving the life of the mother." As necessity is a defence of justification, and justification renders lawful an act which would otherwise be unlawful, was Macnaghten J. impliedly directing the jury on necessity? (See Lord Edmund-Davies in *Southwark London Borough Council v. Williams* [1971] Ch. 734, at 746.)

In *Gillick v. West Norfolk A.H.A.* [1986] A.C. 112, the House of Lords stated that where a doctor prescribed contraceptives for a girl under 16, he would not be guilty of aiding, abetting, counselling or procuring the offence of unlawful sexual intercourse committed by her with a man provided certain circumstances pertained. These were detailed by Lord Scarman as follows—

"Clearly a doctor who gives a girl contraceptive advice or treatment not because in his clinical judgment the treatment is medically indicated for the maintenance or restoration of her health but with the intention of facilitating her having unlawful sexual intercourse may well be guilty of a criminal offence. It would depend, as my noble and learned friend, Lord Fraser of Tullybelton, observes, upon the doctor's intention—a conclusion hardly to be wondered at in the field of the criminal law. . . . He may prescribe only if she has the capacity to consent or if exceptional circumstances exist which justify him in exercising his clinical judgment without parental consent. The adjective 'clinical' emphasises that it must be a medical judgment based upon what he honestly believes to be necessary for the physical, mental, and emotional health of his patient. The bona fide exercise by a doctor of his clinical judgment must be a complete negation of the guilty mind which is an essential ingredient of the criminal offence of aiding and abetting the commission of unlawful sexual intercourse."

Question

If a doctor knows that contraceptives will encourage an underage girl to engage in sexual intercourse but he prescribes them to protect her physically, emotionally and mentally from the trauma of unwanted pregnancy or even abortion, how can his motive in prescribing the contraceptives negate his guilty mind? Is this not in reality a defence of necessity providing a justification for the doctor's act which otherwise would be criminal?

In the case which follows necessity was given recognition by the House of Lords.

Re F. (Mental Patient: Sterilisation)
[1990] 2 A.C. 1
House of Lords

(For the facts of this case see *post*, p. 624.)

LORD GOFF OF CHIEVELEY: That there exists in the common law a principle of necessity which may justify action which would otherwise be unlawful is not in doubt. But historically the principle has been seen to be restricted to two groups of cases, which have been called cases of public necessity and cases of private necessity. The former occurred in the Great Fire of London in 1666. The latter cases occurred when a man interfered with another man's property in the public interest—for example (in the days before we could dial 999 for the fire brigade) the destruction of another man's house to prevent the spread of a catastrophic fire, as indeed occurred when a man interfered with another's property to save his own person or property from imminent danger—for example, when he entered upon his neighbour's land without his consent, in order to prevent the spread of fire onto his own land.

There is, however, a third group of cases, which is also properly described as founded upon the principle of necessity and which is more pertinent to the resolution of the problem in the present case. These cases are concerned with action taken as a matter of necessity to assist another person without his consent. To give a simple example, a man who seizes another and forcibly drags him from the path of an oncoming vehicle, thereby saving him from injury or even death, commits no wrong. But there are many emanations of this principle, to be found scattered through the books. These are concerned not only with the preservation of the life or health of the assisted person, but also with the preservation of his property (sometimes an animal, sometimes an ordinary chattel) and even with certain conduct on his behalf in the administration of his affairs. Where there is a pre-existing relationship between the parties, the intervenor is usually said to act as an agent of necessity on behalf of the principal in whose interests he acts, and his action can often, with not too much artificiality, be referred to the pre-existing relationship between them. Whether the intervenor may be entitled either to reimbursement or to remuneration raises separate questions which are not relevant in the present case.

We are concerned here with action taken to preserve the life, health or well-being of another who is unable to consent to it. Such action is sometimes said to be justified as arising from an emergency; in *Prosser and Keeton, Handbook on Torts*, 5th ed. (1984), p. 117, the action is said to be privileged by the emergency. Doubtless, in the case of a person of sound mind, there will ordinarily have to be an emergency before such action taken without consent can be lawful; for otherwise there would be an opportunity to communicate with the assisted person and to seek his consent. But this is not always so; and indeed the historical origins of the principle of necessity do not point to emergency as such as providing the criterion of lawful intervention without consent. The old Roman doctrine of negotiorum gestio presupposed not so much an emergency as a prolonged absence of the dominus from home as justifying intervention by the gestor to administer his affairs. The most ancient group of cases in the common law, concerned with action taken by the master of a ship in distant parts in the interests of the shipowner, likewise found its origin in the difficulty of communication with the owner over a prolonged period of time—a difficulty overcome today by modern means of communication. In those cases, it was said that there had to be an emergency before the master could act as agent of necessity; though the emergency could well be of some duration. But when a person is rendered incapable of communication either permanently or over a considerable period of time (through illness or accident or mental disorder), it would be an unusual use of language to describe the case as one of "permanent emergency"—if indeed such a state of affairs can properly be said to exist. In truth, the relevance of an emergency is that it may give rise to a necessity to act in the interests of the assisted person, without first obtaining his consent. Emergency is however not the criterion or even a pre-requisite; it is simply a frequent origin of the necessity which impels intervention. The principle is one of necessity, not of emergency.

We can derive some guidance as to the nature of the principle of necessity from the cases on agency of necessity in mercantile law. When reading those cases, however, we have to bear in mind that it was there considered that (since there was a pre-existing relationship between the parties) there was a duty on the part of the agent to act on his principal's behalf in an emergency. From these cases it appears that the principle of necessity connotes that circumstances have arisen in which there is a necessity for the agent to act on his principal's behalf at a time when it is in practice not possible for him to obtain his principal's instructions so to do. In such cases, it has been said that the agent must act bona fide in the interests of his principal: see *Prager v. Blatspiel Stamp & Heacock Ltd* [1924] 1 K.B. 566, 572 *per* McCardie J. A broader statement of the principle is to be found in the advice of the Privy Council delivered by Sir Montague Smith in *Australasian Steam Navigation Co. v. Morse* (1872) L.R. 4 P.C. 222, 230, in which he said.

> "when by the force of circumstances a man has the duty cast upon him of taking some action for another, and under that obligation, adopts the course which, to the judgment of a wise and prudent man, is apparently the best for the interest of the persons for whom he acts in a given emergency, it may properly be said of the course so taken, that it was, in a mercantile sense, necessary to take it."

In a sense, these statements overlap. But from them can be derived the basic requirements, applicable in these cases of necessity, that, to fall within the principle, not only (1) must there be a necessity to act when it is not practicable to communicate with the assisted person, but also (2) the action taken must be such as a reasonable person would in all the circumstances take, acting in the best interests of the assisted person.

(For further extracts from Lord Goff's speech see *post*, pp. 625–628.)

Questions

1. Did Lord Goff recognise necessity as an excuse or justification?
2. The three categories of situation which give rise to a defence of necessity are quite narrow; would the doctors in *Bourne* or *Gillick* be able to bring themselves within any of these categories if charged with a criminal offence?

Note

In *R. v. Bournewood Community and Mental Health NHS Trust* [1998] 3 All E.R. 289, the defence of necessity was recognised and applied by the House of Lords to justify the informal detention and treatment of a mentally incompetent person who had become a danger to himself. The formal procedures under the Mental Health Act 1983 had not been invoked but the House of Lords held that the common law doctrine of necessity applied, Lord Goff of Chieveley stating:

"I have no doubt that all the steps in fact taken ... were in fact taken in the best interests of Mr. L and, in so far as they might otherwise have constituted an invasion of his civil rights, were justified on the basis of the common law doctrine of necessity."

While this case is an example of the defence of necessity being applied, the reasoning of their Lordships does not supply any further explanation of the rationale underpinning the defence nor any further guidance on its ambit and operation.

ii. Duress of circumstances

Note

The categories of situation giving rise to a defence of necessity are very narrow. In recent years, however, the defence of duress has been widened to cover an imminent threat of death or serious injury arising from the circumstances in which the accused finds himself. The earlier cases all involved driving offences where the accused has driven recklessly (see *Willer* (1986) 83 Cr.App.R. 225; *Conway* [1988] 3 All E.R. 1025) or has driven whilst disqualified from driving (see *Martin* [1989] 1 All E.R. 652) or has driven with excess alcohol (see *D.P.P. v. Bell* [1992] Crim.L.R. 176) in order to avoid a threat of death or serious injury to himself or a third party. In *R. v. Pommell* [1995] 2 Cr.App.R. 607 the Court of Appeal confirmed that the defence is not so limited and applies to all crimes except murder, attempted murder and some forms of treason. In cases of duress by threats the party issuing the threats dictates the criminal offence the accused must commit to avoid the threatened harm (see *Cole, ante,* p. 289); in the cases of duress of circumstances which have arisen the accused has chosen to commit a particular crime to avoid the threatened harm but the defence does not appear to be limited to such situations (see *Martin, post,* p. 331). In *Conway* Woolf L.J. explained the rationale of the defence in the following terms (at p. 1029):

"As the learned editors point out in Smith and Hogan *Criminal Law* (6th edn. 1988) p. 225, to admit a defence of 'duress of circumstances' is a logical consequence of the existence of the defence of duress as that term is ordinarily understood, ie 'do this or else'. This approach does no more than recognise that duress is an example of necessity. Whether 'duress of circumstances' is called 'duress' or 'necessity' does not matter. What is important is that, whatever it is called, it is subject to the same limitations as the 'do this or else' species of duress. As Lord Hailsham LC said in his speech in *R. v. Howe* [1987] 1 All ER 771 at 777, [1987] AC 417 at 429:

There is, of course, an obvious distinction between duress and necessity as potential defences: duress arises from the wrongful threats or violence of another human being and necessity arises from any other objective dangers threatening the accused. This, however, is, in my view a distinction without a relevant difference, since on this view duress is only that species of the genus of necessity which is caused by wrongful threats. I cannot see that there is any way in which a person of ordinary fortitude can be excused from the one type of pressure on his will rather than the other."

In *Martin* Simon Brown J. sought to summarise the principles relating to duress of circumstances (at pp. 653–654):

"The principles may be summarised thus: first, English law does, in extreme circumstances, recognise a defence of necessity. Most commonly this defence arises as duress, that is pressure on the accused's will from the wrongful threats or violence of another. Equally however it can arise from other objective dangers threatening the accused or others. Arising thus it is conveniently called 'duress of circumstances'.

Second, the defence is available only if, from an objective standpoint, the accused can be said to be acting reasonably and proportionately in order to avoid a threat of death or serious injury.

Third, assuming the defence to be open to the accused on his account of the facts, the issue should be left to the jury, who should be directed to determine these two questions: first, was the accused, or may he have been, impelled to act as he did because as a result of what he reasonably believed to be the situation he had good cause to fear that otherwise death or serious physical injury would result; second, if so, would a sober person of reasonable firmness, sharing the characteristics of the accused, have responded to that situation by acting as the accused acted? If the answer to both those questions was Yes, then the jury would acquit; the defence of necessity would have been established.

That the defence is available in cases of reckless driving is established by *R. v. Conway* itself and indeed by an earlier decision of the court in *R. v. Willer* (1986) 83 Cr.App.R. 225. *R. v. Conway* is authority also for the proposition that the scope of the defence is no wider for reckless driving than for other serious offences. As was pointed out in the judgment, 'reckless driving can kill' (see [1988] 3 All E.R. 1025 at 1029, [1988] 3 W.L.R. 1238 at 1244).

We see no material distinction between offences of reckless driving and driving whilst disqualified so far as the application and scope of this defence is concerned. Equally we can see no distinction in principle between various threats of death; it matters not whether the risk of death is by murder or by suicide or indeed by accident. One can illustrate the latter by considering a disqualified driver being driven by his wife, she suffering a heart attack in remote countryside and he needing instantly to get her to hospital."

In *Cole* (see *ante*, p. 289) the Court of Appeal stated that a "situation of imminent peril" is a necessary precondition to the defence arising (see further *Abdul-Hussain*, *ante*. p. 286). It is clear, too, that the accused must desist from the commission of the crime as soon as he reasonably can. In *Pommell* the accused was convicted of possessing a prohibited weapon without a firearms certificate. He raised the defence of duress of circumstances, alleging that he had persuaded X, who had visited him in the night, to give him the gun in order to prevent X shooting people who had killed his friend. The trial judge ruled that the accused's failure to take the gun to the police immediately deprived him of the defence. The Court of Appeal held that the question of the reasonableness of the accused's actions, taking into account the surrounding circumstances, ought to have been left to the jury, particularly where, as here, some explanation was offered for the delay in desisting from committing the offence. Only where the delay is such as to make it clear that the duress must have ceased to operate is the judge entitled to withdraw the defence from the jury (see also *D.P.P. v. Bell* (1992) R.T.R. 335 and *D.P.P. v. Jones* (1990) R.T.R. 33).

While the principles applying in duress and duress of circumstances cases are the same, the Court of Appeal in *Abdul-Hussain* (see *ante*, p. 286) drew attention to one issue, proportionality, which may be of greater significance in cases of duress of circumstances where D chooses the offence he commits in response to the perceived threat rather than it being specified by a duressor. The jury have to consider whether the offence D committed was a reasonable and proportionate response to the threat perceived in the circumstances. This forms part of the objective question whether a reasonable person would have done as D did.

A further limitation on pleading duress of circumstances is that the threat D perceives must come from an extraneous source. In *Rodger and Rose* [1998] 1 Cr.App.R. 143 the appellants sought to raise the defence of duress of circumstances on charges of breaking prison claiming they had done so as they had become suicidal in prison. The Court of Appeal affirmed the trial judge's decision not to leave the defence to the jury as the source of the threat was "the thought processes and emotions of the offenders themselves" and not some extraneous to them. To allow such a development "could amount to a licence to commit crime dependent on the personal characteristics and vulnerability of the offender."

Questions

1. The facts of *Pommell* do not disclose any relationship between the accused and those against whom the threatened harm was directed. Is it appropriate to use the language of duress and speak of D's will being overborne in such a case? Would it not be more correctly approached as a defence of necessity? See J.C. Smith [1994] Crim.L.R. 918.

2. When Lord Hailsham stated that "duress is only that species of genus of necessity which is caused by wrongful threats" was he correct and is this statement reconcilable with Lord Goff's speech in *Re F.*, *i.e.* can a genus which is a justification give birth to a species which is an excuse?

3. The Divisional Court in *D.P.P. v. Harris* [1995] 1 Cr.App.R. 170 when applying the *Martin* test stated that a court must "look at all the circumstances, including the nature and extent of the emergency, in order to determine objectively whether in driving as he did a defendant acted reasonably and proportionately". McCowan L.J. went on to consider the potential evil "to be put into the scales". Are these not elements of the defence of necessity in which D makes a rational judgment rather than a test to be applied to the defence of duress? See Law Com. 218, para. 35.5 *post* p. 342.

4. Will the existence of the defence of duress of circumstances assist or obstruct the future development of a general defence of necessity based on the concept of balancing of harms? (*Cf.* American Model Penal Code, s.3.02, *post*, p. 336.)

5. D, driving his car approaches a traffic light which changes to red.

Further along the road he sees a child fall into a river. D drives on both ignoring the traffic light and breaking the speed limit to effect a rescue of the child. On being tried for both driving offences could D plead in his defence either necessity or duress of circumstances (*cf.* Lord Denning in *Buckoke* and *Conway* and *Martin*)?

iii. Necessity, duress of circumstances and homicide

Duress by threats is no defence to a charge of murder (see *Howe, ante,* p. 303) and the same applies to duress of circumstances (see Woolf L.J. in *Conway, ante,* p. 330). Is there a residual defence of necessity to a charge of homicide?

R. v. Dudley and Stephens
(1884) 14 Q.B.D. 273
Queen's Bench Division

D and S and a boy were cast away from a ship on the high seas and drifted for 20 days in an open boat. They had hardly any food or water during that time, and fearing they would all die soon unless they obtained some sustenance D and S killed the boy, who was likely to die first anyway, and ate his flesh. Four days later they were rescued, and were subsequently indicted for the boy's murder. The jury found the facts of the case in a special verdict and the case was adjourned for argument before five judges.

LORD COLERIDGE C.J.: . . . Now it is admitted that the deliberate killing of this unoffending and unresisting boy was clearly murder, unless the killing can be justified by some well-recognised excuse admitted by the law. It is further admitted that there was in this case no such excuse, unless the killing was justified by what has been called "necessity". But the temptation to the act which existed here was not what the law has ever called necessity. Nor is this to be regretted. Though law and morality are not the same, and many things may be immoral which are not necessarily illegal, yet the absolute divorce of law from morality would be of fatal consequence; and such divorce would follow if the temptation to murder in this case were to be held by law an absolute defence of it. It is not so. To preserve one's life is generally speaking a duty, but it may be the plainest and the highest duty to sacrifice it. War is full of instances in which it is a man's duty not to live, but to die. The duty, in case of shipwreck, of a captain to his crew, of the crew to the passengers, of soldiers to women and children, as in the noble case of the *Birkenhead*; these duties impose on man the moral necessity, not of the preservation, but of the sacrifice of their lives for others, from which in no country, least of all, it is to be hoped, in England, will men shrink, as indeed, they have not shrunk. It is not correct, therefore, to say that there is any absolute or unqualified necessity to preserve one's life. "*Necesse est ut eam, non ut vivam*", is a saying of a Roman officer quoted by Lord Bacon himself with high eulogy in the very chapter on necessity to which so much reference has been made. It would be a very easy and cheap display of commonplace learning to quote from Greek and Latin authors, from Horace, from Juvenal, from Cicero, from Euripides, passage after passage, in which the duty of dying for others has been laid down in glowing and emphatic language as resulting from the principles of heathen ethics; it is enough in a Christian country to remind ourselves of the Great Example whom we profess to follow. It is not needful to point out the lawful danger of admitting the principle which has been contended for. Who is to be the judge of this sort of necessity? By what measure is the comparative value of lives to be measured? Is it to be strength or intellect, or what? It is plain that the principle leaves to him who is to profit by it to determine the necessity which will justify him in deliberately taking another's life to save his own. In this case the weakest, the youngest, the most unresisting, was chosen. Was it more necessary to kill him than one of the grown men? The answer must be "No"....

It must not be supposed that in refusing to admit temptation to be an excuse for crime it is forgotten how terrible the temptation was; how awful the suffering; how hard in such trials to keep the judgment straight and the conduct pure. We are often compelled to set up standards we cannot reach ourselves, and to lay down rules which we could not ourselves satisfy. But a man has no right to declare temptation to be an excuse, though he might himself have yielded to it, nor allow compassion for the criminal to change or weaken in any manner the legal definition of the crime. It is therefore our duty to declare that the prisoners' act in this case was wilful murder, that the facts as stated in the verdict are no legal justification of the homicide; and to say that in our unanimous opinion the prisoners are upon this special verdict guilty of murder.

Sentence of death
Commuted later to six months' imprisonment

Question

Consider and compare the following examples often found in textbooks:

A shipwrecked sailor, clinging to a plank which will only support the weight of one man, prevents another from grasping the plank, so that that other dies by drowning.

The man on the plank is pushed off by the swimmer, who takes his place, leaving him to drown.

The lower of two roped rock-climbers slips and falls. The upper is not strong enough to hold him and to save himself from a certain fall, cuts the lower man free, so that he falls to his death.

X, Y and Z are stranded at the foot of a cliff with the tide coming in. A rope ladder is lowered to them which X starts to ascend but fearing heights he stops and clings to it petrified refusing to move up or down. Y, fearing that he and Z will drown, tells Z, who is immediately below X on the ladder, to pull X off. Z does so and X falls to the rocks below where he dies from drowning while Y and Z climb to safety.

Note

In *U.S. v. Holmes* (1842) 25 Fed.Cas. 360, the accused was convicted of the manslaughter of 16 passengers whom he had thrown out of an overcrowded lifeboat. The judge would it seems have allowed a defence of necessity if the choice had been made by the drawing of lots.

The extracts below illustrate the moral and philosophical challenge which necessity as a defence to homicide presents.

Cross "Murder under Duress" (1978) 28 U.T.L.J. 369, at 377

Speaking of the hypothetical case of the two shipwrecked mariners strug-
gling for a plank only large enough for one, [Kant] said: 'A penal law
applying to such a situation could never have the effect intended, for the
threat of an evil that is still uncertain (being condemned to death by a
judge) cannot outweigh the fear of an evil that is certain (being drowned).
Hence we must judge that, although an act of self-preservation through
violence is not inculpable, it is still unpunishable.' . . .

[I]n the context, I find myself wholly unable to distinguish this defence
from that of duress, and I feel bound to say that the English Law Commission has achieved the apotheosis of absurdity by recommending that our
proposed criminal code should provide for a defence of duress while
excluding any general defence of necessity. Surely Lord Simon of Glaisdale was speaking in unanswerable terms when he said in the course of
his dissenting speech in *Lynch* (*ante*, p. 299) 'It would be a travesty of
justice and an invitation to anarchy to declare that an innocent life may
be taken with impunity if the threat to one's own life is from a terrorist
but not when from a natural disaster like ship- or plane-wreck.'

**Kenny, *Freewill and Responsibility* (1978, Routledge & Kegan Paul), pp.
36–38**

In everyday language people are often said to be compelled to do things
when no actual force is used but the actions are performed to avert the
threat of violent action or imminent disaster. These are cases where it will
be natural for the agent to say that he 'had no choice' . . . but in fact the
action is a voluntary one, arising out of a choice between evils. When the
choice . . . is posed as a result of the wrongful threats of another, lawyers
speak of 'duress'; when it arises through the operation of natural causes,
they prefer to speak of 'necessity'. . . . To me the decision [in *Dudley &
Stephens*] seems ethically sound. . . . The principle that one should never
intentionally take innocent life would be contested by supporters of
euthanasia. . . . The decision in *Dudley and Stephens* can be justified by the
narrower principle that one should not take innocent life in order to save
one's own life. This principle seems to me, as it did to Lord Coleridge in
1884, to be correct: it seems likely to reduce the overall number of innocent deaths. Certainly I would rather be in an open boat with companions
who accepted the principle than in company with lawyers who accepted
necessity as a defence to murder.

Williams, *C.L.G.P.*, §237

. . . Where it is merely a case of life for life, the doctrine of necessity must
generally be silent, because the two lives must be accounted equal in the
eye of the law and there is nothing to choose between them. Necessity
cannot justify in such circumstances; but they may go so strongly in alleviation that the accused is discharged without punishment (where this is
possible) or pardoned. The technical conviction merely records that in
the eye of the law the act was wrongful. The necessary and reasonable
consequence of this view is that resistance to the act on the part of the
victim is lawful.

It seems that the position is different where the killing results in a net
saving of life. Here it seems that the killing should be regarded as not
merely excusing from punishment but as legally justifying. We need a
general rule, and one allowing necessity as a defence to homicide where

the minority are killed to preserve the majority is on the whole more satisfactory than the opposite.

A strong instance of this kind of justification is the action of a ship's captain in a wreck. He can determine who are to enter the first lifeboat; he can forbid overcrowding; and it makes no difference that the passengers who are not allowed to enter the lifeboat will inevitably perish with the ship. The captain, in choosing who are to live, is not guilty of killing those who remain. He would not be so guilty even though he kept some of the passengers back from the boat at revolver-point. . . .

J. Horder, "Occupying the Moral High Ground? The Law Commission on Duress" [1994] Crim.L.R. 334, 339

In many of the much-discussed homicide cases in which duress might have been pleaded, there was arguably no direct intention to kill: the actual death of the victim was not, in the eyes of the defendant, intrinsic to a successful conclusion of what she tried to do. Consider the duress of circumstances case in which D, climbing a ladder to safety from a rapidly sinking ship, dislodges the man above him who has been paralysed by terror, in order that he (D) and others may climb to safety. It is sometimes assumed that this is just the kind of case which demonstrates the injustice of denying a defence of duress of circumstances in murder cases. Much might be made to depend, however, on D's direct intention. Although D may well foresee V's death as the virtually certain consequence of his (D's) action in dislodging V, D presumably does not *directly* intend V to die, such that D would (in his eyes) have failed in what he set out to do in pushing V off the ladder if V by chance survives. D presumably directly intends only to dislodge V from the ladder. If D does not directly intend to kill V (and this will commonly be so) one might argue that D should have his defence of duress, because he had not done something that is inexcusable under duress, namely unlawfully and *directly* intentionally killed an innocent.

A.L.I., Model Penal Code, section 3.02

Conduct which the actor believes necessary to avoid a harm or evil to himself or another is justifiable provided that (1) the harm or evil sought to be avoided by such conduct is greater than that sought to be prevented by the law defining the offence charged. . . ."

See also Gross, *A Theory of Criminal Justice* (Oxford, 1979), pp. 26, 27.

Note

The problem of killing in order to save life arose in unusual and traumatic circumstances in the case *Re A (Children) (Conjoined Twins: Medical Treatment) (No.1)* [2000] 4 All E.R. 961, involving the twins Jodie and Mary. The court had to consider whether it would be lawful for doctors to perform an operation to separate the twins the effect of which would be the inevitable death of Mary. The twins shared a common aorta which enabled Jodie's heart to pump the blood she oxygenated through Mary's body as Mary's heart and lungs were deficient and incapable of sustaining her life. Mary's brain was also not fully developed. If an operation to separate them were not performed both twins were expected to die within six months due to the strain being placed on Jodie's heart. If separated the prospects for Jodie's survival were good albeit that she would suffer some disabilities and require further surgery. Mary was incapable of independent existence.

The Court of Appeal was faced with three problems: firstly, what was in the best interests of the children; secondly, if those interests were in conflict, could that conflict be resolved so as to allow one to prevail; and, thirdly, if the prevailing interest was in favour of the operation, could the operation be performed lawfully. The first two questions raised family law issues, the third related to the criminal law. Ward LJ. with whom Brooke L.J. agreed, concluded that while it was in Jodie's best interests for the operation to take place, this was not in Mary's best interests as it would mean her death. He stated that her life "desperate as it is, still has its own ineliminable value and dignity". This conclusion derived from the sanctity of life doctrine which, he said, "compels me to accept that each life has inherent value in itself and the right to life, being universal, is equal for all of us." By contrast Walker L.J. concluded that the operation would be in Mary's best interests as continued life would hold nothing for her except possible pain and discomfort whereas the operation would restore to her, albeit in death, the bodily integrity and autonomy which is her right. For Ward LJ and Brooke L.J. the court's task, where the best interests of the children were in conflict, was to balance the welfare of each child against the other to find the "least detrimental alternative". This balancing exercise would not involve valuing each life but rather the "worthwhilenss" of the proposed treatment. For Mary the treatment was not worthwhile as she had always been "designated for death" due to her disabilities. She was only alive because she was sucking "the lifeblood out of Jodie" and by so doing would ultimately kill her. Only the doctors could save Jodie whereas Mary was beyond help. In those circumstances the balance weighed heavily in Jodies's favour, Ward L.J. stating:

"The best interests of the twins is to give the chance of life to the child whose actual bodily condition is capable of accepting the chance to her advantage even if that has to be at the cost of the sacrifice of the life which is so unnaturally supported. I am wholly satisfied that the least detrimental choice, balancing the interests of Mary against Jodie and Jodie against Mary, is to permit the operation to be performed."

Turning to the criminal law there were two main issues: firstly, whether the operation to separate the twins would involve the intentional killing of Mary; and, secondly, if so whether this could be justified. Both Ward L.J. and Brooke L.J. concluded that the doctors performing the operation would, following the decision of the House of Lords in *Woollin* [1999] 1 A.C. 82 (*ante* p. 103), intend to kill Mary, however much they might not desire that result, as they would recognise her death as being the virtually certain consequence of their acts. (By contrast Walker L.J. adopted the reasoning of Lord Scarman in *Gillick, ante* p. 327, that the bona fide exercise by a doctor of his clinical judgment would negate the guilty mind required for a criminal offence.) The dilemma for the doctors, however, was not just a moral or social one but also a legal one as the failure to operate could amount to a breach of their duty to act in Jodie's best interests. This raised the crucial question in the case, originally framed by Lord Mackay in *Howe* [1987] 1 A.C. 417 (*ante* p. 303) whether 'the law should recognise in any individual in any circumstances, however extreme, the right to choose that one innocent person should be killed rather than another'? As the doctors' duties to Jodie and Mary were in conflict Ward L.J. concluded that "the law must allow an escape through choosing the lesser of two evils" in which case, the operation being justified would involve no unlawful act. Furthermore, as the reality of the situation was that Mary was slowly killing Jodie (even though this unique situation could not be classed as unlawful), the doctors were entitled to come to Jodie's defence to remove the threat of fatal harm Mary presented. Ward L.J. was, however, concerned to point out the very limited extent to which this decision should be regarded as a precedent emphasising the uniqueness of the case. He stated:

> "Lest it be thought that this decision could become authority for wider propositions, such as that a doctor, once he has determined that a patient cannot survive, can kill the patient, it is important to restate the unique circumstances for which this case is authority. They are that it must be impossible to preserve the life of X. without bringing about the death of Y., that Y. by his or her very continued existence will inevitably bring about the death of X. within a short period of time, and that X. is capable of living an independent life but Y. is incapable under any circumstances (including all forms of medical intervention) of viable independent existence."

Brooke L.J. expressly framed the issue as one of necessity. He conducted a comprehensive review of the history and case law relating to this defence concluding that there was no need for an emergency to exist nor need the threat which constitutes the harm be unlawful or constitute "unjust aggression". He overcame the problem of *Dudley* v. *Stephens* (*ante* p. 333) and *Howe* (*ante* p. 303) which would render necessity unavailable as a defence to murder stating:

> "I have considered very carefully the policy reasons for the decision in *R v. Dudley and Stephens*, supported as it was by the House of Lords in *R v. Howe*. These are, in short, that there were two insuperable objections to the proposition that necessity might be available as a defence for the Mignonette sailors. The first objection was evident in the court's questions: Who is to be the judge of this sort of necessity? By what measure is the comparative value of lives to be measured? The second objection was that to permit such a defence would mark an absolute divorce of law from morality.
>
>   In my judgment, neither of these objections are dispositive of the present case. Mary is, sadly, self-designated for a very early death. Nobody can extend her life beyond a very short span. Because her heart, brain and lungs are for all practical purposes useless, nobody

would have even tried to extend her life artificially if she had not, fortuitously, been deriving oxygenated blood from her sister's bloodstream.

It is true that there are those who believe most sincerely—and the Archbishop of Westminster is among them—that it would be an immoral act to save Jodie, if by saving Jodie one must end Mary's life before its brief allotted span is complete . . .. But there are also those who believe with equal sincerity that it would be immoral not to assist Jodie if there is a good prospect that she might live a happy and fulfilled life if this operation is performed. The court is not equipped to choose between these competing philosophies. All that a court can say is that it is not at all obvious that this is the sort of clear-cut case, marking an absolute divorce from law and morality, which was of such concern to Lord Coleridge and his fellow judges."

Brooke L.J. adopted the tests for necessity which Sir James Stephen provided in his *Digest of Criminal Law* (1887):

"(i) the act is needed to avoid inevitable and irreparable evil;
(ii) no more should be done than is reasonably necessary for the purpose to be achieved;
(iii) the evil inflicted must not be disproportionate to the evil avoided."

He concluded that as the principles of family law "point irresistibly to the conclusion that the interests of Jodie must be preferred to the interests of Mary, I consider that all these requirements are satisfied in this case." Walker L.J. was also prepared, if necessary, to extend the defence of necessity to cover the instant case. Brooke L.J.'s adoption of the Stephen test would suggest a more broadly based defence of necessity more closely related to a balancing of harms test as provided in the A.L.I. Model Penal Code (ante p. 336).

As regards the Human Rights Act 1998 and Article 2 of the European Convention, the Court of Appeal was satisfied that the operation would not constitute a breach. Ward LJ took the view that the rights of each child being in conflict and a solution being required, it was inconceivable that the court in Strasbourg would arrive at a different conclusion to the Court of Appeal. Brooke L.J. and Walker L.J. took the view that Article 2(1) which protects individuals from being "intentionally" deprived of life, was not infringed as "intentionally" in this context had to be given its natural and ordinary meaning and thus applied "only to cases where the purpose of the prohibited action is to cause death". Thus as the doctors' purpose would be to save the life of Jodie rather than to cause the death of Mary, the operation would not constitute a violation of Article 2.

Questions

1. Reconsider the questions *ante* p. 334 in light of the decision in *A (Children)*.

2. A, a twin, is terminally and incurably ill having been diagnosed

by doctors to have four to six months to live. A is in a coma but is not connected to a life support machine. B, A's twin brother, is also terminally ill having been diagnosed to have only weeks to live but he could be saved provided a suitable donor of a healthy liver is found. A tissue match is carried out indicating that A's tissue is an exact match for B and further tests establish that A's liver is perfectly healthy. The removal of A's liver would lead to his immediate death but would offer the prospect of saving B's life. Before falling into a coma A signed a consent form to his organs being used for transplant purposes. The doctors treating B apply to the High Court seeking a declaration that an operation to remove A's liver would not be unlawful. How might the court decide such an application? Would it make any difference if A's heart and kidneys were also to be used to save other lives?

3. Ed and Frank are climbing in the Peak District when Frank is hit by a falling rock which knocks him unconscious causing him to slip and fall. He is attached to Ed who loses his foothold and also falls. Miraculously the rope snags on a gnarled tree growing in a crack in the rock face leaving both climbers suspended in space. Dan, a lone climber climbing on the same rock face sees their plight and traverses the rock face to seek to offer assistance. He discovers that the tree is beginning to give way under the strain of the combined weight of the climbers. Dan realises that he will be unable to save both climbers, particularly as Frank is unable to do anything to help himself. Dan determines that he must cut the rope in order to save Ed. He does so resulting in Frank falling to his death but Ed is rescued. Consider whether Dan would be liable for the murder of Frank.

iv. Proposals for Reform

Draft Criminal Law Bill (Law Com. No. 218)

26.—(1) No act of a person constitutes an offence if the act is done under duress of circumstances.

(2) A person does an act under duress of circumstances if—
(a) he does it because he knows or believes that it is immediately necessary to avoid death or serious injury to himself or another, and
(b) the danger that he knows or believes to exist is such that in all the circumstances (including any of his personal characteristics that affect its gravity) he cannot reasonably be expected to act otherwise.

It is for the defendant to show that the reason for his act was such knowledge or belief as is mentioned in paragraph (a).

(3) This section applies in relation to omissions as it applies in relation to acts.

(4) This section does not apply to a person who knowingly and without reasonable excuse exposed himself to the danger known or believed to exist.

If the question arises whether a person knowingly and without reasonable excuse exposed himself to that danger, it is for him to show that he did not.

(5) This section does not apply to—

(a) an act done in the knowledge or belief that a threat has been made to cause death or serious injury to himself or another (see section 25), or
(b) the use of force within the meaning of section 27 or 28, or an act immediately preparatory to the use of force, for the purposes mentioned in section 27(1) or 28(1)."

Legislating the Criminal Code: Offences Against the Person and General Principles, Law Com. No. 218

DURESS OF CIRCUMSTANCES

. . .

The nature of the defence

Authority
35.2 Clause 27 of the Bill accompanying LCCP 122 provided a defence to one who acts to avoid an imminent danger of death or serious injury to himself or another, if in the circumstances he cannot reasonably be expected to act otherwise. The Court of Appeal has recently recognised the existence of such circumstances of defence on a number of occasions, in cases of reckless driving and of driving while disqualified. Nothing in these cases suggests that the defence is of narrower application than the defence of duress by threats. There is also impressive authority in other common law jurisdictions for a general defence.

Relation to duress by threats and to necessity
35.3 *Duress by threats.* Our inclusion of the defence of duress of circumstances in the Draft Code was based on the conviction that '[t]he impact of some situations of imminent peril upon persons affected by them is hardly different in kind from that of threats such as give rise to the defence of duress'. The effect of the situation on the actor's freedom to choose his course of action ought equally to provide him with an excuse for acting as he does. The analogy between 'threats' and other 'circumstances' promising an evil unless a crime is committed likewise influenced the Court of Appeal in naming the new defence 'duress of circumstances', and in modelling it closely upon duress by threats—by limiting the harm to be avoided to death or serious bodily harm and by adopting, with necessary modifications, the model jury direction laid down in *Graham*. Clause 26 of the Criminal Law Bill is generally designed to reflect the analogy with duress by threats.
35.4 *Necessity.* The relationship between duress and necessity is a difficult matter. Duress is sometimes spoken of as if it were a species of necessity, but the law recognises a defence of 'necessity' on a basis quite different from that which underlies the recognition of duress as a defence. The true basis of the duress defences, as we understand them, is that the actor has been in effect compelled to act as he does by the pressure of a human or other threat to which he himself is subject. It is the impact of that pressure on his freedom to choose his course of action that suffices to excuse him from criminal liability. In such cases, the threat must be such that he cannot reasonably be expected to resist it or (as it is put in clause 26 of the Criminal Law Bill in respect of duress of circumstances) to do otherwise than to commit the act that, absent the defence of duress, would be criminal. The gravity of the act committed may be relevant to the question whether the threat (death or serious injury for himself or another) understandably overcame the actor's natural reluctance to commit that

act; but the defences do not depend on an objective comparison between the evil threatened and the harm committed to avoid it.

35.5 By contrast with the defences of duress just discussed, there appear to be some cases, more properly called cases of 'necessity', where the actor does not rely on any allegation that circumstances placed an irresistible pressure on him. Rather, he claims that his conduct, although falling within the definition of an offence, was not harmful because it was, in the circumstances, justified. Such claims, unlike those recognised by the duress defences, do seem to require a comparison between the harm that otherwise unlawful conduct has caused and the harm that that conduct has avoided; because if the latter harm was not regarded as the greater the law could not even consider accepting that the conduct was justified. Nor, fairly clearly, does the defence depend on any claim that the actor's will was 'overborne': on the contrary, the decision to do what, but for the exceptional circumstances, would be a criminal act may be the result of careful judgment, as in the case of the kind of professional decision referred to in the next paragraph.

35.6 Although the English courts have not expressly recognised a general doctrine of 'necessity', a case of high authority, *F v West Berkshire Health Authority* (*ante*, p. 328), provides an example of its operation in connection with the medical treatment of people who are unable to give a valid consent to it. . . . In such cases there is no question of the defence depending on the actor's resistance being overcome . . .; rather, the courts decide that in all the circumstances the actor's, freely adopted, conduct was justified.

35.7 We therefore consider that, as part of the policy of retaining common law defences . . . this specific defence of necessity should be kept open as something potentially separate from duress. That is provided for by clause 36(2) of the Criminal Law Bill, which expressly saves 'any distinct defence of necessity' when abrogating the common law defences of duress by threats and of circumstances.

Some details of the defence

The danger
35.8 The act done must be 'immediately necessary to avoid death or serious injury to [the actor] or another'. The act (reckless driving) in *Conway* was (allegedly) done to save the life of the defendant's passenger; in *Martin* it was claimed that the accused had to drive whilst disqualified to prevent his wife's suicide.

Other matters
35.9 As with duress by threats, the actor's knowledge of, or belief in the existence of, relevant circumstances is crucial. Consistently with that defence, the circumstances that clause 26 of the Criminal Law Bill requires to be taken into account include 'any of his personal characteristics that affect [the gravity of the danger]' (subsection (2)(b)). And a person who has voluntarily exposed himself to a danger cannot rely upon that danger as a ground of this defence (subsection (4)).

Application of the defence

35.10 As in the case of duress by threats, the balance of opinion on consultation was in favour of its application to murder. For the reasons we gave in LCCP 122 . . . we remain of that view, and clauses 24 and 26 of the Criminal Law Bill so provide, by applying the defence to all offences.

35.11 The application of this defence to murder would in effect depart from the law as stated in *Dudley and Stephens*. That famous case, of the shipwrecked men adrift in a small boat without food or drink, who killed one of their number to sustain themselves on his flesh, illustrates the general category of cases in which people are in peril of death or serious harm because of 'duress of circumstances'. The Queen's Bench Division denied the existence of any doctrine of necessity as a defence to murder. Adoption of the clause now proposed would leave it to the jury to say whether in all the circumstances persons in the position of the defendants in *Dudley and Stephens*, assuming they believed their acts to be 'immediately necessary', could reasonably have been expected to act otherwise than as they did. This proposal would appear to stand or fall with the corresponding proposal for duress by threats: and we refer to the relevant discussion in that context.

4. SELF-DEFENCE AND KINDRED DEFENCES

Note

This section covers those situations where force is used by a defendant to protect himself, or his property, or others or to prevent crime. Pleas based on these grounds are not strictly "defences" in the sense that duress is a defence; a successful plea means that the accused's conduct was justified and thus lawful. However the term defence will be used as it appears in the cases and textbooks.

G. Williams, "The theory of excuses" [1982] Crim.L.R. 732 at 739

At any rate, for present English law private defence is clearly a matter of justification, not merely of according mercy to a defender. (Lord MacDermott C.J. referred to it as a 'plea of justification' in *Devlin v. Armstrong* [1971] N.I. 13). If the choice is between injury to an aggressor and injury to a defender, it is better that the injury be suffered by the aggressor, for two reasons. First, it is the aggressor who is the prime cause of the mischief. Secondly, a rule allowing defensive action tends to inhibit aggression, or at least to restrain its continuance, as a rule forbidding defensive action would tend to promote it. It follows that if a person acts against a wrongdoer in the actual necessity of private defence, no one who assists him should be guilty as bringing about a wrongful act, whatever may have been the reason why he lent his assistance.

Winn L.J. stated in *R. v. Wheeler* [1967] W.L.R. 1531, at p. 1533:

". . . wherever there has been a killing, or indeed the infliction of violence not proving fatal, in circumstances where the defendant puts forward a justification such as self-defence, . . . such as resistance to a violent felony, it is very important and indeed quite essential that the jury should understand, and that the matter should be so put before them that there is no danger of their failing to understand, that none of those issues of justification are properly to be regarded as defences: unfortunately there is sometimes a regrettable habit of referring to them as, for example, the defence of self-defence. In particular, where a judge does slip into the error or quasi error of referring to such explanations as defences, it is particularly important that he should use language which suffices to make it clear to the jury that they are not defences in respect of which any onus rests upon the accused, but are matters which the prosecution must disprove as an essential part of the prosecution case before a verdict of guilty is justified."

(Reiterated in R. v. *Abraham* [1973] 1 W.L.R. 1270.)

If D's account of the facts includes matters which, if accepted, could raise a prima facie case of self-defence, that issue should be left to the jury even where D. has not formally relied on self-defence (see *D.P.P. v. Bailey* [1995] 1Cr. App. R.257).

i. Scope of the defences

(a) *Self-defence*

R. v. Scully
(1824) C. & P. 319; 171 E.R. 1213
Gloucester Assizes

The defendant was set to watch his master's premises. He saw a man on the garden wall and hailed him. This man said to another, "Tom, why don't you fire?" The defendant hailed the man on the wall again and he said, "Shoot and be d—d," whereupon he shot at the man on the wall, aiming at his legs. He missed and shot the deceased whom he had not seen. The defendant was charged with manslaughter.

GARROW B.: Any person set by his master to watch a garden or yard, is not at all justified in shooting at or injuring in any way persons who may come into those premises, even in the night: and if he saw them go into his master's hen roost, he would still not be justified in shooting them. He ought first to go and see if he could not take measures for their apprehension. But here the life of the prisoner was threatened and if he considered his life in actual danger, he was justified in shooting the deceased as he had done; but, if not considering his own life in danger, he rashly shot that man, who was only a trespasser, he would be guilty of manslaughter.

Verdict: Not guilty

(b) *Defence of others*

R. v. Rose
(1884) 15 Cox 540
Oxford Assizes

The defendant was a weakly young man of 22; his father was a powerful man. Recently the father had been drinking excessively and whilst intoxicated he was of the opinion that his wife had been unfaithful to him. He had threatened her life and she was so frightened that she had frequently hidden everything in the house that could be used as a weapon. On the night in question the family had retired to separate bedrooms when the father had started abusing and arguing with his wife, threatening to murder her. He rushed from his room, seized his wife, and forced her up against the balusters in such a way as to give the impression that he was cutting her throat. The daughter and the mother shouted "murder", whereupon the defendant ran from his room. He is said to have fired a gun to frighten his father—no trace of his shot was found, and then he fired again, hitting his father in the eye and killing him. On arrest he said, "Father was murdering mother. I shot on one side to frighten him: he would not leave her, so I shot him." He was charged with murder.

LOPES J.: Homicide is excusable if a person takes away the life of another in defending himself, if the fatal blow which takes away life is necessary for his preservation. The law says not only in self-defence such as I have described may homicide be excusable, but also it may be excusable if the fatal blow inflicted was necessary for the preservation of life. In the case of parent and child, if the parent had reason to believe that the life of a child is in imminent danger by reason of an assault by another person, and that the only possible, fair and reasonable means of saving the child's life is by doing something which will cause the death of that person, the law excuses that act. It is the same of a child with regard to a parent; it is the same in the case of husband and wife. Therefore, I propose to lay the law before you in this form: If you think, having regard to the evidence, and drawing fair and proper inferences from it, that the prisoner at the Bar acted without vindictive feeling towards his father when he fired the shot, if you think that at the time he fired that shot he honestly believed, and had reasonable grounds for the belief, that his mother's life was in imminent peril, and that the fatal shot which he fired was absolutely necessary for the preservation of her life, then he ought to be excused, and the law will excuse him, from the consequences of the homicide. If, however, on the other hand, you cannot come to this conclusion, if you think, and think without reasonable doubt, that it is not a fair inference to be drawn from the evidence, but are clearly of opinion that he acted vindictively, and had not such a belief as I have described to you, or had not reasonable grounds for such a belief, then you must find him guilty of murder.

Verdict: Not guilty

R. v. Duffy
[1967] 1 Q.B. 63
Court of Criminal Appeal

The appellant's sister was fighting. It was the appellant's case that she went to rescue her sister and that this was justifiable as self-defence. They were both convicted of unlawful wounding.

EDMUND-DAVIES J.: . . . defending counsel throughout relied upon the plea that the appellant was acting in self-defence, a plea which he submitted extended to the action of the appellant in seeking to rescue her sister. It is established that such a defence is not restricted to the person attacked. It has been said to extend to "the principal civil and natural relations." Hale's Pleas of the Crown, Vol. 1, p. 484, gives as instances master and servant, parent and child, and husband and wife who, if they even kill an assailant in the necessary defence of each other, are excused, the act of the relative assisting being considered the same as the act of the party himself. But no reported case goes outside the relations indicated, although the editor of Kenny's Outlines of Criminal Law, 18th ed. (1962), p. 198, says that ". . . perhaps the courts will now take a still more general view of this duty of the strong to protect the weak." Be that as it may, the judge seems to have found himself limited by the fact that no reported decision extended self-defence to a case where, as here, a sister went to the rescue of a sister, and the direction given to the jury as far as this appellant is concerned was this: "So far as I can see, members of the jury, in this case, the defence of self-defence is not open to Lilian Duffy. There is no suggestion whatever that she personally was attacked and it is my direction to you to approach this case on the footing that it is no defence for Lilian Duffy to say she was going to the assistance of her sister. . . ."

The source of error in this case, as it appears to this court is, as we have said, that everyone, including counsel at the trial and again before us, seems to have overlooked that in reality and in law the case of Lilian Duffy was not trammelled by any technical limitations on the application of the plea of self-defence, and this court is not here concerned to consider what those limitations are. Quite apart from any special relations between the person attacked and his rescuer, there is a general liberty even as between strangers to prevent a felony. That is not to say, of course, that a newcomer may law-fully join in a fight just for the sake of fighting. Such conduct is wholly differ-ent in law from that of a person who in circumstances of necessity intervenes with the sole object of restoring the peace by rescuing a person being attacked. That, credible or otherwise, was the basic defence advanced by the appellant. She herself tied no lawyer's label to her tale. It is true that the judge said: "I need only remind you again that it is Lilian Duffy's case that she was going to the rescue of her sister and that was why she hit Akbar with a bottle, she could not get him off her sister." But his earlier directions had indicated that such a case afforded no defence in law. We think that this was a misdirection. The necessity for intervening at all and the reasonableness or otherwise of the manner of intervention were matters for the jury. It should have been left to them to say whether, in view of the appellant's proved conduct, such a defence could possibly be true, they being directed that the intervener is per-mitted to do only what is necessary and reasonable in all the circumstances for the purpose of rescue. . . .

Appeal allowed

See also *Devlin v. Armstrong, post,* p. 348.

(c) *Defence of property*

R. v. Hussey
(1924) 18 Cr.App.R. 160
Court of Criminal Appeal

The appellant given an invalid notice to quit his rooms by his landlady, refused to do so. The landlady with two friends, armed with a hammer, a spanner, a poker and a chisel, tried to break down the door to the appellant's room which he had barricaded. A panel of the door was broken and the appellant fired through the hole wounding the friends of the landlady. He was charged with unlawfully wounding them and convicted. He appealed on the ground that the distinction between self-defence and defence of one's house had not been drawn to the attention of the jury.

LORD HEWART C.J.: No sufficient notice had been given to the appellant to quit his room, and therefore he was in the position of a man who was defending his house. In Archbold's Criminal Pleading, Evidence and Practice, 26th ed., p. 887, it appears that: "In defence of a man's house, the owner or his family may kill a trespasser who would forcibly dispossess him of it, in the same manner as he might, by law, kill in self-defence a man who attacks him per-sonally; with the distinction, however, that in defending his home he need not retreat, as in other cases of self-defence, for that would be giving up his house to his adversary." That is still the law, but not one word was said about that distinction in the summing-up, which proceeded on the foundation that the defence was the ordinary one of self-defence. The jury, by their verdict, negatived felonious intent, and with a proper direction they might have come to a different conclusion. The appeal must therefore be allowed.

Conviction quashed

Note

The landlady in *Hussey*, above, would now be committing an offence under the Protection from Eviction Act 1977, section 1, and under the Criminal Law Act 1977, section 6. Had the case arisen today, Hussey could have relied on the defence of prevention of crime.

(d) *Prevention of crime*

Criminal Law Act 1967, section 3

"(1) A person may use such force as is reasonable in the circumstances in the prevention of crime, or in effecting or assisting in the lawful arrest of offenders or suspected offenders or of persons unlawfully at large.

(2) Subsection (1) above shall replace the rules of common law on the question when force used for a purpose mentioned in the subsection is justified by that purpose."

Question

Did section 3(1) supersede the common law defences of self-defence, defence of others and defence of property?

Ashworth, Principles of Criminal Law, 3rd ed. 141–144

(d) The Rules and the Principles
A precise statement of English law on the justifications is difficult to locate. The Criminal Law Act 1967, section 3, states that 'a person may use such force as is reasonable in the circumstances in the prevention of crime . . .'. The section was not intended to supplant the common law rules on self-defence, and the courts have continued to develop those rules. It is true that in most situations of self-defence it could be said that the person was preventing crime (*i.e.* preventing an attack which constituted a crime), but that would still leave certain cases untouched— notably, attacks by a child under 10, by a mentally disordered person, or by a person labouring under a mistake of fact. Such aggressors would commit no offence, and so it is the law of self-defence, not the prevention of crime, which governs.

The English law of self-defence, as it is applied by the courts, turns on two requirements: the force must have been necessary, and it must have been reasonable. In dealing with particular cases, however, the courts have, as we shall see, reached decisions which suggest certain sub-rules, but they have generally been reluctant to refer to them as such, preferring to make use of the broad flexibility of the concept of reasonableness. . . .

Both the legislation and judicial decisions prefer to state the law in terms of what is 'reasonable' or 'reasonable and necessary'. . . .

(e) The Proportionality Standard
The requirement that the use of force must be necessary . . . should be combined with a further requirement that the amount of force must be

proportionate to the value being upheld. This shows respect for the rights of the attacker in self-defence cases, and for the rights of suspected offenders in relation to the other justifications. The standard cannot be a precise one: probably the best way of defining it is in terms of what is reasonably proportionate to the amount of harm likely to be suffered by the defendant, or likely to result if the forcible intervention is not made. What is crucial is that it should rule out the infliction or risk of considerable physical harm merely to apprehend a fleeing thief, to stop minor property loss or damage, etc. . . . [T]he proper approach is to compare the relative value of the rights involved, and not to give special weight to the rights of the property owner simply because the other party is in the wrong (i.e. committing a crime). . . .

(f) Aspects of the Necessity Requirement

The necessity requirement forms part of most legal regimes on justifiable force. The first question to be asked is: necessary for what? We have seen that force may be justified for any one of several lawful purposes. The necessity must be judged according to the lawful purpose which the defendant was trying to pursue: for self-defence, purely defensive force will often be all that is necessary; in order to apprehend a suspected offender, on the other hand, a police officer or citizen will need to behave proactively. These differences may become particularly important in cases where there is a suspicion or allegation that the force was used by way of revenge or retaliation rather than in pursuit of a lawful purpose.

Question

D, a nurse in a mental hospital, is attacked by X a patient wielding a meat cleaver. X had escaped from a secure ward for the violently insane. D knowing this nevertheless defends himself with a crutch. He hits X over the head fracturing his skull. If self-defence has been swallowed up by section 3 of the Criminal Law Act 1967, could D plead prevention of crime on a charge under section 20 Offences Against the Person Act 1861 of unlawfully and maliciously inflicting grievous bodily harm?

Notes

1. Smith and Hogan, p. 259, suggest that although section 3 has swallowed up self-defence, in point of policy D in the above situation should have a defence. What would this defence be? Would it be the common law defence of self-defence?!

2. The case *infra* is interesting as it raises not only the issue of the relationship between the common law and section 3 of the Criminal Law Act 1967 (or its Northern Irish equivalent), but also other issues such as the imminence of the threat and defence of others. (This case must be read in light of *R. v. Gladstone Williams, ante,* p. 159).

Devlin v. Armstrong
[1971] N.I. 13
Court of Appeal for Northern Ireland

The case arose out of serious disturbances in Londonderry in August 1969. The appellant exhorted a crowd of people, who had been stoning the police, to build barricades and to fight the police with petrol bombs. Her grounds of appeal against four convictions of riotous behaviour and incitement to riotous behaviour were that she reasonably believed that the police were about to act unlawfully in assaulting people and damaging property and so her behaviour was justified.

LORD MACDERMOTT L.C.J.: with whom Curran and McKeigh L.JJ. agreed, after describing the events in some detail:

The findings of the case indicate that the state of disorder which I have described involved a violent and aggressive resistance to constitutional authority, and if the relevant facts and considerations ended with the tale of events already told, the inescapable conclusion would be that the appellant and those associated with her opposing the police by the means described were participants in a riot and guilty of riotous behaviour.

As I have stated, the answer to this, as advanced on behalf of the appellant, is one of justification. She did what she did, it was submitted, because she believed honestly and reasonably that the police were about to assault people and damage property in the Bogside. The learned resident magistrate did not accept the factual basis of this submission, but that finding has become entwined with one respecting the admissibility of certain evidence which the appellant sought to adduce in support of this plea and I shall, therefore, assume for present purposes that in fact, the appellant did honestly and reasonably believe that the police were about to behave unlawfully in the manner mentioned. Thus arises what I have called the principal issue. Does this plea of justification afford a defence to the charges? At this point I do not need to distinguish between the offences of inciting to riotous behaviour and behaving riotously. If this defence meets one of these offences it must, in the circumstances, meet the other.

The conclusion I have reached on this issue is against the appellant. In my opinion the submission under discussion fails as an answer to any of the charges. Since there is a dearth of authority on the point and various principles have been invoked on one side and the other, I shall enumerate the reasons which, separately and in conjunction, have led me to this view.

1. At any rate one common purpose of the rioters and the appellant was, beyond any question, to keep the police from entering or establishing themselves in the Bogside and to achieve this by force. The appellant's contention that the honesty and reasonableness of her apprehensions (as I have assumed them to be for the sake of the argument) robbed her actions of the *mens rea* necessary to constitute the offences charged must, to my mind, fail once the nature of this common purpose has been demonstrated. If it were conceded that her apprehensions supplied a motive for her actions and incitements, that in itself would fall well short of neutralising her intentions as manifested by the manner of her participation.

2. Reliance was also placed upon the doctrine of self-defence. The general nature of this doctrine may be taken as described in Russell on Crime, 12th ed. (1964) vol. I, p. 680, thus:

"The use of force is lawful for the necessary defence of self or others or of property; but the justification is limited by the necessity of the occasion, and the use of unnecessary force is an assault."

The plea of self-defence may afford a defence where the party raising it uses force, not merely to counter an actual attack, but to ward off or prevent an attack which he has honestly and reasonably anticipated. In that case, however, the anticipated attack must be imminent: see *R. v. Chisam* (1963) 47 Cr.App.R. 130, 134, and the excerpt from Lord Norm-

and's judgment in *Owens v. H.M. Advocate*, 1946 S.C. (J) 119, which is there quoted and which runs:

"In our opinion self-defence is made out when it is established to the satisfaction of the jury that the panel believed that he was in imminent danger and that he held that belief on reasonable grounds. Grounds for such belief may exist though they are founded on a genuine mistake of fact."

That there was a distinction between the right of self-defence and the right to prevent a felony appears from *R. v. Duffy*, (*ante*, p. 345), but the latter right has gone with the abolition of the distinctions between felony and misdemeanour and its place is now taken in this jurisdiction by section 3 of the Criminal Law Act (Northern Ireland), 1967, subsection (1) which says:

"a person may use such force as is reasonable in the circumstances in the prevention of crime. . . ."

However reasonable and convinced the appellant's apprehensions may have been, I find it impossible to hold that the danger she anticipated was sufficiently specific or imminent to justify the actions she took as measures of self-defence. The police were then in the throes of containing a riot in the course of their duty, and her interventions at that juncture were far too aggressive and premature to rank as justifiable effort to prevent the prospective danger of the police getting out of hand and acting unlawfully which, as I have assumed, she anticipated.

3. Where force is used either in exercise of the right of self-defence or, under section 3 of the Act of 1967, in the prevention of crime, it must be reasonable in the circumstances. This consideration alone seems to me fatal to the appellant's plea of justification. Whatever her fears and however genuine they may have been, to organise and encourage the throwing of petrol bombs was, I would hold, an utterly unwarranted and unlawful reaction. The night of August 12 had demonstrated the capacity of these lethal weapons to injure and destroy and nothing that had happened or was likely to happen could excuse the appellant in facilitating and encouraging their use.

4. The plea of justification, whether based on the doctrine of self-defence or the statutory right to prevent crime, appears to me to place a further difficulty when the offence sought to be justified is that of inciting others to riotous behaviour. While there was evidence of a general fear of the police amongst people of the Bogside, there is nothing in the findings or facts of the case to show that those who were exhorted by the appellant to riot were actuated by any honest and reasonable apprehension of unlawful violence on the part of the police such as she is assumed to have had. Her incitements were, therefore, directed to encouraging others to do what for them was prima facie unlawful. It cannot be taken for granted that those she addressed were opposing the police for what she says were her reasons, and this all the more as the rioting had started in opposition to the parade and before the police had entered the Bogside. In my opinion the plea of self-defence cannot be availed of where what is sought to be justified is an incitement to unjustifiable crime. I know of no authority to the contrary, and on this ground as well I would hold that the plea fails.

5. As I understood his argument Sir Dingle Foot at one stage sought, in the alternative, to broaden the appellant's plea of justification by putting it on the basis of a collective right of self-defence arising out of some collective necessity. He frankly admitted that there was no clear authority

of such a concept, but drew our attention to a passage from the judgment of Lord Mansfield in *R. v. Stratton and Ors.* (1779) 21 St.Tr. 1045 at 1224, which is mentioned by Mr. Justice Stephen in his *History of the Criminal Law* (1883), vol. ii, 109, in relation to the plea of compulsion by necessity. In that case the accused, who were charged for deposing Lord Pigot from the Government of Madras, defended themselves on the ground that Lord Pigot's argument had been such that it was necessary for them to do so in the interests of the Madras Presidency. After speaking of cases of natural necessity, such as self-defence, Lord Mansfield continued:

"As to civil necessity, none can happen in corporations, societies, and bodies of men deriving their authority under the Crown and therefore subordinate; no case ever did exist in government to which they can apply, they have a superior at hand, and therefore I cannot be warranted to put to you any case of civil necessity that justifies illegal acts, because the case not existing, nor being supposed to exist, there is not authority in the law books nor any adjudged case upon it. Imagination may suggest, you may suggest so extraordinary a case as would justify a man by force overturning a magistrate and beginning a new government all by force, I mean in India, where there is no superior nigh them to apply to; in England it cannot happen; but in India you may suppose a possible case, but in that case it must be imminent, extreme, necessity; there must be no other remedy to apply to for redress; it must be very imminent, it must be very extreme, and in the whole they do, they must appear clearly to do with a view of preserving the society and themselves—with a view of preserving the whole."

On this aspect Sir Dingle pressed his suit with a delicate circumspection, leaving it to the court to apply such part of Lord Mansfield's words as might be considered appropriate. I need only say that I can find nothing in the passage quoted to justify the actions of the appellant or the rioters whom she incited. It is one thing to act for the best in some case of extreme necessity, where the forces of law and order are absent or have ceased to act in that capacity. It is quite another to fight against and seek to expel a lawfully constituted constabulary while acting as such in the execution of its proper functions.

6. The ambit of the doctrine of self-defence may be wider than it once was, but when considered apart from the statutory right to which I have referred, some special nexus or relationship between the party relying on the doctrine to justify what he did in aid of another, and that other, would still appear to be necessary. Without attempting to define that factor, I cannot accept, on the material available, that it existed as between the appellant and the people of the Bogside. There is nothing to suggest that she belonged to or had property or a home in that district, and her status as a Member of Parliament would not, of itself, afford her protection by supplying a special relationship. It would seem as though she came in as a visitor and made common cause with the rioters, but I cannot regard that as an adequate relationship on which to found a defence of justification by way of self-defence.

7. Finally, the outbreak of rioting on August 12 and 13 imposed a duty on more than the constabulary. The private citizen has authority in law to help in the suppression of riots, and it is his common law duty to assist the constabulary to this end: see Russell on Crime, 12th ed. (1964), pp. 270 *et seq.*, and, in particular, the *Bristol Riots* case (1832) 3 St.Tr. (N.S.) 1 at 4 and 5, and *R. v. Pinney* (1832) 3 St.Tr. (N.S.) 11. That obligation, which rested upon the appellant as well as others, made it impossible, in my

opinion, for her to find any legal justification for her conduct in aiding and encouraging the rioters as she undoubtedly did.

Appeals dismissed

R. v. McInnes [1971] 1 W.L.R. 1600, Edmund-Davies L.J. at p. 1610: "Section 3(1) of the Criminal Law Act 1967 provides that 'A person may use such force as is reasonable in the circumstances in the prevention of crime . . .' and in our judgment the degree of force permissible in self-defence is similarly limited."

ii. The Issues of Imminence and the Pre-Emptive Strike

See *Devlin v. Armstrong, ante,* p. 348.

Attorney-General's Reference (No. 2 of 1983)
[1984] Q.B. 456
Court of Appeal

The defendant's shop in Toxteth had been attacked and damaged by rioters. Fearing further attacks he made some petrol bombs which he intended to use purely as a last resort to repulse raiders from his shop. He was charged with an offence under section 4 of the Explosive Substances Act 1883, namely, of having made an explosive substance in such circumstances as to give rise to a reasonable suspicion that he had not made it for a lawful object. He pleaded that his lawful object was self-defence and the jury acquitted. The Attorney-General referred for the court's opinion the question whether the defence of self-defence was available to a defendant charged with an offence under section 4 of the 1883 Act.

LORD LANE C.J.: . . . Counsel for the Crown argued at trial that self-defence did not provide a valid defence to the respondent on this charge because such a plea is available only to justify actual violence by a defendant. Mr Hill contends that it does not exist as a justification for preliminary and premeditated acts anticipatory of an act of violence by the defendant in the absence of any express statutory provision therefor. . . .

Mr Hill submits that to allow a man to justify in advance his own act of violence for which he has prepared runs wholly contrary to the principle and thinking behind legitimate self-defence and legitimate defence of property. Both are defences which the law allows to actual violence by a defendant, and both are based on the principle that a man may be justified in extremis in taking spontaneous steps to defend himself, others of his family and his property against actual or mistakenly perceived violent attack. It was argued that if a plea of self-defence is allowed to section 4 of the Act of 1883 the effect would be that a man could write his own immunity for unlawful acts done in preparation for violence to be used by him in the future. Rather than that, goes on the argument, in these circumstances a man should protect himself by calling on the police or by barricading his premises or by guarding them alone or with others, but not with petrol bombs. . . .

[In *R. v. Fegan* [1972] N.I. 80 Lord MacDermott C.J. said, at p. 87:]

"Possession of a firearm for the purpose of protecting the possessor or his wife or family from acts of violence, *may* be possession for a lawful object. But the lawfulness of such a purpose cannot be founded on a mere fancy, or on some aggressive motive. The threatened danger must be reasonably and genuinely anticipated, must appear reasonably imminent, and must be of a nature which could not reasonably be met by more pacific means. A lawful object in this particular field therefore falls within a strictly limited category and cannot be such as to justify going beyond what the law may allow in meeting the situation of danger which the possessor of the firearm reasonably and genuinely apprehends."

. . . In our judgment, approaching *a priori* the words "lawful object" it might well seem open to a defendant to say, "My lawful object is self-defence." The respondent in this case said that his intentions were to use the petrol bombs purely to protect his premises should any rioters come to his shop. It was accordingly open to the jury to find that the respondent has made them for the reasonable protection of himself and his property against this danger. The fact that in manufacturing and storing the petrol bombs the respondent committed offences under the [Explosives] Act of 1875 [which prohibits the manufacture and storage of explosives without a licence] did not necessarily involve that when he made them his object in doing so was not lawful. The means by which he sought to fulfil that object were unlawful, but the fact that he could never without committing offences reach the point where he used them in self-defence did not render his object in making them for that purpose unlawful. The object or purpose or end for which the petrol bombs were made was not itself rendered unlawful by the fact that it could not be fulfilled except by unlawful means. The fact that the commission of other offences was unavoidable did not result in any of them becoming one of the respondent's objects. . . .

In the judge's summing up the threatened danger was assumed, as was the respondent's anticipation of it. Also assumed, no doubt upon the basis of the evidence led, was the imminence of the danger. What the judge upon the facts of the case before him left to the jury was the reasonableness of the means adopted for the repulsion of raiders. . . .

In our judgment a defendant is not left in the paradoxical position of being able to justify acts carried out in self-defence but not acts immediately preparatory to it. There is no warrant for the submission on behalf of the Attorney-General that acts of self-defence will only avail a defendant when they have been done spontaneously. There is no question of a person in danger of attack "writing his own immunity" for violent future acts of his. He is not confined for his remedy to calling in the police or boarding up his premises.

He may still arm himself for his own protection, if the exigency arises, although in so doing he may commit other offences. That he may be guilty of other offences will avoid the risk of anarchy contemplated by the reference. It is also to be noted that although a person may "make" a petrol bomb with a lawful object, nevertheless if he remains in possession of it after the threat has passed which made his object lawful, it may cease to be so. It will only be very rarely that circumstances will exist where the manufacture or possession of petrol bombs can be for a lawful object.

For these reasons the point of law referred by Her Majesty's Attorney-General for the consideration of this court is answered by saying: the defence of lawful object is available to a defendant against whom a charge under section 4 of the Act of 1883 has been preferred, if he can satisfy the jury on balance of probabilities that his object was to protect himself or his family against imminent apprehended attack and to do so by means which he believed were no more than reasonably necessary to meet the force used by the attackers.

Opinion accordingly

J. C. Smith, Commentary [1984] Crim.L.R. 290

If the respondent intended to use the bombs only in circumstances in which it would have been lawful to do so, then it seems to follow inevitably that he had them in his possession 'for a lawful object,' and so was not guilty of the offence under the Explosives Substances Act 1883. In determining whether the object was lawful, the court was looking forward to the contemplated actual use of the weapons, so it was not really necessary to decide whether the preparatory acts were lawful or not. So regarded, the decision is a narrow one; and indeed, it seems to have accepted that the respondent was committing an offence of manufacturing and storing explosives without a licence, contrary to the Explosives Act 1875. Nor does any doubt seem to have been cast on *Evans v. Wright* [1964] Crim.L.R. 466 and the other cases under the Prevention of Crime Act 1953 which hold that there is no lawful authority or reasonable excuse for carrying an offensive weapon in a public place for purposes of self-defence, unless there is 'an imminent particular threat affecting the particular circumstances in which the weapon was carried': *Evans v. Hughes* [1972] 3 All E.R. 412 at 415. A person who intends to use an offensive weapon only in reasonable defence has it 'for a lawful object'; yet it seems to be accepted that, unless there is an 'imminent' threat, he commits an offence under the 1953 Act. A taxi-driver might be justified in using the two feet of rubberhose with a piece of metal inserted in the end which he carries for the purposes of self-defence, when he is the victim of a violent attack; but he was committing an offence, at least until the moment when the attack was imminent, by having the article with him in a public place: *Grieve v. Macleod* 1967, S.L.T. 70.

The reasons of policy for such an approach are obvious. The court does not want to create a situation in which the manufacture and carrying of weapons will proliferate. The court says, however, that in their judgment, a defendant was not left in the paradoxical position of being able to justify acts carried out in self-defence but not acts immediately preparatory to it; but the justification is somewhat illusory if, as the court also says, he might at the same time commit other offences.

Self-defence is a defence at common law. It applies not only to common law offences but also to statutory offences, although the statutory definition gives no hint of the existence of any such defence—see, for example, sections 18 and 20 of the Offences Against the Person Act 1861. If the common law defence applies to these offences, why not to other offences such as those under the Explosive Substances Act 1875? If I am being shot at by a dangerous criminal and I pick up the revolver which has been dropped by a wounded policeman and fire it in self-defence, am I really guilty of an offence under the Firearms Act 1968, s. 1, of being in possession of firearms without holding a firearm certificate? It seems strange that the circumstances might justify me in killing my assailant with the revolver and yet not justify me in being in possession of it. If self-defence is justifiable, it surely ought to be a defence to all crimes. If it is not justifiable, it is a defence to none.

Because the only question in the present case was whether the respondent was in possession for a 'lawful object', the question whether the preliminary acts were justifiable did not really arise; but the better view seems to be that at least those acts which are immediately preparatory to the use of reasonable force in self-defence are justifiable to the same extent as the actual use of force.

Question

In the bank robbery example, if Professor Smith was charged with an offence under section 1 of the Firearms Act 1968, could he now plead duress of circumstances?

Note

In *Beckford v. The Queen* [1988] 1 A.C. 130 P.C., Lord Griffiths stated at p. 144:

The common law recognises that there are many circumstances in which one person may inflict violence upon another without committing a crime, as for instance, in sporting contests, surgical operations or in the most extreme example judicial execution. The common law has always recognised as one of these circumstances the right of a person to protect himself from attack and to act in the defence of others and if necessary to inflict violence on another in so doing. If no more force is used than is reasonable to repel the attack such force is not unlawful and no crime is committed. Furthermore a man about to be attacked does not have to wait for his assailant to strike the first blow or fire the first shot; circumstances may justify a pre-emptive strike.

It is because it is an essential element of all crimes of violence that the violence or the threat of violence should be unlawful that self-defence, if raised as an issue in a criminal trial, must be disproved by the prosecution. If the prosecution fail to do so the accused is entitled to be acquitted because the prosecution will have failed to prove an essential element of the crime namely that the violence used by the accused was unlawful.

iii. Is there a duty to retreat?

R. v. Bird
[1985] 1 W.L.R. 816
Court of Appeal

The appellant was charged with unlawful wounding having lunged at a young man with a glass in her hand, injuring him. She claimed that he had slapped and pushed her so that her back was to the wall and that she acted in self-defence without realising until later that she had been holding the glass in her hand. She was convicted.

LORD LANE C.J.: . . . The relevant passages in the summing up are these—first, towards the beginning of the direction to the jury:

"You cannot wrap up an attack in the cloak of self-defence and it is necessary that a person claiming to exercise a right of self-defence should demonstrate by her action that she does not want to fight. At one time it was thought that in order to demonstrate that, that the person seeking to raise a question of self-defence had to retreat. That is not so any longer at all, but there is an obligation to see whether the person claiming to exercise the right of self-defence should have demonstrated that she does not want to fight at all."

Towards the end of the summing up the judge used these words:

"You will have to consider whether in the circumstances of this case self-defence has any application at all. Does it look to you that this lady, who was behaving in this fashion, had demonstrated that she did not want to fight and if she had demonstrated that she did not want to fight, was the use of the glass with a hard blow which broke it, reasonable in the circumstances? All these are matters for you and not for me."

Those words were taken very largely from a decision of this court in *R. v. Julien* [1969] 1 W.L.R. 839. That was an ex tempore judgment by Widgery L.J. to which I was a party as was Karminski L.J. The passage from which the words are taken reads, at p. 842:

"The third point taken by Mr McHale is that the deputy chairman was wrong in directing the jury that before the appellant could use force in self-defence he was required to retreat. The submission here is that the obligation to retreat before using force in self-defence is an obligation which only arises in homicide cases. As the court understands it, it is submitted that if the injury results in death then the accused cannot set up self-defence except on the basis that he had retreated before he resorted to violence. On the other hand, it is said that where the injury does not result in death (as in the present case) the obligation to retreat does not arise. . . .

It is not, as we understand it, the law that a person threatened must take to his heels and run in the dramatic way suggested by Mr McHale, but what is necessary is that he should demonstrate by his actions that he does not want to fight. He must demonstrate that he is prepared to temporise and disengage and perhaps to make some physical withdrawal: and that that is necessary as a feature of the justification of self-defence is true, in our opinion, whether the charge is a homicide charge or something less serious. Accordingly, we reject Mr McHale's third submission."

That decision was to some extent followed later in *R. v. McInnes* [1971] 1 W.L.R. 1600. . . .

The court in *R. v. Julien* was anxious to make it clear that there was no duty, despite earlier authorities to the contrary, actually to turn round or walk away from the scene. But reading the words which were used in that judgment, it now seems to us that they placed too great an obligation upon a defendant in circumstances such as those in the instant case, an obligation which is not reflected in the speeches in *Palmer v. The Queen* [1971] A.C. 814.

The matter is dealt with accurately and helpfully in *Smith and Hogan Criminal Law*, 5th ed. (1983), p. 327:

"There were formerly technical rules about the duty to retreat before using force, or at least fatal force. This is now simply a factor to be taken into account in deciding whether it was necessary to use force, and whether the force was reasonable. If the only reasonable course is to retreat, then it would appear that to stand and fight must be to use unreasonable force. There is, however, no rule of law that a person attacked is bound to run away if he can; but it has been said that—' . . . what is necessary is that he should demonstrate by his actions that he does not want to fight. He must demonstrate that he is prepared to temporise and disengage and perhaps to make some physical withdrawal.' [*R. v. Julien* [1969] 1 W.L.R. 839, 842]. It is submitted that it goes too far to say that action of this kind is *necessary*. It is scarcely consistent with the rule that it is permissible to use force, not merely to counter an actual attack, but to ward off an attack honestly and reasonably believed to be imminent. A demonstration by [the defendant] at the time that he did not want to fight is, no doubt, the best evidence that he was acting reasonably and in good faith in self-defence; but it is no more than that. A person may in some circumstances so act without temporising, disengaging or withdrawing; and he should have a good defence."

We respectfully agree with that passage. If the defendant is proved to have been attacking or retaliating or revenging himself, then he was not truly acting in self-defence. Evidence that the defendant tried to retreat or tried to call off the fight may be a cast-iron method of casting doubt on the suggestion that he was the attacker or retaliator or the person trying to revenge himself. But it is not by any means the only method of doing that.

It seems to us therefore that in this case the judge—we hasten to add through no fault of his own—by using the word "necessary" as we did in the passages in the summing up to which we have referred, put too high an obligation upon the appellant.

Appeal allowed
Conviction quashed

iv. Unknown circumstances of justification

If circumstances actually exist which would justify the use of force against V, must D know of or believe in the existence of these circumstances if he is to plead self-defence or prevention of crime or lawful arrest in respect of a charge arising from his use of force? This problem of "unknown circumstances of justification" arose in *Dadson* (1850) 4 Cox C.C. 358. D, a constable, was on duty watching a copse from which wood had been stolen. V emerged from the copse carrying wood which had been stolen. He ran away when D called to him and D shot him so that he could arrest him. D was convicted of shooting at V with intent to cause him grievous bodily harm. D had sought to raise the justification that he was shooting to arrest an escaping felon. Stealing wood was only a felony where the thief had two previous convictions for that offence. In fact V had several such convictions and thus was a felon but D did not know this. D's conviction was upheld as he was not justified in shooting V as the fact that V was committing a felony was not known to him at the time.

When the Criminal Law Act 1967 was passed it was argued by some that sections 2 and 3 had the effect of reversing *Dadson*. (The Police and Criminal Evidence Act 1984, s.24(4) replaced s.2.) It was argued that if a person actually had committed an arrestable offence an arrest of him would be lawful even though the arresting officer did not know nor suspect on reasonable grounds that he had committed that offence. The Law Commission in its reports on *Codification of the Criminal Law* (Law Com. Nos. 143 and 177) recommended that an accused should be able to rely on unknown circumstances of justification in any case where the use of force was necessary and reasonable (*contra*, see Hogan, "The *Dadson* principle" [1989] Crim. L.R. 679). In *Chapman* (1988) 89 Cr. App. R. 190, the Divisional Court effectively reaffirmed *Dadson* pointing out that if a person is unaware of circumstances justifying an arrest he cannot perform a lawful arrest as he will not be able to comply with section 28(3) of the Police and Criminal Evidence Act

1984 which requires that he inform the suspect of the grounds for the arrest. If an arrest is unlawful it follows that any force used to effect it is likewise unlawful.

Question

D, looking out from his bedroom, spies the head and shoulders of V, his life-long sworn enemy, protruding above a wall 50 metres away. D takes aim with his rifle and shoots V. wounding him. Unknown to D, V was about to depress a plunger wired to an explosive charge below where D was standing which, if it had exploded, would have killed D. D is charged with wounding with intent to do grievous bodily harm contrary to section 18 of the Offences Against the Person Act 1861. Will D succeed on a plea of self-defence or prevention of crime? See Draft Criminal Law Bill, clause 27, *post*, p. 369.

v. To which offences do the defences apply?

R. v. Renouf
[1986] 1 W.L.R. 522
Court of Appeal

The appellant was charged with reckless driving. He had driven his car in pursuit of another vehicle, the occupants of which had assaulted him and damaged his car, he forced the vehicle off the road and rammed it. He was convicted after the trial judge directed that s.3(1) of the Criminal Law Act 1967 was incapable of affording a defence to the charge of reckless driving. He appealed.

LAWTON L.J.: ... The evidence relating to edging the Volvo off the road was what the prosecution alleged amounted to the reckless driving as charged. It did create an obvious and serious risk of causing physical harm to the occupants of the Volvo and of damage to it. On the evidence this was the only risk upon which the allegation of recklessness could be based. There was no risk to oncoming traffic; and nothing more than a tenuous suggestion that there might have been a risk to any traffic there may have been (and there was none) on a side road nearby. ...

This case has to be considered in the light of the evidence which was said to have amounted to reckless driving. This evidence had two facets: one was what the prosecution alleged to be the acts of recklessness; and the other was that these same acts amounted to the use of reasonable force for the purpose of assisting in the lawful arrest of offenders. In our judgment it is only when evidence has these two facets that section 3(1) of the Criminal Law Act 1967 can apply. This being so, the occasions for relying on that section will be rare, certainly not when the reckless acts were antecedent to the use of force. In our judgment the alleged presence of these two facets in the appellant's evidence concerning why he did the acts which the prosecution said were reckless was capable of providing him with a defence. It is no answer for the prosecution to submit, as Mr Clark did, that the wording of sections 1 and 2 of the Road Traffic Act 1972 shuts out any possibility of such a defence because they contained no words such as "lawful excuse". Nor does section 20 of the Offences Against the Persons Act 1861; but section 3(1) had been used to provide a defence to charges under that section.

The only other point which calls for consideration is whether what the appellant said he did amounted to the use of "force". That word is one of ordinary usage in English and does not require judicial interpretation. In that usage a jury might consider that the appellant had forced the Volvo off the road on to the grass verge. The trial judge used the word "force" in this sense in the course of his summing up.

In our judgment, on the unusual evidence in case, the judge should have left to the jury the appellant's defence based on section 3(1) of the Act of 1967. They might have accepted it because they found the appellant not guilty of causing criminal damage to the Volvo when he rammed it in order to stop it moving. They could only have done so because of his defence of "lawful excuse".

Appeal allowed

vi. Reasonable Force

Note

If the prosecution prove beyond reasonable doubt that there was no necessity to use force this will be an end of the matter unless D brings forward some evidence that he was operating under a mistake. Several different situations need to be distinguished. Firstly, if D makes a mistake as to the necessity to use force, the force used is necessarily objectively unreasonable, *i.e.* no force being necessary, any force used would be unreasonable. For example, V in an April Fools Day prank wears a mask, carries an imitation gun and stages an ambush on his friend D who is stalking deer. D, believing V is an armed robber and that his life is at risk, shoots V with his rifle. *R. v. Williams (Gladstone), ante*, p. 159 and *Beckford v. The Queen, ante*, p. 161, established that in such circumstances D must be judged according to his mistaken view of the facts. If D used only such force as was reasonable in the circumstances as he believed them to be, the effect of D's mistake is that he did not intend to use unlawful force and thus lacked the *mens rea* for the offence with which he is charged. Secondly, in any case where force is necessary (or the prosecution have not satisfied the jury that it was not), the reasonableness of that force is to be judged objectively by the jury, see *Palmer v The Queen, infra* and *Att.-Gen. for Northern Ireland's Reference (No. 1 of 1975), infra*. If the force used is excessive the defence will fail. Thirdly, D may make a mistake not as to the need to use force but as to the extent of the necessity, believing that more force is required than the circumstances objectively require—e.g. V attacks D with a knife and D hits V on the head with a brick—the knife, in fact, was a theatrical knife where the blade retracts into the handle when pressure is applied to its tip. There was an assault and probably a battery on D therefore justifying D in using reasonable force to defend himself. The problem is that D anticipated greater danger to himself and used force which would have been appropriate in those anticipated circumstances. In such a situation D believes he is using reasonable force but in fact he is using excessive force. Again, D. will be judged according to the circumstances as he believed them to be, see *Scarlett, infra* and *Owino, infra*. But if D uses more force than is reasonable, his belief that the degree of force he used was reasonable will not be determinative of the issue, see *Owino*. For example, V.

steals chocolate from D's shop and runs off. D takes a gun from under the counter and shouts at him to stop. V continues running and D shoots him in the back killing him. D asserts in his defence that he believes the use of deadly force is reasonable to apprehend shoplifters.

Palmer v. The Queen
[1971] A.C. 814
Privy Council

A group of men, including the appellant went to buy ganja. The accused had a gun. A dispute arose and the men left with the ganja but without paying. A chase ensued and a man was shot. The appellant was charged with murder and claimed self-defence. He was convicted of murder and appealed.

LORD MORRIS OF BORTH-Y-GEST: . . . On behalf of the appellant it was contended that if where self-defence is an issue in a case of homicide a jury came to the conclusion that an accused person was intending to defend himself then an intention to kill or to cause grievous bodily harm would be negatived: so it was contended that if in such a case the jury came to the conclusion that excessive force had been used the correct verdict would be one of manslaughter: hence it was argued that in every case where self-defence is left to a jury they must be directed that there are the three possible verdicts, viz. guilty of murder, guilty of manslaughter, and not guilty. But in many cases where someone is intending to defend himself he will have had an intention to cause serious bodily injury or even to kill, and if the prosecution satisfy the jury that he had one of these intentions in circumstances in which or at a time when there was no justification or excuse for having it—then the prosecution will have shown that the question of self-defence is eliminated. All other issues which on the facts may arise will be unaffected.

An issue of self-defence may of course arise in a range and variety of cases and circumstances where no death has resulted. The tests as to its rejection or its validity will be just the same as in a case where death has resulted. In its simplest form the question that arises is the question: Was the defendant acting in necessary self-defence? If the prosecution satisfy the jury that he was not then all other possible issues remain.

. . .In their Lordships' view the defence of self-defence is one which can be and will be readily understood by any jury. It is a straightforward conception. It involves no abstruse legal thought. It requires no set words by way of explanation. No formula need be employed in reference to it. Only common sense is needed for its understanding. It is both good law and good sense that a man who is attacked may defend himself. It is both good law and good sense that he may do, but may only do what is reasonably necessary. But everything will depend upon the particular facts and circumstances. Of these a jury can decide. It may in some cases be only sensible and clearly possible to take some simple avoiding action. Some attacks may be serious and dangerous. Others may not be. If there is some relatively minor attack it would not be common sense to permit some action of retaliation which was wholly out of proportion to the necessities of the situation. If an attack is serious so that it puts someone in immediate peril then immediate defensive action may be necessary. If the moment is one of crisis for someone in imminent danger he may have to avert the danger by some instant reaction. If the attack is all over and no sort of peril remains then the employment of force may be by way of revenge or punishment or by way of paying off an old score or may be pure aggression. There may no longer be any link with a necessity of defence. Of all these matters the good sense of a jury will be the arbiter. There are no prescribed words which must be employed in or adopted in a summing up. All that is needed is a clear exposition, in relation to the particular facts of the case, of the conception of necessary self-defence. If there has been no attack then clearly there will have been no need for defence. If there has been attack so that defence is reasonably necessary it will be recognised that a person defending himself cannot weigh to a nicety the exact measure of his necessary defensive action. If a jury thought that in a moment of unexpected anguish a person attacked had only done what he honestly and instinctively thought was necessary that would be most potent evidence that only reasonable defensive action had been taken. A jury will be told that the defence of self-defence, where the evidence makes its raising possible, will only fail if the prosecution show beyond doubt that what the accused did was not by way of self-defence. But their Lordships consider, in agreement with the approach in the *De Freitas* case (1960) 2 W.I.R. 523, that if the prosecution have shown that what was done was not done in self-defence then that issue is eliminated from the case. If the jury consider that an accused acted in self-defence or if the jury are in doubt as to this then they will acquit. The defence of self-defence either succeeds so as to result in an acquittal or it is disproved in which case as a defence it is rejected. In a homicide case the circumstances may be such that it will become an issue as to whether there was provocation so that the verdict might be one of manslaughter. Any other possible issues will remain. If in any case the view is possible that the intent necessary to constitute the crime of murder was lacking then that matter would be left to the jury.

Appeal dismissed

Question

Does it follow that because the defendant honestly believed that the force which he used was necessary, a jury will always find that the degree of force which he used was reasonably necessary?

Note

Palmer was followed by the Court of Appeal in *McInnes* [1971] 1 W.L.R. 1600. In the *Attorney-General for Northern Ireland's Reference (No. 1 of 1975)* [1977] A.C. 105, Lord Dilhorne said that where death results from the use of excessive force in prevention of crime or in effecting an arrest, and the accused intended to kill or do grievous bodily harm, he would be guilty of murder and not manslaughter.

In *R. v. Clegg* [1995] 1 A.C. 482, the House of Lords confirmed this position expressing their regret that this was the law but considering that any change in the law was a matter for the legislature. Following this decision the Home Secretary announced a review of the law in this area on January 24, 1995 (see below).

In the case of *R. v. Mackay* [1957] V.R. 560, the Supreme Court of Victoria recognised a qualified defence to murder based on the excessive use of force in circumstances where some force would have been lawful. A killing in such circumstances would result in a manslaughter verdict. This defence was confirmed by the High Court of Australia in *R. v. Howe* (1958) 100 C.L.R. 448 and again in *Viro v. The Queen* (1978) 141 C.L.R. 88. In *Palmer* the Privy Council considered these authorities but decided not to follow them. However, in *Zecevic v. D.P.P.* (1987) 61 A.L.J.R. 375, by a majority of five to two, the High Court of Australia abolished the defence. The majority were motivated by a desire firstly, to simplify the defence of self-defence to make it more readily understandable by juries; secondly, to make for consistency between homicide and other crimes; and thirdly, to bring Australian common law into line with *Palmer*, English common law and the law of the Code States of Australia. Prior to this development there was a rising tide of support in England for the Australian qualified defence; both Smith and Hogan, *Criminal Law* (9th ed. 1999, at p. 263) and Glanville Williams, *Textbook of Criminal Law* (2nd ed., 1983, at pp. 546–547) are in favour of the importation of the defence into the English common law, while the C.L.R.C. (Fourteenth Report, Cmnd. 7844, paragraph 288) and the Law Commission (Law Com. No. 177, Draft Criminal Code Bill, clause 59) and the Select Committee of the House of Lords on Murder and Life Imprisonment (HL Paper 78–1, session 1988–89, paragraph 83) recommended the introduction of a defence similar to the Australian qualified defence.

Report of the Inter-Departmental Review of the Law on the Use of Lethal Force in Self-Defence or the Prevention of Crime (Home Office) 1996

QUESTIONS TO BE ADDRESSED

1) Whether a person who uses excessive force resulting in death in self-defence or the maintenance of law and order should be liable to a charge of murder, manslaughter or some other charge;

2) Whether any specific complete or partial defences should be provided;

3) Whether a new offence or defence should apply only to soldiers and police officers or more generally; and

4) Whether official guidance to soldiers and police officers on the use of firearms should have any status in law.

OVERALL CONCLUSIONS

81. The review recognised that the two existing options—a conviction for murder or an acquittal—might indeed produce a distinction that was too sharp, and arguably artificial, between defendants who were acquitted and those who, having crossed the boundary of an objectively reasonable degree of force, must be convicted of murder. The apparent starkness of that choice had the potential for producing future verdicts which did not command public confidence. It was possible that a police officer, a member of the armed forces or an ordinary civilian would again honestly believe that he or she was faced with circumstances which justified the use of force, yet went beyond what was subsequently regarded as permissible.

82. The review concluded that if a wider choice of options should be made available to the court or jury to deal with that situation, it should be provided by means of a conviction for manslaughter where force used in self-defence or the prevention of crime had been unreasonable in the circumstances honestly believed by the defendant to exist. To deal with

the defendant who was arguably as culpable as others justly convicted of murder, a conviction of murder might be retained for force that was grossly unreasonable. Implementing the change by way of a partial defence reducing murder to manslaughter seemed to offer least disturbance to the current law on murder. Such a change should not be confined to members of the armed forces and police, but should apply to any citizen using lethal force in self-defence or in the prevention of crime.

83. The availability of such a verdict might assist in a comparatively small number of cases in which, previously, the outcome had proved contentious. It might help the jury or court to meet the demands of justice where a defendant had acted sufficiently culpably to deserve a criminal conviction, yet had lacked the evil motive usually associated with murder. The review was not convinced, however, that providing an additional option of manslaughter would enable the court or jury to achieve a result which would necessarily always be seen as just. More options required finer distinctions and judgements to be made. With more borders between cases, there could be more cases that were seen to fall unfairly on the wrong side of the borderline, this time between acquittal and conviction for manslaughter, and between conviction for murder and manslaughter.

84. Whether the introduction of a further option would improve the quality of justice which was perceived to have been achieved in such cases was debatable. At the same time, the review was aware that such a proposal was likely to generate a wish for similar considerations to be given to other cases in which there were argued to be extenuating circumstances—the effect could be a considerable modification to the law on murder. The review recognised that it might be difficult to move in this one area without taking a more fundamental look at the scope and operation of the law on, and the penalty for, murder.

Att.-Gen. for Northern Ireland's Reference
[1977] A.C. 105
House of Lords

The reference was based on a case in which a soldier was charged with murder after shooting at the deceased in the mistaken belief that he was a member of the I.R.A., a proscribed organisation.

LORD DIPLOCK: To kill or wound another person is *prima facie* unlawful. There may be circumstances, however, which render the act of shooting and any killing which results from it lawful; and an honest and reasonable belief by the accused in the existence of facts which if true would have rendered his act lawful is a defence to any charge based on the shooting. So for the purposes of the present reference one must ignore the fact that the deceased was an entirely innocent person and must deal with the case as if he were a member of the Provisional I.R.A. and a potentially dangerous terrorist, as the accused honestly and reasonably believed him to be. . . .

What amount of force is "reasonable in the circumstances" for the purpose of preventing crime is, in my view, always a question for the jury in a jury trial, never a "point of law" for the judge.

The form in which the jury would have to ask themselves the question in trial for an offence against the person in which this defence was raised by the accused, would be: Are we satisfied that no reasonable man a) with knowledge of such facts as were known to the accused or reasonably believed by him to exist b) in the circumstances and time available to him for reflection c) could be of the opinion that the prevention of the risk of harm to which

others might be exposed if the suspect were allowed to escape justified exposing the suspect to the risk of harm to him that might result from the kind of
force that the accused contemplated using?

To answer this the jury would have first to decide what were the facts that
did exist and were known to the accused to do so and what were mistakenly
believed by the accused to be facts. In respect of the latter the jury would
have had to decide whether any reasonable man on the material available to
the accused could have shared that belief. . . .

The jury would have also to consider how the circumstances in which the
accused had to make his decision whether or not to use force and the short-
ness of the time available to him for reflection, might affect the judgment of
a reasonable man. In the facts that are to be assumed for the purposes of the
reference there is material upon which a jury might take the view that the
accused had reasonable grounds for apprehension of imminent danger to
himself and other members of the patrol if the deceased were allowed to get
away and join armed fellow-members of the Provisional I.R.A. who might be
lurking in the neighbourhood, and that the time available to the accused to
make up his mind what to do was so short that even a reasonable man could
only act intuitively. This being so, the jury in approaching the final part of
the question should remind themselves that the postulated balancing of risk
against risk, harm against harm, by the reasonable man is not undertaken in
the calm analytical atmosphere of the court-room after counsel with the benefit of hindsight have expounded at length the reasons for and against the kind
of degree of force that was used by the accused; but in the brief second or
two which the accused had to decide whether to shoot or not and under all
the stresses to which he was exposed.

Note

Part a) of the question to be left to the jury must now be read in
light of *R. v. Gladstone Williams*. This modification has no impact on
the remainder of Lord Diplock's judgment.

R. v. Scarlett
(1994) 98 Cr. App. R. 290
Court of Appeal

D, the landlord of a public house, was convicted of unlawful act manslaughter following his use of force to eject a drunk from the premises.
The jury were directed that if they concluded that D had used unnecessary and unreasonable force, this was unlawful force and that if that
caused V to fall and strike his head, he was guilty of manslaughter. D
appealed on the ground that this was a misdirection.

BELDAM L.J.: . . .

Where one of the issues for the jury is whether the accused is guilty of the
unlawful act of assault in circumstances in which he is entitled to use reasonable force either in self-defence or for the purpose of preventing crime, or as
here in removing a trespasser, the need for a careful direction was stressed
by Lord Lane C.J. in *Williams (Gladstone)*, (*ante*, p. 159).
[His Lordship quoted the first two paragraphs from Lord Lane C.J.'s
judgment reproduced *ante*, pp. 159–160 and continued:]
The issue in the case of *Williams (Gladstone)* was whether the accused
was entitled to be acquitted if he mistakenly believed that he was justified

in using force. The court held that, even if the jury came to the conclusion that the mistake was an unreasonable one, if the defendant may genuinely have been labouring under it, he was entitled to rely upon it.

The reason why he was entitled to be acquitted is because he did not intend to apply unlawful force. The principle we have quoted that the mental element necessary to constitute guilt of an assault is the intent to apply unlawful force to the victim was approved by the Board of the Privy Council in the case of *Beckford v. R.* (*ante*, p. 161).

If the mental element necessary to prove an assault is an intention to apply unlawful force to the victim, and the accused is to be judged according to his mistaken view of the facts whether that mistake was on an objective view reasonable or not, we can see no logical basis for distinguishing between a person who objectively is not justified in using force at all but mistakenly believes he is and another who is in fact justified in using force but mistakenly believes that the circumstances call for a degree of force objectively regarded as unnecessary.

Where, as in the present case, an accused is justified in using some force and can only be guilty of an assault if the force used is excessive, the jury ought to be directed that he cannot be guilty of an assault unless the prosecution prove that he acted with the mental element necessary to constitute his action an assault, that is: ". . . that the defendant intentionally or recklessly applied force to the person of another", *per* James L.J. in *Venna* (1975) 61 Cr.App.R. 310, [1976] Q.B. 421.

Further, they should be directed that the accused is not to be found guilty merely because he intentionally or recklessly used force which they consider to have been excessive. They ought not to convict him unless they are satisfied that the degree of force used was plainly more than was called for by the circumstances as he believed them to be, and, provided he believed the circumstances called for the degree of force used, he is not to be convicted even if his belief was unreasonable.

In this case, the learned judge gave no direction to the jury that the prosecution, to establish an assault, had to prove that the appellant intentionally or recklessly applied excessive force in seeking to evict the deceased. On the contrary, the jury were simply left to say what in the circumstances they considered was reasonable force and directed that if they concluded that what was done involved an unnecessary and unreasonable degree of force they then only had to consider whether the act of unlawful and unnecessary force actually caused the deceased to fall down the steps. And again later:

"So you are left with the situation: how did he meet his death and are you sure that it was the accused's conduct which directly produced it by his unlawful act?"

We are of the opinion that the directions to the jury in the circumstances of this case were inadequate to support a verdict of guilty of manslaughter. The appellant had given clear evidence that he only intended to use sufficient force to remove the deceased from the bar, an act he was lawfully entitled to do. It was not contended, nor were submissions made to the jury on the basis, that he acted recklessly. The direction to the jury was based on the assertion that it was sufficient if they found the force used by the appellant excessive in the circumstances. The learned judge seems to have assumed that this was sufficient to prove that what the appellant did amounted to an assault.

Appeal allowed. Conviction quashed

R. v. Owino
[1996] 2 Cr. App. R. 128
Court of Appeal

D was convicted of assaulting his wife occasioning actual bodily harm. His defence was that the injuries were caused by the use of reasonable force to restrain her and to prevent her from assaulting him. D appealed against his conviction on the ground that the judge had failed to direct the jury that the test of reasonable force was subjective.

COLLINS J.: ... Mr Mendelle [for the appellant] essentially submits that [the trial judge] failed to direct the jury, as he ought to have done, that any force used must be unlawful, in the sense that it must have been excessive—more than was reasonable for self-defence; and further, that the test of what was reasonable was subjective, in the sense that the defendant could not be convicted unless he intended to use force which was more than was necessary for lawful self-defence. He relies on the authority of *Scarlett* (*ante*, p. 364) to support that proposition.

Before I come to the case of *Scarlett* specifically, it is our view that the law does not go as far as Mr Mendelle submits that it does. The essential elements of self-defence are clear enough. The jury have to decide whether a defendant honestly believed that the circumstances were such as required him to use force to defend himself from an attack or a threatened attack. In this respect a defendant must be judged in accordance with his honest belief, even though that belief may have been mistaken. But the jury must then decide whether the force used was reasonable in the circumstances as he believed them to be.

Scarlett was a case where a landlord of a public house had been ejecting, and perfectly lawfully and properly ejecting, a drunken customer from his public house. The allegation was that he had used excessive force in the course of ejecting him so that the customer fell down the steps of the entrance to the pub and unfortunately hit his head and was killed. What Mr Mendelle relies upon in the case of *Scarlett* is a passage ... where Beldam L.J., giving the judgement of the Court, said this:

"Where, as in the present case, an accused is justified in using some force and can only be guilty of an assault if the force used is excessive, the jury ought to be directed that he cannot be guilty of an assault unless the prosecution prove that he acted with the mental element necessary to constitute his action an assault, that is 'that the defendant intentionally or recklessly applied force to the person of another'. Further, they should be directed that the accused is not to be found guilty merely because he intentionally or recklessly used force which they consider to have been excessive. They ought not to convict him unless they are satisfied that the degree of force used was plainly more than was called for by the circumstances as he believed them to be and, provided he believed the circumstances called for the degree of force used, he is not to be convicted even if his belief was unreasonable.

In this case the learned judge gave no direction to the jury that the prosecution, to establish an assault, had to prove that the appellant intentionally or recklessly applied excessive force in seeking to evict the deceased."

The passage which we have cited could, if taken out of context, give rise to a suggestion that the submission by Mr Mendelle is well-founded. But what, in the context, the learned Lord Justice was really saying was, in our view, this: he was indicating that the elements of an assault involved the unlawful application of force. In the context of an issue of self-defence or reasonable restraint, which was what *Scarlett* was essentially about, then clearly a person would not be guilty of an assault unless the force used was excessive; and in judging whether the force used was excessive, the jury had to take account of the circumstances as he believed them to be. That is what is made clear in the first part of the sentence, which we will isolate and read again:

> "They ought not to convict him unless they are satisfied that the degree of force used was plainly more than was called for by the circumstances as he believed them to be and, provided be believed the circumstances called for the degree of force used, he is not to be convicted even if his belief was unreasonable."

So far as the second half of the sentence is concerned, what we understand the learned Lord Justice to have been saying was that, in judging what he believed the circumstances to be, the jury are not to decide on the basis of what was objectively reasonable; and that even if he, the defendant, was unreasonable in his belief, if it was an honest belief and honestly held, that he is not to be judged by reference to the true circumstances. It is in that context that the learned Lord Justice talks about "[belief] that the circumstances called for the degree of force used", because clearly you cannot divorce completely the concept of degree of force and the concept of the circumstances as you believe them to be. In our judgment, that is effectively all that the learned Lord Justice was saying.

What he was not saying, in our view (and indeed if he had said it, it would be contrary to authority) was that the belief, however ill-founded, of the defendant that the degree of force he was using was reasonable, will enable him to do what he did. As Kay J. indicated in argument, if that argument was correct, then it would justify, for example, the shooting of someone who was merely threatening to throw a punch, on the basis that the defendant honestly believed, although unreasonably and mistakenly, that it was justifiable for him to use that degree of force. That clearly is not, and cannot be, the law.

In truth, in the view of this Court, the law was properly and adequately set out in the case of *Williams* (1984) 78 Cr.App.R. 276, (1983) 3 All E.R. 411, which was cited and referred to in *Scarlett* and the Court in *Scarlett* was not going beyond what it set out in *Williams*.

[His Lordship quoted the last three paragraphs of Lord Lane C.J.'s judgment reproduced *ante*, p. 160 and concluded that the trial judge's direction had gone further in favour of the defence than the law made necessary.]

Appeal dismissed.

vii. Fatal Force and the European Convention on Human rights

Note

Article 2 of the European Convention on Human Rights provides:
1. Everyone's right to life shall be protected by law. No on shall be deprived of his life intentionally save in the execution of a sentence of a court following his conviction of a crime for which this penalty is provided by law.
2. Deprivation of life shall not be regarded as inflicted in contraven-

tion of this Article when it results from the use of force which is no more than absolutely necessary:

(a) in the defence of any person from unlawful violence;

(b) In order to effect a lawful arrest or to prevent the escape of a person lawfully detained;

(c) in action lawfully taken for the purpose of quelling a riot or insurrection.

The State could be in contravention of Article 2 where a state official, for example a police officer or a soldier, uses force in circumstances not covered by the exceptions listed in Article 2(2). These exceptions amount to an exhaustive list and in each case the degree of force permitted to be used must be 'no more than absolutely necessary in the circumstances'. In contrast s.3 of the Criminal Law Act 1967 (*ante* p. 347) provides for force being used *inter alia* "in the prevention of crime" and both this provision and the common law on self-defence permit the use of "such force as is reasonable in the circumstances". It is this latter test which may have to be reconsidered by domestic courts following the enactment of the Human Rights Act 1998 when considering fatal force used by state officials. The English case law on the use of force does not distinguish between force used by state officials and that used by private individuals. This will have to be reconsidered in several respects in light of European Convention case law. In *McCann and Others v. United Kingdom* (1996) 21 E.H.R.R. 97, the United Kingdom was found to be in breach of Article 2. Following intelligence information received that a Provisional IRA active service unit was planning a terrorist bomb attack on Gibraltar, SAS soldiers were sent to assist the Gibraltar authorities to arrest them. Three members of the unit were intercepted after they had crossed from Spain into Gibraltar and parked a car. They were shot and killed by the SAS soldiers who believed that they had planted a car bomb which could be detonated by a radio controlled trigger and thus shot them repeatedly to ensure they were unable to trigger the bomb. In fact there was no bomb (although explosives were subsequently discovered in Spain at a property they had rented) nor any radio controlled trigger nor were they armed. The Court emphasised that Article 2 was one of the most fundamental provisions in the Convention. They stated that Article 2(2) did not provide exceptions where it is permissible intentionally to kill but rather instances where it is permissible to use force which may result in the deprivation of life. The crucial point, however, was that the use of force must be no more than "absolutely necessary" for the achievement of one of the purposes set out in Article 2(2). This test would be applied strictly and the Court would scrutinise not only the actions of the individuals who use that force but also all the surrounding circumstances including such matters as the planning and control of the operation to see whether it was organised so as "to minimise, to the greatest extent possible, recourse to lethal force". The Court concluded that in light of the information they had and the instructions they had received, the soldiers did honestly believe, for good reasons, that lethal force was necessary. However, the planning and control of the operation amounted to a breach of

Article 2 as there were errors in the intelligence gathering and the assumptions made about the attack, insufficient allowance had been made for alternative possibilities, and the training of the soldiers giving rise to immediate reflex actions which necessarily did not involve assessments of whether less force might be sufficient, "lacks the degree of caution in the use of firearms to be expected from law enforcement personnel in a democratic society, even when dealing with dangerous terrorists".

The Convention requirement that force be "absolutely necessary" is much more exacting than the domestic test of "reasonable in the circumstances". Where the official using force makes a mistake, the Convention as interpreted in *McCann* (see also *Andronicou and Constantinou v. Cyprus* (1998) 25 E.H.R.R. 491) requires that the beliefs on which the official acted must be based on "good reason" which again is more exacting than the subjective test of honest belief required by *Gladstone Williams* (*ante* p. 159) and *Beckford* (*ante* p. 161). A problem which courts will have to confront is whether an alteration of the law in respect of the fatal use of force by a state official necessitates similar alterations in the law where non-fatal force is used. It would be confusing if one test applied in respect of the amount of force permissible and mistakes thereto where a death ensued and a different test applied where death did not occur. A further issue is whether similar alterations in the law will be necessary where one citizen kills another and seeks to plead self-defence. As a state is under an obligation under the Convention to protect every citizen's right to life from unjustifiable infringement by others (see *A v. U.K.* (1999) 28 E.H.R.R. 603) it could be argued that the same test is necessary as applies to state officials. The argument will doubtless arise in due course and it is difficult to guess how ultimately it will be resolved.

viii. Proposals for Reform

Draft Criminal Law Bill (Law Com. No. 218)

SELF-DEFENCE, PREVENTION OF CRIME, &C.

Justifiable use of force: protection of person or property, prevention of crime, &c.

27.—(1) The use of force by a person for any of the following purposes, if only such as is reasonable in the circumstances as he believes them to be, does not constitute an offence—

(a) to protect himself or another from injury, assault or detention caused by a criminal act;

(b) to protect himself or (with the authority of that other) another from trespass to the person;

(c) to protect his property from appropriation, destruction or damage caused by a criminal act or from trespass or infringement;

(d) to protect property belonging to another from appropriation, destruction or damage caused by a criminal act or (with the authority of the other) from trespass or infringement; or

(e) to prevent crime or a breach of the peace.

(2) The expressions "use of force" and "property" in subsection (1) are defined and extended by sections 29 and 30 respectively.

(3) For the purposes of this section an act involves a "crime" or is "criminal" although the person committing it, if charged with an offence in respect of it, would be acquitted on the ground that—

(a) he was under ten years of age, or
(b) he acted under duress, whether by threats or of circumstances, or
(c) his act was involuntary, or
(d) he was in a state of intoxication, or
(e) he was insane, so as not to be responsible, according to law, for the act.

(4) The references in subsection (1) to protecting a person or property from anything include protecting him or it from its continuing; and the reference to preventing crime or a breach of the peace shall be similarly construed.

(5) For the purposes of this section the question whether the act against which force is used is of a kind mentioned in any of paragraphs (a) to (e) of subsection (1) shall be determined according to the circumstances as the person using the force ("D") believes them to be.
In the following provisions of this section references to unlawful or lawful acts are to acts which are or are not of such a kind.

(6) Where an act is lawful by reason only of a belief or suspicion which is mistaken, the defence provided by this section applies as in the case of an unlawful act, unless—

(a) D knows or believes that the force is used against a constable or a person assisting a constable, and
(b) the constable is acting in the execution of his duty,

in which case the defence applies only if D believes the force to be immediately necessary to prevent injury to himself or another.

(7) The defence provided by this section does not apply to a person who causes conduct or a state of affairs with a view to using force to resist or terminate it.
But the defence may apply although the occasion for the use of force arises only because he does something he may lawfully do, knowing that such an occasion may arise.

Justifiable use of force: effecting or assisting arrest

28.—(1) The use of force by a person in effecting or assisting in a lawful arrest, if only such as is reasonable in the circumstances as he believes them to be, does not constitute an offence.

(2) The expression "use of force" in subsection (1) is defined and extended by section 29.

(3) For the purposes of this section the question whether the arrest is lawful shall be determined according to the circumstances as the person using the force believed them to be.

Meaning of use of force and related provisions

29.—(1) For the purposes of sections 27 and 28—

(a) a person uses force in relation to another person or property not only where he applies force to, but also where he causes an impact on, the body of that person or that property;

(b) a person shall be treated as using force in relation to another person if—

    (i) he threatens him with its use, or

    (ii) he detains him without actually using it; and

(c) a person shall be treated as using force in relation to property if he threatens a person with its use in relation to property.

(2) Those sections apply in relation to acts immediately preparatory to the use of force as they apply in relation to acts in which force is used.

(3) A threat of force may be reasonable although the actual use of force would not be.

(4) The fact that a person had an opportunity to retreat before using force shall be taken into account, in conjunction with other relevant evidence, in determining whether the use of force was reasonable.

CHAPTER 6

DEGREES OF RESPONSIBILITY

1. ACCOMPLICES

i. Principals and Secondary Parties

Notes

The actual perpetrator of a crime or part of a crime, or one who effects it through an innocent agent, is guilty of the crime as principal. One who does not perpetrate a crime but participates in it is punishable as a secondary party if he aids, abets, counsels or procures the principal offender to commit the crime. See Accessories and Abettors Act 1861, section 8, in the judgment of Lord Widgery C.J. in *Att.-Gen.'s Reference (No. 1 of 1975), post*, p. 374, and as to summary offences, Magistrates' Courts Act 1980, section 44. His punishment is the same as that of the principal.

The words "aid and abet, counsel and procure" may all be used together to charge a person who is alleged to have participated in a crime otherwise than as the principal or as accessory after the fact; *Re Smith* (1858) 3 H. & N. 227; *Ferguson v. Weaving, post*, p. 391. Such a person may also be charged as a principal: see *Maxwell v. D.P.P. for Northern Ireland, post*, p. 392. Indeed if two persons are present at the scene of a crime and it is not clear which committed the act and which did no more than help, it is not necessary to show which was the actual perpetrator in order to convict them both: see *Mohan v. R., post*, p. 373. A person charged as an accessory may be convicted as a principal: see *R. v. Cogan & Leak, post*, p. 380.

The terminology has changed over the years, and several terms used in cases before 1967 are now obsolete, a fact which must be borne in mind in reading such cases. The actual perpetrator was called the first principal, or the principal in the first degree. Secondary parties were of two kinds, in felonies principals in the second degree or accessories before the fact, in misdemeanours aiders and abettors, or counsellors and procurers. The technical distinction between the two kinds of secondary party still exists but is not important (see Accessories, *infra*).

Although principal and secondary party are equally guilty, the distinction between them is still of importance because (1) the definition of a crime is almost always in terms applicable only to a principal, and the liability of a secondary party follows from the terms of the Accessories and Abettors Act 1861, section 8, or Magistrates' Courts' Act 1980, section 44; (2) the *mens rea* required of a secondary party is different from that of a principal and (3) not all secondary parties who participate with the appropriate *mens rea* are liable for the offence.

One who aids a criminal *after* the commission of a crime to avoid detection or arrest or trial is not technically a party, although the old term for such a person was accessory after the fact. He may be guilty of one of several offences against the administration of justice, of which the most prominent is assisting an offender, contrary to section 4, Criminal Law Act 1967.

Mohan v. R.
[1967] 2 A.C. 187
Privy Council

D was quarrelling with M, when R, who was D's father, ran out of his house and attacked M with a cutlass. While R was chasing M, D went off and returned with another cutlass. Both struck many blows at M., who collapsed and later died. He was found to be wounded in the back and in the leg. It appeared that death was caused only by the leg wound. D and R were convicted of murder, and appealed on the ground that, as there was no evidence of a pre-arranged plan to attack M, the Crown must show which of them struck the fatal blow.

LORD PEARSON: [The appellants' argument] will be considered on the hypothesis that the death may have been caused solely by the leg wound. The question then arises whether each of the appellants can be held responsible for the leg wound, when it may have been inflicted by the other of them. There is conflicting evidence as to which of them struck the blow on M's leg, the evidence for the prosecution tending to show that the appellant D struck it and the evidence for the defence tending to show that the appellant R struck it. There is uncertainty on that point.

Also it cannot be inferred with any certainty from the evidence that the appellants had a pre-arranged plan for their attack on M.

It is, however, clear from the evidence for the defence as well as from the evidence for the prosecution, that at the material time both the appellants were armed with cutlasses, both were attacking M, and both struck him. It is impossible on the facts of this case to contend that the fatal blow was outside the scope of the common intention. The two appellants were attacking the same man at the same time with similar weapons and with the common intention that he should suffer grievous bodily harm. Each of the appellants was present, and aiding and abetting the other of them in the wounding of M.

That is the feature which distinguishes this case from cases in which one of the accused was not present or not participating in the attack or not using any dangerous weapon, but may be held liable as a conspirator or an accessory before the fact or by virtue of a common design if it can be shown that he was party to a pre-arranged plan in pursuance of which the fatal blow was struck. In this case one of the appellants struck the fatal blow, and the other of them was present aiding and abetting him. In such cases the prosecution do not have to prove that the accused were acting in pursuance of a pre-arranged plan.

Appeals dismissed

Note

The principle in this case does not apply if it is not proved that both were involved in some capacity or other. "Where two people were jointly indicted, and the evidence did not point to one rather than the other, they both ought to be acquitted because the prosecution had not proved its case. The uncertainty could not be resolved by convicting both": *Collins & Fox v. Chief Constable of Merseyside* [1988] Crim.L.R. 247 (D.C.). But where the prosecution can prove that one of the accused committed the offence and the other aided or abetted him, it does not matter that they cannot establish who performed which role: see *R. v. Forman and Ford* [1988] Crim.L.R. 677.

ii. Aiding, Abetting, Counselling or Procuring

Attorney-General's Reference (No. 1 of 1975)
[1975] Q.B. 773
Court of Appeal

The facts appear in the judgment.

LORD WIDGERY C.J.: This case comes before the court on a reference from the Attorney-General, under section 36 of the Criminal Justice Act 1972, and by his reference he asks the following question:

> "Whether an accused, who surreptitiously laced a friend's drinks with double measures of spirits when he knew that his friend would shortly be driving his car home, and in consequence his friend drove with an excessive quantity of alcohol in his body and was convicted of the offence under section 6(1) of the Road Traffic Act 1972, is entitled to a ruling of no case to answer on being later charged as an aider and abettor, counsellor and procurer, on the ground that there was no shared intention between the two, that the accused did not by accompanying him or otherwise positively encourage the friend to drive, or on any other ground."

... The present question has no doubt arisen because in recent years there have been a number of instances where men charged with driving their motor cars with an excess quantity of alcohol in the blood have sought to excuse their conduct by saying that their drinks were "laced," as the jargon has it; that is to say, some strong spirit was put into an otherwise innocuous drink and as a result the driver consumed more alcohol than he had either intended to consume or had the desire to consume. The relevance of all that is not that it entitles the driver to an acquittal because such driving is an absolute offence, but that it can be relied on as a special reason for not disqualifying the driver from driving. Hence no doubt the importance which has been attached in recent months to the possibility of this argument being raised in a normal charge of driving with excess alcohol.

The question requires us to say whether on the facts posed there is a case to answer and, needless to say, in the trial from which this reference is derived the judge was of the opinion that there was no case to answer and so ruled. We have to say in effect whether he is right.

The language in the section which determines whether a "secondary party", as he is sometimes called, is guilty of a criminal offence committed by another embraces the four words "aid, abet, counsel or procure". The origin of those words is to be found in section 8 of the Accessories and Abettors Act 1861, which provides:

"Whosoever shall aid, abet, counsel or procure the commission of any misdemeanor, whether the same be a misdemeanour at common law or by virtue of any Act passed or to be passed, shall be liable to be tried, indicted and punished as a principal offender."

Thus, in the past, when the distinction was still drawn between felony and misdemeanor, it was sufficient to make a person guilty of a misdemeanour if he aided, abetted, counselled or procured the offence of another. When the difference between felonies and misdemeanors was abolished in 1967, section 1 of the Criminal Law Act 1967 in effect provided that the same test should apply to make a secondary party guilty either of treason or felony.

Of course it is the fact that in the great majority of instances where a secondary party is sought to be convicted of an offence there has been a contact between the principal offender and the secondary party. Aiding and abetting almost inevitably involves a situation in which the secondary party and the main offender are together at some stage discussing the plans which they may be making in respect of the alleged offence, and are in contact so that each knows what is passing through the mind of the other.

In the same way it seems to us that a person, who counsels the commission of a crime by another, almost inevitably comes to a moment when he is in contact with that other, when he is discussing the offence with that other and when, to use the words of the statute, he counsels the other to commit the offence.

The fact that so often the relationship between the secondary party and the principal will be such that there is a meeting of minds between them caused the trial judge in the case from which this reference is derived to think that this was really an essential feature of proving or establishing the guilt of the secondary party and, as we understand his judgment, he took the view that in the absence of some sort of meeting of minds, some sort of mental link between the secondary party and the principal, there could be no aiding, abetting or counselling of the offence within the meaning of the section.

So far as aiding, abetting and counselling is concerned we would go a long way with that conclusion. It may very well be, as I said a moment ago, difficult to think of a case of aiding, abetting or counselling when the parties have not met and have not discussed in some respects the terms of the offence which they have in mind. But we do not see why a similar principle should apply to procuring. We approach section 8 of the Act of 1861 on the basis that the words should be given their ordinary meaning, if possible. We approach the section on the basis also that if four words are employed here, "aid, abet, counsel or procure", the probability is that there is a difference between each of those four words and the other three, because, if there were no such difference, then Parliament would be wasting time in using four words where two or three would do. Thus, in deciding whether that which is assumed to be done under our reference was a criminal offence we approach the section on the footing that each word must be given its ordinary meaning.

To procure means to produce by endeavour. You procure a thing by setting out to see that it happens and taking the appropriate steps to produce that happening. We think that there are plenty of instances in which a person may be said to procure the commission of a crime by another even though there is no sort of conspiracy between the two, even though there is no attempt at agreement or discussion as to the form which the offence should take. In our judgment the offence described in this reference is such a case.

If one looks back at the facts of the reference: the accused surreptitiously laced his friend's drink. This is an important element and, although we are not going to decide today anything other than the problem posed to us, it may well be that, in similar cases where the lacing of the drink or the introduction of the extra alcohol is known to the driver quite different considerations may apply. We say that because, where the driver has no knowledge of what is happening, in most instances he would have no means of preventing the offence from being committed. If the driver is unaware of what has happened, he will not be taking precautions. He will get into his car seat, switch on the ignition and drive home, and, consequently, the conception of another procuring the commission of the offence by the driver is very much stronger where the driver is innocent of all knowledge of what is happening, as in the present case where the lacing of the drink was surreptitious.

The second thing which is important in the facts set out in our reference is that, following and in consequence of the introduction of the extra alcohol, the friend drove with an excess quantity of alcohol in his blood. Causation here is important. You cannot procure an offence unless there is a causal link between what you do and the commission of the offence, and here we are told that in consequence of the addition of this alcohol the driver, when he drove home, drove with an excess quantity of alcohol in his body.

Giving the words their ordinary meaning in English, and asking oneself whether in those circumstances the offence has been procured, we are in no doubt that the answer is that it has. It has been procured because, unknown to the driver and without his collaboration, he has been put in a position in which in fact he has committed an offence which he never would have committed otherwise. We think that there was a case to answer and that the trial judge should have directed the jury that an offence is committed if it is shown beyond reasonable doubt that the defendant knew that his friend was going to drive, and also knew that the ordinary and natural result of the additional alcohol added to the friend's drink would be to bring him above the recognised limit of 80 milligrammes per 100 millilitres of blood. . . .

Our decision on the reference is that the question posed by the Attorney-General should be answered in the negative.

Opinion accordingly

Question

How is this decision likely to affect the frequency of the "my drink was laced" plea?

Notes

1. "To procure means to produce by endeavour." If the charge is of procuring only, intention in the accused that the offence shall be committed must be shown, but if the charge is of aiding, abetting, counselling and procuring (as it usually is) recklessness (in the *Cunningham* sense—see, *ante*, p. 116 as to the commission of the offence is sufficient: see *Blakely v. D.P.P.* [1991] R.T.R. 405 (D.C.).

2. In *R. v. Calhaem* [1985] Q.B. 808 (C.A.) it was held that "counsel-

ling," unlike "procuring," needs no causal connection between the counselling and the offence.

3. It has been said that the attempt to give different meanings to the words "aids, abets, counsels, procures" is misguided and useless; see *infra*.

J. C. Smith; "Aid, abet, counsel or procure" in *Reshaping the Criminal Law* (1978, ed. Glazebrook), pp. 122 & 124–125

The formula adopted in section 8 of the Accessories and Abettors Act 1861 and other nineteenth and twentieth century statutes is the most modern in a long line from very early times. . . .

Other earlier and later statutes, however, use different formulae in which the words, 'helping', 'maintaining', 'commanding', 'contriving', 'assisting', 'directing' and 'hiring' and others recur. . . .

Foster (Crown Law, p. 121) agreed that it is true that penal statutes must be strictly construed but said that 'it is equally true that we are not to be governed by the sound, but by the well-known, true, legal import of the words.' He reviewed the large variety of words used in various statutes to describe the activity of accessories and concluded that such words are technical expressions to be given their legal meaning.

> From these different modes of expression, all plainly descriptive of the same offence, I think one may safely conclude, that in the construction of statutes which oust clergy in the case of *Participes Criminis*, we are not to be governed by the bare sound, but by the true legal import of the words. And also, that every person who cometh within the description of these statutes, various as they are in point of expression, is in the judgment of the legislature an accessory before the fact; unless he is present at the fact, and in that case he is undoubtedly a principal.

> According to this highly authoritative view, the actual words used are of no significance once it is clear that they were intended to incorporate the common law concepts of secondary participation. That these are concepts of the common law is clear. It was recognised by Coke, Hale and the subsequent writers of authority that it was not necessary for a statute to provide for the liability of secondary parties. It was sufficient for Parliament to prescribe the offence and liability for secondary participation followed by implication. Yet, for some reason, Parliament sometimes made express provision and sometimes did not. When express provision was made, there was no consistency in the terminology used: but whatever the words, the same concept of the common law applied.

> What then of the words used in section 8 of the Accessories and Abettors Act 1861, and section 35 of the Magistrates' Court Act 1952? According to C. S. Greaves, the editor of the third and fourth editions of *Russell on Crime*, and the draftsman of the 1861 legislation, section 8 'is really only a declaration of the common law on the subject.' This opinion has been followed by the courts on several occasions. It is submitted that this is the right view and that as Sir Francis Adams puts it: 'Nothing is to be gained by attempting to distinguish between the meaning of different words used in this connection.'

Notes

1. In *Ferguson v. Weaving* (for facts, see *post*, p. 391), the defendant, although "absent", was charged with aiding, abetting, counselling and procuring. Lord Goddard C.J.:

"At the hearing an application was made to amend the information against the respondent by the deletion of the words 'aid and abet,' so that the information charged her only with counselling and procuring the commission of the offences. Before us it was contended on her behalf that, even if the facts on which the prosecution relied were accepted, they could only establish a case of aiding and abetting, and that there was no evidence that the respondent in any way counselled or procured the commission of the said offences. It is well known that the words 'aid and abet' are apt to describe the action of a person who is present at the time of the commission of an offence and takes some part therein. He is then described as an aider and abettor, whereas the words 'counsel and procure' are appropriate to a person who, though not present at the commission of the offence, is an accessory before the fact. That all these words may be used together to charge a person who is alleged to have participated in an offence otherwise than as a principal in the first degree was established by *Re Smith* (1858) 3 H. & N. 227. Whether, where the words 'counsel and procure' alone are used, there must be a proof of something more than would establish a case of being an accessory before the fact is not one which we feel necessary to decide in this case. . . . As we are satisfied that the respondent cannot be convicted as a participant, to use a compendious expression, in the offences charged against the persons who consumed the intoxicating liquor, we give no decision on it."

2. Smith, "*Aid, Abet, Counsel or Procure*", *supra*, p. 377: It is submitted that the true position is as follows. The distinction between "aiding and abetting" and "counselling and procuring", like that between principal and accessory, depends on one consideration only, namely whether the defendant was present (again in the large sense in which the common law understood that term) or absent. Notwithstanding the ordinary meaning of the words, the distinction does not turn in any way on the nature of the acts done by the defendant. Any act which would amount to "aiding and abetting" if done while present at the crime would amount to "counselling and procuring" if done while absent. Any act which would amount to "counselling and procuring" when done in the absence of the principal would amount to "aiding and abetting" if done while present at the crime. . . . If it is right to regard the words "aid and abet" as indicative of the liability of a person present and the words "counsel and procure" as indicative of the liability of a person absent, it is obvious that these are highly technical terms. It is inconsistent so to treat the words in one context and yet to regard them as words of ordinary meaning in another.

3. Until 1987, there was one case where a party's liability turned on whether he was present or absent. One who was *absent* could not be convicted of a greater crime than the principal: *R. v. Richards* [1974] Q.B. 776. However this case was overruled by the House of Lords in *R. v. Howe* [1987] A.C. 417, *post*, p. 383.

iii. Proving the principal offence

Note

If B aids or encourages A to commit the *actus reus* of a crime, it may be that A, for some reason personal to himself, is not guilty of the crime. The question of B's liability arises. If A is the "principal" and commits no crime, it would appear that there is no crime to which B can be a secondary party. Sometimes the logic of that has to be accepted: see *Thornton v. Mitchell, infra.* In other cases, the logic is avoided by holding that B is the principal, since he used A as an innocent agent to commit what would be a crime if done by B: see *R. v. Cogan & Leak, infra.* In other cases, it is possible to convict B by holding that although A is not guilty, or not prosecutable, a crime was nevertheless committed by him, in which B was a secondary party: see *R. v. Bourne, R. v. Austin, infra.* Finally, A may be guilty of a lesser offence which has the same *actus reus* as the more serious offence of which B may be convicted: see *Howe, infra.*

Thornton v. Mitchell
[1940] 1 All E.R. 339
King's Bench Division

A bus driver reversed his bus according to the signals of his conductor, who failed to notice some persons standing behind the bus. The driver could not possibly see behind the bus and had to rely on the signals of the conductor. The persons standing behind the bus were injured. The driver was charged with careless driving, and the conductor with aiding and abetting, counselling and procuring the commission of that offence. The charge against the driver was dismissed, but the conductor was convicted. He appealed.

LORD HEWART C.J.: [The justices] say in paragraph 8: "We being of opinion that the conductor [had been very negligent] held that he was guilty of aiding, abetting, counselling and procuring the said Hollindrake to drive without due care and attention, and accordingly we inflicted a fine." In my opinion, this case is *a fortiori* on *Morris v. Tolman* [1923] 1 K.B. 166, to which our attention has been directed. I will read one sentence from the judgment of Avory J. at p. 171: ". . . in order to convict, it would be necessary to show that the respondent was aiding and abetting the principal, but a person cannot aid another in doing something which that other has not done."

That I think is the very thing which these justices have decided that the bus conductor did. In one breath they say that the principal did nothing which he should not have done and in the next breath they hold that the bus conductor aided and abetted the driver in doing something which had not been done or in not doing something which he ought to have done. I really think that, with all respect to the ingenuity of counsel for the respondent, the case is too plain for argument.

Appeal allowed

Note

The reason why the bus conductor could not be convicted of careless driving as principal was because it was impossible to construe the word "drive" in the relevant section of the Road Traffic Act as referring to the conduct of anyone other than the immediate driver. See, Williams, *Textbook,* p. 370. There would seem to be limits beyond which the concept of agency will not stretch, *i.e.* wherever a crime needs personal action by the offender. Rape would appear to be such a crime, but see next case.

R. v. Cogan and Leak
[1976] 1 Q.B. 217
Court of Appeal

L forced his wife to have sexual intercourse with C. C was charged with rape and L was charged with aiding, abetting, counselling and procuring C to commit rape. C was acquitted of rape on it appearing that he did not know that L's wife was not consenting to the intercourse. L was convicted and appealed.

LAWTON L.J.: . . . Leak's appeal against conviction was based on the proposition that he could not be found guilty of aiding and abetting Cogan to rape his wife if Cogan was acquitted of that offence as he was deemed in law to have been when his conviction was quashed: see section 2(3) of the Criminal Appeal Act 1968. Leak's counsel, Mr Herrod, conceded however, that his proposition had some limitations. The law on this topic lacks clarity as a perusal of some of the textbooks shows: see *Smith and Hogan, Criminal Law*, 3rd ed. (1973), pp. 106–109; *Glanville Williams, Criminal Law*, 2nd ed. (1961), pp. 386–390, 406–408; *Russell on Crime*, 12th ed. (1964), vol. 1, p. 128. We do not consider it appropriate to review the law generally because, as was said by this court in *R. v. Quick* [1973] Q.B. 910, 923, when considering this kind of problem:

"The facts of each case . . . have to be considered and in particular what is alleged to have been done by way of aiding and abetting."

The only case which Mr Herrod submitted had a direct bearing upon the problem of Leak's guilt was *Walters v. Lunt* [1951] 2 All E.R. 645. In that case the respondents had been charged, under section 33(1) of the Larceny Act 1916, with receiving from a child aged seven years, certain articles knowing them to have been stolen. In 1951, a child under eight years was deemed in law to be incapable of committing a crime: it followed that at the time the charge had not been proved. That case is very different from this because here one fact is clear—the wife had been raped. Cogan had had sexual intercourse with her without her consent. The fact that Cogan was innocent of rape because he believed that she was consenting does not affect the position that she was raped.

Her ravishment had come about because Leak had wanted it to happen and had taken action to see that it did by persuading Cogan to use his body as the instrument for the necessary physical act. In the language of the law the act of sexual intercourse without the wife's consent was the *actus reus*: it had been procured by Leak who had the appropriate *mens rea*, namely, his intention that Cogan should have sexual intercourse with her without her consent. In our judgment it is irrelevant that the man whom Leak had procured to do the physical act himself did not intend to have sexual intercourse with the wife without her consent. Leak was using him as a means to procure a criminal purpose.

Before 1861 a case such as this, pleaded as it was in the indictment, might have presented a court with problems arising from the old distinctions between principals and accessories in felony. Most of the old law was swept away by section 8 of the Accessories and Abettors Act 1861 and what remained by section 1 of the Criminal Law Act 1967. The modern law allowed Leak to be tried and punished as a principal offender. In our judgment he could have been indicted as a principal offender. It would have been no defence for him to submit that if Cogan was an "innocent" agent, he was necessarily in the old terminology of the law a principal in the first degree, which was a legal impossibility as a man cannot rape his own wife during cohabitation. The law no longer concerns itself with niceties of degrees in participation in crime; but even if it did Leak would still be guilty. The reason a man cannot by his own physical act rape his wife during cohabitation is because the law presumes consent from the marriage ceremony: see Hale, *Pleas of the Crown* (1778), vol. 1, p. 629. There is no such presumption when a man procures a drunken friend to do the physical act for him. Hale C.J. put this case in one sentence, at p. 629:

"... tho in marriage she hath given up her body to her husband, she is not to be by him prostituted to another": see *loc. cit.*

Had Leak been indicted as a principal offender, the case against him would have been clear beyond argument. Should he be allowed to go free because he was charged with "being aider and abettor to the same offence"? If we are right in our opinion that the wife had been raped (and no one outside a court of law would say that she had not been), then the particulars of offence accurately stated what Leak had done, namely, he had procured Cogan to commit the offence. This would suffice to uphold the conviction. We would prefer, however, to uphold it on a wider basis. In our judgment convictions should not be upset because of mere technicalities of pleading in an indictment. Leak knew what the case against him was and the facts in support of that case were proved. But for the fact that the jury thought that Cogan in his intoxicated condition might have mistaken the wife's sobs and distress for expressions of her consent, no question of any kind would have arisen about the form of pleading. By his written statement Leak virtually admitted what he had done. As Judge Chapman said in *R. v. Humphreys* [1965] 3 All E.R. 689, 692:

"It would be anomalous if a person who admitted to a substantial part in the perpetration of a misdemeanour as aider and abettor could not be convicted on his own admission merely because the person alleged to have been aided and abetted was not or could not be convicted."

In the circumstances of this case it would be more than anomalous: it would be an affront to justice and to the common sense of ordinary folk. It was for these reasons that we dismissed the appeal against conviction. . . .
Appeal against conviction dismissed

Notes

1. At the date of this case, a husband could not ordinarily be guilty of personally raping his wife. This is no longer the case following the insertion of a new section 1 to the Sexual Offences Act 1956 by section 142 of the Criminal Justice and Public Order Act 1994 which placed on a statutory footing the effect of the House of Lords decision in *R. v. R.* [1992] A.C. 599.

2. In *R. v. Bourne* (1952) 36 Cr.App.R. 125, the C.C.A. upheld a conviction of a husband for aiding and abetting his wife to commit buggery with a dog, although the facts showed that the wife, who was the only possible principal, would have been able to raise the defence of duress had she been charged with committing buggery with the dog. The reason given was that a plea of duress admits the crime but prays to be excused punishment on the grounds of duress.

3. In *Millward*, [1994] Crim.L.R. 527, M instructed H to drive a tractor and trailer. M knew, but H did not know, that the hitch mechanism

was dangerously defective. As H was driving, the trailer became detached causing a fatal accident. H was acquitted of causing death by reckless driving but M was convicted as he had procured the *actus reus*. While it was not M's purpose to bring about the death, it was his purpose to bring about the reckless driving. The requirement to prove purpose on the part of a procurer seems to be confined to purpose as to the initiating cause of a concequence.

Note

The doctrine employed in *R. v. Bourne, supra*, that although the principal actor may have a complete defence, there is nonetheless a crime, to which secondary participants can be parties, is sometimes less artificial than it was in that case. See next case.

R. v. Austin
[1981] 1 All E.R. 374
Court of Appeal

A child of three years was in the lawful custody of her mother JK RK, the father, got an order from a Maryland Court awarding control of the child to him, which order was not enforceable in England. RK employed A and others to help him take the child by force. RK snatched the child from JK in a street in Winchester, and while A and others confused the pursuit, reached Heathrow and was able to leave the country with the child. A and others were convicted of child stealing and appealed.

WATKINS L.J.: At the close of the case for the Crown in the Crown Court at Winchester counsel for the appellants . . . made a number of concessions on behalf of the appellants. He has repeated them to this court. They are: (1) that each of these appellants aided and abetted King in taking Lara away from the possession of her mother; (2) that the child was taken by King by the use of force on the mother and the child. It was also conceded that they all knew the child was in the lawful possession of the mother, since there was no order in this country which affected her right to that at the material time and the order of the American court could not affect it in any practical way. It was also admitted that they had the intention to deprive the mother of possession of the child.

Having regard to those admissions and the background of this affair, one looks at section 56 of the 1861 [Offences Against the Person] Act which provides:

"Whosoever shall unlawfully . . . by force . . . take away . . . any child under the age of fourteen years, with intent to deprive any parent . . . of the possession of such child . . . shall be liable, at the discretion of the court . . . to be imprisoned: Provided, that no person who shall have claimed any right to the possession of such child, or shall be the mother or shall have claimed to be the father of an illegitimate child, shall be liable to be prosecuted by virtue hereof on account of the getting possession of such child . . ."

. . . A parent who seeks, especially when there is no order of a court in existence affecting the ordinary common law right of possession of parents to a child, to take away that child from the other parent by force will inevitably commit the offence of child stealing under section 56, unless it be shown that at the time there was lawful excuse for the use of the force as a means of taking the child away. Accordingly, apart from the proviso, King on the known facts could have had no defence if charged with this offence.

Undoubtedly King could properly have claimed a right of possession to the child and so have gained the protection of the proviso. What would have been the effect of that? The effect would have been that, although he had committed the offence of child stealing, because he was the child's father and could claim a right to possession of the child, he would not have been prosecuted. It is submitted on the appellant's behalf that the proviso also protects a class of persons wide enough to include those who aid a person such as the father of the child in gaining possession of his child by force. They become his agents for the purpose. Many persons have from time to time the temporary possession of a child as agents of parents. Why are they not protected to the same extent as parents when regaining possession as agents of parents?

In our view the only sensible construction of the proviso allows of its protection being granted to a small class of persons only, which includes the father and the mother of the child, whether the child be legitimate or illegitimate or a guardian appointed by a testamentary document, or by an order conferring the status of guardianship, or a person to whom is granted an order conferring some form of care, control, custody or access. We can think of no other who could claim exemption from prosecution by reason of the proviso.

What of these appellants? They had no good reason for doing what they did. They had no right to assert, and no interest in, the possession of the child. They were the paid hirelings of King to aid him in the commission of a criminal offence, namely stealing a child, and with him they committed it as aiders and abettors. While King may shelter behind the proviso, there is no room there for them. Parliament in its wisdom undoubtedly decided that the mischiefs of matrimonial discord which are unhappily so widespread should not give rise to wholesale criminal prosecutions arising out of disputes about children, about who should have possession and control of them. That and that alone is the reason for the existence of the proviso to section 56. Thus, as we have said, its application is confined to the select class of persons we have endeavoured to define. . . .

Appeals dismissed

R. v. Howe
[1987] AC 417
House of Lords

Lord Mackay of Clashfern: . . .

I turn now to the second certified question [:Can the one who incites or procures by duress another to kill or to be a party to a killing be convicted of murder if that other is acquitted by reason of duress?] In the view that I take on question one the second does not properly arise. However, I am of opinion that the Court of Appeal reached the correct conclusion upon it as a matter of principle.

Giving the judgment of the Court of Appeal Lord Lane C.J. said [1986] Q.B. 626, 641–642:

"The judge based himself on a decision of this court in *Reg. v. Richards* [1974] Q.B. 776. The facts in that case were that Mrs Richards paid two men to inflict injuries on her husband which she intended should 'put him in hospital for a month.' The two men wounded the husband but not seriously. They were acquitted of wounding with intent but convicted of unlawful wounding. Mrs. Richards herself was convicted of wounding with intent, the jury plainly, and not surprisingly, believing that she had the necessary intent, though the two men had not. She appealed against her conviction on the ground that she could not properly be convicted as accessory before the fact to a crime more serious than that committed by the principals in the first degree. The appeal was allowed and the conviction for unlawful wounding was substituted. The court followed a passage from *Hawkins' Pleas of the Crown*, vol. 2. c. 29, para. 15: 'I take it to be an uncontroverted rule that [the offence of the accessory can never rise higher than that of the principal]; it seeming incongruous and absurd that he who is punished only as a partaker of the guilt of another, should be adjudged guilty of a higher crime than the other.'

"James L.J. delivering the judgment in *Reg. v. Richards* [1974] Q.B. 776 said, at p. 780: 'If there is only one offence committed, and that is the offence of unlawful wounding, then the person who has requested that offence to be committed, or advised that that offence be committed, cannot be guilty of a graver offence than that in fact which was committed.' The decision in *Reg. v. Richards* has been the subject of some criticism—see for example *Smith & Hogan, Criminal Law*, 5th ed. (1983), p. 140. Counsel before us posed the situation where A hands a gun to D informing him that it is loaded with blank ammunition only and telling him to go and scare X by discharging it. The ammunition is in fact live, as A knows, and X is killed. D is convicted only of manslaughter, as he might be on those facts. It would seem absurd that A should thereby escape conviction for murder. We take the view that *Reg. v. Richards* [1974] Q.B. 776 was incorrectly decided, but it seems to us that it cannot properly be distinguished from the instant case."

I consider that the reasoning of Lord Lane C.J. is entirely correct and I would affirm his view that where a person has been killed and that result is the result intended by another participant, the mere fact that the actual killer may be convicted only of the reduced charge of manslaughter for some reason special to himself does not, in my opinion in any way, result in a compulsory reduction for the other participant.

iv. Mens Rea of a secondary Party

Note

The secondary party must have knowingly supplied help or encouragement to the principal: see *R. v. Clarkson, infra*. It is sufficient if he knew that the principal was likely to commit the crime; he need not have desired him to do so: see *N.C.B. v. Gamble, infra*. He must have known of the circumstances which made the principal's act criminal, even in the case of a strict liability offence: see *Ferguson v. Weaving, infra*. He need not have foreseen the precise circumstances, *e.g.* time and place of commission, provided that the crime which happened was within his contemplation: see *Maxwell v. D.P.P. for Northern Ireland, infra* and *R. v. Slack, infra*. It follows that if the principal went beyond what the secondary party contemplated, that might serve to excuse the secondary party: see *R. v. English, infra*.

(a) Help or encouragement knowingly supplied

R. v. Clarkson
[1971] 1 W.L.R. 1402
Court-Martial Appeal Court

The accused were charged with aiding and abetting three offences of rape. The evidence was that the accused, who had been drinking heavily, heard a disturbance in a room. They went in and stood watching whilst a woman was raped. They gave neither physical assistance nor verbal encouragement. They were convicted and appealed.

MEGAW L.J.: ... Let it be accepted, and there was evidence to justify this assumption, that the presence of those two defendants in the room where the offence was taking place was not accidental in any sense and that it was not by chance, unconnected with the crime, that they were there. Let it be accepted that they entered the room when the crime was committed because of what they had heard, which indicated that a woman was being raped, and they remained there.

R. v. Coney (1882) 8 Q.B.D. 534, decided that non-accidental presence at the scene of the crime is not conclusive of aiding and abetting. The jury has to be told by the judge, or in this case the court-martial has to be told by the judge advocate, in clear terms what it is that has to be proved before they can convict of aiding and abetting; what it is of which the jury or the court-martial, as the case may be, must be sure as matters of inference before they can convict of aiding and abetting in such a case where the evidence adduced by the prosecution is limited to non-accidental presence.

What has to be proved is stated in *R. v. Coney* by Hawkins J. in a well-known passage in his judgment, at p. 557:

"In my opinion, to constitute an aider and abettor some active steps must be taken by word, or action, with the intent to instigate the principal, or principals. Encouragement does not of necessity amount to aiding and abetting, it may be intentional or unintentional, a man may unwittingly encourage another in fact by his presence, by misinterpreted words, or gestures, or by his silence, or non-interference or he may encourage intentionally by expressions, or gestures, or actions intended to signify approval. In the latter case he aids and abets, in the former he does not. It is no criminal offence to stand by, a mere passive spectator of a crime, even of a murder. Non-interference to prevent a crime is not itself a crime. But the fact that a person was voluntarily and purposely present witnessing the commission of a crime, and offered no opposition to it, though he might reasonably be expected to prevent and had the power so to do, or at least to express his dissent, might under some circumstances, afford cogent evidence upon which a jury would be justified in finding that he wilfully encouraged and so aided and abetted. But it would be purely a question for the jury whether he did so or not."

It is not enough, then, that the presence of the accused has, in fact, given encouragement. It must be proved that the accused intended to give encouragement; that he *wilfully* encouraged. In a case such as the present, more than in many other cases where aiding and abetting is alleged, it was essential that that element should be stressed; for there was here at least the possibility that a drunken man with his self-discipline loosened by drink, being aware that a woman was being raped, might be attracted to the scene and might stay on the scene in the capacity of what is known as a voyeur; and, while his presence and the presence of others might in fact encourage the rapers or discourage the victim, he, himself, enjoying the scene or at least standing by assenting, might not intend that his presence should offer encouragement to rapers and would-be rapers or discouragement to the victim; he might not realise that he was giving encouragement; so that, while encouragement there might be, it would not be a case in which, to use the words of Hawkins J., the accused person "wilfully encouraged."

A further point is emphasised in passages in the judgment of the Court of Criminal Appeal in *R. v. Allan* [1965] 1 Q.B. 130, 135, 138. That was a case concerned with participation in an affray. The court said, at p. 135:

"in effect, it amounts to this: that the judge thereby directed the jury that they were duty bound to convict an accused who was proved to have been present and witnessing and affray if it was also proved that he nursed an intention to join in if help was needed by the side he favoured and this notwithstanding that he did nothing by words or deeds to evince his intention and outwardly played the role of a purely passive spectator. It was said that, if that direction is right, where A and B behave themselves to all outward appearances in an exactly similar manner, but it be proved that A had the intention to participate if needs be, whereas B had no such intention, then A must be convicted of being a principal in the second degree to the affray, whereas B should be acquitted. To do that, it is objected, would be to convict A on his thoughts, even though they found no reflection in his actions."

The other passage in the judgment is at p. 138:

"In our judgment, before a jury can properly convict an accused person of being a principal in the second degree to an affray, they must be convinced by the evidence that, at the very least, he by some means or other encouraged the participants. To hold otherwise would be, in effect, as the appellants' counsel rightly expressed it, to convict a man on his thoughts, unaccompanied by any physical act other than the fact of his mere presence."

From that it follows that mere intention is not in itself enough. There must be an intention to encourage; and there must also be encouragement in fact, in cases such as the present case.

So we come to what was said by the judge advocate. . . . This court has come to the conclusion that the court might have misunderstood the relevant principles that ought to be applied. It might have been left under the impression that it could find these two defendants guilty on the basis of their continuing, non-accidental presence, even though it was not sure that the necessary inferences to be drawn from the evidence included (i) an intention to encourage and (ii) actual encouragement. While we have no doubt that those inferences could properly have been drawn in respect of each defendant on each count, so that verdicts of guilty could properly have been returned, we cannot say that the court-martial, properly directed, would necessarily have drawn those inferences. Accordingly the convictions of the defendants Clarkson and Carroll must be quashed.

Appeals allowed

Questions

1. If B is able to control A's behaviour, and does not do so, with the result, expected by B, that A commits a crime, what is the significance,

on a charge of aiding, abetting, counselling or procuring A's crime, of B's failure?

2. Ought it to make any difference whether B's power to control A is a legal one or merely a physical or psychological one? See *Cassady v. Morris* [1975] Crim.L.R. 398; *Du Cros v. Lambourne* [1907] 1 K.B. 40; *R. v. Harris* [1964] Crim.L.R. 54.

3. B's wife A tells him that she is going to kill herself and their infant children. B protests but does nothing to stop A, who throws her children into a river and jumps in herself, so that they are all drowned. Has B aided, abetted, counselled or procured (i) the murder of the children, (ii) the suicide of A? See Suicide Act 1961, s.2(1), p. 612 (*cf. R. v. Russell* [1933] V.L.R. 59).

(b) Knowledge enough

National Coal Board v. Gamble
[1959] 1 Q.B. 11
Queen's Bench Division

The National Coal Board had an instalment contract with the Central Electricity Authority for a supply of coal to be delivered at a colliery into lorries sent by a carrier on behalf of the authority. In pursuance of this contract W Ltd, a carrier, sent a lorry in the charge of its servant M into the colliery. The method of loading was for a lorry-driver to place his lorry under the Board's hopper and tell the hopper operator to stop when the driver thought he had enough coal on his lorry. The lorry was then driven to the colliery weighbridge which was in the charge of H, a servant of the Board. H, after weighing the lorry and its load, would give the driver a ticket showing the weight of coal loaded, which ticket operated as a delivery note, so that the sale of the load of coal was then complete and the property in the coal passed from the Board to the purchaser.

M went through this procedure, but when H weighed his lorry and load he discovered that they together exceeded the maximum permitted weight for a vehicle being driven on a road. H drew M's attention to this fact, and there was also a large notice at the door of the weighbridge office warning drivers that the Board was not responsible for the use of any vehicle on a road which was loaded beyond its authorised capacity. On being asked by H if he intended to take this load (which he could easily have offloaded) M said that he would risk it. H then handed M the weighbridge ticket and M drove the overloaded lorry out of the colliery onto a road, thereby committing an offence against the Motor Vehicles (Construction and Use) Regulations 1955.

The Board were charged with and convicted of aiding, abetting, counselling and procuring the carrier W Ltd to commit the offence under the Regulations. The Board appealed.

DEVLIN J.: A person who supplies the instrument for a crime or anything essential to its commission aids in the commission of it; and if he does so knowingly and with intent to aid, he abets it as well and is therefore guilty of aiding and abetting. I use the word "supplies" to comprehend giving, lending, selling or any other transfer of the right of property. In a sense a man who gives up to a criminal a weapon which the latter has a right to demand from him aids in the commission of the crime as much as if he sold or lent the article. But this has never been held to be aiding in law: see *R. v. Bullock*

[1955] 1 W.L.R. 1. The reason, I think, is that in the former case there is in law a positive act and in the latter only a negative one. In the transfer of property there must be either a physical delivery or a positive act of assent to a taking. But a man who hands over to another his own property on demand, although he may physically be performing a positive act, in law is only refraining from detinue. Thus in law the former act is one of assistance voluntarily given and the latter is only a failure to prevent the commission of the crime by means of forcible detention, which would not even be justified except in the case of felony. Another way of putting the point is to say that aiding and abetting is a crime that requires proof of *mens rea*, that is to say, of intention to aid as well as of knowledge of the circumstances, and proof of the intent involves proof of a positive act of assistance voluntarily done.

These considerations make it necessary to determine at what point the property in the coal passed from the Board and what the Board's state of knowledge was at that time. If the property had passed before the Board knew of the proposed crime, there was nothing they could legally do to prevent the driver of the lorry from taking the overloaded lorry out onto the road. If it had not, then they sold the coal with knowledge that an offence was going to be committed. (His Lordship repeated the facts as found in the case).

In these circumstances, the property in the coal passed on delivery to the carrier in accordance with Rule 5 of section 18 of the Sale of Goods Act, 1893. If the delivery was complete after loading and before weighing, the Board has not until after delivery any knowledge that an offence had been committed. But where weighing is necessary for the purpose of the contract, as, for example, in order to ascertain the price of an instalment, the property does not pass until the weight has been agreed. . . .

It was contended on behalf of the Board that H had no option after weighing but to issue a ticket for the amount then in the lorry. I think this contention is unsound. In the circumstances of this case the loading must be taken as subject to adjustment; otherwise, if the contract were for a limited amount, the seller might make an over-delivery or an under-delivery which could not thereafter be rectified and the carrier might be contractually compelled to carry away a load in excess of that legally permitted. I think that delivery of the coal was not completed until after the ascertained weight had been assented to and some act was done signifying assent and passing the property. The property passed when H asked M whether he intended to take the load and M said he would risk it and when mutual assent was, as it were, sealed by the delivery and acceptance of the weighbridge ticket. He could, therefore, after he knew of the overload, have refused to transfer the property in the coals.

This is the conclusion to which the justices came. Mr Thompson submits on behalf of the Board that it does not justify a verdict of guilty of aiding and abetting. He submits, first, that even if knowledge of the illegal purpose had been acquired before delivery began, it would not be sufficient for the verdict; and secondly, that if he is wrong about that, the knowledge was acquired too late and the Board was not guilty of aiding and abetting simply because H failed to stop the process of delivery after it had been initiated.

On his first point Mr Thompson submits that the furnishing of an article essential to the crime with knowledge of the use to which it is to be put does not of itself constitute aiding and abetting; there must be proved in addition a purpose or motive of the defendant to further the crime or encourage the criminal. Otherwise, he submits, there is no *mens rea*.

I have already said that in my judgment there must be proof of an intent to aid. . . .

No doubt evidence of an interest in the crime or of an express purpose to assist it will greatly strengthen the case of the prosecution. But an indifference to the result of the crime does not of itself negative abetting. If one man deliberately sells to another a gun to be used for murdering a third, he may be indifferent about whether the third man lives or dies and interested only in the cash profit to be made out of the sale, but he can still be an aider and abettor. To hold otherwise would be to negative the rule that *mens rea* is a matter of intent only and does not depend on desire or motive.

The authorities, I think, support this conclusion, though none has been cited to us in which the point has been specifically argued and decided. . . .

The same principle has been applied in civil cases where the seller has sued upon a contract for the supply of goods which he knew were to be used for an illegal purpose. In some of the authorities there is a suggestion that he could recover on the contract unless it appeared that in addition to knowledge of the purpose he had an interest in the venture and looked for payment to the proceeds of the crime. But in *Pearce v. Brooks* (1866) L.R. 1 Ex. 213, Pollock C.B. stated the law as follows:

"I have always considered it as settled law that any person who contributes to the performance of an illegal act by supplying a thing with the knowledge that it is going to be used for that purpose, cannot recover the price of the thing so supplied. If, to create that incapacity, it was ever considered necessary that the price should be bargained or expected to be paid out of the fruits of the illegal act (which I do not stop to examine), that proposition has been overruled by the cases I have referred to, and has now ceased to be law." . . .

As to Mr Thompson's alternative point, I have already expressed the view that the facts show an act of assent made by H after knowledge of the proposed illegality and without which the property would not have passed. If some positive act to complete delivery is committed after knowledge of the illegality, the position in law must, I think, be just the same as if the knowledge had been obtained before the delivery had been begun. Of course, it is quite likely that H was confused about the legal position and thought that he was not entitled to withhold the weighbridge ticket. There is no *mens rea* if the defendant is shown to have a genuine belief in the existence of circumstances which, if true, would negative an intention to aid; see *Wilson v. Inyang* [1951] 2 K.B. 799; but this argument, which might have been the most cogent available to the defence, cannot now be relied upon, because H was not called to give evidence about what he thought or believed.

Appeal dismissed

Notes

1. Lord Goddard C.J. delivered a concurring judgment. Slade J. dissented on the ground that the alleged aider must have assisted or encouraged the principal offender. "It is not sufficient that the alleged abettor should be proved to have done some act, or to have made some omission, without which the principal offender would not have committed the offence; nor is it sufficient that such act or omission had the effect of facilitating the commission of the offence or that it in fact operated on the mind of the principal offender so as to decide him to commit it. The prosecution must prove that the act or omission upon which they rely as constituting the alleged aiding and abetting

was done or made with a view to assisting or encouraging the principal offender to commit the offence or, in other words, with the
motive of endorsing the commission of the offence." His Lordship
considered that the facts found by the magistrates did not support the
inference that H meant to encourage M in any way.

2. Devlin J.'s discussion becomes heavily involved with the civil law
of sale, the passing of property, and the ability of a seller to sue on a
contract tainted by illegality. It seems inappropriate for the criminal
law to be entangled with the civil law this way. Perhaps Slade J.'s
solution, requiring a positive motive of endorsing the commission of
the offence, is too lax, at any rate where a *serious* crime is *substantially*
facilitated by the accessory's act. But in other cases, the law perhaps
ought to excuse an "indifferent" provider of assistance (*i.e.* one who
knows that a crime may be committed but does not wish it to happen).
In *Gillick* v. *West Norfolk & Wisbech A.H.A.* [1986] A.C. 112, the question
arose whether a doctor who provided contraceptives to a girl under
16 years of age, knowing that that would facilitate her having sexual
intercourse with a man, would necessarily be an accessory to the
man's offence if that intercourse took place. Lord Scarman (at p. 190)
thought that if the provision was a bona fide exercise of his clinical
judgment "it must be a complete negation of the guilty mind which
is an essential ingredient of the criminal offence of aiding and abetting
the commission of unlawful sexual intercourse". Lord Bridge (at p.
194) agreed with the trial judge that the doctor would not be guilty
either because the provision was not directly assisting the offence, or
because the doctor's knowledge of the circumstances of the proposed
offence was not sufficiently specific. (On specificity of knowledge, see,
post, p. 392.)

Questions

Would it be practicable for the law to excuse some "indifferent"
helpers because:

(a) the principal offence is trivial?
(b) the aid supplied is trivial and could easily be got from others?
(c) the aid supplied was in the normal course of a legitimate business?
(d) the secondary party makes known his disapproval of the
offence?
(e) the secondary party was merely "refraining from detinue" (see
Devlin J., *ante*, p. 387)? On this note *Garrett* v. *Arthur Churchill (Glass)
Ltd* [1969] 2 All E.R. 1141 (D.C.). The question was whether B was
knowingly concerned in the export of a valuable goblet without an
export licence. B was holding the goblet as agent for A, who was in
America. B told A that the export needed a licence; but A said that
his agency was terminated and ordered him to hand over the goblet
to a courier at Heathrow. B did so and the courier took the goblet
out of the country. It was held that "albeit there was a legal duty
in ordinary circumstances to hand over the goblet once the agency
was determined, I do not think that an action would lie for breach

of that duty, if the handing over would constitute the offence of being knowingly concerned in its exportation": *per* Lord Parker C.J., at p. 1145.

Ferguson v. Weaving
[1951] 1 K.B. 814
King's Bench Division

Section 4 of the Licensing Act, 1921, made it an offence for any person, except during the permitted hours, to consume on licensed premises any intoxicating liquor. In a large public-house managed by W, customers were found consuming liquor outside permitted hours and were convicted of an offence under the section. There was no evidence that W knew that the liquor was being consumed, which had been supplied by waiters employed by her who had neglected to collect the glasses in time. A charge against W of counselling and procuring the customers' offence was dismissed and the prosecutor appealed.

LORD GODDARD C.J.: There can be no doubt that this court has more than once laid it down in clear terms that before a person can be convicted of aiding and abetting the commission of an offence, he must at least know the essential matters which constitute the offence . . . The magistrate in this case has acquitted the licensee of any knowledge of the matters which constituted the principal offence, but it is said that the cases established that the knowledge of her servants must be imputed to her . . . We now turn to [these] cases . . . It is unnecessary to go through them all because the principle which applies was laid down, not for the first time, in *Linnett v. Metropolitan Police Commissioner* [1946] K.B. 290. All the cases on the subject were quoted, and, in giving judgment, I said: "The principle underlying these decisions does not depend upon the legal relationship existing between master and servant or between principal and agent; it depends on the fact that the person who is responsible in law, as, for example, a licensee under the licensing Acts, has chosen to delegate his duties, powers and authority to another."

We will assume for the purpose of this case that the licensee had delegated to the waiters the conduct and management of the concert room, and if the Act had made it an offence for a licensee knowingly to permit liquor to be consumed after hours, then the fact that she had delegated management and control of the concert room to the waiters would have made their knowledge her knowledge. In this case there is no substantive offence in the licensee at all. The substantive offence is committed only by the customers. She can aid and abet the customers if she knows that the customers are committing the offence, but we are not prepared to hold that knowledge can be imputed to her so as to make her not a principal offender, but an aider and abettor. So to hold would be to establish a new principle in criminal law and one for which there is no authority. If Parliament had desired to make a licensee guilty of an offence by allowing persons to consume liquor after hours it would have been perfectly easy so to provide in the section. But a doctrine of criminal law that a licensee who has knowledge of the facts is liable as a principal in the second degree is no reason for holding that if she herself has no knowledge of the facts but that someone in her employ and to whom she may have entrusted the management of the room did know them, this makes her an aider and abettor. As no duty is imposed on her by the section to prevent the consumption of liquor after hours there was no duty in this respect that she could delegate to her employees. While it may be that the waiters could have been prosecuted for aiding and abetting the consumers, as to which we need express no opinion, we are clearly of opinion that the licensee could not be.

To hold to the contrary would, in our opinion, be an unwarranted extension of the doctrine of vicarious responsibility in criminal law.

Appeal dismissed

Notes

1. For vicarious liability, see, *post*, p. 418.
2. *Callow v. Tillstone* (1900) 83 L.T. 411 (Q.B.D.). B, a veterinary surgeon, negligently examined a carcase and certified it as fit for human consumption, when it was not, as B ought to have known. A, a butcher, was convicted of exposing for sale meat unfit for human consumption. *Held*, B was not guilty of aiding and abetting A's offence.

Question

B's intentional act has facilitated the commission by A of the offence of driving over the blood/alcohol limit.

(i) He knows (intends) that A shall drive, but is merely reckless as to whether he is over the limit;
(ii) He knows that A is over the limit, but is merely reckless as to whether he will drive while in that state.

Is there a relevant difference between these two cases? See *Carter v. Richardson* [1974] R.T.R. 314 as to (i), and *Blakely v. D.P.P.* [1991] R.T.R. 405 as to (ii); and see, *post*, p. 449 *et seq.* as to recklessness as to circumstance in attempts.

(c) Scope of the Common Design

Maxwell v. D.P.P. for Northern Ireland
[1978] 1 W.L.R. 1350 House of Lords

The facts are set out in the speech of Lord Hailsham.

LORD HAILSHAM OF ST MARYLEBONE: My Lords, in my opinion this appeal should be dismissed. The applicant was the owner and driver of the guide car in what subsequently turned out to be a terrorist attack by members of the criminal and illegal organisation known as the Ulster Volunteer Force (UVF) on a public house owned by a Roman Catholic licensee at 40, Grange Road, Toomebridge and known as the Crosskeys Inn. The attack was carried out on the night of January 3, 1976 by the occupants of a Cortina car and took the form of throwing a pipe bomb containing about five pounds of explosive into the hallway of the public house. The attack failed because the son of the proprietor had the presence of mind to pull out the burning fuse and detonator and throw it outside the premises where the detonator exploded either because the fuse had reached the detonator or on contact with the ground.

The appellant was tried on October 13, 1976, on an indictment containing four counts to two of which he pleaded guilty. This appeal is concerned with the remaining two counts (numbered 1 and 2) on which he was convicted at the Belfast City Commission by MacDermott J. sitting without a jury. . . .

The only substantial matter to be discussed in the appeal is the degree of knowledge required before an accused can be found guilty of aiding, abetting, counselling, or procuring. To what extent must the accused be proved to have particular knowledge of the crime in contemplation at the time of his participation and which was ultimately committed by its principal perpetrators? For myself I am content for this purpose to adopt the words of Lord Parker C.J. in *R. v. Bainbridge* [1960] 1 Q.B. 129 when, after saying that it is not easy to lay down a precise form of words which will cover every case, he observed at p. 134 ". . . there must not be merely suspicion but knowledge that a crime of the type in question was intended . . ." and the words of Lord Goddard C.J. in *Johnson v. Youden* [1950] 1 K.B. 544, 546, endorsed by this House in *Churchill v. Walton* [1967] 2 A.C. 224, 236 that "Before a person can be convicted of aiding and abetting the commission of an offence he must at least know the essential matters which constitute that offence." The only question in debate in the present appeal is whether the degree of knowledge possessed by the appellant was of the "essential matters constituting" the offence in fact committed, or, to put what in the context of the instant case is exactly the same question in another form, whether the appellant knew that the offence in which he participated was "a crime of the type" described in the charge.

For that purpose I turn to two passages in the findings of fact of the learned judge. The first is as follows: "In my judgment, the facts of this case make it clear to me that the accused knew the men in the Cortina car were going to attack the Inn and had the means of attacking the Inn with them in their car. The accused may not, as he says, have known what form the attack was going to take, but in my judgment he knew the means of the attack, be they bomb, bullet or incendiary device, were present in that car."

In the second passage MacDermott J. said: "In my judgment, the accused knew that he was participating in an attack on the Inn. He performed an important role in the execution of that attack. He knew that the attack was one which would involve the use of means which would result in danger to life or damage to property. In such circumstances, where an admitted terrorist participates actively in a terrorist attack, having knowledge of the type of attack intended, if not of the weapon chosen by his colleagues, he can in my view be properly charged with possession of the weapon with which it is intended that life should be endangered or premises seriously damaged."

The learned judge also found *inter alia* that the word "job" (as used in the appellant's statements) is "synonymous with military action which raises, having regard to the proven activities of the UVF, the irresistible inference [that] the attack would be one of violence in which people would be endangered or premises seriously damaged."

There was no dispute that there was ample evidence to support all these findings and it follows that the only question is whether the passages contain some self-misdirection in point of law. As to this I agree with the opinion of Sir Robert Lowry C.J. (in the Court of Criminal Appeal for Northern Ireland) when he said [1978] 1 W.L.R. 1363, 1375: "The facts found here show that the appellant, as a member of an organisation which habitually perpetrates sectarian acts of violence with firearms and explosives, must, as soon as he was briefed for his role, have contemplated the bombing of the Crosskeys Inn as not the only possibility but one of the most obvious possibilities among the jobs which the principals were likely to be undertaking and in the commission of which he was intentionally assisting. He was therefore in just the same situation, so far as guilty knowledge is concerned, as a man who had been given a list of jobs and told that one of them would be carried out."

The only argument attacking this passage of any substance directed to your Lordships on the part of the appellant was to the effect that since at the time of the commission of the offence there was no generalised offence of terrorism as such the state of ignorance which must be assumed in favour of the accused as to the precise weapon (*e.g.* bomb, bullets, or incendiary device) or type of violence to be employed in the concerted "job" contemplated was such as to make him ignorant of some or all of the "essential ingredients" of the two offences charged in the particulars of offence in which a "pipe bomb" is specified, and one at least of which, had it been committed, would or at least might have been laid under a separate penal provision.

I regard this point as frankly unarguable. I would consider that bullet, bomb, or incendiary device, indeed most if not all types of terrorist violence, would all constitute offences of the same "type" within the meaning of R. v. *Bainbridge* and that so far as *mens rea* is concerned "the essential ingredients" of all and each of the offences within the other authorities I have cited were each and all contained within the guilty knowledge of the appellant at the time of his participation. The fact that, in the event, the offence committed by the principals crystallised into one rather than the other of the possible alternatives within his contemplation only means that in the event he was accessory to that specific offence rather than one of the others which in the event was not the offence committed. Obviously there must be limits to the meaning of the expression "type of offence" and a minimum significance attached to the expression "essential ingredients" in this type of doctrine, but it is clear that if an alleged accessory is perfectly well aware that he is participating in one of a limited number of serious crimes and one of these is in fact committed he is liable under the general law at least as one who aids, abets, counsels or procures that crime even if he is not actually a principal. Otherwise I can see no end to the number of unmeritorious arguments which the ingenuity of defendants could adduce. This disposes of the present appeal, which seems to me to be as lacking in serious plausibility as it is wholly devoid of substantial merits. . . .

LORD SCARMAN: My Lords, I also would dismiss this appeal. The question it raises is as to the degree of knowledge required by law for the attachment of criminal responsibility to one who assists another (or others) to commit or attempt crime. . . .

I think *R. v. Bainbridge* was correctly decided. But I agree with counsel for the appellant that in the instant case the Court of Criminal Appeal in Northern Ireland has gone further than the Court of Criminal Appeal for England and Wales found it necessary to go in *R. v. Bainbridge*. It is not possible in the present case to declare that it is proved, beyond reasonable doubt, that the appellant knew a bomb attack upon the Inn was intended by those whom he was assisting. It is not established, therefore, that he knew the particular type of crime intended. The Court, however, refused to limit criminal responsibility by reference to knowledge by the accused of the type or class of crime intended by those whom he assisted. Instead, the Court has formulated a principle which avoids the uncertainties and ambiguities of classification. The guilt of an accessory springs, according to the Court's formulation, "from the fact that he contemplates the commission of one (or more) of a number of crimes by the principal and he intentionally lends his assistance in order that such a crime will be committed": *per* Sir Robert Lowry C.J. "The relevant crime," the Lord Chief Justice continues, "must be within the contemplation of the accomplice, and only exceptionally would evidence be found to support the allegation that the accomplice had given the principal a completely blank cheque."

The principle thus formulated has great merit. It directs attention to the state of mind of the accused—not what he ought to have in contemplation, but what he did have: it avoids definition and classification while ensuring that a man will not be convicted of aiding and abetting any offence his principal may commit, but only one which is within his contemplation. He may have in contemplation only one offence, or several:

and the several which he contemplates he may see as alternatives. An accessory who leaves it to his principal to choose is liable, provided always the choice is made from the range of offences from which the accessory contemplates the choice will be made. Although the court's formulation of the principle goes further than in the earlier cases, it is a sound development of the law and in no way inconsistent with them. I accept it as good judge-made law in a field where there is no statute to offer guidance.

Appeal dismissal

(d) Joint enterprise

Note

Where two parties, A and B, embark on an agreed criminal enterprise to commit a particular offence, they have a common criminal purpose. If, in the course of that enterprise, A commits another offence, will B be liable for this as a secondary party? The answer to this question depends upon B's contemplation. It should be noted that the ordinary principles of secondary participation apply in cases of joint enterprise.

R. v. Slack
[1989] 3 All E.R. 90
Court of Appeal

S and B were burgling the flat of an old lady. S passed B a knife "to threaten the old lady with if she starts screaming". While S was out of the room, B cut her throat. S was convicted of murder and appealed.

LORD LANE C.J.: The appellant's case put forward by counsel was simply that, although he was undoubtedly jointly guilty of robbery, he was in no way party to the murder.

Counsel for the appellant submits that the judge misdirected the jury as to the mental element which the prosecution must prove before the secondary participant in a joint enterprise can be convicted of murder, the actual killing having been done by the primary party. . . .

Accordingly it is the written directions on murder which we must examine to see whether they accord with the law. They ran as follows:

"1. Did the Accused intend to kill or cause grievous bodily harm to Mrs Crowder in the sense that he agreed with Buick that in the course of their joint enterprise Mrs Crowder should either be killed e.g., so that she could not give evidence against them or should be caused grievous bodily harm e.g. so that she could not prevent them robbing her and did she die as a result of such conduct by Buick? If so, Accused is guilty of murder. 2. Did the Accused contemplate and foresee that Buick *might* kill or cause grievous bodily harm to Mrs Crowder as part of their joint enterprise and did she die as a result of such conduct by Buick? If so it is open to you to find that he so intended and that he is guilty of murder." (The judge's emphasis.)

It is to the second question that objection is taken, on the ground that it wrongly equates foresight and contemplation with intent. The directions, submits counsel for the appellant, should have been to this effect: assuming that Buick murdered Mrs Crowder, has it been proved to the requisite extent that (a) at the time of the killing Buick and the appellant were taking part in a joint enterprise and (b) the appellant intended that Mrs Crowder be killed or caused really serious harm should the necessity arise?

Some confusion has arisen as to the proper direction to be given to a jury in these circumstances. That seems to be partly due to some of the observations of the Judicial Committee of the Privy Council in *Chan Wing-siu v. R.* [1985] A.C. 168. There three assailants armed with knives burst into the flat of a prostitute, intent it seems on robbery. One of them murdered the prostitute's husband. It could scarcely be doubted that there was a joint agreement to kill or inflict serious injury if necessary. The trial judge's direction in that case, so far as it is relevant, was as follows:

"You may convict . . . of murder if you come to the conclusion . . . that the accused contemplated that either of his companions might use a knife to cause bodily injury on one . . . of the occupants. . . ."

In upholding the conviction Sir Robin Cooke, in the course of delivering the judgment of the Board, said (at p. 175):

"The case must depend rather on the wider principle whereby a secondary party is criminally liable for acts by the primary offender of a type which the former foresees but does not necessarily intend. That there is such a principle is not in doubt. It turns on contemplation or, putting the same idea in other words, authorisation, which may be express but is more usually implied. It meets the case of a crime foreseen as a possible incident of the common unlawful enterprise. The criminal culpability lies in participating in the venture with that foresight."

Their Lordships expressly adopted the principle enunciated by the five-judge court in *R. v. Anderson and Morris* [1966] 2 Q.B. 110 at 118–110, where Lord Parker CJ, delivering the judgment of the court, said:

". . . where two persons embark on a joint enterprise . . . that includes liability for unusual consequences if they arise from the execution of the agreed joint enterprise but (and this is the crux of the matter) . . . if one of the adventurers goes beyond what has been tacitly agreed as part of the common enterprise, his co-adventurer is not liable for the consequences of that unauthorised act. Finally . . . it is for the jury in every case to decide whether what was done was part of the joint enterprise, or went beyond it and was in fact an act unauthorised by that joint enterprise."

The Judicial Committee seems primarily to have been concerned with the problem posed by a conditional agreement, *e.g.* "We do not want to kill or seriously injure, but if necessary we will."

Chan Wing-siu v. R. was considered and approved by this court in *R. v. Ward* (1986) 85 Cr. App. R. 71. The appellant's submissions in that case were that the decisions of the House of Lords in *R. v. Moloney* [1985] A.C. 905 (*ante*, p. 95) and *R. v. Hancock* [1986] A.C. 455 (*ante*, p. 99) had the effect of completely altering the law relating to joint enterprise and that no man can be convicted of murder unless it is specifically decided against him that he had a murderous intent, and since intent had to be read against the decisions in *R. v. Moloney* and *R. v. Hancock* the jury ought to be directed on the basis of those cases.

This court in *R. v. Ward* reiterated the passage from *R. v. Anderson and Morris* cited above and went on to hold that *R. v. Moloney* and *R. v. Hancock* had had no effect on the well-known and well-established principles of joint enterprise.

As counsel for the appellant rightly points out, difficulties have arisen from the decision of another division of this court in *R. v. Barr* (1986) 88 Cr. App. R. 362 [which did not follow the decision in *R. v. Ward*.]

... What the court in that case did was, first, unwittingly to overlook the full effect of the earlier judgment in *R. v. Ward* and, second, to regard the necessary intent to be proved in the case of A, the principal party, as the same as that to be proved in the case of B, the secondary party. A must be proved to have intended to kill or do serious harm at the time he killed. B may not be present at the killing; he may be a distance away, for example, waiting in the getaway car; he may be in another part of the house; he may not know that A has killed; he may have hoped (and probably did) that A would not kill or do serious injury. If, however, as part of their joint plan it was understood between them expressly or tacitly that if necessary one of them would kill or do serious harm as part of their common enterprise, then B is guilty of murder.

As appears from the cases we have cited, the direction may be in a variety of different forms. Provided that it is made clear to the jury that for B to be guilty he must be proved to have lent himself to a criminal enterprise involving the infliction, if necessary, of serious harm or death or to have had an express or tacit understanding with A that such harm or death should, if necessary, be inflicted, the precise form of words in which the jury are directed is not important. As Sir Robin Cooke observed in *Chan Wing-siu v. R.* [1985] A.C. 168 at 179:

"No one formula is exclusively preferable; indeed it may be advantageous in a summing up to use more than one. For the question is not one of semantics."

... In our judgment the second question posed by the judge in the instant case in his written directions to the jury was in accordance with the principles we have endeavoured to express. The question made it clear to the jury that the appellant must have at least tacitly agreed that, if necessary, serious harm should be done to Mrs Crowder, or that he lent himself to the infliction of such harm. There was ample evidence before the jury on which they could come to the conclusion that the prosecution had satisfied them so as to feel sure on these matters so far as the appellant was concerned.

The appeal is accordingly dismissed.

Appeal dismissed

Note

Some doubt having arisen as to whether tacit agreement and lending oneself to the infliction of harm [see last paragraph, above] were alternatives in that either would suffice for conviction, Lord Lane in *R. v. Hyde* [1990] 3 All E.R. 892, 896, took the opportunity to clarify matters:

"It has been pointed out by Professor Smith, in his commentary on *R. v. Wakely* [1990] Crim.L.R. 119 at 120–121, that in the judgments in *R. v. Slack* and also in *R. v. Wakely* itself, to both of which I was a party, insufficient attention was paid by the court to the distinction between on the one hand tacit agreement by B that A should use violence, and on the other hand a realisation by B that A, the principal party, may use violence despite B's refusal to authorise or agree to its use. Indeed in *R. v. Wakely* we went so far as to say:

'The suggestion that a mere foresight of the real or definite possibility of violence being used is sufficient to constitute the mental element of murder is prima facie, academically speaking at least, not sufficient.'

On reconsideration, that passage is not in accordance with the principles set out by Sir Robin Cooke which we were endeavouring to follow and was wrong, or at least misleading. If B realises (without agreeing to such conduct being used) that A may kill or intentionally inflict serious injury, but nevertheless continues to participate with A in the venture, that will amount to a sufficient mental element for B to be guilty of murder if A, with the requisite intent, kills in the course of the venture. As Professor Smith points out, B has in those circumstances lent himself to the enterprise and by so doing he has given assistance and encouragement to A in carrying out an enterprise which B realises may involve murder."

Note

In *Chan Wing-Sui v. R.*, the Privy Council had also to consider the question of what degree of likelihood of the principal crime being committed must the defendant contemplate before it can be said that the crime was within his contemplation.

SIR ROBIN COOKE: ". . . Their Lordships regard as wholly unacceptable any argument that would propose, as any part of the criteria of the guilt of an accomplice, whether on considering in advance the possibility of a crime of the kind in the event actually committed by his co-adventurers he thought that it was more than an even risk. . . . What public policy requires was rightly identified in the submissions for the Crown. Where a man lends himself to a criminal enterprise knowing that potentially murderous weapons are to be carried, and in the event they are in fact used by his partner with an intent sufficient for murder, he should not escape the consequences by reliance upon a nuance of prior assessment, only too likely to have been optimistic.

On the other hand, if it was not even contemplated by the particular accused that serious bodily harm would be intentionally inflicted, he is not a party to murder. . . .

In some cases in this field it is enough to direct the jury by adapting to the circumstances the simple formula common in a number of jurisdictions. For instance, did the particular accused contemplate that in carrying out a common unlawful purpose one of his partners in the enterprise might use a knife or a loaded gun with the intention of causing really serious bodily harm?

The present was such a case. It was not necessary for the trial judge to say more on the subject than he did. . . .

. . . [But] where there is an evidential foundation for a remoteness issue, it may be necessary for the judge to give the jury more help. Although a risk of a killing or serious bodily harm has crossed the mind of a party to an unlawful enterprise, it is right to allow for a class of case in which the risk was so remote as not to make that party guilty of a murder or intentional causing of grievous bodily harm committed by a co-adventurer in the circumstances that in the event confronted the latter. But if the party accused knew that lethal weapons, such as a knife or a loaded gun, were to be carried on a criminal expedition, the defence should succeed only very rarely.

In cases where an issue of remoteness does arise it is for the jury (or other tribunal of fact) to decide whether the risk *as recognised by the accused* was sufficient to make him a party to the crime committed by the principal. Various formulae have been suggested—including a substantial risk, a real risk, a risk that something might well happen. No one formula is exclusive preferable; indeed it may be advantageous in a summing up to use more than one. For the question is not one of semantics. What has to be brought home to the jury is that occasionally a risk may have occurred to an accused's mind—fleetingly or even causing him some deliberation—but may genuinely have been dismissed by him as altogether negligible. If they think there is a reasonable possibility that the case is in that class, taking the risk should not make that accused a party to such a crime of intention as murder or wounding with intent to cause grievous bodily harm. The judge is entitled to warn the jury to be cautious before reaching that conclusion; but the law can do no more by way of definition; it can only be for the jury to determine any issue of that kind on the facts of the particular case."

Note

In *Powell and Daniels* [1999] A.C. 1, the House of Lords had to consider the *mens rea* required of a secondary party to a joint enterprise where one party kills. Counsel for the appellants had argued that the secondary party should only be guilty of murder if he had the full *mens rea* for murder, i.e. an intent to kill or to cause really serious bodily harm. The question certified for their Lordships consideration was:

"Is it sufficient to found a conviction for murder for a secondary party to a killing to have realised that the primary party might kill with intent to do so or must the secondary party have held such intention himself?"

Their Lordships answered the question in the affirmative. Lord Hutton traced the development of the principle which applied through the cases of *Smith (Wesley)* [1963] 1 W.L.R. 1200, *Anderson and Morris* [1966] 2 Q.B. 110, *Chan Wing-Siu* [1985] A.C. 168, *Hyde* [1991] 1 Q.B. 134 and *Hui Chi-ming v. The Queen* [1992] 1 A.C. 34, stating:

"There is therefore a strong line of authority that participation in a joint criminal enterprise with foresight or contemplation of an act as a possible incident of that enterprise is sufficient to impose criminal liability for that act carried out by another participant in the enterprise . . . . [I]t is sufficient to found a conviction for murder for a secondary party to have realised that in the course of the joint enterprise the primary party might kill with intent to do so or with intent to cause grievous bodily harm."

Question

A and B agree to rob a post office, carrying coshes in order to intimidate any person on the scene. B positively forbids A from hitting anyone, but B knows from previous experience that A is excitable while on a raid and that it is possible that he will lose his self-control and hit someone. A does hit a witness V on the head with his cosh and kills him. Is B guilty of the murder of V?

(d) Acts beyond the Common Design

Notes

1. Where A incidentally commits a different offence in performing the common design, B will be liable for this offence. For example, A and B agree that they will burgle a factory and that A will hit V the night-watchman over the head with a cosh to knock him unconscious. If V dies as a result both A and B will be liable for unlawful act manslaughter (see *Baldessare* (1930) 22 Cr.App.R. 70; *Anderson and Morris* [1966] 2 Q.B. 110).

2. Where A deliberately departs from the common design B will not be liable. Hawkins stated the principle as follows (2 P.C. c.29, s.21):

> "But if a man command another to commit a felony on a particular person or thing and he do it on another; as to kill A and he kill B or to burn the house of A and he burn the house of B or to steal an ox and he steal a horse; or to steal such an horse and he steal another; or to commit a felony of one kind and he commit another of quite a different nature; . . . it is said that the commander is not an accessory because the act done varies in substance from that which was commanded."

In *Saunders and Archer* (1573) 2 Plowd 473, S desired to kill his wife and sought the assistance of A who supplied him with poison. S put the poison in an apple and gave it to his wife who ate a little but gave the remainder to their daughter. S witnessed this but did not intervene and his daughter ate the apple and died. S was convicted of murder but A was acquitted as his failure to intervene amounted to a deliberate variation in substance from the common design.

3. A problem which may arise is that of B contemplating harm of the kind inflicted by A but A does so in a fundamentally different way to the manner in which B contemplated it being done. This may arise, in particular, where weapons are used and B contemplates GBH being inflicted, but A uses a different weapon and proceeds to kill the victim. In such circumstances two questions arise: (i) is B a secondary party to murder; and (ii) if not, is B liable to conviction of manslaughter? See the cases which follow.

R. v. English
[1999] A.C. 1
House of Lords

E and W were convicted of murder of a police sergeant, V, on the basis of joint enterprise. Both E and W attacked V with wooden posts. W produced a knife and stabbed V causing his death. The case for the Crown was that even if E did not know that W had a knife, he foresaw that W would cause really serious injury in the attack with the post, and this foresight was sufficient to impose liability for murder. The question certified for the House of Lords by the Court of Appeal was as follows:

> "Is it sufficient for murder that the secondary party intends or foresees that the primary party would or may act with intent to cause grievous

bodily harm, if the lethal act carried out by the primary party is fundamentally different from the acts foreseen or intended by the secondary party?"

LORD HUTTON: . . . Mr. Sallon, for the appellant, advanced to your Lordships' House the submission . . . that in a case such as the present one where the primary party kills with a deadly weapon, which the secondary party did not know that he had and therefore did not foresee his use of it, the secondary party should not be guilty of murder. He submitted that to be guilty under the principle stated in *Chan Wing-Siu* the secondary party must foresee an act of the type which the principal party committed, and that in the present case the use of a knife was fundamentally different to the use of a wooden post.

My Lords, I consider that this submission is correct. It finds strong support in the passage of the judgment of Lord Parker in *Reg. v. Anderson; Reg. v. Morris* [1966] 2 Q.B. 110, 120B . . .:

"It seems to this court that to say that adventurers are guilty of manslaughter when one of them has departed completely from the concerted action of the common design and has suddenly formed an intent to kill and has used a weapon and acted in a way which no party to that common design could suspect is something which would revolt the conscience of people today."

The judgment in *Chan Wing-Siu's* case [1985] A.C. 168 also supports the argument advanced on behalf of the appellant because Sir Robin Cooke stated, at p. 175F:

"The case must depend rather on the wider principle whereby a secondary party is criminally liable for *acts by the primary offender of a type* which the former foresees but does not necessarily intend." (emphasis added).

There is also strong support for the appellant's submission in the decision of Carswell J. (as he then was), sitting without a jury in the Crown Court in Northern Ireland, in *Reg. v. Gamble* [1989] N.I. 268. In that case the four accused were all members of a terrorist organisation, the Ulster Volunteer Force, who had a grievance against a man named Patton. The four accused entered upon a joint venture to inflict punishment upon him, two of them, Douglas and McKee, contemplating that Patton would be subjected to a severe beating or to "knee-capping" (firing a bullet into his kneecap). In the course of the attack upon him Patton was brutally murdered by the other two accused. His throat was cut with a knife with great force which rapidly caused his death. In addition he was shot with four bullets, and two of the bullet wounds would have been fatal had his death not been caused by the cutting of his throat. Douglas and McKee had not foreseen killing with a knife or firing of bullets into a vital part of the body. It was argued, however, on behalf of the prosecution that the joint enterprise of committing grievous bodily harm, combined with the rule that an intent to cause such harm grounded a conviction for murder in respect of a resulting death, was sufficient to make the two accused liable for murder notwithstanding that they had not foreseen the actions which actually caused death. After citing the relevant authorities Carswell J. rejected this argument and stated, at p. 283F:

"When an assailant 'kneecaps' his victim, i.e. discharges a weapon into one of his limbs, most commonly into the knee joint, there must always be the risk that it will go wrong and that an artery may be severed or the limb may be so damaged that gangrene sets in, both potentially fatal complications. It has to be said, however, that such cases must be very rare among victims of what is an abhorrent and disturbingly frequent crime. Persons who take a part in inflicting injuries of this nature no doubt do not generally expect that they will endanger life, and I should be willing to believe that in most cases they believe that they are engaged in a lesser offence than murder.

The infliction of grievous bodily harm came within the contemplation of Douglas and McKee, and they might therefore be regarded as having placed themselves within the ambit of life-threatening conduct. It may further be said that they must be taken to have had within their contemplation the possibility that life might be put at risk. The issue is whether it follows as a consequence that they cannot be heard to say that the murder was a different crime from the attack which they contemplated, and so cannot escape liability for the murder on the ground that it was outside the common design.

To accept this type of reasoning would be to fix an accessory with consequences of his acts which he did not foresee and did not desire or intend. The modern development of the criminal law has been away from such an approach and towards a greater emphasis on subjective tests of criminal guilt, as Sir Robin Cooke pointed out in *Chan Wing-Sui*. Although the rule remains well entrenched that an intention to inflict grievous bodily harm qualifies as the mens rea of murder, it is not in my opinion necessary to apply it in such a way as to fix an accessory with liability for a consequence which he did not intend and which stems from an act which he did not have within his contemplation. I do not think that the state of the law compels me to reach such a conclusion, and it would not in my judgment accord with the public sense of what is just and fitting."

In my opinion this decision was correct in that a secondary party who foresees grievous bodily harm caused by kneecapping with a gun should not be guilty of murder where, in an action unforeseen by the secondary party, another party to the criminal enterprise kills the victim by cutting his throat with a knife. The issue (which is one of fact after the tribunal of fact has directed itself, or has been directed, in accordance with the statement of Lord Parker in *Reg. v. Anderson; Reg. v. Morris* [1966] 2 Q.B. 110, 120B) whether a secondary party who foresees the use of a gun to kneecap, and death is then caused by the deliberate firing of the gun into the head or body of the victim, is guilty of murder is more debatable although, with respect, I agree with the decision of Carswell J. on the facts of that case.

Accordingly, in the appeal of English, I consider that the direction of the learned trial judge was defective (although this does not constitute a criticism of the judge, who charged the jury in conformity with the principle stated in *Hyde*) because in accordance with the principle stated by Lord Parker in *Reg. v. Anderson*, at p. 120B, he did not qualify his direction on foresight of really serious injury by stating that if the jury considered that the use of the knife by Weddle was the use of a weapon and an action on Weddle's part which English did not foresee as a possibility, then English should not be convicted of murder. As the unforeseen use of the knife would take the killing outside the scope of the joint venture the jury should also have been directed, as the Court of Appeal held in *Reg. v. Anderson*, that English should not be found guilty of manslaughter.

On the evidence the jury could have found that English did not know that Weddle had a knife. Therefore the judge's direction made the conviction of English unsafe and in my opinion his appeal should be allowed and the conviction for murder quashed.

Conviction of murder quashed.

R. v. Uddin
Court of Appeal
[1999] 1 Cr.App.R. 319

B was involved in an attack with four other men on V involving the use of sticks and bars. A, one of the five men, produced a knife and stabbed V killing him. A and B were convicted of murder and B appealed on the basis, *inter alia*, that the trial judge had failed to direct the jury that they had to be sure that B had foreseen the use of the knife as a possibility.

BELDAM L.J.: . . . [W]e think that the principles applicable to a case such as the present are:

(i) Where several persons join to attack a victim in circumstances which show that they intend to inflict serious harm and as a result of the attack the victim sustains fatal injury, they are jointly liable for murder; but if such injury inflicted with that intent is shown to have been caused solely by the actions of one participant of a type entirely different from actions which the others foresaw as part of the attack, only that participant is guilty of murder.

(ii) In deciding whether the actions are of such a different type the use by that party of a weapon is a significant factor. If the character of the weapon, e.g. its propensity to cause death is different from any weapon used or contemplated by the others and if it is used with a specific intent to kill, the others are not responsible for the death unless it is proved that they knew or foresaw the likelihood of the use of such a weapon.

(iii) If some or all of the others are using weapons which could be regarded as equally likely to inflict fatal injury, the mere fact that a different weapon was used is immaterial.

(iv) If the jury conclude that the death of the victim was caused by the actions of one participant which can be said to be of a completely different type to those contemplated by the others, they are not to be regarded as parties to the death whether it amounts to murder or manslaughter. They may nevertheless be guilty of offences of wounding or inflicting grievous bodily harm with intent which they individually commit.

(v) If in the course of the concerted attack a weapon is produced by one of the participants and the others knowing that he has it in circumstances where he may use it in the course of the attack participate or continue to participate in the attack, they will be guilty of murder if the weapon is used to inflict a fatal wound.

(vi) In a case in which after a concerted attack it is proved that the victim died as a result of a wound with a lethal weapon, e.g. a stab wound, but the evidence does not establish which of the participants used the weapon, then if its use was foreseen by the participants in the attack they will all be guilty of murder notwithstanding that the particular participant who administered the fatal blow cannot be identified. See *Reg. v Powell* (supra). If, however, the circumstances do not show that the participants foresaw the use of a weapon of this type, none of them will be guilty of murder though they may individually have committed offences in the course of the attack.

(vii) The mere fact that by attacking the victim together each of them had the intention to inflict serious harm on the victim is insufficient to make them responsible for the death of the victim caused by the use of a lethal weapon used by one of the participants with the same or shared intention.

As we have said, in the present case there was no evidence upon which the jury could find that before the attack began the others involved knew that [the principal, A,] was carrying a flick knife.

Appeal allowed. Conviction quashed.
Retrial ordered.

Note

In the above cases the principal, A, has departed from the scope of the joint enterprise by committing a crime of a different type to that contemplated by the secondary party, B, or in a different manner from that foreseen by B. Where A performs the very acts which B foresaw, but does so with the *mens rea* for a more serious crime than any contemplated or foreseen by B, will B be acquitted or be liable to the extent of his contemplation? For example, B contemplates that A might hit V over the head intending ABH but A does the act intending GBH or death, may B be convicted of manslaughter if A is convicted of murder? In *Lovesey and Peterson* [1970] 1 Q.B. 352 Lord Widgery C.J. stated (at p. 356):

> "It is clear that a common design to use unlawful violence, short of the infliction of grievous bodily harm, renders all co-adventurers guilty of manslaughter if the victim's death is an unexpected consequence of the carrying out of that design. Where, however, the victim's death is not the product of the common design but is attributable to one of the co-adventurers going beyond the scope of that design , by using violence which is intended to cause grievous bodily harm, the others are not responsible for that unauthorised act."

This decision was followed in *Dunbar* [1988] Crim. L.R. 693 and *Wan and Chan* [1995] Crim. L.R. 296. By contrast in *Stewart and Schofield* [1995] 1 Cr. App. R. 441 the Court of Appeal took the view that each party to a contemplated unlawful act which caused death should be liable to the extent of their *mens rea*. This decision was recently followed by the Northern Ireland Court of Appeal in the case which follows.

R. v. Gilmour
[2000] 2 Cr.App.R. 407
Court of Appeal of Northern Ireland

The appellant drove two men to a house where they threw a petrol bomb. Three children died in the ensuing fire. The appellant remained in the car throughout but knew that a petrol bomb was to be thrown into the house. He was tried before a judge sitting alone and convicted of three counts of murder and appealed. The Court of Appeal concluded that the trial judge was wrong to conclude that he appreciated that the principals intended to inflict grievous bodily harm and quashed his convictions of murder.

CARSWELL LCJ: . . . The issue then is whether he can be found guilty of manslaughter on the first three counts, on the basis that if the principals had thrown the petrol bomb into the house without the intention of killing or inflicting grievous bodily harm on any person they would have properly been convicted of that offence. It was argued on behalf of the appellant that if he did not share the intention of the principals he should not be found guilty of either murder or manslaughter, in the same way as if the principals go outside the contemplated acts involved in the joint enterprise the accessory cannot be convicted of either offence: see our recent decision in *R. v. Crooks* [1999] NI 226, following the principles laid down in *R. v. Powell* [1999] AC 1.

The issue is discussed in Blackstone's *Criminal Practice*, 2000 ed, para. A5.5 at page 75, in which the example is posed where the principal and accessory agree that the principal will post an incendiary device to the victim, the accessory contemplating only superficial injuries but the principal foreseeing and hoping that the injuries will be serious or fatal. The principal will be guilty of murder and the accessory will not. The editors conclude that the accessory should in such a case be convicted of manslaughter, because the act done by the principal is precisely what was envisaged. In our opinion this is the correct principle to apply in the present case. The appellant foresaw that the principals would carry out the act of throwing a petrol bomb into the house, but did not realise that in so doing they intended to kill or do grievous bodily harm to the occupants. To establish that a person charged as an accessory to a crime of specific intent is guilty as an accessory it is necessary to prove that he realised the principal's intention: see *R. v. Hyde* [1991] QB 134 at 139, per Lord Lane CJ, approved by Lord Hutton in *R. v. Powell* [1999] AC 1 at 27–8. The line of authority represented by such cases as *R. v. Anderson and Morris* [1966] 2 QB 110, approved in *R. v. Powell*, deals with situations where the principal departs from the contemplated joint enterprise and perpetrates a more serious act of a different kind unforeseen by the accessory. In such cases it is established that the accessory is not liable at all for such unforeseen acts. It does not follow that the same result should follow where the principal carries out the very act contemplated by the accessory, though the latter does not realise that the principal intends a more serious consequence from the act.

We do not consider that we are obliged by authority to hold that the accessory in such a case must be acquitted of manslaughter as well as murder. The cases in which an accessory has been found not guilty both of murder and manslaughter all concern a departure by the principal from the actus reus contemplated by the accessory, not a difference between the parties in respect of the mens rea of each. In such cases the view has prevailed that it would be wrong to hold the accessory liable when the principal committed an act which the accessory did not contemplate or authorise. We do not, however, see any convincing policy reason why a person acting as an accessory to a principal who carries out the very deed contemplated by both should not be guilty of the degree of offence appropriate to the intent with which he so acted. It is of course conceivable, as is suggested in Blackstone, *loc. cit.*, that in some cases the nature of the principal's mens rea may change the nature of the act committed by him and take it outside the type of act contemplated by the accessory, but it does not seem to us that the existence of such a possibility affects the validity of the basic principle which we have propounded. A verdict of guilty of manslaughter on this basis was upheld by the Court of Appeal in *R. v. Stewart and Schofield* [1995] 3 All E.R. 159. The judgment has been strongly criticised by Sir John Smith in [1995] Crim.L.R. 296 and [1995] Crim.L.R. 422 and in Smith & Hogan, *Criminal Law*, 9th ed, p. 145. Even if there may be ground for criticism of some of the propositions enunciated in the court's judgment, the principle accepted as its basis is in our view sustainable.

We accordingly allow the appeal, substitute a verdict of not guilty of

murder but guilty of manslaughter on counts 1 to 3 and set aside the verdicts
of guilty on counts 4 to 6.

(e) Withdrawal

R. v. Becerra
(1975) 62 Cr.App.R. 212
Court of Appeal

B broke into a house with C and G, intending to steal. B gave a knife
to C to use if necessary on anyone interrupting them. The tenant of the
upstairs flat L came down to investigate the noise. B said, "There's a
bloke coming. Let's go," jumped out of the window and ran away. C
stabbed L with the knife, killing him. At his trial for murder, B contended that he had withdrawn from the joint adventure before the
attack on L. The jury were directed that his words and departure
through the window were insufficient to constitute a withdrawal. B was
convicted, and sought leave to appeal.

ROSKILL L.J.: Mr Owen [for the appellant] says that in that passage which I
have just read, the learned judge in effect, though perhaps not in so many
words, withdrew the defence of "withdrawal" from the jury, because the
learned judge was saying to the jury that the only evidence of Becerra's suggested "withdrawal" was the remark, if it were made, "Come on let's go",
coupled with the fact of course that Becerra then went out through the
window and ran away and that that could not in those circumstances amount
to "withdrawal" and therefore was not available as a defence, even if they
decided the issue of common design against Becerra. It is upon that passage
in the summing-up that Mr Owen has principally focused his criticism.

It is necessary, before dealing with that argument in more detail, to say a
word or two about the relevant law. It is a curious fact, considering the
number of times in which this point arises where two or more people are
charged with criminal offences, particularly murder or manslaughter, how
relatively little authority there is in this country upon the point. But the principle is undoubtedly of long standing.

Perhaps it is best first stated in *R. v. Saunders and Archer (ante,* p. 400), in a
note by *Plowden,* p. 476, thus: ". . . for if I command one to kill J.S. and before
the Fact done I go to him and tell him that I have repented, and expressly
charge him not to kill J.S. and he afterwards kills him, there I shall not be
Accessory to this Murder, because I have countermanded my first Command,
which in all Reason shall discharge me, for the malicious Mind of the Accessory ought to continue to do ill until the Time of the Act done, or else he shall
not be charged; but if he had killed J.S. before the Time of my Discharge or
Countermand given, I should have been Accessory to the Death, notwithstanding my private Repentance."

The next case to which I may usefully refer is some 250 years later, but over
150 years ago: *R. v. Edmeads and Others* (1828) 3 C. & P. 390, where there is a
ruling of Vaughan B. at a trial at Berkshire Assizes, upon an indictment charging Edmeads and others with unlawfully shooting at game keepers. At the
end of his ruling the learned Baron said on the question of common intent, at
p. 392, "that is rather a question for the jury; but still, on this evidence, it is
quite clear what the common purpose was. They all draw up in lines, and
point their guns at the game-keepers, and they are all giving their counten-
ance and assistance to the one of them who actually fires the gun. If it could
be shewn that either of them separated himself from the rest, and showed

distinctly that he would have no hand in what they were doing, the objection would have much weight in it."

I can go forward over 100 years. Mr Owen (to whose juniors we are indebted for their research into the relevant Canadian and United States cases) referred us to several Canadian cases, to only one of which is it necessary to refer in detail, a decision of the Court of Appeal of British Columbia in *R. v. Whitehouse* (alias *Savage*) (1941) 1 W.W.R. 112. I need not read the headnote. The Court of Appeal held that the trial judge concerned in that case, which was one of murder, had been guilty of misdirection in his direction to the jury on this question of "withdrawal". The matter is, if I may most respectfully say so, so well put in the leading judgment of Sloan J.A., that I read the whole of the passage at pp. 115 and 116: "Can it be said on the facts of this case that a mere change of mental intention and a quitting of the scene of the crime just immediately prior to the striking of the fatal blow will absolve those who participate in the commission of the crime by overt acts up to that moment from all the consequences of its accomplishment by the one who strikes in ignorance of his companions' change of heart? I think not. After a crime has been committed and before a prior abandonment of the common enterprise may be found by a jury there must be, in my view, in the absence of exceptional circumstances, something more than a mere mental change of intention and physical change of place by those associates who wish to dissociate themselves from the consequences attendant upon their willing assistance up to the moment of the actual commission of that crime. I would not attempt to define too closely what must be done in criminal matters involving participation in a common unlawful purpose to break the chain of causation and responsibility. That must depend upon the circumstances of each case but it seems to me that one essential element ought to be established in a case of this kind: Where practicable and reasonable there must be timely communication of the intention to abandon the common purpose from those who wish to dissociate themselves from the contemplated crime to those who desire to continue in it. What is 'timely communication' must be determined by the facts of each case but where practicable and reasonable it ought to be such communication, verbal or otherwise, that will serve unequivocal notice upon the other party to the common unlawful cause that if he proceeds upon it he does so without the further aid and assistance of those who withdraw. The unlawful purpose of him who continues alone is then his own and not one in common with those who are no longer parties to it nor liable to its full and final consequences." The learned judge then went on to cite a passage from 1 Hale's *Pleas of the Crown* 618 and the passage from *R. v. Saunders and Archer* to which I have already referred.

In the view of each member of this Court, that passage, if we may respectfully say so, could not be improved upon and we venture to adopt it in its entirety as a correct statement of the law which is to be applied in this case.

The last case, an English one, is *R. v. Croft* [1944] 1 K.B. 295, a well known case of a suicide pact where, under the old law, the survivor of a suicide pact was charged with and convicted of murder. It was sought to argue that he had withdrawn from the pact in time to avoid liability (as the law then was) for conviction for murder.

The Court of Criminal Appeal, comprising Lawrence J. (as he then was), Lewis and Wrottesley JJ. dismissed the appeal and upheld the direction given by Humphreys J. to the jury at the trial. Towards the end of the judgment Lawrence J. said (pp. 297 and 298): ". . . counsel for the appellant complains—although I do not understand that the point had ever been taken in the court below—that the summing-up does not contain any reference to the possibility of the agreement to commit suicide having been determined or countermanded. It is true that the learned judge does not deal expressly with that matter except in a passage where he says: 'Even if you accept his statement in the witness-box that the vital and second shot was fired when he had gone through the window, he would still be guilty of murder if she was then committing suicide as the result of an agreement which they had mutually arrived at that that should be fate of both of them, and it is no answer for him that he altered his mind after she was dead and did not commit suicide himself.' . . . The authorities, such as they are, show in our opinion, that where a person has acted as an accessory before the fact, he must give express and actual countermand or revocation of the advising, counselling, procuring, or abetting which he had given before."

It seems to us that those authorities make plain what the law is which has to be applied in the present case.

We therefore turn back to consider the direction which the learned judge gave in the present case to the jury and what was the suggested evidence that Becerra had withdrawn from the common agreement. The suggested evidence is the use by Becerra of the words "Come on let's go", coupled, as I said a few moments ago, with his act in going out through the window. The evidence, as the judge pointed out, was that Cooper never heard that nor did the third man. But let it be supposed that that was said and the jury took the view that it was said.

On the facts of this case, in the circumstances then prevailing, the knife having already been used and being contemplated for further use when it was handed over by Becerra to Cooper for the purpose of avoiding (if necessary) by violent means the hazards of identification, if Becerra wanted to withdraw at that stage, he would have to "countermand", to use the word that is used in some of the cases or "repent" to use another word so used, in some manner vastly different and vastly more effective than merely to say "Come on, let's go" and go out through the window.

It is not necessary, on this application, to decide whether the point of time had arrived at which the only way in which he could effectively withdraw, so as to free himself from joint responsibility for any act Cooper thereafter did in furtherance of the common design, would be physically to intervene so as to stop Cooper attacking Lewis, as the judge suggested, by interposing his own body between them or somehow getting in between them or whether some other action might suffice. That does not rise for decision here. Nor is it necessary to decide whether or not the learned judge was right or wrong, on the facts of this case, in that passage which appears at the bottom of p. 206, which Mr Owen criticised: "and at least take all reasonable steps to prevent the commission of the crime which he had agreed the others should commit." It is enough for the purposes of deciding this application to say that under the law of this country as it stands, and on the facts (taking them at their highest in favour of Becerra), that which was urged as amounting to withdrawal from the common design was not capable of amounting to such withdrawal. Accordingly Becerra remains responsible, in the eyes of the law, for everything that Cooper did and continued to do after Becerra's disappearance through the window as much as if he had done them himself.

Application refused

Notes

"A declared intent to withdraw from a conspiracy to dynamite a building is not enough, if the fuse has been set; he must step on the fuse", *per* McDermott J. in *Eldredge v. U.S.*, 62F. 2nd 449 (1932). That leaves the question of what will be enough if it *is* timely. Roskill L.J. appears to indicate that at some stage a point of time will be reached where only physical prevention of the crime, or at least all reasonable steps to prevent it, will exculpate the accessory, leaving open the question of what will suffice before that point of time is reached.

R. v. Grundy [1977] Crim.L.R. 543 (C.A.): Six weeks before a burglary, A gave information to the burglars about the premises to be attacked, the habits of the owner and other matters. For two weeks before the burglary, 'he had been trying to stop them breaking in' [although it does not appear that he warned the householder or the police]. *Held*, his defence of withdrawal should have been left to the jury.

R. v. Whitefield (1983) 79 Cr.App.R. 36 (C.A.); W told G that the occupant of the flat next to his was away; he agreed to break in with G by way of his own flat's balcony and to divide the spoils. Later he told G he would take no part, but on the night in question, he heard G breaking in via the coal chute, and took no steps to stop him. 'In this case there was ... evidence ... that he had served unequivocal notice on G. that if he proceeded with the burglary he would do so without the aid or assistance of the appellant. In his ruling the judge stated that such notice was not enough, and that in failing to communicate with the police or take any other steps to prevent the burglary he remained 'liable in law for what happened, for everything that was done that night.' In the judgment of the court, in making that statement the judge fell into an error of law' (at p. 40).

In *Mitchell and another* [1999] Crim. L.R. 496, M, N and D having desisted from a spontaneous attack on V, D returned to administer a further beating to V as a result of which V died. In quashing the convictions of M and N for murder and ordering a retrial, the Court of Appeal sought to draw a distinction between joint enterprises involving pre-planned violence and those involving spontaneous violence. In the former *Becerra* remains the authority, but in the latter the Court of Appeal suggested that mere withdrawal from the scene without communication could be sufficient. Professor Smith in his *Commentary* on the case is critical of the decision as withdrawal from the scene does not necessarily cancel out the encouragement already offered to the principal by the secondary party's participation in the enterprise up to that point, particularly if the principal is unaware of the secondary party's withdrawal.

In *Robinson*, February 3, 2000, 9903443Y3, D and a group of youths had followed V taunting him. The group looked to D for leadership and called on him to hit V. D did so, whereupon the group joined in the attack. D stood back while they did so but when the attack appeared to be going further than he intended, he intervened and the attack ceased. The Court of Appeal followed *Becerra* holding that in the instant case where violence was not spontaneous communication of withdrawal was necessary. Furthermore, Otton L.J. stated:

"There is a clear line of authority that where a party has given encouragement to others to commit an offence it cannot be withdrawn once the offence has commenced. (See *R v. Whitefield* [1984] 79 C.A.R. 36, *R v. Rook* [1993] 97 C.A.R. 327 and *R v. Pearman* [1996] 1 C.A.R. p. 24)."

His Lordship, who also gave the judgment of the Court in *Mitchell*, quoted from Professor Smith's *Commentary to Mitchell* with approval, and made it clear that *Mitchell* was an exceptional case stating:

"it can only be in exceptional circumstances that a person can withdraw from a crime he has initiated. Similarly in those rare circumstances communication of withdrawal must be given in order to give the principal offenders the opportunity to desist rather than complete the crime. This must be so even in situations of spontaneous violence unless it is not practicable or reasonable so to communicate as in the exceptional circumstances pertaining in *Mitchell* where the accused threw down his weapon and moved away before the final and fatal blows were inflicted."

Dealing with the question of withdrawing where encouragement had been offered, Otton L.J. stated:

"The trial judge's direction that encouragement once given, cannot be withdrawn once the offence has commenced, is in accordance with principle. Once the jury found as a fact that the defendant had encouraged the commission of the violence that ensued it was an accurate direction that by the time the appellant had given his encouragement he had played his part and thereafter he could not escape liability by attempting to withdraw at that stage. . . .
   We have no hesitation in reaching the conclusion that there is no basis upon which it can be said that the verdict of the jury was unsafe. Indeed it would be a very curious state of our law if a person who had encouraged or incited violence by initiating the attack, could stand aside when he was aware that those who were to continue the violence might form the necessary intention to commit (and did commit) an offence of grievous bodily harm and could thereafter escape all responsibility except for assault occasioning actual bodily from the initial blow. Commonsense and the Common Law go hand in hand."

The effect of this judgment appears to limit withdrawal where encouragement has been offered to the period prior to the commencement of the offence. If the attack on the victim which D has initiated commences, it will be too late for him to withdraw and avoid liability.

Questions

1. What ought to be the law's objectives in this area? To encourage repentance, or to encourage efforts to undo the harm done by the initial encouragement?
2. If the latter, is it likely that 'unequivocal notice to the principal that if he goes on it will be without the aid or assistance of the accessory' will often be a significant undoing of the harm done by the initial encouragement?
3. If in *Whitefield*, the telling of G that the flat was unoccupied without any promise of assistance in the actual break-in would be enough to implicate W, why should the making and later withdrawal of the promise make any difference to his liability?

4. Whichever object is to be preferred, need notice to the principal be insisted on if steps are taken to frustrate the enterprise?

5. Ought the requirements for withdrawal to be different if the accessory has supplied the principal with the means for committing the crime? Might it have made a difference in *Becerra* if B had not supplied C with the knife?

Notes

See Lanham, *Accomplices and Withdrawal* (1981) 97 L.Q.R. 575.

v. Secondary Party Not Convictable as a Principal

Sayce v. Coupe
[1953] 1 Q.B. 1
Queen's Bench Division

C. was charged with aiding, abetting, counselling and procuring a person unknown to sell tobacco otherwise than as a licensed retailer of tobacco contrary to section 13 of the Tobacco Act 1842 as amended. It appeared that C. had purchased the tobacco from a person who was not a licensed retailer. The magistrates dismissed the charge, and the prosecutor appealed.

LORD GODDARD C.J.: [Counsel for the accused] has argued that because the statute does not make it an offence to buy, but only makes it an offence to sell, we ought to hold that the offence of aiding and abetting the sale ought not to be preferred or could not be preferred. It is obvious that it can be preferred. The statute does not make it an offence to buy, but obviously, on ordinary general principles of criminal law, if in such case a person knows the circumstances and knows, therefore, that an offence is being committed and takes part in, or facilitates the commission of the offence, he is guilty as a principal in the second degree, for it is impossible to say that a person who buys does not aid and abet the sale.

Appeal allowed

R. v. Tyrrell
[1894] 1 Q.B. 710
Court for Crown Cases Reserved

Tyrrell, a girl aged between 13 and 16, was convicted of aiding and abetting one Ford to commit the misdemeanour of having unlawful carnal knowledge of her, which was an offence under Criminal Law Amendment Act 1885, s.5. (See now, Sexual Offences Act 1956, s.6.)

Counsel for the accused: Under [the Offences Against the Person Act 1861], section 58, a woman is not indictable for administering poison or other noxious thing to herself with intent to procure abortion, unless she is with child when she does so; but she is liable to conviction and punishment if, with the same intent, she administers poison, etc. to another woman, though the other be not with child. . . . *R. v. Whitchurch* (1890) 24 Q.B.D. 420 . . . therefore has no application here. It is impossible that the legislature, in passing the Criminal Law Amendment Act 1885, can have intended that the women and girls for whose protection it was passed should be liable to prosecution and punishment under it.

Part I, in which section 5 comes, is headed "Protection of Women and Girls". A girl under 16 is treated as of so immature a mind as not to be capable of consenting. The Act assumes that she has no *mens rea*, and she cannot, therefore, be treated as capable of aiding and abetting. If a girl is liable to be convicted of aiding and abetting an offence under section 5 she is also liable to conviction for aiding and abetting the felony made punishable by section 4, and she would then be liable to be sentenced to penal servitude for life, because an accessory before the fact to a felony may be punished as a principal. The result would be to render the Act inoperative, because girls would not come forward to give evidence. The Criminal Law Amendment Act, 1885, s.5, created no new offence, and for 600 years it has never been suggested that such an offence as that charged against the defendant could be committed at common law.

LORD COLDERIDGE C.J.: The Criminal Law Amendment Act, 1885, was passed for the purpose of protecting women and girls against themselves. At the time it was passed there was a discussion as to what point should be fixed as the age of consent. That discussion ended in a compromise, and the age of consent was fixed at 16. With the object of protecting women and girls against themselves the Act of Parliament has made illicit connection with a girl under that age unlawful; if a man wishes to have such illicit connection he must wait until the girl is 16, otherwise he breaks the law; but it is impossible to say that the Act, which is absolutely silent about aiding and abetting or soliciting or inciting, can have intended that the girls for whose protection it was passed should be punishable under it for the offences committed upon themselves. I am of opinion that this conviction ought to be quashed.

MATHEW J.: I am of the same opinion. I do not see how it would be possible to obtain convictions under the statute if the contention for the Crown were adopted, because nearly every section which deals with offences in respect of women and girls would create an offence in the woman or girl. Such a result cannot have been intended by the legislature. There is no trace in the statute of any intention to treat the woman or girl as criminal.

Conviction quashed

R. v. Whitehouse
[1977] Q.B. 868
Court of Appeal

W pleaded guilty to a charge of inciting his 15-year-old daughter to commit incest with him. On appeal against sentence, the Court of Appeal gave him leave to appeal against conviction on the view that he may have pleaded guilty to an offence which was unknown to the law.

SCARMAN L.J.: . . . We can turn now to consider whether the indictment disclosed an offence known to the law. The count standing by itself does disclose such an offence because the count merely alleges incitement to commit incest. But when one goes on to the particulars one sees that the defendant is charged with inciting his daughter, a girl aged 15, to commit incest with him. The Crown recognises that there are difficulties in the drafting of the indictment. The Crown recognises that under section 11 of the Sexual Offences Act 1956 a girl aged 15 cannot commit incest. The relevant subsection is (1) and I read it:

"It is an offence for a woman of the age of 16 or over to permit a man whom she knows to be her ... father ... to have sexual intercourse with her by her consent."

It is of course accepted by the Crown that at common law the crime of incitement consists of inciting another person to commit a crime. When one looks at this indictment in the light of the particulars of the offence pleaded, one sees that it is charging the defendant with inciting a girl to commit a crime which in fact by statute she is incapable of committing. If therefore the girl was incapable of committing the crime alleged, how can the defendant be guilty of the common law crime of incitement? The Crown accepts the logic of that position and does not seek in this court to rely on section 11 of the Act of 1956 or to suggest that this man could be guilty of inciting his daughter to commit incest, to use the old phrase, as a principal in the first degree. But the Crown says that it is open to them upon this indictment to submit that it covers the offence of inciting the girl to aid and abet the man to commit the crime of incest upon her. Section 10 of the Act of 1956 makes it an offence for a man to have sexual intercourse with a woman whom he knows to be his daughter, and the Crown says that upon this indictment it is possible to say that the defendant has committed an offence known to the law the offence being that of inciting his daughter under the age of 16 to aid and abet him to have sexual intercourse with her.

... We are prepared to assume, for the purposes of this appeal, that the indictment can be cured, and accordingly we now read the indictment as an indictment charging this man with the offence of inciting a girl of 15 to aid and abet him to commit incest with her.

Is there such an offence known to the law? The difficulty arises from two features of the law to which I have already referred. First, at common law the crime of incitement consists of inciting another person to commit a crime. This was laid down in *R. v. Higgins* (1801) 2 East 5 many years ago and is well described in the very beginning of Chapter 10 of Smith and Hogan, *Criminal Law*, 3rd ed. (1973), p. 172. The authors cite a passage from *S. v. Nkosiyana* 1966 (4) S.A. 655, 658, which includes this sentence: "An inciter is one who reaches and seeks to influence the mind of another to the commission of a crime." The second difficult feature of the law is section 11 of the Act of 1956 to which I have already referred. A woman under the age of 16 cannot commit the crime of incest. But, says the Crown, a man can commit incest, and so they go on to make their submission that a girl of 15 can aid and abet him to do so.

There is no doubt of the general principle, namely, that a person, provided always he or she is of the age of criminal responsibility, can be guilty of aiding or abetting a crime even though it be a crime which he or she cannot commit as a principal in the first degree. There are two famous illustrations in the books of this principle. A woman can aid and abet a rape so as herself to be guilty of rape, and a boy at an age where he is presumed impotent can nevertheless aid and abet a rape. The cases, which are very well known, are first in time *R. v. Eldershaw* (1828) 3 C. & P. 396. In that case Vaughan B., in the course of a six line judgment, the brevity of which I wish I could emulate, says "This boy being under 14, he cannot, by law, be found guilty of a rape, except as a principal in the second degree." So much for the boy.

The position in regard to a woman is stated by Bowen L.J. in one-line-and-a-half in *R. v. Ram* (1893) 17 Cox C.C. 609, where two prisoners, a Mr and Mrs Ram, were indicted jointly for rape upon Annie Edkins of the age of 13. It was submitted that the woman could not be indicted for rape.

Bowen L.J. declined to quash the indictment for rape as against the female prisoner.

Those cases clearly establish, and have been regarded for a very long time as establishing, the general principle to which I have referred.

But what if the person alleged to be aiding and abetting the crime is herself the victim of the crime? This poses the short question with which this appeal is concerned. Before we consider it we would comment that, if indeed it be the law that this girl aged 15 can be guilty of incest as the aider and abettor of a man who is seeking to have intercourse with her, then one has the strange situation that, although she cannot be guilty of the crime of incest under the section which formulates the conditions under which a woman may be found guilty of that crime, yet through this doctrine of aiding and abetting she can be guilty of the offence when it is committed by a man. That is an odd conclusion, but not necessarily to be rejected because of its oddity.

The important matters in our judgment are these. First this girl, aged 15, belongs to a class which is protected, but not punished, by sections 10 and 11 of the Sexual Offences Act 1956, and secondly the girl is alleged to be the victim of this notional crime. The whole question has an air of artificiality because nobody is suggesting either that the father has committed incest with her or that she has aided and abetted him to commit incest upon her. What is suggested is that the father has committed the crime of incitement because by his words and conduct he has incited her to do that which, of course, she never has done.

The question in our judgment is determined by authority. It is, strictly speaking, persuasive authority only because it deals with a different Act of Parliament, but it is a decision by a strong court which has declared a principle which is as applicable to the statutory provision with which we are concerned as to that with which that case was concerned. The case is *R. v. Tyrrell*, [*ante*, p. 411]. [After reciting the facts and quoting the judgment of Coleridge L.C.J.]. In our judgment it is impossible, as a matter of principle, to distinguish *R. v. Tyrrell* from the present case. Clearly the relevant provisions of the Sexual Offences Act 1956 are intended to protect women and girls. Most certainly, section 11 is intended to protect girls under the age of 16 from criminal liability, and the Act as a whole exists, in so far as it deals with women and girls exposed to sexual threat, to protect them. The very fact that girls under the age of 16 are protected from criminal liability for what would otherwise be incest demonstrates that this girl who is said to have been the subject of incitement was being incited to do something which, if she did it, could not be a crime by her.

One can only avoid that conclusion if one can pray in aid the doctrine of aiding and abetting and apply it to a crime committed by a man under section 10. But *R. v. Tyrrell* makes it clear that to do that would be to impose criminal liability upon persons whom Parliament has intended should be protected, not punished.

We have therefore come to the conclusion, with regret, that the indictment does not disclose an offence known to the law because it cannot be a crime on the part of this girl aged 15 to have sexual intercourse with her father, though it is of course a crime, and a very serious crime, on the part of the father. There is here incitement to a course of conduct, but that course of conduct cannot be treated as a crime by the girl. Plainly a gap or lacuna in the protection of girls under the age of 16 is exposed by this decision. It is regrettable indeed that a man who importunes his daughter under the age of 16 to have sexual intercourse with him but does not go beyond incitement cannot be found guilty of a crime. . . . It may be that the legislature will consider it desirable to stop that gap. But in our judgment, applying the principles of the common law relating to the crime of incitement, and taking note of the decision of *R. v. Tyrrell* in relation to legislation similar to the Sexual Offences Act 1956, we have to declare the existence of the lacuna to which I have referred. There was incitement; but it was not incitement to crime. The girl's notional crime—because she never did commit it—is unknown to the law and therefore there can be no offence by him, the inciter. . . .

Appeal against conviction allowed

Notes

1. Section 54 of the Criminal Law Act 1977 now makes it an offence for a man or boy to incite to have sexual intercourse with him a girl under the age of 16 whom he knows to be his grand-daughter, daughter, sister or half-sister.

2. The rationale of *Tyrrell* and *Whitehouse* appears to be that the statute never meant to include under-age girls, because it was passed for their protection. (It may be doubted if that was the reason for section 10 of the Sexual Offences Act 1956, which says nothing about the age of the woman concerned. A more convincing reason is that section 11 makes an under-age girl unconvictable as principal, leading to the conclusion that she is not to be liable as an accessory either.) Other reasons apart from the protection principle could in appropriate cases be advanced for concluding that a statute was not intended to cover particular classes of people, *e.g.* that in penalising the unlicenced sale of tobacco, Parliament must have had both parties to the sale in mind, and the fact that it did not penalise the seller is an indication that it did not want him to be punished. However English law appears, on this question, to take no account of any reason other than the protection principle, see *Sayce v. Coupe, ante,* p. 411.

3. In consultation Paper No. 131, *Assisting and Encouraging Crime* (1993), the Law Commission propose to generalise this reason stating at para. 4103 that "a person [should] not [be] guilty of complicity by assisting an offence if the offence is so defined that his conduct is inevitably incidental to its commission and that conduct is not made criminal by that offence." The Law Commission go on to state at paragraph 4.104 that "the rule will mainly affect what are sometimes regarded as 'regulatory', non-indictable offences, such as offences of sale; but . . . it would also extend to sexual offences of some gravity."

4. On the law as it is at present, apart from the rule of statutory exclusion involved in *R. v. Tyrrell* and *R. v. Whitehouse,* and the rule that a victim cannot be guilty of conspiracy (see Section 2(1) Criminal Law Act 1977, *post,* p. 481, there is no *general* rule that a victim cannot be a party to an offence. For example if A allows B to inflict bodily harm on him without what the law regards as a good reason, he will be an accessory to that crime: see *post* p. 629. But where consent is a defence to the crime, the "victim's" participation may mean that no crime has been committed.

vi. Proposals for Reform

In Consultation Paper No 131, *Assisting and Encouraging Crime* (1993) the Law Commission makes radical proposals for a restructuring of the law on complicity. The Law Commission considers that the haphazard development of the common law has led to substantial uncertainty both as to the mental element in complicity and the conduct which can amount to complicity. The striking feature of the proposals is to abandon the derivative nature of accessorial liability whereby the accessory's liability is derived from the commission of an offence by the principal, and to replace it with an two new inchoate offences of "assisting" and "encouraging" crime. The latter offence would replace the common law offence of incitement. The major effect of this proposed change would be that someone who offers assistance to another to commit a crime, *e.g.* by supplying equipment to be used in the commission of the offence, would be liable to be convicted of the new offence of assisting crime even though the principal offence was not committed. (For a critique of the proposals see K.J.M. Smith, "The Law Commission Consultation Paper on Complicity: (1) A Blueprint for Rationalism [1994] Crim L.R. 239; G. R. Sullivan, "The Law Commission Consultation Paper on Complicity: (2) Fault Elements and Joint Enterprise" [1994] Crim L.R. 252.)

Assisting crime

4.99 (1) A person commits the offence of assisting crime if he

(a) knows or believes that another ("the principal") is doing or causing to be done, or will do or cause to be done, acts that do or will involve the commission of an offence by the principal; and
(b) knows or believes that the principal, in so acting, does or will do so with the fault required for the offence in question; and
(c) does any act that he knows or believes assists or will assist the principal in committing that offence.

(2) Assistance includes giving the principal advice as to commit the offence, or as to how to avoid detection or apprehension before or during the commission of the offence.

(3) A person does not assist the commission of an offence for the purposes of this section if all that he does is to fail to prevent or impede the commission of that offence.

(4) "Offence" in sub-paragraphs (a)-(c) of sub-section (1) above means the breach of a specified prohibition laid down by statute or the common law; but, provided the defendant knows or believes sufficient facts to show that such a breach is taking place or will take place, he need not know the time, place or other details of the offence.

(5) A person also commits an offence under this section if he knows or believes that the principal intends to commit one of a number of offences and does any act that he knows or believes will assist the principal in committing whichever of those offences the principal in fact intends.

Encouraging crime

4.163 (1) A person commits the offence of encouraging crime if he

(a) solicits, commands or encourages another ("the principal") to do or cause to be done an act or acts which, if done, will involve the commission of an offence by the principal; and

(b) intends that that act or those acts should be done by the principal; and

(c) knows or believes that the principal, in so acting, will do so with the fault required for the offence in question.

(2) The solicitation, command or encouragement must be brought to the attention of the principal, but it is irrelevant to the person's guilt whether or not the principal reacts to or is influenced by the solicitation, command or encouragement.

(3) The defendant need not know the identity of the principal, nor have any particular principal or group of principals in mind, provided that he intends his communication to be acted on by any person to whose attention it comes.

(4) "Offence" in sub-paragraphs (a) and (c) of sub-section (1) above means the breach of a specified prohibition laid down by statute or the common law; but for the purposes of this section the defendant may solicit, command or encourage the commission of such an offence without intending that it should be committed at a specific time or place.

Questions

1. D is released from prison having served his sentence following a conviction for obtaining property by deception arising from his forging and selling miniature portrait paintings. He visits his optician, A, complaining that his eyesight has deteriorated while in prison and that he is finding it difficult both to read and to see road signs while driving. A, who is aware of D's criminal career, asks D if he intends to continue forging miniatures. D replies that he probably will as he has no other means of making a living. A performs an eye test and dispenses new spectacles to D aware that these will assist D in making his forgeries. Would A fall within the Law Commission's offence of "assisting crime"? Had A not asked any questions of D but harboured strong suspicions would he have committed the offence of "assisting crime"? If D made no more forgeries would A be guilty of any offence under the current law? Instead of proving knowledge or belief should the proposed offence require proof of an intention to assist the commission of a crime? (see G. R. Sullivan, "Fault Elements and Joint Enterprise" [1994] Crim L.R. 252.)

2. A supplies a gun to D whom he knows to be a bank robber. D assures A that he only wants it to frighten anyone who might seek to obstruct or apprehend him. A believes that D might use the gun to injure or kill anyone who obstructs him. Consider A's liability at this point under the proposed offence of assisting crime and under the current law. If D proceeds to commit a robbery and kill a bank clerk who seeks to apprehend him would A have assisted the crime of murder or merely robbery? What would the position be under the current law?

3. In *R. v. Gianetto, The Times,* July 19, 1996, the Court of Appeal upheld G's conviction of murder on the basis that a conviction of murder was permissible where the jury were satisfied that if G was not the killer he at least encouraged the killing. If the prosecution could not establish which form a defendant's involvement in a killing

took, *i.e.* whether he was the killer or one who assisted or encouraged the killing, would they be able to pursue a prosecution under the Law Commission's proposed offences?

2. VICARIOUS LIABILITY

R. v. Huggins (1730) 2 Strange 869: H, the Warden of the Fleet prison was charged with aiding and abetting B, a turnkey, in the murder of A, a prisoner who was so neglected by B that he died. The jury found a special verdict and the case was argued before all the judges. "It is a point not to be disputed but that in criminal cases the principal is not answerable for the act of the deputy, as he is in civil cases; they must each answer for their own acts and stand or fall by their own behaviour. All the authors that treat of criminal proceedings, proceed on the foundation of this distinction; that to affect the superior by the act of the deputy, there must be the command of the deputy, which is not found in this case. The duress in this case consisted in the first taking him against his consent, and putting him in that room, and the keeping him there so long without necessaries, which was the occasion of his death. Now none of these circumstances are found as against the prisoner. The jury does not say he directed his being put into the room; that he knew how long he had been there, that he was without the necessaries in the indictment, or was ever kept there after the time the prisoner saw him, which was fifteen days before his death. . . ." Judgment: Not Guilty.

Mousell Bros. v. *London and North Western Ry.* [1917] 2 K.B. 836, 845 (C.A.):

ATKIN J.: "I think that the authorities cited . . . make it plain that while prima facie a principal is not to be made criminally responsible for the acts of his servants, yet the legislature may prohibit an act or enforce a duty in such words as to make the prohibition or the duty absolute; in which case the principal is liable if the act is in fact done by his servants. To ascertain whether a particular Act of Parliament has that effect or not regard must be had to the object of the statute, the words used, the nature of the duty laid down, the person upon whom it is imposed, the person by whom it would in ordinary circumstances be performed, and the person upon whom the penalty is imposed."

Notes

1. Discovering the Parliamentary intention involves first asking whether strict liability was intended (on this, see *ante*, p. 184) because on the whole if *mens rea* is required for a conviction, a guiltless master cannot be convicted (although *Mousell's* case is itself an exception, the offence being "giving a false account with intent to avoid tolls," which was held to import vicarious liability). If the statute contains such words as "knowingly", "maliciously", "fraudulently", the master is not usually fixed with the knowledge, malice or fraud of his servant. And if the offence consists of "permitting", "suffering" or "allowing" something to happen, a master does not do so merely because his servant permits, suffers or allows: see *James & Son v. Smee* [1955] 1 Q.B. 78. All this is however, subject to the doctrine of delegation, as to which see *Vane v. Yiannopoulos, infra.*

2. Even if the offence is one of strict liability, much depends on the key verb used in the statute to describe the conduct prohibited: some activities by a servant can be attributed to the master with more plausibility than others. "Using" is apt for vicarious liability, so if a servant uses a vehicle on his master's business, the master will often be held to be using it: see *James & Son v. Smee* [1955] 1 Q.B. 78; *John Henshall (Quarries) Ltd v. Harvey* [1965] 2 Q.B. 233. Compare "driving"—only the actual driver can be said to be doing this: *cf. Thornton v. Mitchell*, *ante*, p. 379.

National Rivers Authority v. Alfred McAlpine Homes East Ltd
[1994] 4 All ER 286
Queen's Bench Division

The respondent company were building houses on a residential development. The NRA inspected a stream close to the building site and discovered a number of dead and distressed fish. Cement had been washed into a stream from the building site. The company's site agent and site manager both accepted responsibility for the pollution. The NRA brought an information against the company alleging that it had caused polluting matter to enter controlled waters contrary to s.85 of the Water Resources Act 1991 which provides:

"A person contravenes this section if he causes or knowingly permits any poisonous, noxious or polluting matter . . . to enter any controlled waters."

The justices held that there was no case to answer and dismissed the information holding that while s.85 appeared to create an offence of strict liability, the NRA had failed to show that the company itself was liable because neither the site agent nor site manager were of a sufficiently senior standing within the company to fall within the category of those whose acts were the acts of the company. The NRA appealed arguing that s.85 could be construed as imposing vicarious liability on the company.

SIMON BROWN LJ: . . .
[Counsel for the company argued, *inter alia*, that:]

(1) A company can only be criminally liable in one of two ways, either (a) by being held vicariously liable for the acts of its servants or agents, or (b) by being identified with individuals held to represent its controlling mind and will—the acts and state of mind of these individuals being deemed to be those also of the company itself.

(2) *Alphacell* (*ante*, p. 199) is properly to be regarded as a category (b) case.

(3) This case is distinguishable from *Alphacell*, there being nothing equivalent here to the storage system designed and operated by the controlling officers of the defendant company there.

(4) Given, as all accept, that neither the site agent nor the site manager can possibly be regarded as exercising the respondent company's controlling mind and will, it can accordingly only be found criminally liable were this court (for the first time, it is suggested) to determine that s. 85 of the 1991 Act should be construed so as to impose vicarious liability upon companies—liability, that is, for their servants or agents. . . .

To my mind the difficulty with this whole elaborate argument is that it breaks down at least as early as stage (2). Assuming, without deciding, that the dichotomy suggested at stage (1) is both sound and absolute, I for my part see *Alphacell* as an illustration of vicarious liability rather than a case where the House of Lords concluded that those representing the directing mind and will of the company had themselves personally caused the polluting matter to escape. The failure in the pumps which was the immediate cause of the pollution was unexplained; but there was certainly nothing to link it to any senior officer in the company. True, none of their Lordships' speeches specifically referred to the company's servants or agents as such; nor did they expressly use the language of vicarious liability. But to my mind the whole tenor of the judgments is consistent only with that approach. How else distinguish *Moses v. Midland Railway Co* (1915) 84 L.J.K.B. 2181 in the way they did? Why else, in discussing *Impress (Worcester) Ltd v. Rees* [1971] 2 All E.R. 357, does Lord Wilberforce speak of "some unauthorised person" having opened the valve "for purposes unconnected with the appellant's business", and "the act of a third person" having interrupted "the chain of causation initiated by the person who owns or operates the installation or plant from which the flow took place"; and Lord Salmon refer to "the active intervention of a stranger, the risk of which could not reasonably have been foreseen"? Why do the speeches stress the clear analogy between this statutory offence of causing pollution and the common law public nuisance cases which plainly recognise a master's liability for his servant's acts? Why, similarly, does Lord Salmon speak of the section as one "which encourages riparian factory owners not only to take reasonable steps to prevent pollution but to do everything possible to ensure that they do not cause it"?

And only such an approach seems to me consistent too with later decisions of the Divisional Court directed to subsequent enactments of this same provision. Take Lloyd LJ's judgment in the Divisional Court in *Welsh Water Authority v. Williams Motors (Cymdu) Ltd* (1988) Times, 5 December, with regard to s. 32(1)(a) of the Control of Pollution Act 1974. There, a delivery company, whilst filling the defendants' storage tank with diesel oil, spilled some oil, which eventually found its way into controlled waters. In upholding the defendants' acquittal, Lloyd LJ said this:

> "[The delivery company] were independent contractors . . . They were not in any sense under the control of the respondents in the way they carried out and fulfilled their functions under the contract . . . It was no different from that of an ordinary domestic householder who finds that his tank has been overfilled by the oil company . . . Giving the word 'cause' its ordinary common sense meaning, as Lord Wilberforce says we must, I can find no positive act in any chain of operations by the respondents here which could be said to have caused the pollution."

The implication from these various dicta is surely unmistakable: an employer is liable for pollution resulting from its own operations carried out under its essential control, save only where some third party acts in such a way as to interrupt the chain of causation.

Is the present case then properly distinguishable from *Alphacell Ltd v. Woodward* [1972] 2 All E.R. 475, [1972] A.C. 824 in point of fact? I believe not, at least not on the evidence as it stood before the justices at the close of the authority's case. I see no difference in principle between the design and maintenance of a storage tank for pollutants (*Alphacell*), and the carrying on of building operations involving the use of pollutants (here, cement to construct a water feature), each occurring on land adjacent to controlled waters. Either system, if ineffectively devised or operated, can result equally in the escape of polluting material into the adjacent stream.

It accordingly seems to me nothing to the point that those in the company's head office here may well have had no direct part in determining the precise system of construction which allowed this cement to wash into the Ditton Stream. It is sufficient that those immediately responsible on site (those who in the event acknowledged what had occurred) were employees of the company and acting apparently within the course and scope of that employment. Certainly it could not be said of them (in contradistinction to the independent contractors responsible for the pollution in the *Welsh Water Authority* case) that "they were not in any sense under the control of the [company] in the way they carried out and fulfilled their functions under the contract". In my judgment, therefore, unless and until the company were themselves to call evidence displacing the clear inference otherwise arising from the facts found—that the pollution resulted directly from the company's own operation in constructing the water feature—it seems to me that the justices could not properly find here no case to answer. On the contrary, there appears to me to have been the clearest possible case.

MORLAND J. . . . Despite the skill and cogency of Mrs Kennedy-McGregor's arguments and her attempt to distinguish *Alphacell Ltd v. Woodward* [1972] 2 All E.R. 475, [1972] A.C. 824 on the basis of the inherent design fault in the pumping system (see Viscount Dilhorne's speech [1972] 2 All E.R. 475 at 479, [1972] A.C. 824 at 836) and that thus the causative act of pollution was by the controlling mind and will of the company, in my judgment, her arguments are fallacious if the relevant words of s. 85(1) of the 1991 Act are given a purposive interpretation.

The object of the relevant words of s. 85(1) and the crime created thereby is the keeping of streams free from pollution for the benefit of mankind generally and the world's flora and fauna. Most significantly deleterious acts of pollution will arise out of industrial, agricultural or commercial activities. The damage occasioned may take years to repair and often at a cost running into thousands or millions of pounds. The act or omission by which the polluting matter enters a stream may result from negligence or may not. It does not matter. In almost all cases the act or omission will be that of a person such as a workman, fitter or plant operative in a fairly low position in the hierarchy of the industrial, agricultural or commercial concern.

In my judgment, to make the offence an effective weapon in the defence of environmental protection, a company must by necessary implication be criminally liable for the acts or omissions of its servants or agents during activities being done for the company. I do not find that this offends our concept of a just and fair criminal legal system, having regard to the magnitude of environmental pollution, even though no due diligence defence was provided for.

In my judgment, the dicta in *Alphacell Ltd v. Woodward* entirely support this interpretation, although the question for the House was whether "knowingly" qualified "causes" in the earlier 1951 Act. . . .

It can be strongly argued that the respondents by their activities directly caused the flow of polluting matter into the stream. It is difficult to see in principle why it should matter whether those activities are essentially mechanical by their plant or essentially manual by their servants or agents. The forbidden result is the same. . . .

Lord Salmon said ([1972] 2 All E.R. 475 at 491, [1972] A.C. 824 at 848–849):

"If this appeal succeeded and it were held to be the law that no conviction could be obtained under the [Rivers (Prevention of Pollution) Act
1951] unless the prosecution could discharge the often impossible onus
of proving that the pollution was caused intentionally or negligently, a
great deal of pollution would go unpunished and undeterred to the
relief of many riparian factory owners. As a result, many rivers which
are now filthy would become filthier still and many rivers which are
now clean would lose their cleanliness. The legislature no doubt recognised that as a matter of public policy this would be most unfortunate.
Hence s. 2(1)(*a*) which encourages riparian factory owners not only to
take reasonable steps to prevent pollution but to do everything possible
to ensure that they do not cause it."

Although Lord Salmon was dealing with an entirely different point,
"mens rea", in my judgment, if, to succeed in such prosecutions, the
authorities had to prove that the company by its "controlling mind and
will" caused the pollution rather than criminal liability vicariously by
some human intervention by their servants or agents in the company's
activities, the effectiveness of the relevant part of s. 85(1) of the 1991 Act
would be lost and the filthiness of rivers increased.

I see no reason why Parliament as a matter of policy should not have
placed on principals, whether companies or others, the responsibility of
environmental protection. They are best placed to ensure that streams are
not polluted during their activities by their servants or agents. They can
do this by training, discipline, supervision and the highest standard of
maintenance of plant . . .

In my judgment if the magistrates had directed themselves correctly in
law they must have found a case to answer.

I would allow the appeal and order that the case be reheard by a fresh
bench of magistrates.

Appeal allowed.

Williams, *Criminal Law: The General Part*, section 96, p. 281 (citations omitted)

. . . It seems we are now to witness the compiling of a new 'judicial dictionary' which will distinguish between those verbs in respect of which
the servant's conduct can be regarded as the master's, and those in which
it cannot. We must take it as settled by authority that a sale or use or
(perhaps) presentation of a play by a servant, if within the general scope
of his authority (though forbidden in the precise circumstances), is a sale
or use or presentation by the master. On the other hand, it has been held
that a representation made by the servant in the course of selling is not a
representation by the master. A servant's 'ill-treating' of an animal cannot
be attributed to his master. A receiving by a servant does not make his
master guilty of 'receiving' stolen goods. So also a giving of credit by a
servant is not a giving of credit by the master, and a demand for an illegal
premium by a servant is not a demand by the master. Although the point
has not been expressly decided, it seems that a master could not be convicted of an offence of 'driving' a vehicle through his servant, for in law
it is only the actual driver who drives. Yet it has been held that a bus
company 'carries' its passenger and is apparently responsible for an
offence in relation to carriage committed by the conductor. . . .

To make the law more difficult still, the same verb may possibly be
construed to create vicarious responsibility in a 'public welfare offence'
but not in one of the traditional crimes. Thus when a servant is in *de*

facto possession of a thing on behalf of his master, the possession may be attributed to the master for the purpose of a public welfare offence, and yet not attributed to him for the purpose of the crime of receiving stolen goods. This way of reconciling the authorities may lead to the somewhat surprising conclusion that the presentation of an unlicensed stage play is a 'public welfare offence.' Again, the context of the verb may modify its meaning: for example, the word 'use' may be restricted by the purport of the section to persons of a particular class.

Notes

1. Where vicarious responsibility is held to exist, it is not, in the absence of some express provision in the statute, any defence to show that the act of the servant was in defiance of the master's instructions: *Coppen v. Moore (No. 2)* [1898] 2 Q.B. 306 (D.C.)

2. Except when the master is a company and the servant a director (as to which see *post*, p. 426), whether or not the offence is one where vicarious liability is held to be intended, it seems that in no case will a master be primarily or vicariously liable for *aiding and abetting* an offence, without personal knowledge of the essential matters constituting the offence. On such a charge, the knowledge of the servant is not imputed to the master (see *Ferguson v. Weaving, ante*, p. 391. *N.C.B. v. Gamble, ante*, p. 387 is not an authority to the contrary because there the master invited the court to identify him with the servant whose acts and knowledge constituted the aiding and abetting: see [1959] 1 Q.B. 26.

Draft Criminal Code

Vicarious liability

29.—(1) Subject to subsection (3), an element of an offence (other than a fault element) may be attributed to a person by reason of an act done by another only if that other is—

(a) specified in the definition of the offence as a person whose act may be so attributed; or
(b) acting within the scope of his employment or authority and the definition of the offence specifies the element in terms which apply to both persons.

(2) Subject to subsection (3), a fault element of an offence may be attributed to a person by reason of the fault of another only if the terms of the enactment creating the offence so provide.

(3) This section does not affect the application in relation to any pre-Code offence (as defined in section 6) of any existing rule whereby a person who has delegated to another the management of premises or of a business or activity may, in consequence of the acts and fault of the other, have the elements of the offence attributed to him.

Commentary on Draft Criminal Code: Law Com. 177

9.49 *Independent contractors*. The reference in paragraph (b) to a person's 'acting within the scope of his authority' extends, of course, to a case in which the person who does the prohibited act is acting for the defendant not as an employee but as an independent contractor. The clause does not distinguish between the person who 'uses' the defendant's vehicle as his employee and the person who 'uses' the defendant's vehicle on a single occasion because the defendant has asked him to do so, whether or not for payment. This does not mean that a person will necessarily be liable for the act of his independent contractor even where the offence employs a verb like 'uses'. The matter remains one for judicial interpretation. It is one thing to hold that a person carrying on a business of supplying milk or heavy building materials 'uses' a vehicle if he employs an independent contractor to supply those things in the contractor's vehicle. It would be quite another thing to hold that a householder 'uses' the removal van owned by the firm of removers whom he engages to carry his furniture to a new residence.

Question

Do you agree that, in the matter of "using" an independent contractor's van, there is a distinction between a person in the business of supplying building materials and a person moving furniture to a new residence?

Note

Under the present law, if the offence involved is not one of strict liability a master without knowledge of what is being done is normally not vicariously liable. To this rule, the doctrine of delegation forms an exception. See *infra*.

Vane v. Yiannopoullos
[1965] A.C. 486
House of Lords

By section 22(1) of the Licensing Act 1961: "If—(a) the holder of a justices' on-licence knowingly sells or supplies intoxicating liquor to persons to whom he is not permitted by the conditions of the licence to sell or supply it . . . he shall be guilty of an offence."

The licensee of a restaurant had been granted a justices' on-licence subject to the condition that intoxicating liquor was to be sold only to persons ordering meals. He employed a waitress, whom he had instructed to serve drinks only to customers ordering meals, but on one occasion, whilst he was on another floor of the restaurant, the waitress served drinks to two youths who did not order a meal. The licensee did not know of that sale. He was charged with knowingly selling intoxicating liquor on the premises to persons to whom he was not permitted to sell, contrary to section 22(1)(a) of the Act. The magistrate dismissed the information and the prosecutor appealed, ultimately to the House of Lords.

LORD EVERSHED (after reviewing many cases cited by the appellant): But the effect of these numerous cases appears to my mind to be that (subject to the exception which follows) where the scope and purpose of the relevant Act is the maintenance of proper and accepted standards of public order in licensed premises or other comparable establishments, there arises under the legislation what Channell J. [in *Emary v. Nolloth* [1903] 2 K.B. 264] called a "quasi-criminal offence" which renders the licensee or proprietor criminally liable for the acts of his servants, though there may be no *mens rea* on his part. On the other hand, where the relevant regulation imports the word "knowingly" as a condition of liability on the part of the licensee or proprietor the result will be different. "Knowledge", that is *mens rea* in a real sense, on the part of the licensee or proprietor should normally be established as a fact if he is to be held liable under the statute. To this second proposition it appears, however, that, for better or worse, it should now be accepted that something further may be added—namely, that in the absence of proof of actual knowledge, nevertheless the licensee or proprietor may be held liable if he be shown, in the language of the judgments to which I have referred, in a real sense, effectively to have "delegated" his proprietary or managerial functions. If it be asked what is meant by delegation, it may be said . . . that the expression will cover cases where the licensee or proprietor has handed over all the effective management of his premises, where he in truth connives at or wilfully closes his eyes to what in fact is being done. But I prefer to attempt nothing further in the way of definition applicable to any of the classes of case which have arisen; for I venture, for my part, to think that in the light of the numerous authorities the answer to any given case will generally depend upon the common sense of the jury or magistrate concerned, in light of what I believe can now be fairly and sensibly derived from the effect of the numerous cases referred to in the argument, to some of which I have alluded. On the one hand, where there is absent from the statutory prohibition the word "knowingly" applied to the licensee, I think that it should now be accepted that he may yet be held, and properly held, liable for breaches of the conditions of the licence committed by his servants in conscious disregard of those conditions, in spite of his own innocence, where a contrary view would, in the language of Viscount Reading C.J. [in *Mousell Brothers, Ltd v. London and North Western Railway Co.* [1917] 2 K.B. 836], be regarded as fairly likely to stultify what, upon its fair construction, was the purpose of the legislation. On the other hand, where statutory liability on the licensee's part is qualified by the word "knowingly" (or some similarly clear term) then actual knowledge—that is, *mens rea*—is prima facie required. But I also think, in the light of the cases which have come before the Divisional Court during the present century, that it is right and sensible to hold that, even in the absence of that knowledge on the licensee's part, he may yet fairly and sensibly be held liable where he has in truth and reality "delegated" his powers, functions and responsibilities in the sense indicated in the examples which I have cited from the authorities. I do not attempt any further definition. As I have said, I think the result in any given case will depend upon the common sense of the jury or magistrate in light of what I think to be the effect of the numerous decisions.

So far, however, as the present case is concerned, I feel no doubt that the decision of the Divisional Court was right. There was clearly no "knowledge" in the strict sense proved against the licensee: I agree also with the Lord Chief Justice that there was no sufficient evidence of such "delegation" on his part of his powers, duties and responsibilities to render him liable on that ground. I would therefore without hesitation dismiss the appeal.

Appeal dismissed

Note

The delegation principle is to be abolished for Code and post-Code offences: Clause 29(2), *ante*, p. 423; but pre-existing cases where it has been held to apply are not to be affected: Clause 29(3).

3. CORPORATIONS

Notes

1. By Interpretation Act 1978, section 5, schedule 1, in every Act, unless the contrary intention appears, "person" includes a body of persons corporate or unincorporate.

2. A corporation is *vicariously* liable to exactly the same extent as a natural person: see last section. However a corporation is also directly liable for acts performed by some natural persons who are identified with it. In such a case the acts and intentions of those who control the corporation are deemed to be those of the corporation itself. There are, however, two limitations to corporate liability identified in *R. v. I.C.R. Haulage Ltd* [1944] K.B. 551. Firstly, there are certain offences which, from their very nature, cannot be committed by corporations, for example, bigamy, rape, incest and perjury. Secondly, a corporation will not be convicted of an offence where the only punishment which may be imposed is physical. Where a corporation is convicted of an offence it will be punished by the imposition of a fine and/or a compensation order.

Tesco Supermarkets Ltd v. Nattrass
[1972] A.C. 153
House of Lords

TS Ltd was charged with an offence under the Trade Descriptions Act 1968. It sought to raise a defence under section 24(1) on the grounds that the commission of the offence was due to the act or default of another person, namely the manager of the store at which it was committed, and it exercised all due diligence to avoid the commission of the offence. The magistrates found that the company had set up a proper system, so it had exercised all due diligence; but the manager, who had failed to carry out his part under the system, was not "another person". The company, on conviction, appealed to the Divisional Court which held that the manager was "another person" but the company had not exercised all due diligence. The company appealed to the House of Lords.

LORD REID: My Lords, the appellants own a large number of supermarkets in which they sell a wide variety of goods. The goods are put out for sale on shelves or stands, each article being marked with the price at which it is offered for sale. The customer selects the articles he wants, takes them to the cashier, and pays the price. From time to time the appellants, apparently by way of advertisement, sell "flash packs" at prices lower than the normal price. In September 1969 they were selling Radiant washing powder in this way. The normal price was 3s. 11d. but these packs were marked and sold at 2s. 11d. Posters were displayed in the shops drawing attention to this reduction in price.

These prices were displayed in the appellants' shop at Northwich on September 26. Mr Coane, an old age pensioner, saw this and went to buy a pack. He could only find packs marked 3s. 11d. He took one to the cashier who told him that there were none in stock for sale at 2s. 11d. He paid 3s. 11d. and complained to an inspector of weights and measures. This resulted in a prosecution under the Trade Descriptions Act 1968 and the appellants were fined £25 and costs.

Section 11(2) provides:

"If any person offering to supply any goods gives, by whatever means, any indication likely to be taken as an indication that the goods are being offered at a price less than that at which they are in fact being offered he shall, subject to the provisions of this Act, be guilty of an offence."

It is not disputed that that section applies to this case. The appellants relied on section 24(1) which provides:

"In any proceedings for an offence under this Act it shall, subject to subsection (2) of this section, be a defence for the person charged to prove—(*a*) that the commission of the offence was due to a mistake or reliance on information supplied to him or to the act or default of another person, an accident or some other cause beyond his control; and (*b*) that he took all reasonable precautions and exercised all due diligence to avoid the commission of such an offence by himself or any person under his control."

The relevant facts as found by the magistrates were that on the previous evening a shop assistant, Miss Rogers, whose duty it was to put out fresh stock found that there were no more of the specially marked packs in stock. There were a number of packs marked with the ordinary price so she put them out. She ought to have told the shop manager, Mr Clement, about this, but she failed to do so. Mr Clement was responsible for seeing that the proper packs were on sale, but he failed to see to this although he marked his daily return "all special offers O.K." The magistrates found that if he had known about this he would either have removed the poster advertising the reduced price or given instructions that only 2s. 11d. was to be charged for the packs marked 3s. 11d.

Section 24(2) requires notice to be given to the prosecutor if the accused is blaming another person and such notice was duly given naming Mr. Clement.

In order to avoid conviction the appellants had to prove facts sufficient to satisfy both parts of section 24(1) of the Act of 1968. The magistrates held that they

"had exercised all due diligence in devising a proper system for the operation of the said store and by securing so far as was reasonably practicable that it was fully implemented and thus had fulfilled the requirements of section 24(1)(*b*)."

But they convicted the appellants because in their view the requirements of section 24(1)(*a*) had not been fulfilled: they held that Clement was not "another person" within the meaning of that provision.

Where a limited company is the employer difficult questions do arise in a wide variety of circumstances in deciding which of its officers or servants is to be identified with the company so that his guilt is the guilt of the company.

I must start by considering the nature of the personality which by a fiction the law attributes to a corporation. A living person has a mind which can have knowledge or intention or be negligent and he has hands to carry out his intentions. A corporation has none of these: it must act through living persons, though not always one or the same person. Then the person who acts is not speaking or acting for the company. He is acting as the company and his mind which directs his acts is the mind of the company. There is no question of the company being vicariously liable. He is not acting as a servant, representative, agent or delegate. He is an embodiment of the company or, one could say, he hears and speaks through the persona of the company, within his appropriate sphere, and his mind is the mind of the company. If it is a guilty mind then that guilt is the guilt of the company. It must be a question of law whether, once the facts have been ascertained, a person in doing particular things is to be regarded as the company or merely as the company's servant or agent. In that case any liability of the company can only be a statutory or vicarious liability.

In *Lennard's Carrying Co. Ltd v. Asiatic Petroleum Co. Ltd* [1915] A.C. 705 the question was whether damage had occurred without the "actual fault or privity" of the owner of a ship. The owners were a company. The fault was that of the registered managing owner who managed the ship on behalf of the owners and it was held that the company could not dissociate itself from him so as to say that there was no actual fault or privity on the part of the company. Viscount Haldane L.C. said, at pp. 713, 714:

"For if Mr Lennard was the directing mind of the company, then his action must, unless a corporation is not to be liable at all, have been an action which was the action of the company itself within the meaning of section 502. . . . It must be upon the true construction of that section in such a case as the present one that the fault or privity is the fault or privity of somebody who is not merely a servant or agent for whom the company is liable upon the footing respondent superior, but somebody for whom the company is liable because his action is the very action of the company itself."

Reference is frequently made to the judgment of Denning L.J. in *H.L. Bolton (Engineering) Co. Ltd v. T.J. Graham & Sons Ltd* [1957] 1 Q.B. 159. He said, at p. 172:

"A company may in many ways be likened to a human body. It has a brain and nerve centre which controls what it does. It also has hands which hold the tools and act in accordance with directions from the centre. Some of the people in the company are mere servants and agents who are nothing more than hands to do the work and cannot be said to represent the mind or will. Others are directors and managers who represent the directing mind and will of the company, and control what it does. The state of mind of these managers is the state of mind of the company and is treated by the law as such."

In that case the directors of the company only met once a year: they left the management of the business to others, and it was the intention of those managers which was imputed to the company. I think that was right. There have been attempts to apply Lord Denning's words to all servants of a company whose work is brain work, or who exercise some managerial discretion under the direction of superior officers of the company. I do not think that Lord Denning intended to refer to them. He only referred to those who "represent the directing mind and will of the company, and control what it does".

I think that is right for this reason. Normally the board of directors, the managing director and perhaps other superior officers of a company carry out the functions of management and speak and act as the company. Their subordinates do not. They carry out orders from above and it can make no difference that they are given some measure of discretion. But the board of directors may delegate some part of their functions of management giving to their delegate full discretion to act independently of instructions from them. I see no difficulty in holding that they have thereby put such a delegate in their place so that within the scope of the delegation he can act as the company. It may not always be easy to draw the line but there are cases in which the line must be drawn. *Lennard's* case was one of them.

In some cases the phrase alter ego has been used. I think it is misleading. When dealing with a company the word alter is I think misleading. The person who speaks and acts as the company is not alter. He is identified with the company. And when dealing with an individual no other individual can be his alter ego. The other individual can be a servant, agent, delegate or representative but I know of neither principle nor authority which warrants the confusion (in the literal or original sense) of two separate individuals. . . .

In the next two cases a company was accused and it was held liable for the fault of a superior officer. In *D.P.P. v. Kent and Sussex Contractors Ltd* [1944] K.B. 146 he was the transport manager. In *R. v. I.C.R. Haulage Ltd* [1944] K.B. 551 it was held that a company can be guilty of common law conspiracy. The act of the managing director was held to be the act of the company. I think that a passage in the judgment is too widely stated, at p. 559:

> "Where in any particular case there is evidence to go to a jury that the criminal act of an agent, including his state of mind, intention, knowledge or belief is the act of the company, and, in cases where the presiding judge so rules, whether the jury are satisfied that it has been proved, must depend on the nature of the charge, the relative position of the officer or agent, and the other relevant facts and circumstances of the case."

. . . I think that the true view is that the judge must direct the jury that if they find certain facts proved then as a matter of law they must find that the criminal act of the officer, servant or agent including his state of mind, intention, knowledge or belief is the act of the company. I have already dealt with the considerations to be applied in deciding when such a person can and when he cannot be identified with the company. I do not see how the nature of the charge can make any difference. If the guilty man was in law identifiable with the company then whether his offence was serious or venial his act was the act of the company but if he was not so identifiable then no act of his, serious or otherwise, as the act of the company itself.

In *John Henshall (Quarries) Ltd v. Harvey* [1965] 2 Q.B. 233 a company was held not criminally responsible for the negligence of a servant in charge of a weighbridge. In *Magna Plant v. Mitchell* (unreported) April 27, 1966, the fault was that of a depot engineer and again the company was held not criminally responsible. I think these decisions were right. In the *Magna Plant* case Lord Parker C.J. said:

> ". . . knowledge of a servant cannot be imputed to the company unless he is a servant for whose actions the company are criminally responsible, and as the cases show, that only arises in the case of a company where one is considering the acts of responsible officers forming the brain, or in the case of an individual, a person to whom delegation in the true sense of the delegation of management has been passed."

I agree with what he said with regard to a company. But delegation by an individual is another matter. It has been recognised in licensing cases but that is in my view anomalous (see *Vane v. Yiannopoullos, ante,* p. 424). . . .

What good purpose could be served by making an employer criminally responsible for the misdeeds of some of his servants but not for those of others? It is sometimes argued—it was argued in the present case—that making an employer criminally responsible, even when he has done all that he could to prevent an offence, affords some additional protection to the public because this will induce him to do more. But if he has done all he can how can he do more? I think that what lies behind this argument is a suspicion that magistrates too readily accept evidence that an employer has done all he can to prevent offences. But if magistrates were to accept as sufficient a paper scheme and perfunctory efforts to enforce it they would not be doing their duty—that would not be "due diligence" on the part of the employer.

Then it is said that this would involve discrimination in favour of a large employer like the appellants against a small shopkeeper. But that is not so. Mr Clement was the "opposite number" of the small shopkeeper and he was liable to prosecution in this case. The purpose of this Act must have been to penalise those at fault, not those who were in no way to blame.

The Divisional Court decided this case on a theory of delegation. In that they were following some earlier authorities. But they gave far too wide a meaning to delegation. I have said that a board of directors can delegate part of their functions of management so as to make their delegate an embodiment of the company within the sphere of the delegation. But here the board never delegated any part of their functions. They set up a chain of command through regional and district supervisors, but they remained in control. The shop managers had to obey their general directions and also take orders from their superiors. The acts or omissions of shop managers were not acts of the company itself.

In my judgment the appellants established the statutory defence. I would therefore allow this appeal.

[Lord Morris of Borth-y-Gest, Viscount Dilhorne, Lord Pearson and Lord Diplock delivered speeches agreeing that the appeal should be allowed.]

Appeal allowed

Note

The state of mind of the controlling officers is *not* the state of mind of the company where those officers are accused of committing a crime against the company: see R. v. *Gomez, post,* p. 703.

Where an offence is one of strict liability, the identification principle is not relevant as the company may be liable for the acts of any of its employees or agents. Where an offence requires *mens rea* a company may only be convicted where a controlling officer who is identified with the company has the requisite state of mind. A problem area is that of manslaughter. For a time it was thought that manslaughter was an offence of which a corporation could not be convicted. This view was rejected in *P. & O. European Ferries Ltd* (1990) 93 Cr. App. R. 72. In the area of safety there may be many failures within a corporation at different levels which may coalesce to result in a major disaster resulting in loss of life. In such a case the issue arises as to whether a prosecution for manslaughter may be based on an aggregation of the differing failures even though the failure of any one individual might not be great enough to be designated "grossly negligent". Clearly, if an offence is one demanding proof of *mens rea* it should not be possible to aggregate the states of mind of several individuals which individually do not satisfy the *mens rea* requirement to conclude that in aggregate they do. In *Armstrong v. Strain* [1952] 1 K.B.232, Devlin J. stated, "You cannot add an innocent state of mind to an innocent state of mind and get as a result a dishonest state of mind." If manslaughter was an offence requiring *mens rea*, this principle should apply. Following the decision of the House of Lords in *Seymour* [1983] 2 A.C. 493, manslaughter demanded proof of recklessness in the *Caldwell/Lawrence sense (see ante* pp. 121–128). In this context the aggregation principle was rejected in *R. v. H.M. Coroner for East Kent, ex p. Spooner* (1988) Cr App.R. 10 and *P. & O. European Ferries Ltd.* Since the decision of the House of Lords in *Adomako* [1995] 1 A.C. 171 (*post* p. 592), however, manslaughter by gross negligence is not an offence requiring *mens rea*. This being so, is it possible to aggregate the negligence of individuals within a corporation to arrive at a finding of gross negligence on the part of the corporation? In *Kite and OLL Ltd* (Winchester Crown Court, December 8, 1994, unreported) the company was convicted of manslaughter but this followed on the conviction of its managing director, the company being a one-man concern. In the case which follows the issue of aggregation was directly addressed.

Attorney General's Reference No 2/1999
Court of Appeal
[2000] Cr.App.R. 207

THE VICE PRESIDENT, ROSE L.J.: The court's opinion is sought in relation to two questions referred by the Attorney General under s.36 of the Criminal Justice Act 1972:

1. can a defendant be properly convicted of manslaughter by gross negligence in the absence of evidence as to that defendant's state of mind?

2. can a non-human defendant be convicted of the crime of manslaughter by gross negligence in the absence of evidence establishing the guilt of an identified human individual for the same crime?

The questions arise from a ruling given by Mr Justice Scott Baker at the Central Criminal Court on 30th June 1999. At the outset of the trial of the defendant train operating company, on an indictment containing seven counts of manslaughter, he ruled that it is a condition precedent to a conviction for manslaughter by gross negligence for a guilty mind to be proved and that where a non-human defendant is prosecuted it may only be convicted via the guilt of a human being with whom it may be identified. It is submitted for the Attorney General that the judge was wrong in both respects.

The prosecution arose from the disastrous collision which occurred at Southall at 1.15 pm on 19th September 1997. The 10.32 high speed train (HST) from Swansea to London Paddington, with approximately 180 passengers and staff on board, operated by the defendant and travelling on the up main line, collided with a freight train crossing from the down relief line to Southall Yard. Seven passengers died. One hundred and fifty one people were injured. Millions of pounds worth of damage was done.

The HST had a driver of considerable experience but no second competent person with him. The power car was fitted with two safety devices independent of the driver. Each was designed to prevent a signal being passed at danger. One system was the Automatic Warning System (AWS) which had been in common use in the United Kingdom since the 1950s. It had been deliberately switched off. The other system was Automatic Train Protection (ATP) which the defendant was piloting for Railtrack and was the only United Kingdom operator using it. It had been switched off. The driver knew that neither AWS nor ATP were operating.

The movement of the train was correctly signalled i.e. the signals on the up main line affecting the HST prior to the junction were set successively at green, double yellow, single yellow and red. The HST driver remembered passing through the green signal but next recalled seeing the red signal. He braked as hard as he could, but, as he was travelling at an average of 116 mph over the 3600 metres immediately preceding the accident, it was too late.

The case for the prosecution was that the cause of the collision was, first, the driver's failure to see or heed the double yellow and single yellow signals warning of impending red and, secondly, the defendant's manner of operating the HST. The case against the defendant was that it owed a duty to take reasonable care for the safety of its passengers, of which it was in grossly negligent breach. Three signals were passed because the AWS and ATP were switched off and there was only one man in the cab. The defendant should not have permitted such a train to operate in such circumstances. Following the judge's ruling, the defendant pleaded guilty to count 8 on the indictment, which alleged failure to conduct an undertaking, namely the provision of transport by rail to members of the public, in such a way as to ensure that they were not exposed to risks to their health and safety, contrary to sections 3(1) and 33(1)(a) of the Health and Safety at Work Act 1974. The defendant was fined £1.5 million for what the judge described as "a serious fault of senior management". No employee of the defendant, apart from the driver, was prosecuted.

For the Attorney General, Mr Lissack Q.C. submitted, in relation to question 1, that involuntary manslaughter can be committed by an unlawful act, gross negligence or subjective recklessness (see Law Commission Paper No 237 paras 2.3, 2.8, and 2.26). The present case rests on gross negligence manslaughter. He submits that, since *R v. Adomako* [1995] 1 A.C. 171, a defendant can be found guilty of such manslaughter in the absence of evidence as to his state of mind. "The ordinary principles of the law of negligence apply to ascertain whether or not the defendant has been in breach of a duty of care towards the victim who has died. If such breach of duty is established the next question is whether that breach of duty caused the death of the victim. If so, the jury must go on to consider whether that breach of duty should be characterised as gross negligence and therefore as a crime. This will depend on the seriousness of the breach of duty committed by the defendant in all the circumstances in which the defendant was placed when it occurred. The jury will have to consider whether the extent to which the defendant's conduct departed from the proper standard of care incumbent upon him , involving as it must have done a risk of death to the patient, was such that it should be judged criminal." (*per* Lord Mackay of Clashfern L.C. in *Adomako* at 187 B-D). Only gross breaches will give rise to criminal liability.

As a result of *Adomako*, Mr Lissack submitted, gross negligence manslaughter can be proved without the need to enquire into the state of the defendant's mind. This proposition is supported by a passage at pages 90 and 91 in the 7th Edition of Smith and Hogan's *Criminal Law*, which culminates in contrasting crimes requiring *mens rea* with crimes of negligence. The *Adomako* test was derived from *Bateman* 19 Cr.App.R. 8, which was an objective test (see Law Commission Consultation Paper 135 para. 32).

For the defendant Mr Caplan Q.C., in relation to question 1, submitted that there is a difference between whether *mens rea* must be proved and whether it may be relevant. He accepted that it need not be proved for gross negligence. But, he said, it may be relevant because the *Adomako* test requires the jury, when deciding if the breach is criminal, to consider it in all the circumstances. Furthermore, in *Adomako* at 187H Lord Mackay went on to say that it was perfectly appropriate to use the word "reckless" in cases of involuntary manslaughter, in its ordinary connotation as in *Stone* [1977] Q.B. 354. At 363F in *Stone* Lord Lane C.J. said that, where a defendant had undertaken a duty of care for the health and welfare of an infirm person the prosecution had to prove "a reckless disregard of danger to the health and welfare. Mere indifference is not enough. The defendant must be proved to have been indifferent to an obvious risk of injury to health or actually to have foreseen the risk but to have determined nevertheless to run it".

On this question, we accept the submissions of both Mr Lissack and Mr Caplan. They lead to the conclusion that question 1 must be answered "Yes". Although there may be cases where the defendant's state of mind is relevant to the jury's consideration when assessing the grossness and criminality of his conduct, evidence of his state of mind is not a pre-requisite to a conviction for manslaughter by gross negligence. The *Adomako* test is objective, but a defendant who is reckless as defined in *Stone* may well be the more readily found to be grossly negligent to a criminal degree.

As to question 2, Mr Lissack accepted that policy considerations arise. Large companies should be as susceptible to prosecution for manslaughter as one-man companies. Where the ingredients of a common law offence are identical to those of a statutory offence there is no justification for drawing a distinction as to liability between the two and the public interest requires the more emphatic denunciation of a company inherent in a conviction for manslaughter. He submitted that the ingredients of the offence of gross negligence manslaughter are the same in relation to a body corporate as to a human being, namely grossly negligent breach of a duty to a deceased causative of his death. It is, he submitted, unnecessary and inappropriate to enquire whether there is an employee in the company who is guilty of the offence of manslaughter who can be properly be said to have been acting as the embodiment of the company. The criminal law of negligence follows the civil law of negligence as applied to corporations: the only difference is that, to be criminal, the negligence must be gross. Of the three theories of corporate criminal liability, namely vicarious liability, identification and personal liability, it is personal liability which should here apply. In the present case, it would have been open to the jury to convict if they were satisfied that the deaths occurred by reason of a gross breach by the defendant of its personal duty to have a safe system of train operation in place. The identification theory, attributing to the company the mind and will of senior directors and managers, was developed in order to avoid injustice: it would bring the law into disrepute if every act and state of mind of an individual employee was attributed to a company which was entirely blameless (see *per* Lord Reid in *Tesco Supermarkets Ltd v. Nattrass* 1972 A.C. 153 at 169 and *per* Estey J. of the Supreme Court of Canada in *Canadian Dredge Co v. The Queen*) 19 D.L.R. 314 at 342). Its origins lay in the speech of Viscount Haldane L.C. in *Lennard's Carrying Co Ltd v. Asiatic Petroleum Co Ltd* 1915 AC 705 at 713, and it was developed by the judgment of Denning L.J. in *Bolton Engineering v. T J Graham & Sons* 1957 1 Q.B. 159 at 172 and [Lord Reid in] *Tesco Supermarkets Ltd v. Nattrass* . . . .

Before turning to Mr Lissack's submission in relation to personal liability it is convenient first to refer to the speech of Lord Hoffmann in *Meridian Global Funds Management v. Securities Commission* [1995] 2 A.C. 500 on which Mr Lissack relied as the lynch pin of this part of his argument. It was a case in which the chief investment officer and senior portfolio manager of an investment management company, with the company's authority but unknown to the board of directors and managing director, used funds managed by the company to acquire shares, but failed to comply with a statutory obligation to give notice of the acquisition to the Securities Commission. The trial judge held that the knowledge of the officer and manager should be attributed to the company and the Court of Appeal of New Zealand upheld the decision on the basis that the officer was the directing mind and will of the company. The Privy Council dismissed an appeal. In a passage at 506C Lord Hoffmann, giving the judgment of the Privy Council, said that the company's primary rules of attribution were generally found in its constitution or implied by company law. But, in an exceptional case, where the application of those principles would defeat the intended application of a particular provision to companies, it was necessary to devise a special rule of attribution. At 507B Lord Hoffmann said:

"For example, a rule may be stated in language primarily applicable to a natural person and require some act or state of mind on the part of that person "himself", as opposed to his servants or agents. This is generally true of the rules of the criminal law, which ordinarily impose liability only for the *actus reus* and *mens rea* of the defendant himself. How is such a rule to be applied to a company? One possibility is that the court may come to the conclusion that the rule was not intended to apply to companies at all; for example, a law which created an offence for which the only penalty was community service. Another possibility is that the court might interpret the law as meaning that it could apply to a company only on the basis of its primary rules of attribution i.e. if the act giving rise to liability was specifically authorised by a resolution of the board or an unanimous agreement of the shareholders. But there will be many cases in which neither of these solutions is satisfactory; in which the court considers that the law was intended to apply to companies and that, although it excludes ordinary vicarious liability, insistence on the primary rules of attribution would in practice defeat that intention. In such a case, the court must fashion a special rule of attribution for the particular substantive rule. This is always a matter of interpretation: given that it was intended to apply to a company, how was it intended to apply? Whose act (or knowledge, or state of mind) was *for this purpose* intended to count as the act etc of the company? One finds the answer to this question by applying the usual canons of interpretation, taking into account the language of the rule (if it is a statute) and its content and policy".

Lord Hoffmann then referred to *Tesco Supermarkets Ltd v. Nattrass* and *In re. Supply of Ready Mixed Concrete (No 2)* [1995] 1AC 456, Viscount Haldane's speech in *Lennards Co* and Denning L.J.'s judgment in *Bolton v. Graham*. Having at 511A referred to the concept of directing mind and will, he went on to say:

"It will often be the most appropriate description of the person designated by the relevant attribution rule, but it might be better to acknowledge that not every such rule has to be forced into the same formula. Once it is appreciated that the question is one of construction rather than metaphysics the answer in this case seems to their Lordships to be . . . the policy of s20 of the Securities Amendment Act 1988 is to compel, in fast-moving markets, the immediate disclosure of the identity of persons who become substantial security holders in public issuers . . ..
What rule should be implied as to the person whose knowledge for this

purpose is to count as the knowledge of the company? Surely the person who, with the authority of the company, acquired the relevant interest. Otherwise the policy of the Act would be defeated. ... The company knows that it has become a substantial security holder when that is known to the person who had authority to do the deal. It is then obliged to give notice'. Lord Hoffmann went onto comment that it was not necessary in that case to inquire whether the chief investment officer could be described as the 'directing mind and will' of the company. At 511H he said "It is a question of construction in each case as to whether the particular rule requires that the knowledge that an act has been done, or the state of mind in which it was done, should be attributed to the company".

Mr Lissack's submission that personal liability on the part of the company is capable of arising in the present case was based on a number of authorities in addition to *Meridian*. In *R v. British Steel Plc* [1995] 1 W.L.R. 1356 the defendant was prosecuted, as was the present defendant, for a breach of sections 3.(1) and 33(1)(a) of the Health and Safety at Work Act 1974. A worker was killed because of the collapse of a steel platform during a re-positioning operation which a competent supervisor would have recognised was inherently dangerous. The defence was that the workmen had disobeyed instructions and, even if the supervisor was at fault, the company at the level of its directing mind had taken reasonable care. An appeal against conviction was dismissed by the Court of Appeal Criminal Division. The judgment was given by Steyn LJ who said this at 1362H

"Counsel for British Steel Plc concedes that it is not easy to fit the idea of corporate criminal liability only for acts of the "directing mind" of the company into the language of s.3(1). We would go further. If it be accepted that Parliament considered it necessary for the protection of public health and safety to impose, subject to the defence of reasonable practicability, absolute criminal ability, it would drive a juggernaut through the legislative scheme if corporate employers could avoid criminal liability where the potentially harmful event is committed by someone who is not the directing mind of the company, ... that would emasculate the legislation".

In a commentary on this decision in [1995] *Criminal Law Review* 655 Professor Sir John Smith said in relation to the "directing mind" argument

"where a statutory duty to do something is imposed upon a particular person (here an employer) and he does not do it, he commits the actus reus of an offence. It may be that he has failed to fulfil his duty because his employee or agent has failed to carry out his duties properly, but this is not a case for vicarious liability. If the employer is held liable, it is because he personally has failed to do what the law requires him to do and he is personally not vicariously liable. There is no need to find someone—in the case of a company the brains and not merely the hands—for whose act the person with the duty be held liable. The duty on the company in this case was to ensure, ie to make certain, that persons are not exposed to risk. They did not make it certain. It does not matter how; they were in breach of their statutory duty and, in the absence of any requirement for mens rea, that is the end of the matter".

Mr Lissack also relied on *In re-supply of Ready Mixed Concrete (No. 2)* where the House of Lords held companies liable for a breach of the restrictive trade practices legislation where their local managers had entered into price fixing and market sharing agreements in defiance of clear instructions from the board of directors and without their knowledge. Lord Templeman said, at 465B, that to permit a company to escape liability by forbidding its employees to do the acts in question would allow it

> "to enjoy the benefit of restriction outlawed by Parliament and the benefit of arrangements prohibited by the courts, provided that the restrictions were accepted and implemented and the arrangements negotiated by one or more employees who had been forbidden to do so by some superior employee, identified in argument as a member of the higher management of the company, or by one or more of the directors of the company identified in argument as the guiding will of the company".

In *R v. Associated Octel* [1996] 1 W.L.R. 1543, in a prosecution under s.3 of the Health and Safety at Work Act 1974 the defendant's conviction was upheld by the House of Lords. Lord Hoffmann, in a speech with which the other members of the House agreed, said, at 1547B, that s.3 imposed a duty towards persons not in employment on the employer himself defined by the conduct of his undertaking. In *R v. Gateway Foodmarkets* [1997] 2 Cr.App.R. 40 the Court of Appeal Criminal Division reached a similar conclusion in relation to s2(1) of the same Act in relation to employees.

Mr Lissack submitted that, in accordance with the speech of Lord Hoffmann in *Meridian*, the choice of the appropriate theory depends on the ingredients of the offence itself; and the requirements of both retribution and deterrence point to corporate liability where death is caused through the company's gross negligence. He relied on a passage in Steyn L.J.'s judgment in the *British Steel* case at 1364A where there is reference to the promotion of "a culture of guarding against the risks to health and safety by virtue of hazardous industrial operations".

Mr Lissack advanced two subsidiary submissions. First, if, contrary to his primary submission, a corporation cannot be convicted unless an employee embodying the company can be identified as guilty of manslaughter, the presence of such an employee can be inferred: he relied on a passage in the speech of Lord Hoffmann in *Meridian* at 510H which seems to us to afford no support whatever for this submission. We reject it. Secondly, he suggested that aggregation has a role to play *i.e.* where a series of venial management failures are aggregated and cumulatively amount to gross negligence, a company may be convicted. There is a tentatively expressed passage in Smith and Hogan 9th Edition at p186, based on an analogy with civil negligence, which supports this suggestion. But there is no supporting and clear contrary judicial authority—see per Bingham L.J. in *R v. HM Coroner ex.p Spooner* 88 Cr.App.R. 10 at 16: "A case against a personal defendant cannot be fortified by evidence against another defendant. The case against a corporation can only be made by evidence properly addressed to showing guilt on the part of the corporation as such". The Law Commission 237 at para. 7.33 are against introducing the concept of aggregation. We reject the suggestion that aggregation has any proper role to play.

For the defendant, Mr Caplan submitted, in relation to question 2, that *Adomako* was not concerned with corporate liability. It is necessarily implicit in the Law Commission's recommendation, in L.C. 237, that Parliament should enact a new offence of corporate killing, that the doctrine of identification still continues to apply to gross negligence manslaughter since *Adomako*. *Tesco v. Nattrass* is still authoritative (see *Seaboard Offshore v.*

Secretary of State for Transport [1994] 1 W.L.R. 541) and it is impossible to find a company guilty unless its alter ego is identified. None of the authorities since *Tesco v. Nattrass* relied on by Mr Lissack supports the demise of the doctrine of identification: all are concerned with statutory construction of different substantive offences and the appropriate rule of attribution was decided having regard to the legislative intent, namely whether Parliament intended companies to be liable. There is a sound reason for a special rule of attribution in relation to statutory offences rather than common law offences, namely there is, subject to a defence of reasonable practicability, an absolute duty imposed by the statutes. The authorities on statutory offences do not bear on the common law principle in relation to manslaughter. Lord Hoffmann's speech in *Meridian* is a re-statement not an abandonment of existing principles: see, for example, Lord Diplock in *Tesco v. Nattrass* at 200H: "There may be criminal statutes which upon their true construction ascribe to a corporation criminal responsibility for the acts of servants and agents who would be excluded by the test that I have stated" (viz those exercising the powers of the company under its articles of association). The Law Commission's proposals were made after *Meridian* and the *British Steel* case. Identification is necessary in relation to the actus reus i.e. whose acts or omissions are to be attributed to the company and *Adomako's* objective test in relation to gross negligence in no way affects this. Furthermore, the civil negligence rule of liability for the acts of servants or agents has no place in the criminal law—which is why the identification principle was developed. That principle is still the rule of attribution in criminal law whether or not mens rea needs to be proved.

Finally Mr Caplan relied on the speech of Lord Lowry in *C. v. DPP* [1996] 1 A.C. 1 and invited this court to reject the prosecution's argument for extending corporate liability for manslaughter. At page 28C Lord Lowry said, with regard to the propriety of judicial law making "(1) If the solution is doubtful, the judges should beware of imposing their own remedy. (2) Caution should prevail if Parliament has rejected opportunities of clearing up a known difficulty or has legislated, while leaving the difficulty untouched. (3) Disputed matters of social policy are less suitable areas for judicial intervention than purely legal problems. (4) Fundamental legal doctrines should not be lightly set aside. (5) Judges should not make a change unless they can achieve finality and certainty". Each of these considerations, submitted Mr Caplan, is pertinent in the present case.

There is, as it seems to us, no sound basis for suggesting that, by their recent decisions, the courts have started a process of moving from identification to personal liability as a basis for corporate liability for manslaughter. In *Adomako* the House of Lords were, as it seems to us, seeking to escape from the unnecessarily complex accretions in relation to recklessness arising from *Lawrence* [1982] A.C. 510 and *Caldwell* [1982] A.C. 341. To do so, they simplified the ingredients of gross negligence manslaughter by re-stating them in line with *Bateman*. But corporate liability was not mentioned anywhere in the submissions of counsel or their Lordship's speeches. In any event, the identification principle is in our judgment just as relevant to the actus reus as to mens rea. In *Tesco v. Nattrass* at 173D Lord Reid said "The judge must direct the jury that if they find certain facts proved then, as a matter of law, they must find that the criminal act of the officer, servant or agent, including his state of mind, intention, knowledge or belief is the act of the Company." In *R v. HM Coroner ex.p Spooner* Bingham L.J. at 16 said "For a company to be criminally liable for manslaughter . . . it is required that the mens rea and the *actus reus* of manslaughter should be established ... against those who were to be identified as the embodiment of the company itself.'' In *R. v. P & O European Ferries* 93 C.A.R. 72 Turner J., in his classic analysis of the relevant principles, said at 83 ''Where a corporation through the controlling mind of one of its agents, does an act which fulfils the pre-requiste of the crime of manslaughter, it is properly indictable for the crime of manslaughter.'' In our judgment, unless an identified individual's conduct, characterisable as gross criminal negligence, can be attributed to the company the company is not, in the present state of the common law, liable for manslaughter. Civil negligence rules eg as enunciated in *Wilsons & Clyde Coal Co v. English* [1938] A.C. 57 are not apt to confer criminal liability on a company.

None of the authorities relied on by Mr Lissack as pointing to personal liability for manslaughter by a company supports that contention. In each, the decision was dependent on the purposive construction that the particular statute imposed, subject to a defence of reasonable practicability, liability on a company for conducting its undertaking in a manner exposing employees or the public to health and safety risk. In each case there was an identified employee whose conduct was held to be that of the company. In each case it was held that the concept of directing mind and will had no application when construing the statute. But it was not suggested or implied that the concept of identification is dead or moribund in relation to common law offences. Indeed, if that were so, it might have been expected that Lord Hoffmann, in *Associated Octel*, would have referred to the ill health of the doctrine in the light of his own speech , less than a year before, in *Meridian*. He made no such reference, nor was *Meridian* cited in *Associated Octel*. It therefore seems safe to conclude that Lord Hoffmann (and, similarly, the members of the Court of Appeal Criminal Division in *British Steel* and in *Gateway Food Market*) did not think that the common law principles as to the need for identification have changed. Indeed, Lord Hoffmann's speech in *Meridian*, in fashioning an additional special rule of attribution geared to the purpose of the statute, proceeded on the basis that the primary ''directing mind and will'' rule still applies although it is not determinative in all cases. In other words, he was not departing from the identification theory but re-affirming its existence.

This approach is entirely consonant with the Law Commission's analysis of the present state of the law and the terms of their proposals for reform in their Report No 237 published in March 1996. In this report, both the House of Lords decision in *Adomako* and the Privy Council's decision in *Meridian* were discussed. In the light of their analysis, the Law Commission concluded (para. 6.27 and following and para. 7.5) that, in the present state of the law, a corporation's liability for manslaughter is based solely on the principle of identification and they drafted a Bill to confer liability based on management failure not involving the principle of identification (see clause 4 of the Draft Bill annexed to their Report). If Mr Lissack's submissions are correct there is no need for such a Bill and, as Scott Baker J put it, the Law Commission have missed the point. We agree with the judge that the Law Commission have not missed the point and Mr Lissack's submissions are not correct: the identification principle remains the only basis in common law for corporate liability for gross negligence manslaughter.

We should add that, if we entertained doubt on the matter, being mindful of the observations of Lord Lowry in *C. v. D.P.P.* at page 28C, we would not think it appropriate for this court to propel the law in the direction which Mr Lissack seeks. That, in our judgment, taking into account the policy considerations to which Mr Lissack referred, is a matter for Parliament, not the courts. For almost 4 years, the Law Commission's draft Bill has been to hand as a useful starting point for that purpose.

It follows that, in our opinion, the answer to question 2 is "No".

Questions

1. Is Rose L.J. correct when he states that Bingham L.J.'s view in *Spooner* is "clear, contrary judicial authority" to the proposition of aggregation in a case of gross negligence manslaughter when the authority governing Bingham L.J. was *Seymour* and the prosecution would have been for reckless manslaughter?

2. Rose L.J. states: "unless an identified individual's conduct, characterisable as gross criminal negligence, can be attributed to the company the company is not, in the present state of the common law, liable for manslaughter. Civil negligence rules . . . are not apt to confer criminal liability on a company." But in *Adomako* Lord Mackay stated that "the ordinary principles of the law of negligence apply to ascertain whether or not the defendant has been in breach of a duty of care towards the victim who has died." Next the jury had to consider causation and then whether the breach was gross enough to constitute a crime. If the operation system was not safe, is Rose L.J. suggesting that this could not amount to civil negligence unless an actual individual was proved to be negligent? If not, why should there be a difference in applying the criminal law to companies as opposed to private individuals? Is there a danger that the more neglectful of safety individuals within a company are (i.e. they do nothing rather than simply doing something incompetently) the less likely the company is to be convicted of manslaughter if death ensues from its operations?

Note

In *Legislating the Criminal Code: Involuntary Manslaughter* (Law Com No. 237) the Law Commission examines the issue of corporate liability for manslaughter. It has not engaged in a full scale review of corporate liability as this was outwith the remit of the project. The Law Commission does not favour the adoption of the aggregation principle stating (at para 7.33):

> "In our view, it would be unsatisfactory to extend the doctrine of identification by introducing a principle of aggregation. In practice, it is often possible to state with confidence what the corporation did or omitted to do without investigating the conduct of individual controlling officers and the information that each of them possessed. The principle of aggregation would not enable this fact to be reflected automatically in a finding that the corporation was therefore liable. It would be no more than a gloss on the identification principle, and would not obviate the need to conduct a detailed investigation into the conduct and state of mind of particular controlling officers; and it might well give rise to difficult (and perhaps insoluble) problems where different controlling officers knew or believed different things."

What it proposes is an adaptation of its proposed offence of killing by gross carelessness to fit the corporate context. The proposed offence focuses on management failure to ensure the health and safety of persons employed in or affected by the corporation's activities rather than on the conduct of individual employees.

Draft Involuntary Homicide Bill

4.—(1) A corporation is guilty of corporate killing if—

(a) a management failure by the corporation is the cause or one of the causes of a person's death; and
(b) that failure constitutes conduct falling far below what can reasonably be expected of the corporation in the circumstances.

(2) For the purposes of subsection (1) above—

(a) there is a management failure by a corporation if the way in which its activities are managed or organised fails to ensure the health and safety of persons employed in or affected by those activities; and
(b) such a failure may be regarded as a cause of a person's death notwithstanding that the immediate cause is the act or omission of an individual.

(3) A corporation guilty of an offence under this section is liable on conviction on indictment to a fine.

(4) No individual shall be convicted of aiding, abetting, counselling or procuring an offence under this section but without prejudice to an individual being guilty of any other offence in respect of the death in question.
. . .
(8) In this section "a corporation" does not include a corporation sole but includes any body corporate wherever incorporated.

Law Commission, *Legislating the Criminal Code: Involuntary Manslaughter*, Law Com No 237

8.2 For the offence of killing by gross carelessness, it must be proved

(1) that the defendant's conduct caused the death,
(2) that the risk of death or serious injury would have been obvious to a reasonable person in her position, and that she was capable of appreciating that risk, and
(3) that her conduct fell far below what could reasonably be expected of her in the circumstances.

FORESEEABILITY OF THE RISK

8.3 In our view, the second of these requirements cannot appropriately be applied to corporations, which . . . are only metaphysical entities. To hypothesise a human being who *could* be in the same position as the corporation is a logical impossibility, and it would therefore be meaningless to enquire, as in the offence of killing by gross carelessness, whether the risk would have been "obvious" to such a person. Moreover, corporations have no "capacity", in the sense in which we use that term in this report in relation to an individual, so that it would be equally impossible to enquire whether the defendant corporation had the capacity to appreciate the risk. It is also, in our view, unnecessary. In judging the conduct of an individual defendant, the law must in fairness take account of such personal characteristics as may make it harder for her to appreciate risks that another person would appreciate; but the same considerations scarcely apply to a *corporate* defendant.

8.4 We have therefore concluded that the foreseeability of the risk, either to a hypothetical person in the defendant's position or to the defendant itself, should not be included in the definition of the corporate offence. This will not prevent juries from finding (in general terms) that the risk was, or should have been, obvious to any individual or group of individuals within the company who were or should have been responsible for taking safety measures, in deciding whether the company's conduct fell below the required standard. Nor would we wish to discourage the jury from approaching its task in that way. We are simply concerned, in formulating the new offence, to remove the *legal* requirement under the present law to identify individuals within the company whose conduct is to be attributed to the company itself.

SERIOUSNESS OF THE DEFENDANT'S CONDUCT

8.5 On the other hand we see no reason why the third requirement for the individual offence, that the defendant's conduct must have fallen *far* below what could reasonably be expected of her in the circumstances, should not apply equally to the corporate offence. This approach . . . is based on our view that the offence ought to be one of last resort, available only when all the other sanctions that already exist seem inappropriate or inadequate, and that, therefore, the negligence in question must have been very serious.

8.6 We have therefore concluded . . . that the new corporate offence should be committed only where the defendant's conduct fell far below what could reasonably be expected of it "in the circumstances". In our view, it would be neither practicable nor desirable to specify in legislation what those "circumstances" should or should not include: in every case it would be for the jury to decide whether the corporation's conduct fell within that description. In many cases this would involve the jury in balancing such matters as the likelihood and possible extent of the harm arising from the way in which the company conducted its operations against the social utility of its activities and the cost and practicability of taking steps to eliminate or reduce the risk of death or serious personal injury.

8.7 The jury might also think it right to take account of the extent (if any) to which the defendant corporation's conduct diverged from practices generally regarded as acceptable within the trade or industry in question. This could not be conclusive, since the fact that a given practice is common does not *in itself* mean that the observance of that practice cannot fall far below what can reasonably be expected; but it might well be highly relevant. The weight to be attached to it, if any, would be a matter for the jury.

CONDUCT OF THE DEFENDANT THAT CAUSES DEATH

8.8 Of the three requirements for the individual offence of killing by gross carelessness, therefore, we envisage that the second . . . should be discarded for the purposes of the corporate offence, whereas the third . . . should be retained. It remains to be determined what should be done about the first, namely that the defendant's conduct should have caused the death. Obviously that requirement must be retained in some form; equally obviously . . . it must be adapted for the purposes of the corporate defendant. There are two aspects to this requirement: first, the defendant must have acted, or omitted to act, in a particular way; and second, the death must have resulted from that act or omission. In the case of an individual defendant it is rarely necessary to distinguish these two aspects: once the facts are known, there is no difficulty in distinguishing the defendant's conduct from someone else's. In the case of a *corporate* defendant, however, this distinction is problematic. Since we have rejected the option of attributing to the corporation *everything* done (or not done) by its agents, we must find a way of identifying that conduct which *can* properly be attributed to it. The question is: in what circumstances can it properly be said, not merely that the conduct of a corporation's *agents* has caused a death, but that the conduct of *the corporation itself* has done so?

Conduct of the defendant

8.9 In answering this question we have not had to start with an entirely clean slate. In the first place we have borne in mind the analogy of the identification principle laid down in *Tesco Supermarkets v Nattrass*, which distinguishes between those agents of a company that qualify as its "controlling minds" and those that do not. As we have explained in Part VII above, we do not think that this principle is in itself sufficient for the imposition of corporate liability in every case of homicide where such liability would be justified; but the main reason for this is that the principle requires the prosecution to identify one or more "controlling minds" who are themselves guilty of a homicide offence. The distinction drawn in the *Tesco* case between things done in the management and organisation of the company on the one hand, and things done at a purely operational level on the other, seems to us to encapsulate the nature of the distinction that we need to draw. The difference between our approach and the identification principle is that we think the distinction should be drawn in terms of the *kind of conduct* that can incur liability, rather than the *status* of the person or persons responsible for it.

8.10 Secondly, we have drawn on the law governing an employer's common law obligation to take care for the safety of employees, and one aspect of that obligation in particular—namely, the employer's duty to provide a safe system of work. This obligation is personal to the employer and is quite distinct from any *vicarious* liability that may arise in respect of injury caused to an employee by a fellow employee in the course of their employment. A breach of this obligation is not just negligence for which the employer is (vicariously) responsible: it is the employer's *own* negligence. The distinction thus corresponds to the distinction that we seek to draw, in the case of a corporate employer, between the conduct of the corporation and the conduct of its employees alone; and it is because of this analogy that we have taken this obligation as a starting-point in defining the kind of conduct that we propose as an element of the new corporate offence. In effect, we propose to use it as a model for the duty of *every* corporation to *all* those (not just employees) who may be affected by the corporation's activities. . . .

8.20 Under our proposals, individuals within the company could be concurrently liable, in respect of an incident for which the company was liable, for the offence of killing by gross carelessness; and, whether or not they were so liable, their conduct might be relevant to the corporate offence as part of the circumstances surrounding that offence. For the purpose of the corporate offence and by contrast with the present law, however, there would be no need to identify the controlling officers of the company. The question would be whether there had been a management failure, rather than, as at present, whether there was blameworthy conduct on the part of any individual or group of individuals which should be attributed to the company.

8.21 To take a simple hypothetical example, if a lorry driver employed by a company causes death by dangerous driving in the course of the company's business, this act would not *of itself* involve a management failure so as to incur corporate liability; nor would the company be *vicariously* liable for the driver's negligence. The company might be liable, however, if the incident occurred because the driver was overtired at the material time in consequence of a requirement to work excessively long hours, or because she consistently worked very long hours in her desire to earn overtime, and the company had no adequate system of monitoring to ensure that this did not happen.

Note

In May 2000 the Home Office published a Consultation Paper, *Reforming the Law on Involuntary Manslaughter: The Government's Proposals* based on the Law Commission Report No. 237 (see pp. 598–603, *post*). The Government accepts the Law Commission's proposal for a new offence of corporate killing subject to its proposed extension of the offence to cover all "undertakings" *i.e.* "any trade or business or other activity providing employment. This would bring within the ambit of the offence "schools, hospital trusts, partnerships and unincorporated charities, as well as one or two person businesses e.g. self-employed gas-fitters. In effect the offence of corporate killing could apply to all employing organisations" (para. 3.2.5).

CHAPTER 7

INCHOATE OFFENCES

Ashworth, *Principles of Criminal Law*, 2nd ed., p. 442

THE CONCEPT OF AN INCHOATE OFFENCE

The word 'inchoate', not much used in ordinary discourse, means 'just begun', 'undeveloped'. The common law has given birth to three general offences which are usually termed 'inchoate' or 'preliminary' crimes—attempt, conspiracy, and incitement. A principal feature of these crimes is that they are committed even though the substantive offence (i.e. the offence it was intended to bring about) is not completed and no harm results. An attempt fails, a conspiracy comes to nothing, words of incitement are ignored—in all these instances, there may be liability for the inchoate crime.

Note

Attempt is now defined and punished in the Criminal Attempts Act 1981, and conspiracy in Part I of the Criminal Law Act 1977, as amended by the Criminal Attempts Act 1981. Incitement remains a common law offence.

1. ATTEMPTS

Criminal Attempts Act 1981, Sections 1, 4(5), 6(1)

Section 1: (1) If, with intent to commit an offence to which this section applies, a person does an act which is more than merely preparatory to the commission of the offence, he is guilty of attempting to commit the offence.

(2) A person may be guilty of attempting to commit an offence to which this section applies even though the facts are such that the commission of the offence is impossible.

(3) In any case where—

(a) apart from this subsection a person's intention would not be regarded as having amounted to an intent to commit an offence; but
(b) if the facts of the case had been as he believed them to be, his intention would be so regarded,

then, for the purposes of subsection (1) above, he shall be regarded as having had an intent to commit that offence.

(4) This section applies to any offence which, if it were completed, would be triable in England and Wales as an indictable offence, other than—

(*a*) conspiracy (at common law or under section 1 of the Criminal Law Act 1977 or any other enactment);

(*b*) aiding, abetting, counselling, procuring or suborning the commission of an offence;

(*c*) offences under section 4(1) (assisting offenders) or 5 (1) (accepting or agreeing to accept consideration for not disclosing information about an arrestable offence) of the Criminal Law Act 1967.

Section 4: (3) Where, in proceedings against a person for an offence under section 1 above, there is evidence sufficient in law to support a finding that he did an act falling within subsection (1) of that section, the question whether or not his act fell within that subsection is a question of fact.

Section 6: (1) The offence of attempt at common law and any offence at common law of procuring materials for crime are hereby abolished for all purposes not relating to acts done before the commencement of this Act.

Notes

1. Section 1 applies to indictable offences only. An attempt to commit a summary offence is only an offence if the statute creating the offence specifically makes it so. In deciding whether such an attempt has been committed, a court will work to the same definition as for an attempt to commit an indictable offence: see section 3(4), (5).

2. In the common law of attempt existing before August 1981, there was much uncertainty surrounding the definition of the *actus reus*, especially in cases where the crime attempted was, for one reason or another, impossible to commit. Some uncertainty also attached to the *mens rea*. The difficulties are outlined in Law Com. No. 102: Attempt, and Impossibility in Relation to Attempt, Conspiracy and Incitement 1980. The Law Commission's proposals for dealing with those difficulties were reproduced, although not exactly, in the Act. The common law of Attempt was abolished: Section 6(1), *supra*. However this did not at first prevent the Courts from referring to many of the pre-Act authorities. For proposals in the Draft Criminal Code, see *infra*, p. 470.

Ashworth, *Principles of Criminal Law*, 3rd ed., pp. 461–463

'The rationale for criminalizing attempts can best be appreciated by drawing a theoretical distinction (which the law itself does not draw) between two kinds of attempt. First, there are incomplete attempts, which are cases in which the defendant has set out to commit an offence but has not yet done all the acts necessary to bring it about. [For] example, ... X put[s] petrol-soaked paper through the door of V's house ...: he has still to strike a match and light the paper. Contrast this with the second kind of attempt, which will be called a complete attempt. Here the defendant has done all that he intended, but the desired result has not followed—Y has driven [a] car at V, intending to injure V, but he failed; and Z has smuggled [a] package into the country, believing it to be cannabis when in fact it is a harmless and worthless substance.

It is easier to justify the criminalization of complete attempts than incomplete attempts, and the two sets of justifications have somewhat different emphases. The justification for punishing complete attempts is that the defendant has done all the acts intended, with the beliefs required for the offence, and is therefore no less blameworthy than a person who is successful in committing the substantive offence. The complete 'attempter' is thwarted by some unexpected turn of events which, to him, is a matter of pure chance—the intended victim jumped out of the way, or the substance was not what it appeared to be. These are applications of . . . 'subjective' principles . . ., the essence of which is that people's criminal liability should be assessed on what they were trying to do, intended to do, and believed they were doing rather than on the actual consequences of their conduct. Rejection of this approach would lead to criminal liability always being judged according to the actual outcome, which would allow luck to play too great a part in the criminal law. Of course luck and chance play a considerable role in human affairs. . . .

However, there is no reason why a human system for judging and formally censuring the behaviour of others should be a slave to the vagaries of chance. The 'subjective principle' would also be accepted by the consequentialist as a justification for criminalizing complete attempts: the defendant was trying to break the law, and therefore constitutes a source of social danger no less (or little less) than that presented by 'successful' harm-doers.

What about incomplete attempts? The subjective principle does have some application here, inasmuch as the defendant has given some evidence of a determination to commit the substantive offence—though the evidence is likely to be less conclusive than in cases of complete attempts. There is one distinct factor present in incomplete attempts, which is the social importance of authorizing official intervention before harm is done. Since the prevention of harm has a central place in the justifications for criminal law, there is a strong case for stopping attempts before they result in the causing of harm. . . .

Once this point has been reached, then the agents of law enforcement may intervene to stop attempts before they go further. The culpability of the incomplete attempter may be less than that of the complete attempter because there remains the possibility that there would have been voluntary repentance at some late stage: after all, it may take greater nerve to do the final act which triggers the actual harm than to do the preliminary acts. But so long as it is accepted that the incomplete attempter has evinced a settled intention to continue, and to commit the substantive offence by doing some further acts, there is sufficient ground for criminalization.

Note

In the Law Commission's view, punishable preparatory acts should be limited to those which a layman would describe as trying to commit an offence (paragraph 2.8). This philosophy, embodied in the use of the ordinary word "attempt" as the name for the offence, confines the ambit of the law more narrowly than some might think desirable from the point of view of public protection. See, as to the *mens rea*, pp. 447 *et seq.*, and as to *actus reus*, Williams, *infra*, p. 468.

i. Mental Element

R. v. Mohan
[1976] Q.B. 1
Court of Appeal

M drove his car straight at a policeman, who managed to jump out of the way. M was convicted of attempting by wanton driving to cause bodily harm to the policeman. The jury were directed that it was sufficient for the prosecution to prove that he was reckless as to whether bodily harm would be caused by his driving. M appealed.

JAMES L.J., for the Court: Mr Bueno's argument for the Crown was that the judge was right in his direction that the Crown did not have to prove, in relation to count 2, any intention in the mind of the defendant. His argument was that where the attempt charged is an attempt to commit a crime which itself involves a specific state of mind, then to prove the attempt the Crown must prove that the accused had that specific state of mind, but where the attempt relates to a crime which does not involve a specific state of mind, the offence of attempt is proved by evidence that the accused committed an act or acts proximate to the commission of the complete offence and which unequivocally point to the completed offence being the result of the act or acts committed. Thus to prove a charge of attempting to cause grievous bodily harm with intent there must be proof that the accused intended to cause grievous bodily harm at the time of the act relied on as the attempt. But, because the offence of causing bodily harm by wanton or furious driving, prescribed by section 35 of the Offences against the Person Act 1861, does not require proof of any intention or other state of mind of the accused, proof of attempt to commit that crime does not involve proof of the accused's state of mind, but only that he drove wantonly and that the wanton driving was proximate to, and pointed unequivocally to, bodily harm being caused thereby.

The attraction of this argument is that it presents a situation in relation to attempts to commit a crime which is simple and logical, for it requires in proof of the attempt no greater burden in respect of mens rea than is required in proof of the completed offence. The argument in its extreme form is that an attempt to commit a crime of strict liability is itself a strict liability offence. It is argued that the contrary view involves the proposition that the offence of attempt includes mens rea when the offence which is attempted does not and in that respect the attempt takes on a graver aspect than, and requires an additional burden of proof beyond that which relates to, the completed offence.

Mr Glass, for the defendant, does not shrink from this anomalous situation. His argument was expressed in words which he cited from *Smith and Hogan, Criminal Law*, 3rd ed. (1973), p. 191.

"Whenever the definition of the crime requires that some consequence be brought about by (the defendant's) conduct, it must be proved, on a charge of attempting to commit that crime, that (the defendant) intended that consequence; and this is so even if, on a charge of committing the complete crime, recklessness as to that consequence—or even some lesser degree of mens rea—would suffice."

That, Mr Glass argued, is an accurate statement of the law.

In support of his argument he cited the words of Lord Goddard C.J. in *R. v. Whybrow* (1951) 35 Cr.App.R. 141, 146:

"Therefore, if one person attacks another, inflicting a wound in such a

way that an ordinary, reasonable person must know that at least grievous bodily harm will result, and death results, there is the malice aforethought sufficient to support the charge of murder. But, if the charge is
one of attempted murder, the intent becomes the principal ingredient
of the crime. It may be said that the law, which is not always logical, is
somewhat illogical in saying that, if one attacks a person intending to
do grievous bodily harm and death results, that is murder, but that if
one attacks a person and only intended to do grievous bodily harm,
and death does not result, it is not attempted murder, but wounding
with intent to do grievous bodily harm. It is not really illogical because,
in that particular case, the intent is the essence of the crime while, where
the death of another is caused, the necessity is to prove malice aforethought, which is supplied in law by proving intent to do grievous
bodily harm."

[After citations from *R. v. Hyam* [1975] A.C. 55, *ante*, p. 93.]

We do not find in the speeches of their Lordships in *R. v. Hyam* anything which binds us to hold that mens rea in the offence to attempt is
proved by establishing beyond reasonable doubt that the accused knew
or correctly foresaw that the consequences of his act unless interrupted
would "as a high degree of probability", or would be "likely" to, be the
commission of the complete offence. Nor do we find authority in that case
for the proposition that a reckless state of mind is sufficient to constitute
the mens rea in the offence of attempt.

Prior to the enactment of section 8 of the Criminal Justice Act 1967, the
standard test in English law of a man's state of mind in the commission
of an act was the forseeable or natural consequence of the act. Therefore
it could be said that when a person applied his mind to the consequences
that did happen and foresaw that they would probably happen he intended them to happen, whether he wanted them to happen or not. So knowledge of the foreseeable consequence could be said to be a form of
"intent". Section 8 reads:

"A court or jury, in determining whether a person has committed an
offence, (*a*) shall not be bound in law to infer that he intended or foresaw a result of his actions by reason only of its being a natural and
probable consequence of those actions; but (*b*) shall decide whether he
did intend or foresee that result by reference to all the evidence, drawing such inferences from the evidence as appear proper in the circumstances."

Thus, upon the question whether or not the accused had the necessary
intent in relation to a charge of attempt, evidence tending to establish
directly, or by inference, that the accused knew or foresaw that the likely
consequence, and, even more so, the highly probable consequence, of his
act—unless interrupted—would be the commission of the completed
offence, is relevant material for the consideration of the jury. In our judgment, evidence of knowledge of likely consequences, or from which
knowledge of likely consequences can be inferred, is evidence by which
intent may be established but it is not, in relation to the offence of attempt,
to be equated with intent. If the jury find such knowledge established they
may and, using common sense, they probably will find intent proved, but
it is not the case that they must do so.

An attempt to commit a crime is itself an offence. Often it is a grave
offence. Often it is as morally culpable as the completed offence which is
attempted but not in fact committed. Nevertheless it falls within the class
of conduct which is preparatory to the commission of a crime and is one

step removed from the offence which is attempted. The court must not strain to bring within the offence of attempt conduct which does not fall within the well-established bounds of the offence. On the contrary, the court must safeguard against extension of those bounds save by the authority of Parliament. The bounds are presently set requiring proof of specific intent, a decision to bring about, in so far as it lies within the accused's power, the commission of the offence which it is alleged the accused attempted to commit, no matter whether the accused desired that consequence of his act or not.

In the present case the final direction was bad in law.

Appeal allowed

Notes

1. *Narrow meaning of Intention*: In rejecting foresight of probable consequences as "intention" in respect of Attempts, the Court distinguished *Hyam v. D.P.P.*, a murder case which laid down that such foresight generally is intention. But see now *R. v. Woollin, ante*, p. 103, which differs from *Hyam v. D.P.P.* on this.

2. *Intention as to Context*: According to James L.J., attempt requires specific intent, "a decision to bring about, in so far as it lies in the accused's power, the commission of the offence which it is alleged the accused attempted to commit". The Law Commission, adopting this dictum, paraphrased it as "an intent to commit the crime attempted", and accordingly section 1, Criminal Attempts Act 1981 uses that expression. However, the phrase is ambiguous, because if an offence requires intention for the *result* of D.'s conduct but is satisfied by recklessness as to the context in which the conduct takes place (*e.g.* rape, obtaining by deception), it can be questioned whether D. "intends to commit the offence", if he is intentional as to the result but only reckless as to context. But see next case.

R v. Khan and Others
[1990] 2 All E.R. 783
Court of Appeal

Six men were charged with rape and attempted rape of a 16-year-old girl. It appeared that some of them had not succeeded in having intercourse with her. The appellants were convicted of attempted rape. On appeal:-

RUSSELL L.J., for the Court: These appeals raise the short but important point of whether the offence of attempted rape is committed when the defendant is reckless as to the woman's consent to sexual intercourse. The appellants submit that no such offence is known to the law . . .

The judge dealt with [the question of consent in] the offence of rape as follows:

"It must first be proved in this case that [the complainant] did not in fact consent. If she did or if in your view she may have done in relation to any of the defendants, you may acquit them without considering the position further. If, however, you decide that she did not in fact consent, the next question is: did the defendant in question know that she was not consenting? If you are unsure about that, go on to ask whether he was reckless as to whether the girl was consenting or not, and reckless in this context could be simply defined . . . as the state of mind of the particular defendant that he could not care less either way whether she consented or not. If you are sure that was his state of mind, then he was behaving recklessly and he would be guilty of the offence . . ."

No complaint is made about this direction. The judge then turned to the charges of attempted rape and said:

". . . As in the case of rape, the principles relevant to consent apply in exactly the same way as in attempted rape. I do not suppose you need me to go through it again. Apply the same principles as to rape."

It is the last three sentences that counsel for the appellants submit amount to a material misdirection, for it is argued that recklessness as a state of mind on the part of the offender has no place in the offence of attempted rape.

We remind ourselves first of the statutory definition of rape to be found in s. 1 (1) of the Sexual Offences (Amendment) Act 1976:

"For the purposes of section 1 of the Sexual Offences Act 1956 (which relates to rape) a man commits rape if—(*a*) he has unlawful sexual intercourse with a woman who at the time of the intercourse does not consent to it; and (*b*) at that time he knows that she does not consent to the intercourse or he is reckless as to whether she consents to it . . ."

Section 1 (1) of the Criminal Attempts Act 1981 created a new statutory offence as follows:

"If, with intent to commit an offence to which this section applied, a person does an act which is more than preparatory to the commission of the offence, he is guilty of attempting to commit the offence."

This section applies to rape.

The impact of the words of s. 1 of the 1981 Act and in particular the words "with intent to commit an offence" has been the subject matter of much debate amongst distinguished academic writers. We were referred to and we have read and considered an article by Professor Glanville Williams entitled "The Problem of Reckless Attempts" [1983] Crim.L.R. 365. The argument there advanced is that recklessness can exist within the concept of attempt and support is derived from *R. v. Pigg* [1982] 2 All E.R. 591, [1982] 1 W.L.R. 762, albeit that authority was concerned with the law prior to the 1981 Act. The approach also receives approval from Smith and Hogan, *Criminal Law* (6th ed., 1988) pp. 287–289.

Contrary views, however, have been expressed by Professor Griew and Mr Richard Buxton QC, who have both contended that the words "with intent to commit an offence" involve an intent as to every element constituting the crime.

Finally, we have had regard to the observations of Mustill LJ giving the judgment of the Court of Appeal, Criminal Division in *R. v. Millard and Vernon* [1987] Crim.L.R. 393. That was a case involving a charge of attempting to damage property. . . .

Mustill L.J. said (and we read from the transcript):

". . . We have come to the conclusion that there does exist a problem in this field [of attempts], and that it is by no means easy to solve, but also that it need not be solved for the purpose of deciding the present appeal. In our judgment two different situations must be distinguished. The first exists where the substantive offence consists simply of the act which constitutes the actus reus (which for present purposes we shall call the "result") coupled with some element of volition, which may or may not amount to a full intent. Here the only question is whether the "intent" to bring about the result called for by s. 1(1) [of The Criminal Attempts Act 1981] is to be watered down to such a degree, if any, as to make it correspond with the mens rea of the substantive offence. The second situation is more complicated. It exists where the substantive offence does not consist of one result and one mens rea, but rather involves not only the underlying intention to produce the result, but another state of mind directed to some circumstance or act which the prosecution must also establish in addition to proving the result. The problem may be illustrated by reference to the offence of attempted rape. As regards the substantive offence the "result" takes the shape of sexual intercourse with a woman. But the offence is not established without proof of an additional circumstance (namely that the woman did not consent), and a state of mind relative to that circumstance (namely that the defendant knew she did not consent, or was reckless as to whether she consented). When one turns to the offence of attempted rape, one thing is obvious, that the result, namely the act of sexual intercourse, must be intended in the full sense. Also obvious is the fact that proof of something about the woman's consent, and something about the defendant's state of mind in relation to that consent. The problem is to decide precisely what that something is. Must the prosecution prove not only that the defendant intended the act, but also that he intended it to be non-consensual? Or should the jury be directed to consider two different states of mind, intent as to the act and recklessness as to the circumstances? Here the commentators differ: contrast Smith and Hogan *Criminal Law* (5th ed., 1983) p. 255 ff. with a note on the Act by Professor Griew in *Current Law Statutes 1981.*"

We must now grapple with the very problem that Mustill L.J. identifies in the last paragraph of the passage cited.

In our judgment an acceptable analysis of the offence of rape is as follows: (1) the intention of the offender is to have sexual intercourse with a woman: (2) the offence is committed if, but only if, the circumstances are that (a) the woman does not consent *and* (b) the defendant knows that she is not consenting or is reckless as to whether she consents.

Precisely the same analysis can be made of the offence of attempted rape: (1) the intention of the offender is to have sexual intercourse with a woman: (2) the offence is committed if, but only if, the circumstances are that (a) the woman does not consent *and* (b) the defendant knows that she is not consenting or is reckless as to whether she consents.

The only difference between the two offences is that in rape sexual intercourse takes place whereas in attempted rape it does not, although there has to be some act which is more than preparatory to sexual intercourse. Considered in that way, the intent of the defendant is precisely the same in rape and in attempted rape and the mens rea is identical, namely an intention to have intercourse plus a knowledge of or recklessness as to the woman's absence of consent. No question of attempting to achieve a reckless state of mind arises; the attempt relates to the physical activity; the mental state of the defendant is the same. A man does not recklessly have sexual intercourse, nor does he recklessly attempt it. Recklessness in rape and attempted rape arises not in relation to the physical act of the accused but only in his state of mind when engaged in the activity of having or attempting to have sexual intercourse.

If this is the true analysis, as we believe it is, the attempt does not require any different intention on the part of the accused from that for the full offence of rape. We believe this to be a desirable result which in the instant case did not require the jury to be burdened with different directions as to the accused's state of mind, dependent on whether the individual achieved or failed to achieve sexual intercourse.

We recognise, of course, that our reasoning cannot apply to all offences and all attempts. Where, for example as in causing death by reckless driving or reckless arson, no state of mind other than recklessness is involved in the offence, there can be no attempt to commit it.

In our judgment, however, the words "with intent to commit an offence" to be found in s.1 of the 1981 Act mean, when applied to rape, "with intent to have sexual intercourse with a woman in circumstances where she does not consent and the defendant knows or could not care less about her absence of consent". The only "intent", giving that word its natural and ordinary meaning, of the rapist is to have sexual intercourse. He commits the offence because of the circumstances in which he manifests that intent, *i.e.* when the woman is not consenting and he either knows it or could not care less about the absence of consent.

Accordingly, we take the view that in relation to the four appellants the judge was right to give the directions that he did when inviting the jury to consider the charges of attempted rape.

Appeals against conviction dismissed

Note

In the case which follows the Court of Appeal, while affirming *Khan*, went further in stretching the realm of liability for attempt by accepting that a person may be convicted of attempt where *Caldwell* recklessness as to a consequence suffices for the full offence.

Attorney-General's Reference (No. 3 of 1992)
[1994] 1 W.L.R. 409
Court of Appeal

The respondents were in a moving car from which a lighted petrol bomb was thrown at an occupied car beside a pavement on which persons were standing. The bomb passed over the car and hit a wall adjacent to the pavement. They were charged with attempted aggravated arson, contrary to section 1 of the Criminal Damage Act 1971. The trial judge ruled that there was no evidence on which the jury could find an intent to endanger life and that on a true construction of the Act, the danger to the life of another was a consequence of the intended damage and as such required a specific intent in relation to that element recklessness being insufficient. Accordingly she directed that the respondents be acquitted. The Attorney-General referred the following point of law for the opinion of the Court of Appeal: "Whether on a charge of attempted arson in the aggravated form contemplated by section 1(2) of the Criminal damage Act 1971, in addition to establishing a specific intent to cause damage by fire, it is sufficient to prove that the defendant was reckless as to whether life would thereby be endangered"

SCHIEMANN J.:

There are three further preliminary matters which need to be mentioned in this context as background, although none is contentious. First, it is common ground that the recklessness here referred to is what has become known as *Caldwell* recklessness: see *Reg. v. Caldwell* (*ante*, p. 121).

Lord Diplock went on to say at p. 354G: "Where the charge is under section

1(2) the question of the state of mind of the accused must be approached in stages, corresponding to paragraphs (*a*) and (*b*)."

The second preliminary matter is this. It is clear that the prosecution are required to prove that the danger to life resulted from the destruction of or damage to property; it is not sufficient for the prosecution to prove that it resulted from the act of the defendant which caused the destruction or damage: *Reg. v. Steer* (*post*, p. 914).

The third preliminary matter is that, although in the present reference the question is posed in relation to arson, it has not been submitted that the presence or absence of fire makes any difference to the answer to the question posed which applies to any form of attempted criminal damage. So we omit any further reference to the element of fire in this judgment.

With those three preliminary matters out of the way, we turn to consider what again is uncontentious, namely, what the prosecution need to prove in each case in order to secure a conviction for the completed offence of arson and aggravated arson.

So far as the completed simple offence is concerned, the prosecution needs to prove (1) property belonging to another was damaged by the defendant; (2) the state of mind of the defendant was one of the following, (a) he intended to damage such property, or (b) he was reckless as to whether any such property would be damaged.

In the case of the completed aggravated offence the prosecution needs to prove (1) the defendant in fact damaged property, whether belonging to himself or another; (2) that the state of mind of the defendant was one of the following, (a) he intended to damage property, and intended by the damage to endanger the life of another, or (b) he intended to damage property and was reckless as to whether the life of another would be thereby endangered, or (c) he was reckless as to whether any property would be damaged and was reckless as to whether the life of another would be thereby endangered.

It is to be noted that the property referred to under (1)—to which we shall hereafter refer as "the first named property" is not necessarily the same property as that referred to in (2)—to which we shall refer as "the second named property" although it normally will be. . . .

The problem which has given rise to this reference . . . amounts to this: whether, if the state of mind of the defendant was that postulated in (2) (b) above, namely, that he intended to damage property and was reckless as to whether the life of another would thereby be endangered, and whilst in that state of mind he did an act which was more than merely preparatory to the offence, he is guilty of attempting to commit that offence. . . .

So far as attempting to commit the simple offence is concerned, in order to convict on such a charge it must be proved that the defendant—(a) did an act which was more than merely preparatory to the commission of the offence—and (b) did an act intending to damage any property belonging to another.

One way of analysing the situation is to say that a defendant, in order to be guilty of an attempt, must be in one of the states of mind required for the commission of the full offence, and did his best, as far as he could, to supply what was missing from the completion of the offence. It is the policy of the law that such people should be punished notwithstanding that in fact the intentions of such a defendant have not been fulfilled.

If the facts are that, although the defendant had one of the appropriate states of mind required for the complete offence, but the physical element required for the commission of the complete offence is missing, the defendant is not to be convicted unless it can be shown that he intended to supply the physical element. This was the state of affairs in *Reg. v. Millard and Vernon* [1987] Crim.L.R. 393, of which we have seen the transcript. There the defendants were convicted of attempting to damage property. The particulars of the offence were that they "attempted to damage a wooden wall at the . . . stadium . . . intending to damage the . . . wall or being reckless as to whether the . . . wall was damaged." The trial judge directed the jury that recklessness was sufficient. Mustill L.J., delivering the judgment of the Court of Appeal, stated:

"The result which would have been achieved if the offence had been taken to fruition was damage to the stand . . . the prosecution had to show . . . that it was this state of affairs which each appellant had decided, so far as in him lay, to bring about."

In consequence, mere recklessness was not sufficient and the convictions were quashed.

We turn finally to the attempt to commit the aggravated offence. In the present case, what was missing to prevent a conviction for the completed offence was damage to the property referred to in the opening lines of section 1 (2) of the Act of 1981, what in the example of a crane, which we gave earlier in this judgment, we referred to as "the first named property." Such damage is essential for the completed offence. If a defendant does not intend to cause such damage he cannot intend to commit the completed offence. At worst he is reckless as to whether the offence is committed. The law of attempt is concerned with those who are intending to commit crimes. If that intent cannot be shown, then there can be no conviction.

However, the crime here consisted of doing certain acts in a certain state of mind in circumstances where the first named property and the second named property were the same, in short where the danger to life arose from the damage to the property which the defendant intended to damage. The substantive crime is committed if the defendant damaged property in a state of mind where he was reckless as to whether the life of another would thereby be endangered. We see no reason why there should not be a conviction for attempt if the prosecution can show that he, in that state of mind, intended to damage the property by throwing a bomb at it. One analysis of this situation is to say that although the defendant was in an appropriate state of mind to render him guilty of the completed offence the prosecution had not proved the physical element of the completed offence, and therefore he is not guilty of the completed offence. If, on a charge of attempting to commit the offence, the prosecution can show not only the state of mind required for the completed offence but also that the defendant intended to supply the missing physical element of the completed offence, that suffices for a conviction. That cannot be done merely by the prosecution showing him to be reckless. The defendant must intend to damage property, but there is no need for a graver mental state than is required for the full offence.

The trial judge in the present case, however, went further than this, and held that not merely must the defendant intend to supply all that was missing from the completed offence—namely, damage to the first named property—but also that recklessness as to the consequences of such damage for the lives of others was not enough to secure a conviction for attempt, although it was sufficient for the completed offence. She held that before a defendant could be convicted of attempting to commit the offence it had to be shown that he intended that the lives of others should be endangered by the damage which he intended.

She gave no policy reasons for so holding, and there is no case which bound her so to hold. The most nearly relevant case is *Reg. v. Khan (ante,* p. 449). . .

An attempt was made in argument to suggest that *Reg. v. Khan (Mohammed Iqbal)* was wrongly decided. No policy reasons were advanced for that view, and we do not share it. The result is one which accords with common sense, and does no violence to the words of the statute.

What was missing in *Reg. v. Khan (Mohammed Iqbal)* was the act of sexual intercourse, without which the offence was not complete. What was missing in the present case was damage to the first named property, without which the offence was not complete. The mental state of the defendant in each case contained everything which was required to render him guilty of the full offence. In order to succeed in a prosecution for attempt, it must be shown that the defendant intended to achieve that which was missing from the full offence. Unless that is shown, the prosecution have not proved that the defendant intended to commit the offence. Thus in *Reg. v. Khan (Mohammed Iqbal)* [1990] 1 W.L.R. 813 the prosecution had to show an intention to have sexual intercourse, and the remaining state of mind required for the offence of rape. In the present case, the prosecution had to show an intention to damage the first named property, and the remaining state of mind required for the offence of aggravated arson. . . .

While the judge in the instant case opined that *Reg. v. Khan (Mohammed Iqbal)* was distinguishable she did not indicate any policy reasons for distinguishing it. We see none, and none has been submitted to us directly.

We now remind ourselves of the precise question posed by the reference:

"Whether on a charge of attempted arson in the aggravated form contemplated by section 1(2) of the Criminal Damage Act 1971, in addition to establishing a specific intent to cause damage by fire, it is sufficient to prove that the defendant was reckless as to whether life would thereby be endangered."

We answer it in the affirmative.

We add that, in circumstances where the first named property is not the same as the second named property, in addition to establishing a specific intent to cause damage by fire to the first named property, it is sufficient to prove that the defendant was reckless as to whether the life of another would be endangered by the damage to the second named property.

Question referred answered in affirmative.

Questions

1. In s. 1(1) of the Criminal Attempts Act 1981 a person is stated to be guilty of attempt where he does a more than merely preparatory act "with intent to commit an offence". Is this the same as an intent "to supply the missing physical element of the completed offence"?

2. Is failure to give thought to an obvious risk rightly described as "the state of mind required by the completed offence"?

3. Professor Ashworth, *Principles of Criminal Law*, 3rd ed., p. 465, speculates that the courts might not stop in their extension of the reach of the criminal law until they create a general law of reckless attempts. He asks:

"Until now English law has resolved the question pragmatically, by creating a few specific offences of endangerment to deal with reckless behaviour on the roads and in other situations where there is a risk but no actual occurrence of serious consequences [*e.g.* causing an explosion likely to endanger life, contrary to Explosives Act 1883, s. 2, possession

of explosives with intent to endanger life, contrary to s. 3, possession of
a firearm with intent to endanger life, contrary to the Firearms Act 1968,
s. 16]. . . . Since we are concerned here with preliminary offences which
go beyond the definitions of substantive crimes, is it not more judicious
to proceed in this piecemeal way, thereby ensuring that the outer
boundaries of the criminal law are carefully regulated?"

Smith, Commentary [1994] Crim. L.R. 350–351

. . . The statement of principle adopted by the court may, however, be
thought to go much too far—and farther, perhaps, than the court
appreciated. . . .

So, D, a man aged 25, attempts to have sexual intercourse with a girl,
V, whom he believes on reasonable grounds to be aged 16 but who is in
fact only 15. D is guilty of an attempt to have sexual intercourse with a
girl under the age of 16, contrary to section 6 of the Sexual Offences Act
1956. He has the state of mind required for the commission of the full
offence—an intention to have sexual intercourse with a girl who is in fact
(whether he knows, or ought to know it, or not) under the age of 16. He
has done his best "to supply what was missing from the completion of
the offence" (a very odd way of putting it!), namely, to have sexual intercourse. And so strict liability is introduced into the law of attempts. And
this *is* the "policy of the law". Really?

There is a logical argument in favour of such an extension of inchoate
liability which the writer propounded in (1957) 70 *Harvard Law Review* 422
at 433 and re-examined in [1962] Crim.L.R. 135 but it never found much
favour—indeed, it was described by a distinguished American lawyer as
"fantastic" and "astounding". With characteristic humility I abandoned
that argument in favour of the less far-reaching theory advocated by
others that, while intention must be proved as to any result which is an
element of the *actus reus*, recklessness (but nothing less) as to any circumstances in the definition of the offence will suffice where such recklessness
is a sufficient fault for the complete offence. It is this theory which is
embodied in the draft Criminal Code and was adopted in relation to rape
in *Khan*.

Well then, it may be said, even if the broad statement of principle in
the present case goes too far, at least the decision is right because the
defendant intended the result and was reckless as to the rest. But not
quite. There is recklessness and "*Caldwell* recklessness". Recklessness as
to circumstances has been thought to be an acceptable *mens rea* for this
inchoate offence because it is a true state of mind, an actual awareness of
the risk of endangering life or whatever the relevant element of the
offence is. That is the sense in which "reckless" is used in the draft Code.
But a person is "*Caldwell* reckless" whether life be endangered even if the
possibility of danger to life never enters his head, where he has in fact
created an obvious risk of danger to life. In fact, he is being held liable
for his negligence in failing to be aware of the obvious risk and to behave
accordingly. If we hold the defendant liable in attempt for his negligence
as to an element of the offence, it is only another short step to imposing
strict liability with respect to circumstances. Another possibility would be
to hold that, in criminal damage and other offences which are satisfied by
Caldwell recklessness, on a charge of attempt, only the first Diplock variety
("he has recognised that there was some risk involved") would suffice;
but that would add an undesirable complexity to an already complex area
of the law.

As is mentioned, there is a case in favour of extending liability in attempt to commit crimes of negligence or strict liability with respect to circumstances; but one suspects that the issue was not fully appreciated or debated on the reference.

Question

Suppose it is an offence to use or attempt to use a motor vehicle which does not comply with the regulations as to, *inter alia*, effective brakes. The offence is strict as to non-compliance with the regulation, *i.e.* no mental state of any kind is required as to that circumstance. A was stopped as he was about to drive off in a borrowed car which had defective brakes, although he did not know and had no means of knowing that fact. Can A be convicted of attempting to use a motor vehicle which does not comply with the regulations?

ii. Actus Reus

Note

There may be many stages between the formulation of an intention to commit a crime and the actual commission of it. At some stage after formulation of intention and before actual commission, the point will be reached at which the actor can be said to have attempted it and so be guilty of the crime of attempt. The common law never succeeded in what is probably an impossible task, namely, formulating a general test which would, on being applied to any set of facts, infallibly indicate whether the crucial point had been reached. About the only two propositions which could be taken as settled were (1) that not all things done on the way to commission of an intended crime were attempts at it (some early steps were regarded as too remote), and (2) that if the accused had done the last act which he knew was needed for full commission, it was an attempt by him.

Various tests were suggested in the cases or in writings, such as the first step on the road to full commission, the final step before full commission (sometimes qualified by the view that even a final step was not enough if the accused could still withdraw from full commission); the doing of an act which unequivocally showed what crime was intended; the taking of a substantial step towards commission of the offence. (For a review of these theories, see Law Com. 102 §§ 2.22–2.37.) None of them yielded satisfactory results across the whole band of possible cases. The only general test consistently quoted in the authorities was that formulated in *R. v. Eagleton* (1855) 6 Cox C.C. 559, 571 by Parke B.: "The mere intention to commit a misdemeanour is not criminal. Some act is required and we do not think that all acts towards committing a misdemeanour are indictable. Acts remotely leading towards the commission of the offence are not to be considered as attempts to commit it, but acts immediately connected with it are . . ." This was usually called the proximity test. Proximity was accepted by the House of Lords in *D.P.P. v. Stonehouse* (1978) A.C. 55 as the true test, although there was little agreement on how to define the concept more exactly, and of course without more exact definition the test is so vague as to be of but limited use.

Ashworth, *Principles of Criminal Law*, 3rd ed., p. 466

Since the effect of the law of attempts is to extend the criminal sanction further back than the definition of substantive offences, the question of the minimum conduct necessary to constitute an attempt has great importance. The issue concerns incomplete attempts: when has a person gone far enough to justify criminal liability? Two schools of thought may be outlined here. First, there is the fault-centred approach, arguing that the essence of an attempt is trying to commit a crime, and that all the law should require is proof of the intention plus any act designed to implement that intention. The reasoning is that any person who has gone so far as to translate a criminal intention into action has crossed the threshold of criminal liability, and deserves punishment. . . .

On the other hand there are two types of act-centred approach. One type bases itself on the argument that one cannot be sure that the deterrent effect of the criminal law has failed until D has done all the acts necessary, since one could regard the law as successful if D did stop before the last act out of fear of detection and punishment. The other type of act-centred approach is adopted by those who see great dangers of oppressive official action—to the detriment of individual liberties—if the ambit of the law of attempts is not restricted tightly. If *any* overt act were to suffice as the conduct element in attempts, wrongful arrests might be more numerous; convictions would turn largely on evidence of D's intention, so the police might be tempted to exert pressure in order to obtain a confession; and miscarriages of justice might increase, especially when inferences from silence are permissible. . . . To safeguard the liberty of citizens and to assure people that justice is being fairly administered, the law should require proof of an unambiguous act close to the commission of the crime before conviction of an attempt. Otherwise, we would be risking a world of thought crimes and thought police.

The choices for the conduct element in attempts might therefore be ranged along a continuum. The least requirement would be 'any overt act', but that would be objectionable as risking oppressive police practices and as leaving little opportunity for an attempter to withdraw voluntarily. The most demanding requirement would be the 'last act' or 'final stage', but that goes too far in the other direction, leaving little time for the police to intervene to prevent the occurrence of harm and allowing the defence to gain an acquittal by raising a doubt as to whether D had actually done the very last act.

Law Com. No. 102

(Footnotes as in the original)

3. Recommendations as to the actus reus

§ 2.45 In the light of the case law, the opinions of writers and the various approaches to the *actus reus* already described, we must make it clear that in our view there is no magic formula which can now be produced to define precisely what constitutes an attempt. . . . Of the various approaches, only the 'proximity' test has produced results which may be thought broadly acceptable. Its disadvantages are that hitherto it has not worked well in some cases, and that it is imprecise. It shares the latter disadvantage with all other approaches but its flexibility does enable difficult cases to be reconsidered and their authority questioned. Further, where cases are so dependent on what are sometimes fine differences of degree, we think it is eminently appropriate for the question whether the conduct in a particular case amounts to an attempt to be left to the jury. This suggests that a relatively similar definition based on the 'proximity' approach is the best which can be hoped for.

(a) *Content of the Actus Reus*

§ 2.46 The first element in a statutory test of proximity should be the drawing of the distinction between acts of preparation and acts which are sufficiently proximate to the offence. This is a truism repeated in many cases including the most recent. It is nonetheless useful because it recognises that certain forms of conduct, in almost all circumstances which can be envisaged, do not amount to an attempt. Possession of implements for the purpose of committing an offence is an obvious example which, as we have noted, is at present dealt with by other means. Reconnoitring the place contemplated for the commission of the intended offence is another example of conduct which it is difficult to regard as more than an act of preparation: it would not ordinarily be called an attempt.

§ 2.47 The definition of sufficient proximity must be wide enough to cover two varieties of cases; first, those in which a person has taken all the steps towards the commission of a crime which he believes to be necessary as far as he is concerned for that crime to result,[27] such as firing a gun at another and missing. Normally such cases cause no difficulty. Secondly, however, the definition must cover those instances where a person has to take some further step to complete the crime, assuming that there is evidence of the necessary mental element on his part to commit it; for example, when the defendant has raised the gun to take aim at another but has not yet squeezed the trigger. We have reached the conclusion that, in regard to these cases, it is undesirable to recommend anything more complex than a rationalisation of the present law.

§ 2.48 In choosing the words to be used to describe this rationalisation of the present law, we have had to bear in mind that they will be the subject of consideration and interpretation by the courts. For this reason we have rejected a number of terms which have already been used with some frequency in reported cases, such as acts which are 'proximate to', or 'closely connected' or 'immediately connected' with the offence attempted. The literal meaning of 'proximate' is 'nearest, next before or after (in place, order, time, connection of thought, causation, etc.).' Thus, were this term part of a statutory description of the *actus reus* of attempt, it would clearly be capable of being interpreted to exclude all but the 'final act'; this would not be in accordance with the policy outlined above. The term 'immediately connected' is in our view inappropriate for the same reason. And acts which may be 'closely connected' in the sense that they have advanced a considerable way towards the completed offence may nonetheless bear no qualitative resemblance to the acts required for completion. For example, it is arguable that what the appellant in *R. v. Robinson* (*post*, p. 462) had done had no close qualitative connection with that remainder to be done—making a claim on the insurance company—

---

[27] This is on the assumption that he is the actual perpetrator; if his part in the commission is a minor one, none of his acts may get beyond the state of preparation: see *D.P.P. v. Stonehouse* [1978] A.C. 55, 86, *per* Lord Edmund-Davies.

even though in terms of quantity his conduct as a whole had advanced far towards his objective. This potential ambiguity therefore precludes use of that term.

§ 2.49 The foregoing considerations lead us to *recommend* as the most appropriate form of words to define the *actus reus* of attempt *any act which goes so far towards the commission of the offence attempted as to be more than an act of mere preparation.*

(b) *Issues of Law and Fact*

§ 2.50 The final element of the offence of attempt which requires consideration in the present context is the respective functions of the judge and jury. We have noted that the 'substantial step' approach would require the judge to direct the jury as a matter of law as to whether particular conduct, if proved, constitutes a substantial step. (§ 2.30) . . . Since then, the majority in *D.P.P. v. Stonehouse* has, as we have noted, approved the decision in *R. v. Cook* in which Lord Parker C.J. stated that, 'while in every case it is for the judge to rule whether there is any evidence capable of constituting an attempt, it is always for the jury to say whether they accept it as amounting to an attempt. That involves . . . a careful direction in every case on the general principle with regard to what acts constitute attempts': (1963) 48 Cr.App.R. 98, 102. We agree with this view: as factual situations may be infinitely varied and the issue of whether an accused's conduct has passed beyond mere preparation to commit an offence may depend upon all the surrounding circumstances, it is appropriate to leave the final issue to be decided as a question of fact, although 'the judge may sum up in such a way as to make it plain that he considers that the accused is guilty and should be convicted.' *D.P.P. v. Stonehouse* [1978] A.C. 55, 80, *per* Lord Salmon. Furthermore, this division of function between judge and jury is in accord with the principle that it is for the judge to tell the jury what the law is, but for the jury to say whether on the facts the accused has been brought within the provisions of the offence with which he has been charged. If the conduct is such that in law it cannot constitute more than an act of preparation the judge must direct the jury to acquit. . . .

Dennis, "The Elements of Attempt" [1980] Crim.L.R. 758, 768

These proposals give rise to a number of misgivings.

1. *Imprecision.* Even given the premise that precise definition is impossible, the Law Commission's test is more open-textured than any of the common law tests which it replaces. The form of words chosen does very little more than indicate that some acts do constitute attempts ('more than preparatory') and some acts do not ('preparatory'). The descriptive words '[an act] which goes so far towards the commission of the offence' do not constitute a qualitative distinction between these two categories: they merely indicate that a scale of conduct is in contemplation, and that at some point along it a line is drawn to fix the threshold of liability.

What the Law Commission have done then is to take a principle—that in order to preserve a balance between the interests of the individual and those of society not all acts towards the commission of an offence should be punishable—and erect it into a rule to be applied by the tribunal to resolve individual cases, but without giving it any further content. How is this principle/rule to be applied?

One radical answer would have been to take the current fashion to extremes, and to turn the whole issue over to the jury, asking them to construe the word 'preparatory' as an ordinary word of the English language. All they would then need to do would be to decide whether the defendant's acts went beyond their understanding of that term. It appears, however, that the Law Commission do not wish to go as far as this. The judge is to retain control in the first instance of the limits of preparation. 'If the conduct is such that *in law it cannot constitute more than an act of preparation* the judge must direct the jury to acquit.' (Emphasis supplied). To this extent then the application of the test is a matter of law, but no guidance is given in the draft Bill on how this question of law should be determined. We may assume that a judge will decide, for example, that evidence of 'reconnoitring the place intended for the commission of the offence' is evidence of an act of preparation only, but on what basis is he to reach the conclusion? Certainly he will be in some difficulty if he turns to the pre-existing common law because the Law Commission have cogently criticised all the common law theories and endeavoured to replace them with the codified offence.

2. *Role of the Jury*. Pursuing this theme, how are the jury to apply the test if the evidence passes the judge? (We may assume that [section 4(3)] does have the effect of requiring the issue of whether D's conduct fell within [section 1(1)] to be left to the jury, although it does not actually say so). They are still being given a very large issue to decide, and it is submitted that the 'question of fact' represents a considerable extension of that term. It normally refers to the finding of primary facts (did D practise a deception?), evaluation of primary facts against a fixed standard (was the force used by D reasonable?), and, more controversially, the determination of statutory words where they are used as ordinary words of the English language (was D dishonest?). In this case the jury are *not* being asked to decide the meaning of the word attempt, or any other word, as a matter of ordinary language. Rather they are being asked expressly to determine whether D's act fell within a subsection of a criminal statute. Putting the matter in these terms connotes a question of interpretation and classification, and it is submitted that it is simply leaving too much to the jury to ask them to perform the task with such an imprecise criterion.

The practical risks involved are those of perverse verdicts and inconsistent verdicts. Perverse verdicts of acquittal may occur where the law is, or should be, clear that a sufficient act of attempt has taken place, as where D has committed the last act he intended to commit. The Law Commission anticipate this objection and argue that the risk can be obviated by clarity in identifying the contested issue and by commenting on the evidence, if necessary in strong terms. Fair enough, but there is still no guidance on how the contested issue could be clarified in a direction, and what benefit is gained by leaving the question open if the answer is clear?

Inconsistent verdicts are a much more serious danger. The Law Commission commented at the beginning of this section of the Report that 'in the absence of any definition of the conduct required for an attempt, there would be little assistance which a judge could give in directing the jury, and this could lead to unacceptable discrepancies and very marked inconsistencies in jury verdicts in similar cases. (§ 2.19) It has been argued that the test in [section] 1(1) does not take the definition of attempt very much further. In the absence of any statutory guidance on how the test is to be interpreted, there is a real risk that different juries may adopt different criteria to deal with essentially similar material facts. Suppose that the facts of *Robinson (infra)* and of *Comer v. Bloomfield (infra)* recur. The judge leaves the issue to the jury in both cases, realising that the Law Commission wished the boundaries of 'preparation' to be altered so that the conduct in these cases was at least capable of amounting to an attempt. Jury

A convict on the facts of *Robinson*, arguing that this was an elaborate deception showing firmness of purpose, and that it was not necessary that the deception should have come to the notice of the intended victim of the fraud. Jury B acquit on the facts of *Comer v. Bloomfield* arguing that the accused had not actually made a claim for the loss of his vehicle and that his enquiry about it was not an act showing clear unlawful purpose. If this example is not far fetched, the result brings the law into disrepute, since the accused in case B had clearly gone further than the accused in case A.

Notes

R. v. Robinson and Comer v. Bloomfield were criticised by the Law Commission as cases where the result, to the man in the street, appears to be contrary to common sense (§ 2.39). Nevertheless, in this scene-setting type of case, the dangers of inconsistent verdicts may have receded, in that the Court of Appeal seems to take the view, contrary to that of the Law Commission, that such cases are not capable of being attempts in law.

R. v. Robinson [1915] 2 K.B. 342. D, a jeweller, insured his stock against theft and contrived to be found tied up, with his safe empty. He told the policeman who found him that he had been the victim of a burglary. Later he confessed that his object was to make a false claim on his insurers. He did not submit any claim. *Held* (C.A.) no attempt at obtaining money by false pretences, the acts done being too remote.

Comer v. Bloomfield (1970) 55 Cr.App.R. 305. D drove his vehicle into the depths of a wood and reported it stolen. He enquired of insurers whether a claim would lie for its loss, but did not make a claim. *Held* (Div. Ct.), no attempt to obtain money by deception. See also *R. v. Ilyas* (1983) 78 Cr.App.R. 17, which was decided after the Criminal Attempts Act had been passed but on facts which required to be judged at common law. The facts were on all fours with those in *Comer v. Bloomfield* and the result was the same.

R. v. Widdowson (1985) 82 Cr.App.R. 314. D, wishing to obtain a van on hire-purchase terms but knowing that he would not be accepted as credit-worthy, filled in a credit enquiries form in the name of another person. *Held* (C.A.) not an attempt to obtain services (the hire-purchase of a van) by deception.

"Assuming that the finance company had responded favourably to proposal, it still remained for the appellant to seek a hire purchase deal from them. To our minds it is that step which would constitute an attempt to obtain the services relied upon in this case. If one asks whether this appellant had carried out every step which it was necessary for him to perform to achieve the consequences alleged to have been attempted, the answer must be that he did not.

Equally, it seems to us, this appellant's acts cannot be described as immediately rather than merely remotely connected with the specific offence alleged to have been attempted. Thus whichever of the tests described in *Ilyas* is applied, what the appellant did cannot reasonably be described as more than merely preparatory."

R. v. Gullefer
(1986) [1990] 3 All E.R. 882
Court of Appeal

The appellant was convicted of attempted theft. During a race at a grey-hound racing stadium the appellant had climbed on to the track in front of the dogs and in an attempt to distract them had waved his arms. His efforts were only marginally successful and the stewards decided it was unnecessary to declare "no race". Had they done so the bookmakers would have had to repay the amount of his stake to any punter, but would not have been liable to pay any winnings to those punters who would have been successful had the race been valid. The appellant told the police he had attempted to stop the race because the dog on which he had staked £18 was losing. He had hoped for a "no race" declaration and the recovery of his stake. The appellant's main ground of appeal was that the acts proved to have been carried out by the appellant were not "sufficiently proximate to the completed offence of theft to be capable of comprising an attempt to commit theft".

LORD LANE C.J. for the Court: [His Lordship referred to ss. 1 (1) and 4 (3) of the 1981 Act:]

Thus the judge's task is to decide whether there is evidence on which a jury could reasonably come to the conclusion that the defendant had gone beyond the realm of mere preparation and had embarked on the actual commission of the offence. If not, he must withdraw the case from the jury. If there is such evidence, it is then for the jury to decide whether the defendant did in fact go beyond mere preparation. That is the way in which the judge approached this case. He ruled that there was sufficient evidence. Counsel for the appellant submits that he was wrong in so ruling.

The first task of the court is to apply the words of the 1981 Act to the facts of the case. Was the appellant still in the stage of preparation to commit the substantive offence, or was there a basis of fact which would entitle the jury to say that he had embarked on the theft itself? Might it properly be said that when he jumped on to the track he was trying to steal £18 from the bookmaker?

Our view is that it could not properly be said that at that stage he was in the process of committing theft. What he was doing was jumping onto the track in an effort to distract the dogs, which in its turn, he hoped, would have the effect of forcing the stewards to declare "no race", which would in its turn give him the opportunity to go back to the bookmaker and demand the £18 he had staked. In our view there was insufficient evidence for it to be said that he had, when he jumped onto the track, gone beyond mere preparation.

So far at least as the present case is concerned, we do not think that it is necessary to examine the authorities which preceded the 1981 Act, save to say that the sections we have already quoted in this judgment seem to be a blend of various decisions, some of which were not easy to reconcile with others.

However, in deference to the arguments of counsel, we venture to make the following observations. Since the passing of the 1981 Act, a division of this court in *R. v. Ilyas* (1983) 78 Cr.App.R. 17 has helpfully collated the authorities. As appears from the judgment in that case, there seem to have been two lines of authority. The first was exemplified by the decision in *R. v. Eagleton* (1855) Dears CC 515. That was a case where the defendant was alleged to have attempted to obtain money from the guardians of a parish by falsely pretending to the relieving officer that he had delivered loaves of bread of the proper weight to the outdoor poor when in fact the loaves were deficient in weight.

Parke B, delivering the judgment of the court of nine judges, said (Dears CC 515 at 538):

"Acts remotely leading towards the commission of the offence are not to be considered as attempts to commit it, but acts immediately connected with it are; and if, in this case, after the credit with the relieving officer for the fraudulent overcharge, any *further step* on the part of the defendant had been necessary to obtain payment, as the making out a further account or producing the vouchers to the Board, we should have thought that the obtaining credit in account with the relieving officer would not have been sufficiently proximate to the obtaining the money. But, on the statement in this case, no other act on the part of the defendant would have been required. It was the last act, *depending on himself*, towards the payment of the money, and therefore it ought to be considered as an attempt." (Parke B's emphasis.)

Lord Diplock in *D.P.P. v. Stonehouse* [1978] A.C. 55 at 68, having cited part of that passage from *R. v. Eagleton* added: "In other words the offender must have crossed the Rubicon and burnt his boats."

The other line of authority is based on a passage in *Stephen's Digest of the Criminal Law* (5th edn, 1894) art 50:

"An attempt to commit a crime is an act done with intent to commit that crime, and forming part of a series of acts which would constitute its actual commission if it were not interrupted."

As Lord Edmund-Davies points out in *D.P.P. v. Stonehouse* at 85–86, that definition has been repeatedly cited with judicial approval: see Byrne J in *Hope v. Brown* [1954] 1 W.L.R. 250 at 253 and Lord Parker CJ in *Davey v. Lee* [1968] 1 Q.B. 366 at 370. However, as Lord Parker CJ in the latter case points out, *Stephen's* definition falls short of defining the exact point of time at which the series of acts can be said to begin.

It seems to us that the words of the 1981 Act seek to steer a midway course. They do not provide, as they might have done, that the *R. v. Eagleton* test is to be followed, or that, as Lord Diplock suggested, the defendant must have reached a point from which it was impossible for him to retreat before the actus reus of an attempt is proved. On the other hand the words give perhaps as clear a guidance as is possible in the circumstances on the point of time at which *Stephen's* "series of acts" begins. It begins when the merely preparatory acts come to an end and the defendant embarks on the crime proper. When that is will depend of course on the facts in any particular case. . . .

Appeal allowed: Conviction quashed

R. v. Jones
[1990] 3 All E.R. 886
Court of Appeal

Jones was convicted of attempted murder in the circumstances outlined in the judgment. He appealed on the ground that the correct test of an attempt was whether the defendant had committed the last act prior to the full offence being committed.

TAYLOR L.J. for the Court: The appellant, a married man, started an affair with a woman named Lynn Gresley in 1985. She lived with him in Australia during 1986. In September 1987, back in England, she began a relationship with the victim, Michael Foreman. She continued, however to see the appellant, to whom she was still very attached. In November 1987 she decided to break off the relationship with the appellant, but he continued to write to her, begging her to come back to him.

On 12 January 1988 the appellant applied for a shotgun certificate, and three days later bought two guns in company with two companions. He bought two more guns a few days later on his own. On 23 January he shortened the barrel of one of them and test fired it twice the following day.

The appellant told a colleague at work that he would be away on Tuesday, 26 January. On 24 January he phoned Lynn Gresley in a distraught state. The next day he apologised, but she again refused his invitation to resume their relationship. The appellant then told his wife that he had packed a bag as he was going to Spain to do some work on their chalet. On 26 January he left home dressed normally for work, saying that he would telephone his wife whether he was leaving for Spain that evening.

That same morning, the victim, Michael Foreman, took his daughter to school by car as usual. After the child left the car, the appellant appeared, opened the door and jumped into the rear seat. He was wearing overalls, a crash helmet with the visor down, and was carrying a bag. He and the victim had never previously met. He introduced himself, said he wanted to sort things out and asked the victim to drive on. When they stopped on a grass verge, the appellant handed over a letter he had received from Lynn. Whilst the victim read it, the appellant took the sawn-off shotgun from the bag. It was loaded. He pointed it at the victim at a range of some ten to twelve inches. He said. "You are not going to like this" or similar words. The victim grabbed the end of the gun and pushed it sideways and upwards. There was a struggle during which the victim managed to throw the gun out of the window. As he tried to get out, he felt a cord over his head pulling him back. He managed to break free and run away, taking the gun with him. From a nearby garage he telephoned the police.

Meanwhile, the appellant drove off in the victim's car. He was arrested jogging away from it carrying his holdall. He said that he had done nothing and only wanted to kill himself. His bag contained a hatchet, some cartridges and a length of cord. He also had a sharp kitchen knife which he threw away. In the appellant's car parked near the school was £1,500 together with a quantity of French and Spanish money. The evidence showed that the safety catch of the shotgun had been in the on position. The victim was unclear whether the appellant's finger was ever on the trigger. When interviewed, the appellant declined to make any comment.

At the end of the prosecution case, after the above facts had been given in evidence, a submission was made to the judge that the charge of attempted murder should be withdrawn from the jury. It was argued that since the appellant would have had to perform at least three more acts before the full offence could have been completed, *i.e.* remove the safety catch, put his finger on the trigger and pull it, the evidence was insufficient to support the charge. The[re] was a discussion as to the proper construction of s.1(1) of the Criminal Attempts Act 1981. After hearing full argument, the judge ruled against the submission and allowed the case to proceed on count 1. Thereafter, the appellant gave evidence. In the result, the jury convicted him unanimously of attempted murder. It follows that they found that he intended to kill the victim.

The sole ground of appeal is that the judge erred in law in his construction of s.1(1) and ought to have withdrawn the case. . . .

Counsel for the appellant puts forward three broad propositions. First, he says that for about a century, two different tests as to the actus reus of attempt have been inconsistently applied by the courts. . . .

[After quoting from Parke B.'s judgment in *R. v. Eagleton* (1855) Dears C.C. 515]: Accordingly, the test deriving from *R. v. Eagleton* was said to be the "last act" test. It was adopted in a number of cases, *e.g. R. v. Robinson* [1915] 2 K.B. 342. In *D.P.P. v. Stonehouse* [1978] A.C. 55 at 68 Lord Diplock referred to *R. v. Eagleton* as the locus classicus, adopted some of the words of Parke B and summarised them in the graphic phrase: "In other words the offender must have crossed the Rubicon and burnt his boats."

The other test referred to by counsel for the appellant derives from *Stephen's Digest of the Criminal Law* (5th edn. 1894) art. 50, where it was stated thus:

"An attempt to commit a crime is an act done with intent to commit that crime, and forming part of a series of acts which would constitute its actual commission if it were not interrupted."

Lord Edmund-Davies noted in *D.P.P. v. Stonehouse* that *Stephen's* definition has been repeatedly cited with approval. He referred to its adoption in *Hope v. Brown* [1954] 1 All E.R. 330 at 332, and *Davey v. Lee* [1968] 1 Q.B. 366. It was also applied in *R. v. Linneker* [1906] 22 K.B. 99, where *R. v. Eagleton* was not cited.

In some cases, including three since the 1981 Act, both tests have been considered, and the court has found it unnecessary to decide between them, holding that the result in those cases would have been the same, whichever applied (see *R. v. Ilyas* (1983) 78 Cr.App.R. 17, *R. v. Widdowson* (1986) 82 Cr.App.R. 314 and *R. v. Boyle* (1986) 84 Cr.App.R. 270).

The second proposition of counsel for the appellant is that s 1(1) of the 1981 Act has not resolved the question which is the appropriate test. Third, he submits that the test deriving from *R. v. Eagleton* should be adopted.

This amounts to an invitation to construe the statutory words by reference to previous conflicting case law. We believe this to be misconceived. The 1981 Act is a codifying statute. It amends and sets out completely the law relating to attempts and conspiracies. In those circumstances the correct approach is to look first at the natural meaning of the statutory words, not to turn back to earlier case law and seek to fit some previous test to the words of the section . . .

This approach was adopted by Lord Lane C.J. presiding over this court in *R. v. Gullefer* . . .

[After quoting the last paragraph reproduced, *ante*, p. 464 of Lord Lane's judgment]. We respectfully adopt those words. We do not accept counsel's contention that s. 1(1) of the 1981 Act in effect embodies the "last act" test derived from *R. v. Eagleton*. Had Parliament intended to adopt that test, a quite different form of words could and would have been used.

It is of interest to note that the 1981 Act followed a report from the Law Commission on *Attempt, and Impossibility in Relation to Attempt, Conspiracy and Incitement* (Law. Com. no. 102). [His lordship quoted paras. 2.47, 2.48, *ante* p. 438].

Clearly, the draftsman of s. 1(1) must be taken to have been aware of the two lines of earlier authority and of the Law Commission's report. The words "an act which is more than merely preparatory to the commission of the offence" would be inapt if they were intended to mean "the last act which lay in his power towards the commission of the offence."

Looking at the plain natural meaning of s. 1(1) in the way indicated by Lord Lane C.J., the question for the judge in the present case was whether there was evidence from which a reasonable jury, properly directed, could conclude that the appellant had done acts which were more than merely preparatory. Clearly his actions in obtaining the gun, in shortening it, in loading it, in putting on his disguise and in going to the school could only be regarded as preparatory acts. But, in our judgment, once he had got into the car, taken out the loaded gun and pointed it at the victim with the intention of killing him, there was sufficient evidence for the consideration of the jury on the charge of attempted murder. It was a matter for them to decide whether they were sure that those acts were more than merely preparatory. In our judgment, therefore, the judge was right to allow the case to go to the jury, and the appeal against conviction must be dismissed.

Appeal against conviction dismissed

K.J.M. Smith, "Proximity in Attempt: Lord Lane's Midway Course" [1991] Crim. L.R. 576, 577.

. . . Lord Lane C.J. saw pre-Act case law as amply illustrating the 'difficulties which abound in this branch of the criminal law,' but that the 'present law is . . . now enshrined in the Criminal Attempts Act . . .' Are we then to take it that references to pre-Act decisions should never cross the lips of counsel in future attempt cases? Well not quite, for a few paragraphs later Lord Lane qualifies his earlier comment by noting: 'So far as the *present* case is concerned, we do not think it is necessary to examine the authorities which preceded the Act of 1981'; the implication being that in some (unspecified) situations admission of common law authorities would be permissible for some (unspecified) purposes. There is little doubt that the subsequent Court of Appeal judgment in *Jones* construed *Gullefer's* relegation of pre-Act cases in this modified sense: 'the correct approach is to look *first* at the natural meaning of the statutory words.' . . .

It, therefore, seems that pre-Act authorities may still be enlisted in *some* circumstances to assist a court in settling what acts may be 'more than merely preparatory.' However, no direct clues are offered by the Court of Appeal in *Gullefer* or *Jones* as to when such earlier case law may be prayed in aid, and to what effect. Yet, if anything is of 'doubtful import', surely the unforthcoming formula set out in the 1981 Act takes a lot of beating: doubt on the proximity question lurks in relation to almost any activity falling short of the unsuccessful defendant's 'last act'."

R. v. Campbell [1991] Crim. L.R. 268 (C.A.) : C appealed against a conviction of attempted robbery. Police had information leading them to believe that an attempt might be made to rob a sub-post office, and watched the premises. On the day in question, C was seen lurking in the vicinity. He rode a motor cycle along the road and walked around. He wore a crash helmet and gloves. He was seen to put on sunglasses and then put his right hand into a pocket which seemed to contain something heavy. He stopped about 30 yards from the post office and took off his sunglasses. He looked around before turning away. Half an hour later he walked back towards the post office. He was arrested in front of the post office. He was searched and an imitation gun, sunglasses and a threatening note were found on him. He admitted that he had been reconnoitring the post office and had intended using the note to frighten the person behind the counter. The trial judge rejected a submission of no case to answer. *Held*, quashing his conviction, the judge should not have made any reference to the previous law; moreover, since several acts remained to be done by C and he had not even gained the place where he would be in a position to carry out the offence, the judge should have withdrawn the case from the jury.

R. v. Geddes, The Times, July 16, 1996 (C.A.) : D. entered a school and, on being found in the boys' toilet by a teacher, he ran away, leaving behind a rucksack containing a knife, lengths of rope and tape. He appealed against his conviction for attempted false imprisonment arguing that the evidence was insufficient in law to support a finding that he had done an act which was more than merely preparatory to the commission of an offence. *Held*: An accurate paraphrase of the statutory test was to ask whether the available evidence, if accepted, could show that a defendant had done an act which showed that he was actually trying to commit the act in question or whether he had only got ready or put himself in a position or equipped himself to do so. Had he moved from the role of intention, preparation and planning into the area of execution or implementation? The court answered in the negative, allowing the appeal and quashing the conviction.

R. v. Tosti [1997] Crim. L.R. 746 (C.A.): D. and E. appealed against convictions of attempted burglary. They had concealed oxyacetylene equipment in a hedge, approached the door of a barn they were intending to burgle and examined the padlock on the door before being arrested. *Held*, upholding the convictions, that the question is one of degree: how close to, and necessary for, the commission of the offence were the acts which the accused did? The acts were not merely preparatory but were essentially first steps in the commission of the offence.

Note

The line to be drawn between preparation and commission appears to be an exceedingly fine one. In *Tosti* examining the padlock appears to have amounted to a crossing of that line even though no attempt was made to break the lock and the oxyacetylene equipment was still hidden in the hedge. It is difficult to see how this differs from *Campbell* but if the line is correctly drawn in *Tosti*, it would appear to have been incorrectly drawn in *Geddes*.

Williams: "Wrong Turnings in the Law of Attempt" [1991] Crim.L.R. 417, 419.

The root problem with the law is that it looks at the facts retrospectively: backwards from the moment when the crime was intended to be committed, instead of forwards from the time when the defendant started to make his criminal intention a reality. . . .

To effect a real reform of this part of the law we need to get away from retrospective reasoning and substitute prospective reasoning. In other words, we need express legislation adopting a 'substantial step' definition of an attempt. Such a reform was embodied in the Model Penal Code of the American Law Institute, which has been widely accepted in legislation in the United States. Section 5.01, after stating the 'substantial step' test in subsection (1), works it out in businesslike detail in subsection (2) (here slightly shortened).

'(1) Conduct shall not be held to constitute a substantial step . . . unless it is strongly corroborative of the actor's criminal purpose . . .'

Pausing there, this obviously means that the conduct must be strongly corroborative not merely of the defendant's criminal inclinations but of his formed purpose to commit this particular crime. Remote preparations, such as enquiries to establish the possibility of committing a particular crime, should be ruled out under this test.

'(2) The following, if strongly corroborative of the actor's criminal purpose, shall not be held insufficient as a matter of law: (*a*) lying in wait, searching for or following the contemplated victim of the crime; (*b*) enticing or seeking to entice the contemplated victim of the crime to go to the place contemplated for its commission; (*c*) reconnoitering the place contemplated for the commission of the crime; (*d*) unlawful entry of a structure, vehicle or enclosure in which it is contemplated that the crime will be committed; (*e*) possession of materials to be employed in the commission of the crime, which are specially designed for such unlawful use or which can serve no lawful purpose of the actor under the circumstances; (*g*) soliciting an innocent agent to engage in conduct constituting an element of the crime.'

This list beautifully clarifies nearly all the matters that have been litigated in England, most of which we have either failed to settle or settled in an impolitic way. (I would add to it: '(*h*) deceiving any person for the purpose of committing the crime,' and (*i*) 'preparing a deception for the purpose of any crime involving deception or fraud' (both of which Robinson did).

The Working Party ... recommended the adoption of a 'substantial step' test in the future code, but the commission rejected it. . . . The following were the reasons that guided the commission, as they eventually surfaced in Law Com. No. 102, together with the answers I would like to make.

(1) It was feared that the substantial step text would widen the law of attempt too much (para. 2.32). Certainly it would widen the law, but no example is given of how it would widen it too much. Perhaps the commission had in mind the serious doubts that were felt about the old 'sus' legislation (now repealed), but the following points may be made. (*a*) The 'sus' legislation enabled evidence to be given of the defendant's previous convictions; this is not proposed for charges of attempt. (*b*) The provision in the Model Penal Code requires proof of an act that is 'strongly corroborative of the actor's criminal purpose.' This should be enough to keep the law of attempt within bounds. (It may be noticed that the requirement is missing from the Draft Code's provision on articles acquired for the purpose of criminal damage, with which the commission appears to be content). (*c*) If desired, the items about reconnoitring and unlawful entry could be omitted from the list of examples in the M.P.C. provision, though I think this would be a mistake. (*d*) All the acts listed in the M.P.C. provision would be overt acts from which a conspiracy could be deduced if they were committed by two people together; why should the fact of numbers make any difference to criminal liability? (The commission proposed no reduction in the scope of conspiracy.)

(2) The commission acknowledged that at one time the proximity rule appeared to be working unsatisfactorily, and it mentioned *Robinson* as such an unsatisfactory case, where 'the result reached would, to the man in the street, appear to be contrary to common sense' (para. 2.39). But the commission offered its opinion that 'the position has changed to some extent since the Working Party reported' (para. 2.33). How the commission thought it had changed, we are not told.

(3) The substantial step test had been criticised because it was incapable of further description or elucidation (para. 2.33). Replies: first, this is not true of the substantial step test: the M.P.C. gave the test a large measure of clarification by means of examples. Secondly, the commission's objection is impressively true of its own test of an act 'going beyond mere preparation,' which is to be left without any statutory examples. The commission of 1989 included examples of attempts in its Report on the Code, but in selecting them it carefully refrained from shedding any glimmer of light on what goes and what does not go beyond mere preparation, in

doubtful cases. Thus it seems that the commission was not interested in further describing or elucidating its own test. (In any case, the commission did not intend its examples to be part of the enacted code.)

(4) Of all the commission's anaemic objections, the feeblest was its idea that if the substantial step test were adopted, the offence could no longer properly be called an attempt. As I have already said, this problem has not prevented the extension of crimes like murder and burglary beyond the scope popularly understood from their names. Anyway, I would not grant the objection. I do not think it an abuse of language to say that Kenneth Jones started his attempt as soon as he set out with his firearm, his disguise and his Spanish money, or even when he acquired the firearm and his disguise with the firm purpose of using it in the offence; nor would there be any linguistic objection to saying that an attempt was committed by various rogues who have got off charges on the proximity issue, such as Robinson. . . .

Draft Criminal Code, Clause 49

Attempt to commit an offence

(1) A person who, intending to commit an indictable offence, does an act that is more than merely preparatory to the commission of the offence is guilty of attempt to commit the offence.

(2) For the purposes of subsection (1), an intention to commit an offence is an intention with respect to all the elements of the offence other than fault elements, except that recklessness with respect to a circumstance suffices where it suffices for the offence itself.

(3) 'Act' in this section includes an omission only where the offence intended is capable of being committed by an omission.

(4) Where there is evidence to support a finding that an act was more than merely preparatory to the commission of the offence intended, the question whether that act was more than merely preparatory is a question of fact.

(5) Subject to section 52(1), this section applies to any offence which, if it were completed, would be triable in England and Wales as an indictable offence, other than an offence under section 4(1) (assisting offenders) or 5(1) (accepting or agreeing to accept consideration for not disclosing information about an arrestable offence) of the Criminal Law Act 1967.

(6) It is not an offence under this section, or under any enactment referred to in section 51, to attempt to procure, assist or encourage as an accessory the commission of an offence by another; but—

(a) a person may be guilty as an accessory to an attempt by another to commit an offence; and
(b) this subsection does not preclude a charge of attempt to incite (under section 47 or any other enactment), or of attempt to conspire (under section 48 or any other enactment), to commit an offence.

2. CONSPIRACY

D.P.P. v. Nock [1978] A.C. 977: "Lord Tucker [in *B.O.T. v. Owen* (*post*, p. 488)] by stressing the 'auxiliary' nature of the crime of conspiracy, and by explaining its justification as being to prevent the commission of substantive offence, has placed the crime firmly in the same class and category as attempts to commit a crime. Both are criminal because they are steps towards the commission of a substantive offence. The distinction between the two is that whereas a 'proximate' act is that which constitutes the crime of attempt, agreement is the necessary ingredient in conspiracy. The importance of the distinction is that agreement may, and usually will, occur well before the first step which can be said to be an attempt. The law of conspiracy thus makes possible an earlier intervention by the law to prevent the commission of the substantive offence.": *per* Lord Scarman.

Note

Conspiracy was a common law offence, consisting of "the agreement of two or more to do an unlawful act, or to do a lawful act by unlawful means": *per* Willes J. in *Mulcahy v. R.* (1868) L.R. 3 H.L. 306. "Unlawful" in this context covered all crimes, even summary offences, some torts, fraud, the corruption of public morals and the outraging of public decency. The aim of the Law Commission (Law Com. No. 76, § 1.111) is to confine conspiracy to agreements to commit crimes. This aim is partially achieved by sections 1 and 5 of the Criminal Law Act 1977 (see *infra*). However, pending a comprehensive review of offences of fraud and of the law relating to obscenity and indecency, conspiracies to defraud, and to corrupt public morals or outrage public decency, are preserved.

i. Statutory Conspiracies

Criminal Law Act 1977, section 1

Section 1: *The offence of conspiracy* (1) Subject to the following provisions of this Part of this Act, if a person agrees with any other person or persons that a course of conduct shall be pursued which, if the agreement is carried out in accordance with their intentions, either—

(*a*) will necessarily amount to or involve the commission of any offence or offences by one or more of the parties to the agreement, or
(*b*) would do so but for the existence of facts which render the commission of the offence or any of the offences impossible,

he is guilty of conspiracy to commit the offence or offences in question. [Substituted by section 5(1) Criminal Attempts Act 1981].

(2) Where liability for any offence may be incurred without knowledge on the part of the person committing it of any particular fact or circumstance necessary for the commission of the offence, a person shall nevertheless not be guilty of conspiracy to commit that offence by virtue of subsection (1) above unless he and at least one other party to the agreement intend or know that that fact or circumstance shall or will exist at the time when the conduct constituting the offence is to take place.

(3) Where in pursuance of any agreement the acts in question in relation to any offence are to be done in contemplation or furtherance of a trade dispute (within the meaning of the Trade Union and Labour Relations Act 1974) that offence shall be disregarded for the purposes of subsection (1) above provided that it is a summary offence which is not punishable with imprisonment.

(4) In this Part of this Act 'offence' means an offence triable in England and Wales.

(a) *Agreement*

Note

Since the forbidden "act" in conspiracy is agreement, and agreement is a mental process, it is more difficult than with most crimes to separate out *mens rea* and *actus reus*.

The agreement must be that a course of conduct will be pursued which, if the agreement is carried out in accordance with their intentions, will necessarily amount to or involve the commission of an offence by one or more parties to the agreement. (Questions of impossibility will be discussed later.) There is no requirement that any conspirator should take any steps towards carrying out the agreement.

Inherent in the kind of agreement required is that D must intend that the agreement be carried out and the projected crime committed by one or more of the conspirators; but the statutory definition does not require D to intend himself to play any part in carrying out the agreement. This was the position at common law, and the Law Commission (Law Com. 76, paragraph 1.38) drafted section 1(1) to ensure that that position should continue. However this intention was frustrated by the next case.

R. v. Anderson
[1986] A.C. 27
House of Lords

D and A, in custody in relation to entirely unconnected offences, spent one night in the same cell. D, who was expecting to be released soon, agreed with A to participate in a scheme to secure A's escape from prison. D was to meet A's brother and another man and supply diamond wire, which they would then smuggle in to A. D was also to do further acts to facilitate the escape. He was to be paid £20,000 for his assistance. He received £2,000 on account from A's brother, but was injured in a road accident before anything further happened. He did not supply the wire, and took no further part in the scheme. D admitted that he had intended to supply the wire on payment of another £10,000 on account, but said he would then have gone abroad and taken no further part in the plan, which he believed was doomed to failure. His submission that he lacked the mental element for conspiracy to effect an escape, in that he did not intend or expect the plan to be carried into effect, was rejected by the judge and by the Court of Appeal, which also held that, even if he was not a principal in conspiracy he could be convicted of aiding abetting counselling and procuring the conspiracy of the other two men (see 80 Cr.App.R. 64, 77). On appeal to the House of Lords on both of these questions:

LORD BRIDGE OF HARWICH: The Act of 1977, subject to exceptions not presently material, abolished the offence of conspiracy at common law. It follows that the elements of the new statutory offence of conspiracy must be ascertained purely by interpretation of the language of section 1(1) of the Act of 1977. For purposes of analysis it is perhaps convenient to isolate the three clauses each of which must be taken as indicating an essential ingredient of the offence as follows: (1) "if a person agrees with any other person or persons that a course of conduct shall be pursued" (2) "which will necessarily amount to or involve the commission of any offence or offences by one or more of the parties to the agreement" (3) "if the agreement is carried out in accordance with their intentions".

Clause (1) presents, as it seems to me, no difficulty. It means exactly what it says and what it says is crystal clear. To be convicted, the party charged must have agreed with one or more others that "a course of conduct shall be pursued." What is important is to resist the temptation to introduce into this simple concept ideas derived from the civil law of contract. Any number of persons may agree that a course of conduct shall be pursued without undertaking any contractual liability. The agreed course of conduct may be a simple or an elaborate one and may involve the participation of two or any larger number of persons who may have agreed to play a variety of roles in the course of conduct agreed.

Again, clause (2) could hardly use simpler language. Here what is important to note is that it is not necessary that more than one of the participants in the agreed course of conduct shall commit a substantive offence. It is, of course, necessary that any party to the agreement shall have assented to play his part in the agreed course of conduct, however innocent in itself, knowing that the part to be played by one or more of the others will amount to or involve the commission of an offence.

It is only clause (3) which presents any possible ambiguity. The heart of the submission for the appellant is that in order to be convicted of conspiracy to commit a given offence the language of clause (3) requires that the party charged should not only have agreed that a course of conduct shall be pursued which will necessarily amount to or involve the commission of that offence by himself or one or more other parties to the agreement, but must also be proved himself to have intended that that offence should be committed. Thus, it is submitted here that the appellant's case that he never intended that Andaloussi should be enabled to escape from prison raised an issue to be left to the jury, who should have been directed to convict him only if satisfied that he did so intend. I do not find it altogether easy to understand why the draftsman of this provision chose to use the phrase "in accordance with their intentions". But I suspect the answer may be that this seemed a desirable alternative to the phrase "in accordance with its terms" or any similar expression, because it is a matter of common experience in the criminal courts that the "terms" of a criminal conspiracy are hardly ever susceptible of proof. The evidence from which a jury may infer a criminal conspiracy is almost invariably to be found in the conduct of the parties. This was so at common law and remains so under the statute. If the evidence in a given case justifies the inference of an agreement that a course of conduct should be pursued, it is a not inappropriate formulation of the test of the criminality of the inferred agreement to ask whether the further inference can be drawn that a crime would necessarily have been committed if the agreed course of conduct had been pursued in accordance with the *several* intentions of the parties. Whether that is an accurate analysis or not, I am clearly driven by consideration of the diversity of roles which parties may agree to play in criminal conspiracies to reject any construction of the statutory language which would require the prosecution to prove an intention on the part of each conspirator that the criminal offence or offences which will necessarily be committed by one or more of the conspirators if the agreed course of conduct is fully carried out should in fact be committed. A simple example will illustrate the absurdity to which this construction would lead. The proprietor of a car hire firm agrees for a substantial payment to make available a hire car to a gang for use in a robbery and to make false entries in his books relating to the hiring to which he can point if the number of the car is traced back to him in connection with the robbery. Being fully aware of the circumstances of the robbery in which the car is proposed to be used he is plainly a party to the conspiracy to rob. Making his car available for use in the robbery is as much a part of the relevant agreed course of conduct as the robbery itself. Yet, once he has been paid, it will be a matter of complete indifference to him whether the robbery is in fact committed or not. In these days of highly organised crime the most serious statutory conspiracies will frequently involve an elaborate and complex agreed course of conduct in which many will consent to play necessary but subordinate roles, not involving them in any direct participation in the commission of the offence or offences at the centre of the conspiracy. Parliament cannot have intended that such parties should escape conviction of conspiracy on the basis that it cannot be proved against them that they intended that the relevant offence or offences should be committed.

There remains the important question whether a person who has agreed that a course of conduct will be pursued which, if pursued as agreed, will necessarily amount to or involve the commission of an offence is guilty of statutory conspiracy irrespective of his intention, and, if not, what is the *mens rea* of the offence. I have no hesitation in answering the first part of the question in the negative. There may be many situations in which perfectly respectable citizens, more particularly those concerned with law enforcement, may enter into agreements that a course of conduct shall be pursued which will involve commission of a crime without the least intention of playing any part in furtherance of the ostensibly agreed criminal objective, but rather with the purpose of exposing and frustrating the criminal purpose of the other parties to the agreement. To say this is in no way to encourage schemes by which police act, directly or through the agency of informers, as agents provocateurs for the purpose of entrapment. That is conduct of which the courts have always strongly disapproved. But it may sometimes happen, as most of us with experience in criminal trials well know, that a criminal enterprise is well advanced in the course of preparation when it comes to the notice either of the police or of some honest citizen in such circumstance that the only prospect of exposing and frustrating the criminal is that some innocent person should play the part of an intending collaborator in the course of criminal conduct proposed to be pursued. The *mens rea* implicit in the offence of statutory conspiracy must clearly be such as to recognise the innocence of such a person, notwithstanding that he will, in literal terms, be obliged to agree that a course of conduct be pursued involving the commission of an offence.

I have said already, but I repeat to emphasise its importance, that an essential ingredient in the crime of conspiring to commit a specific offence or offences under section 1(1) of the Act of 1977 is that the accused should agree that a course of conduct be pursued which he knows must involve the commission by one or more of the parties to the agreement of that offence or those offences. But, beyond the mere fact of agreement, the necessary *mens rea* of the crime is, in my opinion, established if, and only if, it is shown that the accused, when he entered into the agreement, intended to play some part in the agreed course of conduct in furtherance of the criminal purpose which the agreed course of conduct was intended to achieve. Nothing less will suffice; nothing more is required.

Applying this test to the facts which, for the purposes of the appeal, we must assume, the appellant, in agreeing that a course of conduct be pursued that would, if successful, necessarily involve the offence of effecting Andaloussi's escape from lawful custody, clearly intended, by providing diamond wire to be smuggled into the prison, to play a part in the agreed course of conduct in furtherance of that criminal objective. Neither the fact that he intended to play no further part in attempting to effect the escape, nor that he believed the escape to be impossible, would, if the jury had supposed they might be true, have afforded him any defence.

In the result, I would answer the first part of the certified question in the affirmative and dismiss the appeal. Your Lordships did not find it necessary to hear argument directed to the second part of the certified question and it must, therefore, be left unanswered.

Lords Scarman, Diplock, Keith and Brightman agreed.

Appeal dismissed

Notes

1. The House of Lords could have avoided the need to tinker with the *mens rea* of conspiracy if they had upheld D's conviction on the basis that he had aided and abetted the conspiracy as the others involved clearly had the intention that the substantive offence be committed.

2. ". . . An essential ingredient in the crime of conspiring to commit a specific offence . . . is that the accused shall agree that a course of conduct be pursued which he knows must involve the commission by one or more parties to the agreement of that offence. . . . But, beyond the mere fact of agreement, the necessary *mens rea* of the crime . . . is established if, and only if, it is shown that the accused, when he entered into the agreement, intended to play some part in the agreed course of conduct in furtherance of the criminal purpose which the agreed course of conduct was intended to achieve. Nothing less will suffice, nothing more is required."

This dictum was considered and "explained" by the Court of Appeal in *R. v. Siracusa* (1989) 90 Cr.App.R. 340. There was a large and complicated agreement to import various prohibited drugs at various times. The parties were charged with conspiracy to contravene section 170(2)(b) Customs and Excise Management Act 1979, which prohibits the import of various classes of drugs with various penalties attached. In *R. v. Shivpuri* [1987] A.C.1 (*post*, p. 504), the House of Lords held that for this offence the *mens rea* required was an intention to import any prohibited drug, not necessarily one of the class actually imported. In the course of dismissing the appeals in the present case, O'Connor L.J. said:

"[The dictum above quoted] must be read in the context of that case. We think it obvious that Lord Bridge cannot have been intending that the organiser of a crime who recruited others to carry it out would not himself be guilty of conspiracy unless it could be proved that he intended to play some active part himself thereafter. . . . Participation in a conspiracy is infinitely variable; it can be active or passive. If the majority shareholder and director of a company consents to the company being used for drug smuggling carried out in the company's name by a fellow director and minority shareholder, he is guilty of conspiracy. Consent, that is the agreement or adherence to the agreement, can be inferred if it is proved that he knew what was going on and the intention to participate in the furtherance of the criminal purpose is also established by his failure to stop the unlawful activity.

. . . The *mens rea* sufficient to support the commission of a substantive offence will not necessarily be sufficient to support a charge of conspiracy to commit that offence. An intent to cause grievous bodily harm is sufficient to support a charge of murder, but it is not sufficient to support a charge of conspiracy to murder, or of attempt to murder. We have come to the conclusion that if the prosecution charge a conspiracy to contravene section 170(2) of the Customs and Excise Management Act by the importation of heroin, then the prosecution must prove that the agreed course of conduct was the importation of heroin. This is because the essence of the crime of conspiracy is the agreement and, in simple terms, you do not prove an agreement to import heroin by proving an agreement to import cannabis."

3. The defendant must know that what is projected is a crime, otherwise it cannot be said that he agreed to a course of conduct involving the commission of a crime. This is the position even if the *offence* can be committed without full knowledge of a fact or circumstance which makes the conduct criminal. Section 1(2) Criminal Law Act 1977, *ante*, p. 471, provides that in such a case, to be guilty of *conspiring* to commit the offence, D and at least one other party must intend or know that that fact or circumstance shall or will exist at the time when the conduct constituting the offence is to take place. Thus: it is an offence to use in a vehicle fuel on which the appropriate duty has not been paid; to convict D of this offence it is not necessary to show that he knew that the duty had not been paid. But if D is charged with conspiracy to use in a vehicle fuel on which duty has not been paid, it must be shown that he and at least one other party knew that the duty had not been paid. (Compare the similar rule in aiding and abetting, *ante*, p. 376.) It is the offence of rape to have intercourse with a non-consenting person being reckless as to whether s/he is consenting or not. D agrees with C to have intercourse with a woman, who in fact is non-consenting; D does not know this, but could not care less whether she will consent or not. To convict D of conspiracy to rape, it must be shown that both he *and* C knew she would not consent. (Compare *R. v. Khan* and the different rule on attempt, *ante*, p. 449.)

4. But, according to Lord Bridge in *Anderson*, it is not necessary that D should intend that the crime should be carried out; it is sufficient if he knows that another party to the agreement intends to commit it.

Question

The brother of A and B had been murdered, apparently on the orders of P, a dangerous criminal. A and B agreed to meet near P's house on June 14, when they knew that P would be away, and reconnoitre a place to ambush him; on June 16 they would return, lie in wait for P and kill him. At the time of the agreement, each privately thought that the enterprise was too dangerous, and resolved not to be present on the 16th. In order not to appear too fainthearted, each intended to be present on the 14th and assist in fixing a place of ambush, but each intended to arrange some pressing business to keep him away on the day of the attack, which each expected the other to carry out alone. Are they guilty of conspiracy to murder?

Note

The authority of *Anderson* has been thrown further into doubt by the Privy Council decision in *Yip Chiu-Cheung v. R, infra,* which,

although not binding on English courts, is highly persuasive particularly as the committee comprised Lords Griffiths, Browne-Wilkinson,
Mustill, Jauncey of Tullichettle and Slynn of Hadley. *Siracusa* was not
cited but their Lordships addressed issues raised in *Anderson*. The case
arose in Hong Kong where conspiracy is an offence contrary to
common law. There is no apparent distinction between the Hong
Kong common law definition of conspiracy and the statutory definition in s.1(1) of the 1977 Act.

Yip Chiu-Cheung v. The Queen
[1995] 1 A.C. 111
Privy Council

D had been convicted of conspiracy to traffic in heroin contrary to
common-law and to section 4 of the Dangerous Drugs Ordinance. The
conspiracy concerned an agreement between D and N, an American
undercover drug enforcement agent, that he would meet D in Hong
Kong where he would receive from him the supply of heroin which N
would take to Australia. The authorities were aware of the plan and
had agreed not to prevent N proceeding to Australia as his aim was to
identify the others in the drugs ring. N however, missed his flight to
Hong Kong and the plan was abandoned. D argued on appeal that N
could not be a co-conspirator as he lacked the necessary *mens rea* for
conspiracy.

LORD GRIFFITHS delivered the judgment of their Lordships:
   . . . On the principal ground of appeal it was submitted that the trial judge
and the Court of Appeal were wrong to hold that Needham, the undercover
agent, could be a conspirator because he lacked the necessary mens rea or
guilty mind required for the offence of conspiracy. It was urged upon their
Lordships that no moral guilt attached to the undercover agent who was at
all times acting courageously and with the best of motives in attempting to
infiltrate and bring to justice a gang of criminal drug dealers. In these circumstances it was argued that it would be wrong to treat the agent as having any
criminal intent, and reliance was placed upon a passage in the speech of Lord
Bridge of Harwich in *R. v. Anderson (William Ronald)* [1986] A.C. 27, 38–39;
but in that case Lord Bridge was dealing with a different situation from that
which exists in the present case. There may be many cases in which undercover police officers or other law enforcement agents pretend to join a conspiracy in order to gain information about the plans of the criminals, with no
intention of taking any part in the planned crime but rather with the intention
of providing information that will frustrate it. It was to this situation that
Lord Bridge was referring in *R. v. Anderson*. The crime of conspiracy requires
an agreement between two or more persons to commit an unlawful act with
the intention of carrying it out. It is the intention to carry out the crime that
constitutes the necessary mens rea for the offence. As Lord Bridge pointed
out, an undercover agent who has no intention of committing the crime lacks
the necessary mens rea to be a conspirator.
   The facts of the present case are quite different. Nobody can doubt that
Needham was acting courageously and with the best of motives; he was
trying to break a drug ring. But equally there can be no doubt that the method
he chose and in which the police in Hong Kong acquiesced involved the commission of the criminal offence of trafficking in drugs by exporting heroin
from Hong Kong without a licence. Needham intended to commit that offence

by carrying the heroin through the customs and on to the aeroplane bound for Australia.

Neither the police, nor customs, nor any other member of the executive have any power to alter the terms of the Ordinance forbidding the export of heroin, and the fact that they may turn a blind eye when the heroin is exported does not prevent it from being a criminal offence . . .

Naturally, Needham never expected to be prosecuted if he carried out the plan as intended. But the fact that in such circumstances the authorities would not prosecute the undercover agent does not mean that he did not commit the crime albeit as part of a wider scheme to combat drug dealing.

The judge correctly directed the jury that they should regard Needham as a conspirator if they found that he intended to export the heroin.

Appeal dismissed.

(b) *The scope of the agreement*

The defendant must have agreed "that a course of conduct will be pursued which will necessarily amount to or involve the commission of any offence or offences by one or more of the parties to the agreement if the agreement is carried out in accordance with their intentions," section 1(1) of the Criminal Law Act 1977, *ante*, p. 471.

Notes

1. Conduct . . . "which will necessarily amount to or involve" an offence.

Law Com. 76. Draft Bill, Clause 1. Explanatory Note 3

"Subsection 1 requires that the parties must agree on a course of conduct which if carried out will *necessarily* amount to an offence; so, for example, an agreement to beat up a nightwatchman will be a conspiracy to cause grievous bodily harm and not conspiracy to murder, notwithstanding that, if the agreement were carried out and the watchman died, there would be an offence of murder."

2. "if the agreement is carried out"

The agreement need not be to the effect that the course of conduct must necessarily be carried out; only to the effect that, if it is carried out, it will necessarily involve a crime. The fact that the agreement will only be carried out if some condition precedent, *e.g.* it is safe, necessary, expedient, etc., is satisfied, is nothing to the point.

In *R. v. Jackson* [1985] Crim.L.R. 442. A and B agreed that if C, then on trial for burglary, was convicted they would do acts likely to pervert the course of justice. It was held that this was a conspiracy to pervert the course of justice. Planning was taking place for a contingency and if that contingency occurred the conspiracy would necessarily involve the commission of an offence. "Necessarily" is not to be held to mean that there must inevitably be the carrying out of the offence; it means, if the agreement is carried out in accordance with the plan, there must be the commission of the offence referred to in the conspiracy count.

In *R. v. Reed* [1982] Crim.L.R. 819, 820. Donaldson L.J. considered two examples: "In the first A and B agree to drive from London to Edinburgh in a time which can be achieved without exceeding the speed limits, but only if the traffic they encounter is exceptionally light. Their agreement will not necessarily involve the commission of any offence, even if it is carried out in accordance with their intentions, and they do arrive from London to Edinburgh within the agreed time. Accordingly the agreement does not constitute the offence of statutory conspiracy or indeed of any offence. In the second example, A and B agree to rob a bank, if when they arrive at the bank it seems safe to do so. Their agreement will necessarily involve the commission of the offence of robbery if it is carried out in accordance with their intentions. Accordingly they are guilty of the statutory offence of conspiracy."

Question

Can it be said that in the first example, A and B agreed to exceed the speed limit if it proved necessary in order to arrive at Edinburgh on time? If it can, what distinction is there between the two examples, or between the first example and the facts in *R. v. Reed?*

(c) *Parties*

Notes

1. *At least two conspirators.* It takes two to agree, so if A is adjudged not to have agreed with B, it would appear to follow that B has not agreed with A. From this it was thought to be a rule that if A were acquitted of conspiracy with B, a conviction of B for conspiracy with A (if there were no other conspirators involved) could not possibly stand. This alleged rule was abolished by the House of Lords in *D.P.P. v. Shannon* [1975] A.C. 717, where the following passage from *R. v. Andrews-Weatherfoil Ltd* [1972] 1 W.L.R. 118, 125 was approved.

"As long as it is possible for persons concerned in a single offence to be tried separately, it is inevitable that the verdicts returned by the two juries will on occasion appear to be inconsistent with one another. Such a result may be due to differences in the evidence presented at the two trials or simply to the different views which the juries separately take of the witnesses. . . . When inconsistent verdicts are returned by the same jury, the position is usually more simple. If the inconsistency shows that the single jury was confused, or self contradictory, its conclusions are unsatisfactory or unsafe and neither verdict is reliable. Very often, however, an apparent inconsistency reflects no more than the jury's strict adherence to the judge's direction that they must consider each case separately and that evidence against one may not be admissible against the other: for example, where there is a signed confession. So too, where the verdicts are returned by different juries the inconsistency does not, of itself, indicate that the jury which returned the verdict was confused or misled or reached an incorrect conclusion on the evidence before it. The verdict 'not guilty' includes 'not proven'."

The decision in *D.P.P. v. Shannon* was confirmed by Criminal Law Act 1977:

Criminal Law Act 1977

Section 5:(8) The fact that the person or persons who, so far as appears from the indictment on which any person has been convicted of conspiracy, were the only other parties to the agreement on which his conviction was based have been acquitted of conspiracy by reference to that agreement (whether after being tried with the person convicted or separately) shall not be a ground for quashing his conviction unless under all the circumstances of the case his conviction is inconsistent with the acquittal of the other person or persons in question.

(9) Any rule of law or practice inconsistent with the provisions of subsection (8) above is hereby abolished.

2. *Effect of exempt parties.* If A is charged with conspiring with B to commit a crime, and it appears that B would incur no liability for the crime if it were consummated, two questions arise.

The first question is, does B's exemption in respect of the contemplated crime mean that he cannot be convicted of *conspiring* to commit the crime?

If B has some personal exemption which prevents him from being convicted as first principal of the contemplated crime, then, as seen (*ante*, p. 411) this does not always prevent him from being convicted as a secondary party to that crime. There is no reason why he should not be guilty of conspiracy to commit a crime to which he could be a secondary party. But if B could not be guilty either as a principal or as a secondary party, he ought not to be convicted of conspiring to commit the crime. The policy of the law which excluded B from liability as a party to the crime ought, to be consistent, to exclude him from liability for conspiracy to commit the crime. The Law Commission so recommended (see Law Com. No. 76, § 1.56), disapproving of the only authority in favour of liability: *R. v. Whitchurch* (1890) 24 Q.B.D. 420. However the provision giving effect to this recommendation was not adopted by Parliament, as was noted by the Court of Appeal in *R. v. Burns* (1984) 79 Cr.App.R. 173, 179. This was in the course of upholding the conviction of a father of a child conspiring with others to steal it from the mother, although by the terms of section 56 of the Offences Against the Person Act 1861 (*ante*, p. 382) he could not have been prosecuted for child-stealing.

"Accordingly one considers the question of conspiracy and exempt persons on such authority as exists in respect of this little used branch of the criminal law. There is a paucity of it. We find none that leads us to say that it is in any way wrong or unjust for a person who is exempt, in the sense that James Burns was, from prosecution for the substantive offence to be proceeded against for the crime of conspiracy. The dangers of permitting a father of children to collect a posse of men and suddenly to launch a siege of the home of his erstwhile wife, to break in and then snatch away sleeping children are surely self-evident. The criminal law does not in our view permit that sort of conduct. When a father who is exempt under section 56 behaves in that way, it is, in our judgment, not only lawful but right and just that the prosecution should be free to bring a charge of conspiracy against him."

On the question of when personal exemption from liability as a principal entails exemption from accessorial liability, see *ante*, p. 415.

The second question is, does B's exemption from liability for the crime contemplated mean that A is not guilty of conspiracy with him? If B's "exemption" is because he did not know that the crime was to be committed, then the whole agreement between A and B did not involve the commission of the crime, and it must follow that A has not agreed in the terms required by section 1. (See *ante*, p. 471). As to other exemptions, the Law Commission concluded that A should never be guilty of conspiracy with B if B had a personal exemption in respect of the agreed-on crime (§ 1.57). This also was not acted on, and the strictly limited answers to both questions are contained in section 2.

Criminal Law Act 1977, section 2

Section 2—(1) A person shall not by virtue of section 1 above be guilty of conspiracy to commit any offence if he is an intended victim of that offence.

(2) A person shall not by virtue of section 1 above be guilty of conspiracy to commit any offence or offences if the only other person or persons with whom he agrees are (both initially and at all times during the currency of the agreement) persons of any one or more of the following descriptions, that is to say—

(*a*) his spouse;

(*b*) a person under the age of criminal responsibility; and

(*c*) an intended victim of that offence or of each of those offences.

Note

Code Proposals: (1) On the question of B's personal exemption in respect of the contemplated crime protecting him from conviction of *conspiracy* to commit it, the draft Code continues the principle expressed in section 2(1), but instead of "intended victim," (which was thought to be too wide), substitutes the notion of "protected person," *i.e.* one who is not only an intended victim, but also belongs to a class of persons which the enactment of the crime was intended to protect.

(2) On the question of A's liability when his "co-conspirator" B is his spouse or a child under the age of criminal responsibility or the intended victim, the Law Commission has changed its mind: see Commentary on Code, paras. 13.28–13.32). It now disapproves of the rule that spouses cannot conspire with each other, and as to children under age and intended victims, A is to be liable for conspiracy with them just as though they were "normal" persons: see Clause 48(8), *infra*.

Questions

Which of the following persons (a) are under the Criminal Law Act 1977, and (b) would be under the Draft Criminal Code if it were enacted, guilty of conspiracy?

1. A, a foreman, agrees with B, an operative, that B will operate a

dangerous machine in a factory without a guard as required by regulations. This is an offence under the regulations. B is injured as a result.

2. C persuades D, a child of 9 years of age, to walk out of a shop with goods for which C has not paid and does not intend to pay. Does it make any difference whether D knows or does not know that he is doing anything wrong?

Draft Criminal Code, Clause 48

(1) A person is guilty of conspiracy to commit an offence or offences if—

(a) he agrees with another or others that an act or acts shall be done which, if done, will involve the commission of the offence or offences by one or more of the parties to the agreement; and
(b) he and at least one other party to the agreement intend that the offence or offences shall be committed.

(2) For the purposes of subsection (1) an intention that an offence shall be committed is an intention with respect to all the elements of the offence (other than fault elements), except that recklessness with respect to a circumstance suffices where it suffices for the offence itself.

(3) Subject to section 52, 'offence' in this section means any offence triable in England and Wales; and

(a) it extends to an offence of murder which would not be so triable; but
(b) it does not include a summary offence, not punishable with imprisonment, constituted by an act or acts agreed to be done in contemplation of a trade dispute.

(4) Where the purpose of an enactment creating an offence is the protection of a class of persons, no member of that class who is the intended victim of such an offence can be guilty of conspiracy to commit that offence.

(5) A conspiracy continues until the agreed act or acts is or are done, or until all or all save one of the parties to the agreement have abandoned the intention that such act or acts shall be done.

(6) A person may become a party to a continuing conspiracy by joining the agreement constituting the offence.

(7) It is not an offence under this section, or under any enactment referred to in section 51, to agree to procure, assist or encourage as an accessory the commission of an offence by a person who is not a party to such an agreement; but—

(a) a person may be guilty as an accessory to a conspiracy by others; and
(b) this subsection does not preclude a charge of conspiracy to incite (under section 47 or any other enactment) to commit an offence.

(8) A person may be convicted of conspiracy to commit an offence although—

(a) no other person has been or is charged with such conspiracy;
(b) the identity of any other party to the agreement is unknown;
(c) any other party appearing from the indictment to have been a party to the agreement has been or is acquitted of such conspiracy, unless in

all the circumstances his conviction is inconsistent with the acquittal of the other; or

(d) the only other party to the agreement cannot be convicted of such conspiracy (for example, because he was acting under duress by threats (section 42), or he was a child under ten years of age (section 32(1) or he is immune from prosecution).

ii. Common Law Conspiracies

Criminal Law Act 1977

Section 5: *Abolitions, savings, transitional provisions, consequential amendments and repeals.*

(1) Subject to the following provisions of this section, the offence of conspiracy at common law is hereby abolished.

(2) Subsection (1) above shall not affect the offence of conspiracy at common law so far as relates to conspiracy to defraud. [As amended by Criminal Justice Act 1987, section 12, below].

(3) Subsection (1) above shall not affect the offence of conspiracy at common law if and in so far as it may be committed by entering into an agreement to engage in conduct which—

(a) tends to corrupt public morals or outrages public decency, but

(b) would not amount to or involve the commission of an offence if carried out by a single person otherwise than in pursuance of an agreement.

(7) Incitement to commit the offence of conspiracy (whether the conspiracy incited would be the offence at common law or under section 1 above or any other enactment) shall cease to be offences. [As amended by Criminal Attempts Act 1981, section 10.]"

Criminal Justice Act 1987

Section 12: *Charges of and penalty for conspiracy to defraud.*

(1) If—

(a) a person agrees with any other person or persons that a course of conduct shall be pursued; and

(b) that course of conduct will necessarily amount to or involve the commission of any offence or offences by one or more of the parties to the agreement if the agreement is carried out in accordance with their intentions,

the fact that it will do so shall not preclude a charge of conspiracy to defraud being brought against any of them in respect of the agreement.

(2) In section 5 (2) of the Criminal Law Act 1977, the words from 'and' to the end are hereby repealed.

(3) A person guilty of conspiracy to defraud is liable on conviction on indictment to imprisonment for a term not exceeding 10 years or a fine or both.

(a) Conspiracy to defraud

Scott v. Metropolitan Police Commissioner
[1975] A.C. 819
House of Lords

S agreed with employees of cinema owners temporarily to abstract, without permission of the owners, films, without the knowledge or consent of the copyright owners, for the purpose of making infringing copies and distributing them on a commercial basis. He was convicted of conspiracy to defraud the copyright owners, and appealed.

VISCOUNT DILHORNE: The Court of Appeal certified that a point of law of general public importance was involved in the decision to dismiss the appeal against conviction on count one, namely,

"Whether on a charge of conspiracy to defraud, the Crown must establish an agreement to deprive the owners of their property by deception; or whether it is sufficient to prove an agreement to prejudice the rights of another or others without lawful justification and in circumstances of dishonesty."

Before the House Mr Blom-Cooper put forward three contentions, his main one being that which he advanced unsuccessfully before the Court of Appeal and Judge Hines that there could not be a conspiracy to defraud without deceit. . . .

Mr Blom-Cooper's main submission was based on the well known dicta of Buckley J. in *Re London and Globe Finance Corporation Ltd* [1903] 1 Ch. 728, 732:

"To deceive is, I apprehend, to induce a man to believe that a thing is true which is false, and which the person practising the deceit knows or believes to be false. To defraud is to deprive by deceit: it is by deceit to induce a man to act to his injury. More tersely it may be put, that to deceive is by falsehood to induce a state of mind; to defraud is by deceit to induce a course of action."

Mr Blom-Cooper, while not submitting that an intent to defraud necessarily includes an intention to deceive, nevertheless submitted that a man could not be defrauded unless he was deceived. Buckley J.'s definition was, he said, exhaustive and as the conspiracy charged in count one did not involve any deceit of the companies and persons who owned the copyright and the distribution rights of the films which had been copied, the conviction on that count could not, he submitted, stand.

In a great many and it may be the vast majority of fraud cases the fraud has been perpetrated by deceit and in many cases Buckley J.'s dicta have been quoted in charges to juries. It does not, however, follow that it is an exhaustive definition of what is meant by "defraud". Buckley J. had to decide when a prima facie case had been shown "of doing some or one of the acts" mentioned in sections 83 and 84 of the Larceny Act 1861 "with intent to deceive or defraud." He did not have to make or to have to attempt to make an exhaustive definition of what was meant by "defraud."

Stephen, History of the Criminal Law of England (1883), vol. 2, contains the following passage, at p. 121:

"Fraud—There has always been a great reluctance amongst lawyers to attempt to define fraud, and this is not unnatural when we consider the number of different kinds of conduct to which the word is applied in connection with different branches of it. I shall not attempt to construct a definition which will meet every case which might be suggested, but there is little danger in saying that whenever the words 'fraud' or 'intent to defraud' or 'fraudulently' occur in the definition of a crime two elements at least are essential to the commission of the crime: namely, first, deceit or an intention to deceive or in some cases mere secrecy; and, secondly, either actual injury or possible injury or an intent to expose some person either to actual injury or to a risk of possible injury by means of that deceit or secrecy."

Stephen thus recognises that a fraud may be perpetrated without deceit by secrecy and that an intent to defraud need not necessarily involve an intent to deceive. . . .

In the course of the argument many cases were cited. It is not necessary to refer to all of them. Many were cases in which the conspiracy alleged was to defraud by deceit. Those cases do not establish that there can only be a conspiracy to defraud if deceit is involved and there are a number of cases where that was not the case.

[After citing various cases] Indeed, in none of these cases was it suggested that the conviction was bad on the ground that the conspiracy to defraud did not involve deceit of the person intended to be defrauded. If that had been a valid ground for quashing the conviction it is, I think, inconceivable that the point would not have been taken, if not by counsel, by the court. . . .

In the course of delivering the judgment of the Court of Appeal in *R. v. Sinclair* [1968] 1 W.L.R. 1246, where the defendants had been convicted of conspiracy to cheat and defraud a company, its shareholders and creditors by fraudulently using its assets for purposes other than those of the company and by fraudulently concealing such use, James J. said at p. 1250:

"To cheat and defraud is to act with deliberate dishonesty to the prejudice of another person's proprietary right."

Again, one finds in this case no support for the view that in order to defraud a person that person must be deceived.

One must not confuse the object of a conspiracy with the means by which it is intended to be carried out. In the light of the cases to which I have referred, I have come to the conclusion that Mr Blom-Cooper's main contention must be rejected. I have not the temerity to attempt an exhaustive definition of the meaning of "defraud". As I have said, words take colour from the context in which they are used, but the words "fraudulently" and "defraud" must ordinarily have a very similar meaning. If as I think, and as the Criminal Law Revision Committee appears to have thought, "fraudulently" means "dishonestly", then "to defraud" ordinarily means, in my opinion, to deprive a person dishonestly of something which is his or of something to which he is or would or might but for the perpetration of the fraud be entitled. . . .

In this case the accused bribed servants of the cinema owners to secure possession of films in order to copy them and in order to enable them to let the copies out on hire. By so doing Mr Blom-Cooper conceded they inflicted more than nominal damage to the goodwill of the owners of the copyright and distribution rights of the films. By so doing they secured for themselves profits which but for their actions might have been secured by those owners just as in *R. v. Button* (1848) 3 Cox C.C. 229, the defendants obtained profits which might have been secured by their employer.

In the circumstances it is, I think, clear that they inflicted pecuniary loss on those owners.

Reverting to the questions certified by the Court of Appeal, the answer to the first question is in my opinion in the negative. I am not very happy about the way in which the second question is phrased although the word "prejudice" has been not infrequently used in this connection. If by "prejudice" is meant "injure", then I think that an agreement by two or more by dishonesty to deprive a person of something which is his or to which he is or would be or might be entitled and an agreement by two or more by dishonesty to injure some proprietory right of his, suffices to constitute the offence of conspiracy to defraud.

In my opinion this appeal should be dismissed.

Appeal dismissed.

Notes

1. Just as deceit is not necessary for a conspiracy to defraud, neither is an intent (in the sense of purpose) that the victim shall suffer injury in some proprietory right. In *Wai Yu-Tsang v. R.* [1991] 4 All E.R. 664, the following direction by a trial judge was approved by the Privy Council, when upholding a conviction of conspiracy to defraud:

"It is fraud if it is proved that there was the dishonest taking of a risk which there was no right to take, which—to [D's] knowledge at least—would cause detriment or prejudice to another, detriment or prejudice to the economic or proprietary rights of another. That detriment or prejudice to somebody else is very often incidental to the purpose of the fraudsman himself. The prime object of the fraudsmen is usually to gain some economic advantage for themselves, any detriment or prejudice to somebody else is often secondary to that objective, but nonetheless is a contemplated or predictable outcome of what they do. If the interests of some other person—the economic or proprietary interests of some other person are imperilled, that is sufficient to constitute fraud even though no loss is actually suffered and even though the fraudsman himself did not desire to bring about any loss."

In *Adams v. The Queen* [1995] 1 WLR 52, D, a director of E.H.L. agreed with his co-defendants, who comprised the investment team, to set up a complex system by which share transactions could be conducted thereby making for themselves a profit which they concealed from E.H.L. The Privy Council dismissed D's appeal against conviction for conspiracy to defraud, Lord Jauncey of Tullichettle stating (at p. 65):

"Since a company is entitled to recover from directors secret profits made by them at the company's expense, it would follow that any dishonest agreement by directors to impede a company in the exercise of its right of recovery would constitute a conspiracy to defraud. In their Lordship's view a person can be guilty of fraud when he dishonestly conceals information from another which he was under a duty to disclose to that other or which that other was entitled to require him to disclose."

Affirming *Wai Yu-tsang* he stated (at p. 64) that "A person is not prejudiced if he is hindered in inquiring into the source of moneys in which he has no interest. He can only suffer prejudice in relation to some right or interest which he possesses."

2. In *R. v. Ayres* [1984] A.C. 447, 455, Lord Bridge, dealing with section 5 as it existed before amendment by section 12 of the Criminal Justice Act 1987 said "According to the true construction of the Act, an offence which amounts to a common law conspiracy to defraud must be charged as such and not as a statutory conspiracy under section 1. Conversely a section 1 conspiracy cannot be charged as a common law conspiracy to defraud." The extreme width of conspiracy to defraud as defined in *Scott v. M.P.C.* covering agreements to commit crimes, *e.g.* theft or obtaining by deception, meant that these agreements must be charged as conspiracies to defraud, and not as conspiracies to steal, or obtain by deception. It was therefore held that the effect of section 5 was to cut down conspiracy to defraud to agreements which, if carried into effect, would *not* necessarily involve the commission of any substantive criminal offence by any of the conspirators: *R. v. Ayres*, at p. 462. The effect of section 12 of the Criminal Justice Act 1987, *ante*, p. 483, is to restore the offence of conspiracy to defraud to what it was held to be in *Scott v. M.P.C.*. An agreement, *e.g.* to steal, is therefore both a statutory and a common law conspiracy and may be charged as either.

3. The problem remains as to whether conspiracy to defraud could be abolished without leaving unacceptable gaps in the law. The Law Commission, returning to the matter in 1987, reached a provisional view that it could be, but that there would be lost significant procedural and practical advantages of being able to charge the offence, particularly in large scale fraud cases: W.P. 104. In its latest report on this subject, Law Com. No. 228, *Criminal Law: Conspiracy to Defraud* (1994), the Law Commission concluded that simple abolition of conspiracy to defraud, without replacement, would leave undesirable gaps in the law and that the offence should be retained pending the outcome of their comprehensive review of dishonesty offences. (For further discussion see J.C. Smith, "Conspiracy to Defraud: Some comments on the Law Commission's Report [1995] Crim. L.R. 209.)

(4) An agreement to deceive a public official into breaching his duty is a conspiracy to defraud: *D.P.P. v. Withers* [1975] A.C. 842.

(b) *Conspiracies to corrupt public morals or outrage public decency*

Note

Agreements to do these things are certainly criminal conspiracies. They were common law conspiracies before the 1977 Act: see *Knuller v. D.P.P.* [1973] A.C. 435. According to section 5 (3), *ante*, p. 483, an agreement to do either of them is still a common law conspiracy if and insofar as corrupting public morals or outraging public decency is a crime in its own right (*i.e.* a crime if done by one person without any agreement with someone else). They probably are offences in their own right, and thus agreements to commit them are statutory conspiracies to commit those crimes. But it is thought to be open to the House of Lords to hold that they do not exist as offences, in which case agreements to do them would remain as common law conspiracies.

iii. Jurisdiction

Note

Conspiracies are nowadays often international in character. Since "all crime is local" and "The jurisdiction over the crime belongs to the country where the crime is committed . . .": *per* Lord Haldane L.C. in *MacLeod v. Att.-Gen. for New South Wales* [1891] A.C. 455, 458, and since the essence of conspiracy is the agreement, it might be thought that the only question on jurisdiction is whether the agreement was made in this country. However this is not so. For the purposes of discussion, "international" conspiracies may be divided into two classes: (a) Agreement here to do acts abroad and (b) Agreement abroad to do acts here.

(a) Agreement here to do acts abroad

In *Board of Trade v. Owen* [1957] A.C. 602 the House of Lords held that a conspiracy to commit a crime abroad is not indictable in this country unless the substantive offence, if committed, could be tried here. In the aftermath of the Omagh bombing on August 25, 1998, legislation was introduced primarily to deal with terrorism but also giving the courts jurisdiction to try for conspiracy those who plot in England and Wales to commit offences abroad. The Criminal Justice (Terrorism and Conspiracy) Act 1998 inserts a new section 1A into the Criminal Law Act 1977.

Criminal Law Act 1977

1A.—(1) Where each of the following conditions is satisfied in the case of an agreement, this Part of this Act has effect in relation to the agreement as it has effect in relation to an agreement falling within section 1(1) above.

(2) The first condition is that the pursuit of the agreed course of conduct would at some stage involve—

(a) an act by one or more of the parties, or
(b) the happening of some other event,

intended to take place in a country or territory outside the United Kingdom.

(3) The second condition is that that act or other event constitutes an offence under the law in force in that country or territory.

(4) The third condition is that the agreement would fall within section 1(1) above as an agreement relating to the commission of an offence but for the fact that the offence would not be an offence triable in England and Wales if committed in accordance with the parties' intentions.

(5) The fourth condition is that—

(a) a party to the agreement, or a party's agent, did anything in England and Wales in relation to the agreement before its formation, or

(b) a party to the agreement became a party in England and Wales (by joining it either in person or through an agent), or
(c) a party to the agreement, or a party's agent, did or omitted anything in England and Wales in pursuance of the agreement.

(b) *Agreement abroad to do acts here*

The Criminal Law Act 1977 makes no specific reference to this, but see next case.

R. v. Sansom
(1990) 92 Cr.App.R. 115
Court of Appeal

S and others were convicted of conspiracy to evade the prohibition on the import of cannabis. The appeal was dealt with on the footing that they had agreed while abroad to import into Belgium from Morocco half a ton of cannabis resin. The consignment was to be shipped from Morocco in the vessel Lady Rose and trans-shipped in international waters from the Lady Rose into the fishing boat Danny Boy, on which it would be taken into Belgium. One of the conspirators chartered the Danny Boy in England and sailed it out to meet the Lady Rose. It was contended that on these facts the Court had no jurisdiction to try the appellants for conspiracy.

TAYLOR L.J.: . . . A submission was made to the learned judge, and has been repeated on appeal, on behalf of Sansom and Williams that the court had no jurisdiction to try the count of conspiracy. The agreement was alleged to have been made abroad and it was contended that to constitute a triable offence in England there would have to be proven some unlawful act in England in pursuance of the conspiracy. If, as the defence alleged, the Danny Boy was arrested outside territorial waters, no such unlawful act could be proved. The learned judge rejected the submission, basing his decision on *D.P.P. v. Doot* [1973] A.C.807. In that case the House of Lords held that a conspiracy entered into abroad could be prosecuted in England if the parties acted in England in concert and in pursuance of the agreement. . . .
Lord Salmon said, at p. 833F:

"Suppose a case in which evidence existed of a conspiracy hatched abroad by . . . drug pedlars to smuggle large quantities of dangerous drugs on to some stretch of the English coast. Suppose the conspirators came to England for the purpose of carrying out the crime and were detected by the police reconnoitring the place where they proposed to commit it, but doing nothing which by itself would be illegal, it would surely be absurd if the police could not arrest them then and there but had to take the risk of waiting and hoping to be able to catch them as they were actually committing or attempting to commit the crime. Yet that is precisely what the police would have to do if a conspiracy entered into abroad to commit a crime here were not in the circumstances postulated recognised by our law as a criminal offence which our courts had any jurisdiction to try."

At p. 835B-C Lord Salmon went further. There he said:

"It is, unfortunately, by no means unlikely that cases may arise in the future in which there will be conclusive evidence of persons having conspired abroad to commit serious crimes in England and then having done acts here in furtherance of the conspiracy and in preparation for the commission of those crimes yet none of these acts will in itself be unlawful. Although such a case would be very different from the present, if the reasoning upon which I have based this opinion is sound it follows that such persons could properly be arrested and tried for conspiracy in our courts."

That view was supported by the learned authors of *Smith and Hogan on Criminal Law*, 6th ed. (1988), p. 269. They say:

"Whether such a conspiracy is indictable if the parties take no steps in England to implement it has not been decided. It is submitted that the better view is that any of the parties entering the jurisdiction during the continuance of the agreement should be indictable at common law."

In *Somchai Liangsiriprasert v. The Government of the United States of America and Another* [1990] 3 W.L.R. 606, the Privy Council on July 2, 1990 upheld that view. The case concerned a conspiracy to import heroin to the United States from Thailand, the proceeds to be collected in Hong Kong. Lord Griffiths, giving the advice of the Board, stated that in general English criminal law is local in its effect and does not concern itself with crimes abroad. There are exceptions. At p. 614 he said:

"There has as yet however been no decision in which it has been held that a conspiracy entered into abroad to commit a crime in England is a common law crime triable in English courts in the absence of any overt act pursuant to the conspiracy taking place in England. There are however a number of *dicta* in judgments and academic commentaries suggesting that it should be so."

Lord Griffiths then reviewed the authorities and, at p. 620, he continued:

"But why should an overt act be necessary to found jurisdiction? In the case of conspiracy in England the crime is complete once the agreement is made and no further overt act needs be proved as an ingredient of the crime. The only purpose of looking for an overt act in England in the case of a conspiracy entered into abroad can be to establish the link between the conspiracy and England or possibly to show the conspiracy is continuing. But if this can be established by other evidence, for example the taping of conversations between the conspirators showing a firm agreement to commit the crime at some future date, it defeats the preventative purpose of the crime of conspiracy to have to wait until some overt act is performed in pursuance of the conspiracy.

Unfortunately in this century crime has ceased to be largely local in origin and effect. Crime is now established on an international scale and the common law must face this new reality. Their Lordships can find nothing in precedent, comity or good sense that should inhibit the common law from regarding as justiciable in England inchoate crimes committed abroad which are intended to result in the commission of criminal offences in England. Accordingly a conspiracy entered into in Thailand with the intention of committing the criminal offence of trafficking in drugs in Hong Kong is justiciable in Hong Kong even if no overt act pursuant to the conspiracy has yet occurred in Hong Kong."

Although not binding on this Court, the decision of the Privy Council has of course very strong persuasive force especially when coupled with the earlier *dicta* in *D.P.P. v. Doot*. It was argued that *Somchai* referred only to the common law. The present conspiracy was charged as contrary to the Criminal Law Act 1977 which does not in terms deal with extra-territorial conspiracies. We reject that argument for three reasons. First, it cannot have been the intention of Parliament in enacting the 1977 Act to alter the common law rules as to extra-territorial conspiracies without specific words. Secondly, since conspiracies to defraud are not within the scope of the 1977 Act, the appellants' argument would produce the absurdity that the *Somchai* principle would apply to them but not to other conspiracies. Finally, we consider that the Privy Council, knowing that most conspiracies in English law are now covered by the 1977 Act, would specifically have indicated that the important principle they were enunciating in regard to conspiracy only applied to the restricted categories of common law conspiracy now surviving, had that been intended. In our judgment the principle propounded in *Somchai* by Lord Griffiths should now be regarded as the law of England on this point. In the present case there was clear evidence that one of the alleged conspirators, Wilkins, had acted in England in pursuance of the alleged conspiracy which was still subsisting by commissioning the Danny Boy and sailing in her to collect the cannabis from the Lady Rose. . . . This ground of appeal therefore fails.

Sansom's Appeal allowed on other grounds

Note

Part I of the Criminal Justice Act 1993 expands the jurisdiction of courts in England and Wales to try most offences of fraud and dishonesty where an element of the *actus reus* occurs in England and Wales regardless of the whereabouts of the accused at that time. The Act applies to offences under sections 1, 15, 15A,16,17, 19, 20(2), 21, 22 and 24A of the Theft Act 1968, sections 1 and 2 of the Theft Act 1978 and sections 1 to 5 of the Forgery and Counterfeiting Act 1981. The Act also asserts jurisdiction to try conspiracy (or attempt) to commit any of the above offences or conspiracy to defraud regardless of where the conspiracy (or attempt) takes place provided the court would have jurisdiction to try the substantive offence.

3. INCITEMENT

Notes

1. Counselling a crime which is not committed does not make the counsellor an aider and abettor in the counselled crime: *R. v. Gregory* (1867) L.R. 1 C.C.R. 77; but the counsellor is guilty of the offence of incitement. "But it is argued, that a mere intent to commit evil is not indictable, without an act done; but is there not an act done, when it is charged that the defendant solicited another to commit a felony? The solicitation is an act": *per* Lord Kenyon C.J. in *R. v. Higgins* (1801) 2 East 5.

2. The solicitation is an act by the incitor: but no act at all is required from the incitee. "It matters not that no steps have been taken towards the commission of the attempt or of the substantive offence. It matters not, in other words, whether the incitement had any effect at all. It is merely the incitement or the attempting to incite which constitutes the offence": *per* Lord Widgery C.J. in *R. v. Assistant Recorder of Kingston-upon-Hill* [1969] 2 Q.B. 58.

3. If the solicitation reaches the mind of the incitee, it is the full offence of incitement even if the solicitation has no effect on that mind, *e.g.* if the incitee is completely unmoved, or has already decided to commit the crime anyway. Attempting to incite occurs where the solicitation (*e.g.* in a letter) does not reach the mind of the incitee: see *R. v. Ransford* (1874) 13 Cox 9.

4. An incitement made by A to B to commit a crime necessarily involved inciting B to conspire with A, an attempt by A to conspire with B, and an attempt by A to counsel or procure an offence by B. These three offences, being redundant, have been abolished: see section 5 (7) Criminal Law Act 1977; section 1 (4) Criminal Attempts Act 1981, *ante*, p. 445. However it has been held that incitement to incite is still an offence known to the law, *e.g.* where A incites B to incite C to kill V: *R. v. Sirat* (1985) 83 Cr.App.R. 41; *R. v. Evans* [1986] Crim.L.R. 470. *Cf.* Law Com. C.P. No. 131 (para 4.163) *ante*, p. 416.)

(a) Actus Reus

Notes

1. The incitement, which may be addressed to the world in general, may consist in persuasion (*i.e.* urging), or threats or pressure.

R. v. Most (1881) 7 Q.B.D. 244 (C.C.C.R.): M published in London an article in a newspaper urging readers in foreign countries to assassinate their Heads of State. *Held*, incitement to murder under section 4 of the Offences Against the Person Act 1861.

Race Relations Board v. Applin [1973] Q.B. 815, 825 (C.A.): A. sent a circular to W's neighbours, complaining about W's taking coloured foster children. His object was to get W to take white foster children only. The question was whether this was an incitement of W to do an unlawful act under the Race Relations Act 1968. Lord Denning M.R.: "[It was suggested] that to 'incite' means to urge or spur on by advice, encouragement or persuasion, and not otherwise, I do not think the word is so limited, at any rate in the present context. A person may 'incite' another to do an act by threatening or by pressure, as well as by persuasion." A had therefore incited W.

Invicta Plastics v. Clare [1976] R.T.R. 251 (Div. Ct.): I.P. advertised for sale a device which was not illegal to own, but was illegal to operate without a licence, which was unlikely to be given. The device, when operated by a car driver, gave him warning when a police radar trap was set. *Held*, approving Lord Denning's remarks in *Applin's* case (above), I.P. incited readers of the advertisement to commit an offence under the Wireless Telegraphy Act 1949.

2. The incitement must be to do an act which, if done by the incitee, would be a crime by him. In *R. v. Whitehouse* [1977] Q.B. 868 (see *ante*, p. 412) A urged B to commit incest, which B was legally not able to commit as either a principal or an accessory. *Held*, A was not guilty of common law incitement.

3. The fact that B does not know that what he is being urged to do would be a crime by him means that A is not guilty of incitement, although he may be guilty of attempting to commit a crime through an innocent agent.

Question

A urges B to drink V's wine. A knows that V does not and would not consent to this, and thinks that B has similar knowledge. In fact B thinks that V consents to his drinking the wine. Is A guilty of inciting B to steal V's wine?

(b) *Mens Rea*

The incitor must intend the incitee to do an act which would be a crime by him.

R. v. Curr
[1968] 2 Q.B. 944
Court of Appeal

Curr lent money and in return took as security family allowance vouchers which the borrower signed for him. He got another woman to cash these vouchers for him at a Post Office. He was charged with (*inter alia*) soliciting this woman to commit a summary offence under section 9(*b*) of the Family Allowances Act 1945 (see *infra*). Curr appealed against his conviction at quarter sessions.

FENTON ATKINSON J.: The facts shortly were these, that he was in fact a trafficker in family allowance books. His method was to approach some married woman who had a large family of children and lend her money on the security of her family allowance book. A woman would borrow from him, let us say, £6, and would sign three of the vouchers in her family allowance book to the value of, let us say £9, and hand over the book to him as security. He then had a team of women agents whom he sent out to cash the vouchers, and he would pocket the proceeds in repayment of the loans and thereafter return the books. . . . He agreed quite frankly that he knew he was not legally entitled to receive these payments, and that it could be risky. . . .

Count 3 was of soliciting the commission of a summary offence contrary to section 9(b) of the Act of 1945. . . . Mr Kershaw's main point is this, that the offence the commission of which the defendant is said to have solicited is not an absolute statutory offence, but it is one requiring knowledge on the part of the female agent that she is doing something unlawful in receiving the allowance.

Section 9 is headed "Penalty for obtaining or receiving payment wrongfully", and provides:

"If any person—. . . (b) obtains or receives any such sum as on account of an allowance, either as in that person's own right or as on behalf of another, knowing that it was not properly payable, or not properly receivable by him or her; that person shall be liable on summary conviction to imprisonment for a term not exceeding three months or to a fine not exceeding fifty pounds . . ."

Mr Kershaw's argument was that if the woman agent in fact has no guilty knowledge, knowing perhaps nothing of the assignment, or supposing that the defendant was merely collecting for the use and benefit of the woman concerned, then she would be an innocent agent, and by using her services in that way the defendant would be committing the summary offence himself, but would not be inciting her to receive money knowing that it was not receivable by her. He contends that it was essential to prove, to support this charge, that the woman agent in question . . . knew the allowances were not properly receivable by her. [Counsel for the Crown's] answer to that submission was that the woman agent must be presumed to know the law, and if she knew the law, she must have known, he contends, that the allowance was not receivable by her. . . .

The argument is that in no other circumstances [than those set out in the book, *e.g.* during illness] may an agent lawfully collect for the use and benefit of the book holder. . . .

In our view the prosecution argument here gives no effect to the word "knowing" in section 9(b), and in our view the defendant could only be guilty on count 3 if the woman solicited, that is, the woman agent sent to collect the allowance, knew that the action she was asked to carry out amounted to an offence. . . . But the assistant recorder never [dealt] with the question of the knowledge of the woman agents, and in the whole of the summing-up dealing with this matter he proceeded on the assumption that either guilty knowledge in the woman agent was irrelevant, or, alternatively, that any woman agent must be taken to have known that she was committing an offence under section 9(b).

Appeal allowed

Notes and Questions

1. In *Curr*, above, the court said: "In our view the defendant could only be guilty [of incitement] if the woman solicited . . . knew that the action she was asked to carry out amounted to an offence." Since it is never necessary for the incited person to intend to commit the offence, is not the Court stating the wrong test? Should it not be, did Curr know that the act required of the women would be an offence by her? Would the result of the case have been different if it had fallen to be decided under the definition of incitement contained in the Draft Criminal Code, *infra*?

2. In *Shaw* [1994] Crim. L.R. 365, D encouraged a co-employee, K, to obtain cheques from the company for which they worked on the basis of bogus invoices. D alleged that he set up the scheme to disclose to his employers the defects in the company's security arrangements and thereby further his chances of promotion. He did not tell K of his purpose but claimed he would eventually have done so. D's conviction for incitement to obtain property by deception was quashed by the Court of Appeal on the basis that the jury should have been directed that if they found that D did not intend permanently to deprive the owners of the property and make a profit for himself then he should be acquitted.

Smith points out (*Commentary*, [1994] Crim. L.R. 366):

"The court has confused the mens rea of incitement with the mens rea of the offence. . . . It was necessary to show that [D] intended K to act dishonestly and with intention permanently to deprive but quite unnecessary to show that [D] had any such dishonest intention."

Do you agree?

If K had been convicted of the obtaining offence, would the honesty of D's intentions have any relevance to his guilt as a secondary party? (See Chapter 6, *ante*.) Compare the *mens rea* required in conspiracy (see

Yip Chiu-Cheung, ante, p. 477) with that now declared for incitement. If K had agreed with D to pursue the course of action D suggested, could D have been convicted of conspiracy?

In the case which follows the Divisional Court had to wrestle with the problem of the two binding Court of Appeal decisions in *Curr* and *Shaw*.

Director of Public Prosecutions v. Armstrong (Andrew)
November 5, 1999
Divisional Court

J, a police officer, received a telephone call from D who had been put in touch with him unaware of his identity, in which D asked J to supply him with child pornography. J agreed. D was arrested and charged with inciting J to distribute indecent photographs of children. In cross-examination J. indicated that through his work he had access to such material but that he had no intention of supplying D. At the end of the prosecution case D submitted successfully, *inter alia*, that there was no case to answer relying on *Curr* and *Shaw* on the basis that the person incited must have a "parity of *mens rea*" with the inciter. The prosecution appealed by way of case stated.

LORD JUSTICE TUCKEY: ... Before considering the two authorities referred to by the magistrate, it is helpful to analyse the position from first principles, free from authority. Incitement, like attempt and conspiracy, is an "auxiliary" (as Lord Diplock would have it) or "inchoate" (as the authors of text books would have it) offence. It is one of the ways in which criminal responsibility attaches to conduct short of the commission of the full offence. The *actus reus* of the offence is the incitement by the defendant of another to do something which is a criminal offence. He must do so with the intention that if the other person does as he asks he will commit a criminal offence. That is the *mens rea*. On this analysis the intention of the person incited is entirely irrelevant. It is put in *Archbold* at paragraph 33–70 as follows:

"To solicit another to commit a crime is indictable at common law, even though the solicitation or incitement is of no effect."

Blackstone refers also to the fact that the offence may be committed where the person incited flatly refuses to commit the offence.

The nature of the offence of incitement is accurately defined in the draft Criminal Code produced by the Law Commission in their paper No 177 at clause 47 which says:

"A person is guilty of incitement to commit an offence or offences if—
   (a) he incites another to do or cause to be done an act or acts which, if done, will involve the commission of the offence or offences by the other; and
   (b) he intends or believes that the other, if he acts as incited, shall or will do so with the fault required for the offence or offences."

On this analysis of the law there is no principle of parity of *mens rea* of the kind contended for by the respondent and accepted by the magistrate. Were that to be the law, then all the cases about agent provocateur would have been wrongly decided because in each such case (where often the agent provocateur is a policemen) if it were a defence to the defendant to say: "Well, the officer never intended to commit the offence which I asked him to commit", there would be no offence of incitement and many people would be in prison for committing such offences who should not be. . . .

With that analysis of the law free from authority, I turn to see whether the two cases referred to by the magistrate compel one to modify the position.

In *R. v. Shaw* . . . [t]he short report of the case in the Criminal Law Review which we have does not set out the precise terms of the charge but it is clear that it alleged that S dishonestly incited K dishonestly to obtain cheques from the company . . . . The particulars of the offence also said that he had done so with the intention of permanently depriving the company of the cheques. After the jury had been sent out they returned with a note saying that they (or some of them) were not sure whether the prosecution had established that what S had done was with a view to profit for himself. In other words, they (or some of them) were disposed to accept the defence he was running. The Court of Appeal allowed the appeal because the judge, when faced with the note, had not given the jury an adequate direction about that part of the particulars of the offence which alleged that the appellant had done what he had with the intention of permanently depriving his employers by deception. He should have told them that if they thought it possible that S was merely concerned to demonstrate the insecurity of the system the verdict should be not guilty. In a case where the principal issue was dishonesty and the jury were doubtful about whether S had been dishonest one can well understand why the Court of Appeal was concerned with how the judge had dealt with the note. There is nothing in the report which shows why K's *mens rea* was relevant. But it says:

> "Held, allowing the appeal, the jury were concerned with the proof of *mens rea* both of S and of K, since both had to be considered."

It is this sentence which enabled Mr Sharpe to make the submissions he did. It has led to much criticism which can be found in Archbold, Blackstone and in the Commentary which immediately follows in the Criminal Law Report. This Commentary says:

> "The decision seems to be misconceived. If I tell Bill Sikes, the burglar, about the poor state of security of my employer's premises and encourage him to enter and steal therein, I have surely incited him to commit burglary. I have tried to persuade him to do an act which, when done, will, as I know, be the offence of burglary. How can it possibly be said that I have not incited him to commit the offence? . . . .
>
>   The court has confused the *mens rea* of incitement with the *mens rea* of the offence incited."

There is then a reference to *R v. Sang* (1979) 69 Cr.App.R.282 in which Lord Diplock indicated in terms that if a dishonest policeman, anxious to improve his detection record, tries very hard with the help of an agent provocateur to induce a young man with no criminal record to commit a serious crime, and ultimately the young man reluctantly succumbs to the inducement, both the policeman and the informer who had acted together in inciting to commit the crime should both be prosecuted and suitably punished.

Shaw is a decision of the Court of Appeal and therefore binding on us. It can be explained on its facts in the way I have attempted to do but it can also perhaps be explained because the indictment specifically alleged that S had dishonestly incited K to dishonestly obtain. It is not in my judgment therefore general authority for the proposition that the person incited must act with the same parity of *mens rea* as the inciter.

R v. Curr (supra) is also binding on us . . . . It seems to me that all the court is saying in that case is that what the appellant was doing was something short of asking the woman concerned to commit a criminal offence. He was not inciting her to commit an offence because the offence required her knowledge that she was committing an offence. There is nothing in the judgment to suggest that the court was making any general pronouncement upon whether for the offence of incitement it is necessary to prove that not only the inciter but also the person incited had the *mens rea* to commit the full offence.

It follows from what I have said that I do not see anything in either of these two cases which compels me to conclude that the law is not as I stated it to be in the earlier part of this judgment. And it also follows that I do not think the magistrate was correct when he found that the law requires that the person incited must have parity of *mens rea* with the inciter. Applied to the facts of this case, it was not necessary for the prosecutor to show that the officer intended to supply child pornography to the respondent. His intention was irrelevant. The offence of incitement was committed when he was asked to commit the offence of supplying child pornography with the intention on the part of the respondent that in doing so he would be committing a criminal offence.

Decision of magistrate quashed.

Notes

1. The contrived basis for distinguishing *Shaw* was that the indictment alleged that D had acted dishonestly with intention of permanently depriving his employer. The flaw, accordingly, was that the indictment alleged something which it was unnecessary to prove! This seems to be more a procedural point about the drafting of indictments than about the elements of the offence of incitement. The basis for distinguishing *Curr* appears to be equally contrived. Such contrivance, however, is understandable when the Divisional Court is faced with two binding authorities which would, if followed, serve to make a nonsense of the offence of incitement. It is to be hoped that the Court of Appeal will endorse the reasoning of the Divisional Court and consign its previous decisions in *Curr* and *Shaw* to the history books.

2. In Law Com. C.P. No. 131, *Assisting and Encouraging Crime* (1993) the Law Commission propose the abolition of the distinction between the inchoate offence of incitement and secondary liability for crime based on aiding and abetting. They propose a single set of rules to cover all cases of assisting and encouraging crime (see Law Com. C.P. No. 131, chapter 4; the draft text of the new offences is reproduced *ante*, p. (416).

4. IMPOSSIBILITY IN RELATION TO INCHOATE OFFENCES

Note

This section deals with the position where what D attempts to do, or incites another to do, or conspires with another to do, is in some respects impossible. The question is, should that mean that D is not guilty as charged, even if all the other elements of attempt, incitement or conspiracy are present? It is evident that the answer, whatever it is, should not differ depending upon which inchoate offence is involved. The Draft Criminal Code, Clause 50(1) proposes, "A person may be guilty of incitement conspiracy or attempt to commit an offence, although the commission of the offence is impossible, if it would be possible in the circumstances which he believes or hopes exist or will exist at the relevant time." This does not reflect the present law, which has different answers for the various inchoate offences. This is because (1) the leading case, *Haughton v. Smith, infra*, set out the law on impossible attempts in a way which was widely regarded as unsatisfactory; (2) it was subsequently decided that that unsatisfactory law applied to the other inchoate offences also; but (3) statutory attempts to rectify the position apply only to attempts and statutory conspiracy. Common law conspiracy and incitement thus continue to be governed by the principles enunciated in *Haughton v. Smith*.

i. Attempt

Note

No one attempts to do that which he knows to be impossible (the same can be said of inciting and conspiring). Anyone who appears to do so is therefore making a mistake of some sort. The kinds of mistake possibly involved are three.

1. He mistakes the criminal law, and assumes that it prohibits what he is aiming at. Since the criminal law is not interested in his projected conduct, it follows that it will not punish him for achieving what he desires; *a fortiori* if he merely goes some way towards achieving it. The fact that he believes he is defying the law can make no difference. There has never been any liability where this kind of mistake is involved, and that is still the position. An example would be where D, knowing he has English lace, and thinking the law prohibits the import of English lace without payment of duty, attempts to avoid the payment of duty on his lace.

2. Where, because of a mistake about the facts, D believes that the factual result he wishes is possible of attainment. It is necesary to distinguish two situations, namely, inadequacy of means and absolute impossibility. The former arises where, *e.g.* D tries to kill someone with a dose of poison which is too small to kill, or tries to shoot someone out of the range of his gun, or tries to break into a safe which is too strong for the tools he uses. In these cases of "inadequate means", there may be an attempt, but the House of Lords in *Haughton v. Smith, infra* denied that it could be an attempt if what D attempted was absolutely impossible, as where the subject matter did not exist or did not exist in the form he imagined, *e.g.* where D attempted to take money from a pocket or purse which contained no money, or where D attempted to deceive a person who knew the truth and could not be deceived.

3. Where because of a mistake about the facts, D believes that the factual result he wishes is criminal, *e.g.* D wishes to smuggle in French

lace, on which he knows that duty is payable, but the lace in his possession is in fact English lace, on which no duty is payable; or D wishes to handle stolen goods, but the goods involved in his plan are not stolen. There was controversy about this class of mistake, and this handling non-stolen goods problem received different answers in cases from Commonwealth and American jurisdictions. This particular problem was involved in *Haughton v. Smith*, and the House decided that that particular mistake, and all mistakes in this class, prevented D's conduct from being an attempt.

Haughton v. Smith
[1975] A.C. 746
House of Lords

A van load of stolen meat was intercepted by the police, and allowed to continue its journey with two policemen concealed inside. S later did acts amounting to handling the meat. On the view that the goods' restoration to lawful custody meant that they were no longer stolen (see *post*, p. 852), S was not charged with handling stolen goods, but with attempting to handle stolen goods contrary to section 22, Theft Act 1968 (see *post*, p. 850). He was convicted, his appeal was allowed by the Court of Appeal, and the prosecution further appealed.

LORD HAILSHAM OF ST. MARYLEBONE, L.C.: I was at first inclined to think that section 22 of the Theft Act 1968 was drafted in such a way as to permit the construction that to be stolen for the purpose of section 22(1) it was sufficient that the goods had been stolen without continuing to be stolen at the time of the handling, provided, of course, that the accused believed them at the time of the handling to be stolen. I thought that the expression "believed" in the subsection aided the view that it could cover a state of facts where the defendant believed the goods to be stolen when they were not in fact still stolen at that moment of time. But, on consideration, I am sure that this would be a false construction, and that the expression "believed" was inserted to guard against acquittals which had taken place under the former Larceny Act when it was necessary to prove knowledge that the goods were stolen and belief was not enough. If I were not already certain that this was the true meaning of section 22(1), the provisions of section 24, and, in particular, section 24(3), would, I think, clinch the matter. In my view, it is plain that, in order to constitute the offence of handling, the goods specified in the particulars of offence must not only be believed to be stolen, but actually continue to be stolen goods at the moment of handling. Once this is accepted as the true construction of the section, I do not think that it is possible to convert a completed act of handling, which is not itself criminal because it was not the handling of stolen goods, into a criminal act by the simple device of alleging that it was an attempt to handle stolen goods on the ground that at the time of handling the accused falsely believed them still to be stolen. In my opinion, this would be for the courts to manufacture a new criminal offence not authorised by the legislature.

This would be enough to decide the result of this appeal, but both counsel invited us to take a wider view of our obligations, and, since the question was discussed by the Court of Appeal in general terms and since I believe that the result of our decision is to overrule a number of decided cases, at least to some extent, I feel bound to accede to this invitation. The question certified by the Court of Appeal was:

"If stolen goods are returned to lawful custody and thus cease to be stolen by virtue of section 24(3) of the Theft Act 1968 can a person who subsequently dishonestly handles goods believing them to be stolen be guilty of the offence of attempting to handle stolen goods?"

I have already given a negative answer to this question, but the range of the discussion before us demands a wider consideration of the principles involved. . . .

I note that in the New Zealand case of *R. v. Donnelly* [1970] N.Z.L.R. 980, which, except in so far as it relates to the construction of the relevant New Zealand statutes, is very much on all fours with this, Turner J., adopts a six-fold classification. He says, at p. 990:

"He who sets out to commit a crime may in the event fall short of the complete commission of that crime for any one of a number of reasons. *First*, he may, of course, simply change his mind before committing any act sufficiently overt to amount to an attempt. *Second*, he may change his mind, but too late to deny that he had got so far as an attempt. *Third*, he may be prevented by some outside agency from doing some act necessary to complete commission of the crime—as when a police officer interrupts him while he is endeavouring to force the window open, but before he has broken into the premises. *Fourth*, he may suffer no such outside interference, but may fail to complete the commission of the crime through ineptitude, inefficiency or insufficient means. The jemmy which he has brought with him may not be strong enough to force the window open. *Fifth*, he may find that what he is proposing to do is after all impossible—not because of insufficiency of means, but because it is for some reason physically not possible, whatever means be adopted. He who walks into a room intending to steal, say a specific diamond ring, and finds that the ring is no longer there, but has been removed by the owner to the bank, is thus prevented from committing the crime which he intended, and which, but for the supervening physical impossibility imposed by events he would have committed. *Sixth*, he may without interruption efficiently do every act which he set out to do, but may be saved from criminal liability by the fact that what he has done, contrary to his own belief at the time, does not after all amount in law to a crime."

. . . Applying the three principles derived from my primary definitions, I would seek to obtain the following results. (1) In the first case no criminal attempt is committed. At the relevant time there was no *mens rea* since there had been a change of intention, and the only overt acts relied on would be preparatory and not immediately connected with the completed offence. (2) In the second case there is both *mens rea* and an act connected immediately with the offence. An example would be an attempted rape where the intended victim was criminally assaulted, but the attacker desisted at the stage immediately before he had achieved penetration. It follows that there is a criminal attempt. (3) The third case is more difficult because, as a matter of fact and degree, it will depend to some extent on the stage at which the interruption takes place, and the precise offence the attempt to commit which is the subject of the charge. In general, however, a criminal attempt is committed, assuming that the proximity test is passed. (4) In the fourth case there is ample authority for the proposition that, assuming the proximity test is passed, a criminal attempt is committed. But here casuistry is possible. Examples were given in argument of shots at an intended victim which fail because he is just out of range, or because, as in the case of the well known popular novel, *The Day of the*

Jackal, the intended victim moves at the critical moment, or when a dose of poison insufficient to kill is administered with intent to murder. In all these cases the attempt is clearly criminal. (5) The fifth case is more complicated. It is clear that an attempt to obtain money by a false pretence which is not in fact believed, is criminal notwithstanding that the consequences intended were not achieved: see *R. v. Hensler* (1870) 11 Cox C.C. 570. The same would be true of an attempted murder when the victim did not actually die for whatever reason. But I do not regard these as true, or at least not as typical, examples of the fifth class. They belong rather to the fourth, since the criminal had done all that he intended to do, and all that was necessary to complete the crime was an act or event wholly outside his control. *R. v. M'Pherson* (1857) Dears. & B. 197 where the conviction was quashed, may be regarded as simply a case where a man was charged with one thing and convicted of another. But both the facts and the reasoning of the judges are much closer to the example postulated by Turner J. in *R. v. Donnelly* as typical of the fifth class, though Turner J.'s own opinion to the effect that the attempt is criminal depends on the terms of the New Zealand statute and has no application to English law. In *R. v. M'Pherson* the reasoning of the English judges on English law was to the contrary. Cockburn C.J. said, at p. 201:

"Here the prisoner had the *intention* to steal before he went into the house; but when he got there the goods specified in the indictment were not there; how then could he *attempt* to steal those goods? There can be no attempt asportare unless there is something asportare."

Bramwell B., anticipating the decisions in *R. v. Collins* (1864) 9 Cox C.C. 497, said, at p. 201:

"The argument that a man putting his hand into an empty pocket might be convicted of attempting to steal, appeared to me at first plausible; but suppose a man, believing a block of wood to be a man who was his deadly enemy, struck it a blow intending to murder, could he be convicted of attempting to murder the man he took it to be?"

And, in giving judgment, Cockburn C.J. said, at p. 202:

"The word attempt clearly conveys with it the idea, that if the attempt had succeeded the offence charged would have been committed, and therefore the prisoner might have been convicted if the things mentioned in the indictment or any of them had been there; but attempting to commit a felony is clearly distinguishable from intending to commit it. An attempt must be to do that which, if successful, would amount to the felony charged; but here the attempt never could have succeeded, as the things which the indictment charges the prisoner with stealing had already been removed—stolen by somebody else."

And Bramwell B. was equally emphatic.

Clearly Cockburn C.J. and Bramwell B. were of the view that Turner J.'s example of his fifth class of inchoate act was not a criminal attempt. *R. v. M'Pherson*, was followed in *R. v. Collins*, by a court which also included Cockburn C.J. and Bramwell B. and was the identical case postulated by Bramwell B. in the earlier case of a man putting his hand into an empty pocket. . . .

It was not long, however, before the decision in *R. v. Collins* was challenged by Lord Coleridge C.J. in *R. v. Brown* (1889) 24 Q.B.D. 357, 359 as "no longer law", but without giving reasons and in *R. v. Ring* (1892) 17 Cox C.C. 491, 492 (an early "mugging" case on the Metropolitan Railway) with even greater emphasis and even fewer reasons. Since then *R. v. Collins* has generally been held to be bad law. On this I express no concluded opinion, but in general I regard the reasoning in *R. v. M'Pherson* and *R. v. Collins* as sound and in general I would consider that "attempts" in Turner J.'s fifth class of case are not indictable in English law, and I consider that the purported overruling of *R. v. Collins* needs further consideration. In addition to the reported cases, we postulated in argument a number of real and imaginary instances of this class. In *The Empty Room*, Sherlock Holmes' enemy, Colonel Maron, was induced to fire at a wax image of the detective silhouetted in the window, though Holmes prudently rejected Inspector Lestrade's advice to prefer a charge of attempted murder and so the matter was never tested; in *R. v. White* [1910] 2 K.B. 124, a man who put a small quantity of cyanide in a wine glass, too small to kill, was held guilty of attempted murder. This was an example of the fourth of Turner J.'s cases and therefore criminal. But *quaere*, what would have been the position if the glass administered had contained pure water, even though the accused believed falsely that it contained cyanide? We discussed the situation when a would-be murderer attempts to assassinate a corpse, or a bolster in a bed, believing it to be the living body of his enemy, or when he fires into an empty room believing that it contained an intended victim; and we had our attention drawn to an American case where the accused fired at a peephole in a roof believed to be in use by a watching policeman who was in fact a few yards away. In most of these cases, a statutory offence of some kind (*e.g.* discharging a fire-arm with intent to endanger life) would be committed in English law, but in general I would think that a charge of an attempt to commit the common law offence of murder would not lie since, if the contemplated sequence of actions had been completed (as in some of the supposed instances they were) no substantive offence could have been committed of the type corres-ponding to the charge of attempt supposed to be laid. I get some support for this view from the summing up of Rowlatt J. in R. v. *Osborn* (1919) 84 J.P. 63. But I prefer to rest on the principle above stated, since *Osborn* was couched in more popular language than is appropriate to what has become a some-what theoretical discussion. At the end of the day there must be a question of fact for the jury. The judge may direct them what facts, if established, could constitute an attempt, or would be evidence of an attempt. The jury alone can decide whether there was an attempt.

(6) Turner J.'s sixth class of case was where a man efficiently does "without interruption every act which he set out to do, but may be saved from criminal liability by the fact that what he has done, contrary to his own belief at the time, does not after all amount to a crime." . . . I have already explained that I consider that the present appeal fails on the proper construction of section 22 of the Theft Act 1968. But I think that this is a special example of a wider principle, and I agree with Turner J.'s conclusion about it.

"Suppose a man takes away an umbrella from a stand with intent to steal it, believing it not to be his own, but it turns out to be his own, could he be convicted of attempting to steal?"

In *R. v. Villensky* [1892] 2 Q.B. 597 Lord Coleridge C.J. in circumstances not unlike the present, following *R. v. Dolan* (1855) Dears. C.C. 436, held that prisoners could [not] be indicted under the old law for receiving stolen goods, and made no reference to the possibility of a conviction for attempt.

In *R. v. Williams* [1893] 1 Q.B. 320, 321, the same Lord Chief Justice said that a boy below the age at which he could be properly indicted for rape could not be convicted on the same facts for an attempt. I do not agree with the contrary opinion of Hawkins J. in the same case, even though it was possibly supported by the rest of the court. The same reasoning would apply to a case of unlawful carnal knowledge (cf. *R. v. Waite* [1892] 2 Q.B. 600), whether, as there, it was the male who was by reason of age incapable in law of committing the offence, or the female who was in law incapable by reason of her age of having it committed against her, and it would not, in my view, matter in the latter case that the male falsely believed her to be under age. Support for his view is to be found in *D.P.P. v. Head* [1959] A.C. 83, which was a charge of a completed offence in relation to a mental defective, but counsel for the respondent made considerable play with the argument *a silentio* to be derived from the fact that no one suggested the possibility of a conviction for an attempt. In my view, it is a general principle that Turner J.'s sixth class of attempts are not criminal, not because the acts are not proximate or because the intention is absent, but because the second of the three propositions I derive from the two judicial definitions I cited above is not satisfied. The acts are not part of a series "which would constitute the actual commission of the offence if it were not interrupted." In this event the often discussed question whether the legal impossibility derives from a mistake of fact or law on the part of the accused is hardly relevant.

This discussion enables me to deal with the cases cited in the judgment of the Court of Appeal. Like Lord Widgery C.J., I disagree with the decision in *People v. Rojas* (1961) 10 Cal.Rptr. 465 and prefer the decisions in *R. v. Donnelly* [1970] N.Z.L.R. 980 and *People v. Jaffe* (1960) 185 N.Y. 496 (overruling the decisions in the lower courts, *cf.* (1906) 98 N.Y.S. 406). I agree with the decision in *R. v. Percy Dalton (London) Ltd* (1984) 33 Cr.App.R. 102, and particularly with the quotation from Birkett J. cited by Lord Widgery C.J. in the present case, where he said, at p. 110:

> "Steps on the way to the commission of what would be a crime, if the acts were completed, may amount to attempts to commit that crime, to which, unless interrupted, they would have led; but steps on the way to the doing of something, which is thereafter done, and which is no crime, cannot be regarded as attempts to commit a crime."

I would add to the last sentence a rider to the effect that equally steps on the way to do something which is thereafter *not* completed, but which if done would not constitute a crime cannot be indicted as attempts to commit that crime. It is, of course, true that, at least in theory, some villains will escape by this route. But in most cases they can properly be charged with something else—statutory offences like breaking and entering with intent etc., or loitering with intent etc., using an instrument with intent etc., discharging or possessing a firearm with intent etc., or as here, common law offences like conspiring to commit the same offence as that the attempt to commit which is charged, or even committing a substantive offence of a different kind, as here, stealing or attempting to steal.

[Lord Reid, Lord Morris and Viscount Dilhorne delivered speeches dismissing the appeal; Lord Salmon agreed with Lord Hailsham.]

Appeal dismissed

Notes

1. The Law Commission criticised the ratio of *Haughton v. Smith*.

Law. Com. No. 102

§ 2.96: We think it would be generally accepted that if a man possesses the appropriate *mens rea* and commits acts which are sufficiently proximate to the *actus reus* of a criminal offence, he is guilty of attempting to commit that offence. Where, with that intention, he commits acts which, if the facts were as he believed them to be, would have amounted to the *actus reus* of the full crime or would have been sufficiently proximate to amount to an attempt, we cannot see why this failure to appreciate the true facts should, in principle, relieve him of liability for the attempt. We stress that this solution to the problem does not punish people simply for their intentions. The necessity for proof of proximate acts remains.

2. As to the differences between "inadequate means" and absolute impossibility, one of its criticisms centred on the very fine distinctions it required the Court to draw.

Law. Com. No. 102

§ 2.64: In *R. v. Farrance* (1977) 67 Cr.App.R. 136, the defendant had been convicted of attempting to drive when he had a blood alcohol concentration above the prescribed limit contrary to section 6(1) of the Road Traffic Act 1972. The facts were that the clutch of his car had burnt out, so that although the defendant could operate the engine he could not drive the car. The Court of Appeal upheld the conviction on the grounds that a burnt out clutch was only an impediment to the commission of a crime, similar to the inadequate burglar's tool or the would-be poisoner's insufficient dose. It is not clear what the court's answer would have been if the car had had no petrol or if its transmission had completely seized up.

3. The Commission's proposals for rectifying the position were amended during the passage of the Act, and eventually emerged as section 1(2) and (3), *ante*, p. 444. In *Anderton v. Ryan* [1985] A.C. 560, the House of Lords held that the statutory wording had not affected the *ratio* of *Haughton v. Smith*, which was still of authority. However the House speedily reconsidered this position. See *infra*.

R. v. Shivpuri
[1987] A.C. 1.
House of Lords

D was arrested in possession of a suitcase which he believed contained heroin or cannabis. Subsequently the substance in the suitcase was analysed and found to be harmless vegetable matter. D was convicted under s. 1(1) of the Criminal Attempts Act 1981 of attempting to be knowingly concerned in dealing with and in harbouring prohibited drugs contrary to s. 170(1)(b) of the Customs and Excise Management Act 1979. The Court of Appeal dismissed his appeal but certified the following point of law of general public importance:

"Does a person commit an offence under Section 1, Criminal Attempts Act, 1981, where, if the facts were as at that person believed them to be, the full offence would have been committed by him, but where on the true facts the offence which that person set out to commit was in law impossible, *e.g.* because the substance imported and believed to be heroin was not heroin but a harmless substance?"

LORD BRIDGE OF HARWICH: . . .

The certified question depends on the true construction of the Criminal Attempts Act 1981. The Act marked an important new departure since, by section 6, it abolished the offence of attempt at common law and substituted a new statutory code governing attempts to commit criminal offences. It was considered by your Lordships' House last year in *Anderton v. Ryan* after the decision in the Court of Appeal which is the subject of the present appeal. . . .

(After reading section 1, *ante*, p. 444). Applying this language to the facts of the case, the first question to be asked is whether the appellant intended to commit the offences of being knowingly concerned in dealing with and harbouring drugs of class A or class B with intent to evade the prohibition on their importation. Translated into more homely language the question may be rephrased, without in any way altering the legal significance, in the following terms: did the appellant intend to receive and store (harbour) and in due course pass on to third parties (deal with) packages of heroin or cannabis which he knew had been smuggled into England from India? The answer is plainly Yes, he did. Next, did he, in relation to each offence, do an act which was more than merely preparatory to the commission of the offence? The act relied on in relation to harbouring was the receipt and retention of the packages found in the lining of the suitcase. The act relied on in relation to dealing was the meeting at Southall station with the intended recipient of one of the packages. In each case the act was clearly more than preparatory to the commission of the *intended* offence; it was not and could not be more than merely preparatory to the commission of the *actual* offence, because the facts were such that the commission of the actual offence was impossible. Here then is the nub of the matter. Does the "act which is more than merely preparatory to the commission of the offence" in section 1(1) of the 1981 Act (the *actus reus* of the statutory offence of attempt) require any more than an act which is more than merely preparatory to the commission of the offence which the defendant intended to commit? Section 1(2) must surely indicate a negative answer; if it were otherwise, whenever the facts were such that the commission of the actual offence was impossible, it would be impossible to prove an act more than merely preparatory to the commission of that offence and subsections (1) and (2) would contradict each other.

This very simple, perhaps over-simple, analysis leads me to the provisional conclusion that the appellant was rightly convicted of the two offences of attempt with which he was charged. But can this conclusion stand with *Anderton v. Ryan*? The appellant in that case was charged with an attempt to handle stolen goods. She bought a video recorder believing it to be stolen. On the facts as they were to be assumed it was not stolen. By a majority the House decided that she was entitled to be acquitted. I have re-examined the case with care. If I could extract from the speech of Lord Roskill or from my own speech a clear and coherent principle distinguishing those cases of attempting the impossible which amount to offences under the statute from those which do not, I should have to consider carefully on which side of the line the instant case fell. But I have to confess that I can find no such principle.

Running through Lord Roskill's speech and my own in *Anderton v. Ryan* is the concept of "objectively innocent" acts which, in my speech certainly, are contrasted with "guilty acts". A few citations will make this clear. Lord Roskill said [1985] A.C. 560 at 580):

"My Lords, it has been strenuously and ably argued for the respondent that these provisions involve that a defendant is liable to conviction for an attempt even where his actions are innocent but he erroneously believes facts which, if true, would make those actions criminal, and further, that he is liable to such conviction whether or not in the event his intended course of action is completed."

He proceeded to reject the argument. I referred to the appellant's purchase of the video recorder and said [1985] A.C. 560 at 582): "Objectively considered, therefore, her purchase of the recorder was a perfectly proper commercial transaction."

A further passage from my speech stated [1985] A.C. 560 at 582–583):

"The question may be stated in abstract terms as follows. Does s.1 of the 1981 Act create a new offence of attempt where a person embarks on and completes a course of conduct, which is objectively innocent, solely on the ground that the person mistakenly believes facts which, if true, would make the course of conduct a complete crime? If the question may be answered affirmatively it requires convictions in a number of surprising cases: the classic case, put by Bramwell B. in *R. v. Collins* (1864) 9 Cox C.C. 497 at 498, of the man who takes away his own umbrella from a stand, believing it not to be his own and with intent to steal it; the case of the man who has consensual intercourse with a girl over 16 believing her to be under that age; the case of the art dealer who sells a picture which he represents to be and which is in fact a genuine Picasso, but which the dealer mistakenly believes to be a fake. The common feature of all these cases, including that under appeal, is that the mind alone is guilty, the act is innocent."

I then contrasted the case of the man who attempts to pick the empty pocket, saying [1985] A.C. 560 at 583):

"Putting the hand in the pocket is the guilty act, the intent to steal is the guilty mind, the offence is appropriately dealt with as an attempt, and the impossibility of committing the full offence for want of anything in the pocket to steal is declared by [subs. (2)] to be no obstacle to conviction."

If we fell into error, it is clear that our concern was to avoid convictions in situations which most people, as a matter of common sense, would not regard as involving criminality. In this connection it is to be regretted that we did not take due note of para. 2.97 of the Law Commission Report, Criminal Law: Attempt and Impossibility in Relation to Attempt, Conspiracy and Incitement (1980) (Law Com. No. 102) which preceded the enactment of the 1981 Act, which reads:

"If it is right in principle that an attempt should be chargeable even though the crime which it is sought to commit could not possibly be committed, we do not think that we should be deterred by the consideration that such a change in our law would also cover some extreme and exceptional cases in which a prosecution would be theoretically possible. An example would be where a person is offered goods at such a low price that he believes that they are stolen, when in fact they are not; if he actually purchases them, upon the principles which we have discussed he would be liable for an attempt to handle stolen goods. Another case which has been much debated is that raised in argument by Bramwell B. in *R. v. Collins*. If A takes his own umbrella, mistaking it for one belonging to B and intending to steal B's umbrella, is he guilty of attempted theft? Again, on the principles which we have discussed he would in theory be guilty, but in neither case would it be realistic to suppose that a complaint would be made or that a prosecution would ensue."

The prosecution in *Anderton v. Ryan* itself falsified the Commission's prognosis in one of the "extreme and exceptional cases." It nevertheless probably holds good for other such cases, particularly that of the young man having sexual intercourse with a girl over 16, mistakenly believing her to be under that age, by which both Lord Roskill and I were much troubled.

However that may be, the distinction between acts which are "objectively innocent" and those which are not is an essential element in the reasoning in *Anderton v. Ryan* and the decision, unless it can be supported on some other ground, must stand or fall by the validity of this distinction. I am satisfied on further consideration that the concept of "objective innocence" is incapable of sensible application in relation to the law of criminal attempts. The reason for this is that any attempt to commit an offence which involves "an act which is more than merely preparatory to the commission of the offence" but which for any reason fails, so that in the event no offence is committed, must *ex hypothesi*, from the point of view of the criminal law, be "objectively innocent". What turns what would otherwise, from the point of view of the criminal law, be an innocent act into a crime is the intent of the actor to commit an offence. I say "from the point of view of the criminal law" because the law of tort must surely here be quite irrelevant. A puts his hand into B's pocket. Whether or not there is anything in the pocket capable of being stolen, if A intends to steal his act is a criminal attempt; if he does not so intend his act is innocent. A plunges a knife into a bolster in a bed. To avoid the complication of an offence of criminal damage, assume it to be A's bolster. If A believes the bolster to be his enemy B and intends to kill him, his act is an attempt to murder B; if he knows the bolster is only a bolster, his act is innocent. These considerations lead me to the conclusion that the distinction sought to be drawn in *Anderton v. Ryan* between innocent and guilty acts considered "objectively" and independently of the state of mind of the actor cannot be sensibly maintained. . . .

I am thus led to the conclusion that there is no valid ground on which *Anderton v. Ryan* can be distinguished. I have made clear my own conviction, which as a party to the decision (and craving the indulgence of my noble and learned friends who agreed in it) I am the readier to express, that the decision was wrong. What then is to be done? If the case is indistinguishable, the application of the strict doctrine of precedent would require that the present appeal be allowed. Is it permissible to depart from precedent under the 1966 Practice Statement *Note* notwithstanding the especial need for certainty in the criminal law? The following considerations lead me to answer the question affirmatively. Firstly, I am undeterred by the consideration that the decision in *Anderton v. Ryan* was so recent. The 1966 Practice Statement is an effective abandonment of our prevention to infallibility. If a serious error embodied in a decision of this House has distorted the law, the sooner it is corrected the better. Secondly, I cannot see how, in the very nature of the case, anyone could have acted in reliance on the law as propounded in *Anderton v. Ryan* in the belief that he was acting innocently and now find that, after all, he is to be held to have committed a criminal offence. Thirdly, to hold the House bound to follow *Anderton v. Ryan* because it cannot be distinguished and to allow the appeal in this case would, it seems to me, be tantamount to a declaration that the 1981 Act left the law of criminal attempts unchanged following the decision in *Haughton v. Smith*. Finally, if, contrary to my present view, there is a valid ground on which it would be proper to distinguish cases similar to that considered in *Anderton v. Ryan*, my present opinion on that point would not foreclose . . . the option of making such a distinction in some future case. . . .

I would answer the certified question in the affirmative and dismiss the appeal.

Appeal dismissed

Note

Although the whole House agreed with Lord Bridge's speech over-ruling *Anderton v. Ryan* (and therefore that Mrs. Ryan was guilty of attempted handling), Lord Hailsham, with Lord Elwyn-Jones and Lord Mackay, also held that *Anderton v. Ryan* was distinguishable on the ground that the sole intent of Shivpuri was to evade the prohibition on the import of drugs, whereas "the only intention of Mrs. Ryan was to buy a particular video cassette recorder at a knock-down price and the fact that she believed it to be stolen formed no part of that intention" (*per* Lord Hailsham, at p. 337).

It is misleading to describe her intention to buy this particular recorder at a low price as "her only intention", and to say that the fact that she believed it to be stolen was "no part of that intention". A crime is committed intentionally if the forbidden result is *desired* and the circumstances making it forbidden are *known* to the actor. (See Chap. 3.) If the recorder had been stolen, her intention to buy that object knowing it to be stolen would be an intention to handle stolen goods. Section 1(3) provides that, since that would be her intention on the facts as she thinks them to be, it is her intention on the facts as they are.

But in any event section 1(3) is redundant. Intention is a state of mind which does not depend on the facts as they are. Otherwise, as has been pointed out by J. C. Smith [1986] Crim.L.R. 540, as often as the facts change, the defendant's intention will change even though he is unaware of the changes in the facts. His intention cannot be affected by situational changes of which he is unaware. If D intends to handle goods, which are, as he knows, stolen, he intends to handle stolen goods, and it cannot be said that that *intention* is no longer there if, unknown to him, they have ceased to exist as stolen goods.

On the difficulties involved in Lord Hailsham's suggested distinction, see J. C. Smith [1986] Crim.L.R. 539–541.

ii. Conspiracy

Note

In *D.P.P. v. Nock* [1978] A.C. 979, the defendants agreed to extract cocaine from a substance which, unknown to them, contained none. It was held by the House of Lords that "logic and justice seem to require that the question as to the effect of the impossibility of the substantive offence should be answered in the same way, whether the crime charged be conspiracy or attempt" (*per* Lord Scarman, at p. 997). The principles of *Haughton v. Smith, ante*, p. 499, therefore applied and since the result agreed on by the defendants—extraction of cocaine—was absolutely impossible, their agreement was not punishable.

So far as concerns statutory conspiracies, section 1(1) of the Criminal Law Act 1977 (*ante*, p. 471) includes in the definition of conspiracy an agreement which would amount to or involve the commission of an offence but for the existence of facts which render the commission of the offence impossible. However common law conspiracies are unaffected by the section, and are still governed by *D.P.P. v. Nock* and, presumably, the principles laid down in *Haughton v. Smith*.

iii. Incitement

R. v. Fitzmaurice
[1983] Q.B. 1083
Court of Appeal

X asked A to find someone to rob a woman on a certain day while walking between her place of work and a bank by snatching wages from her. A agreed and recruited B, C & D to do the job. Unknown to any of them, the proposed robbery of the woman was a complete fiction, invented by X. His plan was to obtain a reward by telling the police of a raid on a security van calling at the bank at the time of B, C & D's planned raid. B, C & D were arrested by the police under the impression that they were lying in wait for the security van. A was convicted of inciting B, C & D to commit robbery by robbing a woman at Bow. He appealed on the ground, *inter alia*, that he could not be guilty of inciting B, C & D to commit a crime which could not be committed.

NEILL., delivering the judgment of the Court: Incitement is one of three inchoate offences, incitement, conspiracy and attempt. Mr Cocks argued that there was no logical basis for treating the three offences differently when considering their application in circumstances where the complete offence would be impossible to commit, and that therefore the court should apply the principles laid down by the House of Lords in the case of attempts in *Haughton v. Smith* and in the case of conspiracy in *D.P.P. v. Nock*.

Mr Cocks pointed to the fact that though the law as laid down by the House of Lords in those two cases had been altered by statute by section 1(2) and section 5(1) of the Criminal Attempts Act 1981, there had been no change in the law relating to the offence of incitement. Accordingly, he said, the common law rules as to impossibility should be applied.

It is to be observed that the omission of the crime of incitement from the Criminal Attempts Act 1981 followed the recommendations of the Law Commission in their report (1980) Law Com. No. 102 and was in accordance with the draft Bill set out in appendix A to that report. The Law Commission explained the omission of incitement from the draft Bill on the basis that in their view the House of Lords in *D.P.P. v. Nock* was prepared to distinguish the law relating to incitement from that relating to attempts: see paragraphs 4.2 to 4.4. We have had to give careful attention to these paragraphs in the Law Commission's Report. We have also had to consider with care the passage in the speech of Lord Scarman in *D.P.P. v. Nock* [1978] A.C. 979 which appears to have formed the basis for the decision by the Law Commission to exclude incitement from their recommendations for change and from their draft Bill. In *D.P.P. v. Nock* Lord Scarman made reference to two cases which had been cited to their Lordships. He said, at p. 999:

"Our attention was also drawn in two cases, upon which it may be helpful to comment very briefly. In *R. v. McDonough* (1962) 47 Cr.App.R. 37 the Court of Criminal Appeal held that an incitement to receive stolen goods was complete on the making of the incitement even though there were no stolen goods—perhaps even, no goods at all. In *Haggard v. Mason* [1976] 1 W.L.R. 186 the Divisional Court held that the offence of offering to supply a controlled drug was committed, even though the drug in fact supplied was not a controlled drug. Neither of these cases infringes the principle of *Haughton v. Smith*: for in each case, as Lord Widgery C.J. pointed out in *Haggard v. Mason* (p. 189), the offence was complete. In *McDonough* (1962) 47 Cr.App.R. 37 the *actus reus* was the making of the incitement and in *Haggard's* case it was the making of the offer."

We have come to the conclusion that, on analysis, this passage in Lord Scarman's speech does not support the proposition that cases of incitement are to be treated quite differently at common law from cases of attempt or conspiracy.

The decision in *Haggard v. Mason* related to the statutory offence of offering to supply a controlled drug and, as Lord Scarman pointed out, the *actus reus* which the prosecution had to prove was the making of the offer. The explanation of *McDonough's* case, as it seems to us, is that though there may have been no stolen goods or no goods at all which were available to be received at the time of the incitement, the offence of incitement to receive stolen goods could nevertheless be proved because it was not impossible that at the relevant time in the future the necessary goods would be there.

In our view, therefore, the right approach in a case of incitement is the same as that which was underlined by Lord Scarman in *D.P.P. v. Nock* when he considered the offence of conspiracy. In every case it is necessary to analyse the evidence with care to decide the precise offence which the defendant is alleged to have incited. Lord Scarman said, at p. 995:

"The indictment makes plain that the Crown is alleging in this case a conspiracy to commit a crime: and no one has suggested that the particulars fail to disclose an offence known to the law. But the appellants submit, and it is not disputed by the Crown, that the agreement as proved was narrower in scope than the conspiracy charged. When the case was before the Court of Appeal, counsel on both sides agreed that the evidence went to prove that the appellants agreed together to obtain cocaine by separating it from the other substance or substances contained in a powder which they had obtained from one of their co-defendants, a Mr Mitchell. They believed that the powder was a mixture of cocaine and lignocaine, and that they would be able to produce cocaine from it. In fact the powder was lignocaine hydrochloride, an anaesthetic used in dentistry, which contains no cocaine at all. It is impossible to produce, by separation or otherwise, cocaine from lignocaine. . . .

"The trial judge in his direction to the jury, and the Court of Appeal in their judgment dismissing the two appeals, treated this impossibility as an irrelevance. In their view the agreement was what mattered: and there was plain evidence of an agreement to produce cocaine, even though unknown to the two conspirators it could not be done. Neither the trial judge nor the Court of Appeal thought it necessary to carry their analysis of the agreement further. The trial judge described it simply as an agreement to produce cocaine. The Court of Appeal thought it enough that the prosecution had proved 'an agreement to do an act which was forbidden by section 4 of the Misuse of Drugs Act 1971.' Both descriptions are accurate, as far as they go. But neither contains any reference to the limited nature of the agreement proved: it was an agreement upon a specific course of conduct with the object of producing cocaine, and limited to that course of conduct. Since it could not result in the production of cocaine, the two appellants by pursuing it could not commit the statutory offence of producing a controlled drug."

In our view these words suggest the correct approach at common law to any inchoate offence. It is necessary in every case to decide on the evidence what was the course of conduct which was (as the case may be) incited or agreed or attempted. In some cases the evidence may establish that the persuasion by the inciter was in quite general terms whereas the subsequent agreement of the conspirators was directed to a specific crime and a specific target. In such cases where the committal of the specific offence is shown to be impossible it may be quite logical for the inciter to be convicted even though the alleged conspirators (if not caught by section 5 of the Criminal Attempts Act 1981) may be acquitted. On the other hand, if B and C agree to kill D and A, standing beside B and C, though not intending to take any active part whatever in the crime, encourages them to do so, we can see no satisfactory reason, if it turns out later that D was already dead, why A should be convicted of incitement to murder whereas B and C at common law would be entitled to an acquittal on a charge of conspiracy. The crucial question is to establish on the evidence the course of conduct which the alleged inciter was encouraging.

We return to the facts of the instant case. Mr. Cocks submitted that the "crime" which Bonham and the two Browns were being encouraged to commit was a mere charade. The appellant's father was not planning a real robbery at all and therefore the appellant could not be found guilty of inciting the three men to commit it. In our judgement, however, the answer to Mr. Cocks's argument is to be found in the facts which the prosecution proved against the appellant. As was made clear by Mr. Purnell on behalf of the Crown, the case against the appellant was based on the steps he took to recruit Bonham. At the stage the appellant believed that there was to be a wage snatch and he was encouraging Bonham to take part in it. As Mr. Purnell put it, "The appellant thought he was recruiting for a robbery not for a charade." It is to be remembered that the particulars of offence in the indictment included the words "by robbing a woman at Bow." By no stretch of the imagination was that an impossible offence to carry out and it was that offence which the appellant was inciting Bonham to commit.

For these reasons, therefore, we are satisfied that the appellant was rightly convicted. The appeal is dismissed.

Appeal dismissed.

Questions

1. "The appellant (A) thought he was recruiting for a robbery not a charade." Could X have been convicted of inciting A to commit robbery by robbing a woman at Bow?

2. A incites B to handle goods which they both think are stolen. In fact they have already been recaptured by the police, and are no longer stolen goods. Is A guilty of inciting B to handle stolen goods?

Law Com. C.P. No. 131, Assisting and Encouraging Crime (1993)

4.175 Much depends, in the present law of incitement, on the specificity with which the principal crime is envisaged, and on whether that crime is truly impossible. Thus, the conviction in *McDonough* was explained in *Fitzmaurice* on the grounds that "though there may have been no stolen goods or no goods at all which were available to be received at the time of the incitement, the offence of incitement to receive stolen goods could nevertheless be proved because it was not impossible that at the relevant time in the future the necessary goods would be there"; and in *Fitzmaurice* itself the principle that the Court of Appeal recognised did not lead to an acquittal because, although the robbery that D incited P to take part in was (unknown to D) a charade, and never intended to take place, it was not *impossible* for such a robbery to have occurred.

4.176 Such fine distinctions indicate the difficulty of applying the *Fitzmaurice* rule. More fundamentally, however, we question whether the rule is sound as a matter of principle. The same rule, as applied in the case of attempt and of conspiracy, has been reversed by statute; and it seems likely that a similar step would have been taken in respect of incitement but for a mistaken belief that the common law principle enunciated in *D.P.P. v Nock* did not extend to that crime. The rationale of these legislative interventions was that the justification for the existence of inchoate offences lies in the anti-social and criminal intentions or inclinations of the secondary party, which he carries into action; and those intentions are none the less culpable because they are based on mistaken beliefs about the relevant facts. Similarly, the offence of assisting crime is based on the defendant's knowledge or belief that what he does will assist in the commission of a crime; and the offence of encouraging crime on the defendant's intention that a crime should be committed by others. While we invite comment on this point, as at present advised we see no reason why, if the defendant fulfils those requirements, he should escape liability because the commission of that crime is, unknown to him, impossible.

HOMICIDE

Note

The true homicides are murder, manslaughter, infanticide, and causing death by driving (as to the latter see *post*, pp. 471–472). Suicide was an offence until the Suicide Act 1961; some aspects of the crime still remain. Child destruction is a near-homicide which is always dealt with as a homicide. Abortion, similarly, approximates to homicide and is best dealt with in this section.

1. THE ACTUS REUS OF HOMICIDE

Note

The common element in homicides is the *actus reus*, expressed by Coke as follows:

"Unlawfully killing a reasonable person who is in being and under the King's Peace, the death following within a year and a day" Coke, 3 Inst. 47.

The rule that death must occur within a year and a day became increasingly anachronistic. With the development of medical knowledge it is now possible to determine the cause of a person's death even though it may occur a long time after the original injury was inflicted by the defendant. In addition the use of life-support machines in hospitals has meant that patients who may otherwise have died relatively quickly may be kept alive for a considerable length of time in the hope of recovery. In such a case, however, a prosecution for homicide would be precluded if death occurred more than a year and a day after the act which caused it. The Criminal Law Revision Committe's Fourteenth Report on Offences Against the Person (Cmnd. 7844, 1980) suggested that "it would be wrong for a person to remain almost indefinitely at risk of prosecution for murder. A line has to be drawn somewhere and in our opinion the present law operates satisfactorily" (section 39). In its Consultation Paper No. 136, *The Year and a Day Rule in Homicide* (HMSO, 1994) the Law Commission carried out a review of the rule highlighting both the advantages and disadvantages of its retention. The Law Commission recommended its abolition in its report, Law Com. No. 230, *Legislating the Criminal Code: The Year and a Day Rule in Homicide* (HMSO, 1995). Parliament acted promptly in response to its recommendations and the Law Reform (Year and a Day Rule) Act 1996 was passed into law on 17 June 1996. To safeguard against oppressive prosecutions brought several years after the original act causing death was performed, or after the perpetrator has already been convicted of a non-fatal offence in respect of the same incident, the consent of Attorney-General to a prosecution is required in certain circumstances (see s.2).

Law Reform (Year and a Day Rule) Act 1996

Abolition of "year and a day rule"

1. The rule known as the "year and a day rule" (that is, the rule that, for the purposes of offences involving death and of suicide, an act or omission is conclusively presumed not to have caused a person's death if more than a year and a day elapsed before he died) is abolished for all purposes.

Restriction on institution of proceedings for a fatal offence

2. (1) Proceedings to which this section applies may only be instituted by or with the consent of the Attorney General.

(2) This section applies to proceedings against a person for a fatal offence if—

(a) the injury alleged to have caused the death was sustained more than three years before the death occurred, or
(b) the person has previously been convicted of an offence committed in circumstances alleged to be connected with the death.

(3) In subsection (2) "fatal offence" means—

(a) murder, manslaughter, infanticide or any other offence of which one of the elements is causing a person's death, or
(b) the offence of aiding, abetting, counselling or procuring a person's suicide.

(4) No provision that proceedings may be instituted only by or with the consent of the Director of Public Prosecutions shall apply to proceedings to which this section applies.

Short title, commencement and extent

3. (1) This Act may be cited as the Law Reform (Year and a Day Rule) Act 1996.
(2) Section 1 does not affect the continued application of the rule referred to in that section to a case where the act or omission (or the last of the acts or omissions) which caused the death occurred before the day on which this Act is passed.

(3) Section 2 does not come into force until the end of the period of two months beginning with the day on which this Act is passed; but that section applies to the institution of proceedings after the end of that period in any case where the death occurred during that period (as well as in any case where the death occurred after the end of that period).
(4) This Act extends to England and Wales and Northern Ireland.

Questions

1. Should there be a legal definition of death? See *R. v. Malcherek, ante*, p. 58; Williams, T.C.L. pp. 279–285, and C.L.R.C., 14th Report, § 37.
2. What is a life in being? See next case.

R. v. Poulton
(1832) 5 C. & P. 330; 172 E.R. 997
Central Criminal Court

The defendant had given birth to a child. Its body was found with a ligature round its neck. Three medical witnesses called for the prosecution all said that although the child had breathed they could not tell whether the child had been completely born, as breathing can take place during birth. The defendant was charged with murder.

LITTLEDALE J.: With respect to birth the being born must mean that the whole body is brought into the world: and it is not sufficient that the child respires in the progress of the birth. Whether the child was born alive depends mainly upon the evidence of the medical man. None of them say that the child was born alive; they only say that it had breathed. . . .

Not guilty of murder.

Note

The period 1830–40 saw many cases on this point reported by Carrington and Payne, *e.g. R. v. Brain* (1834) 6 C. & P. 349, *R. v. Crutchley* (1837) 7 C. & P. 814 and *R. v. Reeves* (1839) 9 C. & P. 25, which last case added the point that the umbilical cord need not be severed for there to be a life in being. This legal test is not apparently in accord with medical opinion where the emphasis is on breathing; see Stanley B. Atkinson, "Life, Birth and Live Birth" (1904) 20 L.Q.R. 134, 141 *et seq.* As long as the child has "lived" it does not matter that the injuries causing its death occurred while it was still in the womb: *R. v. West* (1848) 2 Car. & Kir. 784; and see *Attorney-General's Reference (No. 3 of 1994)* [1998] A.C. 245, *ante*, p. 180. See also child destruction and abortion, *post*, p. 605ff.

2. MURDER

i. The Penalty for Murder

Note

"The punishment for murder in the old days was a mandatory death sentence; now, by a quirk of language, it was to be a mandatory life sentence" (Williams, T.C.L., p. 247). Capital punishment for murder was abolished by the Murder (Abolition of the Death Penalty) Act 1965 which replaced the unhappy compromise of partial abolition established by the Homicide Act 1957.

The unusual feature of the penalty for murder is that it is mandatory. The judge has no discretion other than to recommend that the convicted person be detained in prison for a specified minimum term of years (1965 Act, s.1(2)). The *Report of the Select Committee of the House of Lords on Murder and Life Imprisonment* (H.L. Paper 78–1, 1989), para. 118, recommended that the mandatory sentence for murder should be abolished (see also *Committee on the Penalty for Homicide* (Prison Reform Trust, 1993). The mandatory sentence, whether death or life, has been a crucial factor in the shaping of the law of homicide, insanity and diminished responsibility. Any discussion of reform of the law of homicide is forced to take account of this. See *post*, p. 614.

ii. The Mental Element in Murder

R. Goff, "The Mental Element in the Crime of Murder" (1988) 104 L.Q.R. 30, 33

I must emphasise that murder is a crime at common law; and that the definition of the mental element is therefore a common law, and not a statutory, definition. . . . The mental element in the crime of murder used to be called 'malice aforethought'. This is, of course, thoroughly misleading; since neither premeditation nor malice towards the victim were necessary. Furthermore, there were three kinds of malice aforethought; express malice, implied malice, and constructive malice. Express malice was simple; that existed where the defendant actually intended to kill his victim. Implied malice existed when he intended to cause 'grievous bodily harm' to his victim and, by so doing, killed him. Constructive malice existed in two circumstances: first, when the defendant killed his victim in the course of, or in furtherance of, committing a felony (as a serious crime was then called); and second, when the defendant killed his victim in the course of, or for the purpose of, resisting an officer of justice, or resisting or avoiding or preventing a lawful arrest, or effecting or assisting an escape or rescue from legal custody. However, we need spend little time on constructive malice, because in English law this category of murder was abolished by section 1 of the Homicide Act 1957.

Homicide Act 1957, section 1

(1) Where a person kills another in the course or furtherance of some other offence, the killing shall not amount to murder unless done with the same malice aforethought (express or implied) as is required for a killing to amount to murder when not done in the course or furtherance of another offence.

(2) For the purposes of the foregoing subsection, a killing done in the course or for the purpose of resisting an officer of justice or of resisting or avoiding or preventing a lawful arrest, or of affecting or assisting an escape or rescue from legal custody, shall be treated as a killing in the course or furtherance of an offence.

R. v. Vickers
[1957] 2 Q.B. 664
Court of Criminal Appeal

The appellant broke into a shop intending to steal. He was seen by the occupant of the living quarters above, an elderly woman of 72. He struck her many blows and kicked her in the face. She died as a result. The appellant was convicted of capital murder.

LORD GODDARD C.J.: . . . The point that has been raised on the appellant's behalf turns entirely on section 1 (1) of the Homicide Act, 1957, which came into force this year.

The marginal note to that section (s.1(1)), which, of course, is not part of the section but may be looked at as some indication of its purpose, is: "Abolition of 'constructive malice'."

"Constructive malice" is an expression which I do not think will be found in any particular decision, but it is to be found in the textbooks, and is something different from implied malice. The expression "constructive malice" is generally used where a person causes death during the course of carrying out a felony which involves violence—that always amounted to murder. There may be many cases in which a man is not intending to cause death, as, for instance, where he gives a mere push and a person falls and strikes his head or falls down the stairs and breaks his neck, and although the push would never have been considered in the ordinary way as an act which would be likely to cause death, yet if it was done in the course of carrying out a felony it would amount to murder. Another illustration of "constructive malice" would be if a man raped a woman, and she died in the course of the struggle. The fact that he may only have used a moderate or even small degree of violence in the struggle would have been no defence to a charge of murder, because if he caused death, he did so during the commission of the felony of rape. . . . Murder is, of course, killing with malice aforethought, but "malice aforethought" is a term of art. It has always been defined in English law as, either an express intention to kill, as could be inferred when a person, having uttered threats against another, produced a lethal weapon and used it on a victim, or implied, where, by a voluntary act, the accused intended to cause grievous bodily harm to the victim and the victim died as the result. If a person does an act which amounts to the infliction of grievous bodily harm he cannot say that he only intended to cause a certain degree of harm. It is called *malum in se* in the old cases and he must take the consequences. If he intends to inflict grievous bodily harm and that person dies, that has always been held in English law, and was at the time this Act was passed, sufficient to imply the malice aforethought which is a necessary constituent of murder.

It will be observed that the section preserves implied malice as well as express malice, and the words "Where a person kills another in the course or furtherance of some other offence" cannot, in our opinion, be referred to the infliction of the grievous bodily harm if the case which is made against the accused is that he killed a person by having assaulted the person with intent to do grievous bodily harm, and from the bodily harm he inflicted that person dies. The "furtherance of some other offence" must refer to the offence he was committing or endeavouring to commit other than the killing, otherwise there would be no sense in it. It was always the English law, as I have said, that if death was caused by a person in the course of committing a felony involving violence that was murder. Therefore, in the present case it is perfectly clear that the words "Where a person kills another in the course or furtherance of some other offence" must be attributed to the burglary he was committing. The killing was in the course or furtherance of that burglary. He killed that person in the course of the burglary because he realised that the victim recognised him and he therefore inflicted grievous bodily harm on her, perhaps only intending to render her unconscious, but he did intend to inflict grievous bodily harm by the blows he inflicted upon her and by kicking her in the face, of which there was evidence. The section goes on: "the killing shall not amount to murder unless done with the same malice aforethought (express or implied) as is required for a killing to amount to murder when not done in the course or furtherance of another offence." It would seem clear, therefore, that the legislature is providing that where one has a killing committed in the course or furtherance of another offence, that other offence must be ignored. What have to be considered are the circumstances of the killing, and if the killing would amount to murder by reason of the express or implied malice, then that person is guilty of capital murder. It is not enough to say he killed in the course of the felony unless the killing is done in a manner which would amount to murder ignoring the commission of felony. It seems to the court, therefore, that in the present case, a burglar attacked a householder to prevent recognition. The householder died as the result of blows inflicted upon her—blows or kicks or both—and if this section had not been passed there could be no doubt that the appellant would have been guilty of murder. He is guilty of murder because he has killed a person with the necessary malice aforethought being implied from the fact that he intended to do grievous bodily harm. . . .

The court desires to say quite firmly that in considering the construction of section 1(1) it is impossible to say that the doing of grievous bodily harm is the other offence which is referred to in the first line and a half of the section. One has to show, independently of the fact that the accused is committing another offence, that the act which caused the death was done with malice aforethought as implied by law. The existence of express or implied malice is expressly preserved by the Act and, in our opinion, a perfectly proper direction was given by Hinchcliffe J. to the jury, and accordingly this appeal fails and is dismissed.

Appeal dismissed

Director of Public Prosecutions v. Smith
[1961] A.C. 290
House of Lords

The appellant was driving a car containing some stolen property when a policeman told him to draw into the kerb. Instead he accelerated and the constable clung on to the side of the car. The car followed an erratic course and the policeman fell in front of another car and was killed. The appellant drove on for 200 yards, dumped the stolen property, and then returned. He was charged with capital murder. The judge directed the jury to consider whether the appellant intended to cause the officer grievous bodily harm. He was convicted but the Court of Criminal Appeal quashed the conviction for capital murder and substituted one for manslaughter. The Crown appealed to the House of Lords, which restored the conviction for capital murder.

VISCOUNT KILMUIR L.C.: . . . The last criticism of the summing-up which was raised before your Lordships was in regard to the meaning which the learned judge directed the jury was to be given to the words "grievous bodily harm". The passages of which complaint is made are the following: "When one speaks of an intent to inflict grievous bodily harm upon a person, the expression grievous bodily harm does not mean for that purpose some harm which is permanent or even dangerous. It simply means some harm which is sufficient seriously to interfere with the victim's health or comfort."

"In murder the killer intends to kill, or to inflict some harm which will seriously interfere for a time with health or comfort."

"If the accused intended to do the officer some harm which would seriously interfere at least for a time with his health and comfort, and thus perhaps enable the accused to make good his escape for the time being at least that would be murder too."

The direction in these passages was clearly based on the well-known direction of Willes J. in *R. v. Ashman* (1858) 1 F. & F. 88 and on the words used by Graham B. in *R. v. Cox* (1818) R. & R. 362 (C.C.R.). Indeed, this is a direction which is commonly given by judges in trials for the statutory offence under section 18 of the Offences Against the Person Act 1861, and has on occasions been given in murder trials: *cf. R. v. Vickers* (*ante*, p. 517).

My Lords, I confess that whether one is considering the crime of murder or the statutory offence, I can find no warrant for giving the words "grievous bodily harm" a meaning other than that which the words convey in their ordinary and natural meaning. "Bodily harm" needs no explanation, and "grievous" means no more and no less than "really serious". . . .

It was, however, contended before your lordships on behalf of the respondent, that the words ought to be given a more restricted meaning in considering the intent necessary to establish malice in a murder case. It was said that the intent must be to do an act "obviously dangerous to life" or "likely to kill". It is true that in many of the cases the likelihood of death resulting has been incorporated into the definition of grievous bodily harm, but this was done, no doubt, merely to emphasise that the bodily harm must be really serious, and it is unnecessary, and I would add inadvisable, to add anything to the expression "grievous bodily harm" in its ordinary and natural meaning.

To return to the summing-up in the present case, it is true that in the two passages cited the learned judge referred to "grievous bodily harm" in the terms used by Willes J. in *R. v. Ashman*, but in no less than four further passages, and in particular in the vital direction given just before the jury retired he referred to "serious hurt" or "serious harm". Read as a whole, it is, I think, clear that there was no misdirection. Further, on the facts of this case it is quite impossible to say that the harm which the respondent must be taken to have contemplated could be anything but of a very serious nature coming well within the term of "grievous bodily harm".

Before leaving this appeal I should refer to a further contention which was but faintly adumbrated, namely, that section 1(1) of the Homicide Act 1957, had abolished malice constituted by a proved intention to do grievous bodily harm, and that, accordingly, *R. v. Vickers* (*ante*, p. 517), which held the contrary, was wrongly decided. As to this it is sufficient to say that in my opinion the Act does not in any way abolish such malice. The words in parenthesis in section 1(1) of the Act and a reference to section 5(2) make this clear beyond doubt.

Appeal allowed

Note

In *R. v. Hyam* [1975] A.C. 55, *ante*, p. 93, the issue whether intention to cause grievous bodily harm constituted malice aforethought, was left in doubt as Lords Diplock and Kilbrandon held that it was not sufficient *mens rea* for murder. Lord Diplock stated:

"[T]he now familiar expression "grievous bodily harm" appears to owe its place in the development of the English law of homicide to its use in 1803 in Lord Ellenborough's Act (43 Geo. 3, c. 58), which made it a felony to shoot at, stab or cut any other person "with intent . . . to murder, . . . maim, disfigure, or disable, . . . or . . . do some other grievous bodily harm . . ." [section 1]. . . . For my part, I am satisfied that the decision of this House in *D.P.P. v. Smith* was wrong in so far as it rejected the submission that in order to amount to the crime of murder the offender, if he did not intend to kill, must have intended or foreseen as a likely consequence of his act that human life would be endangered. . . . I think the reason why this House fell into error was because it failed to appreciate that the concept of "intention to do grievous bodily harm" only became relevant to the common law of murder as a result of the passing of Lord Ellenborough's Act in 1803 and the application to the new felony thereby created of the then current common law doctrine of constructive malice. This led this House to approach the problem as one of the proper construction of the words "grievous bodily harm" which because, though *only* because, of the doctrine of constructive malice had over the past 100 years become part of the standard definition of *mens rea* in murder, as well as part of the statutory definition of *mens rea* in the statutory felony of causing grievous bodily harm with intent to cause grievous bodily harm. I do not question that in the statutory offence "grievous bodily harm" bears the meaning ascribed to it by this House in *D.P.P. v. Smith* but the actual problem which confronted this House in *D.P.P. v. Smith* and the Court of Criminal Appeal in *R. v. Vickers* was a much more complex one. . . ."

Lord Hailsham and Viscount Dilhorne expressly approved *Vickers*. Viscount Dilhorne stated:

"I now turn to the second contention advanced on behalf of the appellant. This has two facets: first, that the reference to the intent to cause grievous bodily harm has been based on the law that killing in the course or furtherance of a felony is murder, and that when the Homicide Act 1957 was enacted abolishing constructive malice it meant that it no longer sufficed to establish intent to do grievous bodily harm; and, secondly, that, if intent to do grievous bodily harm still made a killing murder, it must be intent to do grievous bodily harm of such a character that life was likely to be endangered.

Committing grievous bodily harm was for many, many years, and until all felonies were abolished, a felony. Consequently so long as the doctrine of constructive malice was part of the law of England, to secure a conviction for murder it was only necessary to prove that the death resulted from an act committed in the course of or in furtherance of the commission of grievous bodily harm. But when one looks at the cases and the old textbooks, one does not find any indication that proof of intent to do grievous bodily harm was an ingredient of murder only on account of the doctrine of constructive malice. Indeed, one finds the contrary. . . .

This was recognised in the report of the Royal Commission on Capital Punishment (1953) (Cmnd. 8932). Their five propositions stated in paragraph 76 which were, so the report said, generally accepted to be properly included in the category of murder, were

". . . all cases where the accused either *intended* to cause death or grievous bodily harm or *knew* that his act was likely to cause death or grievous bodily harm".

The Royal Commission went on to recommend the abolition of constructive malice, and in paragraph 123 suggested a clause for inclusion in a Bill to bring that about.

Section 1 of the Homicide Act 1957 is in all material respects similar to the clause proposed. It would, indeed, be odd if the Royal Commission by recommending the abolition of constructive malice had in fact proposed the abolition of intent to do grievous bodily harm as an ingredient of murder when the commission had not intended and did not recommend that. Parliament may, of course, do more by an Act than it intends but if, as in my opinion was the case, intent to do grievous bodily harm was entirely distinct from constructive malice, then the conclusion that Parliament did so by the Homicide Act 1957 must be rejected. In my opinion, *R. v. Vickers* was rightly decided and this House was right in saying that that was so in *D.P.P. v. Smith.*

I now turn to the second facet of the appellant's contention, namely, that the words "grievous bodily harm" are to be interpreted as meaning harm of such a character as is likely to endanger life. . . .

Our task is to say what, in our opinion, the law is, not what it should be. In the light of what I have said, in my opinion, the words "grievous bodily harm" must, as Viscount Kilmuir said [in *D.P.P. v. Smith*] be given their ordinary and natural meaning and not have the gloss put on them for which the appellant contends. . . .

To change the law to substitute "bodily injury known to the offender to be likely to cause death" for "grievous bodily harm" is a task that should . . . be left to Parliament if it thinks such a change expedient . . . I share the view of the majority of the Royal Commission that such a change would not lead to any great difference in the day-to-day administration of the law."

Note

Lord Cross was not prepared to decide on the issue as it had not been fully argued before the House.

The matter was finally resolved in the following case:

R. v. Cunningham
[1981] 2 All E.R. 863
House of Lords

The appellant suspected (wrongly) that the victim was associating with the woman he planned to marry. The victim died from blows struck by the appellant with a chair. He appealed against his conviction for murder on the grounds that to tell the jury that intending really serious harm was sufficient for murder was a misdirection. The Court of Appeal dismissed his appeal but certified that a point of law of general public importance was involved.

LORD HAILSHAM OF ST. MARYLEBONE L.C.: with whom Lords Wilberforce, Simon of Glaisdale and Bridge of Harwich agreed; . . . The real nerve of Lord Diplock's argument [in *R. v. Hyam*], however, does, as it seems to me, depend on the importance to be attached to the passing in 1803 of Lord Ellenborough's Act (43 Geo. 3 c. 58) by which, for the first time, wounding with the intent to inflict grievous bodily harm became a felony. This, Lord Diplock believes, rendered it possible to apply the doctrine of "felony murder" as defined in Stephen's category (c), abolished in 1957, to all cases of felonious wounding, where death actually ensued from the wound. The abolition of

"felony murder" in 1957 was thus seen to enable the judiciary to pursue the
mental element in murder behind the curtain imposed on it by the combined
effect of the statutory crime of felonious wounding and the doctrine of constructive malice, and so to arrive at a position in which the mental element
could be redefined in terms either of an intention to kill, or an intention actually to endanger human life, to correspond with the recommendations of the
Fourth Report of Her Majesty's Commissioners on Criminal Law (March 8,
1839).

It seems to me, however, that this highly ingenious argument meets with
two insuperable difficulties. I accept that it appears to be established that
the actual phrase "grievous bodily harm", if not an actual coinage by Lord
Ellenborough's Act, can never be found to have appeared in print before it,
though it has subsequently become current coin, and has passed into the general legal jargon of statute law, and the cases decided thereon. But counsel,
having diligently carried us through the institutional writers on homicide,
starting with Coke, and ending with East, with several citations from the
meagre reports available, only succeeded in persuading me at least that, even
prior to Lord Ellenborough's Act of 1803, and without the precise label "grievous bodily harm", the authors and the courts had consistently treated as
murder, and therefore unclergiable, any killing with intent to do serious harm,
however described, to which the label "grievous bodily harm", as defined by
Viscount Kilmuir L.C. in *D.P.P. v. Smith* [1961] A.C. 290 at 334 reversing the
"murder by pinprick" doctrine arising from *R. v. Ashman* (1858) 1 F. & F. 88,
could properly have been applied. . . . There is a second difficulty in the way
of treating Lord Ellenborough's Act as providing the kind of historical water-
shed demanded by Lord Diplock's speech and contended for in the instant
appeal by the appellant's counsel. This consists in the fact that, though the
nineteenth-century judges might in theory have employed the felony-murder
rule to apply to cases where death ensued in the course of a felonious
wounding, they do not appear to have done so in fact. No case was cited
where they did so. On the contrary, there appears to be no historical discon-
tinuity between criminal jurisprudence before and after 1803. Stephen never
so treated the matter (either in his text, or except in the last few lines, in his
Note XIV). It was not so treated in the Australian case of *La Fontaine v. R.*
(1976) 136 C.L.R. 62 (after *Hyam*, but in a jurisdiction in which the constructive
malice rule still applied). . . .

Counsel for the appellant used one further ground, not found in Lord
Diplock's opinion, for supporting the minority view in *Hyam*. This was the
difficulty which, as he suggested, a jury would find in deciding what
amounted to an intention to inflict "grievous bodily harm" or "really serious
bodily harm" as formulated in *Smith*. I do not find this argument convincing.
For much more than a hundred years juries have constantly been required to
arrive at the answer to precisely this question in cases falling short of murder
(*e.g.* the s. 18 cases). I cannot see that the fact that death ensues should render
the identical question particularly anomalous, or its answer, though admittedly more important, any more difficult. Nor am I persuaded that a reformul-
ation of murder so as to confine the *mens rea* to an intention to endanger life
instead of an intention to do really serious bodily harm would either improve
the clarity of the law or facilitate the task of juries in finding the facts. On the
contrary, in cases where death has ensued as the result of the infliction of
really serious injuries I can see endless opportunity for fruitless and intermin-
able discussion of the question whether the accused intended to endanger life
and thus expose the victim to a probable danger of death, or whether he
simply intended to inflict really serious injury. . . . In my opinion, *Vickers* was
a correct statement of the law as it was after amendment by the Homicide Act
1957, and in *Smith* and *Hyam* your Lordships were right to indorse *Vickers*. . . .

LORD EDMUND-DAVIES: The minority dissents of Lord Diplock and Lord Kilbrandon, in *Hyam*, above, were based on their conclusions that the law as to intent in murder had been incorrectly stated by this House in *Smith* and that exposure of the error should lead to a quashing of Hyam's conviction for murder. In the present case, on the other hand, your Lordships have unanimously concluded and now reiterate that the law as to murderous intent was correctly stated in *R. v. Vickers.* Even so, is now the time and is this House the place to reveal and declare (so as to "avoid injustice") what ought to be the law and, in the light of that revelation, here and now to recant from its former adoption of *Vickers*?

My lords, I would give a negative answer to the question. I say this despite the fact that, after much veering of thought over a period of years, the view I presently favour is that there should be no conviction for murder unless an intent to kill is established, the wide range of punishment for manslaughter being fully adequate to deal with all less heinous forms of homicide. I find it passing strange that a person can be convicted of murder if death results from, say, his intentional breaking of another's arm, an action which, while undoubtedly involving the infliction of "really serious harm" and, as such, calling for severe punishment, would in most cases be unlikely to kill. And yet, for the lesser offence of attempted murder, nothing less than an intent to kill will suffice. But I recognise the force of the contrary view that the outcome of intentionally inflicting serious harm can be so unpredictable that anyone prepared to act so wickedly has little ground for complaint if, where death results, he is convicted and punished as severely as one who intended to kill.

So there are forceful arguments both ways. And they are arguments of the greatest public consequence, particularly in these turbulent days when, as Lord Hailsham L.C. has vividly reminded us, violent crimes have become commonplace. Resolution of that conflict cannot, in my judgment, be a matter for your Lordships' House alone. It is a task for none other than Parliament, as the constitutional organ best fitted to weigh the relevant and opposing factors. Its solution has already been attempted extra-judicially on many occasions, but with no real success. My Lords, we can do none other than wait to see what will emerge when the task is undertaken by the legislature, as I believe it should be when the time is opportune. . . .

Appeal dismissed.

Note

Similar criticisms to those expressed by Lord Edmund-Davies concerning the grievous bodily harm rule have been made more recently in the House of Lords. In *Attorney-General's Reference No. 3 of 1994* [1998] A.C. 245 (*ante*, p. 180), Lord Mustill stated (at p. 258) that "the grievous harm rule is an outcropping of old law from which the surrounding strata of rationalisations have weathered away." In *Powell (Anthony)* [1999] A.C. 1 (*ante*, p. 399), Lord Steyn said of the rule (at p. 15) that it turned "murder into a constructive crime . . . [resulting] in defendants being classified as murderers who are not in truth murderers. . . . It results in the imposition of mandatory life sentences when neither justice nor the needs of society require the classification of the case as murder and the imposition of the mandatory life sentence." He went on to recommend that "a killing should be classified as murder if there is an intention to kill or an intention to cause really serious harm coupled with awareness of the risk of death". Their

Lordships accepted, however, that the problem was one which only Parliament could resolve.

iii. Proposals for reform

D. A. Thomas, "Form and Function in Criminal Law" in *Reshaping the Criminal Law* (ed. Glazebrook, 1978), pp. 21, 25

"No better example can be found of the failure of all those concerned with development of the criminal law—including Parliament and the appellate judiciary as well as the advisory bodies—to see the substantive law in a functional context than the history of the definition of murder from 1960 to the present day. With few exceptions, discussions of the propriety of the objective test of intention and the proper scope of the offence have proceeded on the same lines for 18 years with only a passing reference to the fact that what was being decided by establishing a definition had utterly changed. In 1960 the questions in issue in *D.P.P. v. Smith* were hanging matters, and Smith was sentenced to death on his original conviction. The Law Commission's Report on Imputed Criminal Intent, which was the first attempt to clarify the implications of the case and propose amending legislation, followed the abolition of the death penalty for murder. The statute which implemented part of the Law Commission's proposals also created the Parole Board. As a result of these two developments the definition of the offence of murder was no longer concerned with the scope of liability to the death penalty, and had become a means of establishing the respective roles of judge and Parole Board in determining the period of time to be served by a person convicted of homicide and (incidentally) the manner in which that decision was to be made. This fundamental change in the nature of what was actually being decided had little obvious impact on the thinking of the House of Lords when the matter was reconsidered in 1974 [*R. v. Hyam, ante*, p. 93], six years after the new system of dealing with murderers had been established. With the exception of Lord Kilbrandon who (with respect) drew the wrong conclusions, their Lordships did not relate their arguments to the realities of the processes of determining the disposal of those convicted of murder and manslaughter. The problem of defining murder was essentially a formal question, to be considered and decided in terms which would have been equally relevant 100 years ago.

The results of maintaining a separation between the development of the substantive criminal law on the one hand and procedure and penal policy on the other is a system of dealing with homicide and grave personal violence which makes no sense at all in functional terms. A man strikes another with a broken glass in a public-house fight in circumstances which would normally lead to a sentence of three or four years' imprisonment for causing grievous bodily harm with intent; fortuitously the victim dies from his injuries, and unless either the prosecution or the jury will relax the law the assailant is convicted of murder and subject to a mandatory sentence of life imprisonment. In another case the defendant makes a determined attempt to kill his victim, using carefully contrived means based on thoughtful preparations; despite his best endeavours his plans miscarry and he is convicted of attempted murder: his sentence is absolutely within the discretion of the sentencing judge. Two men act in concert in the murder of a third. The first is convicted of murder and receives the mandatory sentence of life imprisonment. The second tenders evidence of psychopathic disorder and secures a reduction in his guilt to manslaughter by reason of diminished responsibility: the judge exercises his discretion to sentence him to life imprisonment. Some years pass: the first, having paid his debt (or at least made a down-payment on it) to society, is released by the Home Secretary on the recommendation of the Parole Board. His co-defendant, having established to the satisfaction of the jury—possibly in the face of prosecution evidence to the contrary—that he is suffering from psychopathic disorder—remains in custody, denied parole on the grounds that he is too dangerous to be released. What is counsel's duty in such a case? Should he advise his client to plead guilty as a sane murderer, in the hope of achieving parole within a decade, or aim for an immediate forensic victory which his client may in the long term find to be of the pyrrhic variety? A provision originally intended to mitigate the severity of the law by reducing the scope of liability to the death penalty has, in the context of changes in penal practice, become potentially a trap, at least for the accused person whose defence is based on a condition which is likely to continue and justify precautionary custody.

Other examples abound. The present definition of murder (whatever its precise terms may be) is clearly not a satisfactory basis for selecting offenders for a unique variety of sentencing procedure. In so far as the mandatory life sentence is justified by the special problems of estimating the chances of future violence by those who have killed once, the existence of special defences such as diminished responsibility and provocation, introduced in earlier times for different purposes, undermines the logic of the sentence by excepting from its scope just those offenders who are most likely to prove dangerous for the future. If the justification for the mandatory life sentence is the unique gravity of the offence and the need to emphasise the particular abhorrence of society for the murderer, that justification is at least diluted by the extension of the definition of murder to include the fortuitous killer. The extension of the definition of murder by the felony-murder rule and the recognition of an intention to inflict grievous bodily harm as a sufficient mental state for conviction may have made some sense in the days when the offence was capital, as directing the supposedly unique deterrent effect of the death sentence at the potential offender who was prepared to risk the use of grave violence to achieve his objects. Now that justification has gone, the effect of the extension of the definition of murder beyond intentional killing weakens whatever morally educative force the mandatory life sentence possesses.

A reconstruction of the law of homicide must begin with a decision on the nature of the sentencing structure which is to be attached to the offences concerned. It would clearly be absurd to design a series of definitions on the assumption that a mandatory sentence in some form will continue to exist for murder, and then enact those definitions against the background of a discretionary sentence. The present shape of the law of murder is the product of the process of reducing the scope of the death penalty; a new approach must start with sentencing structure and proceed to establish the graduations and degrees of liability necessary to the rational operation of that structure.

Report of the Advisory Council on the Penal System, "Sentences of Imprisonment" Home Office, 1978

Section 224. Although murder has been traditionally and distinctively considered the most serious crime, it is not a homogeneous offence but a crime of considerable variety. It ranges from deliberate cold-blooded killing in pursuit of purely selfish ends to what is commonly referred to as 'mercy killing'. Instead of automatically applying a single sentence to such an offence, we believe that sentences for murder should reflect this variety with correspondingly variable terms of imprisonment or, in the exceptional case, even with a non-custodial penalty. This is primarily because we do not think that anyone should, without the most specific justification, be subjected to the disadvantages which we see in indeterminate sentencing (see paragraph 226). It is also because we cannot believe that the problems of predicting future behaviour at the time of conviction are inherently more difficult in a murder case than in any other case where there is a measure of instability, or that judges are any less able to make predictions or to assess degrees of culpability in murder cases than in any others. But it is also because efforts to alleviate the harshness of the mandatory penalty have led to complications in legal proceedings for which we believe there can be no proper justification.

Section 225. The efforts at alleviation to which we refer are, first of all, the two special defences of provocation and diminished responsibility which, if successful, reduce the conviction to manslaughter. Although a conviction for manslaughter may be considered less of a stigma than a conviction for murder, to the offender the important difference often is that the lesser conviction avoids the mandatory penalty. The jurisprudence that has developed out of this defence demonstrates the conceptual difficulties of seeking to mitigate a penal consequence via the substantive law. Provocation may be a factor in any crime; it can and does properly affect the sentence passed on the offender, but only in this one case does it reduce the finding of guilt to a lesser offence. Similarly, the legal concept which enables the defence of diminished responsibility, under section 2 of the Homicide Act 1957, to reduce the crime of murder to manslaughter, creates difficulties. If the mental incapacity is not sufficient to negative the requisite mental element for murder, there are problems in describing the offence as any other crime. If judges had discretion in sentencing, the issues of provocation and diminished responsibility could be considered in their proper place, as mitigating factors in the sentencing process.

Report of the Select Committee of the House of Lords on Murder and Life Imprisonment (H.L. Paper 78–1, Session 1988–89), para. 118

Opinion of the Committee

118. The Committee agree with the majority of their witnesses that the mandatory life sentence for murder should be abolished. Among the considerations which carried most weight with the Committee was the weight of judicial opinion in England and Wales. The Lord Chief Justice and 12 out of 19 judges of the High Court and the Court of Appeal were in favour of a discretionary sentence. The Committee also note that the great majority of judges who took part in the vote in the House of Lords in 1965 were in favour of the discretionary sentence.

Note

The Law Commission Draft Criminal Code Bill incorporates, with a few modifications, the recommendations of the Criminal Law Revision Committee, Fourteenth Report, *Offences Against the Person*, Cmnd. 7844 (1980). On the question of the *mens rea* of murder the arguments have centred on whether a state of mind other than an intent to kill should suffice and if so what this should be.

Criminal Law Revision Committee, 14th Report, Offences Against the Person, Cmnd. 7844 (1980), paras. 19–31

Principles

19. It is the mental element in murder which distinguishes it from involuntary manslaughter. If, as we recommend in paragraph 15, murder is to continue to be a crime distinct from manslaughter, we need to define the mental element which will distinguish the gravest from the less grave homicides. We recognise that a mental element defined in terms of the defendant's intention (or, in certain circumstances, recklessness) with respect to the consequences of his act is an imperfect instrument with which to achieve this distinction. Many other factors affect the gravity of the offence. The defendant's motive may be of the greatest significance. An intentional killing done out of compassion may be much less reprehensible than a merely reckless killing committed in the course of a robbery. It is, however, not practicable to provide in the definition of an offence for the wide variety of motives which may induce men to act. It is equally impracticable to take into account other surrounding circumstances which may make the killing more or less heinous. The most that a definition can achieve is that the generality of cases falling within the definition of the graver offence will be more heinous than the generality of cases falling within the definition of the less grave offence. One of the principal reasons for preserving murder as a separate offence is the stigma that attaches to it and the deterrent effect which that stigma may have. It is important that the definition of murder should, so far as possible, ensure that those convicted of murder will be deserving of the stigma. Too wide a law of murder would not only be unjust but would also tend to diminish the stigma to which we (and most of those who commented on our Working Paper) attach value.

Liability where there is no recklessness as to death

20. In our opinion the mental element of murder is too broadly stated in *Hyam*. . . .

[The C.L.R.C. rejected the proposition that it is murder if a person kills by doing an act knowing that serious bodily harm is a [highly] probable result of the act.]

21. . . . [I]t is wrong in principle that a person should be liable to be convicted of murder who neither i'ntended nor was reckless as to the most important element in the offence, namely death. The consequence of that is that an intention to cause serious bodily harm if standing alone should cease to be a sufficient mental element for murder.

22. It is sometimes argued that a person who intends to cause serious bodily harm *must* realise that there is a risk of causing death; but this is not necessarily so. The more serious the injury intended, the more likely it is that the jury will be satisfied that the defendant knew that his act might kill. In principle we do not consider that anything less than the intention to kill should in future suffice for murder (see paragraph 23 below), but we do indeed propose that, additionally, one who intends serious injury foreseeing a risk of death should be guilty of murder (paragraph 28 below). Thus, the escaping robber who has shot at and killed a pursuing police officer would be likely to be convicted of murder even though he claimed that he only intended to stop his victim from

continuing the pursuit. A jury would probably be satisfied that the robber knew that his act might kill; but there are many types of bodily harm which might be considered serious where no one would expect that death might occur. There is no legal definition of 'serious bodily harm' and we do not propose one; but it may be supposed that a jury might find that to break a man's arm would be to cause him serious injury. No doubt a person intentionally inflicting such an injury would deserve severe punishment; but it would seem quite inappropriate to convict him of murder if his victim dies because of some unusual physiological condition he has.

Should all reckless killings be murder?

23. We considered whether to propose a definition of murder in terms of intentional or reckless killing, but it seemed to us such a wide offence that it could not be called murder. It would include many killings that are now manslaughter and would not be generally thought to be murder. Under *Hyam* a person is not guilty of murder unless he foresees a [high] probability of death (or serious injury), whereas a person may be reckless (in the sense in which both the Law Commission and this Committee use the term) if he foresees any possibility of causing death where the risk he is taking is an unreasonable one. A builder who uses a method of construction which he knows might, in some circumstances, be dangerous to life, might be guilty of an unlawful homicide if a fatal accident results; but it would be wrong to hold him guilty of the same offence as the deliberate killer and for him to be subject to a mandatory sentence of life imprisonment. 'We recognise that a very grave result may follow from taking a risk thought to be merely a slight one, for example where thieves cut railway signalling cable and cause a derailment with much loss of life. Such conduct could be severely punished under our proposals, as under the existing law; but it would not generally be regarded as murder and we do not think it should be the same offence in law as those killings which everyone would instantly recognise as murder.'

Should killing with a high degree of recklessness be murder?

24. If reckless conduct causing death is not enough to make a man guilty of murder, why should there not be a conviction for that offence if the defendant knows that there is a high probability or even a mere probability or a serious risk that death will be caused? ... What is a high probability? or a mere probability? Or a serious risk? Some may think that there is a probability if death is more likely than not to result—the 3 to 2 odds on chance—and that there is a high probability if the odds are shorter (but how much shorter?). Others may think that there is a probability when the odds are much longer. Should a man who kills another while playing an adaptation of 'Russian roulette' be guilty of murder if he knows there is a bullet in one of the six chambers of the revolver? Or in two, three, four or five chambers? It has been suggested that, since the outcome of death is so serious, knowledge of a statistically small risk of causing death could be held to be knowledge of probability and even high probability. We do not accept that suggestion, but the fact that it can be made confirms our opinion as to the unsatisfactory nature of the formula.

25. We appreciate that it is difficult to draw the line between what we recommend should be the meaning of intention and the high probability

test mentioned in *Hyam*. To confine intention to wanting a particular result to happen would be too rigid. . . .

Should killing ever be murder when death is not intended?

28. We think that murder should be extended beyond intentional killing in one respect. There is one category of reckless killing where we believe there would be general agreement that the stigma of murder is well merited. That is where the killer intended unlawfully to cause serious bodily injury and knew that there was a risk of causing death. The intention to cause serious bodily injury puts this killing into a different class from that of a person who is merely reckless, even gravely reckless. The offender has shot, stabbed or otherwise seriously injured the victim, and the circumstances are so grave that the jury can find that he must have realised that there was a risk of causing death. For example, he has shot at a pursuer when he is escaping after a robbery, intending only to disable the pursuer but appreciating that there was a risk of wounding him mortally. The line between this and an intentional killing is so fine that both cases are justifiably classified as murder, as they are in the present law. To classify this particular type of risk-taking as murder does not involve the danger of escalation to cases of recklessness in general, since it is tied specifically to circumstances in which the defendant intended to inflict serious injury. . . .

30. In view of the strong public feeling about terrorism, we think it right to reiterate that we recognise that our proposals would not bring within the law of murder some forms of terrorist killing, for example, by those who plant bombs designed to damage property and cause fear (rather than to take life) and therefore timed to explode when it is unlikely that anyone will be around. Such persons may not think it probable that their acts will cause death or serious injury to anyone (and may not therefore be guilty of murder under the existing law). Nor, *a fortiori*, would they have the intent required for murder under our proposals above. Yet they must clearly appreciate that there is some risk that their acts will cause death. It is equally plain that the risk is one which it is unreasonable to take, and that to take it therefore constitutes recklessness in the sense in which we propose that term should be used in the law relating to offences against the person. Under our proposals such conduct would constitute manslaughter, punishable by a maximum penalty of life imprisonment, and would merit and no doubt receive either a life sentence or a long determinate sentence, but on balance we do not think that it should form part of the law of murder. . . .

Recommendations

31. We therefore conclude that it should be murder:

(a) if a person, with intent to kill, causes death and
(b) if a person causes death by an unlawful act intended to cause serious injury and known to him to involve a risk of causing death (paragraphs 19–29).

In addition, if Parliament favours a [further] provision . . . we recommend that it should be on the following lines: that it should be murder if a person causes death by an unlawful act intended to cause fear (of death or serious injury) and known to the defendant to involve a risk of causing death."

Draft Criminal Code Bill

Murder

54.—(1) A person is guilty of murder if he causes the death of another—

(a) intending to cause death; or
(b) intending to cause serious personal harm and being aware that he may cause death,

unless section 56, 58, 59, 62 or 64 applies.

Commentary on Draft Criminal Code Bill, Law Com. No. 177

14.6 The proposals modify the present law in two respects. (i) An intention to cause serious personal harm is at present a sufficient fault for murder. Under the clause, this will not be so unless the defendant is also aware that he may cause death. (ii) At present, the defendant's awareness that it is 'virtually certain' that his conduct will cause death or serious personal harm is only evidence that he intended such a result. Under the Code, the state of mind will be intention. The judge will direct the jury that, if the defendant was aware that, in the ordinary course of events, his act would cause death or serious personal harm, he intended death or serious personal harm.

Report of the Select Committee of the House of Lords on Murder and Life Imprisonment (H.L. Paper 78–1, Session 1988–89), paras. 66–71

66. The Committee consider that the time has come when the law of murder in England and Wales should be defined, as the great majority of crimes already are, by statute. The Committee believe, however, that it is impossible to produce a statutory definition which will infallibly include all the most heinous killings. They agree with the proposition of the CLRC that:

'the most a definition can achieve is that the generality of cases falling within the definition of the graver offence will be more heinous than the generality of cases falling within the less grave offence".

67. The Committee's proposed definition of the crime of murder reflects their opinion that there are two respects in which it would not be appropriate simply to codify the existing common law.

68. First, the Committee agree with those witnesses who argue that a person who intends only to cause serious personal harm and does not foresee even the possibility of death should not be liable to conviction of murder if death happens to result from his act. A person is not generally liable to conviction of a serious crime where the prohibited result was not only unintended but also unforeseen. This seems to the Committee to be a good rule of moral responsibility which should certainly apply to the most serious crime of all, murder. While the law continues to have two categories of homicide, unforeseen but unlawful killings are properly left to the law of manslaughter.

69. Second, the Committee agree with the opinion of the Law Commission that, for the reasons given by the Commission, it is desirable to clarify the meaning of "intention" as stated in the recent cases. The Commission wrote (p. 120):

''The concept of a state of mind that falls short of 'desire or motive' that the result be caused but is something more than foresight that the result is a virtual certainty is difficult for the ordinary person to grasp. The practical effect of *Nedrick* [*ante*, p. 100] seems to be to leave to the jury to characterise the defendant's foresight of the virtual certainty of result as 'intention', or not, as they think right in all the circumstances of the case. We believe that, in appropriate cases, the jury will be better assisted if they are told exactly what the concept of intention embraces as a matter of law, which will be the effect of adopting the definition proposed by the Commission.''

70. Professor Glanville Williams put the same point cogently in a paper submitted to the Committee:

''An intelligent jury may be fogged at being told that they can infer x, when they are not told what x is (but only what it is not)'' (Appendix 7, p. 121).

On the other hand, the Lord Chief Justice stated in evidence to the Committee:

''If, of course the jury come to the conclusion that [the accused] realised that it was almost certain that somebody would be killed, that *is* murder'' (Lord Lane's emphasis).

A direction to that effect would leave the jury in no doubt about the question they must answer.

71. The Committee therefore recommend that murder should be defined on the lines proposed by the Law Commission in their draft Criminal Code, clause 54 (1):

''A person is guilty of murder if he causes the death of another—

(a) intending to cause death; or
(b) intending to cause serious personal harm and being aware that he may cause death . . .''

and that, for the purposes of the law of murder, ''intention'' should be defined on the lines proposed in clause 18 (b) of the draft Criminal Code:

''A person acts 'intentionally' with respect to . . . a result when he acts either in order to bring it about or being aware that it will occur in the ordinary course of events.''

Note

A killing which would otherwise amount to murder will be reduced to manslaughter if the defendant was provoked or suffered from diminished reponsibility.

3. SPECIAL DEFENCES

i. Provocation

Homicide Act 1957, section 3

Where on a charge of murder there is evidence on which the jury can find that the person charged was provoked (whether by things done or by things said or by both together) to lose his self control, the question whether the provocation was enough to make a reasonable man do as he did shall be left to be determined by the jury; and in determining that question the jury shall take into account everything both done and said according to the effect which, in their opinion, it would have on a reasonable man.

(a) *The subjective question*

Notes

1. Although provocation is usually raised by the defence the onus of proof, that the situation was not one of provocation, lies on the prosecution and this must be made clear to the jury, *R. v. Cascoe* [1970] 2 All E.R. 833.

2. Section 3 creates a test which leaves two questions for the jury to consider: (a) whether the defendant was provoked to lose his self-control (the *subjective* question), and (b) whether a reasonable man would have been provoked to lose his self-control and do as the defendant did (the *objective* question). The subjective question remains the same as it did at common law where the leading authority was *Duffy* [1949] 1 All E.R. 932n, where the Court of Appeal approved the summing up of Devlin J. who stated:

"Provocation is some act or series of acts done by the dead man to the accused which would cause in any reasonable person and actually causes in the accused, a sudden and temporary loss of self-control, rendering the accused so subject to passion as to make him for the moment not master of his mind."

Later in his summing up he stated:

"Indeed, circumstances which induce a desire for revenge are inconsistent with provocation, since the conscious formulation of a desire for revenge means that a person has had time to think, to reflect, and that would negative a sudden temporary loss of self-control, which is of the essence of provocation."

These dicta were approved subsequently in *R. v. Ibrams and Gregory* (1981) 74 Cr.App.R. 154.

3. It is crucial to a defence of provocation that the accused should suffer a sudden and temporary loss of self-control (see *Thornton* [1992] 1 All E.R. 306). This need not be immediate upon the last act of provocation but "the longer the delay and the stronger the evidence of deliberation on the part of the defendant, the more likely it will be that the prosecution will negative provocation" (*Ahluwalia* [1993] Crim.L.R. 63). But while the loss of self-control must be sudden, there is no requirement that the provocation be sudden. It may have continued over a long period and the jury are bound to take into account everything done and said according to the effect which, in their opinion, it would have on a reasonable man (see *Thornton* and *Pearson* [1992] Crim.L.R. 193).

4. If there is any evidence to suggest that the accused was provoked to lose her self-control the defence of provocation must be left to the

jury (see *Rossiter* (1992) 95 Cr.App.R. 326 and *Cambridge* [1994] 1 W.L.R. 971). The judge should do so regardless of the defence being run by the accused and even if the accused requests that the defence not be put to the jury (see *Burgess* [1995] Crim.L.R. 425). In leaving the defence to the jury the judge should indicate to them, unless it is obvious, what evidence might support the conclusion that the accused had been provoked to lose her self-control (see *Stewart* [1995] 4 All E.R. 999 and *Humphreys* [1994] 4 All E.R. 1009). This is particularly important where the provocation is not confined to one act but has accumulated over a period time and a range of circumstances (*Humphreys*). Where, for example, the accused is shown to have suffered from battered woman syndrome and she has killed her abuser,

> "[Battered woman syndrome] may form an important background to whatever triggered the *actus reus*. A jury may more readily find there was a sudden loss of control triggered by even a minor incident, if the defendant has endured abuse over a period, on the 'last straw' basis." (*per* Lord Taylor CJ, *Thornton* (No. 2) [1996] 2 All E.R. 1023 at 1030.)

5. While Devlin J. in *Duffy* spoke of an "act or series of acts done by the dead man to the accused," it is clear from section 3 that it is not a requirement of the defence that the victim direct the provocative acts at the accused; the provocation may arise from acts done to third parties. In *Pearson* M. and W. killed their violent and tyrranical father. M. had been subjected to violence and abuse for eight years while W. was away from home. W. returned home to protect M. from further violence becoming, himself, the target for violence. It was held by the Court of Appeal that the whole history of violence against M. was relevant to W.'s defence of provocation.

6. In the following case the court was concerned with what could amount to provocation.

R. v. Doughty
(1986) 83 Cr.App.R. 319
Court of Appeal

The appellant was charged with the murder of his 17-day old son. He raised the defence of provocation based on the baby's persistent crying and restlessness. The judge refused to leave this defence to the jury and the appellant was convicted of murder.

STOCKER L.J., after outlining the facts, referred to the judge's direction to the jury:
"In my judgment the perfectly natural episodes or events of crying and restlessness by a 17 day old baby does not constitute evidence of provocation in relation to the first subjective question. Put another way, the crying and restlessness of a 17 day old baby cannot be utilised as being provocative to enable the defendant to raise the defence of provocation. Though provocation can be constituted by conduct or words which are not unlawful, provocation cannot be founded, in my judgment, on the perfectly natural episodes or events arising in the life of a 17 day old baby. It is notorious that every baby born cries, that every baby can at times be burdensome. It is notorious that a baby of 17 days is incapable of sustaining his own life, that he is defenceless and harmless. These notorious facts are common to every baby who is only

days old. I think that the episodes or events in the life of the baby of 17 days old could not have been in the mind of Parliament when section 3 became the law. The words of section 3, I quote: 'Whether by things done or words said or by both together'—are not, in my judgment, apposite to embrace the perfectly ordinary, certain, and natural episodes or events in the life of a 17 day old baby. Further, common law directions cannot be construed as including these natural and certain episodes that occur in the life of every baby of days old. Finally, I think civilised society dictates that the natural episodes occurring in the life of a baby only days old have to be endured and cannot be utilised as the foundation of subjective provocation to enable his killer to escape a conviction for murder."
. . .

Mr Price submitted that on the proper construction of that section, the judge was bound to leave to the jury the question of provocation, particularly in the light of the admission made by Mr Klevan for the Crown that there was a causal connection between the crying of the baby and the appellant's response. Mr Price submitted that this was a classic case for leaving the issue to the jury and he referred us to the case of the *D.P.P. v. Camplin* (*post*, p. 509). . . .

Mr Price also referred us to Professor Glanville Williams' *Textbook on Criminal Law* (2nd edn, 1983), at p. 534. Professor Williams wrote this: "The Homicide Act, in allowing insults as provocation, inevitably alters the position, because an insult uttered in private is neither a crime nor even a tort. Section 3 contains no restriction to unlawful acts, and the courts seem to be ready to allow any provocative conduct to be taken into consideration, even though that conduct was itself provoked by the defendant. Consequently, there is no longer any reason why the defence should not be available (if the jury uphold it) to the jilted lover who kills the object of his affections or her new lover, or the man who kills a constantly crying baby. Even the rule about lawful blows seems to survive only as a consideration that the jury can take into account when applying the test of reasonableness."
. . . We appreciate the reasons which the learned judge gave for reaching the conclusion that he did, but we are unable to construe section 3 in such a light. The first sentence of section 3 reads: "Where on a charge of murder there is evidence on which the jury can find that the person charged was provoked . . . to lose his self-control." There is no doubt, and it is not in dispute, that there was here evidence upon which the appellant was—I use the word loosely—"provoked" to lose his self-control. Part of that evidence has been cited earlier in this judgment.

The reasoning which the learned judge gave, understandable though it was, involves, in our view, adding in to section 3 words which are not there, presumably by way of restriction. It is accepted by Mr Klevan that there was evidence which linked causally the crying of the baby with the response of the appellant. Accordingly, in our view, it seems inevitable that that being so the section is mandatory and requires the learned judge to leave the issue of the objective test to the jury.

Mr Klevan also referred us to what might, in shorthand, be called the "floodgates proposition", that if the learned judge's direction was wrong it opens up the possibility that in any case in which there is a battered baby allegation and the baby dies, the argument based on provocation may be raised. We feel that even if that submission was right it could not be allowed to dissuade us from putting a construction on section 3 which, in our view, its wording plainly constrains. We also feel that reliance can be placed upon the common sense of juries upon whom the task of deciding the issue is imposed by section 3 and that that common sense will ensure that only in cases where the facts fully justified it would their verdict be likely to be that they would hold that a defendant's act in killing a crying child would be the response of a reasonable man within the section. That matter is, in our view, imposed by Parliament upon the jury, not upon a judge, and the common sense of juries can be relied upon not to bring in perverse verdicts where the facts do not justify the conclusion.

In our view, therefore, though fully understanding his reasons, we are of the view that the learned judge was wrong in not leaving the issue of provocation to the jury.

Appeal allowed in part.
Conviction for murder quashed.
Conviction of manslaughter substituted.
Sentence varied.

Note

In *Davies* [1975] Q.B. 691, the Court of Appeal accepted that provocation may emanate from some person other than the victim.

Question

D returns to his new car parked in a meter bay to discover that someone has driven into it smashing one of the headlights. He is so angry at this that he flares up into a rage and when a traffic warden commences to peruse the meter which is registering "Excess Charge" he hits him with a bottle of wine causing the traffic warden an injury from which he dies. The trial judge refuses to leave provocation to the jury. D appeals. How might the Court of Appeal decide this issue?

Note

The fact that D may have done something to induce the provocative conduct does not preclude him from seeking to raise the defence of provocation. In *Johnson* [1989] 1 W.L.R. 740 Watkins L.J. stated (at p. 744):

"In view of the express wording of section 3 . . . we find it impossible to accept that the mere fact that a defendant caused a reaction in others, which in turn led him to lose his self-control, should result in the issue of provocation being kept outside a jury's consideration. Section 3 clearly provides that the question is whether things done or said or both provoked the defendant to lose his self-control. If there is any evidence that it may have done, the issue must be left to the jury."

(b) *The objective question*

Note

Section 3 of the 1957 Act requires the jury to consider "everything both done and said according to the effect which, in their opinion, it would have on a reasonable man". The fact that D has lost his self-control is not sufficient to result in a manslaughter verdict; the jury should only return such a verdict if they consider the reasonable man might have been provoked and then might have done as D did. The purpose of the provision is to create an objective standard of self-control against which D's actions are measured. There are, however, two problems; firstly, D, due to his character, history or circumstances, may be particularly sensitive to the alleged provocative words or conduct; and secondly, D, due to his youthfulness or some mental impairment, may not be able to exercise the self-control to be expected of the ordinary adult. Should either of these factors have a bearing on the jury's consideration of the objective question?

R. v. Camplin
[1978] A.C. 705
House of Lords

The facts appear in the speech of Lord Diplock, below, in which Lords Fraser of Tullybelton and Scarman concurred.

LORD DIPLOCK: The respondent, Camplin, who was 15 years of age, killed a middle-aged Pakistani, Mohammed Lal Khan, by splitting his skull with a chapati pan, a heavy kitchen utensil like a rimless frying pan. At the time, the two of them were alone together in Khan's flat. At Camplin's trial for murder before Boreham J. his only defence was that of provocation so as to reduce the offence to manslaughter. According to the story that he told in the witness box but which differed materially from that which he had told the police, Khan had buggered him in spite of his resistance and had then laughed at him. Whereupon Camplin had lost his self-control and attacked Khan fatally with the chapati pan.

In his address to the jury on the defence of provocation Mr Baker, who was counsel for Camplin, had suggested to them that when they addressed their minds to the question whether the provocation relied on was enough to make a reasonable man do as Camplin had done, what they ought to consider was not the reaction of a reasonable adult but the reaction of a reasonable boy of Camplin's age. The judge thought that this was wrong in law. So in his summing-up he took pains to instruct the jury that they must consider whether:

"... the provocation was sufficient to make a reasonable man in like circumstances act as the defendant did. Not a reasonable boy, as Mr Baker would have it, or a reasonable lad; it is an objective test—a reasonable man."

The jury found Camplin guilty of murder. On appeal the Court of Appeal (Criminal Division) allowed the appeal and substituted a conviction for manslaughter upon the ground that the passage I have cited from the summing-up was a misdirection. The court held that

"... the proper direction to the jury is to invite the jury to consider whether the provocation was enough to have made a reasonable person of the same age as the defendant in the same circumstances do as he did."

The point of law of general public importance involved in the case has been certified as being:

"Whether on the prosecution for murder of a boy of 15, where the issue of provocation arises, the jury should be directed to consider the question under section 3 of the Homicide Act 1957 whether the provocation was enough to make a reasonable man do as he did by reference to a 'reasonable adult' or by reference to a 'reasonable boy of 15'."

. . .

The doctrine of provocation has a long history of evolution at common law. Such changes as there had been were entirely the consequence of judicial decision until Parliament first intervened by passing the Act of 1957. Section 3 deals specifically with provocation and alters the law as it had been expounded in the cases, including three that had been decided comparatively recently in this House, viz., *Mancini v. D.P.P.* [1942] A.C. 1; *Holmes v. D.P.P.* [1946] A.C. 588 and *Bedder v. D.P.P.* [1954] 1 W.L.R. 1119. One of the questions of this appeal is to what extent propositions as to the law of provocation that are laid down in those cases and in particular in *Bedder* ought to be treated as being of undiminished authority despite the passing of the Act. . . .

[W]ith two exceptions actual violence offered by the deceased to the accused remained the badge of provocation right up to the passing of the Act of 1957. The two exceptions were the discovery by a husband of his wife in the act of committing adultery and the discovery of a father of someone committing sodomy on his son; but these apart, insulting words or gestures unaccompanied by physical attack did not in law amount to provocation. . . .

At least from as early as 1914 (see *R. v. Lesbini* [1914] 3 K.B. 1116) the test of whether the defence of provocation is entitled to succeed has been a dual one; the conduct of the deceased to the accused must be such as (1) might cause in any reasonable or ordinary person and (2) actually causes in the accused a sudden and temporary loss of self-control as the result of which he commits the unlawful act that kills the deceased. But until the Act of 1957 was passed there was a condition precedent which had to be satisfied before any question of applying this dual test could arise. The conduct of the deceased had to be of such a kind as was capable in law of constituting provocation; and whether it was or not was a question for the judge, not for the jury. This House so held in *Mancini v. D.P.P.* [1942] A.C. 1, where it also laid down a rule of law that the mode of resentment, as for instance the weapon used in the act that caused the death, must bear a reasonable relation to the kind of violence that constituted the provocation.

It is unnecessary for the purposes of the present appeal to spend time on a detailed account of what conduct was or was not capable in law of giving rise to a defence of provocation immediately before the passing of the Act of 1957. It had remained much the same as when Stephen was writing in the last quarter of the nineteenth century. What, however, is important to note is that this House in *Holmes v. D.P.P.* [1946] A.C. 588 had recently confirmed that words alone, save perhaps in circumstances of a most extreme and exceptional nature, were incapable in law of constituting provocation.

My Lords, this was the state of law when *Bedder v. D.P.P.* [1954] 1 W.L.R. 1119 fell to be considered by this House. The accused had killed a prostitute. He was sexually impotent. According to his evidence he had tried to have sexual intercourse with her and failed. She taunted him with his failure and tried to get away from his grasp. In the course of her attempts to do so she slapped him in the face, punched him in the stomach and kicked him in the groin; whereupon he took a knife out of his pocket and stabbed her twice and caused her death. The struggle which led to her death thus started because the deceased taunted the accused with his physical infirmity; but in the state of the law as it then was taunts unaccompanied by any physical violence did not constitute provocation. The taunts were followed by violence on the part of the deceased in the course of her attempt to get away from the accused, and it may be that this subsequent violence would have a greater effect upon the self-control of an impotent man already enraged by the taunts than it would have had upon a person conscious of possessing normal physical attributes. So there might have been some justification for the judge to instruct the jury to ignore the fact that the accused was impotent when they were considering whether the deceased's conduct amounted to such provocation as would cause a reasonable or ordinary person to lose his self-control. This indeed appears to have been the ground on which the Court of Criminal Appeal had approved the summing up when they said, at p. 1121:

> "no distinction is to be made in the case of a person who, though it may not be a matter of temperament, is physically impotent, is conscious of that impotence, *and therefore mentally liable to be more excited unduly* if he is 'twitted' or attacked on the subject of that particular infirmity".

This statement, for which I have myself supplied the emphasis, was approved by Lord Simonds L.C. speaking on behalf of all the members of this House who sat on the appeal; but he also went on to lay down the broader proposition, at p. 1123, that

> "It would be plainly illogical not to recognise an unusually excitable or pugnacious temperament in the accused as a matter to be taken into account but yet to recognise for that purpose some unusual physical characteristic, be it impotence or another."

. . . [Section 3 of the 1957 Act] was intended to mitigate in some degree the harshness of the common law of provocation as it had been developed by recent decisions in this House. It recognises and retains the dual test: the provocation must not only have caused the accused to lose his self-control but must also be such as might cause a reasonable man to react to it as the accused did. Nevertheless it brings about two important changes in the law. The first is: it abolishes all previous rules of law as to what can or cannot amount to provocation and in particular the rule of law that, save in the two exceptional cases I have mentioned, words unaccompanied by violence could not do so. Secondly it makes it clear that if there was any evidence that the accused himself at the time of the act which caused the death in fact lost his self-control in consequence of some provocation however slight it might appear to the judge, he was bound to leave to the jury the question, which is one of opinion not of law: whether a reasonable man might have reacted to that provocation as the accused did. . . .

The public policy that underlay the adoption of the "reasonable man" test in the common law doctrine of provocation was to reduce the incidence of fatal violence by preventing a person relying upon his own exceptional pugnacity or excitability as an excuse for loss of self-control. The rationale of the test may not be easy to reconcile in logic with more universal propositions as to the mental element in crime. Nevertheless it has been preserved by the Act of 1957 but falls to be applied now in the context of a law of provocation that is significantly different from what it was before the Act was passed.

Although it is now for the jury to apply the "reasonable man" test, it still remains for the judge to direct them what, in the new context of the section, is the meaning of this apparently inapt expression, since powers of ratiocination bear no obvious relationship to powers of self-control. Apart from this the judge is entitled, if he thinks it helpful, to suggest considerations which may influence the jury in forming their own opinion as to whether the test is satisfied; but he should make it clear that these are not instructions which they are required to follow; it is for them and no one else to decide what weight, if any, ought to be given to them.

As I have already pointed out, for the purposes of the law of provocation the "reasonable man" has never been confined to the adult male. It means an ordinary person of either sex, not exceptionally excitable or pugnacious, but possessed of such powers of self-control as everyone is entitled to expect that his fellow citizens will exercise in society as it is today. A crucial factor in the defence of provocation from earliest times has been the relationship between the gravity of provocation and the way in which the accused retaliated, both being judged by the social standards of the day. When Hale was writing in the seventeenth century, pulling a man's nose was thought to justify retaliation with a sword; when *Mancini v. D.P.P.* [1942] A.C. 1 was decided by this House, a blow with a fist would not justify retaliation with a deadly weapon. But so long as words unaccompanied by violence could not in law amount to provocation the relevant proportionality between provocation and retaliation was primarily one of degrees of violence. Words spoken to the accused before the violence started were not normally to be included in the proportion sum. But now that the law has been changed so as to permit of words being treated as provocation even though unaccompanied by any other acts, the gravity of verbal provocation may well depend upon the particular characteristics or circumstances of the person to whom a taunt or insult is addressed. To taunt a person because of his race, his physical infirmities or some shameful incident in his past may well be considered by the jury to be more offensive to the person addressed, however equable his temperament, if the facts on which the taunt is founded are true than it would be if they were not. It would stultify much of the mitigation of the previous harshness of the common law in ruling out verbal provocation as capable of reducing murder to manslaughter if the jury could not take into consideration all those factors which in their opinion would affect the gravity of taunts or insults when applied to the person to whom they are addressed. So to this extent at any rate the unqualified proposition accepted by this House in *Bedder v. D.P.P.* [1954] 1 W.L.R. 1119 that for the purposes of the "reasonable man" test any unusual physical characteristics of the accused must be ignored requires revision as a result of the passing of the Act of 1957.

That he was only 15 years of age at the time of the killing is the relevant characteristic of the accused in the instant case. It is a characteristic which may have its effects on temperament as well as physique. If the jury think that the same power of self-control is not to be expected in an ordinary, average or normal boy of 15 as in an older person, are they to treat the lesser powers of self-control possessed by an ordinary, average or normal boy of 15 as the standard of self-control with which the conduct of the accused is to be compared?

It may be conceded that in strict logic there is a transition between treating age as a characteristic that may be taken into account in assessing the gravity of the provocation addressed to the accused and treating it as a characteristic to be taken into account in determining what is the degree of self-control to be expected of the ordinary person with whom the accused's conduct is to be compared. But to require old heads upon young shoulders is inconsistent with the law's compassion to human infirmity to which Sir Michael Foster ascribed the doctrine of provocation more than two centuries ago. The distinction as to the purposes for which it is legitimate to take the age of the accused into account involves considerations of too great nicety to warrant a place in deciding a matter of opinion, which is no longer one to be decided by a judge trained in logical reasoning but is to be decided by a jury drawing on their experiences of how ordinary human beings behave in real life. . . .

In my view *Bedder*, like *Mancini v. D.P.P.* [1942] A.C. 1, and *Holmes v. D.P.P.* [1946] A.C. 588, ought no longer to be treated as an authority on the law of provocation.

In my opinion a proper direction to a jury on the question left to their exclusive determination by section 3 of the Act of 1957 would be on the following lines. The judge should state what the question is using the very terms of the section. He should then explain to them that the reasonable man referred to in the question is a person having the power of self-control to be expected of an ordinary person of the sex and age of the accused, but in other respects sharing such of the accused's characteristics as they think would affect the gravity of the provocation to him; and that the question is not merely whether such a person would in like circumstances be provoked to lose his self-control but also whether he would react to the provocation as the accused did.

I accordingly agree with the Court of Appeal that the judge ought not to have instructed the jury to pay no account to the age of the accused even though they themselves might be of opinion that the degree of self-control to be expected in a boy of that age was less than in an adult. So to direct them was to impose a fetter on the right and duty of the jury which the Act accords to them to act upon their own opinion on the matter.

I would dismiss this appeal.

Appeal dismissed.

Note

In *Camplin* the House of Lords drew a distinction between those characteristics (or circumstances) which are relevant to the gravity of the provocation to the accused and those which might affect the accused's powers of self-control. The question of whether there should be any limitations on the characteristics or circumstances which could be relevant to the gravity of the provocation arose in the next case.

R. v. Morhall
[1995] 3 W.L.R. 330
House of Lords

M stabbed the deceased during a fight following persistent taunts by the deceased and others about his addiction to glue-sniffing. The Court of Appeal dismissed his appeal against his conviction for murder on the basis that M's addiction to glue-sniffing was not a characteristic to be attributed to the reasonable man as it was a discreditable characteristic inconsistent with the concept of the reasonable man. The Court of Appeal certified a point of law of general public importance was involved in the decision, namely whether in directing a jury on provocation "the judge should exclude from the jury's consideration characteristics and past behaviour of the defendant, at which taunts are directed, which in the judge's view are inconsistent with the concept of the reasonable man?''

LORD GOFF OF CHIEVELEY: . . .

It is against the background of the decision in *R. v. Camplin* (*ante*, p. 536), and the speeches of their Lordships in that case, that I now turn to consider the problem in the present case, which is whether the defendant's addiction to glue-sniffing should have been taken into account as affecting the gravity of the provocation.

Judging from the speeches in *R. v. Camplin*, it should indeed have been taken into account. Indeed, it was a characteristic of particular relevance, since the words of the deceased which were said to constitute provocation were directed towards the defendant's shameful addiction to glue-sniffing and his inability to break himself of it. Furthermore, there is nothing in the speeches in *R. v. Camplin* to suggest that a characteristic of this kind should be excluded from consideration. On the contrary, in the passage which I have already quoted from his speech Lord Diplock spoke of the jury taking into consideration "all those factors" which would affect the gravity of the taunts or insults when applied to the defendant. Likewise, Lord Simon of Glaisdale said, at p. 727D:

"in determining whether a person of reasonable self-control would lose it in the circumstances, the entire factual situation, which includes the characteristics of the accused, must be considered."

Even so, the Court of Appeal felt that the defendant's addiction to glue-sniffing should be excluded because it was a characteristic which was repugnant to the concept of a reasonable man. It seems to me, with all respect, that this conclusion flows from a misunderstanding of the function of the so-called "reasonable person test" in this context. In truth the expression "reasonable man" or "reasonable person" in this context can lead to misunderstanding. Lord Diplock described it (in *R. v. Camplin* at p. 716G) as an "apparently inapt expression". This is because the "reasonable person test" is concerned not with ratiocination, nor with the reasonable man whom we know so well in the law of negligence (where we are concerned with reasonable foresight and reasonable care), nor with reasonable conduct generally. The function of the test is only to introduce, as a matter of policy, a standard of self-control which has to be complied with if provocation is to be established in law: see *R. v. Camplin*, at p. 716F, *per* Lord Diplock, and p. 726F, *per* Lord Simon of Glaisdale. Lord Diplock himself spoke of "the reasonable or ordinary person", and indeed to speak of the degree of self-control attributable to the ordinary person is (despite the express words of the statute) perhaps more apt, and certainly less likely to mislead, than to do so with reference to the reasonable person. The word "ordinary" is in fact the adjective used in criminal codes applicable in some other common law jurisdictions (as in New Zealand, as to which see *R. v. McGregor* [1962] N.Z.L.R. 1069 and *R. v. McCarthy* [1992] 2 N.Z.L.R. 550, and in Tasmania, as to which see *Stingel v. The Queen* (1990) 171 C.L.R. 312). Indeed, by exploiting the adjective "reasonable" it is easy to caricature the law as stated in section 3 of the Act of 1957 by talking of the test of, for example, the reasonable blackmailer or, nowadays perhaps, the reasonable glue-sniffer; indeed, the sting of the caricature is derived from the implication that the adjective "reasonable" refers to a person who is guided by reason or who acts in a reasonable manner. This is however misleading. In my opinion it would be entirely consistent with the law as stated in section 3 of the Act of 1957, as properly understood, to direct the jury simply with reference to a hypothetical person having the power of self-control to be expected of an *ordinary* person of the age and sex of the defendant, but in other respects sharing such of the defendant's characteristics as they think would affect the gravity of the provocation to him: see *R. v. Camplin* [1978] A.C. 705, 718E–F, *per* Lord Diplock.

I wish, however, to stress two things. First, it is plain that, in the passage from his speech to which I have just referred, Lord Diplock was not attempting to dictate to judges how they should formulate their directions to juries on provocation. This appears from his statement that "a" proper direction to a jury would be "on the following lines". Provided that trial judges direct juries in accordance with the law, they may do so as they think right, tailoring their direction to the facts of the particular case before them. Second, in an appropriate case, it may be necessary to refer to other circumstances affecting the gravity of the provocation to the defendant which do not strictly fall within the description "characteristics", as for example the defendant's history or the circumstances in which he is placed at the relevant time (see *R. v. Camplin*, at p. 717C–D, *per* Lord Diplock, where he referred to "the particular characteristics or circumstances" of the defendant, and at p. 727D, *per* Lord Simon of Glaisdale, who referred to "the entire factual situation", including the characteristics of the defendant.) At all events in the present case, when the judge turned to the second and objective inquiry, he was entitled to direct the jury that they must take into account the entire factual situation (and in particular the fact that the provocation was directed at a habitual glue sniffer taunted with his habit) when considering the question whether the provocation was enough to cause a man possessed of an ordinary man's power of self control to act as the defendant did.

However, the point can be taken further. Among the characteristics stated to be excluded from consideration on the approach favoured by the Court of Appeal is that of being a paedophile. But suppose that a man who has been in prison for a sexual offence, for example rape, has after his release been taunted by another man with reference to that offence. It is difficult to see why, on ordinary principles, his characteristic or history as an offender of that kind should not be taken into account as going to the gravity of the provocation. The point is well made by Professor Smith in his commentary on the present case [1993] Crim.L.R. 957, 958:

> "Suppose that an old lag, now trying to go straight, is taunted with being 'a jailbird'. This might be extremely provoking, especially if it reveals his murky past to new friends or employers unaware of it. It really would not make much sense to ask the jury to consider the effect of such provocation on a man of good character."

In truth, the mere fact that a characteristic of the defendant is discreditable does not exclude it from consideration, as was made plain by Lord Diplock in *R. v. Camplin* when, at p. 717D, he referred to a shameful incident in a man's past as a relevant characteristic for present purposes. Indeed, even if the defendant's discreditable conduct causes a reaction in another, which in turn causes the defendant to lose his self-control, the reaction may amount to provocation: see *Edwards v. The Queen* [1973] A.C. 648, a case concerned with a hostile reaction to his blackmailer by a man whom he was trying to blackmail, and *R. v. Johnson (Christopher)* [1989] 1 W.L.R. 740 in which *Edwards v. The Queen* was followed and applied by the Court of Appeal. These cases are, in my opinion, inconsistent with the decision of the Court of Appeal in the present case.

Of course glue-sniffing (or solvent abuse), like indulgence in alcohol or the taking of drugs, can give rise to a special problem in the present context, because it may arise in more than one way. First, it is well established that, in considering whether a person having the power of self-control to be expected of an ordinary person would have reacted to the provocation as the defendant did, the fact (if it be the case) that the defendant was the worse for drink at the time should not be taken into account, even though the drink would, if taken by him, have the effect of reducing an ordinary person's power of self-control. It is sometimes suggested that the reason for this exclusion is that drunkenness is transitory and cannot therefore amount to a characteristic. But I doubt whether that is right. Indeed some physical conditions (such as eczema) may be transitory in nature and yet can surely be taken into account if the subject of taunts. In *R. v. Camplin* [1978] A.C. 705, 726F, Lord Simon of Glaisdale considered that drunkenness should be excluded as inconsistent with the concept of the reasonable man in the sense of a man of ordinary self-control; but it has to be recognised that, in our society, ordinary people do sometimes have too much to drink. I incline therefore to the opinion that the exclusion of drunkenness in this context flows from the established principle that, at common law, intoxication does not of itself excuse a man from committing a criminal offence, but on one or other of these bases it is plainly excluded. At all events it follows that, in a case such as the present, a distinction may have to be drawn between two different situations. The first occurs where the defendant is taunted with his addiction (for example, that he is an alcoholic, or a drug addict, or a glue-sniffer), or even with having been intoxicated (from any cause) on some previous occasion. In such a case, however discreditable such condition may be, it may where relevant be taken into account as going to the gravity of the provocation. The second is the simple fact of the defendant being intoxicated—being drunk, or high with drugs or glue—at the relevant time, which may not be so taken into account, because that, like displaying a lack of ordinary self-control, is excluded as a matter of policy. Although the distinction is a fine one, it will, I suspect, very rarely be necessary to explain it to a jury. Drunkenness itself may be a not unusual feature of cases raising the issue of provocation, as occurred, for example, in *R. v. Newell* (1980) 71 Cr.App.R. 331, where the drunkenness of the defendant was rightly excluded as irrelevant. But none of the counsel in the present case had any experience, or indeed knowledge, of a case other than the present in which addiction as such was the subject of verbal taunts or insults said to constitute provocation, with the effect that the addiction was therefore relevant as going to the gravity of the provocation. The present case may therefore be compared with *R. v. Newell*, in which the defendant's chronic alcoholism was excluded from consideration because "it had nothing to do with the words by which it is said that he was provoked": see p. 340, *per* Lord Lane C.J. I only wish to add a warning that the court's strong reliance in that case on the judgment of North J. in *R. v. McGregor* [1962] N.Z.L.R. 1069 must be regarded with caution, having regard to the reservations expressed with regard to that judgment by the Court of Appeal of New Zealand in *R. v. McCarthy* [1992] 2 N.Z.L.R. 550, 557–558, *per* Cooke P. delivering the judgment of the court, part of which is quoted by Professor Smith in his commentary on the present case [1993] Crim.L.R. 957, 958. In particular, I wish to record my concern that the Court of Appeal in *R. v. Newell* may have placed too exclusive an emphasis on the word "characteristic," as a result of relying on the judgment of North J. in *R. v. McGregor*, where North J. was construing a statute in which that word was used.

It follows from what I have said that I am, with all respect, unable to accept the reasoning, or the conclusion, of the Court of Appeal. The answer to the question of law posed for consideration by your Lordships' House is apparent from what I have said earlier in this speech. In my opinion, the judge should have directed the jury to take into account the fact of the defendant's addiction to glue-sniffing when considering whether a person with the ordinary person's power of self-control would have reacted to the provocation as the defendant did. The judge failed so to direct the jury. . . . It follows that, since it is accepted that no question of the exercise of the proviso arises in the present case, the conviction of the defendant for murder must be quashed and a conviction of manslaughter substituted. The matter must however be remitted to the Court of Appeal to consider the question of sentence.

[Lords Brown-Wilkinson, Slynn of Hadley, Nicholls of Birkenhead and Steyn concurred.]

Note

Following *Camplin* and *Morhall* it appeared settled that in determining whether the reasonable man might have been provoked the jury should attribute to him or her any of the accused's characteristics, history or circumstances which would be relevant to the gravity of the provocation. With regard to the question whether the reasonable man might have done as the accused did the standard of self-control to be used was that of the ordinary person of the accused's sex and age. A problem which arose, however, in several Court of Appeal cases was that of mental conditions or infirmities which might have a bearing on the gravity of the provocation the accused faced and also his or her ability to exercise self-control. In *Newell* (1980) 71 Cr. App. R. 331, the Court of Appeal upheld the trial judge's decision not to invite the jury to take into account, on the question of provocation, the appellant's condition of chronic alcoholism (which medical evidence indicated may have had a bearing on his powers of self-control) as there was no connection between it and the deceased's derogatory remarks about the appellant's girlfriend and his homosexual overture towards the appellant. In *Ahluwalia* [1992] 4 All E.R. 889, the Court, *obiter*, accepted that battered woman syndrome (BWS) could be a characteristic but it did not suggest that it would be relevant to the issue of the ordinary person's self-control. In *Thornton (No. 2)* [1996] 1 W.L.R. 1174, the Court recognised BWS could be important in helping to explain the killing and may also be a characteristic but did not spell out whether BWS was solely relevant to the question whether a reasonable person might have been provoked or whether it was further relevant to consideration of the degree of self-control to be expected of a reasonable person. In *Dryden* [1995] 4 All E.R. 987, D killed the local authority planning officer who was seeking to enforce an order to demolish a bungalow D had built without planning permission. The Court, *obiter*, considered that the D's obsession with his property and eccentricity were characteristics but dismissed D's appeal as there was no evidence that he had lost his self-control. In *Humphreys* [1995] 4 All E.R. 1008, the Court of Appeal held that D's abnormal immaturity and attention seeking by wrist slashing were characteristics which were relevant to the provocation which took the form of taunts relating to the latter, but it excluded evidence of her explosiveness.

The above cases were considered by the Privy Council in *Luc Thiet Thuan v. R.* [1996] 3 W.L.R. 45. D was convicted of murder having raised both the defences of provocation and diminished responsibility. He adduced medical evidence which showed he suffered from brain damage and was prone to respond to minor provocation by losing his self-control and acting explosively. The trial judge, whose decision was upheld by the Court of Appeal of Hong Kong, had held that this evidence was not relevant to the defence of provocation. Lord Goff delivered the majority opinion concluding that a mental infirmity which impairs an accused's power of self-control was not to be taken into account as it is inconsistent with a person having the power of self-control of an ordinary person who features in the objective test. The mental infirmity of the accused could be taken into account if itself the subject of taunts by the deceased as this would go to the gravity of the provocation. Lord Goff reasoned that this position preserved the distinction between diminished responsibility and provocation which it must have been the intention of the legislature in passing the Homicide Act 1957 to maintain. Furthermore, under the diminished responsibility defence "abnormality of mind" had been given a wide interpretation by the courts which was capable of covering impaired self-control. Lord Steyn dissented expressing the view that the majority position would leave a jury puzzled. He read *Ahluwalia, Dryden, Humphreys* and *Thornton (No. 2)* (along with the first instance decision of *Raven* [1982] Crim.L.R. 51) as supporting the position that mental characteristics which gave rise to impaired self-control should be taken into account when considering whether a reasonable person might have done as the accused did. Lord Steyn's reading of the Court of Appeal decisions was endorsed, *obiter*, by Lord Bingham C.J. in *Campbell* [1997] 1 Cr.App.R. 199 and adopted by the Court of Appeal in *Parker* [1997] Crim.L.R. 760. The issue was considered by the House of Lords in the following case.

R. v. Smith (Morgan)
[2000] 3 W.L.R. 654
House of Lords

D fatally stabbed the deceased in the course of an argument about tools which D alleged the deceased had stolen. At his trial for murder D raised the defence of provocation and adduced medical evidence that he suffered from a depressive illness which impaired his ability to exercise self-control reducing his threshold for erupting with violence. The trial judge accepted the Crown's argument that this evidence was not relevant to the question whether a reasonable man might have lost his self-control. D was convicted of murder and appealed. The Court of Appeal allowed his appeal, substituting a verdict of manslaughter on the ground that his mental impairment was a characteristic to be attributed to the reasonable man not only in assessing the gravity of the provocation but also his reaction to it. The Crown appealed. The Court of Appeal granted leave to appeal and certified the following point of law of general public importance: "Are characteristics other than age and sex, attributable to the reasonable man, for the purpose of section 3 of the Homicide Act 1957, relevant not only to the gravity of the provocation to him but also to the standard of self-control to be expected?" Their Lordships by a majority of three to two answered the question in the affirmative.

LORD HOFFMANN: . . .

2. The defence of provocation
  . . . [Section 3 of the Homicide Act 1957]

plainly changed the law in two ways. First, it provided that if there was evidence that the accused was provoked to lose his self-control (the subjective element) then the question of whether the objective element was satisfied had to be left to the jury. The judge was not entitled, as he could at common law, to withdraw the issue from the jury if he thought there was no evidence upon which a jury could reasonably consider that the objective element might have been satisfied. Secondly, the jury could for this purpose take into account "everything both said and done." This removed any legal restriction on the kind of acts that could amount to provocation, such as the rule in Holmes [1946] A.C. 588 that words alone were insufficient.

[His Lordship considered *Camplin* (*ante* p. 536) and *Luc Thiet Thuan* (*ante*, p. 545), summarised the trial and appeal in the instant case and analysed in detail the historical background to the defence of provocation and the reform proposals of the 1953 Royal Commission on Capital Punishment.]

6. The construction of section 3
  . . . If one approaches the question of construction in the orthodox way, namely by considering the language of the section against the background of the common law of provocation, one has to conclude that the concept of the reasonable man as a touchstone of the objective element could not have been intended to stay the same.

The reasons are to be found in both the other changes expressly made by the section. The first, namely the admission of words as a legitimate source of provocation, I have already mentioned. It was this reason which received the main emphasis in *Camplin*. But the other change, in the respective roles of judge and jury, was equally important. The Royal Commission . . . said (at para. 134) that a change in the law was unnecessary because juries, sometimes in the face of the judge's directions on the law, returned verdicts of manslaughter in cases in which justice appeared to require a concession to human frailty. That is to say, juries arrived at verdicts in favour of the accused which were contrary to law. The traditional way in which judges attempt to deflect the jury from a perverse verdict of this kind is to withdraw the issue. But section 3 was intended to deprive the judge of even this method of control. The jury was to be sovereign and have the power in theory as well as in practice to decide whether the objective element was satisfied.

I do not think it possible to attribute to Parliament, in making this change, any intention other than to legitimate the relaxation of the old law in those cases in which justice appeared to require it and to allow the jury in good conscience to arrive at a verdict which previously would have been perverse. In other words, the jury was given a normative as well as a fact-finding function. They were to determine not merely whether the behaviour of the accused complied with some legal standard but could determine for themselves what the standard in the particular case should be. In this way they could, as the Royal Commission said, "give weight to factors personal to the prisoner" in cases in which it appeared unjust not to do so.

It follows, in my opinion, that it would not be consistent with section 3 for the judge to tell the jury as a matter of law that they should ignore any factor or characteristic of the accused in deciding whether the objective element of provocation had been satisfied. That would be to trespass upon their province. . . . But that did not mean that he was required to leave the jury at large and without any assistance in the exercise of their normative role. He could tell the jury that the doctrine of provocation included the principle of objectivity and that they should have regard to that principle in deciding whether the act in question was sufficiently provocative to be acceptable as a partial excuse. . . .

7. Reg. v. Camplin
[His Lordship looked in detail at Lord Diplock's speech in *Camplin* arriving at the following conclusions:]

(1) Lord Diplock says that youth may be taken into account because the principle of compassion to human infirmity, as a jury drawing on their experience may apply it, requires one to do so. He does not say that the same principle of compassion is incapable of applying to any other characteristics which a jury might on similar grounds think should be taken into account. It would have been easy for him to have said that youth was for this purpose unique.

(2) Lord Diplock expressly rejects the distinction between the effect of age on the gravity of the provocation and on the power of self-control on the grounds that it is "of too great nicety" for application by a jury. Again, there is nothing to suggest that this comment is not equally true of other characteristics. Since *Camplin*, there is a great deal of material which demonstrates that Lord Diplock's scepticism about whether the distinction could be made to work in practice was well founded.

(3) If age were to be the only case in which a particular characteristic could be taken into account as relevant to the expected power of self-control, it would be necessary to explain why it should be so singled out. . . .

[His Lordship went on to consider Lord Diplock's "proper direction to the jury" (*ante*, p. 540).]

The references to age and sex have been taken to mean that in all cases these are the only matters which should be mentioned as relevant to the question of self-control. It seems to me clear, however, that Lord Diplock was framing a suitable direction for a case like *Camplin* [1978] A.C. 705 and not a one-size-fits-all direction for every case of provocation. A jury would be puzzled about why they were being asked to pay particular attention to the age and sex of the defendant if he was an ordinary adult. A number of writers and judges have thought that Lord Diplock was wrong to include the sex of the accused (see for example, *Stingel v. The Queen* (1990) 171 C.L.R. 312, 331) and if the direction had been intended to be of general application, I would agree. But in my view Lord Diplock was only drawing attention to the fact that the hormonal development of male adolescents is different from that of females.

Finally, my Lords, I draw attention to the concluding sentence of Lord Diplock's speech, in which he summed up why he thought it would be wrong to direct the jury that they were not entitled to take into account the youth of the accused. It was because:

"So to direct them was to impose a fetter on the right and duty of the jury which the Act accords to them to act upon their own opinion on the matter."

This, in my view, goes to the heart of the matter and is in accordance with the analysis of the effect of section 3 which I have made earlier in my speech. The jury is entitled to act upon its own opinion of whether the objective element of provocation has been satisfied and the judge is not entitled to tell them that for this purpose the law requires them to exclude from consideration any of the circumstances or characteristics of the accused.

8. The gravity of provocation/self-control distinction.

Although *D.P.P. v. Camplin* [1978] A.C. 705 does not in my opinion provide authoritative support for the distinction between gravity of provocation and powers of self-control, it has been adopted in Australia (*Stingel v. The Queen* (1990) 171 C.L.R. 312) New Zealand (*Reg. v. Campbell* [1997] 1 N.Z.L.R. 16 and *Reg. v. Rongonui* (Court of Appeal, 13 April 2000, unreported); Canada (*Reg. v. Hill* [1986] 1 S.C.R. 313) and by the Privy Council for Hong Kong (*Luc Thiet Thuan v. The Queen* [1997] A.C. 131). It also has a good deal of academic support: see in particular Professor Ashworth's influential article "The Doctrine of Provocation" [1976] C.L.J. 292–320, Jeremy Horder, "Between Provocation and Diminished Responsibility" (1999) 2 K.C.L.J. 143–166 and Professor M.J. Allen, "Provocation's Reasonable Man: A Plea for Self-Control" [2000] Journal of Criminal Law 216–244. It must therefore be considered on its own merits.

The theoretical basis for the distinction is that provocation is a defence for people who are, as Professor Ashworth put it, "in a broad sense mentally normal:" see [1976] C.L.J. at p. 312. If they claim that they had abnormal characteristics which reduced their powers of self-control, they should plead diminished responsibility. There is a clear philosophical distinction between a claim that an act was at least partially excused as normal behaviour in response to external circumstances and a claim that the actor had mental characteristics which prevented him from behaving normally: see Sir Peter Strawson, *Freedom and Resentment*, in *Free Will* (Watson, ed. 1982) at pp. 64–67.

The difficulty about the practical application of this distinction in the law of provocation is that in many cases the two forms of claim are inextricably muddled up with each other. . . .

Besides these practical difficulties in explaining the distinction to the jury, I think it is wrong to assume that there is a neat dichotomy between the "ordinary person" contemplated by the law of provocation and the "abnormal person" contemplated by the law of diminished responsibility. The Act of 1957 made a miscellany of changes of the law of homicide which can hardly be described as amounting to a coherent and interlocking scheme. Diminished responsibility as defined in section 2 ("such abnormality of mind . . . as substantially impaired his mental responsibility for his acts and omissions . . .") is a general defence which can apply whatever the circumstances of the killing and was introduced because of what was regarded as the undue strictness of the defence of insanity. Provocation is a defence which depends upon the circumstances of the killing and section 3 was introduced, as I have suggested, to legitimate the consideration by juries of "factors personal to the prisoner." If one asks whether Parliament contemplated that there might be an overlap between these two defences, I think that the realistic answer is that no one gave the matter a thought. But the possibility of overlap seems to me to follow inevitably from consigning the whole of the objective element in provocation to the jury. If the jury cannot be told that the law requires characteristics which could found a defence of diminished responsibility to be ignored in relation to the defence of provocation, there is no point in claiming that the defences are mutually exclusive.

There are in practice bound to be cases in which the accused will not be suffering from "abnormality of mind" within the meaning of section 2 ("a state of mind so different from that of ordinary human beings that the reasonable man would term it abnormal": *Reg. v. Byrne* [1960] 2 Q.B. 396, 403) but will nevertheless have mental characteristics (temporary or permanent) which the jury might think should be taken into account for the purposes of the provocation defence. The boundary between the normal and abnormal is very often a matter of opinion. . . .

There is however one really serious argument in favour of the distinction between characteristics affecting the gravity of the provocation and characteristics affecting the power of self-control. This is the claim that, despite all its difficulties of application, it is the only way to hold the line against complete erosion of the objective element in provocation. The purpose of the objective element in provocation is to mark the distinction between (partially) excusable and inexcusable loss of self-control. As Lord Diplock said in *D.P.P. v. Camplin* [1978] A.C. 705, 717, the conduct of the accused should be measured against "such powers of self-control as everyone is entitled to expect that his fellow citizens will exercise in society as it is today." If there is no limit to the characteristics which can be taken into account, the fact that the accused lost self-control will show that he is a person liable in such circumstances to lose his self-control. The objective element will have disappeared completely.

My Lords, I share the concern that this should not happen. For the protection of the public, the law should continue to insist that people must exercise self-control. A person who flies into a murderous rage when he is crossed, thwarted or disappointed in the vicissitudes of life should not be able to rely upon his anti-social propensity as even a partial excuse for killing. In *Stingel v. The Queen* (1990) 171 C.L.R. 312, for example, the accused was obsessively infatuated with a woman who had terminated their relationship. He became a stalker, following her about. She obtained a court order restraining him from approaching her. One evening after a party he found the woman in a car with another man. According to his own account, they were having sex. He went back to his own car, fetched a butcher's knife and came back and killed the man. His evidence conformed to the standard narrative which the legal requirement of "loss of control" imposes on such defences:

> "I was all worked up and feeling funny. It was like I was in a rage, almost to the stage where I felt dazed. It was like I really didn"t know what happened until the knife went into him."

The High Court of Australia held that the judge was right to withdraw the issue of provocation from the jury on the ground that such conduct could not raise even a reasonable doubt as to whether the objective element in the defence had been satisfied. I respectfully agree. Male possessiveness and jealousy should not today be an acceptable reason for loss of self-control leading to homicide, whether inflicted upon the woman herself or her new lover. In Australia the judge was able to give effect to this policy by withdrawing issue from the jury. But section 3 prevents an English judge from doing so. So, it is suggested, a direction that characteristics such as jealousy and obsession should be ignored in relation to the objective element is the best way to ensure that people like Stingel cannot rely upon the defence.

9. *The English cases.*

[His Lordship considered the cases of *Newell* (1980) 71 Cr.App.R. 331, *Ahluwalia* [1992] 4 All E.R. 889, *Dryden* [1995] 4 All E.R. 987 and *Campbell* [1997] 1 Cr.App.R. 199, interpreting them as providing "a strong current of authority" for account to be taken of personal characteristics which affect the accused's self-control.]

10. *Guiding the jury*

The effect of section 3 is that once the judge has ruled that there is evidence upon which the jury can find that something caused the accused to lose self-control (compare *Reg. v. Acott* [1997] 1 W.L.R. 306), he cannot tell the jury that the act in question was incapable of amounting to provocation. But that no longer involves any decision by the judge that it would be rational so to decide. [His Lordship cited *Reg. v. Doughty* (*ante* p. 533) as an example.] But [leaving provocation to the jury] does not mean that the judge should tell the jury that the crying of the baby was, in the traditional language, capable of amounting to provocation. This would give the jury the impression that the judge thought it would be rational and in accordance with principle to hold that the crying of the baby constituted an acceptable partial excuse for killing it. The point about section 3 is that it no longer matters whether the judge thinks so or not. He should therefore be able simply to tell the jury that the question of whether such behaviour fell below the standard which should reasonably have been expected of the accused was entirely a matter for them. He should not be obliged to let the jury imagine that the law now regards anything whatever which caused loss of self-control (whether an external event or a personal characteristic of the accused) as necessarily being an acceptable reason for loss of self-control. . . .

11. *The reasonable man*

. . . My Lords, the concept of the "reasonable man" has never been more than a way of explaining the law to a jury; an anthropomorphic image to convey to them, with a suitable degree of vividness, the legal principle that even under provocation, people must conform to an objective standard of behaviour which society is entitled to expect: see Lord Diplock in *Camplin* [1978] A.C. 705, 714. In referring to "the reasonable man" section 3 invokes that standard. But I do not think that it was intended to require judges always to use that particular image, even in cases in which its use is more likely to confuse than illuminate. . . .

In my opinion, therefore, judges should not be required to describe the objective element in the provocation defence by reference to a reasonable man, with or without attribution of personal characteristics. They may instead find it more helpful to explain in simple language the principles of the doctrine of provocation. First, it requires that the accused should have killed while he had lost self-control and that something should have caused him to lose self-control. For better or for worse, section 3 left this part of the law untouched. Secondly, the fact that something caused him to lose self-control is not enough. The law expects people to exercise control over their emotions. A tendency to violent rages or childish tantrums is a defect in character rather than an excuse. The jury must think that the circumstances were such as to make the loss of self-control sufficiently *excusable* to reduce the gravity of the offence from murder to manslaughter. This is entirely a question for the jury. In deciding what should count as a sufficient excuse, they have to apply what they consider to be appropriate standards of behaviour; on the one hand making allowance for human nature and the power of the emotions but, on the other hand, not allowing someone to rely upon his own violent disposition. In applying these standards of behaviour, the jury represent the community and decide, as Lord Diplock said in *Camplin* ([1978] A.C. 717), what degree of self-control "everyone is entitled to expect that his fellow citizens will exercise in society as it is today." The maintenance of such standards is important. As Viscount Simon L.C. said more than 50 years ago in *Holmes v. D.P.P.* [1946] A.C. 588, 601, "as society advances, it ought to call for a higher measure of self-control."

The general principle is that the same standards of behaviour are expected of everyone, regardless of their individual psychological make-up. In most cases, nothing more will need to be said. But the jury should in an appropriate case be told, in whatever language will best convey the distinction, that this is a principle and not a rigid rule. It may sometimes have to yield to a more important principle, which is to do justice in the particular case. So the jury may think that there was some characteristic of the accused, whether temporary or permanent, which affected the degree of control which society could reasonably have expected of *him* and which it would be unjust not to take into account. If the jury take this view, they are at liberty to give effect to it.

My Lords, I do not wish to lay down any prescriptive formula for the way in which the matter is explained to the jury. I am sure that if judges are freed from the necessity of invoking the formula of the reasonable man equipped with an array of unreasonable "eligible characteristics," they will be able to explain the principles in simple terms. Provided that the judge makes it clear that the question is in the end one for the jury and that he is not seeking to "impose a fetter on the right and duty of the jury which the Act accords to them," the guidance which he gives must be a matter for his judgment on the facts of the case. . . .

13. Conclusion.

In my opinion the judge should not have directed the jury as a matter of law that the effect of Smith's depression on his powers of self-control was "neither here nor there." They should have been told that whether they took it into account in relation to the question of whether the behaviour of the accused had measured up to the standard of self-control which ought reasonably to have been expected of him was a matter for them to decide. For the above reasons and those given by my noble and learned friends Lord Slynn of Hadley and Lord Clyde, I would dismiss the appeal.

LORD CLYDE: . . . But if the appellant is correct, it seems to me that there would be a serious risk of injustice being done in some cases where the homicide is due to provocation but the condition of the accused falls short of a mental abnormality. While I fully recognise the importance of not allowing the effects of a quarrelsome or choleric temperament to serve as a factor which may reduce the crime of murder to one of manslaughter, nevertheless I consider that justice cannot be done without regard to the particular frailties of particular individuals where their capacity to restrain themselves in the face of provocation is lessened by some affliction which falls short of a mental abnormality. It does not seem to me that it would be just if in assessing their guilt in a matter of homicide a standard of behaviour had to be applied to people which they are incapable of attaining. I would not regard it as just for a plea of provocation made by a battered wife whose condition falls short of a mental abnormality to be rejected on the ground that a reasonable person would not have reacted to the provocation as she did. The reasonable person in such a case should be one who is exercising a reasonable level of self-control for someone with her history, her experience and her state of mind. On such an approach a jury should be perfectly capable of returning a realistic answer and thus achieve a verdict which would fairly meet any peculiarities of the particular case consistently with the recognition of the importance of curbing temper and passion in the interest of civil order. . . .

LORD HOBHOUSE OF WOODBOROUGH: . . . In the present case the trial judge, Judge Coombe, told the jury that

> "The 'reasonable man' means an ordinary person of either sex, not exceptionally excitable or pugnacious, but possessed of such powers of self-control as everyone is entitled to expect that his fellow citizens will exercise in society as it is today." (p. 17)

The Court of Appeal considered that he was wrong. . . .

Thus, central to the issue of law raised by this appeal is the purpose for which the evidence of mental abnormality is being treated as relevant. It is common ground that s. 3 and the common law of provocation require two questions to be answered. The first is the factual, or as some prefer to call it the "subjective" question: Was the defendant provoked, whether by things said or done to lose his self-control and kill? Since this is a factual question, evidence of any mental or other abnormality which makes it more or less likely that the defendant lost his self-control is relevant and admissible, as is any evidence concerning the defendant which helps the understanding or assessment of the evidence of what occurred. In answering factual questions all relevant evidence is in principle admissible. For such purpose it does not matter whether the evidence relates to something which would be described as a "characteristic" of the defendant. Thus, evidence may be relevant and therefore admissible that the defendant was at the time very drunk or under the influence of a hallucinogenic drug. Such evidence may of course cut either way. It may show that anything said or done did not affect the defendant's conduct which was simply due to his delusions. Or, it may show that something said or done which would not normally cause anyone to lose their self-control may have caused the defendant to do so.

The second question is what is called the "objective" question. It is, in the words of s. 3 "the question whether the provocation was enough to make a reasonable man do as the [defendant] did", taking "into account everything both done and said according to the effect which . . . it would have on a reasonable man." This question itself contains two elements. The first is the assessment of the gravity of the provocation. The second is the assessment how a reasonable man would react to provocation of that gravity. The second element involves applying a standard of self-control. Essential to the understanding of the authorities and the issue on this appeal is the distinction between these two elements. It is well established and not in dispute that in assessing the gravity of the provocation everything both said and done must be taken into account and that this inevitably involves taking into account any peculiarity of the defendant which affects that gravity. What is in dispute on this appeal is whether in applying the standard of self-control the jury should apply a qualified standard to reflect the respondent's lack of capacity to exercise ordinary self-control.

The Court of Appeal accepted the respondent's submission that the standard of self-control should be the qualified one. *Luc Thiet Thuan v The Queen* [1997] A.C. 131 was a case in which this point arose for decision. *Luc Thiet*, although on appeal from Hong Kong was decided on the basis of English law. The opinion of the Privy Council was given by Lord Goff of Chieveley. It was held that the section required the standard of self-control of an ordinary person not that of a person who only had an abnormal and deficient capacity for self-control. Lord Steyn dissented. Lord Steyn stated that he was deciding in accordance with the previous decisions of the English Courts and by implication expressing the opinion that Lord Goff was not. Whether Lord Steyn's dissent did in truth accord with the earlier English authorities is in contention. It is an essential element in the correctness of his view of the law. Later judgments in the Court of Appeal have accepted Lord Steyn's view, referring to the earlier authorities but, it must be said, without themselves undertaking a close examination of what exactly was decided in them. My Lords, in this speech I will re-examine those authorities; I consider that, contrary to the view of Lord Steyn, they show that English law does not require that the jury be directed to visualise an ordinary (reasonable) man with abnormal (unreasonable) mental characteristics.

[His Lordship considered the judgment of North J in *McGregor* [1962] N.Z.L.R. 1069, which superficially appears to conform to Lord Steyn's view in *Luc Thiet Thuan*, pointing out difficulties in the judgment due to some inconsistency and the fact that there is no defence of diminished responsibility in New Zealand.]

Anthropomorphism etc.
My Lords, the view of English law relied upon by the respondent on this appeal is a recent phenomenon. It has emerged gradually from the opinion of North J over little more than a decade. But the seeds from which it has sprung can be detected further back. A root cause is the inveterate (and not wholly unmeritorious) tendency of common lawyers to anthropomorphise concepts. Thus the test of liability in negligence was explained by reference to "the man on the Clapham omnibus". When the phrase "reasonable man" (coming from 19th Century cases such as *Reg. v Welsh* (1869) 11 Cox 336) is used in s. 3, the common lawyer immediately tries to visualise and define some physical human being with identified characteristics (apparently both reasonable and unreasonable) whereas what the phrase is doing is identifying a concept, a standard of self-control. This standard is, as Lord Diplock and your Lordship's House have said in *Reg. v Camplin* [1978] AC 705, 717 those "powers of self-control as everyone is entitled to expect his fellow citizens will exercise in society as it is today". Lord Taylor L.C.J. confirmed the point in *Reg v. Dryden* [1995] 4 All E.R. at 997: "The purpose of taking the reasonable man was to have a yardstick to measure the loss of self-control that will be permitted to found a defence of provocation." In *Reg. v Morhall* [1996] 1 AC at 90, 98, Lord Goff said: "The function of the test is only to introduce as a matter of policy a standard of self-control which has to be complied with if provocation is to be established in law."

It is the anthropomorphic thinking and the artificialities to which it has given rise which have pervaded the more recent judgments of the Court of Appeal and been the primary cause of the confusions and errors which have led to a series of English cases in the decade before the present case came to the Court of Appeal and now a perceived conflict with a considered judgment of the Privy Council. If judges are encouraged or required to sum up to juries in artificial and self-contradictory anthropomorphic terms, it is no wonder that people are confused and critical. One can compare that with the simple and clearly understandable language used by Judge Coombe in the present case which is minimally anthropomorphic. Indeed, there is no complaint that the language of Judge Coombs was in any way obscure or incomprehensible. The complaint is that the jury will have understood his direction too well and therefore have excluded a factor in the respondent's favour which, it is said, they ought to have taken into account. . . .

Construing the Act of 1957 in its context: diminished responsibility
[His Lordship went on to highlight the context in which section 3 was enacted.]

The Act of 1957 was an amending act. It changed the existing law. Sections 1,2 and 3 all emerged from the discussion in the Report of the Royal Commission. Section 1 abolished the concept of "constructive malice" so removing a fiction which was no longer justified. Sections 2 and 3 have clear inter-relation. They both deal with factors which may affect the responsibility of the defendant for the killing. The premise upon which they both proceed is that the defendant has killed or been a party to the killing and has had the *mens rea* requisite to the crime of murder. Sections 2 and 3 provide defences which reduce what would otherwise have been murder to manslaughter, thus disapplying the mandatory sentences applicable to murder. Section 2, diminished responsibility, was a Scottish law concept wholly new to English law. Section 3 was a statutory alteration to an existing common law defence. Section 3, including the retention of the "reasonable man" test, specifically derived from the recommendations of the Royal Commission as part of their review of all aspects of the existence of the death penalty. The Commission did not think that the introduction of the concept of diminished responsibility was justified although they carefully considered and recognised it merits. (See paragraphs 373–413.) Parliament however decided to introduce the defence, hence s.2. Both sections address the same question: the defendant's act was unjustified and unlawful but he may not have been fully responsible for his act.

[His Lordship considered section 2 of the 1957 Act concluding that it covers any kind of abnormality of mind.]

This is important because there seems in some quarters to be an implicit assumption that the assessment by a jury under s.2 is inadequate properly to allow for the defendant's abnormality of mind in relation to any killing which was contributed to by provocation. There is no reason to make this assumption. Further, it is contrary to the drafting of s.2 and to sections 2 and 3 read together. The brain damaged man has an abnormality of the mind. If it is of sufficient severity, in the opinion of the jury, to impair substantially his mental responsibility for killing his provoker, he will be found guilty of manslaughter, not murder, even if his action was not that of a reasonable man (indeed, one could say, *because* his action was not that of a reasonable man).
If the defendant is merely someone with a personality disorder, for example an exceptionally violent or immoral disposition, he will not be able to rely on s.2, nor will he be able to rely on s.3 if his response to the provocation was disproportionate. This is all in accord with the specific

policy of the Act and the ordinary principles of criminal responsibility. Similarly, if the defendant suffered from an abnormality but the jury do not consider it to be sufficient substantially to impair his responsibility, he will not have a defence under s.2. This simply reflects the policy of the statute and it would be contrary to that policy to extend s.3 to give him the defence advisedly denied him by s.2.

One of the errors that have bedevilled some of the recent judicial statements in this part of the English law of homicide is the failure to take account of the interaction of sections 2 and 3 and appreciate that they not only show that the strained construction of s.3 is wrong but also that the perceived injustice which the strained construction is designed to avoid is in fact covered by an application of s.2 in accordance with its ordinary meaning. Section 2 is of course capable of applying in any situation and those situations include a killing by a defendant who has killed after losing his self-control. A defendant in this situation can contend that his conduct was not abnormal and require the prosecution to satisfy the jury that his loss of self-control was not the result of provocation or his response to it was not that of a reasonable man. Or, he can contend and seek to satisfy the jury on the balance of probabilities that he had an abnormality of the mind which in the circumstances substantially reduced his mental responsibility for what he did. A defendant can of course place both contentions before the jury, as the respondent did in this case. The jury can then return a verdict of manslaughter on the one or the other basis. But it is always open to the jury to conclude (as no doubt the jury did in the present case) that the defendant's response was objectively disproportionate and that his abnormality of mind did not suffice to impair his mental responsibility for what he had done. . . .

The defences of diminished responsibility and provocation are both recognised and are capable of operating separately. But, likewise, they can and very often do operate in conjunction. In English law by the Act of 1957 the two defences have been kept separate and are the subject of distinct provision—sections 2 and 3. But the two sections clearly form two parts of a legislative scheme for dealing with defendants who should not be treated as fully responsible for the death they have caused.

The context: the previous law

The "reasonable man" test had been specifically considered by the Royal Commission (paras 141 and following). They discussed the argument that—

> "if the accused is mentally abnormal or is of subnormal intelligence or is a foreigner of more excitable temperament or is for some other reason particularly susceptible to provocation, it is neither fair nor reasonable to judge him by the standard of the ordinary Englishman."

They referred to and adopted the contrary argument that—

> "It is a fundamental principle of the criminal law that it should be based on a generally accepted standard of conduct applicable to all citizens alike, and it is important that this principle should not be infringed. Any departure from it might introduce a dangerous latitude into the law."

They did not recommend any change in the law of provocation in this respect. In reaching this conclusion they expressly mentioned in paragraph 143 the relevance of the Scottish defence of diminished responsibility to the question of a provoked defendant who suffered from some mental abnormality not amounting to insanity, a topic to which they said they would revert (as they did) in a later chapter. The interrelation of the two concepts was not overlooked.

The Act of 1957 follows the same scheme. It preserves the "reasonable man" test unchanged and separately introduces the new defence of diminished responsibility. The argument of the respondent on this appeal raises again the argument rejected by the Royal Commission and seeks to give the Act of 1957 an effect which it is patently not intended to have. Further, if the Legislature had intended to change the law in this respect, one would find some indication of it by a requirement that the jury were to be directed to take into account something which had previously been excluded—a reference to any abnormally deficient powers of self-control of the defendant. Instead the jury are required, in determining the second question, simply to "take into account everything both done and said according to the effect which in their opinion it would have on a reasonable man". . . .

[His Lordship pointed out that the argument of the respondents in the current appeal had been raised and rejected in the cases of Alexander (1913) 9 Cr.App.R. 139 and *Lesbini* [1914] 3 K.B. 1116, which were affirmed by the House of Lords in *Mancini v. D.P.P.* [1942] A.C. 1. The argument was also rejected by the Royal Commission.]

The Legislature in enacting s.3 likewise did not accept the argument in relation to provocation but, by introducing the defence of diminished responsibility in s.2, gave effect to it in a different way and to the extent Parliament thought proper. . . .

Reg. v. Camplin
[Having established that the role of the second question is to provide a standard of ordinary self-control against which the accused's response is compared, his Lordship proceeded to analyse Lord Diplock's speech in *Camplin* which supported this view.]

Lord Diplock stressed that s.3 recognised and retained the dual test for provocation. He also confirmed his agreement with Lord Simon of Glaisdale that evidence is not admissible upon the second question. He then stated, at p. 717 the meaning of the phrase "reasonable man" for the purposes of the law of provocation:

"It means an ordinary person of either sex, not exceptionally excitable or pugnacious" but possessed of such powers of self-control as everyone is entitled to expect that his fellow citizens will exercise in society as it is today." . . .

His opinion was that it was, since the Act, better not to refer juries to what was said in *Bedder* in the interests of avoiding unnecessary complexity. He was clearly of the view that the word "reasonable" was still to be treated as a synonym for ordinary or normal. Thus, in summarising his view as to the appropriate way in which the trial judge should direct a jury on the second question, he said, at p. 718:

"He should explain to them that the reasonable man referred to in the question is a person having *the power of self-control to be expected of an ordinary person* of the sex and age of the accused but *in other respects* sharing such of the accused's characteristics as they think would affect the gravity of the provocation to him; and that the question is not merely whether such a person would in like circumstances be provoked to lose his self-control but also whether he would react to the provocation as the accused did." (emphasis supplied)

As I have emphasised, his formulation is based upon the assumption of the possession of ordinary powers of self-control and it is only *in other respects* that the defendant's abnormal characteristics are to be taken into account. It is also loyal to the drafting of s. 3 which is concerned with the *effect* the provocation would have on the reasonable/ordinary man.

Lord Morris expressly agreed with Lord Diplock's direction and his speech discloses no marked differences. Lord Fraser and Lord Scarman agreed with the speech of Lord Diplock.

Lord Simon, at p. 726, said: "In my judgment the reference to "a reasonable man" at the end of the section means "a man of ordinary self-control"." Thus Lord Simon, like Lord Diplock, equated the concept of the reasonable man with a man with ordinary powers of self control. (See also Lord Simon to the same effect at p. 725D and his express agreement at p. 727 with Lord Diplock's model direction.) All this is loyal to the view of the Royal Commission and the drafting of the section and directly contrary to the respondent's argument in the present case . . ..

[His Lordship went on to examine *Newell* (1980) 71 Cr.App.R. 331 which he found provided no support for the respondent's argument. His Lordship next dispensed with the first instance decision of *Raven* [1982] Crim.L.R. 51, which involved a man of 22 years of age who had a mental age of nine, as one which was at odds with *Camplin* and *Newell* and which should have been decided on the basis of diminished responsibility.]

Lord Taylor of Gosforth C.J.
[His Lordship considered the judgments of Lord Taylor C.J. which the respondents had cited in support of their argument. He found no support in *Ahluwalia* [1992] 4 All E.R. 889, where a retrial was ordered because of new evidence of BWS which disclosed an arguable case of diminished responsibility. His Lordship also found *Dryden* [1995] 4 All E.R. 987 to be an authority against the respondents as although Lord Taylor indicated that the appellant's obsession was relevant to the provocation, he made it clear that his response to it was to be measured against that of a person with the self-control of a reasonable man. His Lordship similarly found no support for the respondent's argument in Lord Taylor's judgment in *Morhall*, in the Court of Appeal, nor in *Thornton* (No. 2) [1996] 1 W.L.R. 1174.]

Reg. v. Morhall
The speech of Lord Goff was agreed to by all the other members of the Committee. The speech rejected the anthropomorphic approach. Lord Goff stressed that the second question was concerned with identifying "a standard of self-control". (p. 98) The law was not concerned to invite the jury to consider a reasonable glue-sniffer. He discussed the law of New Zealand in the light of the later decision in *McCarthy* and the judgment of Cooke P. The thrust of the speech is that there are two aspects of provocation in relation to which a jury might attach significance to an abnormal trait of the defendant. The first, which is permissible, is relevance to the gravity of the provocation to the defendant (point 2). The second,

which is not permissible, is relevance to the standard of self-control required by the law (point 4). The jury should have been directed about this (and had not been). The fact that the trait of the defendant is repugnant to the standard is irrelevant to the question of evaluating the gravity of the provocation.

It is to be observed that this decision is a binding authority in English law. It distinguishes between matters going to the gravity of the provocation and the required standard of self-control. It is in line with the previous authorities but has moved away from treating the judgment of North J. as the place to find all the relevant answers.

Luc Thiet Thuan:

This case raised the question whether a defendant who suffered from brain damage which was irrelevant to the provocation (point 2) but was relevant to his capacity for self-control could rely upon the brain damage in support of his case under the second question in s. 3. Nothing appears to have turned upon the fact that such lack of capacity would be relevant to answering the first, the factual, question whether he did in fact lose his self-control. The opinion delivered by Lord Goff contains nothing new save for a fuller discussion of the law of New Zealand and Australia, the inclusion of quotes from the article of Professor Ashworth [1976] CLJ 292 and an important passage explaining and emphasising the relevance of the defence of diminished responsibility introduced by s. 2 of the Act (p. 1046).

Thus the opinion recites what was decided in *Camplin*, setting the standard. It repeats the distinction between aggravation of the provocation and something which merely impairs the power of self-control. It stresses that the standard of self-control is that of the ordinary person. It points out that it is not open to the courts "either to discard the objective test or to interpret it in a manner inconsistent with the statute." (p. 1039)

The dissent of Lord Steyn postulates situations of greater or lesser emotional content where there is evidence that the defendant suffers from a mental condition which affects her capacity for self-control. This evidence is admissible to deciding upon the answer to be given to the first, the factual, question. He then goes on to postulate that the judge will give the jury a direction upon the second aspect of the second question which is artificial and confusing. This must be contrasted with the simple and easily understood direction that Judge Coombe gave the jury in the present case. The dissent dismisses the inclusion of s. 2 in the statute as an irrelevance, apparently on the ground that "the burden of establishing the defence is on the defendant who raises it"; "it is an optional defence." The reasoning specifically rejects the provisions of s. 2 as being those settled by the Legislature to deal with mental abnormality and asserts that there should be looser criteria. It pays no regard to the fact that the Royal Commission recommended that the "reasonable man" test should be retained and the Legislature chose to do so but with the addition of the diminished responsibility defence. As regards the discussion of the previous authorities, it places wholly inappropriate reliance upon *Raven*. It does not refer to *Newell*. It misstates the decisions in the cases I have analysed as representing the view of Lord Taylor. It fails to give effect to what was decided by *Camplin* and *Morhall*.

My Lords, as I have demonstrated, it is the majority opinion which is in accordance with the English authority not the dissent.

The Later Cases:

[His Lordship pointed out that in *Campbell* [1997] 1 Cr.App.R. 199 the dissent of Lord Steyn in *Luc Thiet Thuan* was supported on the assumption that it accorded with English law as declared by the Court of Appeal. In Parker, February 25, 1997, the Court of Appeal again followed Lord Steyn and *Raven* but failed to consider *Newell*.]

The Court of Appeal

Finally, I come to the Court of Appeal's judgment in the present case. It is a carefully reasoned judgment but it inevitably does not reflect the same thoroughness of review that has been possible for your Lordships. The Court of Appeal were unable to find in s. 3 any support for the view of Judge Coombe. As I have sought to demonstrate, construed in its context, s.3 is in truth only consistent with the prosecution case; put at its lowest it does not provide support for the respondent's case.

As regards the case law, it appears that the relevant cases from *Newell* onwards were cited but the analysis they received seems to have been based upon what was said about them by Lord Steyn in *Luc Thiet*. The Court rejected the distinction between matters which may aggravate the provocation and the objective standard of self-control required by the law even though that distinction can be found not only in *Luc Thiet* but also in the relevant Court of Appeal authorities and *Morhall* and, indeed, is apparent in a quotation which they make from Lord Taylor in Dryden (p. 23 of the transcript).

Like the dissent in *Luc Thiet*, the correctness of the judgment of the Court of Appeal depends upon its having correctly analysed the Court of Appeal authorities. In my view it has not done so.

Conclusion:

The law, as provided in s.3 of the Act of 1957 and held in the authorities down to *Luc Thiet*, establishes that the constituents of provocation are:

(a) The defendant must have been provoked (whether by things done or by things said or by both together) to lose his self-control and kill or do whatever other act is alleged to render him guilty of murder.

(b) This is a factual question upon which all relevant evidence is admissible including any evidence which tends to support the conclusion that the defendant either may have or did not lose his self-control.

(c) If the jury conclude that the defendant may have been provoked to lose his self-control and do as he did, the jury should, as an exercise of judgment, but taking into account all the evidence, form a view as to the gravity of the provocation for the defendant in all the circumstances.

(d) Finally, the jury should decide whether in their opinion, having regard to the actual provocation (a and b above) and their view as to its gravity (c above), a person having ordinary powers of self-control would have done what the defendant did. If some elaboration of the word "ordinary" is thought necessary, it should be along the lines advised by Lord Diplock and used by Judge Coombe in the present case. The phrase "reasonable man" although used in the section is better avoided as not assisting the understanding of the criterion "ordinary powers of self-control". The word "characteristics" should be avoided altogether in relation to (d). It is not used in the section. It is alien to the objective standard of ordinariness and experience has shown that it is a persistent source of confusion. Where relevant the age or gender of the defendant should be referred to since they are not factors which qualify the criterion of ordinariness. But language which qualifies or contradicts such ordinariness must be avoided. It is the standard of ordinary not an abnormal self-control that has to be used.

It is the standard which conforms to what everyone is entitled to expect of their fellow citizens in society as it is.

If the scheme which I have set out above is followed, there should be no difficulty in directing the jury using simple and clearly understandable language. No artificialities are involved and the contradictions involved in the approach contended for by the defendant are avoided. Judge Coombe did this successfully in the present case as have many judges before him. It does less than justice to juries to suggest that they are incapable of understanding directions as simple as the four which I have set out above. If, as will usually be the case where the defence rely upon a mental element, diminished responsibility is also raised, s.2 and the concept of abnormality of mind provides the judge with an opportunity, if he thinks it helpful, to make an illustrative point of contrast with the objective test in s.3.

It is not acceptable to leave the jury without definitive guidance as to the objective criterion to be applied. The function of the criminal law is to identify and define the relevant legal criteria. It is not proper to leave the decision to the essentially subjective judgment of the individual jurors who happen to be deciding the case. Such an approach is apt to lead to idiosyncratic and inconsistent decisions. The law must inform the accused, and the judge must direct the jury, what is the objective criterion which the jury are to apply in any exercise of judgment in deciding upon the guilt or innocence of the accused. Non-specific criteria also create difficulties for the conduct of criminal trials since they do not set the necessary parameters for the admission of evidence or the relevance of arguments. In fairness to those representing the respondent on this appeal, they have not submitted that a non-specific approach is permissible nor that it should be adopted.

The appeal should be allowed. The direction of the Judge was appropriate to the issues at the trial. The conviction was not unsafe.

LORD MILLETT: . . . In *Camplin* [1978] A.C. 705, 726 Lord Simon of Glaisdale stated that "the reasonable man" in section 3 means "a man of ordinary self-control," and Lord Diplock, at p. 717, said that it means:

> "an ordinary person of either sex, not exceptionally excitable or pugnacious, but possessed of such powers of self-control as everyone is entitled to expect that his fellow citizens will exercise in society as it is today."

In the present case Judge Coombe directed the jury in these terms. The Court of Appeal held that he was wrong to do so. There was evidence that the accused suffered from a depressive illness which reduced his powers of self-control. In these circumstances, the Court of Appeal ruled, he should have directed the jury that in his case "the reasonable man" meant a man with the powers of self-control of a person suffering from such an illness; ie. a person with less than normal powers of self-control.

My Lords, this approach requires the accused to be judged by his own reduced powers of self-control, eliminates the objective element altogether and removes the only standard external to the accused by which the jury may judge the sufficiency of the provocation relied on. By introducing a variable standard of self-control it subverts the moral basis of the defence, and is ultimately incompatible with a requirement that the accused must not only have lost his self-control but have been provoked to lose it; for if anything will do this requirement is illusory. It is also manifestly inconsistent with the terms of section 3. It makes it unnecessary for the jury to answer the question which section 3 requires to be left to them, viz. whether the provocation was enough to make a reasonable man do as the accused did. It becomes sufficient that it made the accused react as he did. It substitutes for the requirement that the jury shall take into account everything both done and said according to the effect which in their opinion it would have on a reasonable man a different requirement by reference to the effect which it actually had on the accused. These tests are in truth no tests at all.

It is also inconsistent with Lord Diplock's description of the reasonable man in *Camplin* [1978] A.C. 705, for the reference to "his fellow citizens" (in the plural) is deliberately intended to generalise the test and is plainly not a reference to persons possessing the abnormally reduced powers of self-control of the accused. I respectfully disagree with Lord Hoffmann .... .

[Lord Slynn of Hadley delivered a speech dismissing the appeal.]

Appeal dismissed.

Questions

1. If, as Lord Hoffmann suggests, all characteristics should be left to the jury to weigh up when considering the objective question, is he being inconsistent when he expresses support for "a direction that characteristics such as jealousy and obsession should be ignored in relation to the objective element to ensure that people like Stingel cannot rely upon the defence"? If Smith's depression is relevant why should Stingel's obsession not be?

2. Lord Slynn of Hadley stated (at p. 661) that "The jury must ask whether he [the accused] has exercised the degree of self-control to be expected of someone in his situation." If that "someone" is attributed with the accused's grossly impaired powers of self-control, could a jury ever be satisfied beyond reasonable doubt s/he "might not have reacted as the accused did? If not, has the objective test been emasculated by excessive "subjectivisation"?

3. Lord Clyde stated (at p.684):

"So a concession is made for considerations of age and sex of the accused. But then the problem arises why consideration should not be given to other characteristics. Some groups of people may be seen to be by nature more susceptible to provocation than others. Some races may be more hot-blooded than others. ... Society should require that [the accused] exercise a reasonable control over himself, but the limits within which control is reasonably to be demanded must take account of characteristics peculiar to him which reduce the extent to which he is capable of controlling himself. ... Section 3 requires that the accused should have made reasonable efforts to control himself within the limits of what he is reasonably able to do."

Does this open the way for an accused to tender evidence that due to his race or due to the lack of discipline in his upbringing, his powers of self-control are less than those of other races or those who have had a disciplined upbringing? Is it possible to reconcile the above dictum with the following dictum of North J. in *McGregor* [1962] N.Z.L.R. 1069 (this is part of the passage quoted by Lord Lane C.J. in *Newell*)?

> "[I]f the colour, race or creed of the offender be relied on as constituting a characteristic, it is to be repeated that the provocative words or conduct must be related to the particular characteristic relied upon. Thus, it would not be sufficient, for instance, for the offender to claim merely that he belongs to an excitable race, or that members of his nationality are accustomed to resort readily to the use of some lethal weapon. Here again, the provocative act or words require to be directed at the particular characteristic before it can be relied upon."

4. As a result of the decision of the majority will expert evidence now be called by defendants to inform the jury of the potential effects of various conditions on his or her powers of self-control?

5. In *Camplin* Lord Diplock accepted the relevance of age to the objective test as the law should not "require old heads upon young shoulders." In *Stingel* (1990) 171 C.L.R. 312 the High Court of Australia stated that "the process of development from childhood to maturity . . ., being common to us all, is an aspect of ordinariness." Is impaired self-control due to mental illness an "aspect of ordinariness"?

Note

The reasonable relationship factor

In *Mancini v. D.P.P.* [1942] A.C. 1, the House of Lords held that a judge could decline to leave the defence of provocation to the jury where the "mode of resentment" did not "bear a reasonable relationship to the provocation". This rule could not survive s. 3 of the 1957 Act which recognised that provocation could come from words alone. In *Brown* [1972] 2 Q.B. 229 it was accepted that it is proper for the jury to consider whether a reasonable man would have responded to the provocation in the way that the accused had responded as the relationship between the provocation and the response is an aspect of the objective question. This had been recognised previously by the Privy Council in *Phillips v. R.* [1969] 2 A.C. 130, which rejected the argument that there were not degrees of loss of self-control. Counsel had sought to argue that once self-control was lost "there is no intermediate stage between icy detachment and going berserk". Lord Diplock stated (at p. 137):

> "This premise, unless the argument is purely semantic, must be based upon human experience and is, in their Lordships view, false. The average man reacts to provocation according to its degree with angry words, with a blow of the hand, possibly, if the provocation is gross and there is a dangerous weapon to hand, with that weapon."

The decision in *Smith (Morgan)*, however, leaves the position uncertain as the reasonable (or ordinary) man may now be someone suffering from a mental condition which greatly impairs his powers of self-control such that he may respond with extreme violence in face of minimal provocation.

ii. Diminished Responsibility

Homicide Act 1957, section 2

(1) Where a person kills or is a party to the killing of another, he shall not be convicted of murder if he was suffering from such abnormality of mind (whether arising from a condition of arrested or retarded development of mind or any inherent causes or induced by disease or injury) as substantially impaired his mental responsibility for his acts and omissions in doing or being a party to the killing.

(2) On a charge of murder, it shall be for the defence to prove that the person charged is by virtue of this section not liable to be convicted of murder.

(3) A person who but for this section would be liable, whether as principal or as accessory, to be convicted of murder shall be liable instead to be convicted of manslaughter.

Criminal Procedure (Insanity) Act 1964, section 6

Where on a trial for murder the accused contends

(a) that at the time of the alleged offence he was insane so as not to be responsible according to law for his actions; or
(b) that at the time he was suffering from such abnormality of mind as is specified in subsection (1) of section (2) of the Homicide Act 1957 (diminished responsibility)

the court shall allow the prosecution to adduce or elicit evidence tending to prove the other of those contentions, and may give directions as to the stage of the proceedings at which the prosecution may adduce such evidence.

Note

As with insanity, the onus of proof which the defence have to discharge is on a balance of probabilities: *R. v. Dunbar* [1958] 1 Q.B. 1. This partial defence has largely replaced insanity as a defence to murder. In the years 1989–1998/9 in murder trials there have on average been 64 verdicts per year on the basis of diminished responsibility as opposed to one to two per year of not guilty by reason of insanity (see *Criminal Statistics for England and Wales* 1998, CM4649, Table 4.8, *post*, p. 581). It is noteworthy, however, that the number of findings of diminished responsibility has fallen from a high point of 83 in 1989 to 46 in 1997. (See Appendix 9 of the Butler Report (Cmnd. 6244, 1975) for a table comparing the number of insanity pleas before and after 1957.)

The limitations of the insanity defence have already been discussed, *ante*, p. 218. Williams, T.C.L. 686, says of section 2 both that it "has had highly beneficial results" and that it contains "as embarrassing a formula for a scientifically-minded witness as could be devised". The success of the formula lies in the fact that it uses neither exclusively "legal" nor exclusively "medical" concepts. "Abnormality of mind" is imprecise and has been given wide interpretation by the courts, see *Byrne*, below. "Mental responsibility," as the Butler report comments, is "either a concept of law or a concept of morality; it is not a clinical fact relating to the defendant. . . . [Y]et psychiatrists commonly testify to impaired 'mental responsibility' under section 2" (section 19.5).

S. Dell, "Diminished Responsibility Reconsidered" [1982] Crim.L.R. 809, 813–814

[T]here was disagreement between doctors on the issue of diminished responsibility in no more than 13 per cent of the cases in which the defence was raised. In about half of the cases where there was disagreement, it arose because one of the doctors considered that there was no abnormality of mind. In the other half, there was agreement as to the presence of some mental abnormality, but disagreement as to whether it substantially impaired the offender's mental responsibility.

These two types of disagreement raise different issues. The presence or absence of mental abnormality is a technical psychiatric question, and one on which doctors as experts could on occasion be expected to disagree. In the main their disagreements occurred in relation to the milder cases of mental illness and personality disorder, where there was room for debate on the question of where normality ceases and abnormality begins.

The second area of disagreement—whether mental responsibility was or was not impaired—raises different issues. The Butler Committee pointed out that mental responsibility in the context of section 2 is not a clinical matter on which doctors have expertise, but a legal or a moral question. Glanville Williams has persuasively argued that it cannot sensibly be regarded as a legal question: it is really a moral one. But although the presence or absence of mental responsibility is not a medical matter, doctors grapple with it: and in half the cases where they disagreed with each other on the issue of diminished responsibility, it was on the moral and not the psychiatric aspects of the case that they disagreed. For example, in one case an offender was seen by the prison medical officer and an independent psychiatrist, both of whom found him suffering from an abnormality of mind which they described in virtually identical terms: hysterical psychopathy associated with impulsive and manipulative behaviour. But the independent psychiatrist's report went on to say 'I see no indication to raise a consideration of diminished responsibility,' whilst the prison medical officer wrote 'I would be prepared to say that his responsibility was substantially diminished.' Neither doctor cited in his report any reason for the view he took, and in the event neither was required to give evidence on the matter, as a plea of guilty to diminished responsibility manslaughter was accepted.

There were other cases where the doctors agreed on the presence of mental abnormality, and then disagreed not as to whether there was impairment of mental responsibility, but as to whether it was substantial. For example, a brain-damaged psychopath who killed in the course of a robbery was regarded by the defence as being of substantially diminished responsibility, while the prison medical officer held that his responsibility was diminished 'to a certain extent . . . but this does not amount to a substantial degree of impairment'. Again, the bases of judgments of this kind were not given in the medical reports, and it is not easy to see what they might have been. For, as the Butler Committee pointed out: 'the idea that ability to conform to the law can be measured is particularly puzzling', and doctors have no special qualifications or expertise which fits them to undertake so puzzling a task. That they are nevertheless prepared to undertake it, and that judges (in Butler's view 'surprisingly') are prepared to let them do so, demonstrates the determination of both professions to gloss over the difficulties in section 2 in the interests of making it work.

Note

This Heath Robinson approach to reducing murder to manslaughter is perhaps best explained by the fact that section 2 has two, not always compatible, functions. On the one hand, it is "a device for . . . untying the hands of the judge in murder cases" (Butler Report, section 19.8), while on the other it allows for a display of public sympathy for the domestic, one-off murderer. Problems arise when the sympathy is absent, but the defendant is clearly mentally abnormal within the section. Diminished responsibility is a question of fact but if the jury is perverse in the face of fact and medical evidence, the Court of Appeal will upset the verdict: *R. v. Matheson* [1958] 1 W.L.R. 474, and *Walton v. R., post*, p. 568. Difficulties have also arisen where the court, with the prosecution's consent, agrees to accept the defence plea of diminished responsibility. See *R. v. Vinagre, post*, p. 570 and the discussion following it.

R. v. Byrne
[1960] 2 Q.B. 396
Court of Criminal Appeal

The appellant admitted murder but raised the defence of diminished responsibility. The defence failed and he appealed against the verdict of the jury on the grounds of misdirection in the summing-up.

LORD PARKER C.J.: The appellant was convicted of murder before Stable J. at Birmingham Assizes and sentenced to imprisonment for life. The victim was a young woman whom he strangled in the Y.W.C.A. hostel, and after her death he committed horrifying mutilations upon her dead body. The facts as to the killing were not disputed, and were admitted in a long statement made by the accused. The only defence was that in killing his victim the accused was suffering from diminished responsibility as defined by section 2 of the Homicide Act 1957, and was, accordingly, guilty not of murder but of manslaughter.

Three medical witnesses were called by the defence, the senior medical officer at Birmingham Prison and two specialists in psychological medicine. Their uncontradicted evidence was that the accused was a sexual psychopath, that he suffered from abnormality of mind, as indeed was abundantly clear from the other evidence in the case, and that such abnormality of mind arose from a condition of arrested or retarded development of mind or inherent causes. The nature of the abnormality of mind of a sexual psychopath, according to the medical evidence, is that he suffers from violent perverted sexual desires which he finds it difficult or impossible to control. Save when under the influence of his perverted sexual desires he may be normal. All three doctors were of opinion that the killing was done under the influence of his perverted sexual desires, and although all three were of opinion that he was not insane in the technical sense of insanity laid down in the M'Naghten Rules it was their view that his sexual psychopathy could properly be described as partial insanity.

In his summing-up the judge, after summarising the medical evidence, gave to the jury a direction of law on the correctness of which this appeal turns. He told the jury that if on the evidence they came to the conclusion that the facts could be fairly summarised as follows:

"(1) from an early age he has been subject to these perverted violent desires, and in some cases has indulged his desires; (2) the impulse or urge of these desires is stronger than the normal impulse or urge of sex to such an extent that the subject finds it very difficult or perhaps impossible in some cases to resist putting the desire into practice; (3) the act of killing this girl was done under such an impulse or urge; and (4) that setting aside these sexual addictions and practices this man was normal in every other respect"; those facts with nothing more would not bring a case within the section, and do not constitute such abnormality of mind as substantially to impair a man's mental responsibility for his acts. "In other words," he went on, "mental affliction is one thing. The section is there to protect them. The section is not there to give protection where there is nothing else than what is vicious and depraved."

Taken by themselves these words are unobjectionable, but it is contended on behalf of the appellant that the direction taken as a whole involves a misconstruction of the section, and had the effect of withdrawing from the jury an issue of fact which it was peculiarly their province to decide.

Section 2 of the Homicide Act 1957, is dealing with the crime of murder in which there are at common law two essential elements: (1) the physical act of killing another person, and (2) the state of mind of the person who kills or is a party to the killing, namely, his intention to kill or to cause grievous bodily harm. Subsection (1) of section 2 does not deal with the first element. It modified the existing law as respects the second element, that is, the state of mind of the person who kills or is a party to the killing. . . .

The ability of the accused to control his physical acts by exercise of his will was relevant before the passing of the Homicide Act 1957, in one case only— that of provocation. . . .

It is against that background of the existing law that section 2(1) of the Homicide Act 1957, falls to be construed. To satisfy the requirements of the subsection the accused must show: (a) that he was suffering from an abnormality of mind, and (b) that such abnormality of mind (i) arose from a condition of arrested or retarded development of mind or any inherent causes or was induced by disease or injury and (ii) was such as substantially impaired his mental responsibility for his acts in doing or being a party to the killing.

"Abnormality of mind", which has to be contrasted with the time-honoured expression in the M'Naghten Rules "defect of reason", means a state of mind so different from that of ordinary human beings that the reasonable man would term it abnormal. It appears to us to be wide enough to cover the mind's activities in all its aspects, not only the perception of physical acts and matters, and the ability to form a rational judgment as to whether an act is right or wrong, but also the ability to exercise will-power to control his physical acts in accordance with that rational judgment. The expression "mental responsibility for his acts" points to a consideration of the extent to which the accused's mind is answerable for his physical acts which must include a consideration of the extent of his ability to exercise will-power to control his physical acts.

Whether the accused was at the time of the killing suffering from any "abnormality of mind" in the broad sense which we have indicated above is a question for the jury. On this question medical evidence is no doubt of importance, but the jury are entitled to take into consideration all the evidence, including the acts or statements of the accused and his demeanour. They are not bound to accept the medical evidence if there is other material before them which, in their good judgment, conflicts with it and outweighs it.

The aetiology of the abnormality of mind (namely, whether it arose from a condition of arrested or retarded development or any inherent causes, or was induced by disease or injury) does, however, seem to be a matter determined on expert evidence.

Assuming that the jury are satisfied on the balance of probabilities that the accused was suffering from "abnormality of mind" from one of the causes specified in the parenthesis of the subsection, the crucial question nevertheless arises: was the abnormality such as substantially impaired his mental responsibility for his acts in doing or being a party to the killing? This is a question of degree and essentially one for the jury. Medical evidence is, of course, relevant, but the question involves a decision not merely as to whether there was some impairment of the mental responsibility of the accused but whether such impairment can properly be called "substantial", a matter upon which juries may quite legitimately differ from doctors.

Furthermore, in a case where the abnormality of mind is one which affects the accused's self-control the step between "he did not resist his impulse" and "he could not resist his impulse" is, as the evidence in this case shows, one which is incapable of scientific proof. *A fortiori* there is no scientific measurement of the degree of difficulty which an abnormal person finds in controlling his impulses. These problems which in the present state of medical knowledge are scientifically insoluble, the jury can only approach in a broad common sense way. This court has repeatedly approved directions to the jury which have followed directions given in Scots cases where the doctrine of diminished responsibility forms part of the common law. We need not repeat them. They are quoted in *R. v. Spriggs* [1958] 1 Q.B. 270. They indicate that such abnormality as "substantially impairs his mental responsibility" involves a mental state which in popular language (not that of the M'Naghten Rules) a jury would regard as amounting to partial insanity or being on the borderline of insanity.

It appears to us that the judge's direction to the jury that the defence under section 2 of the Act was not available even though they found the facts set out in Nos. 2 and 3 of the judge's summary, amounted to a direction that difficulty or even inability of an accused person to exercise will power to control his physical acts could not amount to such abnormality of mind as substantially impairs his mental responsibility. For the reasons which we have already expressed we think that this construction of the Act is wrong. Inability to exercise will power to control physical acts, provided that it is due to abnormality of mind from one of the causes specified in the parenthesis in the subsection is, in our view, sufficient to entitle the accused to the benefit of the section; difficulty in controlling his physical acts depending on the degree of difficulty, may be. It is for the jury to decide on the whole of the evidence whether such inability or difficulty has, not as a matter of scientific certainty but on the balance of probabilities, been established, and in the case of difficulty whether the difficulty is so great as to amount in their view to a substantial impairment of the accused's mental responsibility for his acts. The direction in the present case thus withdrew from the jury the essential determination of fact which it was their province to decide.

As already indicated, the medical evidence as to the appellant's ability to control his physical acts at the time of the killing was all one way. The evidence of the revolting circumstances of the killing and the subsequent mutilations as of the previous sexual history of the appellant pointed, we think, plainly, to the conclusion that the accused was what would be described in ordinary language as on the borderline of insanity or partially insane. Properly directed, we do not think that the jury could have come to any other conclusion than that the defence under section 2 of the Homicide Act was made out.

The appeal will be allowed and a verdict of manslaughter substituted for the verdict of murder. The only possible sentence having regard to the tendencies of the accused is imprisonment for life. The sentence will, accordingly, not be disturbed.

Appeal allowed

Note

In *Seers* (1984) 79 Cr.App.R. 261 medical evidence was tendered that D was suffering from chronic reactive depression which constituted an abnormality of mind. The trial judge directed the jury that the test was whether D was partially insane. The Court of Appeal quashed D's conviction of murder and substituted one of manslaughter on the basis that the trial judge's direction was inappropriate. The use of terms such as "partial insanity" is not helpful where the abnormality of mind relied on is not related to any of the generally recognised types of insanity.

Questions

1. In the third question, namely, whether "the abnormality was such as substantially impaired the defendant's mental responsibility for his acts in doing or being a party to the killing?", is the jury being asked to consider the defendant's capacity to comprehend and conform to the standards laid down by the law or are they being asked to consider whether, in light of his abnormality he is morally culpable? In other words, is the issue for the jury one of capacity or liability? See Griew, "The Future of Diminished Responsibility" [1987] Crim. L.R.75.

2. Can it be argued that in *Byrne*, Lord Parker is suggesting that medical evidence is conclusive on "abnormality of mind" but not on whether that resulted in "substantial impairment"? Do the cases below provide any elucidation? See M. D. Cohen, "Medical Evidence and Diminished Responsibility" [1981] N.L.J. 667.

Walton v. The Queen
(1978) 66 Cr.App.R. 25
Privy Council

The appellant was driving home with his girlfriend and her mother when he stopped the car. His girlfriend thought he was "acting funny" and flagged down another car. The appellant shot and killed a passenger in a car which stopped. His defence to murder was diminished responsibility (which, in the Barbadian legislation, was identical with section 2 of the 1957 Act). He called two psychiatrists and a psychologist in his support. The Crown led no medical evidence. There was no evidence of any history of mental disorder. The jury convicted him of murder. The conviction was upheld by the Court of Appeal of Barbados. On appeal to the Privy Council.

LORD KEITH OF KINKEL delivered the judgment of the Board: . . . It was argued by Mr Murray, for the appellant, that in the light of the uncontradicted medical evidence to the effect that the appellant suffered from an abnormality of mind which substantially impaired his mental responsibility for his acts, the jury was bound to accept that the defence of diminished responsibility had been established, and that the trial judge should have so directed them. Mr Murray relied upon *R. v. Matheson* [1958] 1 W.L.R. 474 and *R. v. Bailey* (1978) 66 Cr.App.Rep. 31n. In the first of these cases the accused, who had a long recorded history of conduct indicative of mental abnormality, had killed a 15-year-old boy under peculiarly revolting circumstances. Three medical witnesses testified at the trial that they were satisfied that the accused's mind was so abnormal as substantially to impair his mental responsibility, giving their reasons for that view, and no medical evidence was led in rebuttal. The jury returned a verdict of guilty of murder. The Court of Criminal Appeal quashed that verdict and substituted one of manslaughter. Lord Goddard C.J., delivering the judgment of the Court, having referred to the medical evidence, said (at p. 478): "What then were the facts or circumstances which would justify a jury in coming to a conclusion contrary to the unchallenged evidence of these gentlemen? While it has often been emphasised, and we would repeat, that the decision in these cases, as in those in which insanity is pleaded, is for the jury and not for doctors, the verdict must be founded on evidence. If there are facts which would entitle a jury to reject or differ from the opinions of the medical men, this Court would not, and indeed could not, disturb their verdict, but if the doctor's evidence is unchallenged and there is no other on this issue, a verdict contrary to their opinion would not be 'a true verdict in accordance with the evidence'." After considering other circumstances of the case Lord Goddard continued, at p. 479: "If then there is unchallenged evidence that there is abnormality of mind and consequent substantial impairment of mental responsibility and no facts or circumstances appear that can displace or throw doubt on that evidence, it seems to the Court that we are bound to say that a verdict of murder is unsupported by the evidence."

In *R. v. Bailey* the appellant, who was just 17 years of age at the time, had met a girl aged 16 years and with no apparent motive had battered her to death with an iron bar. In support of a defence of diminished responsibility the evidence of three medical witnesses was led, including a senior prison medical officer. All expressed the opinion that the appellant suffered from epilepsy, which substantially impaired his mental responsibility. The prison medical officer thought it highly probable that the appellant was at the time of the killing in an epileptic upset or fit. The Court of Criminal Appeal substituted a verdict of manslaughter for the jury's verdict of murder. Lord Parker C.J., delivering the judgment of the Court, said (p. 32): "This Court has said on many occasions that of course juries are not bound by what the medical witnesses say, but at the same time they must act on evidence, and if there is nothing before them, no facts and no circumstances shown before them which throw doubt on the medical evidence, then that is all that they are left with, and the jury, in those circumstances, must accept it."

These cases make clear that upon an issue of diminished responsibility the jury are entitled and indeed bound to consider not only the medical evidence but the evidence upon the whole facts and circumstances of the case. These include the nature of the killing, the conduct of the accused before, at the time of and after it and any history of mental abnormality. It being recognised that the jury on occasions may properly refuse to accept medical evidence, it follows that they must be entitled to consider the quality and weight of that evidence. As was pointed out by Lord Parker C.J. in *R. v. Byrne* [*ante*, p. 565], what the jury are essentially seeking to ascertain is whether at the time of the killing the accused was suffering from a state of mind bordering on but not amounting to insanity. That task is to be approached in a broad common sense way.

In the present case their Lordships are of opinion that, in so far as they can judge of the medical evidence from the trial judge's notes, the jury were entitled to regard it as not entirely convincing. Dr Patricia Bannister, whose evidence was subjected to quite lengthy cross-examination, expressed an opinion as to the appellant's state of mind which in terms satisfied the statutory definition. The particular mental abnormality which she identified was that of an extremely immature personality. Mr Browne, the clinical psychologist, found the appellant to be of average intellectual ability with good observational ability and clear thinking. He supported Dr Patricia Bannister's evidence by describing the appellant as having an inadequate personality enhanced by emotional immaturity and a low tolerance level. The evidence of Dr Lawrence Bannister was merely to the effect that he treated the appellant for depression, with disappointing results. It is plain that the quality and weight of this medical evidence fell a long way short of that in *Matheson's* case and in *Bailey's* case. The jury also had before them evidence about the conduct of the appellant before, during and after killing, including that of a number of conflicting statements about it made by him to the police and to Dr Patricia Bannister. They may well have thought there was nothing in that evidence indicative of a man whose mental state bordered on insanity. There was also the appellant's unsworn statement regarding his having suffered in the past from severe headache, blackouts, sleeplessness and lack of memory, supported to some extent by Miss Watson, but no objective evidence of any history of mental disorder. In both these aspects the case is in marked contradistinction to *Matheson's* case.

Having carefully considered the relevant evidence, their Lordships have come to be of opinion that in all the circumstances the jury were entitled not to accept as conclusive the expression of opinion by Dr Patricia Bannister that the appellant's mental condition satisfied the statutory definition of diminished responsibility, and to conclude, as they did, that the defence had not on balance of probabilities been established.

Their Lordships will therefore humbly advise Her Majesty that the appeal should be dismissed.

Appeal dismissed

R. v. Vinagre
(1979) 69 Cr.App.R. 104
Court of Appeal

The appellant, who suspected his wife of infidelity, stabbed her to death. His plea of diminished responsibility was accepted by the trial judge who sentenced him to life imprisonment. It was against this that he appealed. The Court of Appeal considered the wider issue of when such a plea should be accepted.

LAWTON L.J.: . . . In this case there were medical examinations of the accused by psychiatrists. Two medical reports were produced. We find them rather unusual documents, because the substance of them was this, that the appellant at the material time was suffering from a mental condition which was described in picturesque, if inaccurate, language as the "Othello syndrome," which was defined as being "morbid jealousy for which there was no cause". . . .

Such medical evidence as was before the Court came from the Crown. In those circumstances there was not much point in the defence producing any other psychiatric evidence. Indeed there was a danger that they might have produced a hard-headed psychiatrist who would not have had much use for the Othello syndrome.

As a result, when the case came before the trial judge, Mr Baker, on behalf of the accused, was able to tender the plea to manslaughter on the grounds of diminished responsibility on the basis that that was what the Crown themselves were saying. The learned judge, as I have already stated, accepted the plea.

We wish to call attention to the history of the acceptance of pleas on grounds of diminished responsibility. After the passing of the Homicide Act 1957, the question arose as to whether Courts could accept pleas to manslaughter on grounds of diminished responsibility. The Court of Criminal Appeal decided in *R. v. Matheson* [1958] 1 W.L.R. 474, that that was not to be done. After that decision until 1962 in all cases of this kind the verdict of the jury had to be taken. The wording of the Homicide Act 1957 indicates that that may well have been the intention of Parliament, because the burden of proving diminished responsibility was upon the defendant. Between 1957 and 1962 there were distressing cases in which a distraught woman (or sometimes a man but usually a distraught woman) had to sit in the dock listening to hours of evidence of what she had done when she was in a state of mental imbalance. Some judges thought that that was wrong. As a result in 1962 the judges decided that pleas of manslaughter on grounds of diminished responsibility could be accepted.

Thompson J. and I were both judges at the time and we are sure that it was never intended that pleas should be accepted on flimsy grounds. As Scarman L.J. pointed out two or three years ago in *R. v. Ford* (1976) (*unrep.*) cases are tried by the Courts and not by psychiatrists. It seems to us that pleas to manslaughter on the grounds of diminished responsibility should only be accepted when there is clear evidence of mental imbalance. We do not consider that in this case there was clear evidence of mental imbalance. There was clear evidence of a killing by a jealous husband which, until modern times, no one would have thought was anything else but murder.

Be that as it may, Park J. did accept the plea and he listened to the submissions by Mr Baker on behalf of the appellant as to how the case should be disposed of. . . .

Having been told by the psychiatrist that he was satisfied that there would be no recurrence, Mr Baker so informed the learned judge, who was somewhat sceptical about this and in the course of sentencing the appellant he said: "I am told that you are in no danger; you are no longer any danger to the public but for my part, I am not able to say when you will be fit to resume your place in society." . . .

The way things happened has put this Court in a difficulty because if this man is suffering from the Othello syndrome, he may suffer from it again. In other words he is in a state of mental imbalance which may at some future date make him a danger to the public. On the other hand there was some assertion before Park J. that, whatever he may have been suffering from at the time when he killed his wife, he was not likely to suffer from it in the future. That was left unresolved, the judge taking a different view to that which was being urged upon him by Mr Baker.

We feel that we have no alternative but to approach this case on the basis that Mr Baker's instructions were correct. In those circumstances the appellant at the time of the trial, and certainly today, is not suffering from the kind of mental imbalance which would justify keeping him in custody until such time as the Home Secretary and the parole board think that it is safe to release him. Accordingly we quash the sentence of life imprisonment and substitute for it a sentence of seven years' imprisonment. To that extent the appeal against sentence is allowed.

Appeal allowed.
Sentence varied.

Notes

1. In *R. v. Cox* [1968] 1 W.L.R. 308, at 310, Winn L.J. for the Court of Appeal "[F]rom the very outset of the trial it was quite clear . . . that the medical evidence available . . . showed perfectly plainly that [the plea of diminished responsibility] was a plea which it would have been proper to accept. . . . The Court desires to say yet again . . . that there are cases where, on an indictment for murder, it is perfectly proper, where the medical evidence is plainly to this effect, to treat the case as one of substantially diminished responsibility and accept, if it be tendered, a plea to manslaughter on that ground, and avoid a trial for murder."

2. Both the Butler Committee on Abnormal Offenders (Cmnd. 6244, 1975, § 19.19) and the Criminal Law Revision Committee (14th Report, Offences Against the Person, (Cmnd. 7844, 1980, § 95, 96)) recommend that, in clear cases, it should be possible to avoid indicting for murder at all so that the period between committal and trial is not spent under the shadow of an unrealistic charge.

3. Susanne Dell, "Diminished Responsibility Reconsidered" [1982] Crim.L.R. 809, at 812, gives statistics which show that in 80 per cent of cases in which diminished responsibility is raised as a defence, the plea is accepted and in only 20 per cent of cases did the issue go before a jury.

4. The abnormality of the mind must result from arrested or retarded development, or any inherent causes or be induced by disease or injury. In *Vinagre*, above, jealousy, or "Othello syndrome", was accepted as a disease for these purposes. Mercy killings have also resulted in diminished responsibility pleas being successful as in *Price, The Times*, December 22, 1971, where a father placed his severely handicapped son in a river and watched him float away. Pre-menstrual syndrome and post-natal depression have also been accepted as diseases for the purposes of the test (see *Reynolds, The Times*, April 23, 1988 and S. Edwards, "Mad, bad or pre-menstrual?" (1988) 138 N.L.J. 456).

5. However, *Vinagre*, above, and the trial of *Peter Sutcliffe*, the "Yorkshire Ripper" (at the Old Bailey, April-May 1981, *The Times*, May 23, 1981) illustrate the difficulties of, on the one hand, pursuing a humane procedure to protect the mentally disordered and, on the other, striving to preserve the public interest in murderers being convicted as such. Sutcliffe tendered pleas of diminished responsibility to 13 charges of murder. The psychiatric reports were unanimous in suggesting that Sutcliffe was a paranoid schizophrenic. The judge, however, deemed it to be in the public interest that a jury should determine this matter and the trial proceeded. The jury returned convictions for murder. The case highlights, if nothing else, the extent to which murder and manslaughter are divided not by the niceties of legal definitions but by public gut reaction (see further H. Prins, "Diminished Responsibility and the Sutcliffe Case: Legal, Psychiatric and Social Aspects" (1983) 23 *Medicine, Science and the Law* 17). Mercy killers or women suffering from pre-menstrual syndrome or post-natal depression perhaps evoke more sympathy than a paranoid schizo-

phrenic. And this raises the question of the proper roles of prosecution, judge and jury. Who is to be the arbiter of the place which any particular homicide is to take on the scale of heinousness?

Intoxication and diminished responsibility

Note

The problem of discovering the cause of a defendant's abnormality of mind may be complicated by his or her ingestion of alcohol or other drugs.

R. v. Tandy
[1989] 1 W.L.R. 350
Court of Appeal

The appellant, an alcoholic, having drunk nine-tenths of a bottle of vodka strangled her 11-year-old daughter. On her plea of diminished responsibility the judge directed the jury that, if they concluded she had voluntarily taken her first drink of the day, she could not claim that the resultant abnormality of mind was due to the disease of alcoholism. The appellant was convicted of murder and appealed.

WATKINS L.J.: . . . There were three principal areas of conflict between the medical witnesses called at the trial on behalf of the appellant and the medical witness called by the Crown. The first was whether alcoholism is or is not a disease . . . The second area of conflict between the doctors was whether the appellant's drinking on the Wednesday was voluntary or involuntary . . . The third area of conflict in the medical evidence was on the question whether, if the appellant had not taken drink that day, she would have strangled her daughter . . .

The ground of appeal is that there was material misdirection of the jury in regard to the defence of diminished responsibility. The relevant passages in the summing up are where the judge said:

"The choice [of the appellant whether to drink or not to drink on Wednesday 5 March 1986] may not have been easy but . . . if it was there at all it is fatal to this defence, because the law simply will not allow a drug user, whether the drug be alcohol or any other, to shelter behind the toxic effects of the drug which he or she need not have used."

And where he stated earlier:

"If she had taken no drink on 5 March 1986, or if you were satisfied that Dr Wood is right in saying that judgment and emotional response would have been grossly impaired even if no drink had been taken, then the answer would be easy, but clearly she did take drink on 5 March and if she did that as a matter of choice, she cannot say in law or in common sense that the abnormality of mind which resulted was induced by disease."

Mr Stewart, the appellant's counsel, submits that these are misdirections, because (1) the medical evidence had been unanimous that there might be compulsion to drink at least after the first drink of the day; that it was the cumulative effect of the consumption of 90 per cent of the bottle of vodka which caused her to be in the state of intoxication she was in at the time of the killing; by his directions the judge removed the question of compulsion after the taking of the first drink from the jury's consideration; (2) the directions removed from the jury's consideration Dr Wood's evidence that the alcoholism alone produced an abnormal state of mind which substantially impaired her mental responsibility for her acts; (3) the directions removed from the jury the issue which this court in *R. v. Fenton* (1975) 61 Cr.App.R. 261, 263 recognised could arise when an accused person provides such a craving for drink as to produce in itself an abnormality of mind. Lord Widgery C.J.'s actual words were:

"cases may arise hereafter where the accused proves such a craving for drink or drugs as to produce in itself an abnormality of mind; but that is not proved in this case. The appellant did not give evidence and we do not see how self-induced intoxication can of itself produce an abnormality of mind due to inherent causes." ...

The defence of diminished responsibility was derived from the law of Scotland, in which one of the colloquial names for the defence was "partial insanity". Normal human beings frequently drink to excess and when drunk do not suffer from abnormality of mind, within the meaning of that phrase in section 2(1) of the Act of 1957.

Whether an accused person was at the time of the act which results in the victim's death suffering from any abnormality of mind is a question for the jury; and, as the court stated in *R. v. Byrne*, although medical evidence is important on this question, the jury are not bound to accept medical evidence if there is other material before them from which in their judgment a different conclusion may be drawn.

The Court of Appeal in *R. v. Gittens* [1984] Q.B. 698 said that it was a misdirection to invite the jury to decide whether it was inherent causes on the one hand or drink and pills on the other hand which were the main factor in causing the appellant in that case to act as he did. The correct direction in that case was to tell the jury that they had to decide whether the abnormality arising from the inherent causes substantially impaired the appellant's responsibility for his actions. Lord Lane C.J. said, at p. 703:

"Where alcohol or drugs are factors to be considered ... the best approach is that ... approved by this court in *R. v. Fenton*, 61 Cr.App.R. 261.... The jury should be directed to disregard what, in their view, the effect of the alcohol or drugs upon the defendant was, since abnormality of mind induced by alcohol or drugs is not (generally speaking) due to inherent causes.... Then the jury should consider whether the combined effect of the other matters which do fall within the section amounted to such abnormality of mind as substantially impaired the defendant's mental responsibility...."

In the summing up and in the document headed "Questions for the jury", the judge set out the three matters which the defence had to establish on the balance of probability for the defence of diminished responsibility to succeed. No criticism of that part of the summing up or that part of the "Questions for the jury" has been made nor could it have been.

So in this case it was for the appellant to show (1) that she was suffering from an abnormality of mind at the time of the act of strangulation; (2) that that abnormality of mind was induced by disease, namely, the disease of alcoholism; and (3) that the abnormality of mind induced by the disease of alcoholism was such as substantially impaired her mental responsibility for her act of strangling her daughter.

The principles involved in seeking answers to these questions are, in our view, as follows. The appellant would not establish the second element of the defence unless the evidence showed that the abnormality of mind at the time of the killing was due to the fact that she was a chronic alcoholic. If the alcoholism has reached the level at which her brain had been injured by the repeated insult from intoxicants so that there was gross impairment of her judgment and emotional responses, then the defence of diminished responsibility was available to her, provided that she satisfied the jury that the third element of the defence existed. Further, if the appellant were able to establish that the alcoholism had reached the level where although the brain had not been damaged to the extent just stated, the appellant's drinking had become involuntary, that is to say she was no longer able to resist the impulse to drink, then the defence of diminished responsibility would be available to her, subject to her establishing the first and third elements, because if her drinking was involuntary, then her abnormality of mind at the time of the act of strangulation was induced by her condition of alcoholism.

On the other hand, if the appellant had simply not resisted an impulse to drink and it was the drink taken on the Wednesday which brought about the impairment of judgment and emotional response, then the defence of diminished responsibility was not available to the appellant.

In our judgment the direction which the judge gave the jury accurately reflected these principles. There was evidence on which the jury, directed as they were, could reach their verdict. The appellant had chosen to drink vodka on the Wednesday rather than her customary drink of Cinzano. Her evidence was that she might not have had a drink at all on the Tuesday. She certainly did not tell the jury that she must have taken drink on the Tuesday or Wednesday because she could not help herself. She had been able to stop drinking at 6.30 p.m. on the Wednesday evening although her supply of vodka was not exhausted. Thus her own evidence indicated that she was able to exercise some control even after she had taken the first drink, contrary to the view of the doctors. There was the evidence of Dr Lawson that the appellant would have had the ability on that Wednesday to abstain from taking the first drink of the day.

Mr Smith, who appeared for the Crown, pointed out in his submissions that the abnormality of mind described by Dr Wood and Dr Milne was of grossly impaired judgment and emotional responses and it did not include an irresistible craving for alcohol.

The three matters on which the appellant relies in the perfected grounds of appeal for saying that there was a misdirection can be dealt with shortly. As to the first, in our judgment the judge was correct in telling the jury that if the taking of the first drink was not involuntary, then the whole of the drinking on the Wednesday was not involuntary. Further, as we have pointed out, the appellant's own evidence indicated that she still had control over her drinking on that Wednesday after she had taken the first drink.

As to the second, the jury were told correctly that the abnormality of mind with which they were concerned was the abnormality of mind at the time of the act of strangulation and as a matter of fact by that time on that Wednesday the appellant had drunk 90 per cent of a bottle of vodka.

On the third point, we conclude that for a craving for drink or drugs in itself to produce an abnormality of mind within the meaning of section 2(1) of the Act of 1957, the craving must be such as to render the accused's use of drink or drugs involuntary. Therefore, in our judgment the judge correctly defined how great the craving for drink had to be before it would in itself produce an abnormality of mind. In any event, it was not the evidence of the doctors called on behalf of the appellant that her abnormality of mind included, let alone consisted solely, of a craving for alcohol.

For those reasons we find that there was no material misdirection of the jury and we dismiss this appeal.

Appeal dismissed.

Notes and Questions

In *Atkinson* [1985] Crim L.R. 314 (following *Gittens, ante*, p. 574) the Court of Appeal held that where the evidence suggests more than one cause of the abnormality of mind of which one is intoxication, juries should be directed in the following terms:

"Have the defence satisfied you on the balance of probabilities that if the defendant had not taken drink—
  (i) he would have killed as he in fact did? and
  (ii) he would have been under diminished responsibility when he did so?"

It is obvious that alcohol may reduce inhibitions or impair a person's powers of self-control. However, the issue in s.2 is not whether the abnormality of mind caused the killing but rather whether at the time of the killing D was suffering from an abnormality of mind which substantially impaired his responsibility. If D, drunk or sober suffers from, for example, severely arrested or retarded development of mind he is not a responsible actor. If it was alcohol which caused him to lose his inhibitions and kill when otherwise he would not have done so, he remains the same retarded individual who is not a responsible actor. If the *Atkinson* direction applies in all cases it may wreak injustice. In *Egan* [1992] 4 All E.R. 470 the Court of Appeal held that this approach should be applied in all cases including the present one where the accused had a mentality bordering on the subnormal. The defence argued that it was unnecessary to establish a casual link between his abnormality of mind and the killing; that is, that to ask the first of the *Atkinson* questions was not appropriate. This argument failed. Was *Egan* wrongly decided? Should the first question of the *Atkinson* test be left to the jury only where the impairment alleged is D's ability to exercise self-control? (see G. R. Sullivan, "Intoxicants and Diminished Responsibility" [1994] Crim L.R. 156).

Reform

Notes

1. The Butler Committee on Mentally Abnormal Offenders (Cmnd. 6244) put forward two reform proposals. The first, preferred solution, recommended that the mandatory life sentence for murder be abolished leaving the judge with a discretion in passing sentence. As a result, the diminished responsibility defence could be abolished. The Committee stated at paragraph 19.5 of the Report:

"19.5 The wording of section 2, as the Judges readily conceded, is open to criticism from several aspects. 'Abnormality of mind' is an extremely imprecise phrase, even as limited by the parentheses and defined by the Court of Appeal (see the foregoing paragraph). 'Mental responsibility', a phrase not to be found elsewhere in any statute, has created difficulty both for doctors and for jurors. It is either a concept of law or a concept of morality; it is not a clinical fact relating to the defendant. 'Legal responsibility' means liability to conviction (and success in a defence of diminished responsibility does not save the defendant from conviction of manslaughter); 'moral responsibility' means liability to moral censure (but moral questions do not normally enter into the definition of a crime). It seems odd that psychiatrists should be asked and agree to testify as to legal or moral responsibility. It is even more surprising that courts are prepared to hear that testimony. Yet psychiatrists commonly testify to impaired 'mental responsibility' under section 2. Several medical witnesses pointed out to us that the difficulty is made worse by the use of the word 'substantial'. The idea that ability to conform to the law can be measured is particularly puzzling. (See the discussion in paragraph 18.16.) Despite the difficulties of the section in relation to psychiatry the medical profession is humane and the evidence is often stretched, as a number of witnesses remarked. Not only psychopathic personality but reactive depressions and dissociated states have been testified to be due to 'inherent causes' within the section."

If this solution was rejected, the second solution the Committee proposed involved amendment of section 2. The amended defence would not impose a burden of proof on the defendant, and in addition, would allow the prosecution, with the consent of the defence, to indict the defendant for manslaughter where there was evidence that the defence of diminished responsibility could be established. The amended section would provide as follows:

"Where a person kills or is party to the killing of another, he shall not be convicted of murder if there is medical or other evidence that he was suffering from a form of mental disorder as defined in section 4 of the Mental Health Act 1959 and if, in the opinion of the jury, the mental disorder was such as to be an extenuating circumstance which ought to reduce the offence to manslaughter."

2. According to section 1(2) of the Mental Health Act 1983, "mental disorder" means "mental illness, arrested or incomplete development of mind, psychopathic disorder and any other disorder or disability of mind and 'mentally disordered' shall be construed accordingly".

Criminal Law Revision Committee, 14th Report, 'Offences Against the Person,' Cmnd. 7844 (1980), paras. 91–93

Diminished responsibility was introduced into English law as a defence to murder by section 2 of the Homicide Act 1957. . . . The wording of section 2 has created problems for doctors, judges and juries. Psychiatrists are sometimes expected by lawyers to testify in terms that go outside their professional competence. They are required to testify whether the defendant's abnormality of mind substantially impaired his mental responsibility. The section refers to mental responsibility, which is a legal concept not a medical one; and the jury have to consider as a question of fact whether the abnormality of mind, which is a medical concept, has substantially impaired the defendant's mental responsibility. Some jurors probably have difficulty in understanding these concepts. It is the duty of judges to explain the meaning of section 2 to juries: it is not enough for them to read out the section (*Terry* [1961] 2 Q.B. 314).

There can be no doubt that the wording of section 2 of the Homicide Act 1957 is unsatisfactory. We agree that the . . . rewording [suggested by the Butler Committee] . . . provides a more easily recognisable diagnostic framework for doctors giving evidence, and the task of judges would be made easier. However, when we considered the rewording we had two reservations. First, we are concerned about the requirement that the defendant, when he killed, must be suffering 'from a form of mental disorder as defined in section 4 of the Mental Health Act 1959 . . .'. The Butler Committee were of opinion that this rewording would not materially alter the practical effect of the section. Initially, however, we felt some doubt about whether the rewording might be to some extent restrictive and leave outside the revised definition some offenders who are now regarded by the courts as falling within section 2. The kind of case we had in mind was the depressed father who kills a severely handicapped subnormal child or a morbidly jealous person who kills his or her spouse. In our experience such defendants are not necessarily suffering from a mental disorder of such a kind as to justify the making of a hospital order and are commonly dealt with by the courts, following the section 2 verdict, under the ordinary sentencing provisions applicable to manslaughter, for example, by a relatively short custodial sentence or a conditional discharge or probation order. Because of our doubts, this matter was further considered by the medical advisers to the Department of Health and Social Security, who have advised that the proposed rewording would not exclude the kind of cases we had in mind. Having looked at the matter again, we are satisfied that this view is right having regard to the wide terms in which the definition of mental disorder in section 4 of the Mental Health Act 1959 is drafted. We now accept that the types of mental disturbance we had in mind would be within the definition of mental disorder in section 4 of the Act of 1959, and therefore within the rewording proposed by the Butler Committee for section 2 of the Homicide Act 1957, notwithstanding that they fall outside the criteria of section 60 of the Act of 1959 and are not such as to justify the making of a hospital order.

Our other reservation with regard to the Butler Committee's rewording of the section is that we think that in one respect it may be too lax. The new definition recommended provides that a defendant shall not be convicted of murder if there is evidence that he was suffering from a mental disorder 'and if, in the opinion of the jury, the mental disorder was such as to be an extenuating circumstance which ought to reduce the offence to manslaughter'. We appreciate that the concluding words are intended to leave it to the jury to assess whether in all the circumstances the mental disorder is such as ought to reduce the offence to manslaughter, and we agree that any Bill dealing with diminished responsibility should make it clear that the function of the jury extends to this issue as well as to the question whether some degree of mental disorder is present. However, if this formula were implemented a judge would have to direct a jury to consider, first, whether the defendant was suffering from a mental disorder as defined by section 4, secondly, if he was, whether the mental disorder was an extenuating circumstance and, thirdly, whether that extenuating circumstance was such that it ought to reduce the offence from murder to manslaughter. On that final question the judge would have to give some guidance to the jury as to what extenuating circumstances ought to reduce the offence, and in practice that means that the mental disorder has to be substantial enough to reduce the offence to manslaughter. We consider that the definition should be tightened up so as to include that ingredient upon which the jury will have to be directed, which will give to the jury the necessary guidance. A form of wording which in our opinion tightens up the latter part of the proposed definition and which we favour is '. . . the mental disorder was such as to be substantial enough reason to reduce the offence to manslaughter'. But two other ways of dealing with the laxity in the Butler Committee formula are:

(ii) '. . . the mental disorder was of such a degree as to be a substantial reason to reduce murder to manslaughter' or
(iii) '. . . the defendant was suffering from mental disorder to such a degree that he ought not to be held responsible for murder and that in consequence the offence ought to be reduced to manslaughter'.

We have been informed that of our suggested wordings the medical advisers to the Department of Health and Social Security, prefer the first, as we do, since (notwithstanding that similar words are used in section 60 of the Mental Health Act 1959) they consider that phrases like 'such a degree as' in the second and third form of the suggested rewording might present difficulties to doctors as it is not possible to measure degrees of mental disorder. There could therefore be no assurance of comparability between opinions given by different doctors in different cases, which would add to the difficulties of the medical witness.

Note

The Draft Criminal Code Bill adopts in clause 56 the recommendations of the C.L.R.C. with one alteration; the term "mental abnormality" is preferred to "mental disorder" as the latter term is used in clause 36 for the purpose of mental disorder verdicts. (For clause 56 see *infra*, p. 615).

4. INVOLUNTARY MANSLAUGHTER

Notes

1. Manslaughter which has been reduced from murder because of provocation or diminished responsibility (often called "voluntary" manslaughter) has been dealt with in the preceding section. "Involuntary" manslaughter, with which this section is concerned, is a generic term comprising those homicides which occupy "the shifting sands between the uncertain . . . definition of murder and the unsettled boundaries of excusable or accidental death" (Hogan, "The Killing Ground: 1964–73" [1974] Crim.L.R. 387, 391).

2. "Involuntary" manslaughter can be divided into manslaughter by unlawful act and gross negligence manslaughter. The same case will often give rise to a consideration of both: see *R. v. Goodfellow*, *infra*. In *R. v. Larkin* (1944) 29 Cr.App.R. 18, a case where the jury's verdict of manslaughter could have been based on a finding of provocation or of unlawful act, the Court of Criminal Appeal deprecated the practice of asking the foreman to explain the basis of the jury's verdict. Humphreys J., for the court, at p. 27:

"As we in this country think, trial by jury is the best method yet devised for dealing with serious criminal cases, and the jury is the best possible tribunal to decide whether a man is guilty and, if he is guilty, of what he is guilty, subject to the direction in law of the judge; but no one has ever suggested that a jury is composed of persons who are likely to be able to give at a moment's notice a logical explanation of how and why they arrive at their verdict. That was what Oliver, J., was inviting the jury to do in this case, and, as has been already observed, inviting the foreman to do so, and accepting from the foreman something with which, perhaps, the other eleven did not agree. The unhappy result was that the foreman, no doubt thoroughly confused, gave two totally inconsistent answers. That incident cannot, in our opinion, be of any importance whatever from the point of view of this appeal against conviction. It was something which happened after the trial was over, so far as the jury were concerned, and if it has any effect at all, it must be an effect upon the sentence. But it must be understood that this court deprecates questions being put to a jury upon the meaning of the verdict which they have returned. If the verdict appears to be inconsistent, proper questions may be put by a judge to invite the jury to explain what they mean, but where a verdict has been returned which is perfectly plain and unambiguous, it is most undesirable that the jury should be asked any further questions about it at all."

The tables *infra*, pp. 540–541, indicate the frequency with which homicides initially charged as murder result in convictions for manslaughter. About 74 per cent of homicide suspects are ultimately convicted. Of those convicted for the years 1988–1998/9, 45 per cent were convicted of murder, 13 per cent of manslaughter by reason of diminished responsibility, 41 per cent of manslaughter as a result of provocation, an unlawful and dangerous act or recklessness/gross negligence and one per cent of infanticide.

Criminal Statistics, England and Wales, Cm. 4649 (1998)

Table 4.7 Suspects convicted of homicide[1] by type of homicide

England and Wales — Number of persons

Year offence initially recorded	Total indicted for homicide	Convicted of homicide				
		Total	Murder	Section 2 Man-slaughter	Other Man-slaughter	Infanticide
1988	642	493	189	74	222	8
1989	633	458	198	83	176	1
1990	626	443	186	70	183	4
1991	712	502	197	76	224	5
1992	707	503	214	78	205	6
1993	679	499	225	62	207	5
1994	646	490	227	69	191	3
1995	739	548	268	53	224	3
1996	715	528	257	50	217	4
1997	667	488	241	46	198	3
1997/8	656	491	222	47	218	4
1998/9[2]	371	273	131	28	110	4

(1) As at 29 October 1999; figures are subject to revision as cases are dealt with by the police and by the courts, or as further information becomes available.
(2) In addition there were 400 suspects for whom court proceedings were not completed by 29 October 1999.

Criminal Statistics, England and Wales, Cm. 4649 (1998)

Table 4.8 Suspects indicted for homicide by outcome of proceedings[1]
England and Wales

Number of persons

Indictment and outcome	1988	1989	1990	1991	1992	1993	1994	1995	1996	1997	1997/8	1998/9
Indictment[2]												
Murder	556	546	555	630	632	583	562	657	608	559	530	308
Manslaughter	79	87	70	80	72	94	84	81	105	108	125	61
Infanticide	7	–	1	2	3	2	–	1	2	–	1	2
Total	642	633	626	712	707	679	646	739	715	667	656	371
Outcome:												
Not convicted of homicide:[3]												
Not tried—count to remain on file[4]	–	–	–	1	–	1	–	3	11	7	8	3
Found unfit to plead	–	5	–	–	2	–	5	3	2	1	2	1
Found not guilty by reason of insanity	–	2	1	2	3	1	–	1	–	3	3	1
Convicted of lesser offence	37	52	47	39	44	30	27	35	16	26	21	24
Acquitted on all counts	112	116	135	168	155	148	124	149	158	141	131	67
Committed suicide	–	–	–	–	–	–	–	–	–	1	–	2
Total	149	175	183	210	204	180	156	191	187	179	165	98
Convicted of homicide:												
Murder	189	198	186	197	214	225	227	268	257	241	222	131
Sec. 2 Manslaughter	74	83	70	76	78	62	69	53	50	46	47	28
Other Manslaughter	222	176	183	224	205	207	191	224	217	198	218	110
Infanticide	8	1	4	5	6	5	3	3	4	3	4	4
Total	493	458	443	502	503	499	490	548	528	488	491	273
Total	642	633	626	712	707	679	646	739	715	667	656	371

(1) As at 29 October 1999; figures are subject to revision as cases are dealt with by the police and by the courts, or as further information becomes available.
(2) In addition there were 400 suspects for 1998/9, for whom court proceedings were not completed by 29 October 1999.
(3) The offences for which these persons were indicted may nevertheless remain currently recorded as homicide.
(4) This usually implies that the suspect has been dealt with for some less serious offence.

i. Unlawful Act Manslaughter

(a) The act causing death must be unlawful

R. v. Franklin
(1883) 15 Cox 163
Sussex Assizes

The defendant was indicted with manslaughter. He took a box from another man's stall on West Pier, Brighton, and threw it into the sea. The box hit and killed a man who was swimming. The prosecution argued that the question of the defendant's negligence was immaterial, since it was manslaughter where death ensued in consequence of any wrongful act.

FIELD J.: I am of opinion that the case must go to the jury upon the broad ground of negligence and not upon the narrow ground proposed by the learned counsel, because it seems to me—and I may say that in this view my brother Mathew agrees—that the mere fact of a civil wrong committed by one person against another ought not to be used as an incident which is a necessary step in a criminal case. I have a great abhorrence of constructive crime. . . .

Verdict: Guilty.

Note

Counsel in this case had relied upon *R. v. Fenton* (1830) 1 Lew. 179, in which Tindal C.J. had formulated this proposition:

"If death ensues as the consequence of a wrongful act, an act which the party who commits it can neither justify nor excuse, it is not accidental death, but manslaughter. If the wrongful act was done under circumstances which show an attempt to kill, or do any serious injury in the particular case, or any general malice, the offence becomes that of murder. In the present instance the act was one of mere wantonness and sport, but still the act was wrongful, it was a trespass. The only question therefore is whether the death of the party is to be fairly and reasonably considered as a consequence of such wrongful act; if it followed from such wrongful act as an effect from a cause, the offence is manslaughter; if it is altogether unconnected with it, it is an accidental death."

Field J. rejected this harsh rule that a civil wrong could constitute the unlawful act for the purposes of manslaughter. This left undecided what constituted such an unlawful act.

R. v. Church
[1966] 1 Q.B. 59
Court of Criminal Appeal

The appellant was mocked by a woman and fought with her knocking her unconscious. He failed to revive her and in a panic, thinking she was dead, threw her into the river where she drowned. The appellant was acquitted of murder but convicted of manslaughter. He appealed on the ground of a misdirection as to manslaughter.

EDMUND-DAVIES J.: Two passages in the summing-up are here material [to manslaughter by an unlawful act causing death]. They are these: (1) "If by an unlawful act of violence done deliberately to the person of another, that other is killed, the killing is manslaughter even though the accused never intended either death or grievous bodily harm to result. If this woman was alive, as she was, when he threw her into the river, what he did was the deliberate act of throwing a living body into the river. That is an unlawful killing and it does not matter whether he believed she was dead or not, and that is my direction to you", and (2) "I would suggest to you, though it is of course for you to approach your task as you think fit, that a convenient way of approaching it would be to say: What do we think about this defence that he honestly believed the woman to be dead? If you think that is true, why then, as I have told you, your proper verdict would be one of manslaughter, not murder."

Such a direction is not lacking in authority: see, for example, *Shoukatallie v. The Queen* [1962] A.C. 81 and Dr Glanville Williams' *Criminal Law* (2nd edn, 1961), p. 173. Nevertheless, in the judgment of this court it was a misdirection. It amounted to telling the jury that, whenever any unlawful act is committed in relation to a human being which resulted in death there must be, at least, a conviction for manslaughter. This might at one time have been regarded as good law. . . . But it appears to this court that the passage of years has achieved a transformation in this branch of the law and, even in relation to manslaughter, a degree of *mens rea* has become recognised as essential. To define it is a difficult task, and in *Andrews v. D.P.P.* [1937] A.C. 576, Lord Atkin spoke of the "element of 'unlawfulness' which is the elusive factor". Stressing that we are here leaving entirely out of account those ingredients of homicide which might justify a verdict of manslaughter on the grounds of (a) criminal negligence, or (b) provocation, or (c) diminished responsibility, the conclusion of this court is that an unlawful act causing the death of another cannot, simply because it is an unlawful act, render a manslaughter verdict inevitable. For such a verdict inexorably to follow, the unlawful act must be such as all sober and reasonable people would inevitably recognise must subject the other person to, at least, the risk of some harm resulting therefrom, albeit not serious harm. See, for example, *R. v. Franklin*, [*ante*, p. 582]; *R. v. Senior* [1899] 1 Q.B. 283; *R. v. Larkin* [1943] 1 K.B. 174 in the judgment of the court delivered by Humphrey J.; *R. v. Buck & Buck* (1960) 44 Cr.App.R. 213, and *R. v. Hall* (1961) 45 Cr.App.R. 366.

If such be the test, as we adjudge it to be, then it follows that in our view it was a misdirection to tell the jury *simpliciter* that it mattered nothing for manslaughter whether or not the appellant believed Mrs Nott to be dead when he threw her in the river. But, quite apart from our decision that the direction on criminal negligence was an adequate one in the circumstances, such a misdirection does not, in our judgment, involve that the conviction for manslaughter must or should be quashed.

Appeal dismissed.

Notes

1. In *Andrews v. D.P.P.* [1937] A.C. 576, Lord Atkin stated:

"There is an obvious difference in the law of manslaughter between doing an unlawful act and doing a lawful act with a degree of carelessness which the legislature makes criminal. If it were otherwise a man who killed another while driving without due care and attention would *ex necessitate* commit manslaughter."

Thus a manslaughter verdict cannot be based on an act which is unlawful simply because it has been performed negligently; it must be unlawful for some other reason, namely that the defendant had the *mens rea* required for the offence which constituted the unlawful act.

2. The following case makes it clear that *mens rea* for the unlawful act must be established subjectively.

R. v. Lamb

[1967] 2 Q.B. 981

Court of Appeal

The appellant, in fun, pointed a revolver at a friend. He knew that there were two bullets in the chambers, but neither was opposite the barrel. He pulled the trigger and because of the action of the cylinder, which rotated before firing, a bullet was fired and the friend killed. He did not appreciate that the cylinder rotated automatically. The appellant was convicted of manslaughter and appealed against this.

SACHS J.: . . . [I]n the course of his summing-up, the trial judge no doubt founded himself on the part of the judgment of Edmund-Davies J. in *R. v. Church* when he says: "The unlawful act must be such as all sober and reasonable people would inevitably recognise must subject the other person to, at least, the risk of some harm resulting therefrom, albeit not serious harm."

Unfortunately, however, he fell into error as to the meaning of the word "unlawful" in that passage and pressed upon the jury a definition with which experienced counsel for the Crown had disagreed during the trial and which he found himself unable to support on the appeal. The trial judge took the view that the pointing of the revolver and the pulling of the trigger was something which could of itself be unlawful even if there was no attempt to alarm or intent to injure. This view is exemplified in a passage in his judgment which will be cited later.

It was no doubt on that basis that he had before commencing his summing-up stated that he was not going "to involve the jury in any consideration of the niceties of the question whether or not the action of the "accused did constitute or did not constitute an assault"; and thus he did not refer to the defence of accident or the need for the prosecution to disprove accident before coming to a conclusion that the act was unlawful.

Mr Mathew [for the Crown], however, had at all times put forward the correct view that for the act to be unlawful it must constitute at least what he then termed "a technical assault". In this court moreover he rightly conceded that there was no evidence to go to the jury of any assault of any kind. Nor did he feel able to submit that the acts of the defendant were on any other ground unlawful in the criminal sense of that word. Indeed no such submission could in law be made: if, for instance, the pulling of the trigger had had no effect because the striking mechanism or the ammunition had been defective no offence would have been committed by the defendant.

Another way of putting it is that *mens rea*, being now an essential ingredient in manslaughter (compare *Andrews v. D.P.P.* and *R. v. Church*), that could not in the present case be established in relation to the first ground except by proving that element of intent without which there can be no assault.

It is perhaps as well to mention that when using the phrase "unlawful in the criminal sense of that word" the court has in mind that it is long settled that it is not in point to consider whether an act is unlawful merely from the angle of civil liabilities. That was first made in the "Brighton Pier" case (*R. v. Franklin*). . . .

Appeal allowed.

Note

A problem decision in this area, however, is that of *Cato* [1976] 1 W.L.R. 110 (*ante*, p. 46) where the Court of Appeal suggested that the unlawful act need not itself be a crime. Lord Widgery stated, at p. 118:

"Strangely enough, . . . although the possession or supply of heroin is an offence, it is not an offence to take it, and although supplying it is an offence, it is not an offence to administer it . . .

Of course if the conviction on count 2 remains (that is the charge under section 23 of the Offences Against the Person Act 1861 of administering a noxious thing), then that in itself would be an unlawful act. . . .

But . . . had it not been possible to rely on [that] charge, . . . we think there would have been an unlawful act there, and we think the unlawful act would be described as injecting the deceased Farmer with a mixture of heroin and water which at the time of the injection and for the purposes of the injection the accused had unlawfully taken into his possession."

The suggestion that D could be convicted even if the section 23 count was excised from the indictment is *obiter* and appears to be wrong. Possession of heroin is an offence but D's possession of it did not cause the victim's death. This view is confirmed by the fact that in *Dalby* (1982) 74 Cr.App.R. 348, the Court of Appeal expressed the opinion that even the act of supplying a controlled drug to the victim was not an act which *caused* direct harm. The Court affirmed the view that the unlawful act itself must be one which subjects the victim to the risk of some harm; in the instant case it was the victim's own use of the drug in a form and quantity which was dangerous which caused the harm.

Unfortunately the Court of Appeal has recently elaborated further on the error in *Cato* in the case of *Kennedy* [1999] Crim.L.R. 65 where D supplied a syringe filled with heroin to V who injected it into himself and died. In upholding D's conviction for manslaughter the Court of Appeal did so on the basis either that D was guilty of the section 23 offence or that the self-injection of heroin by V was unlawful and D had assisted and wilfully encouraged this. D's voluntary self-injection, however, should be viewed as breaking the chain of causation as he was fully aware of what he was injecting into himself. Even if the causation argument is lost, there was no section 23 offence as again the consumption of heroin was a voluntary act and thus could not constitute an "administration" by D (it would only be such where he had secretly put the poison or noxious thing in something which V was to consume: see *Harley* (1830) 4 C. & P. 396 and *Dale* (1952) Cox C.C. 14). In addition, while possession of heroin may be an offence, consumption of it is not: the thing which D supposedly encouraged or assisted V to do, not being an offence, cannot found a charge of manslaughter.

(b) *The unlawful act must be dangerous*

Church made it clear that there must be an unlawful act and that it must be dangerous. Two issues left unresolved were (i) whether "harm" was limited to physical harm, and (ii) whether the accused had to be aware that his act was dangerous.

In *Dawson* (1985) 81 Cr.App.R. 150, the Court of Appeal resolved the first issue declaring that there must be a risk of physical harm, rather than emotional disturbance, arising from the unlawful act. Watkins L.J. went on to state (at p. 157) that the requirement of proving harm could be satisfied where "the unlawful act so shocks the victim as to cause him physical injury", for example, a heart attack.

The second issue was addressed in the cases which follow.

D.P.P. v. Newbury
[1977] A.C. 500
House of Lords

The appellants, two 15-year-old boys, pushed into the path of an oncoming train a piece of paving stone which some workmen had left on the parapet of a railway bridge. The stone killed the guard of the train. They were convicted of manslaughter and their appeal was dismissed by the Court of Appeal which nevertheless certified the following point of law: "Can a defendant be properly convicted of manslaughter, when his mind is not affected by drink or drugs, if he did not foresee that his act might cause harm to another?"

LORD SALMON, LORDS DIPLOCK, SIMON of GLAISDALE and KILBRANDON agreeing: ... The learned trial judge did not direct the jury that they should acquit the appellants unless they were satisfied beyond a reasonable doubt that the appellants had foreseen that they might cause harm to someone by pushing the piece of paving stone off the parapet into the path of the approaching train. In my view the learned trial judge was quite right not to give such a direction to the jury. The direction which he gave is completely in accordance with established law, which, possibly with one exception to which I shall presently refer, has never been challenged. In *R. v. Larkin* (1944) 29 Cr.App.R. 18, Humphreys J. said, at p. 23:

"Where the act which a person is engaged in performing is unlawful, then if at the same time it is a dangerous act, that is, an act which is likely to injure another person, and quite inadvertently the doer of the act causes death of that other person by that act then he is guilty of manslaughter."

I agree entirely with Lawton L.J. that that is an admirably clear statement of the law which has been applied many times. It makes it plain (a) that an accused is guilty of manslaughter if it is proved that he intentionally did an act which was unlawful and dangerous and that that act inadvertently caused death and (b) that it is unnecessary to prove that the accused knew that the act was unlawful or dangerous. This is one of the reasons why cases of manslaughter vary so infinitely in their gravity. They may amount to little more than pure inadvertence and sometimes to little less than murder.

I am sure that in *R. v. Church* [*ante*, p. 582] Edmund-Davies J. in giving the judgment of the court, did not intend to differ from or qualify anything which had been said in *R. v. Larkin*. Indeed he was restating the principle laid down in that case by illustrating the sense in which the word "dangerous" should be understood. Edmund-Davies J. said at p. 70:

"For such a verdict" (guilty of manslaughter) "inexorably to follow, the unlawful act must be such as all sober and reasonable people would inevitably recognise must subject the other person to, at least, the risk of some harm resulting therefrom, albeit not serious harm."

The test is still the objective test. In judging whether the act was dangerous the test is not did the accused recognise that it was dangerous but would all sober and reasonable people recognise its danger.

Mr Esyr Lewis in his very able argument did not and indeed could not contend that the appellants' act which I have described was lawful but he did maintain that the law stated in *Larkin's* case had undergone a change as a result of a passage in the judgment of Lord Denning M.R. in *Gray v. Barr* [1971] 2 Q.B. 554, 568 which reads as follows:

"In manslaughter of every kind there must be a guilty mind. Without it, the accused must be acquitted [see *R. v. Lamb, supra*]. In the category of manslaughter relating to an unlawful act, the accused must do a dangerous act with the intention of frightening or harming someone, or with the realisation that it is likely to frighten or harm someone, and nevertheless he goes on and does it, regardless of the consequences. If his act does thereafter, in unbroken sequence, cause the death of another, he is guilty of manslaughter."

I do not think that Lord Denning M.R was attempting to revolutionise the law relating to manslaughter if his judgment is read in the context of the tragic circumstances of the case. . . .

R. v. Lamb was referred to by Lord Denning M.R. for the proposition that in manslaughter there must always be a guilty mind. This is true of every crime except those of absolute liability. The guilty mind usually depends on the intention of the accused. Some crimes require what is sometimes called a specific intention, for example murder, which is killing with intent to inflict grievous bodily harm. Other crimes need only what is called a basic intention, which is an intention to do the acts which constitute the crime. Manslaughter is such a crime: see *R. v. Larkin* and *R. v. Church. R. v. Lamb* is certainly no authority to the contrary. . . .

Lawton L.J. had observed that in manslaughter cases, some judges are now directing juries not in accordance with the law as correctly laid down in *R. v. Larkin* and *R. v. Church* but in accordance with the observations of Lord Denning M.R. in *Gray v. Barr* taken in their literal sense. For the reasons I have already given they should cease to do so.

My Lords, I dismiss the appeal.

R. v. Dawson
(1985) 81 Cr.App.R. 150
Court of Appeal

D and E robbed V's filling station wearing masks and armed with a pickaxe handle and replica gun. Shortly afterwards V, who had a serious heart condition, died of a heart attack. D and E were convicted of manslaughter and appealed.

WATKINS L.J.: . . .

We look finally at the direction, "That is to say all reasonable people who knew the facts that you know." What the jury knew included, of course, the undisputed fact that the deceased had a very bad heart which at any moment could have ceased to function. It may be the judge did not intend that this fact should be included in the phrase "the facts that you know". If that was so, it is regrettable that he did not make it clear. By saying as he did, it is argued "including the fact that the gun was a replica" and so on, the jury must have taken him to be telling them that all facts known to them, including the heart condition, should be taken into account in performing what is undoubtedly an objective test. We think there was a grave danger of that.

This test can only be undertaken upon the basis of the knowledge gained by a sober and reasonable man as though he were present at the scene of and watched the unlawful act being performed and who knows that, as in the present case, an unloaded replica gun was in use, but that the victim may have thought it was a loaded gun in working order. In other words, he has the same knowledge as the man attempting to rob and no more. It was never suggested that any of these appellants knew that their victim had a bad heart. They knew nothing about him.

A jury must be informed by the judge when trying the offence of manslaughter what facts they may and those which they may not use for the purpose of performing the test in the second element of this offence. The judge's direction here, unlike the bulk of an admirable summing-up, lacked that necessary precision and in the form it was given may, in our view, have given the jury an erroneous impression of what knowledge they could ascribe to the sober and reasonable man.

For these reasons we see no alternative to quashing the convictions for manslaughter as unsafe and unsatisfactory. The appeal against the convictions for manslaughter is therefore allowed.

R. v. Watson
[1989] 1 W.L.R. 684
Court of Appeal

D and E broke a window and entered the house of Mr Moyler who, unknown to D and E, was aged 87, lived alone and suffered from a serious heart condition. D and E were disturbed by Mr Moyler and abused him verbally and left without stealing anything. Mr Moyler died 90 minutes later. D and E were convicted of manslaughter and appealed contending, *inter alia*, that the sober and reasonable bystander should only be ascribed the knowledge which they had at the moment they entered the house.

LORD LANE C.J.: . . .

The first point taken on behalf of the appellant is this. When one is deciding whether the sober and reasonable person (the bystander) would realise the risk of some harm resulting to the victim, how much knowledge of the circumstances does one attribute to the bystander? The appellant contends that the unlawful act here was the burglary as charged in the indictment.

The charge was laid under section 9(1)(a) of the Theft Act 1968, the allegation being that the appellant had entered the building as a trespasser with intent to commit theft. Since that offence is committed at the first moment of entry, the bystander's knowledge is confined to that of the defendant at that moment. In the instant case there was no evidence that the appellant, at the moment of entry, knew the age or physical condition of Mr Moyler or even that he lived there alone.

The judge clearly took the view that the jury were entitled to ascribe to the bystander the knowledge which the appellant gained during the whole of his stay in the house and so directed them. Was this a misdirection? In our judgment it was not. The unlawful act in the present circumstances comprised the whole of the burglarious intrusion and did not come to an end upon the appellant's foot crossing the threshold or windowsill. That being so, the appellant (and therefore the bystander) during the course of the unlawful act must have become aware of Mr Moyler's frailty and approximate age, and the judge's directions were accordingly correct. We are supported in this view by the fact that no one at the trial seems to have thought otherwise.

Note

The sober and reasonable bystander will also be aware of the background to the unlawful act (which includes preparatory acts done by the accused) as this sets the act in context for the purpose of determining its objective dangerousness. In *Ball* [1989] Crim.L.R. 730, D loaded a shotgun with two cartridges taken from his pocket which contained both live and blank cartridges. He fired the gun at V killing her. Appealing against his conviction of manslaughter, D argued that the objective assessment of the danger of his act should be based on his mistaken belief that he was firing a blank cartridge and not on the actual fact that he was firing a live cartridge. Dismissing the appeal Lord Lane C.J. stated:

"[Once it is] established . . . that the act was both unlawful and that he intended to commit the assaults, the question whether the act is a dangerous one is to be judged not by the appellant's appreciation but by that of the sober and reasonable man, and it is impossible to impute into his appreciation the mistaken belief of the appellant that what he was doing was not dangerous because he thought he had a blank cartridge in the chamber. At that stage the appellant's intention, foresight or knowledge is irrelevant."

Question

Consider D's liability for manslaughter where he fires a blank cartridge and V dies (i) as a result of diving for cover and fracturing her skull on a rock, (ii) as a result of a heart attack, V having no history of heart disease, and (iii) as a result of a cut sustained in diving for cover, V (unknown to D) being a haemophiliac.

(c) *Must the unlawful act be "directed at" the victim?*

R. v. Goodfellow
(1986) 83 Cr.App.R. 23
Court of Appeal

The appellant, who lived in a council house, wished to be rehoused. He set fire to his house while his wife, three children and another woman were in the house. The appellant, using a ladder, rescued two of his children, but the other child, his wife and the other woman all died as the fire spread more rapidly than had been anticipated. The appellant was convicted of manslaughter and appealed.

LORD LANE C.J.: . . . It seems to us that this was a case which was capable of falling within either or both types of manslaughter. On the *Lawrence* aspect [*i.e.* manslaughter by a reckless act] (*post*, p. 591), the jury might well have been satisfied that the appellant was acting in such a manner as to create an obvious and serious risk of causing physical injury to some person, and secondly that he, having recognised that there was some risk involved, had nevertheless gone on to take it.

This was equally, in our view, a case for the "unlawful and dangerous act" direction. Where the defendant does an unlawful act of such a kind as all sober and reasonable people would inevitably recognise must subject another person to, at least, the risk of some harm resulting therefrom, albeit not serious harm and causes death thereby, he is guilty of manslaughter: *Church* (*ante*, p. 542).

Lord Salmon in *D.P.P. v. Newbury* (*ante*, p. 586) approved a dictum of Humphreys J. in *Larkin* [1943] 1 All E.R. 217, 219: "Where the act which a person is engaged in performing is unlawful, then if at the same time it is a dangerous act, that is, an act which is likely to injure another person, and quite inadvertently he causes the death of that other person by that act, then he is guilty of manslaughter." Their Lordships in that case (*Newbury*) expressly disapproved of a passage in the judgment of Lord Denning M.R. in the civil case of *Gray v. Barr* [1971] 2 All E.R. 949, 956, in which he asserted that the unlawful act must be done by the defendant with the intention of frightening or harming someone or with the realisation that it is likely to frighten or harm someone. That decision of the House of Lords is, of course, binding upon us.

It is submitted by Mr Stewart on behalf of the appellant that this was not a case of "unlawful act" manslaughter, because the actions of the appellant were not directed at the victim. The authority for that proposition is said to be *Dalby* (1982) 74 Cr.App.R. 348.

In that case the appellant, a drug addict, supplied a class A drug which he had lawfully obtained to a friend, also an addict. Each injected himself intravenously. After the appellant had left, the friend administered to himself two further injections, the nature of which was unknown. When the appellant returned he was unable to wake up his friend. When medical help eventually arrived, the friend was found to be dead. The appellant was convicted of manslaughter either on the unlawful and dangerous act basis, or alternatively on the basis that he was grossly negligent in not calling an ambulance at an earlier stage.

It was held that since the act of supplying the scheduled drug was not an act which caused direct harm and since the unlawful act of supply of the dangerous drug by Dalby *per se* did not constitute the *actus reus* of the offence of manslaughter, the conviction had to be quashed. Waller L.J., at p. 352, said: "... where the charge of manslaughter is based on an unlawful and dangerous act, it must be an act directed at the victim and likely to cause immediate injury, however slight."

However we do not think that he was suggesting that there must be an intention on the part of the defendant to harm or frighten or a realisation that his acts were likely to harm or frighten. Indeed it would have been contrary to the dicta of Lord Salmon in *D.P.P. v. Newbury* (*supra*) if he was. What he was, we believe, intending to say was that there must be no fresh intervening cause between the act and the death. Indeed at p. 351 he said this: "... the supply of drugs would itself have caused no harm unless the deceased had subsequently used the drugs in a form and quantity which was dangerous"....

The questions which the jury have to decide on the charge of manslaughter of this nature are: (1) Was the act intentional? (2) Was it unlawful? (3) Was it an act which any reasonable person would realise was bound to subject some other human being to the risk of physical harm, albeit not necessarily serious harm? (4) Was that act the cause of death?

Whatever indications the judge may have given earlier as to his intentions, he did in fact direct the jury on this type of manslaughter in the passage which we have already quoted. It is true that he went further and added observations which were more appropriate to the *Lawrence* type of manslaughter. If anything, those passages resulted in a direction which was more favourable to the appellant than if they had been omitted.

Appeal dismissed

Note

The correctness of the decision in *Goodfellow* was confirmed by the decision of the House of Lords in *A-G's Reference (No. 3 of 1994)* [1998] A.C. 245 (*ante* p. 180). Not only is there no requirement for the unlawful act to be directed at the victim, but also there is no requirement that the danger or risk of harm be perceived in respect of the actual victim—a risk of harm to someone else arising from the unlawful act will suffice. Lord Hope of Craighead cited with approval the decision in *Mitchell* [1983] QB 741 where D hit E who was standing in a queue in a post office. E fell against V, an elderly lady, who fell breaking her leg and died thereafter as a result of a pulmonary embolism linked to her fall. The Court of Appeal affirmed D's conviction of manslaughter. Lord Hope also cited with approval *Larkin* and *Newbury* before concluding that the accused in the instant case should have been convicted of manslaughter where he had stabbed M, a pregnant woman, which resulted in the premature birth of her child who in turn died some time later due to problems linked to her premature birth. Lord Hope was satisfied that the stabbing of the mother was an unlawful and dangerous act. Lord Hope stated (at p. 274):

There can be no doubt that all sober and reasonable people would regard that act, within the appropriate meaning of this term, as dangerous. It is plain that it was unlawful as it was done with the intention of causing her injury. As [the accused] intended to commit that act, all the ingredients necessary for *mens rea* in regard to the crime of manslaughter were established, irrespective of who was the ultimate victim of it. The fact that the child whom the mother was carrying at the time was born alive and then died as a result of the stabbing is all that was needed for the offence of manslaughter when *actus reus* for that crime was completed by the child's death. The question, once all the other elements are satisfied, is simply one of causation. The defendant must accept all the consequences of his act, so long as the jury are satisfied that he did what he did intentionally, that what he did was unlawful and that, applying the correct test, it was also dangerous . . .. In my opinion that is sufficient for the offence of manslaughter.

ii. Gross Negligence Manslaughter

Note

The second basis upon which a person may be found guilty of involuntary manslaughter is that of gross negligence. The classic statement of this offence is that of Lord Hewart C.J. in *Bateman* (1925) Cr. App. R. 8 (*post*, p. 594) approved by the House of Lords in *Andrews v. D.P.P.* [1937] AC 576 (*post*, p. 594). The test required there to be a duty of care owed by D to the victim, breach of which caused the victim's death and left it to the jury to determine whether the negligence of D was so gross that it demanded punishment as a crime rather than merely the imposition of civil liability and the payment of compensation. It is a very high degree of negligence which has to be established before criminal liability should ensue and for many years following these decisions the courts used the terms "recklessness" and "gross negligence" interchangeably. In *Seymour* [1983] 2 A.C. 493, a case of manslaughter arising from the reckless driving of a vehicle, the House of Lords declared that no longer would it be appropriate to refer to negligence and that the test for manslaughter was the same as for the statutory offence of causing death by reckless driving contrary to s.1(1) of the Road Traffic Act 1972. This involved the *Caldwell/Lawrence* test of recklessness: a person would be guilty of manslaughter where he did an act which created an obvious and serious risk of causing physical injury to another person and either he was conscious of the risk or he gave no thought to it. In the case which follows the House of Lords reverted to the test of gross negligence.

R. v. Adomako
[1995] 1 A.C. 171
House of Lords

A, an anaesthetist, took over from another anaesthetist during the course of an operation. While he was in charge the endotracheal tube which supplied oxygen to the patient became disconnected. A first became aware that something was amiss when an alarm on the blood pressure monitor sounded some $4\frac{1}{2}$ minutes after the disconnection. A carried out various checks of the equipment and administered atropine to raise the patient's pulse. Approximately 9 minutes after the disconnection the patient suffered a cardiac arrest from which he died. It was only at this point that A discovered the disconnection. The prosecution alleged that A was guilty of gross negligence. A was convicted of manslaughter and appealed. The Court of Appeal dismissed his appeal certifying a point of law of general public importance:

"in cases of manslaughter by criminal negligence not involving driving but involving a breach of duty is it a sufficient direction to the jury to adopt the gross negligence test set out by the Court of Appeal in the present case following *R. v. Bateman* (1925) 19 Cr.App.R. 8 and *Andrews v. Director of Public Prosecutions* [1937] A.C. 576, without reference to the test of recklessness as defined in *R. v. Lawrence (Stephen)* [1982] A.C. 510 or as adapted to the circumstances of the case?"

LORD MACKAY OF CLASHFERN: . . . For the prosecution it was alleged that the appellant was guilty of gross negligence in failing to notice or respond appropriately to obvious signs that a disconnection had occurred and that the patient had ceased to breathe. In particular the prosecution alleged that the appellant had failed to notice at various stages during the period after disconnection and before the arrest either occurred or became inevitable that the patient's chest was not moving, the dials on the mechanical ventilating machine were not operating, the disconnection in the endotracheal tube, that the alarm on the ventilator was not switched on and that the patient was becoming progressively blue. Further, the prosecution alleged that the appellant had noticed but failed to understand the correct significance of the fact that during this period the patient's pulse had dropped and the patient's blood pressure had dropped.

Two expert witnesses gave evidence for the prosecution. Professor Payne described the standard of care as "abysmal" while Professor Adams stated that in his view a competent anaesthetist should have recognised the signs of disconnection within 15 seconds and that the appellant's conduct amounted to "a gross dereliction of care".

On behalf of the appellant it was conceded at his trial that he had been negligent. The issue was therefore whether his conduct was criminal.

The expert witness called on behalf of the appellant at his trial was Dr Monks. His evidence conceded that the appellant ought to have noticed the disconnection. But in his view there were factors which mitigated this failure. He considered that another independent problem either occurred or could have occurred before or at the same time as the disconnection which distracted the appellant's attention and activities. This problem would in his view have caused the patient's blood pressure to drop and may either have been a reaction to the drug being used to paralyse the patient or alternatively may have been caused by an ocular cardiac reflex.

The appellant himself said in evidence that when the alarm sounded on the Dinamap machine his first thought was that the machine itself was not working properly. Having carried out checks on the machine he then thought that the patient had suffered an ocular cardiac reflex for which he administered atropine in two successive doses. Further attempts to administer atropine by intravenous drip and to check the patient's blood pressure followed until the cardiac arrest occurred. It had never occurred to him that a disconnection had taken place. He stated in evidence that "after things went wrong I think I did panic a bit".

In relation to the appellant's actions during this period, Professor Payne had conceded during cross-examination that "given that Dr Adomako misled himself the efforts he made were not unreasonable". The period to which this evidence referred was obviously the period after the alarm had sounded on the Dinamap machine which was, as I have said, apparently some $4\frac{1}{2}$ minutes after the disconnection occurred. . . .

In opening his very cogent argument for the appellant before your Lordships, counsel submitted that the law in this area should have the characteristics of clarity, certainty, intellectual coherence and general applicability and acceptability. For these reasons he said the law applying to involuntary manslaughter generally should involve a universal test and that test should be the test already applied in this House to motor manslaughter. He criticised the concept of gross negligence which was the basis of the judgment of the Court of Appeal submitting that its formulation involved circularity, the jury being told in effect to convict of a crime if they thought a crime had been committed and that accordingly using gross negligence as the conceptual basis for the crime of involuntary manslaughter was unsatisfactory and the court should apply the law laid down in *Seymour* [1983] 2 A.C. 493 generally to all cases of involuntary manslaughter or at least use this as the basis for providing general applicability and acceptability.

Like the Court of Appeal your Lordships were treated to a considerable review of authority. I begin with *R. v. Bateman*, 19 Cr.App.R. 8 and the opinion of Lord Hewart C.J., where he said, at pp. 10–11:

"In expounding the law to juries on the trial of indictments for man-slaughter by negligence, judges have often referred to the distinction between civil and criminal liability for death by negligence. The law of criminal liability for negligence is conveniently explained in that way. If A has caused the death of B by alleged negligence, then, in order to establish civil liability, the plaintiff must prove (in addition to pecuniary loss caused by the death) that A owed a duty to B to take care, that that duty was not discharged, and that the default caused the death of B. To convict A of manslaughter, the prosecution must prove the three things above mentioned and must satisfy the jury, in addition, that A's negligence amounted to a crime. In the civil action, if it is proved that A fell short of the standard of reasonable care required by law, it matters not how far he fell short of that standard. The extent of his liability depends not on the degree of negligence but on the amount of damage done. In a criminal court, on the contrary, the amount and degree of negligence are the determining question. There must be *mens rea*."

Later he said, at pp. 11–12:

"In explaining to juries the test which they should apply to determine whether the negligence, in the particular case, amounted or did not amount to a crime, judges have used many epithets, such as 'culpable', 'criminal', 'gross', 'wicked', 'clear', 'complete'. But, whatever epithet be used and whether an epithet be used or not, in order to establish criminal liability the facts must be such that, in the opinion of the jury, the negligence of the accused went beyond a mere matter of compensation between subjects and showed such disregard for the life and safety of others as to amount to a crime against the state and conduct deserving punishment."

Next I turn to *Andrews v. Director of Public Prosecutions* [1937] A.C. 576 which was a case of manslaughter through the dangerous driving of a motor car. In a speech with which all the other members of this House who sat agreed, Lord Atkin said, at pp. 581–583:

"of all crimes manslaughter appears to afford most difficulties of definition, for it concerns homicide in so many and so varying conditions. From the early days when any homicide involved penalty the law has gradually evolved 'through successive differentiations and integrations' until it recognises murder on the one hand, based mainly, though not exclusively, on an intention to kill, and manslaughter on the other hand, based mainly, though not exclusively, on the absence of intention to kill but with the presence of an element of 'unlawfulness' which is the elusive factor. In the present case it is only necessary to consider manslaughter from the point of view of an unintentional killing caused by negligence, that is, the omission of a duty to take care. . . .
    The principle to be observed is that cases of manslaughter in driving motor cars are but instances of a general rule applicable to all charges of homicide by negligence. Simple lack of care such as will constitute civil liability is not enough: for purposes of the criminal law there are degrees of negligence: and a very high degree of negligence is required to be proved before the felony is established. Probably of all the epithets that can be applied 'reckless' most nearly covers the case. It is difficult to visualise a case of death caused by reckless driving in the connotation of that term in ordinary speech which would not justify a conviction for manslaughter: but it is probably not all-embracing, for 'reckless' suggests an indifference to risk whereas the accused may have appreciated the risk and intended to avoid it and yet shown such a high degree

of negligence in the means adopted to avoid the risk as would justify a conviction. If the principle of *Bateman's* case, 19 Cr.App.R. 8 is observed it will appear that the law of manslaughter has not changed by the introduction of motor vehicles on the road. Death caused by their negligent driving, though unhappily much more frequent, is to be treated in law as death caused by any other form of negligence: and juries should be directed accordingly."

In my opinion the law as stated in these two authorities is satisfactory as providing a proper basis for describing the crime of involuntary manslaughter. Since the decision in *Andrews* was a decision of your Lordships' House, it remains the most authoritative statement of the present law which I have been able to find and although its relationship to *R. v. Seymour* [1983] 2 A.C. 493 is a matter to which I shall have to return, it is a decision which has not been departed from. On this basis in my opinion the ordinary principles of the law of negligence apply to ascertain whether or not the defendant has been in breach of a duty of care towards the victim who has died. If such breach of duty is established the next question is whether that breach of duty caused the death of the victim. If so, the jury must go on to consider whether that breach of duty should be characterised as gross negligence and therefore as a crime. This will depend on the seriousness of the breach of duty committed by the defendant in all the circumstances in which the defendant was placed when it occurred. The jury will have to consider whether the extent to which the defendant's conduct departed from the proper standard of care incumbent upon him, involving as it must have done a risk of death to the patient, was such that it should be judged criminal.

It is true that to a certain extent this involves an element of circularity, but in this branch of the law I do not believe that is fatal to its being correct as a test of how far conduct must depart from accepted standards to be characterised as criminal. This is necessarily a question of degree and an attempt to specify that degree more closely is I think likely to achieve only a spurious precision. The essence of the matter which is supremely a jury question is whether having regard to the risk of death involved, the conduct of the defendant was so bad in all the circumstances as to amount in their judgment to a criminal act or omission.

My Lords, the view which I have stated of the correct basis in law for the crime of involuntary manslaughter accords I consider with the criteria stated by counsel although I have not reached the degree of precision in definition which he required, but in my opinion it has been reached so far as practicable and with a result which leaves the matter properly stated for a jury's determination.

My Lords, in my view the law as stated in *R. v. Seymour* [1983] 2 A.C. 493 should no longer apply since the underlying statutory provisions on which it rested have now been repealed by the Road Traffic Act 1991. It may be that cases of involuntary motor manslaughter will as a result become rare but I consider it unsatisfactory that there should be any exception to the generality of the statement which I have made, since such exception, in my view, gives rise to unnecessary complexity. . . .

I consider it perfectly appropriate that the word "reckless" should be used in cases of involuntary manslaughter, but as Lord Atkin put it, "in the ordinary connotation of that word". Examples in which this was done, to my mind, with complete accuracy are *R. v. Stone* [1977] Q.B. 354 and *R. v. West London Coroner, Ex parte Gray* [1988] Q.B. 467.

In my opinion it is quite unnecessary in the context of gross negligence to give the detailed directions with regard to the meaning of the word "reckless" associated with *R. v. Lawrence* [1982] A.C. 510. The decision of the Court of Appeal (Criminal Division) in the other cases with which they were concerned at the same time as they heard the appeal in this case indicates that the circumstances in which involuntary manslaughter has to be considered may make the somewhat elaborate and rather rigid directions inappropriate. I entirely agree with the view that the circumstances to which a charge of involuntary manslaughter may apply are so various that it is unwise to attempt to categorise or detail specimen directions. For my part I would not wish to go beyond the description of the basis in law which I have already given.

In my view the summing up of the judge in the present case was a model of clarity in analysis of the facts and in setting out the law in a manner which was readily comprehensible by the jury. The summing up was criticised in respect of the inclusion of the following passage:

"Of course you will understand it is not for every humble man of the profession to have all that great skill of the great men in Harley Street but, on the other hand, they are not allowed to practise medicine in this country unless they have acquired a certain amount of skill. They are bound to show a reasonable amount of skill according to the circumstances of the case, and you have to judge them on the basis that they are skilled men, but not necessarily so skilled as more skilful men in the profession, and you can only convict them criminally if, in your judgment, they fall below the standard of skill which is the least qualification which any doctor should have. You should only convict a doctor of causing a death by negligence if you think he did something which no reasonably skilled doctor should have done."

The criticism was particularly of the latter part of this quotation in that it was open to the meaning that if the defendant did what no reasonably skilled doctor should have done it was open to the jury to convict him of causing death by negligence. Strictly speaking this passage is concerned with the statement of a necessary condition for a conviction by preventing a conviction unless that condition is satisfied. It is incorrect to treat it as stating a sufficient condition for conviction. In any event I consider that this passage in the context was making the point forcefully that the defendant in this case was not to be judged by the standard of more skilled doctors but by the standard of a reasonably competent doctor. There were many other passages in the summing up which emphasised the need for a high degree of negligence if the jury were to convict and read in that context I consider that the summing up cannot be faulted.

For these reasons I am of the opinion that this appeal should be dismissed and that the certified question should be answered by saying:

"In cases of manslaughter by criminal negligence involving a breach of duty, it is a sufficient direction to the jury to adopt the gross negligence test set out by the Court of Appeal in the present case following *R. v. Bateman*, 19 Cr.App.R. 8 and *Andrews v. Director of Public Prosecutions* [1937] A.C. 576 and that it is not necessary to refer to the definition of recklessness in *R. v. Lawrence* [1982] A.C. 510, although it is perfectly open to the trial judge to use the word 'reckless' in its ordinary meaning as part of his exposition of the law if he deems it appropriate in the circumstances of the particular case."

... I have reached the same conclusion on the basic law to be applied in this case as did the Court of Appeal. Personally I would not wish to state the law more elaborately than I have done. In particular I think it is difficult to take expressions used in particular cases out of the context of the cases in which they were used and enunciate them as if applying generally. This can I think lead to ambiguity and perhaps unnecessary complexity. The task of trial judges in setting out for the jury the issues of fact and the relevant law in cases of this class is a difficult and demanding one. I believe that the supreme test that should be satisfied in such directions is that they are comprehensible to an ordinary member of the public who is called to sit on a jury and who has no particular prior acquaintance with the law. To make it obligatory on trial judges to give directions in law which are so elaborate that the ordinary member of the jury will have great difficulty in following them, and even greater difficulty in retaining them in his memory for the purpose of application in the jury room, is no service to the cause of justice. The experienced counsel who assisted your Lordships in this appeal indicated that as a practical matter there was a danger in over elaboration of definition of the word "reckless." While therefore I have said in my view it is perfectly open to a trial judge to use the word "reckless" if it appears appropriate in the circumstances of a particular case as indicating the extent to which a defendant's conduct must deviate from that of a proper standard of care, I do not think it right to require that this should be done and certainly not right that it should incorporate the full detail required in *Lawrence*.

[Lords Keith of Kinkel, Goff of Chieveley, Browne-Wilkinson and Woolf agreed with the Lord Chancellor's speech.]

Appeal dismissed

Questions

1. Had the patient in *Adomako* survived but in a persistent vegetative state, would Dr Adomako have been liable to conviction of any other offence?
2. Professor J. C. Smith in his Commentary to *Adomako* [1994] Crim L.R. 757, 758, states, "This welcome decision by the House of Lords removes much unnecessary complication and injustice from the law of involuntary manslaughter." Do you agree?
3. Will the threat of conviction for manslaughter and imprisonment cause similarly positioned anaesthetists not to make mistakes in future?
4. Simon Gardner, "Manslaughter by Gross Negligence" (1995) 111 L.Q.R. 22, 26 states:

> "[Dr Adomako] trained in Russia, and though at the time in question he was in his late forties, his career had consisted entirely of six-month contracts; he was working in the week at one hospital and during the weekends at another; on the morning in question he had started work at 7 o'clock, having got to bed only three-and-a-half hours earlier; at the time of the incident he did not have the assistant whom he was supposed to have."

If the Law Commission's proposed offence of corporate killing (*ante,* p. 439) were to be introduced, would the Hospital Trust or the Local Health Authority be guilty of corporate killing in circumstances such as those pertaining in *Adomako*?
5. If expert evidence discloses that a properly connected endotracheal tube should not become disconnected, would a prosecution for manslaughter of the original anaesthetist who was in charge when the

operation commenced be likely to succeed? What would be the issues a jury would have to consider?

Note

In *Singh (Gurphal)* [1999] Crim. L.R. 582 the Court of Appeal held that whether D owed a duty of care was a question of law for the judge to determine and approved the trial judge's direction that on a charge of gross negligence manslaughter "the circumstances must be such that a reasonably prudent person would have foreseen a serious and obvious risk not merely of injury or even serious injury but of death." Professor J.C. Smith in his commentary to this case at p. 583 states:

> "It seems that the deliberate taking of a high degree of risk of causing serious bodily harm which results in death (formerly murder under *Hyam* [1975] A.C. 55) must now be manslaughter by recklessness. But gross negligence is objective and it is accordingly appropriate that it should be more limited."

This decision clarifies one of the problems with the speech of Lord Mackay in *Adomako* by requiring a risk in respect of which D was negligent to have been one of death rather than any lesser degree of harm. If D, however, is reckless as to a lesser degree of harm and causes V's death, this may amount to reckless manslaughter—a category of manslaughter left open by Lord Mackay which forms the focus of considerable academic speculation although not featuring in the law reports. The circumstances in which manslaughter by recklessness might arise are very narrow (perhaps even non-existent) as most conceivable situations in which D's reckless act causes V's death will fit within the bounds of constructive manslaughter.

iii. Reform of the Law of Involuntary Manslaughter

**Legislating the Criminal Code: Involuntary Manslaughter
Law Commission (Law Com No. 237)**

PART III: WHAT IS WRONG WITH THE PRESENT LAW?

INTRODUCTION

3.1 ... The two major problems relate to the very wide range of conduct falling within the scope of involuntary manslaughter.... The offence encompasses, first, cases involving conduct that falls only just short of murder, where the accused was *aware* of a risk of causing death or serious injury, although he did not *intend* to cause either; second, cases where the accused is a professional person who makes a very serious mistake that results in death; and third, cases where a relatively minor assault ends in death. This leads to problems in sentencing and labelling, including the fundamental problem that many cases currently amounting to unlawful act manslaughter involve only minor fault on the part of the perpetrator, and therefore ought not, perhaps, to be described as manslaughter at all. There are also a number of more specific problems which we consider below.

THE BREADTH OF THE OFFENCE

3.2 ... The width of the present offence can cause problems to judges on sentencing. As Lord Lane C.J. remarked [*Walker* (1992) 13 Cr. App. R. (S) 474, 476]:

"It is a truism to say that of all the crimes in the calendar, the crime of manslaughter faces the sentencing judge with the greatest problem, because manslaughter ranges in its gravity from the borders of murder right down to those of accidental death. It is never easy to strike exactly the right point at which to pitch the sentence."

3.3 There is a strong argument in favour of defining criminal offences in terms of narrow bands of conduct, so that the judge can have the guidance of the jury on important factual questions, such as intention or awareness of risk. We agree with the notion that

"Questions of intention ... involve the application of a test capable of precise definition (even though the task of drawing inferences from the evidence may be difficult). Gradations of culpability based on varying degrees of intention should, therefore, be incorporated into the definition of the offences, so that the issues can be contested with all that that implies in terms of the rules of procedure, evidence and quantum of proof." [D.A. Thomas, "Form and Function in Criminal Law" in *Reshaping the Criminal Law* (ed. Glazebrook, 1978), p. 28.]

The same could be said of awareness of risk.

3.4 Another argument in favour of separate offences follows on from this point about sentencing. It is inappropriate that types of conduct that vary so widely in terms of fault should all carry the same descriptive label. The accused who sets fire to his house so that the council will rehouse him, knowing that his wife and children are asleep inside and that they will almost certainly be killed or seriously injured, is blameworthy in a very different way from the electrician who causes death by miswiring an electrical appliance with a high degree of carelessness. It is arguable that the label "manslaughter" is devalued, and the more serious forms of wrongdoing that it describes might come to be regarded as less serious, because it is also used to describe less heinous crimes. By the same token, juries might be reluctant to convict, for example, a highly incompetent doctor of manslaughter because of the perceived gravity of the offence.

UNLAWFUL ACT MANSLAUGHTER

3.5 The next problem with the present law also relates to the breadth of conduct falling within involuntary manslaughter. ... [I]f a person commits a criminal act that carries a risk of causing *some* harm to another, and by chance he causes death, he will be guilty of unlawful act manslaughter. In some of these cases, the defendant would only have been guilty of a relatively trivial offence if death had not chanced to occur. For example, if D pushes V in a fight, and V staggers but does not fall, D will at most be guilty of causing actual bodily harm under section 47 of the Offences against the Person Act 1861, which carries a maximum sentence of five years' imprisonment. If, however, V loses his balance and falls to the floor, knocking his head on the pavement and thereby sustaining fatal brain injuries, D will be guilty of manslaughter.

3.6 ... [We] consider that it is wrong in principle for the law to hold a person responsible for causing a result that he did not intend or foresee, and which would not even have been *foreseeable* by a reasonable person observing his conduct. Unlawful act manslaughter is therefore, we believe, unprincipled because it requires only that a foreseeable risk of causing *some* harm should have been inherent in the accused's conduct, whereas he is convicted of actually causing death, and also to some extent punished for doing so.

GROSS NEGLIGENCE MANSLAUGHTER AFTER *ADOMAKO*

3.9 The first problem with [the test in *Adomako*] is that it is circular: the jury must be directed to convict the defendant of a crime if they think his conduct was "criminal". In effect, this leaves a question of law to the jury, and, because juries do not give reasons for their decisions, it is impossible to tell what criteria will be applied in an individual case. This must lead to uncertainty in the law. The CPS has told us that prosecutors find it difficult to judge when to bring a prosecution, defendants have difficulty in deciding how to plead, and there is a danger that juries may bring in inconsistent verdicts on broadly similar evidence.

3.10 Other problems arise out of the Lord Chancellor's use of the terminology of "duty of care" and "negligence", and his linkage of the civil and criminal law in his speech. The meanings of these words are not entirely clear in a criminal law context, nor is it clear to what extent they mean the same things in tort and in criminal law.

3.11 As we explained in Consultation Paper No. 135, "negligence" in the context of the crime of manslaughter probably means nothing more than "carelessness": it does not carry the technical meaning that it has in the law of tort, where it depends on the existence of a duty of care owed and a breach of that duty. The Lord Chancellor said in *Adomako* that "the ordinary principles of the law of negligence apply to ascertain whether or not the defendant has been in breach of a duty of care towards the victim who has died". This equation of the civil and criminal law concepts of negligence causes no problems where, as in *Adomako* itself, a death is caused by a badly performed positive act of the accused, because it is virtually certain that both tort and criminal law would hold that a duty was owed to the deceased not to injure him by a *positive act*.

3.12 It is possible, however, that the courts in future cases of *omission* might feel obliged to apply the decision in *Adomako*. If so, they would run into difficulties, because it is by no means certain that the scope of liability for negligent omissions is the same in criminal law as it is in tort. For example, in criminal law it would seem that once someone has voluntarily taken some steps to care for another, he may be liable if his care is not adequate and the other person dies. In tort, however, there is probably no liability if the defendant abandons an effort to care for someone and that person dies, unless he causes harm through his own incompetence.

3.13 It is possible, therefore, that the decision in *Adomako* may have changed the criminal law in relation to liability for omissions, by equating it with the civil law of tort. This may have *restricted* the scope of the duty to act in criminal law, by implicitly overruling *Stone and Dobinson;* on the other hand, there *may* be cases where the law of tort imposes a more stringent duty to act than the criminal law had hitherto. The law on this subject is so unclear that it is difficult to tell whether the effect of Lord Mackay's speech was indeed to change the law, and, if so, what the implications of this change might be. It is, however, clear that the terminology of "negligence" and "duty of care" is best avoided within the criminal law, because of the uncertainty and confusion that surround it.

Note

The Law Commission recommends the creation of two new offences of unintentional killing, one based on recklessness and the other on gross carelessness (paragraph 5.3). They also recommend the abolition of unlawful act manslaughter in its present form (paragraph 5.16) although aspects of this offence appear in the offence of killing by gross carelessness (see clause 2 (1) (c) (ii). The offence retains liability for inadvertent killing but limits this to circumstances where the inadvertence is culpable.

WHAT MAKES INADVERTENCE *CULPABLE*?

. . .

4.18 The first criterion of culpability upon which we must insist is that the harm to which the accused failed to advert was at least *foreseeable*, if not strikingly foreseeable or obvious. If the accused is an ordinary person, she cannot be blamed for failing to take notice of a risk if it would not have been apparent to *an average person in her position*, because the criminal law cannot require an *exceptional* standard of perception or awareness from her. If the accused held herself out as an expert of some kind, however, a higher standard can be expected from her; if she is a doctor, for example, she will be at fault if she fails to advert to a risk that would have been obvious to the average doctor in her position.

4.19 As a matter of strict principle, the accused ought only to be held liable for causing death if the risk to which she culpably failed to advert was a risk of *death*. In practice, however, there is a very thin line between behaviour that risks serious injury and behaviour that risks death, because it is frequently a matter of chance, depending on such factors as the availability of medical treatment, whether serious injury leads to death. Admittedly it is possible for conduct to involve a risk of serious injury (such as a broken limb) though not a risk of death; but intention to cause serious injury constitutes the *mens rea* of murder although the *actus reus* is the causing of death, and we see no compelling reason to distinguish between murder and manslaughter in this respect. We consider, therefore, that it would not be wrong in principle if a person were to be held responsible for causing death through failing to advert to a clear risk of causing death *or* serious injury—subject of course to a second criterion, to which we now turn.

4.20 The second criterion of culpability which we consider to be essential is that the accused herself would have been *capable* of perceiving the risk in question, had she directed her mind to it. Since the fault of the accused lies in her failure to consider a risk, she cannot be punished for this failure if the risk in question would never have been apparent to her, no matter how hard she thought about the potential consequences of her conduct. If this criterion is not insisted upon, the accused will, in essence, be punished for being less intelligent, mature or capable than the average person. . . .

4.22 We consider the position taken in *Elliott v. C (ante,* p. 130) to be highly unsatisfactory. It is hardly to be supposed that a blind person will be held

reckless for inadvertently creating a risk which would have been obvious
to a person with the power of sight; yet a child of 14 was held in this case
to be reckless as a result of thoughtlessly creating a risk which she was
incapable of appreciating, although it would have been obvious to an
adult. A person cannot be said to be morally at fault in failing to advert
to a risk if she lacked the capacity to do so.

4.23 . . . [W]e consider that it is appropriate to impose liability for inadvertently causing harm in cases where the harm risked is *very serious*.
Where a person embarks on a course of conduct which inherently
involves a risk of causing death or serious injury to another, society is
justified in requiring a higher standard of care from her than from someone whose conduct involves a lesser risk or no risk at all. . . .

WHAT MAKES *CONDUCT* CULPABLE?

The conduct led to harmful consequences: "moral luck"

4.30 It is arguable that a person is morally responsible for *all* the consequences that flow from her conduct, and that when these consequences
are harmful it is appropriate for the *law* to hold her liable for them as
well. A philosophical justification for this view is provided by "moral
luck" arguments, which hold that ethics are not separable from *luck*. It
has been suggested that luck influences most aspects of our lives—including the capacities and personalities we are born with—and that, in the
course of a lifetime and throughout a community, good and bad luck are
fairly evenly distributed. Individuals cannot prevent the outcomes of their
actions being influenced by luck, and to the extent that their actions
impinge on others in a harmful way, they are inevitably judged by others
on those outcomes. For example, if a child runs from behind a car into
the path of a van which is being entirely properly driven, and the child
is knocked down and killed, it is commonly said that the death of the
child will be on the conscience of the driver, although everyone accepts
that the death was "an accident". . . .

4.39 Unless one accepts moral luck arguments, it is not clear *why* a person
ought to be held criminally responsible for causing death if death or serious injury were the *unforeseeable* consequences of her conduct, just
because she foresaw, or it was foreseeable, that *some* harm would result.
Surely a person who, for example, pushes roughly into a queue is morally
to blame for the foreseeable consequences of her actions—that a few
people might get jostled, possibly even lightly bruised, and that people
might get annoyed—but not for causing a death if, quite unexpectedly,
she sets in train a series of events which leads to such an outcome. We
consider that the criminal law should properly be concerned with questions of moral culpability, and we do not think that an accused who is
culpable for causing *some harm* is sufficiently blameworthy to be held
liable for the unforeseeable consequence of death.

Draft Involuntary Homicide Bill

Reckless killing

1.—(1) A person who by his conduct causes the death of another is
guilty of reckless killing if—

(a) he is aware of a risk that his conduct will cause death or serious injury; and

(b) it is unreasonable for him to take that risk having regard to the circumstances as he knows or believes them to be.

(2) A person guilty of reckless killing is liable on conviction on indictment to imprisonment for life.

Killing by gross carelessness

2.—(1) A person who by his conduct causes the death of another is guilty of killing by gross carelessness if—

(a) a risk that his conduct will cause death or serious injury would be obvious to a reasonable person in his position;

(b) he is capable of appreciating that risk at the material time; and

(c) either—

    (i) his conduct falls far below what can reasonably be expected of him in the circumstances; or

    (ii) he intends by his conduct to cause some injury or is aware of, and unreasonably takes, the risk that it may do so.

(2) There shall be attributed to the person referred to in subsection (1)(a) above—

(a) knowledge of any relevant facts which the accused is shown to have at the material time; and

(b) any skill or experience professed by him.

(3) In determining for the purposes of subsection (1)(c)(i) above what can reasonably be expected of the accused regard shall be had to the circumstances of which he can be expected to be aware, to any circumstances shown to be within his knowledge and to any other matter relevant for assessing his conduct at the material time.

(4) Subsection (1)(c)(ii) above applies only if the conduct causing, or intended to cause, the injury constitutes an offence.

(5) A person guilty of killing by gross carelessness is liable on conviction on indictment to imprisonment for a term not exceeding [   ] years.

3.—A person is not guilty of an offence under sections 1 or 2 above by reason of an omission unless the omission is in breach of a duty at common law.

Note

The Law Commission provide the following examples of how the offence of killing by gross carelessness would operate.

5.36 *Example 1: D, a climbing instructor, took a group of inexperienced climbers out with inadequate equipment in very bad weather. They got trapped and one of them died.*

In order to convict D, the jury would have to answer "yes" to all the following questions: (1) Would it have been *obvious* to a reasonable climbing instructor in D's place that taking a group of inexperienced climbers out in the prevailing conditions would create a risk of causing death or serious injury to one of them? (2) Was D *capable* of appreciating this risk? and (3) Did his conduct fall *far* below what could reasonably be expected of him in all the circumstances?

5.37 *Example 2: D caused V's death by punching him in the head, not realising that serious injury might result; the impact of the blow caused a blood clot in the brain.*

The jury would have to decide whether it would have been *obvious* to a reasonable person in D's position that punching V as hard as he did would create a risk of causing death or serious injury, and whether D was *capable* of appreciating the risk at the time in question (unless he was incapable due to voluntary intoxication). If the answer to both of these questions is "yes", and if it is satisfied that D intended to cause *some* injury to V, or was reckless as to doing so, the jury must convict. If not, the accused may be convicted of the appropriate non-fatal offence in the alternative.

Questions

D, a surgeon is due to perform two operations: one to remove V's finger and one to remove W's hand. D mistakes the order in which the operations are to take place and, without checking the identity of the patients, amputates V's hand. When V recovers from the anaesthetic he is so shocked and incensed at the incompetence of the medical staff in the hospital that he discharges himself. V's wound becomes infected and he refuses further medical attention with the result that he dies from septicaemia. Expert medical opinion would establish that today the surgical procedure of amputating a hand of an otherwise healthy person would involve no risk of death. If the Draft Involuntary Homicide Bill is enacted would D be liable to conviction for killing by gross carelessness? Would he have been liable to conviction for gross negligence manslaughter? If V had survived would D have been liable to conviction for a non-fatal offence against the person either under the current law or under the Home Office's proposals (see pp. 667–674, *post*)? To what extent do the absence of any proposals in this Report to reform the law relating to causation continue "to compound the effect of luck by giving it legal significance" (paragraph 4.33)?

Note

In May 2000 the Home Office published a Consultation Paper, *Reforming the Law on Involuntary Manslaughter: The Government's Proposals* based on the Law Commission Report No. 237 which the Government largely accepted. The Consultation Paper sought comments on some further possible options. The Home Office endorsed the Law Commission's recommendations of an offence of reckless killing, the abolition of unlawful act manslaughter and its replacement by an offence of killing by gross carelessness. The Home Office sought views on whether an additional homicide offence should be created to cover the situation where a death which was unforeseeable occurs and the following requirements apply (para. 2.11):

- a person by his or her conduct causes the death of another;
- he or she intended to or was reckless as to whether some injury was caused; and

- the conduct causing, or intended to cause, the injury constitutes an offence.

This offence would be narrower than unlawful act manslaughter but liability would still be derived from the consequence of death ensuing. A case such as *Mitchell* (*ante* p. 591) could still arise. The Home Office provides no justification for basing liability on an accidental outcome rather than intention or foresight.

(For the Law Commission's and Home Office's proposals on corporate killing see pp. 439–443, *ante*.)

5. OTHER UNLAWFUL HOMICIDES

i. Infanticide

Infanticide Act 1938, section 1

(1) Where a woman by any wilful act or omission causes the death of her child being a child under the age of twelve months, but at the time of the act or omission the balance of her mind was disturbed by reason of her not having fully recovered from the effect of giving birth to the child or by reason of the effect of lactation consequent upon the birth of the child, then, notwithstanding that the circumstances were such that but for this Act the offence would have amounted to murder, she shall be guilty of felony, to wit of infanticide, and may for such offence be dealt with and punished as if she had been guilty of the offence of manslaughter of the child.

Note

Less than half-a-dozen women are convicted of this offence per year and a custodial sentence is rare.

ii. Child Destruction

Infant Life (Preservation) Act 1929, section 1

(1) Subject as hereinafter in this subsection provided, any person who, with intent to destroy the life of a child capable of being born alive, by any wilful act causes a child to die before it has an existence independent of its mother, shall be guilty of felony, to wit, of child destruction, and shall be liable on conviction thereon to imprisonment for life: Provided that no person shall be found guilty of an offence under this section unless it is proved that the act which caused the death of the child was not done in good faith for the purpose only of preserving the life of the mother.

(2) For the purposes of this Act, evidence that a woman had at any material time been pregnant for a period of twenty-eight weeks or more shall be *prima facie* proof that she was at that time pregnant of a child capable of being born alive.

Note

Neither this offence nor abortion below, are true homicides, see *ante*, p. 487. For a discussion of the proviso to subsection (1), see Abortion, particularly the case of *R. v. Bourne*, below.

iii. Abortion

Offences Against the Person Act 1861, section 58

Every woman being with child, who, with intent to procure her own miscarriage, shall unlawfully administer to herself any poison or other noxious thing, or shall unlawfully use any instrument or other means whatsoever with the like intent, and whosoever, with intent to procure the miscarriage of any woman, whether she be or be not with child, shall unlawfully administer to her or cause to be taken by her any poison or other noxious thing, or shall unlawfully use any instrument or other means whatsoever with the like intent, shall be guilty of felony, and being convicted thereof shall be liable to [imprisonment] for life.

Notes

Complications follow when the woman is not pregnant but does what would otherwise fall within the section. Note the cases of *Whitchurch* (1890) 24 Q.B.D. 42 and *Sockett* (1908) 24 T.L.R. 893 on conspiracy and aiding and abetting respectively, the combined effect of which is to destroy the duality of the offences in section 58. The woman who is not pregnant commits no wrong if she attempts to procure her own miscarriage unaided. If she has help, the helper is guilty under the second part of the section, they are both guilty of conspiracy and the woman herself is guilty of aiding and abetting the helper.

Various acts of preparation are made specifically criminal under the following section:

Offences Against the Person Act 1861, section 59

Whosoever shall unlawfully supply or procure any poison or other noxious thing, or any instrument or thing whatsoever, knowing that the same is intended to be unlawfully used or employed with intent to procure the miscarriage of any woman, whether she be or not be with child, shall be guilty of a misdemeanour, and being convicted thereof shall be liable to [imprisonment] not exceeding five years.

The number of convictions for illegally procuring an abortion has greatly diminished since the Abortion Act 1967 which allows for lawful medical termination.

Abortion Act 1967, as amended by section 37 of the Human Fertilisation and Embryology Act 1990

1. *Medical termination of pregnancy*
(1) Subject to the provisions of this section, a person shall not be guilty of an offence under the law relating to abortion when a pregnancy is termin-

ated by a registered medical practitioner if two registered medical practitioners are of the opinion, formed in good faith—

(a) that the pregnancy has not exceeded its twenty-fourth week and that the continuance of the pregnancy would involve risk, greater than if the pregnancy were terminated, or injury to the physical or mental health of the pregnant woman or any existing children of her family; or
(b) that the termination is necessary to prevent grave permanent injury to the physical or mental health of the pregnant woman; or
(c) that the continuance of the pregnancy would involve risk to the life of the pregnant woman, greater than if the pregnancy were terminated; or
(d) that there is a substantial risk that if the child were born it would suffer from such physical or mental abnormalities as to be seriously handicapped. . . .

(3) Except as provided by subsection (4) of this section, any treatment for the termination of pregnancy must be carried out in a hospital vested in the Secretary of State for the purpose of his functions under the National Health Service Act 1977 or the National Health Service (Scotland) Act 1978, or in a place for the time being approved for the purposes of this section by the Secretary of State.

(4) Subsection (3) of this section, and so much of subsection (1) as relates to the opinion of two registered medical practitioners, shall not apply to the termination of a pregnancy by a registered practitioner in a case where he is of the opinion, formed in good faith, that the termination is immediately necessary to save the life or to prevent grave permanent injury to the physical or mental health of the pregnant woman.

The 1967 Act was in some senses merely a declaration and clarification of the interpretation given by at least one Old Bailey judge to section 58: see the case below.

R. v. Bourne
[1939] 1 K.B. 687
Central Criminal Court

The accused performed an operation on a girl of 14 who was pregnant as a result of a rape. The pregnancy was terminated with the consent of the girl's parents. The accused claimed that to continue the pregnancy would have caused serious injury to the girl.

MACNAGHTEN J. in summing up the case to the jury said: . . . A man of the highest skill, openly, in one of our great hospitals, performs the operation. Whether it was legal or illegal you will have to determine, but he performs the operation as an act of charity, without fee or reward, and unquestionably believing that he was doing the right thing, and that he ought, in the performance of his duty as a member of a profession devoted to the alleviation of human suffering, to do it. That is the case that you have to try today. . . .

The defendant is charged with an offence against section 58 of the Offences Against the Person Act, 1861. . . . But, as in the case of homicide, so also in the case where an unborn child is killed, there may be justification for the act.

Nine years ago Parliament passed an Act called the Infant Life (Preservation) Act, 1929. Section 1, subsection 1 . . . provides for the case where a child is killed by a wilful act at the time when it is being delivered in the ordinary course of nature; but in my view the proviso that it is necessary for the Crown to prove that the act was not done in good faith for the purpose only of preserving the life of the mother is in accordance with what has always been the common law of England with regard to the killing of an unborn child. No such proviso is in fact set out in section 58 of the Offences Against the Person Act, 1861; but the words of that section are that any person who "unlawfully" uses an instrument with intent to procure miscarriage shall be guilty of felony. In my opinion the word "unlawfully" is not, in that section, a meaningless word. I think it imports the meaning expressed by the proviso in section 1, subsection 1, of the Infant Life (Preservation) Act 1929, and that section 58 of the Offences Against the Person Act, 1861, must be read as if the words making it an offence to use an instrument with intent to procure a miscarriage were qualified by a similar proviso.

In this case, therefore, my direction to you in law is this—that the burden rests on the Crown to satisfy you beyond reasonable doubt that the defendant did not procure the miscarriage of the girl in good faith for the purpose only of preserving her life. If the Crown fails to satisfy you of that, the defendant is entitled by the law of this land to a verdict of acquittal. If, on the other hand, you are satisfied that what the defendant did was not done by him in good faith for the purpose only of preserving the life of the girl, it is your duty to find him guilty. It is said, and I think said rightly, that this is a case of great importance to the public and, more especially, to the medical profession; but you will observe that it has nothing to do with the ordinary case of procuring abortion. . . . In those cases the operation is performed by a person of no skill, with no medical qualifications, and there is no pretence that it is done for the preservation of the mother's life. Cases of that sort are in no way affected by the consideration of the question which is put before you today.

What then is the meaning to be given to the words "for the purpose of preserving the life of the mother". There has been much discussion in this case as to the difference between danger to life and danger to health. It may be that you are more fortunate than I am, but I confess that I have found it difficult to understand what the discussion really meant, since life depends upon health, and it may be that health is so gravely impaired that death results. . . . Mr Oliver [for the accused] wanted you to give what he called a wide and liberal meaning to the words "for the purpose of preserving the life of the mother". I should prefer the word "reasonable" to the words "wide and liberal". I think you should take a reasonable view of those words.

It is not contended that those words mean merely for the purposes of saving the mother from instant death. There are cases, we are told, where it is reasonably certain that a pregnant woman will not be able to deliver the child which is in her womb and survive. In such a case where the doctor anticipates, basing his opinion upon the experience of the profession, that the child cannot be delivered without the death of the mother, it is obvious that the sooner the operation is performed the better. The law does not require the doctor to wait until the unfortunate woman is in peril of immediate death. In such a case he is not only entitled, but it is his duty to perform the operation with a view to saving her life.

Here let me diverge for one moment to touch upon a matter that has been mentioned to you, the various views which are held with regard to this operation. Apparently there is a great difference of opinion even in the medical profession itself. Some there may be, for all I know, who hold the view that the fact that a woman desires the operation performed is a sufficient justification for it. Well, that is not the law: the desire of a woman to be relieved of her pregnancy is no justification at all for performing the operation. On the other hand there are people who, from what are said to be religious reasons, object to the operation being performed under any circumstances. That is not the law either. On the contrary, a person who holds such an opinion ought not to be an obstetrical surgeon, for if a case arose where the life of the woman could be saved by performing the operation and the doctor refused to perform it because of his religious opinions and the woman died, he would be in grave peril of being brought before this court on a charge of manslaughter by negligence. He would have no better defence than a person who, again for some religious reason, refused to call in a doctor to attend his sick child, where a doctor could have been called in and the life of the child could have been saved. If the father, for a so-called religious reason, refused to call in a doctor, he is also answerable to the criminal law for the death of his child. I mention these two extreme views merely to show that the law lies between them. It permits the termination of pregnancy for the purpose of preserving the life of the mother.

As I have said, I think those words ought to be construed in a reasonable sense, and, if the doctor is of opinion, on reasonable grounds and with adequate knowledge, that the probable consequences of the continuance of the pregnancy will be to make the woman a physical or mental wreck, the jury are quite entitled to take the view that the doctor who, under those circumstances and in that honest belief, operates, is operating for the purpose of preserving the life of the mother. . . .

Verdict: Not guilty.

Note

The lawfulness of the role of nurses in the conduct of abortions was considered by the House of Lords.

Royal College of Nursing of the United Kingdom v. Department of Health and Social Security
[1981] 1 All E.R. 545
House of Lords

Medical induction has largely replaced the surgical method of terminating pregnancies of over three months. The procedure is in two stages, the second of which is carried out by nurses. The Department issued a circular to the nursing profession stating that no offence was committed by nurses who participated in this stage provided that the person who decided on the termination, initiated it and remained responsible for its overall conduct and control, was a doctor. The Royal College sought a declaration that the advice on the circular was wrong and that nurses would be contravening section 58 of the 1861 Act.

LORD DIPLOCK: The Abortion Act 1967 which it falls to this House to construe is described in its long title as "An Act to amend and clarify the law relating to termination of pregnancy by registered medical practitioners". The legalisation of abortion, at any rate in circumstances in which the termination of the pregnancy is not essential in order to save the mother's life, is a subject on which strong moral and religious convictions are held; and these convictions straddle the normal party political lines. That, no doubt, is why the Act, which incorporates a "conscience clause" that I shall be quoting later, started its Parliamentary life as a private member's Bill and, maybe for that reason, it lacks that style and consistency of draftsmanship both internal to the Act itself and in relation to other statutes which one would expect to find in legislation that had its origin in the office of Parliamentary counsel.

Whatever may be the technical imperfections of its draftsmanship, however, its purpose in my view becomes clear if one starts by considering what was the state of the law relating to abortion before the passing of the Act, what was the mischief that required amendment, and in what respects was the existing law unclear.

In England the law "relating to abortion" which it was the purpose of the Act to amend and clarify, is defined in s.6 of the Act itself as meaning "sections 58 and 59 of the Offences Against the Person Act 1861." [*ante*, p. 564].

. . . It had long been generally accepted that abortion was lawful where it was necessary to save the pregnant woman's life; but what circumstances, if any, short of this, legitimised termination of a pregnancy does not appear to have attracted judicial notice until, in 1938, the matter was put to a sagaciously selected test by Mr Aleck Bourne, a well-known obstetrical surgeon at St Mary's Hospital, London. . . .

The summing-up by Macnaghten J. in *R. v. Bourne* resulted in an acquittal. So the correctness of his statement of the law did not undergo examination by any higher authority. It still remained in 1967 the only judicial pronouncement on the subject.

. . . Such then was the unsatisfactory and uncertain state of the law that the Abortion Act 1967 was intended to amend and clarify. What the Act sets out to do is to provide an exhaustive statement of the circumstances in which treatment for the termination of a pregnancy may be carried out lawfully. That the statement, which is contained in s.1, is intended to be exhaustive appears from s.5(2):

> "For the purposes of the law relating to abortion, anything done with intent to procure the miscarriage of a woman is unlawfully done unless authorised by section 1 of this Act."

This sets aside the interpretation placed by Macnaghten J. in *R. v. Bourne* on the word "unlawfully" in ss.58 and 59 of the Offences Against the Persons Act 1861.

The "conscience clause" which I have already mentioned is also worth citing before coming to the crucial provisions of s.1. It is s.4(1) and so far as is relevant for the present purposes it reads:

> ". . . no person shall be under any duty, whether by contract or by any statutory or other legal requirement, to participate in any treatment authorised by this Act to which he has a conscientious objection . . ."

. . . I have spoken of the requirements of the Act as to the way in which "treatment for the termination of the pregnancy" is to be carried out rather than using the word "termination" or "terminated" by itself, for the draftsman appears to use the longer and the shorter expressions indiscriminately, as is shown by a comparison between subsections (1) and (3) of section 1, and by the reference in the conscience clause to "treatment authorised by this Act". Furthermore, if "termination" or "terminated" meant only the event of miscarriage and not the whole treatment undertaken with that object in mind, lack of success, which apparently occurs in 1 per cent to 2 per cent of cases, would make all who had taken part in the unsuccessful treatment guilty of an offence under section 58 or section 59 of the Offences Against the Person Act 1861. This cannot have been the intention of Parliament.

The requirement of the Act as to the way in which the treatment is to be carried out, which in my view throws most light on the second aspect of its policy and the true construction of the phrase in sub-section (1) of section 1 which lies at the root of the dispute between the parties to this appeal, is the requirement in subsection (3) that, except in cases of dire emergency, the treatment must be carried out in a national health service hospital (or private clinic specifically approved for that purpose by the minister). It is in my view evident that, in providing that treatment for termination of pregnancies should take place in ordinary hospitals Parliament contemplated that (conscientious objections apart) like other hospital treatment, it would be undertaken as a team effort in which, acting on the instructions of the doctor in charge of the treatment, junior doctors, nurses, paramedical and other members of the hospital staff would each do things forming part of the whole treatment which it would be in accordance with accepted medical practice to entrust to a member of the staff possessed of their respective qualifications and experience.

Subsection (1) although it is expressed to apply only "when a pregnancy is terminated by a registered medical practitioner" . . . also appears to contemplate treatment that is in the nature of a team effort and to extend its protection to all those who play a part in it. The exoneration from guilt is not confined to the registered medical practitioner by whom a pregnancy is terminated, it extends to any person who takes part in the treatment for its termination.

What limitation on this exoneration is imposed by the qualifying phrase, "when a pregnancy is terminated by a registered medical practitioner"? In my opinion, in the context of the Act, what it requires is that a registered medical practitioner, whom I will refer to as a doctor, should accept responsibility for all stages of the treatment for the termination of the pregnancy. The particular method to be used should be decided by the doctor in charge of the treatment for termination of the pregnancy; he should carry out any physical acts, forming part of the treatment, that in accordance with accepted medical practice are done only by qualified medical practitioners, and should give specific instructions as to the carrying out of such parts of the treatment as in accordance with accepted medical practice are carried out by nurses or other members of the hospital staff without medical qualifications. To each of them, the doctor, or his substitute, should be available to be consulted or called on for assistance from beginning to end of the treatment. In other words, the doctor need not do everything with his own hands; the requirements of the subsection are satisfied when the treatment for termination of a pregnancy is one prescribed by a registered medical practitioner carried out in accordance with his directions and of which a registered medical practitioner remains in charge throughout.

My noble and learned friend Lord Wilberforce has described the successive steps taken in the treatment for termination of pregnancies in the third trimester by medical induction; and the parts played by registered medical practitioners and nurses respectively in the carrying out of the treatment. This treatment satisfies the interpretation that I have placed on the requirements of section 1 of the Act. I would accordingly allow the appeal and restore the declaration made by Woolf J.

LORDS KEITH OF KINKEL and ROSKILL delivered concurring speeches, LORDS WILBERFORCE and EDMUND-DAVIES dissented.

Appeal allowed.

Question

Lord Diplock states in *Royal College of Nursing of the United Kingdom v. Department of Health and Social Security* that section 5(2) of the Abortion Act 1967 makes it clear that section 1 provides an "exhaustive statement of the circumstances in which the treatment for the termination of a pregnancy may be carried out lawfully". Does this mean that the operation of common law defences is excluded? Consider the following situation: D is a final year medical student. He and his wife, V, are trapped in an isolated cottage by a blizzard and are unable to make contact with the outside world. V is pregnant and develops complications. D honestly believes (and subsequent examination by registered medical practitioners confirms his belief to have been correct) that it is immediately necessary to terminate the pregnancy to save V's life. He is charged with an offence under section 58 of the Offences Against the Person Act 1861 and seeks to plead duress of circumstances. Would D succeed?

iv. Suicide

Suicide Act 1961

Section 1: "The rule of law whereby it is a crime for a person to commit suicide is hereby abrogated."

Section 2: "(1) A person who aids, abets, counsels or procures the suicide of another, or an attempt by another to commit suicide, shall be liable on conviction on indictment to imprisonment for a term not exceeding fourteen years.

(2) If on the trial of an indictment for murder or manslaughter it is proved that the accused aided, abetted, counselled or procured the suicide of the person in question, the jury may find him guilty of that offence."

Homicide Act 1957, section 4

(1) It shall be manslaughter, and shall not be murder, for a person acting in pursuance of a suicide pact between him and another to kill the other or be a party to the other killing himself or being killed by a third person. . . .

(3) For the purposes of this section 'suicide pact' means a common agreement between two or more persons having for its object the death of all of them, whether or not each is to take his own life, but nothing done by a person who enters into a suicide pact shall be treated as done by him in pursuance of the pact unless it is done while he has the settled intention of dying in pursuance of the pact.

Notes

Any doubt as to whether it is an offence to *attempt* to aid, or abet suicide was settled in *R. v. McShane* (1977) 66 Cr. App. R. 97 in which Orr L.J. said, at p. 102:

"[E]very attempt to commit an offence is an offence at common law whether the crime attempted is one by statute or at common law. . . . It follows in our judgment that the appellant was properly charged under count 1 with an offence of attempting to aid or abet, counsel or procure the suicide of Mrs Mott and none the less so because the crime defined in section 2 (1) of the Suicide Act 1961 is itself of the nature of an attempt."

An area surrounded not only by legal doubt but also by difficult, and ultimately insoluble, questions of moral philosophy is that of euthanasia. A person who kills another at the other's request will be liable for murder since consent is no defence. This is mitigated where the killing is in pursuance of a suicide pact (section 4 of the Homicide Act 1957, above), and, possibly, where a doctor administers drugs, which alleviate pain but shorten life. At the trial of Dr Adams in 1957 Devlin J. (as he then was) said that the administration of drugs to relieve pain would not amount to legal causation. This is a grey, untested, area maintained by the turning of a blind eye by prosecuting authorities. See D. Brahams "A Visit to the USA" (1988) 38 N.L.J. 383.

As far as aiding and abetting suicide is concerned the decision to prosecute rests solely with the Director of Public Prosecutions whose consent is required for any proceedings (section 2(4) of the Suicide Act 1961). "Exit", a society campaigning for voluntary euthanasia, published a booklet giving details of methods of committing suicide.

In *Attorney-General v. Able and Others* [1984] 1 Q.B. 795, the Attorney-General sought a declaration that "in specified circumstance" distribution of the guide was an offence under section 2(1) of the Suicide Act 1961. In response the Society sought a declaration that supply of the booklet was lawful. Wolf J. refused to grant either declaration. He held that supply could be an offence where done with the necessary intent but without proof of the necessary intent it could not be said in advance that any particular supply would be an offence. See Smith "Assisting in Suicide—The Attorney-General and the Voluntary Euthanasia Society" [1983] Crim.L.R. 579.

See generally Williams, *The Sanctity of Life and the Criminal Law*, Chap. 8; Williams, "Euthanasia" 41 *Medico Legal Journal* 14; Kennedy, "The Legal Effect of Requests by the Terminally Ill and Aged not to receive further Treatment from Doctors" [1976] Crim.L.R. 21; C.L.R.C. 14th Report, sections 126–129.

v. Causing death by driving

Road Traffic Act 1991, sections 1 and 3

1. Offences of dangerous driving

For sections 1 and 2 of the Road Traffic Act 1988 there shall be substituted—
(1) 'Causing death by dangerous driving.
A person who causes death of another person by driving a mechanically propelled vehicle dangerously on a road or other public place is guilty of an offence.
2. Dangerous driving.
A person who drives a mechanically propelled vehicle dangerously on a road or other public place is guilty of an offence.
2A. Meaning of dangerous driving.
(1) For the purposes of sections 1 and 2 above a person is to be regarded as driving dangerously if (and, subject to subsection (2) below, only if)—
(a) the way he drives falls far below what would be expected of a competent and careful driver, and
(b) it would be obvious to a competent and careful driver that driving in that way would be dangerous.
(2) A person is also to be regarded as driving dangerously for the purposes of sections 1 and 2 above if it would be obvious to a competent

and careful driver that driving the vehicle in its current state would be dangerous.

(3) In subsections (1) and (2) above 'dangerous' refers to danger either of injury to any person or of serious damage to property; and in determining for the purposes of those subsections what would be expected of, or obvious to, a competent and careful driver in a particular case, regard shall be had not only to the circumstances of which he could be expected to be aware but also to any circumstances shown to have been within the knowledge of the accused.

(4) In determining for the purposes of subsection (2) above the state of a vehicle, regard may be had to anything attached to or carried on or in it and to the manner in which it is attached or carried.

3. Causing death by careless driving when under influence of drink or drugs.

Before section 4 of the Road Traffic Act 1988 there shall be inserted—
3A. Causing death by careless driving when under influence of drink or drugs.

(1) If a person causes the death of another person by driving a mechanically propelled vehicle on a road or other public place without due care and attention, or without reasonable consideration for other persons using the road or place, and—

(a) he is, at the time when he is driving, unfit to drive through drink or drugs, or
(b) he has consumed so much alcohol that the proportion of it in his breath, blood or urine at that time exceeds the prescribed limit, or
(c) he is, within 18 hours after that time, required to provide a specimen in pursuance of section 7 of this Act, but without reasonable excuse fails to provide it

he is guilty of an offence.

(2) For the purposes of this section a person shall be taken to be unfit to drive at any time when his ability to drive properly is impaired.

(3) Subsection (1)(b) and (c) above shall not apply in relation to a person driving a mechanically propelled vehicle other than a motor vehicle.

6. REFORM OF THE LAW OF HOMICIDE

The Draft Criminal Code Bill adopts, with a few modifications, the reforms proposed by the C.L.R.C. in their 14th Report (Cmnd. 7844). For reform of the law of involuntary manslaughter see *ante*, pp. 598–605.

Draft Criminal Code Bill

Murder

For clause 54 see *ante*, p. 530.

Manslaughter

55. A person is guilty of manslaughter if—

(a) he is not guilty of murder by reason only of the fact that a defence provided by section 56 (diminished responsibility), 58 (provocation) or 59 (use of excessive force) applies; or

(b) he is not guilty of murder by reason only of the fact that, because of voluntary intoxication, he is not aware that death may be caused or believes that an exempting circumstance exists. . . .

Diminished responsibility

56.—(1) A person who, but for this section, would be guilty of murder is not guilty of murder if, at the time of his act, he is suffering from such mental abnormality as is a substantial enough reason to reduce his offence to manslaughter.

(2) In this section 'mental abnormality' means mental illness, arrested or incomplete development of mind, psychopathic disorder, and any other disorder or disability of mind, except intoxication.

(3) Where a person suffering from mental abnormality is also intoxicated, this section applies only where it would apply if he were not intoxicated.

Evidence of mental abnormality

57.—(1) Whether evidence is evidence of mental abnormality is a question of law.

(2) Where on a charge of murder or attempted murder the defendant has given or adduced evidence of mental disorder, severe mental handicap or automatism, the prosecution may adduce evidence of mental abnormality; but the court may give directions as to the stage of the proceedings at which it may do so.

(3) Where a person is charged with murder (or attempted murder) the prosecution may, with his consent, adduce evidence of mental abnormality at the committal proceedings, whereupon the magistrates' court may commit him for trial for manslaughter (or attempted manslaughter).

(4) Where the defendant has been committed for trial for murder (or attempted murder) the prosecution may, with the consent of the defendant, serve notice in accordance with Rules of Court of evidence of mental abnormality and indict him for manslaughter (or attempted manslaughter).

Provocation

58. A person who, but for this section, would be guilty of murder is not guilty of murder if—

(a) he acts when provoked (whether by things done or by things said or by both and whether by the deceased person or by another) to lose his self-control; and

(b) the provocation is, in all the circumstances (including any of his personal characteristics that affect its gravity), sufficient ground for the loss of self-control.

Use of excessive force

59. A person who, but for this section, would be guilty of murder is not guilty of murder if, at the time of his act, he believes the use of the force which causes death to be necessary and reasonable to effect a purpose referred to in section 44 (use of force in public or private defence), but the force exceeds that which is necessary and reasonable in the circumstances which exist or (where there is a difference) in those which he believes to exist.

Jurisdiction over murder and manslaughter

60. A person is guilty of murder or manslaughter (where section 54 or 55 applies) if—

(a) he causes a fatal injury to another to occur within the ordinary limits of criminal jurisdiction, whether his act is done within or outside and whether the death occurs within or outside those limits;
(b) he causes the death of another anywhere in the world by an act done within the ordinary limits of criminal jurisdiction; or
(c) being a British citizen, he causes the death of another anywhere in the world by an act done anywhere in the world.

Attempted manslaughter

61. A person who attempts to cause the death of another, where section 56, 58 or 59 would apply if death were caused, is not guilty of attempted murder but is guilty of attempted manslaughter.

Suicide pact killing

62.—(1) A person who, but for this section, would be guilty of murder is not guilty of murder but is guilty of suicide pact killing if his act is done in pursuance of a suicide pact between himself and the person killed.

(2) 'Suicide pact' means an agreement between two or more persons having for its object the death of all of them, whether or not each is to take his own life, but nothing done by a person who enters into a suicide pact shall be treated as done by him in pursuance of the pact unless it is done while he has the settled intention of dying in pursuance of the pact.

(3) A person acting in pursuance of a suicide pact between himself and another is not guilty of attempted murder but is guilty of attempted suicide pact killing if he attempts to cause the death of the other.

Complicity in suicide

63. A person is guilty of an offence if he procures, assists or encourages suicide or attempted suicide committed by another.

Infanticide

64.—(1) A woman who, but for this section, would be guilty of murder or manslaughter of her child is not guilty of murder or manslaughter, but is guilty of infanticide, if her act is done when the child is under the age of twelve months and when the balance of her mind is disturbed by reason of the effect of giving birth or of circumstances consequent upon the birth.

(2) A woman who in the circumstances specified in subsection (1) attempts to cause the death of her child is not guilty of attempted murder but is guilty of attempted infanticide.

(3) A woman may be convicted of infanticide (or attempted infanticide) although the jury is uncertain whether the child had been born or whether

it had an existence independent of her when its death occurred (or, in the case of an attempt, when the act was done).

Threats to kill or cause serious personal harm

65. A person is guilty of an offence if he makes to another a threat to cause the death of, or serious personal harm to, that other or a third person, intending that other to believe that it will be carried out.

Abortion

66. A person is guilty of an offence if he intentionally causes the miscarriage of a woman otherwise than in accordance with the provisions of the Abortion Act 1967.

Self-abortion

67.—(1) A pregnant woman is guilty of an offence if she intentionally causes her own miscarriage otherwise than in accordance with the provisions of the Abortion Act 1967.

(2) Notwithstanding section 50 (impossibility) a woman who is not pregnant cannot be guilty of an attempt to commit an offence under this Act.

Supplying article for abortion

68. A person is guilty of an offence if he supplies or procures any article or substance knowing that it is to be used with the intention of causing the miscarriage of a woman otherwise than in accordance with the provisions of the Abortion Act 1967, whether the woman is pregnant or not.

Child destruction

69.—(1) A person is guilty of child destruction if he intentionally causes the death of a child capable of being born alive before the child has an existence independent of his mother, unless the act which causes death is done in good faith for the purpose only of preserving the life of the mother.

(2) The fact that a woman had at any material time been pregnant for twenty-eight weeks or more is *prima facie* proof that she was at that time pregnant of a child capable of being born alive.

(3) A person who is found not guilty of murder or manslaughter (or attempted murder or manslaughter) of a child by reason only of the fact that the jury is uncertain whether the child had been born or whether he had an existence independent of his mother when his death occurred (or, in the case of an attempt, when the act was done) shall be convicted of child destruction (or attempted child destruction).

CHAPTER 9

NON-FATAL OFFENCES AGAINST THE PERSON

1. ASSAULT AND BATTERY

Criminal Justice Act 1988, section 39

Common assault and battery shall be summary offences and a person guilty of either of them shall be liable to a fine not exceeding level 5 on the standard scale,[1] to imprisonment for a term not exceeding six months, or to both.

Notes

1. Section 40 of the same Act nevertheless provides that an indictment may include a count for common assault or battery if it is founded on the same facts or evidence as a count charging an indictable offence or is part of a series of offences of the same or similar character as an indictable offence which is also charged.

If such a count is not included, there can be no conviction of common assault or battery: *R. v. Mearns* [1991] 1 Q.B. 82 (C.A.).

2. Assault and battery are separate statutory crimes: *R. v. Taylor, R. v. Little* [1992] 1 All E.R. 708 (C.A.). An indictment charging assault and battery is bad for duplicity, *i.e.* as charging more than one crime.

3. Although there are many statutory crimes, in the Offences Against the Person Act 1861 and elsewhere, which are based on the concepts of assault and battery, there is no statutory definition of those concepts, the meaning of which must be sought in case law, including civil cases, since both assault and battery are also torts. In the past there has been a practice, in statutes and in judgments, to use the term "assault" as comprehending also a battery (see *Fagan v. M.P.C.*,

---

[1] Section 37 of the Criminal Justice Act 1982 established a standard scale of fines for summary offences. The amounts in the scale are revised from time to time to take account of the decline in the value of money. They are currently as follows:

    Level 1 £200
        2 £500
        3 £1000
        4 £2500
        5 £5000

below). The Draft Offences Against the Person Bill (*post*, p. 670) continues the practice. Now that it is clear that they are two separate crimes which must not be rolled up in one charge, the need for a new terminology is urgent.

i. Actus Reus

Fagan v. Metropolitan Police Commissioner
[1969] 1 Q.B. 439
Divisional Court

Fagan was told by a police officer to park his car at a particular spot. He drove his car on to the policeman's foot. He refused for some time to reverse off. Fagan was convicted by the magistrates of assaulting a police officer in the execution of his duty. On appeal he maintained that the initial driving on the foot was not an assault, because unintentional; nor was the refusal to drive off because this was not an act.

JAMES J. (with whom LORD PARKER C.J. agreed, BRIDGE J. dissenting): In our judgment the question arising, which has been argued on general principles, falls to be decided on the facts of the particular case. An assault is any act which intentionally—or possibly recklessly—causes another person to apprehend immediate and unlawful personal violence. Although "assault" is an independent crime and is to be treated as such, for practical purposes today "assault" is generally synonymous with the term "battery" and is a term used to mean the actual intended use of unlawful force to another person without his consent. On the facts of the present case the "assault" alleged involved a "battery". Where an assault involves a battery, it matters not, in our judgment, whether the battery is inflicted directly by the body of the offender or through the medium of some weapon or instrument controlled by the action of the offender. An assault may be committed by the laying of a hand upon another, and the action does not cease to be an assault if it is a stick held in the hand and not the hand itself which is laid on the person of the victim. So for our part we see no difference in principle between the action of stepping on to a person's toe and maintaining that position and the action of driving a car on to a person's foot and sitting in the car whilst its position on the foot is maintained.

To constitute the offence of assault some intentional act must have been performed: a mere omission to act cannot amount to an assault. Without going into the question whether words alone can constitute an assault, it is clear that the words spoken by the appellant could not alone amount to an assault: they can only shed a light on the appellant's action. For our part we think the crucial question is whether in this case the act of the appellant can be said to be complete and spent at the moment of time when the car wheel came to rest on the foot or whether his act is to be regarded as a continuing act operating until the wheel was removed. In our judgment a distinction is to be drawn between acts which are complete—though results may continue to flow—and those acts which are continuing. Once the act is complete it cannot thereafter be said to be a threat to inflict unlawful force upon the victim. If the act, as distinct from the results thereof, is a continuing act there is a continuing threat to inflict unlawful force. If the assault involves a battery and that battery continues there is a continuing act of assault.

For an assault to be committed both the elements of *actus reus* and *mens rea* must be present at the same time. The *"actus reus"* is the action causing the effect on the victim's mind (see the observations of Parke B. in *R. v. St George*,

(1840) 9 C.P. 483). The "*mens rea*" is the intention to cause that effect. It is not necessary that *mens rea* should be present at the inception of the *actus reus*; it can be superimposed upon an existing act. On the other hand the subsequent inception of *mens rea* cannot convert an act which has been completed without *mens rea* into an assault.

In our judgment the Willesden magistrates and quarter sessions were right in law. On the facts found the action of the appellant may have been initially unintentional, but the time came when knowing that the wheel was on the officer's foot the appellant (1) remained seated in the car so that his body through the medium of the car was in contact with the officer, (2) switched off the ignition of the car, (3) maintained the wheel of the car on the foot and (4) used words indicating the intention of keeping the wheel in that position. For our part we cannot regard such conduct as mere omission or inactivity.

There was an act constituting battery which at its inception was not criminal because there was no element of intention but which became criminal from the moment the intention was formed to produce the apprehension which was flowing from the continuing act. The fallacy of the appellant's argument is that it seeks to equate the facts of this case with such a case as where a motorist has accidentally run over a person and, that action having been completed, fails to assist the victim with the intent that the victim should suffer.

We would dismiss this appeal.

Appeal dismissed

Question

Would the reasoning in *R. v. Miller, ante*, p. 37, provide a more satisfactory way of upholding Fagan's conviction? And see Draft Criminal Code, Clause 31, *ante*, p. 44.

Note

The crucial requirement in assault is that the victim apprehend immediate unlawful violence. For some time the law was unclear whether words alone causing such an apprehension could constitute an assault. This issue has been resolved by the case which follows.

R. v. Ireland; R. v. Burstow
House of Lords
[1997] A.C. 147

The appellant, Ireland, had pleaded guilty to three counts charging him with assault occasioning actual bodily harm contrary to s.47 of the Offences Against the Person Act 1861. The charges arose from the appellant making a large number of unwanted silent telephone calls over a period of several months to three women. As a result of the calls the women suffered significant psychological symptoms, inter alia, palpitations, difficulty in breathing, anxiety, inability to sleep, tearfulness and stress. The Court of Appeal dismissed his appeal certifying the following point of law of general public importance for consideration by the House of Lords, namely: "Whether the making of a series of silent telephone calls can amount in law to an assault."

LORD STEYN: . . . It is to assault in the form of an act causing the victim to fear an immediate application of force to her that I must turn. Counsel argued that as a matter of law an assault can never be committed by words alone and therefore it cannot be committed by silence. The premise depends on the slenderest authority, namely, an observation by Holroyd J. to a jury that "no words or singing are equivalent to an assault:" *Rex v. Meade and Belt* (1823) 1 Lew. 184. The proposition that a gesture may amount to an assault, but that words can never suffice, is unrealistic and indefensible. A thing said is also a thing done. There is no reason why something said should be incapable of causing an apprehension of immediate personal violence, e.g. a man accosting a woman in a dark alley saying, "Come with me or I will stab you." I would, therefore, reject the proposition that an assault can never be committed by words.

That brings me to the critical question whether a silent caller may be guilty of an assault. The answer to this question seems to me to be "Yes, depending on the facts." It involves questions of fact within the province of the jury. After all, there is no reason why a telephone caller who says to a woman in a menacing way "I will be at your door in a minute or two" may not be guilty of an assault if he causes his victim to apprehend immediate personal violence. Take now the case of the silent caller. He intends by his silence to cause fear and he is so understood. The victim is assailed by uncertainty about his intentions. Fear may dominate her emotions, and it may be the fear that the caller's arrival at her door may be imminent. She may fear the possibility of immediate personal violence. As a matter of law the caller may be guilty of an assault: whether he is or not will depend on the circumstance and in particular on the impact of the caller's potentially menacing call or calls on the victim. Such a prosecution case under section 47 may be fit to leave to the jury. And a trial judge may, depending on the circumstances, put a common sense consideration before the jury, namely what, if not the possibility of imminent personal violence, was the victim terrified about? I conclude that an assault may be committed in the particular factual circumstances which I have envisaged. For this reason I reject the submission that as a matter of law a silent telephone caller cannot ever be guilty of an offence under section 47.

LORD HOPE OF CRAIGHEAD: . . . The important question therefore is whether the making of a series of silent telephone calls can amount in law to an assault.

There is no clear guidance on this point either in the statute or in the authorities. On the one hand in *Rex* v. *Meade and Belt* (1823) 1 Lew. 184 Holroyd J. said that no words or singing can amount to an assault. On the other hand in *Reg.* v. *Wilson* [1955] 1 W.L.R. 493, 494 Lord Goddard C.J. said that the appellant's words, "Get the knives" would itself be an assault. The word "assault" as used in section 47 of the Act of 1861 is not defined anywhere in that Act. The legislation appears to have been framed on the basis that the words which it used were words which everyone would understand without further explanation. In this regard the fact that the statute was enacted in the middle of the last century is of no significance. The public interest, for whose benefit it was enacted, would not be served by construing the words in a narrow or technical way. The words used are ordinary English words, which can be given their ordinary meaning in the usage of the present day. They can take account of changing circumstances both as regards medical knowledge and the means by which one person can cause bodily harm to another.

The fact is that the means by which a person of evil disposition may intentionally or recklessly cause another to apprehend immediate and unlawful violence will vary according to the circumstances. Just as it is not true to say that every blow which is struck is an assault some blows, which would otherwise amount to battery, may be struck by accident or in jest or may otherwise be entirely justified so also it is not true to say that mere words or gestures can never constitute an assault. It all depends on the circumstances. If the words or gestures are accompanied in their turn by gestures or by words which threaten immediate and unlawful violence, that will be sufficient for an assault. The words or gestures must be seen in their whole context.

In this case the means which the appellant used to communicate with his victims was the telephone. While he remained silent, there can be no doubt that he was intentionally communicating with them as directly as if he was present with them in the same room. But whereas for him merely to remain silent with them in the same room, where they could see him and assess his demeanour, would have been unlikely to give rise to any feelings of apprehension on their part, his silence when using the telephone in calls made to them repeatedly was an act of an entirely different character. He was using his silence as a means of conveying a message to his victims. This was that he knew who and where they were, and that his purpose in making contact with them was as malicious as it was deliberate. In my opinion silent telephone calls of this nature are just as capable as words or gestures, said or made in the presence of the victim, of causing an apprehension of immediate and unlawful violence.

Whether this requirement, and in particular that of immediacy, is in fact satisfied will depend on the circumstances. This will need in each case, if it is disputed, to be explored in evidence. But that step was not necessary in this case as the appellant was prepared to plead guilty to having committed the offence. I would therefore answer the certified question in the affirmative and dismiss this appeal also.

Appeal dismissed.

Note and Question

As Ireland had pleaded guilty to assault the issue whether the women had actually apprehended unlawful personal violence never had to be considered by a jury. Lord Steyn states that "a trial judge may, depending on the circumstances, put a common sense consideration before the jury, namely what, if not the possibility of imminent personal violence, was the victim terrified about?" If there is no evidence that the victim feared immediate unlawful personal violence should such a question ever be left to the jury bearing in mind the burden of proof on the prosecution? It should be noted that the prosecution in *Ireland* was brought before the Protection from Harassment Act 1997 was enacted. Under this statute it is an offence punishable with up to six months imprisonment to pursue a course of conduct which amounts to harassment of another (see ss.1(1) and 2(1)). A more serious offence punishable with up to five years imprisonment may be committed where the "course of conduct causes another to fear, on at least two occasions, that violence will be used against him" (s.4(1)). There is no requirement under this offence that the fear be of "immediate" violence. The existence of this offence, however, will not preclude the need to rely on the offence of assault or assault occasioning actual bodily harm in some cases. In particular, section 4(1) requires fear to be caused on at least two occasions. This would not cover a case where D telephones V on one occasion with a specific threat of immediate unlawful violence. This could constitute an assault. If, however, D threatens the violence in the future this would not fall under either assault or section 4(1). In addition section 4(1) requires on the part of the victim a fear that violence *will* be used against him. Lord Steyn doubted that the Act would offer protection to the victim of a silent caller where she feared merely that violence *may* be used against her.

Section 43 of the Telecommunications Act 1984 creates the offence of improper use of a public telecommunication system. This offence may be committed, *inter alia*, by a person who (a) makes calls of a "grossly offensive or of an indecent, obscene or menacing character" or who (b) makes persistent calls "for the purpose of causing annoyance, inconvenience or needless anxiety to another". This is a summary offence but there is no requirement of proof of purpose where (a) applies. Ireland's activities came within (a) and probably also within (b) but the prosecution clearly were not satisfied with a summary offence even though Parliament had increased the penalty to a maximum fine at level 5 and/or imprisonment for a maximum term of six months.

ii. Mens Rea

R. v. Venna
[1975] 3 All E.R. 788
Court of Appeal

> D was involved in a struggle with police officers who were attempting to arrest him. He fell to the ground and then proceeded to lash out wildly with his legs. In so doing he kicked the hand of one of the police officers, fracturing a bone. His story was that he was kicking out in an attempt to get up off the ground. D was convicted of assault occasioning actual bodily harm, after the judge had directed the jury that they could find D guilty if they found that he had lashed out with his feet "reckless as to who was there, not caring one iota as to whether he kicked anybody." He appealed.

JAMES L.J. (reading the judgment of the court): ... In *Fagan v. M.P.C.* (*ante*, p. 619), it was said: "An assault is any act which intentionally or possibly recklessly causes another person to apprehend immediate and unlawful personal violence." In *Fagan* it was not necessary to decide the question whether proof of recklessness is sufficient to establish the *mens rea* ingredient of assault. That question falls for decision in the present case. . . .

In our view the element of *mens rea* in the offence of battery is satisfied by proof that the defendant intentionally or recklessly applied force to the person of another. If it were otherwise, the strange consequence would be that an offence of unlawful wounding contrary to section 20 of the Offences Against the Person Act 1861 could be established by proof that the defendant wounded the victim either intentionally or recklessly, but if the victim's skin was not broken and the offence was therefore laid as an assault occasioning actual bodily harm contrary to section 47 of the 1861 Act, it would be necessary to prove that the physical force was intentionally applied.

We see no reason in logic or in law why a person who recklessly applies physical force to the person of another should be outside the criminal law of assault. In many cases the dividing line between intention and recklessness is barely distinguishable. This is such a case. In our judgment the direction was right in law; this ground of appeal fails . . .

Appeal dismissed

Note

Although the *mens rea* of common assault and battery is not dealt with directly in *Savage, post*, p. 662, the implication of the latter decision is that the recklessness sufficient for these offences is *Cunningham* recklessness, and *R. v. Caldwell, ante*, p. 121, is not in point.

iii. Justifications

Note

There are particular justifications for the application of force or threats of force, *e.g.* cases of self-defence, prevention of crime, which were dealt with *ante*, p. 343. Physical contact which is generally acceptable in the ordinary conduct of social life (*e.g.* jostlings in crowds) may also be justified: see *Collins v. Wilcock*, referred to in *Re F.*, below. Necessity to preserve the life or health or well-being of the person to whom the force is applied may be a justification: see next case. Consent may *sometimes* justify: see *post*, p. 629.

(a) Necessity

Re F. (Mental Patient: Sterilisation)
[1990] 2 A.C. 1
House of Lords

F, a 36-year-old mentally handicapped woman with a mental age of a small child, resided as a voluntary patient in a mental hospital. She formed a sexual relationship with a male patient. The hospital staff considered that F would be unable to cope with the effects of pregnancy and giving birth. Since other forms of contraception were unsuitable, and it was thought undesirable to curtail F's freedom of movement in order to prevent sexual activity, it was felt to be in F's best interests for her to be sterilised. F's mother concurred and sought a declaration that sterilisation would not be an unlawful act by reason only of the absence of F's consent. The declaration was granted, and upheld by the Court of Appeal. On further appeal by the Official Solicitor:—

LORD BRANDON OF OAKBROOK: Part IV of the Mental Health Act 1983 contains provisions, which it is not necessary to detail, imposing restrictions or conditions on the giving to mentally disorded persons of certain kinds of treatment for their mental disorder. The Act, however, does not contain any provisions relating to the giving of treatment to patients for any conditions other than their mental disorder. The result is that the lawfulness of giving any treatment of the latter kind depends not on statute but the common law.

At common law a doctor cannot lawfully operate on adult patients of sound mind, or give them any other treatment involving the application of physical force however small ("other treatment"), without their consent. If a doctor were to operate on such patients, or give them other treatment, without their consent, he would commit the actionable tort of trespass to the person. There are, however, cases where adult patients cannot give or refuse their consent to an operation or other treatment. One case is where, as a result of an accident or otherwise, an adult patient is unconscious and an operation or other treatment cannot be safely delayed until he or she recovers consciousness.

Another case is where a patient, though adult, cannot by reason of mental disability understand the nature or purpose of an operation or other treatment. The common law would be seriously defective if it failed to provide a solution to the problem created by such inability to consent. In my opinion, however, the common law does not so fail. In my opinion, the solution to the problem which the common law provides is that a doctor can lawfully operate on, or give other treatment to, adult patients who are incapable, for one reason or another, of consenting to his doing so, provided that the operation or other treatment concerned is in the best interests of such patients. The operation or other treatment will be in their best interests if, but only if, it is carried out in order either to save their lives, or to ensure improvement or prevent deterioration in their physical or mental health.

Different views have been put forward with regard to the principle which makes it lawful for a doctor to operate on or give other treatment to adult patients without their consent in the two cases to which I have referred above. The Court of Appeal in the present case regarded the matter as depending on the public interest. I would not disagree with that as a broad proposition, but I think that it is helpful to consider the principle in accordance with which the public interest leads to this result. In my opinion, the principle is that, when persons lack the capacity, for whatever reason, to take decisions about the performance of operations on them, or the giving of other medical treatment to them, it is necessary that some other person or persons, with appropriate qualifications, should take such decisions for them. Otherwise they would be deprived of medical care which they need and to which they are entitled.

In many cases, however, it will not only be lawful for doctors, on the ground of necessity, to operate on or give other medical treatment to adult patients disabled from giving their consent; it will also be their common law duty to do so.

In the case of adult patients made unconscious by an accident or otherwise, they will normally be received into the casualty department of a hospital, which thereby undertakes the care of them. It will then be the duty of the doctors at that hospital to use their best endeavours to do, by way of either an operation or other treatment, that which is in the best interests of such patients.

In the case of adult patients suffering from mental disability, they will normally, in accordance with the scheme of the Mental Health Act 1983, be either in the care of guardians, who will refer them to doctors for medical treatment, or of doctors at mental hospitals in which the patients either reside voluntarily or are detained compulsorily. It will then again be the duty of the doctors concerned to use their best endeavours to do, by way of either an operation or other treatment, that which is in the best interests of such patients.

The application of the principle which I have described means that the lawfulness of a doctor operating on, or giving other treatment to, an adult patient disabled from giving consent, will depend not on any approval or sanction of a court, but on the question whether the operation or other treatment is in the best interests of the patient concerned. That is, from a practical point of view, just as well, for, if every operation to be performed, or other treatment to be given, required the approval or sanction of the court, the whole process of medical care for such patients would grind to a halt. . . .

LORD GOFF OF CHIEVELEY: My Lords, the question in this case is concerned with the lawfulness of a proposed operation of sterilisation upon the plaintiff F. . . .

I start with the fundamental principle, now long established, that every person's body is inviolate. As to this, I do not wish to depart from what I myself said in the judgment of the Divisional Court in *Collins v. Wilcock* [1984] 1 W.L.R. 1172, and in particular from the statement, at p. 1177, that the effect of this principle is that everybody is protected not only against physical injury but against any form of physical molestation.

Of course, as a general rule physical interference with another person's body is lawful if he consents to it; though in certain limited circumstances the public interest may require that his consent is not capable of rendering the act lawful. There are also specific cases where physical interference without consent may not be unlawful—chastisement of children, lawful arrest, self-defence, the prevention of crime, and so on. As I pointed out in *Collins v. Wilcock*, a broader exception has been created to allow for the exigencies of everyday life—jostling in a street or some other crowded place, social contact at parties, and such like. This exception has been said to be founded on implied consent, since those who go about in public places, or go to parties, may be taken to have impliedly consented to bodily contact of this kind. Today this rationalisation can be regarded as artificial; and in particular, it is difficult to impute consent to those who, by reason of their youth or mental disorder, are unable to give their consent. For this reason, I consider it more appropriate to regard such cases as falling within a general exception embracing all physical contact which is generally acceptable in the ordinary conduct of everyday life.

In the old days it used to be said, for a touching of another's person to amount to a battery, it had to be a touching "in anger" (see *Cole v. Turner* (1794) 6 Mod. 149, *per* Holt C.J.); and it has recently been said that the touching must be "hostile" to have that effect (see *Wilson v. Pringle* [1987] Q.B. 237, 253). I respectfully doubt whether that is correct. A prank that gets out of hand; an over-friendly slap on the back; surgical treatment by a surgeon who mistakenly thinks that the patient has consented to it—all these things may transcend the bounds of lawfulness, without being characterised as hostile. Indeed the suggested qualification is difficult to reconcile with the principle that any touching of another's body is, in the absence of lawful excuse, capable of amounting to a battery and a trespass. Furthermore, in the case of medical treatment, we have to bear well in mind the libertarian principle of self-determination which, to adopt the words of Cardozo J. (in *Schloendorff v. Society of New York Hospital* (1914) 105 N.E. 92, 93) recognises that:

> "Every human being of adult years and sound mind has a right to determine what shall be done with his own body; and a surgeon who performs an operation without his patient's consent commits an assault . . ."

This principle has been reiterated in more recent years by Lord Reid in *S. v. McC. (orse. S.) and M. (D.S. intervener); W. v. W.* [1972] A.C. 24, 43.

It is against this background that I turn to consider the question whether, and if so when, medical treatment or care of a mentally disordered person who is, by reason of his incapacity, incapable of giving his consent, can be regarded as lawful. As is recognised in Cardozo J.'s statement of principle, and elsewhere (see e.g. *Sidaway v. Board of Governors of the Bethlem Royal Hospital and the Maudsley Hospital* [1985] A.C. 871, 882, *per* Lord Scarman), some relaxation of the law is required to accommodate persons of unsound mind. In *Wilson v. Pringle*, the Court of Appeal considered that treatment or care of such persons may be regarded as lawful, as falling within the exception relating to physical contact which is generally acceptable in the ordinary conduct of everyday life. Again, I am with respect unable to agree. That exception is concerned with the ordinary events of everyday life—jostling in public places and such like—and affects all persons, whether or not they are capable of giving their consent.

Medical treatment—even treatment for minor ailments—does not fall within that category of events. The general rule is that consent is necessary to render such treatment lawful. If such treatment administered without consent is not to be unlawful, it has to be justified on some other principle.

Upon what principle can medical treatment be justified when given without consent? We are searching for a principle upon which, in limited circumstances, recognition may be given to a need, in the interests of the patient, that treatment should be given to him in circumstances where he is (temporarily or permanently) disabled from consenting to it. It is this criterion of a need which points to the principle of necessity as providing justification.

[After surveying the principle of necessity (see, *ante*, p. 324).]

On this statement of principle, I wish to observe that officious intervention cannot be justified by the principle of necessity. So intervention cannot be justified when another more appropriate person is available and willing to act: nor can it be justified when it is contrary to the known wishes of the assisted person, to the extent that he is capable of rationally forming such a wish. As a general rule, if the above criteria are fulfilled, interference with the assisted person's person or property (as the case may be) will not be unlawful. Take the example of a railway accident, in which injured passengers are trapped in the wreckage. It is this principle which may render lawful the actions of other citizens—railway staff, passengers or outsiders—who rush to give aid and comfort to the victims: the surgeon who amputates the limb of an unconscious passenger to free him from the wreckage; the ambulance man who conveys him to hospital; the doctors and nurses who treat him and care for him while he is still unconscious. Take the example of an elderly person who suffers a stroke which renders him incapable of speech or movement. It is by virtue of this principle that the doctor who treats him, the nurse who cares for him, even the relative or friend or neighbour who comes in to look after him, will commit no wrong when he or she touches his body.

The two examples I have given illustrate, in the one case, an emergency, and in the other, a permanent or semi-permanent state of affairs. Another example of the latter kind is that of a mentally disordered person who is disabled from giving consent. I can see no good reason why the principle of necessity should not be applicable in his case as it is in the case of the victim of a stroke. Furthermore, in the case of a mentally disordered person, as in the case of a stroke victim, the permanent state of affairs calls for a wider range of care than may be requisite in an emergency which arises from accidental injury. When the state of affairs is permanent, or semi-permanent, action properly taken to preserve the life, health or well-being of the assisted person may well transcend such measures as surgical operation or substantial medical treatment and may extend to include such humdrum matters as routine medical or dental treatment, even simple care such as dressing and undressing and putting to bed.

The distinction I have drawn between cases of emergency, and cases where the state of affairs is (more or less) permanent, is relevant in another respect. We are here concerned with medical treatment, and I limit myself to cases of that kind. Where, for example, a surgeon performs an operation without his consent on a patient temporarily rendered unconscious in an accident, he should do no more than is reasonably required, in the best interests of the patient, before he recovers consciousness. I can see no practical difficulty arising from this requirement, which derives from the fact that the patient is expected before long to regain consciousness and can then be consulted about longer term measures. The point has however arisen in a more acute form where a surgeon, in the course of an operation, discovers some other condition which, in his opinion, requires operative treatment for which he has not received the patient's consent. In what circumstances he should operate forthwith, and in what circumstances he should postpone the further treatment until he has received the patient's consent, is a difficult matter which has troubled the Canadian Courts (see *Marshall v. Curry* (1933) 3 D.L.R. 260, and *Murray v. McMurchy* (1949) 2 D.L.R. 442), but which it is not necessary for your Lordships to consider in the present case.

But where the state of affairs is permanent or semi-permanent, as may be so in the case of a mentally disordered person, there is no point in waiting to obtain the patient's consent. The need to care for him is obvious: and the doctor must then act in the best interests of his patient, just as if he had received his patient's consent so to do. Were this not so, much useful treatment and care could, in theory at least, be denied to the unfortunate. It follows that, on this point, I am unable to accept the view expressed by Neill L.J. in the Court of Appeal, that the treatment must be shown to have been necessary. Moreover, in such a case, as my noble and learned friend Lord Brandon of Oakbrook has pointed out, a doctor who has assumed responsibility for the care of a patient may not only be treated as having the patient's consent to act, but may also be under a duty so to act. . . .

In these circumstances, it is natural to treat the deemed authority and the duty as interrelated. But I feel bound to express my opinion that, in principle, the lawfulness of the doctor's action is, at least in its origin, to be found in the principle of necessity. This can perhaps be seen most clearly in cases where there is no continuing relationship between doctor and patient. The "doctor in the house" who volunteers to assist a lady in the audience who, overcome by the drama or by the heat in the theatre, has fainted away, is impelled to act by no greater duty than that imposed by his own Hippocratic oath. Furthermore, intervention can be justified in the case of a non-professional, as well as a professional, man or woman who has no pre-existing relationship with the assisted persons—as in the case of a stranger who rushes to assist an injured man after an accident. In my opinion, it is the necessity itself which provides the justification for the intervention.

I have said that the doctor has to act in the best interests of the assisted person. In the case of routine treatment of mentally disordered persons, there should be little difficulty in applying this principle. In the case of more serious treatment, I recognise that its application may create problems for the medical profession; however, in making decisions about treatment, the doctor must act in accordance with a responsible and competent body of relevant professional opinion, on the principles set down in *Bolam v. Friern Hospital Management Committee* [1957] 1 W.L.R. 582. . . .

[Lords Bridge of Harwich, Griffiths and Jauncey of Tullichettle agreed with Lords Brandon and Goff.]

Appeal dismissed

Note

The application of force or threats of force may sometimes be justified by the consent of the victim. Where it is so justified, neither common assault nor any statutory crime which involves assault is committed. However, sometimes the statute expressly provides that consent is no defence. Moreover, the common law does not recognise consent as a defence to some assaults, on the footing that "no one can license a crime". This doctrine, and the question of what is consent, need separate treatment.

(b) When consent may justify

R. v. Brown
[1994] 1 A.C. 212
House of Lords

The appellants belonged to a group of sado-masochistic homosexuals who over a 10-year period from 1978 willingly participated in the commission of acts of violence against each other, including genital torture, for the sexual pleasure which it engendered in the giving and receiving of pain. The passive partner or victim in each case consented to the acts being committed and suffered no permanent injury. The activities took place in private at a number of different locations, including rooms equipped as torture chambers at the homes of three of the appellants. Video cameras were used to record the activities and the resulting tapes were then copied and distributed amongst members of the group. The tapes were not sold or used other than for the delectation of members of the group. The appellants were charged with assault occasioning actual bodily harm, contrary to s. 47 of the Offences Against the Person Act 1861, and unlawful wounding, contrary to s. 20 of that Act. The prosecution case was based very largely on the contents of the video tapes. At their trial, following a ruling by the trial judge that it was unnecessary for the prosecution to prove that the victim did not consent to the infliction of bodily harm or wounding upon him, the appellants pleaded guilty. Their appeal against conviction was dismissed by the Court of Appeal, which certified the following point of law of general public importance:—"Where A wounds or assaults B occasioning him actual bodily harm in the course of a sado-masochistic encounter, does the prosecution have to prove lack of consent on the part of B before they can establish A's guilt under s. 20 and s. 47 of the 1861 Offences Against the Person Act?" On further appeal:—

LORD TEMPLEMAN: . . . In the present case each of the appellants intentionally inflicted violence upon another (to whom I refer as "the victim") with the consent of the victim and thereby occasioned actual bodily harm or in some cases wounding or grievous bodily harm. Each appellant was therefore guilty of an offence under s. 47 or s. 20 of the Act of 1861 unless the consent of the victim was effective to prevent the commission of the offence or effective to constitute a defence to the charge.

In some circumstances violence is not punishable under the criminal law. When no actual bodily harm is caused, the consent of the person affected precludes him from complaining. There can be no conviction for the summary offence of common assault if the victim has consented to the assault. Even when violence is intentionally inflicted and results in actual bodily harm, wounding or serious bodily harm the accused is entitled to be acquitted if the injury was a foreseeable incident of a lawful activity in which the person injured was participating. Surgery involves intentional violence resulting in actual or sometimes serious bodily harm but surgery is a lawful activity. Other activities carried on with consent by or on behalf of the injured person have been accepted as lawful notwithstanding that they involve actual bodily harm or may cause serious bodily harm. Ritual circumcision, tattooing, ear-piercing and violent sports including boxing are lawful activities.

In earlier days some other forms of violence were lawful and when they ceased to be lawful they were tolerated until well into the 19th century. Duelling and fighting were at first lawful and then tolerated provided the protagonists were voluntary participants. But where the result of these activities was the maiming of one of the participants, the defence of consent never availed the aggressor; see *Hawkins Pleas of the Crown* (1824), 8th ed., Chapter 15. A maim was bodily harm whereby a man was deprived of the use of any member of his body which he needed to use in order to fight but a bodily injury was not a maim merely because it was a disfigurement. The act of maim was unlawful because the King was deprived of the services of an able-bodied citizen for the defence of the realm. Violence which maimed was unlawful despite consent to the activity which produced the maiming. In these days there is no difference between maiming on the one hand and wounding or causing grievous bodily harm on the other hand except with regard to sentence.

When duelling became unlawful, juries remained unwilling to convict but the judges insisted that persons guilty of causing death or bodily injury should be convicted despite the consent of the victim.

Similarly, in the old days, fighting was lawful provided the protagonists consented because it was thought that fighting inculcated bravery and skill and physical fitness. The brutality of knuckle fighting however caused the courts to declare that such fights were unlawful even if the protagonists consented. Rightly or wrongly the courts accepted that boxing is a lawful activity.

In *R. v. Coney* (1882) 8 Q.B.D. 534, the court held that a prize-fight in public was unlawful. . . .

[A] prize-fight being unlawful, actual bodily harm or serious bodily harm inflicted in the course of a prize-fight is unlawful notwithstanding the consent of the protagonists.

In *R. v. Donovan* [1934] 2 K.B. 498 the appellant in private beat a girl of seventeen for purposes of sexual gratification, it was said with her consent. Swift J. said, at p. 507 that:

> "It is an unlawful act to beat another person with such a degree of violence that the infliction of bodily harm is a probable consequence, and when such an act is proved, consent is immaterial."

In *Att.-Gen.'s Reference (No. 6 of 1980)* [1981] Q.B. 715 where two men quarrelled and fought with bare fists Lord Lane, C.J., delivering the judgment of the Court of Appeal said, at p. 719:

> ". . . It is not in the public interest that people should try to cause, or should cause, each other bodily harm for no good reason. Minor struggles are another matter. So, in our judgment, it is immaterial whether the act occurs in private or in public; it is an assault if actual bodily harm is intended and/or caused. This means that most fights will be unlawful regardless of consent. Nothing which we have said is intended to cast doubt upon the accepted legality of properly conducted games and sports, lawful chastisement or correction, reasonable surgical interference, dangerous exhibitions, etc. These apparent exceptions can be justified as involving the exercise of a legal right, in the case of chastisement or correction, or as needed in the public interest, in the other cases."

Duelling and fighting are both unlawful and the consent of the protagonists affords no defence to charges of causing actual bodily harm, wounding or grievous bodily harm in the course of an unlawful activity.

The appellants and their victims in the present case were engaged in consensual homosexual activities. The attitude of the public towards homosexual practices changed in the second half of this century. Change in public attitudes led to a change in the law.

The Wolfenden Report (Report of the Committee on Homosexual Offences and Prostitution (1957) (Cmnd. 247)) declared that the function of the criminal law in relation to homosexual behaviour "is to preserve public order and decency, to protect the citizen from what is offensive or injurious, and to provide sufficient safeguards against exploitation and corruption of others, particularly those who are especially vulnerable because they are young, weak in body or mind, inexperienced, or in a state of special, physical, official or economic dependence"; paragraph 13 of chapter 2.

In response to the Wolfenden Report and consistently with its recommendations, Parliament enacted s. 1 of the Sexual Offences Act 1967 which provided, *inter alia*, as follows:

"(1) Notwithstanding any statutory or common law provision, . . . a homosexual act in private shall not be an offence provided that the parties consent thereto and have attained the age of 21 years." . . .

By the Act of 1967, Parliament recognised and accepted the practice of homosexuality. Subject to exceptions not here relevant, sexual activities conducted in private between not more than two consenting adults of the same sex or different sexes are now lawful. Homosexual activities performed in circumstances which do not fall within s. 1 (1) of the Act of 1967 remain unlawful. Subject to the respect for private life embodied in the Act of 1967. Parliament has retained criminal sanctions against the practice, dissemination and encouragement of homosexual activities.

My Lords, the authorities dealing with the intentional infliction of bodily harm do not establish that consent is a defence to a charge under the Act of 1861. They establish that the courts have accepted that consent is a defence to the infliction of bodily harm in the course of some lawful activities. The question is whether the defence should be extended to the infliction of bodily harm in the course of sado-masochistic encounters. The Wolfenden Committee did not make any recommendations about sado-masochism and Parliament did not deal with violence in 1967. The Act of 1967 is of no assistance for present purposes because the present problem was not under consideration.

The question whether the defence of consent should be extended to the consequences of sado-masochistic encounters can only be decided by consideration of policy and public interest. Parliament can call on the advice of doctors, psychiatrists, criminologists, sociologists and other experts and can also sound and take into account public opinion. But the question must at this stage be decided by this House in its judicial capacity in order to determine whether the convictions of the appellants should be upheld or quashed.

Counsel for some of the appellants argued that the defence of consent should be extended to the offence of occasioning actual bodily harm under s. 47 of the Act of 1861 but should not be available to charges of serious wounding and the infliction of serious bodily harm under s. 20. I do not consider that this solution is practicable. Sado-masochistic participants have no way of foretelling the degree of bodily harm which will result from their encounters. The differences between actual bodily harm and serious bodily harm cannot be satisfactorily applied by a jury in order to determine acquittal or conviction.

Counsel for the appellants argued that consent should provide a defence to charges under both s. 20 and 47 because, it was said, every person has a right to deal with his body as he pleases. I do not consider that this slogan provides a sufficient guide to the policy decision which must now be made. It is an offence for a person to abuse his own body and mind by taking drugs. Although the law is often broken, the criminal law restrains a practice which is regarded as dangerous and injurious to individuals and which if allowed and extended is harmful to society generally. In any event the appellants in this case did not mutilate their own bodies. They inflicted bodily harm on willing victims. Suicide is no longer an offence but a person who assists another to commit suicide is guilty of murder or manslaughter.

The assertion was made on behalf of the appellants that the sexual appetites of sadists and masochists can only be satisfied by the infliction of bodily harm and that the law should not punish the consensual achievement of sexual satisfaction. There was no evidence to support the assertion that sado-masochist activities are essential to the happiness of the appellants or any other participants but the argument would be acceptable if sado-masochism were only concerned with sex, as the appellants contend. In my opinion sado-masochism is not only concerned with sex. Sado-masochism is also concerned with violence. The evidence discloses that the practices of the appellants were unpredictably dangerous and degrading to body and mind and were developed with increasing barbarity and taught to persons whose consents were dubious or worthless.

A sadist draws pleasure from inflicting or watching cruelty. A masochist derives pleasure from his own pain or humiliation. The appellants are middle-aged men. The victims were youths some of whom were introduced to sado-masochism before they attained the age of 21. In his judgment in the Court of Appeal, Lord Lane C.J. said that two members of the group of which the appellants formed part, namely one Cadman and the appellant Laskey:

"... were responsible in part for the corruption of a youth K ... It is some comfort at least to be told, as we were, that K has now it seems settled into a normal heterosexual relationship. Cadman had befriended K when the boy was 15 years old. He met him in a cafeteria and, so he says, found out that the boy was interested in homosexual activities. He introduced and encouraged K in 'bondage affairs'. He was interested in viewing and recording on videotape K and other teenage boys in homosexual scenes ... One cannot overlook the danger that the gravity of the assaults and injuries in this type of case may escalate to even more unacceptable heights."

The evidence disclosed that drink and drugs were employed to obtain consent and increase enthusiasm. The victim was usually manacled so that the sadist could enjoy the thrill of power and the victim could enjoy the thrill of helplessness. The victim had no control over the harm which the sadist, also stimulated by drink and drugs might inflict. In one case a victim was branded twice on the thigh and there was some doubt as to whether he consented to or protested against the second branding. The dangers involved in administering violence must have been appreciated by the appellants because, so it was said by their counsel, each victim was given a code word which he could pronounce when excessive harm or pain was caused. The efficiency of this precaution, when taken, depends on the circumstances and on the personalities involved. No one can feel the pain of another. The charges against the appellants were based on genital torture and violence to the buttocks, anus, penis, testicles and nipples. The victims were degraded and humiliated, sometimes beaten, sometimes wounded with instruments and sometimes branded. Bloodletting and the smearing of human blood produced excitement. There were obvious dangers of serious personal injury and blood infection. Prosecuting counsel informed the trial judge against the protests of defence counsel, that although the appellants had not contracted AIDS, two members of the group had died from AIDS and one other had contracted an HIV infection although not necessarily from the practices of the group. Some activities involved excrement. The assertion that the instruments employed by the sadists were clean and sterilized could not have removed the danger of infection, and the assertion that care was taken demonstrates the possibility of infection. Cruelty to human beings was on occasions supplemented by cruelty to animals in the form of bestiality. It is fortunate that there were no permanent injuries to a victim though no one knows the extent of harm inflicted in other cases. It is not surprising that a victim does not complain to the police when the complaint would involve him in giving details of acts in which he participated. Doctors of course are subject to a code of confidentiality.

In principle there is a difference between violence which is incidental and violence which is inflicted for the indulgence of cruelty. The violence of sado-masochistic encounters involves the indulgence of cruelty by sadists and the degradation of victims. Such violence is injurious to the participants and unpredictably dangerous. I am not prepared to invent a defence of consent for sado-masochistic encounters which breed and glorify cruelty and result in offences under ss. 47 and 20 of the Act of 1861.

. . . Society is entitled and bound to protect itself against a cult of violence. Pleasure derived from the infliction of pain is an evil thing. Cruelty is uncivilised. I would answer the certified question in the negative and dismiss the appeals of the appellants against conviction.

LORD JAUNCEY OF TULLICHETTLE . . .

The basic argument propounded by all the appellants was that the receivers having in every case consented to what was inflicted upon them no offence had been committed against ss. 20 or 47 of the Offences Against the Person Act 1861. All the appellants recognised however that so broad a proposition could not stand up and that there must be some limitation upon the harm which an individual could consent to receive at the hand of another. The line between injuries to the infliction of which an individual could consent and injuries to whose infliction he could not consent must be drawn it was argued where the public interest required. ...

[His Lordship quoted extensively from *Coney, Donovan* and *Att.-Gen's Reference* (No. 6 of 1980)] Although the reasoning in these [last] two cases differs somewhat, the conclusion from each of them is clear, namely, that the infliction of bodily harm without good reason is unlawful and that the consent of the victim is irrelevant. In the unreported case of *R. v. Boyea* (28 January 1992) (see [1992] Crim.L.R. 23), in which the appellant was convicted of indecent assault on a woman, Glidewell L.J. giving the judgment of the Court of Appeal (Criminal Division) said:

"The central proposition in *Donovan* is in our view consistent with the decision of the court in the *Att.-Gen.'s Reference (No. 6 of 1980)*. That proposition can be expressed as follows: an assault intended or which is likely to cause bodily harm, accompanied by indecency, is an offence irrespective of consent, provided that the injury is not 'transient or trifling'."

Glidewell L.J. went on to point out that having regard to the change in social attitude towards sexual relations "transient and trivial" must be understood in the light of conditions prevailing in 1992 rather than in 1934.

Before considering whether the above four cases were correctly decided and if so what relevance they have to these appeals, I must say a word about hostility. It was urged upon your Lordships that hostility on the part of the inflicter was an essential ingredient of assault and that this ingredient was necessarily lacking when injury was inflicted with the consent of the receiver. It followed that none of the activities in question constituted assault. The answer to this submission is to be found in the judgment of the Court of Appeal in *Wilson v. Pringle* [1987] Q.B. 237 where it was said, at p. 253 that hostility could not be equated with ill will or malevolence. The judgment went on to state:

"Take the example of the police officer in *Collins v. Wilcock* [1984] 1 W.L.R. 1172. She touched the woman deliberately, but without an intention to do more than restrain her temporarily. Nevertheless, she was acting unlawfully and in that way was acting with hostility."

If the appellant's activities in relation to the receivers were unlawful they were also hostile and a necessary ingredient of assault was present.

It was accepted by all the appellants that a line had to be drawn somewhere between those injuries to which a person could consent to infliction upon himself and those which were so serious that consent was immaterial. They all agreed that assaults occasioning actual bodily harm should be below the line but there was disagreement as to whether all offences against s. 20 of the Act of 1861 should be above the line or only those resulting in grievous bodily harm. The four English cases to which I have referred were not concerned with the distinction between the various types of assault and did not therefore have to address the problem raised in these appeals. . . .

I prefer the reasoning of Cave J. in *Coney* and of the Court of Appeal in the later three English cases which I consider to have been correctly decided. In my view the line properly falls to be drawn between assault at common law and the offence of assault occasioning actual bodily harm created by s. 47 of the Offences Against the Person Act 1861, with the result that consent of the victim is no answer to anyone charged with the latter offence or with a contravention of s. 20 unless the circumstances fall within one of the well known exceptions such as organised sporting contests and games, parental chastisement or reasonable surgery. There is nothing in ss. 20 and 47 of the Act of 1861 to suggest that consent is either an essential ingredient of the offences or a defence thereto. . . .

I would therefore dispose of these appeals on the basis that the infliction of actual or more serious bodily harm is an unlawful activity to which consent is no answer. In reaching this conclusion I have not found it necessary to rely on the fact that the activities of the appellants were in any event unlawful inasmuch as they amounted to acts of gross indecency which, not having been committed in private, did not fall within s. 1(1) of the Sexual Offences Act 1967. Notwithstanding the views which I have come to, I think it right to say something about the submissions that consent to the activity of the appellants would not be injurious to the public interest.

Considerable emphasis was placed by the appellants on the well-ordered and secret manner in which their activities were conducted and upon the fact that these activities had resulted in no injuries which required medical attention. There was, it was said, no question of prose-lytising by the appellants. . . .

Be that as it may, in considering the public interest it would be wrong to look only at the activities of the appellants alone, there being no sugges-tion that they and their associates are the only practitioners of homosexual sado-masochism in England and Wales. This House must therefore con-sider the possibility that these activities are practised by others and by others who are not so controlled or responsible as the appellants are claimed to be. Without going into details of all the rather curious activities in which the appellants engaged it would appear to be good luck rather than good judgment which has prevented serious injury from occurring. Wounds can easily become septic if not properly treated, the free flow of blood from a person who is H.I.V. positive or who has AIDS can infect another and an inflicter who is carried away by sexual excitement or by drink or drugs could very easily inflict pain and injury beyond the level to which the receiver had consented. Your Lordships have no information as to whether such situations have occurred in relation to other sado-masochistic practitioners. It was no doubt these dangers which caused Lady Mallalieu to restrict her propositions in relation to public interest to the actual rather than the potential result of the activity. In my view such a restriction is quite unjustified. When considering the public interest potential for harm is just as relevant as actual harm. As Mathew J. said in *Coney* at p. 547:

> "There is however abundant authority for saying that no consent can render that innocent which is in fact dangerous."

Furthermore, the possibility of proselytisation and corruption of young men is a real danger even in the case of these appellants and the taking of video recordings of such activities suggest that secrecy may not be as strict as the appellants claimed to your Lordships. If the only purpose of the activity is the sexual gratification of one or both of the participants what then is the need of a video recording?

My Lords I have no doubt that it would not be in the public interest that deliberate infliction of actual bodily harm during the course of homo-sexual sado-masochistic activities should be held to be lawful. In reaching this conclusion I have regard to the information available in these appeals and [to] such inferences as may be drawn therefrom. I appreciate that there may be a great deal of information relevant to these activities which is not available to your Lordships. When Parliament passed the Sexual Offences Act 1967 which made buggery and acts of gross indecency between consenting males lawful it had available the Wolfenden Report (1957) (Cmnd. 247) which was the product of an exhaustive research into the problem. If it is to be decided that such activities as the nailing by A of B's foreskin or scrotum to a board or the insertion of hot wax into C's urethra followed by the burning of his penis with a candle or the incising of D's scrotum with a scalpel to the effusion of blood are injurious neither to B, C and D nor to the public interest then it is for Parliament with its accumulated wisdom and sources of information to declare them to be lawful.

Two further matters only require to be mentioned. There was argument as to whether consent, where available, was a necessary ingredient of the offence of assault or merely a defence. There are conflicting dicta as to its effect. In *Coney* Stephen J. referred to consent as "being no defence", whereas in *Att.-Gen.'s Reference (No. 6 of 1980)* Lord Lane C.J. referred to the onus being on the prosecution to negative consent. In *Collins v. Wilcock* Goff L.J. referred to consent being a defence to a battery. If it were necessary, which it is not, in this appeal to decide which argument was correct I would hold that consent was a defence to but not a necessary ingredient in assault. . . .

My Lords, I would answer the certified question in the negative and dismiss the appeals.

LORD LOWRY: . . . [After considering *Coney, Donovan, Att.-Gen.'s Reference,* and the judgment of the Court of Appeal in the instant case, and noting that the Court considered that the question of consent was immaterial:] If, as I, too, consider, the question of consent is immaterial, there are prima facie offences against ss. 20 and 47 and the next question is whether there is good reason to add sado-masochistic acts to the list of exceptions contemplated in *Att.-Gen.'s Reference.* In my opinion, the answer to that question is "No".

In adopting this conclusion I follow closely my noble and learned friends Lord Templeman and Lord Jauncey. What the appellants are obliged to propose is that the deliberate and painful infliction of physical injury should be exempted from the operation of statutory provisions the object of which is to prevent or punish that very thing, the reason for the proposed exemption being that both those who will inflict and those who will suffer the injury wish to satisfy a perverted and depraved sexual desire. Sado-masochistic homosexual activity cannot be regarded as conductive to the enhancement or enjoyment of family life or conducive to the welfare of society. A relaxation of the prohibitions in ss. 20 and 47 can only encourage the practice of homosexual sado-masochism and the physical cruelty that it must involve (which can scarcely be regarded as a "manly diversion") by withdrawing the legal penalty and giving the activity a judicial imprimatur. As well as all this, one cannot overlook the physical danger to those who may indulge in sado-masochism. In this connection, and also generally, it is idle for the appellants to claim that they are educated exponents of "civilised cruelty". A proposed *general* exemption is to be tested by considering the likely *general* effect. This must include the probability that some sado-masochistic activity, under the powerful influence of the sexual instinct, will get out of hand and result in serious physical damage to the participants and that some activity will involve a danger of infection such as these particular exponents do not contemplate for themselves. When considering the danger of infection, with its inevitable threat of AIDS, I am not impressed by the argument that this threat can be discounted on the ground that, as long ago as 1967, Parliament, subject to conditions, legalised buggery, now a well-known vehicle for the transmission of AIDS.

So far as I can see, the only counter-argument is that to place a restriction on sado-masochism is an unwarranted interference with the private life and activities of persons who are indulging in a lawful pursuit and are doing no harm to anyone except, possibly, themselves. This approach, which has characterised every submission put forward on behalf of the appellants, is derived from the fallacy that what is involved here is the restraint of a lawful activity as opposed [to] the refusal to relax existing prohibitions in the 1861 Act. If in the course of buggery, as authorised by the 1967 Act, one participant, either with the other participant's consent or not, deliberately causes actual bodily harm to that other, an offence against s. 47 has been committed. The 1967 Act provides no shield. The position is as simple as that, and there is *no legal right to cause actual bodily harm* in the course of sado-masochistic activity. . . .

For all these reasons I would answer "No" to the certified question and would dismiss the appeals.

LORD MUSTILL: This is a case about the criminal law of violence. In my opinion it should be a case about the criminal law of private sexual relations, if about anything at all. Right or wrong, the point is easily made. . . . If the criminality of sexual deviation is the true ground of these proceedings, one would have expected that these above all would have been the subject of attack. Yet the picture is quite different.

The conduct of the appellants and of other co-accused was treated by the prosecuting authorities in three ways. First, there were those acts which fell squarely within the legislation governing sexual offences. These are easily overlooked, because attention has properly been concentrated on the charges which remain in dispute, but for a proper understanding of the case it is essential to keep them in view. Thus, four of the men pleaded guilty either as principals or as aiders and abettors to the charges of keeping a disorderly house. . . .

Laskey also pleaded guilty to two counts of publishing an obscene article. The articles in question were video-tapes of the activities which formed the subject of some of the counts laid under the Act of 1861.

The pleas of guilty to these counts, which might be regarded as dealing quite comprehensively with those aspects of Laskey's sexual conduct which impinged directly on public order attracted sentences of four years reduced on appeal to eighteen months imprisonment and three months imprisonment respectively. Other persons, not before the House, were dealt with in a similar way.

The two remaining categories of conduct comprised private acts. Some were prosecuted and are now before the House. Others, which I have mentioned, were not. If repugnance to general public sentiments of morality and propriety were the test, one would have expected proceedings in respect of the most disgusting conduct to be prosecuted with the greater vigour. Yet the opposite is the case. Why is this so? Obviously because the prosecuting authorities could find no statutory prohibition apt to cover this conduct. Whereas the sexual conduct which underlies the present appeals, although less extreme, could at least arguably be brought within ss. 20 and 47 of the 1861 Act because it involved the breaking of skin and the infliction of more than trifling hurt.

I must confess that this distribution of the charges against the appellants at once sounds a note of warning. It suggests that the involvement of the Act of 1861 was adventitious. This impression is reinforced when one considers the title of the statute under which the appellants are charged, "Offences *Against* the Person". Conduct infringing ss. 18, 20 and 47 of the Act of 1861 comes before the Crown Courts every day. Typically it involves brutality, aggression and violence, of a kind far removed from the appellants' behaviour which, however worthy of censure, involved no animosity, no aggression, no personal rancour on the part of the person inflicting the hurt towards the recipient and no protest by the recipient. In fact, quite the reverse. Of course we must give effect to the statute if its words capture what the appellants have done, but in deciding whether this is really so it is in my opinion legitimate to assume that the choice of the Offences Against the Person Act as the basis for the relevant counts in the indictment was made only because no other statute was found which could conceivably be brought to bear upon them.

In these circumstances I find it easy to share the opinion expressed by Wills J. in *R. v. Clarence (post,* p. 646), a case where the accused had consensual intercourse with his wife, he knowing and she ignorant that he suffered from gonorrhoea, with the result that she was infected. The case is of general importance, since the Court for Crown Cases Reserved held that there was no offence under ss. 47 and 20, since both sections required an assault, of which the wound or grievous bodily harm was the result, and that no assault was disclosed on the facts. For present purposes, however, I need only quote from the report, at p. 30:

> ". . . such considerations lead one to pause on the threshold, and enquire whether the enactment under consideration could really have been intended to apply to circumstances so completely removed from those which are usually understood when an assault is spoken of, or to deal with matters of any kind involving the sexual relation or act."

I too am led to pause on the threshold. Asking myself the same question, I cannot but give a negative answer. I therefore approach the appeal on the basis that the convictions on charges which seem to me so inapposite cannot be upheld unless the language of the statute or the logic of the decided cases positively so demand. Unfortunately, as the able arguments which we have heard so clearly demonstrate, the language of the statute is opaque, and the cases few and unhelpful. To these I now turn. . . .

[After considering the law on Death, Maiming, Prizefighting, "Contact" Sports, Surgery, Lawful Correction, Dangerous Pastimes, Rough Horseplay, Prostitution, and Fighting, and concluding that he would not accept that the infliction of bodily harm, and especially the private infliction of it, is invariably criminal, absent some special factor which decrees otherwise]: For these reasons, I consider that the House is free, as the Court of Appeal in the present case was not . . . free, to consider entirely afresh whether the public interest demands the interpretation of the Act of 1861 in such a way as to render criminal under s. 47 the acts done by the appellants.

[After holding that the general tenor of the decisions of the European Court on the European Convention on Human Rights clearly favoured the right of the appellants to conduct their private lives undisturbed by the criminal law]: The purpose of this long discussion has been to suggest that the decks are clear for the House to tackle completely anew the question whether the public interest requires s. 47 of the 1861 Act to be interpreted as penalising an infliction of harm which is at the level of actual bodily harm, but not grievous bodily harm; which is inflicted in private (by which I mean that it is exposed to the view only of those who have chosen to view it); which takes place not only with the consent of the recipient but with his willing and glad co-operation; which is inflicted for the gratification of sexual desire, and not in a spirit of animosity or rage; and which is not engaged in for profit.

My Lords, I have stated the issue in these terms to stress two considerations of cardinal importance. Lawyers will need no reminding of the first, but since this prosecution has been widely noticed it must be emphasised that the issue before the House is not whether the appellants' conduct is morally right, but whether it is properly charged under the Act of 1861. When proposing that the conduct is not rightly so charged I do not invite your Lordships' House to endorse it as morally acceptable. Nor do I pronounce in favour of a libertarian doctrine specifically related to sexual matters. Nor in the least do I suggest that ethical pronouncements are meaningless, that there is no difference between right and wrong, that sadism is praiseworthy, or that new opinions on sexual morality are necessarily superior to the old, or anything else of the same kind. What I do say is that these are questions of private morality; that the standards by which they fall to be judged are not those of the criminal law; and that if these standards are to be upheld the individual must enforce them upon himself according to his own moral standards, or have them enforced against him by moral pressures exerted by whatever religious or other community to whose ethical ideals he responds. The point from which I

invite your Lordships to depart is simply this, that the state should interfere with the rights of an individual to live his or her life as he or she
may choose no more than is necessary to ensure a proper balance between
the special interests of the individual and the general interests of the individuals who together comprise the populace at large. Thus, whilst
acknowledging that very many people, if asked whether the appellants'
conduct was wrong, would reply "Yes, repulsively wrong", I would at
the same time assert that this does not in itself mean that the prosecution
of the appellants under ss. 20 and 47 of the Offences Against the Person
Act 1861 is well founded.

This point leads directly to the second. As I have ventured to formulate
the crucial question, it asks whether there is good reason to impress upon
s. 47 an interpretation which penalises the relevant level of harm irrespective of consent: i.e. to recognise sado-masochistic activities as falling
into a special category of acts, such as duelling and prize-fighting, which
"the law says shall not be done." This is very important, for if the question were differently stated it might well yield a different answer. In particular, if it were to be held that as a matter of law all infliction of bodily
harm above the level of common assault is incapable of being legitimated
by consent, except in special circumstances, then we would have to consider whether the public interest required the recognition of private
sexual activities as being in a specially exempt category. This would be
an altogether more difficult question and one which I would not be prepared to answer in favour of the appellants, not because I do not have
my own opinions upon it but because I regard the task as one which the
courts are not suited to perform, and which should be carried out, if at
all, by Parliament after a thorough review of all the medical, social, moral
and political issues, such as was performed by the Wolfenden Committee.
Thus, if I had begun from the same point of departure as my noble and
learned friend Lord Jauncey of Tullichettle I would have arrived at a similar conclusion; but differing from him on the present state of the law, I
venture to differ.

Let it be assumed however that we should embark upon this question.
I ask myself, not whether as a result of the decision in this appeal, activities such as those of the appellants should *cease* to be criminal, but rather
whether the Act of 1861 (a statute which I venture to repeat once again
was clearly intended to penalise conduct of a quite different nature)
should in this new situation be interpreted so as to *make* it criminal. Why
should this step be taken? Leaving aside repugnance and moral objection,
both of which are entirely natural but neither of which are in my opinion
grounds upon which the court could properly create a new crime, I can
visualise only the following reasons:

1. Some of the practices obviously created a risk of genito-urinary infection, and others of septicaemia. These might indeed have been grave in
former times, but the risk of serious harm must surely have been greatly
reduced by modern medical science.

2. The possibility that matters might get out of hand, with grave results.
It has been acknowledged throughout the present proceedings that the
appellants' activities were performed as a pre-arranged ritual, which at
the same time enhanced their excitement and minimised the risk that the
infliction of injury would go too far. Of course things might go wrong
and really serious injury or death might ensue. If this happened, those
responsible would be punished according to the ordinary law, in the same
way as those who kill or injure in the course of more ordinary sexual
activities are regularly punished. But to penalise the appellants' conduct
even if the extreme consequences do not ensue, just because they might

have done so would require an assessment of the degree of risk, and the balancing of this risk against the interests of individual freedom. Such a balancing is in my opinion for Parliament, not the courts; and even if your Lordships' House were to embark upon it the attempt must in my opinion fail at the outset for there is no evidence at all of the seriousness of the hazards to which sado-masochistic conduct of this kind gives rise. This is not surprising, since the impressive argument of Mr Purnell Q.C. for the respondents did not seek to persuade your Lordships' to bring the matter within the Act of 1861 on the ground of special risks, but rather to establish that the appellants are liable *under the general law* because the level of harm exceeded the critical level marking off criminal from non-criminal consensual violence which he invited your Lordships to endorse.

3. I would give the same answer to the suggestion that these activities involved a risk of accelerating the spread of auto-immune deficiency syndrome, and that they should be brought within the Act of 1861 in the interests of public health. The consequence would be strange, since what is currently the principal cause for the transmission of this scourge, namely consenting buggery between males, is now legal. Nevertheless, I would have been compelled to give this proposition the most anxious consideration if there had been any evidence to support it. But there is none, since the case for the respondent was advanced on an entirely different ground.

4. There remains an argument to which I have given much greater weight. As the evidence in the present case has shown, there is a risk that strangers (and especially young strangers) may be drawn into these activities at an early age and will then become established in them for life. This is indeed a disturbing prospect, but I have come to the conclusion that it is not a sufficient ground for declaring these activities to be criminal under the Act of 1861. The element of the corruption of youth is already catered for by the existing legislation; and if there is a gap in it which needs to be filled the remedy surely lies in the hands of Parliament, not in the application of a statute which is aimed at other forms of wrongdoing. As regards proselytisation for adult sado-masochism the argument appears to me circular. For if the activity is not itself so much against the public interest that it ought to be declared criminal under the Act of 1861 then the risk that others will be induced to join in cannot be a ground for making it criminal.

Leaving aside the logic of this answer, which seems to me impregnable, plain humanity demands that a court addressing the criminality of conduct such as that of the present should recognise and respond to the profound dismay which all members of the community share about the apparent increase of cruel and senseless crimes against the defenceless. Whilst doing so I must repeat for the last time that in the answer which I propose I do not advocate the de-criminalisation of conduct which has hitherto been a crime; nor do I rebut a submission that a new crime should be created, penalising this conduct, for Mr. Purnell has rightly not invited the House to take this course. The only question is whether these consensual private acts are offences against the existing law of violence. To this question I return a negative response.

Accordingly I would allow these appeals and quash such of the convictions as are now before the House.

LORD SLYNN OF HADLEY: . . . The law has recognised cases where consent, expressed or implied, can be a defence to what would otherwise be an assault and cases where consent cannot be a defence. The former include surgical operations, sports, the chastisement of children, jostling in a crowd, but all subject to a reasonable degree of force being used, tattooing and ear-piercing; the latter include death and maiming. None of these situations, in most cases pragmatically accepted, either covers or is analogous to the facts of the present case.

It is, however, suggested that the answer to the question certified flows from the decisions in three cases [*Coney, Donovan* and *Att.-Gen.'s Reference (No. 6 of 1980)*]. . . .

I do not consider that any of these three cases is conclusive in resolving the present question.

These decisions are not in any event binding upon your Lordships' House and the matter has to be considered as one of principle.

Three propositions seem to me to be clear.

It is ''. . . inherent in the conception of assault and battery that the victim does not consent'' (Glanville Williams [1962] Crim.L.R. 74, 75). Secondly, consent must be full and free and must be as to the actual level of force used or pain inflicted. Thirdly, there exist areas where the law disregards the victim's consent even where that consent is freely and fully given. These areas may relate to the person (*e.g.* a child); they may relate to the place (*e.g.* in public); they may relate to the nature of the harm done. It is the latter which is in issue in the present case.

I accept that consent cannot be said simply to be a defence to any act which one person does to another. A line has to be drawn as to what can and as to what cannot be the subject of consent. . . .

I do not think a line can simply be drawn between ''maiming'' and death on the one hand and everything else on the other hand. The rationale for negating consent when maiming occurred has gone. It is, however, possible to draw the line, and the line should be drawn, between really serious injury on the one hand and less serious injuries on the other. I do not accept that it is right to take common assault as the sole category of assaults to which consent can be a defence and to deny that defence in respect of all other injuries. In the first place the range of injuries which can fall within ''actual bodily harm'' is wide—the description of two beatings in the present case show that one is much more substantial than the other. Further, the same is true of wounding where the test is whether the skin is broken and where it can be more or less serious. I can see no significant reason for refusing consent as a defence for the lesser of these cases of actual bodily harm and wounding.

If a line has to be drawn, as I think it must, to be workable, it cannot be allowed to fluctuate within particular charges and in the interests of legal certainty it has to be accepted that consent can be given to acts which are said to constitute actual bodily harm and wounding. Grievous bodily harm I accept to be different by analogy with and as an extension of the old cases on maiming. Accordingly, I accept that other than for cases of grievous bodily harm or death, consent can be a defence. This in no way means that the acts done are approved of or encouraged. It means no more than that the acts do not constitute as assault within the meaning of these two specific sections of the Offences Against the Person Act 1861.

None of the convictions in the present cases have been on the basis that grievous bodily harm was caused. Whether some of the acts done in these cases might have fallen within that category does not seem to me to be relevant for present purposes. . . .

In the present cases there is no doubt that there was consent; indeed there was more than mere consent. Astonishing though it may seem, the persons involved positively wanted, asked for, the acts to be done to them, acts which it seems from the evidence some of them also did to themselves. All the accused were old enough to know what they were doing. The acts were done in private. Neither the applicants nor anyone else complained as to what was done. The matter came to the attention of the police "coincidentally"; the police were previously unaware that the accused were involved in these practices though some of them had been involved for many years. The acts did not result in any permanent or serious injury or disability or any infection and no medical assistance was required even though there may have been some risk of infection, even injury.

There has been much argument as to whether lack of consent is a constituent of the offence which must be proved by the prosecution or whether consent is simply raised by way of defence. . . .

It has been suggested that if the act done is otherwise unlawful then consent cannot be a defence, but it can be a defence, if the act is otherwise lawful, in respect of injury which is less than really serious injury. That would produce the result in the present case that if these acts are done by two men they would be lawful by reason of s. 1 of the Sexual Offences Act 1967, even though the acts are far away from the kinds of homosexual acts which the Wolfenden Report had in mind (see paragraph 105 of the Report); in that situation, consent, it is said, would be a defence. If on the other hand three men took part, the activity would be unlawful under the Act of 1967 so that there could be no consent to the acts done. But it would also appear to mean that if these acts were done mutatis mutandis by a man and a woman, or between two men and a woman, or a man and two women, where the activity was entirely heterosexual, consent would prevent there being an offence. I do not find that this distinction produces an acceptable result.

My conclusion is thus that as the law stands, adults can consent to acts done in private which do not result in serious bodily harm, so that such acts do not constitute criminal assaults for the purposes of the Act of 1861.

. . . I agree that in the end it is a matter of policy. It is a matter of policy in an area where social and moral factors are extremely important and where attitudes can change. In my opinion it is a matter of policy for the legislature to decide. If society takes the view that this kind of behaviour, even though sought after and done in private, is either so new or so extensive or so undesirable that it should be brought now for the first time within the criminal law, then it is for the legislature to decide. It is not for the courts in the interests of "paternalism", as referred to in the passage I have quoted, or in order to protect people from themselves, to introduce, into existing statutory crimes relating to offences *against* the person, concepts which do not properly fit there. If Parliament considers that the behaviour revealed here should be made specifically criminal, then the Offences Against the Person Act 1861 or, perhaps more appropriately, the Sexual Offences Act 1967 can be amended specifically to define it. Alternatively, if it is intended that this sort of conduct should be lawful as between two persons but not between more than two persons as falling within the offence of gross indecency, then the limitation period for prosecution can be extended and the penalties increased where sadomasochistic acts are involved. That is obviously a possible course; whether it is a desirable way of changing the law is a different question.

Accordingly I consider that these appeals should be allowed and the conviction set aside.

Appeals dismissed

Questions

1. Was the case decided at first instance on the basis that the consents of the "victims" were dubious or worthless as Lord Templeman contends?

2. If, as is alleged, juveniles were corrupted, is this relevant to the issue before the court? Of what relevance is the spectre of AIDS, the use of excrement or the suggestion of bestiality to the issue whether an offence contrary to s.47 had been committed? Is the risk of HIV infection confined to homosexual sado-masochists?

3. If society is entitled to protect itself against a cult of violence, were any unwilling members of society liable to be the victims of the sado-masochists' cult of violence, thereby demanding protection from the law? Are the "victims" calling for protection? Are they any more protected following *Brown* than they were before if, as the Law Commission indicate in *Consent in the Criminal Law* (Consultation Paper No. 139), Part X, sado-masochism is being driven further underground, education and advice on safe SM techniques is being hampered and people are afraid to seek medical assistance if they have problems?

4. It was argued that the line between what was lawful and unlawful should be drawn between actual bodily harm and grievous bodily harm. The House of Lords rejected this as it would cause problems for juries dealing with grievous bodily harm under s.20 of the Offences Against the Person Act 1861 (*post*, p. 657). Are all such problems removed by drawing the line between simple assault occasioning actual bodily harm contrary to s.47?

5. As all three of their Lordships in the majority focused on the homosexual aspect of these sado-masochistic encounters, is the ratio of *Brown* confined to homosexual sado-masochism?

6. In *Att-Gen's Reference (No. 6 of 1980)* 1 Q.B. 715 Lord Lane C.J. stated (at p. 719): ". . . it is not in the public interest that people should try to cause or should cause each other bodily harm for no good reason . . . [I]t is an assault if actual bodily harm is intended and/or caused." This statement was quoted with approval by all three of their Lordships in the majority in *Brown*. A and B are engaging in consensual heterosexual activity. A does something to B to which she consents, which is not intended to but which does cause an injury which is more than transient or trifling. Is A guilty of assault occasioning actual bodily harm or even indecent assault? See *R.v. Boyea* [1992] Crim L.R. 574 (CA); *cf. R. v. Simon Slingsby* [1995] Crim L.R. 570 (Crown Court) and *R. v. Savage* [1992] 1 A.C. 699 (*post*, p. 662).

Note

Following the decision of the House of Lords three of the appellants complained to the European Commission of Human Rights that their convictions violated their right to respect for private life guaranteed by Article 8 of the Convention. In *Laskey, Jaggard and Brown v. United Kingdom* (Case No. 109/1995/615/703–705) the European Court of Human Rights held that while the prosecution of the applicants interfered in their private lives, this was "necessary in a democratic society" in pursuance of a legitimate aim, namely that of the "protection of health."

R. v. Wilson
[1996] 3 WLR 125
Court of Appeal

At his wife's instigation W branded his initials on his wife's buttocks with a hot knife. He was convicted of assault occasioning actual bodily harm contrary to s.47 of the Offences Against the Person Act 1861 and appealed.

RUSSELL L.J.: . . . We are abundantly satisfied that there is no factual comparison to be made between the instant case and the facts of either *R. v. Donovan* [1934] 2 K.B. 498 or *R. v. Brown* [1994] 1 A.C. 212: Mrs. Wilson not only consented to that which the appellant did, she instigated it. There was no aggressive intent on the part of the appellant. On the contrary, far from wishing to cause injury to his wife, the appellant's desire was to assist her in what she regarded as the acquisition of a desirable piece of personal adornment, perhaps in this day and age no less understandable than the piercing of nostrils or even tongues for the purposes of inserting decorative jewellery.

In our judgment *R. v. Brown* is not authority for the proposition that consent is no defence to a charge under section 47 of the Act of 1861, in all circumstances where actual bodily harm is deliberately inflicted. It is to be observed that the question certified for their Lordships in *R. v. Brown* related only to a "sado-masochistic encounter". However, their Lordships recognised in the course of their speeches, that it is necessary that there must be exceptions to what is no more than a general proposition. The speeches of Lord Templeman, at p. 231, Lord Jauncey of Tullichettle, at p. 245, and the dissenting speech of Lord Slynn of Hadley, at p. 277, all refer to tattooing as being an activity which, if carried out with the consent of an adult, does not involve an offence under section 47, albeit that actual bodily harm is deliberately inflicted.

For our part, we cannot detect any logical difference between what the appellant did and what he might have done in the way of tattooing. The latter activity apparently requires no state authorisation, and the appellant was as free to engage in it as anyone else. We do not think that we are entitled to assume that the method adopted by the appellant and his wife was any more dangerous or painful than tattooing. There was simply no evidence to assist the court on this aspect of the matter.

Does public policy or the public interest demand that the appellant's activity should be visited by the sanctions of the criminal law? The majority in *R. v. Brown* clearly took the view that such considerations were relevant. If that is so, then we are firmly of the opinion that it is not in the public interest that activities such as the appellant's in this appeal should amount to criminal behaviour. Consensual activity between husband and wife, in the privacy of the matrimonial home, is not, in our judgment, normally a proper matter for criminal investigation, let alone criminal prosecution. Accordingly we take the view that the judge failed to have full regard to the facts of this case and misdirected himself in saying that *R. v. Donovan* [1934] 2 K.B. 498 and *R. v. Brown* [1994] 1 A.C. 212 constrained him to rule that consent was no defence.

In this field, in our judgment, the law should develop upon a case by case basis rather than upon general propositions to which, in the changing times in which we live, exceptions may arise from time to time not expressly covered by authority.

We shall allow the appeal and quash the conviction. We conclude this judgment by commenting that we share the judge's disquiet that the prosecuting authority thought it fit to bring these proceedings. In our view they serve no useful purpose at considerable public expense.

Appeal allowed with costs.
Conviction quashed.

Questions

1. In what way is there an "aggressive intent" where one partner in a sexual relationship causes pain to the other at the request of the other?

2. In light of the fact that branding was one of the activities carried out by the appellants in *Brown*, would the Court of Appeal have arrived at the same conclusion if (i) Mrs Wilson had requested the branding not for motives of personal adornment but because she found pain enhanced her sexual fulfilment, or (ii) Mr Wilson had confessed that he found it sexually arousing to brand his wife?

3. Russell L.J. stated, "Does public policy or the public interest demand that the appellant's activity should be visited by the sanctions of the criminal law?" How does this approach compare with those of the majority and the minority in *Brown*?

4. Is this decision confined to "consensual activity between husband and wife, in the privacy of the matrimonial home" or would it apply to (i) an unmarried couple, or (ii) a gay or lesbian couple?

5. In *Brown* Lord Mustill included religious mortification in the list of activities to which consent to actual bodily harm is a defence. In the Scottish case *William Fraser* (1847) Ark 280, 302, Lord MacKenzie stated, "In some circumstances, a beating may be consented to, as . . . in a case of a father confessor ordering flagellation; but this is not violence or assault, because there is consent". A and B are priests living together in a homosexual relationship. A requests B to flagellate him for purposes of religious mortification. B whips A's back and buttocks causing cuts and weals which amount to actual bodily harm. Subsequently B requests A to flagellate him as he finds this sexually stimulating. A whips B's back and buttocks causing cuts and weals which amount to actual bodily harm. Do either or both instances of flagellation constitute an offence? If the answer differs what are the public policy issues which support this difference of result? Would the outcome in the second case differ if B had kept his purpose of sexual gratification secret from A and A had whipped him with equal vigour believing it was for the purpose of religious mortification?

Note

In *Emmett, The Independent*, July 19, 1999, D was convicted of two counts of assault occasioning actual bodily harm arising from consensual sexual activity with his fiancée (involving asphyxiation on the first occasion and the use of lighter fluid on the second) as a result of which she suffered "subconjunctival haemorrhages in both eyes and some petechial bruising around her neck" and "a burn, measuring some 6cm × 4cm" on her breast. The trial judge ruled that consent was not available as a defence where the parties foresaw the risk of injury arising from their consensual sexual activities. The Court of Appeal saw no reason in principle "to draw any distinction between sadomasochistic activity on a heterosexual basis and that which is conducted in a homosexual context". The Court of Appeal stated that the "actual or potential damage to which the appellant's partner was exposed in this case, plainly went far beyond that which was established by the evidence in *Wilson*."

(c) What is consent?

R. v. Clarence
(1888) 22 Q.B.D. 23
Court for Crown Cases Reserved

C was charged under both section 20 and section 47 of the Offences Against the Person Act 1861. He had had intercourse with his wife when he was suffering from a venereal disease, which was communicated to her. She would not have consented to intercourse had she known of his condition. He was convicted on both counts. On a case being reserved, a majority of nine to four held that an assault was needed for both of the crimes charged and on the facts there was no assault.

STEPHEN J.: The question in this case is whether a man who knows that he has gonorrhoea, and who by having connection with his wife, who does not know it, infects her, is or is not guilty of an offence either under section 20 of 24 and 25 Vict. c. 100, or under section 47 of the same Act. Section 20 punishes everyone who "unlawfully and maliciously inflicts any grievous bodily harm upon any other person". Section 47 punishes everyone who is convicted of "an assault occasioning actual bodily harm to any person". . . .

If the present conviction is right it is clear that unless some distinction can be pointed out which does not occur to me, the sections must be held to apply, not only to venereal diseases, but to infection of every kind which is in fact communicated by one person to another by any act likely to produce it. A man who knowing that he has scarlet fever or small-pox shakes hands with a friend and so infects him may be said to fall under section 20 or section 47 as much as the prisoner in this case. To seize a man's hand without his consent is an assault; but no one would consent to such a grasp if he knew that he risked small-pox by it, and if consent in all cases is rendered void by fraud, including suppression of the truth, such a gesture would be an assault occasioning actual bodily harm as much as the conduct of the prisoner in this case.

Not only is there no general principle which makes the communication of infection criminal, but such authority as exists is opposed to such a doctrine in relation to any disease. . . .

I now come to the construction of the precise words of the statute. [His Lordship held that section 20 required an assault (but see now *R. v. Burstow, post*, p. 658)].

Is the case, then, within section 47, as "an assault occasioning actual bodily harm"? The question here is whether there is an assault. It is said there is none, because the woman consented, and to this it is replied that fraud vitiates consent, and that the prisoner's silence was a fraud. Apart altogether from this question, I think that the act of infection is not an assault at all, for the reasons already given. Infection is a kind of poisoning. It is the application of an animal poison, and poisoning as already shewn, is not an assault. Apart, however, from this, is the man's concealment of the fact that he was infected such a fraud as vitiated the wife's consent to his exercise of marital rights, and converted the act of connection into an assault? It seems to me that the proposition that fraud vitiates consent in criminal matters is not true if taken to apply in the fullest sense of the word, and without qualification. It is too short to be true, as a mathematical formula is true. If we apply it in that sense to the present case, it is difficult to say that the prisoner was not guilty of rape, for the definition of rape is having connection with a woman without her consent; and if fraud vitiates consent, every case in which a man infects a woman or commits bigamy, the second wife being ignorant of the first marriage, is also a case of rape. Many seductions would be rapes, and so might acts of prostitution procured by fraud, as for instance by promises not intended to be fulfilled. These illustrations appear to shew clearly that the maxim that fraud vitiates consent is too general to be applied to these matters as if it were absolutely true. I do not at all deny that in some cases it applies though it is often used with reference to cases which do not fall within it. For instance, it has nothing to do with such cases as assaults on young children. A young child who submits to an indecent act no more consents to it than a sleeping or unconscious woman. The child merely submits without consenting. The only cases in which fraud indisputably vitiates consent in these matters are cases of fraud as to the nature of the act done. As to fraud as to the identity of the person by whom it is done the law is not quite clear. In *R. v. Flattery* (1877) 2 Q.B.D. 410, in which consent was obtained by reporting the act as a surgical operation, the prisoner was held to be guilty of rape. In the case where consent was obtained by the personation of a husband, there was before the passing of the Criminal Law Amendment Act of 1885 a conflict of authority. The last decision in England, *R. v. Barrow* (1868) L.R. 1 C.C.R. 158, decided that the act was not rape, and *R. v. Dee* (1884) 14 L.R.Ir. 485, decided in Ireland in 1884, decided that it was. The Criminal Law Amendment Act of 1885 "declared and enacted" that thenceforth it should be deemed to be rape, thus favouring the view taken in *R. v. Dee.* I do not propose to examine in detail the controversies connected with these cases. The judgments in the case of *R. v. Dee* examine all of them minutely, and I think they justify the observation that the only acts of fraud which so far destroy the effect of a woman's consent as to convert a connection consented to in fact into a rape are frauds as to the nature of the act itself, or as to the identity of the person who does the act. There is abundant authority to shew that such frauds as these vitiate consent both in the case of rape and in the case of indecent assault. I should myself prefer to say that consent in such cases does not exist at all, because the act consented to is not the act done. Consent to a surgical operation or examination is not a consent to sexual connection or indecent behaviour. Consent to connection with a husband is not consent to adultery. . . .

The woman's consent here was as full and conscious as consent could be. It was not obtained by any fraud either as to the nature of the act or as to the identity of the agent. The injury done was done by a suppression of the truth. It appears to me to be an abuse of language to describe such an act as an assault. . . .

Conviction quashed

Notes

1. There are several problems with the decision in *Clarence*. First, central to the decision is the proposition that an assault must be proved as an element of the offence of inflicting grievous bodily harm contrary to section 20 of the Offences Against the Person Act 1861. Following the decision of the House of Lords in *Burstow* [1998] A.C. 147, the authority of *Clarence* on this point is highly questionable (see p. 658 post). Secondly, the court in *Clarence* focused on whether or not there was consent to sexual intercourse. As Mrs Clarence understood the *nature* of this act there was no question of her husband's concealment of his condition amounting to a fraud as to the nature of the act.

His concealment, rather, related to an attribute of his conduct, namely its capacity to spread infection. The offence charged, however, was not rape to which that attribute would be irrelevant, but was an offence against the person involving harm to which the attribute is relevant. Much of Stephen J.'s judgment confuses these issues and his analysis of instances of sexual intercourse which might become rapes if all frauds, without qualification, vitiated consent, do not bear close scrutiny as they lack close attention to the subject to which the fraud relates. Simester and Sullivan, *Criminal Law: Theory and Doctrine* (1999) state (at p. 611):

> The nature/attributes distinction drawn in *Clarence* is dependent on the category of description employed. If our category of description is the distinction between injurious and non-injurious acts, we would distinguish between sexual intercourse with a person who is HIV-positive and sexual intercourse with a person in good health. If our category is the distinction between sexual acts and non-sexual acts, we would distinguish between bodily contact for sexual gratification and bodily contact for therapeutic purposes. Of course, within the description category of sexual acts, we would distinguish between health-threatening sex and safe sex: *within* that category, the distinction is a difference of attribute and not of nature. On facts such as *Clarence*, if we ask, did V consent to sex and the physical contact attendant upon it, the answer is yes. If we ask, did V consent to a risk of bodily harm, the answer is no. Both descriptions may be perfectly valid for the purposes of the criminal law. If D had been charged with rape . . . the question of consent to a sexual act would have been pertinent. Since the charge under s. 20 . . . related to the infliction of bodily harm, whether V consented to the risk of such harm seems the more relevant question.
>
> The nature/attributes distinction can work properly only if it utilises the offence charged as the relevant category of description. The fact that D is infected with a sexually transmissible disease does not *necessarily* entail that he is guilty of rape or indecent assault should he participate in sexual activity with V, even if V would not have consented had she known of D's condition. But, if the risk of bodily harm is not revealed to V, there seems no reason in principle why V should be held to have consented to D's conduct when analysed in the context of non-sexual offences against the person. The fact that the conduct is sexual does not subsume all other descriptions of that conduct.
>
> It is submitted that *Clarence* does not imply that no criminal charges may follow on the basis of D's failure to reveal his infected condition. Should *Clarence* be understood otherwise, remarkable anomalies would ensue. In *Brown* [*ante* p. 629], the House of Lords decided that, in the course of unconventional sexual activities, V could not consent to actual bodily harm, even if aware of all relevant facts and fully amenable to everything D intended to do. It would be highly anomalous if *Brown* were taken to imply a distinction between covert risks in "conventional" sexual activity and explicit risks of non-conventional forms. The conduct in *Clarence* may not involve *sexual* wrongdoing. But it certainly demonstrates reckless disregard for another person's safety.

2. In *Richardson* [1992] Cr.App.R. 200 D was charged with six counts of assault occasioning actual bodily harm arising from her continuing to practise as a dentist while suspended by the General Dental Council. The trial judge rejected a defence submission, *inter alia*, that the

patients had consented to the treatment albeit that they did not know
D was suspended from practice. D then pleaded guilty to all six counts
and appealed. On appeal it was argued that the patients had been
deceived neither as to the nature of the act nor as to the identity of D.
The Crown did not take issue on the first point but concentrated on
the identity issue. The Court of Appeal allowed the appeal there being
no fraud as the concealment by D of her suspension from practice did
not go to identity. The Court of Appeal was unwilling to extend the
concept of "identity" to cover qualifications or attributes. In the context of medical treatment, however, qualifications are crucial: the
patient is concerned to know that the person treating him or her is
qualified so to do; their attributes, such as name, age, gender, race etc
are of secondary, if of any, import. Perhaps the first point, had the
Crown chosen to pursue it, might have provided a more acceptable
means of engaging with this issue. The qualifications of the actor are
of crucial significance to the question whether what the actor is doing
amounts to 'reasonable surgical interference'. In the absence of circumstances of necessity, the performance of a surgical procedure by
an unqualified person would not be lawful. A fraud as to qualifications to practise medicine necessarily relates to the nature of the acts
which the purported practitioner proposes to perform. Indeed, if the
acts do not amount to medical treatment, applying *A-G's Reference (No.
6 of 1980)* and *Brown*, consent is not an issue if actual bodily harm has
been occasioned.

3. In *Tabassum* [2000] Crim.L.R. 686 D carried out examinations of
three women's breasts purporting to be carrying out a study on breast
cancer. The women believed he was medically qualified and would
not have let him examine them had they known he was not. He was
convicted on three counts of indecent assault and appealed arguing
that consent could only be negatived where there was deception as to
identity or where the nature and quality of the act differed from that
to which the victim had consented. The Court of Appeal dismissed
the appeal and distinguished *Richardson* noting that the appeal in that
case had proceeded solely by reference to the point on identity. In the
present case consent to the touching was given as the victims believed
it was for a medical purpose—they were not consenting to indecent
behaviour. Thus "there was consent to the nature of the act but not
its quality". It should be noted that previous cases stated that fraud
as to the *nature* of the act would vitiate consent. The Court of Appeal
in this case has used the term "nature and quality" (a term used in
the *McNaghten* Rules). What the Court seems to mean here is that the
nature of the act the victims consented to was a touching but they
believed it to be an examination by a medically qualified person and
thus to be performed for a medical purpose rather than performed by
an unqualified person for an indecent purpose. By focusing on the
act the Court negotiated the problem of identity and the relevance of
qualifications thereto. (See further Indecent Assault, below). The
court's analysis in this case fits with Simester and Sullivan's nature/
attributes distinction above, the category of distinction being between
sexual acts and non-sexual acts.

Latter v. Braddell
Common Pleas Division
(1880) 50 L.J.K.B 166

L was a housemaid in the service of Mrs B. Mrs B was convinced that L was pregnant, and on her denying it, Mrs B called a doctor and ordered L to submit to a medical examination. He told her to undress and let him examine her. L protested and wept but took off her clothes and submitted to an examination, which showed that she was not pregnant. L sued Mrs B and the doctor for assault. The trial judge (Lindley J.) withdrew from the jury the case against Mrs B, and the jury found in favour of the doctor. In the Common Pleas Divisional Court, Lindley J. upheld his own decision, Lopes J. dissenting.

LINDLEY J.: . . . The plaintiff's case cannot be put higher than this, namely, that, without consulting her wishes, her mistress ordered her to submit to be examined by a doctor, in order that he might ascertain whether she (the plaintiff) was in the family way, and that she (the plaintiff) complied with that order reluctantly—that is, sobbing and protesting—and because she was told she must, and she did not know what else to do. There was, however, no evidence of any force or violence, nor of any threat of force or violence, nor of any illegal act done or threatened by the mistress beyond what I have stated; nor did the plaintiff in her evidence say that she was in fear of the mistress or of the doctor, or that she was in any way overcome by fear. . . . Under these circumstances I am of opinion that there was no evidence of want of consent as distinguished from reluctant obedience or submission to her mistress's orders, and that in the absence of all evidence of coercion, as distinguished from an order which the plaintiff could comply with or not as she chose, the action cannot be maintained. . . .

Note

The case went to the Court of Appeal, where the judgment of Lindley J. was unanimously upheld: see (1881) 50 L.J.Q.B. 448; but note Lopes J.'s dissenting opinion in the Divisional Court.

". . . A submission to what is done, obtained through a belief that she is bound to obey her master or mistress; or a consent obtained through a fear of evil consequences to arise to herself, induced by her master's or mistress's words or conduct, is not sufficient. In neither case would the consent be voluntarily given: it would be a consent in one sense, but a consent to which the will was not a party. The plaintiff's case is stronger. She swears she did not consent. I know not what more a person in the plaintiff's position could do unless she used physical force. She is discharged without a hearing, forbidden to speak, sent to her room, examined by her mistress's doctor alone, no other female being in the room, made to take off all her clothes, and lie naked on the bed. She complains of the treatment, cries continuously, objects to the removal of each garment and swears the examination was without her consent. Could it be said, in these circumstances, that her consent was so unmistakably given that her state of mind was not a question for the jury to consider? I cannot adopt the view that the plaintiff consented because she yielded without her will having been overpowered by force or fear of violence. That, as I have said, is not, in my opinion, an accurate definition of consent in a case like this . . ."

Questions

1. Do you think that Lopes J.'s view of the matter is preferable?
2. As to "consent to which the will is not a party", if the limits of this are not drawn at force or threats of force, where should they be drawn? At belief in law that one must submit? Or at a fear of "evil consequences"? How are they to be defined?

Note

See note to *R. v. Olugboja, post,* p. 677. That case has, under the supposed influence of statute, made the question of consent in rape correspond to the view taken by Lopes J.

(d) Capacity to consent

Notes

1. There is no age or degree of mental affliction which as a matter of law precludes a person from consenting to the application of force to his body. Ability to consent is a matter of fact, depending on the capacity of the individual. In *R. v. D.* [1984] A.C. 778, 806, a case of kidnapping, an ingredient of which is absence of consent on the part of the person taken or carried away, Lord Brandon said:

"I see no good reason why, in relation to the kidnapping of a child, it should not in all cases be the absence of the child's consent which is material, whatever its age may be. In the case of a very young child, it would not have the understanding or the intelligence to give its consent, so that absence of consent would be a necessary inference from its age. In the case of an older child, however, it must, I think, be a question of fact for a jury whether the child concerned has sufficient understanding and intelligence to give its consent; if, but only if, the jury considers that a child has these qualities, it must then go on to consider whether it has been proved that the child did not give its consent. While the matter will always be for the jury alone to decide, I should not expect a jury to find at all frequently that a child under 14 had sufficient understanding and intelligence to give its consent."

(2) As to consent to medical treatment of minors, see *Gillick v. West Norfolk and Wisbech Area Health Authority* [1986] A.C. 112, where Lord Scarman quoted with approval Addy J. in the Ontario High Court in *Johnston v. Wellesley Hospital* (1980) 17 D.L.R. (3d) 139, 144:

"But, regardless of modern trend, I can find nothing in any of the old reported cases, except where infants of tender age or young children were involved, where the Courts have found that a person under 21 years of age was legally incapable of consenting to medical treatment. If a person under 21 years were unable to consent to medical treatment, he would also be incapable of consenting to other types of bodily interference. A proposition purporting to establish that any bodily interference acquiesced in by a youth of 20 years would nevertheless constitute an assault would be absurd. If such were the case, sexual intercourse with a girl under 21 years would constitute rape. Until the minimum age of consent to sexual acts was fixed at 14 years by a statute, the Courts often held that infants were capable of consenting at a considerably earlier age than 14 years. I feel that the law on this point is well expressed in the volume on *Medical Negligence* (1957) by Lord Nathan (p. 176): 'It is suggested that the most satisfactory solution of the problem is to rule that an infant who is capable of appreciating fully the nature and consequences of a particular operation or of particular treatment can give an effective consent thereto, and in such cases the consent of the guardian is unnecessary; but that where the infant is without the capacity, any apparent consent by him or her will be a nullity, the sole right to consent being vested in the guardian.'''

(3) Capacity to consent, in the case of a fully competent adult, involves a right *not* to consent to treatment, however necessary: see *Re T.* [1992] 4 All E.R. 649 (C.A.) and *St. George's Healthcare N.H.S. Trust v. S.* [1998] 3 All E.R. 673 (C.A.) (in the latter case the right of a pregnant woman to refuse a caesarian operation was upheld even though the operation was necessary to preserve both the mother's life and the life of the unborn child); but no minor, of any age below 18, has power by refusing consent to treatment to override a consent by someone with parental responsibility for the minor and *a fortiori* a consent by the court: *Re J.* [1992] 4 All E.R. 614 (C.A.), *per* Donaldson M.R.

(e) Lawful correction

In *Attorney-General's Reference (No. 6 of 1980)* [1981] Q.B. 715 Lord Lane C.J. included "lawful chastisement or correction" in his list of lawful exceptions to the principle that a person should not cause or try to cause bodily harm to another. There is a fairly clear line of cases establishing that it is lawful for a parent or other person *in loco parentis* to use reasonable force to discipline their children or charges (see *Cleary v. Booth* [1893] 1 Q.B. 465; *Mackie* (1973) 57 Cr.App.R. 453) provided the child is old enough to understand its purpose (*Griffin* (1869) 11 Cox. C.C. 402). But corporal punishment administered out of spite or anger or for gratification, or where the degree of force used is unreasonable, is unlawful (see *Hopley* (1860) 2 F.&F. 202; *Taylor, The Times*, December 28, 1983). Limitations on the defence of lawful chastisement are likely following the decision in *A. v. U.K.* (1999) 27 E.H.R.R. 611 where the European Court of Human Rights held that the United Kingdom was in breach of its obligations under Article 3 of the European Convention on Human Rights in failing to provide adequate protection to children and other vulnerable individuals against treatment or punishment which could constitute "inhuman or degrading treatment". In the instant case the stepfather of the applicant had been prosecuted for assault occasioning actual bodily harm arising out of his chastisement of A using a cane which was applied with considerable force resulting in a number of severe bruises. In his defence he pleaded "reasonable chastisement" and was acquitted by the jury. The finding by the European Court of Human Rights thus places serious doubts over the limits of the defence of reasonable chastisement. The Department of Health has issued a consultation document, *Protecting Children, Supporting Parents: A Consultation Document on the Physical Punishment of Children* (2000) and further legislation to clarify this area of the law is likely to follow.

Note

In *Consent in the Criminal Law* (Consultation Paper No. 139) the Law Commission make the following provisional proposals.

The need for the same principles to be adopted in relation to consent in other criminal offences in which consent is an issue

1. We provisionally propose that the proposals contained in paragraphs 12–30 below should apply not only to offences against the person and sexual offences but also to every other criminal offence in which the consent of a person other than the defendant is or may be a defence to criminal liability.

(Paragraphs 1.24–1.27)

Intentional causing of seriously disabling injury

2. We provisionally propose that the intentional causing of seriously disabling injury (as defined at paragraph 7 below) to another person should continue to be criminal, even if the person injured consents to such injury or to the risk of such injury.

(Paragraphs 4.3–4.6 and 4.47)

Reckless causing of seriously disabling injury

3. We provisionally propose that—

(1) the reckless causing of seriously disabling injury (as defined at paragraph 7 below) should continue to be criminal, even if the injured person consents to such injury or to the risk of such injury; but
(2) a person causing seriously disabling injury to another person should not be regarded as having caused it recklessly unless—
    (a) he or she was, at the time of the act or omission causing it, aware of a risk that such injury would result, and
    (b) it was at that time contrary to the best interests of the other person, having regard to the circumstances known to the person causing the injury (including, if known to him or her, the fact that the other person consented to such injury or to the risk of it), to take that risk.

(Paragraphs 4.7–4.28 and 4.48)

Secondary liability for consenting to seriously disabling injury

4. We provisionally propose that, where a person causes seriously disabling injury to another person who consented to injury or to the risk of injury of the type caused, and the person causing the injury is guilty of an offence under the proposals in paragraphs 2 and 3 above, the ordinary principles of secondary liability should apply for the purpose of determining whether the person injured is a party to that offence.

(Paragraphs 1.20–1.23)

Intentional causing of other injuries

5. We provisionally propose that the intentional causing of any injury to another person other than seriously disabling injury as defined at paragraph 7 below (whether or not amounting to "grievous bodily harm" within the meaning of the Offences Against the Person Act 1861 or to "serious injury" within the meaning of the Criminal Law Bill *post*, p. 628) should not be criminal if, at the time of the act or omission causing the injury, the other person consented to injury of the type caused.

(Paragraphs 4.29 and 4.49)

Reckless causing of other injuries

6. We provisionally propose that the reckless causing of any injury to another person other than seriously disabling injury as defined at paragraph 7 below (whether or not amounting to "grievous bodily harm" within the meaning of the Offences Against the Person Act 1861 or to "serious injury" within the meaning of the Criminal Law Bill) should not be criminal if, at the time of the act or omission causing the injury, the other person consented to injury of the type caused, to the risk of such injury or to the act or omission causing the injury.

(Paragraphs 4.29 and 4.50)

Definition of seriously disabling injury

7. We provisionally propose that for the purpose of paragraphs 2–6 above "seriously disabling injury" should be taken to refer to an injury or injuries which—

(1) cause serious distress, and
(2) involve the loss of a bodily member or organ or permanent bodily injury or permanent functional impairment, or serious or permanent disfigurement, or severe and prolonged pain, or serious impairment of mental health, or prolonged unconsciousness;

and, in determining whether an effect is permanent, no account should be taken of the fact that it may be remediable by surgery.

(Paragraphs 4.29–4.40 and 4.51)

Meaning of consent

8. We provisionally propose that for the purposes of the above proposals—

(1) "consent" should mean a valid subsisting consent to an injury or to the risk of an injury of the type caused, and consent may be express or implied;
(2) a person should be regarded as consenting to an injury of the type caused if he or she consents to an act or omission which he or she knows or believes to be intended to cause injury to him or her of the type caused; and
(3) a person should be regarded as consenting to the risk of an injury of the type caused if he or she consents to an act or omission which he or she knows or believes to involve a risk of injury to him or her of the type caused.

(Paragraphs 4.3–4.28 and 4.52)

Mistaken belief in consent: offences against the person

9. We ask—

(1) whether it should in itself be a defence to an offence of causing injury to another person that—

(a) at the time of the act or omission causing the injury, the defendant believed that the other person consented to injury or to the risk of injury of the type caused, or to that act or omission, and

(b) he or she would have had a defence under our proposals in paragraphs 5 and 6 above if the facts had been as he or she then believed them to be; or

(2) whether such a belief should be a defence *only* if, in addition, *either*—

(a) it would not have been obvious to a reasonable person in his or her position that the other person did not so consent, or

(b) he or she was not capable of appreciating that that person did not so consent.

(Paragraphs 7.1–7.28 and 7.31)

Mistaken belief in consent: sexual offences

10. We provisionally propose that, if (but only if) the defence of mistaken belief in consent to injury, or to the risk of injury, or to an act or omission causing injury, were to be available in relation to offences against the person only where one of the conditions set out in paragraph 9(2) is satisfied, it should similarly be no defence to a charge of rape or indecent assault that the defendant mistakenly believed that the other person consented to sexual intercourse or to the alleged assault unless one of those conditions is satisfied.

(Paragraphs 7.29 and 7.32)

2. ASSAULT OCCASIONING ACTUAL BODILY HARM

Offences Against the Person Act 1861, section 47

Whosoever shall be convicted upon an indictment of any assault occasioning actual bodily harm shall be liable to ... [imprisonment for five years].

Note

This section creates a separate statutory offence which ought to be charged as "contrary to section 47": *R. v. Harrow Justices* [1985] 3 All E.R. 185 (Q.B.D.).

R. v. Chan-Fook
[1994] 1 W.L.R. 689
Court of Appeal

The appellant was convicted of assault occasioning actual bodily harm following the judge's direction to the jury which stated:

"What is meant by 'actual bodily harm'? It does not have to be permanent. It does not have to be serious. It is some actual harm which interferes with the comfort of the individual for the time being, described as any hurt or injury calculated to interfere with the health or comfort of [the victim]. An assault that causes an hysterical or nervous condition is capable of being an assault causing actual bodily harm . . .''

HOBHOUSE L.J.: . . .

[The words "actual bodily harm"] are three words of the English language which require no elaboration and in the ordinary course should not receive any. The word "harm" is a synonym for injury. The word "actual" indicates that the injury (although there is no need for it to be permanent) should not be so trivial as to be wholly insignificant. The purpose of the definition in section 47 is to define an element of aggravation in the assault. It must be an assault which besides being an assault (or assault and battery) causes to the victim some injury.

The danger of any elaboration of the words of the statute is that it may have the effect . . . of altering, or at the least distracting the jury from, the ordinary meaning of the words. . . .

The first question on the present appeal is whether the inclusion of the word "bodily" in the phrase "actual bodily harm" limits harm to harm to the skin, flesh and bones of the victim. Lynskey J. [in *R. v. Miller* [1954] 2 Q.B. 282] rejected this submission. In our judgment he was right to do so. The body of the victim includes all parts of his body, including his organs, his nervous system and his brain. Bodily injury therefore may include injury to any of those parts of his body responsible for his mental and other faculties. The matter was well summarised by Lord Wilberforce in *McLoughlin v. O'Brian* [1983] 1 A.C. 410, 418:

"Whatever is unknown about the mind-body relationship (and the area of ignorance seems to expand with that of knowledge), it is now accepted by medical science that recognisable and severe physical damage to the human body and system may be caused by the impact, through the senses, of external events on the mind. There may thus be produced what is as identifiable an illness as any that may be caused by direct physical impact."

As is pointed out by Lord Wilberforce earlier in his speech the conventional phrase "nervous shock" is now inaccurate and inappropriate. Observations to the like effect are to be found in *Attia v. British Gas Plc.* [1988] Q.B. 304 and *Alcock v. Chief Constable of South Yorkshire Police* [1992] 1 A.C. 310. In *Attia v. British Gas Plc.* the Court of Appeal discussed where the borderline should be drawn between on the one hand the emotions of distress and grief and on the other hand some actual psychiatric illness such as anxiety neurosis or a reactive depression. The authorities recognised that there is a line to be drawn and whether any given case falls on one side or the other is a matter for expert evidence. The civil cases are also concerned with a broader question of the boundaries of the law of negligence and the duty of care, which do not concern us.

Accordingly the phrase "actual bodily harm" is capable of including psychiatric injury. But it does not include mere emotions such as fear or distress nor panic nor does it include, as such, states of mind that are not themselves evidence of some identifiable clinical condition. The phrase "state of mind" is not a scientific one and should be avoided in considering whether or not a psychiatric injury has been caused; its use is likely to create in the minds of the jury the impression that something which is not more than a strong emotion, such as extreme fear or panic, can amount to actual bodily harm. It cannot. Similarly juries should not be directed that an assault which causes an hysterical and nervous condition is an assault occasioning actual bodily harm. Where there is evidence that the assault has caused some psychiatric injury, the jury should be directed that that injury is capable of amounting to actual bodily harm; otherwise there should be no reference to the mental state of the victim following the assault unless it be relevant to some other aspect of the case, as it was in *R. v. Roberts*, 56 Cr.App.R. 95. It is also relevant to have in mind the relationship between the offence of aggravated assault comprised in section 47 and simple assault. The latter can include conduct which causes the victim to apprehend immediate and unlawful violence: *Fagan v. Metropolitan Police Commissioner* [1969] 1 Q.B. 439. To treat the victim's fear of such unlawful violence, without more, as amounting to actual bodily harm would be to risk rendering the definition of the aggravated offence academic in many cases.

In any case where psychiatric injury is relied upon as the basis for an allegation of bodily harm, and the matter has not been admitted by the defence, expert evidence should be called by the prosecution. It should not be left to be inferred by the jury from the general facts of the case. In the absence of appropriate expert evidence a question whether or not the assault occasioned psychiatric injury should not be left to the jury . . .

Appeal allowed
conviction quashed

Note

The decision in *Chan-Fook* was confirmed by the House of Lords in *Ireland and Burstow* [1998] A.C. 147. What is required is proof of a psychiatric condition supported by expert evidence. In *Morris* [1998] 1 Cr.App.R. 386 evidence from V's general practitioner that she suffered anxiety, fear, tearfulness, sleeplessness and physical tenseness was held to be insufficient to establish actual bodily harm.

For the *mens rea* required for this offence, see *R. v. Savage, R. v. Parmenter, post*, p. 662.

3. MALICIOUS WOUNDING AND WOUNDING WITH INTENT

i. Malicious Wounding

Offences Against the Person Act 1861, section 20

Whosoever shall unlawfully and maliciously wound or inflict any grievous bodily harm upon any other person, either with or without any weapon or instrument, shall be guilty of [an offence and liable to a maximum penalty of five years' imprisonment].

Notes

Unlawfully: see Justifications, above.

Wound: In *C. v. Eisenhower* [1984] Q.B. 331 (D.C.), the victim was shot and an airgun pellet hit him near the eye. He sustained a bruise just below the eyebrow and fluid filling the front part of the eye for a time contained red blood cells. *Held*, a wound is a break in the continuity of the whole skin, and an internal rupturing of the blood vessels is not a wound.

Grievous bodily harm: The Court of Criminal Appeal in *R. v. Metharam* [1961] 3 All E.R. 200 adopted the dictum of Viscount Kilmuir in *D.P.P. v. Smith, ante,* p. 518, that "bodily harm" needs no explanation and "grievous" means no more and no less than "really serious."

Inflict: does "inflict" in section 20 have a narrower meaning than "cause" in section 18? In *Clarence, ante,* p. 646, it was held that proof of an assault was required to establish this offence. In *Wilson* [1984] A.C. 242, the issue arose whether, on a trial on indictment for a charge under section 20, a jury, which was not satisfied that the victim had sustained a wound or that the injury inflicted amounted to GBH, could convict the accused of the section 47 offence if satisfied that the harm amounted to actual bodily harm. Section 6(3) of the Criminal Law Act 1967 permitted a jury to convict of another offence where "the allegations in the indictment amount to or include (expressly or by implication) an allegation of another offence". The House of Lords held that an accused could inflict GBH without necessarily committing a technical assault or battery. Thus if the allegation in the indictment for a section 20 offence did not "amount to or include" an assault, a conviction of the section 47 offence as an alternative at that trial was not possible. The option of convicting of the section 47 offence should only be presented where the prosecution had presented evidence which pointed to an assault. *Wilson* established, accordingly, that 'inflict' has a wider meaning than "assault" but did not resolve the issue whether it had as wide a meaning as "cause" in section 18. Their Lordships were content to cite with approval the Australian case of Salisbury [1976] V.R. 452, 461 where it was stated that;

> Grievous bodily harm may be inflicted . . . either where the accused has directly and violently 'inflicted' it by doing something, intentionally, which, though it is not itself a direct application of force to the body of the victim, does directly result in force being applied violently to the body of the victim, so that he suffers grievous bodily harm.

It was left to the following case to resolve the issue.

R. v. Ireland; R. v. Burstow
House of Lords
[1997] A.C. 147

The appellant, Burstow, was obsessed with S and stalked her over a period of several years. B had appeared before the courts on numerous occasions as a result of his behaviour towards S and had served three prison sentences. Between February and July 1995 B had, *inter alia,* sent S menacing letters and photographs, repeatedly telephoned her and visited her home. As a result of his actions S suffered from severe depression which was described as "grievous harm of a psychiatric nature". B was charged with inflicting grievous bodily harm contrary to section 20 of the 1861 Act. The defence argued that the House of Lords decision in *Wilson* dictated that a charge under section 20 was inappropriate there being neither an assault nor any force being applied violently to the body of the victim. The prosecution argued that "inflict upon" meant "impose upon" and that the court was not bound by *Wilson* to follow *Salisbury.* The trial judge ruled that *Salisbury* did not correctly define English law and that a charge under section 20 was appropriate. B pleaded guilty and appealed.

His appeal was dismissed by the Court of Appeal which certified the following point of law of general public importance for the consideration of the House of Lords, namely: "Whether an offence of inflicting grievous bodily harm under section 20 of the Offences Against the Person Act 1861 can be committed where no physical violence is applied directly or indirectly to the body of the victim."

Lord Steyn: . . .

Reg. v. Burstow: the meaning of 'inflict' in section 20

The decision in *Reg.* v. *Chan-Fook* opened up the possibility of applying sections 18, 20 and 47 in new circumstances. The appeal of Burstow lies in respect of his conviction under section 20. It was conceded that in principle the wording of section 18, and in particular the words "cause any grievous bodily harm to any person" do not preclude a prosecution in cases where the actus reus is the causing of psychiatric injury. But counsel laid stress on the difference between "causing" grievous bodily harm in section 18 and "inflicting" grievous bodily harm in section 20. Counsel argued that the difference in wording reveals a difference in legislative intent: inflict is a narrower concept than cause. This argument loses sight of the genesis of sections 18 and 20. [As the different sections in the 1861 Act were derived from different Acts passed at different times and in differing circumstances] the difference in language is therefore not a significant factor.

Counsel for Burstow then advanced a sustained argument that an assault is an ingredient of an offence under section 20. He referred your Lordships to cases which in my judgment simply do not yield what he sought to extract from them. In any event, the tour of the cases revealed conflicting dicta, no authority binding on the House of Lords, and no settled practice holding expressly that assault was an ingredient of section 20. And, needless to say, none of the cases focused on the infliction of psychiatric injury. . . . Counsel's argument can only prevail if one may supplement the section by reading it as providing "inflict by assault any grievous bodily harm." Such an implication is, however, not necessary. On the contrary, section 20, like section 18, works perfectly satisfactorily without such an implication. I would reject this part of counsel's argument.

But counsel had a stronger argument when he submitted that it is inherent in the word "inflict" that there must be a direct or indirect application of force to the body. Counsel cited the speech of Lord Roskill in *Reg.* v. *Wilson (Clarence)* [1984] A.C. 242, 259e–260h, in which Lord Roskill quoted with approval from the judgment of the full court of the Supreme Court of Victoria in *Reg.* v. *Salisbury* [1976] V.R. 452. There are passages that give assistance to counsel's argument. But Lord Roskill expressly stated, at p. 260h, that he was

> "content to accept, as did the [court in *Salisbury*] that there can be the infliction of grievous bodily harm contrary to section 20 without an assault being committed."

In the result the effect of the decisions in *Reg.* v. *Wilson* and *Reg.* v. *Salisbury* is neutral in respect of the issue as to the meaning of "inflict." Moreover, in *Reg.* v. *Burstow* [1997] 1 Cr.App.R. 144, 149, Lord Bingham of Cornhill C.J. pointed out that in *Reg.* v. *Mandair* [1995] 1 A.C. 208, 215, Lord Mackay of Clashfern L.C. observed with the agreement of the majority of the House of Lords: "In my opinion . . . the word 'cause' is wider or at least not narrower than the word 'inflict.' " Like Lord Bingham C.J. I regard this observation as making clear that in the context of the Act of 1861 there is no radical divergence between the meaning of the two words.

That leaves the troublesome authority of the Court for Crown Cases Reserved in *Reg. v. Clarence* (1888) 22 Q.B.D. 23 . . .. The case was complicated by an issue of consent. But it must be accepted that in a case where there was direct physical contact the majority ruled that the requirement of infliction was not satisfied. This decision has never been overruled. It assists counsel's argument. But it seems to me that what detracts from the weight to be given to the dicta in *Reg. v. Clarence* is that none of the judges in that case had before them the possibility of the inflicting, or causing, of psychiatric injury. The criminal law has moved on in the light of a developing understanding of the link between the body and psychiatric injury. In my judgment *Reg. v. Clarence* no longer assists.

The problem is one of construction. The question is whether as a matter of current usage the contextual interpretation of "inflict" can embrace the idea of one person inflicting psychiatric injury on another. One can without straining the language in any way answer that question in the affirmative. I am not saying that the words "cause" and "inflict" are exactly synonymous. They are not. What I am saying is that in the context of the Act of 1861 one can nowadays quite naturally speak of inflicting psychiatric injury. Moreover, there is internal contextual support in the statute for this view. It would be absurd to differentiate between sections 18 and 20 in the way argued on behalf of Burstow. As Lord Bingham C.J. observed in *Reg. v. Burstow* [1997] 1 Cr.App.R. 144, 149f, this should be a very practical area of the law. The interpretation and approach should, so far as possible be adopted which treats the ladder of offences as a coherent body of law. Once the decision in *Reg. v. Chan-Fook* [1994] 1 W.L.R. 689 is accepted the realistic possibility is opened up of prosecuting under section 20 in cases of the type which I described in the introduction to this judgment.

For the reasons I have given I would answer the certified question in *Reg. v. Burstow* in the affirmative.

LORD HOPE OF CRAIGHEAD: . . .

Reg. v. Burstow: "inflict"

In this case the appellant changed his plea to guilty after a ruling by the trial judge that the offence of unlawfully and maliciously inflicting grievous bodily harm contrary to section 20 of the Act of 1861 may be committed where no physical violence has been applied directly or indirectly to the body of the victim. Counsel for the appellant accepted that if *Reg.* v. *Chan-Fook* [1994] 1 W.L.R. 689 was correctly decided, with the result that "actual bodily harm" in section 47 is capable of including psychiatric injury, the victim in this case had suffered grievous bodily harm within the meaning of section 20. But he submitted that no offence against section 20 had been committed in this case because, although the appellant might be said to have "caused" the victim to sustain grievous bodily harm, he had not "inflicted" that harm on her because he had not used any personal violence against her.

Counsel based his submission on the decision in *Reg. v. Clarence*, 22 Q.B.D. 23 . . .. It seems to me however that there are three reasons for regarding that case as an uncertain guide to the question which arises where the bodily harm which has resulted from the defendant's conduct consists of psychiatric injury.

The first is that the judges in *Reg. v. Clarence* were concerned with a case of physical, not psychiatric, injury. They did not have to consider the problem which arises where the grievous bodily harm is of a kind which may result without any form of physical contact. The second is that the intercourse had taken place with consent, as the defendant's wife was ignorant of his venereal disease. So there was no question in that case of an assault having been committed, if there was no element of violence or battery. Also, as Lord Roskill pointed out in *Reg. v. Wilson (Clarence)* [1984] A.C. 242, 260c the judgments of the judges who formed the majority are not wholly consistent with each other. This casts some doubt on the weight which should be attached to the judgment when the facts are entirely different, as they are in the present case.

In *Reg. v. Wilson*, Lord Roskill referred, at pp. 259e–260b, with approval to the judgment of the Supreme Court of Victoria in *Reg. v. Salisbury* [1976] V.R. 452, in which the following passage appears, at p. 461:

> "although the word 'inflicts' . . . does not have as wide a meaning as the word 'causes' . . . the word 'inflicts' does have a wider meaning than it would have if it were construed so that inflicting grievous bodily harm always involved assaulting the victim."

Lord Roskill said [1984] A.C. 242, 260h that he was content to accept, as was the full court in *Reg. v. Salisbury*, that there can be an infliction of grievous bodily harm contrary to section 20 without an assault being committed. But these observations do not wholly resolve the issue which arises in this case, in the context of grievous bodily harm which consists only of psychiatric injury.

The question is whether there is any difference in meaning, in this context, between the word "cause" and the word "inflict." The fact that the word "caused" is used in section 18, whereas the word used in section 20 is "inflict," might be taken at first sight to indicate that there is a difference. But for all practical purposes there is, in my opinion, no difference between these two words. In *Reg. v. Mandair* [1995] 1 A.C. 208, 215b Lord Mackay of Clashfern L.C. said that the word "cause" is wider or at least not narrower than the word "inflict." I respectfully agree with that observation. But I would add that there is this difference, that the word "inflict" implies that the consequence of the act is something which the victim is likely to find unpleasant or harmful. The relationship between cause and effect, when the word "cause" is used, is neutral. It may embrace pleasure as well as pain. The relationship when the word "inflict" is used is more precise, because it invariably implies detriment to the victim of some kind.

In the context of a criminal act therefore the words "cause" and "inflict" may be taken to be interchangeable. As the Supreme Court of Victoria held in *Reg. v. Salisbury* [1976] V.R. 452, it is not a necessary ingredient of the word "inflict" that whatever causes the harm must be applied directly to the victim. It may be applied indirectly, so long as the result is that the harm is caused by what has been done. In my opinion it is entirely consistent with the ordinary use of the word "inflict" in the English language to say that the appellant's actions "inflicted" the psychiatric harm from which the victim has admittedly suffered in this case. The issues which remain are issues of fact and, as the appellant pled guilty to the offence, I would dismiss his appeal.

Appeal dismissed.

Questions

1. Their Lordships considered that *Clarence* was not relevant because it was concerned with physical rather than psychiatric injury. But the certified question covered bodily harm generally. Where does this leave *Clarence*?

2. If, in Lord Steyn's words, the words "cause" and "inflict" are not synonymous, in what way do they differ? Lord Hope"s answer was that the word "inflict implies something which the victim is likely to find unpleasant or harmful". Does this mean that *Brown* needs reconsideration as the "victims" of sado-masochism find pain and injury pleasurable?

3. As a result of this decision and *Ireland* (*ante*, p. 620), is infection by disease or poison (a) an assault? or (b) sufficient for a charge under section 20?

R. v. Savage, R. v. Parmenter
[1992] A.C. 714
House of Lords

Savage intentionally threw beer at Beal, the pint glass left her hand, broke and cut Beal. She was convicted of unlawful wounding, the jury having been directed that if they were sure she deliberately threw the beer but unintentionally let go of the glass, so that Beal was wounded, they could convict of unlawful wounding. On appeal, the Court of Appeal quashed the conviction under section 20, Offences Against the Person Act 1861 but substituted a conviction under section 47. She appealed to the House of Lords.

Parmenter was convicted of inflicting grievous bodily harm, contrary to section 20, on his baby son. His rough handling caused the breaking of the child's arm and leg bones. His case was that he did not realise that his handling of the child would cause injury. The jury were directed that they could convict if they were sure that Parmenter should have foreseen some physical harm, albeit minor, not necessarily grievous bodily harm. On appeal, the Court of Appeal allowed his appeal, but declined to substitute a conviction under section 47. The Crown appealed to the House of Lords. Both appeals were heard together.

LORD ACKNER: after outlining the facts and the certified questions:—My Lords, I will now seek to deal with the issues raised in these appeals seriatim.
. . .

II. *Can a verdict of assault occasioning actual bodily harm be returned upon proof of an assault together with proof of the fact that actual bodily harm was occasioned by the assault, or must the prosecution also prove that the defendant intended to cause some actual bodily harm or was reckless as to whether such harm would be caused?*

Your Lordships are concerned with the mental element of a particular kind of assault, an assault "occasioning actual bodily harm". It is common ground that the mental element of assault is an intention to cause the victim to apprehend immediate and unlawful violence or recklessness whether such apprehension be caused (see *R. v. Venna ante* p. 623). It is of course common ground that Mrs Savage committed an assault upon Miss Beal when she threw the contents of her glass of beer over her. It is also common ground that however the glass came to be broken and Miss

Beal's wrist thereby cut, it was, on the finding of the jury, Mrs Savage's handling of the glass which caused Miss Beal "actual bodily harm". Was the offence thus established or is there a further mental state that has to be established in relation to the bodily harm element of the offence? Clearly the section, by its terms, expressly imposes no such a requirement. Does it do so by necessary implication? It uses neither the word "intentionally" nor the word "maliciously". The words "occasioning actual bodily harm" are descriptive of the word "assault", by reference to a particular kind of consequence.

In neither *R. v. Savage* nor *R. v. Spratt* [1991] 2 All E.R. 210 nor in *R. v. Parmenter* was the court's attention invited to the decision of the Court of Appeal in *R. v. Roberts* (1972) 56 Cr.App.R. 95. This is perhaps explicable on the basis that this case is not referred to in the index to *Archbold's Criminal Pleading, Evidence and Practice* (43rd edn, 1988). The relevant text states (para. 20–117): "The mens rea required [for actual bodily harm] is that required for common assault", without any authority being provided for this proposition.

It is in fact *R. v. Roberts* which provides authority for this proposition. Roberts was tried on an indictment which alleged that he indecently assaulted a young woman. He was acquitted on that charge, but convicted of assault occasioning actual bodily harm to her. The girl's complaint was that while travelling in the defendant's car he sought to make advances towards her and then tried to take her coat off. This was the last straw and, although the car was travelling at some speed, she jumped out and sustained injuries. The defendant denied he had touched the girl. He had had an argument with her and in the course of that argument she suddenly opened the door and jumped out. In his direction to the jury the chairman of quarter sessions stated: "If you are satisfied that he tried to pull off her coat and as a result she jumped out of the moving car then your verdict is guilty."

It was contended on behalf of the appellant that this direction was wrong since the chairman had failed to tell the jury that they must be satisfied that the appellant foresaw that she might jump out of the car as a result of his touching her before they could convict. The court rejected that submission. The test was, said the court (at 102):

"Was it [the action of the victim which resulted in actual bodily harm] the natural result of what the alleged assailant said and did, in the sense that it was something that could reasonably have been foreseen as the consequence of what he was saying or doing? As it was put in one of the old cases, it had got to be shown to be his act, and if of course the victim does something so 'daft', in the words of the appellant in this case, or so unexpected, not that this particular assailant did not actually foresee it but that no reasonable man could be expected to foresee it, then it is only in a very remote and unreal sense a consequence of his assault, it is really occasioned by a voluntary act on the part of the victim which could not reasonably be foreseen and which breaks the chain of causation between the assault and the harm or injury."

Accordingly, no fault was found in the following direction of the chairman to the jury (at 103):

"If you accept the evidence of the girl in preference to that of the man, that means that there was an assault occasioning actual bodily harm, that means that she did jump out as a direct result of what he was threatening her with, and what he was doing to her, holding her coat, telling her that he had beaten up girls who had refused his advances,

and that means that through his acts he was in law and in fact responsible for the injuries which were caused to her by her decision, if it can
be called that, to get away from his violence, his threats, by jumping
out of the car."

Thus, once the assault was established, the only remaining question
was whether the victim's conduct was the natural consequence of that
assault. The words "occasioning" raised solely a question of causation, an
objective question which does not involve inquiring into the accused's
state of mind.

In *R. v. Spratt* [1991] 2 All E.R. 210 at 219, McCowan L.J. said:

"However, the history of the interpretation of the 1861 Act shows that,
whether or not the word 'maliciously' appears in the section in question, the courts have consistently held that the mens rea of every type
of offence against the person covers both actual intent and recklessness,
in the sense of taking the risk of harm ensuing with foresight that it
might happen."

McCowan L.J. then quoted a number of authorities for that proposition.
The first is *R. v. Ward* (1871) L.R. 1 C.C.R. 356, but that was a case where
the prisoner was charged with wounding with intent (s.18) and convicted
of malicious wounding (s.20); next, *R. v. Bradshaw* (1878) 14 Cox C.C. 83,
but that was a case where the accused was charged with manslaughter,
which has nothing to do with a s.47 case. Then *R. v. Cunningham* [1957] 2
Q.B. 396 is quoted, a case under s.23 of the Act concerned with unlawfully
and maliciously administering etc. a noxious thing which endangers life.
And, finally *R. v. Venna, ante*, p. 623 in which there was no issue as to
whether in a s.47 case, recklessness had to extend to actual bodily harm.
Thus none of the cases cited was concerned with the mental element
required in s.47 cases. Nevertheless, the Court of Appeal in *R. v. Parmenter*
[1991] 2 All E.R. 225 at 232, preferred the decision in *R. v. Spratt* to that
of *R. v. Savage* because the former was "founded on a line of authority
leading directly to the conclusion there expressed".

My Lords, in my respectful view, the Court of Appeal in *R. v. Parmenter*
was wrong in preferring the decision in *R. v. Spratt*. The decision in *R. v.
Roberts* was correct. The verdict of assault occasioning actual bodily harm
may be returned upon proof of an assault together with proof of the fact
that actual bodily harm was occasioned by the assault. The prosecution
are not obliged to prove that the defendant intended to cause some actual
bodily harm or was reckless as to whether such harm would be caused.

III. *In order to establish an offence under s.20 of the 1861 Act, must the prosecution prove that the defendant actually foresaw that his act would cause harm, or
is it sufficient to prove that he ought so to have foreseen?*
[His Lordship concluded that the answer is that the prosecution must
prove that the defendant actually foresaw that his act would cause harm.
For his consideration of this question, see *ante*, p. 138]

IV. *In order to establish an offence under s.20 is it sufficient to prove that the
defendant intended or foresaw the risk of some physical harm or must he intend
or foresee either wounding or grievous bodily harm?*
It is convenient to set out once again the relevant part of the judgment
of Diplock L.J. in *R. v. Mowatt* [1968] 1 Q.B. 421 at 426. Having considered
Professor Kenny's statement, which I have quoted above, he then said:

In the offence under s.20 . . . for . . . which [no] specific intent is
required—the word "maliciously" does import . . . an awareness that

his act may have the consequence of causing some physical harm to some other person. That is what is meant by the "particular kind of harm" in the citation from Professor Kenny's Outlines of Criminal Law (18th edn, 1962, para. 158a, p. 202). It is quite unnecessary that the accused should have foreseen that his unlawful act might cause physical harm of the gravity described in the section, *i.e.* a wound or serious physical injury. *"It is enough that he should have foreseen that some physical harm to some person, albeit of a minor character, might result."* (My emphasis.)

Mr Sedley submits that this statement of the law is wrong. He contends that, properly construed, the section requires foresight of a wounding or grievous bodily harm. He drew your Lordships' attention to criticisms of *R. v. Mowatt* made by Professor Glanville Williams and by Professor J. C. Smith in their textbooks and in articles or commentaries. They argue that a person should not be criminally liable for consequences of his conduct unless he foresaw a consequence falling into the same legal category as that set out in the indictment.

Such a general principle runs contrary to the decision in *R. v. Roberts*, which I have already stated to be, in my opinion, correct. The contention is apparently based on the proposition that, as the actus reus of a s.20 offence is the wounding or the infliction of grievous bodily harm, the mens rea must consist of foreseeing such wounding or grievous bodily harm. But there is no such hard and fast principle. To take but two examples, the actus reus of murder is the killing of the victim, but foresight of grievous bodily harm is sufficient and, indeed, such bodily harm need not be such as to be dangerous to life. Again, in the case of manslaughter death is frequently the unforeseen consequence of the violence used.

The argument that, as ss.20 and 47 have both the same penalty, this somehow supports the proposition that the foreseen consequences must coincide with the harm actually done, overlooks the oft-repeated statement that this is the irrational result of this piecemeal legislation. The Act "is a rag-bag of offences brought together from a wide variety of sources with no attempt, as the draftsman frankly acknowledged, to introduce consistency as to substance or as to form" (see Professor J. C. Smith in his commentary on *R. v. Parmenter* ([1991] Crim.L.R. 43)).

If s.20 was to be limited to cases where the accused does not desire but does foresee wounding or grievous bodily harm, it would have a very limited scope. The mens rea in a s.20 crime is comprised in the word "maliciously". As was pointed out by Lord Lane C.J., giving the judgment of the Court of Appeal in *R. v. Sullivan* [1981] Crim.L.R. 46, the "particular kind of harm" in the citation from Professor Kenny was directed to "harm to the person" as opposed to "harm to property". Thus it was not concerned with the degree of the harm foreseen. It is accordingly in my judgment wrong to look upon the decision in *R. v. Mowatt* as being in any way inconsistent with the decision in *R. v. Cunningham*.

My Lords, I am satisfied that the decision in *R. v. Mowatt* was correct and that it is quite unnecessary that the accused should either have intended or have foreseen that his unlawful act might cause physical harm of the gravity described in s.20, *i.e.* a wound or serious physical injury. It is enough that he should have foreseen that some physical harm to some person, albeit of a minor character, might result.

In the result I would dismiss the appeal in *Savage's* case but allow the appeal in *Parmenter's* case, but only to the extent of substituting, in accordance with the provisions of s.3(2) of the Criminal Appeal Act 1968, verdicts of guilty of assault occasioning actual bodily harm contrary to s.47 of the 1861 Act for the four s.20 offences of which he was convicted.

[Lords Keith of Kinkel, Brandon of Oakbrook, Jauncey of Tullichettle and Lowry agreed]

Appeal of Savage dismissed;
appeal of Parmenter allowed
in part and conviction of
assault occasioning actual
bodily harm substituted

ii. Wounding with Intent

Offences Against the Person Act 1861, section 18

Whosoever shall unlawfully and maliciously by any means whatever wound, or cause any grievous bodily harm to any person, with intent . . . to do some grievous bodily harm to any person, or with intent to resist or prevent the lawful apprehension or detainer of any person, shall be guilty of [an offence and shall be liable to imprisonment for life].

Notes

1. The chief difference between the offences in section 18 and section 20 are: (1) in section 20 the *mens rea* resides in the word "maliciously", whereas in section 18, that word "adds nothing" to the definition, since the *mens rea* is defined expressly: *R. v. Mowatt* [1968] 1 Q.B. 421, 426; (2) in section 18 the wound or grievous bodily harm may be caused to "any person" whereas section 20 refers to "any other person" which gives rise to the interesting possibility that D could be prosecuted for the section 18 offence where he causes GBH or a wound to himself, for example, to gain discharge from military service.

2. In *R. v. Bryson* [1985] Crim.L.R. 669, a case in which D's car drove into a group of people, allegedly as a deliberate act by D, a conviction under section 18 followed a direction "that (if he was driving) foresight of probable serious harm, whether he wished it or not, amounted to an intention to cause grievous bodily harm". This was held to be wrong, although in view of the overwhelming evidence of intention, the proviso was applied to uphold the conviction.

Questions

1. What lines should the direction have taken? See *ante*, p. 138.

2. Is it a defence to a charge under section 18 that D did not have the appropriate intention by reason of voluntary intoxication? See *ante*, p. 252.

3. Is intentional infection by disease capable of being an offence under section 18?

R. v. Bentley
(1850) 4 Cox 406
Central Criminal Court

V, a P.C. in plain clothes, but accompanied by others in uniform, informed D that he was arresting him for suspicion of highway robbery. V had no warrant, but reasonably believed that D was guilty. D refused to be arrested unless told why and by what authority he was being apprehended, and resisted, injuring V. At D's trial for wounding with intent to resist lawful apprehension, it was objected on his behalf that it was not shown that he knew the arrest was unlawful.

TALFORD J.: If the apprehension is in point of fact lawful, we are not permitted to consider the question, whether or not he believed it to be so, because that would lead to infinite niceties of discrimination. The rule is not, that a man is always presumed to know the law, but that no man shall be excused for an unlawful act from his ignorance of the law. It was the prisoner's duty, whatever might be his consciousness of innocence, to go to the station house and hear the precise accusations against him. He is not to erect a tribunal in his own mind to decide whether he was legally arrested or not. He was taken into custody by an officer of the law, and it was his duty to obey the law.

Verdict: Guilty

Questions

What is D's position with respect to a charge under section 18 in the following cases?

1. V, seeking lawfully to arrest D, laid hands on him. D, believing that V was a person attempting to rob him, punched V on the jaw, breaking it. D admits that his belief was unreasonable, and that the force he used was more than was reasonably necessary to defend himself, but claims he did not intend or expect to break V's jaw. See Chapter 5, *ante* and *Blackburn v. Bowering* [1995] Crim L.R. 38.

2. D pushes over V in order to resist what they both think is a lawful arrest by V. In the fall, V suffers a broken skull. In fact the arrest is unlawful. See Chapter 3, *ante*.

iii. Proposals for Reform

In 1998 the Home Office issued a consultation paper, *Violence: Reforming the Offences Against the Person Act 1861* together with a Draft Offences Against the Person Bill. The consultation and Bill largely adopted the proposals made by the Law Commission in its Report *Legislating the Criminal Code: Offences Against the Person and General Principles* (Law Com. No. 218).

Violence: Reforming the Offences Against the Person Act 1861
Home Office (1998)

1.2 Reforming the law on violence against the person is not just an academic exercise—criminal cases involving non-fatal offences against the person make up a large part of the work of the courts and cost a great deal of taxpayers money. In 1996 83,000 cases came before the courts. It is therefore particularly important that the law governing such behaviour should be robust, clear and well understood. Unclear or uncertain criminal law risks creating injustice and unfairness to individuals as well as making the work of the police and courts far more difficult and time-consuming. The Government's aim is that the proposed new offences should enable violence to be dealt with effectively by the courts and that the law should be set out in clear terms and in plain, modern language. That is what the draft Bill contained in this consultation paper does. It is intended to help not only practitioners of the law but anyone who find themselves involved in court cases, whether as a defendant, victim or witness. . . .

2.1 This paper sets out the Government's proposals for the reform of the law for dealing with non-fatal violence against the person. It does not deal with the law on murder or manslaughter. It does not attempt to be a full codification of the law in this area, or to replace all the common law offences that relate to violence. Its primary purpose is to replace the outdated offences contained in the Offences Against the Person Act 1861 with a rational and coherent set of new offences. In doing so it is not the Government's intention to alter fundamentally the scope or operation of the law. It does not intend to make the law either tougher or more lenient, but to make it clearer and easier to use. In one or two minor respects the proposals will extend the scope of the present law to fill gaps that have been identified, and a few apparently archaic offences are being retained because they are still useful to the prosecuting authorities. . . .

Background

2.2 The law on Offences Against the Person has long been criticised by judges and lawyers as archaic, confusing, and unhelpful to all those involved in the criminal justice system. Some have also argued that the state of the law in these areas creates unnecessary and expensive appeals arising from wrong decisions on questions of law. It was against this background of general criticism that in November 1993, as a step towards codification of the criminal law, the Law Commission published its report No. 218 "Offences against the Person and General Principles", from which the current proposals are derived. . . .

3.2 Our proposals do not extend to all the issues covered in L.C.218. The Government has taken the view that the outdated offences in the 1861 Act are in the most urgent need of reform. These are the offences which cause the greatest difficulties for the courts, and are most obviously in need of modernisation. The priority in this law reform is therefore to place the main offences against the person on a good foundation. In doing so, we have examined all the relevant provisions in the 1861 Act, and have also taken those other parts of the Law Commission's recommendations that are particularly relevant to offences of violence and included them in the draft Bill. Hence we have taken the Law Commission's recommendations on omissions and supervening fault, and included them in our draft Bill. . . .

The Government's Proposals

. . .

Transmission of illness and disease

3.13 . . . In L.C. 218 the Law Commission were unequivocal that the Offences Against the Person Act 1861 could be used to prosecute the transmission of disease, and recommended that the proposed new offences should enable the intentional or reckless transmission of disease to be prosecuted in appropriate cases. The Government has not accepted this recommendation in full.

3.14 There are few decided cases on this point, so the position in the criminal law is not entirely clear. . . . In reforming the law, the issue of whether and if so how the transmission of disease should fall within the criminal law needs the most careful consideration.

3.15 The Government recognises that this is a very sensitive issue. The criminal law deals with behaviour that is wrong in intent and in deed. The Law Commission's original proposal, which included illness and disease in the definition of injury, would have resulted in the intentional or reckless transmission of disease being open to prosecution. They argued that the width of their proposal would be balanced by the fact that prosecution would only be appropriate in the most serious cases. The Government has considered their views very carefully, but is not persuaded that it would be right or appropriate to make the range of normal everyday activities during which illness could be transmitted, potentially criminal. We think it would be wrong to criminalise the reckless transmission of normally minor illnesses such as measles or mumps, even though they could have potentially serious consequences for those vulnerable to infection.

3.16 An issue of this importance has ramifications beyond the criminal law, into the wider considerations of social and public health policy. The Government is particularly concerned that the law should not seem to discriminate against those who are HIV positive, have AIDS or viral hepatitis or who carry any kind of disease. Nor do we want to discourage people from coming forward for diagnostic tests and treatment, in the interests of their own health and that of others, because of an unfounded fear of criminal prosecution.

3.17 The Government therefore considered whether it should exclude all transmission of disease from the criminal law, and concluded that that too would not be appropriate. The existing law extends into this area, even though it has not been used. There is a strong case for arguing that society should have criminal sanctions available for use to deal with evil acts. It is hard to argue that the law should not be able to deal with the person who gives a disease causing serious illness to others with intent to do them such harm. That is clearly a form of violence against the person. Such a gap in the law would be difficult to justify.

3.18 The Government therefore proposes that the criminal law should apply only to those whom it can be proved beyond reasonable doubt had deliberately transmitted a disease intending to cause a serious illness. This aims to strike a sensible balance between allowing very serious intentional acts to be punished whilst not rendering individuals liable for prosecution for unintentional or reckless acts, or for the transmission of minor disease. The Government believes that this is close to the effect of the present law, and that it is right in principle to continue to allow the law to be used in those rare grave cases where prosecution would be justified. This proposal will clarify the present law which, because it is largely untested is unclear; by doing so the effect of the law will be confined to the most serious and culpable behaviour.

3.19 It is important to emphasise that *this proposal does not reflect a significant change in the law.* Prosecutions for the transmission of disease are very rare for very good reasons. Any criminal charge has to be supported by evidence and proved to a court beyond reasonable doubt. It is very difficult to prove both the causal linkage of the transmission and also to prove that it was done intentionally. To do so beyond reasonable doubt is even more difficult. The Government does not expect that the proposed offence will be used very often, but considers that it is important that it should exist to provide a safeguard against the worst behaviour.

3.20 Clause 15 provides for the intentional transmission of serious injury or disease to be included for the purposes of clause 1 (intentional serious injury), but not for any other purpose. This means that only those who transmit diseases with intent to cause serious injury, will be criminally liable.

Draft Offences Against the Person Bill

1.—(1) A person is guilty of an offence if he intentionally causes serious injury to another.

(2) A person is guilty of an offence if he omits to do an act which he has a duty to do at common law, the omission results in serious injury to another, and he intends the omission to have that result.

. . .

2.—(1) A person is guilty of an offence if he recklessly causes serious injury to another.

. . .

3.—(1) A person is guilty of an offence if he intentionally or recklessly causes injury to another.

. . .

4.—(1) A person is guilty of an offence if—

(a) he intentionally or recklessly applies force to or causes an impact on the body of another, or
(b) he intentionally or recklessly causes the other to believe that any such force or impact is imminent.

(2) No such offence is committed if the force or impact, not being intended or likely to cause injury, is in the circumstances such as is generally acceptable in the ordinary conduct of daily life and the defendant does not know or believe that it is in fact unacceptable to the other person.

. . .

6.—(1) A person is guilty of an offence under this section if he causes serious injury to another intending to resist, prevent or terminate the lawful arrest or detention of himself or a third person.

(2) The question whether the defendant believes the arrest or detention is lawful must be determined according to the circumstances as he believes them to be.

. . .

7.—(1) A person is guilty of an offence if he assaults another intending to resist, prevent or terminate the lawful arrest or detention of himself or a third person.

(2) The question whether the defendant believes the arrest or detention is lawful must be determined according to the circumstances as he believes them to be.

(3) For the purposes of this section a person assaults if he commits the offence under section 4.

. . .

8.—(1) A person is guilty of an offence if he acts as mentioned in subsection (2) and-

(a) he intends to cause serious injury, or
(b) he is reckless whether serious injury is caused.

(2) A person acts as mentioned in this subsection if he—

(a) causes an explosive substance to explode,
(b) places a dangerous substance in any place,
(c) delivers or sends a dangerous substance to a person,
(d) throws a dangerous substance at or near a person, or
(e) applies a dangerous substance to a person.

(3) For the purposes of subsection (2) a dangerous substance is an explosive substance or any other dangerous substance.
(4) In this section "explosive substance" has the same meaning as in the Explosive Substances Act 1883.
. . .

9.—(1) A person is guilty of an offence if he acts as mentioned in section 8(2) and—

(a) he intends to cause injury, or risk injury, or
(b) he is reckless whether injury is caused.
. . .

10.—(1) A person is guilty of an offence if he makes to another a threat to cause the death of, or serious injury to, that other or a third person, intending that other to believe that it will be carried out.
. . .

11.—(1) A person is guilty of an offence if—

(a) he administers a substance to another or causes it to be taken by him and (in either case) he does so intentionally or recklessly,
(b) he knows the substance is capable of causing injury to the other, and
(c) it is unreasonable to administer the substance or cause it to be taken having regard to the circumstances as he knows or believes them to be.
. . .

12.—(1) A person is guilty of an offence if he intentionally inflicts severe pain or suffering on another and he does the act—

(a) in the performance or purported performance of his of official duties as a public official, or
(b) at the instigation or with the consent or acquiescence of a public official who is performing or purporting to perform his official duties.

(2) A person is guilty of an offence if—

(a) he omits to do an act which he has a duty to do at common law,
(b) he makes the omission as mentioned in subsection (1)(a) or (b),

(c) the omission results in the infliction of severe pain or suffering on another, and

(d) he intends the omission to have that result.

(3) The following are immaterial—

(a) the nationality of the persons concerned;
(b) whether anything occurs in the United Kingdom or elsewhere;
(c) whether the pain or suffering is physical or mental.

. . .

Meaning of fault terms and of injury

14.—(1) A person acts intentionally with respect to a result if—

(a) it is his purpose to cause it, or
(b) although it is not his purpose to cause it, he knows that it would occur in the ordinary course of events if he were to succeed in his purpose of causing some other result.

(2) A person acts recklessly with respect to a result if he is aware of a risk that it will occur and it is unreasonable to take that risk having regard to the circumstances as he knows or believes them to be.

(3) A person intends an omission to have a result if—

(a) it is his purpose that the result will occur, or
(b) although it is not his purpose that the result will occur, he knows that it would occur in the ordinary course of events if he were to succeed in his purpose that some other result will occur.

(4) A person is reckless whether an omission will have a result if he is aware of a risk that the result will occur and it is unreasonable to take that risk having regard to the circumstances as he knows or believes them to be.

(5) Related expressions must be construed accordingly.

(6) This section has effect for the purposes of this Act.

15.—(1) In this Act "injury" means—

(a) physical injury, or
(b) mental injury.

(2) Physical injury does not include anything caused by disease but (subject to that) it includes pain, unconsciousness and any other impairment of a person's physical condition.

(3) Mental injury does not include anything caused by disease but (subject to that) it includes any impairment of a person's mental health.

(4) In its application to section 1 this section applies without the exceptions relating to things caused by disease.

Matters affecting liability

16.—(1) Where it is an offence under this Act to be at fault in causing a result by an act and a person lacks the fault required when he does an act that may cause or does cause the result, he nevertheless commits the offence if—

(a) being aware that he has done the act and that the result may occur or (as the case may be) has occurred and may continue, and

(b) with the fault required,

he fails to take reasonable steps to prevent the result occurring or continuing and it does occur or continue.

(2) Where it is an offence under this Act to be at fault in causing a result by an omission and a person lacks the fault required when he makes an omission that may cause or does cause the result, he nevertheless commits the offence if—

(a) being aware that he has made the omission and that the result may occur or (as the case may be) has occurred and may continue, and

(b) with the fault required,

he fails to take reasonable steps to prevent the result occurring or continuing and it does occur or continue.

(3) For the purposes of this section fault is intention or recklessness, and references to a person being at fault must be construed accordingly.

(4) Common law rules relating to matters provided for in this section do not apply to offences under this Act.

17.—(1) This section applies in determining whether a person is guilty of an offence under this Act.

(2) A person's intention, or awareness of a risk, that his act will cause a result in relation to a person capable of being the victim of the offence must be treated as an intention or (as the case may be) awareness of a risk that his act will cause that result in relation to any other person affected by his act.

(3) A person's intention, or awareness of a risk, that his omission will have a result in relation to a person capable of being the victim of the offence must be treated as an intention or (as the case may be) awareness of a risk that his omission will have that result in relation to any other person affected as a result of his omission.

(4) Common law rules relating to matters provided for in this section do not apply to offences under this Act.

18.—(1) The provisions of this Act have effect subject to any enactment or rule of law providing—

(a) a defence, or

(b) lawful authority, justification or excuse for an act or omission.

. . .

19.—(1) For the purposes of this Act a person who was voluntarily intoxicated at any material time must be treated—

(a) as having been aware of any risk of which he would have been aware had he not been intoxicated, and

(b) as having known or believed in any circumstances which he would have known or believed in had he not been intoxicated.

(2) Whether a person is voluntarily intoxicated for this purpose must be determined in accordance with the following provisions.

(3) A person is voluntarily intoxicated if—

(a) he takes an intoxicant otherwise than properly for a medicinal purpose,
(b) he is aware that it is or may be an intoxicant, and
(c) he takes it in such a quantity as impairs his awareness or understanding.

(4) An intoxicant, although taken for a medicinal purpose, is not properly so taken if—

(a) the intoxicant is not taken on medical advice, and the taker is aware that the taking may result in his doing an act or making an omission capable of constituting an offence of the kind in question, or
(b) the intoxicant is taken on medical advice, but the taker fails then or afterwards to comply with any condition forming part of the advice and he is aware that the failure may result in his doing an act or making an omission capable of constituting an offence of the kind in question.

(5) Intoxication must be presumed to have been voluntary unless there is adduced such evidence as might lead the court or jury to conclude that there is a reasonable possibility that the intoxication was involuntary.

(6) An intoxicant is any alcohol, drug or other thing which, when taken into the body, may impair the awareness or understanding of the person taking it.

(7) A person must be treated as taking an intoxicant if he permits it to be administered to him.

Scale of Maximum Penalties

Section	Trial on Indictment	Summary Trial
1	Imprisonment for life	
2	Imprisonment for 7 years	Imprisonment for 6 months or a fine not exceeding the statutory maximum or both
3	Imprisonment for 5 years	Imprisonment for 6 months or a fine not exceeding the statutory maximum or both
4		Imprisonment for 6 months or a fine not exceeding level 5 on the standard scale or both.
6	Imprisonment for life	
7	Imprisonment for 2 years	Imprisonment for 6 months or a fine not exceeding the statutory maximum or both
8	Imprisonment for life	
9	Imprisonment for 14 years	
10	Imprisonment for 10 years	Imprisonment for 6 months or a fine not exceeding the statutory maximum or both
11	Imprisonment for 5 years	Imprisonment for 6 months or a fine not exceeding the statutory maximum or both
12	Imprisonment for life	

Notes and Questions

1. Note that the harm intended or foreseen must now correspond to the offence committed whereas under the current law foresight of a lesser degree of harm, *e.g.* ABH, is sufficient to support a conviction for an offence involving a greater degree of harm, e.g. GBH.

2. The anomaly of a wound being treated as of equal seriousness to inflicting GBH, even though the wound is only minor, is removed.

3. The fault requirements are expressed only to apply to this statute. Should they apply generally to all offences? Is the definition of "intention" as clear and comprehensive as it might be? (See *ante*, pp. 85ff.)

4. In clauses 1 and 2 a distinction in terms of culpability is drawn between serious injury caused intentionally and such an injury caused recklessly. No distinction is drawn in clause 3 between intention and recklessness in respect of "injury". This reflects the view of the Law Commission in Law Com. No.218, para. 13.4 that such a distinction "would over-complicate the law". Is this view supportable or is there a potential for injustice?

5. Note that liability for omissions is limited to intentionally causing serious injury. How does this compare to the current law (see *ante*, pp. 26ff)?

6. The proposals involve the criminalization of the intentional transmission of disease where this involves serious injury. Is there a risk of injustice from reckless transmission of disease leading to serious injury not being criminalized?

7. During the final cricket test match of a five match series between England and Australia, D, the cook at the cricket ground deliberately contaminates the food served to the Australian players causing them sickness and diarrhoea. As a result of their debilitation which lasts for 36–48 hours, the Australian players play very badly and England wins the match and the series. Consider D's criminal liability on the assumption that the Draft Bill has become law where (a) the contaminant used was a chemical purgative, and (b) where the contaminant was a culture of bacteria which cause food poisoning. Is there any difference in either the harm caused, or the culpability of D, in each situation?

4. SEXUAL OFFENCES

i. Rape

Note

The offence of rape was reformed in a major way in 1994. Following the decision of the House of Lords in *R. v. R.* [1991] 1 A.C. 599 where it was held that a husband could be convicted of the rape of his wife, Parliament placed this decision on a statutory footing in section 142 of the Criminal Justice and Public Order Act 1994 which substituted for section 1 of the Sexual Offences Act 1956 a new section 1 containing a new and expanded definition of the offence. For the first time the victim of rape may be either male or female and sexual intercourse may be vaginal or anal. Prior to this enactment anal intercourse with a non-consenting woman did not constitute rape.

Sexual Offences Act 1956

Rape of woman or man
(1) It is an offence for a man to rape a woman or another man.
(2) A man commits rape if—
(a) he has sexual intercourse with a person (whether vaginal or anal) who at the time of the intercourse does not consent to it; and
(b) at the time he knows that the person does not consent to the intercourse or is reckless as to whether that person consents to it.
(3) A man also commits rape if he induces a married woman to have sexual intercourse with him by impersonating her husband.
(4) Subsection (2) applies for the purpose of any enactment.

Sexual Offences (Amendment) Act 1976

1.(2) It is hereby declared that, if at a trial for a rape offence the jury has to consider whether a man believed that a woman or *man* was consenting to sexual intercourse, the presence or absence of reasonable grounds for such a belief is a matter to which the jury is to have regard, in conjunction with any other relevant matters, in considering whether he so believed.

[The words in italics were inserted by s.168(2) and Schedule 10(35) of the Criminal Justice and Public Order Act 1994.]

Actus Reus

Sexual Offences Act 1956

44. Where, on the trial of any offence under this Act, it is necessary to prove sexual intercourse (whether natural or unnatural), it shall not be necessary to prove the completion of the intercourse by emission of seed, but the intercourse shall be deemed complete upon proof of penetration only.

Kaitamaki v. The Queen
[1985] A.C. 147
Privy Council

K penetrated V believing she consented to intercourse. After he had penetrated her he became aware that she did not consent but he did not desist from intercourse. He was convicted of rape and appealed.

LORD SCARMAN: delivered the opinion of the Committee . . .
[This appeal] raises a question as to the true construction of sections 127 and 128 of the Crimes Act 1961. Section 127 defines sexual intercourse and is in these terms:

"For the purposes of this Part of this Act, sexual intercourse is complete upon penetration; and there shall be no presumption of law that any person is by reason of his age incapable of such intercourse."

Section 128 defines rape and, so far as is material, is in these terms: "(1) Rape is the act of a male person having sexual intercourse with a woman or girl—(a) Without her consent; . . ."

Counsel for the appellant took one point only; but he submitted that it was all he needed. He relied on the definition in section 127 to establish the proposition that rape is penetration without consent: once penetration is complete the act of rape is concluded. Intercourse, if it continues, is not rape, because for the purposes of the Act it is complete upon penetration.

The Court of Appeal by a majority rejected the submission, expressing the opinion that the purpose of section 127 was to remove any doubts as to the minimum conduct needed to prove the fact of sexual intercourse. "Complete" is used in the statutory definition in the sense of having come into existence, but not in the sense of being at an end. Sexual intercourse is a continuing act which only ends with withdrawal. And the offence of rape is defined in section 128 as that of "having" intercourse without consent.

Their Lordships agree with the majority decision of the Court of Appeal, and with the reasons which they gave for rejecting the appellant's submission and for construing the two sections in the way in which they did. As Lord Brightman observed in the course of argument before the Board section 127 says "complete," not "completed.".

Appeal dismissed

Question

In *Cooper and Schaub* [1994] Crim L.R. 531 the Court of Appeal adopted the reasoning of *Kaitamaki* but stated "penetration is a continuing act". Does this difference in terminology have any difference in effect?

Note

On the question of what is consent in offences against the person generally, see *ante*, p. 646. As to rape, see the next case.

R. v. Olugboja
[1982] Q.B. 320
Court of Appeal

L raped V, and then took her companion K into an adjoining room in order to rape her. L's companion O told V that he was going to have intercourse with her and asked her to remove her trousers, which she did because she was frightened. She did not struggle or resist when O had intercourse with her. O was convicted of rape and appealed.

DUNN L.J.: delivering the judgment of the court: The question of law raised by this appeal is whether to constitute the offence of rape it is necessary for the consent of the victim of sexual intercourse to be vitiated by force, the fear of force or fraud, or whether it is sufficient to prove that in fact the victim did not consent. The offence of rape was defined for the first time by statute in 1976. [His Lordship read section 1(1) of the Sexual Offences (Amendment) Act 1976]. In this appeal it is not disputed that the appellant had sexual intercourse with Jayne. The only questions for the jury were whether she had consented, and if she had not whether the appellant knew she had not or was reckless whether she consented or not. In this appeal we are only concerned with the *actus reus* and not with the *mens rea* of the appellant. [He summarised the evidence]. . . .

Counsel for the appellant, in a series of very able submissions, said that these statements by the judge constituted a misdirection. She submitted that the statutory definition of rape introduced by the 1976 amendment into section 1 of the Sexual Offences Act 1956 was declaratory only, and had not changed the common law whereby the type of threat that vitiates consent is limited to threats of violence either to the victim or as in duress to some close or near relative. She relied in support of that submission on a number of cases going back to the middle of the last century. . . .

Counsel for the appellant accepted that submission by the victim did not necessarily involve consent, but contended that the submission must be induced because of fear of violence: see *R. v. Day* (1841) 9 C. & P. 722. She submitted that moral or economic pressure or even blackmail causing a woman to submit to sexual intercourse could never be enough to found a charge of rape. Otherwise, she said, the film producer who induced an actress to have sexual intercourse by telling her she would not get a part in his new film if she did not, or the man who induced a woman to have sexual intercourse by telling her that if she did not he would tell her fiancé that she had been a prostitute, would be guilty of rape.

She submitted that those classes of case would constitute offences under section 2 of the 1956 Act. That section provides:

"(1) It is an offence for a person to procure a woman, by threats of intimidation, to have unlawful sexual intercourse in any part of the world . . ."

Although the section was first enacted in the Criminal Law Amendment Act 1885 and was probably intended to deal with a person who procured a woman to have sexual intercourse with a third party, it also applies to a man who causes a woman to have sexual intercourse with himself. Although the section is little used, counsel for the appellant said that it is apt to cover cases of threats and intimidation falling short of threats of death or violence. The maximum penalty under the section is two years' imprisonment as compared with life imprisonment for rape. It is right that the law should confine rape to the most serious cases and that lesser offences should be dealt with under section 2.

Counsel for the appellant submitted that just as the law limits the circumstances in which any person may say he has acted involuntarily [due] to duress, which involves threats of death or violence to that person or a close relative, so it is consistent that the common law has limited the circumstances in which a woman who has had sexual intercourse may say that the act was not consensual.

Counsel submitted finally that to say, as the judge did, that any constraint on Jayne's will could negative consent constituted a misdirection. The word "constraint" includes moral as well as physical pressure and moral pressure is not enough. Even to tell a girl that she would not be taken home until she had sexual intercourse, in the absence of any threat of violence expressed or implied, would not vitiate her consent.

The definition of rape imported into the 1956 Act by the 1976 amending Act makes no mention of force, fear or fraud. It simply defines rape as being unlawful sexual intercourse with a woman who at the time of the intercourse does not consent to it. The 1976 Act by its long title is described as "An Act to amend the law relating to rape." Is it a true amending Act or is it merely declaratory of the common law? To answer that question it is necessary to look at the history of the legislation.

D.P.P. v. Morgan [1976] A.C 182 (*ante*, p. 151) stated the law of rape as

it then stood. Their Lordships were primarily concerned with the necessary mens rea of the offence. They were not concerned with, nor did they
consider, the actus reus. But there is a passage in the speech of Lord
Hailsham which appears to indicate that he was accepting the common
law definition of rape, that is to say sexual intercourse by force, fear or
fraud (see [1976] A.C. 182 at 210).

Following the decision in *Morgan* an advisory group on the law of rape
was set up under Heilbron J. The group reported to the Home Secretary
on 14th November 1975 (Cmnd. 6352). Like the House of Lords in *Morgan*
they were principally concerned in the material part of the report with
the mens rea of the offence. However in a section headed. "The Crime of
Rape" there appear the following paragraphs:

"18. There is no modern definition of the crime of rape and although it
is an offence under section 1 of the Sexual Offences Act 1956, the statute
contains no attempt at a definition. The traditional common law definition, derived from a 17th Century writer (1 Hale 627 ff. 1 East P.C. 434)
and still in use, is that rape consists in having unlawful sexual intercourse with a woman without her consent, by force, fear or fraud.

"19. This definition can be misleading, since the essence of the crime
consists in having sexual intercourse with a woman without her consent
and it is, therefore, rape to have intercourse with a woman who is
asleep or with one who unwillingly submits without a struggle.

"20. As Smith and Hogan point out in their text book on the Criminal
Law (3rd Edn., 1973, p. 326): "Earlier authorities emphasised the use of
force; but it is now clear that lack of consent is the crux of the matter
and this may exist though no force is used. The test is not 'was the act
against her will?' but 'was it without her consent?'"

"21. It is, therefore, wrong to assume that the woman must show
signs of injury or that she must always physically resist before there
can be a conviction for rape. We have found this erroneous assumption
held by some and therefore hope that our recommendations will go
some way to dispel it.

"22. The *actus reus* in rape, which the prosecution must establish for
a conviction consists of (a) unlawful sexual intercourse and (b) absence
of the woman's consent."

Paragraph 84 of the report is in these terms:

"Finally, as rape is a crime which is still without statutory definition,
the lack of which has caused certain difficulties, we think that this legislation should contain a comprehensive definition of the offence which
would emphasise that lack of consent (and not violence) is the crux of
the matter."

That paragraph was incorporated into a recommendation for what was
described as "declaratory legislation.". . .

We have not been persuaded by counsel for the appellant that the position at common law before 1976 was different from that stated in the
report of the advisory group, but whatever it may have been we think
that Parliament must have accepted the group's recommendation in para.
84 of their report and incorporated it in the 1976 Act. Accordingly in so
far as the actus reus is concerned, the question now is simply: at the time
of the sexual intercourse did the woman consent to it? It is not necessary
for the prosecution to prove that what might otherwise appear to have
been consent was in reality merely submission induced by force, fear or
fraud, although one or more of these factors will no doubt be present in
the majority of cases of rape.

We do not agree, as was suggested by counsel for the appellant, that once this is fully realised there will be a large increase in prosecutions for rape. Nor, on the other hand, do we agree with the submission of counsel for the Crown that it is sufficient for a trial judge merely to leave the issue of consent to a jury in a similar way to that in which the issue of dishonesty is left in trials for offences under the Theft Act 1968. In such cases it is sufficient to direct the jury that "dishonest" is an easily understood English word and it is for them to say whether a particular transaction is properly so described or not. Although "consent" is an equally common word, it covers a wide range of states of mind in the context of intercourse between a man and a woman, ranging from actual desire on the one hand to reluctant acquiescence on the other. We do not think that the issue of consent should be left to a jury without some further direction. What this should be will depend on the circumstances of each case. The jury will have been reminded of the burden and standard of proof required to establish each ingredient, including lack of consent, of the offence. They should be directed that consent, or the absence of it, is to be given its ordinary meaning and if need be, by way of example, that there is a difference between consent and submission; every consent involves a submission, but it by no means follows that a mere submission involves consent: see *R. v. Day* (1841) 9 C. & P. 722 at 724, *per* Coleridge J. In the majority of cases, where the allegation is that the intercourse was had by force or the fear of force, such a direction coupled with specific references to and comments on the evidence relevant to the absence of real consent will clearly suffice. In the less common type of case where intercourse takes place after threats not involving violence or the fear of it, as in the examples given by counsel for the appellant, to which we have referred earlier in this judgment, we think that an appropriate direction to a jury will have to be fuller. They should be directed to concentrate on the state of mind of the victim immediately before the act of sexual intercourse, having regard to all the relevant circumstances, and in particular the events leading up to the act, and her reaction to them showing their impact on her mind. Apparent acquiescence after penetration does not necessarily involve consent, which must have occurred before the act takes place. In addition to the general direction about consent which we have outlined, the jury will probably be helped in such cases by being reminded that in this context consent does comprehend the wide spectrum of states of mind to which we earlier referred, and that the dividing line in such circumstances between real consent on the one hand and mere submission on the other may not be easy to draw. Where it is to be drawn in a given case is for the jury to decide, applying their combined good sense, experience and knowledge of human nature and modern behaviour to all the relevant facts of that case.

Looked at in this way we find no misdirection by the judge in this case. . . .

Appeal dismissed

Notes

1. The Court of Appeal created some confusion when it stated that "every consent involves a submission". A person who voluntarily and passionately agrees to sexual intercourse with his or her lover could hardly be described as submitting in the sense of "surrendering". It is right to distinguish consent from submission but misleading to sug-

gest that consent involves submission. In *McAllister* [1997] Crim.L.R. 233 the Court of Appeal made it clear that the dividing line lies between "real consent" on the one hand and 'a lack of consent or mere submission on the other'. In drawing this line, Brooke L.J. stated that:

"The focus of the inquiry in all these cases is based on the sexual autonomy of the complainant. The circumstances of a possibly reluctant consent may be infinitely varied, and on each occasion the jury has to decide whether an alleged agreement to a sexual act may properly be seen as a real consent or whether it should be regarded as a submission founded on improper pressure which this particular complainant could not reasonably withstand from this particular defendant."

2. In proving the *actus reus* of rape, the issue is not whether the complainant dissented or put up some physical resistance but rather whether the prosecution have proved that s/he did not *consent*. The fact that D did not use force, threats or deceit does not establish consent (see *Malone* [1998] 2 Cr.App.R. 447).

3. An apparent consent should not be considered valid where the complainant is not in a position to decide whether or not to consent because their knowledge and understanding are impaired by youth (*Howard* [1965] 3 All E.R. 684), mental deficiency (*Fletcher* (1866) L.R. 1 C.C.R. 39) or intoxication (*Lang* (1975) 62 Cr.App.R. 50). An apparent consent also will be vitiated where it has been obtained by fraud as to the nature of the act. In *Flattery* (1877) 2 Q.B.D. 410, D was convicted of rape having induced V to submit to intercourse by deceiving her that he was performing a surgical operation (see also *Williams* [1923] K.B. 340, *post* p. 687).

4. A problem which has troubled the courts for a long time is the question whether fraud as to the identity of the man who has penetrated the complainant vitiates consent. A series of cases culminating in *Barrow* (1868) 11 Cox C.C. 191, held that obtaining sexual intercourse by impersonation of a woman's husband was not rape. To contrary effect was the case of *Dee* (1884) 15 Cox C.C. 579. *Barrow* was reversed by section 4 of the Criminal Law Amendment Act 1885 which provided:

"Whereas doubts have been entertained whether a man who induces a married woman to permit him to have connexion with her by personating her husband is or is not guilty of rape, it is hereby enacted and declared that every such offender shall be deemed to be guilty of rape."

In the Sexual Offences Act 1956, s.1(2) (as originally enacted) stated:

"A man who induces a married woman to have sexual intercourse with him by impersonating her husband commits rape."

In two cases before the Court of Appeal in 1994 the issue arose whether impersonation of some other man might vitiate consent.

R. v. Elbekkay
September 12, 1994, Lexis Transcript
Court of Appeal

E had sexual intercourse with V, she believing that E was her boyfriend. E was convicted of rape and appealed.

McCOWAN L.J.: . . . The appellant did not give or call evidence, but a submission was made on his behalf at the close of the prosecution case that there was no case to answer, that point being the basis of this appeal. The short point was that counsel for the defence submitted that the actus reus of rape had not been made out since she had consented to the act of sexual intercourse. . . .

Reliance for the appellant here, and indeed before Judge Gordon, was placed on a number of 19 Century authorities culminating in the case of *Barrow* 11 Cox C.C. 191. That case, and the earlier ones, held that the obtaining of intercourse with a woman by the impersonation of her husband did not amount to rape. Fraud, it was held in those cases, could not vitiate her consent. . . .

It is necessary for us next to look at the changes effected by statute. The first of these is to be found in the Criminal Law Amendment Act 1885 [section 4]. . . . To our mind the wording employed seems to indicate a preference for the view of those who decided *Dee* rather than for the view of those who decided *Barrow*.

We pass to the Sexual Offences Act 1956. . . . Of the statutory provisions to which we have so far had regard, Judge Gordon had this to say, in the transcript of his judgment at page 3 F, dealing with s 4 of the Criminal Law (Amendment) Act 1885 he said:

"That section is rightly accepted to be declaratory in nature, that is to say, declaratory of the existing or common law and was in my view, passed in order to avoid future confusion and difference of opinion rather than to make new law. If declaratory and relating to particular confusion then it does no more than resolve that confusion. No inference can be properly drawn from its limited scope, it was all that was required at the time. If it had been a statute making new law then it would have concluded that Parliament intended, thereby, to limit liability of impostors to conviction for rape to those who impersonated husbands, but it was not that type of legislation it was declaratory. At that time, there was no need to include the unmarried because the problem had just not arisen. Indeed, it does not appear to have arisen by 1956, certainly the researches of counsel have not revealed any authority on the point between the late 19th century and 1956 and it is therefore, unsurprising that there was no change to the wording when the Sexual Offences Act was passed. Therefore, the common law position seems to be either unclear and open or as decided by *R. v. Dee* and section 1(2) of the Sexual Offences Act 1956 is limited solely to cases involving the impersonation of a husband."

We certainly think it very unlikely that in 1956 Parliament was deliberately and consciously deciding that it was rape to impersonate a husband, but not, say, a man who had been living with the woman for many years.

In any event the situation was clearly affected by the Sexual Offences (Amendment) Act 1976. Section 1 of that Act deals with the meaning of rape, in other words a definition is now being supplied, and subsection (1) reads, so far as it is relevant:

"For the purposes of section 1 of the Sexual Offences Act 1956 (which relates to rape) a man commits rape if—

(a) he has unlawful sexual intercourse with a woman who at the time of the intercourse does not consent to it; . . ."

The section was applied in the case of *Olugboja* 73 Cr. App. Rep. 344 [*ante*, p. 677]. Giving the judgment of the court at page 350 Lord Justice Dunn said:

" . . . in so far as the actus reus is concerned the question now is simply: 'At the time of the sexual intercourse did the woman consent to it?' "

If that question is asked in the present case the answer must be, on the verdict of the jury, that she did not consent.

Mr Arlidge [for the appellant], very properly, drew our attention to the Fifteenth Report of the Criminal Law Revision Committee on Sexual Offences (1985, Cmnd 9213). The relevant passage there reads:

"We see no reason to distinguish between consent obtained by impersonating a husband and consent obtained by impersonating another man, so that latter case should also constitute rape. All other cases of fraud should be dealt with under section 3 of the 1956 Act and should not amount to rape."

Mr Arlidge acknowledges of course that that passage is against him, but he says that clearly the Committee contemplated the need for legislative action and there has been none. That, he says, is how it should be done, not by judicial decision. Dealing with this aspect of the case, Judge Gordon had this to say at page 5 G:

"I now have to consider whether in 1994 at a time when a wife is no longer under a duty to submit to intercourse with her husband, whether there is such a fundamental difference between a wife agreeing to sexual intercourse with her husband and a fiancée or girlfriend agreeing to sexual intercourse with their regular partner that the law should hold that the consent of the wife, if obtained by fraud, is no consent but the consent of the others is still consent in law. I am bound to say, after careful consideration I can find no justification for so finding. It would be wholly contrary to modern attitudes and values which the law should seek to reflect where possible. It would also very seriously curtail or interfere with the right of women to choose, understanding the true facts, whether to participate or not in the act of sexual intercourse."

We wholly agree. Indeed, we think it would be extraordinary for us to come to any other conclusion in 1994. How could we conscientiously hold that it is rape to impersonate a husband in the act of sexual intercourse, but not if the person impersonated is merely, say, the long-term, live-in lover, or in the even more modern idiom, the "partner" of the woman concerned?

The vital point about rape is that it involves the absence of consent. That absence is equally crucial whether the woman believes that the man she is having sexual intercourse with is her husband or another.

In our judgment no authority or statute obliges us to hold otherwise. . . .

For all those reasons, we conclude that the ruling of the judge was correct and the appeal must be dismissed.

Appeal dismissed.

Note and Questions

In *Linekar* [1995] Q.B. 250, a different panel of the Court of Appeal arrived at the same conclusion *Elbekkay* not having been cited before them. Following these decisions the Criminal Justice and Public Order Act 1994 was enacted which by section 142 substituted a new section 1 into the Sexual Offences Act 1956. Section 1(3) provides that "A man also commits rape if he induces a married woman to have sexual intercourse with him by impersonating her husband." As a husband may be convicted of raping his wife was there any need for this provision if impersonation generally vitiates consent? Is the effect of this provision implicitly to overrule the Court of Appeal decision in *Elbekkay* and dicta in *Linekar*? Further clarification would appear to be necessary.

Mens Rea. See *D.P.P. v. Morgan, ante*, p. 151, and next case.

R. v. Satnam and Kewel
(1983) 78 Cr.App.R. 149
Court of Appeal

S & K were convicted of rape and appealed on the ground of misdirection as to the meaning of "reckless".

BRISTOW J. (delivering the judgment of the court): The judge rightly pointed out that there was no dispute that sexual intercourse had in fact taken place. He went on to deal impeccably with the elements of consent by the girl and the knowledge of the appellants which was relevant to the counts on which they were acquitted. He then turned to the element of recklessness and said this: "Members of the jury, a person is reckless in this context: if there was an obvious reason, in the circumstances as the jury find them to be, if there was an obvious reason that the girl was not in fact willing to have sexual intercourse, that is to say, obvious to every ordinary observer, and the defendant either did not apply his mind to that reason at all, for whatever reason, or, applied his mind to the reason, but carried on having sexual intercourse with her, or trying to, that is recklessness." He then repeated that direction and gave no further direction as to the necessary elements to be proved in the crime of reckless rape.

Two grounds of appeal were relied on in this Court. (1) That the judge should have directed the jury that a genuine though mistaken belief that the girl was consenting offered a defence to a charge of reckless rape; (2) that the judge erred in referring to an "ordinary observer" in his direction as to recklessness, and that he should have directed the jury that it was necessary to prove that each appellant was actually aware of the possibility that the girl was not consenting before they could find him reckless.

So far as the first ground was concerned, it was accepted by Mr Smith for the Crown that he could not support the summing up in the absence of a direction as to belief. In *R. v. Thomas* (1983) 77 Cr.App.R. 63 Lord Lane C.J. said, at p. 65: "In this particular case, the judge should have spelt out in terms that a mistaken belief that the woman was consenting, however unreasonable it may appear to have been, is an answer to the charge, and that it is for the prosecution to eliminate the possibility of such a mistake if they are to succeed. He should then have gone on to deal with the matters set out in section 1(2) of the 1976 Act. As it was the jury were left without any guidance on the matter." The same situation arose here. The jury were left without any guidance on the matter of belief and on that ground alone we would allow the appeal.

We turn now to consider the second ground, *i.e.* the direction as to recklessness.

[His Lordship considered *D.P.P. v. Morgan, ante*, p. 151 and the Report of the Advisory Group on the Law of Rape (The Heilbron Committee) Cmnd. 6352, 1975, and the question whether the test of recklessness formulated in *R. v. Caldwell* was relevant to the offence of rape.]

There followed the Sexual Offences (Amendment) Act 1976, section 1.

[His Lordship read the section]. We think that in enacting those provisions Parliament must have accepted the recommendations of the Heilbron Committee, so that the provisions are declaratory of the existing law as stated in *D.P.P. v. Morgan*.

Any direction as to the definition of rape should therefore be based upon section 1 of the 1976 Act and upon *D.P.P. v. Morgan*, without regard to *R. v. Caldwell* or *R. v. Lawrence*, which were concerned with recklessness in a different context and under a different statute.

The word "reckless" in relation to rape involves a different concept from its use in relation to malicious damage or, indeed, in relation to offences against the person. In the latter cases the foreseeability, or possible foreseeability, is as to the consequences of the criminal act. In the case of rape the foreseeability is as to the state of mind of the victim.

A practical definition of recklessness in sexual offences was given in *R. v. Kimber* (*ante*, p. 157), where the Court was concerned with how far an honest belief in consent constituted a defence to a charge of indecent assault. The defendant said in evidence: "I was not really interested in Betty's" (the victim's) "feelings at all". Lawton L.J. said at [1983] 1 W.L.R. 1123: "We have already set out in this judgment the admissions which he is alleged to have made to the police and relevant parts of his own evidence. In our judgment a reasonable jury would inevitably have decided that he had no honest belief that Betty was consenting. His own evidence showed that his attitude to her was one of indifference to her feelings and wishes. This state of mind is aptly described in the colloquial expression, 'couldn't care less.' In law this is recklessness."

In summing-up a case of rape which involves the issue of consent, the judge should, in dealing with the state of mind of the defendant, first of all direct the jury that before they could convict of rape the Crown had to prove either that the defendant knew the woman did not want to have sexual intercourse, or was reckless as to whether she wanted to or not. If they were sure he knew she did not want to they should find him guilty of rape knowing there to be no consent. If they were not sure about that, then they would find him not guilty of such rape and should go on to consider reckless rape. If they thought he might genuinely have believed that she did want to, even though he was mistaken in his belief, they would find him not guilty. In considering whether his belief was genuine, they should take into account all the relevant circumstances (which could at that point be summarised) and ask themselves whether, in the light of those circumstances, he had reasonable grounds for such a belief. If, after considering those circumstances, they were sure he had no genuine belief that she wanted to, they would find him guilty. If they came to the conclusion that he could not care less whether she wanted to or not, but pressed on regardless, then he would have been reckless and could not have believed that she wanted to, and they would find him guilty of reckless rape.

Appeals allowed: convictions of rape quashed

Questions

Is the recklessness described above the same as *Cunningham* recklessness? See *ante*, p. 119.

2. How will the model summing up suggested by Bristow J. affect
the case of the defendant who never gave a thought to the question
of consent?

Note

See discussion in Mistake, *ante*, p. 150.

ii. Other Offences Involving Sexual Intercourse

Note

In the offences which follow "sexual intercourse" is confined to
intercourse *per vaginam*; it does not include anal intercourse with
either a woman or a man.

Sexual Offences Act 1956

2.—(1) It is an offence for a person to procure a woman, by threats or
intimidation, to have sexual intercourse in any part of the world.

3.—(1) It is an offence for a person to procure a woman, by false pretences or false representations, to have sexual intercourse in any part of
the world.

5. It is felony for a man to have unlawful sexual intercourse with a girl
under the age of thirteen.

6.—(1) It is an offence, subject to the exceptions mentioned in this section, for a man to have unlawful sexual intercourse with a girl under the
age of sixteen.

(3) A man is not guilty of an offence under this section because he has
unlawful sexual intercourse with a girl under the age of sixteen, if he is
under the age of twenty-four and has not previously been charged with
a like offence, and he believes her to be of the age of sixteen or over and
has reasonable cause for the belief.

In this subsection, 'a like offence' means an offence under this section
or an attempt to commit one, or an offence under paragraph (1) of section
five of the Criminal Law Amendment Act, 1885 (the provision replaced
for England and Wales by this section).

7.—(1) It is an offence, subject to the exception mentioned in this section, for a man to have unlawful sexual intercourse with a woman who
is a defective.

(2) A man is not guilty of an offence under this section because he has
unlawful sexual intercourse with a woman if he does not know and has
no reason to suspect her to be a defective.

8. [Repealed]

9.—(1) It is an offence, subject to the exception mentioned in this section, for a person to procure a woman who is a defective to have unlawful
sexual intercourse in any part of the word.

(2) A person is not guilty of an offence under this section because he procures a defective to have unlawful sexual intercourse, if he does not know and has no reason to suspect her to be a defective.

Note

For the relationship between these offences and rape under section 1, see next case.

R. v. Williams
[1923] 1 K.B. 340
Court of Criminal Appeal

W, a singing master, had sexual intercourse with a pupil aged 16 by pretending to her that it was a method of training her voice. The girl made no resistance, as she believed him and did not know that he was having sexual intercourse with her. He was convicted of rape and appealed.

LORD HEWART C.J.: Mr Gorst has today taken one point and one point only on behalf of the appellant—namely, that in view of the evidence the appellant ought not to have been convicted of the crime of rape. In support of that argument the attention of the court has been directed to *R. v. O'Shay* (1898) 19 Cox 76, and to the provisions of the Criminal Law Amendment Act, 1885. There is no doubt that before the passing of the Act of 1885 a man who by fraudulent pretence succeeded in obtaining sexual intercourse with a woman might be guilty of rape. For example, in *R. v. Case* (1850) 4 Cox 220, a medical practitioner had sexual connection with a girl of fourteen years of age upon the pretence that he was treating her medically and the girl made no resistance owing to a bona fide belief that she was being medically treated. It was held that he was properly convicted of an assault and might have been convicted of rape. In *R. v. Flattery* (1877) 2 Q.B.D. 410 the same principle was affirmed. But it has been argued that the position has been changed by the passing of the Criminal Law Amendment Act, 1885. Mr. Gorst, when the question was specifically put to him, did not contend that that Act would prevent the laying of an indictment for rape in such a case as *R. v. Flattery*, but he said that that Act made an indictment for rape impossible in the present case. The argument is based upon the provisions of section 3, subsection (2), of the Act of 1885, which provides that "any person who . . . by false pretences or false representations procures any woman or girl, not being a common prostitute or of known immoral character, to have any unlawful carnal connection, either within or without the Queen's dominions . . . shall be guilty of a misdemeanour . . ." It is obvious that those words go beyond a case of rape. It is easy to imagine a case which would come within the comprehensive scope of those words and yet fail to come within the charge of rape. No doubt in *R. v. O'Shay*, Ridley J. did appear to say that after the passing of Criminal Law Amendment Act *R. v. Flattery* was no longer law. . . . It is, however, quite clear when one looks at the report of the case that the attention of the judge was not directed to section 16 of the Act of 1885. That section makes it plain that the provisions of the statute were not in the least intended to interfere with the liability of a person for an offence punishable at common law, but were intended to supplement the offences punishable at common law. In the opinion of this court the decision in *R. v. O'Shay* was given under a misapprehension.

Reference has been made in the course of the argument to *R. v. Dicken* (1877) 14 Cox 8, which was tried at the Stafford Assizes in 1877. In that case a man was charged with rape upon a girl above the age of twelve and under the age of thirteen years. Mr C. J. Darling (as he then was) argued that the prisoner could not be convicted of felony. He said that the prisoner "was charged with rape. That offence consisted of his unlawfully and carnally knowing the girl against her will, *i.e.* without her consent. But such an offence was now defined in 38 & 39 Vict., c. 94, section 4, and thereby declared to be a misdemeanour. Consequently, with respect to girls between the age of twelve and thirteen the earlier statutes making that offence a felony were repealed." That argument depended upon the words in the statute: "whether with or without her consent". Mellor J., who was the judge trying the case, said: "The carnal abuse of children having excited the attention of the legislature, they have been specially protected by Acts of Parliament. 24 & 25 Vict., c. 100, section 51, enacted that 'Whosoever shall unlawfully and carnally know and abuse any girl being above the age of ten years and under the age of twelve years, shall be guilty of a misdemeanour.' Under this provision an offender was punishable, whether the girl did or did not consent to his act. In 1875 it was thought desirable that further protection should be given to young girls, and the limit of ten years was extended, by 38 & 39 Vict., c. 94, section 4, declaring that 'Whosoever shall unlawfully and carnally know and abuse any girl being above the age of twelve years, and under the age of thirteen, whether with or without her consent, shall be guilty of misdemeanour.' *Ex abundanti cautela* the words 'whether with or without her consent' were inserted in the later enactment; but, save in respect of the alteration in the age of the girl, the law remained exactly as it was previously—that is to say, if she consented, the prisoner might be convicted of the statutory misdemeanour; if she did not, *a fortiori* he might be so. But if she did not consent, his offence would amount also to a higher crime the felony of rape, and he might be indicted and tried for it quite irrespective of the modern statutes throwing special protection around children. The present indictment is for rape, and therefore if the girl consented to the carnal knowledge, the act was not done 'against her will,' and the crime is not made out. It would be preposterous to suppose that Parliament intended to repeal the law of rape as to girls of the very age during which extra statutory protection is cast over them, and I am clearly of the opinion that no such repeal has been effected." . . .

In the present case the argument on behalf of the appellant must amount to this—if it be a sound argument at all—that after the passing of the Act of 1885 it is no longer possible to indict a man for rape in such cases as *R. v. Case* and *R. v. Flattery*. That is to say that inasmuch as there is a statute which makes the obtaining of carnal connection with a woman by false pretences a misdemeanour that offence can no longer be rape. That proposition cannot be the law, for the same reason as that stated by Mellor J. in *R. v. Dicken*, even if section 16 of the Act of 1885 be disregarded, but in view of that section the proposition is obviously untenable. Branson J. stated the law in the course of the summing-up in the present case in accurate terms. He said: "The law has laid it down that where a girl's consent is procured by the means which the girl says this prisoner adopted, that is to say, where she is persuaded that what is being done to her is not the ordinary act of sexual intercourse but is some medical or surgical operation in order to give her relief from some disability from which she is suffering, then it is rape although the actual thing that was done was done with her consent, because she never consented to the act of sexual intercourse. She was persuaded to consent to what he did because she thought it was not sexual intercourse and because she thought it was a surgical operation."

Appeal dismissed

Questions

1. In view of the meaning of consent given in *R. v. Olugboja, ante*, p. 631, what scope is there for the offences in sections 2 and 3?

2. Ought there to be a lower limit below which threats inducing intercourse are insufficient for the offence in section 2? If so, at what point should the line be drawn?

3. Is a bigamist necessarily guilty of an offence under section 3 if he has intercourse with his deluded "wife"?

4. While Alan is having consensual intercourse with Betty, aged 15, Cora, aged 15, acts as lookout to warn them of approaching strangers. Are Betty and Cora guilty as accessories to an offence under section 6? See *R. v. Tyrrell, ante*, p. 411. Are any of the three guilty of conspiracy to commit the offence in section 6? See section 2 of the Criminal Law Act 1977, *ante*, p. 481.

iii. Indecent Assault

Sexual Offences Act 1956

14.—(1) It is an offence, subject to the exception mentioned in subsection (3) of this section, for a person to make an indecent assault on a woman.

(2) A girl under the age of sixteen cannot in law give any consent which would prevent an act being an assault for the purposes of this section.

(3) Where a marriage is invalid under section two of the Marriage Act, 1949, or section one of the Age of Marriage Act, 1929 (the wife being a girl under the age of sixteen), the invalidity does not make the husband guilty of any offence under this section by reason of her incapacity to consent while under that age, if he believes her to be his wife and has reasonable cause for the belief.

(4) A woman who is a defective cannot in law give any consent which would prevent an act being an assault for the purposes of this section, but a person is only to be treated as guilty of an indecent assault on a defective by reason of that incapacity to consent, if that person knew or had reason to suspect her to be a defective.

15.—(1) It is an offence for a person to make an indecent assault on a man.

(2) A boy under the age of sixteen cannot in law give any consent which would prevent an act being an assault for the purposes of this section.

(3) A man who is a defective cannot in law give any consent which would prevent an act being an assault for the purposes of this section, but a person is only to be treated as guilty of an indecent assault on a defective by reason of that incapacity to consent, if that person knew or had reason to suspect him to be a defective.

Notes

1. A maximum penalty of 10 years' imprisonment attaches to both of these offences: Schedule 2, as amended by section 3(3) of the Sexual Offences Act 1985.

2. Indecent assault is used where for some reason a charge involving

sexual intercourse is inapplicable, *e.g.* where a man under 23 has the statutory defence of reasonable belief that a girl under 16 is over that age: see section 6(3), *ante*, p. 686.

3. Both offences may be committed by a woman, and if a woman has sexual intercourse with a boy under 16, she is guilty of indecently assaulting him, at any rate if she does anything active which causes her body to come into contact with his: *R. v. Hare* [1934] 1 K.B. 354; *Faulkner v. Talbot* [1981] 3 All E.R. 468 (D.C.) As for when she remains completely passive, see next note.

4. There must be an assault, from which it follows that genuine consent by the victim may be a complete defence: see *ante*, p. 589. Both sections provide that a person who is under 16 or a defective cannot in law consent; but if D remains passive and allows V to touch his or her body, this cannot be an assault by D, whatever the age of V: see *Fairclough v. Whipp* (1951) Cr.App.R. 138. It may be an offence under the Indecency with Children Act 1960, if V is under 14.

5. The assault must be indecent. There has been controversy over whether the assault must be objectively indecent, or whether a colourless act is indecent if D's motive for the assault is the obtaining of sexual gratification. For a summary of many authorities in this country and in other parts of the Commonwealth, see A. N. Mackesy, "The Criminal Law and the Woman Seducer" [1956] Crim.L.R. 529–542. But see next case.

R. v. Court
[1988] 2 All E.R. 221
House of Lords

D, a shop assistant, pulled a 12-year-old girl visitor to the shop across his knees, and smacked her 12 times on the buttocks outside her shorts for no apparent reason. Asked by the police why he had done so, he said "I don't know: buttock fetish." He pleaded guilty to assault, but denied that the assault was indecent and contended that his statement about his "buttock fetish" should be excluded as evidence because it was merely a secret motive which was not communicated to the victim and it could not make indecent an act which was not overtly indecent. The judge having refused to exclude the evidence, D was convicted of indecent assault and appealed, ultimately to the House of Lords.

LORD ACKNER: . . . It is particularly important to bear in mind that the essential basis of the appeal [in the Court of Appeal] was that the judge was wrong to admit the statement about the "buttock fetish" because, so it was contended, it was merely an admission of the appellant's secret motive, which had not been communicated to the victim of the assault and could not therefore make the assault an indecent one. It was argued that the cause of the wrongful admission of this damaging evidence was the judge's direction that the prosecution had to prove that the accused had an indecent intention in doing what he did. It was accordingly submitted by the appellant that no mental element is required with reference to the indecency ingredient of the offence. It was contended before the Court of Appeal, which contention was maintained before your Lordships, "that the mental element required for indecent assault is that required for common assault, namely that the offender intends to use force on the victim, or is reckless as to the infliction of force, without his or her consent."

As to the admissibility of the appellant's statement about the "buttock fetish", it is apparent from the judgment of the Court of Appeal ([1987] Q.B. 156) that the prosecution contended that, given that the circumstances of the assault were such that the jury *could* hold them to be indecent, then the uncommunicated purpose of the appellant should be taken into account by the jury in deciding whether the circumstances were indecent. It is not, however, apparent from the judgment what were the prosecution's submissions with regard to the mental element required for the proof of the offence. Before your Lordships, counsel for the Crown, consistent with his written case, has argued "that no more need be proved than for common assault, namely that the defendant intends to inflict force or the fear of force on the victim, or is reckless thereto, without the victim's consent" subject to the proviso expressed in these terms "that evidence of the defendant's state of mind is admissible in appropriate cases". This is a surprising submission since, not only does it not support the decision of the Court of Appeal ... in addition, the proviso is, for the reasons I give later, quite inconsistent with the substantive submission. . . .

The Court of Appeal saw no ground for regarding the verdict as unsafe or unsatisfactory, and accordingly it dismissed the appeal but certified that it involved a point of law of public importance, namely:

> "Whether it is correct that on a charge of indecent assault the prosecution must prove:—(a) That the accused intentionally assaulted the victim and (b) that he was aware of the indecent circumstances of what he did, or was reckless as to their existence; but that it is not necessary for the prosecution to prove in addition that the accused had an indecent purpose or intention."

... [T]he appellant maintained his submission made to the Court of Appeal that no mental element is required with reference to indecency. Consistent with his written case counsel rejected the test propounded by the Court of Appeal arguing that "the requirement of proof of knowledge of or recklessness as to the circumstances of indecency is superfluous and confusing." . . . [C]ounsel for the Crown adopted the same line, subject to the proviso that in appropriate cases the jury may have regard to the appellant's state of mind at the time of the assault, where such evidence is probative of the true nature of the circumstances accompanying the assault, adopting the very words of the Court of Appeal quoted above that "the jury were . . . entitled to assess the nature of the appellant's acts by reference to his proved purpose."

[His Lordship quoted section 14(1) of the Sexual Offences Act 1956, and dicta from *Sherras v. De Rutzen, ante*, p. 191 and *Sweet v. Parsley, ante*, p. 186]: It cannot, in my judgment, have been the intention of Parliament that an assault can, by a mere mistake or mischance, be converted into an indecent assault, with all the opprobrium which a conviction for such an offence carries. To take one of the less imaginative examples discussed in the course of the arguments, it may be a common occurrence during travel on the London tube during rush hours for a person suddenly to realise belatedly that the train has stopped at the very station where he wishes to alight, without his having taken the wise precaution of getting close to its doors. Such a person may well in his anxiety to get out, rather than be carried on to the next stop, use unnecessary force in pushing his way through his fellow passengers. If he thus came into contact with a woman, then he would be guilty of having assaulted her. If something that he was carrying, such as an umbrella, became caught up, as it might well do, in her dress as he pushed past, thus tearing away her upper clothing, he would in my judgment be guilty only of an assault. He would not be

guilty of an indecent assault. The contrary result would appear to be possible if the Court of Appeal's test was applied. It would certainly follow,
if the submission made in their cases by counsel both for the appellant
and the prosecution were right, that to establish the mental element in
the offence of indecent assault no more need to be established than for
common assault.

    . . . The judge in assisting the jury in his summing up as to the meaning
of an *indecent* assault adopted, inter alia, a definition used by Professor
Glanville Williams in *Textbook of Criminal Law* (2nd ed., 1983) p. 231:
"'indecent' may be defined as 'overtly sexual.'" This is a convenient shorthand expression, since most, but not necessarily all, indecent assaults will
be clearly of a sexual nature although they, as in this case, may have only
sexual undertones. A simpler way of putting the matter to the jury is to
ask them to decide whether "right-minded persons would consider the
conduct indecent or not." It is for the jury to decide whether what
occurred was so offensive to contemporary standards of modesty and
privacy as to be indecent.

    It also was common ground before your Lordships, as it was in the
Court of Appeal, that, if the circumstances of the assault are *incapable* of
being regarded as indecent, then the undisclosed intention of the accused
could not make the assault an indecent one. The validity of this proposition is well illustrated by *R. v. George* [1956] Crim. L.R. 52. The basis of
the prosecution's case was that the defendant on a number of occasions
removed a shoe from a girl's foot and that he did so, as indeed he admitted, because it gave him a kind of perverted sexual gratification. Counsel
for the prosecution submitted that an assault was indecent if it was committed to gratify an indecent motive in the mind of a defendant, even
though there was no overt circumstances of indecency. Streatfeild J. ruled
that an assault became indecent only if it was accompanied by circumstances of indecency towards the person alleged to have been assaulted,
and that none of the assaults (the removal or attempted removal of the
shoes) could possibly amount to an indecent assault.

    Again it was common ground that if, as in this case, the assault
involved touching the victim it was not necessary to prove that she was
aware of the circumstances of indecency or apprehended indecency. An
indecent assault can clearly be committed by the touching of someone
who is asleep or unconscious.

    As to the facts of this case, it is important to bear in mind that at the
trial not only did the appellant admit that he was guilty of an assault but
his counsel expressly conceded that what had happened *was capable* of
amounting to an indecent assault. That concession was repeated in the
Court of Appeal and accepted by the court as being a correct concession.
Sensibly no attempt was made before your Lordships to withdraw this
concession, for the sound reason that the explanation of this unprovoked
assault could reveal that the assault was an indecent one, as indeed the
girl's father suspected and as the jury so decided.

    The assault which the prosecution seek to establish may be of a kind
which is inherently indecent. The defendant removes, against her will, a
woman's clothing. Such a case, to my mind, raises no problem. Those
very facts, *devoid of any explanation*, would give rise to the irresistible inference that the defendant intended to assault his victim in a manner which
right-minded persons would clearly think was indecent. Whether he did
so for his own personal sexual gratification or because, being a misogynist
or for some other reason, he wished to embarrass or humiliate his victim
seems to me to be irrelevant. He has failed, ex hypothesi, to show any
lawful justification for his indecent conduct. This, of course, was not such

a case. The conduct of the appellant in assaulting the girl by spanking her was only *capable* of being an indecent assault. To decide whether or not right-minded persons might think that assault was indecent, the following factors were clearly relevant: the relationship of the defendant to this victim (were they relatives, friends or virtually complete strangers?), how had the defendant come to embark on this conduct and *why* was he behaving in this way? Aided by such material, a jury would be helped to determine the quality of the act, the true nature of the assault and to answer the vital question: were they sure that the defendant not only intended to commit an assault on the girl, but an assault which was indecent; was such an inference irresistible? For the defendant to be liable to be convicted of the offence of indecent assault, where the circumstances of the alleged offence can be given an innocent as well as an indecent interpretation, without the prosecution being obliged to establish that the defendant intended to commit both an assault and an indecent one, seems to me quite unacceptable and not what Parliament intended.

Much reliance was placed by counsel for the appellant on the definition of "indecent assault" in *Beal v. Kelley* [1951] 2 All E.R. 763 at 764 as approved by Lord Goddard C.J.: ". . . an assault, accompanied with circumstances of indecency on the part of the prisoner." It was submitted to your Lordships that an indecent motive can only become "a circumstance of indecency" if it is communicated to the victim by means of words or gestures at the time of the assault. If the motive is not communicated it is not such a circumstance. However, the definition which Lord Goddard C.J. accepted has not the force of a statute. It was wholly appropriate to the facts of that case, where the defendant had indecently exposed himself to a young boy and, when the boy refused to handle him indecently, he got hold of the boy's arm and pulled him towards himself. In such a case and in many others cited to us the assault in itself was not indecent. It was the combination of the assault with circumstances of indecency that established the constituents of the offence. In the instant case, it is the assault itself, its true nature, an assault for sexual gratification, which was capable of amounting to an indecent assault.

The jury in their question to the judge were concerned with the position of a doctor who carried out an intimate examination of a young girl. Mars-Jones J. dealt with their point succinctly by saying (see [1987] Q.B. 156 at 166):

> "In that situation what is vital is whether the examination was necessary or not. If it wasn't necessary but indulged in by the medical practitioner it would be an indecent assault. But if it was necessary, even though he got sexual gratification out of it, that would not make it an indecent assault."

I entirely agree. If it could be proved by the doctor's admission that the consent of the parent, or if over 16 the patient, was sought and obtained by the doctor falsely representing that the examination was necessary, then, of course, no true consent to the examination had ever been given. The examination would be an assault and an assault which right-minded persons could well consider was an indecent one. I would not expect that it would make any difference to the jury's decision whether the doctor's false representations were motivated by his desire for the sexual gratification which he might achieve from such an examination or because he had some other reason, entirely of his own, unconnected with the medical needs or care of the patient, such as private research, which had caused him to act fraudulently. In either case the assault could be, and I expect would be, considered as so offensive to contemporary standards of modesty or privacy as to be indecent. A jury would therefore be entitled to conclude that he, in both cases, intended to assault the patient and to do so indecently. I can see nothing illogical in such a result. On the contrary, it would indeed be surprising if in such circumstances the only offence that could be properly charged would be that of common assault. No doubt the judge would treat the offence which had been motivated by the indecent motive as the more serious.

Our attention has been drawn to a number of cases, but they do not, except with one exception, focus sharply on the question of the mental element required to be established in this offence. The only exception is *R. v. Pratt* [1984] Crim.L.R. 41. That was a case tried in the Crown Court at Plymouth and presided over by Mr Clive Nicholls Q.C. sitting as an assistant recorder. The facts were very strange. Two 13-year-old boys were engaged in night fishing when they were suddenly threatened by the defendant with a gun. As each boy was forced to undress, the other was obliged to shine a torch on him. The defendant stood some way from the boys and touched neither of them. He gave evidence that his sole motive in causing the boys thus to expose their private parts was to search for cannabis which he thought the boys had taken from him the previous afternoon. The prosecution submitted that the defendant's evidence could not provide a defence to the charges, since it was only necessary for the prosecution to prove a common assault and, having proved a common assault, for there to be circumstances of indecency. It was not relevant for the defendant's state of mind to be further considered. In short, the prosecution needed only to prove intention or recklessness as to the common assault and the jury could then find if there were circumstances of indecency accompanying the assault. The assistant recorder held that it was necessary for the prosecution to prove an indecent intention and he decided to admit the evidence. Contrary to the view taken by the Court of Appeal, I consider that the decision of the assistant recorder on the facts of the case was right. The defendant was entitled to put before the jury his explanation of his strange conduct in order to contend that the prosecution had not established that he intended to commit an assault which was indecent. If the jury thought that his explanation might be true, they might decide that right-minded persons would not think that what he had done in the circumstances was indecent.

I, therefore, conclude that on a charge of indecent assault the prosecution must not only prove that the accused intentionally assaulted the victim, but that in so doing he intended to commit an indecent assault, *i.e.* an assault which right-minded persons would think was indecent. Accordingly, any evidence which tends to explain the reason for the defendant's conduct, be it his own admission or otherwise, would be relevant to establish whether or not he intended to commit, not only an assault, but an indecent one. The doctor's admissions in the two contrasting examples which I have given would certainly be so relevant. The appellant's admission of ''buttock fetish'' was clearly such material. It tended to confirm, as indeed did the events leading up to the assault and the appellant's conduct immediately thereafter, that what he did was to satisfy his peculiar sexual appetite. It was additional relevant evidence. It tended to establish the sexual undertones which gave the assault its true cachet.

If, contrary to my view, the Court of Appeal correctly decided that, in addition to establishing the assault, all the prosecution had to do was to establish that the defendant was aware of the indecent circumstances of what he did or was reckless as to their existence, I cannot follow how his uncommunicated motive could have been relevant and therefore, as the

Court of Appeal held, admissible evidence. As Professor Glanville Williams has pointed out in "What is an Indecent Assault?" (1987) 137 N.L.J. 870 at 872, since there was no evidence that the appellant did anything other than spank the girl as if he was chastising her, there was no evidential basis for suggesting that his explanation of his conduct was relevant because it was "likely to affect the way in which he takes hold of the child and restrains her and then strikes her". Counsel for the Crown has not sought to uphold the court's reasoning. He submits that in the no doubt rare cases where there is evidence of the accused's state of mind which discloses his motive, purpose or intention such evidence is admissible "as probative of the true nature and circumstances accompanying the assault." He submitted that "the defendant's motive is no less a circumstance of indecency towards the complainant, merely because it is secretive." This submission cannot stand side by side with the contention that no mental element is required to be proved with reference to indecency. If all that has to be proved is the intended assault, the evidence of the accused's state of mind relative to the indecent ingredient of the offence must be wholly irrelevant. However, the resolute determination shown by the Crown before your Lordships to establish the admissibility of such evidence underlines the obvious, that it would be an affront to common sense that if such evidence exists it must be concealed from the jury, who must thus be deprived of the answer to the vital question necessary for the proper evaluation of this accused's behaviour: why did he behave like that?

I would accordingly dismiss the appeal and answer the certified question as follows. On a charge of indecent assault the prosecution must prove (1) that the accused intentionally assaulted the victim, (2) that the assault, or the assault and the circumstances accompanying it, are capable of being considered by right-minded persons as indecent, (3) that the accused intended to commit such an assault as is referred to in (2) above. These requirements, as counsel for the Crown confirmed, should give rise to no difficulty or complication.

I would add that evidence, if any, of the accused's explanation for assaulting the victim, whether or not it reveals an indecent motive, is admissible both to support or to negative that the assault was an indecent one and was so intended by the accused.

[Lords Keith and Griffiths delivered speeches in favour of dismissing the appeal. Lord Fraser agreed that the appeal should be dismissed. Lord Goff of Chieveley delivered a dissenting speech to the effect that there is no requirement to prove an indecent motive to establish an indecent assault and, accordingly, that the evidence of the appellants' secret motive was inadmissible.]

Appeal dismissed

Questions

1. Lord Ackner said that if the circumstances of an assault are *incapable* of being regarded as indecent, the undisclosed intention of the accused could not make the assault an indecent one. But in his view, it was rightly conceded that Court's actions were *capable* of amounting to an indecent assault "for the sound reason that the explanation of this unprovoked assault could reveal that the assault was an indecent one, as indeed the girl's father suspected" (*ante*, p. 692). Could not the explanation of George's unprovoked assault by removal of shoes (see *ante*, p. 692) reveal that this assault was an indecent one? What relev-

ant distinction is there between forcibly removing shoes and spanking on the buttocks? Are the victim's father's suspicions relevant?

2. In the following cases, there being nothing in the circumstances to suggest indecency, is evidence of D's motive admissible on a charge of indecent assault?

(i) D seized V by the hand in the street. V thought he was trying to rob her, but his object was to drag her into a nearby abandoned house and rape her.

(ii) D, a burglar, hit V on the head. His object was to render her unconscious so that he could rape her.

(iii) D, a burglar, hit V's husband on the head. His object was to disable him so that he could rape V.

3. D, posing as a doctor, was pretending to treat F in order to obtain money from him. At F's request, D made an intimate examination of F's 8-year-old daughter V. On a charge of indecent assault, is it relevant that D's only motive for examining V was to preserve his pretence of being a doctor?

4. Can the behaviour of the *victim* make a "colourless" assault on him or her indecent? See *R. v. Goss* (1990) 90 Cr.App.R. 400 (C.A.), where a grown woman D gave a "motherly" hug to an underage girl V, while V was sexually stimulating D with her hand. *Held*: "the clearest evidence of an indecent assault by the woman."

5. Is Lord Ackner's support for the decision in *Pratt* consistent with his example of an inherently indecent assault, namely, a man stripping a woman of her clothing against her will? Can it be reconciled with the Court of Appeal's decision in *Sargeant* [1997] Crim.L.R. 50 where D's conviction of indecent assault was upheld where he had grabbed V, aged 16, and forced him to masturbate into a condom, the court holding that while there was no indecent touching of V by D or threat thereof, there was an assault in circumstances capable of being considered indecent by right-minded persons, and D intended to commit the assault in those circumstances.

Note

Tabassum, ante, p. 649, is consistent with *Court* fitting into the second situation identified by Lord Ackner as something inherently indecent regardless of D's purpose or motives. Thus once it was held that D's fraud vitiated consent, the touching, being inherently indecent, constituted an indecent assault as D intended to perform the touching in those circumstances.

iv. Proposals for Reform

In July 2000 the Home Office published *Setting the Boundaries: Reforming the Law on Sex Offences* which is a report to the Home Secretary from the Sex Offences Review which he set up in January 1999. The terms of reference of the review were:

"To review the sex offence in the common and statute law of England and Wales, and make recommendations that will:

- provide coherent and clear sex offences which protect individuals, especially children and the more vulnerable, from abuse and exploitation;
- enable abusers to be appropriately punished; and
- be fair and non-discriminatory in accordance with the ECHR and Human Rights Act."

The Review recommends a large number of reforms. Below are the major recommendations relating to the offences covered in this chapter.

Recommendations:

1: The offence of **rape** should be retained as penile penetration without consent, and extended to include oral penetration.

   This should be defined as penetration of the anus, mouth or genitalia to the slightest extent, and, for the avoidance of doubt, surgically reconstructed male or female genitalia should be included in the definition in law. (Para 2.8.5)

2: **Rape** should not be subdivided into lesser or more serious offences. (Para 2.8.8)

3: There should be a new offence of **sexual assault by penetration** to be used for all other penetration without consent.

   This should be defined as penetration of the anus or genitalia to the slightest extent, and, for the avoidance of doubt, surgically reconstructed genitalia should be included in the definition.

   In circumstances where the means of penetration is not clear, the offence of sexual assault by penetration would apply. (Para 2.9.2)

4: **Consent** should be defined in law as **"free agreement"**. (Para 2.10.5)

5: The law should set out a **non-exhaustive list of circumstances** where consent was not present. (Para 2.10.6)

6: The law should include a non-exhaustive list of **examples of where consent is not present** such as where a person:

   - submits or is unable to resist because of force or fear of force;
   - submits because of threats or fear of serious harm or serious detriment of any type to themselves or another person;
   - was asleep, unconscious, or too affected by alcohol or drugs to give free agreement;
   - did not understand the purpose of the act, whether because they lacked the capacity to understand, or were decieved as to the purpose of the act;
   - was mistaken or deceived as to the identity of the person or the nature of the act;
   - submits or is unable to resist because they are abducted or unlawfully detained;
   - has agreement given for them by a third party.

   (Para 2.10.9)

7: There should be a **standard direction** on the meaning of consent and consideration should be given as to whether this should be placed in statute. (Para 2.11.6)

8: **Rape/sexual assault by penetration** may be committed **intentionally or recklessly** and the definition of recklessness in sex offences should include the lack of any thought as to consent; this can be described as "could not care less about consent". (Para 2.12.6)

9: A defence of **honest belief in free agreement** should not be available where there was self induced intoxication, recklessness as to consent, or if the accused did not take all reasonable steps in the circumstances to ascertain free agreement at the time. (Para 2.13.14)

10: There should be a new offence of **sexual assault** to cover sexual touching (defined as behaviour that a reasonable bystander would consider to be sexual) that is done without the consent of the victim. (Para 2.14.4)

11: There should be a new offence of **assault to commit rape or sexual assault by penetration**. (Para 2.15.3)

12: A new sex offence of **trespass with intent to commit a serious sex offence** should replace burglary with intent to rape. (Para 2.16.3)

13: There should be a new offence of **abduction with intent to commit a serious sex offence**. (Para 2.17.2)

14: There should be an offence of **obtaining sexual penetration by threats or deception** in any part of the world. (Para 2.18.7)

15: An offence of **administering drugs** (etc.) with intent to stupefy a victim in order that they are sexually penetrated should be retained. (Para 2.19.3)

16: There should be new offences of **compelling another to perform sexual acts** with several levels of seriousness depending on the nature of the compelled acts. (Para 2.20.4)

17: As a matter of public policy, the **age of legal consent** should remain at sixteen. (Para 3.5.7)

18: The law setting out specific offences against children should state that **below the age of 13 a child cannot effectively consent** to sexual activity. (Para 3.5.11)

. . .

21: A **mistake of fact in age** should be available as a defence, but with the following restrictions: that it should be limited to honest and reasonable belief and that the defendant has taken all reasonable steps to ascertain age. (para 3.6.13)

22: The **use of the defence** of mistake of fact in age should be limited to raising the defence in court on one occasion only. (para 3.6.14)

23: In principle, the defence of mistake of fact in age should remain **limited by age of defendant**. (Para 3.6.16)

. . .

26: Those recognised as giving help, advice, treatment and support to children and young people in **matters of sexual health** should not be regarded as aiding and abetting a criminal offence, nor should the children and young people who seek help and advice about sexual health matters, including contraception. (Para 3.8.1)

. . .

30: There should be a statutory definition of **capacity to consent** which reflects both knowledge and understanding of sex and its broad implications. We recommend adoption of the definition proposed by the Law Commission. (Para 4.5.13)

31: There should be a specific offence relating to **sexual activity with a person with severe mental disability** who would not have the capacity to consent to sexual relations. (Para 4.6.5)

32: There should be offences of a **breach of a relationship of care** to prohibit:

- sexual relationships between a patient with a metal disorder, whether inpatient or outpatient, and any member of staff, whether paid or unpaid;
- sexual relationships between a person in residential care and a member of staff, whether paid or unpaid;
- sexual relationships between a person receiving certain care services in the community and designated care providers whether paid or unpaid;
- sexual relationships between doctors and their patients, and therapists and clients.

(Para 4.8.15)

The Law Commission's recommendations on capacity to consent, contained in their policy paper, *Consent in Sex Offences*, February 2000, are as follows:

(1) a person should be regarded as lacking capacity to consent if at the material time:

(a) the person is by reason of mental disability unable to make a decision for themselves on the matter in question; or

(b) the person is unable to communicate their decision on that matter because they are unconscious or for any other reason.

(2) a person should be regarded as being unable to make a decision on whether to consent to an act if:

(a) he or she is unable to understand

(i) the nature and reasonably foreseeable consequences of the act; and

(ii) the implications of the act and its reasonably foreseeable consequences; or

(b) being able so to understand, he or she is nonetheless unable to make a decision; and

(3) "mental disability" should mean a disability or disorder of the mind or brain, whether permanent or temporary, which results in an impairment or disturbance of mental functioning.

CHAPTER 10

THEFT AND ROBBERY

THEFT

Notes

1. Before 1969, the law about dishonest acquisition of the property of another was contained in the Larceny Act 1916, which was a codification of a number of common law rules with certain piecemeal statutory amendments mostly occurring in the Victorian era. The principal offence was larceny, but it was a highly technical crime, too narrowly defined to cover certain quite common cases of dishonesty. The crime was tinkered with both by statute and by judicial innovation, but the basis of the crime was such that no amount of tinkering would enable it to cover the whole range of dishonest conduct involving the property of another. The basis of the offence was that the accused should take and carry away property in the possession of another; it therefore failed to cover an accused person who dishonestly misappropriated that of which he already had lawful possession, and the offences of embezzlement and fraudulent conversion had to be invented to fill some of this gap. Moreover, the law's insistence that the crime was a wrong against possession, not against ownership, meant that the law was complicated by the need to reflect the intricacies of the English law of possession. The offence of fraudulent conversion, which, in its modern form, was first created by statute in 1901, was tied neither to taking and carrying away by the accused, nor to possession as the invaded interest of the victim. It consisted essentially of the accused fraudulently converting to his own use or benefit or to the use or benefit of any other person the property of the victim. When it was decided to replace larceny, embezzlement and fraudulent conversion by a single new offence of theft, the offence of fraudulent conversion was the model taken for the new definition in section 1. See Criminal Law Revision Committee's Eighth Report, on Theft and Related Offences, Cmnd. 2977, paras. 15–39.

2. What might be called "swindling", *i.e.* obtaining by false pretences and certain other offences of fraud, was not swept into the new definition, and was treated separately by both the Report, § 38, and the Act, which contains a range of new offences of swindling, which have since been supplemented by additional offences in Theft Act 1978. See next Chapter, which deals with offences of fraud. Various

700

other offences against property—blackmail, handling, burglary—are also contained in the Theft Act 1968 (see Chaps. 12–14), but the Act does not deal with offences of damaging property (see Chap. 15).

3. So far as concerns theft and the other offences contained in the Theft Acts, the Acts are comprehensive and in one sense conclusive. There is nothing left of the old offences, which were all completely swept away. However, this does not mean that cases on the earlier law, and on other branches of the law such as property or contract, can be entirely ignored. Occasionally the Court of Appeal concludes that the draftsman must have had a particular decision in mind in choosing the words used in the Act (see, *e.g. post*, p. 756). Moreover, protecting as it does property interests, theft law cannot easily avoid using the technical terms found in and given meanings by the civil law, *e.g.* "proprietary right or interest", "obligation". But in general the Courts, taking the view that the object of the Theft Act was to simplify the law, resist the introduction of the complexities of the civil law into a trial for theft, and are loath to give the statutory words any technical meaning. The rules of property and contract have sometimes been disregarded in a cavalier fashion, and there has been an increasing tendency to categorise the words in the Act as "ordinary" words and to leave juries to say what they mean. The result is that the law of theft, which because of its subject matter could never be simple, has become more complicated than it need be and indeed, in some places, unprincipled and capricious. See, *e.g. post*, pp. 712, 747, 775.

4. Most of the offences in the Theft Acts appear in the Draft Criminal Code Bill. However, although the Law Commission (Law Com. 177, Commentary 16.4) recognised the existence of criticisms of the Acts and the case law on them, they contented themselves with reproducing the Acts, without any changes of substance. An exception will be found, *post*, p. 891, on the subject of burglary with intent under section 9(1)(*b*), Theft Act 1968. The Law Commission issued a Consultation Paper, *Legislating the Criminal Code: Fraud and Deception* (C.P. No. 155) in 1999 which may lead to reform proposals for some of the deception offences.

Theft Act 1968, section 1

(1) A person is guilty of theft if he dishonestly appropriates property belonging to another, with the intention of permanently depriving the other of it; and 'thief' and 'steal' shall be construed accordingly.

(2) It is immaterial whether the appropriation is made with a view to gain, or is made for the thief's own benefit.

(3) The five following sections of this Act shall have effect as regards the interpretation and operation of this section (and, except as otherwise provided by this Act, shall apply only for purposes of this section).

Note

The *actus reus* of theft is (i) appropriating (ii) property (iii) belonging to another. The *mens rea* is found in the expressions (iv) with the intention of depriving the other of it and (v) dishonestly. All five elements are given extended definitions by sections 2–6.

i. Appropriation

Theft Act 1968, section 3

(1) Any assumption by a person of the rights of an owner amounts to an appropriation, and this includes, where he has come by the property (innocently or not) without stealing it, any later assumption of a right to it by keeping or dealing with it as owner.

(2) Where property or a right or interest in property is or purports to be transferred for value to a person acting in good faith, no later assumption by him of rights which he believed himself to be acquiring shall, by reason of any defect in the transferor's title, amount to theft of the property.

Glanville Williams, *Textbook of Criminal Law* (1st ed.), p. 726

The phrase 'any assumption of the rights of an owner' [in section 3(1), *supra*] is a remarkable juristic invention. Except in special situations that the framers of the Act were probably not thinking of, it is impossible for anyone to 'assume the rights of an owner' by way of theft, in the sense of actually acquiring rights of ownership. Thieves do not normally acquire rights against the owner. One may steal a watch, but one cannot generally steal rights of ownership in the watch. The thief may act in a way that would be lawful *if* he had the rights of an owner, or *if* he were acting by authority of the owner; but he does not by stealing give himself those rights. Obviously the word 'assumption' in this context means, generally, a *usurpation* of rights. (The word 'usurpation' is given as one of the meanings of 'assumption' in the OED). What appears to be intended by this cloudy definition is that an appropriation is (or includes) anything done in relation to property by a non-owner that only the owner could lawfully do or authorise.

Notes

1. As Williams points out (*supra*), it is never necessary that the owner shall lose his rights to the property as a result of D's act (and in most cases he does not). In many cases, the owner loses *possession* to D by the latter's act of appropriation, but even that is not necessary. Nothing is said about "possession" in section 3(1). It seems that if D does something in relation to property which only the owner can do, *e.g.* offer it for sale, it is an appropriation even if the owner's rights are not affected in any way, or even put at risk. Thus if D draws an unauthorised cheque on V's bank account, that is an appropriation of V's rights against the bank (see *R. v. Kohn, post*, p. 732), even though in law any debit entry on V's account which the bank might make on honouring the cheque is a complete nullity, so that V's rights against the bank remain exactly as before: *Chan Man-sin v. Att.-Gen. of Hong Kong* [1988] 1 All E.R. 1 (P.C.). Even if the cheque is never presented, the mere fact of drawing it (a thing which only the owner of the account can do) is an assumption of the rights of the owner and therefore "amounts to an appropriation": *Re Osman* [1989] 3 All E.R. 701 (D.C.). In truth, as Lord Oliver pointed out in *Chan Man-sin*, (at p. 3) the definition of appropriation in section 3(1) is a completely artificial one.

It does not follow that where there is an appropriation there is a complete theft, because there must in addition be an intent to deprive the owner permanently. However, this concept also has an artificial meaning (see *post*, pp. 762ff), and it can exist even if there is no intention that V should be deprived of the property itself. On this see further, p. 711.

2. Glanville Williams's choice of the word "usurpation" as being what "appropriation" means in section 3(1) is no longer entirely appropriate. This is because it contains within it the idea of acting in a way not authorised by the owner. However, although what a thief does is usually unauthorised, it need not be so: see next case, which settled a long-standing conflict of authority.

R. v. Gomez
[1993] 1 All E.R. 1
House of Lords

D was assistant manager of an electrical goods shop. He was approached by B, who asked to be supplied with goods in exchange for two stolen building society cheques. D agreed and asked the shop manager G to authorise the transaction, without telling him the cheques were worthless. In response to G's enquiries on the point, D falsely told him the cheques "were as good as cash". G then authorised the handing over of the goods to B in exchange for the cheques, which were dishonoured. D was convicted of theft of the goods and appealed. His appeal was allowed and the prosecution appealed to the House of Lords.

LORD KEITH OF KINKEL My Lords, this appeal raises the question of whether two decisions of your Lordships' House upon the proper construction of certain provisions of the Theft Act 1968 are capable of being reconciled with each other and, if so, in what manner. The two decisions are *Lawrence v. Metropolitan Police Commissioner* [1972] A.C. 626 and *R. v. Morris* [1984] A.C. 320. The question has given rise to much debate in subsequent cases and in academic writings.

[After reciting the facts] The respondent appealed to the Court of Appeal (Criminal Division) which on 22 April 1991 (Lord Lane C.J., Hutchison and Mantell JJ.) quashed the convictions: ([1991] 1 W.L.R. 1344). Lord Lane C.J., delivering the judgment of the court, after considering *Lawrence* and *Morris*, said at p. 1338:

"What in fact happened was that the owner was induced by deceit to agree to the goods being transferred to Ballay. If that is the case, and if in these circumstances the appellant is guilty of theft, it must follow that anyone who obtains goods in return for a cheque which he knows will be dishonoured on presentation, or indeed by way of any other similar pretence, would be guilty of theft. That does not seem to be the law. *Morris* decides that when a person by dishonest deception induces the owner to transfer his entire proprietary interests that is not theft. There is no appropriation at the moment when he takes possession of the goods because he was entitled to do so under the terms of the contract of sale, a contract which is, it is true, voidable, but has not been avoided at the time the goods are handed over."

And later, at p. 1339:

"We therefore conclude that there was de facto, albeit voidable, contract between the owners and Ballay; that it was by virtue of that contract that Ballay took possession of the goods; that accordingly the transfer of the goods to him was with the consent and express authority of the owner and that accordingly there was no lack of authorisation and no appropriation."

The court later granted a certificate under section 1(2) of the Administration of Justice Act 1960 that a point of law of general public importance was involved in the decision, namely

"When theft is alleged and that which is alleged to be stolen passes to the defendant with the consent of the owner, but that has been obtained by a false representation, has (a) an appropriation within the meaning of section 1(1) of the Theft Act 1968 taken place, or (b) must such a passing of property necessarily involve an element of adverse interference with or usurpation of some right of the owner?"

The Crown now appeals, with leave granted here, to your Lordships' House.

[After quoting sections 1(3), 3(1), 4(1), 7 and 15(1) Theft Act 1968]: It is to be observed that by section 26 of the Criminal Justice Act 1991 the maximum sentence for theft was reduced from 10 to 7 years. The section 15(1) penalty was left unchanged.

The facts in *Lawrence*, as set out in the speech of Viscount Dilhorne, were these:

"The appellant was convicted on December 2, 1969, of theft contrary to section 1(1) of the Theft Act 1968. On September 1, 1969, a Mr Occhi, an Italian who spoke little English, arrived at Victoria Station on his first visit to this country. He went up to a taxi driver, the appellant, and showed him a piece of paper on which an address in Ladbroke Grove was written. The appellant said that it was very far and very expensive. Mr Occhi got into the taxi, took £1 out of his wallet and gave it to the appellant who then, the wallet being still open, took a further £6 out of it. He then drove Mr Occhi to Ladbroke Grove. The correct lawful fare for the journey was in the region of 10s. 6d. The appellant was charged with and convicted of the theft of the £6."

The conviction was upheld by the Court of Appeal (Criminal Division) which in granting leave to appeal to your Lordships' House certified the following questions as involving a point of law of general public importance:

"(1) Whether section 1(1) of the Theft Act 1968 is to be construed as though it contained the words 'without the consent of the owner' or words to that effect and (2) Whether the provisions of section 15(1) and of section 1(1) of the Theft Act 1968 are mutually exclusive in the sense that if the facts proved would justify a conviction under section 15(1) there cannot lawfully be a conviction under section 1(1) on those facts."

Viscount Dilhorne, whose speech was concurred in by Lord Donovan, Lord Pearce, Lord Diplock and Lord Cross of Chelsea, after stating the facts, and expressing some doubts as to what Mr Occhi had meant when he said that he "permitted" the taxi driver to take £6, continued, at p. 631:

"The main contention of the appellant in this House and in the Court of Appeal was that Mr Occhi had consented to the taking of the £6 and that, consequently, his conviction could not stand. In my opinion, the facts of this case to which I have referred fall far short of establishing that Mr Occhi had so consented.

"Prior to the passage of the Theft Act 1968, which made radical changes in and greatly simplified the law relating to theft and some other offences, it was necessary to prove that the property alleged to have been stolen was taken 'without the consent of the owner' (Larceny Act 1916, section 1(1)).

"These words are not included in section 1(1) of the Theft Act, but the appellant contended that the subsection should be construed as if they were, as if they appeared after the word 'appropriates'. Section 1(1) reads as follows: 'A person is guilty of theft if he dishonestly appropriates property belonging to another with the intention of permanently depriving the other of it; and 'thief'and 'steal' shall be construed accordingly.'

"I see no ground for concluding that the omission of the words 'without the consent of the owner' was inadvertent and not deliberate, and to read the subsection as if they were included is, in my opinion, wholly unwarranted. Parliament by the omission of these words has relieved the prosecution of the burden of establishing that the taking was without the owner's consent. That is no longer an ingredient of the offence.

"Megaw L.J., delivering the judgment of the Court of Appeal, said [1971] 1 Q.B. 373, 376 that the offence created by section 1(1) involved four elements; '(i) a dishonest (ii) appropriation (iii) of property belonging to another (iv) with the intention of permanently depriving the owner of it.'

"I agree. That there was appropriation in this case is clear. Section 3(1) states that any assumption by a person of the rights of an owner amounts to an appropriation. Here there was clearly such an assumption. That an appropriation was dishonest may be proved in a number of ways. In this case it was not contended that the appellant had not acted dishonestly. Section 2(1) provides, inter alia, that a person's appropriation of property belonging to another is not to be regarded as dishonest if he appropriates the property in the belief that he would have the other's consent if the other knew of the appropriation and the circumstances of it. A fortiori, a person is not to be regarded as acting dishonestly if he appropriates another's property believing that with full knowledge of the circumstances that other person has in fact agreed to the appropriation. The appellant, if he believed that Mr Occhi, knowing that £7 was far in excess of the legal fare, had nevertheless agreed to pay him that sum, could not be said to have acted dishonestly in taking it. When Megaw L.J. said that if there was true consent, the essential element of dishonesty was not established, I understand him to have meant this. Belief or the absence of belief that the owner had with such knowledge consented to the appropriation is relevant to the issue of dishonesty, not to the question whether or not there has been an appropriation. That may occur even though the owner had permitted or consented to the property being taken. So proof that Mr Occhi had consented to the appropriation of £6 from his wallet without agreeing to paying a sum in excess of the legal fare does not suffice to show that there was not dishonesty in this case. There was ample evidence that there was.

"I now turn to the third element 'property belonging to another'. Mr Back Q.C., for the appellant, contended that if Mr Occhi consented to the appellant taking the £6, he consented to the property in the money passing from him to the appellant and that the appellant had not, therefore, appropriated property belonging to another. He argued that the old distinction between the offence of false pretences and larceny had been preserved. I am unable to agree with this. The new offence of obtaining property by deception created by section 15(1) of the Theft Act also contains the words 'belonging to another.' 'A person who by any deception dishonestly obtains property belonging to another, with the intention of permanently depriving the other of it' commits that offence. 'Belonging to another' in section 1(1) and in section 15(1) in my view signifies no more than that, at the time of the appropriation or the obtaining, the property belonging to another, with the words 'belonging to another' having the extended meaning given by section 5. The short answer to this contention on behalf of the appellant is that the money in the wallet which he appropriated belonged to another, to Mr Occhi.

"There was no dispute about the appellant's intention being permanently to deprive Mr Oochi of the money.

"The four elements of the offence of theft as defined in the Theft Act were thus clearly established and, in my view, the Court of Appeal was right to dismiss the appeal."

In the result, each of the certified questions was answered in the negative.

It will be seen that Viscount Dilhorne's speech contains two clear pronouncements, first that it is no longer an ingredient of the offence of theft that the taking should be without the owner's consent and second, that an appropriation may occur even though the owner has permitted or consented to the property being taken. The answer given to the first certified question was in line with those pronouncements, so even though Viscount Dilhorne was of opinion that the evidence fell short of establishing that Mr Occhi had consented to the taking of the £6 it was a matter of decision that it made no difference whether or not he had so consented.

Morris involved two cases of price label switching in a supermarket. In the first case the defendant had removed the price label from a joint of meat and replaced it with a label showing a lesser price which he had removed from another joint. He was detected at the check-out point before he had paid for the joint and later convicted of theft contrary to section 1(1) of the Theft Act. In the second case the defendant had in similar manner switched price labels on goods in a supermarket but was not arrested until after he had passed the check-out point and paid the lesser prices for the goods. He was charged with two counts of theft contrary to section 1(1) and one count of obtaining property by deception contrary to section 15(1). The jury convicted him on the counts of theft, but by directions of the recorder returned no verdict on the section 15(1) count. Appeals against conviction by both defendants were dismissed by the Court of Appeal (Criminal Division) and by this House. Lord Roskill, in the course of a speech concurred in by Lords Fraser of Tullybelton, Edmund-Davies, Brandon of Oakbrook and Brightman, at p. 331 referred to the *Lawrence* case with apparent approval as having set out the four elements involved in the offence of theft and as having rejected the argument that there could not be theft within section 1(1) if the owner of the property had consented to the defendant's acts. He observed that in *Lawrence* the House did not have to consider the precise meaning of "appropriation" in section 3(1) and continued:

"Mr Denison submitted that the phrase in section 3(1) 'any assumption by a person of *the rights*' (my emphasis) 'of an owner amounts to an appropriation' must mean any assumption of '*all* the rights of an owner'. Since neither defendant had at the time of the removal of the goods from the shelves and of the label switching assumed *all* the rights of the owner, there was no appropriation and therefore no theft. Mr Jeffreys for the prosecution, on the other hand, contended that *the* rights in this context only meant *any* of the rights. An owner of goods has many rights—they have been described as 'a bundle or package of rights.' Mr Jeffreys contended that on a fair reading of the subsection it cannot have been the intention that every one of an owner's rights had to be assumed by the alleged thief before an appropriation was proved and that essential ingredient of the offence of theft established.

"My Lords, if one reads the words 'the rights' at the opening of section 3(1) literally and in isolation from the rest of the section, Mr Denison's submission undoubtedly has force. But the later words 'any later assumption of a right' seem to me to militate strongly against the correctness of the submission. Moreover the provisions of section 2(1)(a) also seem to point in the same direction. It follows therefore that it is enough for the prosecution if they have proved in these cases the assumption by the [defendants] of *any* of the rights of the owner of the goods in question, that is to say, the supermarket concerned, it being common ground in these cases that the other three of the four elements mentioned in Viscount Dilhorne's speech in *Lawrence* had been fully established.

"My Lords, Mr Jeffreys sought to argue that any removal from the shelves of the supermarket, even if unaccompanied by label switching, was without more an appropriation. In one passage in his judgment in *Morris's* case the learned Lord Chief Justice appears to have accepted the submission, for he said [1983] Q.B. 587, 596: 'it seems to us that in taking the article from the shelf the customer is indeed assuming one of the rights of the owner—the right to move the article from its position on the shelf to carry it to the check-out.'

"With the utmost respect, I cannot accept this statement as correct. If one postulates an honest customer taking goods from a shelf to put in his or her trolley to take to the checkpoint there to pay the proper price, I am unable to see that any of these actions involves any assumption by the shopper of the rights of the supermarket. In the context of section 3(1), the concept of appropriation in my view involves not an act expressly or impliedly authorised by the owner but an act by way of adverse interference with or usurpation of those rights. When the honest shopper acts as I have just described, he or she is acting with the implied authority of the owner of the supermarket to take the goods from the shelf, put them in the trolley, take them to the checkpoint and there pay the correct price, at which moment the property in the goods will pass to the shopper for the first time. It is with the consent of the owners of the supermarket, be that consent express or implied, that the shopper does these acts and thus obtains at least control if not actual possession of the goods preparatory, at a later stage, to obtaining the property in them upon payment of the proper amount at the checkpoint. I do not think that section 3(1) envisages any such act as an 'appropriation', whatever may be the meaning of that word in other fields such as contract or sale of goods law.

"If, as I understand all your Lordships to agree, the concept of appropriation in section 3(1) involves an element of adverse interference with or usurpation of some right of the owner, it is necessary next to consider whether that requirement is satisfied in either of these cases. As I have already said, in my view mere removal from the shelves without more is not an appropriation. Further, if a shopper with some perverted sense of humour, intending only to create confusion and nothing more both for the supermarket and for other shoppers, switches labels, I do not think that that act of label switching alone is without more an appropriation, though it is not difficult to envisage some cases of dishonest label switching which could be. In cases such as the present, it is in truth a combination of these actions, the removal from the shelf and the switching of the labels, which evidences adverse interference with or usurpation of the right of the owner. Those acts, therefore, amount to an appropriation and if they are accompanied by proof of the other three elements to which I have referred, the offence of theft is established. Further, if they are accompanied by other acts such as putting the goods so removed and relabelled into a receptacle, whether a trolley or the shopper's own bag or basket, proof of appropriation within section 3(1) becomes overwhelming. It is the doing of one or more acts which individually or collectively amount to such adverse interference with or usurpation of the owner's rights which constitute appropriation under section 3(1) and I do not think it matters where there is more than one such act in which order the successive acts take place, or whether there is any interval of time between them. To suggest that it matters whether the mislabelling precedes or succeeds removal from the shelves is to reduce this branch of the law to an absurdity.''

The answer given to the question certified by the Court of Appeal was this:

"There is a dishonest appropriation for the purposes of the Theft Act 1968 where by the substitution of a price label showing a lesser price on goods for one showing a greater price, a defendant either by that act alone or by that act in conjunction with another act or other acts (whether done before or after the substitution of the labels) adversely interferes with or usurps the right of the owner to ensure that the goods concerned are sold and paid for at that greater price.''

In my opinion Lord Roskill was undoubtedly right when he said in the course of the passage quoted that the assumption by the defendant of any of the rights of an owner could amount to an appropriation within the meaning of section 3(1), and that the removal of an article from the shelf and the changing of the price label on it constituted the assumption of one of the rights of the owner and hence an appropriation within the meaning of the subsection. But there are observations in the passage which, with the greatest possible respect to my noble and learned friend Lord Roskill, I must regard as unnecessary for the decision of the case and as being incorrect. In the first place, it seems to me that the switching of price labels on the article is in itself an assumption of one of the rights of the owner, whether or not it is accompanied by some other act such as removing the article from the shelf and placing it in a basket or trolley. No one but the owner has the right to remove a price label from an article or to place a price label upon it. If anyone else does so, he does an act, as Lord Roskill puts it, by way of adverse interference with or usurpation of that right. This is no less so in the case of the practical joker figured by Lord Roskill than in the case of one who makes the switch with dishonest intent. The practical joker, of course, is not guilty of theft because he has not acted dishonestly and does not intend to deprive the owner permanently of the article. So the label switching in itself constitutes an appropriation and so to have held would have been sufficient for the dismissal of both appeals. On the facts of the two cases it was unnecessary to decide whether, as argued by Mr Jeffreys, the mere taking of the article from the shelf and putting it in a trolley or other receptacle amounted to the assumption of one of the rights of the owner, and hence an appropriation. There was much to be said in favour of the view that it did, in respect that doing so gave the shopper control of the article and the capacity to exclude any other shopper from taking it. However, Lord Roskill expressed the opinion that it did not, on the ground that the concept of appropriation in the context of section 3(1) "involves not an act expressly

or impliedly authorised by the owner but an act by way of adverse interference with or usurpation of those rights". While it is correct to say that
appropriation for purposes of section 3(1) includes the latter sort of act, it
does not necessarily follow that no other act can amount to an appropriation and in particular that no act expressly or impliedly authorised by
the owner can in any circumstances do so. Indeed, *Lawrence* is a clear
decision to the contrary since it laid down unequivocally that an act may
be an appropriation notwithstanding that it is done with the consent of
the owner. It does not appear to me that any sensible distinction can be
made in this context between consent and authorisation.

In the civil case of *Dobson v. General Accident Fire and Life Assurance
Corporation plc* [1990] 1 Q.B. 274 a Court of Appeal consisting of Parker
and Bingham L.JJ. considered the apparent conflict between *Lawrence* and
Morris and applied the former decision. The facts were that the plaintiff
had insured property with the defendant company against inter alia "loss
or damage caused by theft." He advertised for sale a watch and ring at
the total price of £5,950. A rogue telephoned expressing an interest in
buying the articles and the plaintiff provisionally agreed with him that
the payment would be by a building society cheque in the plaintiff's
favour. The rogue called on the plaintiff next day and the watch and the
ring were handed over to him in exchange for a building society cheque
for the agreed amount. The plaintiff paid the cheque into his bank, which
informed him that it was stolen and worthless. The defendant company
denied liability under its policy of insurance on the ground that the loss
of the watch and ring was not caused by theft within the meaning of the
Act of 1968. The plaintiff succeeded in the county court in an action to
recover the amount of his loss, and the decision was affirmed by the Court
of Appeal. One of the arguments for the defendants was that there had
been no theft because the plaintiff had agreed to the transaction with the
rogue and reliance was placed on Lord Roskill's statement in *Morris* at
p. 332 that appropriation

> "involves not an act expressly or impliedly authorised by the owner
> but an act by way of adverse interference with or usurpation of those
> rights."

In dealing with this argument Parker L.J. said, at p. 281:

> "The difficulties caused by the apparent conflict between the decisions
> in *Lawrence* and *Morris* have provided, not surprisingly, a basis for
> much discussion by textbook writers and contributors of articles to law
> journals. It is, however, clear that their Lordships in *Morris* did not
> regard anything said in that case as conflicting with *Lawrence* for it was
> specifically referred to in Lord Roskill's speech, with which the other
> members of the Judicial Committee all agreed, without disapproval or
> qualification. The only comment made was that, in *Lawrence*, the House
> did not have to consider the precise meaning of 'appropriation' in sec-
> tion 3(1) of the Act of 1968. With respect, I find this comment hard to
> follow in the light of the first of the questions asked in *Lawrence* and
> the answer to it, the passages from Viscount Dilhorne's speech already
> cited, the fact that it was specifically argued 'appropriates is meant in a
> pejorative, rather than a neutral, sense in that the appropriation is
> against the will of the owner,' and finally that dishonesty was common
> ground. I would have supposed that the question in *Lawrence* was
> whether appropriation necessarily involved an absence of consent."

[After quoting other criticisms by Parker L.J. of Lord Roskill's speech in
Morris, and noting Bingham L.J.'s suggestion that Viscount Dilhorne's

ruling might be reconciled with the reasoning in *Morris* on the ground that in *Lawrence* the victim might not in fact have consented to the taxi-driver taking anything in excess of the correct fare]:

It was argued for the respondent in the present appeal that the case of *Dobson* was wrongly decided. I disagree, and on the contrary find myself in full agreement with those parts of the judgment of Parker L.J. to which I have referred. As regards the attempted reconciliation by Bingham L.J. of the reasoning in *Morris* with the ruling in *Lawrence* it appears to me that the suggested basis of reconciliation, which is essentially speculative, is unsound. The actual decision in *Morris* was correct, but it was erroneous, in addition to being unnecessary for the decision, to indicate that an act expressly or impliedly authorised by the owner could never amount to an appropriation. There is no material distinction between the facts in *Dobson* and those in the present case. In each case the owner of the goods was induced by fraud to part with them to the rogue. *Lawrence* makes it clear that consent to or authorisation by the owner of the taking by the rogue is irrelevant. The taking amounted to an appropriation within the meaning of section 1(1) of the Theft Act. *Lawrence* also makes it clear that it is no less irrelevant that what happened may also have constituted the offence of obtaining property by deception under section 15(1) of the Act.

In my opinion it serves no useful purpose at the present time to seek to construe the relevant provisions of the Theft Act by reference to the Report which preceded it, namely the Eighth Report of the Criminal Law Revision Committee (1966) Cmnd. 2977. The decision in *Lawrence* was a clear decision of this House upon the construction of the word "appropriate" in section 1(1) of the Act, which had stood for twelve years when doubt was thrown upon it by obiter dicta in *Morris*. *Lawrence* must be regarded as authoritative and correct, and there is no question of it now being right to depart from it. . . .

My Lords, for the reasons which I have given I would answer branch (a) of the certified question in the affirmative and branch (b) in the negative, and allow the appeal.

[Lords Browne-Wilkinson, Jauncey of Tullichettle and Slynn of Hadley agreed that the appeal should be allowed for the reasons given by Lord Keith of Kinkel. Lord Lowry dissented.]

Appeal allowed. Conviction restored.

Questions

Is there a theft, and if so when does it occur, in the following situations—

(a) P lends D his bicycle to go on a two week cycling holiday to France. In fact D intends from the outset to go on from France to live in Spain. After two weeks in France he crosses the border into Spain with the bike.

(b) D, on holiday in France, hires a bicycle. At the end of the hire period D keeps the bicycle and returns to England with it. D offers the bicycle for sale and sells it to V for £100. (See *Atakpu* [1993] 4 All E.R. 215.)

(c) P tells her son D to take from her purse the cost of some groceries he has purchased at her request. P takes £5 but the groceries cost £4—he does this in front of his mother who appears to consent to him pocketing the five pounds. Would it make any difference if P knew the actual cost of the groceries and did not dissent when she saw D take the £5?

(d) D removes items from a supermarket shelf into a wire basket intending to take them to a quiet corner in the store out of sight of the checkout assistant and conceal them in his overcoat. He goes to the corner of the store as planned only to find an assistant restocking shelves. He sets down his basket and leaves.

(e) D buys a car from X believing him to be the lawful owner but in fact it belonged to P. D subsequently discovers that P is the rightful owner of the car but refuses to restore it to P. D sells the car to V for £1,000. (See *Adams* [1993] Crim L.R. 72.)

Note

In *Gomez*, Lord Lowry gave a very strong dissenting judgment in which he argued that D should not be guilty of theft where V has transferred ownership of goods to him even though D's title to the goods is voidable due to his deception. Lord Lowry referred in detail to the Eighth Report of the CLRC, *Theft and Related Offences*, Cmnd. 2977 (1966) upon which the Theft Act was based. His argument was that such a case should be dealt with under the section 15(1) offence of obtaining property by deception. Had the prosecutor charged this in the first place the case before their Lordships would never have arisen.

In *Gomez* the title D obtained to the property he took from the shop was voidable due to the deception. If P, having capacity, makes a gift of property to D, could D by receiving that property be guilty of theft? By gifting property a donor transfers ownership of the property to the donee. However, if there is coercion, undue influence or fraud, the transaction is voidable, that is, it may be avoided by the donor. Could a donee be considered dishonest in accepting a gift, even though there was no coercion, undue influence or fraud on the donee's part, where, for example, the donee is manipulative and takes advantage of a gullible or vulnerable donor? Clearly it would be undesirable for the criminal law to find a donee guilty of theft where the civil law would find that a valid gift had been made and that the allegedly stolen property belonged to the alleged thief. Of course, if the donor lacks the capacity necessary to make a valid gift, the transaction would be void and the property would remain that of the donor.

In *Mazo* [1996] Crim. L.R. 435, D, a maid to Lady S, was convicted of theft having cashed cheques totalling £37,000 made payable to her by Lady S. There was evidence to the effect that Lady S was elderly and suffered from confusion at times and short-term memory lapses. D's convictions were quashed as the trial judge had not given an adequate direction to the jury to consider whether Lady S had capacity to make valid gifts. The Court of Appeal accepted that it was common ground that if the gifts were valid there could not be a theft, Pill L.J. quoting from the speech of Viscount Dilhorne in *Lawrence* [1972] A.C. 626, which was referred to in *Gomez* where he stated at p.632:

"a person is not to be regarded as acting dishonestly if he appropriates another's property believing that, with full knowledge of the circumstances, that other person has in fact agreed to the appropriation."

Adopting a narrow reading of *Gomez*, the Court of Appeal took it to have decided that a transaction which was done with the owner's consent could found a charge of theft if there had been deception.

In *Kendrick and Hopkins* [1997] 2 Cr.App.R. 524, the appellants' convictions for conspiracy to steal were upheld where they had drawn a large number of cheques on the victim's account. The victim, aged 99 and virtually blind, was a resident in a small residential home for the elderly run by the appellants. The Court of Appeal stated that they found it unnecessary to consider whether or not the gloss on *Gomez* adopted in *Mazo* was well-founded, being satisfied in the instant case that the jury had received an adequate direction on the question of the capacity of the victim to make valid gifts.

Mazo and *Kendrick and Hopkins* were not in conflict; a legitimate reading of them would be that liability for theft would not arise where there was a valid *inter vivos* gift. This position has been thrown into disarray by the case which follows.

R. v. Hinks
House of Lords
October 26, 2000

D was convicted of theft of a television set and sums amounting to £60,000 which had been given to her by P, a 53-year-old man of limited intelligence whom she had befriended. The prosecution case had been presented on the basis that she had coerced or unduly influenced P to make the gifts. The prosecution also alleged that P lacked the mental capacity to make gifts. The judge directed the jury that they could convict of theft where D received a valid gift if they were satisfied that her conduct fell short of the standards of ordinary decent people and she realised this. The Court of Appeal upheld her conviction holding that the issue was not whether or not a gift was valid but simply whether there had been an appropriation; a gift might be clear evidence of an appropriation which could occur even though the owner consented to the property being taken. D appealed to the House of Lords.

LORD STEYN: . . .

I. . . . The certified question before the House is as follows:

Whether the acquisition of an indefeasible title to property is capable of amounting to an appropriation of property belonging to another for the purposes of section 1(1) of the Theft Act 1968.

In other words, the question is whether a person can "appropriate" property belonging to another where the other person makes him an indefeasible gift of property, retaining no proprietary interest or any right to resume or recover any proprietary interest in the property.

. . .

III. The appellant appealed to the Court of Appeal. The Court of Appeal (Rose L.J., Vice President, Douglas Brown and Dyson JJ.) dismissed the appeal: *Reg. v. Hinks* [2000] 1 Cr.App.R. 1. . . . After an accurate review of the case law, and in particular the decisions of the House in *Lawrence* [1992] A.C. 626 and *Gomez* [1993] A.C. 442 Rose L.J. concluded, at p. 9:

"In our judgment, in relation to theft, one of the ingredients for a jury to consider is not whether there has been a gift, valid or otherwise, but whether there has been appropriation. A gift may be clear evidence of appropriation. But a jury should not, in our view, be asked to consider whether a gift has been validly made because, first, that is not what section 1 of the Theft Act requires; secondly, such an approach is inconsistent with *Lawrence* and *Gomez*, and thirdly, the state of mind of a donor is irrelevant to appropriation: see, in particular, the speech of Lord Browne-Wilkinson, with which Lord Jauncey agreed, in *Gomez* at 396 and 495H . . .: The authorities, as it seems to us, make clear the importance of maintaining a distinction in relation to theft between the two quite separate ingredients of appropriation and dishonesty. Belief or lack of belief that the owner consented to the appropriation is relevant to dishonesty. But appropriation may occur even though the owner has consented to the property being taken. In the present case, the jury were so directed."

This was the view of a strong Court of Appeal, experienced in this class of criminal work. . . .

V. The starting point must be the words of the statute as interpreted by the House in its previous decisions. The first case in the trilogy is *Reg.* v. *Lawrence* 1971 [1972] A.C. 626 . . .. [His Lordship quoted at length from the speech of Viscount Dilhorne.]

Lord Dilhorne expressly added that belief that the passenger gave informed consent (i.e. knowing that he was paying in excess of the fare) "is relevant to the issue of dishonesty, not to the question whether or not there has been an appropriation": at p. 632D. The appeal was dismissed. The ratio decidendi of *Lawrence*, namely that in a prosecution for theft it is unnecessary to prove that the taking was without the owner's consent, goes to the heart of the certified question in the present case.

The second decision of the House was *Reg.* v. *Morris* in 1983 [1984] A.C. 320 Lord Roskill made an observation, which was in conflict with the ratio of *Lawrence* and had to be corrected in *Gomez*. Lord Roskill said, at p. 332D:

"If one postulates an honest customer taking goods from a shelf to put in his or her trolley to take to the checkpoint there to pay the proper price, I am unable to see that any of these actions involves any assumption by the shopper of the rights of the supermarket. In the context of section 3(1), the concept of appropriation in my view involves not an act expressly or impliedly authorised by the owner but an act by way of adverse interference with or usurpation of those rights."

It will be observed that this observation was not necessary for the decision of the case: absent this observation the House would still have held that there had been an appropriation. Lord Roskill took the view that he was following the decision in *Lawrence*. It is clear, however, that his observation (as opposed to the decision in *Morris*) cannot stand with the ratio of *Lawrence*. And as his observation, cast in terms of "the honest customer", shows Lord Roskill conflated the ingredients of appropriation and dishonesty contrary to the holding in *Lawrence*.

The third decision of the House was in *Reg.* v. *Gomez* in 1992 [1993] A.C. 442. . . . In crystalline terms Lord Keith of Kinkel speaking for all the numbers of the majority ruled at p. 464 C-D: (1) The meaning of the relevant provisions must be determined by construing the statutory language without reference to the report which preceded it, namely the Eighth Report of the Criminal Law Revision Committee on Theft and Related Offences (1966) (Cmnd. 2977). (2) The observations of Lord Roskill in *Morris* [1984] A.C. 320 were unnecessary for the decision of that case; that they were in clear conflict with the ratio of *Lawrence* [1972] A.C. 626; and that they were wrong. (3) *Lawrence* must be accepted as authoritative and correct, and "there is no question of it now being right to depart from it." At the same time Lord Keith, at p. 463 H, endorsed the judgment of Parker L.J. in the civil case of *Dobson v. General Accident Fire and Life Assurance Corporation Plc.* [1990] 1 Q.B. 274 where Parker L.J. highlighted the conflict between *Lawrence* [1972] A.C. 626 and *Morris* [1984] A.C. 320 and chose to follow *Lawrence*. (4) Any act may be an appropriation notwithstanding that it was done with the consent or authorisation of the owner. In *Gomez* [1993] A.C. 442 the House was expressly invited to hold that "there is no appropriation where the entire proprietary interest passes": at 448B. That submission was rejected. The leading judgment in *Gomez* was therefore in terms which unambiguously rule out the submission that section 3(1) does not apply to a case of a gift duly carried out because in such a case the entire proprietary interest will have passed. In a separate judgment (with which Lord Jauncey of Tullichettle expressed agreement) Lord Browne-Wilkinson observed, at pp. 495H–496A:

> ". . . I regard the word 'appropriation' in isolation as being an objective description of the act done irrespective of the mental state of either the owner or the accused. It is impossible to reconcile the decision in *Lawrence* (that the question of consent is irrelevant in considering whether there has been an appropriation) with the views expressed in *Morris*, which latter views in my judgment were incorrect."

In other words it is immaterial whether the act was done with the owner's consent or authority. It is true of course that the certified question in *Gomez* referred to the situation where consent had been obtained by fraud. But the majority judgments do not differentiate between cases of consent induced by fraud and consent given in any other circumstances. The ratio involves a proposition of general application. *Gomez* therefore gives effect to section 3(1) of the Act by treating "appropriation" as a neutral word comprehending "any assumption by a person of the rights of an owner." If the law is as held in *Gomez*, it destroys the argument advanced on the present appeal, namely that an indefeasible gift of property cannot amount to an appropriation.

VI. Counsel for the appellant submitted in the first place that the law as expounded in *Gomez* and *Lawrence* must be qualified to say that there can be no appropriation unless the other party (the owner) retains some proprietary interest, or the right to resume or recover some proprietary interest, in the property. Alternatively, counsel argued that "appropriates" should be interpreted as if the word "unlawfully" preceded it. Counsel said that the effect of the decisions in *Lawrence* and *Gomez* is to reduce the actus reus of theft to "vanishing point" (see *Smith and Hogan, Criminal Law*, 9th ed., (1999) p. 505). He argued that the result is to bring the criminal law "into conflict" with the civil law. Moreover, he argued that the decisions in *Lawrence* and *Gomez* may produce absurd and grotesque results. He argued that the mental requirements of dishonesty and intention of permanently depriving the owner of property are insufficient to filter out some cases of conduct which should not sensibly be regarded as theft. He did not suggest that the appellant's dishonest and repellent conduct came within such a category. . . .

At the extremity of the application of legal rules there are sometimes results which may seem strange. A matter of judgment is then involved. The rule may have to be recast. Sir John Smith has eloquently argued that the rule in question ought to be recast. I am unpersuaded. If the law is restated by adopting a narrower definition of appropriation, the outcome is likely to place beyond the reach of the criminal law dishonest persons who should be found guilty of theft. The suggested revisions would unwarrantably restrict the scope of the law of theft and complicate the fair and effective prosecution of theft. In my view the law as settled in *Lawrence* and *Gomez* does not demand the suggested revision. Those decisions can be applied by judges and juries in a way which, absent human error, does not result in injustice.

Counsel for the appellant further pointed out that the law as stated in *Lawrence* and *Gomez* creates a tension between the civil and the criminal law. In other words, conduct which is not wrongful in a civil law sense may constitute the crime of theft. Undoubtedly, this is so. The question whether the civil claim to title by a convicted thief, who committed no civil wrong, may be defeated by the principle that nobody may benefit from his own civil or criminal wrong does not arise for decision. Nevertheless there is a more general point, namely that the interaction between criminal law and civil law can cause problems: compare Beatson and Simester, "Stealing One's Own Property" (1999) 115 L.Q.R. 372. The purposes of the civil law and the criminal law are somewhat different. In theory the two systems should be in perfect harmony. In a practical world there will sometimes be some disharmony between the two systems. In any event, it would be wrong to assume on a priori grounds that the criminal law rather than the civil law is defective. Given the jury's conclusions, one is entitled to observe that the appellant's conduct *should* constitute theft, the only available charge. The tension between the civil and the criminal law is therefore not in my view a factor which justifies a departure from the law as stated in *Lawrence* and *Gomez*. Moreover, these decisions of the House have a marked beneficial consequence. While in some contexts of the law of theft a judge cannot avoid explaining civil law concepts to a jury (e.g. in respect of section 2(1)(a)), the decisions of the House of Lords eliminate the need for such explanations in respect of appropriation. That is a great advantage in an overly complex corner of the law.

VII. My Lords, if it had been demonstrated that in practice *Lawrence* and *Gomez* were calculated to produce injustice that would have been a compelling reason to revisit the merits of the holdings in those decisions. That is however, not the case. In practice the mental requirements of theft are an adequate protection against injustice. In these circumstances I would not be willing to depart from the clear decisions of the House in *Lawrence* and *Gomez*. This brings me back to counsels' principal submission, namely that a person does not appropriate property unless the other (the owner) retains, beyond the instant of the alleged theft, some proprietary interest or the right to resume or recover some proprietary interest. This submission is directly contrary to the holdings in *Lawrence* and *Gomez*. It must be rejected. The alternative submission is that the word "appropriates" should be interpreted as if the word "unlawfully" preceded it so that only an act which is unlawful under the general law can be an appropriation. This submission is an invitation to interpolate a word in the carefully crafted language of the Act of 1968. It runs counter to the decisions in *Lawrence* and *Gomez* and must also be rejected. It follows that the certified question must be answered in the affirmative. . . .

My Lords, I would dismiss the appeal to the House.

LORD HOBHOUSE OF WOODBOROUGH: . . . The trial judge, rightly, rejected a submission of no case to answer but when he came to sum up he seems to have discarded the way in which the prosecution had founded their case and directed the jury that they could convict the appellant of theft on the simple basis that she had been the recipient of a valid gift provided that the jury were satisfied that the conduct of the appellant fell short of the standards of ordinary and decent people and the appellant realised this. [In the Court of Appeal] . . . Rose LJ said [2000] 1 Cr.App.R. 1 at 9:

> "In our judgment, in relation to theft, one of the ingredients for a jury to consider is not whether there has been a gift, valid or otherwise, but whether there has been an appropriation. *A gift may be clear evidence of appropriation*. But a jury should not, in our view, be asked to consider whether a gift has been validly made . . ." (emphasis supplied)

The dismissiveness of this reasoning is in itself remarkable but the proposition which needs particularly to be examined is that which I have emphasised bearing in mind that the Court of Appeal draws no distinction between a fully effective gift and one which is vitiated by incapacity, fraud or some other feature which would lead both the man in the street and the law to say that the transfer was not a true gift resulting from an actual intention of the donor to give. Another aspect of the Court of Appeal's reasoning which also has to be examined is the relationship of that proposition to the concept of dishonesty. It is explicit in the Court of Appeal judgment that the relevant definition of the crime of theft is to be found in the element of dishonesty and *R. v. Ghosh* [1982] Q.B. 1053 and that this is to receive no greater definition than consciously falling below the standards of an ordinary and decent person and may include anything which such a person would think was morally reprehensible. It may be no more than a moral judgment.

The reasoning of the Court of Appeal therefore depends upon the disturbing acceptance that a criminal conviction and the imposition of custodial sanctions may be based upon conduct which involves no inherent illegality and may only be capable of being criticised on grounds of lack of morality. This approach itself raises fundamental questions. An essential function of the criminal law is to define the boundary between what conduct is criminal and what merely immoral. Both are the subject of the disapprobation of ordinary right-thinking citizens and the distinction is liable to be arbitrary or at least strongly influenced by considerations subjective to the individual members of the tribunal. To treat otherwise lawful conduct as criminal merely because it is open to such disapprobation would be contrary to principle and open to the objection that it fails to achieve the objective and transparent certainty required of the criminal law by the principles basic to human rights.

I stress once more that it is not my view that the resort to such reasoning was necessary for the decision of the present case. I would be reluctant to think that those of your Lordships who favour dismissing this appeal have fallen into the trap of believing that, without adopting the reasoning of the Court of Appeal in this case, otherwise guilty defendants will escape justice. The facts of the present case do not justify such a conclusion nor do the facts of any other case which has been cited on this appeal.

The Act:

. . . [The] structure of sections 1 to 6 has had an unfortunate by-product. It has led to a practice (started by Megaw LJ in the Court of Appeal in *Lawrence*) of construing each of the words or phrases in s.1(1) as if they were independent and not part of a single complex definition. The words and phrases have an inter-relation, the one affecting the meaning of another and of the whole. Lord Browne-Wilkinson warned against this in his speech in *R. v. Gomez* [1993] A.C. 442 at 495:

"But it should not be overlooked that elements (i) and (ii) . . . are inter-linked: element (i) (dishonest) is an adjectival description of element (ii) (appropriation). Parliament has used a composite phrase 'dishonest appropriation'. Thus it is not every appropriation which falls within the section but only an act which answers the composite description. The fact that Parliament used that composite phrase—'dishonest appropriation'—in my judgment casts light on what is meant by the word 'appropriation'."

Another point which has arisen from the general intention of the Act and its drafting is the assumption that all questions arising in connection with the law of theft should now be capable of answer without involving any concept or rule derived from the civil law or using any technical legal terminology. Whilst there can be no doubt about the general intention of the Act, to proceed from such a general intention to that assumption is simplistic and erroneous. It is, of course, part of the duty and function of the judge at the criminal trial to separate the questions of law from the questions of fact and only direct the jury on matters of law so far as the issues in the case make it necessary for them to know the law in order to decide the issues of fact and determine the defendant's guilt or innocence; but, when there are relevant questions of law, they must be recognised and the jury directed accordingly.

The truth is that theft is a crime which relates to civil property and, inevitably, property concepts from the civil law have to be used and questions answered by reference to that law. Lord Roskill (expressing sentiments similar to those voiced by others before and since) was no doubt right in *R v. Morris* [1984] A.C. 320 at 334 to warn in general terms against introducing into the criminal law questions whether particular contracts were void or voidable on the ground of mistake or fraud or whether any mistake was sufficiently fundamental to vitiate a contract. But the Act at times expressly requires civil law concepts to be applied. Section 1(1) uses the expression "belonging to another". Thus, in some criminal cases, it may be necessary to determine whether the relevant property belonged to the alleged victim or to the defendant. In *R v Walker* [1984] Crim.L.R. 112 the case turned upon whether the article in question had been rejected by the buyer so as to revest the title to it in the seller, the defendant. (See also per Bingham LJ in *Dobson v General Accident, Fire and Life Assurance Corporation Plc* [1990] 1 Q.B. 274) This was an issue which had to be answered by reference to the civil law and about which the criminal law had nothing to say except to pose the question. (Another case which illustrated the same need to recognise and give effect to the civil law is *R v Preddy* [1996] A.C. 815 and the consequence of having failed to do so was that the Court of Appeal had then to reconsider a considerable number of wrongly based convictions.)

Section 5: "Belonging to Another":
[His Lordship quoted section 5, post p. 740.]

Section 5 qualifies and defines the expression "belonging to another" and specifically makes use of a number of civil law concepts. Under subsection (1) the jury may have to decide who had the possession of the article or whether someone other than the defendant had a 'proprietary right or interest' including an equitable interest (subject to the stated exception) and receive the requisite direction as to the civil law. Subsections (2) and (3) necessitate the consideration of the law of trusts and the rights of beneficiaries and the law of bailment and agency. Subsection (4) makes provision for the situation "where a person gets property by another's mistake". The criterion which the subsection then applies is whether or not the recipient came under an obligation to make restoration of the property (or its value or proceeds). This is a sophisticated criterion wholly dependant upon distinctions to be drawn from the civil law. Unless the criterion is satisfied this constituent of the crime of theft has not been proved.

It is relevant to look at this example further because it is an example of a person who has acquired a defeasible title. Where the transferor has made a mistake, the mistake can be so fundamental that the transferee acquires no rights at all in respect of the chattel transferred as against the transferor. But there may be cases where the mistake does not have so absolute an effect and the transferor may only have equitable rights (*cf* subsection (1)) or restitutionary rights against the transferee. If, however, the transferee has already had validly transferred to him the legal title to and possession of the chattel without any obligation to make restoration, a later retention of or dealing with the chattel by the transferee, whether or not "dishonest" and whether or not it would otherwise amount to an appropriation, cannot amount to theft. However much the jury may consider that his conduct in not returning the chattel falls below the standards of ordinary and decent people, he has not committed the crime of theft. The property did not belong to another.

Section 5 and, particularly, section 5(4) demonstrate that the Theft Act has been drafted so as to take account of and require reference to the civil law of property, contract and restitution. The same applies to many other sections of the Act. For example, section 6 is drafted by reference to the phrase "regardless of the other's rights"—that is to say rights under the civil law. Section 28, dealing with the restoration of stolen goods, clearly can only work if the law of theft recognises and respects transfers of property valid under the civil law, otherwise it would be giving the criminal courts the power to deprive citizens of their property otherwise than in accordance with the law.

Section 5 shows that the state of mind of the transferor at the time of transfer may be relevant and critical. Similarly, the degree of the transferee's knowledge will be relevant to the section 5 question quite independently of any question under section 2. For instance, where there has been a mistake on the part of the transferor, the position under section 5(4) can be different depending on whether or not the transferee was aware of the mistake.

Further, it will be appreciated that the situations to which section 5 is relevant can embrace gifts as well as other transactions such as transfers for value. The prosecution must be able to prove that, at the time of the alleged appropriation, the relevant property belonged to another within the meaning given to that phrase by section 5. Where the defendant has been validly given the property he can no longer appropriate property belonging to another. The Court of Appeal does not seem to have had their attention directed to section 5. The question certified on the grant of leave to appeal is self-contradictory. The direction of the trial judge approved by the Court of Appeal is inadequate. There is no law against appropriating your own property as defined by section 5.

Section 2: "Dishonestly":
[His Lordship quoted section 2, *post* p. 773.]

Although s.2 is headed "Dishonestly", this quotation shows that it is as much involved with the application of the concepts "appropriation" and "property belonging to another". (a) contemplates that the defendant believes that he has the right to appropriate the property and (b) his belief that he would have the consent of the person to whom the property belongs to appropriate it. If belief in such a right or such consent can prevent the defendant's conduct from amounting to theft (whatever the jury may think of it), how can it be said that his knowledge that he has such a right or the actual consent of the person to whom the property belongs is irrelevant? How can it be said that the right of the defendant to accept a gift is irrelevant—or the fact that the transferor has actually and validly consented to the defendant having the relevant property? Yet it is precisely these things which the judgment of the Court of Appeal would wholly exclude.

Section 2(1) is cutting down the classes of conduct which the jury are at liberty to treat as dishonest. They qualify the *Ghosh* approach and show that in any given case the court must consider whether it is adequate to give an unqualified *Ghosh* direction as the Court of Appeal held to be sufficient in the present case.

Gifts:

The discussion in the present case has been marked by a failure to consider the law of gift. Perhaps most remarkable is the statement of the Court of Appeal that "a gift may be clear evidence of appropriation". The making of a gift is the act of the donor. It involves the donor in forming the intention to give and then acting on that intention by doing whatever it is necessary for him to do to transfer the relevant property to the donee. Where the gift is the gift of a chattel, the act required to complete the gift will normally be either delivery to the donee or to a person who is to hold the chattel as the bailee of the donee; money can be transferred by having it credited to the donee's bank account—and so on. Unless the gift was conditional, in which case the condition must be satisfied before the gift can take effect, the making of the gift is complete once the donor has carried out this step. The gift has become the property of the donee. It is not necessary for the donee to know of the gift. The donee, on becoming aware of the gift, has the right to refuse (or reject) the gift in which case it revests in the donor with resolutive effect. (See *Halsbury's Laws*: Gifts, vol. 20, paras 48–49 and the cases cited.)

What consequences does this have for the law of theft? Once the donor has done his part in transferring the property to the defendant, the property, subject to the special situations identified in the subsections of section 5, ceases to be "property belonging to another". However wide a meaning one were to give to "appropriates", there cannot be a theft. For it to be possible for there to be a theft there will have to be something more, like an absence of a capacity to give or a mistake satisfying section 5(4). Similarly, where the donee himself performs the act necessary to transfer the property to himself, as he would if he himself took the chattel out of the possession of the donor or, himself, gave the instructions to the donor's bank, section 5(1) would apply and mean that that constituent of the crime of theft would at that time have been satisfied.

If one treats the "acceptance" of the gift as an appropriation, and this was the approach of the judge and is implicit in the judgment of the Court of Appeal (despite their choice of words), there are immediate difficulties with section 2(1)(a). The defendant did have the right to deprive the donor of the property. The donor did consent to the appropriation; indeed, he intended it. There are also difficulties with section 6 as she was not acting regardless of the donor's rights; the donor has already surrendered his rights. The only way that these conclusions can be displaced is by showing that the gift was not valid. There are even difficulties with section 3 itself. The donee is not "assuming the rights of an owner": she has them already.

Section 3: "Appropriates":
[His Lordship quoted section 3, *ante* p. 702.]

This is the shortest of the explanatory sections. Its purpose is undoubtedly to get away from some of the technicalities of the law of larceny which arose from the need for the defendant to have *taken* the property. It uses a different concept which does not require an acquisition of possession. The concept is any assumption of the rights of an owner (which has been held to mean "the assumption of *any* of the rights of an owner": *R. v. Morris*). The second part of subsection (1) clearly has to be read with section 5.

Subsection (2) deals with the purchase for value of a defective title and provides a further illustration of two of the points I have already made. It is drafted by reference to the position under civil law. It cross-refers to factors which are primarily relevant to honesty—"good faith" and what the defendant "believed" he had acquired—so demonstrating again the intimate inter-relationship of the drafting of one section with another and with the definition in section 1(1) as a whole.

Section 3 does not use any qualitative expression such as "*mis*appropriates" nor does it repeat the Larceny Act expression "without the consent of the owner". It has thus been read by some as if "appropriates" was a wholly colourless expression. This reading declines to draw any guidance from the context in which the word is used in the definition in section 1(1) and the scheme of sections 2 to 6. It also declines to attach any significance to the use of the word "assumption". This led some curious submissions being made to your Lordships.

It was for example suggested that the garage repair mechanic employed to change the oil of a car would have appropriated the car. The reasoning is that only the owner has the right to do this or tell someone to do it therefore to do it is to assume the rights of the owner. This is an absurdity even when one takes into account that some of the absurd results can be avoided by other parts of the definition of theft. The mechanic is not assuming any right he is merely carrying out the instructions of the owner. The person who accepts a valid gift is simply conforming to the wishes of the owner. The words "appropriate" [property belonging to another] and "assume" [the rights of that other] have a useful breadth of meaning but each of them in its natural meaning includes an element of doing something which displaces the rights of that other person. The rights of that other [the owner] include the right to authorise another [the defendant] to do things which would otherwise be an infringement of the rights of the owner.

For the sake of completeness, I should mention that it is not necessary for the present appeal to consider the questions of timing that may arise in relation to appropriation. A carrier may receive goods of which he intends to deprive the owner at a convenient moment. (*R. v. Skipp* [1975]

Crim.L.R. 114, *R. v. Fritschy* [1985] Crim.L.R. 745.) If goods are entrusted to the defendant for one purpose and he takes possession of them for another, it may well be that he has then and there appropriated them since he is thereby assuming the rights of an owner not those of a bailee. This also helps with understanding the supermarket cases. Putting back an article which has been lifted off the shelf in order to read the label or packet does not without more assume any right of ownership. Nor does taking the article to the check-out in order to offer to buy it; that is merely to comply with an implicit request by the owner (the supermarket). On the other hand to interfere with the price label or to take the article with the purpose of smuggling it out of the shop without paying is an assumption of the rights of an owner. (*R. v. Morris*)

The considerations which I have discussed now at some length all lead to the conclusion that sections 1 to 6 of the Theft Act should be read as a cohesive whole and that to attempt to isolate and compartmentalise each element only leads to contradictions. This vice is particularly clear where alleged gifts are involved. In such a situation greater care in the analysis is required under sections 2, 3 and 5 and it will normally be necessary to direct the jury in fuller terms and not merely ask them if they think that the defendant fell below the standards of an ordinary and decent person and realised that such persons would so regard his conduct.

The Authorities:
The House of Lords:

The appellant has submitted that your Lordships should, if needs be, over-rule *R. v. Lawrence* [1972] A.C. 626 and *R. v. Gomez* [1993] A.C. 442. I do not consider that either case should be over-ruled nor is it necessary for the decision of the present case. Neither is inconsistent with my analysis of the law. What appears to have happened is that some of the language used in the three successive House of Lords decisions (*Lawrence, Morris, Gomez*) has been misread without sufficient regard to the context in which the language in each case was used and without a constructive consideration of the intent of sections 1 to 6 as a whole. . . .

[In] *Lawrence* . . . Viscount Dilhorne with whom the other members of the House agreed said, at p. 632:

"That there was an appropriation in this case is clear. Section 3(1) states that any assumption by a person of the rights of an owner amounts to an appropriation. Here there clearly was such an assumption. That an appropriation was dishonest may be proved in a number of ways. In this case it was not contended that the appellant had not acted dishonestly. Section 2(1) provides, inter alia, that a person's appropriation of property belonging to another is not to be regarded as dishonest if he appropriates the property in the belief that he would have the other's consent if the other knew of the appropriation and the circumstances of it. *A fortiori, a person is not to be regarded as acting dishonestly if he appropriates another's property believing that with full knowledge of the circumstances that other person has in fact agreed to the appropriation.*" (emphasis supplied)

This passage, including the important (but sometimes overlooked) sentence which I have emphasised, supports what I have said above in relation to section 2(1)(b). He added:

"Belief or the absence of belief that the owner had with such knowledge [ie knowledge that £7 was far in excess of the legal fare] consented to the appropriation is relevant to the issue of dishonesty, not to the question whether or not there has been an appropriation."

If one asks the question "was there a dishonest appropriation?" the need to make the distinction disappears. The perceived difficulty only arises because the definition is fragmented. As I have pointed out in relation to section 5(1), where the defendant himself removes the property from the owner, he will be taking property belonging to another. The situation in *Lawrence* is not problematical. The whole transaction was driven and coloured by the taxi-driver's fraud. It does not strain the language to describe what happened as an appropriation of property belonging to another. It was never a case of consent except possibly in a technical Larceny Act sense. The damaging legacy of the *Lawrence* judgment has been the adoption of the fragmented approach and the separation of the statement that consent was not relevant to appropriation from its context and from the accompanying statement that knowledge of actual consent is incompatible with dishonesty. . . .

[In] *Morris* [1984] A.C. 320 . . . Lord Roskill . . . held that an assumption of any of the rights of an owner would suffice and answered the certified question by saying that such conduct did amount to a dishonest appropriation where it "adversely interferes with or usurps the right of the owner to ensure that the goods concerned are sold and paid for" at the full price. Lord Roskill clearly treated the phrase "dishonestly appropriates" as a composite one (a view which seems to have led him to distinguish the example of the practical joker: p. 332).

In the Court of Appeal in *Morris* Lord Lane, C.J. [1983] Q.B. 587, 596 had expressed the opinion that merely taking the goods to the check-out in order there to pay the proper price was an appropriation. Lord Roskill disagreed [1984] A.C. 320, 332. It was not an assumption by the shopper of the rights of the supermarket:

"In the context of s.3(1), the concept of appropriation in my view involves not an act expressly or impliedly authorised by the owner but an act by way of adverse interference with or usurpation of those rights. When the honest shopper acts as I have just described, he or she is acting with the implied authority of the owner of the supermarket to take the goods from the shelf, put them in the trolley, take them to the checkpoint and there pay the correct price at which moment the property in the goods will pass to the shopper for the first time. It is with the consent of the owners of the supermarket, be that consent express or implied, that the shopper does these acts . . ."

Applying the same reasoning to the case of the dishonest shopper who removes goods from the shelf and hides them in her shopping bag intending from the very beginning to steal them, he approved the decision in *R. v. McPherson* [1973] Crim.L.R. 191 that in that situation there was an appropriation.

The contentious part of this decision was (or should have been) the treatment of the assumption of *any* right of an owner as sufficient for section 3. But, given their decision on that point, the decision is wholly consistent with the decision in *Lawrence* and is free from the influence of the language of Visct. Dilhorne which I have criticised. On the same basis, the decision and the speech of Lord Roskill correctly understood the intent of sections 1 to 6 of the Theft Act: this was clearly the view of the remainder of the House and is a view I respectfully share.

However, some of the language used by Lord Roskill itself gave rise to difficulty. It was believed that he had been saying that any consent to the act of the defendant necessarily negatived appropriation and that he was contradicting *Lawrence*: fraudulently induced consent would be as conclusive as any other form of consent or authorisation. This belief was only plausible if the reader of his speech was adopting the mind-set of the Larceny Act. It is clear that Lord Roskill was not intending to contradict the decision in *Lawrence*.

It was in these circumstances that the matter of consent and fraud was brought back before your Lordships' House nine years later in *Gomez* [1993] A.C. 442. . . .

The certified question asked whether there has been an appropriation where "that which is alleged to be stolen passes to the defendant with the consent of the owner, but that has been obtained by a false representation". It therefore starts from the premise that there has been overt and directly relevant dishonesty and that the acquisition comes squarely within section 5(4) and (1). The significance of the argument would again seem to be to whether section 1 or section 15 was the relevant section, a point which had already been disposed of by Lawrence. The question also asked, puzzlingly in view of the premise, but obviously directed at Lord Roskill's choice of words: "Must such a passing of property necessarily involve an element of adverse [interference] with or usurpation of some right of the owner?". It might be thought that to obtain possession of another's goods by fraudulently causing him to allow you to do so would be a clear case of an adverse interference with his rights.

It was in this connection that Lord Keith of Kinkel said, at p. 460:

"While it is correct to say that appropriation for purposes of s.3(1) includes [an unauthorised interference], it does not necessarily follow that no other act can amount to an appropriation and in particular that no act expressly or impliedly authorised by the owner can *in any circumstances* do so. Indeed *R v Lawrence* is a clear decision to the contrary since it laid down unequivocally that an act may be an appropriation notwithstanding that it is done with the consent of the owner. It does not appear to me that any sensible distinction can be made *in this context* between consent and authorisation." (emphasis supplied)

The context is consent or authorisation induced by fraud. That was the subject matter of the primary question asked. That this is the context to which Lord Keith is referring is confirmed by his reference to *Lawrence*. Lord Keith is emphatically not saying that consent or authorisation *not* induced by fraud cannot be relevant to the question of appropriation for the purposes of the definition of theft.

This reading is further confirmed by quotations from the judgment of Parker L.J. in *Dobson v. General Accident Fire and Life Insurance Corporation Plc* [1990] 1 Q.B. 274 which Lord Keith agreed with and adopted at p. 463H:

"Moreover, on general principles, it would in my judgment be a plain interference or usurpation of an owner's rights by the customer if he were to remove a label which the [supermarket] owner had placed on goods or put another label on. It would be a trespass to goods and it would be usurping the owner's rights, for only he would have any right to do such an act and no one could contend that there was any implied consent or authority to a customer to do any such thing. There would thus be an appropriation." (p.461-2)

"I have reached the conclusion that whatever *R v Morris* did decide it cannot be regarded as having over-ruled the very plain decision in *R v. Lawrence* that appropriation can occur even if the owner consents and that *R v. Morris* itself makes it plain that it is no defence to say that the property passed under a voidable contract." (p. 463)

What Parker L.J., and through him Lord Keith, is doing is rejecting the misreading of Lord Roskill's speech. Neither is saying that consent and authorisation are irrelevant to appropriation but, rather, that they do not necessarily exclude the possibility of appropriation. The consent or authority may be limited in its scope and not cover the acts done by the defendant because the defendant has an unauthorised purpose (Parker L.J.; and *Morris*) or the consent or authorisation may have been obtained by fraud (*Lawrence*; and *Gomez*). The fundamental argument which all these authorities are having to battle with is the resurrection of the former possession-based rule that consent negatived larceny, distinguishing between larceny by a trick and obtaining by false pretences. It is clear that the Theft Act declined to adopt that rule and defined theft in terms which were not dependant on it.

Lord Keith's speech includes language which is capable of giving rise to the same difficulties as that upon which I have commented in the speech of Visct. Dilhorne in *Lawrence* and it contains criticisms of the speech of Lord Roskill in *Morris* which for my part I do not consider to have been justified. But its main thrust is that consent or authorisation can be relevant to the question of appropriation though not in circumstances such as those in *Lawrence* and *Gomez*. It does not justify the decision of the Court of Appeal in the present case where *ex hypothesi* there is no fraud.

The speech of Lord Browne-Wilkinson is differently reasoned. He recognises that the Theft Act uses the composite phrase "dishonestly appropriates". But he then proceeds (it may be thought, inconsistently and with a lack of logic) from this to the adoption of a meaning of appropriate "in isolation" which is devoid of any content dependant upon the mental state of the owner or the accused. He goes further than Lord Keith. But he does not refer to any of the difficulties discussed earlier which would arise from that view nor does he consider the elaboration of the criterion "dishonestly" which is necessary in order to preserve the contextual meaning of the composite phrase. If the criterion "appropriates" is to become less discriminating, the criterion "dishonestly" has to become more discriminating in order to retain the meaning of the composite phrase in its context in sections 1 to 6 of the Act.

The dissent of Lord Lowry is based upon the need in his view to preserve the same type of distinction between sections 1 and 15 of the Theft Act as formerly existed between sections 1 and 32 of the Larceny Act. If anything, that disagreement lends force to my reading of the speech of Lord Keith . . ..

The Later Authorities:

[His Lordship considered *Mazo, ante* p. 711.] The Court of Appeal allowed her appeal. Pill L.J. giving the judgment of the Court said, at p. 521:

"It is clear that a transaction may be a theft for the purpose of s.1(1) notwithstanding that it was done with the owner's consent if it was induced by fraud, deception or a false representation: see *Gomez*. It is also common ground that the receiver of a valid gift, *inter vivos*, could not be the subject of a conviction for theft. In *Gomez* reference was made to the speech of Visct. Dilhorne in *Lawrence*. In the course of his speech with which the other members of the House agreed Lord Dilhorne stated [p.632]: 'A fortiori, a person is not to be regarded as acting dishonestly if he appropriates another's property believing that, with full knowledge of the circumstances, that other person has in fact agreed to the appropriation.' It is implicit in that statement that if in all the circumstances, there is held to be a valid gift there can be no theft."

Later in the judgment Pill L.J. referred to the criteria for deciding whether such a gift was valid as explained in *In re. Beaney* [1978] 1 W.L.R. 770, having regard to lack of comprehension and mental incapacity. He concluded, at p. 523 with the timely warning that the summing-up created "a danger that the jury would take a view that the appellant's conduct was not of a moral quality of which they could approve and convict her on that ground rather than on the true basis of the law of theft".

In my judgment, my Lords, the explanation of the law in the judgment in *Mazo* is correct and accurately reflects the scheme and purpose of sections 1 to 6 of the Theft Act and demonstrates a correct understanding of the speech of Lord Keith in *Gomez*.

Mazo was distinguished and not followed in *R. v. Kendrick and Hopkins*, [*ante* p. 712]. . . . On the basis of *Mazo*, the summing-up was criticised as not going sufficiently deeply into the question of validity. These criticisms were rightly rejected; the summing-up was not deficient. The appeal was dismissed.

However, the Court of Appeal also criticised the judgment in *Mazo* as not reflecting what was said in *Gomez* particularly by Lord Browne-Wilkinson: the concept of appropriation was distinct from the concept of dishonesty; appropriation could be looked at "in isolation"; other factors, including the incapacity of the donor and fraud only came in in relation to dishonesty; a simple *Ghosh* direction sufficed.

The Court of Appeal in the present case preferred to follow the judgment in *Kendrick and Hopkins* rather than that in *Mazo*. There was probably no conflict between the actual decisions in the two cases. The Court of Appeal in *Kendrick and Hopkins* were justified in dismissing the appeal and, on an overall assessment, rejecting the criticisms of the summing up in that case and upholding the safety of the convictions. They were in error in their adoption of Lord Browne-Wilkinson's view that appropriation should be looked at in isolation.

The Present Case—Conclusions:
The question certified demonstrates the further step which your Lordships are being asked to take beyond that involved in answering the question in *Gomez*. Does the primary question in *Gomez* receive the same answer if one deletes the words "obtained by false representation"? The Court of Appeal in the present case held that it should. Two strands of reasoning led them to this conclusion. The first was that s.3(1) should be construed in isolation from the remainder of sections 1 to 6. In this they followed the lead given by Lord Browne-Wilkinson and the Court of Appeal judgment in *Kendrick and Hopkins*. I have already explained why I consider that this is wrong.

The second was the view that Lord Keith and Parker L.J. had ruled that consent of the owner is always wholly irrelevant to what acts amount to appropriation. They achieved this position only by standing on its head what Lord Keith and Parker L.J. had said. What Lord Keith and Parker L.J. confirmed was that "consent" (in the Larceny Act sense) will not necessarily negative appropriation. What Rose L.J. has derived from this is that consent can never negative appropriation. (The incomplete quotation by Rose L.J. at [2000] 1 Cr.App.R.1, 8 from Parker L.J. is revealing.)

This leads Rose L.J. directly to the position that a valid gift is fully consistent with theft, a proposition which is seriously inconsistent with the scheme of sections 1 to 6 and with other parts of the Act and which is not a proposition to be derived from any of the House of Lords decisions (with the possible exception of the speech of Lord Browne-Wilkinson in *Gomez*).

To say, as does Rose L.J. at p. 10, that "civil unlawfulness is not a constituent of the offence of theft" is of course true. That expression does not occur in s.1(1) and it is anyway not clear what it encompasses. But to proceed from there to the proposition that the civil law of property is irrelevant is, as I have explained earlier in this speech, a far greater error.

My Lords, if, contrary to my view, your Lordships are to travel down the route adopted by the Court of Appeal, your Lordships are faced with a choice between two options neither of which are consistent with dismissing this appeal. One option is to accept the "Browne-Wilkinson" approach and adopt a sanitised concept of appropriation isolated from any context of or interdependence with the other parts of the definition and sections 1 to 6 (particularly sections 2 and 5) *and* then make the necessary qualifications of the concept of dishonesty when the factual issues raised by an individual case require it. The other is to revert to the law as stated by the majority in *Gomez* and by Visct. Dilhorne and, so far as still relevant, by your Lordships' House in *Morris*, and correctly understood by the Court of Appeal in *Mazo*. It is not an option to do neither as happened in the present case. The unqualified *Ghosh* approach cannot survive in conjunction with the 'Browne-Wilkinson' approach.

In my judgment the correct answer is that adopted by Pill L.J. but if your Lordships are of a different opinion the least that should be done is to draw attention to and confirm the provisions of sections 2 and 5 and their implications for cases where the issue raised is whether the property alleged to have been stolen was transferred to the defendant as a gift. What must be erroneous is to treat as "belonging to another" property which at the time of the alleged appropriation belongs to the defendant in accordance with section 5(4). Similarly it must be wrong to treat as a dishonest "appropriation of property belonging to another" under section 2(1) an appropriation for which the defendant correctly knows (as opposed to mistakenly believes) he actually had (as opposed to would have had) the other's consent, the other knowing of the appropriation and the circumstances of it (as opposed to the other person only hypothetically having that knowledge).

My Lords, the relevant law is contained in sections 1 to 6 of the Act. They should be construed as a whole and applied in a manner which presents a consistent scheme both internally and with the remainder of the Act. The phrase "dishonestly appropriates" should be construed as a composite phrase. It does not include acts done in relation to the relevant property which are done in accordance with the actual wishes or actual authority of the person to whom the property belongs. This is because such acts do not involve any assumption of the rights of that person within section 3(1) or because, by necessary implication from section 2(1), they are not to be regarded as dishonest appropriations of property belonging to another.

Actual authority, wishes, consent (or similar words) mean, both as a matter of language and on the authority of the three House of Lords cases, authorisation not obtained by fraud or misrepresentation. The definition of theft therefore embraces cases where the property has come to the defendant by the mistake of the person to whom it belongs and there would be an obligation to restore it—s.5(4)—or property in which the other still has an equitable proprietary interest—s.5(1). This would also embrace property obtained by undue influence or other cases coming within the classes of invalid transfer recognised in *In re Beaney*.

In cases of alleged gift, the criteria to be applied are the same. But additional care may need to be taken to see that the transaction is properly explained to the jury. It is unlikely that a charge of theft will be brought where there is not clear evidence of at least some conduct of the defendant which includes an element of fraud or overt dishonesty or some undue influence or knowledge of the deficient capacity of the alleged donor. This was the basis upon which the prosecution of the appellant was originally brought in the present case. On this basis there is no difficulty in explaining to the jury the relevant parts of s.5 and s.2(1) and the effect of the phrase "assumption of the rights of an owner". Where the basis is less specific and the possibility is that there may have been a valid gift of the relevant article or money to the defendant, the analysis of the prosecution case will break down under sections 2 and 5 as well as s.3 and it will not suffice simply to invite the jury to convict on the basis of their disapprobation of the defendant's conduct and their attribution to him of the knowledge that he must have known that they and other ordinary and decent persons would think it dishonest. Theft is a crime of dishonesty but dishonesty is not the only element in the commission of the crime.

I would answer the certified question in the negative. But, in any event, I would allow the appeal and quash the conviction because the summing-up failed to direct the jury adequately upon the other essential elements of theft, not just appropriation.

[Lords Slynn of Hadley and Jauncey of Tullichettle concurred in the speech of Lord Steyn. Lord Hutton delivered a speech in favour of allowing the appeal.]

Appeal dismissed

Questions

1. According to Lord Steyn whether or not there is an appropriation may be determined in isolation from the other elements of the offence of theft. If a valid gift is made by P to D, when D takes possession of the relevant property and does to it anything that might constitute an appropriation, whose property is it?

2. As the context in which the three previous cases before their Lordships had arisen involved deception, was Lord Steyn right to construe from these decisions a broader general principle that an appropriation may occur notwithstanding a valid consent to the property being taken.

3. D, a young, attractive escort goes to live with P, an elderly, ill but very rich man, as his maid. P is lonely and appreciates the care and attention D provides him. He knows D is only interested in his money but he considers that as he will soon die D may as well benefit from his wealth. Over a period of several months V makes gifts to D of several hundred thousand pounds, a car and expensive jewellery. He also has conveyed to her full legal and equitable title to his holiday home in the Lake District. P is of sound mind and D has not deceived him, coerced him or exercised undue influence over him. She has, however, taken advantage of P's situation and illness to enrich herself

and she realises many people might regard her actions as reprehensible. Could D be convicted of theft of the money, jewellery and car? Could she be convicted of theft of the holiday home? (see section 4, below). Section 148 of the Powers of Criminal Courts (Sentencing) Act 2000 provides that a court on convicting someone of theft may make an order that the stolen goods be restored to any person entitled to recover them from the thief. If D's title is indefeasible, to whom should the goods be restored? If D had given some of the money and jewellery to her sister, E, who was aware of the circumstances in which D had acquired them, could E be convicted of handling stolen goods? (see sections 22 and 24, *post* p. 850.)

4. Lord Hobhouse stated that the words "appropriate" and "assume" include "an element of doing something which displaces the rights of" the owner. In what way could D above be displacing the rights of P? Does Lord Steyn provide an answer to this conundrum?

5. P, a wealthy resident in a home for the elderly, makes a gift of a cheque for £10,000 to D her nurse. D believes P is not of sound mental capacity but takes the cheque and cashes it. Consider D's liability for theft on the basis that (a) P is not of sound mental capacity' and (b) P is of sound mental capacity.

6. Is it possible to reconcile the decision of the majority with the provisions in section 2(1)(a) and (b) relating to the circumstances in which an appropriation is not to be regarded as dishonest? (see *post* p. 773.) Lord Hutton stated:

"My Lords, it appears contrary to common sense that a person who receives money or property as a gift could be said to act dishonestly, no matter how much ordinary and decent people would think it morally reprehensible for that person to accept the gift. Section 2(1)(b) of the Act recognises the common sense view .... It follows, a fortiori, that a person's appropriation of property belonging to another should not be regarded as dishonest if the other person actually gives the property to him."

7. Does it make for certainty in the law if the civil law relating to ownership of property and the criminal law of theft are inconsistent?

ii. "Property"

Theft Act 1968, section 4

(1) 'Property' includes money and all other property, real or personal, including things in action and other intangible property.

(2) A person cannot steal land, or things forming part of land and severed from it by him or by his directions, except in the following cases, that is to say—

(a) when he is a trustee or personal representative, or is authorised by power of attorney, or as liquidator of a company, or otherwise, to sell or dispose of land belonging to another, and he appropriates the land or anything forming part of it by dealing with it in breach of the confidence reposed in him; or

(b) when he is not in possession of the land and appropriates anything forming part of the land by severing it or causing to be severed, or after it has been severed; or

(c) when, being in possession of the land under a tenancy, he appropriates the whole or part of any fixture or structure let to be used with the land.

For purposes of this subsection 'land' does not include incorporeal hereditaments; 'tenancy' means a tenancy for years or any less period and includes an agreement for such a tenancy, but a person who after the end of a tenancy remains in possession as statutory tenant or otherwise is to be treated as having possession under the tenancy, and 'let' shall be construed accordingly.

(3) A person who picks mushrooms growing wild on any land, or who picks flowers, fruit or foliage from a plant growing wild on any land, does not (although not in possession of the land) steal what he picks, unless he does it for reward or for sale or other commercial purpose.

For purposes of this subsection 'mushroom' includes any fungus, and 'plant' includes any shrub or tree.

(4) Wild creatures, tamed or untamed, shall be regarded as property; but a person cannot steal a wild creature not tamed nor ordinarily kept in captivity, or the carcase of any such creature, unless either it has been reduced into possession by or on behalf of another person and possession of it has not since been lost or abandoned, or another person is in course of reducing it into possession.

Notes

Section 4 replaces the common law definition of things capable of being stolen, which in general included only tangible moveable objects. There are, however, still some things which are not or not completely within the concept of stealable things.

1. *Corpses and body parts*. At common law neither a corpse, nor parts of a corpse, could be stolen as there was no property in a corpse (see *Sharpe* (1857) Dears & B. 160). In *Kelly and Lindsay* [1998] 3 All E.R. 741, the Court of Appeal recognised an exception to this principle in affirming the convictions of the appellants for theft of 35 to 40 body parts which L had removed, at K's request, from the Royal College of Surgeons so that K, a sculptor, could make casts of them. K had retained some of the parts and disposed of others. Rose L.J. stated (at p. 749) that "parts of a corpse are capable of being property . . . if they have acquired different attributes by virtue of the application of skill, such as dissection or preservation techniques, for exhibition or teaching purposes." Rose L.J. went on to state (at p. 750):

"Furthermore, the common law does not stand still. It may be that if, on some future occasion, the question arises, the courts will hold that human body parts are capable of being property for the purposes of s.4, even without the acquisition of different attributes, if they have a use or significance beyond their mere existence. This may be so if, for example, they are intended for use in an organ transplant operation, for the extraction of DNA or, for that matter, as an exhibit in a trial."

2. *Land*. Land, and things attached to or growing on land could not in general be stolen, and although the Criminal Law Revision Committee were pressed to equate land with other property exactly,

in the end they decided that the position should remain broadly as it was previously: Cmnd. 2977, paras. 44, 47.

Questions

1. Is theft involved in any of the following cases?

A moves the fence between his own land and that of his neighbour B, so as to take in a strip of B's land.

C, a licensee of D's land, strips off some antique wooden panelling and sells it as firewood.

E, an outgoing tenant of F, purports to sell some antique panelling in the house to G, the incoming tenant.

H, tenant of J, cuts down a wood on the land and sells it as firewood.

K enters L's land and uproots a Christmas tree growing wild, with intention of taking it home to decorate his own home.

M is given £1. by N to collect enough wild mushrooms from L's land to make a breakfast for N.

2. Is a charge of criminal damage available in any of these cases? Compare section 10(1) of the Criminal Damage Act 1971, *post*, p. 901.

3. *Wild animals*, while alive and free, were not the subject of larceny. Dead animals were larcenable but not, ordinarily, by the person who killed them; in other words, poaching was not larceny. The Committee, on the grounds that poaching was not popularly regarded as stealing and that to make it theft would increase the maximum penalty too greatly, decided against equating wild animals with other things.

Various provisions making summary offences of taking deer and fish were contained in the Larceny Act 1861, which the Theft Act repeals entirely. In order to preserve these offences pending a comprehensive reform of the law of poaching, they were re-enacted substantially unchanged in Schedule 1 to the Theft Act. The provisions relating to deer were superseded by the Deer Act 1980. There are also other poaching statutes, *e.g.* the Salmon and Freshwater Fisheries Act 1975. Moreover, legislation not concerned with protecting anyone's property in the creatures involved protects wild birds, their nests and eggs (Protection of Birds Act 1954) and endangered species (Conservation of Wild Creatures and Wild Plants Act 1975). And see Wildlife and Countryside Act 1981, section 13.

Question

A rounds up wild ponies from the moorland where they are born and reared, in order to sell them at auction. B, who disapproves of this, releases them from the auction pen and one escapes. C captures it and refuses to return it to A or to pay for it. Can the actions of A or B or C amount to theft?

4. *Things in action and other intangible property.* Before the Theft Act, to be stealable, property had to be tangible. Other things of value,

such as a legal right, could not be stolen, and a prosecutor was driven to such shifts as charging the stealing of the piece of paper which evidenced such a right. There is now no need to do that in many cases, as a result of the wide definition of property in section 4(1); but if a piece of paper is involved and changes hands, it may still be convenient to charge the theft of the paper, because the attempt in section 4(1) to widen the concept of stealable property is not without its difficulties.

4a. *Things in action.* A thing in action (or chose in action) is property which does not exist in a physical state, and cannot be enjoyed physically (looked at, listened to, eaten, worn, ridden, etc.), but can only be claimed by legal action. Examples are a debt, shares in a company, a copyright, a trade-mark, insurance cover. These things can be stolen by one who appropriates them with intent to deprive the owner permanently, *e.g.* a trustee or personal representative, the legal owner of shares beneficially owned by X, dishonestly assigning them to Y. A bank account is also a chose in action. The property rights involved in a bank account are often misunderstood.

Lord Goddard C.J. in *R. v. Davenport* [1954] 1 All E.R. 602, 603:

"Although we talk of people having money in a bank, the only person who has money in a bank is the banker. If I pay money into my bank, either by paying cash or a cheque, the money at once becomes the money of the banker. The relationship between banker and customer is that of debtor and creditor. He does not hold my money as an agent or trustee.... When the banker is paying out, whether in cash or over the counter or whether by crediting the bank account of someone else, he is paying out his own money, not my money, but he is debiting me in my account with him. I have a chose in action, that is to say I have a right to expect that the banker will honour my cheque, but he does it out of his own money."

If a customer A has a credit of £500 in bank B, the only property is the chose in action, the right to call on B to honour cheques up to that amount. There is no particular sum in the bank vaults over which this right operates. The consequences are: (1) there is no question of a dishonest A stealing this thing in action from B, because by its nature it never could belong to B. Normally it belongs to A himself [but it may "belong to" someone else if another joint account holder is involved, or if it were obtained subject to an obligation to deal with it in a certain way, or by mistake with an obligation to restore: see section 5(3)(4) and *Att.-Gen.'s Reference (No. 1 of 1983)* [1984] 3 All E.R. 369. If A obtained the right to overdraw up to £500 by fraud, it is not theft by A, because this right (to call on B to honour cheques up to £500) never did or could belong to B: but see Obtaining Pecuniary Advantage by Deception, *post*, p. 821: (2) If A by fraud gets B to honour his cheque by paying £500 to P, it is not theft. The £500 given to P may be property, but A does not appropriate it by his fraud, since he does not assume the rights of ownership over any identifiable property; he merely causes B to assume a duty to pay P £500 out of B's general assets: *R. v. Navvabi* [1986] 3 All E.R. 102; but see Obtaining Services by Deception, *post*, p. 823.

But A's right to call on bank B may be stolen by *someone else*, as where, *e.g.* D is A's cashier with power to draw cheques on A's account, and draws one dishonestly in favour of his own creditor Q. When this cheque is presented and met, A will have lost part of his debt against his banker B. See next case. And even if the cheque is not met, the act of presenting it for payment is an appropriation of one of the rights of the owner, A: *Chan Man-sin v. Att.-Gen. for Hong Kong* [1988] 1 All E.R. 1 (P.C.); *Re Osman* [1989] 3 All E.R. 701 (Div.Ct.).

See also Griew, "Stealing and Obtaining Bank Credits" [1986] Crim.L.R. 356.

R. v. Kohn
(1979) 69 Cr.App.R. 395
Court of Appeal

K was a director of Panelservice Ltd., with authority to make payments on its behalf by drawing cheques against its bank account. He drew cheques against the account for his own purposes. He was charged in respect of each occasion on which he had written a cheque for his own purposes with two counts of theft, the first alleging theft of a thing in action, *viz.* the debt owed by the bank to Panelservice, and the second alleging theft of the cheque itself. The counts related to various dates during which the state of the bank account varied from being in credit, being in overdraft but within the limits of the overdraft facility, and being in overdraft but beyond the limits of the overdraft facility. K was convicted of theft of the things in action which the cheques represented, and of the cheques themselves. He appealed.

GEOFFREY LANE L.J.: . . . So far as the first situation is concerned, when the account is in credit, the prosecution say that, where an account is in credit the relationship of debtor and creditor exists between the bank and the customer, The customer is the creditor, the bank is the debtor. The debt is owing by the bank to the customer. That debt is something which cannot be physically handled, it is not a thing or chose in possession; it is a thing in action, namely something which can only be secured by action and, goes the argument, this is a case of a thing in action par excellence, and if it be proved that the defendant has stolen, in other words appropriated that thing in action, then the offence is made out. [After considering reported decisions on the meaning of "chose in action"]: So the prosecution start off with the advantage of the fact that that expression is plainly one which covers a multitude of matters and over the history of English law has spread really far beyond its original concept. So at first blush it would seem that the appellant's contentions on this point are a little difficult to sustain.

But what Mr Tyrrell submits is this—since we are not sure we have followed the argument, we quote what he says verbatim: "The very act done which is relied on as interfering with the owner's rights destroys the subject matter of the theft and so there has been no appropriation. Nothing has ever come into the possession of the appellant." What he says, we think, is that the thing in action has been destroyed before any appropriation and therefore there has been no theft.

It seems to us that the argument is quite untenable. First of all, is there a thing in action, and the answer is undoubtedly yes. Secondly, has the appellant appropriated it? The answer is yes. Was the intention permanently to deprive the owner, and again there was ample evidence upon which the jury properly directed could come to the conclusion that it was. Was it dishonest? Again there was ample evidence on which the jury could come to that conclusion.

A submission was made at the close of the prosecution case similar to that made to us, which the judge rejected. We think that he was right to reject it.

Mr Tyrrell has frankly said that his researches have brought to light no authorities which give any support to his proposition. In so far as there is authority it is against his contentions. It is contained in the writings of two eminent academic lawyers: first of all Professor Griew in his book *The Theft Acts 1968 and 1978* (3rd ed, 1978), paras. 2–11, where one finds this:

> "The case of an employee (D.) who has authority to draw on his employer's (P.'s) bank account and who dishonestly draws on it for unauthorised purposes seem also to be theft (assuming the account to be in credit), D. has in some manner appropriated the debt owed by the bank to P. Although nothing in the transaction operates as an assignment of that debt to D., it would seem that D. has appropriated the debt or part of it by causing P.'s credit balance to be diminished, or at the very least taking the risk of such diminution. The case is analogous to the theft of a chattel by destruction."

The whole of that passage, and particularly the last sentence, if it is correct, as we think it is, sounds the death knell to this particular submission on behalf of the appellant. . . .

We now turn to the counts which cover the situation where the account was overdrawn, but the amount of the cheque was within the agreed limits of the overdraft. So far as this aspect of the matter is concerned, Mr. Tyrrell submits that the grant of facilities for an overdraft does not create a debt. [After considering authorities holding that specific performance is not possible on a contract to lend money, and holding that to that extent the contract does not constitute a debt] [But] if the account is in credit . . . there is an obligation to honour the cheque. If the account is within the agreed limits of the overdraft facilities, there is an obligation to meet the cheque. In either case it is an obligation which can only be enforced by action and therefore potentially a subject of theft under the provisions of the 1968 Act. The cheque is the means by which the theft of this property is achieved. The completion of the theft does not take place until the transaction has gone through to completion. . . .

[In] *William Rouse v. Bradford Banking Co. Ltd.* [1894] A.C. 586, 596, Lord Herschell L.C. said:

> " . . . It may be that an overdraft does not prevent the bank who have agreed to give it from at any time giving notice that it is no longer to continue, and that they must be paid their money. This I think at least it does; if they have agreed to give an overdraft they cannot refuse to honour cheques or drafts, within the limit of that overdraft, which have been drawn and put in circulation before any notice to the person to whom they have agreed to give the overdraft that the limit is to be withdrawn. . . ."

Finally the passage of Sir John Donaldson P. in *Eckman v. Midland Bank Ltd* [1973] Q.B. 519, 529 a decision of the National Industrial Relations Court, Sir John Donaldson sitting as President with two other lay members:

"If, however, a bank has contracted with the contemnor in terms which the sequestrators are entitled to have transferred to them and which they can operate by authority of the writ of sequestration."

It seems to us, in the light of those authorities and in the light of the wording of the Theft Act 1968, that in this situation, when the order to the bank is within the agreed limits of the overdraft, a thing in action certainly exists and accordingly the judge was right in rejecting the submission. The appeal so far as those particular counts are concerned must fail.

That leads us to the third situation, which affects only count 7, that being, it will be remembered, the count which dealt with the cheque presented to the bank at the time when the account was over the agreed overdraft limit which had been imposed by the bank.

The situation here is that there is no relationship of debtor and creditor, even notionally. The bank has no duty to the customer to meet the cheque. It can simply mark the cheque "Refer to drawer." It can decline to honour the cheque. The reasons for that are obvious. If then a bank declines to honour a cheque, there is no right of action in the customer. If they do as a matter of grace—that is all it can be—honour the cheque then that is a course which does not retrospectively create any personal right of property in the customer and does not create any duty retrospectively in the bank. It seems, therefore, on that bald statement of principle, that this count which alleged a theft of a thing in action when the account was over the agreed limit must be quashed, unless some external reason can be found for saving it. . . .

We turn now to the next matter [theft of the cheques] . . . The case for the appellant is that it was not possible in law for him to steal the cheques as alleged in that: (a) he himself wrote and drew the cheques; (b) there was no possibility of Panelservice Ltd. being permanently deprived of the cheques in their character as pieces of paper since they had that character both before and after the appellant drew them; (c) there was no possibility of Panelservice Ltd. being permanently deprived of the cheques in their character as things in action since they did not acquire that character until the appellant wrote and drew them." . . .

The matter seems to us to become reasonably clear . . ., if one looks at p. 21 of the first volume of the transcript. Here the learned judge said to the jury: "What is represented by the cheque is, of course, the right of the person named in it, the payee, to receive the payment represented by that cheque. So far as that cheque itself is concerned, true it is a piece of paper but it is a piece of paper which changes its character completely once it is paid because then it receives a rubber stamp or, in this case, the perforated stamp saying that it has been paid and it then also ceases to be a thing in action. That is a bill of exchange which is a thing in action as I have told you. The cheque is the same thing. It ceases to be that or, at any rate, it ceases to be in its substance the same thing as it was before. That is an instrument on which payment falls to be made." It seems tolerably clear from that that the judge, counsel and the jury were not considering the cheque in its capacity as a piece of paper *simpliciter*, even if one can view a cheque properly in that light. They were looking at it as a negotiable instrument in the way that the judge described.

Even if that was the way the matter was being considered, said Mr Rose, the drawing of a cheque in favour of a third party does not amount to treating oneself as an owner and therefore there is no appropriation sufficient to satisfy the requirements of section 1.

We do not consider that those submissions can be supported. The way in which the matter should be approached, we think is as Miss Goddard submitted to us, which was this. A cheque is not a piece of paper and no more. In no circumstances, in this type of situation, can it be so considered. It is a piece of paper with certain special characteristics.

The sequence of events in this case can be brought down to a simple series of facts. The defendant starts with a cheque book in his possession. It is the cheque book of the company and he is plainly in lawful possession of that book with cheques inside it. He apparently had the habit, as we have already indicated, at least occasionally, of removing blank cheques from the book, tearing out the cheque leaving the counterfoil in position, putting the cheque in his pocket and filling it in at a later stage. Still nothing wrong at all in that. He is still acting lawfully, although it may be somewhat unusual. He then makes up his mind to fill in a cheque with the amount, then the payee and the date and so on. The third party in whose favour the cheques were being made were *ex hypothesi* not entitled to those sums. The appellant was therefore using the company's cheques and the company's bank account for his own purposes. Miss Goddard suggests that there was a gradual appropriation as the events moved on in this way.

The next stage is this. He says to himself, "I am now going to make the cheque payable to E.P. or Happy Pets or whoever it may be." That action is unknown to Mr Aust. It is *ex hypothesi* once again contrary to the interests of the company. It is contrary to the will of the company and it is dishonest. This is dealing with the cheque not as the agent of the company duly authorised, but is dealing with the cheque as if it were his own. That seems to us is sufficient to amount to an appropriation under the Act.

So when the writing gets on to the cheque, it becomes a bill of exchange and becomes a necessary demand upon the bank to honour the bank's obligations to the customer, which is the company. But that is being done for the defendant's own purposes, and when he sends it on to the company, to Happy Pets or to E.P., it has come to the point where he has made the cheque his own. For the purposes of the Theft Act he has appropriated the cheque, and given that the other elements of the crime are present, which one must assume for purposes of this argument, the offence is complete. Be it noted it is not a matter of what happens to the document thereafter.

Consequently for purposes of these counts, that is to say the even numbered counts, the "cheque" counts rather than the "thing in action" counts, it does not matter whether the account of the company is in credit, it does not matter whether it is within its overdraft limits, it does not matter whether it is outside the overdraft limits, the offence is nevertheless complete.

Now to deal with the further question of whether there is an intent permanently to deprive the owner? Here we would wish to do what the judge did, simply to cite the passage from Megaw L.J.'s judgment in *Duru and Asghar* [[1974] 1 W.L.R. 2] "In the view of this Court there can be no doubt that the intention of both of these appellants, as would necessarily have been found by the jury if the matter had been left to the jury on a proper direction of law (a direction which would no doubt have been given if the pleas of guilty had not been entered), was permanently to deprive the Greater London Council of that thing in action, that cheque; that piece of paper, in the sense of a piece of paper carrying with it the right to receive payment of the sum of £6,002.50 which is the amount concerned in count 3. So far as the cheque itself is concerned, true it is a piece of paper. But it is a piece of paper which changes its character completely once it is paid, because then it receives a rubber stamp on it saying it has been paid and it ceases to be a thing in action, or at any rate it ceases to be, in its substance, the same thing as it was before: that is, an instrument on which payment falls to be made. It was the intention of the appellants, dishonestly and by deception, not only that the cheques should be made out and handed over, but also that they should be presented and paid, thereby permanently depriving the Greater London Council of the cheques in substance as their things in action. The fact that the mortgagors were under an obligation to repay the mortgage loans does not affect the appellant's intention permanently to deprive the council of these cheques."

Consequently so far as the counts involved in these supplementary grounds of appeal are concerned, particulars of which have already been detailed, the appeal must fail. The appellant was assuming the rights of the owner, that is to say the rights of the creditor vis-à-vis the bank, that is the rights of the company to demand that the bank should hand over the money. He is assuming the right to do what he likes with that part of the company's debt with which he is dealing.

The learned Lord Justice then dealt with the further grounds of appeal, discussed them and concluded: For the reasons which we have indicated it seems to us, apart from the conviction on count 7 which must be quashed, this appeal must be dismissed.

Conviction on count 7 quashed. Appeal dismissed on other counts.

Notes

1. Although Geoffrey Lane L.J. (*ante*, p. 733) said that "the completion of the theft does not take place until the transaction has gone through to completion", this was held to be *obiter* in *Chan Man-sin v. A.-G. for Hong Kong* [1988] 1 All E.R. 1 (P.C.) and *Re Osman* [1989] 3 All E.R. 701 (D.C); the giving of instructions to the bank to debit V.'s account is a usurpation of one of the rights of the owner of the account (V.).

2. The Court of Appeal holds that Kohn stole not only the right which Panelservice had against the bank to have their cheques met, but also the cheques themselves (the even-numbered counts). It is held that a cheque is not only a piece of paper but also a chose in action, a right in the drawee (Happy Pets) to be paid the amount of the cheque by Panelservice. Converting a blank cheque into a valid cheque is an appropriation of Panelservice's piece of paper, and so is sending it to Happy Pets; if done with intent to deprive, it is theft. The only question is, how does Kohn permanently deprive Panelservice of the appropriated property, *i.e.* the cheque which will eventually find its way back to Panelservice? One answer is to say that Panelservice has to "buy" it back, by meeting the cheque, by paying Happy Pets the amount specified in the cheque. It is clear that the owner of property is permanently deprived if he is only to get it back by buying it back [see, *post*, p. 762]. However the Court adopts another view (formulated in *R. v. Duru*), that what the owner, Panelservice, gets back is something entirely different from what was taken from it. What was taken was a thing in action, "a piece of paper carrying with it the right to receive payment of a sum of money," and what was returned was a mere piece of paper (a cancelled cheque). The inference is that it has been stripped of all or most of its value to Panelservice. It is not at first sight clear what has been removed from the cheque which is of

value to Panelservice, since its obvious value is a duty in Panelservice to pay a sum of money to the payee. Removal of this "value" does not prejudice Panelservice. The answer appears to be that while it was a cheque, Panelservice could exchange it for goods or other value. Now it has only a worthless piece of paper. However it does not seem accurate to say that Panelservice is deprived of a thing in action, because that thing in action, being a right to sue Panelservice for money, could never have been owned by Panelservice. The better view (see Smith and Hogan, *Criminal Law*, 9th edn, pp. 568–569) is that the cheque is a valuable security, which is a tangible thing of value, and it ceases to be such when it is paid.

The exact status of this part of the Court of Appeals' judgment is in doubt following the House of Lords decision in *Preddy* [1996] 3 All E.R. 481 (*post*, p. 735). Lord Goff of Chieveley, speaking *obiter*, considered that an intention to permanently deprive the owner of a cheque could not be established where the cheque was obtained by deception. On this basis he considered *Duru* and *Mitchell* [1993] Crim L.R. 788, which had applied it, were wrongly decided. This does not establish, however, whether in a situation such as that which pertained in *Kohn*, a charge of theft cannot be supported. In the deception case the cheque which returns to the drawer has on it the writing which he put there. In the *Kohn* situation, however, the cheques which returned to Panelservice had writing on them which Kohn, not they, put there. It is arguable, therefore, that the cheques, as pieces of paper, had been stolen as D's writing on them manifests his intention to, using the words of s. 6(1), "treat the thing as his own to dispose of regardless of the other's rights". (See further pp. 705–711, 741 and 815–816 *post*.)

3. Where a cheque is drawn by P in favour of D, the thing in action which the cheque represents, namely a right in the payee to sue the drawer for £x, belongs to D and thus cannot be stolen by D. However, if D presents the cheque for payment, the effect of this is to diminish by £x (or destroy) P's credit balance in his bank account. Could D be guilty of stealing this? In *Williams*, October 13, 2000 (Case No. 1986/99) D ran a building business and targeted vulnerable elderly householders. D's practice was to charge a modest sum for an initial piece of work to gain the customer's trust and then to charge exorbitant sums for subsequent work. D was charged with sample counts of theft of the customers' credit balances by causing cheques to be drawn in his favour and then presenting them for payment. The trial judge directed the jury that the prosecution had to prove that D had appropriated the credit balances of the customers stating, "If you get a householder to draw a cheque on a bank or building society and cause the cheque to be presented, you cause the householder's credit balance to be diminished, and accordingly take that credit balance for your own use." In upholding D's convictions the Court of Appeal referred to *Kohn* and *Graham, Ali and Others* [1997] 1 Cr.App.R. 302, where the Court had sought to make clear that nothing it said should cast doubt on *Kohn* and 'the principle that theft of a chose in action may be committed when a chose in action belonging to another is destroyed by the defendant's act of appropriation'.

4b. *Other intangible property.* Some intangible things can be valuable, without being a recognised thing in action. Examples are a patent, which is declared by statute to be personal property but not a thing in action: Patents Act 1977 section 30(1); and a trader's assignable export quota was held to be stolen by the person in the trader's organisation who was in charge of buying and selling such quotas when it was sold by him at a gross undervalue to a competitor: *Att.-Gen for Hong Kong v. Nai Keung* [1987] 1 W.L.R. 1339. Other examples are kinds of information: an idea, news, "know-how", a secret, especially a trade secret. Industrial espionage is rife nowadays, and such valuables are often "stolen," in popular parlance at least. However, it seems that information is not anyway comprehended in the statutory phrase "other intangible property".

Oxford v. Moss
(1978) 68 Cr.App.R. 183
Queens Bench Division

The facts appear in the judgment of Smith J.

Smith J.: This is a prosecutor's Appeal by way of Case Stated.

On May 5, 1976, an information was preferred by the prosecutor against the defendant alleging that the defendant stole certain intangible property, namely, confidential information being examination questions for a Civil Engineering Examination to be held in the month of June 1976 at Liverpool University, the information being the property of the Senate of the University, and the allegation being that the Respondent intended permanently to deprive the said Senate of the said property.

The facts can be stated very shortly indeed. They were agreed facts. They are set out in the case and they are as follows. In May 1976 the defendant was a student at Liverpool University. He was studying engineering. Somehow (and this Court is not concerned precisely how) he was able to acquire the proof of an examination paper for an examination in Civil Engineering to be held in the University during the following month, that is to say June 1976. Without doubt the proof, that is to say the piece of paper, was the property of the University. It was an agreed fact, as set out in the case, that the respondent at no time intended to steal what is described as "any tangible element" belonging to the paper; that is to say it is conceded that he never intended to steal the paper itself.

In truth and in fact, and in all common sense, what he was about was this. He was borrowing a piece of paper hoping to be able to return it and not be detected in order that he should acquire advance knowledge of the questions to be set in the examination and thereby, I suppose, he would be enabled to have an unfair advantage as against other students who did not possess the knowledge that he did.

By any standards, it was conduct which is to be condemned, and to the layman it would readily be described as cheating. The question raised is whether it is conduct which falls within the scope of the criminal law.

The learned stipendiary magistrate at Liverpool was of the opinion that, on the facts of the case, confidential information is not a form of intangible property as opposed to the property in the proof examination paper itself, that is the paper and the words printed thereon. He was of the opinion, further, that confidence consisted in the right to control the publication of the proof paper and was a right over property other than a form of intangible property.

Finally, he was of the opinion that by his conduct the respondent had gravely interfered with the owner's right over the paper. He had not permanently deprived the owner of any intangible property. Accordingly, the learned stipendiary magistrate dismissed the charge.

The prosecutor appeals. The question for this Court, shortly put, is whether confidential information can amount to property within the meaning of the Theft Act 1968. By section 1(1) of the statute: "A person is guilty of theft if he dishonestly appropriates property belonging to another with the intention of permanently depriving the other of it . . .";

By section 4(1): "'property' includes money and all other property, real or personal, including things in action and other intangible property."

The question for this Court is whether confidential information of this sort falls within the definition contained in section 4(1). We have been referred to a number of authorities emanating from the area of trade secrets and matrimonial secrets. In particular, we were referred to *Peter Manufacturing Corporation v. Corsets Silhouette Ltd* [1963] 3 All E.R. 402, to *Seager v. Copydex Ltd* [1967] 2 All E.R. 415, to the case of *Argyll v. Argyll* [1965] 2 W.L.R. 790, and *Fraser v. Evans* 3 W.L.R. 1172.

Those are cases concerned with what is described as the duty to be of good faith. They are clear illustrations of the proposition that, if a person obtains information which is given to him in confidence and then sets out to take an unfair advantage of it, the courts will restrain him by way of an order of injunction or will condemn him in damages if an injunction is found to be inappropriate. It seems to me, speaking for my part, that they are of little assistance in the present situation in which we have to consider whether there is property in the information which is capable of being the subject of a charge of theft. In my judgment, it is clear that the answer to that question must be no. Accordingly, I would dismiss the Appeal. (Lord Widgery C.J. and Wien J. agreed.)

Appeal dismissed

Questions

1. It was conceded that Moss never intended to steal the paper itself. On the agreed facts need this concession have been made? See section 6(1), *post*, p. 762, and J. R. Spencer, *The Metamorphosis of section 6 of the Theft Act*, *post*, p. 762.

2. It is not said how Moss obtained the proof. If he had used a collaborator in the University Registry, what would have been his offence? See, *ante*, p. 484.

Notes

The Court held that civil cases on protection of confidential information are of little assistance. Even if a right over something is protected by the law in some ways (*e.g.* by injunction, or by damages for its misuse) it does not follow that the right is intangible property, still less that it is intangible property for all purposes, *i.e.* that it ought to be protected by the criminal law, or by the law of theft specifically. In some areas theft is a blunt instrument where a discriminating tool is required.

5. *Electricity.* This was not stealable at common law. It is not included in the definition of property in section 4 because the dishon-

est use or wasting or diverting of it is made a special offence in section 13. See *Low v. Blease* [1975] Crim.L.R. 513.

6. *Unspecific Property.* If A is charged with stealing a watch, he cannot be convicted of stealing an umbrella (see Cockburn C.J. in *R. v. McPherson* (1858) D. & B. 197, 200). He must be shown to have stolen the specific property he is charged with stealing, although not necessarily the whole of it.

Machent v. Quinn [1970] 2 All E.R. 255 (Q.B.D.). Q was charged with stealing 35 shirts, nine pairs of trousers, four sweaters, two beach sets and two cardigans, to the total value of £199. It was proved that he stole four sweaters only, valued at £25. *Held,* he could be convicted as charged, (but his sentence was to relate to the four sweaters only).

It would be different if all that could be shown was that Q had stolen some articles from the list, but not which articles. However if the articles are identical (or undifferentiated in the indictment, *i.e.* described as "goods"), it is no objection that the stolen ones cannot be identified.

R. v. Tideswell [1905] 2 K.B. 273 (C.C.C.R.). T had permission to help himself to ashes in P's yard, paying for the weight taken. In collusion with P's servant, he took 32 tons 13 cwts., knowing that the servant had recorded the sale as of 31 tons 3 cwts. only. *Held,* T could be convicted on an indictment charging him with larceny of 1 ton 10 cwts.

And if it is impossible to show which particular articles A stole and when, but only that goods or money to a certain total value was appropriated in a certain period (*e.g.* between two stock-takings), he may be charged with, and convicted of, stealing the general deficiency, *R. v. Tomlin* [1954] 2 Q.B. 274.

In charges of attempted theft, or burglary with intent to commit theft, it is not necessary to charge or prove that the accused had any particular property in mind: *Re A.-G.'s References (Nos. 1 and 2 of 1979)* [1980] Q.B. 180 (C.A.).

iii. "Belonging to Another"

Theft Act 1968, section 5

(1) Property shall be regarded as belonging to any person having possession or control of it, or having in it any proprietary right or interest (not being an equitable interest arising only from an agreement to transfer or grant an interest).

(2) Where property is subject to a trust, the persons to whom it belongs shall be regarded as including any person having a right to enforce the trust, and an intention to defeat the trust shall be regarded accordingly as an intention to deprive of the property any person having that right.

(3) Where a person receives property from or on account of another, and is under an obligation to the other to retain and deal with that property or its proceeds in a particular way, the property or proceeds shall be regarded (as against him) as belonging to the other.

(4) Where a person gets property by another's mistake, and is under an obligation to make restoration (in whole or in part) of the property or its proceeds or of the value thereof, then to the extent of that obligation the

property or proceeds shall be regarded (as against him) as belonging to the person entitled to restoration, and an intention not to make restoration shall be regarded accordingly as an intention to deprive that person of the property or proceeds.

(5) Property of a corporation sole shall be regarded as belonging to the corporation notwithstanding a vacancy in the corporation.

Notes

1. A person can only steal what belongs to another. "Belonging to another" is given an extended meaning, and covers persons who have only minor interests in the property (possession, control, any proprietory right or interest). If B has such a minor interest in property, that property can be stolen from him by A, and it matters not whether A is also entitled to a minor (or indeed major) interest in the same property. Moreover, even if A is the entire owner, and B has no interest which the civil law will recognise, it may still be possible for A to steal the property if A got the property under an obligation.

2. Moreover a company is another person *vis-à-vis* its shareholders. Even if A owns all the shares in P Ltd, the property is not his, but "belongs to another," *viz.*, P Ltd, and A can steal that property: *A.-G.'s Reference No. 2 of 1982* [1984] 2 Q.B. 624: *R. v. Philippou* (1989) 89 Cr.App.R. 290. The fact that the defendant is in complete control of the company, and so able to secure its compliance with what he does, affords him no defence. His will is not that of the company when he is engaged in a crime against the company, and anyway the consent of the owner is irrelevant in theft, according to *R. v. Gomez*: see Lord Browne-Wilkinson.

3. The "belonging to another" factor, extended as it is, must exist at the time when the accused did the act which is said to be theft. If *before* he dishonestly does an act with regard to the property, it has ceased to belong to another and belongs to the accused, that act cannot be theft. See *Edwards v. Ddin*, below. But if the dishonest act *results* in the property belonging to the accused, because the victim consents to him becoming its owner, that act is nevertheless an appropriation of property belonging to another, and can be theft; it is sufficient if the property belonged to another at the time of the dishonest act: see *R. v. Gomez, ante*, p. 703 and particularly Viscount Dilhorne in *Lawrence, ante*, p. 704.

Edwards v. Ddin
[1976] 1 W.L.R. 942
Queen's Bench Division

The facts appear in the judgment of Croom-Johnson J.

CROOM-JOHNSON J.: This is an appeal by way of case stated from the magistrates' court sitting at Amersham in which the defendant had an information preferred against him that he stole three gallons of petrol and two pints of oil together of the value of £1.77, the property of Mamos Garage, Amersham, contrary to section 1 of the Theft Act 1968.

On the facts as found by the justices the following things happened. The defendant arrived with a motor car and he asked for some petrol and oil to

be placed in his car. Petrol and oil to the value as stated £1.77, was placed
into the car at his request by the garage attendant. When he ordered the petrol
and oil the defendant impliedly made to the attendant the ordinary representation of an ordinary customer that he had the means and the intention of
paying for it before he left. He was not in fact asked to pay and he did not in
fact pay, but the moment when the garage attendant was doing something
else he simply drove away. The justices also found, as one would think was
perfectly obvious, that whilst the petrol and oil had been placed in the car,
either in the tank or in the sump, it could not reasonably be recovered by the
garage in default of payment.

The questions therefore which have to be resolved in order to satisfy section
1 of the Act were two in number. First of all, was the defendant dishonest? It
appears that the justices must have considered that that was so. Secondly, had
he appropriated property belonging to another with the intention of permanently depriving the other of it? Upon that point the defence submitted successfully that at the time when the car was driven away the petrol and oil which
had got into the tank or sump were in fact not the property of the garage any
more but were the property of the defendant. On that basis the justices said
that that particular essential ingredient of theft under section 1 of the Act had
not been fulfilled and dismissed the information.

The whole question therefore was: whose petrol and oil was it when
the defendant drove away? Property passes under a contract of sale when
it is intended to pass. In such transactions as the sale of petrol at a garage
forecourt ordinary common sense would say that the garage and the
motorist intended the property in the petrol to pass when it is poured
into the tank and irretrievably mixed with the other petrol that is in it,
and I think that is what the justices decided.

But the prosecutor has appealed and has based his appeal on a consideration of the Sale of Goods Act 1893 and the provisions of that Act, and
seeks a ruling that transfer of the petrol was conditional only and that
therefore until payment the petrol remained the property of the garage.

But if one considers the provisions of the Sale of Goods Act 1893 one
comes out at the same answer as common sense would dictate.

The prosecution argument went this way, that when the motorist
arrives at the garage and says "will you fill me up, please?" or "will you
give me two gallons?" then there is a contract for the sale of unascertained
goods by description. In such circumstances when does the property in
the petrol pass? Nothing will have been said between the motorist and
the pump attendant about that, so one is thrown back on section 18 of the
Sale of Goods Act 1893 and rules made under it in order to ascertain the
intention of the parties.

By pouring the petrol into the tank the goods have been appropriated
to the contract with the assent of both parties. If that is done unconditionally, then the property in the petrol passes to the motorist: rule 5(1). The
prosecution argument then goes on that, however, there is a condition
which is waiting to be fulfilled, namely, payment, and says that under
section 19 of the Sale of Goods Act 1893 the garage reserves the right of
disposal of the petrol until the payment has been made and that therefore
the property has not passed under rule 5(1).

It is at this point that the argument breaks down. The garage owner
does not reserve the right to dispose of the petrol once it is in the tank,
nor is it possible to see how effect could be given to any such condition
wherever petrol has been put in and is all mixed up with what other
petrol is already there. Consequently one passes back to rule 5(2) of section 18, which says that where a seller delivers the goods to the buyer
and does not reserve the right to dispose of them, he is deemed to have

unconditionally appropriated the goods to the contract and in those circumstances the property has passed to the buyer in accordance with rule 5(1).

Reference was also made by the prosecutor to section 5 of the Theft Act 1968 which deals with one of the subsidiary definitions arising under section 1, which is the initial section dealing with theft. Section 5, which deals with but is not definitive of the expression "belonging to another", is concerned with all manner of interests in property. It was urged upon us that the motorist is under an implied obligation to retain his car with the petrol in its tank on the garage premises and not to take it away until such time as he has paid for it, and that until that has been done the garage owner retains some proprietary interest in the petrol in the tank.

The relevant part of section 5, which is in subsection (3), reads:

"Where a person receives property from or on account of another, and is under an obligation to the other to retain and deal with that property or its proceeds in a particular way, the property or proceeds shall be regarded (as against him) as belonging to the other."

That section in my view is not apt to cover a case such as the present where there has been an outright sale of the goods and the property in the goods has passed and the seller is only waiting to be paid. Therefore the provisions of section 5 do not affect the conclusion in the present case.

I do not enter into any discussion for the purposes of this judgment of what might have been the position if the charge had been brought under some other section of the Theft Act 1968, or if the appropriation for the purposes of section 1 had been said to have arisen at an earlier stage of events which took place. On the facts as found and on the case as it was presented to the magistrates, in my view the magistrates reached a correct conclusion in law and I would dismiss the appeal.

Appeal dismissed

Questions

1. The Court leaves open the position if the appropriation had been said to have arisen at an earlier stage of the events. *Could* the appropriation have been said to have arisen earlier than the act of driving the car away? If yes, what difference should it have made to the result?

2. Would it have made any difference if the garage had *expressly* reserved the right of disposal pending payment? Consider the effect of the following condition of sale: "The seller supplies petrol on the understanding that from the moment of delivery until the amount supplied has been paid for, the whole of the petrol in the customer's tank shall be the property of the seller."

3. Of what offence could Ddin have been convicted if the facts had occurred in 1979? See, *post*, p. 830.

Notes

1. In *Davies v. Leighton* (1978) 68 Cr.App.R. 4, Lord Widgery C.J. regarded the law as well settled that in a supermarket sale the property in goods does not pass to the customer until he has paid for them, and he applied this rule to a case where the goods were not picked off the shelf by the customer but, being fruit, were weighed, bagged, priced and handed over by an assistant. See J. C. Smith's commentary

on this case at [1978] Crim.L.R. 576 for discussion of many of the different problems which can arise out of shop sales.

2. The introduction of civil law contractual questions into trials for theft has been deprecated, *e.g.* by Lord Roskill in *R. v. Morris* [1984] A.C. 320. However, if the issue is whether the property the subject of an apparent sale "belongs to another" at the time of the alleged theft by D, such questions are inevitable.

R. v. Walker [1984] Crim.L.R. 112. V bought a video recorder from D, which turned out to be defective. V returned it to D for repair and then, not getting any satisfaction, sued D in the County Court for the return of money paid for defective goods. Two days after he was served with the County Court summons, D sold the recorder to P. On D's trial for theft, the judge left it to the jury to decide on the evidence if the recorder belonged to V at the time D sold it to P. *Held*, this was not enough. "The relevant law, which was contained in the sale of Goods Act 1979 was complicated but the judge had made no attempt to explain it. For centuries juries had decided civil actions on points arising under the law of sale of goods. There was no reason why this jury should not have had the relevant law explained to them and in the absence of such an explanation it was impossible for them to do justice in the case." *Appeal allowed.* [The relevant law is that recission of a contract of sale returns the property in the goods to the vendor, and the service of a summons for the return of the purchase price could have amounted to such a recission]

Questions

1. A in a pub approaches B, who works at a local garage, and says he will make it worth B's while if he "forgets" to ask for any money when he fills his vehicle with petrol. B consults his employer, who instructs B to pretend to play A's game and arranges for the police to be present. Next day, A asks B to fill his tank and when that has been done starts to drive off without paying, but is apprehended. Is this theft by A? See *R. v. Gomez, ante*, p. 703.

2. (i) A sees an old car parked on the hard shoulder of a motorway. It is the same model as A's car, for which he has found difficulty in obtaining spares. A removes a part from the parked car, which A thinks has merely broken down but which in fact has been abandoned there by B. Is this theft by A?

(ii) Is it attempted theft by A? See, *ante*, p. 444.

(iii) Would it make any difference if the car had been abandoned in Q's barn? See next case.

R. v. Woodman
[1974] Q.B. 758
Court of Appeal

A was the owner of a disused factory. He sold all the scrap metal in the place to B. B entered the factory and removed all the scrap metal which he could easily reach, but left some which was in such an inaccessible position as to be not worth the trouble of getting. A, who thought that all the metal had been removed by B, then put a barbed wire fence around the factory to exclude trespassers. W entered the factory and removed the remaining metal. He was convicted of theft, and appealed on the ground that no-one had possession or control of the metal.

LORD WIDGERY C.J.: ... The recorder took the view that the contract of sale between English China Clays and the Bird group had divested English China Clays of any proprietary right to any scrap on the site. It is unnecessary to express a firm view on that point, but the court are not disposed to disagree with that conclusion that the proprietary interest in the scrap had passed. The recorder also took the view on the relevant facts that it was not possible to say that English China Clays were in possession of the residue of the scrap. It is not quite clear why he took that view. It may have been because he took the view that difficulties arose by reason of the fact that English China Clays had no knowledge of the existence of this particular scrap at any particular time. But the recorder did take the view that so far as control was concerned there was a case to go to the jury on whether or not this scrap was in the control of English China Clays, because if it was, then it was to be regarded as their property for the purposes of a larceny charge even if they were not entitled to any proprietary interest.

The contention before us today is that the recorder was wrong in law in allowing this issue to go to the jury. Put another way, it is said that as a matter of law English China Clays could not on these facts have been said to be in control of the scrap.

We have formed the view without difficulty that the recorder was perfectly entitled to do what he did, that there was ample evidence that English China Clays were in control of the site and had taken considerable steps to exclude trespassers as demonstrating the fact that they were in control of the site, and we think that in ordinary and straightforward cases if it is once established that a particular person is in control of a site such as this, then prima facie he is in control of articles which are on that site.

... The fact that it could not be shown that they were conscious of the existence of this or any particular scrap iron does not destroy the general principle that control of a site by excluding others from it is prima facie control of articles on the site as well.

There has been some mention in argument of what would happen if in a case like the present, a third party had come and placed some article within the barbed-wire fence and thus on the site. The article might be an article of some serious criminal consequence such as explosives or drugs. It may well be that in that type of case the fact that the article has been introduced at a late stage in circumstances in which the occupier of the site had no means of knowledge would produce a different result from that which arises under the general presumption to which we have referred, but in the present case there was, in our view, ample evidence to go to the jury on the question of whether English China Clays were in control of the relevant time. Accordingly, the recorder's decision to allow the case to go to the jury cannot be faulted and the appeal must be dismissed.

Appeal dismissed

Questions

1. "In my judgment, it is quite clear that a person cannot be said to be in possession of some article which she does not realise is, or may be, in her handbag, in her room, or in some other place over which she had control": *per* Lord Parker C.J., in *Lockyer v. Gibb* [1967] 2 Q.B. 243, a prosecution for the offence of being in possession of a controlled drug. Is this dictum inconsistent with the decision in *R. v. Woodman*?

2. Suppose W, when stripping the factory of metal, had discovered and taken away a cache of controlled drugs abandoned there by X. If, consistent with Lord Parker's dictum English China Clays were held not to have possession of the drugs, could W be convicted of stealing them?

Subsection 1: Possession, control or any proprietary right or interest

R. v. Bonner
[1970] 1 W.L.R. 838
Court of Appeal

B took metal from the house of W, with whom he was in partnership as demolition contractors. B said the metal was partnership property and he took it in order not to deprive W of it permanently but hold it as security for what was due to him from W out of the partnership profits. B was convicted of theft but his appeal was allowed on the ground that the verdict was in all the circumstances unsafe and unsatisfactory. However the Court of Appeal thought it right to deal with the legal point certified by the trial judge, *viz.* whether the jury was misdirected on the law relating to the theft by a partner of partnership property. The direction in question is quoted in the judgment of Edmund-Davies L.J. below.

EDMUND DAVIES L.J.: ... Mr Inglis-Jones has ... submitted that the circumstances of this case a mere taking away of partnership property, even with the intention of keeping the other partner permanently out of possession of it would not *per se* suffice to amount to theft; there would have to be something like destruction of the metal or its sale in market overt, which would have the effect (provided there was innocence in the buyer) of transferring a good title to him and so defeating the title of the deprived partner. Defending counsel summarised the matter by submitting that for there to be an "appropriation" within the Theft Act 1968, there must be a "conversion" of the property by one or other of the foregoing methods, neither of which was resorted to here. Therefore, so it is submitted, there was no theft.

Rejecting that submission, Judge Ranking directed the jury in these terms:

"... even if you are satisfied that there was a full partnership between Webb and Bonner, a partner has no right to take any partnership property with the intention of permanently depriving the other of his share. Therefore, even if Bonner was a partner of Webb, if he took that lead, which was partnership property, intending to deprive Webb permanently of his share and when he did it, he knew perfectly well that he had no legal right to take it, then he is guilty of theft; he is guilty of the theft of the whole property and not just guilty of the theft of Webb's share, because the whole of it was partnership property and it had not been divided ... and if one partner takes it he is guilty of stealing the whole of it."

Was this a misdirection? This court is clearly of the opinion that it was not. Sections 1, 3 and 5 of the Theft Act 1968, are here relevant. ...

Mr Inglis-Jones has boldly submitted that, since the basic requirement of theft is the appropriation of property belonging to another, there can be no such appropriation by one co-owner of property which is the subject matter of the co-ownership or partnership; and that there can be no "assumption ... of the rights of an owner" in a case like the present, where one is dealing with (as Bonner claims) property belonging to a partnership.

The whole object of the Theft Act 1968, was to get away from the technicalities and subtleties of the old law. . . .

The view of this court is that in relation to partnership property the provisions in the Theft Act 1968, have the following result: provided there is the basic ingredient of dishonesty, provided there be no question of there being a claim of right made in good faith, provided there be an intent permanently to deprive, one partner can commit theft of the property of another to whom he is a complete stranger.

Early though these days are, this matter has not gone without comment by learned writers. Professor Smith in his valuable work on the Theft Act 1968, expresses his own view quite clearly in paragraph 80 under the heading "Co-owners and partners" in this way:

"D. and P. are co-owners of a car. D. sells the car without P.'s consent. Since P. has a proprietary right in the car, it belongs to him under section 5(1). The position is precisely the same where a partner appropriates the partnership property."

. . . We thus have no doubt that there may be an "appropriation" by a partner within the meaning of the Act, and that in a proper case there is nothing in law to prevent his being convicted of the theft of partnership property. But this *excursus* is of an academic kind in the present case for we have already indicated our view regarding the unsatisfactory and unsafe nature of the verdicts returned against each of these accused. In these circumstances, all four appeals are allowed.

Appeals allowed

[Three other men who had helped Bonner had been charged with him.]

R. v. Turner (No. 2)
[1971] 1 W.L.R. 901
Court of Appeal

T took his car to a garage to have it repaired. Those repairs having been practically completed, the car was left in the road outside the garage. T called at the garage and told the proprietor that he would return the following day, pay him, and take the car; instead he took the car, using his spare key, without paying for the repairs. Later he lied about the matter to the police. He was convicted of theft of the car.

LORD PARKER C.J.: The words "belonging to another" are specifically defined in section 5 of the Act, subsection (1) of which provides: "Property shall be regarded as belonging to any person having possession or control of it, or having in it any proprietary right or interest." The sole question was whether Mr Brown [the garage proprietor] had possession or control.

This court is quite satisfied that there is no ground whatever for qualifying the words "possession or control" in any way. It is sufficient if it is found that the person from whom the property is taken, or to use the words of the Act, appropriated, was at the time in fact in possession or control. At the trial there was a long argument as to whether that possession or control must be lawful, it being said that by reason of the fact that this car was subject to a hire-purchase agreement, Mr Brown could never even as against the defendant obtain lawful possession or control. As I have said, this court is quite satisfied that the judge was quite correct in telling the jury they need not bother about lien, and that they need not bother about hire purchase agreements. The only question was whether Mr Brown was in fact in possession or control.

The second point that is taken relates to the necessity for proving dishonesty. Section 2(1) provides that: "A person's appropriation of property belonging to another is not to be regarded as dishonest (*a*) if he appropriates the property in the belief that he has in law the right to deprive the other of it, on behalf of himself or of a third person";

The judge said in his summing up: "Fourth and last, they must prove that the defendant did what he did dishonestly and this may be the issue which lies very close to the heart of the case." He then went on to give them a classic direction in regard to claim of right, emphasising that it is immaterial that there exists no basis in law for such belief. He reminded the jury that the defendant had said categorically in evidence: "I believe that I was entitled in law to do what I did." At the same time he directed the jury to look at the surrounding circumstances. He said this: "The prosecution say that the whole thing reeks of dishonesty, and if you believe Mr Brown that the defendant drove the car away from Carlyle Road, using a duplicate key, and having told Mr Brown that he would come back tomorrow and pay, you may think the prosecution are right." On this point Mr Herbert says that if in fact you disregard lien entirely, as the jury were told to do, then Mr Brown was a bailee at will and this car could have been taken back by the defendant perfectly lawfully at any time whether any money was due in regard to repairs or whether it was not. He says, as the court understands it, first that if there was that right, then there cannot be theft at all, and secondly that if and in so far as the mental element is relevant, namely belief, the jury should have been told that he had this right and be left to judge, in the light of the existence of that right, whether they thought he may have believed, as he said, that he did have a right.

The court, however, is quite satisfied that there is nothing in this point whatever. The whole test of dishonesty is the mental element of belief. No doubt, though the defendant may for certain purposes be presumed to know the law, he would not at the time have the vaguest idea whether he had in law a right to take the car back again, and accordingly when one looks at his mental state, one looks at it in the light of what he believed. The jury were properly told that if he believed he had a right, albeit there was none, he would nevertheless fall to be acquitted. This court, having heard all that Mr Herbert has said, is quite satisfied that there is no manner in which this summing-up can be criticised, and that accordingly the appeal against conviction should be dismissed.

Appeal dismissed.

Questions

1. A's car was taken by some person unknown. A few days later, A saw it standing locked on the drive of B's house. Using his spare key, he drove it away. Was this theft by A? Would it make any difference if he thought that the law gave him no right to repossess himself of the car but required him to report the matter to the police and leave them to take steps to get the car back? (Refer to the discussion of "legal impossibility" in regard to attempts, *ante*, p. 498).

2. Is the following case distinguishable from *R. v. Turner (No. 2)*?

In *R. v. Meredith* [1973] Crim.L.R. 253, M's car was impounded by the police while he was at a football match and removed to the police station yard, where it was left locked. When M went to the police station, he found it crowded and so, rather than wait, he took his car away from the yard without contacting any policeman. He was charged with stealing the car. Under the Disposal and Removal of Vehicles Regulations 1968, the owner was liable to pay the statutory charge of £4 if his car had been causing an obstruction. On going to the police he could (i) admit obstruction and pay £4, or (ii) refuse to pay and face prosecution for obstruction, or (iii) agree to pay and receive a bill for £4. In any event he would be allowed to take the car away for the regulations gave the police no power to retain it as against him. It was held by a Crown Court judge that M had no case to answer.

Trust Property

Notes

1. A beneficiary under a trust clearly has a proprietory right or interest in the trust property, and a defaulting trustee may be guilty of stealing that property from him. The object of the special provision in section 5(2) (*ante*, p. 740) is to cover cases such as a charitable trust where there is no defined beneficiary, but the trust is enforceable by someone, *e.g.* the Attorney-General. The trust property "belongs to" that person for the purposes of theft.

2. As to constructive trusts, it was thought that the expression "proprietary interest" covered the interest of one entitled under such a trust (with the single stated exception of an equitable interest arising from an agreement to transfer or grant an interest). However there are divergent decisions of the Court of Appeal on whether to recognise interests under constructive trusts as proprietary interests within the meaning of subsection (1). In *A.-G.'s Reference (No. 1 of 1985)* (*post*, p. 753), a profit obtained by A from the unauthorised use of his employer's premises and facilities was held not to make A a constructive trustee of the profit; but the Court also held that, even if he was a constructive trustee, the trust did not give rise to a proprietary interest of the kind mentioned in subsection (1), because to convict a dishonest servant of stealing if he kept the profit would be far removed from ordinary notions of stealing. However, on the proprietary interest remaining on one who hands over money or property by mistake, see next case and Note 1. p. 757.

R. v. Shadrokh-Cigari
(1988) Transcript by LEXIS
Court of Appeal

S was guardian of his nephew R, whose father in Iran arranged for money to be paid into R's bank account in the United States. By error at the bank, $286,000 was credited to the account instead of $286. The United States bank transferred the larger sum to R's account with the Midland Bank, Sutton Coldfield. S prevailed on R to sign an authority for the issue of bankers drafts in favour of S totalling £197,000. Midland Bank issued the drafts and delivered them to S, who cashed them for his own purposes. He was convicted of theft of the drafts and appealed on the ground that the drafts belonged entirely to him.

SAVILLE J. for the Court: ... In our judgment the error in these submissions lies in the assumption that the entire proprietary interest in the drafts existed and vested in the Appellant leaving the Midland Bank with no rights at all. The fact of the matter is that the drafts would not have been drawn and delivered to the Appellant at all but for the mistake made by the United States bank, which, in turn led the Midland Bank to believe that the amount in question had been duly transferred from the United States for the credit of the account of Ramin. As Mr Phillips put it in evidence, a banker would not issue a banker's draft unless he himself was absolutely certain that he had received the money in payment and that in the instant case (having checked with London that the transfer had in fact been made and having credited the account of Ramin) he regarded the money as belonging to Ramin, who then authorised the issue of the drafts. It could hardly be suggested (and indeed it was not suggested) that if the Midland Bank had known the true position it would, nevertheless, have issued the drafts, since they would then be aware that there was, at the lowest, a substantial risk that the United States bank would be able to reclaim the funds. Indeed, we consider that the latter bank would have been able successfully to do so. See *Chase Manhattan Bank v. Israel-British Bank* [1981] 1 Ch 105. The mistake of the United States bank in the present case, therefore, totally undermined the basic assumption upon which the Midland bank issued the drafts, namely that the funds which had been received could properly be dealt with as directed by the account holder.

In these circumstances, it seems to us that as between the Midland Bank and the Appellant, the transaction falls fairly and squarely within the principles of the law relating to mistake. In *Kelly v. Solari* (1841) 9 M & W 54 and 58, Parke B stated the principle in the following terms:

"I think that where money is paid to another under the influence of a mistake, that is, upon the supposition that a particular fact is true, which would entitle the other to the money, which fact is untrue, and the money would not have been paid if it had been known to the payer that it was untrue, an action will lie to recover it back, and it is against conscience to retain it."

It has been suggested in later cases that the principle is not, in fact, stated widely enough by Parke B. to cover all circumstances where money or property can be recovered after a mistake has been made, but this citation will suffice for present purposes, since in this context we can see no material distinction between money and the drafts in question.

As Lord Wright pointed out in *Norwich Union v. Price* [1934] AC 455 at 463, the mistake must be one in respect of the underlying assumption of the contract or transaction or as being fundamental or basic, but to our minds that is clearly the case here. It is also probably the case that the mistake must be one of fact rather than law, but again we consider that if this is a requirement, it was satisfied in the present case.

The original mistake was clearly one of fact on the part of the United States bank and so far as the Midland Bank were concerned, the latter to our minds were clearly under the factual misapprehension that the former truly intended to transfer and vest in Ramin the entire right, property and interest in the amount remitted.

On this basis, it seems to us that the Appellant came under an obligation to make restoration of the instruments in question on the basis that the Midland Bank retained an equitable proprietary interest in the drafts as a result of the mistake, as in *Chase Manhattan Bank v. Israel-British Bank* (supra). The fact that the choses in action created by the drafts could not be owned by the bank, since they were debts due from the bank, is in our view irrelevant. The bank created the drafts and before delivery they undoubtedly owned them, although at that stage, as promissory notes, they were inchoate and incomplete (see Section 84 of the Bills of Exchange Act 1882). Upon delivery under the mistake, the bank retained an equitable interest in those instruments. It was not disputed that such an equitable interest amounts to property within the meaning of Section 5 (1) of the Theft Act 1968. To that extent, therefore, the drafts continued to belong to the Midland Bank at all material times within the meaning of the Theft Act 1968, so that the suggested difficulty in proving an appropriation does not arise.

In our judgment this conclusion is not only supported by Section 5(4) of the Theft Act 1968, but can be reached by another route through the application of that subsection, which provides as follows:

"Where a person gets property by another's mistake, and is under an obligation to make restoration (in whole or in part) of the property or its proceeds or of the value thereof, then to the extent of that obligation the property or proceeds shall be regarded (as against him) as belonging to the person entitled to restoration, and an intention not to make restoration is to be regarded accordingly as an intention to deprive that person of the property or proceeds."

It is clear from this sub-section that even if it cannot be said that the property belongs to another in the sense of that other having proprietary rights over the property itself, nevertheless (other things being equal) the property is to be regarded for the purposes of theft as belonging to that other even if the person getting it is only under an obligation to restore the proceeds of the property or its value, as opposed to the property itself, though the latter case is, of course, also covered by the sub-section.

We consider that the Appellant did come under an obligation to restore the proceeds or value of the instruments to the Midland Bank on the basis of the principles of civil law to which we have already referred.

On this aspect of the matter Mr Brock submitted that neither an equity in the drafts nor the right to claim their proceeds or value arose unless the Appellant was shown to have been aware that he was not entitled to receive the money in the form of the drafts. Mr Brock cited *Att.-Gen.'s Reference (No. 1 of 1985), post*, p. 753 as authority for this proposition.

So far as the equitable proprietary remedy is concerned, (with which the case cited did not deal) this proposition is clearly wrong, since it is settled law that the beneficiary (i.e. the owner of the equitable interest) can claim the property from an innocent volunteer who has taken it without notice of the equitable interest—see *Re Diplock* [1948] Ch 465 at 539.

So far as rights to claim the property or its proceeds or value on other grounds are concerned, the law is less certain. In the case cited by Mr Brock, of course, the Lord Chief Justice was dealing with a case of theft, where knowledge is essential for another reason, namely to establish dishonesty, so that in that context it is hardly surprising that the Court made the observations upon which Mr Brock places reliance.

We remain unpersuaded that knowledge on the part of the recipient is a necessary pre-condition to a civil obligation on his part to restore the property, its proceeds or value but for the purposes of this appeal we are prepared to make the opposite assumption in favour of the Appellant. Having done so, we take the view that the point is an academic one, for, in fact, the judge did leave this very question to the jury.

Appeal dismissed

*Subsection 3: An obligation to retain and deal with the property or its
proceeds in a particular way*

R. v. Hall
[1973] 1 Q.B. 126
Court of Appeal

H, a travel agent, received money from certain clients as deposits and
payments for air trips to America. He paid the money so received into
his firm's general account. None of the projected flights materialised
and none of the money was refunded. He was convicted of theft. He
appealed on the ground that he had not, within the meaning of section
5(3), been placed under an obligation to retain and deal with in a particular way the sums paid to him.

EDMUND DAVIES L.J.: Two points were presented and persuasively developed
by the appellant's counsel: (1) that, while the appellant has testified that all
moneys received had been used for business purposes, even had he been
completely profligate in its expenditure he could not in any of the seven cases
be convicted of "theft" as defined by the Theft Act 1968; there being no allegation in any of the cases of his having *obtained* any payments by deception,
counsel for the appellant submitted that, having received from a client, say,
£500 in respect of a projected flight, as far as the criminal law is concerned he
would be quite free to go off immediately and expend the entire sum at the
races and forget all about his client . . .
    Point (1) turns on the application of section 5(3) of the Theft Act 1968 . . .
    Counsel for the appellant submitted that in the circumstances arising in
these seven cases there arose no such "obligation" on the appellant. He
referred us to a passage in the Eighth Report of the Criminal Law Revision
Committee which reads as follows: "*Subsection* (3) provides for the special
case where property is transferred to a person to retain and deal with for a
particular purpose and he misapplies it or its proceeds. An example would
be the treasurer of a holiday fund. The person in question is in law the owner
of the property; but the subsection treats the property, as against him, as
belonging to the persons to whom he owes the duty to retain and deal with
the property as agreed. He will therefore be guilty of stealing from them if he
misapplies the property or its proceeds."
    Counsel for the appellant . . . submits that the position of a treasurer of a
holiday fund is quite different from that of a person like the appellant, who
was in general (and genuine) business as a travel agent, and to whom people
pay money in order to achieve a certain object—in the present cases to obtain
charter flights to America. It is true, he concedes, that thereby the travel agent
undertakes a contractual obligation in relation to arranging flights and at the
proper time paying the airline and any other expenses. Indeed, the appellant
throughout acknowledged that this was so, although contending that in some
of the seven cases it was the other party who was in breach. But what counsel
for the appellant resists is that in such circumstances the travel agent "is
under an obligation" to the client "to retain and deal with . . . in a particular
way" sums paid to him in such circumstances.
    What cannot of itself be decisive of the matter is the fact that the appellant
paid the money into the firm's general trading account. As Widgery J. said in
R. v. Yule [1964] 1 Q.B. 5, 10, decided under section 20(1)(iv) of the Larceny
Act 1916: "The fact that a particular sum is paid into a particular banking
account . . . does not affect the right of persons interested in that sum or any
duty of the solicitor either towards his client or towards third parties with
regard to disposal of that sum." Nevertheless, when a client goes to a firm

carrying on the business of travel agents and pays them money, he expects that in return he will, in due course, receive the tickets and other documents necessary for him to accomplish the trip for which he is paying, and the firm are "under an obligation" to perform their part to fulfil his expectation and are liable to pay him damages if they do not. But, in our judgment, what was not here established was that these clients expected them "to retain and deal with that property or its proceeds in a particular way," and that an "obligation" to do so was undertaken by the appellant. We must make clear, however, that each case turns on its own facts. Cases could, we suppose, conceivably arise where by some special arrangement (preferably evidenced by documents), the client could impose on the travel agent an "obligation" falling within section 5(3). But no such special arrangement was made in any of the seven cases here being considered. It is true that in some of them documents were signed by the parties; thus, in respect of counts one and three incidents there was a clause to the effect that the People to People organisation did not guarantee to refund deposits if withdrawals were made later than a certain date; and in respect of counts six, seven and eight the appellant wrote promising "a full refund" after the flights paid for failed to materialise. But neither in those nor in the remaining two cases (in relation to which there was no documentary evidence of any kind) was there, in our judgment, such a special arrangement as would give rise to an obligation within section 5(3).

It follows from this that, despite what on any view must be condemned as scandalous conduct by the appellant, in our judgment on this ground alone this appeal must be allowed and the convictions quashed.

Conviction quashed.

Note

In *Klineberg and Marsden* [1999] 1 Cr.App.R. 427, the appellants sold timeshare apartments. The purchasers paid the purchase price on the understanding that the money would be held by an independent trust company until the apartments were ready for occupation. Only £233 of a total of £500,000 paid was deposited with the trust company. The appellants' convictions of theft were upheld as there was a legal obligation imposed on them to deal with the purchasers' money in a particular way which had been breached. (See also *Re. Kumar* [2000] Crim.L.R. 504. Cf. *Floyd v. D.P.P.* [2000] Crim.L.R. 411 and commentary thereon.)

Attorney-General's Reference (No. 1 of 1985)
[1986] 2 All E.R. 219
Court of Appeal

D, the manager of a tied public house, was obliged by his contract of employment with P Brewery to obtain all liquor from them and pay all takings into their bank account. D secretly bought beer elsewhere and sold this keeping the profits. Three questions arose on the reference: (1) whether the moneys paid by customers in respect of the beer he had secretly obtained from elsewhere were received on account of his employer within the meaning of section 5(3); (2) whether the secret profit he had made using his employer's premises, was subject to a constructive trust in favour of the employer; and (3) if so, whether that constructive trust gave the employer a proprietary right or interest in the secret profit within the ambit of section 5(1)?

LORD LANE C.J.: . . . Counsel for the Attorney-General bases his submission on two of the subsections to s.5 of the 1968 Act. First of all s.5(3) [*ante* p. 681]. . . .

Although, goes the argument, at first sight the money which A receives from selling the beer which he bought seems to belong to him, the effect of this subsection is to make the profit element in the money notionally belong to the employers. Thus when A appropriates the profit, he is guilty of theft, assuming that he is acting dishonestly.

Whether that argument is correct or not depends on whether A can properly be said to have received property (*i.e.* the payment over the counter for the beer he has sold to the customer) "on account of the employers". We do not think he can. He received the money on his own account as a result of his private venture. No doubt he is in breach of his contract with the employers; no doubt he is under an obligation to account to the employers at least for the profit he has made out of his venture, but that is a different matter. The fact that A may have to account to B for money he has received from X does not mean necessarily that he received the money on account of B.

[His lordship referred to s. 17 of the larceny Act 1916 which was the predecessor of s.5(3).]

Section 17 of the 1916 Act was in almost identical terms to s.68 of the Larceny Act 1861. There is a decision on the meaning of that latter section which is in point, *R. v. Cullum* (1873) L.R. 2 C.C.R. 28. That was a case in which the defendant was the captain of a barge and in the exclusive service of its owner. His remuneration was half the earnings of the barge, and he had no authority to take any other cargoes except those appointed for him. It was his duty to account to his master for the proceeds of each voyage which he undertook. On one occasion, although he had been ordered to bring the barge back empty from a certain place, and forbidden to take a particular cargo, he nevertheless loaded such cargo in the barge and returned therewith, being paid by the freight owners for that service. He told his master that the barge had come back empty and he never accounted for the money which he had received. The question was whether the defendant was properly convicted of embezzlement. The Court for Crown Cases Reserved held that on those facts the defendant was not guilty. Bovill C.J. in the course of his judgment said (at 31):

> "The facts before us would seem more consistent with the notion that the prisoner was misusing his master's property, and so earning money for himself, and not for his master. Under those circumstances, the money would not be received 'for' or 'in the name of', or 'on account of', his master, but for himself, in his own name and for his own account. His act, therefore, does not come within the terms of the statute, and the conviction must be quashed."

Blackburn J. said (at 33);

> "Now, in the present case, I cannot see how this was the master's property, or that the servant had authority to carry anything in this barge but the cargo he was directed to convey. He was actually forbidden to load this barge on the return voyage; he did load it, and very improperly earned money by the use of it; but in what sense he can be said to have received this sum for the use of his master I cannot understand. The test of the matter would really be this—if the person to whom the manure belonged had not paid for the carriage, could the master have said, 'There was a contract with you, which you have broken, and I sue you on it?' There would have been no such contract, for the servant never assumed to act for his master, and on that ground his act does not come within the statute. I think that in no case could

he have been properly convicted under the Act unless the money became that of the master."

The other three judges comprising the court agreed with those observations. Counsel for the Attorney-General seeks to distinguish that decision on the grounds that the freight owners would imagine that the man with whom they were dealing, namely the defendant himself, was entitled to the money they paid, because they did not know of the existence of the master, whereas in the instant case the customers, he suggests, would think they were handing over their money to the employers. We doubt whether the customers would pause to consider the destination of their money or whether it would make any difference to the legal situation if they did. Alternatively it is submitted *R. v. Cullum* was wrongly decided. We disagree. The argument based on s. 5(3) of the 1968 Act was a late addition to the reference. We think it is misconceived.

The reference as originally drawn relied solely on arguments based on s. 5(1) [*ante* p. 740].

The argument of the Crown is that A. was a "constructive trustee" of the profit element in the money paid by customers over the bar for the "bought in" beer and that accordingly the money belonged not, as might seem at first, to A. but to the beneficiary of the trust, namely the employers. The result of that, it is said, is that when A. paid the money into his bank account or otherwise appropriated it, he was guilty of theft (assuming dishonesty).

(After referring to various authorities.) We find it impossible to reconcile much of the language used in these decisions. Two matters however do emerge. The first is that if the contentions of the Crown are well-founded, and if in each case of secret profit a trust arises which falls within s.5, then a host of activities which no layman would think were stealing will be brought within the 1968 Act. As this court pointed out in *Dip Kaur v. Chief Constable for Hampshire* [1981] 2 All E.R. 430 at 433, [1981] 1 W.L.R. 578 at 583:

"... the court should not be astute to find that a theft has taken place where it would be straining the language so to hold, or where the ordinary person would not regard the defendant's acts, though possibly morally reprehensible, as theft."

The second matter is this. There is a clear and important difference between on the one hand a person misappropriating specific property with which he has been entrusted, and on the other hand a person in a fiduciary position who uses that position to make a secret profit for which he will be held accountable. Whether the former is within s.5, we do not have to decide. As to the latter we are firmly of the view that he is not, because he is not a trustee. . . .

Lord Wilberforce in *Tarling (No. 1) v. Government of the Republic of Singapore* (1978) 70 Cr.App.R. 77 at 110, said:

"[The transactions] . . . would appear, prima facie, to amount to a case of persons in a fiduciary capacity making a secret profit at the expense of their companies—conduct for which there exists classical remedies in equity. . . . Breach of fiduciary duty, exorbitant profit making, secrecy, failure to comply with the law as to company accounts . . . are one thing: theft and fraud are others."

Next there is the judgment of a powerful Court of Appeal in *Lister & Co. v. Stubbs* (1890) 45 Ch.D. 1. In that case Stubbs was employed by the plaintiffs who were silk spinners, as a foreman to buy for them certain materials which they used in their business. Stubbs corruptly took from one of the firms with whom he was so dealing (Messrs Varley) large sums by way of commission, which he then invested in the purchase of land and other investments. Some of it was retained in the shape of cash. The plaintiff company sought to follow such money into the investments and moved for an injunction to restrain Stubbs from dealing with the investments, alternatively for an order directing him to bring the moneys and the investments into court. Cotton L.J. said (at. p. 12):

"... in my opinion this is not the money of the Plaintiffs, so as to make the Defendant a trustee of it for them, but is money acquired in such a way that, according to all rules applicable to such a case, the Plaintiffs, when they bring the action to a hearing, can get an order against the Defendant for the payment of that money to them. That is to say, there is a debt due from the Defendant to the Plaintiffs in consequence of the corrupt bargain which he entered into; but the money which he has received under that bargain cannot, in the view which I take, be treated as being money of the Plaintiffs, which was handed by them to the Defendant to be paid to Messrs Varley in discharge of a debt due from the Plaintiffs to Messrs Varley on the contract between them."

Lindley L.J. gave judgment in similar terms (at p. 15):

"Then comes the question, as between Lister & Co. and Stubbs, whether Stubbs can keep the money he has received without accounting for it? Obviously not. I apprehend that he is liable to account for it the moment that he gets it. It is an obligation to pay and account to Messrs Lister & Co., with or without interest, as that of debtor and creditor; it is not of trustee and *cestui que trust*. We are asked to hold that it is—which would involve consequences which, I confess, startle me.... If by logical reasoning from the premises conclusions are arrived at which are opposed to good sense, it is necessary to go back and look again at the premises and see if they are sound. I am satisfied that they are not sound—the unsoundness consisting in confounding ownership with obligation."

Bowen L.J. concurred with those judgments.

It seems to us that the draftsmen of the 1968 Act must have had that decision in mind when considering the wording of s.5. Had they intended to bring within the ambit of the 1968 Act a whole new area of behaviour which had previously not been considered to be criminal, they would, in our judgment, have used much more explicit words than those which are to be found in s.5. Nor do we think it permissible to distinguish that decision by saying that bribes are in a different category from such transactions as those in the instant case. There is, in our view, no distinction in principle between the two....

Assuming that, contrary to our views, s.5(1) does import the constructive trust into the 1968 Act, on the facts of the case the employers still obtain no proprietary interest. A trustee is not permitted to make a profit from his trust. Therefore if he uses trust property to make a profit from the trust, he is accountable for that profit. If and when such profit is identified as a separate piece of property, he may be a constructive trustee of it. However, until the profit is identifiable as a separate piece of property, it is not trust property and his obligation is to account only.

A used the employers' property and his own money to make a private profit in breach of contract. He received from customers sums of money which represented in part the cost of the beer he had bought and in part possible profit for which he was accountable to the employers. This profit element, assuming it existed, never became a separate piece of property of which A could be trustee. It remained part of a mixed fund. Therefore there never was a moment at which A was trustee of a definite fund. It follows that there never was a moment when the employers had any proprietary interest in any of the money. The money did not belong to another. There was therefore no theft.

No less difficulty would arise in the proof of dishonesty and guilty intent. A might very well say, and say truthfully, that he knew that he was breaking the terms of his contract, but the idea that he might be stealing from his employers the profit element in this transaction had never occurred to him. There are topics of conversation more popular in public houses than the finer points of the equitable doctrine of the constructive trust.

It is said in answer to that obligation that the employers could, by giving in advance the necessary warnings, instruct their servants what the true meaning of the 1968 Act is. That seems to us to be a good illustration of the objectionability of the proposition. If something is so abstruse and so far from the understanding of ordinary people as to what constitutes stealing, it should not amount to stealing.

For these reasons we think that the submissions based on s.5(1) likewise fail.

The answers to the questions posed in the reference are therefore these: (1) no; (2) if, which we do not believe, it is properly described as a trust, it is not such a trust as falls within the ambit of s.5(1) of the Theft Act 1968; (3) no.

Opinion accordingly

Notes

1. At the time *Att.-Gen.'s Reference (No. 1 of 1985)* was decided the position at civil law was that an employee who took a bribe or made a secret profit by misusing his employer's property or his own position was bound to account to his employer for the profit on the basis of being a debtor. Lord Lane CJ purported to follow *Lister v. Stubbs* (1890) 45 Ch D 1. In *Att.Gen. for Hong Kong v. Reid* [1994] 1 A.C. 324 the Privy Council disapproved of *Lister v. Stubbs* finding that it was inconsistent with pre-existing authorities. The Privy Council was of the view that a person in a fiduciary position who receives a bribe becomes not only a debtor for the amount of the bribe but also holds the bribe (and its proceeds) on constructive trust. If the English courts follow this highly persuasive authority such property, being under s.5(1) "any proprietary . . . interest", could be the subject of theft. This, of course, would involve overruling *Att.-Gen.'s Reference (No. 1 of 1985)* but it would remove the artificial distinction the Court of Appeal has created between constructive trusts and other trusts.

2. This subsection is to a large extent redundant, because in the vast majority of cases where there is an obligation to retain and deal with the property in a certain way, the person to whom the obligation is owed will have a proprietary right or interest in the property. Thus with a bailment, the property "belongs to" the bailor, and with a trust, the property "belongs to" the beneficiary, under subsection 1, and in the case of misappropriation by the bailee or trustee there is no need of subsection 3 to secure a conviction. There are so many difficulties

involved in subsection 3 that it is unwise of a prosecutor to rely on it unless it is absolutely necessary to do so, which is rarely if ever the case.

3. It is said that the obligation must be a legal one, not a merely moral one (see *R. v. Gilks* [1971] 1 W.L.R. 1341: "In a criminal statute, where a person's criminal liability is made dependent on his having an obligation, it would be quite wrong to construe that word so as to cover a moral or social obligation as distinct from a legal one"). However, an obligation arising under a domestic arrangement of a sort which the civil law would say was not enforceable by action has been held to be enough (*R. v. Cullen* 1974, unreported: Smith § 2.76). Even if the accused is under an obligation at the moment of appropriation, he is not within the words of subsection 3 unless he received the property from or on account of the person to whom he now owes the obligation.

4. The obligation must be to retain and deal with *that property or its proceeds* in a particular way. This excludes an obligation to perform some service or do some act in return for being given the property, *e.g.* as in *R. v. Hall, ante,* p. 752, where B paid A money in return for A's promise to supply air tickets. A was not obliged to do anything *with* the money; his obligation was merely to perform his part of the bargain. It is the same, in most cases, if B lends A money. The only obligation in the borrower A is to repay the loan to B, not to do anything with the money lent. A owes B the amount of the loan, but a simple debtor-creditor relationship is not enough. A debtor who dishonestly puts himself in a position in which he is unable to pay his creditor does not commit theft.

The sort of situation which is within subsection 3 is illustrated by *Davidge v. Bunnett* [1974] Crim.L.R. 257 (D.C.). D shared a flat with A, B & C, the expenses being shared. A gas bill having become due, A, B & C gave D cheques for their shares, payable to D's employer, because she herself had no bank account. D cashed the cheques, paid some of the bill, but spent most of the money on Christmas presents. *Held*, D was under an obligation to apply the proceeds of the cheques towards paying the bill and was guilty of theft of the money spent on Christmas presents. A, B & C were not the owners of the money received from cashing the cheques. On the other hand, in no sense could it be said that D merely owed the money to them; what she owed them was a duty to use the fund to pay the gas bill.

In *Wain* [1995] 2 Cr.App.R. 660, the Court of Appeal, disapproving of *Lewis v. Lethbridge* [1987] Crim L.R. 59, D.C., followed *Davidge v. Bunnett*. D had taken part in fundraising for a 'Telethon' held for the charity 'The Telethon Trust'. Events he had organised raised £2,800 which he paid into a separate bank account. Subsequently he transferred this money into his own bank account. D's conviction of theft was affirmed on the basis that he had been under an obligation to retain, if not the actual notes and coins, at least their proceeds for the benefit of the Trust.

5. 'Whether or not an obligation arises is a matter of law, because the obligation must be a legal obligation': *R. v. Mainwaring* (1981) 74 Cr.App.R. 99, 107. Nevertheless, it was said at various places

(including *R. v. Hall, ante,* p. 752) that although a judge could rule that any approved situation did *not* amount to a relevant obligation and direct an acquittal, he could not rule that it *did* amount to such, but must leave it to the jury to say whether the facts did amount to the sort of obligation covered by subsection 3. See also *R. v. Hayes* (1976) 64 Cr.App.R. 82. But in *R. v. Mainwaring,* the Court of Appeal, without reference to the previous cases, said that the judge should direct 'If you find such and such, then I direct you as a matter of law that a legal obligation arose to which section 4(3) applies' (see also *Dubar* [1995] 1 Cr.App. R. 280). This is preferable in confining the jury to finding the facts, which indeed will be difficult enough in many cases. Except where a written document specifies the accused's obligation (which is a matter of construction for the judge), the jury must ask, did the payers *expect* the accused to retain and deal with the property in a particular way: see Edmund Davies L.J. in *R. v. Hall,* (*ante,* p. 752). In many cases, such as *R. v. Hall* itself where the payers were the multitudinous clients of a travel agency, it will be impossible to discover any general expectation, and any proved particular expectation by an individual client might be unreasonable and unassented to by the accused. The normal practice of traders in the accused's line of business would appear to be a better guide; but even if such were proved and was to the effect that clients' money was usually kept separate, it does not follow that the clients knew of the practice and expected the accused to follow it.

Subsection 4: Property got by another's mistake

Note

This subsection was passed in order to deal with a point highlighted in one particular case—*Moynes v. Cooper* [1956] 1 Q.B. 439. It was thought that if property was obtained by A from B by mistake in circumstances where B meant A to become the owner of it then, although A might be under a quasi-contractual obligation to restore the property or its value to B, in most cases B did not have any proprietary interest in the property, which belonged solely to A. The subsection provides that even if A is the only person with an interest in the property, the existence of the obligation to restore makes it theft if A dishonestly resolves not to restore. However, in 1979, it was held, apparently for the first time, in the case of *Chase Manhattan Bank v. Israel-London Bank* [1981] Ch. 105 (Goulding J.), that B has not merely a quasi-contractual right to sue A for the value, but an equitable interest in the property under a constructive trust. This principle was used in *R. v. Shadrokh-Cigari* (*ante,* p. 749) to convict A of theft when he dishonestly appropriated money given to him by mistake. The property belonged to B under subsection (1), and there was no need to have recourse to subsection (4). There is never a need to have recourse to that subsection. It is not every kind of mistake which gives rise to an obligation to restore, but if a mistake does have that effect, it gives rise to a proprietary interest in the person to whom the obligation is owed. There is one case where A is under an obligation to restore within the meaning of subsection (4) although B has no proprietary interest under subsection (1); that is when the property has become lost or consumed or otherwise untraceable under equity's rules. But in such a case, A's dishonest refusal to make good to B can never be theft, because there is no identifiable property for him to appropriate. He is no more than a defaulting debtor.

Although subsection (4) is not needed, it has been used to convict people who have got property by mistake: see *Att.-Gen.'s Reference (No. 1 of 1983)* 3 All E.R. 369.

iv. "With the Intention of Depriving Permanently"

Note

The definition of theft in section 1 requires that the appropriation should be with the *intention of permanently depriving the owner of it*. The italicised words are the same as those in the definition of larceny in section 1 of the Larceny Act 1916.

The intention to deprive must be a settled one at the time of the appropriation. As to an intention to deprive if and only if the goods on examination turn out to be what the taker wants, see next case.

R. v. Easom
[1971] 2 Q.B. 315
Court of Appeal

E took a handbag, searched through it, found nothing to interest him, and left it with contents intact near the owner, who repossessed it. E was convicted of theft of the bag and its detailed contents.

EDMUND DAVIES L.J: . . . In every case of theft the appropriation must be accompanied by the intention of permanently depriving the owner of his property. What may be loosely described as a "conditional" appropriation will not do. If the appropriator has it in mind merely to deprive the owner of such of his property as, on examination, proves worth taking and then, finding that the booty is valueless to the appropriator, leaves it ready to hand to be repossessed by the owner, the appropriator has not stolen. If a dishonest postal sorter picks up a pile of letters intending to steal any which are registered, but on finding that none of them are, replaces them, he has stolen nothing, and this is so notwithstanding the provisions of section 6(1) of the Theft Act 1968. In the present case the jury were never invited to consider the possibility that such was the appellant's state of mind or the legal consequences flowing therefrom. Yet the facts are strongly indicative that this was exactly how his mind was working, for he left the handbag and its contents entirely intact and to hand, once he had carried out his exploration. For this reason we hold that the conviction of the full offence of theft cannot stand. . . .

So once more, one is driven back to consider with what intention the appellant embarked upon the act of taking. This court, in *R. v. Stark* (unreported), October 4, 1967, quashed the conviction for larceny of a man caught in the act of lifting a tool-kit from the boot of a car, the judge having misdirected the jury by telling them: "Was Stark intending, if he could get away with it, and if it was worthwhile, to take the tool-kit when he lifted it out? If he picked up something, saying "I am sticking to this—if it is worthwhile," then he would be guilty." But does it follow from all this that the appellant (as to

whose identity and physical acts the verdict establishes that the jury entertained no doubt) has to go scot-free? Can he not, as the Crown originally
submitted, be convicted at least of attempted theft? Even though the contents
of the handbag, when examined, held no allure for him, why was he not as
guilty of attempted theft as would be the pickpocket who finds his victim's
pocket empty (see *R. v. Ring* (1892) 61 L.J.M.C. 116). Does a conditional intention to steal count for nothing? In his *Criminal Law (The General Part)*, 2nd ed.
(1961), p. 52, para. 23, Professor Glanville Williams says: "A conditional intention is capable of ranking as intention for legal purposes. Thus it is no defence
to an apparent burglar that his intention was merely to steal a certain paper
if it should happen to be there." He then cites the American Model Penal
Code, s.2.02(6) (T.D. No. 4 pp. 14, 129), which states that: "When a particular
purpose is an element of an offence, the element is established although such
purpose is conditional, unless the condition negatives the harm or evil sought
to be prevented by the law defining the offence."

But as to this, all, or, at least, much, depends upon the manner in which
the charge is framed. Thus, "if you indict a man for stealing your watch, you
cannot convict him of attempting to steal your umbrella" (*per* Cockburn C.J.
in *R. v. M'Pherson* (1857) D. & B. 197, 200)—unless, of course, the court of trial
has duly exercised the wide powers of amendment conferred by section 5 of
the Indictment Act 1915. In our judgment, this remains the law and it is unaffected by the provisions of section 6 of the Criminal Law Act 1967. No amendment was sought or effected in the present case, which accordingly has to be
considered in relation to the articles enumerated in the theft charge and nothing else. Furthermore, it is implicit in the concept of an attempt that the person
acting intends to do the act attempted, so that the *mens rea* of an attempt is
essentially that of the complete crime (see *Smith and Hogan, "Criminal Law"*,
2nd ed. (1969), p. 163). That being so, there could be no valid conviction of
the appellant of attempted theft on the present indictment unless it were
established that he was animated by the same intention permanently to
deprive Sergeant Crooks of the goods enumerated in the particulars of the
charge as would be necessary to establish the full offence. We hope that we
have already made sufficiently clear why we consider that, in the light of the
evidence and of the direction given, it is impossible to uphold the verdict on
the basis that such intention was established in this case.

For these reasons, we are compelled to allow the appeal and quash the
conviction.

Appeal allowed

Notes

1. 'What may be loosely described as a conditional appropriation
will not do. If the appropriator has it in mind merely to deprive the
owner of such of his property as, on examination, proves worth taking
and then, finding that the booty is valueless to the appropriator, leaves
it ready to hand to be repossessed by the owner, the appropriator has
not stolen.' For the subsequent history of this dictum of Edmund-
Davies L.J. (*supra*), which caused difficulties in burglary with intent to
steal, see *Att.-Gen's References (Nos. 1 and 2 of 1979)*, *post*, p. 886.

2. Usually, the crime of attempt is available to deal with cases of
this kind. In *Att.-Gen.'s References (Nos. 1 and 2 of 1979)*, Roskill L.J.
(see *post*, p. 828) said of *Easom* 'It seems clear from the latter part of
Edmund Davies L.J.'s judgment that if he had been charged with an
attempt to steal some or all of the contents of that handbag, he could

properly have been convicted.' In a case exactly like *Easom—R. v.
Smith & Smith* [1986] Crim.L.R. 166 (C.A.)—just such a charge was
preferred and the conviction was upheld on appeal. But since Easom
was held not to intend to steal any of the listed contents of the bag, it
seems odd to hold that he intended to steal 'some or all' of the
(unlisted) contents. Listed in the indictment or not, they were all
rejected by him. What he intended to steal was something which was
not there, *i.e.* something which he would have thought worth stealing.
The fact that his attempt to steal something valuable was impossible
is now no bar to his being convicted of attempting to steal; and he is
better dealt with by a charge of 'attempted theft from a handbag',
without any mention of the contents. See *R. v. Shivpuri, ante*, p. 504.

3. Edmund-Davies L.J. says (*ante*, p. 760) that his hypothetical dishonest postal sorter was not guilty of theft 'notwithstanding the provisions of section 6(1) of the Theft Act 1968'. Nevertheless, that section
does apparently make theft of *some* cases of conditional intent to
deprive permanently.

Theft Act 1968, section 6

(1) A person appropriating property belonging to another without meaning the other to lose the thing itself is nevertheless to be regarded as
having the intention of permanently depriving the other of it if his intention is to treat the thing as his own to dispose of regardless of the other's
rights; and a borrowing or lending of it may amount to so treating it it,
but only if, the borrowing or lending is for a period and in circumstances
making it equivalent to an outright taking or disposal.

(2) Without prejudice to the generality of subsection (1) above, where a
person, having possession or control (lawfully or not) of property
belonging to another, parts with the property under a condition as to its
return which he may not be able to perform, this (if done for purposes of
his own and without the other's authority) amounts to treating the property as his own to dispose of regardless of the other's rights.

J. R. Spencer, 'The Metamorphosis of Section 6 of the Theft Act' [1977] Crim.L.R. 653

An "intention to deprive" was, of course an element of the crime of larceny. Over the course of many years, the concept had been interpreted
in numerous cases. Generally, an *intention* to deprive, rather than mere
recklessness, was necessary. Thus abandoning another person's property
knowing there was a risk that he would never get it back was not larceny,
unless the person who did so actually desired the owner to lose it, or
(presumably) foresaw the virtual certainty that he would do so. However,
there were three judge-made extensions of "intention permanently to
deprive" where mere recklessness, or something like it, was sufficient.
(a) There was the "ransom principle," whereby it counted as an intention
permanently to deprive if the idea was to return the property to the owner
only if he was prepared to pay for it. (b) There was the "essential quality
principle," whereby it counted as an intention permanently to deprive if
the idea was to return the property only after it had undergone some
fundamental change of character: a live horse taken but a dead horse
returned, a valid ticket taken but a cancelled ticket returned. And (c) there
was the "pawning principle," where it counted as an intention perman-

ently to deprive if a person pawned another's property without his consent, hoping to be able to redeem the pledge, but knowing he might be unable to do so. The Criminal Law Revision Committee heartily approved of "intention permanently to deprive" as so elaborated by the courts, and it was the one element of larceny which the Committee thought could be transplanted into the new crime of theft without any alteration. The Committee assumed that the old case-law would automatically be applied if the phrase were enacted in the definition of theft without any attempt at further elaboration. It therefore opposed putting a section into the Theft Act elaborating "intention of permanently depriving," and carefully omitted any such clause from the Draft Theft Bill which it appended to its Eighth Report. However, somebody who had the ear of the Government thought otherwise . . . [after tracing the tangled Parliamentary history of the new clause]; Not surprisingly, the courts have so far failed to spot Parliament's real intention through the obscure verbiage in which Parliament has dressed it up. To date, they have been quite mystified by the section. . . .

A fair summary of the Court of Appeal's interpretation of section 6 in [*R. v. Warner*] would be the following.

"The section was enacted to extend "intention permanently to deprive" beyond its previous interpretation; however, it was only meant to do so to some infinitesimal degree, and we are not prepared to say in which direction; any judge who drags section 6 into his summing-up can expect to be reversed on appeal."

It has certainly not crossed anybody's mind that section 6 was designed to *preserve* the existing case law. In *Duru* [1974] 1 W.L.R. 2, the Court of Appeal applied the "essential quality" principle, but did so without reference to section 6. And in *Easom* (*ante*, p. 760) Edmund Davies L.J. indicated that a conditional intention to deprive was insufficient for theft, notwithstanding section 6; whereas the "pawning principle" and the "ransom principle", which section 6 was intended to preserve, are obvious instances of conditional intention.

Thus, as a result of section 6, the present meaning of "intention of permanently depriving" in theft is doubly in doubt. The expression is thought to be extended beyond its literal meaning by section 6, but we do not know how far or in what direction. And we do not know, how far, if at all, the pre-1968 case law on "intention permanently to deprive" can be relied on.

R. v. Lloyd
[1985] Q.B. 829
Court of Appeal

The appellant L was the chief projectionist at a cinema. He removed films from the cinema and passed them to the appellants A and B who made copies of them. All the films were returned to the cinema in a matter of hours. The pirated copies of the films were sold to the detriment of the film distributors. The appellants were convicted of conspiracy to steal and appealed. The issue on appeal was whether there could be an intention permanently to deprive in the circumstances.

LORD LANE C.J.: . . . What then was the basis of the prosecution case and the basis of the judge's direction to the jury? It is said that section 6(1) of the Theft Act 1968 brings such actions as the appellants performed here within the provisions of section 1. The judge left the matter to the jury on the basis that they had to decide whether the words of section 6(1) were satisfied by the prosecution or not. [His Lordship read s. 6(1)] . . .

That section has been described by J.R. Spencer in his article (*ante*, p. 762), as a section which "sprouts obscurities at every phrase," and we are inclined to agree with him. It is abstruse. But it must mean, if nothing else, that there are circumstances in which a defendant may be deemed to have the intention permanently to deprive, even though he may intend the owner eventually to get back the object which has been taken. . . .

In general we take the same view as Professor Griew in *The Theft Act 1968 and 1978*, 4th ed. (1982), p. 47 para. 2–73, namely, that section 6 should be referred to in exceptional cases only. In the vast majority of cases it need not be referred to or considered at all.

Deriving assistance from another distinguished academic writer, namely, Professor Glanville Williams, we would like to cite with approval the following passage from his *Textbook of Criminal Law*, 2nd ed. (1983), p. 719:

> "In view of the grave difficulties of interpretation presented by section 6, a trial judge would be well advised not to introduce it to the jury unless he reaches the conclusion that it will assist them, and even then (it may be suggested) the question he leaves to the jury should not be worded in terms of the generalities of the subsection but should reflect those generalities as applied to the alleged facts. For example, the question might be: 'Did the defendant take the article, intending that the owner should have it back only on making a payment? If so, you would be justified as a matter of law in finding that he intended to deprive the owner permanently of his article, because the taking of the article with that intention is equivalent to an outright taking.'"

Bearing in mind the observations of Edmund Davies L.J. in *R. v. Warner*, [(1970) 55 Cr.App.R. 93] we would try to interpret the section in such a way as to ensure that nothing is construed as an intention permanently to deprive which would not prior to the Act of 1968 have been so construed. Thus, the first part of section 6(1) seems to us to be aimed at the sort of case where a defendant takes things and then offers them back to the owner for the owner to buy if he wishes. If the taker intends to return them to the owner only upon such payment, then, on the wording of section 6(1), that is deemed to amount to the necessary intention permanently to deprive: see, for instance, *R. v. Hall* (1848) 1 Den. 381, where the defendant took fat from a candlemaker and then offered it for sale to the owner. His conviction for larceny was affirmed. There are other cases of similar intent: for instance, "I have taken your valuable painting. You can have it back on payment to me of £X,000. If you are not prepared to make that payment, then you are not going to get your painting back."

It seems to us that in this case we are concerned with the second part of section 6(1), namely, the words after the semi-colon:

> "and a borrowing or lending of it may amount to so treating it if, but only if, the borrowing or lending is for a period and in circumstances making it equivalent to an outright taking or disposal."

These films, it could be said, were borrowed by Lloyd from his employers in order to enable him and the others to carry out their "piracy" exercise.

Borrowing is *ex hypothesi* not something which is done with an intention permanently to deprive. This half of the subsection, we believe, is intended to make it clear that a mere borrowing is never enough to constitute the necessary guilty mind unless the intention is to return the "thing" in such a changed state that it can truly be said that all its goodness or virtue has gone: for example *R. v. Beecham* (1851) 5 Cox C.C. 181, where the defendant stole railway tickets intending that they should be returned to the railway company in the usual way only after the journeys had been completed. He was convicted of larceny. The judge in the present case gave another example, namely, the taking of a torch battery with the intention of returning it only when its power is exhausted.

That being the case, we turn to inquire whether the feature films in this case can fall within that category. Our view is that they cannot. The goodness, the virtue, the practical value of the films to the owners has not gone out of the article. The film could still be projected to paying audiences, and, had everything gone according to the conspirators' plans, would have been projected in the ordinary way to audiences at the Odeon Cinema, Barking, who would have paid for their seats. Our view is that those particular films which were the subject of this alleged conspiracy had not themselves diminished in value at all. What had happened was that the borrowed film had been used or was going to be used to perpetrate a copyright swindle on the owners whereby their commercial interests were grossly and adversely affected in the way that we have endeavoured to describe at the outset of this judgment. That borrowing, it seems to us, was not for a period, or in such circumstances, as made it equivalent to an outright taking or disposal. There was still virtue in the film.

For those reasons we think that the submissions of Mr Du Cann on this aspect of the case are well founded. Accordingly the way in which the judge directed the jury was mistaken, and accordingly, this conviction of conspiracy to steal must be quashed.

Appeals allowed

Notes

1. Lord Lane C.J. said that it might be that the only offence of which Lloyd and his collaborators could be convicted would be conspiracy to commit a breach of the Copyright Act. However, now section 12 of the Criminal Justice Act 1987, *ante*, p. 483, will allow a charge of conspiracy to defraud. See *Scott v. M.P.C., ante*, p. 484.

2. Lord Lane's suggestion that a court should "try to interpret the section in such a way as to ensure that nothing is construed as an intention permanently to deprive which would not prior to the Act of 1968 have been so construed" (*ante* p. 764) appears to confirm Spencer's fear (*ante*, p. 763) that section 6 extends the law only minimally and obscurely, at least where a borrowing or a lending is involved. Nevertheless, since the decision in *Lloyd*, other cases have taken a less restricted view of the section's ambit; and the Court of Appeal in *R. v. Wille* (1988) 86 Cr.App.R. 296, and the Privy Council in *Chan Man-sin v. Att.-Gen. for Hong Kong* [1988] 1 All E.R. 1 read the section quite literally, and had no difficulty in holding that where D knew that V's bank account would not be diminished in any way by his drawing an unauthorised cheque on it, he was "nevertheless to be regarded as having the intention of permanently depriving" V, because he intended "to treat the thing (the bank account) as his own to dispose of regardless of the other's rights."

In *Fernandes* [1996] 1 Cr.App.R. 175, Auld L.J. reading the judgment of the Court of Appeal stated (at p. 188):

"In our view, section 6(1), which is expressed in general terms, is not limited in its application to the illustrations given by Lord Lane C.J. in

Lloyd. Nor, in saying that in most cases it would be unnecessary to refer to the provision, did Lord Lane suggest that it should be so limited. The critical notion, stated expressly in the first limb and incorporated by reference in the second, is whether a defendant intended 'to treat the thing as his own to dispose of regardless of the other's rights'. The second limb of subsection (1), and also subsection (2), are merely specific illustrations of the application of that notion. We consider that section 6 may apply to a person in possession or control of another's property who, dishonestly and for his own purpose, deals with that property in such a manner that he knows he is risking its loss."

3. In *Marshall* [1998] 2 Cr.App.R. 282, the Court of Appeal applied *Fernandes*. The appellants obtained used, but unexpired, tickets from passengers leaving London Underground stations and sold them on to other travellers thereby depriving London Underground of revenue. The appellants were convicted of theft of the tickets and appealed contending that tickets are analogous to cheques in that they represent a chose in action which belongs to the customer, not London Underground and, in so far as the tickets are pieces of paper, these would be returned to the possession of London Underground in due course. The Court of Appeal dismissed their appeals holding that the tickets, as pieces of paper, belonged at all times to London Underground and that the appellants by acquiring and re-selling them had the intention to treat them as their own to dispose of regardless of London Underground's rights, it being irrelevant that the tickets would find their way back into the possession of London Underground. This ruling does not fall within the ransom principle, essential quality principle or the pawning principle. The case has been subjected to criticism by Professor Smith, "Stealing Tickets" [1998] Crim. L.R. 723, who argues that the decision will not necessarily apply to all tickets as the question whether the original vendor of the ticket retains property in the ticket will depend on the terms of the contract. Professor Smith states (at p. 724):

But a person is not bound by a condition printed on a ticket unless reasonable steps have been taken to bring it to his attention. If such steps have not been taken, the condition does not form part of the contract and it cannot be relied on to show that the ownership in the ticket did not pass. Where a ticket is obtained from a machine, the supplier must give reasonable notice to the purchaser before he inserts his money. A term printed on the ticket issued by the machine is too late; the contract is already made.

4. In *Cahill* [1993] Crim.L.R. 142 the Court of Appeal approved the following passage in Smith, *The Law of Theft* (6th edn) p. 73:

It is submitted, however, that an intention to use the thing as one's own is not enough and that "dispose of" is not used in the sense in which a general might "dispose of" his forces but rather in the meaning given by the *Shorter Oxford Dictionary*: "To deal with definitely: to get rid of; to get done with, finish. To make over by way of sale or bargain, sell."

In *D.P.P. v. Lavender* [1994] Crim. L.R. 297, the Divisional Court, without referring to *Cahill*, ruled that the dictionary definition of "dispose of" was too narrow and a disposal could include "dealing with" property. L had been charged with theft of two doors from the council. He had taken the doors from a council property undergoing repair and used them to replace damaged doors in his girlfriend's council flat. The justices had dismissed the information. The Divisional Court allowed the prosecution's appeal and remitted the case to the justices with a direction to convict. If "dispose of" means "deal with", it is difficult to see what purpose the words "to treat the thing as his own" serve; they appear to be superfluous. *Cahill* should be followed.

Questions

1. D, an attendant at the National Gallery, offers to sell to P, a gullible tourist, a Constable painting. If appropriation is an artificial concept and intention permanently to deprive is likewise an artificial concept, could D be convicted of theft of the painting?

2. V carries on the business of dressing skins in his warehouse. V buys undressed skins from A, paying him for the number delivered, and employs B to dress skins, paying him according to the number dressed. The practice is for A to dump skins in V's delivery room; when V has credited them to A, V moves them to the dressing room. Dressed skins, when B's work on them has been credited to him, are moved from the dressing room to the storage room. In order to be paid twice for delivered skins, A moves back a pile of undressed skins from the dressing room to the delivery room. In order to be paid twice for dressing skins, B moves back a pile of dressed skins from the storage room to the dressing room. What is the difference between the positions of A and B, so far as concerns a possible charge of theft?

See *R. v. Hall*, referred to *ante*, p. 752, and *R. v. Manning* (1852) Dears. 21, and compare *R. v. Holloway* (1849) 2 C. & K. 942.

v. "Temporary Deprivation"

Criminal Law Revision Committee's Eighth Report, Cmnd. 2977

§ 56 . . . We considered whether temporary deprivation of property in general should be included in theft or made a separate offence under the Bill. There is certainly a case for making temporary deprivation punishable in circumstances in which it may involve dishonesty comparable with that involved in theft and may cause serious loss or hardship. The taker gets the benefit of the property without payment, and the owner is correspondingly deprived. The property may be lost or damaged, or it may be useless to the owner by the time it is returned. . . . But the committee generally are against extending theft to include temporary deprivation or creating a general offence of temporary deprivation of property. The former course seems to them wrong because in their view an intention to return the property, even after a long time, makes the conduct essentially different from stealing. Apart from this either course would be a considerable extension of the criminal law, which does not seem to be called for by any existing serious evil. It might moreover have undesirable social consequences. Quarrelling neighbours and families would be able to threaten one another with prosecution. Students and young people sharing accommodation who might be tempted to borrow one another's property in disregard of a prohibition by the owner would be in danger of acquiring a criminal record. Further, it would be difficult for the police to avoid being involved in wasteful and undesirable investigations into alleged offences which had no social importance. It is difficult to see how the provision could be framed in a way which would satisfactorily exclude trivial cases and meet these objections. If cases of temporary deprivation should become common, or if it should become too easy a defence to a charge of theft that the intention was to return the property in the end, it might be necessary, notwithstanding these formidable difficulties, to create an offence of temporary deprivation with a high enough maximum penalty for serious cases.

Note

The Committee nevertheless identified two particular cases where temporary deprivation should be an offence. They are articles in places open to the public, and conveyances. Special offences in relation to them appear in sections 11 and 12 of the Theft Act 1968 respectively.

For criticism of the details of both of these special offences, and of the general principle that temporary deprivation should not be theft, see, *post*, p. 715.

(a) Removal of Articles from Places open to the Public

Criminal Law Revision Committee's Eighth Report, Cmnd. 2977

§ 57 A striking recent instance is the removal from the National Gallery of Goya's portrait of the Duke of Wellington. The portrait, before being returned, was kept for four years, during which there was evidence that the man who took it tried to make it a condition of his returning it that a large sum should be paid to charity. He was acquitted of stealing the portrait (but convicted of stealing the frame, which was never recovered and which, if his initial statement was true, he destroyed soon after taking it). In another case an art student took a statuette by Rodin from an exhibition, intending, as he said, to live with it for a while, and returned it over four months later. (Meanwhile the exhibitors, who had insured the statuette, had paid the insurance money to the owners, with the result that the statuette, when returned, became the property of the exhibitors.) Yet another case was the removal of the Coronation Stone from Westminster Abbey. There is obviously a substantial question whether conduct of this kind should be made criminal. Many people may think that taking in cases of these kinds should be punishable, if not as theft, then as a special offence. Churches, art galleries, museums and other places open to the public may contain articles of the greatest importance and value, many of them irreplaceable. They cannot always be protected as well as in private premises and, if removed, may easily be lost or damaged. Against this it can be argued that serious cases of the kind are rare and, judging from the cases mentioned, that offenders are more eccentric than genuinely criminal. Before the Goya case few people would have said that there was an evil unprovided for and serious enough to require the creation of a new offence: and there are objections to extending the criminal law because of isolated occurrences. There may also be the danger that the taker will be less likely to return the property eventually if he is liable to punishment for having removed it. We have come to the conclusion that the situation, especially in view of the Goya case, is serious enough to justify the creation of a special offence in spite of the possible objections. . . .

Note

The Committee felt that the offence ought to be designed as one of criminal damage, so did not draft a clause in their Bill. Nevertheless section 11 was inserted during the Theft Bill's passage through Parliament.

Theft Act 1968, section 11

(1) Subject to subsections (2) and (3) below, where the public have access to a building in order to view the building or part of it, or a collection or part of a collection housed in it, any person who without lawful authority removes from the building or its grounds the whole or part of any article displayed or kept for display to the public in the building or that part of it or in its grounds shall be guilty of an offence.

For this purpose 'collection' includes a collection got together for a temporary purpose, but references in this section to a collection do not apply to a collection made or exhibited for the purpose of effecting sales or other commercial dealings.

(2) It is immaterial for purposes of subsection (1) above, that the public's access to a building is limited to a particular period or particular occasion; but where anything removed from a building or its grounds is there otherwise than as forming part of, or being on loan for exhibition with, a collection intended for permanent exhibition to the public, the person removing it does not thereby commit an offence under this section unless he removes it on a day when the public have access to the building as mentioned in subsection (1) above.

(3) A person does not commit an offence under this section if he believes that he has lawful authority for the removal of the thing in question or that he would have it if the person entitled to give it knew of the removal and the circumstances of it.

(4) A person guilty of an offence under this section shall, on conviction on indictment, be liable to imprisonment for a term not exceeding five years.

(b) Taking Conveyances

Note

If A took goods from B and later abandoned them in a position whence it would naturally be expected that B would eventually recover them, it was difficult to prove that the taking was with intent to deprive B. The fact that abandoned motorcars are invariably returned, through the system of universal registration of motor vehicles, to their registered owners, made it difficult to convict a "joyrider" of larceny of the motor car. The legislature therefore invented a crime for motor vehicles (see section 217 of the Road Traffic Act 1960) which could be described as larceny without intention permanently to deprive. Boats were covered by the Vessels Protection Act 1967, and the offence was widened still further by section 12 of the Theft Act, under which aircraft are covered for the first time.

Theft Act 1968, section 12

(1) Subject to subsections (5) and (6) below, a person shall be guilty of an offence if, without having the consent of the owner or other lawful authority, he takes any conveyance for his own or another's use, or, knowing that any conveyance has been taken without such authority, drives it or allows himself to be carried in or on it.

(2) A person guilty of an offence under subsection (1) above shall be liable on summary conviction to a fine not exceeding level 5 on the standard scale (see scale on p. 618, *ante*) to imprisonment for a term not exceeding six months, or to both.

(3) Offences under subsection (1) above and attempts to commit them shall be deemed for all purposes to be arrestable offences within the meaning of section 2 of the Criminal Law Act 1967.

(4) If on the trial of an indictment for theft the jury are not satisfied that the accused committed theft, but it is proved that the accused committed an offence under subsection (1) above, the jury may find him guilty of the offence under subsection (1).

(5) Subsection (1) above shall not apply in relation to pedal cycles; but, subject to subsection (6) below, a person who, without having the consent of the owner or other lawful authority, takes a pedal cycle for his own or another's use, or rides a pedal cycle knowing it to have been taken without such authority, shall on summary conviction be liable to a fine not exceeding fifty pounds.

(6) A person does not commit an offence under this section by anything done in the belief that he has lawful authority to do it or that he would have the owner's consent if the owner knew of his doing it and the circumstances of it.

(7) For purposes of this section—

(a) 'conveyance' means any conveyance constructed or adapted for the carriage of a person or persons whether by land, water or air, except that it does not include a conveyance constructed or adapted for use only under the control of a person not carried in or on it, and 'drive' shall be construed accordingly; and

(b) 'owner' in relation to a conveyance which is the subject of a hiring agreement or hire-purchase agreement, means the person in possession of the conveyance under that agreement.

(c) Criticism

Glanville Williams: "Temporary Appropriation Should Be Theft" [1981] Crim.L.R. 129

That the law of theft, taken by itself, would be inadequate is recognised not only by the survival of conspiracy to defraud but by the creation of special statutory offences. It is an offence under the Post Office Act 1953, s. 53, unlawfully to take a postal packet in course of transmission by post, without any necessity for an intent to deprive the owner permanently. The same is true for the taking and concealment of judicial documents. It is an offence to take fish even though the angler throws them back immediately upon catching them. Blackmail for the purpose of making a temporary acquisition of property can be punished as blackmail (see *post*, p. 778) but a robbery for the same purpose is not robbery in law, this offence being dependent on the definition of theft. Better-known exceptions are those created by sections 11 and 12 of the Theft Act 1968 (the former inserted in response to the public indignation at the outcome of the *Goya* case). But the exceptions are rather arbitrary. Why should it be an offence to make off temporarily with a cart but not with a horse, or with a statuette from a public museum but not from an auction sale-room when the public have been invited to view the articles or from a private collection that specific people have been invited to view? Why should the statutory offence be committed by going off with a valuable duck from the grounds of a zoo if the zoo houses some of its exhibits in a building open to the public (*e.g.* a parrot-house) but not if the public are left entirely in the open air? Is a church a building 'where the public have access in order to view the building or part of it, or a collection or part of a collection housed in it,' or is it exclusively a place of worship? In *Barr* [1978] Crim.L.R. 244 it was ruled in the Crown Court that public access is given for devotional purposes only, and not 'in order to view'. If that is correct for the ordinary church, what about Westminster Abbey? It may be remembered that during the early hours of Christmas morning, 1950, some Glasgow students took the Stone of Scone from the Abbey, subsequently leaving it at Arbroath Abbey; so the point may not be wholly without practical importance.

The special offences do not mesh with other offences involving the concept of theft. For example, it is not burglary to break into a public museum to remove an exhibit for temporary enjoyment, or to break into a garage and take off a car for a temporary criminal purpose. . . .

Suppose that a person removes a small piece of sculpture from a private exhibition or a valuable book from a University library, and returns it after a year. During that time it has of course been lost to its owner; and both the owner and the police have been put to trouble. (If the owner has made a claim upon an insurer or bailee, and been compensated on the basis of total loss, he may even find that the insurer or bailee claims the right to sell the article when it is recovered, so that the owner loses it). The taker of the article may use it in such a way as to put it at risk, or he may make a profit from it, or he may return it in an impaired condition; and if he is a person of no substance the owner's civil remedy against him will be an insufficient penalty. . . .

As in the case of the missing Goya, the temporary removal of a thing may be done with the intention of causing loss to the owner, or with an intention that necessarily involves such loss. Another example of this relates to copyright and industrial espionage. It is not theft or any other offence to remove a paper that is due to be set in an examination in order to read it and then return it (See *Oxford v. Moss, ante,* p. 738) even though the result is that the examining body has to go to the expense of setting another paper. Nor is it an offence to remove a film unlawfully in order to make pirated copies, or to remove a secret document in order to copy it and sell the copy to a trade rival. A conspiracy to do these things may be punished as a conspiracy to defraud (see *Scott v. M.P.C., ante,* p. 484), but is it right that the criminal law should take no notice of this behaviour by individuals? . . .

Yet it is not only a question of the risk of *losing* the article. When an article is unlawfully taken, even if only for a temporary purpose and without substantial risk of permanent loss of the article, the owner suffers an immediate loss, namely in respect of the use of it. . . .

One of the principal arguments for changing the law is that the value of articles lies in their use. More and more things are used by way of hiring, for longer or shorter periods, instead of by ownership. Many articles of use have comparatively short useful 'lives'. In a few years they wear out or become unfashionable or technically obsolete. Therefore, to deprive the owner of the article even for a short period is to deprive him of an appreciable part of its utility. Besides, the owner is in the dilemma of either being without the article for that time or putting himself to the expense of buying another—an expense that may turn out to have been unnecessary if the article is returned. The loss of the article will be particularly annoying if the owner has relied upon having the article for a particular purpose, which becomes frustrated. . . .

Particular trouble is caused to the police and others when dangerous articles are taken, as when in 1966 a Cobalt 60 isotope was taken from a factory by someone who broke in and then dumped it in a barrel of water in the factory area; shortly afterwards the same isotope was taken again. The fact that such a dangerous article is returned reduces but by no means eliminates the danger to the public and the nuisance of those responsible for the article when it is unlawfully carried off. . . .

Only two arguments against making the proposed extension of the Theft Act are worth consideration. The first, that it would be contrary to tradition, or that people would not recognise temporary appropriations as theft, can perhaps be answered by pointing to the legal systems that have this concept already. Many of the illustrations given in this article would, I think, readily be regarded as theft by many people. For example, it would, I am sure, generally be regarded as theft for a person to take a bicycle, use it for several weeks, and then abandon it on the street, even if the owner eventually recovers it. In the debate on the Theft Bill in the House of Lords, Viscount Dilhorne made the interesting point that none of the definitions of the word 'steal' in the *Oxford English Dictionary* required an intent to deprive the owner permanently; they spoke only of the dishonest taking or appropriating of the property of another. In one respect the definition of theft has always gone far beyond popular usage; the slightest moving of the article with the necessary intent is traditionally theft, though the ordinary man would not regard the theft as complete at that stage. Under the Theft Act it seems to be sufficient merely to touch the article, since touching is one of 'the rights of an owner' within section 3(1). It is strange to swallow this camel while straining at the gnat of saying that it is theft to decamp with someone's valuable article and to conceal it from him dishonestly for what may be a considerable period of time.

It may be that the reader, while accepting some of the arguments in this article, has throughout been afflicted by one other doubt. Is it seriously suggested that trivial cases of dishonestly using the property of another should be subject to prosecution as theft?

The argument about trivial cases is frequently used to oppose extensions of the law, but it is never conclusive in itself, because practically every offence covers *some* trivial matters. If an offence is needed to deal with serious misconduct, that is sufficient to justify it. Even the present law could be abused by prosecuting for trivial thefts, but in practice a sensible discretion is generally exercised. The Canadian experience bears out the view that a law of *furtum usus* is unlikely to be used oppressively. . . . The question has generally arisen in Canada in connection with people who walk off with articles of furniture from beer parlours or hotels; and I see no injustice or oppression in convicting them of theft, even though they aver, after being found out, that they were about to come back with the article. . . .

My main legislative proposal is that the word 'permanently' should be repealed in section 1(1) of the Theft Act 1968. It should also be repealed in section 15(1), since it was put there only out of supposed logical necessity after being put in section 1(1). There is no reason of policy why a cheat who obtains the hire of a car by deception should not be guilty of obtaining property by deception. The fact that this conduct can now be brought, somewhat awkwardly, within the offence of obtaining services under the Theft Act 1978, s.1 is no argument for not making this change in the Act of 1968. . . ."

vi. "Dishonestly"

Theft Act 1968, section 2

(1) A person's appropriation of property belonging to another is not to be regarded as dishonest—

(a) if he appropriates the property in the belief that he has in law the right to deprive the other of it, on behalf of himself or of a third person; or
(b) if he appropriates the property in the belief that he would have the other's consent if the other knew of the appropriation and the circumstances of it; or
(c) (except where the property came to him as trustee or personal representative) if he appropriates the property in the belief that the person to whom the property belongs cannot be discovered by taking reasonable steps.

(2) A person's appropriation of property belonging to another may be dishonest notwithstanding that he is willing to pay for the property.

Criminal Law Revision Committee, Eighth Report, Cmnd. 2977

§ 39 The word 'dishonestly' in the definition in clause 1(1) is very important, as dishonesty is a vital element in the offence. The word replaces the requirement in 1916 section 1(1) that the offender should take the property 'fraudulently and without a claim of right made in good faith'. 'Dishonestly' seems to us a better word than 'fraudulently'. The question 'Was this dishonest?' is easier for a jury to answer than the question 'Was this fraudulent?' 'Dishonesty' is something which laymen can easily recognise when they see it, whereas 'fraud' may seem to involve technicalities which have to be explained by a lawyer. The word 'dishonestly' could probably stand without a definition and some members of the committee would have preferred not to define it. But we decided to include the partial definition in clause 2 in order to preserve specifically two rules of the present law. The first is the rule mentioned above that a 'claim of right made in good faith' is inconsistent with theft; this rule is preserved in different language in paragraph (a) of clause 2(1). The second is the rule in 1916 section 1(2)(d) that a finder of property cannot be guilty of stealing it unless he 'believes that the owner can be discovered by taking reasonable steps'; this rule is reproduced in slightly different language in paragraph [c] of clause 2(1).

Note

Paragraph (*b*) of section 2(1) clarified what was not clear before, namely, that it is not an offence where the accused knows that he has no consent to what he is doing but believes that he would have been given consent if the owner had been asked.

Question

In *R. v. Thurborn* (1849) 1 Den. 387, T found in the street a banknote with no means of identification on it. As soon as he picked it up, he resolved to appropriate it to his own use, but before he could spend it, he was told who the owner was. He nevertheless disposed of the note and was held not guilty of larceny, because he did not, at the time he found the note, know how the owner could be found. In view of sections 2(1)(*c*) and 3(1) (*ante*, pp. 702, 773) would T today be guilty of theft? At what stage did he assume the rights of an owner?

Note

The definition in section 2 is not a complete one. The section instances three cases where the defendant's belief means that his appropriation is not to be regarded as dishonest, but is silent or inconclusive on other cases. One situation not covered is the case of a person who takes property (*e.g.* money) without any colour of right, knowing that the owner does not and would not consent, but intending to restore the equivalent (*e.g.* other coins to the value of the money taken). Section 2(2) covers the case but not conclusively, saying that such an appropriation *may* be dishonest. See next case.

R. v. Feely
[1973] Q.B. 530
Court of Appeal

F was the manager of a bookmaker's betting shop. His employers wrote to all their managers stating that the practice of borrowing from tills was to stop. He nevertheless took £30 for his own purposes. He claimed that he always meant to return the money. He was convicted of stealing the money and appealed.

LAWTON L.J: The appeal raises an important point of law, namely, can it be a defence *in law* for a man charged with theft and proved to have taken money to say that when he took the money he intended to repay it and had reasonable grounds for believing and did believe that he would be able to do so? The trial judge, Judge Edward Jones, adjudged that such a defence is not available. . . .

In section 1(1) of the Act of 1968, the word "dishonestly" can only relate to the state of mind of the person who does the act which amounts to appropriation. Whether an accused person has a particular state of mind is a question of fact which has to be decided by the jury when there is a trial on indictment, and by the magistrates when there are summary proceedings. The Crown did not dispute this proposition, but it was submitted that in some cases (and this, it was said, was such a one) it was necessary for the trial judge to define "dishonestly" and when the facts fell within the definition he had a duty to tell the jury that if there had been appropriation it must have been dishonestly done.

We do not agree that judges should define what "dishonestly" means.

This word is in common use whereas the word "fraudulently" which was used in section 1(1) of the Larceny Act 1916, had acquired as a result of case law a special meaning. Jurors, when deciding whether an appropriation was dishonest can be reasonably expected to, and should, apply the current standards of ordinary decent people. In their own lives they have to decide what is and what is not dishonest. We can see no reason why, when in a jury box, they should require the help of a judge to tell them what amounts to dishonesty. We are fortified in this opinion by a passage in the speech of Lord Reid in *Cozens v. Brutus* [1973] A.C. 854, a case in which the words "insulting behaviour" in section 5 of the Public Order Act 1936, had to be construed. The Divisional Court had adjudged that the meaning of the word "insulting" in this statutory context was a matter of law. Lord Reid's comment was as follows, at p. 861: "In my judgment that is not right. The meaning of an ordinary word of the English language is not a question of law. The proper construction of a statute is a question of law. If the context shows that a word is used in an unusual sense the court will determine in other words what that unusual sense is. But here there is in my opinion no question of the word 'insulting' being used in any unusual sense. . . . It is for the tribunal which decides the case to consider, not as law but as fact, whether in the whole circumstances the words of the statute do or do not as a matter of ordinary usage of the English language cover or apply to the facts which have been proved."

When this trenchant statement of principle is applied to the word "dishonestly" in section 1(1) of the Theft Act 1968, and to the facts of this case, it is clear in our judgment that the jury should have been left to decide whether the defendant's alleged taking of the money had been dishonest. They were not, with the result that a verdict of guilty was returned without their having given thought to what was probably the most important issue in the case. . . .

Appeal allowed

Note

This case was thought by some to lay down a purely objective test of dishonesty, *i.e.* whatever the jury thought it was, without reference to what the defendant thought. That was felt to be too hard on the defendant, and inconsistent with the three specific cases of honesty in section 2(1), all of which are made to depend on the defendant's belief. On the other hand, making the test purely subjective (what view the defendant took of his own conduct) would be a charter of immunity for those with low or idiosyncratic moral viewpoints, *e.g.* Robin Hood seeing no wrong in robbing the rich to feed the poor. There followed discordant decisions, under which the meaning of dishonesty was held to be different depending upon which crime was involved or, in the case of obtaining by deception, which part of the crime was involved. See next case, which achieves a significant degree of reconciliation, but does not remove all problems.

R. v. Ghosh
[1982] Q.B. 2053
Court of Appeal

G, a consultant surgeon, obtained money by falsely pretending that it was owing as an anaesthetist's fee. He was convicted of dishonestly obtaining the money by deception, contrary to section 15, Theft Act 1968 (see, *post*, p. 734) and appealed.

LORD LANE C.J.: The grounds of appeal are simply that the judge misdirected the jury as to the meaning of dishonesty. What the judge had to say on that topic was as follows:

"Now, finally dishonesty. There are, sad to say, infinite categories of dishonesty. It is for you. Jurors in the past and, whilst we have criminal law in the future, jurors in the future have to set the standards of honesty. Now it is your turn today, having heard what you have, to consider contemporary standards of honesty and dishonesty in the context of all that you have heard. I cannot really expand on this too much, but probably it is something rather like getting something for nothing, sharp practice, manipulating systems and many other matters which come to your mind."

. . . *R. v. Feely* (*ante*, p. 774) . . . is often treated as having laid down an objective test of dishonesty for the purpose of section 1 of the Theft Act 1968. But what it actually decided was (i) that it is for the jury to determine whether the defendant acted dishonestly and not for the judge, (ii) that the word "dishonestly" can only relate to the defendant's own state of mind, and (iii) that it is unnecessary and undesirable for judges to define what is meant by "dishonestly".

It is true that the court said, at pp. 537–538:

"Jurors, when deciding whether an appropriation was dishonest, can be reasonably expected to, and should, apply the current standards of ordinary decent people."

It is that sentence which is usually taken as laying down the objective test. But the passage goes on:

"In their own lives they have to decide what is and what is not dishonest. We can see no reason why, when in a jury box, they should require the help of a judge to tell them what amounts to dishonesty."

The sentence requiring the jury to apply current standards leads up to the prohibition on judges from applying *their* standards. That is the context in which the sentence appears. It seems to be reading too much into that sentence to treat it as authority for the view that "dishonesty can be established independently of the knowledge or belief of the defendant". If it could, then any reference to the state of mind of the defendant would be beside the point.

This brings us to the heart of the problem. Is "dishonestly" in section 1 of the Theft Act 1968 intended to characterise a course of conduct? Or is it intended to describe a state of mind? If the former, then we can well understand that it could be established independently of the knowledge or belief of the accused. But if, as we think, it is the latter, then the knowledge and belief of the accused are at the root of the problem.

Take for example a man who comes from a country where public transport is free. On his first day here he travels on a bus. He gets off without paying. He never had any intention of paying. His mind is clearly honest; but his conduct, judged objectively by what he has done, is dishonest. It seems to us that in using the word "dishonestly" in the Theft Act 1968, Parliament cannot have intended to catch dishonest conduct in that sense, that is to say conduct to which no moral obloquy could possibly attach. This is sufficiently established by the partial definition in section 2 of the Theft Act itself. All the matters covered by section 2(1) relate to the belief of the accused. Section 2(2) relates to his willingness to pay. A man's belief and his willingness to pay are things which can only be established subjectively. It is difficult to see how a partially subjective definition can be made to work in harness with the test which in all other respects is wholly objective.

If we are right that dishonesty is something in the mind of the accused (what Professor Glanville Williams calls "a special mental state"), then if the mind of the accused is honest, it cannot be deemed dishonest merely because members of the jury would have regarded it as dishonest to embark on that course of conduct.

So we would reject the simple uncomplicated approach that the test is purely objective, however attractive from the practical point of view that solution may be.

There remains the objection that to adopt a subjective test is to abandon all standards but that of the accused himself, and to bring about a state of affairs in which "Robin Hood would be no robber": *R. v. Greenstein*. This objection misunderstands the nature of the subjective test. It is no defence for a man to say "I knew what I was doing is generally regarded as dishonest; but I do not regard it as dishonest myself. Therefore I am not guilty." What he is however entitled to say is "I did not know that anybody would regard what I was doing as dishonest." He may not be believed; just as he may not be believed if he sets up "a claim of right" under section 2(1) of the Theft Act 1968, or asserts that he believed in the truth of a misrepresentation under section 15 of the Act of 1968. But if he *is* believed, or raises a real doubt about the matter, the jury cannot be sure that he was dishonest.

In determining whether the prosecution has proved that the defendant was acting dishonestly, a jury must first of all decide whether according to the ordinary standards of reasonable and honest people what was done was dishonest. If it was not dishonest by those standards, that is the end of the matter and the prosecution fails.

If it was dishonest by those standards, then the jury must consider whether the defendant himself must have realised that what he was doing was by those standards dishonest. In most cases, where the actions are obviously dishonest by ordinary standards, there will be no doubt about it. It will be obvious that the defendant himself knew that he was acting dishonestly. It is dishonest for a defendant to act in a way which he knows ordinary people consider to be dishonest, even if he asserts or genuinely believes that he is morally justified in acting as he did. For example, Robin Hood or those ardent anti-vivisectionists who remove animals from vivisection laboratories are acting dishonestly, even though they may consider themselves to be morally justified in doing what they do, because they know that ordinary people would consider these actions to be dishonest.

Cases which might be described as borderline, such as *Boggeln v. Williams* [1978] 1 W.L.R. 873, will depend upon the view taken by the jury as to whether the defendant may have believed what he was doing was in accordance with the ordinary man's idea of honesty. A jury might have come to the conclusion that the defendant in that case was disobedient or impudent, but not dishonest in what he did.

So far as the present case is concerned, it seems to us that once the jury had rejected the defendant's account in respect of each count in the indictment (as they plainly did), the finding of dishonesty was inevitable, whichever of the tests of dishonesty was applied. If the judge had asked the jury to determine whether the defendant might have believed that what he did was in accordance with the ordinary man's idea of honesty, there could have only been one answer—and that is no, once the jury had rejected the defendant's explanation of what happened.

In so far as there was a misdirection on the meaning of dishonesty, it is plainly a case for the application of the proviso to section 2(1) of the Criminal Appeal Act 1968.

Appeal dismissed

Questions

1. Does this case dispose of the 'Robin Hood defence", as Lord Lane suggests (*ante*, p. 777)? D, accused of stealing from his bookmaker, says in evidence "Bookmakers are a race apart; it would be dishonest if your grocer gave you too much change and you kept it, knowing that he had made a mistake. But it is not dishonest in the case of a bookmaker." (See *Gilks* [1971] 1 W.L.R. 1341). Must he not be acquitted if (i) the jury think it is not dishonest to diddle bookmakers? or (ii) the jury do not think so but think that D may have thought that reasonable people may have thought so?

2. "Dishonesty is something which laymen can easily recognise when they see it" (C.L.R.C. § 39, *ante*, p. 773). Does this mean that 12 jurors will always agree in describing some transaction as honest or dishonest? and that successive juries dealing with similar transactions will agree in the same way? If so, do you agree? Is it possible to forecast the view of a jury on the honesty of, *e.g.* a taking of experimental animals in order to save them from vivisection? If juries did usually hold that such a taking was not theft, how could this be reconciled with the law which allows properly licensed vivisection?

3. Is (a) good motive, or (b) necessity, generally a defence to crime? See *ante*, Chaps. 3 and 5.

4. The judge needs to direct the jury to apply the double test of dishonesty laid down by Lord Lane (*ante*, p. 777) (was D's conduct dishonesty by ordinary standards, and if so did he realise it was so?) only where dishonesty is a live issue, *i.e.* only where D is in effect saying that he thought what he was doing was not dishonest. In other cases it is potentially misleading to direct on these matters: *R. v. Price* (1989) 80 Cr.App.R. 409.

5. In Victoria, under a statute in all material respects identical to the Theft Act, the Supreme Court, rejecting the reasoning in *Feely*, has held that the meaning of "dishonestly" is a matter of law for the judge, and that meaning is "with disposition to withhold from a person what is his right": *R. v. Salvo* [1980] V.R. 401, 432; *R. v. Brow* [1981] V.R. 738; *R. v. Bonollo* [1981] V.R. 633.

Note

The Law Commission issued a consultation in 1999 which considered the question whether a general fraud offence based on dishonesty should be introduced. It provisionally concluded that there should not be such an offence. In the course of its deliberations it analysed the test of dishonesty formulated in *Ghosh*.

**Legislating the Criminal Code: Fraud and Deception
Law Commission Consultation Paper No. 155 (1999)**

An unusual kind of requirement

5.11 The *Ghosh* approach requires fact-finders to set a moral standard of honesty and determine whether the defendant's conduct falls short of that standard. The argument in *Feely* (which first laid down the approach developed in *Ghosh*) is that this is a purely *semantic* enquiry: "dishonestly" is an ordinary English word, and, as presumably competent users of English, fact-finders can be expected to know what it means. But it is also a *moral* enquiry, and requires the making of a moral judgment. To say that something is dishonest is to characterise the existing facts, not add another fact. This, we believe, is an unusual kind of requirement in English criminal law. Traditionally, offences consist of objectively defined conduct (or circumstances, or events) and mental states (or other fault elements, such as negligence), subject to objectively defined circumstances of justification or excuse (such as self-defence or duress). In general the fact-finders' task is to determine whether the defendant's conduct falls within the legal definition of the offence, not whether they think it sufficiently blameworthy to be an offence. A requirement that the conduct in question fall short of an undefined *moral* standard is out of keeping with this approach.

5.12 It is true that fact-finders often have to make judgments on matters of degree. Driving, for instance, becomes an offence if it falls below a certain level of competence or diligence. But dangerous driving is defined by statute in terms which render it a factual question, and the same is true of careless driving as a matter of case law. Thus, in these offences, the role of the fact-finders is to determine whether the defendant's conduct falls below a legally defined standard. They are not required to decide whether conduct which does fall below that standard is sufficiently blameworthy to be criminal.

5.13 A closer analogy to *Ghosh* dishonesty, perhaps, is gross negligence manslaughter. The law requires the jury to determine whether the defendant's conduct was careless enough to be criminal, but does not tell them how careless it needs to be. It therefore requires the jury not just to *apply* a standard, but also to *set* it. Arguably this is no different in principle from the kind of enquiry required by *Ghosh*. But in one sense it is more objective, because the riskiness of a person's conduct is more quantifiable than its dishonesty. Given enough facts, risk can be mathematically assessed: the relative dangerousness of different forms of conduct is at bottom a question of fact. A 30 per cent risk of death is greater than a 10 per cent risk. In the case of dishonesty, however, even this degree of objectivity does not exist. Dishonesty is not quantifiable, even in theory. ... The fact-finders are required not merely to place the defendant's conduct at an appropriate point on the scale, but to construct their own scale.

5.14 We suggest, therefore, that the task allocated to juries and magistrates by the *Ghosh* test is a very unusual one. It is as if juries were directed, in relation to the defence of self-defence: "It is for you to decide whether the defendant's response to the force used by the victim was justified or not. 'Justified' is an ordinary English word, which you must define and apply for yourselves." Some juries would apply the same standard that the law now applies. Others might adopt a pacifist position and say that no force was justified, even in self-protection. Others again might consider that, having started the fight, the victim deserved a good beating. And there would be no way of rationally adjudicating the competing moral outlooks revealed.

Inconsistency

5.15 That like circumstances should be treated alike is fundamental to fairness and the rule of law. The result of our analysis of dishonesty is that the use made of the concept in the law must result in endemic inconsistency.

5.16 Central to *Feely* and *Ghosh* is the insistence that "dishonesty" is an ordinary English word. But even if it is an ordinary word in the English language, there is no guarantee that all speakers of the language will agree as to its application, particularly in marginal cases. . . . Individuals can reasonably differ in the application of a word. The point of the paraphrase provided by a definition is to bring users of the word together. Where the law defines a term, the process goes further: the meaning is, for the purposes of the provision, prescribed. Thereafter, any divergence in application from the prescribed meaning is an error. But fact-finders considering dishonesty are given no such assistance.

5.17 The test in *Ghosh* provides a way for fact-finders to apply the "ordinary standards of reasonable and honest people", presumably by applying their common understanding of the word. But this amounts to an appeal to a unified conception of honesty which we do not think is workable in modern society. We live in a heterodox and plural society which juries (and to a lesser extent magistrates) presumably replicate. To assume that there is a single community norm or standard of dishonesty, discernible by twelve (or even ten) randomly selected people of any age between 18 and 65, and of widely varied class, cultural, educational, racial and religious backgrounds, is unrealistic. How juries cope with these problems we cannot tell, given the prohibition on research into jury discussions. It seems inconceivable, however, that different juries do not come to different decisions on essentially similar facts. These are not *perverse* verdicts, because individually they are the result of the jury correctly applying the law. Such verdicts have been described as "anarchic", because they are the result of the jury being asked "a question of moral estimation without guidelines".

. . .

5.20 Our provisional view is that juries and magistrates should not be asked to set a moral standard on which criminal liability essentially depends. As a general rule, the law should say what is forbidden, and that should be informed by moral insights. A jury or magistrates should then be asked to apply the law by coming to *factual* conclusions, not moral ones.

The potential ambit of a general dishonesty offence

5.21 A general dishonesty offence may extend the reach of the criminal law too far, rendering criminal that which should not be. It is the essence of such an offence that it cannot be said with any certainty what conduct will or will not attract criminal liability. Any restriction of the right of fact-finders to treat particular conduct as dishonest would be inconsistent with the very idea of a general dishonesty offence.

The criminalisation of otherwise lawful conduct

5.24 The dangers of allowing the ambit of a criminal offence to be determined entirely by *Ghosh* dishonesty are illustrated by the present state of the law of theft, which (as a result of the decision in *Gomez* that even an authorised dealing with property is an "appropriation" of it) effectively now consists of doing something "dishonest" with another's property with the intention of permanently depriving the other of it. Recent decisions make it clear that theft may be committed where the defendant's conduct does not even give rise to a remedy in civil law. [The Law Commission proceeded to examine the Court of Appeal decisions in *Kendrick and Hopkins* [1997] 2 Cr.App.R. 524 (*ante* p. 712) and *Hinks* [1998] Crim. L.R. 904.]

. . .

5.28 In our provisional view, this is an unsatisfactory state of affairs. In general, we believe that the criminal law should take a robust view of what is to be allowed in the market place; and in particular we think it wrong that conduct which is not actionable (that is, which gives rise to no remedy in civil law) should be regarded as a substantive crime of dishonesty. The proper role of the criminal law of dishonesty, in our view, is to provide additional protection for rights and interests which are already protected by the civil law of property and obligations. To apply it to conduct which gives rise to no civil liability is to extend it beyond its proper function. We therefore do not believe that it should be criminal to accept a gift, or a transfer of property for consideration, *merely* because some people would regard it as a dishonest thing to do.

2. ROBBERY

Theft Act 1968, section 8

(1) A person is guilty of robbery if he steals, and immediately before or at the time of doing so, and in order to do so, he uses force on any person or puts or seeks to put any person in fear of being then and there subjected to force.

(2) A person guilty of robbery, or of an assault with intent to rob, shall on conviction on indictment be liable to imprisonment for life.

Notes

1. *Theft*. Without a theft (or attempted theft in the case of assault with intent to rob) there is no robbery. Theft is complete as soon as there is an appropriation with intent to steal. See Appropriation, *ante*, p. 702, and *Corcoran v. Anderton* (1980) 71 Cr.App.R. 104 (D.C.), where it was held that wrestling with the owner for possession of an article is an assumption of the rights of the owner and therefore theft and, if accompanied by force, robbery.

In *R. v. Robinson* [1977] Crim.L.R. 173 (C.A.) it was held that the law as laid down in *R. v. Skivington* [1968] 1 Q.B. 166 had not been altered by the Theft Act. In *R. v. Skivington*, S threatened with a knife his wife's employer in order to collect wages due to her which he had her authority to collect. The judge directed the jury that before S could maintain a defence to a charge of robbery, they must be satisfied that he had an honest belief that he was entitled to take the money in the way in which he did take it. Lord Goddard C.J.: "In the opinion of this court the matter is plain, namely that a claim of right is a defence to robbery . . . and that it is unnecessary to show that the defendant must have had an honest belief also that he was entitled to take the money in the way that he did."

Conviction quashed

Question

Is robbery involved in the following cases?

A is lent a lawnmower by his neighbour B. When B asks for its return, A drives him away with blows, saying he is going to keep it.

C, needing the use of a car to escape pursuit by the police, takes D's car from him at gunpoint.

E, needing the use of a car for a smash and grab raid on a shop, takes F's car from him at gunpoint. See below.

2. Force immediately before or at the time of the theft

Andrews, "Robbery" [1966] Crim.L.R. 524, 525

Another advantage of the new definition is that the crime of robbery is not restricted to stealing from the person or in the presence of the person against whom force is used or threatened. . . . However a problem does arise even under the new definition. Let us take the case of a defendant who assaults and binds someone and then proceeds to his victim's property some distance away where minutes or even hours later he steals. Is he guilty of robbery? The fact that the theft is away from the presence of the victim would no longer be a problem, but the new definition does restrict the scope of robbery to circumstances where the defendant 'immediately before or at the time of [stealing] wilfully uses force on any person or wilfully puts or seeks to put any person in fear of being then and there subjected to force'. Has the force been used 'immediately before' in our example? Does immediate mean seconds, minutes or hours? Presumably it is not intended to cover the situation where the violence precedes the stealing by a matter of days. Nor can one argue that the force or fear is a continuing factor if the victim remains under continuing fear or restraint, because what must be immediate is the wilful use of force not the continuing effect of it, or alternatively the putting of the person in fear or seeking to put him in fear must be immediate, not merely the continuing fear. The matter might be better put if the words 'immediately before or at the time of doing so' were left out of the definition. The crime of robbery would still be limited to where the person uses force or fear 'in order to [steal].' To further restrict it in terms of temporal proximity of force and theft is to make a defence of the criminal's divorcing in time the violence and the stealing and there seems no great reason in that. The real issue should surely be whether the force or threat of force was used *in order to steal*.

R. v. Hale
(1978) 68 Cr.App.R. 415
Court of Appeal

H and M entered the house of Mrs C wearing stocking masks. H put his hand over her mouth to stop her screaming. M went upstairs and came back with her jewellery box. They then tied up Mrs C and threatened harm to her child if she told the police within five minutes of their leaving. H was convicted of robbery and appealed.

EVELEIGH L.J.: . . . On behalf of the appellant it is submitted that the learned judge misdirected the jury in that the passages quoted above could indicate to them that if an accused used force in order to effect his escape with the stolen goods that would be sufficient to constitute the crime of robbery. In so far as the facts of the present case are concerned, counsel submitted that the theft was completed when the jewellery box was first seized and any force thereafter could not have been "immediately before or at the time of stealing" and certainly not "in order to steal". The essence of the submission was that the theft was completed as soon as the jewellery box was seized. . . .

Section 8 of the Theft Act 1968 begins: "A person is guilty of robbery if he steals. . . ." He steals when he acts in accordance with the basic definition of theft in section 1 of the Theft Act; that is to say when he dishonestly appropriates property belonging to another with the intention of permanently depriving the other of it. It thus becomes necessary to consider what is "appropriation" or, according to section 3, "any assumption by a person of the rights of an owner". An assumption of the rights of an owner describes the conduct of a person towards a particular article. It is conduct which usurps the rights of the owner. To say that the conduct is over and done with as soon as he lays hands upon the property, or when he first manifests an intention to deal with it as his, is contrary to common-sense and to the natural meaning of words. A thief who steals a motor car first opens the door. Is it to be said that the act of starting up the motor is no more a part of the theft?

In the present case there can be little doubt that if the appellant had been interrupted after the seizure of the jewellery box the jury would have been entitled to find that the appellant and his accomplice were assuming the rights of an owner at the time when the jewellery box was seized. However, the act of appropriation does not suddenly cease. It is a continuous act and it is a matter for the jury to decide whether or not the act of appropriation has finished. Moreover, it is quite clear that the intention to deprive the owner permanently, which accompanied the assumption of the owner's rights, was a continuing one at all material times. This Court therefore rejects the contention that the theft had ceased by the time the lady was tied up. As a matter of common-sense the appellant was in the course of committing theft; he was stealing.

There remains the question whether there was robbery. Quite clearly the jury were at liberty to find the appellant guilty of robbery relying upon the force used when he put his hand over Mrs Carrett's mouth to restrain her from calling for help. We also think that they were also entitled to rely upon the act of tying her up provided they were satisfied (and it is difficult to see how they could not be satisfied) that the force so used was to enable them to steal. If they were still engaged in the act of stealing the force was clearly used to enable them to continue to assume the rights of the owner and permanently to deprive Mrs Carrett of her box, which is what they began to do when they first seized it. . . .

Appeal dismissed

Compare C.L.R.C.'s Eighth Report, Cmnd. 2977, § 65; *infra*. See also *Gregory* (1981) 77 Cr.App.R. 41 and *Lockley* [1995] Crim.L.R. 656.

3. *Force on any person*

Criminal Law Revision Committee, Eighth Report, Cmnd. 297

§ 65 But the force will have to have been used for the purpose of stealing; force used only to get away after committing a theft does not seem naturally to be regarded as robbery (though it could be charged as a separate offence in addition to the stealing). We should not regard mere snatching of property, such as a handbag, from an unresisting owner as using force for the purpose of the definition, though it might be so if the owner resisted. In the case of robbery by putting in fear the draft requires the fear to be that of being then and there subjected to force. This seems to us to correspond to what should be the essence of the offence. A threat to accuse a person of an offence comes more naturally under blackmail than under property.

R. v. Dawson
(1976) 64 Cr.App.R. 170
Court of Appeal

D and two others came alongside a sailor, and nudged him from side to side. While he was trying to keep his balance, one of the three was enabled to take his wallet. They were convicted of robbery and appealed.

LAWTON L.J.: Mr Locke had submitted at the end of the prosecution's case that what had happened could not in law amount to the use of force. He called the learned judge's attention to some old authorities and to a passage in *Archbold* ... based on the old authorities, and submitted that because of those old authorities there was not enough evidence to go to the jury. He sought before this Court to refer to the old authorities. He was discouraged from doing so because this Court is of the opinion that in these cases what judges should now direct their attention to is the words of the statute. This had been said in a number of cases since the Theft Act 1968.

The object of that Act was to get rid of all the old technicalities of the law of larceny and to put the law into simple language which juries would understand and which they themselves would use. That is what has happened in section 8 which defines "robbery". That section is in these terms: "A person is guilty of robbery if he steals and immediately before or at the time of doing so, and in order to do so, he uses force on any person or puts or seeks to put any person in fear of being then and there subjected to force."

The choice of the word "force" is not without interest because under the Larceny Act 1916 the word "violence" had been used, but Parliament deliberately on the advice of the Criminal Law Revision Committee changed that word to "force". Whether there is any difference between "violence" or "force" is not relevant for the purposes of this case; but the word is "force". It is a word in ordinary use. It is a word which juries understand. The learned judge left it to the jury to say whether jostling a man in the way which the victim described to such an extent that he had difficulty in keeping his balance could be said to be the use of force. The learned judge, because of the argument put forward by Mr Locke, went out of his way to explain to the jury that force in these sort of circumstances must be substantial to justify a verdict.

Whether it was right for him to put that adjective before the word "force" when Parliament had not done so we will not discuss for the purposes of this case. It was a matter for the jury. They were there to use their common sense and knowledge of the world. We cannot say that their decision as to whether force was used was wrong. They were entitled to the view that force was used.

Other points were discussed in the case as to whether the force had been used for the purpose of distracting the victim's attention or whether it was for the purpose of overcoming resistance. Those sort of refinements may have been relevant under the old law, but so far as the new law is concerned the sole question is whether the accused used force on any person in order to steal. That issue in this case was left to the jury. They found in favour of the Crown.

We cannot say that this verdict was either unsafe or unsatisfactory. Accordingly the appeal is dismissed.

Appeal dismissed

R. v. Clouden [1987] Crim.L.R. 56 (C.A.): C was seen to follow a woman who was carrying a shopping basket in her left hand. He approached her from behind and wrenched the basket down and out of her grasp with both hands and ran off with it. He was charged in two counts with robbery and theft respectively and convicted on the first count of robbery. He appealed on the grounds (i) that there was insufficient evidence of resistance to the snatching of the bag to constitute force on the person under section 8 of the Theft Act 1968; and (ii) that the learned judge's direction to the jury on the requirement of force on the person was inadequate and confused.

Held, dismissing the appeal, the old cases distinguished between force on the actual person and force on the property which in fact causes force on the person but, following *Dawson*, the court should direct attention to the words of the statute without referring to the old authorities. The old distinctions have gone. Whether the defendant used force on any person in order to steal is an issue that should be left to the jury. The judge's direction to the jury was adequate. He told the jury quite clearly at the outset what the statutory definition was, though thereafter he merely used the word "force" and did not use the expression "on the person".

Questions

1. What exactly did *Dawson* purport to decide on the question of "force?" What did the Court in *Clouden* treat it as deciding?

2. If a pickpocket "lifts" a wallet, for it to be "force on a person" need the victim feel the movement? Need the pickpocket realise that the victim might feel the movement?

3. Is it justifiable to treat a "non-violent" removal of a bag from the victim's presence so much more seriously than simple theft if the victim is actually holding it at the time?

4. In view of the other offences necessarily involved in a robbery situation, do we need a separate crime of robbery at all?

FRAUD

Note

The law of larceny did not, even in its latter-day expanded form, cover all offences of dishonesty connected with property. The law always drew a distinction between a thief and a swindler, the former being one who took the goods of another without any colour of consent and the latter being one who fraudulently persuaded the victim to make him (the swindler) the owner. The swindler was originally not punished by the common law at all in ordinary cases, and when statute invented the crime of obtaining by false pretences to cover him, it maintained a sharp distinction between the thief and the swindler, the former being in all cases a felon while the latter, except in cases where personation or forged documents were involved in the swindle, was guilty of misdemeanour only. By 1916, there was a range of offences covering various forms of swindling, see, *e.g.* the Forgery Act 1861, section 3; the Debtors Act 1869, section 13; the False Personation Act 1874, section 1, and the Larceny Act 1916, section 32, the principal offence being obtaining by false pretences under section 32(1) of the Larceny Act 1916.

Criminal Law Revision Committee's Eighth Report, Cmnd. 2977

§ 38 The sub-committee for a considerable time proposed that the general offence of theft should be made to cover the present offence of obtaining by false pretences under 1916, s.32(1). It might seem appropriate to extend theft in this way in order to make it cover as many ways as possible of getting property dishonestly. But in the end the sub-committee gave up the idea (to the regret of some members), and the full committee agreed. In spite of its attractions, it seemed to the majority of the committee that the scheme would be unsatisfactory. Obtaining by false pretences is ordinarily thought of as different from theft, because in the former the owner in fact consents to part with his ownership; a bogus beggar is regarded as a rogue but not as a thief, and so are his less petty counterparts. To create a new offence of theft to include conduct which ordinary people would find difficult to regard as theft would be a mistake. The unnaturalness of including obtaining by false pretences in theft is emphasised by the difficulty of drafting a satisfactory definition to cover both kinds of conduct. . . .

Notes

1. In spite of this declaration that theft and obtaining by deception are recognisably different, the scheme of the Committee's proposals, and of the Act which followed them, is that the two offences are equally reprehensible, and that in most situations it should make no difference whether the property was taken without any colour of right or by deceiving the victim into transferring it to the fraudulent person. Thus, the maximum penalty for theft and obtaining property by deception was to be the same (10 years' imprisonment—but since then the maximum for theft has been lowered to seven years: section 26 Criminal Justice Act 1991); for the purposes of handling, it makes no difference whether the goods were originally stolen or obtained by deception (s.24(4), *post*, p. 850); for the purpose of going equipped, it makes no difference whether the defendant has the article with him for use in a theft or an obtaining by deception (section 25(1), *post*, p. 893). Moreover there is nothing in the Theft Act making the offences mutually exclusive alternatives, *i.e.* it is no defence to a person charged with one crime to say that his offence is really the other. Indeed, as a result of the decision in *R. v. Gomez, ante*, p. 703, in almost all cases of obtaining, a charge of theft would be equally appropriate; that case decides that where A by fraud induces B to make him the owner of the property, that is an appropriation of property belonging to another.

2. The principal crime is obtaining property by deception: see *infra*. The problem of how to deal with the swindler who obtains not property but some valuable service was a troublesome one for the law. After a false start largely represented by the offence in section 16(2)(*a*) of the Theft Act 1968 of obtaining pecuniary advantage by reducing or evading or deferring a debt or charge (now repealed), a range of offences was introduced by the Theft Act 1978. They overlap with each other, and also with section 15 of 1968 Act. For example, if A, intending never to pay, induces B to let him have some goods by dishonestly giving a worthless cheque, he obtains property by deception (section 15/1968), but also obtains services (the delivery of the goods) by deception (section 1/1978) and evades liability by inducing B to wait for payment (section 2(1)(*b*)/1978). Moreover, as a result of *R. v. Gomez*, he steals the goods under section 1/1968.

3. Apart from crimes in the Theft Acts, there is a wide range of offences in other Acts covering frauds involving forgery, trading by companies, misleading investors, revenue frauds and social security frauds. There is also the offence of conspiracy to defraud (*ante*, p. 484), covering all these and any other conceivable frauds, provided that more than one person is involved. A similarly wide general offence of fraud committable by one person has been mooted: Law Commission W.P. 104 (1987).

1. OBTAINING PROPERTY BY DECEPTION

Theft Act 1968, section 15

(1) A person who by any deception dishonestly obtains property belonging to another, with the intention of permanently depriving the

other of it, shall on conviction on indictment be liable to imprisonment for a term not exceeding ten years.

(2) For purposes of this section a person is to be treated as obtaining property if he obtains ownership, possession or control of it, and 'obtain' includes obtaining for another or enabling another to obtain or to retain.

(3) Section 6 above shall apply for purposes of this section, with the necessary adaptation of the reference to appropriating, as it applies for purposes of section 1.

(4) For purposes of this section 'deception' means any deception (whether deliberate or reckless) by words or conduct as to fact or as to law, including a deception as to the present intentions of the person using the deception or any other person.

Note

This is the principal swindling crime, and differs from the others dealt with in this chapter in that *property* is obtained *with intent to deprive permanently.*

i. Obtaining Property Belonging to Another with Intention Permanently to Deprive

Notes

1. By section 34(1) "property" in this offence is given the same meaning as that given by section 4(1) for the purposes of theft (*ante*, p. 728). The limitations and exceptions as to land and wild animals imposed by section 3(2)–(4) relating to theft have no application to the present offence. "Belonging to another" is given the same meaning as that given by section 5(1) for the purposes of theft (*ante*, p. 740). The problems which this phrase can give rise to in the context of banking transactions executed as a result of fraud are highlighted in the House of Lords' decision in *Preddy, infra*. The remaining subsections of section 5 do not apply to the present offence.

2. On intention permanently to deprive, see *ante*, pp. 760–767. The need for this intention means that obtaining by lies the *loan* of an article which one intends to return is not an offence under this section. It is different with a loan of money, however, because there is usually no intention to return the precise coins or notes lent. In such a case the question of guilt will turn on what view the jury take of the accused's honesty. (See *post*, p. 819.)

R. v. Preddy, Slade and Dhillon
[1996] 3 All E.R. 481
House of Lords

At a time when house prices were rising rapidly the appellants obtained a substantial number of mortgage advances from building societies to purchase houses. They intended to repay the mortgages when, as they hoped, they sold the houses at a profit. All the mortgage applications contained false representations. The mortgage advances were sometimes paid by telegraphic transfer, sometimes by the CHAPS system and sometimes by cheque. The appellants were convicted of obtaining property by deception contrary to s. 15(1) of the Theft Act 1968. Their appeals to the Court of Appeal were dismissed. The Court of Appeal certified, inter alia, the following question: (i) whether the debiting of a bank account and the corresponding credit of another's bank account brought about by dishonest misrepresentation amounts to the obtaining of property within section 15 of the Theft Act 1968?

LORD GOFF OF CHIEVELEY: . . . [His Lordship examined the legislative history of the Theft Act 1968. Clause 12 of the Bill, which became section 15 of the Act, originally contained a provision, cl. 12(2), which made it an offence to obtain credit by fraud which would have covered the facts of the instant case. During its parliamentary stages clause 12(2) was dropped leaving clause 12(1) which became s.15(1) of the 1968 Act.]

. . . It is legitimate to comment that it is improbable that obtaining a loan such as a mortgage advance by deception should have been intended to fall within s.15(1) of the 1968 Act when s.15(2), as proposed, provided for a separate offence of dishonestly obtaining credit by deception in terms wide enough to include obtaining credit in respect of the repayment of a loan.

The first question

Against the above background, I now turn to the first question which your Lordships have to consider, which is whether the debiting of a bank account and the corresponding crediting of another's bank account brought about by dishonest misrepresentation, amount to the obtaining of property within s 15 of the 1968 Act.

Under each count, one of the appellants was charged with dishonestly obtaining, or attempting to obtain, from the relevant lending institution an advance by way of mortgage in a certain sum. In point of fact it appears that, when the sum was paid, it was sometimes paid by cheque, sometimes by telegraphic transfer, and sometimes by the CHAPS (Clearing House Automatic Payment System) system. However, in the cases where the sum was paid by cheque the appellants were not charged with dishonestly obtaining the cheque. A useful description of the CHAPS system is to be found in the Law Commission's Report *Criminal Law: Conspiracy to Defraud* (Law Com. No. 228) (1994) p. 39, n. 83. It involves electronic transfer as between banks, and no distinction need be drawn for present purposes between the CHAPS system and telegraphic transfer, each involving a debit entry in the payer's bank account and a corresponding credit entry in the payee's bank account.

The Court of Appeal in the present case concentrated on payments by the CHAPS system. They considered that the prosecution had to prove that the relevant CHAPS electronic transfer was "property" within s.15(1) of the 1968 Act. They then referred to the definition of property in s.4(1) of the Act as including "money and all other property, real or personal, including things in action and other intangible property"; and they concluded, following the judgment of the Court of Appeal in *R. v. Williams* (1993) *Times*, 18 August, that such a transfer was "intangible property" and therefore property for the purposes of s.15(1).

The opinion expressed by the Court of Appeal in *R. v. Williams* on this point was, in fact, obiter. The case related to a mortgage advance, the amount having been paid by electronic transfer. The court however concluded that a sum of money represented by a figure in an account fell within the expression "other intangible property" in s.4(1), and that the reduction of the sum standing in the lending institution's account, and the corresponding increase in the sum standing to the credit of the mortgagor's solicitor's account, constituted the obtaining of intangible property within s.15(1).

In holding that a sum of money represented by a figure in an account constituted "other intangible property", the court relied upon the decision of the Privy Council in *A-G of Hong Kong v. Nai-Keung* [1987] 1 W.L.R. 1339, in which an export quota surplus to a particular exporter's requirements, which under the laws of Hong Kong could be bought and sold, was held to constitute "other intangible property" within s.5(1) of the Hong Kong Theft Ordinance (Laws of Hong Kong, 1980 rev, c. 210) (identical to the English 1968 Act). I feel bound to say that that case, which was concerned with an asset capable of being traded on a market, can on that basis be differentiated from cases such as the present. But in any event, as I understand the position, the Court of Appeal were identifying the sums which were the subject of the relevant charges, as being sums standing to the credit of the lending institution in its bank account. Those credit entries would, in my opinion, represent debts owing by the banks to the lending institution which constituted choses in action belonging to the lending institution and as such fell within the definition of property in s. 4(1) of the 1968 Act.

My own belief is, however, that identifying the sum in question as property does not advance the argument very far. The crucial question, as I see it, is whether the defendant obtained (or attempted to obtain) property *belonging to another*. Let it be assumed that the lending institution's bank account is in credit, and that there is therefore no difficulty in identifying a credit balance standing in the account as representing property, *i.e.* a chose in action, belonging to the lending institution. The question remains, however, whether the debiting of the lending insitution's bank account, and the corresponding crediting of the bank account of the defendant or his solicitor, constitutes obtaining of that property. The difficulty in the way of that conclusion is simply that, when the bank account of the defendant (or his solicitor) is credited, he does not obtain the lending institution's chose in action. On the contrary, that chose in action is extinguished or reduced pro tanto, and a chose in action is brought into existence representing a debt in an equivalent sum owed by a different bank to the defendant or his solicitor. In these circumstances, it is difficult to see how the defendant thereby obtained *property belonging to another*, *i.e.* to the lending institution.

Professor Sir John Smith, in his commentary on the decision of the Court of Appeal in the present case, has suggested that:

"Effectively, the victim's property has been changed into another form and now belongs to the defendant. There is the gain and equivalent loss which is characteristic of, and perhaps the substance of, obtaining." (See [1995] Crim. L.R. 564 at 565–566.)

But even if this were right, I do not for myself see how this can properly be described as obtaining property belonging to another. In truth, the property which the defendant has obtained is the new chose in action constituted by the debt now owed to him by his bank, and represented by the credit entry in his own bank account. This did not come into existence until the debt so created was owed to him by his bank, and so never belonged to anyone else. True, it corresponded to the debit entered in the lending institution's bank account; but it does not follow that the property which the defendant acquired can be identified with the property which the lending institution lost when its account was debited. In truth, s. 15(1) is here being invoked for a purpose for which it was never designed, and for which it does not legislate.

I should add that, throughout the above discussion, I have proceeded on the assumption that the bank accounts of the lending institution and the defendant (or his solicitor) are both sufficiently in credit to allow for choses in action of equivalent value to be extinguished in the one case, and created in the other. But this may well not be the case; and in that event further problems would be created, since it is difficult to see how an increase in borrowing can constitute an extinction of a chose in action owned by the lending institution, or a reduction in borrowing can constitute the creation of a chose in action owned by the defendant. It may be that it could be argued that in such circumstances it was the lending institution's bank whose property was "obtained" by the defendant; but, quite apart from other problems, that argument would in any event fail for the reasons which I have already given. For these reasons, I would answer the first question in the negative.

Payment by cheque
Before I leave this topic, I wish to turn briefly to cases in which a mortgage advance has been made, not by telegraphic or electronic transfer, but by cheque. It appears that, in the case of some of the mortgage advances made in the present cases, the money was in fact advanced by cheque. Strictly speaking, cases concerned with payment by cheque do not fall within the scope of the three questions posed for your Lordships' consideration, and they were not considered by the Court of Appeal. Even so, they provide a common alternative to cases of payment under the CHAPS system and raise very similar problems. It would, therefore, be unrealistic to ignore them and, since they were the subject of argument before the Appellate Committee, I propose to consider them.

None of the appellants was charged with obtaining the cheques themselves by deception. They were, even in the cases in which payment was made by cheque, charged with the obtaining by deception of the relevant advance. But whether they had been charged with obtaining the cheques by deception, or (as they were) with obtaining the advances by deception, the prosecution was, in my opinion, faced with the same insuperable difficulty as that which I have already discussed, *viz.*, that the defendant must have obtained property belonging to another to be convicted of obtaining property by deception under s. 15(1) of the 1968 Act.

The point in question has been much discussed in the literature on the subject, and there now appears to be a broad consensus on the point, with which I find myself to be in agreement. I can therefore consider the point relatively shortly.

I start with the time when the cheque form is simply a piece of paper in the possession of the drawer. He makes out a cheque in favour of the payee, and delivers it to him. The cheque then constitutes a chose in action of the payee, which he can enforce against the drawer. At that time, therefore, the cheque constitutes "property" of the payee within s. 4(1) of the 1968 Act. Accordingly, if the cheque is then obtained by deception by a third party from the payee, the third party may be guilty of obtaining property by deception contrary to s. 15(1).

But if the payee himself obtained the cheque from the drawer by deception, different considerations apply. That is because, when the payee so obtained the cheque, there was no chose in action belonging to the drawer which could be the subject of a charge of obtaining property by deception. This was decided long ago in *R. v. Danger* (1857) Dears & B. 307, 169 E.R. 1018. There, the defendant was charged with obtaining a valuable security by false pretences, on the basis that he had presented a bill to the prosecutor who accepted it and returned it to the defendant, his acceptance having been induced by false pretences on the part of the defendant. The court held that in these circumstances the defendant was not guilty of the offence with which he was charged because, before the document came into his possession, the prosecutor had no property in the document as a security, nor even in the paper on which the acceptance was written. Lord Campbell CJ, delivering the brief judgment of the court, said ((1857) Dears & B. 307 at 324, 169 E.R. 1018 at 1025):

> ". . . we apprehend that, to support the indictment, the document must have been a valuable security while in the hands of the prosecutor. While it was in the hands of the prosecutor it was of no value to him, nor to any one else unless to the prisoner. In obtaining it the prisoner was guilty of a gross fraud; but we think not of a fraud contemplated by this Act of Parliament [7 & 8 Geo. 4 c. 29, s. 53]."

Unfortunately, this authority does not appear to have been cited in *R. v. Duru* [1973] 3 All E.R. 715, [1974] 1 W.L.R. 2. There, the defendants were involved in mortgage frauds perpetrated on a local authority. The advances were made by cheque, and the defendants were charged with obtaining the cheques by deception. The principal question for consideration was whether there was an intention on the part of the defendants to deprive the council of the property. The Court of Appeal held that there was such an intention. Megaw L.J., who delivered the judgment of the court, had this to say ([1973] 3 All E.R. 715 at 720, [1974] 1 W.L.R. 2 at 8):

> "So far as the cheque itself is concerned, true it is a piece of paper. But it is a piece of paper which changes its character completely once it is paid, because then it receives a rubber stamp on it saying it has been paid and it ceases to be a thing in action, or at any rate it ceases to be, in its substance, the same thing as it was before: that is, an instrument on which payment falls to be made. It was the intention of the appellants, dishonestly and by deception, not only that the cheques should be made out and handed over, but also that they should be presented and paid, thereby permanently depriving the Greater London Council of the cheque in substance as their things in action."

That decision was followed and applied by the Court of Appeal in *R. v. Mitchell* [1993] Crim. L.R. 788.

Both these decisions have been the subject of academic criticism, notably by Professor Smith in his commentary on *Mitchell* in the Criminal Law Review (in which he withdrew the support which he had previously given to the decision in *Duru*). The point is simply that, when the cheque was obtained by the payee from the drawer, the chose in action represented by the cheque then came into existence and so had never belonged to the drawer. When it came into existence it belonged to the payee, and so there could be no question of his having obtained by deception "property belonging to another". This is the point which was decided in *Danger*. The case of a cheque differs from *Danger* only in the fact that the cheque form, unlike the paper on which the bill was written in *Danger*, did belong to the drawer. But there can have been no intention on the part of the payee permanently to deprive the drawer of the cheque form, which would on presentation of the cheque for payment be returned to the drawer via his bank.

For these reasons I am satisfied that *Duru* and *Mitchell* are to this extent wrongly decided, and that the prosecution of the appellants in cases where the advance was made by cheque would have been equally flawed if they had been charged with obtaining the cheque in question by deception, as they were when charged with obtaining the advance itself by deception, contrary to s 15(1). Whether they could have been charged with dishonestly procuring the execution of a valuable security by deception contrary to s 20(2) of the 1968 Act does not arise for consideration in the present appeals. . . .

Obtaining services by deception
    In *R. v. Halai* [1983] Crim. L.R. 624, the defendant who had committed a mortgage fraud was convicted on four counts contrary to s. 1 of the 1978 Act and one count contrary to s. 15 of the 1968 Act. It is not necessary for present purposes to explore in detail each of these counts. It is enough to refer to three counts—counts 2, 3 and 4—under each of which he was convicted of obtaining or attempting to obtain services by deception, and his convictions were quashed by the Court of Appeal on the ground that no service had been obtained. The services which the defendant was alleged to have obtained, or to have attempted to obtain, were respectively: the opening of a savings account; a mortgage advance; and the increase of an apparent credit balance in a savings account. For present purposes, the most relevant conclusion was that the provision of a mortgage advance was not a service for the purposes of s. 1 of the 1978 Act.
    This decision has been strongly criticised, both by Sir John Smith in *The Law of Theft* (7th ed., 1993) paras. 4–70ff and by *Griew* pp. 171–172, para 8.08. It has also been criticised by the Law Commission in their report, *Criminal Law: Conspiracy to Defraud* pp. 39–40, paras 4.30–4.33, and described by Lord Lane C.J. in *R. v. Chuah* (*Teong Sun*), *R. v. Chuah* (*Teong Tatt*) [1991] Crim. L.R. 463 at 464 as bearing "all the hallmarks of being per incuriam". I hope that I do not do injustice to these criticisms if I epitomise them as founded essentially upon s. 1(2) of the 1978 Act, which provides that it is an obtaining of services "where the other is induced to confer a benefit by doing some act . . . on the understanding that the benefit has been or will be paid for". It is said that, in the present context, the act is the making of the advance, and that that act is plainly to be paid for because interest is to be charged for the advance.
    There is considerable force in this criticism; and certainly, if accepted, it would close a manifest gap in our criminal law. I feel bound to comment however that, although a wide definition of "services" appears to have been intended (see *Smith* p. 112), nevertheless if sub-s (2) were to be construed in the literal manner which is understandably urged upon us in the literature on the subject, it would follow that the ambit of s. 1 of the 1978 Act would be remarkably wide. It would stretch far beyond what is ordinarily included in the notion of services as generally understood. In particular, although we have become used to the expression "financial services" as describing a range of services available from those involved in that service industry, it is not altogether natural to think of the simple making of a loan upon interest as itself constituting a service. Moreover, on this approach it is, I suppose, arguable that for example the supply of goods (at an underpayment) or procuring the execution of a valuable security might also fall within this section, which could lead to an overlap between the section and ss. 15(1) and 20(2) of the 1968 Act. The effect is that s. 1 of the 1978 Act is exposed to some of the criticisms which led to the rejection of cl. 12(3) of the Criminal Law Revision Committee's original Bill, though its scope is restricted by the requirement that the relevant benefit should be conferred on the understanding that it has been or will be paid for.
    The Appellate Committee was invited to hear argument on this point, and to rule upon it; but in the end they resisted the temptation to do so. This was because the question did not arise, even indirectly, in the appeals

before your Lordships. In so ruling, the committee had to recognise the fact that this left prosecuting authorities in a difficult position. While *Halai* stands, its effect is that they can hardly charge defendants, alleged to have committed mortgage frauds, with the offence of obtaining services by deception; and yet they cannot obtain an authoritative ruling whether *Halai* is right or wrong, because it is not practicable to launch a prosecution on a basis which the Court of Appeal has held to be wrong in law, and an Attorney-General's reference to the Court of Appeal under s 36 of the Criminal Justice Act 1972 is only available in cases where a defendant has been charged and acquitted. However the Law Commission has addressed the problem and, following a recommendation made in its previous report (Law Com. No. 228, para 4.33), has prepared a simple two-clause Bill which could be introduced as a matter of urgency, under which it is made clear that dishonestly inducing another to make a loan, or to cause or permit a loan to be made, could constitute the offence of dishonestly obtaining services by deception contrary to s. 1 of the 1978 Act. This solution would appear to provide the most effective means of dealing rapidly with the particular problem. In these circumstances, I do not think it necessary or appropriate for your Lordships to say anything more on the subject.

[Lords Mackay of Clashfern, L.C., Jauncey of Tullichettle, Slynn of Hadley and Hoffman concurred in the speech of Lord Goff of Chieveley.]

Appeals allowed. Convictions quashed.

Note

The decision in *Preddy* sent shock waves through the banking world. The Law Commission quickly produced a Report, *Offences of Dishonesty: Money Transfers* (Law Com. No. 243), in which it recommended, *inter alia*, (i) the insertion into the Theft Act 1968 of a new section 15A, creating an offence of dishonestly obtaining a money transfer by deception; (ii) that the new offence should extend to payments made by cheque as well as those made electronically; (iii) the insertion into the Theft Act 1968 of a new section 24A (see *post*, p. 872), supplementing the law on handling, creating an offence of retaining a credit from a dishonest source; and (iv) that any money dishonestly withdrawn from an account to which a wrongful credit has been made should, to the extent that it derives from that credit, be regarded as stolen goods. Parliament responded rapidly and enacted the Law Commission's draft Bill as the Theft (Amendment) Act 1996. This Act also adopted one of the Law Commission's recommendations from its Report on *Conspiracy to Defraud* (Law Com No. 228), namely that the decision in *Halai* [1983] Crim. L.R. 624 be reversed and the obtaining of a loan by deception be recognised as an offence contrary to s.1 of the Theft Act 1978 (see *post*, p. 823).

Theft Act 1968, section 15A

Obtaining a money transfer by deception

(1) A person is guilty of an offence if by any deception he dishonestly obtains a money transfer for himself or another.

(2) A money transfer occurs when—
  (a) a debit is made to one account,
  (b) a credit is made to another, and
  (c) the credit results from the debit or the debit results from the credit.

(3) References to a credit and to a debit are to a credit of an amount of money and to a debit of an amount of money.

(4) It is immaterial (in particular)—

  (a) whether the amount credited is the same as the amount debited;
  (b) whether the money transfer is effected on presentment of a cheque or by another method;
  (c) whether any delay occurs in the process by which the money transfer is effected;
  (d) whether any intermediate credits or debits are made in the course of the money transfer;
  (e) whether either of the accounts is overdrawn before or after the money transfer is effected.

(5) A person guilty of an offence under this section shall be liable on conviction on indictment to imprisonment for a term not exceeding ten years.

ii. Deception

Note

Deception is needed for this crime, as it is also for obtaining pecuniary advantage (*post*, p. 821) obtaining services (*post*, p. 823), and evasion of liability (*post*, p. 824). The definition in section 15(4) is made to apply to these other offences by the Theft Act 1968, s.16(3) and the Theft Act 1978, s.5(1). The principal offence of obtaining pecuniary advantage was that contained in the Theft Act 1968, s.16(2)(*a*). This provision was repealed by the Theft Act 1978, s.5(5), a fact which must be borne in mind in considering some of the cases following, which are reproduced as authorities on deception and on the need for the deception to cause the obtaining.

Director of Public Prosecutions v. Ray
[1974] A.C. 370
House of Lords

R, and others, entered a restaurant and ordered a meal. R did not have enough money to pay, but one of his companions agreed to lend him enough to pay. After eating the meal, while the waiter was still in the dining room, the men decided not to pay and to run out of the restaurant. Ten minutes later they did so while the waiter was absent in the kitchen. The Divisional Court quashed R's conviction for obtaining a pecuniary advantage by deception contrary to section 16(2)(*a*) of the Theft Act (since repealed). The prosecution appealed to the House of Lords.

LORD MACDERMOTT: . . . Two questions [are left] for consideration. First, do the facts justify a finding that the respondent practised a deception? And secondly, if he did, was his evasion of the debt obtained by that deception?

The first of these questions involves nothing in the way of words spoken or written. If there was deception on the part of the respondent it was by his conduct in the course of an extremely common form of transaction which, because of its nature, leaves much to be implied from conduct. Another circumstance affecting the ambit of this question lies in the fact that, looking only to the period *after* the meal had been eaten and the respondent and his companions had decided to evade payment, there is nothing that I can find in the discernible conduct of the respondent which would suffice in itself to show that he was then practising a deception. No doubt he and the others stayed in their seats until the waiter went into the kitchen and while doing so gave all the appearance of ordinary customers. But, in my opinion, nothing in this or in anything else which occurred *after* the change of intention went far enough to afford proof of deception. The picture, as I see it, presented by this last stage of the entire transaction, is simply that of a group which had decided to evade payment and were awaiting the opportunity to do so.

There is, however, no sound reason that I can see for restricting the inquiry to this final phase. One cannot, so to speak, draw a line through the transaction at the point where the intention changed and search for evidence of deception only in what happened before that or only in what happened after that. In my opinion the transaction must for this purpose be regarded in its entirety, beginning with the respondent entering the restaurant and ordering his meal and ending with his running out without paying. The different stages of the transaction are all linked and it would be quite unrealistic to treat them in isolation.

Starting then, at the beginning one finds in the conduct of the respondent in entering and ordering his meal evidence that he impliedly represented that he had the means and the intention of paying for it before he left. That the respondent did make such a representation was not in dispute and in the absence of evidence to the contrary it would be difficult to reach a different conclusion. If this representation had then been false and matters had proceeded thereafter as they did (but without any change of intention) a conviction for the offence charged would, in my view, have had ample material to support it. But as the representation when originally made in this case was not false there was therefore no deception at that point. Then the meal is served and eaten and the intention to evade the debt replaces the intention to pay. Did this change of mind produce a deception?

My Lords, in my opinion it did. I do not base this conclusion merely on the change of mind that had occurred for that in itself was not manifest at the time and did not amount to "conduct" on the part of the respondent. But it did falsify the representation which had already been made because that initial representation must, in my view, be regarded not as something then spent and past but as a continuing representation which remained alive and operative and had already resulted in the respondent and his defaulting companions being taken on trust and treated as ordinary, honest customers. It covered the whole transaction up to and including payment and must therefore, in my opinion, be considered as continuing and still active at the time of the change of mind. When that happened, with the respondent taking (as might be expected) no step to bring the change to notice, he practised, to my way of thinking, a deception just as real and just as dishonest as would have been the case if his intention all along had been to go without paying.

Holding for these reasons that the respondent practised a deception, I turn to what I have referred to as the second question. Was the respondent's evasion of the debt obtained by that deception?

I think the material before the justices was enough to show that it was. The obvious effect of the deception was that the respondent and his associates were treated as they had been previously, that is to say as ordinary, honest customers whose conduct did not excite suspicion or call for precautions. In consequence the waiter was off his guard and vanished into the kitchen. That gave the respondent the opportunity of running out without hindrance and he took it. I would therefore answer this second question in the affirmative.

I would, accordingly, allow the appeal and restore the conviction.

LORD MORRIS OF BORTH-Y-GEST: For a deception to take place there must be some person or persons who will have been deceived. "Deception" is a word which is well understood. As Buckley J. said in *Re London and Globe Finance Corporation Ltd* (1903) 1 Ch. 728, 732:

> "To deceive is, I apprehend, to induce a man to believe that a thing is true which is false, and which the person practising the deceit knows or believes to be false."

In the present case the person deceived was the waiter. Did the respondent deceive the waiter as to what were his intentions? Did the respondent so conduct himself as to induce the waiter to believe that he (the respondent) intended to pay his bill before he left the restaurant whereas at the relevant time he did not so intend? . . .

The situation may perhaps be unusual where a customer honestly orders a meal and therefore indicates his honest intention to pay but thereafter forms a dishonest intention of running away without paying if he can. Inherent in an original honest representation of an intention to pay there must surely be a representation that such intention will continue.

In the present case it is found as a fact that when the respondent ordered his meal he believed that he would be able to pay. One of his companions had agreed to lend him money. He therefore intended to pay. So far as the waiter was concerned the original implied representation made to him by the respondent must have been a continuing representation so long as he (the respondent) remained in the restaurant. There was nothing to alter the representation. Just as the waiter was led at the start to believe that he was dealing with a customer who by all that he did in the restaurant was indicating his intention to pay in the ordinary way, so the waiter was led to believe that the state of affairs continued. But the moment came when the respondent decided and therefore knew that he was not going to pay: but he also knew that the waiter still thought that he was going to pay. By ordering his meal and by his conduct in assuming the role of an ordinary customer the respondent had previously shown that it was his intention to pay. By continuing in the same role and behaving just as before he was representing that his previous intention continued. That was a deception because his intention, unknown to the waiter, had become quite otherwise. The dishonest change of intention was not likely to produce the result that the waiter would be told of it. The essence of the deception was that the waiter should not know of it or be given any sort of clue that it (the change of intention) had come about. Had the waiter suspected that by a change of intention a secret exodus was being planned, it is obvious that he would have taken action to prevent its being achieved. . . .

The final question which arises is whether, if there was deception and if there was pecuniary advantage, it was by the deception that the respondent obtained the pecuniary advantage. In my view, this must be a question of fact and the magistrates have found that it was by his deception that the respondent dishonestly evaded payment. It would seem to be clear that if the waiter had thought that if he left the restaurant to go to the kitchen the respondent would at once run out, he (the waiter) would not have left the restaurant and would have taken suitable action.

The waiter proceeded on the basis that the implied representation made to him (*i.e.* of an honest intention to pay) was effective. The waiter was caused to refrain from taking certain courses of action which but for the representation he would have taken. In my view, the respondent during the whole time that he was in the restaurant made and by his continuing conduct continued to make a representation of his intention to pay before leaving. When in place of his original intention he substituted the dishonest intention of running away as soon as the waiter's back was turned, he was continuing to lead the waiter to believe that he intended to pay. He practised a deception on the waiter and by so doing he obtained for himself the pecuniary advantage of evading his obligation to pay before leaving. That he did so dishonestly was found by the magistrates who, in my opinion, rightly convicted him.

I would allow this appeal.

LORD PEARSON: . . . The essential feature of this case, in accordance with the magistrates' findings and opinions as I understand them, is that there was a continuing representation to be implied from the conduct of the respondent and his companions. By 'continuing representation' I mean in this case not a continuing effect of an initial representation, but a representation which is being made by conduct at every moment throughout the course of conduct. The course of conduct consisted of: (i) entering the restaurant, sitting down at a table and probably looking at the menu; (ii) giving to the waiter an order for a main course to be served; (iii) eating the main course; (iv) remaining at the table for about 10 minutes. The remaining at the table for that time was consistent in appearance with continuing their conversation and deciding whether or not to order another course. In my opinion all those actions can properly be regarded as one course of conduct continuing up to but not including the running out of the restaurant without paying. That is where the course of conduct was broken off. Up to the moment of running out they were behaving ostensibly as ordinary customers of the restaurant, and the ordinary customers of such a restaurant intend to pay for their meals in the appropriate manner before leaving the restaurant. . . .

In my view, the magistrates could and did reasonably imply from the course of conduct a representation by the respondent that he had a present intention of paying for his meal before leaving the restaurant. It was a continuing representation in the sense that I have indicated, being made at every moment throughout the course of conduct. Insofar as it was being made before the decision to run out without paying, it was according to the magistrates' finding a true representation of the respondent's then present intention. Insofar as it was being made after that decision, it was a false representation of the respondent's then present intention, and of course false to his knowledge. That false representation deceived the waiter, inducing him to go to the kitchen, whereby the respondent with his companions, was enabled to make his escape from the restaurant and so dishonestly evade his obligation to pay for his meal. Thus by deception he obtained for himself the pecuniary advantage of evading the debt.

In my opinion, the respondent was rightly convicted by the magistrates. I would allow the appeal and restore the conviction and sentence.

Appeal allowed

Questions

1. Is the misrepresentation of a person in Ray's position (a) that he intends to pay for the meal, or (b) that his original representation that

he would pay for the meal is still true? Can it ever matter which it is?

2. A after consuming his meal, discovers that his wallet is empty and realises that he cannot pay. Is he under a duty at once to own up to the waiter? If not, how is he to be distinguished from Ray?

3. Does it follow from *D.P.P. v. Ray* that failure to correct a mistaken impression in the other party before he transfers property to the accused counts as a deception? A, a private person, orders goods from P, a wholesaler, making no representation express or implied as to his own status. During the negotiations, he becomes aware that P thinks that he (A) is a retailer and will only sell to retailers. A fails to correct the misapprehension. Is he guilty of obtaining the goods by deception? See also the following case.

R. v. Rai
[2000] 1 Cr.App.R. 242
Court of Appeal

D applied to the council for a grant to provide a bathroom downstairs in his house for the use of his mother who was infirm. The grant was approved but two days after D's notification of this, his mother died. D did not inform the council of this fact and the building work went ahead. D was charged with obtaining services by deception contrary to section 1(1) of the Theft Act 1978. D sought to argue that his silence or inactivity could not amount to a deception. The trial judge ruled against him and D pleaded guilty and appealed against his conviction.

JUDGE DAVID CLARKE Q.C. (The Recorder of Liverpool): . . . The central issue before us was whether, on the facts of the present case, there was conduct capable of constituting that deception and in particular the circumstances in which an omission to act or silence can amount to such conduct . . ..

The learned judge gave a reasoned judgment, deciding this issue in favour of the Crown and ruling that his silence in those circumstances did amount to conduct sufficient to constitute a deception on the local authority. It seems to us that, in effect, he found it was capable of amounting to such conduct. Whether it did would have been, no doubt, an issue for the jury.

The underlying facts which underpinned that finding were, not only that the appellant did not tell the council, but that—as was undisputed—this was his house and at all material times he lived there. When, after the learned judge's ruling, the appellant pleaded guilty, he did so on the specific factual basis that his only relevant conduct was his failure to inform the council of the death of his mother. He did not acknowledge any other conduct on his part by which the council might have been deceived.

The learned judge, in his reasoned ruling, based his decision principally on an analogy with the somewhat different facts of the House of Lords case of *Director of Public Prosecutions v. Ray* [1974] A.C. 370 [*ante* p. 795]. He accurately summarised the facts of that case . . .. The relevant continuing conduct was staying in the restaurant; that was the basis for the finding by the majority in the House of Lords that there was sufficient conduct in that particular case to amount to a deception. The students had changed their minds about paying. They did so whilst sitting at the table in the restaurant. They continued to sit there for a time, and, in that sense, their conduct was continuing because they were then sitting there with their newly formed intention not to pay for their meals, thus falsifying their earlier implied representation that they would pay.

This, in the opinion of the House of Lords, amounted to sufficient conduct to satisfy that essential element of the offence.

The basis in the present case of the learned judge's ruling was that this appellant's conduct was equivalent to that conduct on the part of those students, and the question for this Court is whether that was correct.

Mr Cowley makes the point, cogently and clearly, that, in this case, there was no act or continuing act on the part of the appellant. He submits that the appellant in the present case was not playing a similar role or occupying a similar role to that occupied by the students in the case of *Director of Public Prosecutions v. Ray*, but that there was no act identified as representing conduct by which the local authority were deceived.

The learned judge held, however, in his ruling, that by simply sitting there doing nothing and allowing the work to be done, the appellant was committing a straightforward deception, because, as he was aware, the local authority were still of the mind that the mother would occupy the premises. He was living there at all material times. In the judgment of this Court, that, against the background of it being his home and he having made the application, was conduct sufficient to amount to conduct within the terms of section 15(4) of the 1968 Act. In our judgment the approach of the learned judge was correct, albeit on the basis of a feature of this case, that it was his house and that he was living in it continuously, which was not apparent to this Court on our first reading of the papers. But, on a common-sense and purposive construction of the word "conduct", it does, in our judgment, cover positive acquiescence in knowingly letting this work proceed as the appellant did in the present case . . ..

That being said . . . we are satisfied that, in the present case, there was conduct capable of amounting to the deception alleged by the prosecution. Accordingly, the learned judge's ruling was, in our judgment, correct, and there is thus no basis for this Court to hold that the plea of guilty entered by the appellant is in any way wrong or that the conviction should be regarded as unsafe. For those reasons, the appeal against conviction is dismissed.

Appeal dismissed.

Notes

1. Omissions in a statement which cause it to convey a false impression make the statement a false one: *R. v. Lord Kylsant* [1932] 1 K.B. 442. It has also been held that omission to make any statement at all is a deception if the situation is such that it is incumbent upon D to make a statement and failure to do so gives a false impression: *R. v. Firth* [1991] Crim.L.R. 326 (C.A.), which concerned evasion of liability, *post*, p. 768. See also *R. v. Shama* [1990] 2 All E.R. 602 (C.A.)—false accounting, where D did not, as his duty required, fill in a blank form recording a transaction.

2. *Deliberate or reckless*: In *R. v. Staines* (1974) 60 Cr.App.R. 160 (C.A.), a case of A signing cheques on B's behalf not *knowing* that B's account was overdrawn, James L.J. said (at p. 162) "This Court accepts the contention put forward that in this section 'recklessly' does mean more than being careless, does mean more than being negligent, and does involve an indifference to or disregard of the feature of whether a statement be true or false."

Compare "recklessly" in other parts of the law, *ante*, pp. 119, 121.

Griew, *The Theft Acts 1968 and 1978*, 7th ed.

§ *Need P believe the representation?* 'To deceive is, I apprehend, to induce a man to believe that a thing is true which is false.' This well-known statement by Buckley J. in *Re London and Globe Finance Corporation* [1903] 1 Ch. 728 at 832, was cited with approval in *D.P.P. v. Ray* (*ante*, p. 795). It appears at first sight to state the obvious and require no elaboration. Yet there is, on reflection, a good deal of uncertainty attaching to the notion of 'believing that a thing is true'; and there has been no judicial consideration of what amounts to 'believing' for this purpose. It is submitted that, if indeed 'believing' is an appropriate word in this context, it should not be understood only in the sense of firmly accepting the truth of the statement in question. The deception offences can hardly be limited to cases in which P. is induced to hold a strong positive belief. P. may be well aware he does not know D., that there are rogues and liars abroad and that D. may be one of them. He may act 'on the strength' of D.'s assertion and in reliance upon it, but without any positive sense either believing or disbelieving it. If D. is lying, P. is surely 'deceived' for the purposes of section 15. It may in fact be better to abandon the word 'believe' and say that to deceive is to induce a man to act in reliance upon a false representation."

Note

The deception must be "as to fact or as to law". There were two kinds of representations which were not enough for the pre-1968 crime of obtaining by false pretences. One was the making of a false promise: *R. v. Dent* [1955] 2 Q.B. 590 (C.A.). That is now covered by the words in subsection 4 "including a deception as to the present intentions of the person using the deception." The other was the expression of a dishonest opinion: *R. v. Bryan* (1957) D. & B. 265 (C.C.C.R.).

J. C. Smith: *The Law of Theft*, 8th ed., § 4–31

The Theft Act gives no guidance as to whether a misrepresentation of opinion is capable of being a deception. In principle there is no reason why it should not be, where the opinion is not honestly held. A vendor's description of his tenant as 'a most desirable tenant' when the rent was in arrears and, in the past, had only been paid under pressure was held by the Court of Appeal to be a sufficient misrepresentation to found an action in deceit.

> "In a case where the facts are equally well-known to both parties, what one of them says to the other is frequently nothing but an expression of opinion. . . . But if the facts are not equally well-known to both sides, then a statement of opinion by one who knows the facts best involves very often a statement of a material fact, for he impliedly states that he knows facts which justify his opinion." *Smith v. Land and House Property Corporation* (1884) 28 Ch.D. 7, 15.

The way seems open to the courts, if they so wish, to hold that "deception" extends to this kind of case. The use of that term frees them from the fetters of false pretences. A view of commercial morality very different from that of the majority of the judges in *Bryan* now prevails and deliberate mis-statements of opinion would today be generally condemned as dishonest, no less dishonest, indeed, than mis-statements of other facts—for whether an opinion is held or not is a fact—and the law should follow the changed attitude. It may, moreover, be a significant fact that at the time *Bryan* was decided, it was not possible for the prisoner to give evidence in his own defence.

Against this view, it might be argued that, since the Act has expressly removed one limitation on false pretences (representations as to intention) and has said nothing about this limitation, Parliament's intention is to allow it to continue. It is submitted that this would be a quite unjustifiable assumption. Parliament, in fact, has left it to the judges and, by the use of new terminology, given them a more or less free hand. The question now ought to be not "Is it a matter of opinion?" but, "If it is a matter of opinion, was it D's real opinion?" If the opinion is not honestly held there is, in truth, a misrepresentation of fact for the accused's state of mind is a question of fact. The Act indeed recognises this by holding false promises to be deception. If "I intend . . ." (not intending) is a deception, is not "I believe . . ." (not believing) equally a deception?

<h3 style="text-align:center">R. v. Silverman</h3>
(1988) 86 Cr.App.R. 213
Court of Appeal

D was known to two elderly sisters because he and his firm had done building work for their family for many years. On the occasions the subject of his prosecution, he grossly overcharged them for building work, and was convicted of obtaining the money they paid him by deception, namely by representing that the sum involved was a fair and reasonable charge for the work. On appeal:—

WATKINS L.J. for the Court: [Counsel for D.] has argued, first, that the appellant made no representations to the complainants. He has not shrunk from conceding that the appellant was dishonest. He has submitted that the appellant quoted the sisters for the work to be done but that it was open to them either to accept or reject the quotation upon such advice as they might seek and perhaps in the light of tenders by others, and that the appellant was in much the same position as anyone else who is asked to quote for work to be done. He has argued that it is a dangerous concept to introduce into the criminal law that an excessively high quotation amounts to a false representation under section 15(1) of the Theft Act 1968. In certain circumstances that submission may we think be well founded. But whether a quotation amounts to false representation must depend upon the circumstances.

It seems clear to us that the complainants, far from being worldly wise, were unquestionably gullible. Having left their former home, they relied implicitly upon the word of the appellant about their requirements in their maisonette. In such circumstances of mutual trust, one party depending upon the other for fair and reasonable conduct, the criminal law may apply if one party takes dishonest advantage of the other by representing as a fair charge that which he but not the other knows is dishonestly excessive. . . .

As to directing the jury upon what the prosecution had to prove and the circumstances in which they might succeed, we find no fault whatever in the way in which the judge directed them. There was material for a finding that there had been a false representation although it is true that the appellant had said nothing at the time he made his representations to encourage the sisters to accept the quotations. He applied no pressure upon them, and apart from mentioning the actual prices to be charged was silent as to other matters that may have arisen for question in their minds.

On the matter of representation we have been referred to *D.P.P. v. Ray, ante* p. 795, which concerned someone leaving a restaurant without paying for a meal. At [1974] A.C. 379 Lord Reid said: "So the accused, after he changed his mind, must have done something intended to induce the waiter to believe that he still intended to pay before he left. Deception, to my mind, implies something positive."

Mr Hopmeier submits that nothing positive was done in this case. Lord Reid continued (*ibid.*): "It is quite true that a man intending to deceive can build up a situation in which his silence is as eloquent as an express statement."

Here the situation had been built up over a long period of time. It was a situation of mutual trust and the appellant's silence on any matter other than the sums to be charged were, we think, as eloquent as if he had said:

"What is more, I can say to you that we are going to get no more than a modest profit out of this."

There is, we think, no foundation for the criticism of the judge in the first ground of appeal nor any substance in this ground in law. . . .

Appeal allowed on other grounds

iii. The Obtaining must be by the Deception

Note

It must be shown that the victim, because he was deceived, made the transfer complained of.

It appears from *Davies v. Flackett* [1973] R.T.R. 8 (D.C.) that deception needs a human victim, and it is impossible to practice a deception on a machine.

R. v. Collis-Smith [1971] Crim.L.R. 716 (C.A.) A drove his private car into a service station and asked for petrol, which was put into his tank. The attendant then asked if he was paying for it, and A said it was to be booked to his employer although, as A well knew, he had no authority to pledge his employer's credit for petrol. He was convicted of obtaining the petrol by deception, the deception being that his employer would pay. His appeal was allowed; the petrol had already been obtained before the deception took place. The court emphasised that it was dealing with a particular situation where petrol had been put in the tank of a vehicle, and would be difficult to recover, and not with different situations, such as a person putting goods into a shopping basket and being stopped before leaving the shop.

Questions

1. Why would it make a difference if the property, instead of being petrol in the tank of a car, had been goods in a shopping basket in a shop? See *Edwards v. Ddin, ante*, p. 741.

2. If the deception alleged had been an implied representation that he (the defendant) would pay, might the result have been different? (cf. *Coady* [1996] Crim.L.R. 518, C.A.)

R. v. Mills (1857) 8 Cox 263: (C.C.C.R.): M claimed money from P for work done which had not been done as M well knew. P also knew this but sent the money to M for the purpose of entrapping him. Held, the

representation was not what caused P to send the money, but the desire
to entrap M.

R. v. Lince (1873) 12 Cox 451 (C.C.C.R.): D obtained a quantity of pota-
toes from P after stating that he was the nephew of a man in P's employ
(which was true) and that he lived at a certain beer house (which was
false). P said in evidence that both facts influenced him. Bovill C.J.: "It
has long been settled that it is immaterial that the prosecutor was influenced by other circumstances than the false pretence charged. If that were
not so, an indictment for false pretences could scarcely ever be maintained, as a tradesman is generally more or less influenced by the profit
he expects to make on the transaction." *Conviction affirmed.*

R. v. Laverty [1970] 3 All E.R. 432 (C.A.): A reconstructed an old car and
substituted for the original number plates, plates from another car he had
broken up. A sold the car with the false plates to B. The deception alleged
was that the car bore its original number plates. B said in evidence that
what induced him to part with his money was the representation that A
had a title to sell. Lord Parker C.J.: "The proper way of proving these
matters is through the mouth of the person to whom the false representation is conveyed, and further it seems to the court in the present case that
no jury could say that the only inference was that B parted with his money
by reason of this false representation. B may well have been of the mind
as he stated he was, namely that what operated on his mind was the belief
that the appellant was the owner. Provided that the appellant was the
owner it may well be that B did not mind that the car did not bear its
original number plates. At any rate, as it seems to the court, it cannot be
said that the only possible inference here is that it actuated on B's mind."
Appeal allowed.

Question

Is it possible to reconcile the decision in the following case with
those in the cases noted above?

R. v. Miller (1992) 95 Cr.App.R. 421: D represented himself to be a
licensed taxi-driver and picked up foreign passengers at airports. He was
convicted of three counts of obtaining property by deception. In each case
be charged a fare far in excess of the normal fare. At the time of paying
the fare, however, each passenger had realised that D's car was not a taxi
but paid because they felt obliged to do so or because they feared what
might happen if they did not. D applied for leave to appeal arguing that
there could not be an offence of obtaining where the victim had ceased to
believe the initial lie by the time when payment was made. The Court of
Appeal refused the application, Lord Lane C.J. stating (at p. 424):

"[I]t is not legitimate to isolate the moment when the money was
handed over from the rest of the story. If on the whole story it could
legitimately be said that the various deceptions alleged in the indictment were the cause of the money being handed over it was irrelevant
that at the final moment the victim suspected or even believed that he
had been swindled."

Would a charge of attempt to obtain by deception or even of theft
have been more appropriate in such circumstances?

Note

Laverty was a case where the victim's evidence did not support the prosecution's case. Often, in the nature of the case, there will be no evidence by any victim and the question of whether anyone was influenced will have to be decided by inference. The necessary inference was not drawn in *Laverty*, but see next case.

R. v. Doukas
[1978] 1 W.L.R. 372
Court of Appeal

D, a waiter at a hotel, was found with bottles of wine not of a type sold by the hotel. He admitted that he intended, when a customer ordered wine, to substitute his own bottle for his employer's, make out a separate bill and pocket the money paid by the customer. He was convicted of going equipped to cheat, contrary to section 25 of the Theft Act 1968. He applied for leave to appeal against conviction.

GEOFFREY LANE L.J.: . . . The offence of going equipped to cheat is to be found in section 25 of the Theft Act 1968. It reads:

"(1) A person shall be guilty of an offence if, when not at his place of abode, he has with him any article for use in the course of or in connection with any burglary, theft or cheat . . . (5) For purposes of this section . . . 'cheat' means an offence under section 15 of this Act."

Section 15 concerns obtaining property by deception. . . .

Combining those two sections of the Theft Act—section 25 and section 15—which are apposite, one reaches this result: a person shall be guilty of an offence if, when not in his place of abode, he has with him any article for use in the course of or in connection with any deception, whether deliberate or reckless, by words or conduct, as to fact or as to law, for purposes of dishonestly obtaining property belonging to another with the intention of permanently depriving the other of it.

If one analyses that combined provision, one reaches the situation that the following items have to be proved. First of all, that there was an article for use in connection with the deception: here the bottles. Secondly, that there was a proposed deception: here the deception of the guests into believing that the proffered wine was hotel wine and not the waiter's. Thirdly, an intention to obtain property by means of the deception, and the property here is the money of the guests which he proposes to obtain and keep. Fourthly, dishonesty. . . . Fifthly, there must be proof that the obtaining would have been, wholly or partially, by virtue of the deception. The prosecution must prove that nexus between the deception and obtaining. It is this last and final ingredient which, as we see it in the present case, is the only point which raises any difficulty. . . .

We have, as in the notice of appeal, been referred to the decision in *R. v. Rashid* [1977] 1 W.L.R. 298, which was a decision by another division of this court. That case concerned not a waiter in a hotel, but a British Rail waiter who substituted not bottles of wine for the railway wine but his own tomato sandwiches for the railway tomato sandwiches; and it is to be observed that the basis of the decision in that case was that the summing up of the judge to the jury was inadequate. On that basis the appeal was allowed. But the court went on to express its views obiter on the question whether in those circumstances it could be said that the obtaining was by virtue of deception, and it came to the conclusion, as I say obiter, that the answer was probably no.

Of course each case of this type may produce different results according to the circumstances of the case and according, in particular, to the commodity which is being proffered. But, as we see it, the question has to be asked of the hypothetical customer, "Why did you buy this wine, or, if you had been told the truth, would you or would you not have bought the commodity"? It is, at least in theory, for the jury in the end to decide that question.

Here, as the ground of appeal is simply the judge's action in allowing the case to go to the jury, we are answering that question, so to speak, on behalf of the judge rather than the jury. Was there evidence of the necessary nexus fit to go to the jury? Certainly so far as the wine is concerned, we have no doubt at all that the hypothetical customer, faced with the waiter saying to him: "This of course is not hotel wine, this is stuff which I imported into the hotel myself and I am going to put the proceeds of the wine, if you pay, into my own pocket," would certainly answer, so far as we can see, "I do not want your wine, kindly bring me the hotel carafe wine." Indeed it would be a strange jury that came to any other conclusion, and a stranger guest who gave any other answer for several reasons. First of all, the guest would not know what was in the bottle which the waiter was proffering. True, he may not know what was in the carafe which the hotel was proffering, but he would at least be able to have recourse to the hotel if something was wrong with the carafe wine, but he would have no such recourse with the waiter; if he did, it would be worthless.

It seems to us the matter can be answered on a much simpler basis. The hypothetical customer must be reasonably honest as well as being reasonably intelligent and it seems to us incredible that any customer, to whom the true situation was made clear, would willingly make himself a party to what was obviously a fraud by the waiter upon his employers. If that conclusion is contrary to the obiter dicta in *R. v. Rashid* then we must respectfully disagree with those dicta. . . .

Application refused

Note

'It seems to us incredible that any customer . . . would willingly make himself a party to what was obviously a fraud by the waiter on his employers.' Although the inference that all customers are bound to be honest and unwilling to participate in fraud has not proved irresistable to all judges (see, *e.g. R. v. Rashid*, and Lord Bridge in *R. v. Cooke* [1986] A.C. 909, 921), the notion has proved useful in securing convictions in the not-uncommon case where A obtains things from B by proffering a cheque and cheque card, or a credit card, when the bank has withdrawn his authority to use the card. Since the giving of an ordinary unbacked cheque by A implies a representation that he has funds or an arrangement with his bank under which the cheque will be honoured, B will obviously rely on the representation of creditworthiness in deciding whether to give A goods or credit. If he makes a mistake he will lose. The obtaining is thus clearly caused by the representation in all ordinary cases. But where a cheque and apparently valid cheque card, or an apparently valid credit card, is presented by A, B will be paid anyway whatever the state of A's finances, and it becomes difficult to say that B relies on the representation of credit-worthiness in giving A goods on credit. It is now recognised that the relevant representation in this sort of case is not as to credit-worthiness (which may well be a matter of indifference to B), but as to *authority to present the card*, which, so it is held in the next case, cannot be a matter of indifference to B.

R. v. Lambie
[1981] 2 All E.R. 776
House of Lords

L obtained a credit card from a bank giving her credit facilities up to a limit of £200. The bank entered into contracts with retailers by which the bank guaranteed any purchase made with the credit card provided the retailer complied with certain conditions relating to the validity of the card. L, when well over her credit limit of £200, purchased goods from a shop using her credit card. The shop complied with the conditions of a credit card purchase and, since the amount involved was less than the amount for which special authorisation was required from the bank, made no enquiry of the bank as to L's credit standing. L was charged with obtaining a pecuniary advantage by deception contrary to section 16(1) of the Theft Act 1968. The judge asked the jury whether the shop keeper relied on the presentation of an apparently valid credit card as being due authority to use the card. The jury convicted, L's appeal to the Court of Appeal was allowed, and the prosecution appealed to the House of Lords.

LORD ROSKILL: ... My Lords, at the close of the case for the prosecution, learned counsel for the respondent invited the learned judge to withdraw both counts from the jury on, it seems, from reading the learned judge's clear ruling upon this submission, two grounds, first, that as a matter of law there was no evidence from which a jury might properly draw the inference that the presentation of the card in the circumstances I have described was a representation by the respondent that she was authorised by the bank to use the card to create a contract to which the bank would be a party, and secondly, that as a matter of law there was no evidence from which a jury might properly infer that Miss Rounding [the departmental manager at Mothercare] was induced by any representation which the respondent might have made to allow the transaction to be completed and the respondent to obtain the goods. The foundation for this latter submission was that it was the existence of the agreement between Mothercare and the bank that was the reason for Miss Rounding allowing the transaction to be completed and the goods to be taken by the respondent, since Miss Rounding knew of the arrangement with the bank, so that Mothercare was in any event certain of payment. It was not, it was suggested, any representation by the respondent which induced Miss Rounding to complete the transaction and to allow the respondent to take the goods.

My Lords, the learned judge rejected these submissions. He was clearly right to do so, as indeed was conceded in argument before your Lordships' House, if the decision of this House in *Commissioner of Police for the Metropolis v. Charles* [1977] A.C. 177 is of direct application. In that appeal this House was concerned with the dishonest use, not as in the present appeal of a credit card, but of a cheque card. The appellant defendant was charged and convicted on two counts of obtaining a pecuniary advantage by deception, contrary to section 16 of the Theft Act 1968. The Court of Appeal (Criminal

Division) and your Lordships' House both upheld those convictions. Your Lordships unanimously held that where a drawer of a cheque which is accepted in return for goods, services or cash, uses a cheque card he represents to the payee that he has the actual authority of the bank to enter on its behalf into the contract expressed on the card that it would honour the cheque on presentation for payment.

My Lords, I venture to quote in their entirety three paragraphs from the speech of my noble and learned friend, Lord Diplock, at pages 182 and 183 of the report, which as I venture to think, encapsulate the reasoning of all those members of your Lordships' House who delivered speeches:

"When a cheque card is brought into the transaction, it still remains the fact that all the payee is concerned with is that the cheque should be honoured by the bank. I do not think that the fact that a cheque card is used necessarily displaces the representation to be implied from the act of drawing the cheque which has just been mentioned. It is, however, likely to displace that representation at any rate as the main inducement to the payee to take the cheque, since the use of the cheque card in connection with the transaction gives to the payee a direct contractual right against the bank itself to payment on presentment, provided that the use of the card by the drawer to bind the bank to pay the cheque was within the actual or ostensible authority conferred upon him by the bank.

By exhibiting to the payee a cheque card containing the undertaking by the bank to honour cheques drawn in compliance with the conditions endorsed on the back, and drawing the cheque accordingly, the drawer represents to the payee that he has actual authority from the bank to make a contract with the payee on the bank's behalf that it will honour the cheque on presentment for payment.

It was submitted on behalf of the accused that there is no need to imply a representation that the drawer's authority to bind the bank was actual and not merely ostensible, since ostensible authority alone would suffice to create a contract with the payee that was binding on the bank; and the drawer's possession of the cheque card and the cheque book with the bank's consent would be enough to constitute his ostensible authority. So, the submission goes, the only representation needed to give business efficacy to the transaction would be true. This argument stands the doctrine of ostensible authority on its head. What creates ostensible authority in a person who purports to enter into a contract as agent for a principal is a representation made to the other party that he has the actual authority of the principal for whom he claims to be acting to enter into the contract on that person's behalf. If (1) the other party has believed the representation and on the faith of that belief has acted upon it and (2) the person represented to be his principal has so conducted himself towards that other party as to be estopped from denying the truth of the representation, then, and only then, is he bound by the contract purportedly made on his behalf. The whole foundation of liability under the doctrine of ostensible authority is a representation, believed by the person to whom it is made, that the person claiming to contract as agent for a principal has the actual authority of the principal to enter into the contract on his behalf."

If one substitutes in the passage at page 182G the words "to honour the voucher" for the words "to pay the cheque", it is not easy to see why *mutatis mutandis* the entire passages are not equally applicable to the dishonest misuse of credit cards as to the dishonest misuse of cheque cards.

But the Court of Appeal in a long and careful judgment delivered by

Cumming-Bruce L.J. felt reluctantly impelled to reach a different conclusion. The crucial passage in the judgment which the learned Lord Justice delivered reads thus:

"We would pay tribute to the lucidity with which the learned judge presented to the jury the law which the House of Lords had declared in relation to deception in a cheque card transaction. If that analysis can be applied to this credit card deception the summing-up is faultless. But, in our view, there is a relevant distinction between the situation described in *Charles* and the situation devised by Barclays Bank for transactions involving use of their credit cards. By their contract with the bank, Mothercare had bought from the bank the right to sell goods to Barclaycard holders without regard to the question whether the customer was complying with the terms of the contract between the customer and the bank. By her evidence Miss Rounding made it perfectly plain that she made no assumption about the appellant's credit standing at the bank. As she said 'the Company rules exist because of the Company's agreement with Barclaycard'. The flaw in the logic is in our view demonstrated by the way in which the Judge put the question of the inducement of Miss Rounding to the jury:

'Is that a reliance by her, Miss Rounding of Mothercare, upon the presentation of the card as being due authority *within the limits as at that time* as with count one?'

In our view, the evidence of Miss Rounding could not found a verdict that necessarily involved a finding of fact that Miss Rounding was induced by a false representation that the appellant's credit standing at the bank gave her authority to use the card."

I should perhaps mention, for the sake of clarity, that the person referred to as the appellant in that passage is the present respondent.

It was for that reason that the Court of Appeal (Criminal Division) allowed the appeal, albeit with hesitation and reluctance. That court accordingly certified the following point of law as of general public importance, namely:

"In view of the proved differences between a cheque card transaction and a credit card transaction, were we right in distinguishing this case from that of *Commissioner of Metropolitan Police* v. *Charles* [1977] A.C. 177 upon the issue of inducement?"

My Lords, as the appellant says in paragraph 9 of his printed case, the Court of Appeal Criminal Division laid too much emphasis upon the undoubted, but to my mind irrelevant fact that Miss Rounding said she made no assumption about the respondent's credit standing with the bank. They reasoned from the absence of assumption that there was no evidence from which the jury could conclude that she was "induced by a false representation that the appellant's credit standing at the bank gave her authority to use the card." But, my Lords, with profound respect to the learned Lord Justice, that is not the relevant question. Following the decision of this House in *Charles*, it is in my view clear that the representation arising from the presentation of a credit card has nothing to do with the appellant's credit standing at the bank but is a representation of actual authority to make the contract with, in this case, Mothercare on the bank's behalf that the bank will honour the voucher upon presentation. Upon that view, the existence and terms of the agreement between the bank and Mothercare are irrelevant, as is the fact that Mothercare, because of that agreement, would look to the bank for payment.

That being the representation to be implied from the respondent's actions and use of the credit card, the only remaining question is whether Miss Rounding was induced by that representation to complete the transaction and allow the respondent to take away the goods. My Lords, if she had been asked whether had she known the respondent was acting dishonestly and, in truth, had no authority whatever from the bank to use the credit card in this way, she (Miss Rounding) would have completed the transaction, only one answer is possible—no. Had an affirmative answer been given to this question, Miss Rounding would, of course, have become a participant in furtherance of the respondent's fraud and a conspirator with her to defraud both Mothercare and the bank. Leading counsel for the respondent was ultimately constrained, rightly as I think, to admit that had that question been asked of Miss Rounding and answered, as it must have been, in the negative, this appeal must succeed. But both he and his learned junior strenuously argued that, as my noble and learned friend, Lord Edmund-Davies, pointed out in his speech *Charles* at pages 192 and 193 of the report, the question whether a person is or is not induced to act in a particular way by a dishonest representation is a question of fact, and since what they claimed to be the crucial question had not been asked of Miss Rounding, there was no adequate proof of the requisite inducement. In her deposition, Miss Rounding stated, no doubt with complete truth, that she only remembered this particular transaction with the respondent because someone subsequently came and asked her about it after it had taken place. My Lords, credit card frauds are all too frequently perpetrated, and if conviction of offenders for offences against sections 15 or 16 of the Theft Act 1968 can only be obtained if the prosecution are able in each case to call the person upon whom the fraud was immediately perpetrated to say that he or she positively remembered the particular transaction and, had the truth been known, would never have entered into that supposedly well-remembered transaction, the guilty would often escape conviction. In some cases, of course, it may be possible to adduce such evidence if the particular transaction is well remembered. But where as in the present case no one could reasonably be expected to remember a particular transaction in detail, and the inference of inducement may well be in all the circumstances quite irresistible, I see no reason in principle why it should not be left to the jury to decide, upon the evidence in the case as a whole, whether that inference is in truth irresistible as to my mind it is in the present case. In this connection it is to be noted that the respondent did not go into the witness box to give evidence from which that inference might conceivably have been rebutted.

My Lords, in this respect I find myself in agreement with what was said by Humphreys J. giving the judgment of the Court of Criminal Appeal in *R. v. Sullivan* (1945) 30 Cr.App.R. 132 at 136:

"It is, we think, undoubtedly good law that the question of the inducement acting upon the mind of the person who may be described as the prosecutor is not a matter which can only be proved by the direct evidence of the witness. It can be, and very often is, proved by the witness being asked some question which brings the answer: 'I believed that statement and that is why I parted with my money'; but it is not necessary that there should be that question and answer if the facts are such that it is patent that there was only one reason which anybody could suggest for the person alleged to have been defrauded parting with his money, and that is the false pretence, if it was a false pretence."

It is true that in *R. v. Laverty* (*ante*, p. 804), Lord Parker C.J. said that the Court of Appeal Criminal Division was anxious not to extend the principle in *Sullivan* further than was necessary. Of course, the Crown must always prove its case and one element which will always be required to be proved in these cases is the effect of the dishonest representation upon the mind of the person to whom it is made. But I see no reason why in cases such as the present, where what Humphreys J. called the direct evidence of the witness is not, and cannot reasonably be expected to be available, reliance upon a dishonest representation cannot be sufficiently established by proof of facts from which an irresistible inference of such reliance can be drawn. My Lords, I would answer the certified question in the negative and would allow the appeal and restore the conviction of the respondent upon the second count in the indictment which she faced at Bedford Crown Court.

Appeal allowed: Conviction restored

Note

Charles and Lambie were convicted of obtaining a pecuniary advantage contrary to section 16(2)(a) of the Theft Act 1968 which was repealed by the Theft Act 1978. The appropriate offence to charge now is evasion of liability by deception, in particular, securing the remission of an existing liability to make a payment contrary to section 2(1)(a) of the 1978 Act (*post* p. 824). Where D has no authority to use a credit card and does so to purchase goods, a charge of obtaining property by deception is possible. The appropriate question to ask the shop assistant would be, "Would you have sold the goods to D by means of a credit card (or debit card or cheque guarantee card) transaction if you had known that D had no authority to use the card?" If the shop assistant answers "No" this supplies the evidence that the goods have been obtained by means of the deception. It is crucial, however, that the right question is asked of the shop assistant. Below the Law Commission give further consideration to the problem of credit/debit and cheque cards

Legislating the Criminal Code: Fraud and Deception
Law Commission Consultation Paper No. 155 (1999)

Constructive Deception

8.8 The law requires first that there be a deception, and secondly that the deception be a cause of the obtaining. The current state of the law, however, sometimes conflates the two stages. A person is regarded as having been deceived where he or she does not in fact *believe* something to be true, if that person would have acted differently had he or she known that it was not. In these circumstances, a person is *said* to be deceived, and that deception is said to be operative in causing the obtaining, where there is in fact no mental state corresponding to deception, and the person concerned may even deny that he or she was in fact deceived. It seems appropriate to call this "constructive deception".

Cheque, credit and debit cards

8.9 Constructive deception has principally arisen in connection with the obtaining of property or other benefits by means of a credit card or a cheque backed by a cheque card. It is hardly surprising that the criminal misuse of cheque cards or credit cards is not happily dealt with in the Theft Acts, as it is a comparatively modern problem. It was not until 1965 that the banks began issuing cheque cards; Barclaycard was launched in 1966 and Access in 1972. . . .

8.10 The use of such cards reassures the trader that the bank will honour payment if the conditions on the card are satisfied. This will be so even if the customer is acting without the bank's authority because his or her account is overdrawn or a credit limit has been exceeded. The bank has made it unnecessary for the trader to enquire into the state of the customer's bank account, or his or her credit limit, by promising that payment will be made. However, the courts have proved reluctant in some cases to acknowledge what is likely to be the trader's real state of mind with regard to such a transaction. . ..

8.13 In neither case [*Charles* and *Lambie*] could it fairly be said, in our view, that the alleged victim *believed* (or even assumed) something to be true which was in fact false. The nature of payment cards is such that the fraudster has no need to instil such a belief. There can be a causal link between the fraudster's misuse of the card and his or her obtaining of the property (or other benefit) despite the absence of any real, operative deception. It may, however, be assumed that, had the trader known the truth in each case (namely that the user of the card was not authorised to use it), he or she would not have accepted it: to do so would have implicated him or her in the fraud, and thus disentitled him or her to payment. That state of mind—knowledge of the truth—would have broken the causal chain between the misuse of the card and the obtaining of the benefit. The effect of the House of Lords' reasoning is that, even if the trader is indifferent to the state of the card user's bank account or credit limit (and thus cannot properly be described as having been deceived), he or she can be *treated* as having been deceived if, had he or she happened to know that the account was overdrawn or the credit limit exceeded, he or she would not have accepted that form of payment. A statement about causation is thus used to attribute to the trader a state of mind which he or she does not in fact have.

8.14 This approach, which we call "constructive" deception, has the advantage that it is *capable* of rendering criminal a very prevalent abuse. Its disadvantage is that it does so by resorting to artificiality, which can cause practical problems. It is said to be difficult to persuade a jury to convict where the trader has given evidence that he or she was not concerned about the true state of affairs—an admission likely to be secured in a high proportion of real cases.

8.15 There are two facets to this problem. The first is that the jury may acquit "wrongly", in the sense of not properly applying the law. It has traditionally been thought that juries are suspicious of constructive liability of any sort. Even if a jury try to apply the directions they are given, the artificiality of the legal analysis involved is likely to result in misunderstandings. Such problems are likely to be at their most acute in inchoate offences such as attempt or going equipped for "cheat" (as going equipped to obtain by deception is known).

8.16 Secondly, the facts may be such that, under the law, the jury are *right* to acquit. The trader may say that it would have made no difference if he or she had known that the defendant was not authorised to use the card; or the jury might conclude that that is what the trader meant by saying that he or she did not care one way or the other. And they might be right to think so. If a customer says to a shop assistant "I'm overdrawn, so I had better use my cheque card just in case", it would be a rare shop assistant who replies "Well, in that case I am afraid I cannot accept payment by cheque, even with a card". We believe that deception should be understood as the inducing of a false belief—a psychological fact—rather than as something which by abstruse legal analysis can be *deemed* to have occurred.

Imposing liability on a third party

8.17 If deception were so understood, however, an offence based on deception would not catch the fraudulent use of payment cards. We therefore suggest that misuse of payment cards should form the subject matter of a new offence. Such an offence would properly identify the actual wrongdoing and the real victim, namely the bank (or other card provider).The bank gives the card-holder a tool which enables him or her to fix the bank with liability. The wrongdoing lies in the fraudulent misuse of this tool to the bank's detriment. The customer mentioned in the previous paragraph, who is honest about his or her overdraft, does the same wrong to the bank (if the card is accepted) as the customer who says nothing, or lies about the state of his or her account.

8.18 The essence of the suggested offence is that one person causes another to become indebted to a third, without any legal right to do so. A similar offence has been proposed by Professor Sir John Smith:

> A person commits an offence if he intentionally causes a legal liability to pay money to be imposed on another, knowing that the other does not consent to his doing so and that he has no right to do so. [(1996) 28 Bracton L.J. 27, 40–41]

The requirement that the defendant should have no "right" to impose liability on the other should, in our view, mean that his or her conduct must be actionable at the other's instance. Clearly the offence could not extend to cases where one person is legally free to impose liability on another.

8.19 An alternative approach would be to define the offence by specific reference to payment cards. But to do so would involve definitions which might quickly become out of date, as payment instruments develop under the impact of new technology and greater commercial sophistication. Focusing on the legal effect of what is done, rather than the commercial machinery by which it is done, would minimize the risk of technical points being taken as to the precise circumstances in which the rule applies. Our provisional preference, therefore, is for a broader offence of the kind proposed by Sir John Smith. . . .

The mental element

8.24 Sir John Smith's formulation of the offence requires a threefold mental element:

(1) intention to impose the liability on the other;

(2) knowledge that the other does not consent to the imposition of the liability;

and

(3) knowledge that, in those circumstances, the defendant has no right to impose it.

8.25 While we provisionally accept the second and third of these requirements, our provisional view is that the requirement of *intention* to impose liability is too strict. While there are some offences which require the bringing about of a particular consequence with the intention of bringing it about, in general it is sufficient that the defendant was aware of the risk of the specified consequence but nevertheless unreasonably went ahead with the conduct that brought it about. This state of mind is known as recklessness. We are not convinced that there is any reason why the offence we propose should be an exception to this general principle.

8.26 Moreover, a requirement of intention is likely to be misunderstood. The fraudulent user of a payment card does not care whether anyone else incurs liability for the debt, as long as he or she does not have to pay it; and it might therefore be thought that there is no *intention* to impose liability on another. The theoretical answer to this argument is that there is a difference between intention and purpose. To say that D intends V to become indebted to a third party does not mean that D *cares* whether V becomes indebted. A person can intend a consequence without desiring it to come about. But this is a somewhat subtle distinction. Many non-lawyers would say that the fraudster does not intend to impose liability on the bank, only to get the property or services. We believe that it would be unwise to require proof of an element as to which fact-finders are likely in doubt, even when in law it clearly exists. We therefore provisionally conclude that it should not be necessary to prove that the defendant intended to impose liability on another, only that he or she was reckless whether this occurred.

Presumed consent

8.27 It is worth considering whether it is indeed right that all unauthorised use of payment cards should be criminal. The case which in our view should arguably *not* be criminalised is that in which, in the context of an ordinary, continuing banking relationship, a person knows that by making a purchase he or she will cause his or her bank account to become overdrawn without authority, but nevertheless goes ahead and uses a cheque card to make the purchase. Such a person is no doubt in breach of the terms of his or her contract with the bank, but in the context of a continuing relationship where it will be understood by both parties that the overdraft will be repaid in due course. Indeed, in such a case, one would not ordinarily expect the bank to take any action.

8.28 Problems may, however, arise in excluding such a case without also excluding clear cases of true fraud. One could limit the offence to cases where the card was stolen or temporarily appropriated, and the individual had never had a right to use it. But that would probably exclude a person who applies for payment cards in order to run up unauthorised debts and then abscond. There would be an offence in such a case if the bank account or payment card were obtained by deception, but this will not necessarily be so. We think it would also be right to criminalise the *use* of the card.

8.29 The point could perhaps be met by including within the new offence a negative dishonesty element, thus excluding a defendant whom the fact-finders consider not to be morally culpable. But it is in such cases that the *unreliability* of dishonesty, even as a negative element, is relevant. It *might* have the desired effect, but equally it might not. And it would provide those who *should* be convicted with a chance of acquittal - resulting in unnecessary trials where there would otherwise be a guilty plea, and unnecessarily prolonged trials where there was another, real, issue.

8.30 An at least partial alternative would be to include in the offence a defence analogous to that provided by section 2(1)(b) of the Theft Act 1968. A person would not commit the offence by imposing a liability on a third party without authority where he or she believes that the third party *would* have authorised the imposition of the liability if that party had known all the material circumstances. Thus if the defendant said in evidence "I believed that if I had telephoned my bank and explained the situation, they would have said I could make the purchase", and the fact-finders thought this might be true, an acquittal would follow. Our provisional view is that this approach is right in principle, and would serve to exclude cases involving no real moral blame.

8.31 **We provisionally propose**

(1) that a person should commit an offence if he or she intentionally or recklessly causes a legal liability to pay money to be imposed on another, knowing that the other does not consent to his or her doing so and that he or she has no right to do so; and

(2) that the other should not be regarded as consenting to the imposition of the liability if his or her consent is procured by deception; but

(3) that a person should not commit the offence if, at the time of causing the liability to be imposed, he or she believes that the other would have consented to his or her doing so if the other had known all the material circumstances.

R. v. Clucas
[1949] 2 K.B. 226
Court of Criminal Appeal

C induced a bookmaker to bet with him by falsely representing that he was acting as agent for many people at his place of work. The bet was successful and C was paid the winnings. C was convicted of obtaining money by false pretences.

LORD GODDARD C.J.: The main point which arises in the case . . . may be stated this way: Does a man who induces a bookmaker to bet with him by making false pretences as to his identity or as to the capacity in which he is putting on the bets, obtain money by false pretences if he is fortunate enough, having made those pretences, to back a winning horse so that the bookmaker pays him? The case as it was argued originally before a court consisting of three judges raised this point, and the court showed when they adjourned the hearing, that there was not unanimity at that stage, consequently they adjourned it to be heard before a full court, for which reason five judges have now heard it.

In the opinion of the court it is impossible to say that there was an obtaining of the money by false pretences which were alleged, because the money was obtained not by reason of the fact that the people falsely pretended that they were somebody else or acting in some capacity which they were not; it was obtained because they backed a winning horse and the bookmaker paid because the horse had won. No doubt the bookmaker might never have opened an account with these men if he had known the true facts, but we must distinguish in this case between one contributing cause and the effective cause which led the bookmaker to pay the money.

The effective cause which led the bookmaker to pay the money was the fact that these men had backed a winning horse. . . . Although these two men induced the bookmaker to bet with them by means of a false pretence, what the court cannot see is that the false pretence was the false pretence which led to the payment of the money. What led to the payment of the money was the fact that these men backed a winning horse by inducing the bookmaker to bet with them. They put themselves in the position that if they backed the horse and lost, they had to pay the bookmaker and if they backed the horse and won they were entitled to receive the money. In the opinion of the court, therefore, it cannot be said that the money was obtained by false pretences within the meaning of section 32, subsection (1), of the Larceny Act, 1916.

Mr Boileau has called the attention of the court to certain cases, and no doubt the nearest case to this one and the only one which I think it is necessary to mention is *R. v. Button* [1900] 2 Q.B. 597. In that case the defendant, by representing that he was a person of the name Sims, who was a very moderate performer in athletic sports and was not known as a likely winner of races, managed to obtain from the committee of some athletic sports which were to be held in Lincoln a very substantial handicap in a race. He was in fact a man who had won a great many races and had the truth been known he would have received either no handicap at all or a very moderate handicap instead of the very substantial handicap which he obtained. Indeed, after the race was won by him he repeated the false pretence to the secretary and obtained a prize, but it was not only on account of the repetition of the false pretence that he obtained the prize. The court held that by falsely representing himself to be someone he was not, thereby obtaining a substantial handicap, he obtained the prize on false pretences because it was a matter directly connected with the winning or not winning of the prize. He obtained for himself a winning chance. He got the handicap which he would not otherwise have got, and thereby enabled himself to win the race. We think that that case on the facts is clearly distinguishable from this case.

Conviction on this count quashed

Note

In fact Button did not actually receive the prize and the charge was attempting to obtain property by false pretences.

The distinction between the two cases appears to be that in *Clucas* the placing of the bet was merely a *causa sine qua non* of the obtaining; without making the bet, he could not have received any winnings, but that applies equally to all sorts of other factors such as the fact that the bookmaker had a telephone which enabled C to get in touch with him and place the bet; these are merely contributing causes; the *causa causans*, the one cause which above all others produced the payment of winnings was the fact that the horse that C backed was first past the post. But in *Button*, the one effective cause, the *causa causans* was the fact that he had been given a big start in the race. Since the false pretences produced the *causa causans* it can be said that (had the crime been complete) the false pretence produced the handing over of the prize.

Questions

B by lies obtains a three yard start, wins by five yards, claims and is given the prize. Is B, on the view adopted in *Clucas*, guilty of obtaining the prize by deception? Is he guilty of attempting to gain the prize by deception?

R. v. King
[1987] 1 All E.R. 547
Court of Appeal

K and S, falsely representing they were from a famous firm of tree surgeons, falsely represented to an elderly householder that it was necessary to remove trees on her property to prevent damage to gas mains and house foundations. They said the work would cost £470, and she agreed to them doing the work. The police arrested K and S before they could go any further, and they were subsequently convicted of attempting to obtain £470 from the householder by deception. They appealed.

NEILL L.J.: gave the judgment of the Court: In support of the appeal against conviction counsel for the appellants argued that the judge erred in rejecting the motion to quash the indictment, or alternatively the submission that there was no case to answer. The argument was developed on the following lines: (1) that, as the appellants were charged with an attempt, it was incumbent on the prosecution to prove that if the relevant conduct had been completed it would have constituted a criminal offence; (2) that if the appellants had received £470 for cutting down the trees they would have been paid by reason of the work they had done, and not by reason of any representation they had made to secure the work; (3) that since the decision in *R. v. Lewis* (January 1922, unreported) it had been generally recognised that conduct of the kind complained of in the present case did not constitute the criminal offence of obtaining property by false pretences or by deception because, as a matter of causation, the relevant property was obtained by reason of the work carried out rather than by reason of any representation or deception. Our attention was directed to statements on the subject in some leading textbooks . . .

In order to examine these arguments it is necessary to start by setting out the particulars of offence as stated in the indictment, as amended. The particulars read as follows:

> "David King and Jimmy Stockwell on the 5th day of March 1985 in Hampshire, dishonestly attempted to obtain from Nora Anne Mitchell, £470 in money with the intention of permanently depriving the said Nora Anne Mitchell thereof by deception, namely by false oral representations that they were from J. F. Street, Tree Specialists, Pennington, that essential work necessary to remove trees in order to prevent damage to the gas supply and house foundations would then have to be carried out."

. . . The argument advanced on behalf of the appellants on causation or remoteness was founded on the decision in *R. v. Lewis*, and on commentaries on that decision by academic writers. The report of the decision in *R. v. Lewis* is scanty and, as far as we are aware, is contained only in a footnote in *Russell on Crime* (12th ed., 1964), vol. 2, p. 1186, n. 66).

In that case (which was a decision at Somerset Assizes in January 1922) a schoolmistress obtained her appointment by falsely stating that she possessed a teacher's certificate. She was held to be not guilty of obtaining her salary by false pretences, on the ground that she was paid because of the services she rendered, and not because of the false representation.

It was submitted on behalf of the appellants that the principle underlying the decision in *R. v. Lewis* could be applied in the present case. It was further submitted that the authority of *R. v. Lewis* was implicitly recognised by the enactment of para. (*c*) of s.16(2) of the Theft Act 1968. Section 16 is concerned with the obtaining of a pecuniary advantage by deception; s.16(2) provides:

"The cases in which a pecuniary advantage within the meaning of this section is to be regarded as obtained for a person are cases where . . . (*c*) he is given the opportunity to earn remuneration or greater remuneration in an office or employment . . ."

It is to be observed, however, that Professor Glanville Williams in his *Textbook of Criminal Law* (2nd ed., 1983) p. 792 has this to say of the decision in *R. v. Lewis*:

"Yet *Lewis* would not have got the job and consequently her salary, if it had not been for the pretence. Her object in making the pretence was to get the salary. Assuming, as is likely, that her employer would not have made her any payment of salary if a lie had not been operating on his mind, there was certainly a factual causal connection between the lie and the obtaining of salary. Why should it not be a causal connection in law? We have seen that when the defendant produces a consequence intentionally, it is generally regarded as imputable to him. Why should it not be so here?"

Furthermore, the learned author of *Russell on Crime* p. 1187 (immediately after the footnote already referred to) continued:

"But it is submitted that cases of this kind could be placed beyond doubt if the indictment were worded carefully. The essential point in this crime is that in making the transfer of goods the prosecutor must have been influenced by the false pretence as set out in the indictment."

We have given careful consideration to the argument based on causation or remoteness and have taken account of the fact that some support for the argument may be provided by the writings of a number of distinguished academic lawyers. Nevertheless, we have come to the conclusion that on the facts of the present case the argument is fallacious.

In our view, the question in each case is: was the deception an operative cause of the obtaining of the property? This question falls to be answered as a question of fact by the jury applying their common sense.

Moreover, this approach is in accordance with the decision of the Court for Crown Cases Reserved in *R. v. Martin* (1867) L.R. 1 C.C.R. 56, where it was held that a conviction for obtaining a chattel by false pretences was good, although the chattel was not in existence at the time that the pretence was made, provided the subsequent delivery of the chattel was directly connected with the false pretence. Bovill C.J. said:

"What is the test? Surely this, that there must be a direct connection between the pretence and the delivery—that there must be a continuing pretence. Whether there is such a connection or not is a question for the jury."

The decision in *R. v. Martin* was referred to with approval in *R. v. Moreton* (1913) 8 Cr.App.R. 214, where Lord Coleridge J. said:

"*Martin* leaves the law in no doubt; it was held there that the fact that the goods were obtained under a contract does not make the goods so obtained goods not obtained by a false pretence, if the false pretence is a continuing one and operates on the mind of the person supplying the goods."

In the present case there was, in our judgment, ample evidence on which the jury could come to the conclusion that had the attempt succeeded the money would have been paid over by the victim as a result of the lies told to her by the appellants. We consider that the judge was correct to reject both the motion to quash the indictment and the submission that there was no case to answer.

For the reasons which we have set out, we consider that the appellants were rightly convicted in this case, and the appeals must therefore be dismissed.

Appeals dismissed

Question

1. D, by using a false reference, obtained employment as a teacher. When the lie was discovered, she was dismissed and charged with obtaining her last month's salary by deception. Is it relevant

(i) that since appointment she had been promoted?
(ii) she held the post for ten years but consistently performed her duties less well than would be expected if the reference had been genuine and true?

Note

Nowadays persons in the position of Clucas and Lewis commit the offence of obtaining by deception a pecuniary advantage (the opportunity to win money by betting, to earn remuneration in an office or employment, respectively; see section 16(2), *post*, p. 821. This may be thought a more appropriate way of dealing with such cases, reflecting more accurately what it is which is got by deception. However section 16 only covers a few particular cases. It was conceded in *King* that the offence did not cover what happened there because King was not given an opportunity to earn remuneration "in an office or employment". [but see now *R. v. Callendar*, *post* p. 822. The C.L.R.C. proposed a general offence of dishonestly, with a view to gain, by deception inducing a person to do or refrain from any act, but this was rejected by Parliament as being too broad.

iv. Dishonesty

Criminal Law Revision Committee's Eighth Report, Cmnd. 2977

§ 88 The provision in [section 15(1)] making a person guilty of criminal deception if he 'dishonestly obtains' the property replaces the provision in 1916, s.32(1), making a person guilty of obtaining by false pretences if he 'with intent to defraud, obtains' the things there mentioned. The change will correspond to the change from 'fraudulently' to 'dishonestly' in the definition of stealing which is discussed in § 39. 'Dishonestly' seems the right word to use in relation to criminal deception also. Owing to the words 'dishonestly obtains' a person who uses deception in order to obtain property to which he believes himself entitled will not be guilty; for though the deception may be dishonest, the obtaining is not. In this respect also the offence will be in line with theft, because a belief in a legal right to deprive an owner of property is for the purpose of theft inconsistent with dishonesty and is specifically made a defence by the partial definition of 'dishonesty' in [section] 2(1). The partial definition in [section] 2(1) is not repeated in [section 15(1)]. It would be only partly applicable to the offence of criminal deception, and it seems unnecessary and undesirable to complicate the Bill by including a separate definition in [section 15]). The fact that a claim of right will be a defence to a charge under [section 15(1)] is probably in accordance with the present law of obtaining by false pretences; for the existence of a claim of right to the property obtained is regarded as inconsistent with that of an 'intent to defraud' for the purpose of 1916, s.32(1).

Notes

This desire to avoid complication in the Bill has resulted in "claim of right" not being a defence in law to a charge of obtaining. Once the question of dishonesty was held to be one of fact for the jury (see *R. v. Feely, ante*, p. 774, *R. v. Ghosh, ante*, p. 775), then with the failure of section 15 to include the three cases which in theft are legally not to be regarded as dishonest by section 2(1), there are no such cases in obtaining. The *Ghosh* directions are all that are needed in every case of obtaining in which honesty is in issue.

R. v. Woolven
(1983) 77 Cr.App.R. 231
Court of Appeal

D was convicted of attempting dishonestly to obtain money by deception. In trying to withdraw money from a bank account he pretended to be the owner of the account. In evidence he admitted that most people would think his behaviour was dishonest, but insisted that he thought he was acting on the instructions of the owner of the account. The direction to the jury followed the guidelines in *Ghosh*, but contained no reference to claim of right.

LEONARD J.: In the judgment of this Court any direction based on the concept of claim of right as set out in section 2(1)(*a*), or otherwise, would have added nothing to what the learned judge in fact said. Indeed a direction based on *Ghosh* seems likely to us to cover all occasions when a section 2(1)(*a*) type direction might otherwise have been desirable.

Our attention was drawn to *R. v. Falconer-Atlee* (1973) 58 Cr.App.R. 348—a case of theft to which section 2(1)(*a*) therefore applied. A claim of right was raised by the evidence. The learned judge directed the jury as to the elements which the prosecution had to prove in order to establish the offence. In dealing with the element of dishonesty he said: "The all important word ... in those four elements is "dishonestly," but of course, it may well be that you may not have much difficulty in deciding that if somebody in circumstances such as are alleged here appropriated property belonging to another with the intention of permanently depriving the other of it, then it was done dishonestly, but that is a matter for you. It is for you to decide whether whatever was done was done dishonestly. If you are not satisfied that it was, then you could not convict. . . ."

In delivering the judgment of this Court, Roskill L.J. (as he then was) said at p. 359: "To give the jury the limited direction which the learned judge gave, impeccable so far as it went in relation to "dishonestly," but on the facts of this case not to go on to tell them what section 2(1)(*a*) expressly provided was *not* to be regarded as "dishonest" was to omit what was an extremely important direction."

In contrast, the summing-up in the present case clearly brought home to the jury that they must consider the appellant's own account of events and what he said about his state of knowledge and if, on that basis, they thought he might have regarded his actions as honest, they must acquit.

At pp. 32–33 the trial judge summarised the matters which were put forward by the appellant as part of his case. . . . The jury, in all probability, considered them in the context of Roberts's [an accomplice] version which imputed some knowledge of the true state of affairs to the appellant.

The jury in the present case had the facts before them. The appellant eventually conceded that ordinary people would, on the basis of his own version, have found his behaviour to be dishonest. He maintained that he himself had not thought it to be dishonest at the time. In the view of this Court it was inevitable that the jury would disbelieve the last proposition, even if they believed the appellant's account otherwise.

There is in our view nothing unsafe or unsatisfactory about this conviction. Accordingly, for the reasons stated, the appeal is dismissed.

Appeal dismissed

Question

A and B both have what they think are justifiable claims to be paid £10 by P. A, by force, takes £10 from P; B, by lies, gets P to give him £10. Should there be, and is there, any difference in the way the issue of their honesty should be summed up to the juries who are trying them for theft and obtaining by deception respectively?

2. OBTAINING PECUNIARY ADVANTAGE BY DECEPTION

Theft Act 1968, section 16

(1) A person who by any deception dishonestly obtains for himself or another any pecuniary advantage shall on conviction on indictment be liable to imprisonment for a term not exceeding five years.

(2) The cases in which a pecuniary advantage within the meaning of this section is to be regarded as obtained for a person are cases where—

(a) [repealed by Theft Act 1978, Section (5)]
(b) he is allowed to borrow by way of overdraft, or to take out any policy of insurance or annuity contract, or obtains an improvement of the terms on which he is allowed to do so; or
(c) he is given the opportunity to earn remuneration or greater remuneration in an office or employment, or to win money by betting.

(3) For the purposes of this section "deception" has the same meaning as in section 15 of this Act.

Notes

No pecuniary advantage need in fact be obtained. If the situation comes within the two cases in subsection 2 a pecuniary advantage 'is to be regarded as obtained'. On the other hand, the two cases are exhaustive, and no other case of a *de facto* pecuniary advantage is comprehended in the offence. See *D.P.P. v. Turner* [1974] A.C. 357.

2. For 'deception', 'dishonestly', and the need for the deception to cause the obtaining, see *ante*, pp. 787–821.

Case (b)

R. v. Waites [1982] Crim.L.R. 369 (C.A.) W, who was issued with a cheque book and cheque card, but with no power to overdraw, wrote cheques to pay for purchases. By contract with the shopkeepers, the bank was obliged to meet the cheques, so that W's account went into overdraft to the extent of £850. *Held*: she was "allowed to borrow" in that she was allowed to use the card which carried the power (albeit in breach of contract with the bank) to commit the bank to meeting her cheques and thereby creating an overdraft.

Question

Did W obtain the *power to commit the bank* by deception?

R. v. Watkins [1976] 1 All E.R. 578 (Crown Ct.) D, as a result of lies, was granted overdraft facilities but did not draw on them.

Held: subsection 2(*b*) referred in its alternatives to the *granting* of facilities or improved facilities, not to the use of them. D's offence was complete.

Question

D, by lies, was given insurance cover over the phone. No policy was issued, or claim made, before D's lies were uncovered. Is he guilty of an offence under section 16(2)(*b*)?

Case (c)

R. v. Callender [1992] 3 All E.R. 51 (C.A.): D, by pretending to be a qualified accountant, obtained "employment" in helping small businessmen to prepare their tax and VAT returns. *Held:* "employment" was not limited to a master and servant relationship. The dictionary meaning, which covered D's situation, was what Parliament intended.

Note

The principal case of obtaining pecuniary advantage was until 1978 contained in section 16(1)(*a*). It was the case where "any debt or charge for which he makes himself liable or is or may become liable (including one not legally enforceable) is reduced or in whole or part evaded or deferred". This short passage caused such difficulties of interpretation that it was repealed by the Theft Act 1978. Its replacement, founded on the 13th Report of the Criminal Law Revision Committee, (Cmnd. 6733) but amended in Parliament, consists of the three offences mentioned below. The first two are punishable on indictment by imprisonment for 5 years, the third by imprisonment for 2 years.

3. OBTAINING SERVICES BY DECEPTION

Theft Act 1978, section 1

(1) A person who by any deception dishonestly obtains services from another shall be guilty of an offence.

(2) It is an obtaining of services where the other is induced to confer a benefit by doing some act, or causing or permitting some act to be done, on the understanding that the benefit has been or will be paid for.

Notes

1. For "deception", "dishonestly" and the need for the deception to cause the obtaining, see *ante*, pp. 787–821, and on the offence generally see Smith, §§ 225–236, and Spencer, "The Theft Act 1978" [1979] Crim.L.R. 26–30.

2. The services provided can include the delivery of property, where a charge under section 15 of the 1968 Act is more appropriate. But it is an offence under this section also: *R. v. Widdowson* (1986) 82 Cr.App.R. 314, 318, (*ante*, p. 462).

3. There must be an understanding that the benefit has been or will be paid for. The deception need not be as to the payment; the reference to an understanding of payment is merely to exclude gratuitous conferment of benefit from the definition of services. But it is the doing of an act or causing or permitting an act to be done which must be on this understanding.

Questions

Are the following cases offences under section 1?

(1) A, by pretending that his dog is an entrant for a championship dog show to be held next day, gets B, a vet, to examine and prescribe for it, for an agreed sum of £20, which A intends to pay.

(2) B, by pretending to be a vet, gets A to allow him to examine and prescribe for his dog, for an agreed payment of £20.

(3) A, by falsely pretending that he has no money with him, induces B, a taxi-driver, to give him a free ride. And see, section 2(1)(c) below.

(4) A, a non-resident using the restaurant at a hotel, by representing that he is a resident guest, persuades a waiter to allow him to enter the television room and to watch the television, services which are available only to resident guests.

Note

In *Halai* [1983] Crim.L.R. 624, the appellant's conviction of obtaining services by deception, where he had obtained a mortgage advance, was quashed by the Court of Appeal. O'Connor L.J., giving the judgment of the court, stated:

"In our judgment, a mortgage advance cannot be described as a service. A mortgage advance is the lending of money for property and can properly be charged under section 15 of the 1968 Act, if the facts support it. This count should never have been in the indictment."

The House of Lords' decision in *Preddy, Slade and Dhillon* (*ante* p. 788) made it clear that a charge under s. 15 is not appropriate in any case where a loan is advanced by any means other than cash. In his commentary on this decision Professor Sir John Smith states (at p. 626):

"[S]urely it is undeniable that when a building society is induced to make a mortgage advance it "is induced to confer a benefit by doing some act . . . on the understanding that the benefit . . . will be paid for". There is clearly an act, there is no doubt that it confers a benefit and it is certainly going to be paid for by the interest charged. In that case it is an obtaining of services within the section."

The Law Commission, *Criminal Law: Conspiracy to Defraud* (Law Com. No. 228) considered that *Halai* is wrong stating (at para. 4.31) "the court appears to have applied the ordinary meaning of the word "services" rather than the extremely wide statutory definition." They recommended statutory action to make it clear that the dishonest obtaining of loans falls within the s. 1 offence suggesting that a new subsection (3) be added to s. 1. They repeated this recommendation in *Offences of Dishonesty: Money Transfers* (Law Com. No. 243). Parliament adopted this recommendation and by s.4(1) of the Theft (Amendment) Act 1996 inserted a new sub-section into s.1 of the Theft Act 1978 in the following terms:

(3) Without prejudice to the generality of subsection (2) above, it is an obtaining of services where the other is induced to make a loan, or to cause or permit a loan to be made, on the understanding that any payment (whether by way of interest or otherwise) will be or has been made in respect of the loan.

In *Legislating the Criminal Code: Fraud and Deception* (Consultation Paper No. 155) the Law Commission recommend an extension of the offence of obtaining services by deception to cover two situations (see paras 7.31–7.34): firstly, a deception which results in the usual payment being waived and thus the service being provided on the understanding that it will not be paid for; and, secondly, where the service provided is not paid for directly but the provider confers it with a view to gain either for himself or someone else. The example given of the latter situation was *Halai*, *ante*, where it was held that D had not obtained a service by deception where he opened a building society account using a bad cheque as building societies do not charge for opening accounts.

4. EVASION OF LIABILITY BY DECEPTION

Theft Act 1978, section 2

(1) Subject to subsection (2) below, where a person by any deception—

(a) dishonestly secures the remission of the whole or part of any existing liability to make a payment, whether his own liability or another's; or

(b) with intent to make permanent default in whole or in part on any existing liability to make a payment, or with intent to let another do so, dishonestly induces the creditor or any person claiming payment on behalf of the creditor to wait for payment (whether or not the due date for payment is deferred) or to forgo payment; or

(c) dishonestly obtains any exemption from or abatement of liability to make a payment;

he shall be guilty of an offence.

(2) For purposes of this section 'liability' means legally enforceable liability; and subsection (1) shall not apply in relation to a liability that has not been accepted or established to pay compensation for a wrongful act or omission.

(3) For purposes of subsection (1)(b) a person induced to take in payment a cheque or other security for money by way of conditional satisfaction of a pre-existing liability is to be treated not as being paid but as being induced to wait for payment.

(4) For purposes of subsection (1)(c) "obtains" includes obtaining for another or enabling another to obtain.

Note

For 'deception', 'dishonestly' and the need for the deception to cause the remission, inducement or obtaining, see, *ante*, pp. 787–821.

Spencer, The Theft Act 1978 [1979] Crim.L.R. 34

There seems little practical need for 2(1)(a). Where it applies, D. has been fraudulent and dishonest, but his conduct is unlikely to have done P. any harm. In theory harm has been caused: P. used to own a debt against D.; by deceiving P. into waiving it, D. has deprived him of it. So, it may be said, D. ought to be punished just as if he had deprived P. of any other item of his property—his car, for example—by deception. But the analogy is false. Where D. obtains P.'s car by deception, P. once had a car, and is left with a civil remedy against D. which usually is worthless. Where D. secures the remission of a debt by deception, P. is also left with a probably worthless civil remedy. He can rescind the remission for fraud, and then enforce the debt—but D. probably has no assets with which to pay it. However, in this case what did P. have *before* D. deprived him of it by deception? Merely a debt—a right to sue D. for the money. It is possible that D. had the money to pay at the time of the deception, and spent it on beer after the debt was remitted; but this is most unlikely. Usually, the reason why D. deceived P. will be that D. had no money but lacked the effrontery to say so. Therefore, as a result of D.'s deception, P. is unlikely to be any the worse off. The only result of fining and imprisoning D. if he is caught will be to make P.'s civil remedy against D. worthless in the rare case where D. was, before the prosecution, worth powder and shot.

Section 2(1)(b) seems to have little more rhyme or reason to it. It is said to be aimed mainly at those who knowingly write dud cheques in purported settlement of existing liability—conduct which frequently does the creditor good rather than harm [because the creditor can sue on the cheque as well as on the debt]. It is harmful in only two ways. First, the payee may unsuspectingly draw against the cheque and so overdraw his own bank account. If this is the mischief aimed at, however, 2(1)(b) is too narrow, because the offence is only committed where D. intends never to pay, and P. is equally likely to overdraw whatever D.'s intentions. Secondly, tendering the cheque may enable D. to disappear without trace. However, the mischief here is only the same as that involved in "making off without payment." Why should running away after telling lies carry a sentence of five years' imprisonment under 2(1)(b), when running away without telling lies—which is more harmful, because D. is likely to be harder to trace—only carries a sentence of two years under section 3? Furthermore, as against any dubious benefits to society which 2(1)(b) may provide, there is the uncomfortable fact that because of it, anyone who, however innocently, tenders a cheque which is dishonoured, can be threatened with a prosecution which is likely to get past the committal stage.

The only part of section 2 which seems to strike accurately at an evil worthy of criminal sanction is 2(1)(c), which applies to the evasion of future liability by deception. Although originally intended partly to cover obtaining services cheap or free by deception, and now in that respect redundant, [because section 1 as finally enacted has a wider scope than clause 1 as proposed by the C.L.R.C.], it still covers conduct which is really harmful to the victim and amounts to no other criminal offence. Take for example the case of the council-house tenant who by deception has his rent halved by way of rent rebate. The council will thereafter fail to collect half his rent as it would otherwise have fallen due. If the fraud is not discovered for several years, the council may lose thousands of pounds. On discovery of the fraud, the council will have in theory a right to sue the tenant for the money, but whereas he could have paid it in instalments over the years, the chance of his ever finding it now—in addition to future rent at the proper rate—is remote. This sort of conduct surely does deserve a prosecution.

A final criticism of section 2 is that it is complicated. Long, expensive hours will be spent in the courts discussing arid procedural questions resulting from a failure to specify what the relationship between the three main clauses is, and whether they are three offences or one. It is an ill wind of legal change which blows no barrister any good.

Note

The gloomy prognostication in the last paragraph above has not been fully borne out. The cases below demonstrate that the Courts have a relaxed attitude about evasion of liability. Without going to the length of holding that it is all one offence, they are unsympathetic to appeals claiming that the wrong sub-paragraph was charged.

R. v. Holt and Lee
[1981] 2 All E.R. 854
Court of Appeal

The appellants consumed meals costing £3.65 in a restaurant. They were overheard by an off duty police officer planning to evade payment by the pretence that a waitress had removed a £5 note which they had placed on the table. When presented with the bill by a waiter they advanced this pretence. They were arrested and charged with attempting to evade liability by deception contrary to section 2(1) of the Theft Act 1978. The particulars of the offence made it clear that the attempt charged was on to commit the paragraph (b) offence. They were convicted and appealed.

LAWSON J.: . . . At the close of the prosecution case in the Crown Court counsel who has also conducted this appeal, made a submission which was overruled, the main point of which was that assuming the facts as we have recounted them to be correct, the attempt to evade thus emerging was an attempt to commit an offence not under section 2(1)(*b*) as charged but under section 2(1)(*a*) of the 1978 Act since, he submitted, had the attempt succeeded, the appellants' liability to pay for their meals would have been "remitted" and not just "forgone", to use the contrasting terms contained in the respective subsections.

Counsel further developed his submission before us. As we understand it, he submits that the vital differences between the two offences defined in the first two paragraphs of section 2(1) of the Act are that "remission" involves that, first, the creditor who "remits" the debtor's existing liability must communicate his decision to the debtor and, second, the legal consequence of the "remission" is to extinguish the debt, whereas the "forgoing of an existing liability", to use the words of subsection 2(1)(*b*), need not be communicated to the debtor and has not the consequence in law of extinguishing such liability. We find great difficulty in introducing these concepts into the construction of the subsection. We will later return to the matter.

Counsel further submitted that the effect of section 2(1) of the Act was to create three different offences but conceded that there could be situations in which the conduct of the debtor or his agent could fall under more than one of the three paragraphs of section 2(1).

The elements of the offence defined by section 2(1)(*b*) of the Act relevant to the present case are clearly these: first, the defendant must be proved to have the intent to make permanent default on the whole or part of an existing liability. This element is unique to section 2(1)(*b*); it has no application to the offences defined in section 2(1)(*a*) or (*c*). Second, given such intent, he must use deception. Third, his deception must be practised dishonestly to induce the creditor to forgo payment.

It must always be remembered that in the present case, whatever offence was being attempted, the attempt failed. The creditor was not induced by the dishonest deception and did not forgo payment. It is clear on the evidence that the appellants' conduct constituted an attempt to evade liability by deception, and the jury, who were properly directed, clearly concluded that the appellants' conduct was motivated by the intent to make permanent default on their supper bill. Thus, all the elements needed to enable an attempt to commit the offence defined in section 2(1)(*b*) were found to be present, so that the appellants were rightly convicted as charged.

Reverting to the construction of section 2(1) of the Act, as to which the commentators are not at one, we are not sure whether the choice of expressions describing the consequences of deception employed in each of its paragraphs, namely in paragraph (*a*) "secures the remission of any existing liability", in paragraph (*b*) "induces a creditor to forgo payment" and in paragraph (*c*) "obtains any exemption from liability", are simply different ways of describing the same end result or represent conceptual differences.

Whilst it is plain that there are substantial differences in the elements of the three offences defined in section 2(1), they show these common features: first, the use of deception to a creditor in relation to a liability, second, dishonesty in the use of deception, and third, the use of deception to gain some advantage in time or money. Thus the differences between the offences relate principally to the different situations in which the debtor-creditor relationship has arisen.

The practical difficulty which counsel's submissions for the appellants failed to confront is strikingly illustrated by cases of attempting to commit an offence under section 2(1)(*a*) or section 2(1)(*b*). If, as he submits, section 2(1)(*a*) requires communication of remission to the debtor, whereas section 2(1)(*b*) does not require communication of the "forgoing of payment" but, as the case is a mere attempt, the matter does not *end* in remission of liability or forgoing of payment, then the prosecution would be in a dilemma since it would either be impossible to charge such an attempt or the prosecution would be obliged to charge attempts in the alternative in which case, since any attempt failed, it would be quite uncertain which of the alternatives it was.

These appeals are accordingly dismissed.

Applications for leave to appeal granted. Appeals dismissed

R. v. Jackson [1983] Crim.L.R. 617 (C.A.) D used a stolen credit card to pay for petrol. He was convicted of evading liability by securing the remission of an existing liability, contrary to section 2(1)(*a*). He appealed on the ground that he should have been charged under section 2(1)(*b*).

Held, dismissing the appeal, that although in *Holt, supra*, it was held that the element under section 2(1)(*b*) of an intent to make permanent default on the whole or part of an existing liability was unique to sub-paragraph (*b*), that judgment was not authority for the proposition that the elements in sub-paragraphs (*a*), (*b*) and (*c*) of section 2(1) were mutually exclusive. The transaction of tendering a stolen credit card and having it accepted by a trader who forthwith would look to the authority issuing the card for payment and not to the person tendering the card, meant that that person had dishonestly secured the remission of an existing liability. It was not necessary to consider whether a charge in respect of that transaction could be brought under section 2(1)(*b*). In the circumstances the matter was not wrongly charged under section 2(1)(*a*).

R. v. Sibartie [1983] Crim.L.R. 470 (C.A.) D "flashed" at a ticket inspector a pass which did not cover the journey he was making. He was convicted of attempted evasion of liability by obtaining exemption from liability to make a payment, contrary to section 2(1)(*c*).

Held, dismissing the appeal that the correct method of approach was to ask whether, taking the words of section 2(1)(*c*) in their ordinary meaning, one would say that what the appellant was attempting to do fell within the ambit of the words. The jury by their verdict must have been satisfied that the appellant dishonestly used his season ticket, which did not in fact cover the journey he was making, in an attempt to persuade the ticket inspector that they did cover the journey. Did that amount to an attempt to obtain exemption from liability to make a payment for the journey he was making or had made? He was saying, albeit tacitly, by waving the supposed season ticket in the air that he was the holder of a ticket authorising him to be making the journey without further payment and consequently he was not under any liability to pay any more. In the ordinary meaning of words that was dishonestly obtaining an exemption from the liability to pay the excess which, had he been honest, he would have had to pay. There might be a degree of overlap between section 2(1)(*a*), (*b*) and (*c*), and the fact that what the appellant did might also have been an attempt to commit an offence under section 2(1)(*b*) was neither here nor there.

J. C. Smith, [1983] Crim.L.R. 471, commenting on this case: "If he was guilty of three offences, does not this look like a case of overkill on the part of the legislator? Some overlap of offences is reasonable and to be expected; but it must surely be assumed that Parliament intended each offence to have some function. If the broadest construction is put upon each offence there seems to be nothing for paragraph (b), in so far as it relates to forgoing payment, to do.

Paragraphs (a) and (c) do not require proof of an intent to make permanent default and, if they cover cases of forgoing payment, Parliament's evident intention, that one who merely induces a creditor to forgo payment should not be guilty unless he has an intent to make permanent default, is defeated. It is no answer to this argument that there was evidence of an intent to make permanent default in the present case. Such an intent was no part of the offence of which the appellant was convicted.

There is, however, an interpretation of the section which avoids this result, and which requires nothing more extravagant than a literal reading of the words of the section. Offence (a) is not committed unless the defendant 'secures the remission' of a liability. Offence (c) is not committed unless the defendant obtains an 'exemption from . . . liability to make a payment'. Assuming again that the defendant had succeeded in deceiving the inspector in the present case, the inspector would have had no intention to 'remit' an existing liability because he would have been persuaded that there was no liability to remit, nor would he in law have remitted any liability. The defendant's liability to pay the proper fare would unquestionably have continued unimpaired. Similarly, the inspector would not have intended to exempt the defendant from any liability to make a payment, existing or otherwise, being persuaded that there was no liability, and the defendant would not have been exempted from any liability. . . .

What the defendant would have succeeded in doing if he had deceived the inspector was to induce him to forgo payment of an unremitted, still existing liability to pay the full fare, from which no one intended to exempt him and from which he was not exempted."

R. v. Andrews & Hedges [1981] Crim.L.R. 106 (C.C.Ct.): Mr Recorder Sherrard Q.C.: Defendants were charged with inducing creditors to wait for payment by deception contrary to section 2(1)(b) of the Theft Act 1978. The creditors had in the course of dealing supplied large quantities of meat to the defendants on credit terms of up to three weeks for which payments were duly made by cheques which were met. The dishonesty relied upon by the prosecution was that thereafter having obtained meat from suppliers in a later period the defendants issued cheques unsupported by funds in their bank account which were not met on presentation, and induced the creditors to wait for payment. The deception relied on in each case was the false representation that the cheque in question was a good and valid order and that in the ordinary course, the cheque would be met.

Held, there was no inducement to wait for payment where the parties had traded together previously and where credit terms had been allowed and where payment by cheque was accepted in the ordinary course of dealing between the parties; for section 2(1)(b) only applied where a creditor is induced to accept a cheque instead of cash, and only then did section 2(3) operate as a matter of law to treat the creditor as having been induced to wait for payment. There was no evidence that the creditors had asked for cash and no evidence that they had been induced to accept cheques or to wait for payment. Accordingly, there was no case to answer.

5. MAKING OFF WITHOUT PAYMENT

Theft Act 1978, section 3

(1) Subject to subsection (3) below, a person who, knowing that payment on the spot for any goods supplied or service done is required or expected from him, dishonestly makes off without having paid as required or expected and with intent to avoid payment of the amount due shall be guilty of an offence.

(2) For the purposes of this section 'payment on the spot' includes payment at the time of collecting goods on which work has been done or in respect of which service has been provided.

(3) Subsection (1) above shall not apply where the supply of the goods or the doing of the service is contrary to law, or where the service done is such that payment is not legally enforceable.

(4) Any person may arrest without warrant anyone who is, or whom he, with reasonable cause, suspects to be, committing or attempting to commit an offence under this section.

Note

No deception is needed; only dishonesty. Nor is it material whether ownership of goods has been transferred to the defendant, nor whether he was dishonest before or after any goods were supplied or service done. Many difficulties in the way of a prosecution for theft or obtaining property by deception are thus avoided, but the wording of the present offence is not without its own difficulties, *e.g.* as to "on the spot", "goods supplied", "makes off" "without having paid".

Questions

1. A travels on a train without first buying a ticket, as the regulations require. When challenged at the exit barrier at his destination, he runs away. Is he still "on the spot" when he makes off? Yes, according to *Moberley v. Alsop, The Times*, December 13, 1991 (D.C.).

2. A, in a self-service store, picks up an article, puts it in his pocket and dishonestly departs without paying for it. Can the article be described as "goods supplied"?

3. A, having eaten a meal at B's restaurant, persuades B to let him go without paying by falsely promising to return next day with the money. Is this "making off" by A? See *R. v. Brooks & Brooks, infra.*

4. On facts such as occurred in *R. v. Lambie, ante,* p. 807, where a credit card is dishonestly presented to a supermarket cashier, does the customer make off "without payment"?

5. A, having consumed a meal, absent-mindedly leaves without paying. On being followed out into the street by the waiter, he realises his omission, but decides not to pay and runs away. Has A dishonestly made off? See *R. v. Brooks & Brooks, infra.*

6. A, having consumed a meal, discovers he has no money. To avoid a fuss, he slips out of the restaurant, intending to return next day with the money. Has A made off "with intent to avoid payment of the amount due"? See *R. v. Allen, infra.*

In *R. v. Brooks & Brooks* (1983) 76 Cr.App.R. 66, 68 (C.A.), the meaning of "makes off" was considered:

We have been referred to a fuller examination of the definition of the offence which has been made in the academic field, notably by Professor Smith in *The Law of Theft* (4th ed. 1979) paragraph 242 and Mr J. R. Spencer in an article entitled 'The Theft Act 1978', [1979] Crim.L.R. 24, in particular at p. 37 thereof. Thus Professor Smith comments that the words 'makes off' should be construed in a pejorative sense and includes both a sudden and secret departure but excludes departure consented to by means of a deception. Mr Spencer relies upon one meaning given to the term 'makes off' in the *Shorter Oxford Dictionary*, namely 'to depart suddenly, often with a disparaging implication, to hasten away; to decamp.'

Pausing there, it is plain that the learned compilers do not suggest that the words must always be construed in the pejorative sense. In any case it is an unnecessary construction, for the words do not stand alone. The making off must be dishonest.

Mr Spencer is of the opinion that the term suggests a sudden and unexpected departure. In so doing he fails to consider one of the alternatives given in the dictionary, namely to 'decamp,' which may be an exercise accompanied by the sound of trumpets or a silent stealing away after the folding of tents. Obviously, the term covers a wide variety of modes of departure. Nevertheless, we strongly deprecate the involvement of a jury in any philosophic study, however interesting it may be to lawyers and academics. Nor do we adopt the attitude feared by Mr Spencer of simply saying it is 'all a question of fact for the jury.'

In our opinion, the words 'dishonestly makes off' are words easily understandable by any jury which, in the majority of cases, require no elaboration in a summing-up. The jury should be told to apply the words in their ordinary natural meaning and to relate them to the facts of the case. We agree with the decision in *R. v. McDavitt* [1981] Crim.L.R. 843 that 'making off' involves a departure from the spot where payment is required.

R. v. Allen
[1985] A.C. 1029
House of Lords

A, who had incurred a bill of £1286 at an hotel, left without paying. Two days later, he rang to explain that he was in financial difficulties, he expected to be able to pay soon, and offered to return and deposit his passport as security. When he did return he was arrested and charged with making off without payment. In answer to a question from the jury, the judge directed them that the intent to avoid payment in section 3(1) did not have to be permanent but need only apply to the date on which A had avoided the payment on the spot that had been required or expected from him by the hotel. His conviction having been quashed by the Court of Appeal, the prosecution appealed to the House of Lords.

LORD HAILSHAM OF ST. MARYLEBONE: Despite some (though not unanimous) text book opinions in an opposite sense . . . I consider [the judge's] answer to be clearly erroneous. [His Lordship read section 3(1).]

The appellant's contention was that the effect of this section is to catch not only those who intend permanently to avoid payment of the amount due, but also those whose intention is to avoid payment on the spot, which, after all, is the time at which, *ex hypothesi*, payment has been "expected or required", and the time, therefore, when the "amount" became "due".

The judgment of the Court of Appeal, with which I agree, was delivered by Boreham J. He said [1985] 1 W.L.R. 50, 57:

"To secure a conviction under section 3 the following must be proved: (1) that the defendant in fact made off without making payment on the spot (2) the following mental elements—(a) knowledge that payment on the spot was required or expected of him; and (b) dishonesty; and (c) intent to avoid payment [sc. 'of the amount due']."

I agree with this analysis. To it the judge adds the following comment:

"If (c) means, or is taken to include, no more than an intention to delay or defer payment of the amount due it is difficult to see what it adds to the other elements. Anyone who knows that payment on the spot is expected or required of him and who then dishonestly makes off without paying as required or expected must have at least the intention to delay or defer payment. It follows, therefore, that the conjoined phrase 'and with intent to avoid payment of the amount due' adds a further ingredient—an intention to do more than delay or defer—an intention to evade payment altogether."

My own view, for what it is worth, is that the section thus analysed is capable only of this meaning. But counsel for the appellant very properly conceded that, even if it were equivocal and capable of either meaning, in a penal section of this kind any ambiguity must be resolved in favour of the subject and against the Crown. Accordingly the appeal falls to be dismissed either if on its true construction it means unambiguously that the intention must be permanently to avoid payment, or if the clause is ambiguous and capable of either meaning. Even on the assumption that, in the context, the word "avoid" without the addition of the word "permanently" is capable of either meaning, which Boreham J. was inclined to concede, I find myself convinced by his final paragraph, which reads:

"Finally, we can see no reason why, if the intention of Parliament was to provide, in effect, that an intention to delay or defer payment might suffice, Parliament should not have said so in explicit terms. This *might* have been achieved by the insertion of the word 'such' before payment in the phrase in question. It *would* have been achieved by a grammatical reconstruction of the material part of section 3(1) thus, 'dishonestly makes off without having paid and with intent to avoid payment of the amount due as required or expected'. To accede to the Crown's submission would be to read the section as if it were constructed in that way. That we cannot do. Had it been intended to relate the intention to avoid 'payment' to 'payment as required or expected' it would have been easy to say so. The section does not say so. At the very least it contains an equivocation which should be resolved in favour of the appellant."

There is really no escape from this argument.... In order to give the section now under consideration the effect required the section would have to be remodelled in the way suggested by Boreham J. in the passage quoted above, or the word "and" in the ultimate phrase would have to be read as if it meant "that is to say" so that the required intent would be equated with "dishonestly" in the early part of the subsection.

Apart from a minor matter not relevant to the judgment there is nothing really to be added to the judgment delivered by Boreham J.

The minor matter to which I have just referred was the disinclination of the Court of Appeal to consider the 13th Report of the Criminal Law

Revision Committee, Section 16 of the Theft Act 1968 (1977) (Cmnd. 6733), which led to the passing of the Act of 1978. In accordance with present practice, this, for the purpose of defining the mischief of the Act but not to construe it, their Lordships in fact have done. The "mischief" is covered by paragraphs 18 to 21 of the report and it is significant that the report was accompanied by a draft Bill, section 3 of which is in terms identical with section 3 of the Act, save that the proposed penalty was three years instead of two. Though we did not use it as an aid to construction, for the purpose of defining the mischief to be dealt with by the section, I consider it to be relevant. The discussion had originated from the decision in *D.P.P. v. Ray, ante*, p. 795, and the committee defined the mischief in the following terms (paragraph 18):

> "there was general support for our suggestion that where the customer knows that he is expected to pay on the spot for goods supplied to him or services done for him it should be an offence for him dishonestly to go away without having paid *and intending never to pay."* (Emphasis mine.)

From this it is plain beyond doubt that the mischief aimed at by the authors of the report was precisely that which the Court of Appeal, construing the section without reference to the report, attributed to the section by the mere force of grammatical construction.

(Lords Scarman, Diplock, Bridge and Brightman agreed.)

Prosecution's appeal dismissed

Note

Griew § 12.18, commenting on this case: "Section 3 turns out not to do the whole job it ought to do. In the case of sellers and suppliers of services who undertake very small transactions on the basis of immediate payment, the mischief to be controlled is the very act of making off. . . . The decision in *Allen* threatens an increase in the number of contested cases as bilkers run bogus, but possibly just plausible, defences of 'I was going to go back and pay later.' "

BLACKMAIL

Theft Act 1968, section 21

(1) A person is guilty of blackmail if, with a view to gain for himself or another or with intent to cause loss to another, he makes any unwarranted demand with menaces; and for this purpose a demand with menaces is unwarranted unless the person making it does so in the belief—

(a) that he has reasonable grounds for making the demand; and
(b) that the use of the menaces is a proper means of reinforcing the demand.

(2) The nature of the act or omission demanded is immaterial, and it is also immaterial whether the menaces relate to action to be taken by the person making the demand.

(3) A person guilty of blackmail shall on conviction on indictment be liable to imprisonment for a term not exceeding fourteen years.

i. Demand with Menaces

Notes

Neither "demand" nor "menaces" is defined by the Act. "Menaces", where it was used in the statutory predecessor of the present section (*i.e.* section 29(1) of the Larceny Act 1916) had acquired a definite meaning, being exactly synonymous with threat.

Thorne v. Motor Trade Association [1937] A.C. 797: Lord Atkin (at p. 806), "If the matter came to us for decision for the first time I think there would be something to be said for a construction of 'menace' which connotes threats of violence and injury to person or property, and a contrast which might be made between 'menaces' and 'threats,' as used in other sections of the various statutes. But in several cases it has been decided that 'menace' in this subsection and its predecessors is simply equivalent to threat."

Lord Wright (at p. 817),

"I think the word 'menace' is to be liberally construed and not as limited to threats of violence but as including threats of any action detrimental to or unpleasant to the person addressed. It may also include a warning that in certain events such action is intended."

But "threat" was regarded as too wide by the draftsmen of the Theft Act 1978.

Cmnd. 2977, § 123: "We have chosen the word 'menaces' instead of 'threats' because notwithstanding the wide meaning given to 'menaces' in *Thorne's* case . . . we regard that word as stronger than 'threats' and the consequent slight restriction of the scope of the offence seems to us right."

R. v. Lawrence and Pomroy
(1971) 57 Cr.App.R. 64
Court of Appeal

L and P were convicted of blackmail in that on January 20, with a view to gain for themselves they made an unwarranted demand of £70 from T with menaces. P had done some work for T. T, not being satisfied with the work, had paid part only of the contract price and had indicated that the balance of £70 would be paid when the work was completed to his satisfaction. On January 16, P had asked T for the £70 and, on being refused, said that unless T paid up, he had better look over his shoulder whenever he went out. On January 20, P again visited T, this time in company with L, a big man. The conversation on that occasion is set out in the judgment of Cairns L.J., below. L and P appealed on the grounds that the judge failed to give (a) a definition of menaces and (b) a direction on proviso (*b*) of section 21(1).

CAIRNS L.J.: Detective Constable Walters said that in company with other officers he was concealed behind the door of Thorn's house when the appellants arrived on January 20. He heard a conversation about the £70 which ended with Lawrence saying: "Now listen, I've got an interest in the £70, see," and then after a pause: "Come out of the house and we'll sort this lot out now." Thorn said: "No" and Lawrence said: "Come on mate, come outside." The police officers then revealed themselves and Walters said that he saw the appellants outside the door. He said to Lawrence: "What is your name?" and Lawrence said: "Leave off, what do you want to know for?" Pomroy said: "Yes it's all right, we only want my money." Lawrence said: "Leave me out, I've only come to help my mate," and when asked gave his name to the police. The appellants were told that they were being arrested for demanding money from Thorn. After caution Lawrence said: "That's nice, we've been well set up." Pomroy said: "But he does owe me money. . . ."

The first point we deal with is the contention that the judge gave the jury no definition of what constitutes a menace. It is said that they should have been directed in accordance with *R. v. Clear* [1968] 1 Q.B. 670, that they must consider what the effect would be in the mind of a reasonable man of the words and actions of the two defendants. The word "menaces" is an ordinary English word which any jury can be expected to understand. In exceptional cases where because of special knowledge in special circumstances what would be a menace to an ordinary person is not a menace to the person to whom it is addressed, or where the converse may be true, it is no doubt necessary to spell out the meaning of the word. But, in our view, there was no such necessity here. The judge made it abundantly clear that the issue for the jury was whether the two men had gone to Thorne's house merely to ask reasonably for payment, on Pomroy's part to ask reasonably for payment and on Lawrence's part merely as a companion, or whether they had gone to threaten and frighten him into paying. That was quite a sufficient explanation of what is meant by menaces.

Next, should the judge have directed the jury on the proviso to section 21(1)(b) of the Theft Act: that is to say, as to whether the accused believed that what they did was a proper way of enforcing the debt? Neither of them suggested at the trial that, if menaces were used by them, it was a proper means of enforcement. It is true that the police evidence was that when Pomroy's statement was read to him, Lawrence said: 'That's about it, what's wrong with that?' but he repudiated that in his evidence and said that his reaction had been 'It's a lot of nonsense.'

Where on the face of it the means adopted to obtain payment of a debt is not the proper way of enforcing it and where the accused does not at his trial set up the case that he believed it to be, there is no need for any direction to be given on the proviso. . . .

Appeals dismissed

Note

As to the exceptional cases mentioned by Cairns L.J. where it is necessary to spell out the meaning of 'menaces', the Court of Appeal in *R. v. Garwood* [1987] said:

"It seems to us that there are two possible occasions on which a further directive on the meaning of the word menaces may be required. The first is where the threats might have affected the mind of an ordinary person of normal stability but did not affect the person actually addressed. In such circumstances that would amount to a sufficient menace: see *R. v. Clear* [1968] 1 Q.B. 670. The second situation is where the threats in fact affected the mind of the victim, although they would not have affected the mind of a person of normal stability. In that case, in our judgment, the existence of the menaces is proved providing that the accused man was aware of the likely effect of his actions on the victims."

R. v. Harry [1972] Crim.L.R. 32 (Crown Ct.): H sent letters to 115 local shopkeepers asking them to buy immunity posters by contributing to a Student Rag Appeal in aid of charity. The purpose of the poster was to "protect you from any Rag Activity which could in any way cause you inconvenience". The poster read "These premises are immune from Rag '73 activities whatever they may be." In directing an acquittal of blackmail, Judge Petre said "Menaces is a strong word. You may think that menaces must be of a fairly stern nature to fall within the definition."

Treacy v. Director of Public Prosecutions
[1971] A.C. 537
House of Lords

T wrote and posted in England a letter addressed to a woman in Germany, which letter contained a demand. T argued that he was not triable in England, not having made the demand in England.

LORD DIPLOCK: . . . Arguments as to the meaning of ordinary everyday phrases are not susceptible of much elaboration. The Theft Act, 1968, makes a welcome departure from the former style of drafting in criminal statutes. It is expressed in simple language as used and understood by ordinary literate men and women. It avoids so far as possible those terms of art which have acquired a special meaning understood only by lawyers in which many of the penal enactments which it supersedes were couched. So the question which has to be answered is: Would a man say in ordinary conversation: "I have made a demand" when he had written a letter containing a demand and posted it to the person to whom the demand was addressed? Or would he not use those words until the letter had been received and read by the addressee?

My answer to that question is that it would be natural for him to say "I have made a demand" as soon as he had posted the letter, for he would have done all that was in his power to make the demand. He might add, if it were the fact: "but it has not reached X yet", or: "I made a demand but it got lost in the post." What, at any rate, he would not say is: "I shall make a demand when X receives my letter," unless he contemplated making some further demand after the letter had been received.

I see nothing in the context or in the purpose of the section to indicate that the words bear any other meaning than that which I have suggested they would bear in ordinary conversation. . . .

As respects the purpose of the section, I see no reason for supposing that Parliament did not intend to punish conduct which is anti-social or wicked— if that word is still in current use—unless the person guilty of the conduct achieves his intended object of gain to himself or loss caused to another. The fact that what a reasonable man would regard as an unwarranted demand with menaces after being posted by its author goes astray and never reaches the addressee, or reaches him but is not understood by him, or because of his unusual fortitude fails to disturb his equanimity, as was the case in *R. v. Clear* [1968] 1 Q.B. 670, may be a relevant factor in considering what punishment is appropriate but does not make the conduct of the author himself any less wicked or anti-social or less meet to be deterred.

My Lords, all that has to be decided upon this aspect of the instant appeal is whether the appellant "made a demand" when he posted his letter to the addressee. In the course of the argument many other and ingenious ways in which a blackmailer may choose to send his demand to his victim have been canvassed, and many possible, even though unlikely, events which might intervene between the sending of the demand by the blackmailer and its receipt and comprehension by the victim have been discussed. These cases which so far are only imaginary may fall to be decided if they ever should occur in real life. But unless the purpose of the new style of drafting used in the Theft Act, 1968, is to be defeated they, too, should be decided by answering the question: "Are the circumstances of this case such as would prompt a man in ordinary conversation to say: 'I have made a demand'?"

For both the reasons which I have given I would dismiss this appeal.

Appeal dismissed

Notes

1. A possible danger in "the new style of drafting used in the Theft Act, 1968", is illustrated by the fact that of the five Law Lords concerned in *Treacy's* case, three thought that posting a letter containing a demand was making a demand, but two thought that no demand was made until the letter reached the addressee. A technical term at least has the merit that its meaning is precise and can be the subject of a precise direction to the jury.

2. Both demand and menaces may be implicit, rather than explicit. See next case.

R. v. Collister and Warhurst
(1955) 39 Cr.App.R. 100
Court of Criminal Appeal

C and W, who were police officers, were charged with demanding money with menaces, under section 30 of the Larceny Act 1916. C told

W, in the presence of P, that P had been importuning him. The prosecutor protested, but W said to him, "This is going to look very bad for you." They arranged to meet him on the next day, W telling C in P's hearing to type out a report on the matter but to hold it up and use it only if P failed to keep the appointment. When they met next day, W asked P whether he had brought anything with him, and P handed over five one pound notes.

PILCHER J. directed the jury: What you have got to be satisfied with in this case is that these two men, working in concert, intended to convey, and did in fact convey, to Mr Jeffries in the first place that they, being police officers, intended to take him to the West Central Police Station on a charge of importuning, or to put in a report about him, unless Jeffries then or later paid them money. That, I think, is putting it as simply as I can put it. You need not be satisfied that there was an express demand for money in words. You need not be satisfied that any express threats were made, but if the evidence satisfies you that, although there was no such express demand or threat, the demeanour of the accused and the circumstances of the case were such that an ordinary reasonable man would understand that a demand for money was being made upon him and that that demand was accompanied by menaces— not perhaps direct, but veiled menaces—so that his ordinary balance of mind was upset, then you would be justified in coming to the conclusion that a demand with menaces had been made. . . .

> *They were convicted and on appeal this direction*
> *was held to be perfectly proper*

ii. Unwarranted

Criminal Law Revision Committee: Eighth Report, Cmnd. 2977

§ 118 As to the illegality of making the demand we are decidedly of the opinion that the test should be subjective, namely whether the person in question honestly believes that he has the right to make the demand. This means in effect adopting the test of whether there is a claim of right, as in 1916, s.30, and not the test whether there is in fact a reasonable cause for making the demand, as in 1916, s.29(1)(i). Since blackmail is in its nature an offence of dishonesty, it seems wrong that a person should be guilty of the offence by making a demand which he honestly believes to be justified. Moreover to adopt the objective test seems to involve almost insuperable difficulty. It would be necessary either to set out the various kinds of demand which it was considered should be justified or to find an expression which would describe exactly these kinds but not others. The former course might in theory be possible; but the provision would have to be very elaborate, and it would involve the risk which attends any attempt to list different kinds of conduct for the purpose of a criminal offence—that of including too much or too little. Moreover there is much room for disagreement as to what kinds of demand should or should not be treated as justified. The latter course seems impossible having regard to the results which have followed from making liability depend on the absence of a 'reasonable and probable cause.' Any general provision would probably have to use some such uninformative expression, and it would be almost bound to cause similar difficulty and uncertainty.

§ 119 It is in relation to the question when it is permissible to employ threats in support of a demand that differences of opinion become most acute. Several situations are possible. A. may be owed £100 by B. and be unable to get payment. Perhaps A. needs the money badly and B. is in a

position to pay; or perhaps A. can easily afford to wait and B. is in difficulty. Should it be blackmail for A. to threaten B. that, if he does not pay,
A. will assault him—or slash the tyres of his car—or tell people that B. is
a homosexual, which he is (or which he is not)—or tell people about the
debt and anything discreditable about the way in which it was incurred?
On one view none of these threats should be enough to make the demand
amount to blackmail. For it is no offence merely to utter the threats without making the demand (unless for some particular reason such as breach
of the peace or defamation); nor would the threat become criminal merely
because it was uttered to reinforce a demand of a kind quite different
from those associated with blackmail. Why then should it be blackmail
merely because it is uttered to reinforce a demand for money which is
owed? On this view no demand with menaces would amount to blackmail, however harsh the action threatened unless there was dishonesty.
This is a tenable view, though an extreme one. In our opinion it goes too
far and there are some threats which should make the demand amount
to blackmail even if there is a valid claim to the thing demanded. For
example, we believe that most people would say that it should be blackmail to threaten to denounce a person, however truly, as a homosexual
unless he paid a debt. It does not seem to follow from the existence of a
debt that the creditor should be entitled to resort to any method, otherwise non-criminal, to obtain payment. There are limits to the methods
permissible for the purpose of enforcing payment of a debt without
recourse to the courts. For example, a creditor cannot seize the debtor's
goods; and in *Parker* (1910) 74 J.P. 208, it was held . . . that a creditor who
forged a letter from the Admiralty to a sailor warning him to pay a debt
was guilty of forgery notwithstanding the existence of the debt.

§ 120 If it is agreed that some threats should make a demand amount
to blackmail, the difficulty is to draw the line between different kinds of
threats in a way which would be generally accepted. It may be thought
that a threat to cause physical injury or damage to property should always
be sufficient, even though one does not ordinarily think of such threats in
connection with blackmail. A threat to injure a person in relation to his
business, for example by cutting off supplies to a retailer if he will not
pay a debt or persists in breaking an agreement, would probably not be
regarded as rightly included in blackmail. Some might think that any
threat to disclose a matter not connected with the circumstances giving
rise to the debt should be included; but opinion may differ widely about
threats to disclose some discreditable conduct which resulted in the debt
being incurred. Probably most people would say that the offence should
not extend to a threat to disclose the existence of a debt. For example, it
is not blackmail to threaten to post the name of a betting defaulter at
Tattersalls (see *Russell on Crime*, 12th ed., pp. 881–882). As in the case of
demands, the possible courses seem to be to lay down a subjective test,
depending on whether the person who utters the threat believes in his
right to do so, or an objective test, whether by specifying the kinds of
threats which should or should not be permissible or by means of a general provision to cover the latter. For reasons similar to those given in
paragraph 118 concerning the demand we think that the only satisfactory
course would be to adopt a subjective test and to make criminal liability
depend on whether the person who utters the threat believes in the propriety of doing so.

§ 122 At first we proposed to include a requirement that a person's
belief that he has reasonable grounds for making the demand or that the
use of the menaces is proper should be reasonable belief. There would be
a case for this in policy; for it may be thought that a person who puts

pressure on another by menaces of a kind which any reasonable person would think ought to be blackmail should not escape liability merely because his moral standard is too low, or his intelligence too limited, to enable him to appreciate the wrongness of his conduct. The requirement might also make the decision easier for the jury; for if they found that the demand was unwarranted or that the menaces were improper, they would not have to consider whether the accused believed otherwise. But we decided finally not to include the requirement. To require that an honest belief, in order to be a defence, should be reasonable would have the result that the offence of blackmail could be committed by mere negligence (for example, in not consulting a lawyer or, as did Bernhard, in consulting the wrong kind of lawyer). [See *R. v. Bernhard* [1938] 2 K.B. 264.]"

Sir Bernard MacKenna, "Blackmail: a Criticism" [1966] Crim.L.R. 466

5. A man's belief that he has reasonable grounds for making a demand depends on two matters:

(a) his belief that the facts of the case are such-and-such; and
(b) his opinion upon these facts that it would be reasonable to make the demand.

In a particular case one man's belief that there are reasonable grounds for making a demand may differ from another's because of a difference in their beliefs about the facts (one believing the facts to be X., the other to be Y.), or because of a difference in their opinions upon the same facts (one opinion that those facts give a reasonable ground for making the demand, the other that they do not).

6. 'Reasonable grounds' in [section 21(1)(a)] cannot be limited to such as are believed to give a legally enforceable claim. To many it would seem reasonable to demand satisfaction of a claim recognised by the law as valid though unenforceable by legal action for some technical reason, such as the want of a writing or the expiration of the period of limitation. To some it would seem equally reasonable to demand payment of a claim incapable in any circumstances of being enforced by action, such as the claim to be paid a winning bet. There may be many other cases in which a moral, as distinct from a legal, right would seem to some at least a reasonable ground for making a demand. On these questions there could be differences of opinion, particularly as to whether on the facts of the case the person demanding had a moral right to the thing demanded. There could be similar 'moral' differences about the propriety of using threats.

7. The Committee intend that the test shall be subjective in both the respects indicated in 5 above: (i) the facts shall be taken to be those which the defendant believed to exist, and (ii) his opinion as to whether those facts gave him a reasonable ground for making a demand (or made it proper for him to use threats) will be the only relevant one. His own moral standards are to determine the rightness or wrongness of his conduct. This appears from a sentence in paragraph 122 where the Committee discuss (and dismiss) the possible objection to [section 21(1)(a)] that 'it may be thought that a person who puts pressure on another by menaces of a kind which any reasonable person would think ought to be blackmail should not escape liability merely because his moral standard is too low, or his intelligence too limited, to enable him to appreciate the wrongness of his conduct.'

8. That a sane man's guilt or innocence should depend in this way on his own opinion as to whether he is acting rightly or wrongly is, I think, an innovation in our criminal law.

9. The claim of right which excuses a taking that might otherwise be theft under section 1 of the Larceny Act 1916, may of course be a mistaken claim, and the mistake may be one of law or of fact. A man's mistaken belief that the rules of the civil law make him the owner of a certain thing is as good an excuse as his mistaken belief that the thing is X. when it is in fact Y. But [section 21(1)] goes further than this, and gives efficacy to the defendant's moral judgments whatever they may be. That is surely something different. It is one thing to hold that the defendant is excused if he believes the civil law to be X. when it is Y. It is another to excuse him in any case where he thinks that what he is doing is morally right, though according to ordinary moral notions he may be doing something very wrong."

R. v. Harvey
(1980) 72 Cr.App.R. 139
Court of Appeal

H and others paid £20,000 to S for what was thought to be a consignment of cannabis, but in fact was a load of rubbish. They kidnapped S's wife and small child and told S they would maim and kill his family unless he gave them their money back. They were convicted of blackmail and appealed.

BINGHAM J.: The learned judge in his direction to the jury quoted the terms of the subsection and then continued as follows: "Now where the defence raise this issue, in other words, where they say that the demand is warranted and where they say they believe they had reasonable cause for making the demand and that the use of the menaces was a proper way of reinforcing the demand, it is for the prosecution to negative that allegation. It is not for the defendants to prove it once they have raised it. It is for the prosecution to prove that they had no such belief. Now is that clear? It is not easy and I do not want to lose you on the way. It has been raised in this case so you have got to ask yourself this. Has the prosecution disproved that these defendants or those who have raised the matter believed that they had *reasonable* grounds for making the demand? Certainly you may say to yourselves that they have been ripped off to the tune of £20,000. They had been swindled.... As I say, on this question of reasonable ground for making a demand, you may say to yourselves: 'Well, they did have reasonable ground for making the demand in this sense, that they had put money into this deal, they had been swindled by Scott, and it was reasonable to demand the return of their money.' So you may say: 'Well, the prosecution have not negatived that but what about the second leg of the proviso, the belief that the use of menaces is a proper method of reinforcing the demand?' Now it is for you to decide what, if any, menaces were made, because that is a question of evidence. If you decide that the threats or menaces made by these accused, or any of them, were to kill or to maim or to rape, or any of the other matters that have been mentioned in evidence—I mention about three that come into my mind—then those menaces or threats are threats to commit a criminal act, a threat to murder, a threat to rape, or a threat to blow your legs or kneecaps off, those are threats to commit a criminal offence and surely everybody in this country, including the defendants, knows those are criminal offences. The point is that this is a matter of law. It cannot be a proper means of reinforcing the demand to make threats to commit serious criminal offences. So I say to you that if you look at these two counts of blackmail and you decide that these defendants, or any of them, used menaces, dependent upon the menaces you decide were used, the threats that were used, but if you decide that these threats were made by these men to commit criminal offences against Scott, they cannot be heard to say on this blackmail charge that they had reasonable belief that the use of those threats was a proper method of reinforcing their demand."

Later, when prosecuting counsel drew attention to the learned judge's erroneous reference to "reasonable" belief, he added the following: "I do not think it affects the point I was seeking to make, that where the demand or the threat is to commit a criminal offence, and a serious criminal offence like murder and maiming and rape, or whatever it may be, it seems hard for anybody to say that the defendants had a belief that was a proper way of reinforcing their demand. That is the point."

For the appellants it was submitted that the learned judge's direction, and in particular the earlier of the passages quoted, was incorrect in law because it took away from the jury a question properly falling within their province of decision, namely, what the accused in fact believed. He was wrong to rule as a matter of law that a threat to perform a serious criminal act could never be thought by the person making it to be a proper means. While free to comment on the unlikelihood of a defendant believing threats such as were made in this case to be a proper means, the judge should nonetheless (it was submitted) have left the question to the jury. For the Crown it was submitted that a threat to perform a criminal act can never as a matter of law be a proper means within the subsection, and that the learned judge's direction was accordingly correct. Support for both these approaches is to be found in academic works helpfully brought to the attention of the Court.

The answer to this problem must be found in the language of the subsection, from which in our judgment two points emerge with clarity: (1) the subsection is concerned with the belief of the individual defendant in the particular case: "... a demand with menaces is unwarranted unless *the person making it* does so in the belief ..." (added emphasis). It matters not what the reasonable man, or any man other than the defendant, would believe save in so far as that may throw light on what the defendant in fact believed. Thus the factual question of the defendant's belief should be left to the jury. To that extent the subsection is subjective in approach, as is generally desirable in a criminal statute. (2) In order to exonerate a defendant from liability his belief must be that the use of the menaces is a "proper" means of reinforcing the demand. "Proper" is an unusual expression to find in a criminal statute. It is not defined in the Act, and no definition need be attempted here. It is, however, plainly a word of wide meaning, certainly wider than (for example) "lawful." But the greater includes the less and no act which was not believed to be lawful could be believed to be proper within the meaning of the subsection. Thus no assistance is given to any defendant, even a fanatic or a deranged idealist, who knows or suspects that his threat, or the act threatened, is criminal, but believes it to be justified by his end or his peculiar circumstances. The test is not what he regards as justified, but what he believes to be proper. And where, as here, the threats were to do acts which any sane man knows to be against the laws of every civilised country no jury would hesitate long before dismissing the contention that the defendant genuinely believed the threats to be a proper means of reinforcing even a legitimate demand.

It is accordingly our conclusion that the direction of the learned judge was not strictly correct. If it was necessary to give a direction on this aspect of the case at all (and in the absence of any evidence by the defendants as to their belief we cannot think that there was in reality any live issue concerning it) the jury should have been directed that the demand with menaces was not to be regarded as unwarranted unless the Crown satisfied them in respect of each defendant that the defendant did not make the demand with menaces in the genuine belief both—(a) that he had had reasonable grounds for making the demand; and (b) that the use of the menaces was in the circumstances a proper (meaning for present purposes a lawful, and not a criminal) means of reinforcing the demand.

The learned judge could, of course, make appropriate comment on the unlikelihood of the defendants believing murder and rape or threats to commit those acts to be lawful or other than criminal.

On the facts of this case we are quite satisfied that the misdirection to which we have drawn attention could have caused no possible prejudice to any of the appellants. Accordingly, in our judgment, it is appropriate to apply the proviso to section 2(1) of the Criminal Appeal Act 1968, and the appeals are dismissed.

Appeals against conviction dismissed

Questions

1. On the C.L.R.C.'s proposal for a subjective test of propriety, Sir Bernard MacKenna comments: 'That a sane man's guilt or innocence should depend this way on his own opinion as to whether he is acting rightly or wrongly is, I think, an innovation in our criminal law' (*ante*, p. 784). Has not the law reached this position with regard to theft? See *Ghosh, ante*, p. 720.

2. 'No act which was not believed to be lawful could be believed to be proper within the meaning of the subsection. . . . The test is not what he regards as justified, but what he believes to be proper':— Bingham J., above. Is this consistent with the subjective test of propriety proposed by the C.L.R.C., *ante*, p. 839, § 120?

3. Can mistake of law be relevant in this connection?

4. In the following cases, D, on trial for blackmail, contends that his request and threat were perfectly justified. How ought the judge to deal with the issue in his directions to the jury?

(a) D, with his entourage, arrives in England from a country where it is common for thieves to have their right hands cut off. D discovers that a member of his entourage, P, has been stealing money from him. He warns P that unless he returns the money, D will cut off his right hand.

(b) D, who uses his car daily to get to work, discovers that his road fund licence has expired. Not having the money to renew it, he asks P, his mother, for the money. When P refuses D says; 'Driving an unlicensed car is a crime. Unless you give me the money, I will certainly commit this crime every day. You wouldn't want that on your conscience, would you?'

Note

Williams, *Textbook*, p. 837: 'A factor of prime importance in a black-mail case will frequently be the secrecy or the openness of the transaction. A man who thinks he is acting properly in making a threat will not try to conceal his identity, and demand that money should be left in used pound notes at a telephone kiosk. Again, it is in practice impossible for a defendant both to argue that he did not utter the menaces and that if he did they were justified. So, if he chooses merely to deny the menaces, and the jury find against him and the menaces are prima facie improper, the judge need not direct the jury on the unscrupulous mental element.'

iii. With a View to Gain, etc.

Theft Act 1968, section 34

. . . (2) For the purposes of this Act—

(a) 'gain' and 'loss' are to be construed as extending only to gain or loss in money or other property, but as extending to any such gain or loss whether temporary or permanent; and

(i) 'gain' includes a gain by keeping what one has, as well as a gain by getting what one has not; and

(ii) 'loss' includes a loss by not getting what one might get, as well as a loss by parting with what one has.''

R. v. Parkes [1973] Crim.L.R. 358 (Sheffield Crown Court). D was charged with blackmail (*inter alia*). The evidence adduced by the prosecution showed that in one instance the money demanded was undoubtedly money owed to D by the complainant and, indeed, long overdue. In the other instance there was some issue as to whether or not the money demanded was a debt but the submission was made and ruled upon the basis that it *was* a debt owing by the complainant to D.

It was submitted that to demand what is lawfully owing to you was not a demand "with a view to gain" within the meaning of section 21(1) of the Theft Act 1968, as interpreted by section 32(2)(a) of that Act. Judge Dean Q.C. ruled that by demanding money lawfully owing to him D did have a view to "gain." Section 34(2)(a)(i) defines gain as including "getting what one has not"; by intending to obtain hard cash as opposed to a mere right of action in respect of the debt D *was* getting more than he already had and accordingly the submission failed.

R. v. Bevans [1988] Crim.L.R. 236 (C.A.): D, suffering from osteoarthritis, went to a doctor's surgery, produced a gun and threatened to shoot the doctor if he did not give him an injection of a pain-killing drug. *Held*, upholding his conviction of blackmail, the drug was property; the demand involved gain for D; the fact that his ulterior motive was relief from pain rather than economic gain was immaterial.

Note

If the immediate object is to get property, the motive for making an unwarrantable demand with menaces is irrelevant: see *Bevans, supra.* But if D's immediate object is to get a service rather than property or money, it may still be blackmail if his *motive* is financial. The words *"with a view* to gain" are capable of comprehending an ulterior motive of gain, *e.g.* D demands that V vote for him in an election for a company directorship, *so that* D will gain director's fees. See next case which concerned a different crime but one which also requires a view to gain or intent to cause loss.

R. v. Golechha and Choraria
(1990) 90 Cr.App.R. 241
Court of Appeal

G and C were convicted of falsification of accounts, contrary to section 17(1) Theft Act 1968, in that they dishonestly and with a view to gain for themselves or with intent to cause loss to another falsified certain bills of exchange. Their object was alleged to be to obtain a bank's forbearance to enforce against them certain other bills which had matured. On appeal:—

LORD LANE C.J. for the Court: ". . . When he came to sum up, the learned judge . . . directed the jury as follows:

"Going back to count one, you will see that after the word 'dishonestly' we get 'and with a view to gain for themselves.' Now you may not have thought that this required a great deal of your consideration, but there are certain things that have to be proved. The dishonest falsification, if you find that there was such a thing, must be with a view to gain for the person or persons who are doing the falsifying. As a matter of law I will tell you that the mere fact that Johnson Matthey credited the dollar current account of Berg [a company owned and run by Golechha] with a sum which represented the discounted value of the bill does not amount to gain if you stop there. All that has happened is that there has been a paper plus put on the account and that does not amount to gain if you stop there. But if you decide that what the defendant Golechha and the defendant Choraria or either of them had in view—there is the word 'with a view to gain'—went further than just getting a credit, a paper plus on Berg's account, but that what they were after was that Golechha should be able to turn that credit to practical use by drawing on it, converting it to cash in order to raise hard finance to buy goods, confirm deals and so forth, if you come to that view or that decision I should say, and you decide that that was the view that these people or either of them had in mind, members of the jury, that would amount to gain. That is a matter of fact for you."

. . . Mr Blair Q.C. for the Crown submitted, rightly in our view, that in the passage we have cited from the summing up the learned judge was . . . directing the jury [that] the mere crediting of the account . . . was not in law a gain; but if they concluded that the object of the defendants was to turn that paper credit, by drawing on it, to cash for the purposes of trade, that would amount to gain. Mr Blair submits that the judge's interpretation of the section was perfectly reasonable and indeed correct. Parliament deliberately chose the words "with a view to gain"—a phrase plainly admitting of some flexibility—precisely in order to cover cases such as the present.

As to the distinct argument to the effect that a mere forbearance to sue cannot in any event constitute a gain, Mr Blair contended that here too the judge was correct to regard his interpretation as affording an answer to it. He argued that even if all that was sought to be achieved by means of putting in place the last three bills was a forbearance on the part of the bank from suing on the earlier bills, the appellants were by that means trying to keep what they had in the sense that they were seeking to preserve a facility upon which they could in practice draw, whether or not it was enforceable in law.

In his reply to these submissions Mr Marshall-Andrews for Golechha . . . concentrated on two submissions only: first, that the judge's interpretation of section 17 is incorrect, and second that, even if it be correct, it does not meet the forbearance to sue point.

Mr Marshall-Andrews developed the first point in this way. He argued that the words "with a view to gain" must refer to the gain sought to be obtained by the falsification. They were included so as to incorporate temporary gain and keeping what you have, but there was in truth no distinction between the expressions "with a view to gain" and the expression "with intent to obtain property." It was not legitimate to look at the property into which that which was obtained might be converted. . . .

We see the attractions, from a practical common sense point of view, of the judge's interpretation of the section, while at the same time appreciating the force of Mr Marshall-Andrews' argument against it. However we find it unnecessary in the present case further to examine or to seek to resolve this matter, because we have reached the clear conclusion that Mr Marshall-Andrews' . . . second answer to Mr Blair's submissions is conclusive in favour of the appellants.

Put in its simplest form, the prosecution's argument on forbearance to sue amounts to this: that even if all that the appellants sought to achieve was forbearance on the part of the bank to enforce their rights under an earlier bill, they were seeking by that means to preserve the facility. This argument is superficially attractive, but fallacious. Even if it be assumed in favour of the Crown that the first two bills reflected genuine trade transactions—as to which there was no evidence one way or the other— all that had been brought into existence was a debt owed by Berg to the bank: a debt which existed at all times. To speak of "preserving the facility" by means of the placing of the falsified bills is to attribute to the facility characteristics which it does not possess. A debtor is not possessed of any proprietary rights: he does not have money, and the chose in action represented by the debt is owned by the creditor. Accordingly, while it may well be that the three falsified bills were falsified with a view to securing the bank's forbearance from enforcing their rights on the earlier bills, this did not and could not constitute falsification with a view to gain (that is gain by keeping money or other property). It was designed simply to postpone the enforcement of an obligation.

If it be accepted for present purposes that the learned judge's construction of the words "with a view to gain" was correct, and that it is therefore legitimate to see how funds sought to be obtained on the strength of a falsified bill would be used by the defendant, that cannot avail the prosecution in a case where all that the defendant had in view was the forbearance to enforce an existing indebtedness. If the desired forbearance is obtained, this neither gives to the defendant nor allows him to retain anything on which he can draw or which he can convert into cash or goods. Such a case is quite distinct from one in which the object in view is to obtain an advance.

If, which we do not, we had any doubts as to the correctness of this analysis, they would be dispelled by the reflection that section 16 of the 1968 Act or section 2 of the 1978 Act are entirely apt to found charges based on the sort of conduct we have been considering.

It follows that, since it was at the very least a distinct possibility that the appellants' object in falsifying the bills in question was merely to obtain the bank's forbearance, the judge's failure to invite the jury to consider whether that was the position and to direct them that if it was the defendants were not guilty of the offence charged was a misdirection.

Accordingly these appeals must on that ground be allowed.

Convictions quashed

Note

Blackmail is a sort of inchoate offence in that the making of the unwarranted demand with menaces is the full crime, even if the demand is not acceded to and no property is got as a result. If property *is* got as a result, then theft and robbery may also be committed. But blackmail is also a "fall-back" offence, in that if property is got but claim of right prevents a conviction of theft or robbery (see *R. v. Skivington, ante,* p. 781) it will be blackmail if the jury think D knew the menaces used were improper. As *Parkes, ante,* p. 844, shows, the fact that D is or thinks he is entitled to what he gets does not mean that he does not act "with a view to gain." Similarly if the menaces used do not amount to the use of force on a person or the putting or seeking to put a person in fear of imminent force, it cannot be robbery but can be blackmail.

The extracts which follow highlight a problem with the offence of blackmail in terms of its breadth.

James Lindgren, "Unravelling the Paradox of Blackmail" (1984) 84 Col. L.R. 670

In blackmail, the heart of the problem is that two separate acts, each of which is a moral and legal right, can combine to make a moral and legal wrong. For example, if I threaten to expose a criminal act unless I am paid money, I have committed blackmail. Or if I threaten to expose a sexual affair unless I am given a job, once again I have committed blackmail. I have a legal right to expose or threaten to expose the crime or affair, and I have a legal right to seek a job or money, but if I combine these rights it is blackmail. If both a person's ends—seeking a job or money—and his means—threatening to expose—are otherwise legal, why is it illegal to combine them? Therein lies what has been called the "paradox of blackmail.". . .

Not surprisingly, drawing the line between legitimate and illegitimate threats has proved impossible without an accepted theory. . . .

One group of theories examines different parts of the blackmail transaction, postulating that the wrongfulness of blackmail consists in what the blackmailer threatens to do if not paid, in what he offers to do if paid, in what he is seeking or in what he is selling. These theories fail chiefly because no single part of the blackmail transaction, taken separately, is necessarily wrong. Since the conduct these theories identify may be wrong in blackmail but legitimate elsewhere, they fail to adequately distinguish legitimate from illegitimate behavior. A second group of theories centers on the purpose served by a law of blackmail—either to discourage invasions of privacy or to prevent the waste of economic resources. These theories fail because they do not explain either why blackmail is forbidden where these harms are absent or why we do not prohibit many other activities that create the same harms. . . .

III. A NEW THEORY OF BLACKMAIL

A. Distinguishing Legitimate from Illegitimate Threats
We now turn to the main problem—distinguishing blackmail from legitimate bargaining. Merely identifying the element of threat will not solve the problem. Even highly coercive threats are present in many types

of legitimate economic bargaining. For example, an injured potential plaintiff may threaten to sue unless a settlement is reached. A seller may threaten to sell to someone else unless the buyer agrees to pay the price demanded. Or a bank may threaten to foreclose on a loan that will destroy a business as well as someone's way of life. The problem is to distinguish legitimate threats from illegitimate ones; we must explain why the same threat when made by one person can be permissible, but when made by another person in different circumstances can be blackmail.

Let us first examine informational blackmail. Here the blackmailer threatens to tell others damaging information about the blackmail victim unless the victim heeds the blackmailer's request, usually a request for money. The blackmailer obtains what he wants by using extra leverage. But that leverage belongs more to a third person than to the blackmailer. The blackmail victim pays the blackmailer to avoid involving third parties; he pays to avoid being harmed by *persons other than the blackmailer*. When the reputation of a person is damaged, he is punished by all those who change their opinion of him. They may "punish" him by treating him differently or he may be punished merely by the knowledge that others no longer respect him.

Thus when a blackmailer threatens to turn in a criminal unless paid money, the blackmailer is bargaining with the state's chip. The blackmail victim pays to avoid the harm that the state would inflict; he pays because he believes that he can thereby suppress the state's potential criminal claim. Of course, this does not effect a legally binding settlement, but the leverage is effective precisely to the extent that the victim believes that he has reached an effective settlement. Likewise, when a blackmailer threatens to expose damaging but noncriminal behavior unless paid money, he is also turning third-party leverage to his own benefit. What makes his conduct blackmail is that he interposes himself parasitically in an actual or potential dispute in which he lacks a sufficiently direct interest. What right has he to make money by settling other people's claims?

At the heart of blackmail, then, is the triangular nature of the transaction, and particularly this disjunction between the blackmailer's personal benefit and the interests of the third parties whose leverage he uses. In effect, the blackmailer attempts to gain an advantage in return for suppressing someone else's actual or potential interest. The blackmailer is negotiating for his own gain with someone else's leverage or bargaining chips.

This misuse of another's leverage is perhaps seen most clearly in noninformational blackmail, in situations where a formal agency relationship exists—for instance, where a labor union leader threatens to cause a strike unless he is given a personal payoff. There the labor leader is turning group power and a group dispute to personal benefit. The pressure on the blackmail victim would be the same if the blackmailer's agency relationship were merely informal—for instance, where an influential businessman threatens to cause a strike unless he is given a personal payoff. Notice that the victim of blackmail probably does not care whether the threatener is a labor leader or an influential businessman, an authorized agent or an unauthorized one. What the victim fears is a strike. Whoever seeks a personal payoff by credibly wielding the power of a third party to harm the victim is a blackmailer. . . .

What emerges from these examples is the observation that blackmail is the misuse of an informal (or formal) power of agency or representation. Under my theory, blackmail is the seeking of an advantage by threatening to press an actual or potential dispute that is primarily between the blackmail victim and someone else. The blackmailer threatens to bring others into the dispute but typically asks for something for himself; he turns someone else's power, usually group power, to personal benefit. The bargaining is unfair in that the threatener uses leverage that is less his than someone else's.

Thus in a general sense, the law of blackmail promotes principled negotiations by outlawing a particular kind of unfair bargaining. A blackmailer uses a type of extra leverage to exact unearned payments, convert causes of action to cash, or resolve disputes other than on their merits. The law of blackmail tries to compel people to resolve their disputes by means the legal system provides or prefers, such as civil suits. It also discourages the settlement of disputes by persons who are neither parties to those disputes nor agents for those parties. Thus blackmail law is a manifestation of a core principle of our legal system, the assignment of enforcement rights to the victim: an individual enforces a private wrong and the state enforces a public wrong. This enforcement principle is extremely broad. It applies in civil law and criminal law, in public law and private law. It has been justified by economic analysis and doctrines of individual liberty, by natural law and constitutional law. It is fundamental to the organization of our courts and to our system of procedure.

But the exclusive assignment principle is not monolithic—quite the contrary. It takes different forms in tort, contract and criminal law, and its configurations have changed over time. For example, in torts and contracts different people are assigned enforcement rights today than were assigned such rights before the decline of privity doctrines. Criminal claims are assigned to the state. Tort and contract claims are assigned to the victim of those kinds of wrongdoing. And claims that would be nonredressable in court, such as the right to change one's opinion of someone, are assigned to the person who would change his mind. . . .

Conclusion

Thus blackmail differs from ordinary bargaining and threats because the leverage used belongs less to the threatener than to a third party. It becomes clear why, in the paradoxical case, otherwise legitimate conduct becomes illegitimate in blackmail. The problem is not with anything intrinsic to the threat, or any other aspect of the conduct, which may remain legitimate when taken in isolation. Rather, the problem essentially is that the wrong person is making the threat; the blackmailer's own interest is not sufficient to justify his using that leverage. Thus the leverage being used, while legitimate in the hands of another, is illegitimate in the hands of the blackmailer.

HANDLING

Theft Act 1968, section 22

(1) A person handles stolen goods if (otherwise than in the course of stealing) knowing or believing them to be stolen goods he dishonestly receives the goods, or dishonestly undertakes or assists in their retention, removal, disposal or realisation by or for the benefit of another person, or if he arranges to do so.

(2) A person guilty of handling stolen goods shall on conviction on indictment be liable to imprisonment for a term not exceeding fourteen years.

Note

The offence created by this section replaces the offence of receiving stolen goods contained in section 33 of the Larceny Act 1916 and section 97 of the Larceny Act 1861. The present offence is wider than the former. Receiving was confined to cases where a man took into his possession goods which he knew had been obtained unlawfully. Handling, however, "will punish not only receivers, but also those who knowingly convey stolen goods to any place after the theft, those who take charge of them and keep them on their premises or hide them on the approach of the police, those who negotiate for the sale of the goods and the like. The definition will also include a person who in the course of his otherwise innocent employment knowingly removes the goods from place to place, for example a driver employed by dishonest transport owners. If the driver knows that the goods are stolen and that in conveying them he is helping in their disposal, it seems right that he should be guilty of the offence. The fact that he is acting in the course of his ordinary employment may go in mitigation." (Cmnd. 2977, 128.)

If, as is often the case, what is done by any of the above persons is a dishonest appropriation of the property with intent permanently to deprive the owner (see Chap. 10), it will also be theft.

i. Stolen Goods

Theft Act 1968, section 24

(1) The provisions of this Act relating to goods which have been stolen shall apply whether the stealing occurred in England or Wales or else-

where, and whether it occurred before or after the commencement of this Act, provided that the stealing (if not an offence under this Act) amounted to an offence where and at the time when the goods were stolen; and references to stolen goods shall be construed accordingly.

(2) For purposes of those provisions references to stolen goods shall include, in addition to the goods originally stolen and parts of them (whether in their original state or not)—

(a) any other goods which directly or indirectly represent or have at any time represented the stolen goods in the hands of the thief as being the proceeds of any disposal or realisation of the whole or part of the goods stolen or of goods so representing the stolen goods; and
(b) any other goods which directly or indirectly represent or have at any time represented the stolen goods in the hands of a handler of the stolen goods or any part of them as being the proceeds of any disposal or realisation of the whole or part of the stolen goods handled by him or of goods so representing them.

(3) But no goods shall be regarded as having continued to be stolen goods after they have been restored to the person from whom they were stolen or to other lawful possession or custody, or after that person and any other person claiming through him have otherwise ceased as regards those goods to have any right to restitution in respect of the theft.

(4) For the purposes of the provisions of this Act relating to goods which have been stolen (including subsection (1) to (3) above) goods obtained in England or Wales or elsewhere either by blackmail or in the circumstances described in section 15(1) of this Act shall be regarded as stolen; and 'steal,' 'theft' and 'thief' shall be construed accordingly.

Theft Act 1968, section 34

(2) For the purposes of this Act—

(b) 'goods,' except in so far as the context otherwise requires, includes money and every other description of property except land, and includes things severed from the land by stealing.

Notes

1. It has to be shown that "goods" within the meaning of section 34(2)(*b*), were stolen (or obtained by blackmail or deception: section 24(4)) by someone (who may be the present defendant: see *post*); that the property the subject of the charge is either those goods or represents them (section 24(2)); and that, at the time of the alleged handling, the goods were still stolen goods (section 24(3)).

2. Section 24(2) was explained by the C.L.R.C., § 138 as follows, "It may seem technical; but the effect will be that the goods which the accused is charged with handling must, at the time of the handling or at some previous time, (i) have been in the hands of the thief or of a handler, and (ii) have represented the original stolen goods in the sense of being the proceeds direct or indirect, of a sale or other realisation of the original goods."

3. As to the definition of "goods", compare "property" in section 4(1), *ante*, p. 728.

Attorney-General's Reference (No. 1 of 1974)
[1974] Q.B. 744
Court of Appeal

The facts appear in the Court's opinion

LORD WIDGERY C.J.: This is a reference to the court by the Attorney-General on a point of law seeking the opinion of the court pursuant to section 36 of the Criminal Justice Act 1972. . . .

The facts of the present case, which I take from the terms of the reference itself, are these:

"A police constable found an unlocked, unattended car containing packages of new clothing which he suspected, and which in fact subsequently proved to be stolen. The officer removed the rotor arm from the vehicle to immobilise it, and kept observation. After about ten minutes, the accused appeared, got into the van and attempted to start the engine. When questioned by the officer, he gave an implausible explanation, and was arrested."

Upon those facts two charges were brought against the respondent: one of stealing the woollen goods, the new clothing, which were in the back of the car in question and secondly and alternatively of receiving those goods knowing them to be stolen. The trial judge quite properly ruled there was no evidence to support the first charge, and that he would not leave that to the jury, but an argument developed as to whether the second count should be left to the jury or not. Counsel for the respondent in the court below had submitted at the close of the prosecution case that there was no case to answer, relying on section 24(3) of the Theft Act 1968. That provides as follows:

". . . no goods shall be regarded as having continued to be stolen goods after they have been restored to the person from whom they were stolen or to other lawful possession or custody. . . ."

The rest of the subsection is not relevant and I do not read it. It was therefore contended in the court below on the facts to which I have already referred that by virtue of section 24(3) the goods had been restored to other lawful possession or custody, namely the custody or possession of the police officer before the respondent appeared on the scene and sought to drive the car away. If that argument was sound of course it would follow that there was no case for the respondent to answer, because if in fact the police constable had restored the stolen goods to his own lawful possession or custody before the act relied upon as an act of receiving occurred, it would follow that they would not be stolen goods at the material time.

After hearing argument, the judge accepted the submission of the respondent and directed the jury that they should acquit on the receiving count. That has resulted in the Attorney-General referring the following point of law to us for an opinion under section 36 of the Criminal Justice Act 1972. He expresses the point in this way:

"Whether stolen goods are restored to lawful custody within the meaning of section 24(3) of the Theft Act 1968 when a police officer, suspecting them to be stolen, examines and keeps observation on them with a view to tracing the thief or a handler."

One could put the question perhaps in a somewhat different way by asking whether upon the facts set out in the reference the conclusion as a matter of law was clear to the effect that the goods had ceased to be stolen goods. In other words, the question which is really in issue in this reference is whether the trial judge acted correctly in law in saying that those facts disclosed a defence within section 24(3).

Subsection (3) is not perhaps entirely happily worded. It has been pointed out in the course of argument that in the sentence which I have read there is only one relevant verb, and that is "restore." The section contemplates that the stolen goods should be restored to the person from whom they were stolen or to other lawful possession or custody. It is pointed out that the word "restore" although it is entirely appropriate when applied to restoration of the goods to the true owner, is not really an appropriate verb to employ if one is talking about a police officer stumbling upon stolen goods and taking them into his own lawful custody or possession.

We are satisfied that despite the absence of another and perhaps more appropriate verb, the effect of section 24(3) is to enable a defendant to plead that the goods had ceased to be stolen goods if the facts are that they were taken by a police officer in the course of his duty and reduced into possession by him.

Whether or not section 24(3) is intended to be a codification of the common law or not, it certainly deals with a topic upon which the common law provides a large number of authorities. I shall refer to some of them in a moment, although perhaps not all and it will be observed that from the earliest times it has been recognised that if the owner of stolen goods resumed possession of them, reduced them into his possession again, that they thereupon ceased to be stolen goods for present purposes and could certainly not be the subject of a later charge of receiving based on events after they had been reduced into possession. It is to be observed that at common law nothing short of a reduction into possession, either by the true owner or by a police officer acting in the execution of his duty, was regarded as sufficient to change the character of the goods from stolen goods into goods which were no longer to be so regarded.

I make that assertion true by a brief reference from the cases to which we have been referred. The first is *R. v. Dolan* (1855) 6 Cox C.C. 449. The facts there were that stolen goods were found in the pocket of a thief by the owner. The owner sent for a policeman, and the evidence given at the subsequent trial showed that after the policeman had taken the goods from the thief, the thief, the policeman and the owner went towards the shop owned and occupied by the prisoner at which the thief had asserted that he was hoping to sell the stolen goods. When they got near the shop the policeman gave the goods to the thief, who then went on ahead into the shop with a view to selling the goods, closely followed by the owner and the policeman, who proceeded to arrest the shop keeper. It was held there

"that the prisoner was not guilty of feloniously receiving stolen goods; inasmuch as they were delivered to him under the authority of the owner by a person to whom the owner had bailed them for that purpose."

Put another way, one can explain that decision on the broad principle to which I have already referred: the goods had already been returned to the possession of the owner before they were then released by him into the hands of the thief in order that the thief might approach the receiver with a view to the receiver being arrested. The principle thus enunciated is one which, as I have already said, is to be found in the other authorities to which we have been referred.

The next one which is similar is *R. v. Schmidt* (1866) L.R. 1 C.C.R. 15. The reference in the headnote suffices:

"Four thieves stole goods from the custody of a railway company, and afterwards sent them in a parcel by the same company's line addressed to the prisoner. During the transit the theft was discovered; and, on the arrival of the parcel at the station for its delivery, a policeman in the employ of the company opened it, and then returned it to the porter whose duty it was to deliver it, with instructions to keep it until further orders. On the following day the policeman directed the porter to take the parcel to its address, when it was received by the prisoner, who was afterwards convicted of receiving the goods knowing them to be stolen, . . ."

And it was held by the Court for Crown Cases Reserved "that the goods had got back into the possession of the owner, so as to be no longer stolen goods and that the conviction was wrong." Again unquestionably they had been reduced into the possession of the owner by the hand of the police officer acting on his behalf. They had not been allowed to continue their course unaffected. They had been taken out of circulation by the police officer, reduced into the possession of the owner or of the officer, and it matters not which, and thus had ceased to be stolen goods for present purposes. . . .

Then there is a helpful case, *R. v. Villensky* [1892] 2 Q.B. 597. Again it is a case of a parcel in the hands of carriers. This parcel was handed to the carriers in question for conveyance to the consignees, and whilst in the carriers' depot it was stolen by a servant of the carriers who removed the parcel to a different part of the premises and placed upon it a label addressed to the prisoners by a name by which they were known and a house where they resided. The superintendent of the carriers on receipt of information as to this and after the inspection of the parcel, directed it to be placed in the place from which the thief had removed it and to be sent with a special delivery receipt in a van accompanied by two detectives to the address shown on the label. At that address it was received by the prisoners under circumstances which clearly showed knowledge on their part that it had been stolen. The property in the parcel was laid in the indictment in the carriers and an offer to amend the indictment by substituting the names of the consignees was declined. The carriers' servant pleaded guilty to a count for larceny in the same indictment. It was there held by the Court for Crown Cases Reserved

"that as the person in which the property was laid"—that is the carriers—"had resumed possession of the stolen property before its receipt by the prisoners, it had then ceased to be stolen property, and the prisoners could not be convicted of receiving it knowing it to have been stolen."

On p. 599 there is a brief and valuable judgment by Pollock B. in these terms:

"The decisions in *Dolan,* and *Schmidt,* are, in my judgment, founded on law and on solid good sense, and they should not be frittered away. It is, of course, frequently the case that when it is found that a person has stolen property he is watched; but the owner of the property, if he wishes to catch the receiver, does not resume possession of the stolen goods; here the owners have done so, and the result is that the conviction must be quashed."

We refer to that brief judgment because it illustrates in a few clear words what is really the issue in the present case. When the police officer discovered these goods and acted as he did, was the situation that he had taken possession of the goods, in which event, of course, they ceased to be stolen goods? or was it merely that he was watching the goods with a view to the possibility of catching the receiver at a later stage? I will turn later to a consideration of those two alternatives.

Two other cases should, I think, be mentioned at this stage. The next one is *R. v. King* [1938] 2 All E.R. 662. We are now getting to far more recent times. The appellant here was convicted with another man of receiving stolen goods knowing them to have been stolen. A fur coat had been stolen and shortly afterwards the police went to a flat where they found the man Burns and told him they were enquiring about some stolen property. He at first denied that there was anything there but finally admitted the theft and produced a parcel from a wardrobe. While a policeman was in the act of examining the contents of the parcel, the telephone bell rang. Burns answered it and the police heard him say: "Come along as arranged." The police then suspended operations and about 20 minutes later the appellant arrived, and, being admitted by Burns, said "I have come for the coat. Harry sent me." This was heard by the police, who were hiding at the time. The coat was handed to the appellant by Burns, so that he was actually in possession of it. It was contended that the possession by the police amounted to possession by the owner of the coat, and that, therefore, the coat was not stolen property at the time the appellant received it. Held by the Court of Appeal: that the coat had not been in the possession of the police and it was therefore still stolen when the appellant received it. . . .

The most recent case on the present topic, but of little value in the present problems is *Haughton v. Smith* [*ante*, p. 499], in the House of Lords. The case being of little value to us in our present problems, I will deal with it quite briefly. It is a case where a lorry load of stolen meat was intercepted by police, somewhere in the North of England, who discovered that the lorry was in fact full of stolen goods. After a brief conference they decided to take the lorry on to its destination with a view to catching the receivers at the London end of the affair. So the lorry set off for London with detectives both in the passenger seat and in the back of the vehicle, and in due course was met by the defendant at its destination in London. In that case before this court it was conceded, as it had been conceded below, that the goods had been reduced into the possession of the police when they took possession of the lorry in the North of England, so no dispute in this court or later in the House of Lords was raised on that issue. It is, however, to be noted that three of their Lordships, when the matter got to the House of Lords, expressed some hesitation as to the propriety of the prosecution conceding in that case that the goods had been reduced to the possession of the police when the lorry was first intercepted. Since we cannot discover on what ground those doubts were expressed either from the report of the speeches or from the report of the argument, we cannot take advantage of that case in the present problem.

Now we return to the present problem again with those authorities in the background: did the conduct of the police officer, as already briefly recounted, amount to a taking of possession of the woollen goods in the back seat of the motor car? What he did, to repeat the essential facts, was: that seeing these goods in the car and being suspicious of them because they were brand new goods and in an unlikely position, he removed the rotor arm and stood by in cover to interrogate any driver of the car who might subsequently appear. Did that amount to a taking possession of the goods in the back of the car? In our judgment it depended primarily on the intentions of the police officer. If the police officer seeing these goods in the back of the car had made up his mind that he would take them into custody, that he would reduce them into his possession or control, take charge of them so that they could not be removed and so that he would have the disposal of them, then it would be a perfectly proper conclusion to say that he had taken possession of the goods. On the other hand, if the truth of the matter is that he was of an entirely open mind at that stage as to whether the goods were to be seized or not and was of an entirely open mind as to whether he should take possession of them or not, but merely stood by so that when the driver of the car appeared he could ask certain questions of that driver as to the nature of the goods and why they were there, then there is no reason whatever to suggest that he had taken the goods into his possession or control. It may be, of course, that he had both objects in mind. It is possible in a case like this that the police officer may have intended by removing the rotor arm both to prevent the car from being driven away and to enable him to assert control over the woollen goods as such. But if the jury came to the conclusion that the proper explanation of what had happened was that the police officer had not intended at that stage to reduce the goods into his possession or to assume the control of them, and at that stage was merely concerned to ensure that the driver, if he appeared, could not get away without answering questions, then in that case the proper conclusion of the jury would have been to the effect that the goods had not been reduced into the possession of the police and therefore a defence under section 24(3) of the Theft Act 1968 would not be of use to this particular defendant.

In the light of those considerations it has become quite obvious that the trial judge was wrong in withdrawing the issue from the jury. As a matter of law he was not entitled to conclude from the facts which I have set out more than once that these goods were reduced into the possession of the police officer. What they should have done in our opinion would have been to have left that issue to the jury for decision, directing the jury that they should find that the prosecution case was without substance if they thought that the police officer had assumed control of the goods as such and reduced them into his possession. Whereas on the other hand, they should have found the case proved, assuming that they were satisfied about its other elements, if they were of the opinion that the police officer in removing the rotor arm and standing by and watching was doing no more than ensure that the driver should not get away without interrogation and was not at that stage seeking to assume possession of the goods as such at all. That is our opinion.

Opinion accordingly

Note

It is not always a question of fact whether the owner or police have reduced the goods into possession. In *M.P.C. v. Streeter* (1980) 71 Cr.App.R. 113, the owner's security officer initialled the goods and alerted the police, who kept watch and followed the defendant when he picked up the goods. It was held by the Divisional Court that the magistrates were wrong to conclude that this was a reduction into the possession of the owner, and the case was sent back with a direction to convict.

ii. Otherwise than in the Course of Stealing

R. v. Pitham and Hehl
(1986) 65 Cr.App.R. 45
Court of Appeal

P and H were charged with burglary along with M. M was convicted of burglary but P and H were acquitted, when it appeared that M had invited them into the victim's house and offered them the victim's furniture. They paid him for it and took it away. P and H were also charged with handling stolen goods and were convicted of this. They appealed on the ground that the handling was not "otherwise than in the course of stealing."

LAWTON L.J.: . . . What was the appropriation in this case? The jury found that the two appellants had handled the property *after* Millman has stolen it. That is clear from their acquittal of these two appellants on count 3 of the indictment which had charged them jointly with Millman. What had Millman done? He had assumed the rights of the owner. He had done that when he took the two appellants to 20 Party Road, showed them the property and invited them to buy what they wanted. He was then acting as the owner. He was then, in the words of the statute, "assuming the rights of the owner." The moment he did that he appropriated McGregor's goods to himself. The appropriation was complete. After this appropriation had been completed there was no question of these two appellants taking part, in the words of section 22, in dealing with the goods "in the course of the stealing."

It follows that no problem arises in this case. It may well be that some of the situations which the two learned professors envisage and discuss in their books may have to be dealt with at some future date, but not in this case. The facts are too clear.

Mr Murray suggested the learned judge should have directed the jury in some detail about the possibility that the appropriation had not been an instantaneous appropriation, but had been one which had gone on for some time. He submitted that it might have gone on until such time as the furniture was loaded into the appellants' van. For reasons we have already given that was not a real possibility in this case. It is no part of a judge's duty to give the jury the kind of lecture on the law which may be appropriate for a professor to give to a class of undergraduates. We commend the judge for not having involved himself in a detailed academic analysis of the law relating to this case when on the facts it was as clear as anything could be that either these appellants had helped Millman to steal the goods, or Millman had stolen them and got rid of them by sale to these two appellants. We can see nothing wrong in the learned judge's approach to this case and on that particular ground we affirm what he did and said. . . .

Appeal dismissed

Questions

1. Does it follow that Millman, the thief, was also guilty of handling? See forms of handling below.

2. If he was guilty, is that a satisfactory result? See *infra*.

Criminal Law Revision Committee's Eighth Report, Cmnd. 2977

§ 131 [Justifying the phrase 'otherwise than in the course of the stealing']
Under the definition a thief may be liable for handling if, after the theft
is complete, he does some of the things mentioned in the definition for
someone else, for example if he helps a receiver to dispose of the goods.
Since it might be thought too severe to make a thief guilty of handling in
such a case, we thought of providing that a thief should not be guilty of
handling by reason of doing any of the things mentioned in the definition
in respect of goods which he has himself stolen. But we decided not to
include the provision. If after the theft is complete the thief takes part in
a separate transaction for the disposal of the goods, it seems right that he
should be guilty of handling like anybody else involved in the transaction.

Notes

1. This compromise by the C.L.R.C. is not without its awkwardness
in practice. The offences of theft and handling are not entirely mutually exclusive, in that D can be guilty of both if, after the theft is
complete, he takes part in a separate transaction for the disposal of
the goods. But apart from the difficult question of what is a separate
transaction, as to which see *R. v. Pitham and Hehl, supra,* in practice in
many cases where D is inferentially guilty of handling, by being in
possession of goods which have recently been stolen by someone,
there will be nothing to suggest one way or the other whether he was
the thief and his possession arose out of the stealing. Although separate counts for theft and handling may be included in one indictment,
the difficulty remains that the jury may well be sure that D is guilty
of either theft *or* handling, but are not sure which. In such a case, they
may not convict of either. Their duty is to consider the theft which
made the goods stolen goods, and if they are satisfied that D committed it, to convict him of theft. If they are not so satisfied, they must
acquit him of theft and go on to consider whether he handled the
goods with guilty knowledge. They are not entitled to say, "We are
satisfied he committed one or the other", and then go on to convict of
the offence which seems more probable: see *Att.-Gen. for Hong Kong v.
Yip Kai-Foon* [1988] 1 All E.R. 153 (P.C.).

2. Of course many (though not all) acts of handling are themselves
appropriations of property belonging to another with intent to deprive
the owner permanently. Any handler who deals with the goods himself (as opposed to merely "arranging", or "assisting" someone else),
commits theft when he does so, and if the alternative count for theft
is drafted sufficiently widely to cover both the original taking and the
subsequent dealing with the goods, then even if there is doubt about
whether the original theft was by him and his act of handling was in
the course of that theft, he may still, on a suitably careful direction,
be convicted of theft in respect of the appropriation in the act of handling. See *Stapylton v. O'Callaghan* [1973] 2 All E.R. 782.

Question

Were Pitham and Heyl rightly acquitted of burglary? (See, *post,*
Chap. 14.) When they took the goods from Millman, did not they

dishonestly appropriate property belonging to the victim? Did they not enter the victim's house as trespassers with the intent to commit that theft? See next case.

R. v. Gregory (1981) 77 Cr.App.R. 41 (C.A.) The jury were allowed to convict D of burglary if they thought that he had gone to V's house at the invitation of A and B with the intention of buying V's goods which they had stolen. D appealed on the ground that since, according to *R. v. Pitham & Heyl*, the theft of the goods by A & B would have been complete by the time D. dealt with them, his offence was handling, not burglary. In upholding the conviction, the Court of Appeal distinguished *R. v. Pitham & Heyl* as being a case of "what might be called instantaneous appropriation. But not every appropriation need be or indeed is instantaneous."

[After quoting Eveleigh L.J. in *R. v. Hale, ante*, p. 783]

"Nor do we think that in a given criminal enterprise involving theft there can necessarily be only one 'appropriation' within section 3(1) of the Theft Act 1968. It seems to us that the question of whether, when and by whom there has been an appropriation of property has always to be determined by the jury having regard to the circumstances of the case. The length of time involved, the manner in which it came about and the number of people who can properly be said to have taken part in an appropriation will vary according to those circumstances. In a case of burglary of a dwelling-house and before any property is removed from it, it may consist of a continuing process and involve either a single appropriation by one or more persons or a number of appropriations of the property in the house by several persons at different times during the same incident. If this were not a correct exposition of the law of appropriation, startling and disturbing consequences could arise out of the presence of two or more trespassers in a dwelling-house. Thus a person who may have more the appearance of a handler than the thief can nevertheless still be convicted of theft, and thus of burglary, if the jury are satisfied that with the requisite dishonest intent, he appropriated, or took part in the appropriation, of another person's goods."

Question

To uphold the conviction, was it necessary to distinguish *R. v. Pitham & Heyl*?

iii. Forms of Handling

Notes

1. The offence is not confined to 'receiving', as before 1968. It can be committed either by 'receiving' or by 'undertaking or assisting in the goods' retention, removal, disposal or realisation by or for the benefit of another person', or 'arranging' to do any of these things.

2. If the goods are not in fact stolen goods when any of these forms of handling is done, it is not the full offence (see *Haughton v. Smith, ante,* p. 499), although it may be an attempt to handle (see *R. v. Shivpuri, ante,* p. 504). An 'arrangement' to receive or to undertake or

assist in the goods' retention etc. entered into before they are stolen, may well be conspiracy to handle, but it is not the full offence (see *R. v. Park* (1988) 87 Cr.App.R. 164, C.A.), unless, presumably, the arrangement is ratified or confirmed in some way after the theft has taken place.

3. Receiving, or arranging to receive, may be entirely on the accused's own account; but if the form of handling alleged is one of the other matters mentioned in section 22(1), it must be 'by or for the benefit of another person'. On the meaning of this expression, see *R. v. Bloxham, post*, p. 864.

R. v. Pitchley
(1972) 57 Cr.App.R. 30
Court of Appeal

P's son handed P £150 in order that P should look after it for him. According to P, he paid it into his post office savings account, and then later became aware that the £150 was stolen. Because he did not wish to give his son away, P did nothing about the money in the account until he was interviewed some days later by the police. He was convicted of "dishonestly handling goods, namely the sum of £150 . . . knowing or believing the same to be stolen goods." He appealed.

CAIRNS L.J.: The indictment . . . simply charged handling stolen goods without specifying whether it was under the first limb or under the second limb, and if the latter, under which part of the second limb of section 22(1) of the Theft Act; but the case that was presented by the prosecution at the trial was clearly presented in the alternative, that it was either under the first limb of receiving, or under the second limb for assisting in the retention of stolen goods. . . .

The main point that has been taken by Mr Kalisher, who is appearing for the appellant in this court, is that, assuming that the jury were not satisfied that the appellant received the money knowing it to have been stolen, and that is an assumption which clearly is right to make, then there was no evidence after that, that from the time when the money was put into the savings bank, that the appellant had done any act in relation to it. His evidence was, and there is no reason to suppose that the jury did not believe it, that at the time when he put the money into the savings bank he still did not know or believe that the money had been stolen—it was only at a later stage that he did. That was on the Saturday according to his evidence, and the position was that the money had simply remained in the savings bank from the Saturday, to the Wednesday when the police approached the appellant. It is fair to say that from the moment when he was approached he displayed the utmost frankness to the extent of correcting them when they said it was £100 to £150 and telling them where the post office savings book was so that the money could be got out again and restored to its rightful owner.

But the question is: Did the conduct of the appellant between the Saturday and the Wednesday amount to an assisting in the retention of this money for the benefit of his son Brian? The court has been referred to the case of *Brown* (1969) 53 Cr.App.R. 527 which was a case where stolen property had been put into a wardrobe at the appellant's house and when the police came to inquire about it the appellant said to them: "Get lost". The direction to the jury had been on the basis that it was for them to consider whether in saying: "Get lost", instead of helping the police constable, he was dishonestly assisting in the retention of stolen goods. This court held that that was a misdirection but there are passages in the judgment in the case of *Brown* (*supra*) which, in the view of this court, are of great assistance in determining what is meant by "retention" in this section. I read first of all from p. 528 setting out the main facts a little more fully: "A witness named Holden was called by the prosecution. He gave evidence that he and others had broken into the café and had stolen the goods, and that he had brought them to the appellant's flat, where, incidentally, other people were sleeping, and had hidden them there; and he described how he had taken the cigarettes out of the packets, put them in the plastic bag and hidden them in the wardrobe. Holden went on to say that later and before the police arrived he told the appellant where the cigarettes were; in other words, he said that the appellant well knew that the cigarettes were there and they had been stolen." There was no evidence that the appellant had done anything active in relation to the cigarettes up to the time when the police arrived. The Lord Chief Justice, Lord Parker, in the course of his judgment at p. 530 said this: "It is urged here that the mere failure to reveal the presence of the cigarettes, with or without the addition of the spoken words 'Get lost', was incapable itself of amounting to an assisting in the retention of the goods within the meaning of the subsection. The court has come to the conclusion that that is right. It does not seem to this court that the mere failure to tell the police, coupled if you like with the words 'Get lost', amounts in itself to an assisting in their retention. On the other hand, those matters did afford strong evidence of what was the real basis of the charge here, namely, that knowing that they had been stolen, he permitted them to remain there or, as it has been put, provided accommodation for these stolen goods in order to assist Holden to retain them." Having said that the direction was incomplete the Lord Chief Justice went on to say: "The Chairman should have gone on to say: 'But the fact that he did not tell the constable that they were there and said "Get lost" is evidence from which you can infer, if you think right, that this man was permitting the goods to remain in his flat, and to that extent assisting in their retention by Holden.'" In this present case there was no question on the evidence of the appellant himself, that he was permitting the money to remain under his control in the savings bank book, and it is clear that this court in the case of *Brown* regarded such permitting as sufficient to constitute retention within the meaning of retention. That is clear from the passage I have already read, emphasised in the next paragraph, the final paragraph of the judgment, where the Lord Chief Justice said (at p. 531): "It is a plain case in which the proviso should be applied. It seems to this court that the only possible inference in these circumstances, once Holden was believed is that this man was assisting in their retention by housing the goods and providing accommodation for them, by permitting them to remain there." It is important to realise that that language was in relation to a situation where there was no evidence that anything active had been done by the appellant in relation to the goods.

In the course of the argument, Nield J. cited the dictionary meaning of the word "retain"—keep possession of, not lose, continue to have. In the view of this court, that is the meaning of the word "retain" in this section. It was submitted by Mr Kalisher that, at any rate, it was ultimately for the jury to decide whether there was retention or not and that even assuming that what the appellant did was of such a character that it could constitute retention, the jury ought to have been directed that it was for them to determine as a matter of fact, whether that was so or not. The court cannot agree with that submission. The meaning of the word "retention" in the section is a matter of law in so far as the construction of the word is necessary. It is hardly a difficult question of construction because it is an ordinary English word and in the view of this court, it was no more necessary for the Deputy Chairman to leave the jury the question of whether or not what was done amounted to retention than it would be necessary for a judge in a case where goods had been handed to a person who knew that they had been stolen for him to direct the jury it was for them to decide whether or not that constituted receiving.

We are satisfied that no complaint of the summing-up which was made can be sustained and that there is no ground on which this verdict could be said to be unsafe or unsatisfactory. The appeal is therefore dismissed.

Appeal dismissed

R. v. Kanwar
[1982] 2 All E.R. 529
Court of Appeal

K's husband brought home stolen goods. K., knowing they were stolen, used them to furnish the house. Later she told lies to police officers about the goods in order to persuade them that they were not stolen. She was convicted of handling stolen goods by dishonestly assisting in their retention, and appealed.

CANTLEY J.: In *R. v. Thornhill*, decided in this court on May 15, 1981 (unreported), and in *R. v. Sanders* (see *infra*), it was held that merely using stolen goods in the possession of another does not constitute the offence of assisting in their retention. To constitute the offence, something must be done by the offender, and done intentionally and dishonestly, for the purpose of enabling the goods to be retained. Examples of such conduct are concealing or helping to conceal the goods, or doing something to make them more difficult to find or to identify. Such conduct must be done knowing or believing the goods to be stolen and done dishonestly and for the benefit of another.

We see no reason why the requisite assistance should be restricted to physical acts. Verbal representations, whether oral or in writing, for the purpose of concealing the identity of stolen goods may, if made dishonestly and for the benefit of another, amount to handling stolen goods by assisting in their retention within the meaning of section 22 of the Theft Act 1968.

The requisite assistance need not be successful in its object. It would be absurd if a person dishonestly concealing stolen goods for the benefit of a receiver could establish a defence by showing that he was caught in the act. In the present case, if, while the police were in one part of the house, the appellant, in order to conceal the painting had put it under a mattress in the bedroom, it would not alter the nature of her conduct that the police subsequently looked under the mattress and found the picture because they expected to find it there or that they caught her in the act of putting it there.

The appellant told these lies to the police to persuade them that the picture and the mirror were not the stolen property which they had come to take away but were her lawful property which she had bought. If that was true, the articles should be left in the house. She was, of course, telling these lies to protect her husband, who had dishonestly brought the articles there but, in our view, she was nonetheless, at the time, dishonestly assisting in the retention of the stolen articles.

In his summing up, the judge directed the jury as follows:

"It would be quite wrong for you to convict this lady if all she did was to watch her husband bring goods into the house, even if she knew or believed that they were stolen goods because, no doubt, you would say to yourselves, 'What would she be expected to do about it?' Well, what the Crown say is that she knew or believed them to be stolen and that she was a knowing and willing party to their being kept in that house in those circumstances. The reason the Crown say that, and we shall be coming to the evidence, is that when questioned about a certain number of items, [the appellant] gave answers which the Crown say were not true and that she could not possibly have believed to be true and that she knew perfectly well were untruthful. So, say the prosecution, she was not just an acquiescent wife who could not do much about it, she was, by her conduct in trying to put the police officers as best she could off the scent, demonstrating that she was a willing and knowing party to those things being there and that she was trying to account for them. Well, it will be for you to say, but you must be satisfied before you can convict her on either of these counts, not only that she knew or believed the goods to be stolen, but that she actively assisted her husband in keeping them there; not by just passive acquiesence in the sense of saying, 'What can I do about it?' but in the sense of saying, 'How nice to have these things in our home, although they are stolen goods.'"

In so far as this direction suggests that the appellant would be guilty of the offence if she was merely willing for the goods to be kept and used in the house and was thinking that it was nice to have them there, although they were stolen goods, it is a misdirection. We have considered whether on that account the conviction ought to be quashed. However, the offence was established by the uncontradicted evidence of the police officer which, looked at in full, clearly shows that in order to mislead the officer who had come to take away stolen goods, she misrepresented the identity of the goods which she knew or believed to be stolen. We are satisfied that no miscarriage of justice has occurred and the appeal is accordingly dismissed.

Appeal dismissed

R. *v. Sanders* (1982) 75 Cr.App.R. 84 (C.A.): A, who owned a garage, stole some equipment. It was found in the garage being used by D, the son of A, who was employed there. He admitted he knew it was stolen. *Held*, mere use of goods knowing them to be stolen was not enough to found a conviction of assisting in the retention of them; he must have concealed, disguised, or held the goods pending disposal.

R. *v. Coleman* [1986] Crim.L.R. 56 (C.A.): D and his wife purchased a flat in their joint names with money the wife had stolen, as D well knew. *Held*, the *actus reus* was assisting in the disposal of the money, not getting the benefit, and the fact that D had benefited from what his wife did was no proof that he had assisted her. There had to be evidence of helping or encouraging. On a proper direction, the jury could properly have inferred that D told his wife to use the stolen money or agreed that she should do so; but they were not so directed, and it was impossible to say whether they would have done so; they might have inferred that the wife acted without assistance.

Questions

1. A, after stealing a gold watch, deposits it in the potting shed of his friend B. Later B and C, another friend, notice the watch, recognise it as stolen, and guess that A will return and remove it when he has the opportunity. Because they do not wish to 'shop' A, both B and C reply 'Get lost' when asked by a policeman if they have seen the watch. On this evidence, can either of them be convicted of handling?

2. A gives a fur coat to his wife B. He later tells her that he had

stolen it in a burglary, but she continues to wear it. Is B guilty of handling?

3. A gives a fur coat to his wife B. When he later tells B that he bought the coat with the proceeds of a burglary he had committed, B sells the coat to a friend. Does B undertake the disposal or realisation of the coat for the benefit of another? See next case.

R. v. Bloxham
[1982] 1 All E.R. 582
House of Lords

B agreed to buy a car which, unknown to him, had been stolen. Several months later, he became convinced that it had been stolen, because his vendor failed to produce the registration documents. B therefore sold the car to a man he did not know who was prepared to buy it without the documents. B was charged with handling stolen goods contrary to section 22 of the Theft Act 1968. After a ruling by the trial judge that the sale was a dishonest realisation of the car for the benefit of another person, B pleaded guilty. He appealed on the ground that the judge's ruling was wrong in law.

LORD BRIDGE OF HARWICH: The critical words to be construed are "undertakes ... their ... disposal or realization ... for the benefit of another person." Considering these words first in isolation, it seems to me that, if A sells his own goods to B, it is a somewhat strained use of language to describe this as a disposal or realisation of the goods for the benefit of B. True it is that B obtains a benefit from the transaction, but it is surely more natural to say that the disposal or realisation is for A's benefit than for B's. It is the purchase, not the sale, that is for the benefit of B. It is only when A is selling as agent for a third party C that it would be entirely natural to describe the sale as a disposal or realisation for the benefit of another person.

But the words cannot, of course, be construed in isolation. They must be construed in their context.... The ... words contemplate four activities (retention, removal, disposal, realisation). The offence can be committed in relation to any one of these activities in one or other of two ways. First, the offender may himself undertake the activity *for the benefit* of another person. Second, the activity may be undertaken *by* another person and the offender may assist him.... If the analysis holds good it must follow, I think, that the category of other persons contemplated by the subsection is subject to the same limitations in whichever way the offence is committed. Accordingly, a purchaser, as such, of stolen goods cannot, in my opinion, be "another person" within the subsection, since his act of purchase could not sensibly be described as a disposal or realisation of the stolen goods *by* him. Equally, therefore, even if the sale to him could be described as a disposal or realisation for his benefit, the transaction is not, in my view, within the ambit of the subsection....

Appeal allowed: conviction quashed

Question

What offence was committed by Bloxham if (i) the purchaser from him knew or believed that the car was stolen, (ii) the purchaser did not know or believe that?

Note

Where A and B are jointly charged in one count on an indictment with handling "by or for the benefit of another person", the other person must be someone other than the co-accused. In *Gingell* [2000] 1 Cr.App.R. 88, Gingell was convicted of handling and the particulars of the offence were as follows:

"Andrew Camper and Stewart Matthew Albert Gingell on a day between the 20th day of April 1997 and the 30th day of April 1997 dishonestly undertook or assisted in the retention removal disposal or realisation of stolen goods namely a Vauxhall L22 RPU belonging to Stephen Bate by or for the benefit of another or dishonestly arranged so to do knowing or believing the same to be stolen goods."

In respect of Gingell the other person was alleged to be Andrew Camper, his co-accused. In quashing Gingell's conviction Waller L.J. stated:

"As a matter of plain language this count charged Camper and Gingell with undertaking or assisting 'for the benefit of another'. As a matter of plain language that must be someone other than Camper or Gingell. That being so, as it seems to us, in this case the appellant Gingell was in fact convicted of an offence which was not the offence proved by the Crown and that being so his appeal against conviction must be allowed."

iv. Knowing or Believing them to be Stolen Goods

Notes

1. *R. v. McCullum* (1973) 57 Cr.App.R. 645: M was charged with handling by assisting in the retention of stolen guns and ammunition. The guns and ammunition were in a suitcase in her possession. Part of her case was that she did not know what was in the suitcase. A direction by the trial judge that knowledge or belief that the suitcase contained stolen goods without knowledge of the nature of the goods was sufficient, was upheld by the Court of Appeal, even though the indictment had specified the goods as guns and ammunition.

2. *R. v. Hulbert* (1979) 69 Cr.App.R. 243: (C.A.): H was charged with handling stolen clothes. H admitted to the police that she bought them at low prices in public houses from persons who told her they were stolen. *Held*, the information from the sellers was evidence that she knew they were stolen, but not evidence that they were stolen (being hearsay). However, her appeal was dismissed because the *circumstances*, admitted by her, (namely purchases in public houses at low prices) were prima facie evidence that the goods were stolen.

3. The previous law required the accused to receive 'knowing' that the goods were stolen. The C.L.R.C., Cmnd. 2977 § 134, justified the addition of the alternative "or believing" as follows:

"It is a serious defect of the present law that actual knowledge that the property was stolen must be proved. Often the prosecution cannot prove this. In many cases indeed guilty knowledge does not exist, although the circumstances of the transaction are such that the receiver ought to be guilty of an offence. The man who buys goods at a ridiculously low price from an unknown seller whom he meets in a public house may not *know* that the goods were stolen, and he may take the precaution of asking no questions. Yet it may be clear on the evidence that he *believes* that the goods were stolen. In such cases the prosecution may fail (rightly, as the law now stands) for want of proof of guilty knowledge. We consider that a person who handles stolen goods ought to be guilty if he believes them to be stolen. A purchaser who is merely careless, in that he does not make sufficient inquiry, will not be guilty of the offence under the new law any more than under the old."

4. The prosecution must prove that the requisite knowledge or belief existed at the time the *actus reus* was performed (*Williams* [1994] Crim.L.R. 934). Where handling by receiving is charged the relevant point in time is when D receives or acquires the goods; if he only acquires this knowledge or forms this belief some time later, this will not suffice (*Brooks* [1993] Crim.L.R. 455). But note that dishonest retention may constitute theft or an offence contrary to s. 93B of the Criminal Justice Act 1988.

5. *R. v. White* (1859) 1 F. & F. 665: W was charged with receiving lead, he well knowing it to have been stolen. Bramwell B. (to the jury): "The knowledge charged in this indictment need not be such knowledge as would be acquired if the prisoner had actually seen the lead stolen; it is sufficient if you think the circumstances were such, accompanying the transaction, as to make the prisoner believe that it had been stolen." Since a receiver or handler can only rarely 'know' about the history of the goods, this direction may be thought to be only common sense. The question is, what is added by the inclusion of the words 'or believing' in section 22?

6. *Haughton v. Smith* [1975] A.C. 485 (H.L.) (*ante*, p. 499): Viscount Dilhorne, at p. 503: 'It is, in my opinion, clear that section 22(1) of the Theft Act 1968 does not make the handling of goods which are not stolen goods an offence if a person believes them to have been stolen. The offence created by that section is in relation to goods which are stolen and it is an ingredient of the offence that the accused must know or believe them to have been stolen. The word "believing" was, I think, inserted to avoid the possibility of an accused being acquitted when there was ample evidence that he believed the goods stolen, but no proof that he knew they were.'

R. v. Forsyth
[1997] 2 Cr.App.R. 299
Court of Appeal

D was convicted of handling £400,000 knowing or believing that it had been stolen from Polly Peck International by its chairman and chief executive, Asil Nadir. D appealed on the ground, *inter alia*, that the judge had misdirected the jury as to knowledge or belief by directing them that the shutting of eyes to the obvious was equivalent to belief.

BELDAM L.J.: . . .
6. *The judge's direction on "knowing or believing" that the money was stolen.*
The judge based his direction on the case of Hall (1985) 81 Cr.App.R. 260 at 264. The judge said:

> "Knowing or believing are words of ordinary usage in the English language. A person may be said to know the money is stolen when she is told by someone with first hand knowledge, such as the thief, that such is the case. Belief of course is something short of knowledge. It may be said to be the state of mind of a person who says to himself 'I cannot say I know for certain that this money is stolen, but there can be no other reasonable conclusion in the light of all the circumstances, in the light of all that I have heard and seen'.
> Either of these two states of mind is enough to establish guilt. It is sufficient to constitute belief even if the defendant says to herself: 'Despite all that I have heard I refuse to believe what my brain tells me is obvious'. You cannot shut your eyes to the obvious. But what is not enough to establish guilt is mere suspicion, i.e.: 'I suspect that this money may be stolen but it may be on the other hand that it is not.' This state of mind does not fall within the words 'knowing or believing'".

The judge had this direction typed out and given to each member of the jury. The appellant objected and urged that the jury should simply be directed in the words of the section without further elaboration and particularly without the gloss suggested.

The appellant criticised this direction. The prosecution had to prove that the appellant actually knew or actually believed that the money she handled in Geneva was stolen. The words "knowing" or "believing" cover the state of mind of those who are subjectively sure of the unlawful provenance of the goods. Whilst an accused's belief that goods are stolen may be inferred by the jury from all the circumstances of the transaction, the word "belief" does not import an objective test nor is belief the same as "shutting one's eyes to the obvious". The judge's direction blurred the distinction between actual belief and evidence from which it may be inferred by indicating that it could be constituted:

(a) By unreasonable uncertainty and
(b) By a refusal to believe the obvious.

Further, by contrasting these states with "mere" suspicion, the direction suggested that real or weighty suspicion may be enough to constitute belief. Belief is not to be equated with suspicion or even great suspicion and the jury may have been left with the impression that it was. That impression could have been reinforced when, towards the end of the summing-up, the judge returned to the subject after reminding the jury that the appellant had said in evidence that she did not know the money was stolen or believe it to be, nor did she suspect it was stolen. Commenting on these answers the judge said:

> "What the prosecution have to prove on this aspect is at the time she handled the money or the chose in action the defendant either knew or believed that it was stolen but mere suspicion would not be enough."

It is beyond question that even great suspicion is not to be equated with belief. Ever since the judgment of Lord Widgery C.J. in *Atwal v. Massey*

(1971) 56 Cr.App.R. 6, references to suspicion in exegesis of the word "believing" in sec. 22 of the Theft Act have given rise to difficulty. In that case Lord Widgery emphasised that the question was a subjective one and he posed it in these terms:

"... was the appellant aware of the theft or did he believe the goods to be stolen or did he, suspecting the goods to be stolen, deliberately shut his eyes to the consequences?"

But as James L.J. said in *Griffiths* (1974) 60 Cr.App.R. 14:

"There is a danger in the adoption of the passage cited from the judgment in *Atwal v Massey* as the direction to the jury unless great care is taken to avoid confusion between the mental element of knowledge or belief and the approach by which a jury may arrive at the conclusion as to knowledge or belief. To direct the jury that the offence is committed if the defendant, suspecting the goods were stolen, deliberately shut his eyes to the circumstances as an alternative to knowing or believing the goods were stolen is a misdirection. To direct the jury that, in common sense and in law, they may find that the defendant knew or believed the goods to be stolen because he deliberately closed his eyes to the circumstances is a perfectly proper direction."

James L.J. thus stressed the difference between evidence from which a jury might infer belief and their being directed that shutting the eyes to circumstances of suspicion is equivalent to belief. In *Moys* (1984) 79 Cr.App.R.72 , 74 this Court had to consider a direction which included the passage:

"Thirdly, the prosecution has to satisfy you so that you are sure that at the time the horse came into his possession the defendant knew or believed that it was stolen. 'Believed' in that sense means that he suspected very strongly that it was stolen and shut his eyes to that possibility altogether ...."

The Court held this to be a misdirection. The judge had told the jury that suspicion coupled with a deliberate shutting of eyes was not merely an alternative but was equivalent to belief. That was incorrect and a material misdirection. Lord Lane C.J., after reviewing the cases referred to in *Griffiths* and the case of *Grainge* (1973) 59 Cr.App.R. 3, said at p.6 that mistakes in this branch of the law were frequent and suggested a direction in these terms:

"The question is a subjective one and it must be proved that the defendant was aware of the theft or that he believed the goods to be stolen. Suspicion that they were stolen, even coupled with the fact that he shut his eyes to the circumstances, is not enough, although these matters may be taken into account by the jury when deciding whether or not the necessary knowledge or belief existed."

Old concepts, however, tend to recur. In *Hall* (1985) 81 Cr.App.R. 260, Boreham J. giving the judgment of the Court over which Lord Lane presided said at p.264 after dealing with knowledge:

"Belief, of course, is something short of knowledge. It may be said to be the state of mind of a person who says to himself: 'I cannot say I know for certain that these goods are stolen, but there can be no other reasonable conclusion in the light of all the circumstances, in the light of all that I have heard and seen.' Either of those two states of mind is enough to satisfy the words of the statute. The second is enough (that is, belief) even if the defendant says to himself: 'Despite all that I have seen and all that I have heard, I refuse to believe what my brain tells me is obvious'. What is not enough, of course, is mere suspicion. 'I suspect that these goods may be stolen, but it may be on the other hand that they are not'. That state of mind, of course, does not fall within the words 'knowing or believing' ".

In subsequent cases (*Harris (Martin)* (1987) 84 Cr.App.R. 75 and *Toor* (1987) 85 Cr.App.R. 116) the appellant complained of a failure by the judge to follow the judgment in *Hall* but as Lawton L.J. said at p.79 in *Harris (supra):*

> "It may well be that in many cases, depending on how the case for the Crown is conducted, it is necessary to give the kind of direction to which Boreham J. referred in *Hall;* but we doubt whether it is necessary is every case."

It is a trite observation that every summing-up should be tailored to the circumstances of the particular case the jury have to decide. It seems to us it was incumbent on the judge to do so in this case. The judge devoted a long passage in his summing-up to the many questions put to the appellant when she was interviewed asking her why she had not enquired where the £400,000 had come from and what she imagined was the purpose of the transaction in which she had taken part. These questions were clearly aimed at highlighting circumstances of suspicion which should have put her on enquiry. In essence the appellant's defence was that she completely trusted Mr Nadir and having regard to his immense wealth and enormous income it did not occur to her to question this particular transaction. She had on one previous occasion been asked to handle a sum of £200,000 though not in these circumstances. Colloquially it might be said that her state of mind was "I could not believe that somebody like Mr Asil Nadir would need to steal money or would involve me in a dishonest transaction". We think that in such a case it was a mistake to embark on an attempt to give examples of particular states of mind which might be regarded as equivalent to belief. The ordinary meaning of belief is the mental acceptance of a fact as true or existing. In the context of this case it meant that the appellant had in fact accepted that the money she was asked to handle had been stolen. We doubt whether a jury unversed in legal dialectics would be likely to subject the direction they were given to the careful analysis required to differentiate the concepts of "not knowing for certain", "there being no other reasonable conclusion" and "refusing to believe what my brain tells me is obvious". This last concept appears to contain the paradox that it refers to a person whose mind does not in fact believe but whose brain sends him the message that it does. Whilst it is true that the direction as a whole is couched in subjective terms, we think it is open to misinterpretation. The appellant had said that she could not believe the money was stolen in spite of all the circumstances of suspicion suggested to her. Although it might have been obvious to others, it was not to her because of her trust and confidence in the integrity of Mr Nadir. We think the form of the directions may have left the jury with the impression that the appellant was guilty even though in her mind she could not accept that the goods were stolen. Thus the jury may have concluded that the appellant was guilty if they were satisfied that there were circumstances of great suspicion from which the only conclusion which could reasonably be drawn was that the goods were stolen but which the appellant because of her knowledge of and faith in Mr Nadir could not bring herself to believe so that her eyes had been closed to what was obvious. We doubt whether on a charge of handling it is necessary or helpful to attempt an exposition of the meaning of the word "belief" by equating it with different and less easily understood states of mind. Between suspicion and actual belief there may be a range of awareness. In the present case, to say that mere suspicion is not enough could have been taken by the jury to imply that great suspicion, coupled with an inability to believe that the money was stolen, was equivalent to belief which it plainly is not. If the judge thought that the jury might find difficulty with the concept of "belief", it seems to us that he ought to have made it clear to them that they had to be satisfied that the appellant actually believed that the money was stolen. In our view the judge ought to have followed the guidance given in *Moys* (*supra*) which is clear and more readily understandable by a jury and avoids the potential for confusion inherent in a *Hall* direction.

On this crucial issue the judge's direction could have led the jury to find the appellant guilty without finding that she actually believed the money was stolen. Accordingly we think he misdirected them.

Appeal allowed.
Conviction quashed.

v. Dishonesty

Notes

1. Dishonesty must exist at the time of the act alleged to constitute handling. On Dishonesty in Theft, see *ante*, p. 773.

2. In a case at York Assizes in 1971, it was held by Shaw J. that a person who, on instructions from the owner, arranged with the thieves for the return of the goods, was not guilty of *dishonestly* assisting in the goods' disposal. See Harvey, 'What Does Dishonesty Mean?' [1972] Crim.L.R. 213. In *R. v. Roberts* (1985) 84 Cr.App.R. 117, a case on dishonesty generally, one ground of appeal was that dishonest in section 22 meant dishonest in relation to the loser of the goods and not dishonest in a more general way. The Court of Appeal held that the York case was no authority for this, but as Roberts was not acting for the owner, the question of whether dishonesty must be *vis-à-vis* the owner did not really arise. But in the York case, D was acting throughout for the owner, who had recruited him for the purpose of recovering the goods. Smith comments, [1986] Crim.L.R. 123:

> "It is very difficult to see how the sole owner of the stolen property could be said to be dishonest for the purposes of handling; and, as the defendant was identified with her, it seems to follow that he could not be held to be dishonest either. The same act may frequently constitute [both theft and handling]. The House of Lords held in *Morris* (*ante*, p. 657) that theft 'involves not an act expressly or impliedly authorised by the owner but an act by way of adverse interference with or usurpation of the owner's rights.' Probably a similar principle ought to apply to handling. This suggests that the true test of dishonesty is whether there is dishonesty *vis-à-vis* the owner (or one of the owners, if there is more than one). Who else is there in respect of whom the act specified in section 22 could be dishonest? Since they are all acts of dealing with property, it seems that they could only be dishonest with respect to someone with a proprietary interest. Perhaps the court has the public

in mind but it is noteworthy that in the 1972 case Shaw J. did not find considerations of public policy to be of assistance. The public interest in matters of this kind is defended by the offences of perverting the course of justice and those contained in sections 4 and 5 of the Criminal Law Act 1967 as well as section 23 of the Theft Act 1968 (Advertising rewards for return of goods stolen or lost)."

Questions

1. In *R. v. Matthews* [1950] 1 All E.R. 137, M received what he well knew were stolen goods, intending to hand them over to the police. Later, he changed his mind and did not hand them over. It was held that this did not amount to receiving stolen goods. If a similar case arose today, would M be guilty of handling? See forms of handling, *supra*.

2. B owed A £10. Being short of cash, A broke into B's desk and helped himself to £10. He later admitted to the police that he knew he had no right to do this. A shared the money with C. C knew how A got the money, but thought that since B owed A £10, A was entitled to help himself. A was convicted of theft. Ought C to be convicted of handling?

vi. Dishonestly retaining a wrongful credit

Note

The decision of the House of Lords in *Preddy* [1996] 3 W.L.R. 255 (*ante*, p. 788) had further ramifications for the law of handling. These were identified by the Law Commission.

Law Commission, *Offences of Dishonesty: Money Transfers* (Law Com. No 243)

6.2 Section 24(4) provides that goods are "stolen" if they are obtained, in England or Wales or elsewhere, by blackmail or in the circumstances described in section 15(1). Before *Preddy* it would have been generally assumed that a credit balance resulting from an inter-account transfer procured by deception was stolen goods, because it was obtained in the circumstances described in section 15(1). On this assumption, the offence of handling would be committed if, knowing or believing the funds to be stolen goods, a person dishonestly receives them or deals with them in any of the other ways set out in section 22(1). According to *Preddy*, however, the funds are not obtained in the circumstances described in section 15(1); therefore they are probably not stolen goods, and subsequent dealings with them fall outside section 22(1).

6.3 Moreover, even if the funds in question *were* stolen goods, there would be a further difficulty in applying section 22(1) to them where they are transferred to another account. Before *Preddy* it had been held by the Court of Appeal in *Attorney-General's Reference (No 4 of 1979)* [1981] 1 W.L.R. 667 that a person who dishonestly accepts a transfer of stolen funds from another's account into his or her own account is "receiving" stolen goods within the meaning of section 22(1). But it is hard to see how this reasoning can survive *Preddy*. It assumes that the funds received by the transferee are the *same* funds as those that, before the transfer, were in the transferor's account; and according to *Preddy* this is not so.

6.4 It might be argued that the funds received are " stolen" by virtue of section 24(2) of the 1968 Act [*ante*, p. 850] . . . .

6.5 But this rule applies only to goods which represent (or have represented) the stolen goods *in the hands of the thief or of a handler*; and in the case of stolen funds which are transferred to another account, this requirement is not satisfied. According to *Preddy*, the funds obtained by the transferee have never been in the hands of the thief at all; and the transferee, in whose hands they are, cannot be regarded as a handler until it has first been determined that the funds received are stolen goods. It would obviously be circular to argue (a) that those funds are stolen goods, (b) that the transferee is therefore a handler of stolen goods, (c) that the requirements of section 24(2)(b) are therefore satisfied, and (d) that the funds received are therefore stolen goods.

6.6 Moreover, even if the funds obtained by the transferee could some-how be brought within the terms of section 24(2), so that they were stolen goods once the transferee had received them, it would still be hard to see how the transferee could be said to have *received stolen goods:* that expression would seem to mean that the goods received must have been stolen goods *before* the transferee received them, not that it is sufficient if they *became* stolen goods once the transeree *had* received them.

6.7 It is true that this problem existed even before *Preddy*: it appears to extend to any case where stolen goods in the hands of the thief are converted into other goods in the hands of another, for example where the thief pays stolen cash into another's bank account. However, before *Preddy* it appeared not to extend to the case where a stolen credit balance is moved from one account to another, because the *Attorney-General's Reference* assumed the property to be the same property throughout. If this is not the case, as *Preddy* makes clear it is not, the lacuna is now a great deal more serious than was previously thought.

Note

The Law Commission recommended the creation of a new offence which Parliament enacted in s.2 of the Theft (Amendment) Act 1996 which inserted a new s.24A into the Theft Act 1968.

Theft Act 1968, section 24A

Dishonestly retaining a wrongful credit

(1) A person is guilty of an offence if—
(a) a wrongful credit has been made to an account kept by him or in respect of which he has any right or interest;
(b) he knows or believes that the credit is wrongful; and
(c) he dishonestly fails to take such steps as are reasonable in the circumstances to secure that the credit is cancelled.

(2) References to a credit are to a credit of an amount of money.

(3) A credit to an account is wrongful if it is the credit side of a money transfer obtained contrary to section 15A of this Act.

(4) A credit to an account is also wrongful to the extent that it derives from—

(a) theft:
(b) an offence under section 15A of this Act;
(c) blackmail; or
(d) stolen goods.

(5) In determining whether a credit to an account is wrongful, it is immaterial (in particular) whether the account is overdrawn before or after the credit is made.

(6) A person guilty of an offence under this section shall be liable on conviction on indictment to imprisonment for a term not exceeding ten years.

Note

In Law Com. No. 243, paragraph 6.20, the Law Commission provide the following examples of how the new offence will operate:

(1) A, by deception, dishonestly obtains a transfer of funds from V's account into his own. A is guilty of obtaining a money transfer by deception, and also (unless he has an immediate change of heart and returns the money) of retaining a credit from a dishonest source— though we doubt that any sensible prosecutor would charge the latter, because it would be harder to prove and would confuse a jury.

(2) A steals funds from V's account by transferring them into his own. (He may, for example, be authorised to draw on V's account.) A is guilty of theft and also (unless he returns the money) of retaining a credit from a dishonest source.

(3) A blackmails V into transferring funds from V's account into his own. A is guilty of blackmail and also (unless he returns the money) of retaining a credit from a dishonest source.

(4) A, by deception, theft or blackmail, obtains a transfer of funds from V's account into B's. A is guilty of obtaining a money transfer by deception or of theft or blackmail (as the case may be). The credit to B's account is therefore wrongful. B is guilty of retaining a credit from a dishonest source if, knowing or believing the credit to be wrongful, she dishonestly fails to take reasonable steps to cancel it.

(5) A, by deception, theft or blackmail, obtains a transfer of funds from V's account into his own, and transfers the proceeds to B's. B's position is the same as in example (4). If B transfers the proceeds to C's account, the same rules apply in respect of C's liability; and so on, ad infinitum.

(6) A steals banknotes (or obtains them by deception or blackmail) and pays them into B's account. B, if she knows the circumstances but does not take steps to cancel the credit, is guilty of retaining a credit from a dishonest source.

(7) A obtains a money transfer by deception, theft or blackmail, withdraws the proceeds from his account and hands the cash to B.

The cash is stolen goods. If B knows or believes this, she is guilty of handling.

(8) A obtains a money transfer by deception, theft or blackmail and transfers the proceeds to B's account. B dishonestly withdraws the proceeds and hands the cash to C. The cash is stolen goods, and C is guilty of handling if he knows or believes this. If he pays the cash into D's account, the credit is wrongful, and D is guilty of retaining a credit from a dishonest source if she knows or believes this but takes no steps to cancel it.

CHAPTER 14

BURGLARY AND KINDRED OFFENCES

1. BURGLARY

Theft Act 1968, section 9, as amended by Criminal Justice Act 1991, section 26(2)

(1) A person is guilty of burglary if—

(a) he enters any building or part of a building as a trespasser and with intent to commit any such offence as is mentioned in subsection (2) below; or

(b) having entered any building or part of a building as a trespasser he steals or attempts to steal anything in the building or that part of it or inflicts or attempts to inflict on any person therein any grievous bodily harm.

(2) The offences referred to in subsection (1)(a) above are offences of stealing anything in the building or part of a building in question, of inflicting on any person therein any grievous bodily harm or raping any woman therein, and of doing unlawful damage to the building or anything therein.

(3) A person guilty of burglary shall on conviction on indictment be liable to imprisonment for a term not exceeding—

(a) where the offence was committed in respect of a building or part of a building which is a dwelling, fourteen years;

(b) in any other case, ten years.

(4) References in subsections (1) and (2) above to a building, and the reference in subsection (3) above to a building which is a dwelling, shall apply also to an inhabited vehicle or vessel, and shall apply to any such vehicle or vessel at times when the person having a habitation in it is not there as well as at times when he is.

Note

The range of conduct prohibited by this section was before the Theft Act distributed between the offences of burglary, housebreaking and sacrilege, and the law was found in sections 25, 26 and 27 of the Larceny Act 1916. There were many intricate and confusing differences between the different offences; burglary proper needed a dwelling-house, a breaking and entering, and an intention to commit a felony, and it had to be committed in the night. The present offence may take place at any time of day. Any kind of building is now covered, and vehicles and vessels are also covered provided they are inhabited. Burglary in such a vehicle or vessel, or in a dwelt-in building, attracts a higher maximum penalty.

i. Entry

Note

Breaking, round which a great number of technicalities clustered, is no longer necessary, but entry is still required. This, too, was a highly technical concept, and as entry is not defined in the Act, it remains a question to that extent the pre-existing meaning is still operative. In that meaning, the law made a distinction between entry by the defendant's body and entry by an instrument wielded by him.

R. v. Hughes
(1785) 1 Leach 406
Old Bailey Sessions

H with intent to steal property from a house, inserted a centre bit into a door near the bolt. The end of the bit penetrated the door but no part of the prisoner's body entered the house. He was indicted for burglary. On the question of whether there was an entry:

COUNSEL FOR THE PRISONER: It has been held that the smallest degree of entry whatever is sufficient to satisfy the law. Putting a hand, or a foot, or a pistol over the threshold of the door, or a hook or other instrument through the broken pane of a window . . . have been decided to be burglarious entries; but the principle of all these new determinations is, that there has been such a previous breaking of the castle of the proprietor, as to render his property insecure. . . . And in those cases where an instrument has formed any part of the question, it has always been taken to mean, not the instrument by which the breaking was made, but the instrument, as a hook, a fork or other thing by which the property was capable of being removed, introduced subsequent to the act of breaking. . . . In the present case, the introduction of the instrument is part of the act of breaking, but it is impossible to conceive that it was introduced for the purpose of purloining property, for it is incapable of performing such an office.

The prisoner was acquitted

Note

But the insertion of any part of the body was an entry, whether the purpose of the insertion was to commit the ulterior felony or merely to effect entry: see *R. v. Bailey* (1818) R. & R. 341.

However a remark in *R. v. Collins*, below, by Edmund Davies L.J. that the defendant had to have made "an effective and substantial entry" has proved problematic. In *R. v. Brown* [1985] Crim.L.R. 212, (C.A.), it was held that whether there has been an entry is a question of fact for the jury. In this case D leaned through a broken shop window and stole goods. The Court of Appeal did not think that the word "substantial" was of any assistance. This left the problem, however, that entry of part of the body could be effective for one ulterior offence, as in this case for stealing, but not for another such as rape. While a charge of attempted burglary would be available for cases where partial entry would not be "effective" to commit the ulterior offence, this is not really a satisfactory solution. As Professor J.C. Smith, *The Law of Theft* (7th ed.) points out (at para 11–03):

> "Yet it cannot have been intended that D should have got so far into the building as to be able to accomplish his unlawful purpose. The intending rapist is guilty of burglary when he enters through the ground floor window though his victim is on the fourth floor. 'Effective' seems no more helpful than 'substantial'. Probably the safest and best course is to assume the continued existence of the common law rule."

In the most recent case, *R. v. Ryan* [1996] Crim.L.R. 320, D was found by an elderly householder trapped with his head and arm inside a window. He was convicted of burglary but appealed contending that his actions could not constitute an "entry" as he could not have stolen anything as he was firmly stuck. The Court of Appeal held, following *Brown*, that entry of part of his body could constitute an entry and it was irrelevant whether or not he was capable of stealing anything. The Court did not go so far as to declare that the insertion of any part of D's body is sufficient to constitute an entry preferring to leave the matter to juries to decide. It is likely that the question of "effectiveness" is now no longer relevant but a firmer declaration of the law by the Court of Appeal would have resolved the matter once and for all. Furthermore, by leaving the issue to the jury to decide, rather than expressly affirming the common law rule, similar cases may end up being decided differently by different juries.

Question

Suppose D puts a child under 10 through a window, not to steal but to open a door and admit D who will himself steal. Is that entry by D?

ii. As a Trespasser

R. v. Collins
[1973] 1 Q.B. 100
Court of Appeal

C was convicted of burglary with intent to commit rape in the circumstances outlined in the judgment below.

EDMUND-DAVIES L.J.: . . . Let me relate the facts. Were they put into a novel or portrayed on the stage, they would be regarded as being so improbable as to be unworthy of serious consideration and as verging at times on farce. At about 2 o'clock in the early morning of Saturday, July 24, 1971, a young lady of 18 went to bed at her mother's home in Colchester. She had spent the evening with her boyfriend. She had taken a certain amount of drink, and it may be that this fact affords some explanation of her inability to answer satisfactorily certain crucial questions put to her at the trial.

She has the habit of sleeping without wearing night apparel in a bed which is very near the lattice-type window of her room. At one stage in her evidence she seemed to be saying that the bed was close up against the window which, in accordance with her practice, was wide open. In the photographs which we have before us, however, there appears to be a gap of some sort between the two, but the bed was clearly quite near the window.

At about 3.30 or 4 o'clock she awoke and she then saw in the moonlight a vague form crouched in the open window. She was unable to remember, and this is important, whether the form was on the outside of the window sill or on that part of the sill which was inside the room, and for reasons which will later become clear, that seemingly narrow point is of crucial importance.

The young lady then realised several things: first of all that the form in the window was that of a male; secondly, that he was a naked male; and thirdly, that he was a naked male with an erect penis. She also saw in the moonlight that his hair was blond. She thereupon leapt to the conclusion that her boyfriend, with whom for some time she had been on terms of regular and frequent sexual intimacy, was paying her an ardent nocturnal visit. She promptly sat up in bed, and the man descended from the sill and joined her in bed and they had full sexual intercourse. But there was something about him which made her think that things were not as they usually were between her and her boyfriend. The length of his hair, his voice as they exchanged what was described as "love talk", and other features led her to the conclusion that somehow there was something different. So she turned on the bed-side light, saw that her companion was not her boyfriend and slapped the face of the intruder, who was none other than the defendant. He said to her, "Give me a good time tonight", and got hold of her arm, but she bit him and told him to go. She then went into the bathroom and he promptly vanished.

The complainant said that she would not have agreed to intercourse if she had known that the person entering her room was not her boyfriend. But there was no suggestion of any force having been used upon her, and the intercourse which took place was undoubtedly effected with no resistance on her part.

The defendant was seen by the police at about 10.30 later that same morning. According to the police, the conversation which took place then elicited these points: He was very lustful the previous night. He had taken a lot of drink. . . . He went on to say that he knew the complainant because he had worked around her house. On this occasion, during sexual intercourse—and according to the police evidence he added that he was determined to have a girl, by force if necessary, although that part of the police evidence he challenged—he went on to say that he walked around the house, saw a light in an upstairs bedroom, and he knew that this was the girl's bedroom. He found a step ladder, leaned it against the wall and climbed up and looked into the bedroom. He could see through the wide-open window a girl who was naked and asleep. So he descended the ladder and stripped off all his clothes, with the exception of his socks, because apparently he took the view that if the girl's mother entered the bedroom it would be easier to effect a rapid escape if he had his socks on than if he was in his bare feet. That is a matter about which we are not called upon to express any view, and would in any event find ourselves unable to express one.

Having undressed, he then climbed the ladder and pulled himself up on to the window sill. His version of the matter is that he was pulling himself in when she awoke. She then got up and knelt on the bed, she put her arms around his neck and body, and she seemed to pull him into the bed. He went on: "I was rather dazed because I didn't think she would want to know me.

We kissed and cuddled for about 10 or 15 minutes and than I had it away with her but found it hard because I had had so much to drink."

The police officer said to the defendant: "It appears that it was your intention to have intercourse with this girl by force if necessary, and it was only pure coincidence that this girl was under the impression that you were her boyfriend and apparently that is why she consented to allowing you to have sexual intercourse with her." It was alleged that he then said, "Yes, I feel awful about this. It is the worst day of my life, but I know it could have been worse." Thereupon the officer said to him—and he challenges this: "What do you mean, you know it could have been worse?," to which he is alleged to have replied: "Well, my trouble is drink and I got very frustrated. As I've told you, I only wanted to have it away with a girl and I'm only glad I haven't really hurt her."

Then he made a statement under caution, in the course of which he said: "When I stripped off and got up the ladder I made my mind up that I was going to try and have it away with this girl. I feel terrible about this now, but I had too much to drink. I am sorry for what I have done."

In the course of his testimony, the defendant said that he would not have gone into the room if the girl had not knelt on the bed and beckoned him into the room. He said that if she had objected immediately to his being there or his having intercourse he would not have persisted. While he was keen on having sexual intercourse that night, it was only if he could find someone who was willing. He strongly denied having told the police that he would if necessary, have pushed over some girl for the purpose of having intercourse. . . .

Now, one feature of the case which remained at the conclusion of the evidence in great obscurity is where exactly Collins was at the moment when, according to him, the girl manifested that she was welcoming him. Was he kneeling on the sill outside the window or was he already inside the room, having climbed through the window frame, and kneeling upon the inner sill? It was a crucial matter, for there were certainly three ingredients that it was incumbent upon the Crown to establish. Under section 9 of the Theft Act, 1968, which renders a person guilty of burglary if he enters any building or part of a building as a trespasser and with the intention of committing rape, the entry of the accused into the building must first be proved. Well, there is no doubt about that, for it is common ground that he did enter this girl's bedroom. Secondly, it must be proved that he entered as a trespasser. We will develop that point a little later. Thirdly, it must be proved that he entered as a trespasser with intent at the time of entry to commit rape therein.

The second ingredient of the offence—the entry must be as a trespasser—is one which has not, to the best of our knowledge, been previously canvassed in the courts. . . .

What does that involve? According to the editors of *Archbold Criminal Pleading Evidence & Practice*, 37th ed. (1969), para. 1505: "Any intentional, reckless or negligent entry into a building will, it would appear, constitute a trespass if the building is in the possession of another person who does not consent to the entry. Nor will it make any difference that the entry was the result of a reasonable mistake on the part of the defendant, so far as trespass is concerned." If that be right, then it would be no defence for this man to say (and even were he believed in saying), "Well, I honestly thought that this girl was welcoming me into the room and I therefore entered, fully believing that I had her consent to go in." If *Archbold* is right, he would nevertheless be a trespasser, since the apparent consent of the girl was unreal, she being mistaken as to who was at her window. We disagree. We hold that, for the purposes of section 9 of the Theft Act, a person entering a building is not guilty of trespass if he enters without knowledge that he is trespassing or at least without acting recklessly as to whether or not he is unlawfully entering.

A view contrary to that of the editors of *Archbold* was expressed in Professor Smith's book on *The Law of Theft*, 1st ed. (1968), where, having given an illustration of an entry into premises, the author comments, at paragraph 462: "It is submitted that . . . D. should be acquitted on the ground of lack of *mens rea*. Though, under the civil law, he entered as a trespasser, it is submitted that he cannot be convicted of the criminal offence unless he knew of the facts which caused him to be a trespasser or, at least, was reckless."

The matter has also been dealt with by Professor Griew, who in paragraph 4–05 of his work *The Theft Act 1968* has this passage: "What if D. wrongly believes that he is not trespassing? His belief may rest on facts which, if true, would mean that he was not trespassing: for instance, he may enter a building by mistake, thinking that it is the one he has been invited to enter. Or his belief may be based on a false view of the legal effect of the known facts: for instance, he may misunderstand the effect of a contract granting him a right of passage through a building. Neither kind of mistake will protect him from tort liability for trespass. In either case, then, D. satisfies the literal terms of section 9(1): he 'enters . . . as a trespasser.' But for the purposes of criminal liability a man should be judged on the basis of the facts as he believed them to be, and this should include making allowances for a mistake as to rights under the civil law. This is another way of saying that a serious offence like burglary should be held to require *mens rea* in the fullest sense of the phrase: D. should be liable for burglary if he knowingly trespasses or is reckless as to whether he trespasses or not. Unhappily it is common for Parliament to omit to make clear whether *mens rea* is intended to be an element in a statutory offence. It is also, though not equally, common for the courts to supply the mental element by construction of the statute."

We prefer the view expressed by Professor Smith and Professor Griew to that of the editors of *Archbold*. In the judgment of this court there cannot be a conviction for entering premises "as a trespasser" within the meaning of section 9 of the Theft Act unless the person entering does so knowing that he is a trespasser and nevertheless deliberately enters, or, at the very least, is reckless as to whether or not he is entering the premises of another without the other party's consent.

Having so held, the pivotal point of this appeal is whether the Crown established that this defendant at the moment that he entered the bedroom knew perfectly well that he was not welcome there or, being reckless as to whether he was not welcome or not, was nevertheless determined to enter. That in turn involves consideration as to where he was at the time that the complainant indicated that she was welcoming him into her bedroom. If, to take an example that was put in the course of argument, her bed had not been near the window but was on the other side of the bedroom, and he (being determined to have her sexually even against her will) climbed through the window and crossed the bedroom to reach her bed, then the offence charged would have been established. But in this case, as we have related, the layout of the room was different, and it became a point of nicety which had to be conclusively established by the Crown as to where he was when the girl made welcoming signs, as she unquestionably at some stage did.

How did the judge deal with this matter? We have to say regretfully that there was a flaw in his treatment of it. Referring to section 9, he said "There are three ingredients. First is the question of entry. Did he enter into that house? Did he enter as a trespasser? That is to say, was the entry, if you are satisfied that there was an entry, intentional or reckless? And, finally, and you may think this is the crux of the case as opened to you by Mr. Irwin, if you are satisfied that he entered as a trespasser, did he have the intention to rape this girl?

The judge then went on to deal in turn with each of these three ingredients. He first explained what was involved in "entry" into a building. He then dealt with the second ingredient. But here he unfortunately repeated his earlier observation that the question of entry as a trespasser depended on "was the entry intentional or reckless?" We have to say that this was putting the matter inaccurately. This mistake may have been derived from a passage in the speech of counsel for the Crown when replying to the submission of "no case". Mr. Irwin at one stage said: "Therefore, the first thing that the Crown have got to prove, my Lord, is that there has been a trespass which may be an intentional trespass, or it may be a reckless trespass." Unfortunately the judge regarded the matter as though the second ingredient in the burglary charged was whether there had been an intentional or reckless entry, and when he came to develop this topic in his summing up that error was unfortunately perpetuated. The judge told the jury: "He had no right to be in that house, as you know, certainly from the point of view of the girl's parent. But if you are satisfied about entry, did he enter intentionally or recklessly? What the prosecution say about that is, you do not really have to consider recklessness because when you consider his own evidence he intended to enter that house, and if you accept the evidence I have just pointed out to you, he in fact did so. So, at least, you may think, it was intentional. At the least, you may think it was reckless because as he told you he did not know whether the girl would accept him."

We are compelled to say that we do not think the judge by these observations made sufficiently clear to the jury the nature of the second test about which they had to be satisfied before this young man could be convicted of the offence charged. There was no doubt that his entry into the bedroom was "intentional". But what the accused had said was, "She knelt on the bed, she put her arms around me and then I went in." If the jury thought he might be truthful in that assertion, they would need to consider whether or not, although entirely surprised by such a reception being accorded to him, this young man might not have been entitled reasonably to regard her action as amounting to an invitation to him to enter. If she in fact appeared to be welcoming him, the Crown do not suggest that he should have realised or even suspected that she was so behaving because, despite the moonlight, she thought he was someone else. Unless the jury were entirely satisfied that the defendant made an effective and substantial entry into the bedroom without the complainant doing or saying anything to cause him to believe that she was consenting to his entering it, he ought not to be convicted of the offence charged. The point is a narrow one, as narrow maybe as the window sill which is crucial to this case. But this is a criminal charge of gravity and, even though one may suspect that his intention was to commit the offence charged, unless the facts show with clarity that he in fact committed it he ought not to remain convicted.

Some question arose as to whether or not the defendant can be regarded as a trespasser *ab initio*. But we are entirely in agreement with the view expressed in *Archbold*, again in paragraph 1505, that the common law doctrine of trespass *ab initio* has no application to burglary under the Theft Act, 1968. One further matter that was canvassed ought perhaps to be mentioned. The point was raised that, the complainant not being the tenant or occupier of the dwelling house and her mother being apparently in occupation, this girl herself could not in any event have extended an effective invitation to enter, so that even if she had expressly and with full knowledge of all material facts invited the defendant in, he would nevertheless be a trespasser. Whatever be the position in the law of tort, to regard such a proposition as acceptable in the criminal law would be unthinkable.

We have to say that this appeal must be allowed on the basis that the jury were never invited to consider the vital question whether this young man did enter the premises as a trespasser, that is to say knowing perfectly well that he had no invitation to enter or reckless of whether or not his entry was with permission. . . .

Appeal allowed

R. v. Jones and Smith
[1976] 3 All E.R. 54
Court of Appeal

J and S were convicted of burglary contrary to section 9(1)(*b*) of the Theft Act 1968. They had entered the house of S's father and stolen two television sets. S's father had reported the theft to the police at the time, but at the trial, he gave evidence to the effect that he had given S unreserved permission to enter the house, stating that S "would not be a trespasser in the house at any time". J and S appealed.

JAMES L.J.: The next ground of appeal relied on by Counsel for the appellants in his argument is that which is put forward in the first of each of the defendants' grounds. It is the point upon which Counsel had laid the greatest stress in the course of his argument. The argument is based upon the wording of the Theft Act 1968, section 9(1)(*b*) . . .

The important words from the point of view of the arguments in this appeal are "having entered any building . . . as a trespasser." This is a section of an Act of Parliament which introduced a novel concept. Entry as a trespasser was new in 1968 in relation to criminal offences of burglary. It was introduced in substitution for, as an improvement upon, the old law which required considerations of breaking and entering and involved distinctions of nicety which had bedevilled the law for some time.

Counsel for the appellants argued that a person who had a general permission to enter premises of another person cannot be a trespasser. His submission is as short and as simple as that. Related to this case he says that a son to whom a father has given permission generally to enter the father's house cannot be a trespasser if he enters it even though he had decided in his mind before making the entry to commit a criminal offence of theft against the father once he had got into the house and had entered that house solely for the purpose of committing that theft. It is a bold submission. Counsel frankly accepts that there has been no decision of the court since this Act was passed which governs particularly this point. He has reminded us of the decision in *Byrne v. Kinematograph Renters Society Ltd* [1958] 1 W.L.R. 762, which he prays in aid of his argument. In that case persons had entered a cinema by producing tickets not for the purpose of seeing the show, but for an ulterior purpose. It was held in the action, which sought to show that they entered as trespassers pursuant to a conspiracy to trespass, that in fact they were not trespassers. The important words in the judgment are (at p. 776): "They did nothing that they were not invited to do. . . ." That provides a distinction between that case and what we consider the position to be in this case.

Counsel has also referred us to one of the trickery cases, *R. v. Boyle*,

[1954] 2 Q.B. 292, and in particular to a passage in the judgment of that case (at p. 295). He accepts that the trickery cases can be distinguished from such a case as the present because in the trickery cases it can be said that that which would otherwise have been consent to enter was negatived by the fact that consent was obtained by a trick. We do not gain any help in the particular case from that decision.

We were also referred to *R. v. Collins* [*ante*, p. 877], and in particular to the long passage of Edmund Davies L.J., where he commenced the consideration of what is involved by the words "the entry must be 'as a trespasser'". Again it is unnecessary to cite that long passage in full; suffice it to say that this court on that occasion expressly approved the view expressed in Professor Smith's book on the Law of Theft, and also the view of Professor Griew in his publication on the Theft Act 1968 on this aspect of what is involved in being a trespasser.

In our view the passage there referred to is consonant with the passage in the well known case of *Hillen and Pettigrew v. I.C.I. (Alkali) Ltd* [1936] A.C. 65 where, in the speech of Lord Atkin, these words appear:

> "My Lords, in my opinion this duty to an invitee only extends so long as and so far as the invitee is making what can reasonably be contemplated as an ordinary and reasonable use of the premises by the invitee for the purposes for which he has been invited. He is not invited to use any part of the premises for purposes which he knows are wrongfully dangerous and constitute an improper use. As Scrutton L.J. has pointedly said (*The Calgarth, the Ontarama* [1927] P. 93 at 110) 'When you invite a person into your house to use the stair case you do not invite him to slide down the banisters.'"

The decision in *R. v. Collins* in this court, a decision on the criminal law, added to the concept of trespass as a civil wrong only the mental element of *mens rea*, which is essential to the criminal offence. Taking the law as expressed in *Hillen and Pettigrew v. I.C.I. (Alkali) Ltd* and *R. v. Collins*, it is our view that a person is a trespasser for the purpose of section 9(1)(*b*) of the Theft Act 1968 if he enters premises of another knowing that he is entering in excess of the permission that has been given to him to enter, providing the facts are known to the accused which enable him to realise that he is acting in excess of the permission given or that he is acting recklessly as to whether he exceeds that permission, then that is sufficient for the jury to decide that he is in fact a trespasser.

In this particular case it was a matter for the jury to consider whether, on all the facts, it was shown by the prosecution that the appellants entered with the knowledge that entry was being effected against the consent or in excess of the consent that had been given by Mr Alfred Smith to his son Christopher. The jury were, by their verdict, satisfied of that. It was a novel argument that we heard, interesting but one without, in our view, any foundation. . . .

Finally, before parting with the matter, we would refer to a passage of the summing-up to the jury which I think one must read in full. In the course of that the recorder said:

> "I have read out the conversation they had with Detective Sergeant Tarrant and in essence Smith said, 'My father gave me leave to take these sets and Jones was invited along to help.' If that account may be true, that is an end of the case, but if you are convinced that that night they went to the house and entered as trespassers and had no leave or licence to go there for that purpose, and they intended to steal these sets and keep them permanently themselves, acting dishonestly, then

you will convict them. Learned counsel for the prosecution did mention the possibility that you might come to the conclusion that they had gone into the house with leave or licence of the father and it would be possible for you to bring in a verdict simply of theft but, members of the jury, of course it is open to you do to that if you felt that the entry to the house was a consequence of the father's leave or licence, but what counts of course for the crime of burglary to be made out is the frame of mind of each person when they go into the property. If you go in intending to steal, then your entry is burglarious, it is to trespass because no one gave you permission to go in and steal in the house."

Then the recorder gave an illustration of the example of a person who is invited to go into a house to make a cup of tea and that person goes in and steals the silver and he went on:

"I hope that illustrates the matter sensibly. Therefore you may find it difficult not to say, if they went in there they must have gone in order to steal because they took elaborate precautions, going there at dead of night, you really cannot say that under any circumstances their entry to the house could have been other than trespass."

In that passage that I have just read the recorder put the matter properly to the jury in relation to the aspect of trespass and on this ground of appeal as on the others we find that the case is not made out, that there was no misdirection, as I have already indicated early in the judgment, and in those circumstances the appeal will be dismissed in the case of each of the appellants.

Appeals dismissed

Questions

1. Smith was not residing with his father at the time of the theft. Would it have made any difference if he had been so residing?

2. A knocks on the door of his neighbour, Miss B. Miss B, recognising him and thinking his call is purely social, invites him in, and he goes in. In fact A's intention is to rape Miss B. On the question of whether A is guilty of burglary, do the cases of *Collins*, and *Jones and Smith* give different answers?

3. Does it follow from *Jones and Smith* that an intending shoplifter necessarily commits burglary as soon as he walks through the door of the shop? Consider the following from Dawson J. in *Barker v. R.* (1983) 57 A.L.J.R. 426, 440 (High Court of Australia):

"It is essential to recognise that the offence consists both of an intentional entry as a trespasser and an intent to steal at the time of entry. The distinction must be maintained because a person accused of burglary may enter premises with an intention to steal but nevertheless in the belief that he is entitled to enter. A person who enters premises with apparent consent but with intent to steal, such as an ordinary shoplifter, is likely to believe at the time he enters the premises that he has the same right of entry as other persons notwithstanding the criminal purpose for which he enters. If interrupted before attempting to steal anything, no doubt he would say that he had done nothing wrong and was entitled to be on the premises. And if he believed that to be so, as he very well might, the mental element required to prove entry as a trespasser would be lacking, notwithstanding evidence of that other aspect of intent required for burglary, an intent to steal at the time of entry. Before there can be a burglary there must be an entry as a trespasser with intent to enter as a trespasser as well as with intent to steal."

4. If A, while in a shop, forms the intent to steal, that is no offence. If he attempts to steal or actually steals, he is liable to 7 years imprisonment. But whether or not he steals or attempts to steal, if he formed the intent to steal before entering the shop, he is (subject to Dawson J.'s remarks above) liable to 10 years imprisonment. What policy of the law can be thought to demand this extra punishment?

iii. Buildings or Parts of Buildings

Notes

1. The word "building" in statute law has had many different meanings given to it. Under the Malicious Damage Act 1861, the word was held to cover a house which was unfinished but substantially complete and with a roof on; *R. v. Manning* (1871) L.R. 1 C.C.R. 338. In *Stevens v. Gourlay* (1859) 7 C.B. (N.S.) 99, the C.C.C.R. held that both the ordinary meaning and the presumed intention of the legislature must be looked at. Thus a wooden structure intended as a shop was held to be a building for the purposes of the Metropolitan Building Act 1855, the court holding that an object of the Act was to prevent the metropolis from being covered by combustible structures. The ordinary meaning was held to require a structure of considerable size and intended to be permanent or at least to endure for a considerable time. This dictum was apparently used in *B. and S. v. Leathley* [1979] Crim.L.R. 314 (Carlisle Crown Court) to hold that burglary applied to a freezer container, 25 feet long with 7ft. square cross-sections, left standing in a farm yard for two or three years, notwithstanding that it was portable. It seems to be agreed that tents are not buildings (the C.L.R.C. did not envisage that they were: Cmnd. 2977, § 78), and that portability alone does not prevent a structure from being a building. Apart from that, little can be said with confidence, and puzzles such as a bandstand, or telephone kiosk, will have to be elucidated as and when cases arise.

2. Entry as a trespasser into a "part" of a building, *either* with intent to commit a relevant crime in that part, *or* followed by the commission of a relevant crime in that part is also burglary, even if there is no trespassory entry of the building as a whole. Most "parts" of buildings, *e.g.* rooms, cause no difficulty, but doubt might be caused by less differentiated areas, *e.g.* separate counters in a department store. It seems that there must be at least some physical demarcation for an area to be a "part" for the purposes of the law of burglary.

R. v. Walkington (1979) 1 W.L.R. 1169, 1175: W was convicted of burglary by entering a part consisting of a movable three-sided enclosure round a till in a department store. On appeal: Geoffrey Lane L.J. One really gets two extremes, as it seems to us. First of all you have the part of the building which is shut off by a door so far as the general public is concerned, with a notice saying "Staff Only" or "No admittance to customers." At the other end of the scale you have for example a single table in the middle of the store, which it would be difficult for any jury to find properly was a part of the building, into which the licensor prohibited customers from moving.

Here, it seems to us, there was a physical demarcation. Whether there was sufficient to amount to an area from which the public were plainly excluded was a matter for the jury. It seems to us that there was ample evidence on which they could come to the conclusion (a) that the management had impliedly prohibited customers entering that area and (b) that this particular defendant knew of that prohibition.

iv. Intent to Commit an Offence in the Building

Attorney General's References (Nos. 1 and 2 of 1979)
[1980] Q.B. 180
Court of Appeal

The references arose out of two cases in each of which the judge directed an acquittal.

In Case 1, A was discovered ascending the stairs to the private rooms above a grocer's shop, where he had no right to be. He said he was looking for money to steal. He was charged with burglary with intent to steal.

In Case 2, B at 3.15 a.m. was discovered by a householder trying to force the french windows of her house. He said he wasn't going to damage anything, only to see if there was anything lying around. He was charged with attempting to enter the house with intent to steal therein.

Roskill L.J.: The matters arising for determination are of wide general importance for the administration of justice both in the Crown Court and in magistrates' courts. There appears from what we have been told by counsel and from an admirable memorandum prepared by the Law Commission for the assistance of the court on these references, to be a question of law which is causing and has caused considerable confusion, and has led to what would appear to be unjustified acquittals as a result of circuit judges or their deputies in the Crown Court and also magistrates' courts acceding to submissions that there was no case to answer, the submissions being based on a single sentence in the judgment of this court in *R. v. Husseyn* (Note) (1977) 67 Cr.App.R. 131, decided on December 8, 1977, the court consisting of Viscount Dilhorne, Lord Scarman and the late Cusack J. The Attorney-General has referred two such cases decided in the Crown Court to this court in order that a decision may be obtained whether the acquittals with which we are immediately concerned, and also certain other acquittals of which we have been told, were in fact justified.

The question referred to in Reference No. 1 is:

"Whether a man who has entered a house as a trespasser with the intention of stealing money therein is entitled to be acquitted of an offence against section 9(1)(a) of the Theft Act 1968 on the grounds that his intention to steal is conditional upon his finding money in the house."

The answer of this court to this question is "No". In the second reference the question is:

"Whether a man who is attempting to enter a house as a trespasser with the intention of stealing anything of value which he may find therein is entitled to be acquitted of the offence of attempted burglary on the ground that at the time of the attempt his said intention was insufficient to amount to 'the intention of stealing anything' necessary for conviction under section 9 of the Theft Act 1968.''

The answer of this court to this question is also ''No.'' . . .

[In *R. v. Husseyn* Viscount Dilhorne expressed strong disapproval of the use of ''conditional intention. In their memorandum the Law Commission stated that'' conditional intention ''means that the accused does not know what he is going to steal but intends that he will steal whatever he finds of value or worthwhile stealing.'']

We respectfully agree with Viscount Dilhorne's stated strong disapproval of the phrase, but if it is to be used, it should only be used for that limited purpose set out in the last sentence which I have read. In paragraph 13 the [Law Commission memorandum] goes on:

''The doctrine finds its first expression in the statement of Lord Scarman in *R. v. Husseyn*, that 'it cannot be said that one who has it in mind to steal only if what he finds is worth stealing has a present intention to steal.' *R. v. Husseyn* was a case of attempted theft and, taken literally, the statement means that a conditional intent to steal in the sense of an intention to steal whatever the accused may find worth stealing or of value is insufficient to ground a charge of attempted theft. It follows from this that a charge or indictment for attempted theft must necessarily be quashed as bad in law if it specifies the mental element as 'intending, at that time, to steal whatever he might find worth stealing (or of value) therein.' Thus, wherever the prosecution has to establish an intention to steal as one of the constituents of a theft-related offence, it must prove a fixed and settled intention, contemporaneous with the act forming the other (actus reus) element of the offence, on the part of the accused permanently to deprive someone of a specified identifiable object which either exists or is believed by the accused to exist in or near the scene of his operations (or 'the target', as the references aptly describe it). This is self-evident in cases of completed theft or 'successful' burglary or robbery where, *ex hypothesi*, the accused is charged with having appropriated a specific identifiable object. The importance of the doctrine lies in the field of attempted theft or other cases where, although an intention to steal is required, the relevant *actus reus* does not postulate that anything should necessarily have been appropriated. These offences include burglary, attempted burglary, assault with intent to rob, or, as a suspected person, loitering with intent to steal or rob.''

Thus the so called doctrine of ''conditional intention'' is described.

It will be useful to go through some of the cases to show how this so called doctrine has developed and to explain, as each member of this court is satisfied is the position, that the whole problem arises from a misunderstanding of a crucial sentence in Lord Scarman's judgment, which must be read in the context in which it was uttered, namely an indictment which charged an attempt to steal a specific object.

[His Lordship then considered *R. v. Stark* (unreported, October 5, 1967), *R. v. Easom* (*ante*, p. 760), *R. v. Husseyn*, and continued] Lord Scarman [in *R. v. Husseyn*] dealt with the law relating to attempts at p. 132 and said that in that respect there was no misdirection by the judge. But his Lordship then went on:

''Very different considerations apply when one comes to consider the way the learned judge summed up the issue of intention. The learned judge said that the jury could infer that what the young men were about was to look into the holdall and, if its contents were valuable, to steal it. In the view of this court that was a misdirection. What has to be established is an intention to steal at the time when the step is taken, which constitutes or which is alleged to constitute, the attempt. Edmund Davies L.J. put the point in *R. v. Easom* [*ante,* p. 760]: 'In every case of theft the appropriation must be accompanied by the intention of permanently depriving the owner of his property. What may be *loosely* described as a "conditional" appropriation will not do. If the appropriator has it in mind merely to deprive the owner of such of his property as, on examination, proves worth taking and then, finding that the booty is valueless to the appropriator, leaves it ready to hand to be repossessed by the owner, the appropriator has not stolen.' The direction of the learned judge in this case is exactly the contrary. It must be wrong, for it cannot be said that one who has it in mind to steal only if what he finds is worth stealing has a present intention to steal."

We were asked to say that either that last sentence was wrong or that it was *obiter.* We are not prepared to do either. If we may say so with the utmost deference to any statement of law by Lord Scarman, if this sentence be open to criticism, it is because in the context it is a little elliptical. If one rewrites that sentence, so that it reads: "It must be wrong, for it cannot be said that one who has it in mind to steal only if what he finds is worth stealing has a present intention to steal *the specific item charged,"* (our emphasis added), then the difficulties disappear, because, as already stated, what was charged was attempted theft of a specific object just as what had been charged in *R. v. Easom* had been the theft of a number of specific objects.

[His Lordship then considered *R. v. Hector* (1978) 67 Cr.App.R. 224, and continued]. So we have these four cases: *Stark, Easom, Husseyn* and *Hector.* In each the charge related to specific objects and in each the conviction was quashed because there had been a misdirection or because the Crown was not in a position to prove that there was on the part of the accused person or persons at the relevant time an intent to steal or to attempt to steal the specific objects which were the subject of the charges or for both those reasons. None of those cases is authority for the proposition that if a charge is brought under section 9(1) of entering any building or part of a building as a trespasser with intent to steal, the accused is entitled to acquittal unless it can be shown that at the time he entered he had the intention of stealing specific objects.

The last case to which it is necessary to refer is *R. v. Walkington* [1979] 1 W.L.R. 1169. Mr Tudor Price for the Attorney-General and Mr. Simon Brown, who has appeared as *amicus curiae,* both agree that if *R. v. Walkington* is right, as they submitted and as we think it clearly is, that decision is conclusive as to the answer in Reference No. 1, for the reasons given by Geoffrey Lane L.J. in giving the judgment of the court. . . .

In *R. v. Walkington* the indictment was for burglary. At the beginning of his judgment Geoffrey Lane L.J. set out the indictment, at p. 1171:

"Statement of offence: Burglary, contrary to section 9(1)(a) of the Theft Act 1968. Particulars of offence: Terence Walkington on January 15th, 1977, entered as a trespasser part of a building known as Debenhams Store with intent to steal therein."

Be it noted there was no averment in those particulars of any intention to steal any specific or identified objects. Geoffrey Lane L.J., after dealing with the first point which is presently irrelevant, dealt with the second and relevant point, at p. 1176:

... "These submissions are based upon the decision of this court in *R. v. Husseyn*: if we may say so respectfully, a most powerful court, because it consisted of Viscount Dilhorne, Lord Scarman and Cusak J."

The Lord Justice then read the headnote and the passage—in Lord Scarman's judgment upon which we have already commented. Geoffrey Lane L.J. said, at pp. 1177–1178:

"What Mr Osborne suggests to us is that that last passage—the last two sentences—meets the situation in this case and that if the facts were that the defendant in this case had it in mind only to steal if what he found was worth stealing, then he had no intention to steal. That is the way he put it. First of all we would like to say that the particulars of offence in *R. v. Husseyn* were that the two men . . . 'attempted to steal a quantity of sub-aqua equipment'. Plainly what considerations have to be applied to a charge of attempting to steal a specific article are different considerations from those which have to be applied when one is considering what a person's intent or intention may be under section 9 of the Theft Act 1968. That, we feel, is sufficient to distinguish our case from *R. v. Husseyn*."

Then the Lord Justice read what Lord Scarman himself had said about *R. v. Husseyn* in *D.P.P. v. Nock* [1978] A.C. 979. I will return to this shortly—and said, at p. 1178:

"In this case there is no doubt that the defendant was not on the evidence in two minds as to whether to steal or not. He was intending to steal when he went to that till and it would be totally unreal to ask oneself, or for the jury to ask themselves, the question, what sort of intent did he have? Was it a conditional intent to steal if there was money in the till or a conditional intention to steal only if what he found there was worth stealing? In this case it was a cash till and what plainly he was intending to steal was the contents of the till, which was cash. The mere fact that the till happened to be empty does not destroy his undoubted intention at the moment when he crossed the boundary between the legitimate part of the store and the illegitimate part of the store. The judge's direction which we have cited already covered that point, and the matter was accurately left to the jury.

It has again been pointed out to us, and it is right that we should make reference to it, that that decision in *R. v. Husseyn* has apparently been causing some difficulty to judges of the Crown Court."

The Lord Justice then referred to two cases reported in the Criminal Law Review and said that the brief report in the latter case would suffice to demonstrate the difficulties which had arisen. After reading that report Geoffrey Lane L.J. went on, at p. 1179:

"A reading of that would make the layman wonder if the law had taken leave of its senses, because, if that is the proper intepretation to be applied to section 9(1)(a), there will seldom, if ever, be a case in which section 9(1)(a) will bite. It seems to this court that in the end one simply has to go back to the words of the Act itself which we have already cited, and if the jury are satisfied, so as to feel sure, that the defendant has entered any building or part of a building as a trespasser, and are satisfied that at the moment of entering he intended to steal anything in the building or that part of it, the fact that there was nothing in the building worth his while to steal seems to us to be immaterial. He nevertheless had the intent to steal. As we see it, to hold otherwise would be to make nonsense of this part of the Act and cannot have been the intention of the legislature at the one when the Theft Act 1968 was passed. Nearly every prospective burglar could no doubt truthfully say that he only intended to steal if he found something in the building worth stealing.

So, whilst acknowledging that these recent decisions do provide difficulties which have been pointed out to us clearly by Mr. Osborne, it seems to us in the end that one must have regard to the wording of the Act. If that is done, the meaning, in our view, is clear."

I come back to what Lord Scarman himself said in *D.P.P. v. Nock* [1978] A.C. 979. The relevant passage is at pp. 999 to 1000. His Lordship, after referring to the decision of the House of Lords in *Haughton v. Smith* [*ante*, p. 499] said at p. 1000:

"We were invited by the Crown to express an opinion as to the correctness or otherwise of three decisions of the Court of Appeal, *R. v. Easom, Partington v. Williams* (1975) 62 Cr.App.R. 220 and *R. v. Husseyn. Easom* and *Husseyn* (to which I was a party) were, I think, correctly decided: but each, like every other criminal appeal, turned on its particular facts and on the way in which the trial judge directed the jury on the law. In *Easom* Edmund Davies L.J. emphasised that in a case of theft the appropriation must be accompanied by the intention of permanently depriving the owner of his property. This, of course, follows from the definition of theft in section 1(1) of the Theft Act 1968. All that *Husseyn* decided was that the same intention must be proved when the charge is one of attempted theft unfortunately in *Husseyn* the issue of intention was summed up in such a way as to suggest that theft, or attempted theft, could be committed by a person who had not yet formed the intention which the statute defines as a necessary part of the offence. An intention to steal can exist even though, unknown to the accused, there is nothing to steal: but, if a man be in two minds as to whether to steal or not, the intention required by the statute is not proved."

We venture to draw particular attention to the opening part of that last sentence: "An intention to steal can exist even though, unknown to the accused, there is nothing to steal. . . ."

We had an interesting discussion, with the help of Mr Tudor Price and Mr Simon Brown, how, in these cases of burglary or theft or attempted burglary or theft, it is in future desirable to frame indictments. Plainly it may be undesirable in some cases to frame indictments by reference to the theft or attempted theft of specific objects. Obviously draftsmen of indictments require the maximum latitude to adapt the particulars charged to the facts of the particular case, but we see no reason in principle why what was described in argument as a more imprecise method of criminal pleading should not be adopted, if the justice of the case requires it, as for example, attempting to steal some or all of the contents of a car or some or all of the contents of a handbag. The indictment in *R. v. Walkington* is in no way open to objection. There is no purpose in multiplying further examples. It may be that in some cases further particulars might be asked for and if so the prosecution could in a proper case no doubt give them without difficulty. The important point is that the indictment should correctly reflect that which it is alleged that the accused did, and that the accused should know with adequate detail what he is alleged to have done.

Taking as an example the facts in *R. v. Easom*, plainly what the accused intended was to steal some or all of the contents of the handbag if and when he got them into his possession. It seems clear from the latter part of Edmund Davies L.J.'s judgment that if he had been charged with an attempt to steal some or all of the contents of that handbag, he could properly have been convicted, subject of course to a proper direction to the jury.

It follows that this court respectfully and whole-heartedly adopts Geoffrey Lane L.J.'s judgment on the second question in *R. v. Walkington* which, as I have already said, is conclusive of the answer in the first reference.

So far as the answer in the second reference is concerned, it would, as Mr Simon Brown very properly agreed, be very strange if a different answer had to be given in the second reference, which is concerned with attempted burglary, from that given in the first reference. In our view, notwithstanding the argument that Mr Shepherd attempted to advance in the first of the two Divisional Court cases, it is impossible to justify giving different answers according to whether the charge is burglary or attempted burglary, theft or attempted theft or loitering with intent to commit an arrestable offence, which in most cases will be theft. In our view both principle and logic require the same answers in all these cases.

For those reasons the answers in the two references will be, as I have already indicated, "no" in the first and "no" in the second.

Opinions accordingly

Note

On conditional intent in theft, see *ante*, p. 760.

v. The Ulterior Offence

Notes

1. It will be noted that the list of possible ulterior offences is different according to whether the charge is entering with intent under section 9(1)(*a*) or entering and committing under section 9(1)(*b*). Thus if A enters B's house as a trespasser with the intention of quarrelling with B, and in the course of the quarrel he deliberately breaks B's priceless Ming vase, A is not guilty of burglary, but he *is* guilty of burglary if he punches B and breaks his nose. And he is guilty of burglary if, when he entered, he intended to do either of these two things.

2. The wording of section 9(1)(b) does not require that, after tres-passory entry, D should commit the *offence* of inflicting grievous bodily harm on any person in the building, only that he should inflict grievous bodily harm. It is thus possible on the wording for D to be guilty of burglary if he enters as a trespasser and *accidently*, even *lawfully*, inflicts grievous bodily harm. This was not intended, and the Draft Criminal Code Bill, cl. 147(b) puts right the mistake by requiring D to commit *an offence* of theft, attempted theft, or causing or attempting to cause serious bodily harm.

3. The only dishonest offence in either list is theft: fraudulent abstraction of electricity under section 13 of the Theft Act is not covered: *Low v. Blease* [1975] Crim.L.R. 513. Nor is obtaining property

by deception, but, as a result of *R. v. Gomez, ante,* p. 703, most cases of obtaining are also theft.

2. AGGRAVATED BURGLARY

Theft Act 1968, section 10

(1) A person is guilty of aggravated burglary if he commits any burglary and at the time has with him any firearm or imitation firearm, any weapon of offence, or any explosive; and for this purpose—

(a) 'firearm' includes an airgun or air pistol, and 'imitation firearm' means anything which has the appearance of being a firearm, whether capable of being discharged or not; and
(b) 'weapon of offence' means any article made or adapted for use for causing injury to or incapacitating a person, or intended by the person having it with him for such use; and
(c) 'explosive' means any article manufactured for the purpose of producing a practical effect by explosion, or intended by the person having it with him for that purpose.

(2) A person guilty of aggravated burglary shall on conviction on indictment be liable to imprisonment for life.

Notes

1. *"At the time."* The time is the time of the burglary charged. In the case of entry with intent under section 9(1)(*a*), it is the time of entry as a trespasser. In the case of an ulterior offence after trespassory entry under section 9(1)(*b*), it is the time of the ulterior offence. In *R. v. Francis* [1982] Crim.L.R. 363 (C.A.), A and B banged on V's door with sticks, and then entered as trespassers. They discarded their sticks, but later stole articles in the house. The judge directed that the prosecution had to prove that they were armed when they entered. *Held,* if a person entered a building as a trespasser and stole under section 9(1)(*b*), he committed burglary at the moment he stole and he committed aggravated burglary only if he had with him a weapon of offence at the time when he stole.

Question

When D enters as a trespasser with intent to steal, he is not armed with a weapon of offence. Once inside the house, he picks up a golf-club in case he is disturbed by the occupier. Being disturbed by the occupier, he threatens him with the club and then steals a valuable clock. Is D guilty of aggravated burglary? See *R. v. O'Leary* (1986) 82 Cr.App.R. 341, and *R. v. Kelly* (1992) 97 Cr.App.R. 245.

2. *"Has with him"*: This means "knowingly" has with him: *R. v. Cugullere* [1961] 1 W.L.R. 858, and one who has forgotten that he has the article with him is not "knowing" for this purpose: *R. v. Russell* (1984) 81 Cr.App.R. 315 (*ante,* p. 116). It is an open question whether it must be shown that D, who knowingly has an article, also knows that it is a weapon of offence: see *R. v. Warner* [1969] 2 A.C. 256; *R. v.*

Pierre [1963] Crim.L.R. 513, decided under different statutes, which suggest the answer "No." The words "has with him" do not require that D should be actually carrying the weapon of offence at the time of the offence: *R. v. Kelt* (1977) 3 All E.R. 1099, 1102 (C.A.); an accomplice may be carrying it. Where the offence is being carried by an accomplice, however, the offence of aggravated burglary will only be committed where the accomplice enters the building (see *Klass* [1998] 1 Cr.App.R. 453) as the gravamen of the offence is entry into a building with a weapon; if the accomplice carrying the weapon remains outside the burglary would not be an aggravated one.

3. *"Made or adapted for use for causing injury or incapacitation"*: If D at the relevant time has with him such an article, it is immaterial whether he intends it for such use. As to whether an article is so made or adapted, if it is one about which a realistic question can arise, it is for the jury to decide: *R. v. Williamson* (1977) 67 Cr.App.R. 35 (C.A.), *e.g.* a sheath knife, where it would depend on the sort of knife in the sheath. But with a flick knife, the jury must take judicial notice that it is so made: *R. v. Simpson* [1983] 3 All E.R. 789 (C.A.).

4. *"Intended by the person having it with him for such use."* If an article is not made or adapted for use for causing injury to or incapacitating a person, it is nevertheless a weapon of offence if "intended by the person having it with him for such use." The intended use need not be with respect to the particular burglary D is engaged in: *R. v. Stones* (1989) 89 Cr.App.R. 26 (C.A.). If A has with him a coil of rope with which he intends to tie up a watchman on the premises, the rope is a weapon of offence and if burglary is involved it will be aggravated burglary. But suppose A has with him an article, not otherwise a weapon of offence, which he does not intend to use on this or any other occasion, for injuring or incapacitating, but which, perhaps on the spur of the moment, he does in fact use for such purposes. A has a rope which he intends to use to lower stolen goods out of a window, but on being surprised by a watchman B, uses the rope to tie B up. Does A have with him an article intended for such use? In *R. v. Kelly* (1992) 97 Cr.App.R. 245, it was held that it was sufficient that he had it with him at the time when he used it (distinguishing cases on similar wording in the Prevention of Crime Act 1953, s. 1).

3. GOING EQUIPPED

Theft Act 1968, section 25

(1) A person shall be guilty of an offence if, when not at his place of abode, he has with him any article for use in the course of or in connection with any burglary, theft or cheat.

(2) A person guilty of an offence under this section shall on conviction on indictment be liable to imprisonment for a term not exceeding three years.

(3) Where a person is charged with an offence under this section, proof that he had with him any article made or adapted for use in committing a burglary, theft or cheat shall be evidence that he had it with him for such use.

(4) Any person may arrest without warrant anyone who is, or whom

he, with reasonable cause, suspects to be, committing an offence under this section.

(5) For the purposes of this section an offence under section 12(1) of this Act of taking a conveyance shall be treated as theft, and 'cheat' means an offence under section 15 of this Act.

i. Has with him

Note

See the cases cited on similar wording in section 10(1) (aggravated burglary), *supra*.

Question

A and B are apprehended while trying to break into a warehouse at night. When B is searched he is found to possess a banker's credit card which does not apparently belong to him. There is no evidence that A knew that B was carrying this article. Are A and B guilty of an offence under section 25? Would it make any difference if the article was not a credit card, but a jemmy? See next case.

R. v. Lester and Byast
(1955) 39 Cr.App.R. 157
Court of Criminal Appeal

L and B were convicted of being found by night having in their possession implements of housebreaking. Most of the implements were found in the boot of a car owned and driven by B, but some were found on B's person. L was a passenger in the car. The police had seen both L and B in the act of stealing petrol from another car, but there was no evidence of joint participation on their part in any enterprise of housebreaking.

HALLETT J.: It seems to us that the housebreaking implements found in the boot of the car were found in the possession of Byast within the meaning of section 28 [of the Larceny Act 1916], and we would refer to what was said in *Thompson* (1869) 11 Cox 362, more particularly in the interpolations at p. 364, where Lush J. says, "Or if a burglar were to hire a little boy to carry his implements, could he not be convicted under [the relevant section]?" and Blackburn J. says, "Or if the implements were in a pannier on an ass's back, could the donkey be said to be in possession of them?" The case was decided by a very powerful court, and those two interpolations seem to us to indicate what the learned judges concerned would have thought to be the true view when the implements were being carried, not by a little boy or by an ass, but by the more modern method of a boot of a motor-car....

With regard to Lester, on the other hand, somewhat different considerations arise. As we understand it, the case made against him is twofold. In the first place it is said that the implements of housebreaking which were found in the car were in his possession as well as in the possession of Byast. There was, however, a distinction between the facts proved in the case of Byast and those proved in the case of Lester. Whatever suspicions may be entertained—and certainly strong suspicions can be entertained—the only evidence is that Lester was a passenger in the car belonging to and driven by Byast, in the cubbyhole of which were two pairs of gloves and a piece of celluloid, and in the boot of which were other housebreaking implements. In our view, the *mere* fact that a man is a passenger in a car which contains housebreaking implements is not sufficient to show that he is in possession of them, whatever may be the case as regards the owner and driver of the car.

The alternative ground on which it is suggested that Lester should have been found guilty is that he was a participant with Byast in a housebreaking expedition, and that in such a case, where one of the participants is found in possession of housebreaking implements, his possession can be attributed in law to the other participant also, the authority for that proposition being *Thompson, supra*. We do not doubt that, if a common participation in a housebreaking expedition had been established by the evidence, the principle of *Thompson, supra*, would apply and the conviction of Lester would be upheld on that ground. The difficulty which we all feel in this case is that ... there is ... a lack of evidence, ... that the common enterprise in which Lester was engaged with Byast was an enterprise of housebreaking. It may very well have been, but we can see no evidence to establish that it was.

Byast's appeal dismissed
Lester's conviction quashed

Note

In *Re McAngus* [1994] Crim.L.R. 602, a case arising out of extradition proceedings, the Divisional Court held that the offence could be made out where the applicant took undercover agents to a bonded warehouse and displayed to them counterfeit clothing. This case seems to stretch to the limits the meaning of "has with him" as the section was not intended to cover mere possession (see CLRC Eighth Report, *Theft and Related Offences* (Cmnd 2977) para. 150). As the applicant was "not at his place of abode" and, when he lifted shirts to display them to the agents he had the shirts with him at that point, he committed the offence. In his commentary to *McAngus* Professor Smith states:

> "So the offence was presumably committed on the occasion of the visit to the warehouse and was not a continuing offence. But if the warehouse belongs to the defendant, then he is in possession of the offending articles. Is the mere possession then a continuing offence? It is submitted that it is not: 'has with him' implies physical presence. Is it enough then that he is present gloating over his potential profit-earners? Again it is submitted that it is not."

ii. When Not at his Place of Abode

R. v. Bundy [1977] 2 All E.R. 382 (C.A.). B was convicted under section 25 of the Theft Act, in respect of articles found in a car he was driving. He appealed on the ground that for several weeks he had been living in the car, which was therefore his place of abode.

LAWTON L.J. (at 384): We must construe the phase in the context in which it appears in section 25(1) of the Theft Act 1968. In that context it is manifest that no offence is committed if a burglar keeps the implements of his criminal trade in his "place of abode". He only commits an offence when he takes them from his "place of abode". The phrase "place of abode", in our judgment, connotes, first of all, a site. That is the ordinary meaning of the word "place". It is a site at which the occupier intends to abide. So, there are two elements in the phrase "place of abode", the element of site and the element of intention. When the appellant took the motor car to a site with the intention of abiding there, then his motor car on that site could be said to be his "place of abode", but when he took it from that site to move it to another site where he intended to abide, the motor car could not be said to be his "place of abode" during transit.

When he was arrested by the police he was not intending to abide on the site where he was arrested. It follows that he was not then at his "place of abode". He may have had a "place of abode" the previous night, but he was away from it at the time of his arrest when in possession of articles which could be used for the purpose of theft. It follows, in our judgment, that there is no substance in the point. . . .

iii. Any Article

Smith, *The Law of Theft,* **8th ed.**

12–02 The *actus reus* consists in the accused's having with him any article. Clearly the article need not be made or adapted for use in committing one of the specified offences. It is sufficient that the *mens rea* is proved in respect of the article, that is, that the accused intended to use it in the course of, or in connection with, one of the specified offences. Thus, it might be a tin of treacle, intended for use in removing a pane of glass; a pair of gloves to be worn so as to avoid leaving fingerprints; a collecting box marked "Oxfam" when the possessor did not represent that organisation; and so on. There may occasionally be difficulty in deciding what is an "article." Does it include blacking on the face to prevent recognition, or "Bostik" on the fingers to prevent fingerprints? Having regard to the mischief at which the section is aimed, it is arguable that a substance so applied to the body, remains an "article".

12–03 The offence is thus very wide in its scope. But there must be some limits. Thus D. can hardly be committing an offence because he is wearing his trousers when on his way to do a burglary. Yet he intends to wear them while he is committing the burglary and would not dream of undertaking such an enterprise without them. Similarly, he can hardly be committing an offence by wearing his shoes or any other item of everyday apparel. Yet it was stated above that gloves for the avoidance of fingerprints would entail liability. This suggests that the article must be one which D. would not be carrying with him but for the contemplated offence. If it is something which he would carry with him on a normal, innocent expedition, it should not fall within this section. So there might be a difference between a pair of rubber gloves and a pair of fur-lined gloves which D. was wearing to keep his hands warm on a freezing night, even though he did intend to keep them on so as to avoid leaving fingerprints. The latter pair of gloves is hardly distinguishable, for this purpose, from D.'s overcoat which seems to fall into the same category as his trousers. If D. is carrying a pair of plimsolls in his car to facilitate his cat-burgling, this seems a plain enough case; but what if he has simply selected his ordinary crepe-sole shoes for wear because they are less noisy than his hob-nails?

Question

D is out at night looking for a suitable house to break into to rape the occupant. He has with him a condom which he intends to wear to minimize the risk of being detected by means of forensic tests. Is he liable to conviction for the section 25 offence. Would it make any difference if evidence was tendered that D always carried a packet of condoms with him following the "safe sex" advertising campaign. (See further *Ellames*, below.)

iv. For Use in the Course of or in Connection with any Burglary, Theft or Cheat

R. v. Ellames
[1974] 3 All E.R. 130
Court of Appeal

After a robbery had taken place, E disposed of a bag containing articles used in the robbery, including a sawn-off shotgun, and ammonia in spray containers. He was charged under section 25 Theft Act. The judge directed that the fact that the theft was over did not prevent him from having the articles for the purpose of theft. E was convicted and appealed.

BROWNE J.: In our judgment the construction of the section suggested by the Crown would produce many problems, anomalies and absurdities, and it is impossible to give it that construction having regard to the words used.

In our judgment, the words in section 25(1) of the 1968 Act: "has with him any article for use" mean "has with him for the purpose" (or "with the intention") "that they will be used". The effect of section 25(3) is that if the article is one "made or adapted for use in committing a burglary, theft or cheat", that is evidence of the necessary intention, though not of course conclusive evidence. If the article is not one "made or adapted" for such use, the intention must be proved on the whole of the evidence—as it must be in the case of an article which is so made or adapted, if the defendant produces some innocent explanation. We agree with the learned authors of Smith and Hogan's Criminal Law (3rd ed., p. 484) that section 25 is directed against acts preparatory to burglary, theft or cheat; that

> "Questions as to D.'s knowledge of the nature of the thing can hardly arise here, since it must be proved that he intended to use it in the course of or in connection with [burglary, theft or cheat]";

and that the *mens rea* for this offence includes "an intention to use the article in the course of or in connection with any of the specific crimes."

An intention to use must necessarily relate to use in the future. If any support is needed for this view, we think it is found in the recent decision of this court in *R. v. Allamby*, *R. v. Medford* [1974] 3 All E.R. 126, decided under the Prevention of Crime Act 1953. It seems to us impossible to interpret section 25(1) of the 1968 Act as if it read: "has with him any article for use or *which has been used* in the course of or in connection with any burglary, theft or cheat." Equally, it is impossible to read section 25(3) as if it said: "had it with him for *or after* such use."

In our judgment the words "for use" govern the whole of the words which follow. The object and effect of the words "in connection with" is to add something to "in the course of". It is easy to think of cases where an article could be intended for use "in connection with" though not "in the course of" a burglary, etc., *e.g.* articles intended to be used while doing preparatory acts or while escaping after the crime (see Smith and Hogan).

In our view, to establish an offence under section 25(1) the prosecution must prove that the defendant was in possession of the article, and intended the article to be used in the course of or in connection with some future burglary, theft or cheat. But it is not necessary to prove that he intended it to be used in the course of or in connection with any *specific* burglary, theft or cheat; it is enough to prove a general intention to use it for *some* burglary, theft or cheat; we think that this view is supported by the use of the word "any" in section 25(1). Nor, in our view, is it necessary to prove that the defendant intended to use it himself; it will be enough to prove that he had it with him with the intention that it should be used by someone else. For example, if in the present case it had been proved that the defendant was hiding away these articles, which had already been used for one robbery, with the intention that they should later be used by someone for some other robbery, he would be guilty of an offence under section 25(1).

It follows from our conclusion as to the true construction of section 25(1) that in our judgment the judge should have upheld the appellant's submission of no case on count 2 and that the conviction must be quashed.

We come to this conclusion with some regret. But our conclusion that a person who is in possession only after a burglary, theft or cheat of articles which had been used in the crime is not guilty of an offence under section 25(1) of the 1968 Act, does not mean that he cannot be guilty of some other offence—the obvious possibility is an offence under section 4 of the Criminal Law Act 1967 of impeding apprehension or prosecution. It may be that if this appellant had been charged under that section he could properly have been convicted, but he was not charged under that section.

Accordingly, this appeal must be allowed and the conviction quashed.

Appeal allowed; conviction quashed

Notes

1. "The prosecution must prove that the defendant was in possession of the article and intended the article to be used in the course of or in connection with some future burglary theft or cheat": Browne J., *supra*. However it has been held that if D comes into possession of the article after he has embarked on an offence and intends to use it in the course of that offence, that is enough: *Minor v. D.P.P.* (1987) 86 Cr.App.R. 378 (D.C.).

2. The offence in prospect must not be too remote. In *R. v. Mansfield* [1975] Crim.L.R. 101 (C.A.), D was in possession of a driving licence and other documents belonging to another, with intent to obtain a job which would give him the opportunity to steal. *Held*, he did not have them with him "in connection with" the contemplated thefts.

3. Moreover, one who has not decided whether to use the article in the course of or in connection with any burglary theft or cheat does not have it with him for such use: *R. v. Hargreaves* [1985] Crim.L.R. 243. However, a conditional intent to use it (*e.g.* if the opportunity or need arises) ought to be enough.

4. For what must be proved if the contemplated offence is cheat, *i.e.* obtaining property by deception, see *R. v. Doukas* [1978] 1 W.L.R. 372, *ante*, p. 805 approved in *R. v. Cooke* [1986] A.C. 909, 934 (H.L.). These

and other cases concentrate on whether the victim would be influenced to part with his property by D's deception, but the true question, it has been suggested [Griew 16.11, Smith 12–07], is whether D *intended* to influence the victim.

CHAPTER 15

CRIMINAL DAMAGE

Note

The principle offences concerned with damage to property are contained in Criminal Damage Act 1971. The previous law was mostly in the Malicious Damage Act 1861, which made it an offence unlawfully and maliciously to commit any damage to a large number of specifically mentioned types of property. The Act of 1971 creates only a small number of wide, general, offences. The Draft Criminal Code Bill proposes no substantial changes, except as to "Lawful Excuse": see *post.*

1. DESTROYING OR DAMAGING PROPERTY

Criminal Damage Act 1971, sections 1 and 4

Section 1: (1) A person who without lawful excuse destroys or damages any property belonging to another intending to destroy or damage any such property or being reckless as to whether any such property would be destroyed or damaged shall be guilty of an offence.

(2) A person who without lawful excuse destroys or damages any property, whether belonging to himself or another:

(a) intending to destroy or damage any property or being reckless as to whether any property would be destroyed or damaged; and
(b) intending by the destruction or damage to endanger the life of another or being reckless as to whether the life of another would be thereby endangered;

shall be guilty of an offence.

(3) An offence committed under this section by destroying or damaging property by fire shall be charged as arson."

Section 4: "(1) A person guilty of arson under section 1 above or of an offence under section 1(2) above (whether arson or not) shall on conviction on indictment be liable to imprisonment for life.

(2) A person guilty of any other offence under this Act shall on conviction on indictment be liable to imprisonment for a term not exceeding ten years.

Notes

1. If the damage or destruction is by fire, the offence must be charged as arson. Moreover, since a heavier penalty is provided, it is

900

a different offence from criminal damage, and if arson is charged, there can be no conviction on that indictment of criminal damage in either of its forms: see *R. v. Cooper & Cooper* [1991] Crim.L.R. 524 (C.A.)

2. As to criminal damage, there are two offences in section 1, a simple offence and an aggravated one. The differences between them are connected with the expressions "belonging to another" and "without lawful excuse" (see *infra*), and with the additional *mens rea* required for the aggravated offence. The common features are the destroying or damaging of any property. "Property" is defined in section 10, below, but neither "destroy" nor "damage" is defined. Destroy may be surplusage, since it is hardly possible to destroy property without damaging it.

Criminal Damage Act 1971, section 10

(1) In this Act 'property' means property of a tangible nature, whether real or personal, including money and:

(a) including wild creatures which have been tamed or are ordinarily kept in captivity, and any other wild creatures or their carcasses if, but only if, they have been reduced into possession which has not been lost or abandoned or are in the course of being reduced into possession; but (b) not including mushrooms growing wild on any land or flowers, fruit or foliage of a plant growing wild on any land.

For the purpose of this subsection, 'mushroom' includes any fungus and 'plant' includes any shrub or tree.

[Compare the definition of property in section 4 of the Theft Act 1968, *ante*, p. 728].

R. v. Whiteley
(1991) 93 Cr.App.R. 25
Court of Appeal

D was a computer hacker, who gained unauthorised access to a computer network and altered data contained on discs in the system. Charged under Section 1(1) Criminal Damage Act 1971, he was convicted on counts in which the crown case was that he caused damage to the discs by way of alteration of the state of the magnetic particles on them so as to delete and add files. The discs themselves were not physically damaged, but the jury were directed that once the particles were written on the disc, they formed part of it and were therefore capable of sustaining damage. On appeal:—

LORD LANE C.J., for the Court: The evidence before the jury was that the discs are so constructed as to contain upon them thousands, if not millions, of magnetic particles. By issuing commands to the computer, impulses are produced which magnetise or demagnetise those particles in a particular way. By that means it is possible to write data or information on the discs and to program them to fulfil a variety of functions. By the same method it is possible to delete or alter data, information or instructions which have previously been written on to the disc. The argument advanced on behalf of the appellant, when reduced to its essence, seems to us to be this. That since the state of the magnetic particles on the disc is not perceptible by the unaided human senses, for instance of sight or touch, therefore the appellant's admitted activities only affected the "intangible information contained" on the disc itself. Even if the absence of such a perceptible change is not fatal to the prosecution, goes on the submission, interference with the particles cannot amount to damage in law.

It seems to us that that contention contains a basic fallacy. What the Act requires to be proved is that tangible property has been damaged, not necessarily that the damage itself should be tangible. There can be no doubt that the magnetic particles upon the metal discs were a part of the discs and if the appellant was proved to have intentionally and without lawful excuse altered the particles in such a way as to cause an impairment of the value or usefulness of the disc to the owner, there would be damage within the meaning of section 1. The fact that the alteration could only be perceived by operating the computer did not make the alterations any the less real, or the damage, if the alteration amounted to damage, any the less within the ambit of the Act.

We have been referred to a number of authorities which to a greater or lesser extent bear upon this problem. *Fisher* (1865) L.R. 1 C.C.R. 7: Here the defendant was convicted of damaging a steam engine. He had plugged up the feed-pipe and displaced other parts so as to render it temporarily useless and potentially explosive. There was no removal of any part, no cutting, no breaking and no lesion (as it was put). The conviction was upheld by the Court of Crown Cases Reserved. Pollock C.B. put the matter as follows at p. 9:

> "It is like the case of spiking a gun, where there is no actual damage to the gun, although it is rendered useless. . . . Surely the displacement of the parts was a damage . . . if done with intent to render the machine useless."

It should however be noted that the charge was brought under the Malicious Damage Act 1861 which provided by section 14 as follows:

> "Whosoever shall unlawfully and maliciously cut, break, or destroy, or damage with intent to destroy or to render useless, . . . any machine or engine. . . ."

In *Tacey* (1821) Russ. and Ry. 452, the allegation was that the defendant had mischievously damaged a frame used for stocking-making, by unscrewing and taking away a part of the machine, so rendering the whole useless. The judge reserved the point of whether mere removal of a part in these circumstances could amount to "damaging." It was held that it could. These two cases seem to demonstrate that no actual lesion to the tangible object is necessary. In *Henderson and Batley* (unreported, November 29, 1984), this Court had to consider the meaning of "damage" in section 1(1) of the 1971 Act. The property allegedly damaged was a development land site upon which the defendants had dumped 30 lorry loads of rubble, which the owners had to remove at a cost of some £2,000. The argument advanced by the defendants was that what they had done could not be said to have damaged the land. The trial judge ruled against them and his decision was upheld on appeal, on the grounds that damage can be of various kinds and that the definition found in the *Concise Oxford Dictionary*, (6th ed., p. 256) namely "injury impairing value or usefulness," was appropriate to cover the facts of the case. It was a question for the jury to decide whether damage had been proved.

That decision was cited by Stephen Brown L.J. in the Divisional Court decision of *Cox v. Riley* (1986) 83 Cr.App.R. 54, where the facts were not altogether dissimilar from those in the instant case. A disgruntled employee had erased from the printed circuit card a computer program which controlled a computerised saw belonging to his employers. The saw was thereby put out of action. He was charged with damaging the circuit card. It was contended on behalf of the prosecutor that by removing the information stored upon the card, the defendant had damaged the card within the meaning of section 1(1). On behalf of the defendant it was argued that the program in question did not exist in a tangible form and therefore was not property within the meaning of section 10(1), and secondly, that erasing a program from the printed circuit card did not amount to damage. "Damage", it was contended, should be given its "original meaning". This argument was amplified by counsel on the basis that because the program could not be seen or touched in the ordinary physical sense, the removal of the program could not amount to causing damage.

Stephen Brown L.J. in rejecting that argument in the course of his judgment at pp. 56, 57, 58, said this:

"It has to be observed that the property referred to in the charge was the plastic circuit card, which undoubtedly . . . is property of a tangible nature . . . the only possible argument which [counsel] could put forward is that there was no damage within the meaning of the Act. . . . The defendant . . . wished to put out of action, albeit temporarily, the computerised saw, and he was able to do that by operating the computer blanking mechanism in order to erase from the printed circuit card the relevant programs. That made it necessary for time and labour and money to be expended in order to replace the relevant programs on the printed circuit card. . . . It seems to me to be quite untenable to argue that . . . this . . . did not amount to causing damage to property."

We respectfully agree with those conclusions. *Morphitis v. Salmon* [1990] Crim.L.R. 48 was another decision of the Divisional Court. The facts of the case are immaterial, but in the course of delivering his judgment, with which Lloyd L.J. agreed, Auld J., in the transcript of the judgment, having cited the decision in *Cox v. Riley (supra)*, said this:

"The authorities show that the term 'damage' for the purpose of this provision, should be widely interpreted so as to include not only permanent or temporary physical harm, but also permanent or temporary impairment of value or usefulness."

The effect of those various decisions, in our judgment, is as follows: Any alteration to the physical nature of the property concerned may amount to damage within the meaning of the section. Whether it does so or not will depend upon the effect that the alteration has had upon the legitimate operator (who for convenience may be referred to as the owner). If the hacker's actions do not go beyond, for example, mere tinkering with an otherwise "empty" disc, no damage would be established. Where, on the other hand, the interference with the disc amounts to an impairment of the value or usefulness of the disc to the owner, then the necessary damage is established . . .

Appeal dismissed

Note

This case remains of authority as to audio or video recorders or tapes, but as to computers, section 3(6) Computer Misuse Act 1990 provides that a modification of the contents of such shall not be regarded as damaging any computer or computer storage medium unless the modification affects or impairs the physical condition of the computer or storage medium. Persons like Whiteley or Riley would now be guilty of unauthorised modification of computer material: section 3(1) *ibid*.

See Wasik, "The Computer Misuse Act 1990" [1990] Crim.L.R. 767.

Roe v. Kingerlee [1986] Crim.L.R. 735 (Div.Ct.). D smeared the walls of a police cell with mud, which cost £7 to clean off. The Magistrates held that there was nothing amounting to damage, but on appeal by the prosecutor, *Held*: What constitutes criminal damage is a matter of fact and degree and it is for the justices, applying their common sense, to decide whether what occurred was damage or not. It is not necessary that the damage should be permanent before an act can constitute criminal damage. . . . In the circumstances of the present case, what occurred so far as the walls of the cell were concerned could amount to criminal damage. The justices were wrong to take the view that as a matter of law it could not. . . . The application of graffiti to a structure will not necessarily amount to causing criminal damage. That must be a question of fact and degree for the tribunal of fact.

A. The Simple Offence: Without Danger to Life

i. Belonging to Another

Criminal Damage Act 1971, section 10

(2) Property shall be treated for the purposes of this Act as belonging to any person:

(a) having the custody or control of it;
(b) having in it any proprietary right or interest (not being an equitable interest arising only from an agreement to transfer or grant an interest); or
(c) having a charge on it.

(3) Where property is subject to a trust, the persons to whom it belongs shall be so treated as including any person having a right to enforce the trust.

(4) Property of a corporation sole shall be so treated as belonging to the corporation notwithstanding a vacancy in the corporation.

Note

Before the Act, a person was criminally responsible for destroying or damaging his or her own property, if he or she did so with the intention of defrauding anyone. But see next case, and *R. v. Smith, post*, p. 911.

R. v. Denton
[1982] 1 All E.R. 65
Court of Appeal

D employed at a cotton mill, set fire to the mill and machinery in it because he thought his "employer" T had asked him to do so, saying "There is nothing like a good fire for improving the financial circumstances of a business." After submissions by him were rejected, he pleaded guilty, but appealed.

LORD LANE C.J.: The certificate given by the judge reads:

"As to Count 2 the defendant's defence was that he believed he had not only the permission but the encouragement of the proprietor of the business for which he worked, to set fire to the goods of that business with a view to obtaining insurance monies for that proprietor by fraud. After hearing submissions of Counsel at the conclusion of the evidence, I ruled that the word 'entitled' in section 5(2) the Criminal Damage Act 1971, despite the proprietorial basis of the Criminal Damage Acts, carried a connotation of general lawfulness in addition to private title. On the basis that the proprietor could not be said to be 'entitled' to consent to damage for a fraudulent purpose, the defendant changed his plea to guilty."

It was agreed on all hands for the purpose of this case that T. was the person who, any evil motives apart, was entitled to consent to the damage. It was likewise conceded that the defendant honestly believed that T. occupied that position and was entitled to consent.

It is plain from the way that the judge put the matter in his certificate that he had come to the conclusion that the word "entitled" was in some way qualified by a word which does not appear in the section, namely "honestly". It is on that basis that counsel for the Crown here seeks to support the judge's direction.

In order perhaps to see what the scheme of the Criminal Damage Act 1971 entails, it is necessary to have regard to the earlier Act, namely the Malicious Damage Act 1861. Under that Act, certainly by section 3, and also by two other sections (sections 13 and 59), a man's right to do what he liked to his own property was restricted, and it was, amongst other things, an offence to set fire to certain buildings if there was an intent to injure or defraud, even if those buildings were in the possession of the defendant. It is very striking to observe that the words "with intent to injure or defraud" are absent from the terms of the 1971 Act which I have just read. It is quite apparent from that, indeed in this court it is not argued to the contrary, that in so far as the 1971 Act is concerned it is not an offence for a man to damage or injure or destroy or set fire to his own premises.

One therefore turns to see what the situation would have been had T. made a confession in the same, or similar, terms as that made by the defendant, and to see what would have happened on the Crown's argument if the two of them, T. and the defendant, stood charged under section 1(1) of the 1971 Act in the Crown Court. It is not an offence for a man to set light to his own property. So T. would have been acquitted. But if the Crown is correct, the defendant, the man who had been charged with the task of actually putting the match to the polystyrene, and setting the fire alight, would have been convicted.

Quite apart from any other consideration, that is such an anomalous result that it cannot possibly be right. The answer is this: that one has to decide whether or not an offence is committed at the moment that the acts are alleged to be committed. The fact that somebody may have had a dishonest intent which in the end he was going to carry out, namely a claim from the insurance company, cannot turn what was not originally a crime into a crime. There is no unlawfulness under the 1971 Act in burning a house. It does not become unlawful because there may be an inchoate attempt to commit fraud contained in it; that is to say it does not become a crime under the 1971 Act, whatever may be the situation outside of the Act.

Consequently it is apparent to us that the judge, in his ruling in this respect, was wrong. Indeed it seems to us, if it is necessary to go as far as this, that it was probably unnecessary for the defendant to invoke section

5 of the 1971 Act at all, because he probably had a lawful excuse without it, in that T. was lawfully entitled to burn the premises down. The defendant believed it. He believed that he was acting under the directions of T. and that on its own, it seems to us, may well have provided him with a lawful excuse without having resort to section 5.

The result is that the plea of guilty to count 2 in the indictment was based on a wrong view of the law by the judge. Consequently, despite the plea of guilty, the conviction on count 2 must be quashed and the appeal allowed.

Appeal allowed

Note

This case proceeds on the ground that T, who was variously described as D's 'employer', and 'the proprietor', was the owner of the mill. In fact the mill was owned by Leslie Fink & Co., Ltd. The assumption that T was the person who was entitled to consent to the damage was therefore of doubtful validity. In *R. v. Appleyard* (1985) 81 Cr.App.R. 319 (C.A.) a managing director charged with burning down a store belonging to the company was not allowed to use the assumption in *R. v. Denton* to argue that as managing director he was entitled to consent to the damage.

Questions

1. Ought not a person in Appleyard's position to be able to argue at least that he *thought* he was entitled to consent to the damage?

2. Is a person who damages his own property in order to defraud his insurers guilty of attempt to obtain money from them by deception? See *ante*, p. 462.

ii. Without Lawful Excuse

Criminal Damage Act 1971, section 5

(1) This section applies to any offence under section 1(1) above and any offence under section 2 or 3 above other than one involving a threat by the person charged to destroy or damage property in a way which he knows is likely to endanger the life of another or involving an intent by the person charged to use or cause or permit the use of something in his custody or under his control so to destroy or damage property.

(2) A person charged with an offence to which this section applies shall, whether or not he would be treated for the purpose of this Act as having a lawful excuse apart from this subsection, be treated for those purposes as having a lawful excuse:

(a) if at the time of the act or acts alleged to constitute the offence he believed that the person or persons whom he believed to be entitled to consent to the destruction or damage to the property in question had so consented, or would have so consented to it if he or they had known of the destruction or damage and its circumstances; or

(b) if he destroyed or damaged or threatened to destroy or damage the property in question or, in the case of a charge of an offence under section 3 above, intended to use or cause or permit the use of something to destroy or damage it, in order to protect property belonging to himself or another or a right or interest in property which was or which he believed to be vested in himself or another, and at the time of the act or acts alleged to constitute the offence he believed:

(i) that the property, right or interest was in immediate need of protection; and

(ii) that the means of protection adopted or proposed to be adopted were or would be reasonable having regard to all the circumstances.

(3) For the purpose of this section it is immaterial whether a belief is justified or not if it is honestly held.

(4) For the purpose of subsection (2) above a right or interest in property includes any right or privilege in or over land, whether created by grant, licence or otherwise.

(5) This section shall not be construed as casting doubt on any defence recognised by law as a defence to criminal charges.

Notes

1. All the offences in the Act must be committed "without lawful excuse". But as to the simple offence (not the aggravated offence) section 5 gives particular cases of beliefs which count as lawful excuse. None of the beliefs need be reasonable, provided they are generally held. But see *R. v. Hill*, below.

2. The definition of lawful excuse is not exhaustive: see section 5(5). Thus any other defence to the use of force will avail, *e.g.* duress, prevention of crime, arrest of offenders, self-defence. However these, defences are only effective if the measures taken by D are objectively reasonable: see *ante*, p. 343. The test under section 5(2) is subjective. In *Chamberlain v Lindon* [1998] 1 W.L.R. 1252 the Divisional Court upheld the decision of the Nuneaton Justices to acquit D of criminal damage where he had demolished a wall built by D on C's land as D honestly believed such action was reasonably necessary in the circumstances to protect his right of vehicular access across C's land and that delay would prejudice his rights. The court also held that section 5(2) did not contain any requirement that the defendant had to exhaust any alternative remedies, for example, in the civil courts, before self-redress was permitted as the longer the wall remained, the more urgent was the need to remove it to avoid any suggestion of acquiescence in the obstruction; this supported D's belief that his property (*i.e.* the right of way) was in immediate need of protection.

3. In *Merrick* [1996] 1 Cr.App.R. 130 counts of simple criminal damage were dismissed on the basis of lawful excuse but the trial proceeded for the counts under s.1(2) where, according to the Court of Appeal, "the defence of lawful excuse did not apply". There was no investigation of who actually owned the cabling and the trial proceeded on the basis that the householder did and could consent to its removal. If this was so, D was not placing reliance on s.5(2)(a) but rather on the fact of consent which is an "excuse apart from this subsection" (see *R. v. Denton, ante*, p. 904; Professor J.C. Smith, Commentary, *Merrick* [1995] Crim.L.R. 804). The suggestion is that more should have been made of the excuse point on appeal in *Merrick* and that the dictum of the Court of Appeal is obiter and wrong.

4. The fact that subsections 2 and 3 deal specifically with mistaken belief in the consent of the owner and mistaken belief in a right to be protected has been held to mean that such mistakes can ground a defence even though they arise as a result of self-induced intoxication: see *Jaggard v. Dickinson* [1980] 3 All E.R. 716. See *ante*, p. 271.

Question

D, whose trousered leg is being attacked by P's small dog, brains the dog with his walking stick. If D is prosecuted under the Act for killing the dog, what difference might it make whether D acted to prevent injury to his leg or to prevent damage to his trousers?

R. v. Hill
(1988) 89 Cr.App.R. 74
Court of Appeal

Hill was apprehended outside a U.S. Naval Base in Dyfed in possession of a hacksaw blade. She admitted that she intended to use it to cut the perimeter fence of the base. She was convicted of having the blade with intent without lawful excuse to use it to damage property belonging to another, contrary to Section 3 Criminal Damage Act 1971 (see *post*, p. 860). She said that she feared that the presence of the base would at some future time attract a nuclear strike by Soviet missiles, which would damage her property in the vicinity. The object of her proposed activity was to make the U.S. authorities close the base. She claimed that she was acting with lawful excuse in that her property was in immediate need of protection and that the means of protection proposed would be reasonable having regard to all the circumstances. The judge in effect directed the jury to convict. [Another woman was also convicted on the same charge in precisely similar circumstances]. On appeal:-

LORD LANE C.J. for the Court:—The learned judge ... directed the jury to convict on two bases. The first basis was this, that what the applicant did or proposed to do could not, viewed objectively, be said to have been done to protect her own or anyone else's property under section 5(2)(b) which I have just read. It is simply, he concluded, part of a political campaign aimed at drawing attention to the base and to the risks as she described them raised by the presence of the base in Pembrokeshire. It aimed further at having the base removed. He came to the conclusion that the causative relationship between the acts which she intended to perform and the alleged protection was so tenuous, so nebulous, that the acts could not be said to be done to protect viewed objectively.

The second ground was with reference to the provision that the lawful excuse must be based upon an immediate need for protection. In each case the judge came to the same conclusion that on the applicant's own evidence the applicant could not be said to have believed under the provisions of section 5(2)(b)(i) that the property was in immediate need of protection ...

The judge in each case relied upon a decision of this Court in *Hunt* (1978) 66 Cr.App.R. 105. We have the advantage also of having that report in transcript. We also have before us a more recent decision of this Court in *Ashford and Smith* (unreported) decided on May 26, 1988, in which very similar considerations were raised to those which exist in the present case. It also has the advantage of having set out the material findings of the Court in *Hunt* which were delivered by Roskill L.J. I am referring to p. 4 of the transcript in *Ashford and Smith*, and it will help to set out the basis of the decision not only in *Ashford and Smith* but also in *Hunt* if I read the passage. It runs as follows:

"The judge relied very largely upon the decision of this Court in *Hunt* (1978) 66 Cr.App.R. 105. That was a case in which the appellant set fire to a guest room in an old people's home. He did so, he said, to draw attention to the defective fire alarm system. 'He was charged with arson, contrary to section 1(1) of the Criminal Damage Act 1971. He sought to set up the statutory defence under section 5(2) by claiming to have had a lawful excuse in doing what he did and that he was not reckless whether any such property would be destroyed. The trial judge withdrew the defence of lawful excuse from the jury and left the issue of recklessness for them to determine. The jury by a majority verdict convicted the appellant. On appeal," "Held, that, applying the objective test, the trial judge had ruled correctly because what the appellant had done was not an act which in itself did protect or was capable of protecting property; but in order to draw attention to what in his view was an immediate need for protection by repairing the alarm system; thus the statutory defence under section 5(2) of the Act was not open to him; accordingly, the appeal would be dismissed."

"Giving the judgment of the Court Roskill L.J. said, at p. 108: 'Mr Marshall-Andrews' submission can be put thus: if this man honestly believed that that which he did was necessary in order to protect this property from the risk of fire and damage to the old people's home by reason of the absence of a working fire alarm, he was entitled to set fire to that bed and so to claim the statutory defence accorded by section 5(2). 'I have said we will assume in his favour that he possessed the requisite honest belief. But in our view the question whether he was entitled to the benefit of the defence turns upon the meaning of the words 'in order to protect property belonging to another.' It was argued that those words were subjective in concept, just like the words in the latter part of section 5(2)(*b*) which are subjective. 'We do not think that is right. The question whether or not a particular act of destruction or damage or threat of destruction or damage was done or made in order to protect property belonging to another must be, on the true construction of the statute, an objective test. Therefore we have to ask ourselves whether, whatever the state of this man's mind and assuming an honest belief, that which he admittedly did was done in order to protect this particular property, namely the old people's home in Hertfordshire? 'If one formulates the question in that way, in the view of each member of this Court, for the reason Slynn J. gave during the argument, it admits of only one answer: this was not done in order to protect property; it was done in order to draw attention to the defective state of the fire alarm. It was not an act which in itself did protect or was capable of protecting property.'"

Then the judgment in *Ashford and Smith*, delivered by Glidewell L.J. continued as follows: "In our view that reasoning applies exactly in the present case. *Hunt* is, of course, binding upon us. But even if it were not, we agree with the reasoning contained in it."

Now it is submitted by Mr Bowyer to us that the decision in *Hunt* and the decision in *Ashford and Smith* were wrong and that the test is a subjective test. In other words the submission is that it was a question of what the applicant believed, and accordingly it should have been left to the jury as a matter of fact to decide what it was the applicant did believe.

We are bound by the decision in *Hunt* just as the Court in *Ashford and*

Smith were bound, unless that case can be demonstrated to have been wrongly decided in the light of previous authority. Mr Bowyer endeavoured to persuade us that the decision which I have read of Roskill L.J. flew in the face of the decision of the House of Lords in *Chandler v. Director of Public Prosecutions* [1964] A.C. 763. [After rejecting this submission]

That leaves us with the fact that we are bound by the decision in *Hunt*. But we add that we think that *Hunt* was correctly decided, for this reason. There are two aspects to this type of question. The first aspect is to decide what it was that the applicant, in this case Valerie Hill, in her own mind thought. The learned judge assumed, and so do we, for the purposes of this decision, that everything she said about her reasoning was true. . . . Up to that point the test was subjective. In other words one is examining what is going on in the applicant's mind.

Having done that, the judges in the present cases—and the judge particularly in the case of Valerie Hill—turned to the second aspect of the case, and that is this. He had to decide as a matter of law, which means objectively, whether it could be said that on those facts as believed by the applicant, snipping the strand of the wire, which she intended to do, could amount to something done to protect either the applicant's own home or the homes of her adjacent friends in Pembrokeshire.

He decided, again quite rightly in our view, that that proposed act on her part was far too remote from the eventual aim at which she was targeting her actions to satisfy the test.

It follows therefore, in our view, that the judges in the present two cases were absolutely right to come to the conclusion that they did so far as this aspect of the case is concerned, and to come to that conclusion as a matter of law, having decided the subjective test as the applicants wished them to be decided.

The second half of the question was that of the immediacy of the danger. Here the wording of the Act, one reminds oneself, is as follows: She believed that "the property . . . was in immediate need of protection".

Once again the judge had to determine whether, on the facts as stated by the applicant, there was any evidence on which it could be said that she believed there was an immediate need of protection from immediate damage. In our view that must mean evidence that she believed that immediate action had to be taken to do something which would otherwise be a crime in order to prevent the immediate risk of something worse happening. . . . The evidence given by this woman (and the evidence given by the other applicant was very similar) drives this Court to the conclusion, as they drove the respective judges to the conclusion, that there was no evidence on which it could be said that there was that belief . . .

Appeal dismissed

Questions

1. The words "in order to protect property" are suggestive of the purpose behind the acts of destruction or damage. Can a purpose exist "objectively" or is it something which, to use Professor J.C. Smith's words, can "only exist in someone's mind—and, in this context, that must be the mind of the defendant"? If that is so of what relevance should be evidence as to the remoteness of the damage from the achievement of protection or the inefficacy of the damage to effect protection? (*cf.* Lord Lane C.J.'s dictum in *R. v. Williams (Gladstone)*,

ante, p. 159 on the evidential relevance of the reasonableness or unreasonableness of D's beliefs.)

2. Who decides generally whether a defendant's state of mind amounts to "intention" and is this a question of fact or of law? How does this compare to the Courts' decisions regarding "purpose" under this provision? Is the fact that "purpose" arises in the context of a defence a plausible explanation of any difference of approach? (*cf.* duress and see *Valderrama-Vega, ante,* p. 287.)

Note

The provisions on lawful excuse are sorted out and extended to defence of person by clauses 184, 184 Draft Criminal Code Bill, below, which apply to the "simple" offences and not to the "aggravated" offences. The definition of "lawful excuse" is still not to be exhaustive; common law defences preserved by Clause 45(c) may apply.

Draft Criminal Code Bill

184. A person does not commit an offence to which this section applies if—

(a) he knows or believes that the person whom he believes to be entitled to consent to the destruction or damage has so consented; or
(b) he believes that that person would so consent if he knew of the destruction or damage and its circumstances.

185.—(1) A person does not commit an offence to which this section applies by doing an act which, in the circumstances which exist or which he believes to exist, is immediately necessary and reasonable—

(a) to protect himself or another from unlawful force or injury; or
(b) to prevent or terminate the unlawful detention of himself or another; or
(c) to protect property (whether belonging to himself or another) from unlawful appropriation, destruction or damage.

(2) Section 44(3) (meaning of 'unlawful') applies for the purposes of this section.

iii. Intending to Destroy or Damage any such Property

R. v. Smith
[1974] Q.B. 354 Court of Appeal

S, a tenant of a flat, installed some stereo equipment and, with the consent of the landlord, put in certain roofing, wall panels and flooring to mask the electric wiring. These fixtures thereupon belonged to the landlord by law, but S. did not know this. When he was given notice to quit he damaged the fixtures in order to remove the wiring. He said he thought he was damaging his own property. He was convicted of an offence under section 1(1) Criminal Damage Act 1971, and appealed.

JAMES L.J.: The appellant's defence was that he honestly believed that the damage he did was to his own property, that he believed that he was entitled to damage his own property and therefore he had lawful excuse for his actions causing the damage. In the course of his summing up the deputy judge directed the jury in these terms:

"Now, in order to make the offence complete, the person who is charged with it must destroy, or damage that property belonging to another, 'without lawful excuse,' and that is something that one has got to look at a little more, members of the jury, because you have heard here that, so far as each defendant was concerned, it never occurred to them, and you may think, quite naturally never occurred to either of them, that these various additions to the house were anything but their own property. . . . But members of the jury, the Act is quite specific, and so far as the defendant David Smith is concerned lawful excuse is the only defence which has been raised. It is said that he had a lawful excuse by reason of his belief, his honest and genuinely held belief that he was destroying property which he had a right to destroy if he wanted to. But, members of the jury, I must direct you as a matter of law, and you must, therefore, accept it from me, that belief by the defendant David Smith that he had the right to do what he did is not lawful excuse within the meaning of the Act. Members of the jury, it is an excuse, it may even be a reasonable excuse, but it is not, members of the jury a lawful excuse, because, in law, he had no right to do what he did. Members of the jury, as a matter of law, the evidence, in fact, discloses, so far as David Smith is concerned, no lawful excuse at all, because, as I say, the only defence which he has raised is the defence that he thought he had the right to do what he did. I have directed you that that is not a lawful excuse, and, members of the jury, it follows from that that so far as David Smith is concerned, I am bound to direct you as a matter of law that you must find him guilty of this offence with which he is charged."

It is contended for the appellant that that is a misdirection in law, and that, as a result of the misdirection, the entire defence of the appellant was wrongly withdrawn from the jury. . . .

The offence created [by s.10] includes the elements of intention or recklessness and the absence of lawful excuse. There is in section 5 of the Act a partial "definition" of lawful excuse. . . .

[After reading section 5(2), (3), (5), his Lordship continued]

It is argued for the appellant that an honest, albeit erroneous, belief that the act causing damage or destruction was done to his own property provides a defence to a charge brought under section 1(1). The argument is put in three ways. First, that the offence charged includes the act causing the damage or destruction and the element of *mens rea*. The element of *mens rea* relates to all the circumstances of the criminal act. The criminal act in the offence is causing damage to or destruction of "property belonging to another" and the element of *mens rea*, therefore, must relate to "property belonging to another". Honest belief, whether justifiable or not, that the property is the defendant's own negatives the element of *mens rea*. . . .

It is conceded by Mr Gerber [for the Crown] that there is force in the argument that the element of *mens rea* extends to "property belonging to another". But it is argued, the section creates a new statutory offence and that it is open to the construction that the mental element in the offence relates only to causing damage to or destroying property. That if in fact the property damaged or destroyed is shown to be another's property the offence is committed although the defendant did not intend or foresee damage to another person's property.

We are informed that so far as research has revealed this is the first occasion on which this court has had to consider the question which arises in this appeal.

It is not without interest to observe that, under the law in force before the passing of the Criminal Damage Act 1971, it was clear that no offence was committed by a person who destroyed or damaged property belonging to another in the honest but mistaken belief that the property was his own or that he had a legal right to do the damage. In *R. v. Twose* (1879) 14 Cox C. C. 327 the prisoner was indicted for setting fire to furze on a common. Persons living near the common had occasionally burned the furze in order to improve the growth of grass but without the right to do so. The prisoner denied setting fire to the furze and it was submitted that even if it were proved that she did she could not be found guilty if she *bona fide* believed she had a right to do so whether the right were a good one or not. Lopes J. ruled that if she set fire to the furze thinking she had a right to do so that would not be a criminal offence.

Upon the facts of the present appeal the charge, if brought before the Act of 1971 came into force, would have been laid under section 13 of the Malicious Damage Act 1861, alleging damage by a tenant to a building. It was a defence to a charge under that section that the tenant acted under a claim of right to do the damage.

If the direction given by the deputy judge in the present case is correct, then the offence created by section 1(1) of the Act of 1971 involves a considerable extension of the law in a surprising direction. Whether or not this is so depends upon the construction of the section. Construing the language of section 1(1) we have no doubt that the *actus reus* is "destroying or damaging any property belonging to another." It is not possible to exclude the words "belonging to another" which describes the "property." Applying the ordinary principles of *mens rea*, the intention and recklessness and the absence of lawful excuse required to constitute the offence have reference to property belonging to another. It follows that in our judgment no offence is committed under this section if a person destroys or causes damage to property belonging to another if he does so in the honest though mistaken belief that the property is his own, and provided that the belief is honestly held it is irrelevant to consider whether or not it is a justifiable belief.

In our judgment, the direction given to the jury was a fundamental misdirection in law. The consequence was that the jury were precluded from considering facts capable of being a defence to the charge and were directed to convict. . . .

Appeal allowed

Questions

1. In *Jaggard v. Dickinson* (*ante*, p. 271), the accused, because she was drunk, thought that the owner of the property had consented to her damaging it. It was held that since the case came under section 5(2)(a), she was entitled to be acquitted notwithstanding that her mistake was due to self-induced intoxication. But in *R. v. Smith*, the Court rejected the argument that his case came under section 5. Does this mean that if Miss Jaggard thought it was her *own* window she was breaking, her drunken mistake would not have saved her?

iv. Being Reckless as to Whether any such Property would be Destroyed or Damaged

See *R. v. Caldwell; Elliott v. C.; R. v. Stephen Malcolm R., R. v. Sangha, ante*, pp. 121, 130, 133, 135 on recklessness.

Note

The Intention or Recklessness must be with regard to "any such property" (s.1(1), *ante*, p. 900), *i.e.* property belonging to another.

Question

Is the simple offence involved in the following cases?

(a) D intends to damage P's property and unexpectedly damages Q's property.
(b) D is reckless as to harm to P and unexpectedly damages P's property.

B. *The Aggravated Offence: With Danger to Life*

Note

See section 1(2), and *R. v. Caldwell, ante*, p. 121. Since the gravamen of the offence is danger to life, the property damaged need not belong to the accused. The extended meaning of "without lawful excuse" in section 5 does not apply, and in addition to the *mens rea* required for the simple offence he must intend to endanger the life of another or be reckless as to whether another's life is endangered.

R. v. Steer
[1988] A.C. 111
House of Lords

S fired a shot through a window pane behind which Mr & Mrs G were standing. The pane was broken by the shot, but they were not hurt. It was accepted that S did not intend to endanger their lives. He was charged, *inter alia*, with damaging property being reckless whether the life of another would be endangered. On the judge's ruling against his submission that the endangering must by the damage to the window, not by the act which caused damage to the window, he pleaded guilty to the charge. His appeal against the ruling was allowed by the Court of Appeal. The prosecution further appealed.

LORD BRIDGE OF HARWICH: We must, of course, approach the matter on the footing, implicit in the outcome of the trial, that the respondent, in firing at the bedroom window, had no intent to endanger life, but accepts that he was reckless whether life would be endangered.

Under both limbs of section 1 of the 1971 Act it is the essence of the offence which the section creates that the defendant has destroyed or damaged property. For the purpose of analysis it may be convenient to omit reference to destruction and to concentrate on the references to damage, which was all that was here involved. To be guilty under subsection (1) the defendant must have intended or been reckless as to the damage to property which he caused. To be guilty under subsection (2) he must additionally have intended to endanger life or been reckless whether life would be endangered "by the damage" to property which he caused. This is the context in which the words must be construed and it seems to me impossible to read the words "by the damage" as meaning "by the danger or by the act which caused the damage". Moreover, if the language of the statute has the meaning for which the Crown contends, the words "by the destruction or damage" and "thereby" in subsection 2(b) are mere surplusage. If the Crown's submission is right, the only additional element necessary to convert a subsection (1) offence into a subsection (2) offence is an intent to endanger life or recklessness whether life would be endangered simpliciter.

It would suffice as a ground for dismissing this appeal if the statute were ambiguous, since any such ambiguity in a criminal statute should be resolved in favour of the defence. But I can find no ambiguity. It seems to me that the meaning for which the respondent contends is the only meaning which the language can bear.

The contrary construction leads to anomalies which Parliament cannot have intended. If A. and B. both discharge firearms in a public place, being reckless whether life would be endangered, it would be absurd that A., who incidentally causes some trifling damage to the property, should be guilty of an offence punishable with life imprisonment, but that B., who causes no damage, should be guilty of no offence. In the same circumstances, if A. is merely reckless but B. actually intends to endanger life, it is scarcely less absurd that A should be guilty of the graver offence under section 1(2) of the 1971 Act, B. of the lesser offence under section 16 of the Firearms Act 1968.

Counsel for the Crown did not shrink from arguing that section 1(2) of the 1971 Act had created, in effect, a general offence of endangering life with intent or recklessly, however, the danger was caused, but had incidentally included as a necessary, albeit insignificant, ingredient of the offence that some damage to property should also be caused. In certain fields of legislation it is sometimes difficult to appreciate the rationale of particular provisions, but in a criminal statute it would need the clearest language to persuade me that the legislature had acted so irrationally, indeed perversely, as acceptance of this argument would imply.

It was further argued that to affirm the construction of section 1(2)(b) adopted by the Court of Appeal would give rise to problems in other cases in which it might be difficult or even impossible to distinguish between the act causing damage to property and the ensuing damage caused as the source of danger to life. In particular, it was suggested that in arson cases the jury would have to be directed that they could only convict if the danger to life arose from falling beams or similar damage caused by the fire, not if the danger arose from the heat, flames or smoke generated by the fire itself. Arson is, of course, the prime example of a form of criminal damage to property which, in the case of an occupied building, necessarily involves serious danger to life and where the gravity of the consequence which may result as well from recklessness as from a specific intent fully justifies the severity of the penalty which the 1971 Act provides for the offence. But the argument in this case is misconceived. It is not the match and the inflammable materials, the flaming firebrand or any other inflammatory agent which the arsonist uses to start the fire which causes danger to life, it is the ensuing conflagration which occurs as the property which has been set on fire is damaged or destroyed. When the victim in the bedroom is overcome by the smoke or incinerated by the flames as the building burns, it would be absurd to say that this does not result from the damage to the building.

Counsel for the Crown put forward other examples of cases which he suggested ought to be liable to prosecution under section 1(2) of the 1971 Act, including that of the angry mob of striking miners who throw a hail of bricks through the window of the cottage occupied by the working miner and that of people who drop missiles from motorway bridges on passing vehicles. I believe that the criminal law provides adequate sanctions for these cases without the need to resort to section 1(2) of the 1971 Act. But, if my belief is mistaken, this would still be no reason to distort the plain meaning of that subsection. . . .

[Lords Griffiths, Ackner, Oliver and Goff agreed]

Appeal dismissed

Note

The damage by which D intended to endanger life or was reckless as to endangering life is the damage he intended to cause or was reckless as to causing, not the damage he actually caused. The fact that he was not intentional or reckless about the damage actually caused endangering life, and the fact that that damage involved no danger to life, are both immaterial: *R. v. Dudley* [1989] Crim.L.R. 57.

R. v. Asquith, Webster and Seamans
[1995] 1 Cr.App.R. 492
Court of Appeal

The appellants pushed a coping-stone from the parapet of a railway bridge on to a passenger train passing below. The stone landed on the bulkhead of a carriage, showering the passengers with glass fibre and polystyrene from the roof, but did not fall into the compartment. No one was injured. The appellants were convicted of criminal damage intending to endanger life.

LORD TAYLOR C.J.: . . . As to the dropping of stones from bridges, the effect of the statute may be thought strange. If the defendant's intention is that the stone itself should crash through the roof of a train or motor vehicle and thereby directly injure a passenger or if he was reckless only as to that outcome, the section would not bite. That would follow from the ratio in *Steer* and is no doubt why Lord Bridge made the comment he did about missiles from motorway bridges. If, however, the defendant intended or was reckless that the stone would smash the roof of the train or vehicle so that metal or wood struts from the roof would or obviously might descend upon a passenger, endangering life, he would surely be guilty. This may seem to many a dismal distinction.

Unfortunately, the learned judge was not referred to *R. v. Steer*. In his summing up, he directed the jury as follows at p. 52E-G:

"If a man pushed, deliberately pushed, a coping-stone weighting about 2 cwt over a railway bridge, timing it to fall so as to strike the roof of a passing train, the very pushing, the weight, the depth of the fall, the timing, entitle you to presume that there was an intention on the part of the pusher to do the damage to the roof of the train for a start, and having regard to what a dangerous act you may think it was, you could judge an intention in the mind of the pusher to endanger the life of any passenger upon whom such a heavy object, having penetrated the roof, might well fall."

Clearly, having regard to the decision in *Steer*, the last few words of that passage amounted to a misdirection. If the intention was that the stone itself should endanger the life of the passengers, then the "pusher" would not be guilty of this offence. Had the learned judge, instead of the last few words he used, said; "You could judge an intention in the mind of the pusher to endanger the life of any passengers by causing the roof to descend on such passengers following the impact of the falling stone", he would properly have left an issue to the jury to consider. The learned judge also left the issue of recklessness to the jury.

In our view, by convicting each of the appellants on count one after the learned judge's direction, the jury must be taken to have found (a) that the appellants jointly pushed the stone over and (b) that each of them intended the stone itself to crash through the roof and endanger life. The conviction on that basis cannot be sustained. However, the jury's finding of an intent by each appellant to endanger life by causing the stone itself to penetrate the roof, must, in common sense, carry the implication that they were each reckless as to endangering life by whatever damage the stone might do when it fell. If the intention was for the stone to penetrate the roof, there was clearly an obvious risk that it might endanger life by bringing parts of the roof down into the compartment. In these circumstances, we consider the proper course is for us to squash the conviction on count one but, pursuant to section 3 of the Criminal Appeal Act 1968, to substitute in each case a conviction on count two of "being reckless as to whether the life of another would be thereby endangered". This we do.

Questions

1. As the jury did not return a verdict on the basis of recklessness as to endangering life, does it necessarily follow, as the Court of Appeal concluded, that their finding of intention (following a misdirection) implied that they were satisfied also of recklessness?

2. D is on top of a cliff and drops a large stone on to a tent below which he believes to be unoccupied. The stone penetrates the canvass and seriously injures V. Has D committed the section 1(2) offence or any other offence against the person?

3. D fills up a lemonade bottle with a clear liquid weed-killer which is poisonous to humans and leaves it in a cupboard in his kitchen realising that there is a risk that someone might drink it in mistake for lemonade but not caring whether or not they do. Has D committed any offence at this point?. If there had been 50mls of lemonade in the bottle when D added the weed-killer would your answer differ? Is the danger any different in the latter situation? Is D's behaviour any more or less culpable in the latter situation? Would it make any difference in the latter situation if D had not thought about the danger, D being a fourteen-year-old child of well below average intelligence (see *Elliott v. C (A Minor), ante*, p. 130).

4. Should there be an offence of intentionally or recklessly endangering life regardless of how the endangerment may be intended or foreseen to arise?

2. OTHER OFFENCES

Criminal Damage Act 1971, sections 2 and 3

2. A person who without lawful excuse makes to another a threat, intending that that other would fear it would be carried out—

(a) to destroy or damage any property belonging to that other or a third person; or

(b) to destroy or damage his own property in a way which he knows is likely to endanger the life of that other or a third person;

shall be guilty of an offence.

3. A person who has anything in his custody or under his control intending without lawful excuse to use it or cause or permit another to use it—

(a) to destroy or damage any property belonging to some other person; or

(b) to destroy or damage his own or the user's property in a way which he knows is likely to endanger the life of some other person;

shall be guilty of an offence.

Notes

1. As with section 1, both of these sections have a pair of offences, a simple offence and an aggravated offence, *i.e.* one referring to danger to life (although the maximum penalties—10 years imprisonment— are the same). With the offences in sections 2(*a*) and 3(*a*), but not with the offences in sections 2(*b*) and 3(*b*), the lawful excuse provisions in section 5 apply, and the threatened property must belong to someone else.

2. There need be no intention to carry out the threat in section 2, merely an intention that the person to whom it is made would fear that it would be carried out. If there is such an intention, it makes no difference that such a fear is not aroused in that person.

3. For the offence in section 3, "in his possession" was rejected by the Law Commission on account of the difficulties centred round the question of when a person can be said to be in possession of something without knowing: see *Warner v. Commissioner of Police* [1969] A.C. 256.

Questions

1. That question can be said to be purely academic with regard to section 3. Why is this?

2. D, looking for a "squat" to sleep in, has in his custody a jemmy so that he can break into a suitable house if he cannot get in in any other way. Is he guilty of an offence in section 3? See discussion of conditional intent in theft, *ante*, p. 760, and burglary, *ante*, p. 886, and *R. v. Buckingham* (1976) 63 Cr.App.R. 159 (C.A.).

INDEX